ENGLISH PLACE-NAME SOCIETY
VOLUME LXVII/LXVIII/LXIX
FOR 1989-90, 1990-1 & 1991-2

General Editor

KENNETH CAMERON

THE PLACE-NAMES OF RUTLAND

ENGLISH PLACE-NAME SOCIETY
COUNTY VOLUMES

I. Part 1:	Introduction to the Survey of English Place-Names.
Part 2:	The Chief Elements Used in English Place-Names.
II.	The Place-Names of Buckinghamshire.
III.	The Place-Names of Bedfordshire and Huntingdonshire.
IV.	The Place-Names of Worcestershire.
V.	The Place-Names of the North Riding of Yorkshire.
VI, VII.	The Place-Names of Sussex, Parts 1 and 2.
VIII, IX.	The Place-Names of Devon, Parts 1 and 2.
X.	The Place-Names of Northamptonshire.
XI.	The Place-Names of Surrey.
XII.	The Place-Names of Essex.
XIII.	The Place-Names of Warwickshire.
XIV.	The Place-Names of the East Riding of Yorkshire and York.
XV.	The Place-Names of Hertfordshire.
XVI.	The Place-Names of Wiltshire.
XVII.	The Place-Names of Nottinghamshire.
XVIII.	The Place-Names of Middlesex.
XIX.	The Place-Names of Cambridgeshire and the Isle of Ely.
XX-XXII.	The Place-Names of Cumberland, Parts 1, 2, and 3.
XXIII, XXIV.	The Place-Names of Oxfordshire, Parts 1 and 2.
XXV, XXVI.	English Place-Name Elements, Parts 1 and 2.
XXVII-XXIX.	The Place-Names of Derbyshire, Parts 1, 2, and 3.
XXX-XXXVII.	The Place-Names of the West Riding of Yorkshire, Parts 1-8.
XXXVIII-XLI.	The Place-Names of Gloucestershire, Parts 1-4.
XLII, XLIII.	The Place-Names of Westmorland, Parts 1 and 2.
XLIV-XLVIII.	The Place-Names of Cheshire, Parts 1-4, 5.I:i.
XLIX-LI.	The Place-Names of Berkshire, Parts 1-3.
LII, LIII.	The Place-Names of Dorset, Parts 1 and 2.
LIV.	The Place-Names of Cheshire, Part 5.I:ii.
LV.	The Place-Names of Staffordshire, Part 1.
LVI/LVII.	Cornish Place-Name Elements.
LVIII.	The Place-Names of Lincolnshire, Part 1.
LIX/LX.	The Place-Names of Dorset, Part 3.
LXI.	The Place-Names of Norfolk, Part 1.
LXII/LXIII.	The Place-Names of Shropshire, Part 1.
LXIV/LXV.	The Place-Names of Lincolnshire, Part 2.
LXVI.	The Place-Names of Lincolnshire, Part 3.
LXVII/LXVIII/	
LXIX.	The Place-Names of Rutland.

All communication concerning the Society and membership should be addressed to:

THE HON. SECRETARY, English Place-Name Society,
The University, Nottingham NG7 2RD

ENGLISH PLACE-NAME SOCIETY
VOLUME LXVII/LXVIII/LXIX
FOR 1989-90, 1990-1 & 1991-2

THE PLACE-NAMES
OF RUTLAND

By

BARRIE COX

ENGLISH PLACE-NAME SOCIETY

1994

Published by the English Place-Name Society

© English Place-Name Society 1994

ISBN: 0 904889 17 3

Printed in Great Britain
by Woolnough Bookbinding, Irthlingborough

For

Kenneth Cameron

The Camera-ready Copy of this volume
has been produced by Mrs Esmé Pattison
on equipment provided
by
Messrs Allied Breweries plc
and by
Messrs Advent Desktop Publishing Limited

ACKNOWLEDGEMENTS

The publication of this volume has been greatly assisted by generous grants from the British Academy and by a handsome gift from a member of the Rotary Club of Rutland.

PREFACE

This survey of the place-names of Rutland has been many years in the making. As early as 1959, J.E.B. Gover had prepared a short study of the county's major names, based on a collection of materials made by Sir Allen Mawer and himself and had handed the collection to the late F.T. Wainwright to develop as part of an old-style English Place-Name Survey volume for Leicestershire. A copy of Gover's typescript of Rutland's major names survived in the Survey's archive at Nottingham but Gover's and Mawer's materials and any which Wainwright may have added to them were lost at Wainwright's death.

In 1967, therefore, I began researching the place-names of Leicestershire and Rutland completely afresh, eventually producing a study of the major and minor names of these counties as a doctoral thesis in 1971. Professor Kenneth Cameron, Honorary Director of the English Place-Name Survey, had supervised this research and asked me to develop it as the Survey's volumes for Leicestershire and Rutland. Since only a fraction of the materials which I had collected had been used for my Ph.D. thesis, I agreed to this but found that the demands of lecturing and administration in the next fifteen years were such that I had little opportunity for sustained research. From 1987, however, with only a part-time teaching post in the University of Nottingham to occupy me, I was able to turn my hand to completing the survey for Rutland.

Mr John Field undertook to collect post-1800 field-names and to extract from nineteenth and twentieth century printed directories. His principal source for late field-names was a detailed survey for the county made by the Home Guard in 1943. Since Rutland possessed no Record Office of its own, this had the advantage of being a very accessible quarry but because of late creation, contained a fair percentage of field-names in some parishes consisting only of acreage. These 'acreage names' have been retained, however, for historical accuracy. As a medievalist by inclination and education, I am extremely grateful for Mr Field's application to a task that would have proved onerous for me. His expertise as a field-names specialist was particularly valuable in his preliminary comments on some of the more arcane modern formations and in his observations on the completed text.

Another significant contributor to this Rutland survey was Dr Mark Bateson who, as the English Place-Name Survey's research assistant, meticulously collected a substantial amount of eighteenth and nineteenth century material from various county and London archives. Mr D. Tew, formerly of Langham, later of Oakham, made available field-name forms from modern deeds in private hands. Mrs L. Worrall of Barrowden collected materials from documents in the Burghley Estate Office and Mr G.A. Chinnery of Hungarton extracted forms from selected Glebe Terriers on microfiche in the County Record Office, Leicester.

My thanks are also due to His Grace the Duke of Rutland who gave me complete access to the superb collection of medieval and later manuscripts in his archives at Belvoir Castle and to his library and to cartularies normally kept on public display in his galleries. They are due in addition to the staffs of the County Record Office, Leicester, of the Lincolnshire Archives Office, Lincoln and of the University Archives, Nottingham, for their untiring assistance in the provision of documents housed therein. I am also grateful to the Trustees of the Burghley Estate for access to the Burghley Estate archive and to the Trustees of The Leverhulme Trust for a research grant to enable me to complete the collection of materials for the survey and to make many field-trips to Rutland to clear up problems best dealt with by a personal examination of local topography.

Mrs M.D. Pattison, the Secretary of the English Place-Name Society, prepared my necessarily complicated text for press. I am greatly in her debt and am truly sorry for the many headaches which I must have created for her.

Above all, I must express my deepest gratitude to my mentor and friend, Professor Kenneth Cameron, who kindled and encouraged my interest in the Anglo-Saxon world. He has scrutinized this survey at every stage of its preparation. His wise and patient counsel has been without price.

Barrie Cox

University of Nottingham

CONTENTS

Introduction	xiii
Abbreviations and Bibliography	lxvi
Phonetic Symbols	lxxix
Notes on the Phonology of Rutland Place-Names	lxxx
Notes on Arrangement	lxxxiv
Rutland	1
River-Names	1
District-Names	3
The Place-Names of Alstoe Hundred	4
The Place-Names of Oakham Soke Hundred	64
The Place-Names of East Hundred	130
The Place-Names of Martinsley Hundred	171
The Place-Names of Wrangdike Hundred	231
The Elements in Rutland Place-Names and Field-Names	308
Notes on the Distribution and Usage of some Elements	397
Pre-English Names	411
French Place-Names and Elements	411
Categories of Field- and Minor Names	412
Personal Names in Rutland Place-Names and Field-Names	433
The Surnames recorded in Rutland Minor Names and Field-Names	435
The Names of identified Persons or Families	446
Index of the Place-Names of Rutland	463
Maps 1-8	in pocket at end

INTRODUCTION
to
THE PLACE-NAMES OF RUTLAND

1.   TERRITORY, GEOLOGY AND LANDSCAPE.

Rutland comprises a triangle of land with its apex to the south. It
is bounded on the south-east from Caldecott to Tinwell by River
Welland. Stamford's town lands north of R. Welland to its
confluence with R. Gwash were no doubt once part of Rutland's
territory. The rivers here are its natural boundaries. Beyond R.
Gwash, the easterly bulge of the parishes of Ryhall and Essendine
encompasses in part low-lying ground which stretches into the fen-
lands of Lincolnshire. Towards the extreme eastern tip of
Essendine, Rutland's boundary is demarcated by a linear earthwork
of the Bronze Age. In the south-west, from Caldecott to Belton,
the county boundary is formed by Eye Brook, but from Belton
north to Langham there is no natural feature to constitute a
frontier, the boundary crossing hill country which was once well
wooded. Flitteris, on the county boundary in Oakham parish,
indicates by its name (Old English *(ge)flit* 'strife, dispute' plus *hrīs*
'brushwood', hence 'brushwood-covered region of disputed ownership') that there were early problems with border definition along
this stretch. At Whissendine, the frontier swings east. There is no
physical boundary here obvious today, but in earlier times what was
marshy moorland lying across the north-east of Whissendine and
across Teigh to the rise of the Market Overton escarpment once
formed a significant barrier. This was *Rutmore* 'Rōta's moor', no
doubt named from the same Anglo-Saxon overlord after whom the
whole territory was called, that is 'Rōta's land or domain'. From
Market Overton on its higher ground, the county boundary runs
due east to meet Roman Ermine Street which it follows south for a
short way before turning eastward again across the limestone flat-
lands via Stretton and then south-east to Essendine.

Physically, Rutland falls roughly into two parts, a raised
plateau in the west and north-west, lower land in the east and
south-east. Its landscape is one of undulations rather than of
dramatic heights. In the north-west, the broad plateau is divided by

the Vale of Catmose, giving the Cottesmore Upland to its east and to its west a stretch of high ground along the Leicestershire border rising to over 400 feet. A number of streams which flow eastward to R. Welland have cut into this high ground, producing a series of inter-fluvial ridges. In the far west, the upland is covered by Boulder Clays of the Upper Lias which produce intractable, heavy soils, repellent to early settlement. The hill and vale country further to the south comprises the series of inter-fluvial ridges just mentioned, which fall from west to east. Towards the west, these are of iron-bearing Northampton Sands and further east of Jurassic Limestone, both of which give light, porous soils. Here are sited such important settlements as Ridlington, Uppingham, Glaston and Seaton. The Upper Lias clays of the river valleys were avoided.

The Vale of Catmose has a floor of marlstone of the Middle Lias from which water springs. It provides the finest soils in the county, bright red-brown and very fertile. The sandstone and marlstone of the Middle Lias were attractive to early settlement. Oakham, Ashwell and Whissendine are located on this formation. At Belton, Stoke Dry and land to the south of Oakham, glacial sands and gravels make tractable soils, while post-glacial gravels at Caldecott and Thorpe by Water also provide light, clean earth.

East of the Vale of Catmose rises the imposing escarpment of an outcrop of Northampton Sands ironstone, the Cottesmore Upland, running south from Market Overton to Burley. Further south, this same rock forms the great hill of Hambleton (OE *hamol-dūn* 'the flat-topped hill'), once probably the *caput* of the Anglian kingdom of Rutland. Empingham, North Luffenham and Barrowden, all important early major settlements, also stand on outliers of the Northampton Sands formation. This outcrop was a significant source of water supply since springs are located at its junction with the impervious Upper Lias clays, both at its main outcropping and at its southern subsidiaries.

The east of the county is largely uniform and covered by Jurassic limestones which produce the good, light soils exploited by the villa estates of Rutland's Romano-British landowners.

Rutland once had major areas of woodland. The Domesday Survey of 1086 shows most of the recorded woodland to be in the north and west of the county, particularly on the Liassic and Boulder Clays in the west and on the Northampton Sands of the Cottesmore Upland.[1] Woodland is also recorded in the Domesday

Survey in small scattered patches in the Welland Valley. The heaviest concentrations in the north were in the area bounded by Market Overton, Greetham, Whitwell and Oakham. In the west, the Leighfield Forest region was heavily wooded south to Stoke Dry and Lyddington. In the east of the county, woodland was notable east of Ermine Street.

The early place-name evidence echoes this Domesday distribution except for in the Welland Valley. Indeed, early woodland names are virtually absent from what was to become Wrangdike Hundred, except in Lyddington and Stoke Dry in the south-west. One of the common elements signifying woodland is OE *lēah* 'woodland, a woodland clearing' and this occurs predominantly in the west and south-west, in what was once the Leighfield Forest and Beaumont Chase region and also in the Burley, Exton, Barnsdale area at the southern end of the Cottesmore Upland. OE *wudu* 'a wood' is distributed most heavily to the east of the Roman roads Sewstern Lane and Ermine Street in the north-east of the county where *lēah* is rare. It is also well represented in the south-west from Leighfield to Stoke Dry.

2. PREHISTORIC RUTLAND

The problem of the age of Rutland as a recognizable territory is an intriguing one. Charles Phythian-Adams has argued for at least an Iron Age origin for some of its bounds, viewing Rutland as reflecting the extent of an early tribal unit. He notes that the important Romano-British settlements at Great Casterton and Thistleton lie beside Roman roads at locations close to where they cross territorial boundaries in a way which is closely matched elsewhere in England. As parallels in the immediate region, he cites the Romano-British settlements at Medbourne on the Gartree Road where it crosses from Leicestershire into Northamptonshire, that at Willoughby on the Wolds where the Fosse Way leaves Nottinghamshire for Leicestershire and the town at Chesterton beside the boundary between Northamptonshire and the former Huntingdonshire. He suggests that the Romans may have planted important settlements 'beside *pre*-existing divisions between the Iron Age peoples in question in order to control both feuding and marketing between the tribes concerned'.[2]

The position of sacred shrines in relation to early borders may also be relevant in dating Rutland's boundaries. In this connection it is to be noted that at Thistleton, an important Romano-British market site, a Roman temple was dedicated to the Celtic deity Veteris. This temple had a precursor dating to the first century AD.[3] The name of the settlement at Willoughby on the Wolds was Vernemetum: this contains the Celtic word *nemeton* 'a sacred grove', indicating an important religious site, probably antedating the Roman conquest. In the churchyard at Braunston, a border parish on Rutland's western boundary, stands the monolithic figure of a mother goddess which is certainly pre-Germanic, either of Iron Age or, more likely, of Romano-British date. It is probable that there was an ancient border shrine at Braunston which in some way may have conditioned the siting of the later Christian church. The positions of both the Braunston and the Thistleton shrines lend support to the notion of a pre-Roman date for Rutland's boundaries.

The place-names of the county may well throw additional light on the problem of its possible pre-Roman territorial origins, in particular those in which OE *beorg* 'a burial mound' is compounded. As early as 1922 Grundy, writing on the boundary features contained in the Anglo-Saxon charters of Hampshire, noted that 'in no single case is there any real reason to suppose that *beorg* means anything but a barrow. The evidence of the Berkshire and Wiltshire charters tends more definitely to the same conclusion'.[4] Later work by Grinsell and O'Neil in Gloucestershire reinforced Grundy's observations.[5] Modern research by Della Hooke concludes that 'recent studies seem to indicate that Old English terms [i.e. for tumuli] were used with a much greater degree of precision than has previously been thought. Although a number of terms such as *beorg* ... and *hlæw* have been used to refer to natural hills, they appear to have been used much more often than formerly realised to refer to specific burial features'. In particular, the Anglo-Saxons employed *beorg* to name prehistoric barrows, burial mounds already ancient in their day. They used the word *hlāw/hlæw* to refer to their own pagan burial mounds.[6]

Although, as would be expected, names with *beorg* are found occasionally in the inland parishes of Rutland, such as the surviving Wing Burrows in Bisbrooke, *Broken Barrow* in Empingham (possibly signifying a burial mound robbed in antiquity) and perhaps *Barrow leayes* in Exton, their distribution otherwise is confined exclusively to the border parishes.[7]

Typical is Barrowden overlooking R. Welland in the south-east of the county. Barrowden is OE *beorga-dūn* 'the hill with the burial mounds upon it'. Barrowden is one of the very early types of OE topographical name.[8] The barrows on this hill were old when the pagan Anglo-Saxons settled. They are recorded independently in the parish from c1275 as *le Berues*. South-west from Barrowden, *the Barrows* in Morcott, The Barrows in Seaton, *le Norberwe* and *le Beru* in Thorpe by Water and *The Barrows* in Lyddington lined the high ground above the river. It is possible that *The Pimpole* in low-lying Caldecott at the southernmost point of Rutland (with early Modern English *pimpel* 'a pimple' used topographically) also refers to an erstwhile boundary burial mound.

The western border parishes lie on the Boulder Clay, avoided by early settlers because of its intractable soils. This region was once well wooded, yet here we find *Barrowe Hill* in Belton, *Risberwe* in Leighfield, *Netherborrows* in Braunston and Ranksborough in Langham. As the frontier line was not clear-cut in this stretch of hill country, it seems as if the builders of the barrows placed them specifically to signal their territorial limits. In the west of Barleythorpe, south of Ranksborough, *le Spellow* 'the speech mound' lay on the county boundary with Leicestershire. This Anglo-Saxon local moot-site may well have been another example of a prehistoric border barrow, one of the series under discussion. Its position would so indicate.

Across the north-east of Whissendine and across Teigh lay *Rutmore*, an area of marshy moorland. It seems that the ancient northern frontier ran just to the south of this. In Whissendine are *Gosborough* and *Greensborough*, in Teigh is *Rush Barrow* (no doubt so named because of marshland flora) and to their east is Barrow itself on the Northampton Sands escarpment overlooking *Rutmore*. The line of this northern frontier apparently continued into Greetham where we find *Budborow*. Both *Budborow* and Ranksborough have OE personal names as their first elements, perhaps indicative of secondary pagan Anglo-Saxon burials in existing prehistoric grave mounds.

In the east of the county, no names with *beorg* survive. It may be that the intensive farming of its good, light soils from the Romano-British period onwards early destroyed its barrows. But barrows do survive as crop marks. When the crop marks of ring-ditches are plotted, we again find the expected few scattered in the inland parishes: however, the vast majority lines the county boundary in the low-lying parishes of Essendine, Ryhall, Ketton and Tixover. More appear on the boundary in Lyddington, Beaumont Chase, Whissendine, Teigh and Greetham on those stretches of the ancient frontier already traced.[9]

Surviving barrows are few but where they do survive, they too relate to Rutland's frontiers. Hence, in the south-west, burial mounds overlook Eye Brook at Wardley and in the extreme south-west corner of Ridlington parish. The burial mound at Barrow survived into the twentieth century as did the mound on the border at Essendine. Significantly, that at Essendine relates to a triple-ditched linear earthwork of the Bronze Age which forms the county boundary there.

There are obvious problems and pitfalls in evaluating the various types of evidence drawn upon in analysing the barrows pattern and to avoid overburdening this introduction, they are itemized elsewhere in this study.[10] However, all in all, it may be tentatively argued that barrows once defined the borders of a territory which we recognize as Rutland.[11] These barrows were old when the Anglo-Saxons migrated. There would have been no need to create, define and proclaim a new territory under the Pax Romana in Rome's province of Britannia, so we must look back at least to the Iron Age for the erection of these grave mounds. However, Iron Age barrows are extremely rare and special in this country, virtually unknown in the Midlands. The era of the barrow was the Bronze Age and it must therefore be proposed that as a territory, Rutland originated during that period. Such a proposition is not unreasonable. An important parallel is the Bronze Age territory recently recognized near Scarborough, where Bronze Age barrows were erected. in immediate relationship with a Bronze Age linear earthwork to signal the limits of a land-unit.[12]

In pagan Ireland it was believed that a dead ancestor maintained an interest in the possession of the territory of his descendants; future claimants were therefore instructed to enter their lands over the barrows of the dead who lay upon the boundaries.[13] It may be that the dead Rutland chieftains of the Bronze Age were thought to protect their erstwhile homeland by their very presence and the motives which caused their people to erect their grave mounds on its boundaries were both to proclaim the territory and to defend it.

Archaeologists no longer argue in terms of waves of Iron Age invaders into this island displacing resident Bronze Age peoples, but rather view Bronze Age and Iron Age technologies and styles as being absorbed by an indigenous population which remained in place from the advent of the first Neolithic farmers to this island, through Bronze Age, Iron Age, Roman and sub-Roman Britain to their displacement and absorption by Anglo-Saxon newcomers.[14] Colin Renfrew summarizes such modern perspectives succinctly:

'Archaeologists today are much more inclined to think in terms of models of interaction, where contact between neighbouring and politically independent communities proved influential for the development of customs and beliefs. Such peer-polity interactions were probably responsible for the development of the networks of contacts which facilitated the custom of using beaker drinking vessels as prestige objects around 2300 BC. This is seen today as a more acceptable explanation than migrations of 'Beaker Folk', for which in reality there is no good evidence.

In recent years the earlier view that the British Isles were profoundly influenced in the Iron Age by a series of migrations from the continent has been almost universally abandoned. There is no good archaeological evidence for such migrations, although there were clearly important cross-channel political and trading contacts which had significant effects. The local insular development of the British variant of the La Tène art style no doubt came about through the effect on the islanders and their smiths of the prestige objects in the La Tène style which were traded to Britain. It is not necessary to go further than this.'[15]

Such continuity in prehistoric population reinforces the notion of continuity of territories and thus of territorial boundaries.

It must be stressed, however, that detailed research needs to be undertaken on the field-names and archaeology of the boundary parishes in the counties marching *with* Rutland before the premise suggested here can be substantiated. But at present the notion of Rutland's origin being of Bronze Age date looks promising.

Of course, no identifiable place-names survive from such antiquity. In fact, apart from the barrows, only a poor scatter of axeheads and two founders' hoards are known from the Bronze Age in Rutland, except that at Glaston were discovered Bronze Age beakers, a cup, an urn and potsherds in the same sand pit which

produced the pagan Anglo-Saxon inhumation cemetery there.[16] The
Iron Age has provided only a little more. During excavations
preceding the creation of Empingham Reservoir, now Rutland
Water, two domestic sites were found in the valley to the west of
Empingham, while at Thistleton, coins, pottery and the earliest
phase of the border shrine already mentioned may date from
before the Roman conquest of Britain.[17] But no great Iron Age
oppidum such as that beyond the Leicestershire border at Burrough
on the Hill is known. If, as Phythian-Adams argues, Rutland may
have been the territory of an Iron Age tribal unit, an obvious site
for its *caput* would have been the hill of Hambleton at the head of
the Empingham valley, but nothing earlier than Roman pottery has
been identified there to date.[18]

3.   THE ROMAN CONQUEST
AND ROMANO-BRITISH RUTLAND

The arrival of the Romans initiated developments which made a
lasting mark on the territory. In particular, the roads which the
Romans built were to dictate the pattern of the pagan Anglo-Saxon
settlement of Rutland and consequently, the pattern of place-names
which survives today.[19] In the north-east, Ermine Street slices
through the angle of the county, entering it south-west of Stamford
and leaving in the north at Stretton (OE *stræt-tūn* 'the farmstead on
the Roman road'). In what is now Greetham parish, Sewstern Lane
branched from Ermine Street north-west to cross the border at
Thistleton. From Sewstern Lane at Thistleton, a road led
westwards past Market Overton, Teigh and Whissendine to meet the
Fosse Way at Syston in Leicestershire. In the extreme south of the
county, a road branching east from Gartree Road at Medbourne cut
through Caldecott parish before crossing R. Welland to join Ermine
Street at Durobrivae (Water Newton).

Two more roads are indicated, one discovered from crop
marks and the other postulated from field- and minor names. A
stretch of road has been photographed from the air in the south of
Ketton parish, following the line of the river valley towards Tixover.
Presumably it ran south from the Roman town at Great Casterton
to serve the complex of villas in Tixover parish. Whether it crossed
R. Welland is uncertain but wooden piles, possibly part of the
structure of an ancient bridge, have been observed in the river at

Tixover at SP 971 996.[20]

A further Roman road may well have run from Ermine Street south through Empingham, Normanton, Edith Weston, North Luffenham, Morcott and Barrowden to cross R. Welland at Turtle Bridge. Names with OE *stræt*, a word used in place-names chiefly to distinguish such a road, occur in Barrowden, Morcott and North Luffenham.

It is of interest to note that modern parish boundaries relate only minimally to the known lines of Roman roads. This perhaps indicates that, especially in the north and east of the territory, these land-units may be of pre-Roman origin. Only at the eastern edge of Thistleton and at the south of Stretton are there significant co-incidences. At Thistleton, the county/parish boundary runs along Ermine Street. In the west of the parish, the county/parish limit marches for a little way with Sewstern Lane. These conformities lend support to the suggestion made above (note 11) that in the Anglo-Saxon period, an ancient frontier on the Teigh, Barrow, Greetham line was pushed north to embrace the land of Market Overton, Thistleton, Stretton and Clipsham. The Thistleton bounds and a southern stretch of those of Stretton postdate the Roman roads. The only other internal modern parish limit which follows Ermine Street is a short stretch between Horn and that northern portion of Empingham which now embraces Hardwick. Clearly some redrawing of boundaries has taken place here too, possibly following the later demise as settlements of Horn and Hardwick which are both now deserted medieval villages.

It is also interesting to note the comparative sizes of Rutland parishes.[21] Those of the north-eastern half of the county are in general more extensive than those of the south-western half. This perhaps reflects both the survival of Romano-British or earlier land-units in the north-east and a combination of the dismember-ment of early estates (such as seems to have taken place in the Ayston, Wing, Bisbrooke, Glaston area) and the difficult assarting of the forested west and south-west of the territory.

A Roman fort was early established at Great Casterton on Ermine Street and another at Market Overton at the northern end of the Cottesmore Upland escarpment beside the road running west to the Fosse Way. An important civil settlement developed beside the Great Casterton fort and eventually superseded it, while another settlement was encouraged to grow at the junction of the western

road with Sewstern Lane at Thistleton. It was in the north-eastern
half of the territory served by the road system that the villa estates
were established, farming the good, light, easily worked soils on the
limestone. Villas are known at Ryhall, Great Casterton, Tinwell,
Ketton, Tixover (2), Empingham (2), Whitwell, Clipsham and
Thistleton, while another is probable at Essendine. A kiln at
Greetham indicates an undiscovered habitation site there too.
Scatters of Roman pottery show that much other land in the county
was being worked during this period.[22] Hence, along the western
road, Roman pottery occurs in Market Overton, Teigh and
Whissendine parishes. On the Cottesmore Upland it is found in
Barrow, Cottesmore and Burley. The important site of Hambleton
has also produced such pottery, as has Oakham. To these can be
added spreads in the fields of Pilton and Barrowden. Clearly the
soils of the Northampton Sands and marlstone of the Middle Lias
were also attractive to Romano-British farmers. The late
Romano-British inhumation burial at Glaston and the coin hoard
from Uppingham are also on the ironstone of the Northampton
Sands. Only the forested south-west of Rutland has to date
produced no indication of Romano-British settlement and
exploitation.

With so much evidence for the widespread cultivation of the
territory's soils, it is surprising that so little survives of the place-
names of pre-Anglian Rutland. Only the river-names Chater, Glen
and Welland are extant from this period. It is significant that the
names of the two important Romano-British settlements at Great
Casterton and Thistleton are lost and that no words taken directly
from Latin, such as *camp, ecles, funta* and *wīc* (in the compound
wīc-hām), are found in Rutland place-names.[23] Nor are there any
place-names with OE *walh* 'a Briton' to signify a surviving Celtic
population.[24] The Anglo-Saxon settlement of Rutland appears to
have been heavy, with Old English replacing comprehensively any
other languages used formerly in the territory. Place-name evidence
for Romano-British/Anglo-Saxon contact is minimal.

4.   THE ANGLO-SAXON SETTLEMENT
                AND THE MIDDLE ANGLIAN KINGDOM

It is believed that the first major presence of Germanic peoples in this country dates from the early fifth century AD with the planned settlement of *foederati* or *laeti* within the Roman and sub-Roman framework of Britain. As friendly barbarians, they protected the eastern parts of the island against hostile incursions of their own kind in return for land to farm. It is suggested that the recruitment of such Germanic mercenaries continued long after 410 AD when the British were advised to take measures for their own defence. Two kinds of archaeological materials especially have been proposed as the earliest evidence for such a presence. One is the so-called Romano-Saxon pottery, mass-produced wheel-thrown ware decorated in Germanic taste;[25] the other is a developed form of provincial Roman military gear in Germanic style which archaeologists term late military metalwork.[26]

Three sites in Rutland have produced such materials. At the Roman villa at Clipsham were discovered both Romano-Saxon pottery and late Roman provincial military equipment. From the excavation of the villa at Great Casterton has come Romano-Saxon pottery dated to post- 375, while in the pagan Anglo-Saxon cemetery at North Luffenham (in use from c400), late military metalwork was also found.[27] Two of the land-units where this material was discovered developed names in *hām*, an early Anglo-Saxon habitation-name type discussed below, while all three sites are directly related to the network of Roman roads.

Of course, we cannot be certain that the users of the Romano-Saxon ware and the provincial military gear were Anglo-Saxons: but with pagan Anglo-Saxon burials, we are on surer ground. Six cemeteries have been discovered in Rutland, five in parishes lying on known Roman roads.[28] At Great Casterton, a town site occupied into the fifth century AD, the cemetery outside the north-west ramparts contained not only late Romano-British inhumations but also Anglo-Saxon cremation burials in urns and inhumations. *The Urns*, a field-name here of 1876, may record a further lost cremation cemetery. Beside the fortified Roman site at Market Overton, two Anglo-Saxon cemeteries have been found about 400 yards apart, one with inhumations only and one with both cremations and inhumations. At Empingham, another two cemeteries have been excavated, one of which, dating from the sixth through to the early seventh century, contained 132 graves. Both were closely related to the villa sites in Empingham parish, one spreading on each side of a Roman boundary ditch. At North

Luffenham, an important early mixed rite cemetery is known, in use from c400 to the end of the sixth century. This contained the buckles and harness equipment of late military type specified above. Only at Glaston is a pagan Anglo-Saxon cemetery, in this case of the inhumation rite, not related to a Roman road for which there is physical or toponymic evidence; but as we have seen, the soils of this parish were long cultivated as the Bronze Age finds mentioned earlier and the late Romano-British inhumation burial towards the east testify.[29] There once must have been a minor route (roughly on the line of the modern A47 road) along the inter-fluvial ridge through Glaston to Uppingham, itself an early settlement site where a Roman coin hoard and a gold coin of Arcadius (395-408 AD) have been found.

There are also isolated finds in the county which nevertheless may represent pagan Anglo-Saxon cemeteries. From the Cottesmore Upland, north of what was once heavy woodland in the Burley/Exton area, are urns from Barrow, Cottesmore and Burley parishes. A solitary urn is known from the north of Essendine parish, while as recently as 1988, an Anglo-Saxon urn and inhumation burial have been discovered at Seaton, a settlement close to the old crossing of R. Welland at Turtle Bridge.

What is clear is that these pagan Anglo-Saxon burial sites are closely related to the network of Roman roads, to the Romano-British settlements, to the long-cultivated soils of the Northampton Sands formations and to those of the Lincolnshire Limestone. The Anglo-Saxons appear to have settled in Rutland within a recognized Romano-British framework.

The pattern of Rutland place-names is illuminating and this pattern is overwhelmingly of Anglo-Saxon creation. An analysis of place-names appearing in Old English records to 730 AD indicates that of those surviving in Rutland, the following may be considered to be very early: habitation names in *hām* 'a village, an estate' and nature names in *dūn* 'a large hill'.[30] Place-names in which *-inga-*, the genitive plural of the folk-name-forming suffix *-ingas*, is compounded (especially as *-ingahām*) may be only slightly later than these.[31]

In the east on Ermine Street and Sewstern Lane are Clipsham and Greetham, while Luffenham (the present parishes of North and South Luffenham no doubt represent a former single land-unit) lies on the postulated Roman road running south to Turtle Bridge.[32]

Two names with -inga-, Empingham (from -ingahām) and Tinwell (from -ingawella) also lie on these roads. Uppingham (again from -ingahām) seems isolated, but an original large estate with a name in hām, i.e. Thornham, appears to have lain to its north and east.[33] The Glaston pagan Anglo-Saxon cemetery may have related to this lost estate. Clipsham, Empingham and Tinwell are also villa locations, while Greetham has a Roman kiln which probably represents an as yet undiscovered Romano-British habitation site. The three Rutland names in dūn, Hambleton, Lyndon and Barrowden, march with parishes with names in hām. Hambleton, of course, may well have been the location of the Anglian caput of the entire territory. Ketton is also early. With its name probably based on a pre-Anglian root, this parish lies astride the Great Casterton to Tixover Roman road and is surrounded by names in hām, dūn and -inga-.

The comparatively small parishes of Normanton and Edith Weston (which shall be returned to later), long and narrow east to west, no doubt comprised or were part of a divided earlier land-unit. It was here that an offshoot of the ancient folk-group, the Hwicce, may have been settled. Their name seems to be recorded in Witchley Warren in Edith Weston and in that of the former Witchley Wapentake. This supposed enclave of the Hwicce was on the Roman road south to Turtle Bridge and its location is surrounded by a cluster of Rutland's earliest English place-names. Another place-name possibly based on the folk-name Hwicce is Whissendine in the north-west. Together with the local Wichley Leys, it is located on the Roman road which ran westwards from the major Romano-British settlement at Thistleton to the Fosse Way at Syston in Leicestershire. Whissendine parish is sited on the attractive soils of the Middle Lias formation and scattered Roman pottery there indicates that it was exploited early. The designation Hwicce is obscure, but it is a very ancient type of folk-name. It has no English cognate and it may well date back to the pre-migration period. The Hwicce seem in the main to have been an Anglian folk who eventually moved by way of the Avon valley into Worcestershire and north Gloucestershire.[34] They were settled in the Cotswolds following 577 and by c660 were named in the Tribal Hidage as tributary to the Mercian kings. By c680, a bishopric was created for them at Worcester. It is likely that small groups of the Hwicce settled very early in Rutland via its Roman road network.

In Northamptonshire, another enclave of this folk may have been located at Whiston, close to the Roman road which ran south-westwards from Durobrivae (Water Newton) through Irchester.[35]

Also in the north-west of Rutland, two more place-names may be identified as early; these are Oakham and Langham. Oakham is most probably a name in *hām*, although *hamm* 'a water meadow' is just possible, while Langham may be compounded with either *hamm* or *hām*. The narrow strip of Barleythorpe parish was probably carved from Oakham's lands. Hence Whissendine, Langham and Oakham originally formed an early contiguous series, while Oakham was eventually separated from Hambleton by Egleton whose name is of the late manorial type. This estate may have been carved from Hambleton's territory in the tenth or eleventh century after Hambleton had lost its old status as the *caput* of Rutland. Given the position of the Romano-British villas at Empingham and Whitwell and the rubbish pit containing Roman pottery found at Oakham, together with Oakham's early Old English name-type, it seems reasonable to suppose that at least a local road of the Roman period led from Empingham westward between the high ground of Burley and Hambleton to Oakham, presumably on the line of the modern A606, although no evidence for such a road has survived physically or in local field-names.

Of the nature names in the north-eastern half of the county, those with *wella* 'a spring, a stream' as their generics may be slightly later than place-names with *hām* and *dūn*.[36] A case in point is Tinwell, a name formed with -*inga*-, a structure also thought to belong to names a little later than those in *hām*.[37] Ashwell and Whitwell may belong here too. However, the other nature names such as Barrow, Cottesmore, Horn, Essendine, Ryhall and Tixover could well have been created in the earliest phase of the Anglo-Saxon settlement. Essendine, Ryhall and Tixover are all sites of Roman villa estates.

Three Rutland parishes have names with the generic *cot* 'a cottage, a shelter'. A.H. Smith suggests of *cot* that 'it would appear to belong to the late OE period.'[38] The element certainly does not figure as a generic in names appearing before c730.[39] However, as habitation sites with names in *cot* were obviously once unimportant, it is unsurprising that the element should not appear as a generic in the place-names of the early charters and in those recording sites of early important events. But it is noteworthy that all three Rutland examples which are now the names of parishes are located on Roman roads and all were vills in the Domesday Survey. Tickencote and Morcott march with land-units with names in *dūn*, *hām* and *-inga-*. Caldecott is a special instance; it was 'a shelter for travellers' at a time when the Roman road upon which it stands still functioned as a viable route.

It is probable that settlement names in *worð* 'an enclosure' belong to the eighth century and later.[40] Although frequent in OE charters, they do not appear before c730. The only name of this type surviving as a parish in Rutland is Pickworth in the far northeast of the county. It borders Clipsham, Greetham, Ryhall and the *territorium* of the Romano-British town at Casterton and is compounded with an OE personal name Pīca which is of the early monothematic type. The minor name Littleworth in Belton is not recorded until very late and if not simply an uncomplimentary nickname may date only from the development of Belton itself with the ·clearance of woodland at the Rutland boundary. A similar name to these is Teigh, which is OE *tēag* 'a close, a small enclosure'. To which settlement this enclosure originally related and at which date it was established are debatable. Presumably it originated after *Rutmore* became firmly a part of Rutland at a time when the ancient frontier was moved further to the north. This territorial adjustment may date to the dominion of the eponymous Rōta.

Nothing historically is known of Rōta, at what date he lived or whether he was a king or an important land-holding thegn. Certainly, no other land-unit of such size in England is named after one man and such a phenomenon implies a degree of greatness. However, one or two observations can be made from such crumbs of evidence that have survived. The personal name of Rōta is of the early monothemàtic type. It was in the later Anglo-Saxon period that it was normal for the aristocracy to use dithematic names such as Æðelstān of Ayston and Ecgwulf of Egleton. The monothematic names continued in use into the later Anglo-Saxon period, but the fact that Rōta does not survive as a figure in Anglo-Saxon records of any sort must favour an early date for him, and his name-type also accords with an early date.

It is reasonable to assume that *Rutmore*, a marshy moorland which extended from the north-east of Whissendine to the escarpment of the Northampton Sands ironstone at Market Overton, took its name from this Rōta. It is also reasonable to assume that the name *Rutmore* was created by Anglo-Saxons living beyond the northern frontier, that is to say Rōta was recognized outside his territory as a wielder of power. This was a portion of the Rutland boundary specifically associated with him. It has been suggested in the discussion of names in *beorg* above, that the northern boundary was moved further northwards from the Teigh, Barrow, Greetham line early in the Anglo-Saxon period to absorb the important market site of Overton/Thistleton and the iron-working industrial complexes in Thistleton and Clipsham. It is precisely north of the ancient frontier from *Rutmore* eastwards that the nucleus of the northern group of place-names in *tūn* is situated. We can date such names roughly to the eighth century AD and later.[41] It is only here, too, that parish boundaries make use of the lines of the Roman roads, indicating a redrawing of the limits of more ancient land-units which predated the routes of these roads. It would seem that to move a territorial boundary for such accruing benefits implies an overlord with significant military muscle at a time when Anglo-Saxon territories were fragmented and unstable.

If he were an independent minor king, it is difficult to believe that Rōta could have exercised enough power to move a border during the reign of Offa (757-796) or in that of the earlier Penda (c632-654) or at any time during the supremacy of Mercia. Perhaps, tentatively, one may suggest that Rōta was a minor king among the early Middle Angles who held sway in the sixth or early seventh century and who refashioned his northern frontier for economic advantage in unsettled times. It may be, as we shall see, that it was he who, in the period before the rise of Mercia, made such provision for that defence of the territory which some minor names and the locations of some boundary defensive earthworks hint at, so that his land assumed his name in perpetuity.

Place-names with generics in *tūn* 'a farmstead', later 'an estate', and *lēah* 'a clearing in woodland' are the commonest of all in England. They belong especially to the eighth century, to a time when the Anglo-Saxons were expanding from areas of ancient cultivation and earliest settlement into land which needed major clearance for exploitation.[42] Place-names with *tūn* and *lēah* continued to be coined, however, until the end of the Anglo-Saxon period and in the case of *tūn*, certainly, for some time after the Norman Conquest.[43] A particular category, that in which *tūn* is compounded with the connective particle -*ing*- and a personal name as first element, giving the sense 'farmstead or estate named from or associated with *x*', may be particularly assigned to the eighth and ninth centuries since place-names of this type can be related to a number of identified historical personages of this period.[44]

The distribution of place-names in *tūn* in Rutland, with a few scattered exceptions, shows two well-defined groupings.[45] The principal spread is in the south-western quarter of the county, away from the areas of known Romano-British exploitation. A smaller group of names in *tūn* lies in the north on the Northampton Sands ironstone of the Cottesmore Upland. There are also isolated examples in the east which appear *not* to be the result of an expansion of land use.

The three parishes in the north of the county with names in *tūn* were vills in the Domesday Survey and thus of some importance. They are Market Overton, Thistleton and Stretton. It is probably significant that these constitute with Clipsham just that territory north of the postulated ancient border line of Teigh, Barrow, Greetham which it has been suggested was acquired for Rutland earlier in the Anglo-Saxon period. Redrawing of boundaries has certainly taken place with reference to the Roman roads here and these names in *tūn* no doubt represent a change in the fashion of naming settlements rather than indicating colonization of new land. After all, Market Overton/Thistleton had been an important strong point, trading and industrial centre, although the thistles growing on the phosphates produced by the rubbish of early house sites indicate that at least in Thistleton, the early occupation area had been abandoned. As well as the major names in *tūn* of these two parishes, in Market Overton were also two farmsteads with geographically related, late names in *tūn* recorded only in the fourteenth century, *Norton* and *Southton*, while in Thistleton was an *Islington*, documented for the first time as late as 1633. This may represent another lost settlement in *tūn*. In Clipsham is *Harton* 'farmstead on the boundary', recorded initially in 1687. South of the ancient northern frontier, but still on the Cottesmore Upland, is the lost *Wenton* in the north of Cottesmore parish, possibly another renamed early habitation site. However, Exton (with Burley, to which we shall return later) does seem to record the clearance of ancient woodland at the southern end of the plateau of Northampton Sands ironstone. Part of this woodland survived as the medieval hunting park of Barnsdale.

In the far east of the county, the modern parishes of Great and Little Casterton represent the small *territorium* of the former defended Romano-British township.[46] The old British name must have fallen out of use with the demise of town life there and, while recognizing the *cæster*, the Anglo-Saxons renamed the land-unit as a *tūn* in the current fashion. The small settlement at Geeston in Ketton may also represent a renamed habitation site in an area of ancient and continuing cultivation.

West of Ketton and still in the east of the county are two other important names in *tūn*, Normanton and Edith Weston. They are later in date than all of the names in *tūn* so far discussed and must be returned to in due course. Suffice it to say at this point that they appear together to represent a former single land-unit, possibly one defining that group of the Hwicce recorded by Witchley Warren in Edith Weston. Here, either *tūn* replaced the name of an earlier estate or the Normanton/Edith Weston land block was cut out of Hambleton itself.

It is unsafe to attempt a relative chronology of the creation of the names in *tūn* in the south-west quarter of the county. Certainly these names do not represent a uniformly progressive movement south-westwards and westwards through ancient woodlands to the territorial boundaries. The establishment of Ayston is known from the only Anglo-Saxon charter with bounds to survive for Rutland. Here at least we have the sure date of 1046 AD. The personal name compounded in Ayston, Æðelstān, as would be expected, is of the later dithematic type. Ayston is thus strictly an estate of the late manorial kind. Three other parishes have names which indicate that they also belong to a time earlier or later in the development of manorial organization. These are Lyddington, Ridlington and Egleton. Lyddington, with its outlying *stoc* 'dairy farm' at Stoke Dry above the pastures of Eye Brook, and Ridlington were both major settlements. Both appear to have names in *-ingtūn* 'estate named after or associated with *x*'. Ridlington was a royal vill at the time of the Domesday Survey (together with Hambleton and Oakham), having seven dependent outliers. Its compounded personal name Rēdel is a shortened form of the later dithematic names in Rēd-/Ræd-, while Hlyda of Lyddington is a personal name of the earlier monothematic type. Egleton appears to be a manorial name in *tūn* which parallels

Ayston in formation. It is perhaps significant that Egleton lies between the probable early Anglian *caput* of Rutland at Hambleton and the later royal vill of Oakham. It may once have been part of a great Hambleton estate which was subdivided to form also Normanton and later Edith Weston. Tentatively one could assign Ridlington and Lyddington to the ninth century, before the Scandinavian incursions, while the name at least of Egleton may well belong to the eleventh century with Ayston. The origin of Egleton as an estate, of course, may be earlier.

Three of the names in *tūn* in the south-west are formed with the earlier monothematic type of OE personal name in the genitive singular. They are Braunston, Manton and the lost *Snelston* in Caldecott, the *tūnas* of Brant, Manna and Snell respectively. Braunston on its tiny patch of marlstone soil, with its forest shrine to the ancient mother goddess and its pre-Saxon quern find[47] evidently had a Romano-British (or earlier) antecedent of some kind, but *Snelston* is likely to have been an assart in well-wooded country on the south-western boundary. Manton, however, may also be a renaming, this of an earlier *Luffewyke*, an old outlying *wīc* 'dairy farm' of the Luffa of Luffenham, two miles to the east. Above R. Welland in the south is Seaton, probably containing the personal name *Sæga*, a shortened form of later dithematic names such as Sægeat and Sægeard. Between the old settlements of Barrowden and Uppingham, Seaton stands on an outcropping of the valued soils of the Northampton Sands ironstone and again may well be a manorially renamed early settlement. A Roman brooch was found near the rectory[48] which suggests a settlement hereabouts at least as early as the period of the pagan Anglo-Saxons. Pilton, on the clays of the valley of R. Chater, appears to be a new farm whose land was carved from the original territory of Lyndon. Preston, 'the estate of the priests', the revenues of which were set aside for the endowment of clergy, obviously postdates the conversion to Christianity of the Middle Angles c653 AD, but at just what date its name was given we cannot know. Belton on the Boulder Clay of the west but also with glacial sands and gravels, whose name may simply record an open space in woodland, seems to have retained its original toponym.

The only other major place-name in *tūn* in Rutland is Glaston. This is of late formation. Its compounded personal-name appears to be a Norwegian Glaðr and for this reason will be discussed principally in relation to the Scandinavian settlements in the Midlands following the apportioning of land in the region by a Viking army in 877.

As a generic in the names of settlements, *lēah* 'woodland, a woodland glade, a clearing in woodland' occurs only three times in Rutland.[49] Burley represents a major stretch of woodland, probably related to an early royal *burh* on the hill at Hambleton. Leighfield on the county's western boundary was originally a simplex place-name in *lēah*, here also meaning 'woodland'. As tree clearance progressed, *feld* 'open country' was suffixed to *lēah*. The village of Leigh barely survived into the post-medieval period but its earth-works lie beside Leigh Lodge. Wardley, again on the county boundary, probably represents 'a woodland glade' or 'a clearing'. Its first element may be OE *weard* 'watch' so that the site high on its hillside could have originated as a border look-out place against incursions from the west. All three names appear to be no later than the eighth century AD. A concentration of minor names in *lēah* lies in a narrow band from Leighfield across to Lyddington. Only at Prestley Hill in Lyddington is there any other indication of a habitation, since the earliest form surviving, that of 1249, records one Willelmus de Presteley. This *lēah* was 'the woodland of the priests', revenues of which were set aside for the endowment of clergy, as were those of Preston a little to the north.

Only two other OE parish names remain to be commented upon in this south-western half of the county, Brooke and Bisbrooke. As a place-name-forming element, *brōc* 'a stream' does not appear in documents before c730. The word used as a generic to denote a stream in recorded early place-names was *burna*.[50] Thus both of these names fall into the general pattern of later OE place-names in the south-western half of Rutland. But it is possible that both of these parish names in *brōc* are the result of renaming processes. Bisbrooke may well have been part of a larger land-unit comprising at least itself, Glaston and Wing, perhaps the *Thornham* of *þornham broc* in the Ayston Charter bounds of 1046. Glaston's Bronze Age, Romano-British and pagan Anglo-Saxon burials certainly indicate that it had desirable soils for early farmers and a *hām* in this area would be unsurprising. That Glaston contains a Norwegian personal name suggests the land's continuing popularity after the Scandinavian arrivals. Bisbrooke marches too, it should be noted, with manorial Ayston with its own possibly redrawn boundaries. Brooke similarly has common bounds with both a manorial Egleton and a Scandinavian Gunthorpe. Martins-thorpe which also borders Brooke may itself be a renaming, that of OE *Martines-stoc 'Martin's outlying secondary settlement'. It is interesting to speculate on the location of Martin's lost *primary* settlement in this area. Whether Martinsthorpe, Gunthorpe and Brooke formerly constituted a land-unit with dispersed habitation sites which was later divided is impossible to say, but at least there seems to be a similarity with the Bisbrooke, Glaston, Wing grouping in relation to a parish name in *brōc.*

In summary, the older OE place-names belong in general to the north-eastern half of Rutland where are found the material remains of the Roman and Romano-British exploitation of the ter-ritory. The younger OE place-names belong to the south-western half of the county where one finds a complex combination of the toponymic results of the later development of less desirable soils and more difficult terrain and some renaming of prized lands which had long been farmed.

5. THE FRONTIERS AND DEFENCES OF
THE ANGLIAN KINGDOM

It is suggested above that as a territory, Rutland has existed with only minor changes to its frontiers since the Bronze Age. If, as seems to be the case, Rutland formed for some time an independ-ent Anglian kingdom with its *caput* at Hambleton, it is reasonable to suppose that its early Anglo-Saxon rulers took measures for the protection of its frontiers and that evidence for such measures may survive both physically on the ground in the form of fortified sites and in the place-names of the border parishes. Lack of excavation of Rutland's border earthworks is a problem, of course, since later development of a particular site may have disguised its original nature.

Such may be the case of the *Moorhall* in Whissendine in the far north-west. Here survive the imposing earthen defences of a medieval manor house referred to in documents from the early fourteenth century.[51] However, it is located on low-lying ground near the northern border, at the opening of a north-facing valley and immediately to the west of the beginning of the marshy

Rutmore, the natural frontier barrier which stretched across Teigh parish to the escarpment of the Cottesmore Upland. It is an odd place for a late domestic site to be positioned but would make sense as an original Anglo-Saxon fortification protecting the frontier and guarding against an inroad to the west of the marshland. It may be paralleled in the north-east corner of the Rutland triangle by the fortified site at Essendine which also survives as a medieval earthwork. Beside the *Moorhall*, a Bronze Age barrow signals the more ancient demarcation. In Whissendine also is an unlocated field-name *Chester*. This may be a very late use of OE *ceaster* 'an old fortification' relating to a once recognized defensive position on the border here.

In Teigh, *Rutmore* formed a natural barrier. Bronze Age border barrows lie beside it. But here again there is evidence of a fortified Anglo-Saxon border strongpoint in *Burstall' medewe* of the late thirteenth century, from OE *burh-stall* 'the site of a fortification'.

Barrow on the Cottesmore Upland to the east of Teigh may be the line of the ancient frontier which Rōta himself, perhaps, moved further north. At the eastern end of Barrow parish is Bussack (Barn) which could be the modern reflex of the *Burghsyk'* recorded here from 1294 onwards. This was another OE *burh* 'a fortified place'. Bussack Barn at the northern boundary of the parish used to stand on rising ground which slopes down to Roman Sewstern Lane about a mile to the east where it crossed into the original territory of Rutland. There was a small rectangular earthwork just to its south (marked on the Ordnance Survey 2½" map Sheet SK 91 of 1951). Sadly all is now levelled as part of the airfield runways of R.A.F. Cottesmore.

North of Barrow, Market Overton's northern boundary is the later march of Rutland. The Roman fort in which Market Overton church now stands has not been excavated. It was possibly reused as a frontier stronghold by the Anglo-Saxons to replace the *burh* in Barrow. Here too is *Wakehull* of 1363, OE *wacu-hyll* 'look-out hill, watch hill' overlooking Sewstern Lane where it crossed the new frontier, an easy route across dry upland into the territory from the north.

In Stretton, the refashioned northern frontier is recorded by Morkery (Leys), OE *mearc-rīð* 'boundary stream', with the first element later Scandinavianized to *mǫrk*, also meaning 'a boundary', while in Clipsham *Mott Close* of 1687 from ME *mote* 'a moat, a protective ditch, an embankment' may record an unlocated fortified site also on the later border.

At Pickworth we are back on the line of the ancient territorial boundary. The slight earthworks of Castle Dike here are now outside the county limits in Newell Wood, but the border at this point makes a plainly artificial right-angled detour to exclude the site from modern Rutland. The natural line of the boundary, however, makes Castle Dike an obvious fortification on Rutland's ancient limits. The earthworks (the original Pickworth?) are heavily overgrown and could be of Iron Age date, but an Anglo-Saxon strongpoint would fit perfectly at this point since the sites at *Moorhall* (Whissendine), Bussack (Barrow), Castle Dike and Essendine are roughly equidistant from each other across the extent of the earlier northern boundary which, topographically, is not strongly demarcated.

Essendine is the remaining fortified site on the northern frontier. The parish forms the north-eastern angle of the Rutland triangle. On high ground which falls sharply down to the territorial boundary are the earthworks of an impressive Norman motte and bailey castle.[52] But again, the position of this fortification is significant. Its location suggests that it had a predecessor thus sited as a border *burh* on a line which has little obvious physical demarcation. As at Whissendine's *Moorhall*, next to Essendine Castle there are Bronze Age barrows which once signalled the ancient frontier.

R. Gwash to its confluence with R. Welland and then R. Welland as far as Caldecott in the extreme south formed a natural boundary and barrier. Stamford's lands north of R. Welland were no doubt once part of the ancient territory of Rutland. Ermine Street crossed the river at this point on its stone-bottomed ford and one can reasonably expect there to have been an early Anglian strongpoint to command the crossing. It has not yet been discovered, however, but the subsequent development of the Danish borough indicates that the Scandinavians merely accepted and perhaps improved what was already to hand.

To the south-west, the next crossing point of the river, overlooked as it is by high ground, was at Turtle Bridge in Barrowden. Here the lost Roman road which ran south from Empingham via North Luffenham and Barrowden passed close to a hilltop used by wardens to guard against possible incursions from the south. Turtle Bridge, recorded as early as 1298, and its neighbouring *Tirtle Meare* seem both to derive from OE *tōt-hyll* 'a look-out hill', marking a site that parallels *Wakehull* in Market Overton beside Sewstern Lane in the north. In the south of Morcott parish, *Arberry Gate*, perhaps from OE *eorð-burh* 'a stronghold with ramparts of earth' and *Castle Thorns* may refer to a lost fortification commanding the road near its river crossing.

At Caldecott, Eye Brook flows from the north-west to form the territorial boundary as far as Belton. In Beaumont Chase, Castle Hill stands at the head of a valley rising from Eye Brook. The valley is a natural route for incursions from the south-west into the valued hinterlands of Uppingham, Ayston and Ridlington. At Castle Hill, on a promontory of the westward-facing escarpment, is a large motte and bailey castle; a few yards to the east is another concentric ditch across the same promontory, surviving only as a crop mark. This may not relate to the medieval stronghold.[53] As at Essendine, the site is a logical strongpoint for border defence and may well have had an early Anglo-Saxon origin.

Wardley commands a superb position on high ground looking westward across the valley of Eye Brook. As already suggested, it probably has OE *weard* 'watch, ward' as its first element and the village may have originated as a place in a woodland glade or clearing from which constant watch to the west and south could be kept. There is also in the parish a lost *Turtle Slade* which is formed from OE *tōt-hyll* 'a look-out hill', a feature already encountered in Barrowden.

The south-western point of Ridlington parish forms a spur of land that runs down to margin Eye Brook. A valley between this headland and the Wardley promontory reaches almost to Ridlington village itself. On the west side of the village is an oval enclosure defended by a bank and ditch.[54] Again this site is unexcavated, but one would favour an early Anglo-Saxon origin for an earthwork in this part of Rutland rather than one of Iron Age date. The stronghold fits into the pattern of Anglian border defences.

Adjoining Wardley is Belton which forms a small angle of land where Eye Brook turns west. The territorial boundary runs north from here across what was once inhospitable hill country covered by Boulder Clay and dense woodland. The first element of the name Belton is obscure, but it could be OE *bēl* 'a beacon fire' which would be appropriate to the settlement's siting on a carefully supervised frontier. Littleworth, here, may have been a defensive strongpoint.

North of Belton, the heavy forest would have prevented large-scale incursions from the west. However, at a point where R. Chater provided some access through forested land into Rutland and no doubt close to where the woodland ceased, *Toteshul,* now Twitch Hill, provided a fine vantage point. This is yet again OE *tōt-hyll* 'a look-out hill', another protective feature related to the Anglian kingdom's borders. North of this to Whissendine no other defensive sites, either recognized on the ground or recorded in place-names, survive. Even so, the weight of the evidence argues strongly for an early Anglian defended frontier for the whole of Rutland, which maintained the tradition of the respected and signalled boundary apparently established by the barrow builders of the Bronze Age.

6.   RUTLAND AND THE SCANDINAVIANS

We learn from the Anglo-Saxon Chronicle how in 877 a Danish army first apportioned the kingdom of Mercia: '*Þa on herfeste gefor se here on Myrcena land and hit gedældon sum and sum Ceolwulfe sealdon*'.[55] Ceolwulf II, an erstwhile thegn of Burgred, King of Mercia, had received temporary rule of the kingdom in 874 from the Danish host so that '*hit him gearo wære swa hwilce dæg swa hi hit habban woldon*'.[56] Following 877, the Scandinavians settled in the Mercian East Midlands north of Watling Street, especially in Lincolnshire, Leicestershire and Nottinghamshire and to a lesser extent in Derbyshire and Northamptonshire. The counties surrounding Rutland are notable for an impressive distribution of Scandinavian place-names. Especially relevant to the situation of Rutland are their concentrations in the east of Leicestershire and in the south-west of Lincolnshire.[57] What is remarkable is the dearth of Scandinavian settlement-names in Rutland itself.

Research published by Professor Kenneth Cameron between 1965 and 1971 established a relative chronology for Scandinavian settlement-name types.[58] The earliest, those representing the initial settlement by men from the Danish army, are the so-called Grimston-hybrids, place-names in which a Scandinavian personal name is compounded with OE *tūn.* Such a name indicates the appropriation of an already existing Anglo-Saxon estate by a Scandinavian and its renaming to reflect his ownership. Place-names

which have Scandinavian *bȳ* 'a farmstead, a village' as their generics
are later than the Grimston-hybrids and indicate Scandinavian
colonization. Many of the founders of these new settlements must
have come as immigrants during the space of two generations in
which Watling Street remained the demarcation between Scandinavian and Anglo-Saxon England. The land upon which settlements in *bȳ* were founded was often inferior to that occupied by
English-named villages and to those renamed as Grimston-hybrids.
The final stage of settlement-name creation with Scandinavian
generics is represented by place-names in *þorp* 'a dependent outlying
farmstead, a secondary settlement'. These belong to a period when
greater integration had taken place between Anglo-Saxons and
Scandinavians. Indeed, the personal names compounded with *þorp*
may be Scandinavian *or* Old English. Such settlements are usually
sited on the poorest soils. They were very much last-comers.

Rutland has no names strictly of the Grimston-hybrid type.
Glaston certainly is a compounding of the Scandinavian personal
name Glaðr with OE *tūn* but the personal name is Norwegian
rather than Danish. It is reasonable to assume that Glaðr was
closely associated with or descended from the Norwegians who
settled at Normanton. It is not necessary to suppose that Glaston
received its name immediately following the dispersal of the Danish
army in 877. In fact, it seems only to be part of the land of a
dismembered early Anglo-Saxon estate called *Thornham* which may
have comprised at least the present parishes of Glaston, Wing and
Bisbrooke. Wing, from Scandinavian. *vengi* 'a field', as its name
implies did not begin its existence as a settlement but was originally
part of something larger. It is possible that Glaston is a late manorial name. Of course, a man called Glaðr in the eleventh century,
if that was when *Thornham* was split up, need not necessarily have
been a Scandinavian. The C and D versions of the Anglo-Saxon
Chronicle for the year 1004 tell us that Ulfcytel, who bore a Scandinavian name, was recognized by the Danes as one of their most
formidable opponents.

Normanton does represent the settlement of Scandinavians in
Rutland, but these were Norwegians rather than Danes. The place-
name is English rather than Scandinavian, however, and indicates
that these Norwegians were notable within an Anglo-Saxon population. It may be significant that their settlement was established
beside Hambleton, the old Anglian *caput* of the territory. Indeed, it

seems possible that Normanton was carved out of a larger Hambleton than now exists and originally comprised the land of the present parishes of Normanton *and* Edith Weston. Both lie on the attractive soils produced by the Northampton Sands ironstone as does Hambleton itself. That Normanton was so located suggests that the Norwegians on arrival were in a position to dictate their choice of land.[59]

There are no major place-names in *bȳ* representing the colonization phase of Scandinavian settlement to be found in the territory. There is a lost *Birchaby* recorded from 1624 in Belton parish in what was woodland immediately on the county boundary with strongly Scandinavian Leicestershire. Here the first element appears to be OE *bryce* 'land newly broken up for cultivation'. Such a hybrid is likelier to represent the impact of the Scandinavian language from beyond the border rather than colonization. *Birchaby* was never more than a farmstead in any case, and even so there is some doubt whether this is indeed a name in *bȳ* rather than one in *lēah* 'a clearing in woodland' and whether one has OE *birce* 'a birch tree' as the specific rather than *bryce*.

Hooby (Lodge) lies in Stretton parish in the north of the county close to heavily Scandinavian-settled Lincolnshire. Again the initial recording is late, here 1633. If this name is not a family name, which it well may be, then it is another hybrid, with OE *hōh* 'a spur of land' as the specific. But as with *Birchaby*, even if this is a place-name, it is likelier to represent linguistic impact from beyond the border rather than the settlement of Danish colonists; and again as with *Birchaby*, Hooby has never been more than an isolated farmstead.

There are fourteen thorpes recorded in the county, but only five of these appear as vills in the Domesday Survey.[60] These are the lost *Alsthorpe* in Burley, Belmesthorpe in Ryhall, Sculthorpe in North Luffenham, Tolethorpe in Little Casterton and Thorpe by Water. Only Belmesthorpe and Thorpe by Water survive as modern villages. The latter seems never to have had its own church: its inhabitants attended the church at Lyddington from which estate the land of Thorpe by Water was taken. The personal names compounded in the Domesday Survey thorpes are OE (E)alhstān (*Alsthorpe*) and Beornhelm (Belmesthorpe), Scandinavian Skúli (Sculthorpe) and Tóli (Tolethorpe). Thus the personal names are balanced equally between Old English and Scandinavian origins, reflecting the formation of the place-names in a period of integration. Barleythorpe, Gunthorpe and Martinsthorpe survive as modern parishes, although Martinsthorpe is now only the territory of a deserted medieval village. As noted above, its name appears to be a late refashioning of OE *Martines-stoc 'Martin's outlying farmstead', so that Scandinavian þorp may simply have replaced OE stoc of similar meaning. Its forms with þorp do not appear until thirty years after those with stoc. Gunthorpe at the edge of a tiny patch of ironstone soil, a name compounded with the Scandinavian personal name Gunni, is also unrecorded until the beginning of the thirteenth century. So is Barleythorpe at the margin of the marlstone, originally a simplex name in þorp, whose land appears to have been taken from Oakham's before Oakham became a royal vill. The remaining thorpes are grouped principally around the Danish borough of Stamford. They too are recorded in the main comparatively late. In Ketton parish, they comprise the lost Fregsthorpe (compounded with the Scandinavian personal name Friðgestr and with forms from 1322), Kilthorpe (with Scandinavian Ketill and forms from c1250), the lost Manthorpe (probably with the Scandinavian personal name Manni; a Scandinavian or OE genitive plural manna 'of the men', i.e. 'communally owned' is unlikely as the first element; forms are recorded only from 1677) and the lost Soulthorpe (perhaps with a Scandinavian by-name Súla as first element; the initial recording is as late as 1919). The two remaining Rutland thorpes are Ingthorpe in Tinwell (probably with the Scandinavian personal name Ingi and with forms from 1189) and the late Westhorpe at the western edge of Wing village (with forms from 1296). The distribution of names in þorp is largely confined to the borders of Rutland; the composition of such names and their apparent general date (roughly 1050 to 1250) indicate that in the main they reflect only Scandinavian linguistic influence on the early Middle English dialect and personal name stock of the East Midlands rather than any direct settlement by Scandinavians in the territory from beyond its borders.[61]

An analysis of the field-names and minor names of the county emphasizes that there was no concentration of Scandinavian settlers anywhere in the territory. Scandinavian influence in Rutland consisted primarily of linguistic echo across its frontiers, especially via the market towns of Oakham, Overton and Stamford. Scandinavian elements in the field-names progressed only slowly from the borders towards the centre of the territory during the course of the Middle Ages.[62]

The place-name evidence as a whole indicates that Scandinavians were excluded politically from Rutland at the time of the disbanding of the Danish army in the East Midlands in 877, the indicator of whose settlement is the Grimston-hybrid name-type, and excluded also during the subsequent colonization phase which is recorded by place-names in *bỹ*. There are no Grimston-hybrids in the real sense in Rutland and no names in *bỹ* compounded with Scandinavian personal names, a remarkable contrast with the surrounding territories.

It is probable that from the bargaining with the Danish army and division of the Mercian kingdom in 877, Ceolwulf retained the territory of Rutland intact as an Anglo-Saxon royal possession. It may be that prior to the Scandinavian incursions, Rutland had been the dower land of the queens of Mercia and its later becoming that of the queens of England merely perpetuated its reginal demesne status.[63] For this reason, the Danes would have appropriated none of its territory and stayed strictly outside its borders.

By 894, however, Rutland appears either to have passed into or to be about to pass into the control of the Scandinavians of York rather than of the Five Boroughs. In Æthelweard's Chronicle, we find that in that year Ealdorman Æthelnoth

adit in hostes Euoraca urbe, qui non parua territoria pandunt in Myrciorum regno loci in parte occidentali Stanforda. Hoc est inter fluenta amnis Vueolod et condenso syluæ quæ uulgo Ceostefne nuncupatur.[64]

The territory so described is obviously Rutland, the streams of R. Welland being its tributaries the Eye Brook and the rivers Chater and Gwash. It is possible that the Norwegian Scandinavians of York took possession of the territory and maintained by negotiation the continuing exclusion of the Danes. This would explain the establishment of a Norwegian settlement at the prime location of Normanton on the fine soils of the Northampton Sands ironstone next to the former *caput* of the Anglian kingdom (land which may well have been appropriated from its ancient great estate), that *caput* from which Rutland perhaps continued to be administered. It may be the reason why Glaston, the only hybrid *tūn* in Rutland, and again on very desirable land, had as its lord a man with a Norwegian personal name and the reason why in the boundary parish of Tixover, *Normandale* 'the valley of the Norwegians' was so identified. Possibly it was a Norwegian Viking York which continued to hold sway over Rutland until the reconquest of the territory by Edward the Elder in 918 and York which negotiated the transfer of a small portion of its original territory north of R. Welland to the growing Danish borough of Stamford in exchange for continuing immunity from the men of that powerful stronghold. That Stamford was part of Rutland until a relatively late date, incidentally, is indicated by the Domesday Survey which records that Stamford contained outlying dependencies of Hambleton, including the church of St Peter with attached lands and that Queen Edith, wife of Edward the Confessor, had held seventy residences in that part of Stamford still regarded as Rutland, as well as forty-five acres of meadow there.[65]

Following the reconquest of the Danelaw by Edward the Elder between 918 and 921, possession of Rutland must have passed to the throne of a unified England and what was once the dower land of the queens of Mercia became that of the queens of a united realm. As a memory of this royal dower land, the name of Edith (Ēadgӯð), the wife of Edward the Confessor (1042-66), became prefixed to Weston. Weston is a typically late *tūn* of the geographically related type, to be compared with *Norton* and *Southton* in Market Overton parish. Edith Weston was to develop as the western estate dependent on the royal manor of Ketton to its east. Its lands seem to have been carved out of those of a more extensive Normanton, but in any case were probably once part of a greater estate of Hambleton. A large proportion of the land of the Norwegians at Normanton must have been appropriated for the royal estate of Weston at some date after the reconquest of the Danelaw, when power passed from the Scandinavians and any remaining link with the kingdom of York was severed.

7.   THE NORMAN CONQUEST

The final effect of the Norsemen on the place-names of Rutland was the result of the invasion of England from Normandy in 1066 by William the Bastard, culminating in his conquest of the realm. Only one major name in the county resulted, Beaumont Chase. This is typical of major Norman-French names in England: these relate principally to military and ecclesiastical sites and to hunting regions. Nor did the developing feudal system have any lasting impact on Rutland's toponyms. To many village names in England are affixed the family names of their feudal lords (as Croxton *Kerrial*, Melton *Mowbray* and *Neville* Holt in neighbouring Leicestershire). This feature is absent from Rutland's place-names. The surname of John le *Bolour* who is mentioned in connection with Oakham in 1200 is prefixed to two surviving forms for Barleythorpe in the early thirteenth century (*Bolaresthorp* 1203, *Bolarysthorp* e13th) and *Folville* to two fifteenth century forms for Teigh. Otherwise, no such feudal affixes exist. Presumably this is the result of the smallness of the territory where scribal confusion over the identity of vills would be unlikely. Barleythorpe (originally a simplex name in *þorp*) and the simplex Thorpe by Water were the only two estates which could cause confusion in early records and this may explain the need to distinguish between them, with *Bolaresthorp* the outcome. The king held both Casterton and Luffenham at the date of the Domesday Survey so that when each of these vills was divided, they were distinguished in the case of Casterton by Great- (forms from 1218) and Little- (forms from 1254) and in that of Luffenham by North- (forms from 1179) and South- (forms from 1210). Two other place-names common to the East Midlands received identifying affixes: Overton (Market-, forms from 1200) and Weston (Edith-, forms from 1263).

8.   AN ANALYSIS OF RUTLAND'S EARLY
PLACE-NAME TYPES

In general, the ratio of habitation names to nature names in the county is 2:1, the exact inverse of the situation in Berkshire whose place-name survey was the most recently completed.[66] If the names of hundreds and of rivers are excluded, the following figures result.
(i) The Rutland Domesday Survey: Old English habitation names 20 + Scandinavian 5 = 25, OE nature names 14 + Scand 0 = 14. Here the numbers are somewhat distorted, however, since the villages/estates of the Martinsley Hundred are subsumed under three royal vills only, i.e. Hambleton with 7 unnamed berewicks, Oakham with 5 and Ridlington with 7. (ii) The names of modern parishes (excluding the Norman Beaumont Chase and treating both

Casterton (Great- and Little-) and Luffenham (North- and South-)
as two units only): OE habitation names 31 + Scand 5 = 36, OE
nature names 19 + Scand 0 = 19. (iii) The tally of major names
both extant and lost (and here 'major' signifies those early names
given particular treatment in the text of this survey, with Beaumont
Chase, Casterton and Luffenham treated as above): OE habitation
names 50 + Scand 17 = 67, OE nature names 35 + Scand 1 =
36. There are problems in categorizing one or two of the names
such as Barrow and Wing but in each case above, the ratio remains
approximately 2 habitation names to 1 nature name.

In the Domesday Survey the most numerous habitation
generics are: OE *tūn* 10 (of which 2 are *-ingtūn* formations), *hām* 4
(of which 2 are *-inga-*), *cot* 3, Scand *þorp* 5. The most numerous
nature generics are: OE *wella* 3 (of which 1 is *-inga-*), *denu* 2 (of
which 1 is doubtfully *-inga-*), *dūn* 2. For the modern parishes the
most numerous habitation generics are: OE *tūn* 18 (of which 2 are
-ingtūn), *hām* 6 (? 7, of which 2 are *-inga-*), *cot* 3, Scand *þorp* 4.
The most numerous nature generics are: OE *wella* 3 (of which 1
is *-inga-*), *dūn* 3, *lēah* 3, *brōc* 2, *denu* 2 (of which 1 is doubtfully
-inga-). The figures for the major names extant and lost are as
follows: the most numerous habitation generics are OE *tūn* 23 (of
which 2 are *-ingtūn*), *hām* 7 (? 8, of which 2 are *-inga-*), *cot* 4, *hall*
2, *stoc* 2, *worð* 2, *wīc* 2, Scand *þorp* 14; and of the nature generics,
OE *lēah* 10, *dūn* 3, *wella* 3 (of which 1 is *-inga-*), *brōc* 2, *denu* 2
(of which 1 is doubtfully *-inga-*), *mōr* 2.

One is struck by the dominance of only 3 habitation generics,
i.e. *hām, tūn, þorp* and only 3 nature generics, i.e. *dūn, lēah, wella.*
Of these 6, only *hām* and *dūn* are of the types shown to be
ancient.[67] There are only 3 (+ 1 doubtful) names in *-inga-*. Names
in *-ingas* are absent. The *-ingtūn* formation signifying 'estate
associated with or named from *x*' is rare, with only 2 instances,
surprising in a territory with so many names in *tūn*. Although
habitation names predominate at a ratio of 2:1, in (i) above they
are formed from only 7 different generics, whereas nature generics
have much more variety, as would be expected, numbering 10 different elements; and so throughout, as in (ii) the ratio is 9:11 and
in (iii) 17:20.

Personal names are compounded with nature generics hardly
at all. Only the following are found: Cott (Cottesmore), Rōta
(*Rutmore*), Esa (Essendine), Tȳni (Tinwell) and the Norman-

imported Bernard (Barnsdale). Byttel is possible in Bisbrooke but the word *bitel* 'a beetle' is more likely as first element. A personal name Hwicce is also possible in Whissendine and Witchley, but the folk-name Hwicce is likelier in these also. A significant word is normally the specific in the nature names. In contrast, in the habitation names, personal names are roughly equal in number to significant words as the specifics.

The personal names compounded in the OE major place-names are predominantly of the early monothematic type. Only Rēdel, Sæga and Tyni are hypocoristic, while Æðelstān, Beornhelm, (E)ahlstān and Ecgwulf are the sole representatives of the later dithematic form, and of these, two are compounded with Scand *þorp*. Martin is a borrowing of the Christian period from Latin into Old English.

The general impression given by the style of Rutland place-names is of a territory settled heavily by the English early in the Anglo-Saxon period, but whether settlement was predominantly dispersed or nucleated is impossible to tell from this type of evidence. There is no indication that in Rutland OE nature names were created earlier than habitation names or vice versa. Presumably the style of the territory's early toponyms resulted from the nature and condition of the landscape which the Anglo-Saxons found and from the cultural framework within which they settled. However, the preponderance of habitation names suggests that they came to what had been, or was, an intensively cultivated countryside.

It appears that there was some renaming of estates in the later manorial phase of Anglo-Saxon Rutland and a number of marginal farmsteads were created principally during the eleventh and twelfth centuries when such sites were styled *þorp*, a Scandinavian word which had become part of the East Midlands dialect of these centuries. Of Rutland's 14 names in *þorp*, 10 are compounded with personal names, of which 3 are OE and 7 of Scandinavian origin. 2 thorpes are simplex and 2 have significant words as first themes.

9.   THE RUTLAND HUNDREDS AND
THE INTEGRITY OF THE TERRITORY

In the Domesday Survey, only two wapentakes form *Roteland* as it

is recognized there, namely Alstoe and Martinsley. The rest of the
Roteland whose boundaries have been traced from Bronze Age territory to Anglian kingdom is styled Witchley Wapentake and is
counted as an integral part of Northamptonshire. The tenants in
chief of Alstoe and Martinsley are listed on the folio of Nottinghamshire landholders under *Roteland* and the three columns of the
Roteland schedule are an appendix to Nottinghamshire. Alstoe
Wapentake is divided into two unnamed 'hundreds' which are
attached to the contiguous Broxtowe and Thurgarton Wapentakes of
Nottinghamshire and both Alstoe and Martinsley are regarded as
part of the Sheriffdom of Nottingham for the purpose of the king's
geld. Domesday *Roteland* has also close links with Lincolnshire.
Stamford in Ness Wapentake has seventy residences in *Roteland* and
itself contains outlying dependencies of Hambleton. Eight of the
twelve lands in Alstoe Wapentake are duplicated in the Lincolnshire
folios.

The progress of Rutland in the two hundred years or so from
the 877 division of Mercia by the Viking host to its condition as
described in the Domesday Survey of 1086 is deeply obscure. It
seems that it maintained its integrity from 877 to 894 when the
record of Æthelnoth's expedition to York indicates that by this date
it had become a possession of the York Scandinavians. The 1086
Survey shows it divided and separately administered from Nottinghamshire and Northamptonshire. Charles Phythian-Adams argues[68]
that · it was between Æthelnoth's visit to York in 894 and the
reconquest of the territory by Edward the Elder in 918 that control
of Rutland from Scandinavian York was replaced by its control
from Scandinavian Nottinghamshire and Northamptonshire. He
believes that this shift of control was the result of a bargain struck
between the West Saxon king, whose emissary Æthelnoth had been,
and the men of the Danelaw. This safeguarded the interests of the
West Saxon queens whose dower land Rutland was in the process
of becoming. For the security of Rutland, the West Saxons as quid
pro quo guaranteed the continuing integrity of the Danelaw.
Phythian-Adams suggests that Æthelflæd, Lady of the Mercians and
daughter of Alfred the Great, was the first West Saxon bride to
acquire what may have been the dower lands of the earlier Mercian
queens. Because of its nature as royal dower land and because of
the West Saxon-Scandinavian pact, it survived the creation of the
Five Boroughs and the eleventh century extension of the new shire

system to this region. It continued as the dower land of in succession Eadgifu, wife of Edward the Elder, Ælfthryth, wife of King Edgar, Emma, wife of Æthelred the Unready and Edith, wife of Edward the Confessor.

It is difficult to see why it was that Nottinghamshire and Northamptonshire received control of Rutland rather than, say, Leicestershire or Lincolnshire. If Phythian-Adams's hypothesis is correct, then presumably much depended on the stages in development of the individual Boroughs when such a transfer of control took place. But Northampton was not one of the Five Boroughs and indeed Lincolnshire did have an interest in *Roteland* as the duplicate entries in the Domesday Survey show. Alstoe was considered as part of Lincolnshire. The discrepancies between the duplicate entries for each vill indicate that it may have been surveyed twice, once from Nottinghamshire and once from Lincolnshire.

In any event, at the death of Queen Edith in 1075, William the Conqueror probably retained *Roteland* for himself. The Pipe Roll for 1130 shows that with the exception of Stamford, *Roteland* included all the territory which had formed the small Anglian kingdom. The Pipe Roll for 1156 indicates the continuing imperfect detachment of its lands from the neighbouring counties since its returns are still included with those of Nottinghamshire and Northamptonshire. However, Witchley is no longer considered to be part of Northamptonshire in the twelfth century Survey of that county. In the Pipe Roll for 1166, Rutland is described as a 'bailiwick', but in 1204 King John gave it to Isabella in dower and in this grant it is described as a *comitatus* 'a county'. By the time of the earliest Feudal Aids at the end of the thirteenth century, it is fully independent.

As for the individual hundreds,[69] Alstoe is recorded as a wapentake from 1086 to 1185 and then as a hundred from 1195. The site of the hundred-moot was near Alstoe House in Burley parish. Significantly, Alstoe would have been the central point of an area comprising the Alstoe Wapentake *less* the additional territory north of the ancient northern border which, it has been argued, was moved northwards in the period of the Anglian kingdom of Rutland to embrace the lands of Market Overton, Thistleton, Stretton and Clipsham. This suggests a long history for the territory's hundredal system.

Martinsley also appears first as a wapentake from 1086 to

1188 and then from 1199 is described as a hundred. The hundred-moot no doubt met at the lost *Martinsley* in Martinsthorpe parish. This too would have been at the centre of the area of the original hundred. The Martinsley Wapentake was eventually divided to give a new Martinsley Hundred and the Oakham Soke Hundred. A *Hundreda de Okeham cum Martynesley* is recorded in 1428 and although as a *soke* Oakham Soke appears in the Domesday Survey, it is not until 1522 that it is styled unambiguously a hundred in its own right. The hundred was formed from the villages and manors held by the castle and manor of Oakham and its court was presumably conducted in the hall of the castle. Clipsham, a part of Oakham Soke, is the only parish in Rutland separated from the body of its hundred.[70] It is reasonable to speculate whether this isolation had its origin in Clipsham's position north of the ancient border and whether, because important for its iron-working, it early became an Anglian royal possession and thus eventually a berewick of the royal vill of Oakham via the old *caput* of Hambleton. It is unfortunate that Clipsham is not named in the Domesday Survey but it is presumably included there as one of the anonymous berewicks of either Hambleton or Oakham. Whether *Martinsley* continued as the moot-site of the refashioned Martinsley Hundred is unknown.

Witchley is the name of two 'hundreds' in the Northamptonshire Geld Roll of ante 1075, i.e. *Hwicceslea east hundred* and *Hwiccleslea west hundred.* In the Domesday Survey of 1086, these are treated as a single unit, variously termed hundred or wapentake. Witchley Wapentake is no longer recorded after 1086. Doubtlessly, the moot-site of its long, narrow territory was at Witchley at the junction of the parishes of North Luffenham, Ketton and Edith Weston. Again, this would have been the central point of this rather attenuated land-unit. The old Witchley Wapentake was divided after 1086 into East Hundred and Wrangdike Hundred. East Hundred is a continuation of the area and name of Witchley East Hundred of the Northamptonshire Geld Roll. Where its hundred-court met is unknown, but at the centrally located ancient town site at Casterton is possible. Forms for East Hundred are recorded only from 1166. The new Wrangdike Hundred is also recorded from 1166. Any moot-site this may have had is unknown, but the *Syrepol* in Seaton parish may indicate its proximity, if the first element of this name is indeed *sclr* 'shire, administrative district'. Of course, none of the refashioned hundreds may have acquired a tranditional open-air Anglo-Saxon moot-site, but if so, it is difficult to understand how Wrangdike Hundred got its name since that name is topographical.

10. OAKHAM AND THE RUTLAND MARKETS

The market sites of Rutland are all close to its borders, emphasizing the exclusivism of the territory which has been such an important feature of its development. The most ancient sites are those assumed to have existed under the Roman occupation. The presence of a market at the Romano-British settlement on the Thistleton/Market Overton boundary has already been touched upon. British coins here and the Iron Age predecessor of the temple to Veteris indicate an ancient trading site before its development as an industrial and market centre in the Roman period. Market Overton was its natural successor in the Anglo-Saxon era. The style *Market-* is recorded only from 1200 but obviously there was continuity here. The market site simply moved a little way south-west, possibly to the protection of the fortified site in which the pre-Conquest church was eventually built. This stronghold was probably Roman in origin, but may well have been refashioned by the Anglo-Saxons as a border fortification. Market Overton was ideally placed for trade. It is positioned on the dry plateau of Northampton Sands ironstone which stretches from Burley northwards. Along this high ground runs the Roman Sewstern Lane. The village is also beside the Roman road which ran westwards to the Fosse Way at Syston in Leicestershire. It is possible that the postulated ancient border at Barrow was moved north early in the period of the Anglian kingdom in part to absorb this market site into the territory and thus to control its revenues.

One must assume, of course, another market to have existed in the Roman period at the town at Great Casterton. This naturally died when urban life there withered but it was replaced eventually by the market at Stamford two miles away which developed with the growth of the Danish Borough. · In the Domesday Survey, the town land of Stamford north-west of R. Welland in what used to be Rutland territory is called *Portland*, from OE *port* 'a market town, a market'. Field-names in

south-eastern and eastern parishes of Rutland in the late eighteenth
and early nineteenth centuries record cattle roads or drift ways
along which livestock was herded to Stamford market. Thus *drift*
features in names in Caldecott, Seaton, Barrowden and Ketton,
indicating a lengthy droveway north-east beside R. Welland. The
feature is recorded also in Essendine, Pickworth and Ryhall,
referring to another route, this time south to Stamford market.
Some driftways no doubt were local, relating to movement of cattle
from outlying pastures, as perhaps was that in Thistleton recorded
as early as 1633, but the south-eastern and eastern examples appear
to relate firmly to routes to Stamford.

Uppingham is not as naturally placed as Market Overton/
Thistleton and Stamford/Great Casterton to have developed as a
market centre for trade across Rutland's frontiers. It had a rather
more parochial focus. The earliest place-name reference to a
market there is dated 1510; but *Portegate*, a 14th century name from
Glaston parish and *Portgate* mentioned in a rental for Seaton of the
reign of Henry IV (1399-1413), both meaning 'the road to the
market (town)' indicate that the market at Uppingham was in being
one hundred years earlier than its initial recording as a name. The
markets were natural points of entry for the Scandinavian language
into a territory which had excluded Danish settlement. It is significant that it is in the Rutland parishes surrounding Stamford and in
those of Market Overton and Oakham that the impact of the
Scandinavian language is earliest and most strongly felt, not in
Uppingham.[71] Uppingham does not feature particularly in the
spread of Scandinavian in the south of the territory. This reinforces
the impression of Uppingham's comparatively late development as a
market site.

Oakham grew as an important market in part because of its
proximity to the dense Scandinavian settlement of the Wreake
Valley of Leicestershire to its north-west. The weight of
Scandinavian elements in the early minor and field-names of the
town and parish illustrates this.[72] Presumably the defunct royal
centre of Hambleton was replaced by Oakham with a king's reeve
to control the revenues of the market. Oakham's market and gaol
are first recorded in post-Conquest sources but probably the growth
of the market belongs to the earlier eleventh century.[73]

The town developed as a defended site with the expansion of
this market. At the northern end of the market place was con-

structed the castle with a later hall built by Wakelin de Ferrers c1180-90. It is not strictly a castle, more a fortified manor house. It was surrounded by a bank of earth and a ditch and does not seem to have received stone encircling walls before the thirteenth century. The absence of a keep or wall-towers is unusual. A gatehouse to the south of its enceinte, with a bridge crossing the castle ditch, gave into the market place. The moat between castle and market place is recorded as *le Casteldyk'* in 1373 and the bridge over it is referred to in the phrase *iuxta pontem castri* in 1374. Across the southern end of the market place ran an east to west through street, possibly called the Bargate, joining the two recorded gatehouses of the fortified town. The West Bar survived to be illustrated by Speed on his plan of the town published in 1610. It survived because William Flore incorporated it into his house, now 34 High Street, by converting its upper floor into an attached private apartment in 1373. We learn of his 'solar built over the gate called *Le Westbarreyate'*. The narrowing of High Street at this point because of the former bar can still be seen in Victorian photographs.[74] The East Bar, first recorded as *atte Barre orientale* in 1305, was close to the lost Bull Inn from which Bull Lane, now a cul-de-sac, was named. Bull Lane was the beginning of the road to Stamford. The inn, the *messuag' iacet apud Estbarreʒate voc' le Bulle*, was conveniently situated for travellers arriving at the town from the direction of Ermine Street.

The little town was certainly defended by a surrounding ditch, since we know of *le Barredyk'* recorded in 1377. It is not clear whether the East or West Bar is alluded to in this reference, but it is obvious from it that the whole enceinte, castle and town, was defended in this way. Nor do we know whether the town was eventually provided with a surrounding wall to replace a probable earlier earthen rampart and wooden palisade. As the West Bar with its archway was indeed stone-built, one must at least reckon with a surrounding wall for Oakham, castle and town together.

How the defences were organized to the south is obscure. There is no record of a South Bar to the town unless the name *Thresholdgate* implies a road lying across the threshold of a southern entrance: but the early town was surely too small for a third gateway. *Thresholdgate* (1632) survives as the name of a furlong in the old southern open-field. It is likely to refer to a road running across the southern limit of the early enceinte, possibly on the line of the eastern section of South Street.

To the south-east of the early market town was an enclosure now remembered in the name of Hayne House and earliest recorded by *Heynes lane* in 1494. This is from OE *hægen* 'an enclosure'. It may be that here was sited a stockyard related to the market. To the west of this, but recorded at a much later date, was *the Penn Close* of 1718, a name surviving in modern Penn Street. Both names may record an early arrangement with enclosures across the southern limits of the market town.

The Domesday Survey of 1086 tells us that Oakham had a priest and a church. Presumably, this church lay within what was to become the defended area. The surviving medieval church was built outside the western line of the early town enceinte. Its oldest fabric belongs to the early thirteenth century. The church was erected in what became Deanshold or Church Manor. The line of demarcation between Castle Manor and Church Manor marks the western limit of the Norman town. It is not clear whether the siting of the new church in the early thirteenth century indicates that the town defences were obsolete by this date. But the castle appears to have received stone walls only in the thirteenth century. The castle ramparts and the nature of the West Bar, stone-built and surviving into the nineteenth century, suggest that Oakham as a whole may have had stone defences in the later Middle Ages, although if so, it is surprising that no traces of curtain walling for the town itself have been identified.

11. RELIGIONS AND SUPERSTITIONS

Research into the distribution of place-names relating to pagan faiths in England locates such names in areas far from the centres of government (which were the natural objects of Christian proselytizing missions) and also in regions difficult of access.[75] The pagan place-names of Rutland are to be found in precisely such a region, in the heavily wooded south-west, on the boundary with a possibly hostile Anglian people in what became Leicestershire. Here are Holyoaks, originally an OE singular *hálig-ác* 'the sacred oak-tree', *Þureslege* 'the sacred grove of Þunor, god of thunder' in Ayston (one of seven known examples in England) and the shrine of the earlier Romano-British mother goddess whose effigy survives at

Braunston. It was in this area, of course, that the medieval hermitages of Wardley and Stockerston were established, perhaps in response to continuing manifestations of pagan cults hereabouts.

Apart from these major centres of heathen worship, pagan superstitions have left their marks on the local names of Rutland. OE *þyrs* 'a demon, a giant' occurs in several names in the south-east. There is a *Thirspit* or *Tyrespyt* 'the demon's pit' in Barrowden, Empingham and Glaston. In Barrowden also, *Robynilpit* may refer to the same demon who later became the hobgoblin Robin Goodfellow or Robin-a-Tiptoe, whose name survives in nearby Robin-a-Tiptoe Hill in Tilton, Leicestershire. Robin was the drudging goblin whose tasks were carried out in the dead of night while the farmer and his household slept.[76] It is possible that *Hob Hole* in Greetham refers to another such hobgoblin, associated here with a pothole in the limestone. OE *scucca* 'a demon', perhaps of the open places, may be present in *Shockmore* in South Luffenham and *Shucheved* in Little Casterton.

A scatter of benificent or sacred springs is spread across the county. It is, of course, impossible to tell whether or not these are pre-Christian in origin. Thus in Leighfield is *Botwell* 'the healing spring' from OE *bōt* 'help, remedy' and in Oakham and Teigh are examples of *Helwell* of similar meaning, from OE *hæl* 'good fortune' or *hǽlu* 'health, healing'. That in Oakham may later have become associated with the Virgin Mary and restyled Our Lady's Well, while in Ryhall, Tibba's Well is named from a seventh century Anglo-Saxon religieuse, Tibba, '*sanctissima et piissima*', who reputedly lived a large part of her life there. *Annwell* in Egleton may have been a spring thought to aid fertility and therefore dedicated to St Anne, a patroness of wells, who interceded for the childless. It has even been suggested that Anne in well-names replaced a more ancient name of similar sound, referring to a Celtic mother goddess such as Anu, a goddess of prosperity.[77] Unassociated holy wells are found in field-names in Barleythorpe, Barrowden, Hambleton, Manton and Seaton.

No major religious houses were founded in Rutland. The largest was Brooke Priory, established before 1153 for Augustinian canons. The Priory at Edith Weston was a small alien cell of the Benedictine Abbey of St George de Boscherville in Normandy. It passed to the Carthusian house of St Mary and St Anne of Coventry in 1390. At Tinwell there may have been a small convent

called Grace Dieu of nuns of the Cistercian order, but no traces of
it remain in field-names in the parish.

The two military orders of Knights Hospitallers and Knights
Templars held land in Rutland and both appear to have left their
marks on the county's field-names. The Knights Templars had a
preceptory at South Witham just over the border in Lincolnshire.
This was discovered and excavated as recently as 1966-7. The lands
at Temple Barns in Stretton and *Temple Peyse* in Greetham were
doubtlessly administered from there. The Knights Hospitallers,
otherwise the Knights of St John of Jerusalem, held the manor of
Stoke Dry and Holyoaks. The local name (*The*) *Fronald* in Stoke
Dry and Lyddington may be a memory of them, possibly deriving
from *freren-holde 'the holding of the brothers of the military
order'. In nearby Wardley, the unusual late field-name *Hospital*
may also relate to them, as may *St John's Peice* in Greetham, *Saint
John's Land* in Little Casterton and *the landes called Sct. Johns* in
Uppingham, although this last group may have alternative impli-
cations.

Crosses on village greens and roadside crosses were a
common feature of the medieval countryside. The broken stumps
of many of these survive, as did *Stompstone* in Cottesmore in 1422
and *Stump Cross* in Edith Weston in 1746. In Preston, the *crucem
ad finem oriental' ville* is recorded in 1556 and now remembered in
Cross Lane. In Lyddington the stump of *alt' Crucem in villa de
lidyngton'* (1510) still remains on The Green. Roadside crosses are
recorded in Barrow (*le Crossegate* c1295), in Great Casterton
(*Crosse Way* 1634), in Greetham (*Fiue Mile Crosse* 1610) and in
Stoke Dry (*Crossegate* 1274). Occasionally, the names of individuals
were attached to crosses, such as *ad crucem Benedicti* of the early
thirteenth century in North Luffenham and *Ravens Crosse* of 1667 in
Barleythorpe. In Barrowden, *Hallewellescros* of the early fourteenth
century stood at a sacred well or spring as did, no doubt, the cross
at *Crosswell* (1749) in Manton. *Salters Crosse* (1615) in South
Luffenham is possibly associated with a lost salt-merchants' route;
otherwise it could contain a family name as does *Hooby Crosse*
(1633) in Wardley. Perhaps the most poignant relic of Rutland's
medieval crosses is that of Ingthorpe in Tinwell parish. Beside the
cross lived *Henricus ad crucem* in 1292 and in 1347 *Ricardus ad
crucem*. All that remains is part of the cross shaft built into a field
wall near the farmyard there. In sum, early crosses are recorded in

twenty-two of Rutland's fifty-eight modern parishes.

12.   DESERTED AND SHRUNKEN MEDIEVAL VILLAGES

Even in so small a county as Rutland, there are some thirty settlements which since the earlier Middle Ages have been abandoned or
have shrunk so that now all that remains is a name attached to a
country house or to a copse. In some cases, not even a name survives. Often, however, their earthworks do.[78]
        Assuming that the identification of the Domesday Survey
Harduic is correct, there are six vills of 1086 which no longer survive as major settlements. They are the lost *Alsthorpe* (Burley),
Hardwick (Empingham), Holyoaks (now in Stockerston, Leicestershire), Horn, Sculthorpe (North Luffenham) and the lost *Snelston*
(Caldecott). Four settlements not appearing in the Domesday Survey remain as parish names, although nowadays they are represented only by a single house, ruinous or otherwise. They are
Gunthorpe, Leighfield, Martinsthorpe and Normanton. To these
may be added a number of settlements which do not appear in the
Domesday Survey and are not the names of modern parishes. They
survive only as the names of isolated houses, woods and in one case
that of a bridge. They are: Bredcroft (Tinwell), *Cotes* (remembered in Coach Bridge, Seaton), Geeston and Kilthorpe (Ketton),
Nether Hambleton (Hambleton), Tolethorpe (Little Casterton),
Stocken (Stretton), Westhorpe (Wing), Woodhead (Great Casterton)
and Woolfox (Greetham). To these may perhaps be added Hooby
(Stretton). Totally lost are *Birchaby* (Belton), *Fregsthorpe,
Manthorpe, Newbottle* and *Soulthorpe* (Ketton), *Hide* (Egleton),
Norton and *Southton* (Market Overton) and *Wenton* (Cottesmore).
        Only rarely do we know at what precise dates settlements
ceased to exist. So, for example, in 1764 Sir Gilbert Heathcote
moved the inhabitants of Normanton to Empingham so that he
could raze the village to build his great Palladian house in
Normanton Park. The last harvest of the thirty inhabitants of
Holyoaks was in 1496, after which Sir Robert Brudenell evicted
them in favour of his sheep. Concerning these villagers we learn:
'They have departed thence and are either idle or have perished.'
        Of the thirty identified sites, only five have nature names
and it is significant that ten of the twenty-five habitation names are

thorpes, those latecoming settlements on the poorest soils in the territory. It is not surprising that either they failed to grow or failed completely. Martinsthorpe was, no doubt, a restyled OE *stoc* which is probably the reason for its surviving so long to give its name to a parish. It was not a latecomer.

13.   FOREST AND PARK

The royal Forest of Rutland was probably created soon after William the Conqueror retained *Roteland* for himself at the death of Queen Edith in 1075. It occupied half of the area of the modern county. One must remember, however, that 'forest' was a legal entity where Forest Laws applied, aimed at the preservation of game and the promotion of hunting. The Norman-French name Beaumont Chase in the extreme south-west emphasizes the concept of the chase, the hunt. It is only in Leighfield's ancient woodland that we find the wolf recorded in a toponym and it is in this area that in the late sixteenth and early seventeenth centuries the hunting lodges were established such as Lambley Lodge and Leigh Lodge in Leighfield, Park Lodge in Ridlington and King's Hill Lodge in Beaumont Chase. In its earliest form, the royal forest was the Forest of Rutland; hence such phrases occur as in *foresta regis de Roteland* 1231. Later the forest was limited to the south-west of the county and became the Forest of Leighfield as in *in foresta regis de Lyfelde* 1491.

Apart from the royal forest, a number of parks for the breeding and preservation of game for hunting and for the table were established. Several of these continued in being for some four hundred years, as Barnsdale (1206-1602), Flitteris (1252-1610) and the royal park of Ridlington (1238-1638). The Bishops of Lincoln enclosed a park at Lyddington, recorded as early as 1227, and built a small palace there. The park at Exton was established as early as 1185. At Essendine, the park to the east of the castle served the castle's keepers. The *parcus de Esindene* is recorded from 1296. Market Overton had its own park recorded from 1269 and at Hambleton *le Park* is known from 1360. Cantor lists a park at Stretton which he suggests originated in the thirteenth century, but place-name forms for a park there have only been discovered in research for this survey from 1637 onwards.[79]

No place-name evidence survives for Cantor's listed park in Greetham, again postulated as having been established in the thirteenth century, while that which he proposes for Whissendine from the late twelfth century has left no trace in toponyms either. However, perhaps Buck Hill in neighbouring Ashwell remembers deer in the vicinity, but Whissendine's *The Park* does not occur in records until 1864. In addition to Flitteris Park in Oakham, there was a small park attached to Oakham Castle recorded from 1285 to the early eighteenth century. Whether this is the park called *Stone Park* (1461) which the historian James Wright mentions in his *History and Antiquities of the County of Rutland* of 1684 is uncertain. A *further parke lyinge towardes Barleythorpe Mault myll* is recorded in Oakham in 1611. It is remembered in the local Park Lane.

From the second half of the sixteenth century and from the seventeenth century further parks are recorded in Rutland. *Park Ford* of 1566 in Egleton clearly relates to a park at Burley, independently recorded from 1651 in local toponyms. In Uppingham was *Lawnde Park* 1572, *Vppingham parke* 1610. There were two small parks in Brooke, *Brooke Parke* also called Town Park of 1682 and *Red deere Parke* of 1685. To these may be added Clipsham Park of 1687. *Park Leyes* of 1634 in Edith Weston appears to record another local park of this period. Later parks include *The Park* 1748 in Lyndon, Sir Gilbert Heathcote's *Normanton Park* 1758 and *New Park* in Hambleton of the early nineteenth century.

In the medieval romance *Sir Gawain and the Green Knight*, the three classic hunts of Sir Bertilak de Hautdesert are for the deer, the boar and the fox. All three animals appear in Rutland minor names of the hunting country. The wild boar and the deer gave toponyms in Lyddington where these quarries were the sport of the Bishops of Lincoln. As well as in Brooke which had its own deer park in the seventeenth century, deer may also be referred to in Buck Hill in Ashwell, mentioned above, and in *Rascalhill* in Manton.

The fox has given local names in fifteen Rutland parishes. Many of these names, of course, belong to the development of fox-hunting as a sport for the gentry from the eighteenth century onwards. To this end, many gorses and fox coverts were created.[80] Local names with *dogge-kenel* also date from this era and refer to accommodation for hunting packs.

Other game creatures, no doubt for lesser mortals, that have produced toponyms are the hare in Stretton, Horn and Essendine in the east and, especially trapped in the Middle Ages, the woodcock which is recorded in the west of the county in Leighfield, Oakham, Uppingham and Whissendine. Rabbits, of course, have long been an important source of food and warrens were established from the Middle Ages onwards to provide an unfailing supply. Only seven rather late warrens appear in Rutland minor names, however, the earliest recorded being Tickencote Warren of 1673, with only three more to 1750. Strictly speaking, warrens were game preserves, some artifically constructed and maintained. The natural rabbit warren was the *coninger* (cf. ME *coni* 'a rabbit', giving ModE *coney*). Instances from 1315 onwards are recorded in Barrowden, Bisbrooke, Egleton, Glaston, South Luffenham, Seaton, Teigh and Whissendine.

14.   THE EIGHTEENTH AND NINETEENTH CENTURIES

Two features of these centuries affected the place-names of Rut-land: first, agricultural experiment and improvement and second, the development of roads, canals and railways.

The introduction of mechanical aids to agriculture is reflected in the field-names. Thus *Engine Close* 1732 in North Luffenham and *Horse Drills* 1761 in Barleythorpe signal the arrival of farm machinery. *Wheelhouse Close* 1838 in Ashwell records the use of the horsewheel for motive power for threshing machines, while *Pump Close* 1723 in Stretton, 1844 in Teigh, marks the application of mechanical means to the distribution of water. *Seedgrass Close* 1723 in Stretton, *Nursery Close* and *Evidence* both of the eighteenth century in Little Casterton, and presumably also *Invention Meadow* 1790 in Egleton, suggest attention to the improvement of crops. In the late eighteenth and early nineteenth centuries, care was given to the breeding of better strains of cattle. This is reflected in the names of local inns such as *The Hereford Ox* 1850 and *The Durham Ox* 1863, both of South Luffenham. There was a *Durham Ox Inn* also in Gunthorpe which was converted into a farm c1900. Such names celebrated particularly famous animals such as the renowned Brocklesby Ox of 1810, bred at Bonby on the Lincolnshire Wolds and remembered in the names of the inns at

Ulceby and Glanford Brigg.

Roman Ermine Street and Sewstern Lane remained major routes throughout the Middle Ages in the east and north-east of the territory. In the seventeenth century, we are reminded of the horse staging-posts along these ancient highways with such names as *The Post Way* 1633 in Thistleton and *Post Way Furlong* 1652 in Greetham. However, in the eighteenth century came the growth of long distance traffic and timetabled stagecoaches. Turnpike trusts were established for the maintenance and improvement of the coach roads. Originally, the turnpike was a spiked barrier placed across a road as a defence against attack, especially by men on horseback. Eventually it came to mean a barrier placed across a road to stop passage until a toll was paid. In effect, it became a toll-gate. Field-names with the element *turnepike* are present from 1763 in Empingham, Ketton, South Luffenham, Lyddington, Morcott, Ryhall and Uppingham. The earliest turnpike to feature in local names is that in Uppingham, while those which survive in modern field-names are now anachronistic. In addition to names with *turnepike*, we find *toll-bar* compounded in local names in Ayston, Burley, Ryhall and Tinwell. The Ram Jam Inn on Ermine Street near Stretton takes its name from a potent drink, *Ram Jam*, concocted from a recipe brought back from India by an eighteenth century landlord, Charles Blake. He sold it as a winter warmer to coach passengers travelling on what had become the Great North Road.

The Oakham Canal was an extension of the Wreake Navigation. Its construction began in 1794 and it was opened in 1802 with wharves at Market Overton, Cottesmore and Oakham. A poor water supply was always its shortcoming and only a few names have resulted from its construction and brief life, such as *The Navigation* in Market Overton and *Navigation Close* in Barrow. *Barrow Wide Hole* in Barrow and *Wide Hole* in Cottesmore were broadenings of the canal to allow the turning of narrowboats. At Market Overton, *The Wharf* is recorded in 1846. *Canal Hole* and *Channel Meadow* both of 1844 in Teigh appear to be the result of popular etymology playing on the local *Charnellhoale* of 1612, obviously a toponym resulting from the discovery of an early group burial there. Given the position of Teigh on the territorial boundary, one is induced to speculate about the presence of an ancient battle cemetery.

The successors of the Inland Navigators who built the canals were the navvies who constructed the railways, especially in the nineteenth century. *Navvys Yard* 1844 in Whissendine was established for the workmen on the expansion of the Midland Railway from Melton Mowbray via Oakham to Stamford. Later, the Welland Viaduct carried the Midland Railway across the valley of R. Welland on eighty-two arches. It was built between the years 1876 and 1878, while Glaston Tunnel which conducted the line towards it was driven through between 1875 and 1880. The navvies who built the tunnel and viaduct established a temporary village called *Cyprus* in Seaton parish. Cyprus was much in the news in these years, with Disraeli's aggressive imperial policy in the Mediterranean securing control of the Suez Canal for Britain in 1875 and Cyprus itself from the Turks in 1878. The development of the railway system in Rutland has given field-names such as *Spoil Banks* in Pilton, *Over the Line* in Barrow and Essendine, *The Line Field* and *Railway* in Ketton, *Railway Fields* in Morcott and *Station Fields* in North Luffenham.

15. THE TWENTIETH CENTURY

Two events have occurred to affect Rutland's place-names in this century, one major, one minor. Principally, more than 3000 acres of Rutland's landscape (that is some 5% of its surface area) were drowned by the creation of Empingham Reservoir, now Rutland Water, to supply water to Peterborough, Corby, Northampton and Milton Keynes. The reservoir was completed in 1977. And on 1st April 1974, Rutland was absorbed into Leicestershire and currently no longer functions as an independent county. From this annexation the name 'Belton in Rutland' has already developed, perhaps to some extent as an indication of the local sense of the territory's unique place in the making of England.

NOTES

1.   *Domesday Book: Rutland*, ed. F. Thorn, Chichester 1980; *The Domesday Geography of Midland England*, ed. H.C. Darby and I.B. Terret, Cambridge 1954, 372-4. See also Map 7.

2.   C. Phythian-Adams, 'Rutland reconsidered', *Mercian Studies*, ed. A. Dornier, Leicester 1977, 78; C. Phythian-Adams, 'The emergence of Rutland and the making of the realm', *Rutland Record* 1 (1980), 6.

3   P. Liddle, *Leicestershire Archaeology, the present state of knowledge*, Vol. 1, Leicester 1982, 35; for Veteris or Vitiris, see I.A. Richmond, *Roman Britain*, London 1955, 207, R.B. Collingwood and J.N.L. Myres, *Roman Britain and the English Settlements*, 2nd ed., Oxford 1949, 268-9.

4.   G.B. Grundy, 'On the meanings of certain terms in Anglo-Saxon charters', *English Association Essays and Studies* 8 (1922), 42.

5.   L.V. Grinsell, 'Berkshire barrows', *Berkshire Archaeological Journal* 42 (1937), 102-16; L.V. Grinsell, *Dorset Barrows*, Dorchester 1959; H. O'Neil and L.V. Grinsell, 'Gloucestershire barrows', *Transactions of the Bristol and Gloucestershire Archaeological Society* 79 (1960), 3-148.

6.   Della Hooke, 'Burial features in West Midland charters', *Journal of the English Place-Name Society* 13 (1980-1), 1-40; see also D.J. Bonney, 'Pagan Saxon burials and boundaries in Wiltshire', *The Wiltshire Archaeology and Natural History Magazine* 61 (1966), 25-30.

7.   Map 2.

8.   Barrie Cox, 'The place-names of the earliest English records', *Journal of the English Place-Name Society* 8 (1975-6), 12-66.

9.   J. Pickering and R.F. Hartley, *Past Worlds in a Landscape: Archaeological Crop Marks in Leicestershire*, Leicester 1985, 60-74.

10.   See **beorg** in Notes on the Distribution of some Elements.

11.   The northern frontier appears to have been moved further north to embrace the important market site at Market Overton/Thistleton and the iron-producing industrial complexes in Thistleton and Clipsham. This movement may belong to the development of an early Anglian kingdom of Rutland. For ancient iron-working at Clipsham, see *Journal of Roman Studies* 45 (1955), 89.

12.   At Scamridge Dikes, Trouts Dale. Information from Dr P.W. Dixon FSA of the Department of Classical and Archaeological Studies, University of Nottingham.

13.   T.M. Charles-Edwards, 'Boundaries in Irish law' in *Medieval Settlement*, ed. P.H. Sawyer, London 1976.

14.   J.G.D. Clark, 'The invasion hypothesis in British prehistory', *Antiquity* 40

(1966), 172-89.

15.   C. Renfrew, *Archaeology and Language*, London 1987, 236.

16.   A.E. Brown, *Archaeological Sites and Finds in Rutland: a Preliminary List*, Leicester 1975, 11-12.

17.   Liddle, op.cit., 35.

18.   Brown, op.cit., 14.

19.   Map 3.

20.   Brown, op.cit., 26.

21.   Map 1.

22.   Map 3.

23.   M. Gelling, *Signposts to the Past*, 2nd ed., London 1988, .63-86.

24.   K. Cameron, 'The meaning and significance of Old English *walh* in English place-names', *Journal of the English Place-Name Society* 12 (1979-80), 1-53.

25.   J.N.L. Myres, *Anglo-Saxon Pottery and the Settlement of England*, Oxford 1969. See also J.N.L. Myres, *The English Settlements*, Oxford 1986, especially 74-103.

26.   S.C. Hawkes, 'Soldiers and settlers in Britain, fourth to fifth century', *Medieval Archaeology* 5 (1961), 1-70.   For arguments against this interpretation of late military metalwork and Romano-Saxon pottery, see for example S. Johnson, *Later Roman Britain*, London 1980, 135-8.

27.   Brown, op.cit.; T.McK. Clough, A. Dornier and R.A. Rutland, *A Guide to the Anglo-Saxon and Viking Antiquities of Leicestershire including Rutland*, Leicester 1975.

28.   Clough, op.cit.; and Map 3.

29.   Brown, op.cit., 12.

30.   Cox, 'The place-names of the earliest English records', op.cit.

31.   Barrie Cox, 'The significance of the distribution of English place-names in *hām* in the Midlands and East Anglia', *Journal of the English Place-Name Society* 5 (1972-3), 15-73.

32.   Map 4.

33.   See 'The Ayston Charter' following the Ayston parish names.

34.   A.H. Smith, *The Place-Names of Gloucestershire*, Part 4, English Place-Name Society Vol. 41, Cambridge 1965, 31-43.

35.   J.E.B. Gover, A. Mawer and F.M. Stenton, *The Place-Names of Northamptonshire*, English Place-Name Society Vol. 10, Cambridge 1933, 152.

36.   Cox, 'The place-names of the earliest English records', op.cit., 65.

37.   Cox, 'The significance of the distribution of English place-names in *hām*', op.cit., 47-9.

38.   A.H. Smith, *English Place-Name Elements*, Part 1, English Place-Name Society Vol. 25, Cambridge 1970, 109.

39.   Cox, 'The place-names of the earliest English records', op.cit.
40.   Barrie Cox, 'Aspects of place-name evidence for early medieval
settlement in England', *Viator* 11 (1980), 43-4.
41.   Cox, 'The place-names of the earliest English records', op.cit.
42.   Cox, 'The place-names of the earliest English records', op.cit.; Margaret
Gelling, 'Some notes on Warwickshire place-names', *Transactions of the
Birmingham and Warwickshire Archaeological Society* 86 (1974), 65-9.
43.   A.H. Smith, *English Place-Name Elements*, Part 2, English Place-Name
Society Vol. 26, Cambridge 1970, 18-22, 188-98.
44.   Smith, *Elements*, Part 1, op.cit., *s.v.* -ing[4] § 4(b), 293-4.
45.   Map 5.
46.   This *territorium* may once also have included Tickencote, Tinwell and the
Stamford town lands north of R. Welland.   Map 3.
47.   Brown, op.cit., 3.
48.   ibid. 23.
49.   Map 7.
50.   Cox, 'The place-names of the earliest English records', op.cit.; A. Cole,
'*Burna* and *brōc*: problems involved in retrieving the OE usage of these place-
name elements', JEPNS 23 (1990-1), 26-47, argues that *burna* is not necessarily
earlier than *brōc* as a name-forming generic.
51.   R.F. Hartley, *The Mediaeval Earthworks of Rutland*, Leicester 1983, 47.
52.   Hartley, op.cit., 15 and 18.
53.   Hartley, op.cit., 7.
54.   Pickering and Hartley, op.cit., 7.
55.   *Anglo-Saxon Chronicle* 877: *Two of the Saxon Chronicles Parallel*, ed. C.
Plummer, 2 vols., Oxford 1892-9, 1 74; 'then in the harvest season the army
went away into Mercia and shared out some of it and gave some to Ceolwulf'
(*The Anglo-Saxon Chronicle: A Revised Translation*, ed. D. Whitelock *et al.*,
London 1961; revised 1965, 48).
56.   *Anglo-Saxon Chronicle* 874: *Two Chronicles*, ed. Plummer 1 73; 'that it
should be ready for them on whatever day they wished to have it', (*Anglo-Saxon
Chronicle*, ed. Whitelock *et al.* 48).
57.   See particularly the distribution maps in Gillian Fellows-Jensen,
Scandinavian Settlement Names in the East Midlands, Copenhagen 1978, 246-63.
58.   The relevant papers are: (i) 'Scandinavian settlement in the territory of
the Five Boroughs: the place-name evidence'. Inaugural lecture, University of
Nottingham 1965; (ii) 'Scandinavian settlement in the territory of the five
boroughs: the place-name evidence. Part II, place-names in thorp', *Medieval
Scandinavia* 3 (1970), 35-49; (iii) 'Scandinavian settlement in the territory of the
five boroughs: the place-name evidence. Part III, the Grimston-hybrids',

England before the Conquest. Studies in Primary Sources presented to Dorothy Whitelock, ed. P. Clemoes and K. Hughes, Cambridge 1971, 147-63. These three studies are conveniently collected in *Place-Name Evidence for the Anglo-Saxon Invasion and Scandinavian Settlements. Eight Studies*, ed. K. Cameron, Nottingham 1975, 115-71.

59.   For a discussion of the distribution and significance of place-names with OE *Norðman* 'a Norwegian', see Fellows-Jensen, op.cit., 261-7.

60.   Map 6.

61.   Barrie Cox, 'Rutland and the Scandinavian settlements: the place-name evidence', *Anglo-Saxon England* 18 (1989), 135-48.

62.   Barrie Cox, 'Rutland in the Danelaw: a field-names perspective', *Journal of the English Place-Name Society* 22 (1989-90), 7-22. Also, Barrie Cox, 'Furze, gorse and whin: an aside on Rutland in the Danelaw', *Journal of the English Place-Name Society* 20 (1987-8), 3-9.

63.   Charles Phythian-Adams, 'The emergence of Rutland and the making of the realm', *Rutland Record* 1 (1980), 10-11.

64.   *The Chronicle of Æthelweard*, ed. A. Campbell, London 1962, 51. Campbell translates thus: 'In the city of York he contacted the enemy who possessed (*pandunt*) large territories in the kingdom of the Mercians, on the western side of the place called Stamford. This is to say, between the streams of the river Welland and the thickets of the wood called Kesteven by the common people.' Campbell's translation of *pandunt* is questioned by S. Keynes and M. Lapidge in their *Alfred the Great. Asser's 'Life of King Alfred' and other Contemporary Sources*, London 1983. They offer as an alternative version of this passage, 'At the city of York he comes upon the enemy who are plundering no small territories in the kingdom of the Mercians to the west of Stamford; that is, between the waters of the river *Weolod* (Welland) and the thickets of the wood which is commonly called Kesteven' (page 190). They note that: 'The transmitted *pandunt* is nonsense, and Campbell's translation of it ("possessed", literally "opened out") is impossible: *pando* is intransitive and cannot govern the accusative *territoria*. We suggest emending to *praedantur* "they plunder"' (page 137). However, Æthelweard most frequently uses the verb *vastare* when he refers to plundering and the verb *pandere* is indeed commonly transitive. Although we may ponder Æthelweard's exact meaning, his verb *pandere* is correctly inflected in its context and consistent with his style.

Whether the York Vikings already held sway over Rutland at this date or whether they were overrunning it prior to taking it into their possession, the territory appears to be regarded by Æthelweard as English and still part of the kingdom of Mercia. Certainly it does not seem to be a province occupied by Danes. It is most unlikely that Scandinavians of York would be plundering the possessions and settlements of fellow Scandinavians living in the East Midlands. Hugh Pagan has suggested that after the 877 division of Mercia, Ceowulf still controlled Lincoln (*Anglo-Saxon Monetary History*, ed. M.A.S. Blackburn, Leicester 1986, 63 and n.33). This is difficult to accept. Even so, the conventional historical wisdom that when Mercia was divided in 877, Ceolwulf retained only the western part of the kingdom and the Danes took the entire East Midlands must now be held in serious question. At just what date Stamford, whose town lands north of R. Welland were once so obviously part of the ancient territory of Rutland, became a Danish borough also remains a problem.

65.   Thorn, *Domesday Book: Rutland*, op.cit., R21 and Lc2.

66.   Margaret Gelling, *The Place-Names of Berkshire*, Part 3, English Place-Name Society Vol. 51, Nottingham 1976, 833.

67.   Cox, 'The place-names of the earliest English records', op.cit.

68.   Phythian-Adams, 'The emergence of Rutland and the making of the realm', op.cit.

69.   Map 1.

70.   Map 1.

71.   Cox, 'Rutland in the Danelaw: a field-names perspective', op.cit.

72,   ibid.

73.   *Victoria County History of Rutland*, Vol. 2, ed. W. Page, London 1931, 7, 8, 13.

74.   *Oakham in Rutland*, ed. R. Traylen, Rutland Local History Society 1982, 65.

75.   Margaret Gelling 'Further thoughts on pagan place-names' in *Otium et Negotium, Studies ... presented to Olof von Feilitzen*, ed. F. Sandgren, Stockholm 1973, 109-28; reprinted in *Place-Name Evidence for the Anglo-Saxon Invasion*, ed. K. Cameron, op.cit., 99-114.

76.   Bruce Dickins, 'Yorkshire hobs', *Transactions of the Yorkshire Dialect Society* 7, pt. 43 (1942), 9-23.

77.   J. Scherr, 'Names of springs and wells in Somerset', *Nomina* 10 (1986), 85-7; P. MacCana, *Celtic Mythology*, rev. ed., London 1983, 132; *The Place-Names of Roman Britain*, ed. A.L.F. Rivet and C.C. Smith, London 1979, 250 *s.n.* Anava.

78.   Hartley, *The Mediaeval Earthworks of Rutland*, op.cit., passim.

79.   L.M. Cantor, 'The medieval hunting grounds of Rutland', *Rutland Record* 1 (1980), 13-18.

80.   Cox, 'Furze, gorse and whin', op.cit.

ABBREVIATIONS AND BIBLIOGRAPHY

Abbreviations printed in roman type refer to printed sources and those in italic to manuscript sources.

a.	*ante.*
AAS	Reports and Papers of the Associated Architectural Societies.
Abbr	*Placitorum Abbrevatio* (RC), 1811.
AC	*Ancient Charters* (PRS 10), 1888.
AD	*Catalogue of Ancient Deeds* (PRO), in progress.
AddCh	Additional Charters in the British Library.
AddRoll	Additional Roll 15250 in the British Library.
adj.	adjective.
Æthelweard	*The Chronicle of Æthelweard*, ed. A. Campbell, 1962.
al.	*alias.*
AllS	*Catalogue of the Archives in the Muniments Room of All Souls' College*, ed. C.T. Martin, 1877.
AN	Anglo-Norman.
Anc	Earl of Ancaster's MSS, Lincolnshire Archives Office, Lincoln.
Angl	Anglian dialect of Old English.
ASC	*The Anglo-Saxon Chronicle*, ed. B. Thorpe (RS), 1861; *Two of the Saxon Chronicles Parallel*, ed. C. Plummer, 1892-9.
ASE	*Anglo-Saxon England.*
Ass	Assize Rolls in various publications.
Ass	Assize Rolls in PRO.
Asw	Aswarby MSS, Lincolnshire Archives Office, Lincoln.
ASWills	*Anglo-Saxon Wills*, ed. D. Whitelock, 1930.
ASWrits	*Anglo-Saxon Writs*, ed. F.E. Harmer, 1952.
Banco	*Index of Placita de Banco 1327-8* (PRO Lists and Indexes 32), 1909.
BCS	*Cartularium Saxonicum*, ed. W. de G. Birch, 3 vols., 1885-93.
BelCartA	Small Cartulary of Belvoir Priory (Add MS 98), Duke of Rutland's Muniments Room, Belvoir Castle.
BelCartB	Large Cartulary of Belvoir Priory (Add MS 105), Duke of Rutland's Muniments Room, Belvoir Castle.
BHS	Browne's Hospital, Stamford MSS, Lincolnshire Archives

Office, Lincoln.

Bir	Miscellaneous deeds in Birmingham City Library.
Bk	Buckinghamshire; *The Place-Names of Buckinghamshire* (EPNS 2), 1925.
Blore	Thomas Blore, *History and Antiquities of the County of Rutland*, 1811.
BM	British Museum.
BM	*Index to the Charters and Rolls in the Department of Manuscripts, British Museum*, ed. H.J. Ellis and F.B. Bickley, 2 vols., 1900-12.
BPR	*The Register of Edward the Black Prince* (PRO), 1930-3.
Bracton	*Henricus de Bracton, Note Book*, ed. F.W. Maitland, 1887.
Braye	Braye MSS, Leicester Muniments Room, Leicester Museum.
Brit	British.
Brk	Berkshire; *The Place-Names of Berkshire* (EPNS 49-51), 1973-6.
BrownArchSites	A.E. Brown, *Archaeological Sites and Finds in Rutland*, Leicester 1975.
Bru	Brudenell MSS, Northamptonshire Record Office, Northampton.
Burghley	Miscellaneous MSS in the Burghley Estate Office, Stamford.
c	*circa.*
C	Cambridgeshire; *The Place-Names of Cambridgeshire and the Isle of Ely* (EPNS 19), 1943.
Camden	W. Camden, *Britannia*, ed. R. Gough, 3 vols., 1789.
Cand	*The Chronicle of Hugh Candidus*, ed. W.T. Mellows, 1949.
CartAnt	*The Cartae Antiquae Rolls* 1-20 (PRS NS 17, 33), 1939 and 1960.
cent.	century.
cf.	compare.
Ch	*Calendar of Charter Rolls* (PRO), 6 vols., 1903-27.
Ch	Cheshire; *The Place-Names of Cheshire* (EPNS 44-7), 1970-2 (EPNS 48, 54), 1981.
ChancR	Chancellor's Rolls (as footnotes to *Pipe Rolls* (PRS), in progress).
ChancW	*Calendar of Chancery Warrants* (PRO), in progress.
Chap	*Chapter Acts, Lincoln Cathedral* (LRS 12, 13, 15), 1915-20.
Chas 1, Chas 2	Regnal date, t. Charles I, t. Charles II.
Chat	Deeds deposited by R. Chatterton, Solicitor, Lincolnshire

Archives Office, Lincoln.

ChR   *Rotuli Chartarum* (RC), 1837.

Churchwardens

     Accts   Churchwardens' Accounts in private hands.

Cl   *Calendar of Close Rolls* (PRO), in progress.

Cl   Close.

ClR   *Rotuli Litterarum Clausarum* (RC), 1833-44.

CN   *Carte Nativorum - a Peterborough Abbey Cartulary* (NRS 20), 1960.

Comp   Compotus Rolls, Duke of Rutland's Muniments Room, Belvoir Castle; Leicester Muniments Room, Leicester Museum; in Middleton MSS, Nottingham University Archives.

Conant   Conant MSS, Leicestershire Record Office, Leicester.

CoPleas   Common Pleas in various publications.

CPT   *Clerical Poll Taxes in the Diocese of Lincoln 1377-81*, ed. A. McHardy (LRS 81), 1992.

CR   *Churches of Rutland*, Rutland Local History Society, 1988.

Crop Marks   J. Pickering and R.F. Hartley, *Past Worlds in a Landscape: Archaeological Crop Marks in Leicestershire*, 1985.

Ct   Court Rolls in Hazlerigg MSS and Winstanley MSS, Leicestershire Record Office, Leicester; in Middleton MSS, Nottingham University Archives; in PRO.

Cu   Cumberland; *The Place-Names of Cumberland* (EPNS 20-2), 1950-2.

Cur   *Curia Regis Rolls* (PRO), in progress.

Curtis   J. Curtis, *A Topographical History of the County of Leicester*, 1831.

D   Devon; *The Place-Names of Devon* (EPNS 8-9), 1931-2.

Dane   F.M. Stenton, *Documents illustrative of the Social and Economic History of the Danelaw*, 1920.

dat.   dative.

Db   Derbyshire; *The Place-Names of Derbyshire* (EPNS 27-9), 1959.

DB   Domesday Book; *Domesday Book: Rutland*, ed. F. Thorn, 1980.

DC   Dean and Chapter MSS, Lincolnshire Archives Office, Lincoln.

Deed   Miscellaneous deeds in Leicestershire Record Office,

	Leicester; in Leicester Muniments Room, Leicester; in Lincolnshire Archives Office, Lincoln; in private collections.
DEG	Danby, Epton and Griffiths, Solicitors; deeds relating to the County Hospital, Lincoln, Lincolnshire Archives Office, Lincoln.
Denb	*The Manuscripts of the Earl of Denbigh* (HMC), 1911.
DEPN	E. Ekwall, *The Concise Oxford Dictionary of English Place-Names,* 4th ed., 1960.
dial.	dialect(al).
DKR	*Reports of the Deputy Keeper of the Public Records* (PRO).
Do	Dorset.
Dom	*Rotuli de Dominabus et Pueris et Puellis* (PRS 35), 1913.
Du	Dutch.
DuDCCh	Durham Cathedral Dean and Chapter charters, Durham County Record Office, Durham.
Dugd	W. Dugdale, *Monasticon Anglicanum,* 6 vols. in 8, 1817-30.
DuLa	Duchy of Lancaster deeds in PRO.
E.	east.
e	early.
ECP.	*Early Chancery Proceedings* (PRO Lists and Indexes 1-10).
ed. ′	edition; edited by.
EDD	J. Wright, *The English Dialect Dictionary,* 6 vols., 1898-1905.
Edw 1, Edw 2 etc.	Regnal date, t. Edward I, t. Edward II etc.
EETS	Publications of the Early English Text Society.
Ekwall Studies[2]	E. Ekwall, *Studies on English Place-Names,* Stockholm 1936.
Ekwall Studies[3]	E. Ekwall, *Etymological Notes on English Place-Names,* Lund 1959.
el.	place-name element.
Elements	A.H. Smith, *English Place-Name Elements* (EPNS 25-6), 1956.
ELiW	*Early Lincoln Wills,* ed. A. Gibbons, 1888.
eModE	early Modern English.
EnclA	Unpublished Enclosure Awards, Leicestershire Record Office, Leicester.
EpCB	*An Episcopal Court Book for the Diocese of Lincoln, 1514-20* (LRS 61), 1967.
EPNS	Publications of the English Place-Name Society.
esp.	especially.
et freq	*et frequenter* (and frequently (thereafter)).

et passim	and occasionally (thereafter).
ExchDep	Exchequer Special Depositions in PRO.
ExchSpC	Exchequer Special Commissions in PRO.
Extents	Ancient Extents in PRO.
FA	*Feudal Aids* (PRO), 6 vols., 1899-1920.
FacCh	*Facsimiles of Early Charters* (NRS 4), 1930.
Farnham	G.F. Farnham, *Leicestershire Medieval Village Notes*, 6 vols., 1929-33,
Fd	Field.
Fees	*The Book of Fees* (PRO), 3 vols., 1920-31.
Feilitzen	O. von Feilitzen, *The Pre-Conquest Personal Names of Domesday Book*, Uppsala 1937.
fem.	feminine.
FF	Feet of Fines in various publications.
FF	Feet of Fines in PRO.
FH	Finch-Hatton MSS, Northamptonshire Record Office, Northampton.
Finch	Finch MSS, Leicestershire Record Office, Leicester.
Fine	*Calendar of Fine Rolls* (PRO), in progress.
FineR	*Excerpta e Rotulis Finium* (RC), 2 vols., 1835-6.
Flor	Florence of Worcester's Chronicle in MHB.
Fm	Farm.
f.n., f.ns.	field-name(s).
For	*Select Pleas of the Forest*, ed. F.J. Turner (Selden Society 13), 1901.
For	Forest Proceedings in PRO.
Forsberg	R. Forsberg *A Contribution to a Dictionary of Old English Place-Names*, Uppsala 1950.
France	*Calendar of Documents preserved in France* (PRO), 1800.
Fransson	G. Fransson, *Middle English Surnames of Occupation*, Lund 1936.
freq.	frequent.
G	Unattributed 19th cent. forms collected by J.E.B. Gover.
GeldR	Northamptonshire Geld Roll in *Anglo-Saxon Charters*, ed. A.J. Robertson, 1939.
gen.	genitive.
GildR	Merchant Gild Rolls in *Register of the Freemen of Leicester, 1196-1770*, ed. H. Hartopp, 1927.
Gl	Gloucestershire; *The Place-Names of Gloucestershire* (EPNS 38-41), 1964-5.

Gt.	Great.
Ha	Hampshire.
Harl	Harley MSS in British Library.
Hastings	*The Manuscripts of the late Reginald Rawdon Hastings of the Manor House, Ashby de la Zouch*, Vol. 1, (HMC), 1928.
Hazlerigg	Hazlerigg MSS, Leicestershire Record Office, Leicester.
HMC	(Report of) The Historical Manuscripts Commission.
HMCVar	*Historical Manuscripts Commision, Reports on MSS in Various Collections*, 1901-23.
Ho.	House.
Hotchkin	Deeds deposited by N.S. Hotchkin of Woodhall Spa, Lincolnshire Archives Office, Lincoln.
Hrt	Hertfordshire; *The Place-Names of Hertfordshire* (EPNS 15), 1938.
HT	Rutland Hearth Tax assessments in PRO.
Hu	Huntingdonshire.
Hy 1, Hy 2 etc.	Regnal date, t. Henry I, t. Henry II etc.
ib, *ib*	*ibidem.*
Icel	Icelandic.
Inqaqd	*Inquisitiones ad quod Damnum* (RC), 1803.
Ipm	*Calendar of Inquisitiones post mortem* (PRO), in progress.
IpmR	*Inquisitiones post mortem* (RC), 4 vols, 1802-28.
ISLR	F.A. Greenhill, *The Incised Slabs of Leicestershire and Rutland*, 1958.
JEPNS	*Journal of the English Place-Name Society.*
KCD	*Codex Diplomaticus Aevi Saxonici*, ed. J.M. Kemble, 6 vols., 1839-48.
Kelly	Kelly's *Directory of the Counties of Leicester and Rutland*, 1932.
l	late.
L	Lincolnshire, *The Place-Names of Lincolnshire*, Pt. 1 (EPNS 58), 1985, Pt. 2 (EPNS 64, 65), 1991.
La	Lancashire.
LAHS	*Transactions of the Leicestershire Archaeological and Historical Society.*
LCDeeds	Leicester Corporation Deeds, Leicester Muniments Room, Leicester Museum.
LCh	Leicestershire Charters, Leicester Muniments Room, Leicester Museum.

Lei	Leicestershire; Barrie Cox, *The Place-Names of Leicestershire and Rutland*, unpublished Ph.D. thesis, Nottingham University, 1971.
LeiW	*Leicester Wills*, ed. H. Hartopp, 2 vols., 1902 and 1920.
Leland	*The Itinerary of John Leland*, ed. L. Toulmin-Smith, 5 vols., 1907-10.
Letter	Unpublished letters in local and private collections.
LHEB	K. Jackson, *Language and History in Early Britain*, 1953.
LindBN	E.H. Lind *Norsk-Isländska Personbinamn*, Uppsala 1920-1.
LinDoc	*Lincoln Diocese Documents*, ed. A. Clark (EETS, OS 149), 1914.
LML	*Lincoln Marriage Licences 1598-1628*, ed. A. Gibbons, 1888.
LN	*Liber Niger Scaccarii*, ed. T. Hearne, 1728.
LNPetr	*Liber Niger Monasterii S. Petri de Burgo* in *Chronicon Petroburgense* (Camden Society 47), 1849.
Löfvenberg	M.T. Löfvenberg, *Studies on Middle English Local Surnames*, Lund 1942.
LP	*Letters and Papers Foreign and Domestic, Henry VIII* (PRO), 1864-1933.
LRS	Publications of the Lincolnshire Record Society.
Lt.	Little.
LWills	*Lincoln Wills* (LRS 5, 10, 24), 1914-30.
m	mid.
Map	Various printed maps.
Map	Unpublished maps in local and private collections.
masc.	masculine.
Mdw(s)	Meadow(s).
ME	Middle English.
MedLat	Medieval Latin.
MER	R.F. Hartley, *The Mediaeval Earthworks of Rutland*, 1983.
MHB	*Monumenta Historica Britannica*, ed. H. Petrie, 1848.
MiD	Middleton MSS, Nottingham University Archives.
Midl	Midlands.
MilS	The Military Survey of Rutland 1522 in *The County Community under Henry VIII*, ed. J. Cornwall, Rutland Record Series 1, 1980.
MinAcc	Ministers' Accounts (PRO Lists and Indexes).
MinAcct	Ministers' Accounts in PRO.
MisAccts	Miscellaneous accounts in local and private collections.
Misc	*Calendar of Inquisitions Miscellaneous* (PRO), in progress.

Mkt.	Market.
MktHPR	Market Harborough Parish Records, Leicester Muniments Room, Leicester Museum.
ModE	Modern English.
Monson	Lord Monson's Muniments, Lincolnshire Archives Office, Lincoln.
Moulton	*Palaeography, Genealogy and Topography: Selections from the collection of H.R. Moulton*, 1930.
MR	Manorial Rolls, Westminster Abbey Muniments Room.
MS, MSS	Manuscript(s).
Mx	Middlesex; *The Place-Names of Middlesex* (EPNS 18), 1942.
N.	north.
Nb	Northumberland.
NCy	North Country.
n.d.	undated.
NED	*A New English Dictionary*, ed. J.A.H. Murray and others, 1888-1933.
neut.	neuter.
Nf	Norfolk; *The Place-Names of Norfolk*, Pt. 1 (EPNS 61), 1989.
NI	*Nonarum Inquisitiones in Curia Scaccarii* (RC), 1807.
Nichols	J. Nichols, *The History and Antiquities of the County of Leicester*, 4 vols. in 8, 1795-1811.
NMidl	North Midlands.
nom.	nominative.
Norw	Norwegian.
NRS	Publications of the Northamptonshire Record Society.
NS	New Series in a run of periodicals or publications.
Nt	Nottinghamshire; *The Place-Names of Nottinghamshire* (EPNS 17), 1940.
Nth	Northamptonshire; *The Place-Names of Northamptonshire* (EPNS 10), 1933.
O	First edition Ordnance Survey 1" maps.
O	Oxfordshire.
OblR	*Rotuli de Oblatis et Finibus* (RC), 1935.
ODan	Old Danish.
OE	Old English.
OFr	Old French.
OG	Old German.
OHG	Old High German.

OIcel	Old Icelandic.
OIr	Old Irish.
ON	Old Norse.
ONFr	Old Northern French.
OR	*Oakham in Rutland*, ed. R. Traylen, Rutland Local
.	History Society, 1982.
OS	Original Series in a run of periodicals or publications.
O.S.	Ordnance Survey.
OScand	Old Scandinavian.
OSurv	*The Oakham Survey of 1305*, Rutland Record Society, 1988.
OSut	*The Rolls and Register of Bishop Oliver Sutton.* (LRS 39, 43, 48, 52, 60), 1948-65.
p.	page.
(p)	place-name used as a personal name or surname.
P	*Pipe Rolls* (PRS), in progress.
Pap	*Calendar of Entries in the Papal Registers* (PRO), in progress.
Pat	*Calendar of Patent Rolls* (PRO), in progress.
PatR	*Rotuli Litterarum Patentium* (RC), 1835.
Peake	Peake MSS (Neville of Holt), Leicestershire Record Office, Leicester.
perh.	perhaps.
pers.n., pers.ns.	personal name(s).
P.H.	Public House.
Piers Plowman B	W. Langland, *Piers Plowman* (B text), ed. J.A.W. Bennet, 1972.
pl.	plural.
Plan	Unpublished plans in local and private collections.
PleaR	Plea Rolls, Nottingham University Archives.
Pleas	*Select Civil Pleas A.D. 1200-3* (Selden Society 3), 1890.
p.n., p.ns.	place-name(s).
PN -ing	E. Ekwall, *English Place-Names in -ing*, 2nd ed., Lund 1962.
Polyolbion	M. Drayton, *Polyolbion*, ed. J.W. Hebel, 1961.
poss.	possible, possibly.
p.part.	past participle.
PR	Parish Registers in various publications.
PRep	*The Register of Bishop Philip Repingdon* (LRS 57-8), 1963.
PRO	Public Record Office.

prob.	probably.
PRS	Publications of the Pipe Roll Society.
PrWelsh	Primitive Welsh.
PSJ	Deeds deposited by Peake, Snowe and Jendwin, Solicitors, Lincolnshire Archives Office, Lincoln.
Queen's	Rentals and surveys of the lands of the Bishop of Lincoln, Queen's College, Oxford, MS 366.
q.v.	*quod vide.*
QW	*Placita de Quo Warranto* (RC), 1818.
RBE	*Red Book of the Exchequer* (RS), 3 vols., 1896.
RBT	The Red Book of Thorney Abbey, Cambridge University Library, Add MS 3021.
RC	Publications of the Record Commission.
Rd	Road.
Reaney	P.H. Reaney, *A Dictionary of British Surnames*, 1958.
Recov	Recovery Rolls in PRO.
Reg	*Regesta Regum Anglo-Normannorum*, 3 vols., 1913, 1956, 1968.
RegAnt	*Registrum Antiquissimum of the Cathedral Church of Lincoln* (LRS 27-9, 51), 1931-58.
Rental	Rentals in local and private collections.
RFinib	*Rotuli de Oblatis et Finibus in Turri Londinensi* (RC), 1835.
RGrav	*Rotuli Ricardi Gravesend Episcopi Lincolniensis* (LRS 20), 1925.
RGros	*Rotuli Roberti Grosseteste Episcopi Lincolniensis* (LRS 11), 1914.
RH	*Rotuli Hundredorum* (RC), 2 vols., 1812-8.
RHug	*Rotuli Hugonis de Welles Episcopi Lincolniensis* (LRS 3, 6), 1912-3.
RN	E. Ekwall, *English River-Names*, 1928.
r.n.	river-name.
RotNorm	*Rotuli Normanniae in Turri Londinensi* (RC), 1835.
RS	Rolls Series.
RTemple	Rothley Temple Deeds, Leicester Muniments Room, Leicester Museum.
Ru	Rutland.
Rut	Duke of Rutland's MSS, Muniments Room, Belvoir Castle.
S	P.H. Sawyer, *Anglo-Saxon Charters*, 1968.
S.	south.

s.a.	*sub anno.*
SAL	Society of Antiquaries, London, MS 60.
Sale	Records of local sales, Lincolnshire Archives Office, Lincoln.
Sandred	Karl Inge Sandred, *English Place-Names in -stead*, Uppsala 1963.
Saxton	Saxton's Map of Rutland, 1576.
sb.	substantive.
Scand	Scandinavian.
sg.	singular.
ShR	Shangton Records, Leicester Muniments Room, Leicester Museum.
Signposts	M. Gelling, *Signposts to the Past*, 2nd ed., 1988.
Slater	*Slater's Royal National Commercial Directory*, 1850.
SlCart	Slawston Cartulary, Leicestershire Record Office, Leicester.
SM	*Stamford Mercury.*
SMED	G. Kristensson, *A Survey of Middle English Dialects 1290-1350*, Lund 1967.
SMETT	G. Kristensson, *Studies on Middle English Topographical Terms*, Lund 1970.
s.n.	*sub nomine.*
SP	State Papers Domestic in PRO.
Speed	John Speed, *The Theatre of the Empire of Great Britain*, 1610.
SPNLY	G. Fellows-Jensen, *Scandinavian Personal Names in Lincolnshire and Yorkshire*, Copenhagen 1968.
SR	Lay Subsidy Rolls in various publications, esp. The Lay Subsidy for Rutland 1524 and 1525 in *The County Community under Henry VIII*, ed. J. Cornwall, Rutland Record Series 1, 1980.
SR	Lay Subsidy Rolls in PRO.
Sr	Surrey; *The Place-Names of Surrey* (EPNS 11), 1934.
surn.	surname.
Surv	Surveys in PRO and in local and private collections.
s.v.	*sub voce.*
Swaff	Robert de Swaffham's footnotes to his transcript of the Chronicle of Hugh Candidus in *The Chronicle of Hugh Candidus*, ed. T. Mellows, 1949.
Sx	Sussex; *The Place-Names of Sussex* (EPNS 6-7), 1929-30.
t.	*tempore.*

TA	Tithe Awards, Leicestershire Record Office, Leicester.
Tax	*Taxatio Ecclesiastica Angliae et Walliae c.1291* (RC), 1802.
TB	Tryon of Bulwick MSS, Northamptonshire Record Office, Northampton.
Templar	*Records of the Templars in England in the Twelfth Century,* ed. B.A. Lees, 1935.
Terrier	Terriers in local and private collections.
TT	Deeds relating to the accession of Terricus Tyers of Cologne, burgher of Stamford, in PRO.
UR	*Uppingham in Rutland,* Rutland Local History Society, 1982.
v.	*vide.*
Val	*The Valuation of Norwich,* ed. W.E. Lunt, 1926.
VCH	*The Victoria County History of Rutland,* 2 vols., 1908 and 1935.
VE	*Valor Ecclesiasticus* (RC), 1810-34.
VR	*The Villages of Rutland,* 2 vols., Rutland Local History Society, 1979.
W	Wiltshire.
WDB	Westminster Domesday Book, Westminster Abbey Muniment Book 11, Westminster Abbey Muniments Room.
We	Westmorland; *The Place-Names of Westmorland* (EPNS 42-3), 1967.
WFris	West Frisian.
Whit	Whitfield MSS, Lincolnshire Archives Office, Lincoln.
White	W. White, *History, Gazetteer and Directory of Leicestershire and Rutland,* 1846, 1863, 1877.
Will	Unpublished wills in local and private collections.
Win	Winstanley MSS, Leicestershire Record Office, Leicester.
wk.obl.	weak oblique.
Wm 1, Wm 2	Regnal date, t. William I, t. William II.
WoCart	John de Wodeford's Cartulary, MS Claudius A XIII, British Library.
WR	D. Henry, *Wind and Watermills of Rutland,* 1988.
Wright	J. Wright, *The History and Antiquities of the County of Rutland,* 1684-8.
Wülcker	T. Wright, *Anglo-Saxon and Old English Vocabularies,* 2nd ed., ed. R.P. Wülcker, 1884, reprinted Darmstadt 1968.
Wyg	Wyggeston Hospital Records, Leicester Muniments Room,

Leicester Museum.

YE	Yorkshire East Riding; *The Place-Names of the East Riding of Yorkshire and York* (EPNS 14), 1937.
YN	Yorkshire North Riding; *The Place-Names of the North Riding of Yorkshire* (EPNS 5), 1928.
YW	Yorkshire West Riding; *The Place-Names of the West Riding of Yorkshire* (EPNS 30-7), 1961-3.
2½"	Ordnance Survey 2½" maps, editions of 1950-5.
6"	Ordnance Survey 6" maps, editions of 1958-71.
*	a postulated form.

PHONETIC SYMBOLS

p	*p*ay	j	*y*ou	ɔ	p*o*t
b	*b*ay	x	lo*ch* (Scots)	ɔ:	s*aw*
t	*t*ea	h	*h*is	ɔi	*oi*l
d	*d*ay	m	*m*an	e	r*e*d
k	*k*ey	n	*n*o	ei	fl*ay*
g	*g*o	ŋ	si*ng*	ɛ	jam*ais* (Fr.)
ʍ	*wh*en	r	*r*un	ɛ:	th*ere*
w	*w*in	l	*l*and	i	p*i*t
f	*f*oe	tʃ	*ch*ur*ch*	i:	b*ea*d
v	*v*ote	dʒ	*j*u*dg*e	ou	l*ow*
s	*s*ay	ɑ:	f*a*ther	u	g*oo*d
z	*z*one	ɑu	c*ow*	u:	b*oo*t
ʃ	*sh*one	a	m*a*nn (German)	ʌ	m*u*ch
ʒ	a*z*ure	ai	fl*y*	ə	ev*er*
þ	*th*in	æ	c*a*b	ə:	b*ir*d
ð	*th*en			?	wa*t*er (Cockney, glottal stop)

Phonetic symbols are enclosed in square brackets: [   ].

The symbols used in the expression of Brit and PrWelsh forms are those used in LHEB.

NOTES ON THE PHONOLOGY
OF RUTLAND PLACE-NAMES

1.   OE *æ* normally becomes ME *a* as in Alstoe, Ashwell, Ayston and *Asshelounde*. There are occasional 13th century spellings
with *e* for Ashwell.

2.   OE *ǽ* regularly becomes ME *ē* as in Seaton and Stretton.
Stretton (with early shortening) also has spellings in *a* (1086-1503).
In field- and minor names, e.g. *the Strete* (Mkt. Overton), ME *ē* is
usual, but ME *a* occurs also, as in *Ladiakre* (Gt. Casterton) and *le
Lady Wong* (Lt. Casterton).

3.   OE *al* followed by a consonant usually remains in ME, as in
Caldecott, *Caldwell* (Mkt. Overton), *Calvercroft* (Cottesmore) and
Kalkeleys (Leighfield). Only very occasionally is ME *o* found, as in
Foldhaluacre (Mkt. Overton) and *le Oldefelde* (Lt. Casterton).

4.   OE *a* before nasals remains ME *a* in major names such as
Hambleton, Langham, Manton, Ranksborough and Wrangdike.
However, field-names frequently show both OE and ON *a* rounding
to ME *o*, as in *Longwrangelondes, Wdebindthornwong* (Cottesmore),
Morwong, Northlongfurlong (Mkt. Overton), *Wrongedich* (N. Luffen-
ham) and *Wrongelond* (Wing).

5.   OE, ON *a* remains as in Glaston, Ryhall and Catmose.

6.   OE *ā* usually remains as ME *a* as in Bredcroft, Holyoaks,
Bradbek (Ashwell) and *Hallewellescros* (Barrowden). But ME *ō* is
also found as in Bore Hill (Lyddington), Broadeng (Tinwell),
Broddole (Thorpe by Water) and *le Brodemor* (Barrowden). ON *á*
becomes ME *ō* in *le Wro* (Lt. Casterton).

7.   OE *e* remains in ME as in Egleton, Empingham, Essendine,
Exton and *Snelston*. ON *e* remains in ME, as in Wing (but with *ie,
ye* spellings in 1203, *ee* 1208, 1346, *ey* 1390, 1409 and *y* from 1294)
and in field-names such as *Beclane* (Hambleton) and *Hesilgate*
(Barrowden).

8.   OE *ē* remains in ME as in Ridlington (with eventual shortening here to *e* and *i* before *-dl-*), *Estrewellewong* (Mkt. Overton)
and *Grenehowe* (Cottesmore).

9.   ME *e* in the final element of Essendine and Whissendine is
lengthened and diphthongized to [ai]: Essendine (*-dyne* 1617),
Whissendine (*-dyne* 1506), cf. Mickledine (*-danes* 1691, Barleythorpe).

10.   OE *ea* becomes ME *a* as in Armley and *Armslades* (Barley-

thorpe).

11.　　OE *ea* becomes ME *ē* as in East Hundred, Edith Weston, Leighfield and Teigh.

12.　　ON *ei* gives ME *ē* in *Brethesik* (Caldecott) and probably in *Bleksike* (Mkt. Overton).

13.　　OE *eo* becomes ME *e* as in Barrow, Barrowden, Belmesthorpe and Hardwick.

14.　　OE *ēo* becomes ME *ē* as in Greetham, Deepdale and The Freewards. In Prestley and Preston, early shortening takes place.

15.　　ME *er* gives *ar* as in Barrowden (from 1428), Barrow (from 1485), Barnsdale (from 1610) and Hardwick (from 1610).

16.　　OE, ON *i* remains in ME in Thistleton, Tickencote, Tixover, The Wisp and Ingthorpe. Flitteris shows a few *e* spellings in the late 13th and 14th centuries, cf. *le welugate* (c1275, Barrowden).

17.　　OE *ī* remains in ME but is eventually shortened in compounds, as in Pickworth, Swintley and Whitwell.

18.　　OE *o* remains in ME, as in Cottesmore, Oakham, Stocken and Stoke Dry.

19.　　OE, ON *ō* remains in ME, as in Brooke, Morcott, Rutland, *Rutmore* and Tolethorpe.

20.　　ME *ō* is sometimes raised and shortened to [u] as in Brooke, Rutland (*Rut-* 1396) and *Rutmore* (*Rut-* 1363).

21.　　OE, ON *u* remains as in Burley, Gunthorpe, Luffenham, *Luffewyke*, Uppingham, Woodhead etc., with occasional *o* spellings to the end of the 14th century.

22.　　OE, ON *ū* often remains, as in Sculthorpe, *Suthfeld* (Oakham) and Woolfox. If shortened, it is represented by ME *o* in names from **dūn** and **tūn**.

23.　　OE, ON *y* appears in ME as *i (or y)*, as in Bisbrooke, Clipsham, Geeston, Rushpit, Ryhall, *Linges* (Lt. Casterton) etc. But ME *u*, as in *Punfold* (Egleton), *Ruddyngdykefurlang* (Cottesmore), *Wakehull, Willeshulles* (Mkt. Overton) and occasionally ME *e*, as in *Wyueleshell'* (Mkt. Overton), also appear.

24.　　OE *ȳ* appears as ME *ī (or ȳ)* in Tinwell and Stoke Dry. It is shortened early to *i (or y)* in Lyddington.

25.　　OE *b* is unvoiced to *p* by dissimilation in some late forms for Bisbrooke.

26.　　OE *hw* normally gives ME *w*, as in Whissendine, ·Whitwell and Witchley. But it remains as ME *wh* in many forms for Whitwell, in *Wheytlondes* (Cottesmore) and in occasional forms for

Witchley.

27.   OE *t* gives ME *th* in some forms for Rutland and Teigh. ON initial *t* appears as *th* in some spellings for Tolethorpe as late as 1610. OE, ON medial *t* is occasionally voiced to *d* as in Braunston, Cottesmore and Kilthorpe.

28.   ME *t* is lost from the 16th century onwards from the group *-ston* as in Braunston, Egleton, Geeston, Glaston and *Snelston*. In Leicestershire also this feature is regular.

29.   OE *þ* remains as ME *th*, as in Thistleton and *Thirspit* (Barrowden, Glaston). OE, ON *þ* frequently gives ME *t* in early ME forms for *-thorpe* as in Gunthorpe, Ingthorpe, Kilthorpe, Martinsthorpe, Thorpe by Water etc.

30.   OE, ON *ð* is always lost in later ME due to contraction. It is occasionally represented by ME *d* as in early forms for Alstoe, Ayston, Glaston and *Fridwod* (Ridlington).

31.   OE *w* is aspirated in some early forms for River Gwash. ME *w* is aspirated in some early forms for Wing.

32.   Intrusive *g* appears when *-ing-* spellings are created by analogy with p.ns. derived from **-inga-** and **-ing-**[4] constructions, as in forms for Essendine and Tickencote.

33.   Metathesis with *r* occurs in Casterton in early forms and from the 16th century in forms for *Alsthorpe*, Belmesthorpe and Westhorpe. In Clipsham, *-il-* becomes *-li-* (*Kilpes-* 1203, *Clipes-* 1286).

34.   Contractions are common as in Alstoe, Ayston, Barnsdale, Belmesthorpe, Egleton etc.

35.   AN features include *au* spellings for *a* in Braunston, *a* spellings for *e* in Scapwell (Barrowden) and *ch* spellings for the voiceless stop [k] in Tixover.

36.   Grammatical forms of interest include: (i) a secondary gen.pl. form *exna* (for OE *oxna*) in Exton; (ii) the northern ME gen.sg. ending *-is, -ys* which occurs in Barnsdale, Clipsham, Egleton, Kilthorpe, Martinsthorpe and *Snelston*; (iii) the inflected weak genitival form *-an* which survives in Essendine.

37.   An early recurring Rutland dialect form is *hell* for *hill*, as *Helle* (c1300, Lt. Casterton), *Wyueleshell'* (1363, Mkt. Overton), *lytle hell* (1566, Egleton), *Hell Hill* (1631, Morcott). Spellings in *furr* for *far* occur in the 17th century, e.g. *Furhill* (1630, Oakham), *Furr Close* (1691 Lyndon, 1729 Hambleton, 1744 Mkt. Overton). *Gorse* is shortened to *gosse* from the 17th century, as in *Gosse Hedge*

(1652, Greetham), *Gosborough* (1748, Whissendine). 17th and 18th century shortening of *sheep* to *ship* occurs, as in spellings for *the Sheepe close* (Glaston), Sheep Coat Hollow (Oakham) and *Shipland Furlong* (Barrow).

1.   The county-name, river-names and district-names are discussed first. After these, the place-names are treated within the divisions of the old Hundreds. The Hundreds are dealt with in the following order: the north, the west, the east, the central west and then the south. Within each Hundred, the civil parishes are treated in alphabetical order and within each parish, the parish-name is followed by names of primary historical or etymological interest, also arranged in alphabetical order. At the end of these sections, all the remaining names on the 1958-71 6" O.S. maps are listed with such early forms and etymological comment as can be provided; these names, however, are usually of obvious origin or ones about whose history it is unwise to speculate. The final section of each parish lists field-names, divided into modern (i.e. post-1800) and earlier. The pre-1800 field-names are printed in italic.

Street-names are given immediately after the interpretation of a town-name, in alphabetical order according to the modern forms. In parishes with a large number of inn-/tavern-names, surviving or defunct, these names are collected in a separate section following the major names, or in the case of towns, following a section dealing with the names of buildings.

2.   Place-names believed to be no longer current are marked '(lost)', e.g. 'ALSTHORPE (lost)'. This does not necessarily mean that the site to which the name was once applied is unknown. We are dealing primarily with names, and it is the names which are lost. These names are printed in italic when referred to elsewhere in the text and in the index. Place-names marked '(local)' are believed to be current locally.

3.   The local pronunciation of the place-names is given, when it is of interest, in phonetic script within square brackets, e.g. 'Glaston [gleistən]'.

4.   In explaining the various place-names and field-names, summary reference is made, by printing the elements in bold type, to the detailed account of these elements in *English Place-Name Elements* (EPNS 25, 26) and JEPNS 1, e.g. 'Ashwell, *v.* **æsc, wella**'.

5.   In the case of all spellings of place-names for which reference has been made to unprinted sources, the fact is indicated

by printing the abbreviation for the source in italic, e.g. '1322 *Wyg*' denotes a form derived from a manuscript, in contrast to '1326 Pat' which denotes one taken from a printed text.

6.   Where two dates are given for a source, e.g. '1189 (1332)', the first is the date at which the document purports to have been composed; the second is that of the copy which has come down to us.   Dates of the form '12', '13', 'e14', etc. refer to the century of the document or manuscript and 'Hy 1', 'Edw 2', etc. to a monarch's reign; the date '1154-60' means that the form belongs to a particular year within those limits but cannot be more precisely dated.

7.   '(p)' after a reference to a source indicates that the spelling given is that of a person's surname, not primarily a reference to a place.   Thus '*Caldecote* 1198 FF (p)' refers to one *Hugo de Caldecote*, bearing *Caldecote* as a surname.

8.   Where a letter in an early place-name form is placed within brackets, forms with and without that letter are found, e.g. '*This(s)leton*' means that the forms *Thisleton* and *Thissleton* are found.

9.   Where an entry reads e.g. 'POOR CLOSE COVERT, 1806 Map', the place-name appears in its modern spelling in the source quoted.

10.   All elements are normally quoted in the form of the headword in *English Place-Name Elements* where the dialectal variants are given.   The Anglian forms are, of course, the only ones found in the place-names of Rutland.   These elements are quoted without asterisks in the case of postulated forms.

11.   When a p.n. is compared with an example from another county, that county is indicated, e.g. 'cf. Ridlington Nf'.   Where no such indication is given, the comparative p.n. belongs to Rutland.

ADDENDA

p. 105 *s.n.* FINKEY ST. Professor Richard Coates in a forthcoming article 'A breath of fresh air through Finkle Street' argues that this street-name is indeed based on ME *fen(e)kel* 'fennel', but that it did not identify a place where fennel grew or was sold. He believes, rather, that *fen(e)kel* indicated a badly smelling thoroughfare. He points out that according to pre-Renaissance medical texts, fennel was much used as a cure for flatulence in encouraging the breaking of wind through the anus. Hence, Finkle Street was a name given to a street that continuously stank. Coates suggests that the name was coined initially in York and spread in the Danelaw area because of traders' activity. Oakham, because of its market, would have been especially receptive to such a linguistic innovation.

p. 193 *s.n.* *Goslyms* (Lyndon) and p. 264 *s.n.* *Goslin(g) Lane* (N. Luffenham). A possible alternative source for these names in adjoining parishes is dialectal *goslin(g)* 'the blossom or catkin of the willow', *v.* EDD, *s.v.*

pp. 28, 52, 149, 220, 228, 262, 285 *s.n.* Water Furrows (in its various forms). Mr J. Field believes that the frequently accepted interpretation of this common field-name (i.e. 'land where water tends to lie in the furrows') is unsatisfactory. He writes, 'Various explanations have been offered for the name, e.g. spade- or plough-cuts across the furrows to facilitate drainage, but the most persuasive is that these were deeper furrows so ploughed in order to carry off surface water. They were conspicuous enough to pass into field-names, confirming that not every furrow (as might be concluded from some definitions) was a water-furrow.' *v.* J. Field, *A History of English Field-Names*, London 1993, p. 50.

RUTLAND

Roteland(e) 1053-66 (12) ASWrits 94 (S 1138), 1086 DB,
 1080-7 Reg, 1155, 1159 P et freq to 1436, 1437 Peake et
 passim to 1552, 1554 Conant, -landa 1130, 1156 P et passim
 to 1177 ib, -laund' 1241, 1244 Cl et passim to 1293 ib,
 -lond(e) 1221 MiD, 1243 Cl, 1368 Pat, 1439 Cl
Roteland sokene c1377 Piers Plowman B
Rotheland 1294, 1337 Cl, Ruthland 1466 Pat
Rut(t)eland(e) 1396, 1397 Cl et passim to 1471 Peake, 1511 FH,
 1586 DuLa, -lond 1555 Conant
Rutland(e) 1416 Wyg, 1442 Rut, 1449 WoCart, 1492 MktHPR et
 passim to 1535 VE, -lond' 1460 Cl, 1497 Braye et passim to
 1540, 1556 Conant
Ruthelandshire c1545 Leland

'Rōta's land', v. land, sōcn. The OE pers.n. Rōta appears to
be a by-name meaning 'the pleasant or cheerful one', from the adj.
rōt 'glad, cheerful, bright'. For reference to the original soke of
Rutland, v. VCH 1 121-36. For minor forms which also record the
Anglo-Saxon Rōta, v. Rutmore in Teigh.

River-Names

CHATER (rises east of Halstead Lei and flows for fifteen
 miles past Ketton to R. Welland north of Stamford L.)
Chatere 1263, 1286 Ass
Chater c1545 Leland, 1610 Speed

This is a pre-English r.n. of uncertain etymology and
meaning. Ekwall DEPN postulates that it is Brit cēto-dubron 'forest
stream', v. cēd 'a wood', dußr 'water'.

EYE BROOK (rises at Tilton Lei and from above Allexton Lei to
 its confluence with R. Welland at Caldecott forms the
 boundary between Rutland and Leicestershire.)
Litelhe 1218, 1227 For, 1227 ClR, Litele 1290, 1299 For, 1300 DC,

Litelye 1276 RH
Lytele 1269 For, *Lytelee* 1376 *For*
Litilhe 1218 Pat, *Lytylhe* 1414 *Conant*
Littleye 1276 RH
Litle Eye c1545 Leland, *Little Ey* 1610 Speed

'The little river', *v.* **lytel, ēa.**

GLEN (rises south-east of Grantham L and flows through the
    extreme eastern tip of Rutland to R. Welland below
    Spalding L.)
Glenye 1276 RH
Glen 1365 Pat, *la Glene* 1435 ib

Ekwall RN 176 suggests that this is from the Brit base
*glanjo- or *glanja-, a derivative of *glano-, Welsh *glan* 'clean, holy,
beautiful, fair'. *Glanjo-* would give PrWelsh *Glen, becoming OE
Glene. Its meaning is 'the clean one', cf. R. Glen Nb, *v.* LHEB
602.

GWASH (rises near Owston Lei and flows twenty miles through
    Rutland to R. Welland below Stamford L.)
le Whasse c1230 RN, *aquam que vocatur le Whasse* 14 *DuDCCh*
Wesse 1263 *Ass*
Wass 1269 For, *Wasse* 1198 FF, 1276 RH, c1300 Blore, 1307
    AD, *Wase* 1266 *For*
Washe c1545 Leland, *Wash* 1613 Polyolbion
Wasch(e) c1545 Leland
Gwash 1586 Camden, *Guash* 1610 Speed, 1684 Wright, 1695 *Map*

The late form *Gwash* is a quasi-Welsh spelling. The name
appears to be OE **(ge)wæsc** 'a washing, a flood'.

WELLAND (rises near Sibbertoft Nth and flows seventy miles to
    The Wash.)
Weolud c924 (s.a. 921) ASC A
Vueolod l10 (e11) Æthelweard
Welund a1118 (s.a. 919) Flor
Weland(e) 1218, 1228 *For*, 1230 Cl, 1247 *Ass*, 1287 *Peake et
    passim* to 1610 Speed

Welond(*e*) 1227 ClR, 1247 *Ass,* 1276 RH, 1312 *Peake et passim*
    to 1411 Pat, 1445 Cl
Weiland 1199 (1330), *Weyland* 1200 Ch, 1263 *Ass,* 1365, 1366
    Pat, *Wailand*(*e*) 1394, 1399 Cl, *Weylaund* 1281 QW, 1285
    Ipm, 1286 *Ass*
Wi-, Wyland 1422, 1466 *Peake,* c1545 Leland, *Wylond* 1377 BM,
    Wylondiam 1351 *Peake*
Welland 1505, 1553 Pat

    A pre-English r.n. of uncertain etymology and meaning.
Jackson, LHEB 221, considers that even a 'Celtic origin is
doubtful'. The change from OE *Wēolud* to ME *Weland* may be due
to Scand influence. Many Scand r.ns. have a participial ending
-and, a form unknown in OE examples.

District-Names

RUTLAND FOREST

    Much of the county once lay within the royal forest of
Rutland (*in foresta de Rotheland'* 1190 CartAnt, *in foresta* (*nostra*)
de Roteland' 1219, 1221 ClR, *in foresta regis de Rotel'* 1231 Cl, *v.*
forest). Later, the forest was restricted to the south-west of the
county and became known as Leighfield (*in foresta regis de Lyfelde*
1491 *For*), *v.* Leighfield.

VALE OF CATMOSE

    The val of Catmouse 1576 Saxton, *The Vale of Catmouse*
    1610 Speed, *Vale of Catmus* 1613 Polyolbion, 1684 Wright,
    Vale of Catmose 1684 ib, 1695 *Map, Vale of Catmoss* 1801
    Map.

    Evidently 'wild-cat marsh', *v.* **cat(t), mos.** The feature was
no doubt much more restricted in area than the region so called
today. The low-lying ground on the streams to the south-east and
east of Oakham (for which a *Fengate* 'road to the marsh' is
recorded) may well have been the original location, *v.* Catmose,
Catmouse mill and also Catmouse in Burley f.ns. (b).

4

ALSTOE HUNDRED

Alfnodestou 1086 DB, *Alnodestou* 1195 P, *Alnethestouwe* 1208 *FF*,
  Alnathestowe 1263, 1286 *Ass*
Alnestow(e) 1184, 1185 P, 1196 ChancR, 1286 *Ass et freq* to 1327
  SR, Alnastowe 1263 *Ass*, 1296 *SR*
Alstowe 1535 VE, *Allstoe* 1610 Speed, *Alstoe* 1695 *Map*

'Ælfnōð's place of assembly', *v.* **stōw**. The site of the
hundred moot was beside Alstoe House in Burley parish. The
division is styled *-wapentac* 1086 DB, *-wapentagio* 1184, 1185 P but
-hundred 1195 P and thereafter, *v.* **vápnatak, hundred**.

Ashwell

ASHWELL
  Exewelle 1086 DB
  Essewell(e) 1202 Ass (p), 1264 (p), 1274 RGrav (p)
  Assewell(e) 1209 P, 1243 RGros *et passim* to 1286, 1294
    Ass et freq to 1353 *ib*, 1357 Cl *et passim* to 1407 *FF*
  Asshewell(e) c1291 Tax, 1312 Pat *et freq* to 1336 *Ass et*
    passim to 1516 *FF*, 1535 VE
  Ashwell 1610 Speed

'The ash-tree stream or spring', *v.* **æsc, wella**.

ASHWELL CHURCH, *Church (St Mary)* 1846 White. ASHWELL
GRANGE, 1932 Kelly, *v.* **grange**. ASHWELL HALL, 1932 ib is
Ashfield Hall 1879 VCH. ASHWELL HILL. ASHWELL LODGE.
LANGHAM PLACE (local), formerly *The Tambourine Inn* - VR.
LOUDAL LANE (local), *Louedale, Loudall* 1610 Speed, *Lowdale*
1838 *TA*, 1897 *Deed, Loodle* 1943 *Map*; the first element is obscure,
v. **dalr**. MANOR FM. MANOR HO., 1932 Kelly. MAYCROFT
(local), possibly from the local surname *May*, cf. John *Maye* 1522
MilS of Teigh,· John *Maye* 1522 ib of Langham and William *May*
1524 SR also of Langham, *v.* **croft**. MERE LANE (local), *v.*
(ge)mære. OLD HALL, 1897 *Deed*, cf. *Hall Close* 1838 *TA*.
THE RECTORY, 1846, 1863 White, 1932 Kelly. SALTERS FORD

LANE (local), *Salterford* 1634 *Terrier*, *Far* -, *Great* -, *Top Salterford*, *Salterford Meadow* 1838 *TA*, 'the saltmerchants' ford' which was at SK 870 119, a point at which the parishes of Ashwell, Burley and Langham meet, cf. Salterford in Burley f.ns. (a), *v.* **saltere, ford**. WESTFIELD is *West Field House* 1897 *Deed*, *Field House* 1846, 1863 White, possibly an antiquarian revival of the name of one of the village's great open-fields, *v. Westfeld* in f.ns. *infra.* WOODSIDE, 1932 Kelly.

Field-Names

The undated forms in (a) are 1897 *Deed* (per Mr D. Tew); those dated 1838 are *TA*; 1883 and 1913 are *Deed* (per Mr D. Tew), 1943 are *Map*. Early forms dated 1371 are *Rental*, 1634 are *Terrier*, while 1650 and 1696 are *Deed*.

(a) Half Acre 1838, 1897, Two Acres 1838, 1897, Three -, Five -, Six Acres 1943, Long Ten -, Near Ten Acres 1838, Ten Acres 1897, 1943, Twelve -, Thirteen Acres 1943, Fourteen Acres 1897, 1943, Eighteen -, Twenty Acres (x2) 1943, Seventy-eight Acre 1943 (*v.* **æcer**); Appletree Moor 1943 (*v.* Board's Cl *infra*); Far -, First Bargate (perh. Angl *bercet* 'a birch copse', cf. Bargate Hill in Braunston f.ns. (a)); Beck Cl or Cow Cl 1838, 1897 (*v.* **bekkr**); Bedshaws (a corrupt form of Redshaws *infra*); Big Fd 1943; Bircham 1943 (poss. 'birch copse', *v.* **bircen**[1]); Colonel Blair's (Big Fd) 1943 (alluding to Lt-Col. F.G. *Blair* of Ashwell Hall 1932 Kelly); Boards Cl or Appletree Moor 1897 (the first f.n. from the surn. *Board*); Bottom Fd 1943; Boundary Corner 1943; Boy Fd and Hasty Cl 1943 (cf. Boyfields Cl in neighbouring Teigh f.ns. (a); Mr J. Field suggests that the name may be from the surn. *Boys*); Brickkiln Cl; Bridge Cl 1838 (1751 *Deed*); Bridge Leys, - Mdw 1838, 1893, Bridge Leys or Dry Leys 1897 (cf. *atte Brygge* 1402 Pat (p), *atte· Brigg* 1403 ib (p), *v.* **brycg**); Broadback Eight Acres, - Ten Acres, - Spring Piece 1838, Broad Buck 1897 (*Bradbek'* 1371 *Rental*, 'broad stream', *v.* **brād, bekkr**); Great -, Broadholme 1897, Big -, Little -, Middle Broadholme 1943 (*v.* **brād, holmr**); Bromley's Cl 1838, 1897, Bromley Land 1883, Bromley Leys 1943 (from the surn. *Bromley*); Buck Hill Cl 1838 (either with *bucca* 'a he-goat' or *bucc* 'a male deer'; although Ashwell was never part of the Forest of Rutland, neighbouring Whissendine may have had a park in the late 12th cent. which could account for *bucc* here); Bulls Cl 1838; Little -, Burnsike 1897, 1943 (*Burneseeke* 1634, *v.* **burna, sik**); Nether -, Over Bush Cl 1838, 1897; Butchers Hill 1943 (from the surn. *Butcher*, cf. *Butcher's Close* in Burley f.ns. (b)); Upper Catten Hills 1897, Upper Catterhills 1943 ('hills frequented by wild cats', *v.* **catte** (**cattena** gen.pl.)); Chapman's Cl 1838, 1897; Church Yard 1838; Far -, Clarks Cl 1838, 1897 (from the surn. *Clark(e)*, cf. William *Clarke* 118 *Surv* of neighbouring Burley); Cooks Cl 1838, 1897; Cottagers Pastures 1838, Cottage - 1897 (*v.* **cotager**); Cottesmore Road Fd 1943; Cow Cl 1838; Four -, Cow Mdw; Cow Gait ('pasturage for a single cow', *v.* **cow-gate**); Cow Pastures 1979 VR; Cross Lane Cl 1838, Crosslands Cl 1897; Crowcut Hades, The Crockadeds 1897 (*Crodicke Hades alias Crodicke Leyes* 1650 *Deed*, *Crodykehades* 1667 *ExchDep*, 'headlands at Crodyke, i.e. the ditch in the nook of land', *v.* **crōh**[2], **dīk**, **hēafod**, **lēah**); Dalby Cl 1838, 1897 (from the surn. *Dalby*, cf. *Dalbies house garden and orchard* in neighbouring Burley f.ns. (b) and Dolby Great Cl in Langham f.ns. (a)); Day's Hill Fd 1838, - High Fd 1897, 1943; Daisy's Fd 1943; Debdales 1943 ('deep valley', *v.* **dēop, dalr**); Eastwell Yard; Far Grass (*v.* **gærs**); Far Mdws; Near -, Fartowns Cl, Presgraves Far Towns 1838 (from the surn. *Presgrave*, poss. a family originating in the lost *Prestgrave* in Neville Holt Lei, cf. *presgraves close* in Oakham f.ns. (b), *v.* **tūn**); Fawcets 1838 (from the surn. *Fawcet(t)*); Fishpond Cl 1838, 1897 (for the fishpond on record here in 1370, *v.* VCH 2 109b; what may be a medieval fish-pond survives at SK 8628 1383, *v.* MER 5); Fossits Cl (perh. identical with Fawcets *supra*); Foxholes (*v.* Rough Cl *infra*); Freeholds Cl 1838, Freeholds 1943; Front of the Hall (cf. Hall Cl *infra*); Garth ('small plot of ground near a house', *v.* **garðr**); Glebe (- Thirty Acre, - Forty Acre) (*v.* **glebe**); Greatholme (*v.* **holmr**); Hall Cl 1838, 1897; Hasty Cl (*v.* Boy Fd *supra*); Herd Cl; Highway Cl 1943, Middle Highway or Ivy Cl 1897, 1943 (Mr J. Field notes that *Ivy* may have been based on a mishearing of (unaspirated) *Highway*); Near -, Nether -, Upper -, Highway Cl; Hill Cl(s) 1897, 1943; Hills Cl and Bogg 1838 (*v.* **bog**); Upper Hog Cl; Holme Cl (*v.* **holmr**); Home Cl 1838 (x8) (1650 *Deed*, *v.* **home**); Home Fd 1943; Capt. Hornsby's Cl; Horse Cl; Hovel Cl (*v.* **hovel**); Inmans Cl (from the surn. *Inman*, cf. Wright *Hinman* 1678 *Anc*, Philip *Hinman* 1758 *Surv* of Stretton and Hinmans in Barrow f.ns. (a)); Nether -, Upper -, Lambhog Cl 1838, 1897 (*Farre Close or Lamb Hogg Close* 1688 *Deed*, alluding to shearling lambs or *hogs*, cf. Upper Hog Cl *supra*); Land Cl 1897, 1943 (*Land Feild or Land Close* 1650 *Deed*, an enclosure consolidating selions of the old open-fields, *v.* **land**); Lingmoor Cl 1838, Great -, Little Lingmore Cl 1883 (*Lingmore* 1650 *Deed*, 'heather-covered moor', *v.* **lyng, mōr**[1]); Littledale; Little Fd (Thirteen Acres) 1943; Long Cl 1913; Long Mdw; Loose Dogs 1943 (prob. with *docce* 'the dock plant' and reference to soil texture); Middle Cl 1943; Middle Fd; Middle Mdw 1943; Middle -, Near -, Upper Molson's Cl 1838, 1897; Monks Cl 1897, 1943; Oakham Way Cl 1838, Oakham Road Fds 1943; Upper Old Cl 1838, Old Cl 1897; The Old Pasture 1943; Osier Bed 1943 (*v.* **oyser, bedd**); Paddock; Pan Cl 1838, 1897 (poss. 'land in a circular depression', *v.* **panne**); Great Park and Warren 1838, 1897, Small

Park and Warren 1897, The Park 1943; Pen(n) Cl 1838, 1897, Pen(n) Mdw 1838, 1897, 1943 (v. **penn²**); Pig Pens 1943; Philpots Cl 1838, 1897 (from the surn. *Phillpot*, cf. William *Phellypot* 1522 MilS of• neighbouring Langham); Potterhills 1838, Potter Hill 1897, Potter's Hill Forty-one Acres 1943 (from the surn. *Potter*, cf. *Potter's Close* in neighbouring Burley f.ns. (b)); Redshaws 1838 (a surn., cf. Redshaw's farmyard in Lyddington f.ns. (a)); Rippins Bottom Fd (from the surn. of John *Rippin* 1932 Kelly); Near -, Rook Cl 1897, 1943 (v. **hrōc**); Rough Cl or Foxholes 1838, Rough Cl 1897, 1943 (v. **rūh¹**); Sandy Leys; Little Seeks 1838 (v. **sīk**); Slad's Cl 1838, 1943, Slade Cl 1897 (v. **slæd**); Smith's Cl; Spring Piece (v. **spring, pece**); Stackyard Fd (v. **stak-ʒard**); Stadfolds and Pingle 1838, Far -, Near Studfolds 1897 (*Stadfoulde* 1634 Terrier, v. **stōd-fald, pingel**); Steeple Cl (perh. alluding to an endowment for the maintenance of church fabric, cf. *Steeple Acre* in Lyddington f.ns. (b) and Steeple Fd in Pickworth f.ns. (a)); Stockwell Bridge 1838; Stonepit Cl, Three Acres or Stone Pit Cl 1897; Three Nook'd Cl 1838 (referring to a triangular piece of land, v. **nooked**); Far -, Near Town Cl (v. **tūn**); Upper Cl 1897, 1943; Far Wake Cl or Big Wright's, Near Wake Cl or Little Wright's 1943, Near -, Upper Wakeleys 1838, Near Walkleys 1897, Near Walk Cl 1897 (alluding to a sheep-walk, v. **walk**); Wards Cl 1838, 1897; Wheelhouse Cl(s) 1838, 1897 (a *wheelehouse* was a building containing a horsewheel as motive power for threshing machines etc.); Whissendine (Whissendine parish adjoins to the west); Whittles 1838; The Wilderness 1838.

(b) *Bikerwode* 1371 ('a wood subject to dispute', v. **biker, wudu**); *Bridge Leyes Close* 1650 (v. **brycg, lēah**); *Bushy Close* 1650, *Byshy Close* 1696 (v. **busshi**); *Cow Close* 1634; *Farre Close* 1650 (v. **feor**); *Godyehades* n.d. VCH (from the surn. *Goody*, v. **hēafod**); *le Haye* 1371 (v. **(ge)hæg**); *Roychards Crofte* n.d. VCH (from the surn. *Richard(s)*, v. **croft**); *Shipman Wong close* 1634 (perh. from the surn. *Shipman*, but in local 17th cent. dial. *sheep > ship*, so that we may have here 'the sheep-man's in-field', cf. *Shipland Furlong* in Barrow f.ns. (b) and *The Shypdike* s.n. Washdyke Cl in Exton f.ns. (a), v. **vangr**); *South Orchard* 1650 (v. **orceard**); *atte Well(e)* 1371 Extent (p), 1379 Pat (p) (v. **wella**); *Westfeld* 1345 MinAcct ('the west field', one of the great open-fields of the village, v. **west, feld**).

Barrow

BARROW
Berc 1197 (p), 1206 Cur, 1208 *FF et passim* to 1296 *SR et freq*
to 1319 Pat, *Berk* 1263 *Ass*, 1276 RH *et passim* to 1319 Pat

Bergh 1316 Ipm, 1322 *FF,* 1327 *SR et passim* to 1428 FA
Berugh 1324 *FF,* 1329 *Deed, Berogh'* 1417 *ib*
Berew(e) 1305 *Deed,* 1376, 1403 Cl, 1405 *FF, Beruwe* 1362 *Deed*
Bargh 1485 *Deed*
Barow 1510 *Deed, Barrowe* 1535 VE, 1539 LP, 1553 Pat, 1610
    Speed, *Borowe* 1522 *Rut*

'The burial mound', *v.* **beorg.** Barrow village stands at the
crest of a steep hillside which rises to 480 ft above sea-level. At
the hill crest near The Green is a tumulus which was once clearly
visible from the valley bottom. It was no doubt this tumulus rather
than the hillside which gave Barrow its name, *v.* VCH 2 120.

BUSSACK BARN (2½"), cf. *Bushock Furlong* 1652 *Terrier, Bussock*
- 1767 *ib.* At first sight, this appears to be an OE **buscuc* 'a place
overgrown with bushes' as in Bussock, Brk 277 (*v.* **busc, -uc**). But
the earlier local forms *Bursyke* c1295 *Deed, Burghsyk'* 1362 *ib,*
Borowsikegate 1294 *ib* may belong here. Bussack Barn was almost a
mile to the east of the village and less than a mile from the Roman
road, Sewstern Lane, further to the east. A fortified site related to
this important routeway into Rutland and to the ancient northern
frontier that appears to have run south of Market Overton,
Thistleton and Stretton would be reasonable and the distance of
such a **burh** from the village would explain the **gata** 'road' of the
1294 form. However, in neighbouring Teigh parish to the west of
Barrow is a lost **burh-stall** 'site of a fortification' (cf. *Burstall'*
medewe in Teigh f.ns. (b)) and these early Barrow forms may relate
to this. Bussack Barn has been demolished and its site is now part
of Cottesmore Airfield. The 2½" O.S. map shows a rectangular
earthwork 500 yards to the south of Bussack Barn at SK 902 153, *v.*
burh, sík, gata.

BARROW HO., cf. *Barrow House Fields* 1943 *Map.* BARROW
WIDE HOLE (local), a former turning place for barges on the
disused Melton Mowbray-Oakham canal. GLEBE FM, *v.* **glebe.**
THE GREEN (local), 1935 VCH, *v.* **grēne**[2].

Field-Names

The undated forms in (a) are 1943 *Map*; those dated 1801 are *Surv*. Early forms dated 1294, c1295, 1305, 1318, 1339, 1362, 1417 and 1687 are *Deed*, while those of 1652 and 1767 are *Terrier*.

(a) Four -, Six Acre (x2), Eight -, Ten -, Twelve -, Fourteen Acre, Twenty-six Acres (*v.* **æcer**); Far -, Home Allotment 1801 (*v.* **allotment**); Allotments (referring to allotment gardens); Barn Fd; Bottom Mdw; Brig Cl (*v.* **brycg**, here in a Scandinavianized form); Broad Cl; Bull's Nook (*v.* **bula, nōk**, cf. *Bulls Nook* in Lyddington f.ns. (b), Bull Nook in Teigh f.ns. (a) and *v.* We 1 30 which notes that "according to Caxton, *The game and playe of chesse* (1474), 112, 'a grete bole is suffisid with right litil pasture', and after the enclosures this seems to have been the view of the local farmers"); Christian's Cl 1801 (from the surn. *Christian*, cf. John-, Robert- and William *Cristian* 1522 MilS, 1524 SR); Clarks Cl; Cow Hill; Hardy's, Hardy's Rayces (*Rayces* is prob. from the surn. *Rayse, Royse* of an earlier owner, cf. John *Rasse* 1522 MilS of Thistleton, Richard *Raysse* 1524 SR of Egleton and Richard *Royse* 1524 ib of neighbouring Greetham); Great Hawkshill 1801 (prob. a corrupted form of *Hawkswell infra*); Hinmans (a surn., cf. Inmans Cl in Ashwell f.ns. (a) and *Philip Hinmans Close* in Stretton f.ns. (b)); Home Cl 1801, 1943 (*v.* **home**); Land Cl (*v.* **land**); Leason's Cl 1801, Leasons 1943; Leaverlands (a surn., cf. William *Leaverland* 1846, 1877 White); Little Cl 1801; Big -, Little Maddison's; Navigation Cl (alluding to the disused Melton Mowbray-Oakham canal); Over the Line (i.e., land 'on the far side of the railway'); Parson's; Robleys (a surn., ultimately from Rabley Hrt or Robley Ha); Rye-grass Cl 1801, Ryegrass 1943 (*v.* **rye-grass**); Stackhills; Stackyard Cl (*v.* **stak-ȝard**); Top Cl; Tow Cl (perh. from *Tolands infra*, but an allusion to the tow-path of the disused canal cannot be discounted); The Two Wongs (*v.* **vangr**).

(b) *Barrow Feild* 1652 (*v.* **feld**); *Borowsikegate* 1294, *Bursyke* c1295, *Burghsyk'* 1362 (*v.* **burh, sík, gata**); *Bryar Bush Furlong* 1652, *Brierbush* - 1767 (*v.* **brēr, busc**); *Caleueldale* c1295 (*v.* **calu, wella, dalr**); *in campo occidental'* c1295 (the old west open-field of the village, later called *Cow Hill Feild, v.* **west, feld**); *in campo orientali* c1295, 1339 (the old east open-field, later called *Mare Bush Feild, v.* **ēast, feld**); *Cow Hill Feild, Cow Hill Furlong* 1652 (*v.* **cū, hyll**); *Crakepornfurlong'* c1295 ('(furlong at the) thorn tree frequented by crows', *v.* **craca, þorn, furlang**); *Crap Land* 1652 (*v.* **crappe, land**); *le Crossegate* c1295 (*v.* **cros, gata** and cf. *Kettles Close infra*); *Dedemansforlang* 1305 (perh. referring to the discovery of an ancient burial in a barrow here, *v.* **dede-man, furlang** and cf.

Deadmans Holme in Barrowden f.ns. (a)); *ad ecclesiam de Berk'* c1295 (*v.* **cirice**); *Emedw* 1417 ('meadow beside a stream', *v.* **ēa, mǣd**); *Fisshepool ʒerd'* 1417 (*v.* **fisc-pōl, geard**); *Gluckffurlang* 1294, *le Glugg* 1417, *Long Lug Furlong* 1652 (prob. ME **glug** 'a clod', alluding to heavy ground, *v.* **furlang**); *Greene Huske Furlong* 1652 (unexplained, cf. *Green Huske Furlong* in Whissendine f.ns. (b) and Stone husk furlong in Lyddington f.ns. (a) and in Thorpe by Water f.ns. (a)); *atte Halle* 1406 Pat (p) (*v.* **hall**); *Hawkswell Close* 1687 (*v.* **hafoc, wella**); *Longhesil* 1339, *Long Hassells* 1652 (*v.* **lang¹, hesli**); *Heseldal'* c1295 (second el. either **dalr** or **deill**, *v.* **hesli**); *Hesilgate* 1417 (*v.* **hesli, gata**; the road ran into Cottesmore parish, cf. *Hesyllgate* in Cottesmore f.ns. (b)); *Barrow Heath Piece* 1787 *Surv, New Heath, Old Heath Furlong* 1652 (*v.* **hǣð**); *le Hilgate* 1318 (*v.* **hyll, gata**); *Holes* 1417 (*v.* **hol¹**); *North -, Sowth -, Hollow Furlong* 1652 (*v.* **holh**); *The Horse Way* 1652 (*v.* **weg**); *Linge Furlong* 1652 (*v.* **lyng**); *Kettles Close or Crosse Close* 1687 (*v.* **cros**); *Mare Bush Feild, North -, South Mare Bush Furlong* 1652 (either referring to a bush acting as a boundary marker or to 'scrubland at the boundary', *v.* **(ge)mǣre, busc**); *The Meere* 1652 (*v.* **(ge)mǣre**); *Meredel* 1417 (also from **(ge)mǣre** 'a boundary'; according to Elements 1 129, OE **dell** 'a dell, a valley' does not occur in the Midl or NCy, so perh. the second el. is Scand **deill** 'a portion of land' (but cf. perh. *Thurndel Ley* in Morcott f.ns. (b))); *Middle Furlong* 1767, *Middle Piece* 1767 (*v.* **pece**); *Midilsyke* 1318 (*v.* **middel, sík**); *Milnewongk'* c1295, *Mill Furlong* 1652, cf. *iuxta molendinum abbat' de Valle Dei* 1318 (the *Abbot of Vaudey* still possessed lands here in 1522 MilS, *v.* **myln, vangr**); *The Neather Close* 1687 (*v.* **neoðera**); *Overbothtys* c1295 (perh. naming a furlong 'above both enclosures', with the final el. the plural of OE **tēag** 'a small enclosure'; but Mr J. Field suggests that the form may be a scribal error for *Overbothys* 'above the booths', with ME **bothe** 'a temporary shelter'); *le Rydale* 1318 (second el. either **dalr** or **deill**, *v.* **ryge**); *Shipland furlong* 1652 ('sheep land', *v.* **scēap, land**); *Stonehill Furlong* 1652 (*v.* **stān, hyll**); *Stone Pitt Furlong* 1652 (*v.* **stān-pytt**); *Stonwongk'* c1295 (*v.* **stān, vangr**); *le Strete* c1295, 1417, *the Streete Way* 1652 (referring to the Roman road now called Sewstern Lane, *v.* **strǣt**); *Swallow Hole Furlong* 1652, 1767, *v.* **swalg, hol¹**); *Tolands* 1417 (*v.* **twēgen, land**); *Upper Furlong in the Middle of the Field* 1767; *The Waste Way* 1652 ('the road to the manorial waste', *v.* **waste, weg**).

Burley

BURLEY

Burgelai 1086 DB, 1179 P, *Burgel'* 1206, 1230, 1231 Cur, *Burgalai* c1150 Dane

Burghele 1288 *Ass*
Burglegh 1286 *Ass*, *-le* 1301 Cl, 1327 *SR*
Burghle 1294 *Ass*, 1301 Pat (p), 1314 ib, 1328 Banco *et passim*
    to 1383 Pat, *-ley* 1393 *FF*, *Burghley al. Byrley* 1548 *ib*
Burle 1218 For, 1276 RH *et passim* to 1369 Pat *et freq* to 1380
    ib *et passim* to 1406 PRep, *-lega* 1202 *FF*, *-legh* 1312, 1316
    Pat *et passim* to 1363 AD, *-ley(e)* 1316 Inqaqd, 1341 NI *et*
    passim to 1428 FA *et freq* to 1610 Speed
Borle 1294 *Ct, Boroule* 1296 *SR, Borowle* 1304 Ipm, *Bor(o)ughle*
    1305 FA, 1353 Ipm

'Woodland belonging to or near to a stronghold', *v.* **burh, lēah**.
The **burh** compounded in this name was most probably Hambleton,
the possible *caput* of an early Anglian kingdom constituting the
territory which was to become modern Rutland.

ALSTHORPE (lost)

Alestanestorp 1086 DB, *Alestanthorp* 1282 IpmR, *Alstanthorp*
    Edw 1 Ipm
Alestorp(e) 1232 RHug, 1234 Pat, *-thorp(e)* 1300 Ipm *et freq* to
    1319, 1334 Pat, 1350 Ipm
Alstorp 1202 Ass, *-thorp(e)* 1297 *Ass*, 1324 *FF et passim* to 1428
    FA
Austhorpe 1610 Speed, *-trop* 1548 Pat, *Awstroppe alias Alstroppe*
    1677 *Deed*

'(E)alhstān's outlying farmstead', *v.* **þorp**. The DB form shows a
glide-vowel *e* which has replaced medial *h*. For the OE pers.n., *v.*
Feilitzen 152-3. The settlement seems to have disappeared by the
middle of the sixteenth century, probably as the result of enclosure.
For field-names arising from the name of this lost settlement which
lay near Chapel Farm, *v.* f.ns. (a) *infra*.

ALSTOE HO. is *Mount Alstoe House* 1780 *Map, Alstoe House Farm*
1846 White, *Alstoe Farm* 1932 Kelly; the site of the hundred
meeting-place, *v.* Alstoe Hundred *supra* and Mount Alstoe *infra*.
BOTTOM MILL COVERT is *Mill Gorse* c1800, 1806 Map, *Mill
Cover* 1824 O, *v.* **gorst, cover(t)**. BRICK KILN SPINNEY (-

COVERT 2½"), cf. *Brick Kiln Close* 1943 *Map.* BROOKE FM, *Burlebroke* c1200 *WDB, Brooke furlong* 1634 *Terrier, v.* **brōc.** BROWNSWELL'S COVERT, cf. *Brownwell Close* 1943 *Map.* BURLEY BUSHES, *v.* **busc.** BURLEY ON THE HILL, *Burleigh on the Hill* 1682 *Deed, Burley on the Hill* 1695, 1780 *Map,* 1863 White, 1932 Kelly, *Burley alias Burleigh House* 1677 *Deed, Burley Hall* 1846 White. BURLEY PARK, *Burleigh Park(e)* 1677, 1694 *Deed,* 1801 Map, *Burley Park* c1800 ib, *The Park* e18 *Rental,* cf. *The Upper Park* c1700 *ib, v.* **park.** BURLEY WOOD, *boscus de Burlega* 1208 *FF, Burley Wood* 1610 Speed, *v.* **wudu.** CHAPEL FM, *Chapel F.* 1824 O, *Chapel Farm* 1826 G, 1846 White, probably named from the chapel of *Alsthorpe* which was endowed with land there by Nicholas de Segrave in 1312, *v.* VCH 2 112. CHESTNUT FM (local) was *The Finchs Arms,* named from the *Finch* family of Burley on the Hill and closed e19 - VR. COW CLOSE FM, 1846 White, *Cow Close* 1729 *Surv,* 18 *Map,* 1824 O, 1826 G, (*The*) *Great Cow Close* c1685, e18 *Rental.* CROW SPINNEY. DOG KENNEL SPINNEY, cf. *Dog Kennell Close* 1729 *Surv, Dog Kennell Yard* 1729 *ib, Dog Kennel* 1824 O, once housing the hounds of the local hunt. EGG SPINNEY, cf. *Eggwonge* 1652 VCH, either referring to shape or to the snowberry (*Symphoricarpus racemosus*), a shrub of the elder family which bears large white berries (dial. *egg*), *v.* **vangr.** EIGHT RIDING TREE, *v.* **ryding.** ENGINE POND was created to supply water for the house and formal gardens at Burley on the Hill. It was equipped with a wind pump which was connected up to drive the water in 1703, *v.* MED 10. EXTON GRANGE, *v.* **grange.** FLINT'S COVERT, cf. Flint's Fields in neighbouring Cottesmore f.ns. (a). GATE HOUSE BRIDGE. GLEBE FARM HO. (local), *v.* **glebe.** THE HERMITAGE, a summer-house built by Lord Winchelsea in 1807, *v.* VCH 2 113. HOLLOW CLOSE COVERT is *Hawleys Plantation* 1824 O, cf. *Hollow Close* 1943 *Map, v. Haleys Close* in f.ns. (b) *infra.* HORSE AND GROOM P.H. (lost), 1850 Slater. MILLFIELD SPINNEY, cf. *Mill Close* 1682 *Deed,* 1729 *Surv,* 18 *Map, v.* **myln.** MOUNT ALSTOE, 1801 Map, *Mt. Alstoe* 1780 *Map,* the surviving motte of an early castle. PARK FM is *Burley Farm* 1824 O, *Park Farm* 1846 White. PARK LODGE, 1846 ib. POOR CLOSE COVERT, 1806 Map, *Powers Close* 1652 VCH, probably referring to a charitable endowment: *power* is a 17th century spelling for *poor.* PURVEYOR'S COVERT, *Purveyor's Cover* 1824 O, cf. *Purvers Close* c1685 *Deed,* e18 *Rental, Purveyors Close* 1729 *Surv,* 18 *Map, Bottom* -, *Top Purveyors* 1943 *ib*; a purveyor was a steward, manager or domestic officer who arranged supplies for a great personage, *v.* **cover(t)**. SOLOMON'S HUT, from the surname *Solomon*, cf. Solomon's Grave in Mkt. Overton f.ns. (a). TOLL BAR (lost), 1846, 1863 White. TURNOVER BRIDGE. THE VICARAGE, cf. *vicaridge furlong* 1634 *Terrier.* WATKIN'S GORSE, 1824 O, *v.* **gorst.**

Field-Names

Undated forms in (a) are 1943 *Map.* Early forms dated 1294, 1295, 1296, 1297, 1298 and 1299 are *Ct*; 1596, 1598, 1601, 1616, 1632, c1660, 1662, 1677, 1682, c1685, 1694 and 17 are *Deed*; 1634 are *Terrier*; c1700, e18 and 1781 are *Rental*; those dated 1729 and 118 are *Surv,* while those dated 18 are *Map.*

(a) Three -, Six -, Nine -, Ten -, Thirteen Acres, Eleven Acre (*v.* **æcer**); Bottom -, Middle -, Top -, Austrip's (*Allesthorp(e)land* 1540 *MinAcct*, 1551 Pat, *Awstropp Landes* or *Awstrop Feildes* 1616, *Austroppe Feilds* alias *Awlstropp(e) Pastures* 1677, 1694, *Nether Alsthorpe* 1596, *Middle Awstropp, Over Alsthorpe* or *Mr Farnehams Closse* 1601, *Ostroppe Close, Ostroppe Field* 1652 VCH, *Fishers* -, *Great Austorpe* c1685, *The Austorp(e)* e18, *Austhorpe Grove* 1610 Speed, *v. Alsthorpe supra*); Barn Cl; Barn Mdw; Booth's Cl (*Booths Close* 17, e18, 1729, *Booth Close* 18, *Booth's Close and Meadow* 18, from the surn. *Booth*); Bosomes Cl (*Bossoms Close* 1601, 1634, *Bosom Close* 1729; perh. from the surn. *Bossom* but OE *bōs* (*bōsum* dat.pl.) 'a cow-stall' is also poss., cf. Boswick Cl in Teigh f.ns. (a)); Burley Fds; Campion's Gorse c1800, 1806 Map (*v.* **gorst**), Campion's Lodge 1806 ib, Campion Plantation c1800 ib (from the surn. *Campion*); Coleseed Cl (*Cole-seed Close* 1729, 18, land on which rape was grown; *Brassica campestris oleifera* was cultivated for the 'sweet oil' obtained from its seeds, *v.* **coleseed**); Top Cottage Cl; Cottager's Spinney 1824 O (*Cottiers Close* 1601, 17, *Cotthers* - c1685, *Cotchers* - e18, *Cottagers* - 1729, *Cottager's* - 18, *v.* **cottere, cotager**); Cottesmore Furlong (near the boundary with Cottesmore parish which adjoins to the north); Galls (*The Galls* 1634, *(The) Gauls* 1729, 18, *v.* **galla**); Glebe (*v.* **glebe**); Gorse Cover 1824 O (*v.* **gorst, cover(t)**); Healy's Cl; Little Hell (a dial. form of *hill*, cf. Big -, Little Hell in Mkt. Overton f.ns. (a)); Henton Gorse c1800 Map, Hentons - 1806 ib (*v.* **gorst** and Henton in Cottesmore f.ns. (a)); Hill Cl (17, e18, 1729, 18, *Nether* - 18, *Nether Hill Close Meadow* 1781); Home Cl (1729, 18, *v.* **home**); Horse Cl; Laxton's Cl (from the surn. *Laxton*, cf. Robert *Laxston* 1522 MilS, husbandman of Greetham); Longslang ('long, narrow strip of land', *v.* **slang**), Longstaffe's Cl; Mill Cl, - Fd; North Cl; Rough Cl (18, *v.* **rūh**[1]); Bridge -, Salterford (*Salterford* 1601, 1634, 1729, 1781, *East* -, *Middle* - 1601, *Old* - c1685, e18, *Salterford(e) Close* 1634, 1682, 1729, - *Closes* 1684 *Anc, Salterfords* 18, *Salterford Mead* 1729, 18; for the location of 'the salt-merchants' ford', *v.* Salter Ford Lane in Ashwell); Bottom -, Middle Seeds (an area of sown grass, *v.* **sǣd**); Smith's Fd, - Mdw (*Smiths Close* 1682, *Smith's* - 18, *Smiths Close and Mead* 1729, *Smith's Close Meadows* 18); Spring Cl (*v.* **spring**); Stile Cl (1729, 18, *v.* **stigel**); Water Wongs (*Waterwoongs* 1729, *Water-Wongs* 18, *waterwongs leas* 1634, *v.* **wæter, vangr, lēah**); White Leys (*White Ley(e)s* 1601, 1729, - *Leas(e)* 1634, 1682; dial. *white* can denote 'dry pasture' and this may pertain here, *v.* **hwīt, lēah**); Winterton's Cl (*Winterton Close* 1729, held by Samuel *Winterton* 1729); Wright's Cl.

(b) *Alsto(e) Closes* 1729, 18 (*v.* Alstoe Ho. *supra*); *The Avenue* 118 (*v.* **avenue**); *Boddilie Meadow* 1652 VCH, *Bodilys Meadow* c1685, c1700, e18; *Brinkleys Cottage* c1685 (with the surn. *Brinkley*); *Bulimore* 1729 (a surn., cf. Bullimore's in neighbouring Oakham f.ns. (a), Bullemores Cl in Langham f.ns. (a)); *Burley Parke Wall* 1632, *Park Wall Close* 1781, *Within the Park Walls* 1729 (*v.* **park**); *Burtons Close* c1685, e18 (from the surn. *Burton*); *Butchers Close* 1729, *Butcher's* - 18 (from the surn. *Butcher*); *Catmouse* c1685, e18, *Catmose* 118, *Catmos Close* 1729, *Catmus Mead,* c1700 (*v.* **cat(t), mos** and Vale of Catmose); *Chamberlains' Close* c1685, *Chamberlins* - e18 (from the surn. *Chamberlain*, cf. Robert *Chamberlyn* 1522 MilS, - *Chamberlen* 1524 SR of neighbouring Cottesmore); *Christians Close* c1685, e18 (from the surn. *Christian*, cf. Christian's Cl in Barrow f.ns. (a)); *Clarkes Paddock* 118 (held by Wm. *Clarke* 118); *Coles Cottage* c1685, 18, - *and Ground* 18 (in the possession of Widow *Cole* c1685); *Comptons Close* c1685, e18, 1729, *Compton* - 18 (from the surn. *Compton*); *Corn Close* 1729, 18; *Cotsmore Lane,* - *Close* 1729, *Cottesmore Lane Close* 18 (Cottesmore parish adjoins to the north); *Coxes Close* c1685, e18 (from the surn. *Cox,* cf. Cox's Cl in Teigh f.ns. (a)); *ate Crosse* 1295 (p), *nether crospond* 1634 (*v.* **cros, ponde**); *Cure Close* 1729, 18 (perh. a pound for sick animals); *Dalbies Ground, Dalbies house garden and orchard* c1685 (from the surn. *Dalby, v.* **grund**); *Den Ecre* 1298 (the first el. may be **denn** 'a den, a pit', *v.* **æcer**); *Drie Close* 1652 VCH, *Dry* - c1700, (*v.* **drȳge**); *Edgeton Padock,* - *2 Padock* 1729 (named from Egleton parish which adjoins to the south); *Exton Cow Close* 1729 (Exton parish adjoins to the east); *Fancutts Cottage* c1685 (from the surn. *Fancourt,* cf. Fancourts Cl in Stretton f.ns. (a)); *ate Fenne* 1294 (p) (*v.* **fenn**, cf. *Catmouse supra*); *Old* -, *New Fish Pond Padock* 1729, *Eastward* -, *Middle* -, *Westward Fishpond Paddock* 118 (the fishpond is now drowned in Rutland Water); *Fosters Close* 1729; *Goddemade* n.d. FF (poss. from the OE pers.n. *Godda,* but an early form of the surn.

Good may also be thought of, cf. the following f.n., *v.* **mǣd**); *Goods Paddock* 118 (from the surn. *Good*); *Grasse Ground* 1601 (*v.* **gærs, grund**); (*The*) *Grove End* 1601, 1729, 18 (*v.* **grǣf, ende**[1]); *The Hall Grounds* 1601 (referring to an early hall, since the predecessor of Burley on the Hill was built by the first Duke of Buckingham c1620-30, *v.* **hall, grund**); *Haleys Close* 1729 (in the possession of Sam. *Hauley* 1729, *v.* Hollow Close Covert *supra*); *The Heigh Feild* 1601, *highefeilde* 1634, *High Field* 18, *Highfield Close* 1729 (*v.* **hēah**[1], **feld**); *Hippisley's Close* 18 (Toby *Hippesley* is cited in 1716 *Deed*); *Jacksons Close* 1685, *Jacson's* - e18; *Ladie Close* 1652 VCH, *Lady Meadow* c1700, e18, 1729 (alluding either to Our Lady, the Virgin Mary, or to a female proprietor or to a dowager or to the lady of the manor, *v.* **hlǣfdige**); *Land Close* c1685, c1700, e18, 1729, 18 (*v.* **land**); *in la Lane* 1294 (p), *in the Lane* 1297 (p) (*v.* **lane**); *Lodg(e) Closes* 1729, 18; *Long Close* c1700, 1729; *Long Meadow* c1685, c1700, e18, 1729; *Longthorne leas, Short longthorne furlong* 1634 (*v.* **lang**[1], **þorn, lēah**); *Masons Close* c1685, e18 (from the surn. *Mason*, cf. Masons Yard Pasture in Teigh f.ns. (a)); *Meadow Close* 1729; *Meakin's Close* c1685, *Meakins* - e18; *ate Mere* 1295 (p) (*Ricardus ate Mere* in this instance is likely to be 'Richard at the Pool', with reference to a mere which was fashioned into the fishpond, formerly on the southern boundary of the parish, before its destruction by the spread of Rutland Water, *v.* **mere**[1]); *Middle Close* 1729, *Midle Pasture* 1682; *Mydilfeld* 1346 Cl (*v.* **middel, feld**); *New Close* c1685, 17, e18, 1729, *Nether -, Upper -* 18; *Newfeild* 1601, 1662, e18, *Newfield Close(s)* 1729, 18 (*v.* **nīwe, feld**); *New Woods* c1685, c1700, e18, *Newwood Close, Newwood Padock* 1729; *The North Feild* 1601, *Northffield* 17, *Northfeild Close* c1685, e18, 1729, *Northfield Closes* 18 (*v.* **norð, feld**); *Henrie Okehams Closse, Okhams Close* 1601; *Orgins Close* c1685, e18, *Organs* - 1729, *Organ's* - 18 (poss. land endowed for the upkeep of the church organ, but more likely is the surn. *Organ* which is recorded from the 13th cent.); *Owens Close* c1685, e18; *Padbrok'* 1299 ('brook frequented by toads', *v.* **padde, brōc**); *The Paddocks* c1700; *The Pann(e)* 1601, *The Pan*, c1685, e18, *Nether -, Upper Pan* 18, *Pann Closes* 1729 (perh. alluding to land in a circular depression, *v.* **panne**); *Pepinherse* 1296 (from the ME surn. *Pepin* (from OFr *pepin* 'a gardener') with a second el. which is either OE *herse* 'a hill top' or OE *ears* 'a buttock' used of some topographical feature resembling the human posterior); *Pond Close* c1685; *Potter's Close* 18 (with the surn. *Potter*); *Rason Close* 1729 (held by Robt. *Rason* in 1729); *Redmills Cottage* 17, *Red Mills Cottage* c1685, 18, *- and Ground* c1685 (from the surn. *Redmile*, poss. a family originating in Redmile Lei); *Rileys House* c1685; *Ruffs Close* 17, 1729, *a close late Ruffs* c1685 (Barbara *Ruffe* is cited in the deed of c1685); *Rushpitt* c1700 (*v.* **risc, pytt**); *Sett Closse* c1660 (*v.* **(ge)set**); *The Shirewood* 1652 VCH (prob. **scīr**[1] 'an administrative district', especially since the Alstoe Hundred moot-site was in the parish, *v.* **wudu**); *Six Acre* 1729, *- Acres* 18; *Smythlond* 1295 (Willelmus *Faber* was in possession in 1295, *v.* **smið, land**); *Smeeth More* 1598, *Smithie More* 1601, *Smithmore furlong* 1634, *The Smidmore* 1682, *Smithemore* 1729, *Smithmore* 18 (prob. 'smooth, level moorland' rather than 'the smithy moor', *v.* **smēðe**[1], **mōr**[1]); *Squires Close* e18 (prob. with the surn. *Squire(s)*); *Stone Pitt Paddock* 1729; *Starr Close* 1652 VCH, *Starrs -* 1662 (prob. **storr** 'bent-grass', cf. Star Fd in Ryhall f.ns. (a)); *Stevens Cottage* c1685; *Storeys House* c1685; *Three Corner Close* 1729 (referring to its triangular shape); *Toppers Close* c1685, e18 (with the surn. *Topper*); *Townes end* 1652 VCH, *Townsend Plot(t)* c1685, e18, *Townsend Close* 1729, *Town-end Closes* 18 (*v.* **tūn, ende**[1]); *Upper Close* 1729, 18; *Wall Paddock* 1729; *Waters Close* c1685, e18 (poss. the surn. *Waters*); *West Feild* 1601 (*v.* **west, feld**); *Wingfield Close* 1729, *Wingfield's -* 18 (held by a Mr *Wingfield* in 1729); *Woods Close* e18.

Cottesmore

COTTESMORE

> *Cottesmore* 971-83 ASWills (S 1498), *Cottesmor(e)* 1202 *FF*, 1206
> P *et passim* to 1338 *MiD*, 1352 Cl *et freq* to 1610 Speed
> *Cotesmore* 1086 DB, *Cotesmor(e)* 1205 ClR, 1208 ChR *et passim*
> to 1225 Cur *et freq* to 1400 Pat *et passim* to 1535 VE
> *Cod(d)esmor(e)* 1217 ClR, 1219 Bracton, 1266 Pat, 13 *MiD*
> *Cotsmore* 1610 Speed, 1640 *FF*, 1684 Wright, 1695 *Map*

'Cott's moor', *v.* **mōr**[1], cf. Cotesbach Lei, Cottesbrook Nth. The OE pers.n. *Cott* occurs in *Cottes hyrst* 962 (10²) BCS 1085 (S 703).

WENTON (lost)

> *Weneton'* 1200 Cur, *-tun* 1246 AD
> *Wenton(e)* 1229 RHug, 1235, 1238 AD *et passim* to 1301 Cl *et*
> *freq* to 1443 ib, 1507 AD, 1535 VE, 1610 Speed, *Wenton*
> *alias Wainton* 1683 *Recov*
> *Wempton* 1327 *SR*

The first element is difficult. It could possibly be an OE pers.n. *Wenna* (as in Wennington Hu) or OE *wenn* 'a wen, a tumour' used topographically, perhaps of a mound resembling such an excrescence; but if so, one would expect the occasional spelling in *-nn-*. If the form *Wainton* of 1683 is phonologically significant, then likelier is OE *wǽn* 'a waggon, a cart', with the regular local dialectal development of OE *æ* to ME *ē*, hence 'the farmstead where the waggons are kept'. The place is referred to as the *grangia de Weneton* 1336 *Ass*. By 1507 it is described as 'land called Wenton in the parish of Cottesmore'. *Wenton* may have been the victim of early enclosure. It lay at about SK 891 143, *v*. **tūn, grange** and BrownArchSites 7.

THE ANCHORAGE P.H., 1932 Kelly. BLACKTHORN COVERT is *Foxearth Gorse* 1824 O, *v*. **gorst.** COTTESMORE BRIDGE. COTTESMORE CHURCH, *Church (St Nicholas)* 1863 White. COTTESMORE GORSE is *Jacksons Gorse* c1800, 1806 Map, *Laxton's Gorse* 1824 O, cf. *Jacksons Close* and Laxton's Cl in neighbouring Burley f.ns. (b) and (a), *v*. **gorst.** COTTESMORE GRANGE, 1932 Kelly, *v*. **grange.** COTTESMORE HALL, *The Hall* 1806 Map, 1846, 1863 White, demolished 1974 - VR. COTTESMORE HO., *Cotsmore House* 1801 Map. COTTESMORE LODGE. COTTESMORE WOOD, 1610 Speed, c1800 Map, *Cotsmoore Wood* 1610 Speed, 1715 Map. FOUNTAIN'S BARN, 1943 *Map*, from the surn. *Fountain*, cf. William *Fountain* 1846 White, Richard *Fountain* 1932 Kelly. FOX AND HOUNDS P.H. (lost), 1846, 1863 White. GLEBE HO, cf. *Glebe House Field* 1943 *Map*, *Glebe Farm* 1932 Kelly, *v*. **glebe.** IVY BRIDGE. IVY COTTAGE. THE LEAS (local), *v*. **lēah.** LIMEKILN SPINNEY. MILL LANE, cf. *Mill Nooks* 1943 *Map*. THE PINFOLD (local), *v*. **pynd-fald.** THE RECTORY, 1846, 1863 White. ROGUES LANE. THE ROOKERY. THE SUN P.H., 1932 Kelly. WARREN FM, cf. *Warren Gorse* c1800, 1806 Map, 1826 G, *v*. **wareine, gorst.**

Field-Names

Undated forms in (a) are 1943 *Map*. Early forms dated 1422, 1702 and 1767 are *Terrier*. The early f.ns. of Cottesmore and *Wenton* are treated separately in (b).

(a) Four Acre, Six -, Nine - (x2), Ten - (x3), Eleven -, Thirteen - (x2), Fifteen - (x2), Sixteen -, Seventeen Acres, Eighteen Acre, Nineteen Acres,

Twenty-five Acre, Twenty-six Acres, Thirty-one -, Thirty-three Acre (v. æcer); Abbey's Cl; America (a transferred name, usually for a remote field); Ashwell Road Cl; Back Fd; Bancroft's Big Fd; Barrow Hill (named from the adjoining parish of Barrow, formerly a chapelry of Cottesmore); Bridge Cl (near Cottesmore Bridge); Bridle Road Fd (cf. *Bridle-gate Furlong* 1767, v. **brigdels, gata**); Little -, Brown's Cl (cf. Samuel *Browne* 1676 *Anc* and Elizabeth *Brown* 1713 *BHS* of nearby Stretton); Butchers Cl (from the surn. *Butcher*, cf. *Butcher's Close* in neighbouring Burley f.ns. (b)); Cottage Cl; The Cottagers Cl (v. **cotager**); Cover Cl (v. **cover(t)**); Cresswell's; Cup's Cl; Debdale (v. **dēop, dalr**); Drive Fd; Dry Cl (v. **drȳge**); Far Fd; Flint's Fds (from the surn. *Flint*, cf. John *Flint* 1846, 1877 White); Glover's Barn Fd Nineteen Acres; Great Cl; Greetham Road Cl; Heath Cl (cf. *Heath Field* 1767, one of the open-fields of Cottesmore, v. **hǣð**); Henton (cf. Henton Gorse in Burley f.ns. (a); prob. a surn. *Henton*, but a lost habitation site, OE *(æt þām) hēan tūne 'high farmstead', is poss.); Hilly Bank; Home Fd (v. **home**); Horse Pastures; House Cl (x2); Hovel Cl (v. **hovel**); Idle's Cl (from the surn. *Idle*); Ironstone Cl, - Fds, - Mdw (referring to adjacent ironstone workings); Little Mdws; Lock's Cl (with the surn. *Lock*, cf. Robert *Loke* 1522 MilS, 1524 SR of Exton and Lock's Cl in Greetham f.ns. (a)); Long Mdw; Mrs Noel's Fd (cf. Mrs *Noel* 1932 Kelly; *Noel* is the family name of the Earls of Gainsborough, major landowners in this area); Nether Cl; New Cl; Parker's Cl (cf. William *Parker* 1706 *Terrier* of Greetham); Pilkington's (a surn., cf. John-, Richard- and William *Pylkyngton* of Barleythorpe 1522 MilS); Pond Cl; Priestwells (*Priestwells Furlong* 1767, v. Priestwells in neighbouring Greetham f.ns. (a)); Road Fd; Roadside Fd; Robinson Cl; Rough Cl; Smith's Fd; Stonepit Cl; Three Corner Fd (referring to its triangular shape); Ploughed -, Tofts (cf. *Toft hyll* 1422, *Toftessike* n.d. AD, v. **toft, hyll, sík**); Top Fd; Townend Fd (v. **tūn, ende**[1]); Wenton (v. *Wenton supra* and VCH 2 130); Wide Hole (cf. Barrow Wide Hole in Barrow); Wood Bridge; Wood Fd (*The Woodfeild* 1702, 1767, one of the open-fields of the village, adjoining Cottesmore Wood).

(b) Cottesmore: *uppon Allesthorp' mere* 1422 (v. **(ge)mǣre** and *Alsthorpe* in Burley); *Ash Furlong* 1767; *over Barrow-dale* 1767 (Barrow parish adjoins to the north, v. **dalr**); *Booths-close Furlong* 1767 (with the surn. *Booth*, cf. Booth's Cl in neighbouring Burley f.ns. (a)); *Broad Roods Furlong* 1767 (v. **brād, rōd**[3]); *Brook Furlong* 1767 (v. **brōc**); *Bruseslonde* 1387 Cl (from the surn. *de Brus*; Bernard *de Brus* held land in neighbouring Exton in 1280 Cl, v. **land** and Barnsdale); *Furlong that butts on Burley Field* 1767 (Burley parish adjoins to the south); *Bylleshegge* 1422 (from the surn. *Bill(s)/Billes*, v. **hecg**); *Clarks headland Furlong* 1767 (v. **hēafod-land** and cf. William *Clarke* 118 *Surv* of Burley); *Cob-thorn Furlong* 1767 ('pollarded thorn tree', v. **copped, þorn**, cf. Cobdenhill Hrt 60);

Dod-moor Furlong 1767 (*v.* Dodmore in Greetham f.ns. (a)); *Extongate* 1422, *Exton-way Furlong* 1767 (Exton parish adjoins to the south-east, *v.* **gata**); *Feernegate* 1422 (*v.* **fearn, gata**); *Feernsyke* 1422 (*v.* **fearn, sīk**); *First Furlong* 1767; *ad Fontem* 1341 NI (p) (*v.* **wella**); *Greetham Townships Furlong* 1767 (Greetham parish adjoins to the east, *v.* **tūn-scipe**); *Grenehowe* 1422 (*v.* **grēne**[1], **haugr**); *Grescroft* n.d. AD (*v.* **gærs, croft**); *Furlong on the side of the Heath* 1767 (*v.* **hǣð**); *Hesyllgate* 1422 (the 'road lined with hazels' ran into Barrow parish, *v.* **hesli, gata** and cf. *Hesilgate* in Barrow f.ns. (b)); *Over the Hollow, Over the Long -, Short Hollow* 1767 (*v.* **holh**); *in venella de Cottesmor* 1305 Deed (p), *in the Lane* 1354 Ipm (p), *Lanes-end Furlong* 1767 (*v.* **lane, ende**[1]); *Lyngefurlonges* 1422, *Dale-lings* - (*v.* **dalr**), *West-lings Furlong* 1767 (*v.* **lyng, furlang**); *Middle Furlong* 1767; *Mill nook upper Furlong* 1767 (*v.* **myln, nōk**); *Money Furlong* 1767 (from the surn. *Money*, cf. Thomas *Monee* 1522 MilS of nearby Teigh and Richard *Money* 1732 *Anc* of Stretton); *Musgroseslonde* 1387 Cl (Robert *de Mucegros* held land in Cottesmore from 1276 Cl, *v.* **land***); Pedderstyle* 1422 (*v.* **peddere, stigel**); *Peyseland'* 1422 (*v.* **pise, land**); *Longwrangelondes* 1422, *Long -, Short Ranglands Furlong* 1767 (*v.* **lang**[1], **wrang, vrangr, land**); *Ruddyngdykefurlang* 1422 (*v.* **ryding, dīk, furlang**); *ouer Stamfordgate* 1422 ('(furlong) above the road to Stamford L', *v.* **ofer**[3], **gata**); *Stanbryghyll'* 1422, *Stone Bridge hill Furlong* 1767 (*v.* **stān, brycg, hyll**); *Stompstone* 1422 (prob. referring to a broken cross shaft, *v.* **stump, stān**); *Stone-gals Furlong* 1767 (*v.* **stān, galla**); *Stye3* 1422 (*v.* **stigu**); *Wellegate* 1422 (*v.* **wella, gata**); *Westfeld'* 1422, *Great Westfeild* 1702, *Westfeild* 1767 (one of the open-fields of the village, *v.* **west, feld**); *Westwode3* 1422, *Westwoods Furlong* 1767 (*v.* **west, wudu**); *Wheytlondes* 1422 (*v.* **hwǣte, land**); *Wodegate* 1422 (*v.* **wudu, gata**); *Wyllowong* 1422 (*v.* **wilig, vangr**); *atte Yard* 1341 NI (p) (*v.* **geard**).

Wenton: *Blakmyld'* 1417 Deed (*v.* **blæc, mylde**); *Calvercroft* 1235 AD (*v.* **calf,** (**calfra** gen.pl.), **croft**); *Wdebindthornwong* 1417 Deed (*v.* **wudubinde, þorn, vangr**).

. Exton

EXTON

Exentune 1086 DB
Exton(e) 1107 Reg, 1185, 1192 P *et passim* to 1207 ib *et freq* to 1610 Speed
Exston 1326, 1330 Pat *et passim* to 1535 VE

Probably 'the ox farm', *v.* **oxa, tūn**. Ekwall DEPN suggests that the first element is a secondary genitive plural form *exna* (influenced by the nominative plural *exen*) of the regular gen.pl. *oxna*.

BARNSDALE, - AVENUE, - HILL, - LODGE, - WOOD

Bernardeshull(e) 1202 *Ass*, 1208 *FF*, 1256 *For*, 1263 *Ass*, 1280 Cl, 1294 *Ass*

Bernardishill' 1201 FF, 1286 QW, *Bernerdishil'* 1298 *FH* (p)

Barnardeshull' 1202 *Ass*

Bernardeshell 1518-20 ECP

Barinsdale 1610 Speed, *Barndalle* 1634 *Terrier*, *Barnsdale* 1695 *Map*

'Bernard's hill', *v.* **hyll**. OFr *Bernart*, OG *Bernard* is likelier than OE *Beornh(e)ard* as the source of the pers.n. Barnsdale was a deer park held by *Bernard* de Brus in 1280 Cl. His predecessor may well have borne the same name. Minor recorded forms are *Barnsdale Park* 1602, 1607 Map, 1710 *Deed*, *Barnsdale Hill* 1806 Map, *Barnshill Lodge* 1806 ib, *Barnsdale Lodge* 1846 White, *Barnsdale Wood* c1800, 1806 Map.

ARMLEY WOOD

Armele 1337 *Deed*, *Armlye* 1634 *Terrier*, *Harmley Wood* c1800, 1806 Map, *Armley Wood* 1824 O

The first element presents difficulty. The OE adjective **earm** 'poor, wretched' is possible, as for Armley YW and Yarmley D. Smith notes (YW **3** 211) that this word has almost invariably a personal reference so that the meaning 'poor, wretched wood' is unlikely. Ekwall DEPN also proposes **earm** for Armley YW but with the sense 'outlawed', hence 'the wood of the outlaw(s)'. Such a signification is to be discounted for the Rutland example which is so close to the important centres of Hambleton and Oakham. An unrecorded OE pers.n. *Earma* (a by-name from **earm**) may also be thought of, as Smith proposes for the YW example: but if the D, Ru and YW place-names all have the same origin, three compounds of *Earm(a)* plus *lēah* (and the pers.n. is otherwise unknown) must be rejected as highly improbable. On balance, **earm** with the sense 'poor quality' seems likeliest here, *v.* **earm**, **lēah**.

TUNNELEY WOOD
> *Todyngley* 15 VCH, *Tarringley wood* 1610 Speed bis, 1715 Map,
> *Turnely Wood* c1800 ib, *Turneley Wood* 1806 ib, *Tunnely
> Wood* 1824 O
> *Tunneley Wood* 1846 White, 1943 *Map*

This was possibly a medieval deer park. There are references to
a park at Exton in 1185, 1207, 1218 and 1269, *v.* VCH 2 128, 130,
253. Little can be made of this name without earlier forms, *v.*
lēah.

WESTLAND WOOD
> *Westerlant* 1373 *For, Westland* 1634 *Terrier, Westland Woode*
> 1610 Speed, *Westland Wood* 1715, c1800, 1806 Map

'The western land', *v.* **wester, land.**

ASH PLANTATION. BLACKSMITHS LANE (local). BROOK
FM, 1826 G, 1846 White, cf. *northside the brooke, southsyde brookes*
1634 *Terrier, v.* **brōc.** BURLEY BUSHES. COCKED HAT
SPINNEY, so called from its tricorne shape. CUCKOO FM, 1932
Kelly. CUCKOO SPINNEY, cf. *Cuckoo Fields* 1943 Map.
EXTON CHURCH, *Church (St Peter and St Paul)* 1846 White.
EXTON HALL, *The Hall* 1846, 1877 ib, *Exton House* 1684 Wright.
EXTON PARK, 18 *Plan,* 1806 Map, 1846, 1877 White, 1932 Kelly.
THE FIRS. FOX AND HOUNDS P.H. FOX BRIDGE, 1826 G,
named from an early inn called *The Fox* sited near the bridge and
functioning as late as 1863 - VR. THE GRANGE, 1932 Kelly, *v.*
grange. THE GREEN (local), *v.* **grēne².** HALL FM, 1846, 1877
White. HAWKSWELL SPINNEY, HAWKSWELL SPRING, cf.
Hawxwell Corner 1634 *Terrier, Hawkwell Leas* 1943 *Map, v.* **hafoc,
wella, corner.** HIGHMOOR FM, formerly Glebe Farm - VR, *v.*
High Moor in Empingham *infra.* HORN MILL, *Hornemill* 1610
Speed, *Horne Mill* 1701 *Deed, the Horn Mills* 1706 ib (prob. to be
identified with *molendin' de Bradewater* 1286 *Ass, v.* **brād, wæter),**
cf. *Horn Mill House* 1795, 1818 *Anc, v.* **myln.** Four mills are
recorded for Horn in DB. KEEPER'S COTTAGE, a gamekeeper's
house. LITTLE EXTON (local). MILL DAM. NEW FIELD

ROAD, *New Field* 1943 *Map.* NEW GARDEN SPINNEY, 1943 *ib.*
OLD HALL, cf. *ad aulam* 1296 *SR* (p), *atte Halle* 1327 *ib* (p), 1328
Banco (p), *v.* **hall.** PUDDING BAG END (local). PUDDING
BAG LANE. RATTLING JACK SPINNEY, 1943 *Map, v.* Rattling
Jack in f.ns. (a) *infra.* THE RECTORY, 1846 White. ROBIN
HOOD'S CAVE, a small medieval moated site now drowned in
Rutland Water; the moat may have surrounded a lodge for the
keeper of the medieval deer park of Barnsdale, cf. *atte Parke* 1327
SR (p), *v.* **park** and MER 17, 19. RUSHPIT WOOD, *Rushepitt
Wood* 1610 Speed, *Rush Pit Wood* c1800, 1806 Map, *v.* **risc, pytt,
wudu.** RY GATE PLANTATION, *Rygate* 1634 *Terrier, cf. Ryegate
Head* 1943 *Map, v.* **ryge, gata, hēafod.** STAMFORD END (local),
cf. West End *infra.* STONE PIT, 1943 *Map.* TOP LODGE.
TYLER'S CORNER (local), named from the *Tyler* family who were
woodsmen on the Exton Park estate - VR. WEST END (local),
i.e. the west end of the village in contrast to Stamford End *supra,*
as Stamford lies to the south-east. THE WILLOWS, cf. *Long
Willows* 1943 *Map.* YEW TREE HO. is *Yew Tree Cottage* 1932
Kelly.

Field-Names

The undated forms in (a) are 1943 *Map.* The forms in (b) are 1634 *Terrier.*

(a) Five -, Six -, Eight -, (Top) Nine -, Ten -, Thirteen - (x2), Fourteen -;
Sixteen -, Seventeen -, Eighteen -, Twenty-four Acre (*v.* **æcer**); Allotments
(referring to allotment gardens); Ash Tree Cl; Avenue Cl or Thistle Graves
(prob. **græf** 'a digging', with reference to thistle-filled excavations, cf. Solomon's
Grave in Mkt. Overton f.ns. (a) and *Jackson's Grave* in Greetham f.ns. (a) *s.n.*
East -, West Jackson's Cl); Barn Fd; Barracks (cf. The Barracks in neighbouring
Horn f.ns (a), perh. alluding to Second World War military accommodation,
although ModE dial. *barrack* 'a temporary shelter, a hut' is poss.); Bell's Hovel
(from the surn. *Bell,* cf. Edward Charles *Bell* 1932 Kelly, *v.* **hovel**); Below the
Garden Fd (adjoins allotment plots); Big Fd (Mr J. Field notes that it is 70
acres in area); (West) Burley Fd; Bush Cl; Captain's Cl, - Mdw; Coach Road Fd
(adjoins main road); Crowden's Fd (from the surn. *Crowden,* cf. Crowden's Mdws
in Seaton f.ns. (a)); Mother Dane's Fd; Big Dodmoor (*v.* Dodmore in Greetham
f.ns. (a)); Footpath Fd; Fountain's Barn (from the surn. *Fountain,* cf. Fountain's
Barn in Cottesmore); Fowler's Park (from the surn. *Fowler,* cf. Willoughby *Fowler*

1846 White, Willingham *Fowler* 1877 ib); Fox's Fd, Fox's Keeper's Fd (*v.* Fox Bridge and Keeper's Cottage *supra*); Goodfeed's Barnsdale or Annecy's Well (from the surn. *Anness*, cf. William *Annes* 1524 SR of Belton; *Goodfeed* may well be a complimentary name given to rich pasture rather than a surn.); Greetham Bushes 1824 O (named from the neighbouring parish of Greetham, *v.* **busc**); Highmoor Grass (*v.* **gærs**); Hills and Hales ('land covered in hillocks and hollows'; Mr J. Field notes that this is a frequent name, with variants, in this area; such land may be, like Hills and Holes in Barnack Nth (now Cambs.), the site of former stone quarrying, cf. Stone Pit *supra*); Home Cl, Home Paddock (*v.* **home**); Horse Fd; Horseshoe Fd (Mr J. Field observes that the actual shape is conventionally rectangular); House Cl; King's Cl; Limepit Fd; Merriman's (cf. Merrimans Platt in Brooke f.ns. (a)); Messons Fd (from the surn. *Masson*, cf. Thomas *Masson* the smith 1522 MilS); Middle Fd; New Head (*v.* **hēafod**); Neward Cl (perh. an alteration of New Head, cf. the preceding f.n.); Noels Cl 1979 VR (from the surn. *Noel*); Old Farm; Paddock; Planting Cl or Avenue Cl (with reference to a plantation, cf. Plantation Fd or Planting Cl in Teigh f.ns. (a)); Rattling Jack (perh. alluding to bird-scaring by means of a rattle or clapper, especially as the field is beside Rattling Jack Spinney *supra*, poss. a refuge for wood-pigeons); Reservoir Fd; Rose's Fd (from the surn. *Rose*, cf. Cecil *Rose* 1932 Kelly); Stackyard (*v.* **stak-ȝard**); Bottom Stocking (*v.* **stoccing**); Sykes (cf. *le southsyk'* 1368 *Wyg*, *v.* **sūð**, **sík**); Three Corner Fd (named from its triangular shape); Washdyke Cl or Sheepdyke Cl (*The Shypdike* 1634 *Terrier*, a ditch used as a sheep-dip, *v.* **scēap**, **dík**); Westland Wood Fd (*v.* Westland Wood *supra*); Whitwell Corner, - Four Acre, - Six Acre, - Twelve Acre, Whitwell Road Fd (Whitwell parish adjoins to the south); First -, Second Wright's (from the surn. *Wright*, cf. William Edward *Wright* 1877 White).

(b) *Allstrops felde*, *Allstrops gate* (referring to *Alsthorpe* in Burley, *v.* **feld**, **gate**); *Bandlandes* (*v.* **bēan**, **land**); *Barrow leayes* (if not the surn. *Barrow* (cf. Robert *Borow* 1522 MilS of Braunston), then referring to a prehistoric burial mound; but cf. *Harbuck leas infra*, *v.* **beorg**, **lēah**); *Burlye gate* (Burley parish adjoins to the west, *v.* **gata**); *Burnman Bush* (prob. with the surn. *Burnman* and referring to ground covered with scrub, *v.* **busc**); *Cottismore* (Cottesmore parish adjoins to the north-west); *Harbuck leas* (prob. with the surn. *Harbuck*, since in this county - *Leys* is commonly prefixed by a surn., *v.* **lēah**); *Haye gatte* (prob. 'the hay road' in contrast to 'the rye road', *v.* **hēg**, **gata** and cf. Ry Gate Plantation *supra*); *Ingresdale Slade* (perh. from the Scand pers.n. *Ingvarr*, *v.* **dalr**, **slæd** and cf. *Ingersdale* in Empingham f.ns. (a), the adjoining parish to the south-east); *the Mault Mill* 1706 *Deed* (*v.* **malte-mylne**); *North Feilde* (one of the great open-fields of the village, *v.* **norð**, **feld**); *Nunesland* 1551 Pat (poss. from

the surn. *Nunn*, but there is fragmentary evidence for a foundation for
Cistercian nuns at Tinwell, cf. None Stalls in Braunston f.ns. (a), *v.* **nunne,
land**); *above Rygate, under Rygate* (*v.* Ry Gate Plantation *supra*); *de la Sale* 1284
Blore (p), *a la Sale* 1288 *Deed* (p) (perh. Scand **salr** 'a hall', but this is rare in
English p.ns. and unlikely in the context of predominantly Anglo-Saxon Rutland;
otherwise OE **salh** 'sallow, willow'); *South Feilde* (one of the great open-fields of
the village, *v.* **sūð, feld**); *Stamford Ashe, beneath the Ashe* (referring to an ash
tree beside the old road to Stamford L, *v.* **æsc**); *Vicar Pyttes* (*v.* **vikere, pytt**);
West Feld (one of the great open-fields, *v.* **west, feld**); *under Westland* (*v.*
Westland Wood *supra*); *Westmore* (*v.* **west, mōr**[1]); *Whyttwell more* (Whitwell
parish adjoins to the south, *v.* **mōr**[1]).

Greetham

GREETHAM
> *Gretham* 1086 DB, 1185 Templar, 1202 Ass, 1205 ClR, 1206 P
> > *et freq* to 1610 Speed
> *Greotham* 1369 Ipm, 1397 Cl, 1399 *Bir*
> *Greteham* 1398 Pat, 1428 *FF et passim* to 1535 VE
> *Greatham* 1608 *FF*
> *Greetham* 1610 Speed

'The village or estate on gravelly or stony soil', *v.* **grēot, hām**, cf.
Greetham L. The settlement stands on an outcrop of Northampton
Sands ironstone.

WOOLFOX WOOD, - LODGE
> *Wulfhus* 1224 *FF, Wlfhus* 1224 Bracton, *Wulfhous* 1301 Ipm
> *Wolfhous* 1296 MinAcct, 1338 Pat (p), *Wolfehows(s)e* 1489 Ipm,
> > 1527 *Surv*
> *Wolveshous* 1507 Ipm
> *Wool(l)fox alias Wo(o)lf(e)house* 1626 *Deed*, 1696, 1697, 1723
> > *Anc*
> *Woolfehouse alias Woolfox Wood* 1635 *Anc*
> *Woolfox Lodge* c1800, 1806 Map

The first el. is probably the OE pers.n. *Wulfa*, as in *Wulfandun*
708 (12) BCS 120 (S 78) but the el. **hūs** 'a house' is rarely

compounded with personal names. By 1527 *Surv*, the settlement seems to have disappeared, since we learn of *pastur' vocat' Wolfehowsse*, *v.* hūs. The south-east projection of Greetham parish beyond Ermine Street may encompass the original bounds of Woolfox.

Greetham Inns and Taverns

BLACK HORSE, 1846 White. CROWN AND ANCHOR (lost), 1846 ib, 1932 Kelly, closed in the 1930s - VR. NEW INN (lost), 1780 Map, *Greetham New Inn* c1800, 1806 ib. OAK (lost - now Oak Ho.), *Oak Inn* 1824 O, 1846 White, closed in the 1920s - VR. PLOUGH. RAM JAM INN, 1801 Map, 1846 White, *The Ram Jam House* 1750 BM; a part of Stretton village, but just within the Greetham parish boundary. The inn reputedly takes its name from a potent drink, *Ram Jam*, concocted from a recipe brought back from India by an 18th century landlord, Charles Blake (died 1791), who sold it to coach passengers travelling on the Great North Road. WHEATSHEAF.

ASH WOOD. CHURCH LANE. THE COPPICE, 1652 *Surv*, *v.* copis. EAST END (local), cf. West End *infra*. GLEBE FM, 1932 Kelly, *v.* glebe. GREAT LANE. GREETHAM CHURCH, *Church* (*St Mary*) 1863 White, cf. *Churchfeilde* in f.ns. (b). GREETHAM HO, 1846 ib. GREETHAM WOOD FAR, - NEAR, *Greetham Wood* 1610 Speed, *Twin Woods* 1780, 1801 Map, 1824 O, *v.* wudu. HEATH LODGE, HEATH SPINNEY, *The Heath* 1525 *Rental*, 1652 *Surv*, *v.* hǣð. HIGH STREET. MANOR HO. The foundations of the medieval manor house are north-west of the church at SK 923 147, *v.* MER 21. A park attached to the house is recorded in 1446 (*v.* VCH 2 136), but the park pale has not been traced, *v.* BrownArchSites 13. MILL HO., *The Mill House* 1787, 1790, 118 *Surv*, cf. *molendino de Grettaham* 1185 Templar, *molendino de Gretham* 14 *RBT*, *le Newmill* 1525 *Rental*, *firma molendini ... de nouo construct' voc' le Newmill* 1527 *Surv*, *Crosse Mill* 1610 Speed (cf. *Five Mile Cross* in f.ns. (b) *infra*), *Greetham Mill* 1824 O: only one mill is recorded for Greetham in DB, *v.* nīwe, myln, cros. MOUNT PLEASANT (local), usually having a favourable meaning, but sometimes used ironically. NEW INN FM, cf. *New Inn Wood*, c1800, 1806 *Map*, v. New Inn *supra*. OLD WINDMILL, cf. *Windmill Furlong* 1652 *Surv*, 1706 *Terrier*, *Windmill Field* 1943 *Map*. POND LANE. SHARMAN'S LODGE, *Shermans Lodge* 1717 LML; Thomas *Shereman* is cited in 1665 *HT*. SHEEPDYKE LANE, alluding to a sheep-dip, cf. *Washdyke Close or Sheepdyke Close* in neighbouring Exton f.ns. (b), v. scēap, dīk. STOCKEN FM, *Stocking Farm* 1846 White, v. stoccing. THE TERRACE, *East -, Middle -, Small Terrace* 1943 *Map*. THE VICARAGE, 1863 White. WALKER'S LODGE, George *Walker* and family are cited in 1665 *HT*, cf. *Walkers Farm* in f.ns. (b) *infra*. WATER MILL, *Water Corn Mill* 1787, 118 *Surv*. WEST END (local), cf. East End *supra*.

Field-Names

Undated forms in (a) are 1943 *Map*. Those dated c1840 are *TA*. Those of 1908 and 1955 are *Deed* (per Mr D. Tew). Early forms dated 1556, 1633 and 1706 are *Terrier*; 1635, 1637, 1670, 1676, 1691, 1695, 1696, 1697, 1707, 1711, 1712, 1714, 1716, 1733, 1739, 1745, 1754, 1757, 1785 and 1795 are *Anc*; 1652, 1758, 1787, 1790 and 118 are *Surv*; 1686 and 1795 are *Rental*; 1626, 1683 and c1733 are *Deed*; 18 are *Plan*.

(a) Barn Cl; Bellases Hollow (from the surn. *Bellaers*, cf. John *Bellaers* 1845 *BHS* of neighbouring Stretton); Berry's Platt (v. plat^2 and cf. Berry's Plott Fd in Stretton f.ns. (a)); Between Gates (*Tweene gates* 1633, *Tween Gates Furlong* 1652, *Tweengate* - 1706, 1714, 1739, 1745, 1754, 'land with roads on two boundaries', v. betwēonan, gata); Big Lane, - Fd; Black Piece (*Black Peice fur'* 1652, *Black Piece* 18; in eModE, *black* 'fertile' is contrasted to *white* 'infertile', although the allusion here may simply be to the colour of the soil, v. pece); Bottom Fd; Bradwell Dale; East -, West Brooks 1869, 1870, First -, Second - (or West -) Brook Fd 1943 (*The Brook(e)* 1739, 1745, 1758, *Bro(w)kefurlong* 1556, *Brook(e) Furlong* 1652, 1706, v. brōc); Bull Fd 1979 VR; Burnt Cl; Bush Wong (1787, 1790, 118, v. busc, vangr); Cake Maker (v. *Capp Maker* in (b) *infra*); Chancery Lane (prob. a corrupted form of *chantry*, cf. *Chantry Close infra*, and attracted ironically to London's Chancery Lane); Chapman's; Cheesecake Cl 1908 (dial. *cheesecake* is used of the fruit of such wild plants as the common mallow (*Malva sylvestris*) and the bird's foot trefoil (*Lotus corniculatus*)); Church Cl; East -, West Clash Wongs (*Plash Wong* 18, *Clash Wong* 1787, 1790, 118, - *Nook*

1787, 1790, v. plæsc, vangr, nōk); Cleves Cl 1955 (either with the surn. *Cleve* or from *clif* 'a steep hillside'); Clover Cl; Cluf Cl (as this is limestone country, prob. *clough* 'a deep valley or ravine', v. clōh); Collins Cl; Corner Fd; Cow Commons or Pastures (*Cow Pastures* 1637, 1652, 1733, v. pasture); Cross Hills (*Cross Hill Cowpasture* 1787, 1790, 118, alluding to *Five Mile Cross* in (b) *infra*); Crossroad Fd; North -, South -, Dikeham (the second el. is prob. Scand holmr rather than OE hamm in origin, v. dīk); North -, South -, Dodmore (*Dodmore* 1652, 1787, 1790, 118, - *Fur'* 1652, *Short Dodmore* 1652, - *Furlong* 1706, *Longdodmore* 1706, - *Furlong* 1714, 1739, 1745; the first el. may well be dēad 'infertile' rather than dodde 'the rounded summit of a hill', forming a likelier compound with mōr 'moorland', cf. *Deadmoore, Dudsemoore* in Belton f.ns. (b), *Dod-moor* in neighbouring Cottesmore f.ns. (b), Dodmoor in Exton f.ns. (b) and *Deadmore* in Manton f.ns. (b), v. mōr¹); Donkey Paddock 1908, 1955; Dry Cl 1908 (18, v. drȳge); East Cl 1908; Exton Way (1652, 1739, *Aboue Exton Way* 1652, *Furlong East Side of Exton Way* 1758; Exton parish adjoins to the south-west); Far Fallow Fd (v. falh); Far Fd; Front Fd; East -, West -, Gorse Hedges (*Goss(e) Hedge* 1652, 1787, - *fur'* 1652, *Gorse Hedge* 1790, 118, *Goss Hedge Close* 18, v. gorst, hecg); Grass Fd (v. gærs); Great Piece (v. pece); Halliday (a surn., cf. John *Halliday* 1776 *BHS* of neighbouring Stretton); Hay Cl; Hazel's (*Hasells fur', Long Hasells, - fur', Short Hasells, Neather -, Upper Hasells fur'* 1652, *Far -, Near Hasles* 1787, 1790, 118, v. hæsel); Highfield Cl 1908, 1955; High Pasture (1787, 1790, 118); Holylane Fds 1979 VR; Home Cl (1652, 1733, v. home); Far -, Near Hooby (*Hooby Hedge Furlong* 1652, referring to the boundary hedge of Hooby (Lodge) in Stretton, v. hecg); House Cl ('formerly Wall Cl and Lime Kiln Cl' 1908); East -, West Jackson's Cl (cf. *Jackson's Grave, Jackson's Meer* 118, v. græf, (ge)mære, cf. Solomon's Grave in Mkt. Overton f.ns. (a), Becky's Grave in Empingham f.ns. (a)); Little One (or Inn) (*Little Ing* 1652, *Littleing* 1706, *Littlelin* 1787, *Little Lin* 1790, 118, *Littling fur'* 1652, v. lytel, eng); Locks Cl 1908 (with the surn. *Lock*, cf. Robert *Loke* 1522 MilS, 1524 SR of Exton and Lock's Cl in Cottesmore f.ns. (a)); Long Acre (*Long Acre fur'* 1652, v. æcer); First -, Second -, Long Cl (*Long Close* 1787, 1790, 118); Longham 1869, 1870, 1908 (v. lang, hamm); Middle Fd; Middle Hill (*Northeastward -, Northwestward -, Southeastward -, Southwestward Middle Hill* 1787, 118); Milking Fd ('land on which cows are milked', v. milking); Money Holes (*Money Hole* 1787, *Moneyhole* 1790, 118; perh. from the surn. *Money* (cf. Richard *Money* 1678 *Anc*, Widow *Money* 1723, 1724, 1732 *ib* and Thomas *Money* 1758 *Surv* of neighbouring Stretton) but it is possible that the reference is to the finding of a coin-hoard at this site, cf. *Money Pit* in Ketton f.ns. (b), v. hol¹); Great North Fd (*North Fylde* 1556, *North Fielde* 1633, *North Feilde* 1683, 1706, *Great North Field* 1787, 1790, 118, *The feild called the South and the North Feild* 1652, *North*

Feild Way fur' 1652, *Over Northfeild Way* 1652; North Field was one of the great open-fields of the village, *v.* **norð, feld**); Old Pasture; Far -, South Paddock; Pear Tree Cl 1908 (1707, *v.* **pertre**); Pheasant Fd (prob. from the surn. *Pheasant, cf. Anna Phesant* 1572 PR and Dorcas *Phesant* 1576 ib of N. Luffenham); Big Pit Cl; Pit Fox Cl; Pond Fd; Priestwells 1908 (*Preistwell* 1652, *Preistwells* 1714, 1739, *Priestwells* 1739, 1745, *Priest Wells* 1754, *Preistwell End* 1652, *Preistwell fur'* 1652, *v.* **prēost, wella, ende**[1], cf. Priestwells in neighbouring Cottesmore f.ns. (a)); Remington Heath 1955 (cf. Bottom -, Top Rimmington in Langham f.ns. (a), Remington Hold Cl in S. Luffenham f.ns. (a), *Rimyngton Furlonge* in Barleythorpe f.ns. (b) and Rimmingtons Hoole in Morcott f.ns. (a)); Saltwells (*Salt Wells* 1733, *Great* - 1758, 1785, *Saltwells Close* 1626, 1733, 1795, *The Ne(a)ther Close alias Salt(e)well Close* 1676, 1695, *v.* **salt**[2], **wella**); Sandy Cl; South Dale (*Sowthe Dale* 1556, *South* - 118, *v.* **sūð, dalr**); South Fd (*Sowthe Fylde* 1556, *South Fielde* 1633, *South Feild* 1706, 1739, 1745, *South Field* 1714, 1739, 1787, 118, one of the great open-fields, *v.* **sūð, feld**); Little Spinney Fd (or Windmill Fd); Stable Cl; Stonepit Cl 1869, 1870, 1943, Middle Stonepit Cl 1869, 1870 (*Stone Pitt,* - *Furlong* 1652, *v.* **stān-pytt**); Upper Street Fd (alluding to the Roman Ermine Street, *v.* **strǣt**); Stretton Cl, - Fd, - Twenty Acre (First -, Second -, Third Stretton Fd 1908, 1955) (Stretton parish adjoins to the north); Stubbs Cl; Swallow Hole 1908, 1955 (*v.* **swalg, hol**[1], cf. Swallow Hole Cl in Stretton f.ns. (a)); Three Corner Cl, - Fd (referring to triangular shape); Treadwell (Mr J. Field suggests 'land with firm soil'); Two Cl; Walker's Cl (cf. Walker's Lodge *supra*); Long -, Short Water Furrows (*Waterfurrowes* 1633, *Water Furrows,* - *fur'*, *Water Thoroughs* 1652, 'land where water tends to lie in the furrows', *v.* **wæter, furh**); West Cl 1908; The Great -, Little Wood c1840.

(b) *Ash Tree Furlong* 1706, *Barrow Way* 1652 (Barrow parish adjoins to the north-west); *Beadles fur'* 1652 (perh. from *beadle* 'a parish constable', otherwise from the surn. *Beadle, v.* **bydel**); *Betes furlong* 1706, *Bettes Baulke* 1633, *Betts Balke* 1652 (from the surn. *Bett,* cf. Stephen *Bett* 1522 MilS of Greetham, John *Bett* 1522 ib, 1524, 1525 SR of neighbouring Cottesmore, *v.* **balca**); *Betweene Dikes* 1706 (*v.* **dik**); *atte Brigge* 1341 NI (p) (*v.* **brycg**); *Bryer Bush* 1652 (*v.* **brēr, busc**); *Budborow* 1556, *Badborough* 1787, 1790, 118, *Budborough Dale* 1652, *Badborrow Dale* 1706, *Budborough Dale fur'*, *Badborough Dale fur-* 1652 (the first el. appears to be a pers.n., perh. OE *Bud(d)a,* cf. Ranksborough in Langham, where an OE pers.n. is compounded with **beorg**, suggesting a pagan Anglo-Saxon burial in an earlier tumulus; a ring-ditch crop mark at SK 933 142 may indicate the site of a ploughed-out barrow (Crop Marks 60-1), *v.* **beorg, dalr**); *Bullock Close* 1733, 1758, 1785 (*v.* **bulluc**); *Butcher's Close* 18 (from the surn. *Butcher*); *The Butts* 1652 (*v.* **butte**); *Calves Closes* 1707; *Capon Acres* 1652, - *Acre* 1706, -

Acres fur' 1652 (either the surn. *Capon, Capoun* or OE *capun* 'a capon' from which it is derived, *v.* æcer and cf. *Capun More* in neighbouring Stretton f.ns. (b)); *Capp Maker, Capp Makers Furlong* 1652, *Cake Makers* 1787, 118, *Cakemakers* 1790 (the seemingly unrelated *Capon Acres supra* and *Capp Maker(s)* were both in the old North Field, the latter prob. a corrupted version of the former; the 18th cent. spellings appear to be an attempt by popular etymology to make sense of the corrupted name, with reference perhaps to sticky soil, fit only for making mud cakes); *Chantry Close* 1782, 1790, 118 (alluding to land endowed for the maintenance of a chantry in the parish church *v.* chaunterie); *Kyrke Fylde* 1556, *Churchfielde* 1633, *Church Feild* 1652, 1706, 1739, 1745, - *Field* 1714, 1739, 1754, one of the great open-fields of the village, *v.* cirice, kirkja, feld); *Church Hedlond* 1556, - *Headland* 1652, - *Had(d)land* 1706, 1714, 1739, 1745, 1754 (*v.* hĕafod-land); *Charitys Home Close* 1787 (in the possession of Thomas *Charity* in 1787); *East Clarkes Close* 1787 (from the surn. *Clarke*); *Clipsham Gàte Close* 1626, 1716, 1733, c1733, 1795 (Clipsham parish lies to the north-east, *v.* gata); *Kokelstone furlong* 1556, *Cockleston,* - *fur',* Short *Cocklestone, Long Cocklestone fur'* 1652, *North Cocklestone* 1706, *Cugglestones* 1787, *Far* -, *Near* - 1787, 1790, 118 (referring to limestone soil containing an abundance of fossil molluscs, *v.* cockle-stone); *Cockepitt Wong* 1652 ('an in-field with a pit for cock-fighting', *v.* cockpit, vangr); *The Common* 1706 (*v.* commun); *Coatesmoore Meare* 1652 (Cottesmore parish adjoins to the west, *v.* (ge)mǣre 'a boundary'); *Cottage Meadow* 1787, 1790, 118; *Cow Close Hill* 1787, 1790, 118, *Old Cow Close Hill* 18, *Old Cow Close* 1787, 1790, 118, 18; *Crabbtree Balke furlong, Crabb Tree fur'* 1652 (*v.* crabtre, balca); *Crosse Horne fur'* 1652, *The Two Crosshornefurlong* 1706, *The Three Crosshorn Furlong* 1714, 1739, 1745, 1754 (prob. 'lying athwart Horn', *v.* cros², but may refer to *Five Mile Cross infra*); *Robert Cumbreys Hadelond* 1739, 1745, 1754, 1758, *v.* hĕafod-land); *Dawes's Close* 1787, *Dawes* - 1790, 118 (from the surn. *Dawes,* cf. Elizabeth *Dawes* 1522 MilS of nearby Langham); *Debdale* 1706, *Dibdale* -, *Debdale fur'* 1652 (*v.* dēop, dalr); *East Dale* 1787 (*v.* dalr); *Ellis Nooke* 1652 (from the surn. *Ellis, v.* nōk); *Exton Meyre* 1556 (Exton parish adjoins to the south-west, *v.* (ge)mǣre); *Farding Green Furlong* 1706 (*v.* feorðung, grēne²; 'farthing' is perh. used here in its sense 'a quarter of an acre'); *Far Wood* 1787, 118; *Fauldal(l) Wood* 1610 Speed, *Feldale* 1623, *Faldall* 1627, 1694 (*v.* fald, dalr); *Five Lands fur'* 1652 (*v.* land); *Fiue Mile Crosse* 1610 Speed, *Five Mile Cross* 1695 Map, 18, *5 Mile Cross* 1780 Map (a wayside cross on Ermine Street, prob. at the point where Sewstern Lane joins it, some five miles from Stamford L, *v.* cros); *Fulwood* 1623, *Fullwood(e)* 1578 (1684) Wright, 1627, 1633, 1652, 1694 (prob. 'foul, dirty wood', *v.* fūl, wudu); *Gadman fur'* 1652, *Gadman Thoroughs, Gadman Furrows fur'* 1652, *Goodman Furrows* 1787, 1790, 118 (perh. from *gadman* 'a goadsman', because difficult soil here made his efforts with the oxen of the ploughteam very necessary, v. **furh**, cf. Gedding Furrows in neighbouring Stretton f.ns. (a); *Gadman* as a ME occupational surname is unrecorded, while *Goodman*, a nickname for the Devil, seems unlikely here, although the surn. *Goodman* does occur in the county, cf. Robert- and Thomas *Goodman* 1522 MilS of N. Luffenham and Goodman's Nether Cl in Lyndon f.ns. (a); cf. also *Goodmans Snowte* in Wardley f.ns. (b), Goodman's or Pick's Cl in Teigh f.ns. (a)); *Gibb Lane End* 1652; *Gil(l)sons Home Close* 1787, 118 (William *Gilson* was in possession in 1787 *Surv*); *Goose Green* 1711, 1733, 1758, - *Close* 1626, 1733, 1795 (v. **gōs, grēne²**); *Great Wood* 1712; *The Green* 1652 (v. **grēne²**); *Grymes Wong Furlong* 1683, *Grimes's Wong* 1787, *Grimes* - 118 (from the surn. *Grimes*, cf. *Grimesholme* in neighbouring Empingham f.ns. (b), v. **vangr**); *Hall Dale Close, Hall Dall Wood* 1652 (v. **hall, dalr**); *Hardwick(e)(s) Close* 1626, 1696, 1697, 1733, c1733, 1795, *Hardwick Gate Close* 1733, 1758, 1785, *Hardwicke grounds* 1676 (named from Hardwick in Empingham *infra*, v. **gata, grund**); *Hawkeslands, - fur', Haukelands fur'* 1652, *Short Hauk(e)land(e)s* 1556, 1714, 1739, 1745, *Short Hawkelands fur', Long Hawkelands* 1652 (in ME surn. creation, *hauoc* 'hawk' was sometimes used by metonomy for 'a hawker' but it was also used with reference to the holding of land by providing hawks for the lord and that may be its use here; alternatively, the f.n. may simply refer to land especially frequented by hawks, v. **hafoc, land**); *Heath fur'* 1652, *Far Heath* 1787, 118, - *fur'* 1652, *Long Heath* 1652, 1787, 118, - *fur'* 1652, *Short Heath fur', New Heath, - fur'* 1652, *Heath Side* 1652, *the North Heath against the Meer* 1706 (v. **hǣð, sīde, (ge)mǣre** and Heath Lodge *supra*); *Betweene the Hedges* 1706 (v. **hecg**); *Heif(f)er Close* 1733, 1758, *Heifers* - 1785 (v. **hēah-fore**); *Henn Hill fur'* 1652 (v. **henn**); *High Bush fur'* 1652 (v. **hēah¹, busc**); *Hob Hole* 1706, 1787, 1790, 118, *Hobb Hole fur'* 1652, *Hobhale furlong* 1706 (poss. *hobb(e)* 'a tussock, a hummock' but *hob* 'a hobgoblin' may also be thought of, v. **hol¹**); *Northeastward -, Northwestward -. Southeastward -, Southwestward Hill Close* 1790; *Great -, Little Holme* 1787, 1790, 118 (v. **holmr**); *Horn Lane* 18 (an 18th cent. local name for the Great North Road, otherwise Ermine Street, cf. Horn Lane Spinney in Horn *infra*); *Horse Pasture* 1787, 1790; *The House* 1758, *House Close* 1758, *The House Ground* 1626, 1733, 1795 (the last f.n. refers to *a close of pasture in Woolfox*, so that the house in question was prob. Woolfox Lodge or its predecessor, v. **grund**); *of the Hull* 1341 NI (p) (v. **hyll**); *Jewel(l) Pool Close* 1787, 1790, 118 (descriptive of a highly prized, constant source of water); *Kite fur', Kite -, Kyte Hill fur'* 1652 (v. **cȳta, hyll**); *Lane Close* 1652, *Little -, Lane End* 1652, *Little Lane Way* 1652; *Laxmore fur'* 1652 (cf., perh., the two examples of Lax Hill, one in Hambleton and the other in Barrowden, for which dial. *lax* 'loose in texture, loosely compacted' is suggested, alluding to the nature of the soil); *Laxton Balke* 1706 (from the surn. *Laxton*, cf. Robert *Laxston*, husbandman in Greetham, 1522 MilS, v. **balca**); *Lesser Wood*

1697, c1733 (*v.* **lesser**); *Leys Close* 1714, 1739, 1745 (*v.* **lēah**); *Lyme Kilne fur'*
1652 (*v.* **lim-kilne**); *Lyngcolne Strete* 1556, *Lincolne Way fur'* 1652 (referring to the
Roman Ermine Street, otherwise Great North Road, leading to Lincoln, *v.* **strǣt**);
Long Borowe fur' 1652, *Longborough Nook, Longborrow Nooke* 1652, 1706,
Longborough Nook fur' 1652 (poss. referring to a lost Neolithic long barrow on
the limestone here, but such a site has not yet shown up as a crop.mark, *v.*
lang[1], **beorg, nōk**); *Longemore* 1556, *Long Moore* 1652, - *fur'* 1652, - *Furlong*
1706, *Longemore Hedge Furlong* 1556 (*v.* **lang**[1], **mōr**[1], **hecg**); *Lull Hill* 1787, 1790,
118 (may contain the OE pers.n. *Lulla*, cf. Lullhaugh Cl in Whissendine f.ns.
(a)); *Far -, Near Lumber Nook* 1787, 1790, 118 (*v.* **lumber, nōk**); *Maniwell Spring*
1652, *Maniwells fur'* 1652, *Mannell Flatt* 1706 ('a spring welling up in several
places', *v.* **manig, wella, spring, flat**); *Meare Wong* 1652, *Meere Wong fur'* 1652 (*v.*
(ge)mǣre, vangr); *Mid(d)le Close* 1626, 1676, 1733, 1758, 1795 (*v.* **middel**); *Middle
Furlong* 1706; *Beneath the Mills* 18 (referring to both the watermill and windmill),
Mill Close 1652, 118, *Mill Dam* 1787, 118, *Mill Dam Close* 1787, 1790, 118, *Mylne
Furlong* 1556, *Mill Holme* 1652, *Mill Meadow* 1787, 1790, 118 (*v.* **myln, damme,
holmr**); *Eastward-. Westward Mortar Pits* 1787, 1790, 118, *Morter Pitts fur'* 1652,
Mortar Pitts Furlong 1706 (*v.* **morter-pytt**); *Near Wood* 1787, 118; *Neather Close
alias Saltewell Close* 1676, *Nether Close alias Saltwell Close* 1695 (*v.* Saltwells
supra); *New Close* 1626, 1733, 1758, 1795, *North New Close* 1676; *Furlong next the
New Dyke* 1652 (*v.* **dīk**); *Nottyngham Strete* 1556, *Nottingham Street fur'* 1652
(referring to the Roman road now called Sewstern Lane, *v.* **strǣt**); *The Parsonage*
1525 *Rental* ('land adjacent to the parsonage, or for the use of the parson', *v.*
personage); *Pickworth Gate Close* 1626, 1691, 1733, 1795, *South Pickworth Grounds*
1676 (Pickworth parish adjoins to the east, *v.* **gata, grund**); *The Pinfold* 1787, 118
(*v.* **pynd-fald**); *Pingle* 1787, 118 (*v.* **pingel**); *Piper -, Pyper Pitt Furlong* 1556, 1652
(poss. an unrecorded OE *pipere* 'a spring', cognate with ODan *pipr-* 'spring,
stream' which is found in several Danish nature names with a first el. *Peber-*, cf.
Piper Hole in Harby Lei, Peppering and Peppering Eye Sx, *v.* **pytt**); *Popples
Farm* 1686 (perh. from OE **popel** 'pebble' referring to stony ground, rather than
from a surn.); *Post Hades* 1706 ('headlands abutting on the post-road, i.e.
Sewstern Lane', *v.* **hēafod**); *Post Way fur'* 1652 (cf. *The Post Way* in Thistleton
f.ns. (b), *v.* **post-way**); *Preist Wood* 1652 (for the endowment of clergy, *v.* **prēost,
wudu**); *Northward -, Southward -, Westward Priorage Close* 1787, 1790, 118 (a
construction comparable with *parsonage* but based on *prior*, the Prior of Warwick
was parson of Greetham in 1522 MilS); *Revel(l)s Close* 1626, 1711, 1733, 1758,
1795 (prob. from the surn. *Revel*); *Rice Furlong* 1652, 1706 (*v.* **hrīs**); *Royse fur'*
1652 (from the surn. *Royse*, cf. Richard *Royse* of Greetham 1524 SR); *Old
Saintfoin Close* 1787, 1790 (*Onobrychis sativa* or *sainfoin* was much grown as a
forage plant in the 18th cent.); *St Johns Peice* 1706, - *Piece* 1787, 118 (prob.

alluding to the Knights of St John but may poss. record the site of the local bonfire on St John's Day, 24th June); *Salley Tree Leas*, - *Leys* 1706, *Sallow Tree Leys* 1739, 1757, 1795, *Swallow Tree Leys* 1745, 1754, *Salow Tre Leyes Furlong* 1556, 1652, *Far* -, *Near Sallow Tree Leys* 1787, 1790, 118, *Sallow Tree fur'* 1652, *Little Sallow Tree Close* 1787, 1790, 118, *Salley Leys* 1706 (*v.* **salh, trēow, lēah**); *Salter Leys*, - *fur'* 1652 (a common pattern in Rutland is for - *Leys* to be preceded by a surn. with or without genitival *s* and *Salter* here may well be a surn.; but as Greetham is on Ermine Street, the pasture may have been associated with grazing for the pack-horses of itinerant salt merchants, *v.* **saltere, lēah**); *Sandye Peece fur'* 1652 (*v.* **sandig, pece**); *Sharpe Pitt fur'*, *Sharpe Pitt Haides fur'* 1652 (from the surn. *Sharpe, v.* **pytt, hēafod**); *Sheapeheards Haides fur'* 1652 (from the surn. *Shepherd, v.* **hēafod**); *Shirt Pole Dale* 1652 (perh. with OE **scite** 'dung' made more delicate, *v.* **pōl[1], dalr**); *Short fur'* 1652 (*v.* **sc(e)ort**); *Sowthe Gate* 1556 (*v.* **sūð, gata**); *Sprouridge* 1637, *Sprowridge* 1556, 1652, 1670, 1706, *Greetham Sprow Ridge* 1733, *Sprowridge Crosse* 1556, *Sprowridge Furlong* 1652, 1706 (*v.* **sprogh, hrycg, cros**); *North Stockings* 1787 (*v.* **stocc ing**); *Stock Pasture* 118, *Stocke Wong*, - *fur'* 1652, *Stockwong Furlong* 1706 (*v.* **stocc, vangr**); *Stone Wong fur'* 1652 (*v.* **stān, vangr**); *Street Ende, Street fur'* 1652 (referring to Ermine Street, *v.* **strǣt, ende[1]**); *Stretton Gate* 1556, - *Crosse* 1556, *Stretton Way(e)* 1556, 1652, *Strattons Way fur'* 1652, *Stretton Meyre* 1556 (Stretton parish adjoins to the north-east, *v.* **gata, cros, (ge)mǣre**); *Swine Tree fur'* 1652, *Swinetree Hedge* 1652, *Swynetre Hedge Furlong* 1556, *Swine Tree Hedge fur'* 1652 (prob. alluding to an oak beneath which pigs foraged for acorns, *v.* **swīn[1], trēow, hecg**); *Temple Peyse* 1556, *Temple Hedge fur'* 1652 (referring to the Knights Templars, a preceptory of whose order was excavated at nearby South Witham L in 1966-7, cf. Temple Barns in neighbouring Stretton f.ns. (a), *v.* **temple, pece, hecg**); *Thicke Moore* 1652, *Thickmore* 1578 (1684) Wright, 1706, *Thicke Moore fur'* 1652, *Thyckemore Grene* 1556 (*v.* **þicce[1], mōr[1], grēne[2]**); *Thistleton Heath, Thistleton Way* 1652 (Thistleton parish adjoins at Greetham's north-west corner, *v.* **hǣð**); *Three Bush Furlong, Three Bush Holme fur'* 1652, *Thre Buske Wong* 1556, *Three Bush Wong Furlong* 1706 (*v.* **þrēo, busc, buskr, holmr, vangr**); *Townes End*, - *Close* 1652 (*v.* **tūn, ende[1]**); *Town Side fur'* 1652 (*v.* **tūn, sīde**); *Tythe Close* 1787, 1790, 118, *William Parkers Tyth Close* 1706, *The Tythe House* 1787, - *Barn* 118 (*v.* **tēoða**); *Upper Close* 1652; *Wades Lane* 1652, *New Wades Close* 1697, c1733 (William *Wade* was a tenant in 1652); *Water Corn Mill* 1787, 118; *Walkers Farm* 1686 *Rental* (from the family name of George *Walker* 1665 HT); *The Waste* 118 ('(land enclosed from) the manorial waste', *v.* **waste**); *Water Wong fur'* 1652 (*water* is no doubt used here in the sense 'wet', *v.* **wæter, vangr**); *West Furlong* 1706; *Wheat(e) Moore* 1706, - *fur'* 1652 (the forms indicate *hwǣte* 'wheat', but this seems unlikely compounded with **mōr** 'moorland', so prob. **wēt** 'wet, damp' is present here, cf. *le wetlondes* in N. Luffenham f.ns. (b), *v.* **mōr**[1]); *Windmill* 1706, *Wind Mill fur'* 1652, *Windmill Hill Cowpasture* 1787, 1790, 118, *Windmill Hill fur'* 1652; *Witham Way fur'* 1652 (South Witham L lies due north of Greetham); *The Woods* 1706, *Wood Close* 1787, 1790, 118; *Wood Fylde* 1556, *Woodfielde* 1633, *Woodfeild* 1652, 1706, 1739, 1745, *Wood Field* 1714, 1739 (one of the great open-fields, *v.* **wudu, feld**); *Wood Haides* 1652 (*v.* **hēafod**); *Wood Side* 1652 (*v.* **sīde**); *Wood Way fur'* 1652.

Horn

HORN

(*on*) *hornan* 852 (12) BCS 464 (S 1440)
Horne 1086 DB, 1221 *FF*, 1234 RHug *et passim* to 1377 Cl *et freq* to 1610 Speed
Horn 1229 RHug, 1238 RGros *et passim* to 1285 Pat *et freq*

The name is from **horna**, a weak form of OE **horn** 'a horn'. Used topographically, the word described a horn-shaped feature such as the sharp bend of North Brook and its valley a half mile to the north of Horn House. Horn no longer exists as a village, but its earthworks survive, *v.* **horna**.

CROWS SPINNEY. FISH POND, cf. *The Troutery* 1943 *Map*. FORT HENRY is a Gothick summer-house of the late 18th century beside the dammed North Brook. HORN HO. is *Horne Lodge* 1780, 1801 Map. HORN LANE SPINNEY, cf. *Horn Lane* 1780 ib, 1795 *Anc*, 1801 Map, 1818 *Anc*, 1824 O, 1846, 1877 White, an 18th century name for the local stretch of the Great North Road, otherwise Ermine Street. NORTH ROAD SPINNEY, referring to the Great North Road. PUG'S PARK SPINNEY, with dial. *pug* 'a hare', cf. Hare Park in Stretton f.ns. (a).

Field-Names

The undated forms in (a) are 1943 *Map*.

(a) Avenue Fd; The Barracks (cf. Barracks in neighbouring Exton f.ns. (a)); Burnt Cl; Burnt Land (*v.* **brende**[2], **land**); Colt's Fd (*v.* **colt**); Great Horse Cl;

Long Cl; Stonepit; (Hibbitt's -) Thirty-six Acre (from the surn. *Hibbitt, cf.* Amos, Robert and William *Hibbitt* 1846 White, Frederick, Cecil and Arthur *Hibbitt* 1932 Kelly, all of Exton).

(b) *Redbroke* 16 Blore (prob. 'reedy brook', an earlier name for North Brook, Empingham, although since that village stands on a thin outcropping of ironstone, rēad 'red' is also poss., *v.* hrēod, rēad, brōc.

Market Overton

MARKET OVERTON
    Overtune 1086 DB
    Ouerton(e), *-v-* 1200 Cur, 1202 Ass *et passim* to 1286 *Ass et freq*
       to 1610 Speed
    Orton 1535 LP *et passim* to 1642 *Recov*

The affix is normally added as:
    Market(t)es -, -is - 1200 Cur, 1280 OSut, 1339 *Deed et passim* to
       1372 Ipm
    Market - 1267 Ch, 1286 *Ass et passim* to 1388 Pat *et freq*

'The village on the ridge', *v.* ofer^2, tūn. The settlement's market function is recorded as early as 1200 Cur, *v.* market. The flat-topped ridge is formed by the Northampton Sands ironstone which enters Rutland from the north. The Romano-British settlement on the parish boundary with neighbouring Thistleton, with its temple dedicated to the god Veteris, was no doubt the market site which preceded Market Overton's. Hundreds of Roman coins have been found here, as well as some British, suggesting a market location on this upland in the Iron Age also. The temple enclosure on Market Overton's boundary would have offered a site for periodic markets where the honesty of traders could be guaranteed by the god. Overton's market seems only to represent a movement of the market site one mile further south-west, possibly to the protection of the fortified precinct within which the parish church now stands.

BLACK BULL P.H., *The Bull Inn* 1846, 1863 White. CORDLE SPRING, *Caldwell', Calwell'* 1346 *MinAcct, Calwhel* 1363 *ib,* cf.

Caldewellemed', *Caldewellesik'* 1363 *ib*, v. **cald, wella, mæd, sík.**
THE GREEN, 1935 VCH, v. **grēne**[2]. LAVENDER FM, 1935 ib.
THE LODGE, 1846 White. MARKET OVERTON CHURCH,
Church (St Peter and St Paul) 1846 ib, an Anglo-Saxon foundation,
built within the bounds of what is probably a Roman camp,
although BrownArchSites 18 (followed by MER. 26) regards the
earthworks as of medieval provenance. MARKET OVERTON
QUARRY. NEW ROW. OLD HALL, *atte Halle* 1411 *Comp* (p),
cf. *Hallesik'* 1346 *MinAcct*, *Alsik* 1363 *ib*, v. **hall, sík.** PINFOLD
LANE 1906 Map, v. **pynd-fald.** THE RECTORY, cf. *Rectory Field*
1943 *Map*. SPRINGFIELD LANE (local). THREE HORSE
SHOES P.H., *The Horse Shoe* 1846 White, *The Three Horse Shoes*
1863 ib. THE WHARF, 1846 ib, cf. *Wharf Fields* 1943 *Map*, beside
the disused Melton Mowbray - Oakham Canal.

Field-Names

Undated forms in (a) are 1943 *Map*. Early forms dated 1345, 1346, 1363 and
1371 are *MinAcct*; 1673, 1760 and c1760 are *Deed*.

(a) Four Acres, Five Acre (x2), Six -, Seven -, Top Eight -, Nine and a
Half -, Ten -, Ten and a Half -, Eleven Acre (x3), Twelve -, Twelve and a Half
-, Thirteen -, Fourteen Acre (x2), Road Fourteen Acre, Fifteen -, The Sixteen
Acre, Eighteen Acres (x3), Nineteen -, The Twenty -, The Thirty Acre (*v.* **æcer**);.
Allotment Fd, Allotments (referring to allotment gardens); Big -, Little Bandale
(*Bandal(e)* 1363, 1371, *Bandaleleyes* 1363, *Bandalls Close* 1673, with either **dalr** or
deill, *v.* **bēan, lēah**); Barfoot Cl (with the surn. *Barfoot*, cf. Rev. H. *Barfoot* 1830
OR of Lyddington and Barfoots Wood in Leighfield f.ns. (a)); Barn Cl; First -,
Second Barrow Fd, Barrow Platt (abutting Barrow parish, *v.* **plat**[2]); Berrybushes
1979 VR; Black Holmes 1906 Map (*Black Holme* 1672 VCH; in eModE, *black*
'fertile' is contrasted with *white* 'infertile', but the colour of the soil may be
indicated here, *v.* **holmr**); Black Wong 1906 Map (cf. Black Holmes *supra*, *v.*
vangr); Middle -, Buildings Fd; Bussocks Fd (bordering Bussock Barn in
neighbouring Barrow); Cheriton's Land; Christian Cl (from the surn. *Christian*,
cf. John-, Robert- and William *Cristian* 1522 MilS, 1524 SR of neighbouring
Barrow); Clark's Cl; Cottles (the surn. *Cottle*, cf. The Cottles in Whissendine
f.ns. (a)); Crabtree (*v.* **crabtre**); Crow Cl; Damade (prob. 'meadow with a dam',
v. **damme, mæd**, cf. *Damfeild* in neighbouring Thistleton f.ns. (b)); Davis's Cl;
Ding Hades 1979 VR (from the surn. *Ding*, cf. John *Dyng*, husbandman of

neighbouring Teigh, 1522 MilS, 1524 SR and Robert *Dyng*, labourer of Teigh, 1522 MilS, *v.* **hēafod**); Engine Fd (land on which agricultural or other machines were sited; Mr J. Field notes that this example adjoins ironstone workings); Fish Pond; Football Fd; Freeby's Cl; Goddins (*Godwin's Close* c1760, cf. *Godwynnisdon* 1346, *Godewynesmed'* 1363, prob. from the OE pers.n. *Gōdwine*; DB records that Godwine held 1½ carucates of land in neighbouring Teigh in the reign of Edward the Confessor, *v.* **dūn, mǣd**); The Gorse Pit (*v.* **gorst**); Far -, Half Mile, Half Mile Edge; Hall Cl; Big -, Little Hell (prob. with the local form of **hyll** 'a hill' rather than a derogatory name for a field with difficult soil); High Bushes; Hill Fd; Holgate (*Hollgate* 1550 *Ct*, *v.* **hol², gata**); Honey Hole (prob. referring to sticky soil); Hopkinson's Gorse 1824 O (*v.* **gorst**); Kew Cl; Kirk Hole 1906 Map (1672 VCH, 'church hollow', *v.* **kirkja, hol¹**); Land Cl (an enclosure consolidating selions of an open-field, *v.* **land**); Limekiln, - Fd; Little 'Uns (*Liteleng* 1346, *Lit(t)lehengg*, *Litling* 1363, *Litelinge* 1371, *v.* **lȳtel, eng**); Marriotts (a surn., cf. Marriott's Cl in Thistleton f.ns. (a) and John *Mariet* 1522 MilS of Lyddington); The Meadow; Mill Fd (cf. *Mellewong'* 1363, *v.* **myln, vangr**; a windmill stood at SK 9025 1713 (BrownArchSites 18)); Mortar Pits; Netherlands ('selions further from the village or lower in elevation', *v.* **neoðera, land**); Nolhills (*Northwell Hill Closes alias Norrell-hill Closes* 1760, *v.* **norð, wella, hyll** and *Northwell infra*); Overton Fd; Overton Mill 1824 O; Parks (cf. *le wong apud Parkassh'* 1363, *Parkwall'* 1346, a deer park, first recorded in 1269 (MER 27), *v.* **park, æsc, wall**); Peasland (*v.* **pise, land**); Pit Fd; River Cl; The Slip (*v.* **slipe**); Smith's; Solomon's Grave (adjoins a quarry, cf. Solomon's Hut in Burley, *v.* **græf**); Spa Cl (*Spaw Close* c1760, *the part of Spaw Close cut off by the Navigation* c1760 (referring to the old Melton Mowbray - Oakham Canal), *v.* **spa**); Spring Cl (*v.* **spring**); First -, Second Stamford Road Fds; Stonepit Fd; Syke ('meadow beside a stream', *v.* **sík**); Bottom -, Tin Hovel Fd ('land containing a shed made of corrugated iron sheets', *v.* **hovel**); Turner's Barn Fd (cf. Turners Fd in neighbouring Stretton f.ns. (a)); Waltham Clays (cf. *Waltham Croft'* 1363, *- Crofts* 1744 *Asw*, from the surn. *Waltham*, cf. John *Waltham*, husbandman of neighbouring Teigh, 1522 MilS, 1524 SR, Laurence *Waltham*, husbandman of Teigh, 1522 MilS, 1524 SR, Lawrence *Waltham* of Ashwell 1525 ib and Richard *Waltham*, also of Teigh, 1522 MilS, 1524 SR, *v.* **clǣg, croft**); Winsell (*Winsell Close* c1760, *v.* **hvin, hyll**); First -, Second Wong (*The Wong* 1672 VCH, *v.* **vangr**); Bottom -, Top Wood Fd.

(b) *Archdales* 1363 (the first el. is obscure, *v.* **deill**); *Bentle* 1346 (*v.* **beonet, lēah**); *Bleksik* 1345, 1346, 1363 (poss. with ON **bleikr** 'bleak, bare of vegetation', *v.* **sík**); *le Brech(e)* 1346, 1363 (*v.* **brēc**); *Brendhoutecroft* 1363, *Brentoutcroft'* 1371 (*v.* **brende², ūt(e), croft**); *Brendeȝerdes* 1363 (*v.* **brende²,

geard); *Buttes atte Parkwall* 1346 (*v.* **butte** and Parks *supra*); *Church Close* 1629
Bir (*v.* **cirice**, cf. Mkt. Overton Church *supra*); *Cottagers Close alias Synnams*
1673 (*v.* **cotager** and *Senholm infra*); *de la Dale* 1363 (p) (*v.* **dalr**); *Estholm* 1346
(*v.* **ĕast, holmr**); *Estmor* 1363 (*v.* **ĕast, mōr**[1]); *Estrewellewong* 1363 (*v.* **ĕstre, wella,**
vangr); *Foldehaluacre* Hy 3 *Surv* (*v.* **fald, half, æcer**); *The Furr Close, - Lane*
1744 *Asw* (*v.* **feor**); *Ganns Close* 1673 (from the surn. *Gann,* cf. John *Ganne*
1524 SR of Ryhall and Gan's Cl in neighbouring Stretton f.ns. (a)); *Gascoignes*
1363, *Gascoyn(es)* 1371 (the surn. *Gascoigne*); *atte Gate* 1363 (p) (*v.* **gata**);
Halffmylle Busk 1551 *Ct* (*v.* **half, mīl, buskr**); *Harris's Close* c1760; *Holmsik'* 1345,
1363, 1371 (*v.* **holmr, sīk**); *le Lampe* 1550 Pat (a piece of land endowed for the
maintenance of a lamp above the altar in the village church, *v.* **lampe**);
Langmerewong 1346 (*v.* **lang**[1], **(ge)mǣre, vangr**); *Long(e)wong* 1346, 1363 (*v.*
lang[1], **vangr**); *le Mor* 1363, *Morwong* 1345, 1346, *Moore Closes* 1760 (*v.* **mōr**[1],
vangr); *Northholm* 1363 (*v.* **norð, holmr**); *Northlongfurlong* 1346 (*v.* **norð, lang**[1],
furlang); *Norton' Wod'* 1363 ('the wood by the northern farmstead', cf. *Southton*
infra, v. **norð, tūn, wudu**); *Ouertonewood* 1371 (*v.* **wudu**); *Rutmor* 1363 ('Rōta's
moor' which stretched westwards through Teigh into Whissendine, *v. Rutmore* in
Teigh); *Senholm* 1346, *Synnams* 1763 ('water-meadow subject to dispute', *v.*
sænna, holmr, cf. *Sanam* in Hambleton f.ns. (b) and Sanham House in Frisby
Lei 290); *Ssortwong'* 1346 (*v.* **sc(e)ort, vangr**); *Snarlings* 1673 ('brushwood-covered
land', cf. Snarlings in neighbouring Thistleton f.ns. (a), *v.* **snār, land**); *Southton',*
-wong 1363 ('the southern farmstead', *v.* **sūð, tūn, vangr**, cf. *Norton' Wod' supra*);
Stratonegate 1371 (Stretton lies to the east of Mkt. Overton, *v.* **gata**); *le wong be*
west the Strete 1363 (the road alluded to here is the Roman Sewstern Lane, *v.*
strǣt); *Swynpit, Swynpitwong* 1346 ('pit where swine forage', *v.* **swīn, pytt, vangr**);
Two Yard Land 1760 (*v.* **gerd-landes**); *Wakehull* 1363, *Wakehilleies* 1346 ('the
look-out hill', appropriate to a settlement on the northern border of the ancient
kingdom of Rutland and near a Roman road running into it, *v.* **wacu, hyll,**
lēah); *Walescroft* 1363 (from the surn. *Wales/Wallis,* cf. *terre quondam Willelmi*
Waleys 1371, *v.* **croft** and Reaney *s.n.*); *Walwortwong'* 1346, 1363 (*v.* **walhwyrt,**
vangr); *Westfeld'* 1363 (*v.* **west, feld**); *be Westgate* 1363 ('(the furlong) beside the
west road', *v.* **west, gata**); *Willeshulles* 1346, *Wyueleshell', Wyueleshelleyes* 1363
(from the OE pers.n. *Wifel, v.* **hyll, lēah**).

Stretton

STRETTON
   Stratune 1086 DB
   Straton(e) 1086 DB, 1208 P, 1224 Cur, *Stratton'* 1107 Reg, c1200

Templar, 1208 P, 1221 RHug *et passim* to 1503 Cl, (*Est* -)
1306 ib
Stretton(e) 1176, 1177 P, 1254 Val *et passim* to 1280 Pat *et freq*
to 1610 Speed, (- *bithe Strete*) 1315 Pat, (- *in the Strete*)
1400 Cl, 1402 Pat, (- *in le Strete*) 1543 LP

'The farm beside the Roman road', *v.* **strǣt, tūn.** Stretton is on
Ermine Street. The affix *ēast* 'east' distinguished this Stretton from
Great - and Little Stretton Lei to the west. The affixes - *bithe
Strete,* - *in the Strete* were added when the significance of the village
name had been forgotten.

HOOBY LODGE

Hooby(e), Hoobie, the dividable Hoobye 1633 *Bru*
The Hubyes 1646 *Deed, Hoobies* 1707 *Anc, Far -, Hither -,*
Middle Hoobys 1758 *Surv,* 1785 *Anc, Far Hobys* 1776, 1830,
1847 *BHS, Greens Far Hoby* 1776, 1830, 1847 *ib, Greens
Hither Hoby Close* 1776, 1830, 1847 *ib, Hoby Closes* 1776,
1830, 1847 *ib, Hooby Gate Close* 1904 *Anc,* - *Closes* 1908
Deed, Hooby Fields 1904 *Anc,* 1908 *Deed*
Hooby Hedge Furlong 1652 *Surv, Hoby Furlong* c1720, 1776,
1830, 1846 *BHS*
Hooby Lodge 1806 Map, 1845 *BHS,* 1846, 1863 White, 1904
Anc, Hoby Lodge c1800 Map

The earliest surviving recording of Hooby is as a field-name of
neighbouring Thistleton parish. Possibly it signifies 'the farmstead
at the spur of land', *v.* **hōh, bȳ.** There is a low ridge (*hōh*) to the
south-east of the site of the present lodge. If this interpretation is
correct, Hooby is one of only two possible recorded examples of
p.ns. in -bȳ in Rutland, the other being *Birchaby* in Belton. The
name Hooby, however, may well be manorial, a family name taken
from Hoby in the Wreake Valley in east Lei (cf. John *Hoby* 1522
MilS, 1524 SR of Brooke, Hooby Farm in Thistleton and Hoby
Cross in Wardley f.ns. (a)). If indeed a p.n. in -bȳ, it is
significantly a hybrid formation with an OE specific and Scand
generic, indicating minimal Norse influence within Rutland's
boundaries. It would also be one of a string of three p.ns. in -bȳ
sited between the Roman roads Ermine Street and Sewstern Lane,

including Gunby and Stainby beyond the county boundary in Lincs. Both of these, however, are totally Scand formations, compounded with Norse personal names. The form *Hooby Hedge* (*v.* **hecg**) indicates that, at least in 1652, Hooby had a recognized boundary. The present shape of Stretton parish suggests that formerly Hooby was a self-contained territory west of Ermine Street.

MORKERY LEYS

Morcary Leys 1723, 1749 *Anc*, 1845 *BHS, Money Morcary Leys*
    1723, 1724, 1732 *Anc, Ashwells Nether Morcary Leys,*
    - Upper - 1723, 1724, 1732 *ib*
Mawkery Leys 1758, 1785 *Anc*
Mockery Leys 1785 *Anc*
Morcrow Leys 1804 *BHS, Nether* - 1847 *ib, Morcray Leys* c1840
    TA, 1842 *Anc*
Morkery Leys 1904 *Anc*, 1908 *Deed*

Possibly an OE compound of **mearc** 'a boundary' and **rīð** 'a stream'. If this is correct, the first el. was later Scandinavianized to **mǫrk** 'border, boundary'. Morkery Leys line the county boundary, with East and West Morkery Woods lying beyond the border in Castle Bytham L. A small stream forms the county boundary for a short stretch north of Stocken Hall. In the reign of Edward the Confessor, Morcar, brother of Edwin, earl of Mercia, held the estate of Casterton some six miles to the south-east. If his name survives here, it is difficult to see what the final el. of Morkery could be. On the other hand, early 18th century antiquarianism may well be responsible for the approximation to Morcar in the spellings recorded in the Ancaster MSS.

Money Morcary Leys were in the possession of Widow *Money* in 1723 *Anc*, while *Ashwells Nether* -, - *Upper Morcary Leys* record the family of Henry *Ashwell*, resident in Stretton in 1637 *ib*.

STOCKEN HALL

le Stokkyng 1326 Ipm, *Stocking(s)* 1678, 1723 *Anc*, 1758 *Surv*,
    1801 Map
Stretton Stocking(e) 1633 *Conant*, 1684 Wright, 1695 *Map*,
    - *Stockings* 1676, 1678, 1723 *Anc*

The Ould Stockinges 1627 *Bir,* New *Stocking(s)* 1637, 1678, 1733 *Anc*
Stockin(g) Hall 1684 Wright, 1702 *Anc, Stockins alias Stocking Hall* 1723 *ib, Stockings Hall* 1824 O, *Stocken Hall* 1845 *BHS,* 1846, 1863 White, 1904 *Anc*
Stocking Wood 1723, 1749 *Anc,* c1800, 1806 Map, *Stocken Wood* c1840 *TA,* 1845 *BHS*

'A piece of ground cleared of tree-stumps', *v.* **stoccing.** For later field-names arising, *v.* f.ns. (a) *infra.* The hall was probably built by John Brown in the early 17th century, *v.* MER 40.

THE COTTAGE. FISH POND, *Fishpond* 1749 *Anc,* 1758 *Surv, Fish Pools* 1904 *Anc,* 1908 *Deed.* LADY WOOD, 1904 *Anc,* 1908 *Deed, v.* **hlæfdige.** THE RECTORY, 1846, 1863 White. STOCKEN PARK, 1908 *Deed, v.* Stocken Hall *supra* and Park Leys in f.ns. (a) *infra.* STRETTON LODGE, 1824 O, 1846, 1863 White, 1904 *Anc,* 1908 *Deed.* STRETTON WOOD, 1610 Speed, 1687 *Map,* 1804, 1825, 1845 *BHS,* 1904 *Anc,* 1908 *Deed, v.* **wudu.** WHEAT SHEAF P.H. (lost), 1845 *BHS.* WHITE HORSE P.H. (lost), 1846 White.

Field-Names

Undated forms in (a) are 1943 *Map.* Forms dated 1804, 1825, 1830, 1837, 1845, 1847, 1869 and 1870 are *BHS;* c1840 are *TA;* 1842, 1852, 1865 and 1904 are *Anc;* 1908 and 1955 are *Deed* (per Mr D. Tew). Early forms dated 13, 1331, 1713, c1713, c1720, c1743, 1746, c1746 and 1776 are *BHS;* 1627 are *Bir;* 1637, 1676, 1678, 1695, 1702, 1704, 1707, 1716, 1723, 1724, 1732, 1733, 1736, c1740, 1749, 1750, 1779, 1780 and 1785 are *Anc;* 1758 are *Surv.*

(a) Three Acres 1842, 1845, 1904, 1908, Three Acres Cl alias Seed Grass Cl 1804 (*Three Acres Close* 1713, c1713, *Three Acre Close or Seed Grass Close* 1746, c1746, *v.* Seed Grass Cl *infra*), Four Acre c1840, - Acres 1908, Five Acre, Seven Acres 1845, Far Seven - 1845, 1904, 1908, Top -, Eight Acres 1904, 1908, East -, Far -, West -, c1840, 1845, 1904, Nine Acres 1845, 1908, Ten Acres 1845, 1904, 1908, - Acre 1943 (*Ten Acre Close* 1749, 1779), Eleven Acre, Twelve Acres 1842, 1845, 1908, - Acre 1943 (*Twelve Acres Close* 1750), Thirteen Acres 1904, 1908, - Acre 1943, Fourteen Acres 1842, 1845, 1908, - Acre 1943 (*v.* The Platt *infra*),

(The) Thirty Acres, The Forty Acres 1904, 1908 (v. æcer); Adder Wood Cl
c1840, 1842, 1845, 1904, 1908, Addah's Wood Cl 1955 (Stretton Great Adowe, -
Little - 1627, v. Addah Wood in Clipsham); Alfin's Cl 1842, Alpins Cl 1845,
Alfins Cl 1943 (cf. Alfin's House 1824 in Normanton f.ns. (a)); Allens Cl 1804,
Allen's - 1825; Allotments on the Warren 1908 (v. The Warren infra); Askews Cl
c1840, 1845, Askew's - 1842; Bakers Cl c1840, 1845, Baker's - 1842; Bannister's
Cl 1804, Bannisters - 1825 (cf. John Banyster 1522 MilS of Lyddington);
Beadhouse Croft and Hovel 1845 (v. hovel), Bedehouse Ley 1842, Beadhouse Ley
in Wards Cl c1840, Beadhouse Ley 1845, 1869, 1870 (v. lēah), Beadhouse
Orchard c1840, 1845 (the Warden of the Almshouse of Stamford had an annuity
from certain lands in Stretton 1522 MilS, v. bed-hūs); a close late Bellaers
c1840, Bellaers Cl 1845 (John Bellaers is cited in 1845, cf. Bellases Hollow in
Greetham f.ns. (a)); Berry's Plot, Berrys Plott Fd 1845, Berry's Plot(t) Fd 1842,
1904, 1908, Berry's Plate Fd 1955, North -, South Berry's c1840, 1842, 1870, -
Berrys 1845, 1869 (Berriffs Plat(t) 1702, 1707, - Plot 1785, Beriffs Platts 1758,
from the surn. Beriff, v. plat²); Blacksmiths Cl 1845, 1904, Blacksmith's - 1908;
Bottom Cl c1840, 1904, 1908; Breach Furlong 1830 (c1720, 1776, The Breach
c1720, v. brēc); Breeder Leys c1840, 1842, 1908, Breder - 1845 (Breether Leyes
1627, Breeders Leyes 1723, 1758, Breeders Leys Close 1723, 'pasture assigned to
the breeding of livestock', v. brēder, lēah); Broadhouse Croft c1840 (perh. an
erroneous form of Beadhouse Croft supra); Broadwell Furlong 1830, 1847 (Broad
Wells, Broadwell Close 1785, Brodewell Gate, Broadwell Gate Furlong, Brodewell
Way Furlong c1720, Broadwell Furlong 1776, v. brād, wella, gata); Brook Cl
c1840, 1845; Bushy Cl c1840, 1908; Camms Cl 1904, 1908; The Canada 1904,
1908 (a transferred name for a piece of land remote from the village); Cart
Run 1943, - Fd c1840, 1842, 1845, 1908, Little Cart Run c1840, 1842, 1908, - Fd
1845 (Carter Hurn 1758, Carters - 1758, Little Carter Hurn 1707, 1758, prob. from
the surn Carter, cf. Carterplase in Whissendine f.ns. (b) and Carter's Close in
Egleton f.ns. (b), v. hyrne); Church Yard c1840; Clarke's Cl 1804, 1825, 1845,
1908, Clarkes - 1842 (Widowe Clarkes Close 1678, Clark(e)s Close 1749, 1758,
1785); Clay Fd c1840, 1842, '1845, 1869, 1870, 1908, Nether -, Upper - 1842, 1845,
Nether -, Upper Clay Ground c1840, Nether -, Top Clay Cl 1845, 1869, 1870,
Little West Fd also the Clay Fd 1830, 1847 (The Clay Field 1702, 1758, 1779,
The Great Clay Feild 1707, Great Clay Field 1758, The Little - 1707, Little West
Feild alias the Clay Feild c1720, - field 1776, v. clæg); Clipsham Dale Furlong
1830, 1847 (1776, Clipsham parish adjoins to the east, v. Clipsham Dale infra);
East -, West Clipsham Platt c1840, - Plott 1842, 1845, 1908 (v. plat²); Common
Wood Cl c1840, 1842, 1845, South - 1842, formerly Common Wood Cl now
Money's Cl 1804, 1825 (The Common Wood Closes 1627, 1678, Common Wood
Close 1713, c1713, 1723, 1746, c1746, 1758, Ashwells - 1723, 1724, 1732 (cf. Henry

Ashwell of Stretton 1637), *Blazes* - 1724, 1732 (cf. John *Blayes* 1678 and Stephen *Blaze* 1732, both of Stretton), *Ne(a)ther* - 1724, 1732, *Redishes* - 1723, 1724 (cf. Thomas *Reddish* of Stretton 1678), *Rubbins* - 1724, 1732 (cf. John *Rubbins* of Stretton 1678), *Scotneys* - 1723 (cf. John *Scotney* of Stretton 1678), *Storers* - 1723, 1724 (cf. Humphrey-and Robert *Storer* of Stretton 1678), *Upper* - 1723, 1732, *Widow Moneys* - 1723, 1724, 1732 (cf. Richard *Money* of Stretton 1678), *Bacons East* -, - *West* - 1723, 1724, 1732 (cf. Bernard *Bacon* of Stretton 1678), *Richmonds East* -, - *West* - 1723, 1724, 1732 (cf. Robert *Richmond* of Stretton 1678), *Skillingtons East* -, - *West* - 1723, 1724, 1732 (cf. John- and Robert *Skillyngton*, husbandmen of Stretton 1522 MilS (- *Skelyngton* 1524 SR), William *Skillington* of Stretton 1678)), Common Wood Furlong 1830, 1847 (*v. Common Wood infra*); Cow Cl 1830, 1842, 1845, 1847, 1908 (1776, *v. cū*); Cottage Plantation 1869; Crewyard, Crewyard Lane 1899 (*v.* **crew-yard**); The Croft 1852 (*v.* **croft**); Croke Hill Furlong 1830, 1847, Crooke - 1837 (*Crokehill Furlong* c1720, 1776, prob. from ME *crōk* 'a bend, a secluded nook'); Dove Coat Cl 1830, 1847 (*Dove Coat Close* 1723, c1740, 1758, 1776, *Dovecoat* - 1707, 1723, *v.* **dove-cot(e)**)); East Cl (x2) c1840, 1842, 1845; Little East Fd also Scotneys Fd 1830, 1847 (*Little East Feild alias Scotneys New Feild* c1720, 1776, John *Scotney* held land in Stretton 1678); Eastowe Furlong 1830, 1847 (*Eastow(e) Furlong* c1720, c1743, 1776, perh. to be identified with *le Esthawe infra*); Ell Cl 1908, Ell Plantation 1904, 1908 ('L-shaped piece of land'); Elsons Cl 1904, Elson's - 1908 (cf. Elsons Moor in Teigh f.ns. (a)); Fancourts Cl 1904, Fancourt's - 1908 (from the surn. *Fancourt*, cf. *Fancutts Cottage* c1685 in Burley f.ns. (b) and Lionel *Fancourt* 1698 *Terrier* of Empingham); Far Fd 1842, 1845, 1904, 1908; Foal's Cl 1804, Foals - 1825, Foal - c1840, 1842, 1845 (*Foal Close* 1723, 1724, 1732, *Foals* - 1749, 1758, *Wards Foals Close* 1785 (cf. William *Ward* of Stretton 1758), *v.* **fola**); Fisher Gate Furlong 1830, 1847 (*Fishers Gate* c1720, *Fishergate Furlong* c1720, 1776), Fishers Cl 1830, Fisher's - 1847 (*Fishers Close* 1776, from the surn. *Fisher*); Five Acres Plot 1908; Five Oaks Furlong 1830, 1847 (c1720, *v.* **āc**); Gan's Cl 1804, Gans - 1825, Ganns - 1845, Gann's - 1908 (*Ganns Closes* 1678, *Gan(n)s Close* 1678, 1723, c1740, 1758; from the surn. *Gann*, cf. John *Ganne* 1524 SR of Ryhall and *Ganns Close* in Mkt. Overton f.ns. (b)); Big -, Little Garden Fd 1904, 1908; Gedding Furrows 1904, 1908, Top Gadden Furrows 1830, 1847, Nether Gedding 1842, 1845, 1943, Upper - 1904, 1908 (*Gadman Furrows* 1707, *Goodman Furrows* 1758, *Bottom Gadman Furrows* 1776, *Top Gadden Furrows* 1776, *v. Gadman fur'* in neighbouring Greetham f.ns. (b)); Glebe Cl 1842, 1845, 1908 (*v.* **glebe**); Bottom -, Top Gossey Cl 1904, - Gassey - 1908, Bottom -, Top Gosby 1943 (*v.* **gorstig**); Grants Platt 1830, 1847 (1702, 1776, *Grants Plot(t)* 1758, 1785, cf. Henry *Grantes Closes* 1678, John *Grantes Closes* 1678, *v.* **plat**^{2}); Great Cl 1908; Great Casterton Fd also the Wood Fd

1830, 1847 (*v.* Wood Fd *infra*); North -, South Green Cl 1842, 1845, 1899, 1908; Grindstone 1865, 1899, Grindlestone 1943, Grindstone Cl 1845, Grindstone Wood c1840, 1845 (*v.* **grindel-stān**); Hack's Cl 1904, 1908; Nether Hall Cl 1943, Hall Fd 1830, 1847, 1908, 1955, Bottom -, Top Hall Fd 1908, Middle Hall Fd c1840, 1842, 1845, Ne(i)ther Hall Fd 1830, c1840, 1842, 1845, 1847, Upper - c1840, 1842, 1845 (*The Hall New Feilds* 1707, *Lower Hall Field* 1758, 1785, *Neither Hall Field* 1776, *Upper Hall Field* 1758, 1776, 1785), First -, Second Hall Platt 1830, 1847 (1776, *v.* **plat**^{2}) (all with reference to Stocken Hall *supra*); Hallidays Home 1830, 1847 (*Hallidays Holme* 1776; John *Halliday* was resident in Stretton 1776, *v.* **holmr**); Hare Park 1830, 1842, 1845, 1847, 1908 ((*The*) *Hare Park* 1702, 1758, *Hare Parks* 1707, 1776, 1785), Hare Park Plantation c1840, 1845, 1904 (a patch of land frequented by hares, *v.* **hara**, **park**); East -, West Heath Cl 1830, 1847 (1776, *Heath Close* 1776); North Heathdale 1842, 1845, South - 1842, 1845, 1943 (*v.* **deill**); Heath Furlong 1830, 1847 (*The Heath Furlong* c1720, 1776); High Cl c1840, 1842, 1845, 1943; High Fd 1904, 1908; High Mdw 1830, 1842, 1845, 1847, 1904, 1908 ((*The*) *High Meadow* 1702, c1720, 1723, 1724, 1732, 1758, 1776, 1785), North -, South High Mdw c1840, 1842, 1845, High Meadow Cl 1830, c1840, 1847 (*Highmeadow Close* 1702, c1720, 1776, *High Meadow Close Hedge* c1720); Hoar Fd 1979 VR, (perh. with **hār**^{2} in its sense 'a boundary'); Holdykes Furlong 1830, 1847 (*Holdikes* 1695, *Holdykes now called Wards Plat* 1702 (cf. William *Ward* of Stretton 1758), *Holdikes* -, *Holdykes Furlong* c1720, 1776, *Holdikes Peice* c1720, *v.* **hol**^{2}, **dīk**, **pece**); Holliwell Hill Furlong 1830, 1847 (c1720, 1776, the hill looking over to Holywell L to the east); Holm Fd 1842, Home - 1830, 1847 (*the Holm* 13, *The Holme*(*s*) 1702, 1758, *The Holme Feild* c1720, - *Field* 1776, *Home New Feild* 1702, 1707, *Holme New Field* 1758, 1785, originally one of the great open-fields of the village, *v.* **holmr**); Home Cl 1842, 1847, 1908 (*v.* **home**); Horn Lane 1846 (a local name for Ermine Street, otherwise the Great North Road, cf. Horn Lane Spinney in Horn); Horse Mdw or Cleeve (*v.* **clif**); Horse Pasture; House Cl c1840, 1842, 1845, 1908; Hovel Cl 1904, 1908, Hovel Fd 1908 (*v.* **hovel**); Keepers Cl 1904, Keeper's - 1908, (i.e. a gamekeeper's close); King's Cl 1904, 1908; Lady Wood Pastures (cf. Lady Wood *supra*); Little Cl c1840, 1842, 1845 (*The Little Close* 1678); Little Wood c1840, 1834; Long Cl c1840, 1842, 1845 (1707, 1749, 1758, 1785); Long Hedge Furlong 1830, 1847 (c1720, 1776, *v.* **hecg**); Merry's Fds, - Cl c1840; Middle Furlong 1830, 1847 (*Midle Furlong in Holme Feild* c1720, *Middle Furlong in ye West Feild* c1720, 1776); Money's Cl 1804, 1825, c1840, 1869, 1870, Near Money Cl c1840, 1842, 1845 (*Richard Moneyes Closes* 1678, *Money Close* 1723, 1724, 1732), Moneys Fd 1904, 1908, Moneys Plat(t) 1830, c1840, Money's - 1847, Moneys Plott 1845, Money's - 1842 (*Moneys Plat*(*t*) 1776, *Monys Platts* 1776, from the surn. of Widow *Money* 1723 and Richard *Money* 1732, landowners in the village, *v.* **plat**^{2}); Moor Cl c1840, 1842, 1845, Moore

Furlong 1830, 1847 (*The More* 1637, *The Moor* 1716, *Mo*(*o*)*re Furlong* 1646, c1720, 1776, *v.* **mōr**[1]); Nether Cl 1842, 1845, 1869, 1870, 1904, 1908; New Cl 1830, c1840, 1845, 1847 (1776); New Fd 1908, Neither -, Upper New Fd 1830, 1842, 1845, 1847 (1776), Top New Fd 1908; New Hills c1840, 1842, 1845, Bottom -, Top New Hill(s) 1904, 1908; New Wong c1840, 1908 (*The New Wong*(*e*) 1637, 1716, 1733, 1758, 1776, 1785, *New Wong Furlong* c1720, 1776, *v.* **vangr**); Newel Hills c1840, 1842 (*Neuell Hills* 1678, *Newell Hills* 1749, *Newill Hills* 1758, *Newelhiles Close* 1678, *Upper* -, *Neather Newell Hill Close* 1723, *v.* **nīwe, wella**); Old Heath 1904, 1908; Old Moor 1908, - Platt 1943 (*v.* **plat**[2]); Orton Gate Furlong 1830, 1847 (c1720, 1776, *Overtonegatforlong* 13; Mkt. Overton parish adjoins to the west, *v.* **gata, furlang**); (The) Paddock(s) 1904, 1908 (*The Paddock* 1723, c1740, 1758); Park Leys 1842, 1845, 1908, - Leas 1943 (*The Park Leaze* 1702, - *Lees*(*e*) 1707, 1776, - *Leas* c1720, - *Ley*(*e*)*s* 1758, 1785, *v.* **lēah**), Park Lees Furlong 1830, 1847 (*Park Leas Furlong* c1720), The Parks 1842, 1845 (1707, 1758, 1785), High Park 1908, Top of Park 1943 (*v.* **park**); The Pit 1845, Long Pit(t) Furlong 1830, 1847 (*Long Pi*(*t*) *Furlong*(*e*) 1646, c1720, 1776, *v.* **pytt**); The Platt or Fourteen Acre, Far -, Near Platt (*v.* **plat**[2]); The Plott 1904, 1908, Old Plott Fd 1845, Old Plotts 1845, Plott Fd 1904, 1908 (*The Plott* 1758, 1785, *The Plot*(*t*)*s* 1758, 1785, *v.* **plot**); Pond Cl 1904, 1908 (*Little Pond Close* 1678; there are two early fishponds at SK 956 178, *v.* MER 40); Pulpit Dale Furlong 1830, 1847 (*Pul*(*l*)*pitt Dale Furlong* c1720, c1743, *Pulpit* - 1776, prob. 'the pit with a pool', with either **dalr** or **deill**, *v.* **pull, pytt**); The Rectors Stackyard 1845 (*v.* **stak-ʒard**); Rectory Fd (*v.* The Rectory *supra*); Red Hills c1840, 1842, 1845, - Cl 1845 (*Great*(*e*) -, *Little Red*(*d*) *Hills* 1678, 1723, c1740, 1758, alluding to the colour of the soil on an outcropping of ironstone, *v.* **rēad**); Ridings Furlong 1830, 1842 (c1720, 1776, *v.* **ryding**); The Rookery c1840, 1842, 1845, 1908 ('land on which are trees with rooks' nests'); Scotia Cl 1904, 1908 (a transferred name from Nova Scotia; Mr J. Field notes that the field adjoins The Canada *supra*); Scrape Hills 1842, 1845, 1908 (1749, 1758, *Scrape Hills Close* 1723, 1732, *Scrape Hill Gate* c1720, from *scrape, sheep-scrape* 'a bare place on a steep hillside where turf has been scraped off by the feet of sheep'; the earliest citation in NED is for 1848, *v.* **scrape, gata**); Seed Grass Cl 1804 (*Seedgrass Close* 1723, c1740, 1749, 1758, *The Three Acre Close or Seed Grass Close* c1746, an area of sown grass, *v.* **sǣd**); Shop End Cl 1904, 1908 (*shop* here in its sense 'shed', *v.* **sc**(**e**)**oppa, ende**[1]); Small Plantation 1904; Smiths Cl 1904, Smith's - 1908; The Spinney; Square Plantation 1904, 1908; Stable Cl c1840, 1845; Stable Wood 1845, 1904; Stackyard c1840, - Cl 1904, 1908, - Fd 1904 (*v.* **stak-ʒard**, cf. The Rectors Stackyard *supra*), formerly Stanhope's Cl now Stanley's Cl 1804, 1825 (*Stanhopes Close* 1749, 1758, *v.* The Seven Leys *infra*), Stanleys Cl c1840, 1842, 1845, 1869, 1870 (1723, 1724, 1732); Stocken Cl 1804, 1825, c1840, 1842, 1845, 1908

ALSTOE HUNDRED

45

(*Stockin(g) Close* 1723, 1724, 1732, 1749, 1758, *North Stocking* 1704), Stocking Wood Cl c1800, 1806 (*Stockings Wood Close* 1723) (v. Stocken Hall *supra*); Stonepit Cl c1840, 1842, 1845, 1908 (*Stonepitt Close* 1678, 1723, *Stone Pit Close* c1740, 1758), Stone Pit Piece 1830, 1847 (1776, v. **pece**), Old Stone Pit 1904, 1908 (v. **stān-pytt**); Stone Quarry 1845; Street Furlong 1830, 1847 (c1720, c1743, 1776, alluding to the Roman road Ermine Street, v. **strǣt**); Stretton Wood Fd; Sturgess Cl 1904, Sturgess' Fd (from the surn. *Sturgess*); Swallow Hole Cl 1904, 1908 (v. **swalg, hol**[1]); Taylor's Fd 1842, 1845, 1904, 1908 (*Taylors Field* 1758, 1785); Temple Barns 1842, 1845, - Barn 1904, 1908, Hovel Temple Barn 1904, 1908 (v. **hovel**), Top Temple Barn 1904, 1908 (*Temple Barn(e)s* 1578 (1684) Wright, 1707, 1758, 1785, *Temple Field* 1758, - *Fields* 1578 (1684) Wright, *Temple Field Close* 1758, 1785), Temple Hedge Furlong 1830, 1847 (c1720, 1726, v. **hecg**), a preceptory of the Knights Templars was excavated in adjoining South Witham L in 1966-7, cf. *Temple Peyse* in neighbouring Greetham f.ns. (b), v. **temple**); Ten Acre Mdw; Thistleton Fds (Thistleton parish adjoins to the west); Todds Cl c1840, 1845, 1865, 1908; Torkington's Corner c1840, 1845 (James *Torkington* was resident in Stretton in 1845, v. **corner**); Triangle Cl c1840, 1842, 1845 (*Mills's Triangle Close* 1723, 1724, 1732, cf. Nicholas *Mills* of Stretton 1678); Turners Fd 1904, 1908 (cf. Turner's Barn Fd in neighbouring Mkt. Overton f.ns. (a); Thomas *Turner* held land in Stretton in 1678); Upper Cl 1842, 1845, 1869, 1870, 1943; Vicar Cl 1830, 1847 (*Vicars Close* c1720, - *Closes* 1785, *Vicar Close* 1776, - *Closes* 1707, 1758, v. **vikere**); Bottom -, Top Wade's Cl 1904, 1908 (William *Wade* held land in the parish in 1758); Wall Cl or Long Cl 1904, 1908, 1943; Ward's Cl 1804, Wards - 1825, 1830, c1840, 1842, 1845, 1870 (*John Ward(e)s Close* 1678, *Wards Close* 1746, c1746), Wards Homestead 1830, 1847 (1776, cf. William *Ward* 1758); The Warren c1840, 1842, 1845, 1904, 1908 (1707, *The Two Warrens* 1758, 1785, v. **wareine**); Water Hill 1830, 1847; Well Fd c1840; Wells Cl 1842 (cf. Robert *Wells*, husbandman of Stretton, 1522 MilS); West Cl c1840, 1842, 1845 (1758); West Fd 1830, 1845, 1847 (*The Great West Field* 1702, *The Great Plough'd Westfeild* 1707, *West Field* c1720, 1758, 1776, 1785, originally one of the open-fields of the village, v. **west, feld**); Little West Fd also the Clay Fd 1830, 1847 (*Little West Feild alias the Clay Feilds* c1720, - *Field* 1776); New Wong 1830, 1842, 1845, 1847, 1904, 1908, - Furlong 1830, 1847, West Wong c1840, 1842, 1845, 1904, 1908, The Wongs 1943 (v. **vangr**); Winkleys Cl c1840 (*the Close of Edward Inckleys, - Inkleys* 1678, *Winckleys Close* 1723, c1740, *Winckley Close* 1758; the surn. presumably derived originally from Hinckley Lei); Witham Cl 1904, 1908 (North - and South Witham lie beyond the county boundary in L); Wood Cl c1840, 1842, 1845, 1908, Nether - c1840, 1845, North -, South - 1830, 1847 (*Maxeys Wood Close* 1723, cf. William *Maxy* of Stretton 1678); Wood Fd 1830, 1908, Great East Fd also Wood Fd 1830, 1847

(*Easthawfeild now called the Woodfeild* 1702, *Woodfeild* 1707, *Great East Feild alias the Woodfeild* c1720, 1776, *Wood Field* 1758, 1785, one of the open-fields of the village, *v.* čast, haga[1], wudu, feld); *Upper Wyles Cl* c1840, 1842, 1845, 1908, *Nether -* 1842, 1845, 1908 (cf. Thomas *Wyles* of Stretton 1758); *Yard Plott* c1840, 1845 (*v.* plot).

(b) *Acre Close* 1758; *Acre Land Leas* c1720 (*v.* land, lčah); *Thomas Andrewes Close* 1678; *Henry As(h)wells Closes* 1678, *Aswells Plot* 1758, *As(h)well(s) Plott(s)* 1758, 1785 (cf. Henry *Ashwell* of Stretton 1637, 1678, *v.* plot); *Bernard Bacons Closes* 1678, *Bacons Close* 1723; *Christopher Beltons Closes* 1678; *Byteleyes* 1627 (*v.* bita, lčah); *Bytenooke* 1627, *Bitenooke* 1749, *Bite Nook* 1758, 1785, *Boyalls Bite Nooke* 1723, *Boyalls North Bite Nooke, - South -* 1723, *Boyalls North Bite Nooke Closes* 1723 (from the surn. *Boyall,* cf. John *Boyeall* 1524 SR of Ketton), *Long Bite Nooke, - Close* 1723, *Maxseys Bite Nooke* 1723 (cf. William *Maxy* of Stretton 1678), *North Bite Nooke* 1723, *Sivers his Bite Nook* 1702, *Sivers's Bite Nooke Close* 1724 (Stephen *Sivers* held land in the parish in 1724), *Skillingtons Bite Nooke* 1702, 1723, *Skillingtons Bite Nook(e) Close* 1723, 1724, 1732 (cf. John- and Robert *Skillyngton* 1522 MilS, - *Skelyngton* 1524 SR of Stretton, William *Skillington* 1678), *South Bite Nooke* 1723 (*v.* bita, nōk); *Blackholme* c1720, c1743 (in eModE *black* 'fertile' is contrasted with *white* 'infertile' but the colour of the soil may perh. be referred to here, *v.* holmr); *John Blayes Closes* 1678; *Browns Close* c1740, *Widow Brown(e)s Close* 1723, 1724, 1732, *Widdo(w) Brownes Meadow* 1723, 1724, 1732 (perh. the daughter-in-law of Samuel *Browne,* landowner in Stretton in 1676); *Brushfield(s) -, Brush Field Close* 1785 (*v.* brusshe); *Richmonds Bush Close* 1723, 1724 (cf. Robert *Richmond* of Stretton 1678); *Scotneys Butcher(s) Close* 1723 (with the local surn. *Butcher* (cf. f.ns. with this surn. in Ashwell, Burley, Cottesmore and Greetham) and cf. John *Scotney* of Stretton 1678); *Capun More* 1331 (prob. from the ME surn. *Capon, Capoun,* cf. *Capon Acres* in Greetham f.ns. (b), *v.* mōr[1]); *Calves Close* 1758, 1785 (*v.* calf); *Cawshaws Close* 1758, 1785; *Cheesecake Close* 1758, 1785 (dial. *cheesecake* is used of the fruit of such wild plants as the common mallow (*Malva sylvestris*) and the bird's foot trefoil (*Lotus corniculatus*)); *Clems Close(s)* 1749, 1758 (perh. from an abbreviated form of the forename of *Clement* Blunfield of Stretton 1758); *Mills's Clerk Close* 1723, *Mill(e)s Clerk(e) Close* 1724, 1732 (with the local surn. *Clark(e)* (cf. f.ns. with this surn. in Ashwell, Burley and Cottesmore) and cf. Nicholas *Mills* of Stretton 1678); *Clipsham Dale* c1720, 1776 (*v.* dalr), *Clipsham Hedge* c1720 (*v.* hecg) (Clipsham parish adjoins to the east); *Common Wood* 1749, 1758, *Brown's -* 1736 (cf. Elizabeth *Brown* of Stretton 1713, Widow *Brown* 1724), *Fishpond -* 1749, 1758, *Mills's -* 1736, 1758 (cf. Nicholas *Mills* 1678 and John *Mills* 1724 both of Stretton), *Upper -* 1749, 1758, *Common Wood Cowpasture* 1678, *Common Wood Furlong* c1720, 1776, *Common Wood Hedge* c1720, *Common Wood Pasture* 1627 ('the wood held by the community', *v.* **commun, wudu**); *Cumbry and Boyalls Closes* 1723, *Cunbrys and Boyals Close* 1723 (cf. *Robert Cumbreys Hadeland* 1739 in Greetham f.ns. (b) and John *Boyeall* 1525 SR of Ketton); *Draycot House* 1758; *Dry Close* 1758 (*v.* **drȳge**); *Eight and Twenty Acres* 1695, 1704, 1750; *le Esthawe* 1326 Ipm, 1331 *BHS*, 1368 Ipm (*v.* **ēast, haga**[1] and *Wood* Fd *supra*); *Stephen Estwicks Closes* 1678; *Fifteen Acres* 1750, *The Fifteen Acres Close* 1750, 1776; *Gore Peice* c1720 (*v.* **gāra, pece**); *Greetham Meere* c1720 (Greetham parish adjoins to the west, *v.* **(ge)mǣre** 'a boundary'); *Hanging Peice* c1720 ('a piece of land on a steep slope', *v.* **hangende, pece**); *Hellewelgate* 1331 ('the road to Holywell L', *v.* **gata**); *Herbertmer* 13 (from the OFr pers.n. *Herbert* (DB records that Stretton was held by Countess Judith who was the feudal mistress of one *Herbert* who held land from her in Whitwell), *v.* **(ge)mǣre**); *Heynwyk'* 1331 ('farm on a high spot', *v.* **hēah**[1] (**hēan** wk.obl.), **wīc**); *Hillside Close* 1678; *Philip Hinmans Close* 1678; *Holgate* 1331 (*v.* **hol**[2], **gata**); *Home Meadows* 1678 (*v.* **home**); *del Hulle* 1341 NI (p) (*v.* **hyll**); *Hursts Close, Hursts East* -, - *Middle Close* 1723; *Jordens Corner* c1720 (from the surn. *Jordan*, cf. John *Jordan* 1522 MilS, - *Jurden* 1524 SR of Oakham, Hew- and John *Jorden* 1524 ib of Barleythorpe, *v.* **corner**); *Land Close* 1707, 1758, 1785, *Lower* - 1758, 1785 (enclosures which consolidated selions of an open-field, *v.* **land**); *Lyttilhawe* 13 (*v.* **lȳtel, haga**[1]); *Little Meadow* 1723; *William Maxyes Closes* 1678; *The Meadow* 1723, 1740; *Meadow Close* 1749, 1758; (*The*) *Meer Close, two closes called The Meer* 1758, 1785 (*v.* **(ge)mǣre**); *Nicholas Mills Close* 1678, *Mill(e)s Long Close* 1723, 1732, *Mills's* - 1724, *Mills's Meadow* 1723, 1724, *Millesmeadow* 1732 (cf. Nicholas *Mills* of Stretton 1678); *le Milnetymbermede* 1326 Ipm (*v.* **myln, timber, mǣd**); *Widow Moneys Meadow* 1723, 1724, 1732; *Thomas Naylors Close* c1720; *Nether Furlong* c1720; *Shermans Nooke* 1723, - *Nook(e) Close* 1723, 1724, 1732 (Thomas *Sherman* was resident in the village in 1678, *v.* **nōk**); *The North Feilde* 1637; *North Meadow* 1723, 1732; *Northwode* 13 (*v.* **norð, wudu**); *Orton Meere* c1720 (Mkt. Overton parish lies to the west, but its boundary no longer adjoins that of Stretton, *v.* **(ge)mǣre**); *The Park(e) Feild* 1637, 1733 (*v.* **park**); *Pauls Closes* 1707, - *Close* 1758, 1785 (from the surn. *Paul*, cf. *Paul's* Fd in Stoke Dry f.ns. (a)); *Peartree Close* 1758; *The Three Plowed Closes* 1678, - *Ploughed* - 1702; *Pipers Pit Close* 1758, 1785 (cf. *Piper Pytt Furlong* in Greetham f.ns. (b)); *Pump Close* 1723, c1740, 1758, 1785 (a close with a water-pump, *v.* **pumpe**); *Ratcliff(e)s Close* 1723, 1724, 1732, 1758 (from the surn. *Ratcliffe*); *Thomas Reddishes Close* 1678; *Robert Richmondes Close* 1678; *John Rubbins Close* 1678, *Rubbins('s) Long Close* 1723, 1724, 1732, *Rubbins('s) Meadow* 1723, 1724, 1732; *John Scotneys Closes* 1678; *The Seven Leys or Severall Leys* 1713, c1713, *The Seven Leas or Severall Leas but now called Stanhopes Close* 1746, *The Seven Leas now called Stanhopes Close* c1746 (*v.* **severall, lēah**); *Sewerby(e')s Headland* c1720 (from the surn. *Sewerby*, *v.* **hēafod-land**); *The Sheepe*

Walke 1646 (unfenced sheep pasture, *v.* **sheep-walk**); *Thomas Shermans Closes* 1678, *Shermans Close* 1723, 1732, *Sharemans* - 1724, *Sharmans* - 1749, 1758, 1785, *Shermans Middle Close* 1723, 1732, *Sharemans* - 1724; *William Skillingtons Close* 1678, *Henry Skillingtons Close* c1720; *Side Hills* 1723, 1733, c1740, 1758, *Side Hill Close* 1702 (from either **sīd** or **sīde**); *Smith Fields* 1758; *Stone Hill Furlong* c1720 (an allusion to the nature of the ground); *Stone Pitt Hill* c1720 (*v.* **stān-pytt**); *Humphrey Storers Close, Robert Storers Close* 1678; *Thistleton Heath, Thistleton Meer* c1720 (Thistleton parish adjoins to the north-west, *v.* **hǣð, (ge)mǣre**); *Thomas Turners Close* 1678; *Vicker* -, *Vickar Lane* c1720, c1743, *Vicar Lane Close* 1758 (*v.* **vikere**); *Wadkins Close* 1749, *Watkīns* - 1758, 1785 (from the surn. *Watkins*); *Holdykes now called Wards Plot* 1702, *Wards Platt* 1707, 1780, *Ward Plotts* 1758, *Wards Plot* 1785 (from the family name of John *Ward* 1678 and William *Ward* 1758, *v.* Holdykes Furlong *supra* and **plat²**); *Waterfall Dale* c1720 (*v.* **dalr**), *Waterfall Hill* c1720, c1743, 1776 (*v.* **wæter-gefall**); *Westhawewong* 13 (*v.* **west, haga¹, vangr**); *The Woods* 1678; *Easthawfeild now called the Woodfeild* 1702, *Woodfeild* 1707, *Wood Field* 1758, 1785, *Woodfield Close* 1702, 1758 (*v.* *Easthawfeild supra*).

Teigh

TEIGH [ti:]
  Tie 1086 DB
  Ti 1202 Ass (p), *Ty* e13 (1449) *WoCart*, 1254 *Val et passim* to
    1295 *Deed*, 1303 (1449) *WoCart et freq* to 1349 AD *et passim*
    to 1513 CoPleas, (- *Foluile*) 1449 *WoCart*, *Tye* 1282 OSut,
    c1291 Tax *et passim* to 1449 *WoCart*
  Thy 1201 Ass (p), 1263 Pat *et passim* to 1327 *SR*, 1341 NI
  Tygh(*e*) 1434 Pat, 1436 Fine *et passim* to 1538 *Finch*, 1539
    Recov, 1610 Speed, (- *Folvyle*) 1468 Cl
  Teigh(*e*) 1605 *Recov*, 1629 LML

'The small enclosure', *v.* **tēag**. The manor belonged to the fee of *de Folville* in the fifteenth century (cf. Ashby Folville Lei). The early field-name *Burstall' medewe* 113 (1449) *WoCart* is recorded for the parish, from **burh-stall** 'the site of a fortification', cf. *Burghsyk'* in neighbouring Barrow f.ns. (b). The 'enclosure' may have once related to this lost fortified site.

RUTMORE (lost), *Rotemor* 113 (1449) *WoCart, Rotemore* 1377 Ipm, 1377 Fine, *Rutmor* 1363 *MinAcct, Rutmore* 1449 *WoCart,* 'Rōta's moor', *v.* **mōr**[1]. No doubt this marshland takes its name from the Anglo-Saxon *Rōta* who gave his name to the whole territory of Rutland. The 1363 form occurs in the f.ns. of neighbouring Market Overton to the east and that of 1377 Ipm in those of Whissendine immediately to the west. That *Rutmore* lies along this northern boundary of Rutland suggests recognition of the unity of Rōta's holding by peoples beyond the frontier.

CATMOS LODGE, a late creation, *v.* Vale of Catmos. THE RECTORY, 1846, 1863 White. TEIGH CHURCH, *Church (Holy Trinity)* 1846, 1863 ib. TEIGH COTTAGES, cf. *The Cottage* 1846, 1863 ib. TEIGH GATE HO. is *Lodge* 1824 O. It is sited at the crossing of the Melton Mowbray - Oakham railway line and the Whissendine - Teigh road, but perhaps more importantly, also at the point where the parish boundary is crossed by this road. The name may have alluded earlier to a gate in the parish boundary fence rather than to a later railway-crossing gate. TEIGH HILL (local). TEIGH LODGE. YEW TREE FM, formerly Ivy House Farm - VR.

Field-Names

Undated forms in (a) are 1844 *TA.* Those dated 1823 are *Terrier;* 1897 are *Deed* and 1943 *Map.* Early forms dated 1612, 1702, 1721, 1723, 1730, 1733, 1736, 1739 and 1744 are *Terrier;* 1661 are *Deed.* All forms from *Terrier* were extracted by Mr G.A. Chinnery.

(a) Acre Riggs 1844, - Rigs 1943 ('ridged arable land', alluding perh. to remains of ancient ridge and furrow cultivation; *acre* here means 'an individual plot of arable land', *v.* **æcer, hryggr**); Four Acre 1943 (*Four acres* 1702), Ten Acre, - Cl 1943, Eleven -, Twenty Acre 1943 (*v.* Big House Park *infra*), Twenty-one Acre 1943 (*v.* House Cl, Lane Cl *infra*), Twenty-four Acre 1943 (*v.* Stackyard Cl *infra*); Ash Fd 1943; Old -, Ashams (*Asholme* 1661, - *Close* 1661, 'a water-meadow with ash tree(s)', *v.* **æsc, holmr**); Backer's Cl 1943; Baileys Mdw, - Moor (*v.* **mōr**[1]); Barn Cl, Near Barn, Barn Fd, Marley's - 1943; Barrow Leies 1823, Nether -, Upper Barrow Leys (*Barrow Leighs* 1702, 1721, 1723, 1730, 1733, 1736, - *Leies* 1739, - *Lees* 1744; Barrow parish adjoins to the south-east, *v.* **lēah**);

Bennett's Fd 1943; Birchnells Cl, Birchnells Mdw or Land Mdw (v. **land**); Boswick Cl (v. **bōs, wīc**); Boyfields Cl, - Mdw (cf. Boy Fd in neighbouring Ashwell f.ns. (a)); Bridge Cl, - Nook (v. **nōk**); Brinckleys Cl, Upper Brinckley Mdw (from the surn. *Brinkley*, cf. *Brinkleys Cottage* in Burley f.ns. (b)); Bull Nook (v. **bula, nōk**, cf. Bull's Nook in Barrow f.ns. (a) and *Bulls Nook* in Lyddington f.ns. (b)); Bumble Bee 1943 (Mr J. Field notes that perh. this indicates land on which there was an abundance of bees); Burdens Home Cl; Burshalls Home Cl 1844, Burshal Cl 1943 (*Burschals Close* 1744; this may perh. be identified with *Burstall' medewe infra*); Canal Hole 1844, Channel Hole 1943, Channel Mdw 1844 (*Charnellhoale* 1612 'a hollow used as a burial place for the dead', v. **charnel, hol**[1]; if these belong together, then a name approximated later by popular etymology to allude to the Melton Mowbray - Oakham canal); Cat Cl or Pump Cl (a close with a water pump, v. **pumpe, cat(t)**); Church Yard; Clay Piece (v. **pece**); Cottage Pasture; Cottagers Cl (v. **cotager**); Cow Cl (1702, 1721, 1723, 1730, 1733, 1736, 1739, 1744); Cox's Cl, - Mdw; Dovecote Cl; Down Croft (v. **dūne, croft**); Drove Cl or Stackyard (v. **drāf, stak-ȝard**); Dry Cl (v. **drȳge**); North -, South Eatons Cl; Edmondthorpe or Hunt Cl 1943 (adjoins Edmondthorpe Lei, beyond the county boundary); Elsons Moor (from a local surn., cf. Elson's Cl in Stretton f.ns. (a), v. **mōr**[1]); Fishpond Cl (the tithe map shows a string of fishponds running from SK 8610 1580 to SK 8587 1556; these no longer survive, but there is now a rectangular fishpond formed by a dam at SK 8600 1563, v. BrownArchSites 24); Flax Hole Mdw (may refer to *gig-holes* or pools in which flax was retted, v. **fleax, hol**[1]); Fowlers Cl; Gascoignes Cl (from the surn. *Gascoigne*, cf. *Gascoignes* in Mkt. Overton f.ns. (b)); Goodman's or Pick's Cl 1932; Gorse Cl (v. **gorst**); Great Cl, Ashams - 1943 (v. Ashams *supra*); Great Ground (v. **grund**); Hall Cl; Hames Moor (v. **mōr**[1] and cf. Great Hames in Tixover f.ns. (a)); Haremouth Cl (*haremouth* 1612, poss. referring to an opening into woodland, the opening frequented by hares; alternatively, the reference may be to the particular split shape of an enclosure (*hare-lip* is recorded from 1567 NED), v. **hara, mūða**); Herrings Mdw (from the surn. *Herring*, cf. Richard *Heryng* 1522 MilS, 1524 SR of Ashwell and Thomas *Heryng* 1522 MilS of Cottesmore); Highway Cl; Home Cl, - Fd, - Plot, South Home Plot, Home Park 1943 (v. **home**); Horse Park, Nether -; House Platt 1844 (is House Cl or Twenty-one Acre 1943) (v. **plat**[2]); Big House Park or Twenty Acres 1943; Hunts Cl (cf. Edmondthorpe Cl *supra*); Lane Cl or Twenty-one Acre 1943; Lane Fd, - Mdw 1943; Little Cl; Long Mdw 1844, 1897, Second - 1943; Masons Yard Pasture (from the surn. *Mason*, cf. *Masons Close* in Burley f.ns. (b)); The Meadow; Merry Acres (*mery acres* 1612, *Merryacres* 1744, adjoins the county boundary so that *(ge)mǣre* 'a boundary, a border' is poss., although the forms rather suggest *myrge* 'pleasant, sweet, agreeable'); Middle Plot or Barn

Cl; Middlings (*Great Midlongs* 1702, *Gossy* - 1702 (*v.* gorstig), *Two midlongs*
1721, 1723, 1730, 1733, *v.* middel, eng); Mill Cl or Hayes Cl (*Mill Close* 1661),
Mill Cl South, Mill Holme (*v.* myln, holmr); Nether -, Top -, Upper Moor 1844
(*Upper Moor Close* 1661), Big -, Little Moor 1943 (*v.* mōr¹); Morris Acre or the
Meadow (if not with a surn., then once used for morris dancing); Nether Cl, -
Mdw; (Plovers) New Fd (*New Feild* 1661, - *field* 1774, *v.* plover); Nether
Overton Cl (Mkt. Overton parish adjoins to the east); Palmers Moors 1943 (cf.
Nicolis *Palmer* 1522 MilS of Langham and Henry *Palmer* 1524 SR of Barrow, *v.*
mōr¹); Pingel or Paddock (*v.* pingel); Plantation Fd or Planting Cl; Pond Cl;
Great Queens Cl 1823, Lower -, Upper Queen's Cl 1943 (*the Queens close* 1744;
Mr J. Field notes that 'if the queen ... was Anne, who had died only in 1714,
this field may be, like Queen Anne's Bounty (Hailey O) and Queen Ann's
Bounty Fd (Willaston Ch), connected in some way with that fund.' (The name
applied to a perpetual fund of first-fruits and tenths granted by a charter of
Queen Anne for the augmentation of the livings of the poorer Anglican
clergy.)); Ram Fd 1943 (*v.* ramm); Road Plat (*v.* plat²); Roberts Plat, Roberts
Moor (from the surn. *Roberts*, *v.* plat², mōr¹); East -, West Rush Barrow
(recording a prehistoric tumulus; Crop Marks 60 identifies two probable barrows
in Teigh, *v.* risc, beorg); Seed Moor 1844, - Fd 1943 (alluding to an area of
sown grass, *v.* sǽd, mōr¹); South Mdw; Spring Mdw, Spring Piece, Spring Wells
(*v.* spring, pece, wella); Stackyard Cl or Twenty-four Acre 1943 (*v.* stak-ʒard);
Staffords Cl (from the surn. *Stafford*, cf. *Staffords Quicke* in neighbouring
Whissendine f.ns. (b)); Templeman Mdw (the surn. *Templeman* originally denoted
'a servant of the Templars'; the Knights Templars held land in nearby Greetham
and Stretton); Thompsons Market Overton Cl 1943 (Mkt. Overton parish adjoins
to the east); Three Corner Fd 1943; Well Cl or Brinkleys Cl (with the surn.
Brinkley); Well Plat (*v.* wella, plat²); Wheel House Cl 1897 (a *wheelhouse* was a
building containing a horsewheel as motive power for threshing machines etc., cf.
Wheel House Closes in adjoining Ashwell f.ns. (a)); Wright's Cl.

(b) *Burstall' medewe* 113 (1449) WoCart ('meadow with or near to the site of
a fortification', *v.* burh-stall, mǽd and Burshalls *supra*); *cunningree feelde,*
cunningree hill, cunningree nooke 1612 (*v.* coninger, nōk, cf. *The northfeelde infra*);
fleetefurlong 1612 (*v.* flēot, cf. *Sowyt Flet* and *Tyflet infra*); *Hellwell medowe* 1612
('the healing spring' or 'the wishing well', cf. *Helwell'* in Oakham f.ns. (b) and
Holywell L, *v.* hǽl, hǽlu, wella); *Hill Close, Litle meadow* 1721, 1723, *Little* -
1730, 1733, 1736, 1739, 1744; *Long Close* 1702, 1721, 1723, 1730, 1733, 1739;
Midlebrinkes Meadow 1661 (*v.* middel, brink); *Middle close* 1744; *The Midlefeeld*
1612 (one of the open-fields of the village, *v.* middel, feld); *Midleyes* 1739 (*v.*
midd, lēah); *The northfeelde called cuningree feelde* 1612 (one of the open-fields

of the village, v. norð, feld and *cunningree feelde supra*); *Seavenacres* 1661 (v. seofon, æcer); *Southfeld* 1612 (one of the open-fields of the village, v. sūð, feld); *Southleche* 1303 (1449) *WoCart* (v. sūð, læc(c)); *Sowyt Flet* 14 (1449) *ib* (v. sūðeweard, flēot); *sparrowmore* 1612 (v. spearwa, mōr[1]); *sydehome* 1612 (v. sīd, side, holmr); *thackham medowe* 1612 (the first el. OE þæc 'thatch, materials for thatching' has prob. been influenced by ON þak of the same meaning, v. þæc, hamm); *Tyflet* 14 (1449) (perh. 'the enclosure stream', v. tēag, flēot, but at the date of the name's coining, the first el. may have already become the p.n. Teigh, hence 'Teigh stream'); *the waterforowes* 1612 (perh. of land where water tended to lie in the furrows, otherwise *water* used with the sense 'wet', v. wæter, furh).

Thistleton

THISTLETON
  Tisteltune 1086 DB, *Tystelton'* 1286 QW
  Thy-, Thisteltun 1212 Fees, 1241 Cl, *-ton(e)* 1226 RHug, 1249
    RGros *et passim* to 1300 Ipm *et freq* to 1535 VE, 1610
    Speed
  Thy-, Thistilton' 1262 *FF*, 1265 Misc *et passim* to 1340 Pat (p)
  Thustelton 1286 *Ass*
  This(s)leton 1535 VE, 1670 *FF*
  Thistleton 1610 Speed

'The farm where thistles abound', v. þistel, tūn. For the archaeologist, thistles are associated with deserted habitation sites because high phosphate content in the soil encourages their growth. There is a large Romano-British settlement site a half mile south-west of the parish church and thistles growing there may well have given the later settlement site its name.

BOTTOM FM. CHURCH LANE. CLAYPITHILL BARN, *Clapehill* 1633 *Bru*, *Clape Hill* c1635 *Map*, *Claypit Hill* 1826 G, *Clay Pit Hill* 1942 *Deed*. The two early forms are presumably corrupt, v. cley-pytt. FOSSE LANE, 1906 Map, also known as Sewstern Lane; a Roman road and therefore Fosse Lane by analogy with Fosse Way, v. foss[1]. GRANGE FM, v. grange. HOOBY FM, in Thistleton village and thus indicating either a late creation echoing

Hooby Lodge in Stretton or a family name. MIDDLE FM.
PEARTREE LANE, 1942 *Deed,* cf. *Peartree Close* 1943 *Map.*
ROMAN WELL, cf. *Well Close* 1942 *Deed,* l943 *Map.*
THISTLETON CHURCH, *Church* (*St Nicholas*) 1846, 1863 White.
THISTLETON GAP, 1831 Curtis, 1942 *Deed, v.* **gappe.** TOP
HOUSE FM.

Field-Names

Undated forms in (a) are 1943 *Map;* those dated 1899 and 1904 are *Anc,* 1942
are *Deed.* Early forms dated 1519, 1607, 1609 and 1633 are *Bru;* 1634 are
Terrier (forms extracted by Mr G.A. Chinnery), c1635 are *Map* while 1717 are
Asw.

(a) Four Acres (*The Four Acres* 1717), (Top) Five -, Six -, Seven Acres,
Eight Acre, Nine Acres 1942 (x2), Nine Acre (Cl) 1943, Ten Acres 1942, - Acre
1943, (Top) Eleven Acre, (Far) Twelve -, Thirteen -, Fourteen Acres, (The)
Eighteen Acres 1942, Eighteen Acre 1943, Top Twenty Acres 1942, - Acre 1943
(*v.* **æcer**); Back Paddock 1942; Barn Cl 1942, 1943; Black Holme 1942, - Holm
1943 (the field containing the Romano-British settlement site; in eModE, *black*
'fertile' is contrasted with *white* 'infertile' and prob. the fertility of the site stems
from ancient settlement deposits; also, no doubt, the soil colour is specified, *v.*
blæc, holmr); Blue Gate Cl 1942, 1943; Bridle Road Cl; Brown's Cl (cf. Samuel
Browne 1676 *Anc* and Elizabeth *Brown* 1713 *BHS* of neighbouring Stretton); Corn
Cl; Corner Cl; Cow Cl; Cross Lane Fd (cf. *the New Cross* 1634, *v.* **cros**); Dickies
Fd (prob. with the surn. *Dickie*); Dry Fd (*v.* **drȳge**); Drywell Head 1942 (*v.*
welle-heved, cf. Roman Well *supra*); Farmhouse 1942; Forster's Cl 1942; Glebe
Fd (*v.* **glebe**); Goodacres (a surn.); Gordon's Fm 1942; Green Cl (*ye Greene,*
Green end peece 1633, *v.* **grēne**[2], **ende**[1], **pece**); East Paddock 1942; Halliday's Cl
1942 (cf. John *Halliday* 1776 *BHS* of Stretton); Hallidor's Top Cl (sic) 1943;
Home Cl (*v.* **home**); Horse Cl; Hovel Cl 1942 (*v.* **hovel**); Lamas Pen 1942,
Lammas - 1943 (*v.* **lammas, penn**[2]); Lank's Lane Cl; Limekiln Cl 1942, 1943;
Long Cl; Long Mdw 1942, 1943; Marriott's Cl 1942 (cf. Marriotts in Mkt.
Overton f.ns. (a) and John *Mariet* 1522 MilS of Lyddington); Middle Cl; Middle
Hooby (*Hooby*(*e*), *Hoobie, ye devid*(*e*)*able Hooby*(*e*), *ye dividable Hooby, Hooby*
Close 1633, *v.* Hooby Lodge in Stretton); Mill Dale (*The Mill Dale* 1633, *v.* **myln,**
dalr); Bottom -, Top Mitcheson; Bottom -, Top Moor Head 1942, 1943 (*Moor*
heads 1633, *v.* **mōr**[1], **hēafod**); Top Morkery Wood Cl 1899, - Morcary - 1904
(West Morkery Wood lies to the east, beyond the county boundary in Castle

Bytham L, *v.* Morkery Leys in Stretton); (Far) Old Ground (*v.* **grund**); Old Piece (*v.* **pece**); Orchard 1942; Ormonds (the surn. *Ormand,* cf. Joseph *Ormand* 1871 WR of Whissendine); Parker's Well Head 1942, 1943 (*the wellhead* 1634, *v.* **welle-heved,** cf. Roman Well *supra*); Pettifer's Far Mdw, - Near Mdw 1942; Pond or Barn Cl; Redcap Hill (poss. referring to a stratum of ironstone at the hill's top); North Road Cl 1942, (Top) Road Cl 1943; Scotland Voyage 1942, 1943 (on the edge of the parish, the name alluding to its remoteness); (Far) Sheep Dyke (referring to a sheep-dip, *v.* **scēap, dīk**); Sissons Cl (cf. Big -, Middle -, Top Sisson in nearby Clipsham f.ns. (a), Sissons in Langham f.ns. (a)); Smith's Home Cl (*v.* **home**); Snarlings (*Snare-lands* 1633, 'ground covered by brushwood', *v.* **snār, land,** cf. *Snarlings* in neighbouring Mkt. Overton f.ns. (b)); Sneath's Fd (cf. Robert *Sneth* 1522 MilS, 1525 SR of nearby Cottesmore); Spinney Cl 1942; Stackyard, - Fd 1943 (*v.* **stak-ȝard**); Stokes' Cl 1942, 1943; Stone Pit (Cl) 1942, Stonepit Cl 1943 (cf. *Stonpitt Furlong* 1633, *v.* **stān-pytt**); Swallow Pit Cl 1942, Swallowpit (Cl) 1943 (*v.* **swalg, pytt,** cf. Swallow Hole Cl in Stretton f.ns. (a)); Three Corner Cl (referring to a triangular shape); Tomlins Mdws; Top Paddock; Town End Cl (*v.* **tūn, ende**[1]); Vote Land 1899, 1904 (referring to land whose seasonal use depended on the agreement of a group of interested parties, *v.* **wote**); Wades Hill (William *Wade* held land in neighbouring Stretton in 1758 *Surv,* cf., however, Wade's Hill in Ayston f.ns. (a)); Walker's Cl; Water Cl 1942; White's Fd; Wood Leys 1942, 1943 (*Woodleyes* 1576 *ExchDep, Wood Leas* 1607, 1633, *Woode Leyes* 1609, 1633, c1635, *v.* **wudu, lēah**).

(b) *Beck Leas* 1633, *the Beck furlong* 1634 (*v.* **bekkr, lēah**); *Bole howe* 1519 ('hill with a place on top where (?iron) ore was smelted', *v.* **bole, haugr**); *Brend Dike* 1633 (*v.* **brende**[2], **dīk**); *Broad Ditch* 1717 (*v.* **brād, dīc**); *The Cowpasture* 1633; *Cranmere Bushes* 1634 (poss. the surn. *Cranmer, v.* **busc**); *Damfeild* 1633, *Damwongs, Dam-Woungs Feilde* 1633, c1635, *Damwange* 1634 (*v.* **damme, vangr, feld**); *The Drift Way* 1633, c1635 (a track along which cattle were driven, *v.* **drift**); *Eastfeild* 1634 (one of the open-fields of the village, *v.* **ēast, feld**); *Greens land end* 1634 (from the surn. *Green,* cf. William *Grene* of Thistleton, labourer, 1522 MilS, *v.* **land, ende**[1]); *The Heath, Heath Feilde* 1633, *the Heathside* 1634 (*v.* **hǣð**); *High Street* 1633 (prob. referring to Ermine Street, *v.* **strǣt**); *Islington* 1633 (poss. recording an early farmstead); *Kirke Meadow* 1633 (*v.* **kirkja, mǣd,** cf. Thistleton Church *supra*); *the Leane wonge bush* 1634 (the first el. is poss. *leyne* 'a tract of arable land', *v.* **vangr, busc**); *Litill ȝard* 1633 (*v.* **lȳtel, geard**); *Long Hedge* 1633 (*v.* **lang**[1], **hecg**); *Longlands* 1717 (*v.* **lang**[1], **land**); *Meg Crafte* 1634 (the first el. is either the pers.n. *Meg* or a surn. derived from it (both ultimately from *Margaret*), *v.* **croft**); *Michell dale* 1634 (with either **dalr** or **deill**, *v.* **micel**); *The Mill, Milfeild, Millfield* 1633 (*v.* **myln, feld**); *Moneis Peice* 1717 (the *Money* family was resident in neighbouring Stretton in the 17th and 18th centuries, cf. also William *Money* of Teigh 1524 SR, *v.* **pece**); *Moor-Close, Moore furlong* 1634 (*v.* **mōr**[1]); *Mr Nixes Home Peice* 1717 (*v.* **home, pece**); *Northfeild* 1634 (one of the open-fields of the village, *v.* **norð, feld**); *Nottingham streete* 1634 (referring to the Roman road Sewstern Lane as it passes through the parish on its way towards Nottingham, *v.* **strǣt**); *Ouerton feld', Orton feld'* 1519, *Orton gate* 1634 (Mkt. Overton parish adjoins to the west, v. **feld, gata**); *ye Pasture, Pasture Leyes* 1633 (*v.* **pasture, lēah**); *Peaze hill* 1634 (*v.* **pisc**); *Pich Close* 1633 (*v.* **piche**); *Pitt -, Pytt Close* 1519 (*v.* **pytt**); *ye Postgapp, The Post Way* 1633 (referring to Sewstern Lane and its crossing of the county boundary at what is now Thistleton Gap, *v.* **gappe, post-way**); *Raslingdike* 1634 (*v.* **dīk**); *Redhill* 1576 VCH, 1633, *Red-hill* 1634 (cf. Redhills in Stretton f.ns. (a) and Redcap Hill *supra, v.* **rēad**); *Sealy Bush* 1634 (from the surn. *Seal(e)y* and prob. referring to scrubland, *v.* **busc**); *Sleadike Lease* 1634 (the first el. is perh. *slēa* 'a grassy slope', *v.* **dīk, lēah**); *smalstones* 1634 (describing a narrow strip of stony ground, *v.* **smæl, stān**); *stone cross dale* 1634 (*v.* **stān, cros, dalr,** cf. Cross Lane Fd *supra*); *Stonegravehill* 1576 VCH (poss. referring to the quarry in Stonepit Cl *supra, v.* **stān, græf, hyll**); *Stonhill* 1633, *stone-hill* 1634 (an allusion to the character of the ground, *v.* **stān, hyll**); *Stretton Closes* 1633, *Stretton Feld* 1519, *Stretton Hole, Stretton Holm* 1633 (Stretton parish adjoins to the south-east, *v.* **feld, hol**[1]**, holmr**); *Thorntre ʒard* 1519 (*v.* **þorn, trēow, geard**); *Vich Close* 1633 (vetch was grown for forage, *v.* **veche**); *the well rundell* 1634 (*v.* **rynel** and Roman Well *supra*); *Westfeild* 1634 (one of the open-fields of the village, *v.* **west, feld**); *The Wind Mill* 1633 (*v.* **wind-mylne**; originally at SK 9209 1740, but nothing survives, *v.* BrownArchSites 25); *Witham Moore* 1633 (South Witham L lies beyond the county boundary to the north, *v.* **mōr**[1]); *Wood Feilde, Woodfeild* 1633 (*v.* **wudu, feld**).

Whissendine

WHISSENDINE

Wichingedene 1086 DB

Wy-, Wissingden(e) 1265 Pat, 1297 *Ass et passim* to 1343 Cl, *Wisingheden* 1266 For

Wy-, Wissenden(e) 1203, 1212, 1214 Cur *et passim* to 1297 Cl *et freq* to 1453 Fine *et passim* to 1610 Speed, *-dena* 1176 P

Wy-, Wissinden' 1238 RGros *et passim* to 1349 Ipm, *Wyssynden* c1291 Tax, 1318 Pat *et passim* to 1498 Ipm

Whittsonden 1491 ISLR, *Whytsondyne* 1506 Nichols, *Whitsondine* 1613 LML, *Whitsendine* 1627 ib, *Whitsundine* 1629, 1719 ib

Why-, Whissendyne 1539 *MinAcct,* 1561 *FF, Whissendine* 1695
Map

This place-name is based on OE *Hwicce* but whether *Hwicce* here is the well-known major folk-name or an unrecorded personal name derived from it is uncertain. If the DB form of the p.n. is significant, then we have as the prototheme a minor folk-name **Hwiccingas* 'the people of a man called Hwicce'. But surviving spellings also allow a likelier original **Hwiccena-denu* 'valley of the Hwicce'. The name *Hwicce,* be it the folk-name or a pers.n., appears to survive elsewhere in the parish in the late-recorded Wichley Leys, *v.* f.ns. (a) *infra. Hwicce* occurs also in the name of the early Rutland hundred of Witchley (*v.* Witchley Warren) and in nearby Whiston Nth, some twenty miles to the south. These p.ns., situated in such close proximity, whether based on a pers.n. or on the folk-name *Hwicce,* suggest that the Anglo-Saxon Hwicce, later centred in Worcestershire, had an early presence in the Rutland region, *v.* Gl **4** 42 ff. The village lies near a Roman road which ran westwards from the important Romano-British settlement at Thistleton to Syston Lei on Fosse Way. Thus the presence of an early folk group of the Hwicce here in the north-west of Rutland is perfectly acceptable and Roman pottery from the parish indicates that there was some pre-Germanic settlement in the neighbourhood. Witchley Warren in Edith Weston is also close to a Roman road.

The early spellings for Whissendine show *ch* > *ss* due to AN influence; hence we have either 'the valley of the Hwiccingas' or 'the valley of the Hwicce', *v.* **-inga-, denu**.

MOORHALL (lost), *le Morhalle* 1325 Ipm, 1377 Cl, *Morehall* 1410, 1543 *FF, Moorhall* 1704 *Recov,* 1748 *Terrier,* 'the hall on moorland', *v.* **hall, mōr**[1]. The rectangular earthworks of this medieval manor house are in the north-east of the parish, only a half-mile from the county boundary, in the field now called The Pound (*v.* f.ns. (a) *infra*). Marshy moorland is an abnormal site for a manor house. Although in a low-lying position, the fortification may have originated as a north-western defensive border stronghold of the Anglian kingdom of Rutland. This was possibly paralleled in the north-east by a stronghold on the site of the later castle at Essendine whose position also appears to be related to the frontiers of Rutland.

Whissendine Inns and Taverns

GREYHOUND (lost), 1846, 1863 White, closed c1900 - VR.
NOEL ARMS (lost), named from the *Noel* family of Exton, closed
c1850 - VR. ROSE AND CROWN, 1846 White, 1861 *Anc*, 1863
White. THREE HORSESHOES. WHITE LION, 1846 ib.

BLAKEWELL COTTAGE, *Blakewell* 1943 *Map*. BROWNE'S
LODGE, 1932 Kelly, *Lodge* 1863 White, cf. Thomas *Browne* 1522
MilS, 1524 SR and Henry *Browne* 1592 VCH, both of Whissendine.
DUNSTALL PLANTATIONS, *Dunstan Plantation* 1861 *Anc*, *Great*
-, *Little* -, *Long Dunstan* 1861 *ib*, *Dunstall, Big Dunstalls* 1943 *Map*,
Dunston Close 1748 *Terrier*, probably from OE **tūn-stall** 'the site of
a farmstead', cf. *Dunston* in Empingham f.ns. (b), *Dunston Hedge* in
Lyddington f.ns. (b) and Great Dunston Cl in Ketton f.ns. (a) where
forms vary principally between *Dunston* and *Dunstall*. FORD,
Staney Ford Willows 1677 *Terrier*, '(the willows at) the ford with the
stony bottom', *v.* **stānig, ford, wilig**. GREEN'S LODGE.
GRANGE FM (local). HOLLY HO., 1932 Kelly. HORTONS
LANE (local). THE HURN (local), *v.* **hyrne**. THE LAURELS,
1932 ib. MANOR FM, 1932 ib. MANOR HO. MOOR LANE,
The Moor 1943 *Map*, *Far* -, *Lawrence* -, *Middle* -, *Top Moor, Farr* -,
Near Moor Close 1748 *Terrier*, *v.* **mōr**[1] and *Moorhall supra*, cf.
Richard *Laurens*, husbandman of Whissendine, 1524 SR and John
Laurence, husbandman of neighbouring Langham, 1522 MilS (-
Laurens 1524 SR). MOUNT PLEASANT, usually having a
favourable meaning in a rural situation, but can be used ironically.
PARK HO., 1932 Kelly, cf. *The Park* 1861 *Anc*, 1943 *Map*. THE
POPLARS, 1932 Kelly. RED HO., 1932 ib. ST. ANDREW'S
CHURCH. STATION RD, leading to the local railway station
beyond the county boundary in Lei. THOMAS HILL, 1861 *Anc*,
1943 *Map*, cf. *Thomas Hill Meadow* 1861 *Anc*, *St Thomas* 1943
Map, possibly to be associated in origin with either father or son
recorded in Whissendine as *Thomas filius Thomas* 1296 SR. THE
VICARAGE, 1932 Kelly is *The Rectory* 1861 *Anc*. VICARAGE
COTTAGE. VICARAGE HO., 1932 Kelly. VICARAGE LODGE,

1932 ib. WHISSENTHORPE seems to be a late fabrication, not
appearing as a site or name on the first edition of the O.S. map of
the county of 1824. WINDMILL, cf. *Milne Furlong* 1677 *Terrier,
Mill Furlong* 1703 *PSJ*, 1861 *Anc*, 1943 *Map, Mill Leyes* 1861 *Anc, v.*
myln.

Field-Names

Undated forms in (a) are 1943 *Map*; those dated 1861, 1867, 1880, 1909 and
1914 are *Anc*; 1869 and 1870 are *BHS*. Early forms dated Edw 3 are *Rental*,
1661, 1779 and 1791 are *Deed*; 1677 and 1748 are *Terrier*; 1703 are *PSJ*.

(a) Half Acre; Two Acres; Five Acres 1861, - Acre 1943; Six Acre(s); Seven
Acres; Eight Acres 1914, 1943; Nine Acre, Ten Acres, Eleven -, Fourteen Acre,
Seventeen Acres, Eighteen Acre (*Eighteen Acres* 1748), Twenty Acre (*v.*
æcer); Acres Cl 1861; Adcock's Covert 1861, Adcocks - 1867, 1869, 1870 (from the surn.
Adcock, v. **cover(t)**); Alley Wong 1861, 1867, 1869, 1870 (*Allouwongholmis* Edw 3,
v. **alor, vangr,** holmr); Ashwell Hedge 1861, - Hedges 1943 (adjoins the parish
boundary with Ashwell to the east, *v.* **hecg**); Back Mdw 1861, 1943; Barley Wood
Sick 1861 (*v.* **sík**); Barn Cl 1861, 1943, Little - 1943, Barn Fd; Little Beck 1861
(*Little Becke* 1703, - *Furlong* 1677, *v.* **bekkr**); Bellamy Cl 1861 (cf. Robert *Bellamy*
of Whissendine 1522 MilS); Best Cl, Big -, Little -; Blakemiles 1861 (either a
surn. *Blakemile* or else alluding to very dark soil, *v.* **blæc, mylde**); Bottom Mdws;
Breach, - Mdw 1861, The Ploughed Breetches, Rough Breetches 1943 (*Breach*
1703, *Breach Feild* 1677, 1703; one of the open-fields of the village, *v.* **hēafod**);
Brecklands, - Seeke, - Syke 1943, Bretland 1861, 1867, - Sick 1861, Bretlands
1869, 1870 (*Bretland* 1703, - *Feild* 1677, 1703, - *Field* 1779, one of the open-fields
of the village; the first el. is obscure, but poss. Angl *brēc* 'land broken up for
cultivation', *v.* **land, sík,** cf. Bretland in Ryhall f.ns. (a)); Briery Wong 1861, 1943
(*v.* **brērig, vangr**); Bridge Mdw 1861; Old Broadway 1870 (*v.* **brād, weg**); The
Brook 1869, 1870, Part of Brook 1867, Brook Mdw 1943 (*v.* **brōc**); Bushy Cl;
Butt Leys 1861 (*v.* **butte, lēah**); Chester (unlikely as a surn., so perh. *ceaster* 'an
old fortification', although Angl *cæster* is the form used in Rutland's Casterton
and in other East Midland major p.ns. with this el.; however, a later use of
chester applied to a recognizable fortified site may be thought of and appropriate
to this frontier parish; crop marks of rectangular enclosures have been recorded
at SK 825 162, SK 838 134 and SK 841 141 (*v.* Crop Marks 60-1), one of which
may relate to this f.n.); Church Leys 1861, Big - 1943 (cf. St Andrew's Church
supra); Coachgate 1861, Coach Gate 1943 (*Coach Gate* 1703, apparently '(the

close beside) the coach road', but cf. Coach Bridge in Seaton where *coach* is the reflex of *cotes* 'the cottages' and cf. the Ru dial. *cotch* 'cottage', *cotcher* 'cottager', *v.* **gata**); Cock Leys 1861 (*Cockley Close* 1748, *v.* **cocc²**, **lēah**); Common Leys 1861, 1867 (*v.* **commun**, **lēah**); Conger Hill 1861 (*v.* **coninger**); Corner Fd; Cottage Pasture 1861; The Cottles (from the surn. *Cottle*, cf. Cottlès in Mkt. Overton f.ns. (a)); Cow Closes 1861 (1748); Cow Lair 1861 ('a barn, a resting place for cows', *v.* **lair**); Cowpit Holme 1861 (*Colepit Holme* 1677, from **col-pytt** 'a place where charcoal is made', *v.* **holmr**); Cow Pasture; Cricket Fd (referring to the game of cricket); Cross Hedges 1861, 1943 (perh. 'hedges lying athwart ...', *v.* **cross²**, **hecg**); Dogwell 1943, - Cl 1861 (*v.* **docce**, **wella**); Duck Pond; Dutmore Land 1861 (may well be a copyist's error for *Rutmore, v. Rotemore* in f.ns. (b) *infra*); Edward's Cl 1861; Eldern Stumps (*v.* **ellern, stump**); Big -, Little Elgate (poss. 'road lined with elder-trees', *v.* **ellern, gata**); Far Fds; Faulkener's Cl 1861 (with the common Ru surn. *Falkener*); The Flats (*v.* **flat**); Flax Leys 1861 (**fleax, lēah**); Flower's Cl (cf. Roger *Flower* 1522 MilS of Oakham); Fox Holes (*v.* **fox-hol**); Front Fd (land in front of a house); Garner's (a surn., cf. Garners Cl, - Mdw in Essendine f.ns. (a)); Gasby Sick 1861 (*Gosborough Seyke* 1748; the first el. is prob. **gorst** 'gorse', with 17th cent. Ru dial. shortening *gorse* > *goss, v.* **beorg, sík**); Left -, Right Hand Gate Cl (adjoining Teigh Gate Ho., *v.* Teigh f.ns. (a)); Gibson's Big Cl; Glover's Fd (cf. William *Glover* 1522 MilS); Gravel Pit Cl; Great Cl 1861, 1943; Great Mdw 1861; Greensborough 1861, Green's Borough 1943 (prob. with **beorg** 'a tumulus'); Green's Cl (from the surn. *Green*); Grindle 1861, 1867, 1943 (*Grindall Seeke* 1677; Grindle is the name of a close beside the parish's principal stream, *v.* **grendel, sík**, cf. *Grindle* in Barleythorpe f.ns. (b) and Grindles Cl in Langham f.ns. (a), presumably referring to the same 'stream with a gravelly bed'); Hall Cl 1861, 1943, Mason's - 1861, Hall Fd 1943, Hall Ground 1861, 1943, Hall Wong 1861 (*Hall Wongs* 1748, *v.* **hall, grund, vangr**); Ham 1861 (*Ham Furlong* 1677, *v.* **hamm**); Hassock's Holme 1861, Hassock - 1943 ('meadow covered with clumps of coarse grass' *v.* **hassuc, holmr**); High Leys 1861, - Lees 1943 (*High Leas* 1677, *v.* **hēah¹, lēah**); High Mill 1861 (*v.* **myln**); Big -, Little Hill; Hill Cl 1861; Holborn 1861, 1867, 1880 (poss. 'stream running in a hollow', *v.* **hol², burna**); Hollow Leys 1861 (*v.* **holh, lēah**); Home Cl 1861, 1867, 1870, 1943 (1748), Home Fd 1943 (*v.* **home**); Horse Cl 1861; Horse Crofts 1861 (1703, *v.* **croft**); Horse Holm 1861 (*v.* **holmr**); Horse Pit 1979 VR; Hovel Cl (*v.* **hovel**); Howgate 1861, 1867 (*v.* **haugr, gata**); Hudson's; Humps and Hollows (cf. Hills and Hales in Exton f.ns. (a)); Ireland's Pingle 1861, Island Pingle 1943 (from the surn. *Ireland*, cf. *Irelands House* 1634 *Conant* in Lyndon and George *Ireland* of Hambleton 118 *Surv, v.* **pingel**); Irnhouse Sick 1861 (*v.* **hyrne, hūs, sík**); Bottom -, Top Jacksons 1943, Jackson's Cl 1861; Jersey Hill (Mr J. Field notes that this is poss. a transferred name from the island of Jersey indicating remoteness, since the land is on the parish boundary); Keeper's Cottage 1861 (a gamekeeper's cottage); Lady's Mdw 1861, Ladies - 1943 (v. hlǣfdige); Lammas Cl 1861, 1943 (cf. *Lammas Grounds* 1748, v. lammas, grund); Langham Gate, Langham Hill (Langham parish adjoins to the south, v. gata); Leesthorpe Fd (adjoins the boundary of Leesthorpe Lei to the west); Big Leighs; Little Ing 1861, 1867, - Ings 1869, 1870 (*Littleing Furlong* 1677, v. lȳtel, eng); Little Mdw 1861; Lodge Fm 1861; Long Mdw 1861; Nether -, Upper Loodale 1861, Ashwell -, Little -, Stanhope Loodle 1943 (*Loudell Furlong* 1677, cf. Loudal Lane in Ashwell (Ashwell parish adjoins to the west) and cf. Stanhope's Cl *infra*); Lullhaugh Cl 1861 (if this records an early name, then 'Lulla's enclosure', v. haga[1] and cf. *Lull Hill* in Greetham f.ns. (b)); Madge Piper 1861 (perh. simply the name of a female owner of the close, one *Margaret Piper, Madge* being a pet-form of *Margaret,* but as *madge* is also a dial. form for 'magpie', earlier spellings are needed); Mathew Yard 1861 (from the surn. *Matthew(s)*, v. geard); Bottom -, Top Melton Gate 1861, 1867, Melton Gate 1943 (*Melton Gate* 1677 '(field beside) the road to Melton Mowbray Lei', v. gata); Middle Cl; Middle Fd; Milking Cl 1861, 1943 ('land on which cows are milked', v. milking); Musson's Cl; The Mushroom Cl; Navvys Yard (created in 1844 to house navvies working on the construction of the Midland Railway); Nether Cl 1861, 1943; Neather Mdw 1861 (v. neoðera); New Close Mdw 1861, - Mdws 1943; Nineteen Acre Swimmingford; Nob Bridge Fd (prob. alluding to stone balls on the balustrades of the bridge); The Nook 1979 VR (v. nōk); North Field Hades 1861 (*North Feild* 1677, 1703, one of the open-fields of the village, v. norð, feld, hēafod); Oat Cl 1861; Oakhame Gate 1861 (*Okeham Gate* 1703, '(field beside) the road to Oakham', v. gata); Big Olran (perh. 'growing with alders', v. alren); Over Cl; Top Paddock 1861; Pan Cl 1861 (either 'pan-shaped close' or 'close lying in a circular hollow', v. panne); Upper Pasture 1861, Pasture Cl 1869, 1870, 1909, Pasture Covert 1861, Pasture Fd 1869, 1870 (v. cover(t)); Peache's Cl 1861; Peaseland Sick 1861, - Sich 1861, 1867 (v. pise, land, sīk, sīc); Big Pickard's; Pingle, - Leys 1861, Pinglees 1943 (*Pingle Leys Seeke* 1703, v. pingel, lēah, sīk); Nether Plantation 1861; Old Ploughed Cl; Ploughed Home Fd; The Ploughed Fd; Pound's Cl 1861, The Pound 1943 (alluding to the earthworks of the medieval manor house called *Moorhall supra,* v. pund); The Pretties (cf. Willm. *Pretty* 1663 *Asw* of Glaston, Pretty Gorse and Prettys in Ayston f.ns. (a)); Priest Wong 1861 (v. vangr); Quake Fen 1861 (*Quackfen Furlong* 1677, 'a marshy place which shakes when walked upon, a stretch of quake-ooze', v. quake, fenn); Ranglands 1861, Ringlands 1943 (*Wrang Lands* 1703, v. wrang, vrangr, land); Red Gore 1861, 1943, Far - 1943, Red Gore Mdw 1861, 1943 (v. gāra); Richmond Leys 1861 (from the surn. *Richmond,* cf. Robert *Richmond* 1678 *Anc* of Stretton); Road Cl, - Fd; Roe Cl 1861 (*Rowe Close*

1703), Roe Lane 1861; Rommell's Cl, Rommell's Fd (both apparently with a surn., although not a local one; the date of these f.ns. (i.e. 1943) suggests an ironical allusion to Field Marshal Erwin *Rommel*, the Second World War German panzer commander, cf. Tank Cl in Lt. Casterton f.ns. (a) and adjoining Ryhall f.ns. (a), both of 1943 also; perh. all were used as tank parks in the Second World War, although *tank* could obviously refer to something as mundane as a water container); Rough Fd 1943, Rough Ground 1861, Rough Hill 1943 (*Rough Meadow* 1743, v. rūh¹, grund); Sandpits; Top Seed Fd, Seeds, - Fd (areas of sown grass, v. sǣd); Sewstern Hill 1861, 1943, Ploughed - 1943 (Sewstern Lei lies on high ground some four miles north-east of Whissendine and no doubt Sewstern Hill provides a prospect of it); Shaft Nooks (perh. an allusion to a pole acting as a boundary marker, v. sceaft, nōk, but cf. *Shafts Furlong* in Belton f.ns. (b) where the surn. *Shaft* occurs); Side Cuttings 1861; Silver Diggings (Mr J. Field notes that this is an ironical name for intractable land); The Slip (v. slipe); Spinney Fd, Big -, Little -; Stackyard Fd, Back - (v. stak-ʒard); Standlands (perh. 'stony selions', v. stān, land); Stapleford Dyke 1861, 1943 ('the ditch forming the boundary with Stapleford Lei', v. dīk); Spring Hades 1861 (1703, v. spring, hēafod); Stanhope's Cl, - Mdw 1861 (from the surn. *Stanhope*, cf. Stanhope's Cl in Stretton f.ns. (a)); Stony Lands 1861; Stover Hill 1861 (poss. 'boundary-post hill', v. stæfer, cf. Shaft Nooks *supra*); Stray Lands (prob. with *stray* 'a piece of unenclosed common pasture'; as an alternative, Mr J. Field suggests OFr *estraieure* 'possessions left without an heir and which passed to the lord'); Tennis Court; Teigh Lane (Teigh parish adjoins to the north-east); The Three Mdws; Thistley Gore 1861 (*Thislegoare Furlong* 1677, v. þistlig, gāra); The Tithe Yard 1861 (v. tēoða, geard); Towell Hill (perh. 'two springs (hill)', v. twēgen, wella); Town End Cl 1861, Townsend 1943, - Cl 1861 (*Wyers Towns End Close* 1779 (poss. with *weyour* 'a pond'), v. tūn, ende¹); Town Leys 1861 (v. tūn, lēah); Waffs, Bottom -, Top - (Mr J. Field suggests 'nooks of land', v. hvarf); Water Leys 1861, 1867 (*Middle Waterly Furlong* 1703, v. wæter, lēah); West Ings 1861, 1867, 1943 (*Westings Furlong* 1677, v. west, eng); Top Westlands; White Headlands 1861, 1867, 1943 (*Whites Head Land* 1677, from a surn., either *White* or *Wayte* (cf. John- and Richard *Wayte* 1522 MilS, 1524 SR of Whissendine), v. hēafod-land); White's Barn Land; Whissendine Pastures 1824 O; Wilker Mdw 1861 (*Wilcocke Meadow* 1748, from the surn. *Wilcock(s)*, cf. John *Wilkokes* 1522 MilS and Robert *Wilcokes* 1522 ib, - *Wylkok* 1524 SR of neighbouring Ashwell); Wichley Leys 1861 (evidently containing the same prototheme as Whissendine and Witchley Warren in Edith Weston, v. lēah).

(b) *Appelmede* 1336 Ipm (v. æppel, mǣd); *Bandlands Furlong* 1677 (v. bēan, land); *pontem de Wissendene* 13 HMCVar (v. brycg); *Bridges Close alias Metcalfes*

Close 1748; *Carterplase* Edw 3 (from the surn. *Carter*, v. **place**); *East Feild* 1677, - *Field* 1779 (one of the open-fields of the village, v. **ēast, feld**); *Estmor*(e) 1336, 1349, 1353, 1355 Ipm (v. **ēast, mōr**[1]); *The Flashes* 1748 (v. **flasshe**); *le Flaxeyerde* Edw 3 (v. **flax-yerde**); *Green Huske Furlong* 1677 (unexplained, cf. *Greene Huske Furlong* (1652) in Barrow f.ns. (b) and Stone husk furlong in Lyddington f.ns. (a) and Thorpe by Water f.ns. (a)); *House Gate Furlong* 1677; *Heckleyn Seeke* 1677 (v. **hæc(c), leyne, sīk**); *Hogg Home* 1703 (poss. from dial. *hog* 'a shearling lamb', otherwise from *hogg* 'a pig', v. **holmr**); *Jekes plase* Edw 3 (from the surn. *Jakes/Jeeks*, v. **place**); *le Kirkmedou* Edw 3 (v. **kirkja, mæd**, cf. St Andrew's Church *supra*); *Long Leys* 1677 (v. **lēah**); *Mickleton Hill Furlong* 1677 (poss. OE *micel-dūn* 'great hill' with a Scandinavianized first el. and unvoicing of *d* > *t* in the second el., v. **micel, mikill, dūn**); *Metcalfes Close, Metcalfs Leys* 1748 (v. **lēah**); *North Feild* 1677, 1703 (one of the open-fields of the village, v. **norð, feld**); *Odmelmedou* Edw 3, *Oadmeale Furlong* 1748 (evidently 'oatmeal meadow' in the earlier f.n., perh. with reference to the nature of the soil, cf. the later *Oatemeale Meadowe* in Hambleton f.ns. (b), v. **ote-mele, mæd**); *Orson Meadow* 1748; *Osbernholm* 1353 Ipm (the first el. is either an original Scand pers.n. *Asbjǫrn*, borrowed into late OE as *Ōsbern*, or its ME reflex *Osbern*, or the surn. *Osborn* derived from it, v. **holmr**); *The Over Pasture* 1791 (v. **uferra**); *Peasewell seeke* 1677 (v. **pise, wella, sīk**); *Perotesmersh* 1336 Ipm, *Perottesmersh* 1349 ib, *Perot Mersh* 1353 ib, *Perotmerssh* 1355 ib (from the surn. *Perot*(t), v. **mersc**); *Rigged Baulke* 1748 ('a bank or unploughed strip of ground marked by ridges', v. **hrycg, hryggr, balca**); *Rotemore* 1377 Ipm ('Rōta's moorland', v. *Rutmore* in Teigh); *The Sheepewalke* 1661 (unfenced sheep pasture, v. **sheep-walk**); *Shovelboards Furlong* 1677 (v. **scofl-brǣdu**); *South Feild* 1677, 1703 (one of the open-fields of the village, v. **sūð, feld**); *Staffords Quicke* 1677 (from the surn. *Stafford*, cf. Staffords Cl in neighbouring Teigh f.ns. (a), v. **cwic**); *Town Close* 1748 (v. **tūn**); *Tythstacke Seeke* 1677 ('tithe-rick field', v. **tēoða, stakkr, sīk**); *The Water Meadows* 1748; *Wellheadland Field* 1748 (v. **wella, hēafod-land**); *West Ends* 1703 (perh. a corrupted form of West Ings *supra*, otherwise from **ende**[1]); *le Westmers*(s)h 1336, 1355 Ipm (v. **west, mersc**, cf. *Perotesmersh supra*).

Whitwell

WHITWELL

 Wy-, Witewell(e) 1086 DB, 1184 (p), 1195 P (p) *et passim* to
  1326 ChancW

 Why-, Whitewell(e) 1197 P, 1226, 1257 FF, 1263, 1286 *Ass et
  passim* to 1305 Pat *et freq* to 1394 *Rut* (p) *et passim* to

1553 Pat, *Qwytewelle* 1286 *Ass*
Why-, Whitwell(e) 1382 Cl, 1394 *Rut* (p) *et passim*

'The white spring or stream', *v.* **hwīt, wella.** A small stream
rises here.

HIGH MOOR FM, - SPINNEY, *Great* -, *Little Highmoor* 1943
Map, v. **hēah**[1], **mōr**[1]. HOME FM. NOEL'S ARMS P.H., *Noel's
Arms (Inn)* 1846 White, 1932 Kelly; *Noel* is the family name of the
Earls of Gainsborough, major landowners in this area. OLD HALL
FM, cf. *The Hall Orchard* 1723 (1822) *DEG, v.* **hall.** THE
RECTORY, 1846, 1863 White is *ye Parsonage House* 1723 (1822)
DEG, v. **personage.** WHITWELL CHURCH, *Church (St Michael)*
1846, 1863 White. WOODLANDS FM.

Field-Names

Undated forms in (a) are 1943 *Map.* Early forms dated 1631, 1667 and 1682
are *Deed*; 1632 are *Terrier*; 1723 (1822) are *DEG.*

(a) Six -, Eight -, Nine -, Twelve - (x2), Fifteen -, The Twenty-one Acre,
The Thirty-two Acres (*v.* Oakham Road Cl *infra*), The Thirty-four Acres, Forty
Acre (*v.* **æcer**); Ash Cl (1723, *v.* **æsc**); Bill's Fd; Black Mould (*v.* **blæc, molde**);
Branston Fd; Bull's Cl; Cottage Cl; Cow Cl (1723); Dixon's Gorse Fd (*v.* **gorst**);
Dixon's Mdws; Empingham Cl (Empingham parish adjoins to the east); Forest
Fd; Hanging Bulk or Balk (*v.* **hangende, balca**); Horses Cl; Oakham Road Cl or
The Thirty-two Acres; Pond Fd; Second Fd; Tuckers Fd; Top Yard Fd (*v.*
geard).

(b) *Brake Hill* 1723 (*v.* **bræc**[1]); *brooke side close* 1623 (*v.* **brōc, sīde**); *Church
Close* 1723; *The Common Field* 1723 (*v.* **commun**); *Conie Close* 1631, *Conye* -
1667 (*v.* **coni**); *Dents Hill* 1631, 1667, *Dench Hill* 1723 (prob. with the surn. *Dent*;
Ekwall in DEPN *s.n.* derives Dent YW and Dent Cu from a British word
related to OIr *dind* 'a hill' but this is most unlikely here, even though the name
of a hill); *Dovecoat Close* 1631, 1667 (*v.* **dove-cot(e)**); *Eight Lease close* 1632,
Eight Leas 1723 (*v.* **lēah**); *Feild Close* 1682 (*v.* **feld**); *Fourteen Leas* 1723 (*v.*
lēah); *The Lower Ground* 1723 (*v.* **grund**); *Middle Close* 1723; *Nixe's Close* 1723
(cf. Mr *Nixe* 1717 *Asw* of nearby Thistleton); *Pasture Closes* 1682 (*v.* **pasture**);

Roluesmedowe 1290 Abbr (prob. with the surn. *Rolf,* derived from the Scand pers.n. *Hrolfr,* otherwise with the pers.n. itself, *v.* **mǣd**); *Skirtly's Close,* - *Meadow* 1723; *Smith's Close* 1682; *Whitwell Field* 1723.

OAKHAM SOKE HUNDRED

Oakham Soke Hundred was formerly part of Martinsley Hundred. The earliest recorded mention is *Hundreda de Okeham cum Martynesley* 1428 FA. By 1522, Oakham Soke is unambiguously a hundred in its own right: *the five Hundreds of County Rotlond, viz. Alstow Hundred, Mertley Hundred, Wrandyke Hundred, Okam Sokon and the Esthundred* 1522 MilS. Later, *soca de Okeham* 1535 VE, *Oukhamsook Hundred* 1610 Speed, *Okeham Soak Hundred* 1695 *Map, v.* **sōcn** 'a district over which a right of jurisdiction is exercised'. The hundred was formed of the townships and manors held by the castle and manor of Oakham. This no doubt accounts for the isolated position of Clipsham parish, which is in the north-east of the county, in relationship to the rest of the hundred. As a soke rather than as a hundred, Oakham Soke appears earliest as *ad socam de Ocheham* 1086 DB.

Barleythorpe

BARLEYTHORPE
  Thorp juxta Ocham, -k- c1200 *WDB,* 1275 *FF,* 1300 Ipm
  Bolaresthorp 1203 *FF, Bolarysthorp* e13 VCH
  Barlicthorp' 1334 *MR, Barlikthorp* 1338 *FF,* 1340 *MR,* 1377
    MinAcct
  Barlithorp, -y- 1286 *Ass,* 1316 FA *et passim* to 1411 *MR,* 1412
    Cl
  Barlethorp 1430 Pat, 1557 *FF*
  Barleythorpe 1496 *MR,* 1619, 1621 LML, 1695 *Map*

Originally 'the outlying farmstead (next to Oakham)'; also known by the family name of John *le Bolour* or *Bulur* who is mentioned in connection with Oakham in 1200 *WDB*. Later **bærlic** 'barley' replaced the family name, possibly through the association of sound, *v.* **þorp**. Barleythorpe as a land-unit appears to have been carved from Oakham's early territory.

BARLEYTHORPE HALL, 1825 OR, 1850 Slater, cf. *Hall leas* 1681 *Ct*, *Hall Leys* 1761 *ib*, *Hallhills* 1665 *ib*, *v.* **hall, lēah, hyll**. BLACK HORSE P.H. (lost), 1846 White. DAIRY FM, cf. *Dairy Field* 1943 *Map*. THE HALL. HORSE AND GROOM P.H. (lost), 1846 White, 1850 Slater. LONSDALE HO., named from Hugh Cecil Lowther, 5th Earl of *Lonsdale* (1857-1944), who sponsored boxing's first Lonsdale Belt and developed Barleythorpe Stud, *v.* Stud Ho. *infra*. MANOR FM. MANOR LANE. MILL HILL is *Muley Hill* 1610 Speed, 1780, 1801 Map, *Mill Hill* 1943 *Map*, *v.* **myln, lēah, hyll**. PASTURE LANE, cf. *(the) Cow Pasture* 1776, 1800 *Ct*, *Barleythorpe Pasture* 1797 *ib*. SPRINGFIELD HO., cf. *under the Spring* 1761 *ib*, *Spring Close* 1943 *Map*. STUD HO. (2½"), 1932 Kelly, cf. *Studhouse Fields* 1943 *Map*, *v.* **stōd**.

Field-Names

Undated forms in (a) are 1943 *Map*; those dated 1803 are *Ct*. Early forms dated 1334, 1340, 1376, 1402, 1408, 1411, 1424, 1446, 1460 and 1500 are *MR*; those of 1410, 1611, 1628, 1630, 1632, 1634, 1638, 1665, 1667, 1671, 1674, 1676, 1679, 1681, 1691, 1698, 1702, 1723, 1726, 1730, 1736, 1742, 1746, 1755, 1761, 1763, 1773, 1776, 1780 and 1797 are *Ct*; those dated 1770 are *Anc*.

(a) Four Acre, Twelve - (x2), Sixteen -, Eighteen Acre (*v.* **æcer**); Baines' (the surn. *Baines*, cf. Thomas *Banes* 1522 MilS of Braunston and Thomas *Banys* 1524 SR of Manton); Barleythorpe Grove 1803 (1755, 1773, *le Grove* 1723, *the Grove* 1780, *v.* **grāf**); Bett's Barn (cf. John *Bett* 1522 MilS of Cottesmore and Stephen *Bett* 1522 ib of Greetham); Best Cl; Blood Cl (from the surn. *Blood*, cf. Blood's Cl in neighbouring Langham f.ns. (a), Johane *Blood* 1522 MilS and John *Bloode* 1524 SR, both of Ryhall); Box Paddock; Bradshaw's; Casterton Mdw; First -, Second Clay Hill (*Cleyhill* 1667, *Clayhill* 1679, 1681, 1761, *v.* **clæg, hyll**); Cold Overton Road Mdws (the adjacent parish of Cold Overton is to the west, beyond the county boundary in Lei); Cricket Fd (referring to the game of cricket); Dennison's Fd; Gunby's (from the surn. *Gunby*, cf. John *Gunby* 1522

MilS, 1524 SR of Gt. Casterton and Robert *Gunby* 1522 MilS, 1524 SR of Oakham); Hill Fd; Holgate Road Cl; Horse Drills (1761, a field evidently named from the early use of the horse-drill, a machine for sowing seeds in 'drills' or small furrows); Far -, Near Klondyke (a name indicating remoteness or some quality (hard work or poss. great profit) associated with the gold-rush in Canada in and after 1896; the name appears also in Beaumont Chase, Hambleton and Wardley f.ns. (a)); Langham House Fd (from Langham House in the adjacent parish of Langham); The Meadows; Mickledine (*Mickledens, Short Mickledanes* 1691, *mikeldenslade* 1411, *v.* **mikill, denu, slæd**); Big -, Middle -, Road Munday (prob. from the surn. *Munday*); Oakham Road Fd; Pinfold Cl 1803 (1726, 1773, *le Pinfeild Close* 1671, *le pinfold close* 1730, *v.* **pynd-fald**); Pocket Nook (*v.* **poket, nōk**); Priestwell's (poss. 'the priest's spring or stream', *v.* **prēost, wella**, cf. *Prestlands infra*); Racecourse; Ring Fd; Seeds (referring to an area of sown grass, *v.* **sǣd**); Sharp's Hill Fd (cf. Thomas *Sharpe* 1522 MilS and Harry *Sharp* 1932 Kelly, both of nearby Egleton); Sharp's Long Cl or Lady Cl (*v.* **hlǣfdige**); Shuttlewood (perh. with *scyt(t)els* 'a bolt, a bar', denoting woodland secured by a fence and gate, or a wood where shuttles or arrows were got, cf. Shutlanger Nth 106); The Slip (a narrow strip of land, *v.* **slipe**); Stall Cl 1862 *Will* (*v.* **stall**); The Top Fd.

(b) *Armslades* 1665, 1773 (*v.* **earm, slæd**, cf. Armley Wood in Exton); *Barlythorpe Mault myll* 1611 *Deed* (*v.* **malte-mylne**); *le Upper Barne* 1667 (*v.* **bere-ærn**); *Branston hedge* 1679 (referring to a parish boundary hedge of Braunston which adjoins to the south, *v.* **hecg**); *iuxta pontem ad finem orientalem ville de Barlithorp'* 1411 (*v.* **brycg**); *Brinkes* 1674, *Brinks* 1691, 1702, 1730, 1742, 1746, 1761, 1773 (*v.* **brink**); *aboue the brook* 1402 (p), 1408 (p), 1424 (p), *att(e) Brok(e)* 1446 (p), 1460 (p), 1500 (p) (*v.* **brōc**); *Brushfeild* 1702 (*v.* **brusshe, feld**); *Bullgrassefurlong* 1674, *Bul(l)grass Furlong* 1726, 1761, 1773 (*v.* **bula, gærs**); *Burleigh Brook(e)s* 1674, 1761, *Burly brookes* 1691, *Burley Brooks* 1730, 1761, *Short Burleigh Brookes* 1674, *Short Burly Brooks* 1698 (Burley parish lies to the east, *v.* **brōc**); *Callewell Leas* 1691, *Short and Long Callyway Leys* 1674, 1730, 1761 (*v.* **calu, wella, lēah**); *Child furlong* 1746 (prob. **cild** 'a young person' rather than the surn. *Child*, cf. Child Furlong in S. Luffenham f.ns. (a)); *the new closing* 1628, *le closeing* 1691, *(le) Closeingside* 1674, 1679, *Closingside* 1667, *Closeing Side* 1676, *Closeingesides* 1674, *le Closes side* 1691 (*v.* **closing, side**); *le Crab Tree in le Millfield* 1730 (*v.* **crabtre**); *Doris Close apud finem occidentalem ville de Barlithorpe* 1634 (from the surn. *Doure,* cf. John *Doure,* husbandman of nearby Cottesmore 1524 SR and *Dures furlonge* in Caldecott f.ns. (b)); *(le) East field* 1730, 1761; *Flitteriss Corner* 1797 (from Flitteris Park in the adjacent parish of Oakham, *v.* **corner**); *Garbridge Furlong* 1674, *Garbidge* 1742 (*v.* **gorebrode**; strips in the gore of the common arable field were broad rather than long in order to produce worthwhile allotments of land in these wedge-shaped areas); *le Gooseberry Bush* 1667 (*v.* **goseberry, busc**); *le Grasse Ends* 1676 (*v.* **gærs, ende**[1]); *Grenegate* 1410, *Greengate* 1681 (*v.* **grēne**[1], **gata**); *Greenhill* 1665 (*v.* **grēne**[1], **hyll**); *Grindle* 1761, *Grindle Syke* 1679 (*v.* **grendel, sīk**, cf. Grindle in Whissendine f.ns. (a) and Grindells in Langham f.ns. (a)); *Hay Hill* 1691; *hold furrows* 1691, *Hole Furrow* 1746, 1763 (*v.* **holh, furh**); *Hollywell slades* 1665 (*v.* **hālig, wella, slæd**); *Homesteads or Old Inclosures* 1776 (*v.* **hām-stede, inclosure**); *horse dales* 1691 (*v.* **hors, deill**); *le upper Houel* 1667 (*v.* **hovel**); *Le Lammas close* 1691 (*v.* **lammas**); *Langham mear* 1691 (*v.* **(ge)mǣre**), *Langham Way* 1691, 1702, 1746, 1773 (Langham parish adjoins to the north); *Lea pounde* 1691 (*v.* **lēah, pund**); *Light Ground* 1761 (referring to light as opposed to heavy soil, *v.* **lēoht, grund**); *South Longland(s)* 1674, 1742, 1773, *South Long Land* 1761 (*v.* **lang**[1], **land**); *Long Roods* 1761 (*v.* **rōd**[3]); *Mault Milne way* 1665 (*v.* **malte-mylne**, cf. *Barlythorpe Mault myll* supra); *le Mere* 1665, *Barlithorpe Meare* 1681, *Barlythorpe Meare* 1761, *Meare Furlong(e)* 1674, 1742, *le Meare hedge* 1681 (*v.* **(ge)mǣre, hecg**); *les Mesnes* 1632, 1638, *les meanes* 1763 (*v.* **mesne**); *le middle feild* 1679, *the middle field* 1742 (*v.* **middel, feld**); *Middletons Lands* 1730, 1797 (from the surn. *Middleton*, cf. John *Middleton* 1522 MilS of Langham); *molendini de Barlicthorp'* 1334, *molend' de Barlikthorp'* 1340, *molendini apud Barlythorp* 1376 (*v.* **myln**); *le Mil(l)feild* 1628, 1665, 1674, 1726, (*le*) *Millfield* 1730, 1742, 1763, *Mill Field* 1746, 1761 (*v.* **myln, feld**); *Narrow Points* 1665, 1761 (*v.* **nearu, point**); *le Nether Close* 1632; *le Netherfield* 1628, 1674, 1679, *le Neitherfeild* 1665, 1667, 1691, *le Neather feild* 1674, *le Neatherfeild* 1730, *le Nether field* 1726, 1742, (*the*) *Nether Field* 1746, 1761, 1763, 1776, 1780 (*v.* **neoðera, feld**); *le New Orchard* 1674, *le Upper Orchard* 1667; *ouerdykes* 1679, *ouerdikes* 1691 (*v.* **ofer**[3], **dīk**); *ouergates* 1674, 1679, 1691, *Over Gates* 1730, *Overgates* 1761, *Short Overgates* 1691, 1773 (*v.* **ofer**[3] 'over, above', used elliptically of '(land) over or across something', *v.* **gata**); *ouerholmes* 1691 (*v.* **ofer**[3], **holmr**); *Partridge Furlong* 1698 (from the surn. *Partridge*, a John *Partridge* was miller of nearby Whissendine in 1814 WR); *le Pingle* 1679 (*v.* **pingel**); *Prestlands* 1674, *Presland* 1698, *Priest Lands* 1742 (*v.* **prēost, land**); *Ravens Crosse* 1667, 1674, *Rauens Crosse* 1698, *Ravenscross* 1742 (if the first el. is a pers.n., then either OE *Hræfn* or Scand *Hrafn*, but *Raven* may be a surn., cf. Hoby Cross in Wardley f.ns. (a)); *Redmiles* 1761 (prob. the surn. *Redmile*, a family which may originally have come from Redmile Lei); *Rimyngton Furlonge* 1611 (from the surn. *Rimmington*, cf. Bottom -, Top Rimmington in neighbouring Langham f.ns. (a), Remington Heath in Greetham f.ns. (a) and Remington Hold Cl in S. Luffenham f.ns. (a)); *Rye furlong* 1665, 1691, 1730, 1746, 1761 (*v.* **ryge**); *le Southfeild* 1691 (*v.* **sūð, feld**); *South Hill* 1665, 1674, 1726, 1746, 1761, 1763, 1773, (*le*) *Southhill* 1667, 1674, 1679 (*v.* **sūð, hyll**); *le*

Spellow 1679, 1691, (*le*) *Spellowfeild* 1679, 1681, 1691, *Spellow Field* 1730, 1742, 1746, 1761 (records a local moot-site; either a Bronze Age barrow surviving near the territorial boundary and used as a convenient meeting place or a mound raised by the Anglo-Saxons specifically as a 'speech-mound', cf. Spellow L, La, Nth, *v.* **spell, hlāw**); *le Stakeyard* 1667 (*v.* **stak-ȝard**); *stubbe furlonge* 1665, *Stub(b) Furlong* 1691, 1702, 1730, 1746, 1761, 1763 (*v.* **stubb**); *le thorn in campo occidentali* 1411 (*v.* **þorn**); *Vppingham Way* 1698 ('(land beside) the road to Uppingham'); *Watergaules* 1674, *Water Galls* 1761 (*v.* **wæter, galla**); *le Wedare furlong* 1698 (*v.* **weðer**); *le West Close* 1723, 1730; *in campo occidentali* 1411, *Campo Occidental' de Barlythorpe* 1674, *le Westfeild* 1674, *West Field* 1742, 1746, 1797 (one of the great open-fields of the village, *v.* **west, feld**); *West lands* 1665 (*v.* **west, land**); *Wheatleas* 1691 (perh. 'wet pasture', since wheat pertains to arable, cf. *le wetlondes* (> *Wheatlands*) in N. Luffenham f.ns. (b), *v.* **wēt**); *Far Wherles* 1665, *Farrwhales* 1679, *Far Whalles* 1691, *hitherwhails, Hither Wharles* 1674, *Hither Walls* 1761, *Whailes Land* 1770, 1773 (poss. *hwerfel* 'a circular or round-topped hill' but the surn. *Wales* cannot be discounted); *Wool Slades* 1746 (perh. dial. *wool* 'thistledown', cf. *Woole Elders* in Bisbrooke f.ns. (b), *v.* **slæd**); *parcell' terr' vocat' le yard roome* 1674 (*v.* **geard, rūm**[1]).

Belton

BELTON

> *Belton(e)* Wm 1 Dugd, 1205 P, 1205 RFinib, 1232 Pat *et passim* to 1295 (p), 1310 *Peake* (p), 1311 *Rut et freq, -tuna* 1080-7 Reg
> *Beleton* 1243 RGros
> *Bealton* 1167 P, *Baealton'* 1205 ib
> *Beuton'* 1244 Fees, 1266 *FF*, 1266 *For*
> *Beautone* c1200 RBE, 1237 Fees
> *Beulton'* 1340 *Peake*

The first theme of the name is obscure. Elements suggests OE **bēl**[1], meaning 'a beacon' in p.ns., but this does not really seem satisfactory in combination with OE **tūn** 'farmstead' and Ekwall NoB xlv 139 wonders if this word appears in any p.ns. discussed by Smith in Elements *s.v.* **bēl**[1]. For detailed treatment of Belton, *v.* Ekwall Studies[2] 159-63 where it is suggested that the element is *bel-* which may be cognate with ON *bil*, Swedish dial. *bil*, Danish dial. *bil*, *boel* 'interval, space'. This word or a derivative *bilan* or the like, Ekwall suggests, might have developed a meaning such as 'open land in a forest' or 'a piece of dry land in a fen'. In the period of the opening up of the west of Rutland, the countryside around Belton would have been heavily wooded. Indeed, the parish was formerly within the bounds of Leighfield Forest. An interpretation 'farmstead on open ground in woodland' would suit the place well, but the idea of a border beacon site next to Wardley (*q.v.*) is also attractive, *v.* **tūn**.

Because of the reorganization of the counties in 1974, the village is now (1991) officially known as 'Belton in Rutland' to distinguish it from Belton Lei.

BIRCHABY (lost), *Burtchbie Sale* 1624 *Deed, Berchby Sale al's Berchby Quarter al's Berchley Laund Sale al's Birchley Coppice* 1677 *ib, Birchby Sale al's Birchley Coppice* 1694 *ib, Birchby Closes* 1729 *Surv, Bruchby Close* e18, 1748 (119) *Whit, Birchby Close, - Meadow* 18 *Surv, Burchaby Close* 1822 (1878) *Whit, Great -, Little Burchaby* 1842 *Asw, Birchaby* 1943 *Map*, perhaps 'farm on land newly broken up for cultivation', *v.* **bryce, bý**. Only minor and field-names represent what may have been a farmstead in cleared woodland on the Rutland border with Lei, *v.* **sale, quarter, launde, copis**. The hybrid OE/Scand formation of the name would not indicate primary Scand settlement and there evidently developed some early confusion with **birce** 'a birch tree' and **lēah** 'a woodland clearing used for pasture or arable'. The only other possible p.n. with Scand **bý** in the county is also at the Rutland boundary, *v.* Hooby Lodge in Stretton.

FINCHLEY BRIDGE, 1801 Map; earlier it is *Fynchefordebrig* 1375 Nichols, *Fynchefordebrigge* 1376 *For*, cf. *Finchesford'* 1227 ClR, *Fincheford* 1266, 1269 *For*, Hy 3 Nichols, *atte brigge* 1377 (p), *atte brugge* 1377 SR (p). Originally 'the ford frequented by finches', *v.* **finc, ford, brycg**. The modern form may be a corruption of the older name, or may represent an undocumented Finchley nearby.

BACKSIDE LANE, *v.* **ba(c)ksyde**. BAPTIST CHAPEL, 1863, 1877 White, 1932 Kelly. BELTON CHURCH, *Church (St Peter)* 1846,

1863, 1877 White, 1932 Kelly. BELTON HO., 1846 White, 1850 Slater, 1863, 1877 White, 1932 Kelly. BLACK HORSE P.H. (lost), 1850 Slater, 1863 White, 1932 Kelly, *Inn called Black Horse* 19 *Whit*, closed c1973 - VR. GRAVEL PIT, cf. *Gravel Pit Furlong* 1786 *Surv*. THE HALL, 1877 White. THE LAMB P.H. (lost), closed a.1880 - VR. LITTLEWORTH, a settlement site which may well be ancient although no early spellings survive. The hamlet appears on the first edition of the Ordnance Survey map of the county of 1824, but no name is attached to it, *v.* lȳtel, worð. A late uncomplimentary nickname is, of course, a possibility. NETHERFIELD HO., 1932 Kelly. THE OLD HALL, 1932 ib. PARKFIELD, (*The*) *Parke Feilde* 1619, 1633 *Terrier*, (*the*) *Park Field* 1733 (119), 1734, 1756, 1756 (119) *Whit*, 1786 *Surv*, 1815 *Whit*, 1943 *Map*, originally one of the great open-fields of the village, *v.* park, feld. THE SUN P.H., 1846, 1863 White. THE VICARAGE, 1846, 1877 ib, 1932 Kelly, cf. *the parsonage* 1619 *Terrier*, *The Parsonage House* 1733 (119), 1734, 1756 (119), 1822 (1878), 1869 *Whit*. WESTBOURNE HO., 1932 Kelly.

Field-Names

Undated forms in (a) are 1943 *Map*. Those dated 1800 (119), 1822 (1878), 1840, 1869, 1871, 1872 and 19 are *Whit*; those of 1842 are *Asw* while 1874 are *Deed*. Those dated 1917 are *Sale* (per Mr D. Tew). Early forms dated 1619 and 1633 are *Terrier*, 1707 are *Deed*, 1730 (119), 1733 (119), 1734, 1748 (119), 1756, 1756 (119), 1793 (1878) and 118 are *Whit*; c1780, 1786 and 18 are *Surv*.

(a) Allen Cl; Back Mdw (*v.* back); Bottom Mdw 1874; Bradley's (named from the local *Bradley* family, cf. James *Bradley* 1932 Kelly); New -, Old Breach Cl 1874, Breach Mdw 1874 (*Breache Furlong* 1619, *Breaches* 1743 *Will*, *Breech Furlong*, *Breech Meadow* 1786, *v.* brēc); Bridge Foot Mdw 1822 (1878), 1869; Bridge Footway 19; Browns Ploughed Fd; Burtin's Cl 1822 (1878), Big Burton's 1943 (*Burton's Close* 1756, 1793 (1878), *Burtons* - 1756 (119)); Cord-hill Mdws 1822 (1878), Cordhill Mdws 1869, - Mdw 19 (*Cawdwell Meadowe* 1619, *Caudle Meadow* 1786, *Caudle Furlong*, *Cadwell Leys* 1786, *v.* cald, wella); Corner Fd; Cricket Fd (referring to the game of cricket); Cuckoo (Mr J. Field notes that *cuckoo* was sometimes used of fields which cropped early); Bottom -, Middle -, Top Endless (perh. a derogatory name for fields where work must go on for ever to get worthwhile returns; but a disguised *-leys* may also be thought of, cf.

Willoughby Waterless < *Waterleys,* Lei 475); Finchleys Cl 1869, Finchley's - 19, Finchley Fd 1943 (*v.* Finchley Bridge *supra*); Fishpond Cl 1871 (cf. *Fishpool Furlong, Fishpools* 1786); (The) Folly 1842, 1871 (*v.* **folie**); Top -, Fourteen Lands, First and Second Fourteen Lands 1943 (a consolidation of fourteen selions of an open-field, *v.* **land**); The Great Mdw 1874; The Great Yard Land 1822 (1878) (1756, 1756 (119), 1793 (1878), *v.* **gerd-landes**); Bottom Greens 1943, Green's Rye Hill 1917; Hollow Corner (Mdw) 1917, Hollow Corners 1943 (*Hollow Corner* 1619, 1633, *v.* **holh, corner**); Home Cl 1917, 1943 (c1780), - Paddock 1917 (*v.* **home**); Hop Yard (*Beneath the hopyard* 1619, *v.* **hop-yard**); Hovel Cl (*v.* **hovel**); Kiln Cl 1822 (1878), 1869, 19 (*Kiln Close Leys* 1786); Lambley Fd (cf. *Lamley Hill* 1619, *Lambley Hill, Lambley hill Furlong, Lambley Leys* 1786, *v.* Lambley Lodge in Leighfield); (the) Lane Mdw 1869, 1872, 19; Langings (*Langlandes* 1619, *Longlandes* 1633, *Langlands* c1780, 1786, *Langlandes Furlonge* 1619, *Langlands Furlong* 1786, *v.* **lang^1, land**); Launde Lees 1917, Lount - 1943 (*Belton Lound* 1344 *For, the Lownt* 1619, *The Lounde* 1633, *The Lount* 18, *Long Lownt* 1619, *- Lounte* 1633, *Upper Long Lount* 1786, *Lount Coppice Meadow* 18, *the Lownt Leies* 1619, *Lownte Leyes* 1633, *Lower -, Upper Lount Leys* 1786, *Lount Pond* 18, *v.* **lundr**); MacTurk's; East Mickling 1800 (119), 1822 (1878), 1869, East Mickling now called the Tithe Mdw 1869, East Mickling or Tithe Mdw 19 (*Est Miklengs* 1684 Wright, *v.* **ēast, mikill, eng**); Middle Cl; Mill Cl 1822 (1878), 1869, 19 (*pro clauso molendini* 1333 *Rental, v.* **myln**); Mill Fd 1822 (1878), 1871, 1943 (*Milne Feild* 1619, *The Milne Feilde* 1633, *Miln Field* 1726 *Terrier, Mill Field* 1786, *v.* **myln, feld**, one of the open-fields of the village); Parsons Leys 1874; Pilleys; Big -, Rialls, Little Rye Hill 1917 (*Rye Hill* 1619, *Upper -, Ryehill Furlong, Ryehill Piece* 1786, *v.* **ryge, hyll, pece**); Rickstead (*Rickstead Close* c1780, *v.* **rickstead** 'a rickyard', occurring also in Braunston f.ns. (b) *s.n. Brackles Reekstead,* in Egleton f.ns. (b) *s.n. Ricksteads fur'* and in Gunthorpe f.ns. (b) *s.n. Gunthorpe rickstede,* all in this hundred. The compound is not listed in K.I. Sandred, *English Place-Names in -stead,* Uppsala 1963); Shawgate Close Pasture 1840 (*Furlong under Shoulgate Hedge* 1786); Spring Cl (c1780), Spring Mdw 1871 (*v.* **spring**); Stonepit Leas (*Stone Pit Leys* c1780, 1786); Sturrock's Nooks (*Stirwood* 1610 Speed, *Steerwood* 1684 Wright, *the Stirwode syde* 1619, *Stirwood close* 1616 Deed, *Stirwood Leyes* 1619, *Lower -, Upper Stirwood, Upper Stirwood Meadow* 18 Surv, *Stirwood Nook* 1786, *Stir Close Nook, Stirs Close* c1780, 'wood subject to regulation and/or to penalties', *v.* **stȳr, wudu, lēah, nōk**); (the) Swarth Mdw 1822 (1878), 1869, 1871, 19 (*Swath Meadow, - Furlong* 1786, *v.* **swǣð**); Big -, Little Swingler's (named from the *Swingler* family, cf. Albert *Swingler* 1932 Kelly); Tithe Mdw 1822 (1878), 1869, 1871, 19 (*the Tyth(e) Meadow* 1733 (119), 1756, 1756 (119), *the Tithe Meadow* 1793 (1878), *v.* **tēoða**); Turner's Home Cl, Turner's Mdw (from the surn. *Turner,* cf. John and

Robert *Turner* 1932 Kelly, graziers in Belton); Turnpike Fd (adjoins a lane to the main road to Uppingham); Tuth Leys 1822 (1878) (poss. from a surn., cf. Alexander *Tyth* 1524 SR of Barrowden, *v.* lêah); Westfield 1871 ((*The*) *West Feilde* 1619, 1633, *West Field* 1726 *Terrier*, 1786, one of the old open-fields of the village); Williamson's Wood Cl 1917 (cf. George Henry *Williamson* 1932 Kelly, grazier in Belton); Windmill Hill; Walter Wright's, Wright's Plough Fd.

(b) *Allaxton Brooke* 1619, *Allexton Milne Holmes* 1633 (Allexton Lei adjoins to the south, beyond Eye Brook which forms the county boundary, *v.* brôc, myln, holmr); *Ash(e)gate* 1610 Speed (*v.* æsc, gata); *Ashslade Ford, Ashslade Furlong* 1786 (*v.* æsc, slæd); *Banner's Piece* 1786 (*v.* pece); *Barrowe Hill* 1619 (*v.* beorg, prob. referring to a burial mound since Ru hill-names with *barrow* occur principally on the county boundary); *Beebies Baulk(e)* 1619 (named from Henry *Beebie* of Belton 1619, *v.* balca); *Blakroodes* 1619, *Blackroods Piece, Lower -, Middle -, Upper Blackroods Furlong* 1786 (*v.* blæc, rōd³, pece); *Bondesmore* 1619, *Boundesmoore* 1633 (from the surn. *Bonds/Bounds, v.* mōr¹); *Brakehill Furlonge* 1619, *Brakhill* - 1633, *Brakehill Furlong* 1786 (*v.* brǣc¹, hyll); *Brendegate* 1371 IpmR ('road to the place cleared by burning', *v.* brende¹, gata); *Brockholes Furlonge* 1619 (*v.* brocc-hol); *Brown's Close* c1780, 1786, *Brown's Orchard* 1786; *Butthedge Furlong, Long Butt Furlong, Lower Butt Furlong* 1786 (*v.* butte, hecg); *Callywell* 1619 (*v.* calu, wella); *Cannons Close* 1707; *Cherrytree Close* c1780, 1786; *Clipston Bushe* 1619, *Clipston's Bush, - Furlong, Upper Clipstons Bush Furlong* 1786 (prob. with the surn. *Clipston* and referring to scrubland, *v.* busc); *Coppice Leys* c1780 (*v.* copis, lêah); *Crabtree Furlonge* 1619 (*v.* crabtre); *Crosegate Furlonge* 1619 (*v.* cros, gata, cf. Hoby Cross in neighbouring Wardley f.ns. (a)); *Deadmoore furlong(e)* 1619, 1633 ('(furlong beside) the infertile moorland', *v.* dêad, mōr¹); *Dogkennell Furlong* 1786 (*v.* dogge-kenel); *Dovecoat Close* 1756, 1756 (119) (*v.* dove-cot(e)); *Dudsemoore Furlong* 1619 (prob. the same name as *Deadmoore supra*, cf. Dodmore in Greetham f.ns. (a)); *Fair Ash Close* 1685 *Terrier, Flemings Land* 1756 (119) (from the surn. *Fleming*); *the Forrest hedge* 1619 (alluding to the boundary of Leighfield Forest, *v.* forest, hecg); *Fulwell* 1786, *Fullwell Sick* 1619, *Fulwellseek* 1786 (*v.* fûl, wella, sîk); *The Furres Leies* 1619, *The Furres Peice* 1619, *The Furze, Furze Furlong* 1786 (*v.* fyrs, lêah, pece); *The Glebe Lands* 1733 (119) (*v.* glebe); *Godfreyes headland* 1619 (held by William *Godfrey* 1619, *v.* hêafod-land); *Gotsholme furlonge* 1633 (poss. from the surn. *Gott, v.* holmr); *Griffins Yard Land* 1733 (119), 1756, 1756 (119) (from the surn. *Griffin, v.* gerd-landes); *Grinley -, Grynley Corner, Grinley Leyes or Rye Hill, Grinley Sicke* 1619 ('green woodland grove', *v.* grêne¹, lêah, corner, sîk, cf. *Greenly Road* in Leighfield f.ns. (b)); *the haies* 1619 (*v.* (ge)hæg); *Haslewoods Lands or the Old Yard Lands* 1756, 1756 (119) (from the family name of Thomas *Haselwood* (died

1559), whose son Thomas was one-time keeper of Leighfield Forest (VCH 2 28), cf. *Thomas Hayslewood* of Belton 1619, *v.* **gerd-landes**); *hillie meadowe* 1619, *Hilles meadow* 1633; *Hilton Leys* 1786 (*v.* **lēah**); *Holegate furlong* 1633, *Hogate Furlong* 1786 (*v.* **hol²**, **gata**); *ye holme* 1726 *Terrier, the Holmes* 1730 (119), *the Holme* 1786 (*v.* **holmr**); *Hoose Piece* 1786 (*v.* **hūs, pece**); *Under Innammes* 1619 (*v.* **innām**); *Lammas Close* c1780, 1786 (*v.* **lammas**); *Langmeadowe* 1619, *Lang Meadow* 1786, *Langmeadow doles* 1619 (*v.* **lang¹, mǣd, dāl**); *Lugmoor* 1786 (the first el. is perh. *lug* in its late dial. sense 'a projection, a protuberance' and indicating a small stretch of moorland at the edge of the parish, *v.* **mōr¹**); *Maple stubbe* 1633 (*v.* **mapel, stubb**); *Midle -, Over -, Neather Micle Hill* 1619, *Midle muckle hill, Overmicle hill, Nether micle hill* 1633, *Middle -, Upper Micklehill* 1786 (*v.* **micel, mikill, hyll, middel, uferra, neoðera**); *Midle Furlong* 1619, *Middle - 1786* (*v.* **middel**); *Mill Holmes* 1756, 1756 (119), *Mill Leys* 1786 (*v.* **myin, holmr, lēah**); *Muncks hill Baulke* 1619 (*v.* Monks Hill in Wardley f.ns. (a) and **balca**); *Near Wood Leys* 1786 (*v.* **lēah**); *Neatherd Close* 1734 (*v.* **neetherd**); *Needhams Farm House* 1733 (119), 1756, 1756 (119) (with the surn. *Needham*); *neither closse* 1619, *Nether Close* 1638 *Deed,* 1786, *the Neather Close* 1733 (119), 1734, *the Neither meadowe* 1619, *Neather Middowe* 1633, *ye neather meadow* 1726 *Terrier* (*v.* **neoðera**); *Newton's Fountain* 1786; *Under Norgat hedge* 1619, *Norgate Hedge* 1633, *Northgate Hedge, North Gate Hedge Leys* 1786 (*v.* **norð, gata, hecg, lēah**); *Ogdens Half Yard Land* 1733 (119), 1756, 1756 (119) (from the family name of John *Ogden* of Belton 1619, *v.* **gerd-landes**); *The Old Yard Lands* 1756, 1756 (119) (*v. Haslewoods Lands supra*); *The Orchard* c1780, 1786; *the parke baulke* 1619, *Park Balk Furlong* 1786, *Park Close* 1748 (119), 118, Parkhill Furlong 1786, *the parke sick* 1619, *The Park sike* 1633, *Parkseek, Park Seek* 1786 (cf. Parkfield *supra, v.* **balca, sīk**); *The Parlour* 1786 (*v.* **parlur**); *the parsonage hedge* 1619, *the parsonage land, the personage land* 1619 (cf. The Vicarage *supra, v.* **personage**); *Pool Close* 1786, *Pool's Close* c1780; *Pounce Pits* 1786 (perh. *pounce* 'a hole cut out for the purposes of decoration', fancifully applied to a group of small excavations; otherwise, pits for the extraction of clay for the manufacture of *pounce*, a powder used in preparing parchment); *Edmund Reeves Landes* 1619; *Respas Springe* 1619, 1633, *Respas Leyes* 1619, *Raspberry Spring Furlong, Raspberry Spring Leys* 1786 ('the spring where raspberries grow', *v.* **respas, spring, lēah**); *Reynold's Furlong* 1786 (from the surn. *Reynold(s)*); *the Sandpitt* 1619 (*v.* **sand-pytt**); *Shafts Furlong* 1786 (from the surn. *Shaft*); *Sharpes Furlonge* 1619 (from the surn. *Sharp(e)*); *Sills Mill Furlong* 1786 (from the surn. *Sill(s)*); *the Slash* 1756, 1756 (119) (*v.* **slash**); *Smear Hill* c1780, *Smeerhill Furlong* 1786 (*v.* **smeoru, hyll**); *Smith's Gate Furlong* 1786; *Stilton meadowe, Stilton meadow doles* 1619 (*v.* **dāl**), *Stiltons Way* 1633, *Over Stiltonway* 1786 (poss. *Stilton* was the name of an early farmstead since the f.n. *Stiltons* (1539) also occurs in neighbouring Loddington Lei, but such an identification is uncertain since late spellings with *St-* occur for Tilton (on the Hill) Lei which also borders Loddington and lies five miles to the north-west of Belton); *Taylors Close* 1786; *William Thompsons baulk* 1619 (*v.* **balca**); *John Tokeyes headland* 1619 (*v.* **hēafod-land**, cf. Jane *Toky* 1522 MilS and Henry *Tokey* 1524 SR, both of Seaton); *Townsend Leys* 1786 (*v.* **tūn, ende**[1], **lēah**); *Twopenny Lands Furlong* 1786 (prob. alluding to a twopenny rent, *v.* **land**); *Under Endhams Furlong* 1786; *Upper Furlong* 1786; *Upper Meadow* 1786; *Walkers half yard Land* 1786 (*v.* **gerd-landes**); *Watermill* 1628 *Deed* (*v.* **water-mylne**, cf. *Allexton Milne Holmes supra*); *Websters Leies and Landes* 1619, *Websters Laeyes* 1633 (from the surn. *Webster*, *v.* **lēah, land**); *the west Brooke* 1619 (referring to Eye Brook, *q.v.*); *West Sickes Furlonge* 1619, *West seek Leys* 1786 (*v.* **west, sīk, lēah**).

Braunston

BRAUNSTON
Branteston(e) 1167 P, 1201 Ass, 1203 *FF et passim* to 1218
    Abbr, 1304 *For*
Braunteston 1256, 1263 *For et passim* to 1299 For
Braundeston' 1231 RegAnt, 1277 Pat, 1311 *FF*, 1327 *SR et*
    passim to 1410 Cl
Braunston' 1300 Ipm, 1301 Cl *et passim* to 1352 *Finch*, 1359
    ELiW *et freq*
Braunson 1566 FF, *Brawnson* 1566 AAS

'Brant's farm', *v.* **tūn**, cf. Branston Lei and Braunstone Lei. The pers.n. *Brant* is OE. Spellings in *au* are due to AN influence.

THE WISP, *Wisp* 1218 Nichols, 1227 ClR, 1266 *For*, 1269 For, Hy 3 Nichols, *le Wysp(e)* 1256 *For*, 1375 Nichols, *le Whipse* 1373 *For, le Wysbe* 1376 ib, *le Wispe* 1611 SP, *The Wisp(e)* 1610 Speed, 1684 Wright, 1780, 1801 Map, 'the thicket or the brushwood', *v.* **wisp**. OE *wisp, wips* 'a wisp' was most likely used topographically in an extended sense such as 'thicket, brushwood', cf. WFris *wisp* 'a twig'.

BLUE BALL P.H., 1846, 1863 White, *Blue Bell* 1877 ib.

BRAUNSTON CHURCH, *Church* (*All Saints*) 1846, 1863, 1877 ib, 1932 Kelly; on an ancient religious site, to judge from the surviving monolithic figure of the Celtic or Romano-British mother goddess now preserved beside the church tower. BROOKE HOUSE FM is *Brooke House* 1932 ib. CEDAR ST. CHAPTER FM, 1932 ib, once belonged to the Dean and *Chapter* of Lincoln Cathedral, patrons of the living, *v.* VCH 2 36. CHESELDYNE HO. is *Cheseldyne Farm* 1604 VCH, *Cheseldyne House* 1932 Kelly. The *Cheseldine* family is associated with Braunston as early as Robert *Chesilden* 1392 Cl. A memorial brass to Kenelm *Cheselden* (died 1596) is in the parish church. CHESTNUT FM, 1932 Kelly. CHURCH ST. THE ELMS. THE GREEN (local), *v.* grēne². GREEN LANE (local). HIGH HO., cf. *the High Hall* 1682 *Deed, High Hall farm* 1682 *ib.* HIGH ST. MANOR HO., 1846, 1863, 1877 White. OLD LEICESTER LANE (local), 1935 VCH, *Leicester Lane* 1913 *Sale.* OLD PLOUGH P.H., *Plough* 1846, 1863 White, *Old Plough Inn* 1932 Kelly. PACEY'S LODGE (BRAUNSTON LODGE 2½"). RATTS LANE (local) is named from George *Ratt,* baker - VR; cf. the f.n. *George Rats* 1943 *Map.* SOUTH LODGE FM (BRAUNSTON SOUTH LODGE 2½") is *Braunston Lodge* 1824 O, 1846 White. THE VICARAGE. WOOD LANE.

Field-Names

Undated forms in (a) are 1943 *Map.* Forms dated 1807 are *EnclA*; those dated 1797, 1822, 1860, 1868 are *Deed.* 1913 are *Sale* and 1925 are *Deed* (both per Mr D. Tew). Undated forms in (b) are 1682 *Terrier.* Those dated 1622 are *AddRoll,* 1627 are Moulton, 1725 are *Hotchkin* and 1726 are *Asw.*

(a) Five -, Six -, Seven -, The Eight -, Nine -, The Sixteen Acre (*v.* æcer); Angel Hill; The Ashes 1925, Ashes 1943 (*at ye Ashes* 1682, *v.* æsc); Bargate Hill (*Barkett hill* 1682, cf. *Berkett Sale* 1677, 1694 *Deed,* Angl *bercet* 'a birch copse', *v.* bercet, sale); Back Barn Cl 1913, 1943, - Mdw 1913, Front Barn Cl 1913, Back -, Barn Fd 1943; Beadman's, - Poultry Fm (named from the *Beadman* family, cf. George *Beadman* 1932 Kelly, grazier in Braunston); Bob's (Bob Atton) (naming three adjacent closes; the alternative explanatory f.n. contains the local surn. *Atton,* cf. Edward, Luke and Mark *Atton* 1932 Kelly, graziers in Braunston and note also Robert Edward *Atton* 1932 ib, grazier in Brooke); Bridge Cl; The

Brinks (*ye Brinkes* 1682, *v.* **brink**); Burley View (referring to Burley on the Hill); Church Headlands (*ye Church headland* 1682, *the Church hadland* 1726, *v.* **hēafod-land**); Clover Fd; Colley Seek (*Colly Seeke* 1682, *Collis Sike* 1726, *v.* **sīk**); Cooper's, - Glebe (cf. Coopers Cl in neighbouring Brooke f.ns. (a), *v.* **glebe**); The Cottages; 1st -, 2nd -, 3rd Cow Fd; Cundict (Mr J. Field notes that the close is near to Oakham waterworks, *v.* **cundite**); Dickman's (the surn. *Dickman*, cf. Robert *Dickman*, husbandman, 1522 MilS, - *Dykman* 1524 SR); Bottom Dry Slight, Top Dryslight (*v.* **drȳge, slæget**); 1st -, 2nd -, 3rd Fast's; Feeding Fd (grazing ground, pasturage, *v.* **feeding**); Field Premises 1913; Fleet Mdw 1868, - Mdws 1943 (a stream flows through the field, *v.* **flēot**); Little Flitteris Cl, Great Flitteris Mdw 1913 (cf. *Fleetris feild* 1622, *Flittris Field* 1682, *Flitteris Feild* 1726, one of the open-fields of the village, *v.* Flitteris Park); Harry Freeman's (cf. *Harry Freeman* 1932 Kelly); Guide Post (Mr J. Field observes that this field is at a road junction); High Mdw 1822, 1860, 1943 (1797); Back of the Hill; Hills, Hill's Fd (named from the family of John *Hill* 1932 Kelly, grazier in Braunston); 1st -, 2nd Hog's Hole (*Hogshole* 1682, *v.* **hogg, hol**[1]); Home Cl, - Fd (*v.* **home**); Horse Cl; Inholmes 1807, Innems 1943 (*v.* **innām**); Kington (prob. a surn.); 1st -, 2nd Leas (*v.* **lēah**); Lewin's (cf. George *Lewin* 1910 OR of neighbouring Oakham and Lewin's in Oakham f.ns. (a)); Little Mdw; Merrill's (a surn., cf. William *Meryell*, husbandman, 1524 SR); Middle Fd 1807, 1943 (1797); Big Needham's (from the surn. *Needham*, cf. *Needhams Farm House* in nearby Belton f.ns. (b) and Roland *Needham* 1932 Kelly of Oakham); Nether Fd 1807, Grass Neither Fd 1943 (*Neather Field* 1682, *the Neather Feild* 1726, *v.* **neoðera**; originally one of the open-fields of the village); None Stalls (*Nunstalls* 1682; poss. alluding to a possession of a nunnery; there is fragmentary evidence for a foundation for Cistercian nuns at Tinwell, cf. *Nunesland* in Exton f.ns. (b), *v.* **nunne, stall**); Norton's (named from the local *Norton* family, cf. Arthur *Norton* 1932 Kelly); Ox Liver (so called from its triangular shape); Padfields (prob. 'fields where toads abound', *v.* **padde**, cf. Padholme in neighbouring Brooke f.ns. (a)); Nether Ploughed Fd; Pond Lane Mdw 1913; Pond Wheat Cl 1913; Rawson (named from the family of Fred *Rawson* 1932 Kelly); Roadley's Cl, - Mdw 1913, Roadley's 1943; 2nd Roberts; Robinson's Top Cl; Round Fd (Mr J. Field notes that this is now rectangular); Seed Acre, - Cl, Big -, Great Seeds (areas of sown grass, *v.* **sǣd**); The Seek (*v.* **sīk**); Simpson's (named from the local *Simpson* family, cf. George *Simpson* 1932 Kelly); Slip ('a narrow strip of land', *v.* **slipe**); Sluice; South Fd, - Mdw; Spinney Fds; Springwell Cl 1913 (*v.* **spring, wella**); Stonepit (Cl); Top Cl; Wallends; The Warrens (*v.* **wareine**); Middle West Cl 1913; The Whisp Land 1932 Kelly, Big Wisp 1943 (*v.* The Wisp *supra*; Mr J. Field notes that this was sixteen acres of land, for the common good of all freeholders having common rights, and for the maintenance of a preacher); Big -, Bottom Wilson's (named from the *Wilson* family, cf. *Bernard Wilson* 1932 Kelly); Wood Fd 1807, Woodfield 1860 (*Wood Field* 1682, *Woodfeild* 1726, one of the open-fields of the village, v. **wudu, feld**).

(b) *Arme Strong Sheepcoate* (from the surn. *Armstrong*, cf. *Robert Armystrong* 1522 MilS of neighbouring Oakham, v. **scēap-cot**); *Barlythorpe way* ('the road to Barleythorpe', v. **weg**); *Bastarde close* 1627 (*bastard* often alludes to abnormal shape although dial. *bastard* means 'unproductive, poor, barren' as in Bastard Leys in Edith Weston f.ns. (a)); *George Bates's Backside* 1726 (v. **ba(c)ksyde**); *Beckwellston* (v. **bekkr, wella**; the final el. appears to be OE *stān* 'a stone' rather than *tūn* 'farmstead'); *Brackendale* 1682, *Bracken Dale* 1726 (v. **brakni**; the generic is either **dalr** or **deill**); *Brackles Reekstead* (v. **rickstead** and Rickstead in Belton f.ns. (a)); *Braunston high meadow* 1684 Wright (v. **hēah**[1], **mǣd**); *ye Brooke* (v. **brōc**); *Broxabush* (v. **busc**); *Butt furlong* 1726 (v. **butte**); *Cathole* (v. **cat(t), hol**[1]); *Mr Chiseldines Sike*, - *Wong* (v. **sik, vangr** and Cheseldyne Ho. supra); *Cobdale furlong* (v. **cobb(e)**; the generic is either **dalr** or **deill**); *Codslane end* (perh. from the surn. *Codd*, v. **lane, ende**[1]); *Cowpitt* (v. **col-pytt**); *Crofte Hill Close* 1627 (v. **croft**); *Dovecoate Close alias Dovecoate Yard* 1726 (v. **dove-cot(e)**); *Forest Close* 1725 (alluding to Leighfield . Forest); *in quodam venella in Braunston vocat' Fosters* 1622 (v. **lane**); *Fouldhill* (v. **fald, hyll**); *atte Hall de Braunston* 1305 OSurv (p), *atte Halle* 1300 Ipm (p), Edw 3 *Rental* (p) (v. **hall**); *Ingsdale* 1726, *Ingsdale Hill* 1682, 1726, *Ingsdale Sike* 1682 (poss. with a much reduced Scand pers.n. in Ing- such as *Ingvarr* (cf. .*Ingersdale* in Empingham f.ns. (b)), but ON *eng* 'meadow, pasture' cannot be discounted; the generic is either **dalr** or **deill**, v. **sik**); *Knoston way* 1682, 1726 (the road to Knossington Lei, v. **weg**); *Leasewell Seeke* (v. **lǣs, wella, sik**); *Little dale* (with either **dalr** or **deill**, v. **lytel**); *Loscoat(e)s* (cf. *Loscott sale* in neighbouring Leighfield f.ns. (b) and Losecoat Field in Empingham, v. **hlōse, cot**); *the Mill* 1726; *Millam Bridg* 1682 (v. **myln, hamm, brycg**); *Morehead* (v. **mōr**[1], **hēafod**); *Netherborrowes* (prob. recording a prehistoric burial mound or mounds, v. **beorg**); *Nuthatch* (v. **hnutu, hæc(c)**); *Oakeham Ridgg, Oakham Rigg* ('the ridge towards Oakham', v. **hrycg**); *Okestead Close* 1725 (v. **āc, stede**); *Orton Gate* 1682, 1726 (the road to Cold Overton Lei, v. **gata**); *Parsonage Close, the Parsonage Piece* (v. **personage, pece**); *Pocket Piece* (v. **poket, pece**); *Porters wong* (from the surn. *Porter*, v. **vangr**); *Quintrey lane* 1726 (poss. a scurrilous name for a lovers' lane, from ME *queinte, quaynte* 'the female pudendum', with the ME substantive-forming suffix -*erie* in its force 'that which is characteristic of, all that is connected with', used commonly with contemptuous implication, cf. Quaintery Way Db 652; related forms are *Quaintree Hall* a.1835, *The Quaintrees* 1835-97 (now The Quaintree Hall House)); *Rancksborough Hill* 1726 (v. Ranksborough Hill in Langham); *Randale Baulke* (the first el. is either OE **răn** 'a boundary strip' or OE **rand** 'an edge, a border' with Scand **dalr** or **deill**, v. **balca**); *Ranglands* (v. **wrang, vrangr, land**); *Redespires* 1373 *For* ('the reed-bed(s)', v. **hrēod, spīr**); *Rhode Sike* 1726 (v. **rod**[1], **sīk**); *Sinderlands* ('land set apart for some special purpose, detached land', v. **sundor-land**); *Smallhill* (v. **smæl, hyll**); *Thurn dike* (v. **þyrne, dīk**); *The Tith Barne and Close* (v. **tēoða**); *Whitthele* 1300 *DC*, *Whithill* 1682, *White Hill* 1726 (v. **hwīt, hyll**); *Windmill* (v. **wind-mylne**; there is a poss. mill-mound at SK 837 072 just to the north of the road to Oakham, v. MER 10); *Wispp way* ('the road to The Wisp', v. **weg** and The Wisp *supra*); *Woodstyle Close* 1627 (v. **wudu, stigel**).

Brooke

BROOKE

> *Broc* 1176 (p), 1177 P (p), 1190 *CartAnt et passim* to 1202 Ass *et freq* to 1236 Fees, 1298 *Peake* (p)
> *Brok(e)* 1242, 1248 RGros *et passim* to 1290 *For*, 1296 (p), 1306 *Peake* (p) *et freq* to 1551 Pat
> *Brook(e)* 1375 *Peake* (p), Edw 3 *Rental* (p), 1410 PRep, 1607 LML, 1610 Speed

'The brook', v. **brōc**. The name refers to the upper reaches of R. Gwash.

AMERICA LODGE (BROOKE LODGE 2½"), *Lodge* 1877 White, named America Lodge in 1900 - VR. This is a 'remoteness' name, indicating a site near to the parish boundary. BRIDGE FM. BROOKE CHURCH, *Church* (*St Peter*) 1846, 1863, 1877 White. BROOKE HALL, 1685 *Anc*, 1824 O, v. **hall**. BROOKE LODGE WEST. BROOKE MILL, 1824 ib, *Brookmyll* 1389 Pat, *Brook Mill* 1684 Wright, v. **myln**. The windmill mound, with traces of the mill which was burned down in the 19th century, is sited in the small spinney at SK 853 070, v. MER 10. BROOKE PRIORY, *Priory* 1846, 1863 White, cf. *Priory Farm* 1877 ib. The original Brooke Priory was a house of Augustinian Canons founded a.1153. THE BUNGALOW, 1932 Kelly. HIBBITS LODGE. HOLLYTREE COTTAGE. HOME FM, (v. **home**). PRIOR'S COPPICE, *Pryors Copyce* 1611 SP, *Brooke Wood or Priors Copy* 1806 Map, *Priors Coppice* 1772, 1785, 1841, 1920 *Anc*, v. **prior, copis**. The coppice evidently once belonged to the Prior of Brooke. RECTORY FM. SHORNE HILL, at the head of a stream which flows into R. Chater; possibly from OE *scearn* 'dung, muck', alluding to wet ground. TOWN PARK (local), 1943 *Map*, *Brooke Parke* 1685 *Anc*, *The Park* 1840 *TA*, v. tūn, park.

Field-Names

Undated forms in (a) are 1840 *TA*; those dated 1943 are *Map*. Early forms dated 1744, 1749, c1780 and 1787 are *Terrier*. (All forms from *Terrier* extracted by Mr G.A. Chinnery.)

(a) 3 -, 4 Acre (x2), 5 -, 7 -, 8 Acre (x3), 9 Acre (x2), (Far) 10 Acre, Middle 14 Acre, 17 Acre 1943 (v. æcer); Acre Aston Dale 1943 (v. deill, found frequently in this parish); Big Dale 1943 (v. deill); Black Acres 1943; Bottom Fd 1943; Boyers Nook (from the surn. *Boyer*, v. nōk); Bramton Piece (poss. with the surn. *Brampton*, cf. John *Brampton* 1522 MilS of Barrowden, v. pece, frequent in this parish); Burkes Mdw (from the surn. *Burke*); Bush Cl 1840, Bushy - 1943; Cindrell 1943 (poss. a late form of Cinderhill, v. sinder); Common Cl; Cookes Cl; Coopers Cl (from the surn. *Cooper*, cf. Cooper's, - Glebe in neighbouring Braunston f.ns. (a)); Corner Cl; Coundries Cl; Bottom -, Top Cunnington 1943; High -, Low Dale, Great -, Dales Cl (v. deill); Double Long Cl; Fant's Dale 1943 (from the surn. *Fant*, v. deill); Fishpond Park 1943, Fishpond Fourteen Acre 1943; Gorse Cl 1943 (v. gorst); Gunthorpe Cl, - Mdw (Gunthorpe parish adjoins to the east); High Fd, - Mdw; Hoe Bank; Home Cl (x3) (v. home); Homestead (v. hām-stede); Great Horn Cl; Hutton Mdw 1943; Johnson Cl; Knoll 1943 (v. cnoll); Land Cl (1744, 1749, c1780, 1787, consolidating selions of a former open-field, v. land); Nether Langley Cl; Long Cl (x2); Long -, Little Mdw; First -, Meadow Cl, Meadow Cls; Merrall's Fd 1943 (from the surn. *Merrill*, cf. William *Meryell* 1524 SR of Braunston); Great -, Merrimans Platt, (Nether -, Upper -) Merrymans (from the surn. *Merriman*, cf. Merriman's in Exton f.ns. (a), v. plat^2); Middle Fd 1943; Mill Cl, Great -, Little Mill Fd 1840, Mill Fd or Bottom High Fd 1943, Mill Field Mdw, Mill Piece, Next Mill Piece (v. pece), Mill Road 1840 (v. Brooke Mill *supra*); Nether Ground (Mdw); New Fd; New Platt Piece (v. plat^2, pece); Oakham Side (*Okeham side* 1685 *Anc*; Oakham parish adjoins to the north, v. sīde); Old Fourteen Acre 1943; Old Home Cl (v. home); Old Plough Cl 1943; Ox Piece (x2) (v. oxa, pece); Padholme (v. padde, holmr, cf. Padfields in Braunston f.ns. (a)); Bottom Palmer's 1943 (from the surn. *Palmer*, cf. Palmers Mdw in neighbouring Leighfield f.ns. (a)); Park Mdw, -

Piece (v. **pece** and Town Park *supra*); The Pasture (1787), Pasture Cl (x2) (1744,
1749, c1780), Pasture Piece (v. **pece**); Other Pasture; Pen Mdw 1943; Pingles
(*the pingel* 1787, v. **pingel**); East -, Far -, Nether -, Upper - (x2), West Platt,
Middle Platt and High Oak 1840, (Big -, Lane -) Platts 1943 (v. **plat**^{2});
Ploughed Dales (v. **deill**); New Ploughed Fd; Great Pond Cl (cf. *the Pond
Ground* 1685 *Anc*, v. **ponde, grund**); Rawson's Dale 1943 (v. **deill**, cf. Fred
Rawson 1932 Kelly of Braunston); Part of Red Deer Park, Park Platt (*Red deere
parke* 1685 *Anc*, v. **park, plat**^{2}, evidently separate from Town Park *supra*);
Robinson's Dale (v. **deill**, cf. Robinson's Top Cl in neighbouring Braunston f.ns.
(a)); Rough Dale 1943 (v. **rūh**^{1}, **deill**); Round Piece (v. **pece**); Side Fd 1943,
Side Mdw 1840; Sleath Lane 1943 (perh. from the surn. *Sleath*, cf. Sleath's in
Oakham f.ns. (a)); Sweet Leys 1943 (a complimentary name, v. **lēah**); Thorpes
Mdw (both Gunthorpe and Martinsthorpe adjoin to the east); Top Fd 1943;
Twitch Hill 1943 (v. Twitch Hill Fm in Ridlington); Little -, Middle Wards,
(Great -, Little -) Wards Cl, Wards Great Cl, Wards West Cl (from the surn.
Ward, cf. Thomas *Ward* 1522 MilS, 1524 SR and William *Ward* 1524 ib of
Brooke); Whitehall Cl; Wolney Cl.

(b) *Brok close* 1530 LWills (v. **clos(e)**); *Brokefeld'* 1484 *MR* (v. **feld**); *capell'
de Brok'* 1276 *ib* (v. **chapel(e)**); *grangea de Brok* 1276 *ib* (v. **grange**); *Oxe livers*
1687 *Anc* (so called from its triangular shape, cf. Ox Liver in neighbouring
Braunston f.ns. (a)); *the Parke Pale* 1682 *Deed* (v. **pale**, cf. Town Park and (Part
of) Red Deer Park *supra*); The Wood Close 1744, 1787 (v. **wudu**); *Woods Close*
1749, c1780.

Clipsham

Clipsham is a detached parish of Oakham Soke Hundred, lying
between Alstoe Hundred and East Hundred in the north-east of the
county.

CLIPSHAM
    Ky-, Kilpesham 1203 *FF*, 1203 Cur *et passim* to 1225 ib *et freq*
        to 1327 Pat *et passim* to 1375 *Peake*, Edw 3 *Rental,*
        Kilpisham 1268 Abbr, 1275 RGrav *et passim* to 1316 FA,
        Kylpysham 1458 Pat
    Chylpesham 1266 *For*
    Ky-, Kilpsham 1254 Val, 1327 Banco *et passim* to 1377 *Peake,*
        1385 Cl
    Clipesham 1286 *Ass*, *Cly-, 'Clippesham* 1346 FA, 1416 *Wyg*, 1428

FA, *Clipisham* 1471, 1472 Pat
Cly-, Clipsham 1329, 1337 Pat, 1366 *LCh et passim*

Perhaps 'Cylp's village or estate', *v.* **hām.** The first element appears to be an unrecorded OE pers.n. *Cylp,* possibly a by-name related to Norw *kylp* 'a small sturdy fellow'. Clipsham is one of a series of early Anglo-Saxon place-names in **hām** related to the earlier pattern of Romano-British settlements and routeways. The Roman villa site in the parish has produced late Roman military metalwork which has been associated with Germanic *foederati,* as well as so-called Romano-Saxon pottery, *v.* BrownArchSites 6.

ADDAH WOOD, 1687 *Map,* 1838 *TA, Adder Wood* 1824 O, cf. *Adowe* 1627 *Bir.* BIDWELL'S LODGE, cf. *East -, West Bidwell* 1687 *Map, Bidwell* 1838 *TA,* probably 'a spring or well provided with a (drinking) vessel or tub', *v.* **byden, wella** and *Nomina* 12, 123-30, cf. Lt. Bidwell in N. Luffenham f.ns (a). BRADLEY FISH POND, BRADLEY LANE, cf. *Addah -, Bytham -, East -, North -, West Bradly* 1687 *Map, Bradley* 1838 *TA,* 1943 *Map, Addah -, Six Acres -, Ploughed -, Twelve Acres -, Fourteen Acres Bradley* 1838 *TA, v.* **brād, lēah;** for *Addah Bradl(e)y,* cf. Addah Wood *supra,* while *Bytham Bradly* alludes to Castle Bytham L which adjoins Clipsham to the north-east. CLIPSHAM CHURCH, *Church (St Mary)* 1846, 1863, 1877 White, cf. *Kyrkelane* 1553 Pat, *v.* **kirkja, lane.** CLIPSHAM HALL, 1932 Kelly, *The Hall* 1846, 1863, 1877 White. It is *Mannor House* 1688 *Map, v.* **maner.** CLIPSHAM LODGE, 1824 O. CLIPSHAM PARK, *The Park* 1687 *Map,* 1838 *TA, v.* **park.** CLIPSHAM PARK WOOD is *Nordwude, Norewode* 1227 RHug, *North Wood* 1687 *Map, Clipsham Wood* c1800, 1806 Map, *Clipsham North Wood* 1824 O, *Park Wood or North Wood* 1838 *TA, Clipsham Park Wood* 1943 *Map, v.* **norð, wudu.** COW CLOSE PLANTATION, *Cow Close* 1687 *Map, Bottom -, Top Cow Close* 1838 *TA, v.* **cū, clos(e).** LITTLE PITS WOOD, cf. *The Pits* c1800 Map, *Pit House* c1800, 1806 ib. MOOR PLANTATION, cf. *The Moors* 1687 *Map, v.* **mōr**[1]. NEW QUARRY FM. OLD QUARRY FM, *The Quarries* 1687 *ib, Clipsham Quarries* 1824 O, *Old Quarry Piece* 1838 *TA, v.* **quarriere.** OLIVE BRANCH P.H., 1846, 1863, 1877 White. OSBONALL WOOD, 1687 *Map,* 1824 O, 1838 *TA, Osburneall Wood* 1610 Speed bis, *Osburnall Wood* 1610 ib: the first

el. is either the OScand pers.n. *Ásbjǫrn* which appears in late OE
as *Ōsbern*, or its ME reflex *Osbern*. THE RECTORY, 1877 White,
Rectory House 1846, 1863 ib. Its predecessor was *Parsonage* 1688
Map, v. MER 12-13. WESTERN FM.

Field-Names

Undated forms in (a) are 1943 *Map;* those dated 1838 are *TA.* Undated forms
in (b) are 1687 *Map;* forms dated 1553 are Pat and those of 1688 are *Map.*

(a) The Two Acres 1838, 2 Acres 1943; 3 Acres; 6 Acre (x2); The Seven
Acres (x2) 1838; The Eight Acres 1838, 8 Acre 1943; 9 Acres; The Ten Acres or
Dry Fd 1838 (*North -, South -, West Dry Field* 1687, *v.* drȳge); The Ten Acres or
Fox Cl 1838; The Fourteen Acres; The Fourteen Acres or Cut Cl 1838, 14 Acre
or Cut Cl 1943 (*Cutt Close* 1687, *v.* cutte[1]); 15 Acre; 19 Acres; 27 Acre; The
Forty Acres 1838 (sometimes used of very small fields in Ru, but this had an
area of about 27 acres (information from Mr J. Field)); Allens Pasture 1838,
1943; Asketrow 1838 (*v.* askr, trēow; the Scand first el. prob. replaced OE æsc);
Bidwell Cl 1943 (*v.* Bidwell's Lodge *supra*); Blank Piece 1838 (the first el. is
poss. dial. *plank* 'a narrow strip of cultivated land', *v.* pece); Bottom Fd 1838;
Breeder Leys (this field adjoins Breeder Leys in Stretton f.ns. (a)); Brown -,
Top Broom; Burnt Cl 1838, 1943; Cottage Fd; Crossdales 1838 (*Crosdales* 1687,
cf. *atte Crosse* 1386 Fine (p), *v.* cros, deill); Dickenham 1838 (poss. a variant of
the following f.n.); Dikeham (x2) 1838, Dikeham North, - South 1943 (*North -,
South -, Way Dikeham* 1687, final el. prob. holmr, cf. Dikeham in Greetham f.ns.
(a), *v.* dik, weg); Dry Cl North, - South 1838; Far Cl (x2) 1838, Far Cl North,
- South 1838, Far Cl or Harley's Cl 1943 (*Farr Close* 1678, *v.* feor); Fox Cl
1838 (*East -, West Fox Close* 1687); Glebe Cl (x3), West - 1838 (*The East Glebe*
1684 *Terrier, The West Glebe* 1684 *ib, West Gleab* 1687, *v.* glebe); Footpath Cl
(x2) 1838; Gardens 1838; Gravel Pit Cl 1838; Greengate 1838 (*East -, North -,
South -, West Green Gate* 1687, *v.* grēne[1], gata); Grubwoods (pasture) 1838
(*Middle -, West Groobwood* 1687, *Middle -, West Grubwood* 1688; the first el. is
from the verb *to grub* (OE *grybban*) in the sense 'to clear the ground of roots
and stumps'); Handkerchief Cl 1838 (prob. alluding to its small size); Far -,
First Hanex 1838, Far -, Near Enochs 1943 (*Hanex Field* 1687, *v.* inhōke);
Harleys Cl 1838 (cf. Far Cl *supra*); Harton (x2) 1838 (1687; prob. 'farmstead on
the boundary', *v.* hār[2], tūn); Home Cl (x2) 1838, Home Cl or Quanbury Cl
1838 (*Quanbury Close* 1687, with the surn. of John *Queneborow* 1522 MilS (-
Quenyborough 1524 SR) of Stretton, Thomas *Queneborow* 1522 MilS and William

Queneborow 1522 ib (- *Quenyborough* 1524 SR), both of Teigh; members of this family originated from Queniborough Lei); Home Cl or Spring Cl 1838; Home Fd 1838 (1687, *v.* **home**); Horse Cl 1838, 1943; Bottom -, Top -, House Cl 1838; Hovel Cl (*v.* **hovel**); Bottom -, Top -, Land Fd (*The Land Field* 1687, evidently consolidating selions of a former open-field, *v.* **land**); Little Dale; Long Cl 1838, 1943 (1688, *v.* **lang**[1]); Longdales 1838 (*v.* **lang**[1], **deill**); Luffs Cl 1838 (from the surn. *Luff*, cf. John *Luffe* 1524 SR of Gt. Casterton and John *Luffe* 1524 ib of Empingham); Matthews' Fd; The Meadow 1838; Far -, Near Mill Fd 1838 (*Mill Field* 1687, *v.* **myln**; a windmill was sited at SK 9635 1604, the low mill mound still visible, *v.* BrownArchSites 6); Middle Fd 1838 (1687); Mortar Pit Cl 1838 (*v.* **morter-pytt**); Nook Cl 1838 (*v.* **nōk**); Old Pasture 1838, 1943 (1687); Old Stone Pit (x2) 1838; Phillips's Cl 1838 (*Phillips Close* 1687); The Pinfold or Common Pound 1838 (*v.* **pynd-fald**); Pingle Plantation (cf. *Pingle Close* 1687, *v.* **pingel**); The Plantation (x2) 1838, Plantation Fd 1943; Quarry Dale 1838 (*Quarrie Dale* 1687, *v.* **quarriere**); Sandwells 1838, Sandy Wells 1943 (*Middle -, North -, South Sandwells* 1687, *v.* **sand**, **wella**); Bottom -, Grass -, Middle Sandwich 1838 (perh. a variant of Sandwells *supra*); Sheep Walk 1838, - Walks 1943 (*v.* **sheep-walk**); Bottom -, Middle -, Top Sisson 1838 (from the surn. *Sisson*, cf. Sissons Cl in nearby Thistleton f.ns. (a)); Sivers Cl 1838 (cf. Stephen *Sivers* 1724 *Anc* of neighbouring Stretton); Spring Cl 1838 (1687, *v.* **spring**); Stable Cl 1838, 1943; Three-Cornered Pightle 1838 (*v.* **pightel**); Top Fd 1838; Bottom -, Middle -, Top Wales 1838 (prob. from the surn. *Wales/Wallis*, cf. *Walescroft* in Mkt. Overton f.ns. (b)); Water Cl 1838 (1687, *v.* **wæter**); Wet Fd 1838; Wood Cl 1838; Wood Fd 1838, 1943 (1687, *v.* **wudu**).

(b) *Barn Close; Bayliffe Close* (either from the surn. *Bayliffe* or from *baillie* 'a bailiff, a steward'); *Cack Close* 1687, *Cock Close* 1688; *Calf Close; le Chauntryhouse* 1552 (*v.* **chaunterie**); *East Close; le Eastfelde* 1553 (one of the open-fields of the village, *v.* **ēast**, **feld**); *Farr Field* (*v.* **feor**); *heremitagium de Nordwude, heremitagium de Norewode* 1227 RHug (*v.* **hermitage** and Clipsham Park Wood *supra*); *Farr Lound, Hither Lownd* (*v.* **lundr**); *Middle Pasture; Mott Close* (perh. to be compared with The Motts in N. Luffenham f.ns. (a)); *North Close; North Field; Quarrie Pastures* (*v.* **quarriere**); *East -, Little -, West Stone Meadow* (*v.* **stān**); *South Close; le Southefeld* 1553, *South Field* 1687 (originally the name of one of the open-fields of the village, *v.* **sūð**, **feld**); *Apple Tree Stockin, Bush Stockin* (*v.* **busc**), *Crab Tree Stockin* (*v.* **crabtre**), *Crook -* (*v.* **krōkr**), *Crow -* (*v.* **crōh**[2]), *North Emmanuel -, South Emmanuel -* (with the surn. *Emmanuel*), *Kidd -* (with the surn. *Kidd*), *Lane -* (*v.* **lane**), *Little -, Long -, Oake - (v.* **āc**), *Pasture -, Pitt - (v.* **pytt**), *Pole - (v.* **pōl**[1]), *Sharp -, Swingler -* (with the surn. *Swingler*), *Tray -, Wood - (v.* **wudu**), *Wool Fox Stockin* (alluding to Woolfox

Wood in adjacent Greetham parish) (*v.* **stocing**); *le Westfelde* 1553, *West Field* 1687 (originally one of the great open-fields of the village, *v.* **west, feld**); *West Pasture.*

Egleton

EGLETON
   Egoluestun' 1218 For
   *Egeliston·*1243 Fees, 13 (1377) *CPT, Egleston* 1319, 1334 Pat
   Egelinton 1257 *FF*
   Egelton' c1225 GildR (p), 1231 *Deed,* 1231 RegAnt, 1272 *WDB
      et passim* to 1388 Misc, *Eggelton* 1240 *FF,* 1286 *Ass*
   Egiltun' 1209 *For,* 1218 For, *-ton'* 1263 *Ass,* 1272 *WDB,* 1275
      RH, 1296 *SR et passim* to 1461 Pat
   Egiston 1400 *Ct,* 1498 Ipm, *Eggiston* 1409 ELiW, 1409 PRep
   Egeton 1494 *Finch, Eggeton* 1534 Chap, *Edgeton* 1610 Speed
   Egleton al. Egelton al. Egeston 1565 *FF, Egleton al. Edgeston*
      1667 *ib, Eggleton* 18 *Terrier*
   Edgson 1614 *Deed*

'Ecgwulf's estate', *v.* **tūn.** The name parallels exactly the form of Ayston. It is no doubt also of the late manorial type.

HIDE (lost), *Hide* 1301 Cl, 1316 Pat, *Egilton Hyde* 1312, 1317 ib, *Hida* 1319 ib, cf. *de la Hide* 1263 *Ass* (p), 1335 Ipm (p), *atte Hyde* 1345 (p), 1349 Fine (p) *et passim* to 1375 Pat (p), *atte Hide* 1346 Cl (p), 1346 Fine (p) *et passim* to 1375 Pat (p), *ad Hydam* 1296 *SR* (p), 'the hide of land', *v.* **hīd.**

BARNETTS FM. BROOK FM. EGLETON CHURCH, *Church (St Edmund)* 1846, 1863, 1877 White. FINCHS ARMS P.H. (lost), named from the *Finch* family of Burley on the Hill; closed c1860 - VR. HOG POND (local). HOME FM. MANOR HO., 1846 White. ORCHARD CLOSE. PINFOLD (local), *Ponfold'* 1374 *Rental, Punfold'* 1376 *MinAcct, The Pinfold* 1790 *Surv, v.* **pynd-fald.** THE RAMPARTS (local), the name of the lane from the church north towards Oakham: dial. **rampart** 'a causeway'.

Field-Names

Undated forms in (a) are 1943 *Map*. Early forms dated 1553 are *Ct*, those dated 1566, 1651, 1790 and 118 are *Surv*.

(a) 3 Acre(s), 5 -, 9 Acre (*Nine Acres* 1790, 118), 11 Acre, 15 -, 15½ -, 25 -, 27 Acre (*v.* **æcer**); Middle -, Top Baines (from the local surn. *Baines,* cf. Thomas *Banes* 1522 MilS of Braunston, Hew *Banys* 1524 SR of Wing and Thomas *Banys* 1524 ib of Manton); Best Cl; Bradshaw's Paddock (named from the *Bradshaw* family, cf. Mrs F. *Bradshaw* and John Robert *Bradshaw* 1932 Kelly); Bridge Cl; Bullock Cl (1790, 118, *v.* **bulluc**); Cow Pastures; Dale's (*Dales fur'* 1651, *est Dalles* 1566, *East Dales fur', North Dales,* - *fur'* 1651, *West dale* 1566, *West Dales fur', Long* -, *Short Westdales fur', Longdales,* - *fur'* 1651, *Long Dale* 1790, 118, *Shortdales,* - *fur'* 1651, *Short Dale* 1790, 118, *v.* **deill**); Dixon's; Drop Hills (*Drop(p)wells fur'* 1651, *Drophalls* 1790, 118, *Eastward* -, *Westward Drophall Meadow* 1790, 118, *v.* **dropi, wella**); Gatehouse Fd; The Glebe (*v.* **glebe**); Gravel Pit (*Gravel Pit Close* 1790, 118); (Top) Home Cl (x2) (*Home Close* 118, *v.* **home**); Holme (*Homes* 1566, *Holme,* - *fur'* 1651, *Holme Meadow* 1790, 118, *v.* **holmr**); Honey Holme (1651, 1790, 118, - *fur'* 1651, *v.* **hunig, holmr**; f.ns. with *honey* frequently indicate sticky soil, but a complimentary name for good land is also conceivable); House Cl (cf. *House Holme* 1651, *v.* **hūs, holmr**); Hovel (*v.* **hovel**); Lounds (*Lownds* 1566, *The Lounds,* - *fur1,* *Under the Lounds* 1651, *Under Lount* 1790, 118, *Little Lounds fur'* 1651, *Tomson's Lount* 1790, *Tomsons* - 118, *v.* **lundr** and cf. Thomas *Tomson* 1790); Milking Cl (1790, 118, *v.* **milking**); Millway (*Mill Way* 1790, 118, *v.* **myln, weg**); Parkwall, Ploughed Parkwall (*att the Parkwall, Burley Park Wall* 1651, *Eastward* -, *Middle* -, *Westward Park Wall Close* 1790, 118, alluding to the wall of neighbouring Burley Park, *v.* **park**); Old Ploughed Cl (*Plough'd Close* 1790, *Ploughed Close* 118, *Eastward* -, *Northward Plough'd Close* 1790, - *Ploughed* - 118); Pond Paddock; Long Rotten (1790, 118, *v.* **graten Forll'** in f.ns. (b) *infra*); The Roost (*the Rosse* 1566, *the Roose, Roose fur'* 1651, *Roost* 1790, *Roosts* 118, *v.* **hrōst**); Between Seeks (*Between the Syches* 1651, *Between Seek* 1790, 118, *v.* **sīc, sīk**); Sharp's 9 Acres (named from the local *Sharp* family, cf. Thomas *Sharpe*, husbandman, 1522 MilS and Harry *Sharp*, grazier, 1932 Kelly); Back Wall; Watergauls (*watergalles* 1566, *Watergalls,* - *fur'* 1651, *Water Gauls* 1790, 118, *v.* **wæter, galla**).

(b) *the abutes close* 1566, *Abbots Close* 1790, 118, *the abuttes leas* 1566 (*v.* **abbat, clos(e), lēah**); *Acrecroft* 1651 (*v.* **æcer, croft**); *an well' Brige, Anwell Bryg'* 1566, *An(n)well Bridge, Annwell Bridge fur'* 1651 (*Annwell* may be an example of a sacred spring dedicated to St Anne, a patroness of wells, who interceded for the childless and who therefore was thought appropriate as a dedicatee for those springs which were believed to aid fertility; but as there is here neither indication of *saint* nor genitival construction of ME form, then perh. the OE masc. pers.n. *Anna* is to be preferred as the prototheme, v. **wella, brycg**); *arnat hyll* 1566, *Arnot hill*, - *fur'* 1651 (eModE dial. *arnut, ernut* 'pig-nut, ground-nut', v. **hyll**); *Asker Syke, Asker Syche*, - *fur'* 1651 (a notable instance of dial. *asker* 'a newt'; its earliest citation in NED is for 1674, v. **sīk, sīc**); *Barn Close* 1651, 1790, 118; *lytle Bedsycke* 1566, *Little Bed Syche*, - *fur'* 1651 (v. **bedd, sīk, sīc**); *Biggs's Close* 1790, *Biggs* - 118 (from the surn. *Biggs*); *blake Roudes* 1566, *Black Roods*, - *fur'* 1651, *Lytle Blackrowdes* 1566 (in eModE, *black* 'fertile' is contrasted with *white* 'infertile', v. **rōd³**); *miyddle borowes, mydle borowes* 1566, *Middle Boroughs, Middle Borroughs fur'*, - *Burroughs* - 1651 (prob. with **beorg**, v. **middel**); *Breaches, -fur'* 1651, *Breach* 1790, 118, *le breche leys* 1553, *brach Leas* 1566, *Breach Leyes fur'* 1651 (v. **brēc, lēah**); *Brooke furlong, Brook Meare*, - *fur'* 1651 (Brooke parish adjoins to the south-west, v. **(ge)mǣre**); *Brownes Willow* 1651 (from the surn. *Brown*, v. **wilig**); *Bull Grass fur'* 1651 (v. **bula, gærs**); *Burley Brok'* 1566, *Burley Brook fur'* 1651, *Burley way* 1566, *Burley Way fur'* 1651 (named from neighbouring Burley parish, v. **brōc, weg**); *Burtons hedge Nook* 1651 (from the surn. *Burton*, v. **hecg, nōk**); *Carter's Close* 1790, *Carters* - 118 (held by Ann *Carter* 1790); *Cartley fur'*, *North Cartley* 1651 ('the wood which provides timber for carts', v. **cræt, lēah**, cf. *Cartley* in Oakham f.ns. (b), no doubt referring to the same feature); *Cawdwell fur'* 1651, *caudle gat'* 1566, *Caudwell gate*, - *fur'* 1651, *cawdle leas* 1566 (v. **cald, wella, gata, lēah**); *Church Close* 1651, *Churche Forl'* 1566, *Church fur'* 1651 (v. **cirice, furlang**); *Church Leyes* 1651 (v. **lēah**); *Churchside fur'* 1651 (v. **sīde**); *the Churcheyard* 1566; *cleay hill'*, - *hyll* 1566, *Clayhill*, - *fur'*, *Great Clayhill*, - *fur'*, *Little Clayhill*, - *fur'* 1651, *Longcleay hyll* 1566, *Nether clayhill fur'* 1651, *ouer cleay hyll'* 1566, *Overclayhill fur'* 1651 (v. **clǣg, hyll**); *Long(e) clotes* 1566, *Long Clotts*, - *furl'* 1651, *Northward* -, *Southward Long Clots* 1790, 118 (v. **lang¹, clot(t)**); *Coke stawpe*, - *stowppe* 1566, *Cock Stirrop fur'*, *Cock Stirrop Balk fur'*, *Cockstrupp Balk fur'* 1651 (prob. **cocc¹** 'a hillock' with **staup** 'a steep declivity', but **stīg-rāp** 'a stirrup' used figuratively of some feature of the hill cannot be discounted, cf. *Styrrup* Nt, v. **balca**); *Co(a)lts fur'* 1651; *Coneygrey Close* 1651, *Gunnery* 1790, *Gunnerey* 118 (v. **coninger**); *Cop, (the) Copps, Copp Closes* 1651, *Cop's Close* 1790, *Cops Close* 118, *Copp fur'* 1651, *Cope leas, Cope well, cope well Dyche* 1566 (v. **copp, lēah, wella, dīc**); *Cophill but fur'* 1651 (v. **copp, hyll, butte**); *Cox balk fur'* 1651 (from the surn. *Cox*, cf. *Coxes Close* in neighbouring Burley f.ns. (b), v. **balca**); *Coxhill Bank fur'* 1651 (from the surn. *Cox*, v. **banke**); *Dike* -, *Dyke fur'* 1651 (v. **dīk**); *est syck* 1566 (v. **ēast, sīk**); *ester syke* 1566 (v. **ēasterra, sīk**); *Field Gate Close* 1651 (v. **feld, gata**); *Flealscroft* 1566, *Fleales Croft fur'*, *Great Fleales Croft fur'* 1651, *lytle Flealscrafte or Hyghe medow* 1566, *Neather*

Fleales Croft fur', Over Fleales Croft fur', Upper Fleal Croft 1651 (*v.* **croft**); *flet landes* 1566, *Fleet Lands fur'* 1651 (*v.* **flēot, land**); *Flush fur'* 1651 (*v.* **flasshe**); *Fram(e)less fur'* 1651 (poss. earlier *Frameleys, indicating meadowland containing cloth-stretching frames or tenters, cf. *Frame furlong* in Caldecott f.ns. (b); in some eastern counties, *-leys* > *-less* as in Westley Waterless C and Willoughby Waterless Lei); *Fulcrofte* 1566, *Broad -, Narrow -, Eastward -, Westward Full Croft* 1790, 118, *Fulcroft Hades* 1566, *Full Crofts Nook* 1790, 118 (*v.* **fūl, croft, hēafod, nōk**); *Neather -, Upper Garbroads, Garbroad(e)s fur'* 1651 ('broad strips of land in the triangular corner of the common field', *v.* **gorebrode**); *Gauge Close* 1790, 118 (perh. reflecting 18th cent. agricultural improvement, but if so, the type and function of the gauge referred to remains doubtful); *Gipsey Close* 1651 (*v.* **gypsey**); *graten Forll', grotten forll'* 1566, *Great -, Little -, Long -* (*v.* Long Rotten in f.ns. (a) *supra*), *Short -, Over -, Upper Gratton fur', - Grotton -* 1651 (referring to sandy or gravelly soil, *v.* **groten, furlang**; in the surviving modern reflex Long Rotten in f.ns. (a) *supra*, popular etymology seems to have been at work so that *rotten* is taken to describe crumbly soil); *Great Close* 1790, 118; *atte Grene* 1305 OSurv (p), *Green fur'* 1651, *Green Lands fur'* 1651 (*v.* **grēne²**, **land**); *Guilton fur', Great -, Little Guilton fur'* 1651, *Nether gyltyn Forl'* 1566 (perh. 'golden' because of wild flowers or other vegetation, *v.* **gylden**); *Gunthorpe* 1651, *gonthorpe Hyghe waye, Gonthorpe waye* 1566, *Gunthorpe Way fur', Gunthorpe Gate* 1651, *gonthorpe Homes* 1566 (named from adjoining Gunthorpe parish to the south, *v.* **weg, gata, holmr**); *North Hadles fur'* 1651 (*v.* **hēafod, lēah**); *Hambleton Mear(e) fur'* 1651, *Hambleton waye* 1566, *Hambleton Way fur'* 1651 (named from adjoining Hambleton parish to the east, *v.* **(ge)mǣre, weg**); *Hartes acres* 1566, *Harts Acres* 1790, *- Acre* 118, *Harts Acres fur'* 1651 (from the surn. *Hart*, cf. Harts Cl in Gunthorpe f.ns. (a) and *Harts Close* in Hambleton f.ns. (b), *v.* **æcer**); *smalheasell, smalheasels* 1566, *Small Has(s)ells, - fur'* 1651 (*v.* **hæsel**); *lytle hell* 1566, *Hell fur', Great Hell fur'* 1651 (*v.* **hyll**); *Herne Meadow* 1790, 118 (*v.* **hyrne**); *High Bank* 1651, 1790, 118, *- Banks* 1790 (*v.* **banke**); *the Hyghe meddowe, Hyghe medow* 1566, *High Meadow* 1651 (*v.* **hēah¹, mǣd** and *Flealscroft supra*); *Highway Close* 1651; *the Hyll* 1566 (*v.* **hyll**); *Hill Barn fur'* 1651; *Home Ground* 1790, 118 (*v.* **home, grund**); *Invention, - Meadow* 1790, 118 (prob. alluding to 18th cent. agricultural improvement); *Ireland Hill, - Meadow* 1790 (from the surn. *Ireland*; George *Ireland* held land in neighbouring Hambleton 118 *Surv*); *Jarvis's Close* 1790, *Jarves's - 118* (from the surn. *Jarvis*, cf. Henry *Jervis* 1522 MilS, *- Jarves* 1524 SR of neighbouring Oakham); *Kiln Close* 1790, 118; *Lames fur'* 1651 (*v.* **lammas**); *Little Syche* 1651 (*v.* **sic**); *Longate furlong* 1651 ('a long (narrow) strip of ground', *v.* **langet**); *Long Close* 1790, 118; *long Landes* 1566, *Longlands* 1651, *Long Lands* 1790, 118, *Longlands fur'* 1651 (*v.* **lang¹, land**); *Long Lane, - Close, Long Lane End* 1651; *long syk* 1566 (*v.* **sik**);

mayde Crofte, mad crafte 1566, *Mad(e)croft* 1651, *Matcroft* 1790, 118, *Mad(e)croft fur'* 1651 (the first el. is poss. *mægðe* 'may-weed' rather than *mægð* 'a maiden', *v.* **croft**); *Manton Way fur'* (Manton lies to the south-east beyond Gunthorpe parish, *v.* **weg**); *Mapeley Cross furlong* 1651 (*v.* **mapel, lēah, cros**); *the Meadow* 1651; *Meadows's Lane* 1790, *Meadow's* - 118, *Meadow's Nine Acres* 1790 (named from Edward *Meadows* 1790); *the mear, mear forl'* 1566, *Mear(e) fur'* 1651 (prob. referring to the pool at the north-eastern boundary with Burley parish, cf. *ate Mere* (p) in Burley f.ns. (b), although *(ge)mǣre* 'a boundary' is also poss., *v.* **mere**[1]); *the Mill,* - *fur',* att *the Mill* 1651 (*v.* **myln**); *more landes* 1566, *Moore Land(s),* - *fur'* 1651 (*v.* **mōr**[1], **land**); *Mortar Pits* 1790, - *Pitts* 118, *Morterpitt Close* 1651 (*v.* **morter-pytt**); *Narrow Close* 1790, 118; *Narrow Syche* 1651 (*v.* **sīc**); *New Close* 1651; *Newfield* 1651; *north endes* 1566, *Eastward* -, *Westward North End Close* 1790, 118, *North End Leys* 1790, 118 (*v.* **norð, ende**[1], **lēah**); *Northerns .Leys* 1651 (perh. from the surn. *Northern*, cf. *Northerens Town End* in N. Luffenham f.ns. (a) s.n. The Townsend; otherwise belonging to the previous f.n., *v.* **lēah**); *in campo borial'* 1553 *Ct,* *the northe Felde* 1566, *Northfield* 1651 (one of the great open-fields of the village, *v.* **norð, feld**); *Northings Close, Northings fur'* 1651 (*v.* **norð, eng**); *oke Forl'* 1566 (*v.* **āc, furlang**); *Okeham field side, Okeham way fur', Over Okeham Way* 1651 (Oakham parish adjoins to the north-west, *v.* **sīde, weg**); *Osborn's Close* 1651, *Osbands* - 118 (from the surn. *Osborn*); *Great* -, *Little Padholme, Padholme fur', Nether* -, *Over Padholme fur'* 1651 (*v.* **padde, holmr**); *Park Ford* 1566, *Park(s) fur'* 1651, *Park Furlong* 1790, 118, *Little Park fur', Parkway fur'* 1651 (alluding to Burley Park, *v.* **park, ford, weg**); *Peas(e)lands fur'* 1651 (*v.* **pise, land**); *Piece Briggs* 1651 (the second el. is Scandinavianized, *v.* **brycg**); *Piggs Holme* 1651 (*v.* **pigga, holmr**); *The Pingle* 1651, *Pingle* 1790, 118 (*v.* **pingel**); *Pottacres* 1566, *Pott Acres* 1651, *nether pottacres* 1566, *Over* -, *Pott Acres fur'* 1651 (perh. referring to land where ancient potsherds were littered, *v.* **pot(t), æcer**); *Priests brink fur'* 1651 (*v.* **brink**); *Ricksteads fur', Little Ricksteds fur'* 1651 (*v.* **rickstead** and Rickstead in Belton f.ns. (a)); *the Rigg, Rigg furlong* 1651 (*v.* **hryggr** and 1st -, 2nd Ridge in Oakham f.ns. (a) where the early spelling shows the OE form *hrycg*); *Rippin's Close* 1790, *Rippings* - 118 (held by Alice *Rippin* 1790); *Sandpitts,* - *fur'* 1651, *sande Pytes hades, sandpytthades* 1566 (*v.* **sand-pytt, hēafod**); *Seed Close* 1790, 118 (a close of sown grass, *v.* **sǣd**); *the Syche* 1651, *Seek* 1790, 118, *Syche fur'* 1651 (*v.* **sīc, sīk**); *Sheepcoate,* - *fur'* 1651, *Sheep Cutt Close* 1790, 118 (*v.* **scēap-cot**); *Side of the Hill* 1651 (*v.* **sīde**); *le Slathouse upon the Smythie Grene* 1549 Pat (*v.* **slate, hūs**; the nearest slate quarries were at Swithland Lei, but limestone roofing slates may be referred to here); *le Smythie Grene* 1549 ib (*v.* **smiððe, grēne**[2]); *in campo austral'* 1553 *Ct,* *the southe feld* 1566, *Southfield* 1651 (one of the open-fields of the village, *v.* **sūð, feld**); *Sponge fur', Spong waye* 1566, *Sponge way* -, *Sponghway fur'* 1651 (OE **spang** 'a clasp, a buckle' used in a topographical sense such as that of dial. *spong* 'a long narrow strip of ground', v. **weg**); *Stamford Way fur*' 1651 ('furlong beside the road to Stamford L', v. **weg**); *Stomacher Close* 1790, 118 (eModE **stomacher** 'a triangular panel in a woman's dress' and 'a kind of waistcoat worn by men' used here of an enclosure of similar shape); *ston fall* 1566 (v. **stān, (ge)fall**); *Stone Pit Close* 1790, 118 (v. **stān-pytt**); *Tan Yard* 1790, 118 (v. **tan-yard**); *Tonglandes* 1566, *Tongue Lands fur*' 1651 (v. **tunge, land**); *Town Close* 1651, 1790, 118 (v. **tūn**); *Towne end close* 17 Deed, *Townsend Close* 1651 (v. **tūn, ende**[1]); *the Waste* 1790, 118 (v. **waste**); *in campo occidental*' 1566 Ct, *the West Fe(i)ld* 1566, *Westfield* 1651 (one of the great open-fields of the village, v. **west, feld**); *West Meades fur*' 1651 (v. **mǣd**); *west mydow* 1566, *West Meadow* 1651, 1790, 118,, - *fur*' 1651 (v. **west, mǣd**); *le White howse* 1566 (v. **hwīt, hūs**); *White Roods, - fur*' 1651 (in eModE, white 'infertile' is contrasted with *black* 'fertile', v. **rōd**[3]); *Wipesnest -, Wypesnest fur*' 1651 (v. **wǣps, nest**); *Wonge Forll*' 1566 (v. **vangr, furlang**); *Yule Cake hills* 1651 (on the Oakham parish boundary, v. *yulecake hill* in Oakham f.ns. (b)).

Gunthorpe

GUNTHORPE

Gunetorp' 1200 Abbr, 1200 Cur, 1200 Pleas, 1202 Ass, 1218 For, -*thorp*' 1223 Cur, 1262 RGrav (p)

Gunnethorp 1269 Pat

Guntorp' 1208 PatR (p), 1231 *Deed*, 1231 RegAnt, -*thorp(e)* 1225 *FF*, 1231 RegAnt *et passim* to 1538 *Finch*, 1610 Speed

'Gunni's outlying farmstead', v. **þorp**, cf. Gunthorpe Nth, L. The OScand pers.n. *Gunni* is a short form of names in *Gunn-*, v. SPNLY 116-7.

THE BUNGALOWS. DURHAM OX FM was The Durham Ox Inn which closed c1900 - VR. GUNTHORPE HALL, 1850 Slater is *Gunthorpe Lodge* 1846 White.

Field-Names

Undated forms in (a) are 1943 *Map*. Those dated 1837 and 1906 are *Anc*. Those of 1939 are *Deed* (per Mr D. Tew). Early forms dated 1632 are *Terrier*,

1637 and 1653 are *Conant*; those dated 1699, 1717, 1785 and 1795 are *Anc*; those of 1796 are *Surv*.

(a) 6 -, 10 -, 63 Acre (*v.* æcer); Approach Road 1939; Barn Close 1837, 1906, 1939 (1717, 1785, 1796); Black Mdw; Bottom Fd 35 Acres; Bridge Cl 1837, 1906, 1939 (1785, 1796, *Bridg Close* 1717, referring to a foot-bridge over R. Gwash); Clements Nook 1837, 1906, 1939, Clement's - 1943 (*Clements Noock* 1717, - *Nook* 1785, *Clement's Nook* 1796, *v.* nōk, cf. John-, Thomas- and William *Clement* 1522 MilS, 1524 SR of Belton); Corn Fd; Eayr's Far Fd (from the name of the local *Eayr* family, cf. Geoffrey V. *Eayr* and William F. *Eayr* of Burley 1932 Kelly); Ford Fd; Front Fd; Furze Cl, - Mdw 1837 (*Furze Close, Furze Close Meadow* 1796, *v.* fyrs); Gunthorpe Gorse c1800, 1806 Map, 1824 O (*v.* gorst); Harts Cl 1837, 1906, 1939 (*Hart's Close* 1796, from the surn. *Hart*, cf. *Hartes acres* in neighbouring Egleton f.ns. (b)); Highway Cl 1837, 1906, 1939 (1796, referring to the Oakham-Uppingham road); East Holme 1837, West - 1837, 1906, 1939 (*East* -, *West Holme* 1796, *v.* holmr); Home Cl 1906, 1939 (*Home Close (called the Nursery)* 1796, *v.* home, nursery); House Cl 1837 (1717, 1785, 1796, referring to Gunthorpe Hall); Nether -, Upper Long Mdw 1837, 1906, 1939 (*Long Meadow* 1796); Middle Ground 1837, 1906, 1939 (1796, *v.* grund); Nether Cl 1837, 1906, 1939 (1717, 1785, 1796); Nether Fd; Nether Mdw 1837 (1796); North Barn 1939, - Cl 1906; Osier Bed Fd (*v.* oyser, bedd); Philpott's (from the surn. *Philpot*, cf. William *Phellypot* 1522 MilS of Langham); Piece by the Railway 1906; Rams Cl 1837, 1906, 1939 (*Ram Close* 1717, 1796, *v.* ramm); Redwells, - Cl 1837 (*Redwells* 1795, *Redwell Close, Redwell Meadow* 1796, *Redwells Spring* 1717, prob. with hrēod 'a reed, a reed-bed', although since Gunthorpe stands on a small outcropping of ironstone, rēad 'red' cannot be discounted; cf. *Redwell* in neighbouring Manton f.ns. (b), *v.* wella); North -, South Road Cl; Round Hill; Sanctuary 1837, 1906, 1939 (*Sanctuary Meadow* 1796, on the parish boundary beside R. Gwash; either of land endowed for the upkeep of the sanctuary of a parish church (although not that of Gunthorpe which lacks a church) or a complimentary name for a place of peace and security); Side Hill; Smith's Mdw 1837, 1939, 1943, Smiths - 1906 (*Smith's Meadow* 1796); Spring Mdw 1837, 1906, 1939 (*Spring Medow* 1717, - *Meadow* 1785, 1796, named from *Redwells Spring supra*); Stable Fd; Stimpsons Mdw 1837, 1906, Stimpson's - 1939, 1943 (*Stimsons Meadow* 1796; William *Stimson* held land in the adjoining parish of Hambleton 1785 *Surv*); Stone Pit 1906; Top Cl 1906, 1939; Upper Mdw 1837, 1906, 1939 (*Upper Medow* 1717, - *Meadow* 1785, 1796, *the Over Meadow, the Over or Upper Meadow* 1795); Wash Dike Nook 1837 (1796, alluding to a sheep-dip, *v.* wæsce, dīk, nōk).

(b) *The Bridge Piece* 1717 (*v.* **pece**); *gonthorpe close* 1632 (*v.* **clos(e)**); (*the*) *Middle Gunthorpe* 1653, 1717, 1795, *Nether Gunthorpe* 1637, 1795, *the Over* -, *Upper* -, *Scotneys Gunthorpe* 1795 (cf. *Scotneys Plot infra*); *Gunthorpe rickstede* 1632 (*v.* **rickstead** and Rickstead in Belton f.ns. (a)); *Gunthorpe Wood otherwise Gunthorpe Coppice* 1795; *The Meadow* 1795; *Middle Meadow* 1653, 1795; *Planke Meadow* 1785 (referring to a plank bridge, *v.* **planke**, cf. Plank Cl in neighbouring Burley f.ns. (a)); *Scotneys Plot* 1795 (*Scotney* was a Ru surn., cf. John *Scotney* 1687 *Anc* of Stretton and *Scotneys Cottage* 1785 *ib* in Empingham f.ns. (b), *v.* **plot**); *Timsons Close* 1653, *Timpsons* - 1795, *Timpsons Meadow* 1699 (either from a surn. *Timpson* or from earlier forms of the surn. *Stimpson* as in Stimpsons Mdw *supra*); *Wards Close* 1699, 1717 (from the surn. *Ward*); *Wood Close* 1699.

Langham

LANGHAM

> *Langeham* Hy 2 Dugd, 1263 Pat (p), 1298 Ipm *et passim* to 1334 Pat (p)
> *Langham* 1202 Ass, 1231 RegAnt, 1248 RGros, 1272 *FF et passim* to 1320 Pat, 1330 *Deed* (p) *et freq*
> *Longhame* 1536 LP

Perhaps 'the long water-meadow or low-lying pasture', *v.* **lang**[1], **hamm**. There are no early spellings in *-hamme*, *-homme*, *-hom* so that we cannot be certain here of distinguishing **hamm** from **hām** 'a village, an estate'. However, the settlement extends at length on level ground on both sides of a meandering stream, while the medieval church stands in a long shallow loop of the watercourse. This stretch of land hemmed in by the stream may be the original **hamm**.

RANKSBOROUGH, - HILL, RANKSBOROUGH GORSE, *Rankesberwe* 1227 ClR, *Rankesborowe Hill* 1610 Speed, *Rankesbro Hill* 1780 Map, *Ranksborough Hill* 1801 ib, cf. *Ranksborough Hill Covert* c1800, 1806 ib, 'Ranc's barrow or hill', *v.* **beorg**, cf. Ronksley Db. The OE pers.n. *Ranc* is a by-name, cf. OE *ranc* 'proud, noble'. Ranksborough Hill is an imposing eminence on the county boundary and has given its name to a small settlement lying between the hill and Langham. Ranksborough is one of a series of names in **beorg** surviving in the boundary parishes of Rutland. It is possible that it records the secondary burial of a pagan Anglo-Saxon called *Ranc* in a prehistoric barrow on the hill-top, cf. *Budborow* in Greetham f.ns. (b).

BACK LANE. BAPTIST CHAPEL, *Particular Baptist Chapel* 1846 White. BLACK HORSE P.H., 1932 Kelly. BRIDGE ST. CHURCH ST. COTTAGE FM. THE GRANGE, 1877 White, *v.* **grange.** HAREWOOD HO., 1932 Kelly. HOLBECK LODGE, *Hobeck* 1630 Ipm, *Holbeck* 1694 *Recov*, 'stream lying in a hollow', *v.* **hol², bekkr**; the stream forms the county boundary to the west. HORSE AND JOCKEY P.H. (lost), 1850 Slater. LANGHAM BREWERY, 1877 White, 1932 Kelly; the home of Ruddles Ales and established in 1858. LANGHAM CHURCH, *Church (St Peter and St Paul)* 1846, 1863, 1877 White. LANGHAM LODGE, 1824 O is *Chapmans Lodge* c1800, 1806 Map. LANGHAM PLACE. MANOR HO., 1846, 1863 White, 1932 Kelly. MIDDLE ST. MILL FIELD MANOR (local) may well take its name from a former water-mill. There are a mound and curved leet at SK 8385 1070 which may be the remains of such a mill, *v.* MER 24. NOEL ARMS P.H., 1877 White, *Noel's Arms* 1850 Slater, named from the *Noel* family of Exton. OLD HALL, 1932 Kelly. ROCOTT HO., ROCOTT SPINNEY, *Rocote* c1800 Map, *Rocart* 1806 ib, 1824 O, 1826 G, *Rocott House* 1877 White, 'the cottage on the boundary', *v.* **rá², cot**; both Rocott House and - Spinney lie beside the western boundary of Rutland. SCHOOL LANE. WELLS ST., cf. *ad fontem* 1305 OSurv (p), *v.* **wella.** WESTMOOR LANE, WESTMOOR LODGE, *Westmore* 1694 *Recov*, cf. *West Moor Close* 1842 *TA*, 'the west moorland', *v.* **west, mōr¹**. WHEATSHEAF P.H., 1850 Slater, *Wheat Sheaf* 1877 White, *Wheatsheaf Inn* 1932 Kelly.

Field-Names

Undated forms in (a) are 1943 *Map*; forms dated 1808, 1810, 1838, 1851 and 1906 are *Anc*; those of 1842 are *TA*; 1925 are *Deed* and 1972 are from oral information per Mr D. Tew. Early forms dated 1285, 1374, 1375, 1376 and 1380 are *MinAcct*; those dated 1305 are OSurv, 1326 are *Ct* and 14 are *Rental*; those of 1684 and 1720 are *Anc*, 1712 and 1718 are *Deed*; those dated 1744 are *Asw*.

(a) The Three Acres 1842, 6 -, 7 -, 8 -, 9 Acre 1943, Ten Acre 1943, - Cl 1842, 12 -, 14 -, 15 Acre 1943, Bottom 15 Acres 1943, 16 -, 20 -, 30 Acre 1943 (*v.* **æcer**); Nether -, Aldney Cl 1842 (cf. Long Holdney Cl, Oldney Banks *infra*); Allotment Fd 1972; Almond's 8 Acre; Ancaster (the Earls of *Ancaster* held land in Langham); Great -, Ashton Cl 1842; Ashwell Cl, Ashwell Road Piece 1842 (named from the neighbouring parish of Ashwell); Back Cl 1842; Barley Thorpe Mere 1842 (Barleythorpe parish adjoins to the south, *v.* **(ge)mǣre**); Barn Cl 1810, 1838, 1842, 1906, - Fd or Big Barn Cl 1943; Bartram's Rough 1943 (from the surn. *Bartram*, *v.* **rūh**^{2}); Baxters Cl 1842; Beavers Cl (with the surn. *Beaver*, cf. Thomas *Beaver* 1712 *Deed* of Empingham); Bell Piece 1842 (poss. endowed for the maintenance of the parish church bell, *v.* **pece**); Beran's; Blood's Cl (with the surn. *Blood*, cf. Blood Cl in neighbouring Barleythorpe f.ns. (a), Johane *Blood* 1522 MilS and John *Bloode* 1524 SR, both of Ryhall); Brewery Cl (adjoining Ruddles Brewery); Brick Fd 1842; Boy Bridge Cl 1842; Bridge Cl, Bridge Yard 1842; Brindle's; Bromley Cl 1842; Bullemores Cl (x2), Other Bullemores Cl 1842 (from the surn. *Bullimore*, cf. Bullimore's in Oakham f.ns. (a)); Bull Acre 1943, - Cl 1842; Bulls (Ten Acre) Cl 1842; Far Burley Cl, Burley Lane, Burley Lane Cl (Other) 1842 (named from adjoining Burley parish); Burtons 11 -, 12 Acre 1972; Bushey Cl 1842; Butchers Cl 1842 (from the surn. *Butcher*, cf. Butchers Hill in neighbouring Ashwell f.ns. (a) and *Butcher's Close* in neighbouring Burley f.ns. (b)); Butlers Cl; Chapel Cl 1842; Cheese Cake Cl 1842, Cheesecake 1943 (dial. *cheesecake* is used of the fruit of such wild plants as the common mallow and the bird's foot trefoil); Clay Hill Cl 1842 (*Clay Hill* 1684, *v.* **clæg, hyll**); Cole's Mdw (with an old Ru surn., cf. Widow *Cole* c1685 *Deed* of neighbouring Burley); Coopers Holm(e) (x3), Other Coopers Holm 1842 (*v.* **holmr**); Cow Pasture Cl, - Corner (*v.* **corner**), - Piece 1842, Old Cow Pasture 1943; Cow (Post) Piece 1842 (*v.* **pece**); Cox's 1943, 1972 (cf. *Coxes Close* in neighbouring Burley f.ns. (b)); Cricket Fd (alluding to the game of cricket); Cross Post Cl 1842; Far -, Lower -, Upper Dale Cl 1842 (*v.* **dalr**); Dams 1972; Darby Cl (x3) 1842; Dolby Great Cl, Dolby Mdw 1842 (from the surn. *Dalby*, cf. Dalby Cl in neighbouring Ashwell f.ns. (a)); Dormon's (from the surn. *Dorman*); Dove House Cl 1842 (*v.* **dove-house**); First -, Upper Dry Cl 1810, 1838, 1842, 1906 (*Dry Close* (x2) 1684, *Neather -, Upper Dry Close, Dry Close Meadow* 1712, *v.* **dryge**); Edgson's 21½ Acre 1943, Edgsons 1972 (named from the *Edgson* family, cf. Robert *Egyston* 1524 SR and William *Edgson* 1932 Kelly; the surn. in its modern spelling is a late form of the local p.n. Egleton *q.v.*); Nether Fallow 1842; Far Cl, - Fd 1842; Farm Mdws; Flat Mdw 1972; Fox Hills

30 Acre 1943, Fox Holes 1810, 1838, 1842, 1906 (Mr J. Field notes that these are a number of separate closes, each of one acre), Foxholes Mdw 1810, 1838, Fox Holes Mdw 1842 (*Foxhoales* 1684, *Foxholes* 1720, *v.* **fox-hol**); Glebe 1842 (*v.* **glebe**); Grass Crofts 1842 (*Grasscroft* 1684, *v.* **gærs, croft**); Great Cl 1842; Grindells, Great Grindle Cl (West End), Grindles Cls (x3) 1842 (*v.* **grendel** 'a gravelly place or stream' and cf. Grindle in Whissendine f.ns. (a) and Barleythorpe f.ns. (a)); Gundels Cl 1842 (prob. belongs with the previous f.n.); Harris's Top (named from the *Harris* family, cf. Philip *Harris* 1932 Kelly, grazier in Langham); Hay Croft 1842 (*v.* **croft**); Lower -, Upper Hell Holes 1943, Hell Holes 1972 (either a derogatory name for inferior land or a form of Hell's Hales in Oakham f.ns. (a), Hills and Hales in Exton f.ns. (a), *hell* being a local dial. form of *hill*); High Mdw (- North, - South) 1842; Far -, Nether Hill Cl 1842; Over Hill, Hill Cl, - Fd 1943, Hill Top Fds 1943; Hingley Cl 1842 (poss. a surn. originating from the p.n. Hinckley Lei); (Brook -, South -) Holbeck, Holbeck Cl, Holbecks Cl South 1842 (*v.* Holbeck Lodge *supra*); Long Holdney Cl 1842 (cf. Aldney Cl *supra*); Holmes Great Cl, Holmes Mdw 1842 (*in le Holm(e)* 1305 (p), 14 (p), *in the Holm(e)* 1374 (p), 1376 (p), 1380 (p), *of the holm* 1375 (p), *v.* **holmr**); Home Cl(s), - Piece 1842, - Cl 1943 (*the Homeclose* 1744, *v.* **home**); Hoods Cl 1842; Hornby Cl 1842, Hornsby 1972 (from the surn. *Hornsby*, cf. William *Horneby* 1524 SR of Empingham and Capt. *Hornsby* 1943 *Map* of neighbouring Ashwell); Horse Cl 1842, 1972; Little House Cl 1842 (*the House Close* 1684); Hovel 15 Acre (*v.* **hovel**); How Cl East, - West, Little -, Upper Howe Cl, The Howes, Middle -, Over Howes 1842 (perh. from **haugr** 'a mound'); Big Hubbard's, Hubbard's Ploughed Fd (named from the *Hubbard* family, cf. Thomas- and John *Hubbard* 1522 MilS, Richerd *Hubbard* and Henry *Hubbert* 1524 SR, husbandmen, Herbert *Hubbard* 1932, grazier, all of Langham); Humphreys 1972; Isaac's Barton (*v.* **bere-tūn**), - Top Fd 1943, Isaacs 1972 (named from the *Isaac* family, cf. Alice *Isaac* 1932 Kelly of Langham and William *Isak* 1524 SR of Braunston); Jones'; Jordans Cl 1842 (from the surn. *Jordan*, cf. John *Jorden* 1522 MilS, 1524 SR of Barleythorpe); Kennels Fd (beside the kennels of the Cottesmore Hunt); Kirk Leys 1925 (*v.* **kirkja, lēah** and Stone Galls *infra*); Land Cl 1842 (*v.* **land**); Lodge Cl 1810, 1838, 1842, 1906, 1920 (divided like Fox Holes *supra*, *v.* Langham Lodge *supra*); Little Lodge Cl 1906; Long Cl 1842; West -, Lows Plat 1842 (*v.* **plat**^{2}); Marks Paddock 1972; Marshalls, Marshalls 8 Acre 1972; Marsham's (11 Acre, - Under Cover (*v.* **cover(t)**)); Little Mead 1842, Little Mdw 1810, 1838, 1842, 1906, Big Mdw 1943, Meadow Cl, The Meadows 1842; Meere Piece, Mere Cl 1842 (*the Meers* 1684, *v.* **(ge)mǣre**); Back -, Home -, Long Mickley 1943, First -, Little Mickley Cl, Mickley Cl (Middle), Mickleys (- Cl, - Mdw) 1842 (poss. the surn. *Mackley* or *Mickley*, cf. Mackley in Ridlington f.ns. (a)); Middle Cl 1842, 1943, - Piece 1842;

Mill Cl (x2) 1842, - Fd 1842, 1943, - Syke 1842 (v. sīk) (v. Mill Field Manor *supra*); Mortar Pit Cl 1842 (v. **morter-pytt**); Mouters 1972; Second -, Nelsons Cl 1842; Nether Cl 1842; Nettleships 1972 (prob. the surn. *Nettleship*); New Nook 1842 (v. **nōk**); North Cl 1842; Oakham Lane Cl 1842 (*Okeham Lane* 1744); Oldney Banks 1842, Holybanks 1972 (*Ould Ley Bankes* 1684, *Old Ley Banks* 1720, v. **ald, lēah, banke** and cf. Aldney Cl *supra*); The Orchard 1842; Over Piece (v. **pece**); (Bottom -, Top -) Over Seek 1943, Great -, Little Over Syke 1842 (v. **sīk**); Paddock (x7) 1842, Paddocks 1943; Pasture Cl 1842, Pastures 1972; Pensons Mdw 1810, 1838, 1842, 1906 (*Pansham Mead or Spansham Mead* 1684, v. **hamm, mǣd**; Pensons Mdw is divided like Fox Holes *supra*); Pightle 1842 (v. **pightel**); Pilkingtons Cl 1842; Ploughed Piece 1842, Old Ploughed Fd 1943; Proctor's Cl 1842, Proctor 1972 (with the surn. *Proctor*, cf. Richard *Proctor* 1524 SR of neighbouring Oakham); Raiterleys Cl 1842; Ranksborough Cl (x6), - Hill, - Piece, Upper Ranksborough 1842 (v. Ranksborough *supra*); Reed Spire Mdw 1842 (v. **spīr**, *spire* is a dial. word for 'reeds, rushes'); Ridlingtons 1842; Bottom -, Top Rimmington, Rimmington's 1943 (from the surn. *Rimmington*, cf. *Rimyngton Furlonge* in Barleythorpe f.ns. (b), Remington Heath in Greetham f.ns. (a), Remington Hold Cl in S. Luffenham f.ns. (a) and Rimmingtons Hoole in Morcott f.ns. (a)); Road Piece, - Cl 1842 (v. **pece**); Rohers Cls 1842; Rudkin's, - Big Fd, Rudkins Cl 1943 (named from the *Rudkin* family, cf. William *Rudkin* 1932 Kelly, farmer in Langham); Nether -, Over Russell Cl 1842; Rylands Cl 1842, Long -, Rylands 1943 (v. **ryc-land**); Shaftnooks 1972 (v. **nōk**); Sharmans 28 Acre 1972 (with the old Ru surn. *Sharman*, cf. Thomas *Shereman* 1665 *HT* of Greetham, Thomas *Sherman* 1678 *Anc* of Langham); Big -, Top Sharrads 1943, Sharrads 1972; Sissons 1972 (a surn., cf. Sissons Cl in Thistleton f.ns. (a), Sisson in Clipsham f.ns. (a)); Smith's (the surn. *Smith*, cf. William Henry *Smith* 1932 Kelly, grazier in Langham); Smith's Heaven 1808, 1851 (a complimentary name for a close of land); Bottom -, Over Speller, The Spellers 1842, Speller 1972 (v. *le Spellow* in neighbouring Barleythorpe f.ns. (b)); The Spinney 1842, Spinney Cl 1943; Spring Cl; Stackyard Cl (v. **stak-ȝard**); Bottom -, Top Stafford's Parlour 1943, Stafford 1972 (v. **parlur** 'a small piece of ground'; prob. from a family formerly associated with the parish, cf. the name John William *Stafford* Smith 1932 Kelly and *Staffords Quicke* in neighbouring Whissendine f.ns. (b)); Steadfast Syke 1842 (evidently a complimentary name for a reliable watercourse, v. **sīk**); Steel's Big Fd 1943, Steeles 1972; Stone Galls 1842, 1943, - or Kirk Lees 1925, Stonegalls 1972 (*Stone Galls or Kirk Leys* 1744, v. **stān, galla, kirkja, lēah**); Stone Quarry Cl 1842, Quarry Fd 1943; Swans Cl 1842; Tenters Cl 1842 (v. **tentour**); Thorpes Meere Nook 1842 (alluding to the Barleythorpe parish boundary, v. (ge)**mǣre, nōk**); The Thackhams 1842 (the first el. OE **þæc** 'thatch, materials for thatching' has prob. been influenced by Scand **þak** of the same meaning, v. **þæc**, hamm); Three Acre Mdw 1842; Turls Cl 1842; Two Field Piece 1842; The Two Pieces 1842 (*v.* pece); Wadmill Cl 1842 (*v.* wadmill 'a building in which woad is processed'); Walker's Top, - Bottom (named from the *Walker* family, cf. John *Walker* 1932 Kelly, grazier in Langham); Wang Road Piece, Ploughed Wang, (Great) Wood -, West Wood Wang, Second Wang Mdw 1842 (*v.* vangr); Waste Piece 1842 (*v.* waste, pece); Wilderness 1972; Williamson's 9 Acre, - 10 Acre (named from the local *Williamson* family, cf. Christopher and Fred *Williamson* 1932 Kelly, graziers in Langham).

(b) *Benethegate* 1305 (p), 14 (p) (*v.* beneoðan, gata); *Langham Brook* 1795 Nichols; *the East Feild* 1601 *Deed* (one of the open-fields of the village, *v.* ēast, feld); *a la Grene* 1305 (p), *atte Grene* 1305 (p), 1326 (p), *ad Grenam* 1305 (p), 14 (p) (*v.* grēne²); *Heybryggeholm* 1374, *Heybriggeholm(e)* 1375, 1380, *Heybrigholm'* 1376 (*v.* (ge)hæg, brycg, holmr); *atte Hull'* 1374 (p) (*v.* hyll); *Katherines Close, - yard* 1718 (a surn., cf. John *Caterns* 1522 MilS of nearby Oakham, Clement *Catterens* 1617 PR of N. Luffenham); *ad venellam* 1285 (p), *atte Lane* 1305 (p), 14 (p), *attelane* 1326 (p), *in la Lane* 1305 (p), 14 (p) (*v.* lane); *Langham Lane* 1724; *Moregore* 1375 (*v.* mōr¹, gāra); *Norbrooke* 1684, *Norbrookes or Dry Close* 1684 (*v.* norð, brōc); *terre fabri* 1376 ('the smith's land', *v.* smið, land); *ad lap'* 1305 (p), 14 (p) ('the stone' must have been a local landmark of some kind, *v.* stān); *molendinum ventriticum de Langham* 1305, *Langham Windmill* 1824 O (*v.* wind-mylne).

Leighfield

Leighfield was formed from the central part of the Forest of Rutland at its disafforestation c1630. It was enclosed and declared to be extra-parochial.

LEIGHFIELD

Leghe 1266 *For,* 1286 *Ass, Leye* 1275 *Abbr,* 1276 *Pat,* c1291 *Tax et freq* to 1319 *Pat et passim* to 1385 *Fine, Leya* 1256 *For, Lee* 1474 *Pat et passim* to 1507 *ib, Lee al' Leigh* 1582 *FF Lighe* 1266 *For, Lye* 1296, 1327 *SR,* 1371 *FF et passim* to 1453 *Cl*

Lee al' Leefeld(e) 1501, 1505 *Cl,* 1538 *Hastings, Leygh al' Leygfeld* 1532 *ib, Lye al' Lyefeld* 1513 *ib*

le Leyfeld in villa de Lye c1318 *FH*

Leyefeld' 1369, 1372 For, (*le*) *Leyfeld* 1388, 1462, 1485 Pat,
   Leefeld(*e*) 1399, 1466 ib *et passim* to 1507 Pat, *Ly*(*e*)*feld*
   1373 Ipm, 1391 Pat *et passim* to 1505 ib, *Lyghfeld* 1475 ib,
   Lighfeld 1510 LP
foresta regis de Lyfelde 1491 *For, forest of Ly* c1545 Leland,
   Leefeilde Forest 1610 Speed, *Lea Forest* 1618 LML, *Forest
   of Leighfeild al's Leefeild al's Rutland* 1677 *Deed, Leighfield
   Forest al' Rutland Forest* 1711 *Recov*

Originally OE **lēah** in its early sense 'woodland'. Later, OE **feld**
'open country' or 'land for pasture or cultivation' was added when
the forest began to be cleared, *v.* **lēah, feld**. The earthworks of the
deserted medieval village are sited east of Leighfield Lodge at SK
830 040, *v.* MER 25-6.

SWINTLEY LODGE, *Swyncliffe in Lee* 1371 IpmR, *Swynclif* 1371
Ipm, *Swynclyf* 1373 ib, 1375 Fine, 1376 *For*, 1379, 1385 Fine,
Swinclife 1611 SP, *Swinclif*(*fe*) *coppice* 1611 *ib*, *Swintley Sale al's
Swincliffe al's Swincliffe Coppice* 1677 *Deed, Swintlye Sale al's
Swincliffe al's Swincliffe Coppice* 1694 *ib*, *Neather Swintly* 17 *ib*,
Upper Swintl(*e*)*y* c1685 *ib*, 1729, 18 *Surv, Upper Swintly Sale* 17
Deed, Swintly 18 *Surv, Swintly Cop, - Meadow* 1729, 18 *ib*, *Swinthley
Lodge* 1824 O, 'swine bank', *v.* **swīn**[1], **clif**. The name, no doubt,
records the feeding of pigs on acorns fallen from the forest oaks.
The forms show the typical sound change [nk] > [nt] before *l*. In
the minor names arising, dial. **sale** is used of 'a division or
"quarter" of a wood, of which the underwood is cut down and sold'.
It is common in the old woodland areas of Beaumont Chase and
Leighfield (*v.* f.ns. *infra*) in Rutland and is found also in various
early minor names in Northants., *v.* Nth 157 and EDD *s.v.* It is
unclear whether the late minor forms *Swintly Cop, Swintly Cop
Meadow* contain an abbreviated *coppice* (which occurs earlier) or
OE *cop* 'the top of a hill' (or its dial. reflex *cop* 'a mound, an
embankment') since both spellings are from surveys. These
documents tended to accumulate copied forms and hence sometimes
obscure former abbreviations, *v.* **copis**.

LAMBLEY LODGE, *Lamley Lodge* 1610 Speed, 1620 Map, 1624

Deed, 1780, 1801 1825 Map, *Lambley Lodge* 1846, 1863 White, 1932 Kelly, cf. *Lamlye Wood* 1564 *For, Lamley Sale* 1624 *Deed, Lamby Sale al's Lamley Quarter al's Lamley Sale Coppice al's Lamley Coppice* 1677 *ib, Lamby Sale al's Lamley quarter al's Lamley Coppice* 1694 *ib, Lambley Close* e18, 1748 (119) *Whit, Lambly Close* 1822 (1878) *ib,* probably 'woodland pasture for lambs', cf. *Lambyngecrofte infra, v.* **lamb, lēah.** For the minor names arising, *v.* **loge, quarter, copis.**

LEIGHFIELD LODGE (LEIGH - 1"), *Lee Lodge* 1567 LAHS, 1610 Speed, 1615 Moulton, 1616 *Deed,* 1620 Map, 1634 *Terrier,* 1684 Map, 1747 *Anc, Lye Lodg(e)* 1579 Saxton, 1602, 1607 Map, *Leigh Lodge* 1613 Moulton, 1685 *Anc,* 1749 *Terrier,* 1785 *Anc,* 1846, 1863 White, *Lea Lodge* 1780 Map, *Leafield Lodge* 1801 ib, cf. *ye Lodgeclosse, ye lodge Closse* 1567 LAHS, *le lodge close* 1611 *SP, (the) Lodge Close* 1661, 1661 (18), 1680, 1747, 1772, 1781, 1784, 1785, 1841 *Anc, v.* **loge, clos(e).**

KALKELEYS (lost), *Calkeleghes* 1369 For, *Calkelyes* 1371 Ipm, *Kalkeleis* 1371 IpmR, *Kalkeleyes* 1373 Ipm, *Calkeleyes* 1375 Fine, *Kalkeleys* 1379, 1385 ib; the first el. is OE **calc** which has the range of meanings 'chalk, limestone, coarse sand mixed with pebbles, heavy clay'. The last signification seems most appropriate in this area, hence 'the woodland clearings with heavy clay ground', *v.* **calc, lēah.** It is possible that *Cockleys* (*v.* f.ns. (b) *infra*) is a later development of this name.

BUSHY WOOD (BUSHY CLOSE 2½"), *Bushy Close* 1824 O, 1826 G, *v.* **busshi.** COLE'S LODGE, *Coles Lodge* 1806, 1820, 1822 Map, 1846, 1863, 1877 White, perhaps to be associated with descendants of Thomas *Cole* 1266 *For.* COLLEGE FM is *College Lodge* 1846, 1863, 1877 White, 1932 Kelly, belonging to the Collegiate Church of Westminster. HAYCOCK SPINNEY. HORSEPOOL LODGE, 1932 Kelly. OLDSALE WOOD, *Brown's Old Sale Wood* 1862 *Will, Browns* - 1918 *Deed, v.* **ald, sale.**

Field-Names

Undated forms in (a) are 1841 *Anc*; those dated 1822 (1848) and 1869 are *Whit*, those of 1842 are *Asw* and 1855 are *Anc*, while those dated 1845 and 1861 are *Deed*. Early forms dated 1256, 1373, 1376 and 1575 are *For*, those of 1611 are *SP*, those of 1623, 1624, 1626, 1677, c1685, 1694 and 17 are *Deed*; those dated 1661, 1661 (18), 1680, 1685, 1747, 1772, 1781, 1784 and 1785 are *Anc*; those of 1670 and 18^1 are *Rental*, 1726 are *Hotchkin*, 1728 are *Asw*; those dated 1729 and 18^2 are *Surv*; those of e18, 1733 (119), 1748 (119) and 1756 (119) are *Whit*.

(a) Bank's Ground 1841, Far -, First -, Little Banks Ground 1855, Bank's Mdw 1841 (*Banks's Ground* 1772, 1785, *Bankes Ground* 1781, *Old Banks's Meadow* 1772, *Banks's Old Meadow* 1781, *Bank's Old Meadow* 1785, v. **grund**); Barfoots Wood 1806 Map (from the surn. *Barfoot*, cf. Rev. H. *Barfoot* of Lyddington 1830 OR); Barn Close Mdw (1772, 1781, 1785), Little Barn Cl (*Little -, Barn Close* 1772, 1781, 1785); Bombast Lane c1800, 1806 Map (from eModE **bombast** 'the soft down of the cotton plant'); Bottom Paddock 1855; Brights Copy c1800 Map (from the surn. *Bright*, v. **copis**); Bushy Park Wood 1839 *TA* (v. **busshi**); East -, West Dry Hill, Dry Hill Mdw (*Dryhill* 1661, 1661 (18), 1680, 1694, 1729, 1747, *Dry Hills* 17, 18^1, 18^2, *East Dry Hill* 1772, 1785, *West -* 1772, 1784, 1785, *Dry Hill Meadow* 1772, 1785, *Dryhill al's Dryhill Coppice* 1677, *Dryhill Leaze* 1661, 1661 (18), 1680, Dryhills Leaze 1747, *Dryhill sale* 1611, v. **drȳge, hyll, copis, lēah, sale**); Lower Eight Acres; Feather Bed Lane 1806 Map (dial. *feather-bed* 'a quagmire'); Far -, Goose Pasture 1842; The Hundred Acres 1845, The Hundred or Under Acres 1861 (Mr J. Field notes that this is an example of the ironic use of 'Hundred Acres' to denote a small field, this close having an area of only a little over two acres; the alternative in the 1861 form is probably a rationalization); Leigh Leys, Upper Leigh Leys, - Mdw 1841, Leigh Leys Lower Mdw, - Upper - 1841, 1855 (*Lee Leez* 1567 LAHS, *le leighe leaze, le Leigh leyes, lighe leaze* 1611, (*the*) *Leigh Lays* 1772, 1781, 1785, *Leigh Leys, Lower -, Upper Leigh Leys* 1785, (*the*) *Leigh Lay(s) Lower Meadow, - Upper -* 1772, 1781, 1785, v. **lēah** and Leighfield *supra*); Middle Cl, ((*the*) *Middle Close* 1772, 1781, 1785); New Mdw ((*the*) *New Meadow* 1772, 1781, 1784, 1785, *Little new meadow* 1772); Palmers Mdw (*Palmers Close* 1661, 1661 (18), 1680, 1747, 1772, 1784, *Palmer's -* 1785, *Palmers close meadow* 1772, *Palmer's Meadow* 1785, from the surn. *Palmer*, cf. Bottom Palmer's in neighbouring Brooke f.ns. (a)); New -, Pen Mdw (*Pen Meadow* 1772, 1784, 1785, v. **penn**^{2}); Rail Mdw, Nether -, Upper Rail 1841, Great Rail Mdw 1855 (*Lawnde rayles* 1575, *le rail close* 1611, (*the*) *Raile* 1661, 1661 (18), 1772, *the Rayle* 1680, 1747, *the Lower Rail* 1785, (*the*) *Nether Rail* 1781, 1785, (*the*) *Upper Rail* 1772, 1781, 1785, *Rail Meadow* 1772, 1784, 1785, referring to the fence of Launde Park, which no doubt formed the county boundary with Lei at this point, v. **raile**); Sharpes Cl 1869 (*Sharp's Close* 1733 (119), from the surn. *Sharp(e)*, cf. *Sharpes Rode infra*, Sharp's Hill Fd and Sharp's Long Cl in nearby Barleythorpe f.ns. (a), Thomas *Sharpe* 1522 MilS of nearby Egleton, Harry *Sharp* 1932 Kelly also of Egleton); Straw Gates; Lower -, Middle ten acre Cl 1842; Tingle Mdw (1772, *Tingle Meadow otherwise Pingle Meadow* 1785, *Pingle Meadow* 1784, 1785, v. **pingel**); Wash Pit Mdw 1855 (referring to a sheep-dip, v. **wæsce, pytt**); the Wood Cls 1869 (*Wood Closes* 1733 (119), *the Wood Close* 1722 (119), 1756 (119)).

(b) *the two Acre Close* 1726; *Bedlam Meadow* 18^2 (Mr J. Field notes that this alludes to the Royal Bethlehem Hospital for the insane in London and to discharged patients therefrom; hence, a derogatory name for a piece of poor land); *Bittewell* 1610 Speed, *Bicklewell* 1677, 1694, *Bittlewell sail* 1684 Wright (the first el. is prob. *bitela* 'a beetle' used of the water-beetle, hence 'beetle-infested stream', v. **bitela, wella, sale**); *Botewell Wood* 1677, 1694 (prob. 'the healing spring', v. **bōt, wella**, cf. Botwell Mx 40); *Branston Sale al's Braniston Quarter al's Braniston Sidewood al's Branston Side Sale al's Branston Sidewood Sale al's Botewell Wood* 1677, *Branston Sale or Braniston quarter or Braniston Side Wood or Braniston side sale or Botewell wood* 1694 (naming woodland near Braunston, v. **sale, quarter, sīde**; for *Botewell Wood*, v. *supra*); *Branston Thins al's Branston Coppice* 1677, *Branston Thins or Branston Coppice* 1694 (naming woodland near Braunston, v. **þynne, copis**); *Brook Meadow* 18^2 (i.e., 'the meadow beside Brooke'); *Mr Cheseldines closes* 1661, *Mr Chisledine his Closes* 1680, *Chesledines closes* 1747 (by 1747, these closes were the property of Joseph *Cheselden*); *claus' olim voc'* ... *Cockleys* ... *modo voc' le lodge Close* 1611, *Cockleyes Sale al's Cockleys Quarter al's Cockleyes Coppice* 1677, *Cockly Sale* 1684 Wright, *Cockleys Coppice* 1694 (if not a later form of *Kalkeleys supra*, then 'the woodland glades or clearings frequented by woodcock', v. **cocc**^{2}, **lēah** and **sale, quarter, copis**); *Coldlees* 1610 Speed, *Coldeleyes* 1610 ib, 1645 Map (v. **cald, lēah**); *(the) Coppice* 1661, 1661 (18), 1680, 1747 (a close so called, v. **copis**); *Crooked Hasels* 1611, *Crooked hasels al's Todeholes leyes* 1611, *Crooked Hasell al's Todales Sales al's Crocked Hasell* 1677, *Toodale Sales al's Crocked Hasell* 1694 (v. **croked, hæsel** and *Todhole infra*); *Fair Ash Sale* 1677, c1685, 1688, 18^1 (v. **fæger, æsc, sale**); *Flat Seeks* 1729 (v. **flat, sīk**); *The Forest Close* 1726 Asw (v. **forest**); *Freewoods* 17, 1729, 18^1, *Middle Freewoods al's Rough Close, Northward Freewoods* 18^2, *Freewood Leaze* 1661, 1661 (18), 1680, *Freewoods Leaze* 1747, *Freewood Meadow* 18^2, *Free Wood Sale* 1611, *Freewood Sale al's Freewood al's Freewood Quarter Coppice* 1677, 1694 ('the free wood', v. **frēo, wudu**, cf. The Freewards in Essendine, evidently woodland in which commoners once enjoyed certain rights,

such as wood gathering, *v.* also **lĕah, sale, quarter, copis**); *Great Meadow* 18[2];
Greenly Road 1733 (119), 1756 (119) (cf. *Grinley Corner* in neighbouring Belton
f.ns. (b)); *Highway Close, Highway Meadow* 18[2]; *House Meadow* 18[2]; *Huntswood*
1651, *Hunts Wood* 17, 1729, 18[2], *East -, West Hunts Wood* 1729, *Great -, Little
Hunts Wood* 18[2], *Hounts Wood Meadow* 18[2], *Hunts Sale al's Huntswood al's
Huntwood Coppice* 1677, 1694 (evidently from the surn. *Hunt, v.* **sale, copis**);
Lambyngecrofte 1567 LAHS (*v.* **lambing, croft**); (*the*) *Lane Close* 1661, 1661 (18),
1680, 1747; *Lane Meadow* 1784; *Langele* 1314 Pat (*v.* **lang**[1], **lĕah**); (*the*) *Little
Meadow* 1781, 1785, 18[2]; *Loscott sale al's Loscott Wood al's Loscott Coppice al's
Loscott Quarter* 1677, *Losscott wood al's Losscott Coppice al's Losecott quarter*
1694, *Loscott Sale* 1733 (119), 1756 (119) ('pig-sty cottage or shelter', reflecting
the practice of feeding pigs on forest mast, *v.* **hlōse, cot** and **sale, quarter, copis**,
cf. Losecoat Field in Empingham and *Loscoat(e)s* in neighbouring Braunston f.ns.
(b)); *Lower Meadow* 18[2], *The Meadow* 1781, 1785, *Meadow Close, Middle Meadow*
18[2]; *Nook Meadow* 18[2] (*v.* **nōk**); *Le parke Dales* 1611 (*v.* **park, deill**); *boscus de
Riseberwe* 1266 *For* (in this border location, the generic is surely **beorg** 'a
barrow' rather than **bearu** 'a wood' (an el. alien to Ru) despite the *boscus* 'a
wood' of the extended form (cf. the parallel development of **beorg** in
Ranksborough Hill in Langham), *v.* **hris**, cf. Riseborough YN 77, Risborough Bk
177); *Branston Rode* 1677, 1694 ('Braunston clearing', *v.* **rod**[1] and Braunston);
Brooke Rode 1677, *Brookrode* 1694 ('Brooke clearing', *v.* **rod**[1] and Brooke);
Clagett Rode 1677, 1694 (perh. 'the clearing at the clay place', *v.* **clæg, -et(t)**,
rod[1]); *Gillians al's Julians Rode* 1677, *Gillian -* 1694 (*v.* **rod**[1]), *the High Rodes*
1677, 1694 (*v.* **hĕah**[1], **rod**[1]), *Kokerode* 1373 *For* (*v.* **cocc**[2], **rod**[1]); *Sharpes Rode*
1677, 1694 (from the surn. *Sharp(e)*, cf. Sharpes Cl *supra, v.* **rod**[1]); *Rosell sale,
Rosoo sale* 1611, *Rush Hill* 18[2] (*v.* **sale**); *Rough Close* 18[2]; *the Sheep Walk in the
Forrest of Lee* 1705, 1720 *Terrier* (*v.* **sheep-walk**); *Strickland Lodge* 1780, 1787
Map (from the surn. *Strickland*, cf. John *Stryckland* 1524 SR of Lyddington and
Edmunde *Strykland* 1524 ib of Barrowden); *Todhols* 1611, *Todalls* 17, *Toodales*
18[1], *Toad holes* 1729, *Toad Hole* 18[2], *Todales al's Todhill Coppice al's Cro(c)ked
Hasell al's To(o)dale Sales' al's Crocked Hasell* 1677, 1694, *Todeholes leyes* 1611,
Toad Hole Meadow 18[2], from **tod-hole** 'a fox-hole', *v.* **copis, lĕah** and *Crooked
Hasels supra*); *Toft Seeke* c1685, *Toftseeke* 17, *Tofft Seek* 18[1], *Toftsike al's Toftsike
Sale al's Tostock Coppice al's Toftsike Quarter* 1677, *Toft Sike al's Toft Sike sale
al's Toft Sike Coppice al's Toftsike quarter* 1694 (*v.* **toft, sik, copis, quarter**);
Upper Meadow 18[2]; *Water Lease al's Water Leaze Coppice* 1677, 1694 (*v.* **wæter,
lĕah, copis**); *Withcock Sale* 1623, 17, *Whitthcote Sale* 18[1] (named from Withcote
beyond the county boundary in Lei, *v.* **sale**); *Woolfit* 17, 18[1], *Woolf Pitt* 1729,
Lower -, Upper Wolfs Pits 18[2], *Woolfitt Sale al's Woolfrett Wood al's Woolfleet
Coppice* 1677 (*v.* **wulf-pytt, sale, copis**); *Youngwood Sale* 1677, 1694 (*v.* **geong,**

wudu, sale).

Oakham

OAKHAM

Ocheham 1086 DB bis

Occham c1154 Rut

Ocham(e), -k- 1067 BM, 1154 WDB, 1202 Ass, 1205 P et freq
    to 1400 Pat et passim to 1454 ShR, Hocham(e), -k- 1152
    BM, 1166 RBE et passim to 1328 Fine (p)

Okeham' 1190 CartAnt, 1231 RegAnt et passim to 1369 ELiW
    et freq to 1551 Pat et passim to 1610 LML, 1703 PSJ

Ockham 1252 IpmR, 1263 Ass et passim to 1388 Cl, Ockeham
    1260 Cl

Okam 1208 PatR, 1269 Cl et passim to 1349 Wyg (p), Hokam
    1317 ib (p)

Owkeham 1519 EpCB, Oukeham 1519 LWills, Oukham 1610
    Speed, Owkham 1608, 1615 LML

Oakeham 1685 FF, Oakham 1846 White

Probably 'Oc(c)a's village or estate', v. hām. Both the OE
pers.n. forms Oca and Occa are recorded in Anglo-Saxon charters.
Roman pottery found at SK 853 089 indicates an early settlement
site, v. BrownArchSites 20.

Street-Names

ASHWELL RD, 1803 Ct, 1846, 1863 White, Ashwell waie 1626 Ct, -
Way 1691, 1698, 1702 ib, 18 Terrier, Aswellway 1671 Ct, Aswell Way
1705 ib, v. Ashwell.

BARLEYTHORPE RD, 1932 Kelly is langhamgate 1412, 1509 Ct,
Langham way 1679 ib, v. gata, Barleythorpe and Langham.

BRAUNSTON RD, 1932 Kelly is Bramstongate 1624 Ct, Branston
gate 1630 ib, 1632 Terrier, 1676, 1683, 1691, 1702, 1723, 1733-6, 1776

Ct, Branson Gate 1702 *ib, v.* **gata** and Braunston.

BROOKE RD, 1846 White, 1932 Kelly is *Brokewaie* 1624 *Ct, Brookeway* 1630, 1632, 1636 *ib, Brooke Abby way* 1634 *ib, Brook Abbey Highway* 1691 *ib, Brookabby way* 1698 *ib, Brook Abby Way* 1702 *ib, Brooke highway* 1739-42 *ib, Brook Way* 18 *Terrier, Abbey way* 1632 *ib, the abby Way* 18 *ib.* The religious foundation at Brooke was a priory of Augustinian Canons, never an abbey, *v.* Brooke.

BUCKINGHAM RD, named from the 1st Duke of *Buckingham* who built the predecessor of neighbouring Burley House, otherwise Burley on the Hill, between 1620 and 1630 and who also purchased Oakham Lordshold or Castle Manor in 1616.

BULL LANE, 1846 White, *the Bull Lane* 1744 *Asw,* took its name from a lost hostelry called *the Bulle Inne,* recorded as early as 1494, which stood near the eastern gateway of the town (*messuag' iacet apud Estbarreʒate voc' le Bulle inter viam voc' Neugate et Heynes lane* 1494 *Finch*). Before becoming a cul-de-sac, Bull Lane was the beginning of the road to Stamford. The Bull Inn was thus conveniently placed for travellers at the eastern entrance to the town, *v.* Inns and Taverns *infra.*

BURLEY RD, 1846, 1863 White. It is *Burley Gate* 1632 *Terrier, Burleigh Gate* 1702 *Ct, Burley Way* 18 *Terrier, Burley horse way* 1723 *Ct, v.* **gata** and Burley. The stretch of Burley Rd beside the castle ramparts is *le Parklane* 1326 *Ct, the parke lane* 1614 *Deed* and (*the*) *Castle Lane* 1632 *Terrier,* 1638, 1691 *Ct,* 1767 *Deed,* with the stretch beyond, it is *Lady Well way* 1636, 1683 *Ct, Ladyeswellway* 1671 *ib, Ladys Well way* 1681 *ib, Ladyes Well Way* 1705 *ib, v.* Little Park *s.n.* The Castle *infra* and Our Lady's Well *infra.*

CATMOS ST, 1846, 1863 White, *Catmose St* 1932 Kelly is *le Neugate* 1374, 1375 *MinAcct,* (*le*) *Newgate* 1381 *ib,* 1388 *Misc,* 15

VCH, *Newegate* 1410 *Finch, viam voc' Neugate* 1494 *ib, Newgate Street* 1614, 1708, 1744 *Asw*, 1787 Map, 'the new road', *v.* **nīwe, gata.** It was also known as *le gebett gate* 1512 *MR, Gibbet Gate* 1610 Speed, 'the road to the gallows', *v.* **gibet, gata.** The gallows stood at Mount Pleasant, *v.* Catmose *infra.*

CHURCH ST, 1846, 1863, 1877 White, *Church Lane* 1850 Slater, 1873 OR. It is *le kirkgate* 1411 *Ct, v.* **kirkja, gata.**

COLD OVERTON RD, 1877 White, 1889 OR, 1932 Kelly, leads to Cold Overton Lei.

CROSS ST, 1846 White, 1932 Kelly.

DEAN'S ST is *Deans Lane* 1610 Speed, 1770-3 *Ct*, 1780 Map, 1827 OR, 1846, 1863 White, *Dean's Lane* 1863 ib, *the Deanes Lane* 1758-61 *Ct, Deans or Dead Lane* 1770-3 *ib.* It is *le Dedelane* 1498 *Ct, the dedelane* 1590 *ib, dedlane* 1504, 1544 *ib, deade lane* 1607 *ib,* (*le*) *dead lane* 1624, 1630, 1641 *ib, le Dead Lane* 1634, 1667 *ib, Dead Lane* 1763, 1800, 1803 *ib.* The earlier name is from the OE adj. **dēad** 'dead' but with what significance is unclear. Usually the el. in p.ns. refers to the place of a violent death or to the discovery of human bones. It may be also used of a lane with a dead-end (cf. Dead Lane, Ch 1 313). Speed's map of Oakham of 1610, which is the earliest extant, shows *Deans Lane* as a thoroughfare. The alternative later name is from ME **den** 'a dean' and relates to Oakham Deanshold or Church Manor.

DIGBY DRIVE is named from the *Digby* family of Stoke Dry.

FERRERS CLOSE is named from the *Ferrers* family. Wakelin de Ferrers built the hall of Oakham Castle c1180-90 and endowed Brooke Priory.

FINCH AVENUE is named from the family name of Daniel *Finch*, 2nd Earl of Nottingham, who rebuilt Burley on the Hill between 1694 and 1705.

FINKEY ST, *Finkle street* 1610 Speed, 1780 Map, *Finkhill streete* 1620 *Ct*, *Finkill Street* 1628 *ib*, *Finkehill Street* 1630 *ib*, *Finkhill street* 1632, 1671, 1723, 1733-6 *ib*, *Finkell Lane* 1667, 1785-97 *ib*, *Fynkell lane* 1683 *ib*, *Finkey Lane* 1730, 1739-42, 1763, 1803 *ib*, 1850 Slater; a common street-name in medieval towns in NMidl and NCy. Ekwall Studies[3] 47-53 suggests that Finkle Street was an obscene name for a lovers' lane, perhaps representing an unrecorded ME **finkle* 'to cuddle, to pet'. However, the common northern ME herb-name *fen(e)kel* 'fennel' seems a more acceptable source (cf. the parallel *Le Fennell Street* 1624 in Loughborough Lei), *v.* YE 286, Nt 16-7, Cu 47-8, We 1 116, L 1 65, *v.* Addenda p. lxxxvi.

GAOL ST, 1932 Kelly, *the Goal Lane* (sic) 1716 *Deed*, *Gaol Lane* 1850 Slater, 1868, 1889 OR, cf. *the house of Correction* 1716 *Deed*.

HANBURY CLOSE is named from the *Hanbury* family of Braunston Manor. From 1900, Mr E. Hanbury supplied Oakham with water piped from his springs at Brooke.

HARRINGTON WAY, named from the family of Sir John *Harrington* of Burley on the Hill, who purchased Oakham Lordshold or Castle Manor in 1596.

HIGH ST, 1831 OR, 1846, 1863 White, 1907 *Deed*. The early name of the eastern portion of High St is uncertain but was possibly Bargate, a name later transferred to the West Bar itself. Its western reach may be the road recorded as *a certayne streete called without the west barr gates* 1614 *Deed*, *v.* The Town Gates *infra*.

JOHN ST, *John Street newly formed from Simpers Close* 1825 *Deed,* *John St* 1846, 1863 White.

KILBURN RD is *Cemetery Road* 1971 *Map,* cf. *Cemetery* 1877 White.

LONSDALE WAY, named from Hugh Cecil Lowther, 5th Earl of *Lonsdale* (1857-1944), who sponsored boxing's first Lonsdale Belt and developed Barleythorpe Stud.

MARKET PLACE, MARKET ST, *The Market* 1610 Speed, 1780 Map, *the Markett place* 1614 *Deed, Market place* 1846, 1863 White, *Markett streete* 1611 *Deed, Market St* 1846 White, 1932 Kelly, *v.* **market.**

MELTON RD, 1846, 1863 White; the road to Melton Mowbray Lei.

MILL ST is *Malt mill stret* 1610 Speed, *Malt Mill Street* 1780 Map, *Mylnes Streete* 1611 *Deed, Mill st* 1846, 1863 White, *The Mill Street* 1896 *Anc, v.* **malte-mylne.**

NEW ST, 1846, 1863 White.

NOEL AVENUE, named from the *Noel* family of Exton, Earls of Gainsborough.

NORTHGATE ST is *le Northgate* 1501 *Ct, northe gate* 1590 *ib, Norgate* 1610 Speed, 1704 *Deed,* 1736 *Ct, Northgate* 1620, 1691 *ib,* 1715 *Deed,* 1763, 1773 *Ct,* 1780 Map, 1797, 1800 *Ct, northgatestrete* 1590 *ib, Northgate Street* 1797, 1803 *ib,* 'the north road', *v.* **norð, gata.**

PARKFIELD RD, cf. *le Parkefeild* 1630 *Ct*, *v*. **park**.

PARK LANE, leading . to *the further parke lyinge towardes Barlythorpe Mault myll* 1611 *Deed*, *v*. **park, malte-mylne**.

PENN ST, 1932 Kelly, cf. *Penn Close* 1718 *Deed*, *The Pen Close* 1790 *ib*, *v*. **penn²** 'a small enclosure, a fold'; cf. Hayne House *infra*, which records another enclosure to the south of the early town.

SIMPER ST, 1829, 1831 OR, 1846 White, 1850 Slater, cf. *Simpers Close* 1718, 1724, 1825 *Deed*, from the surn. *Simper*.

SOUTH ST, 1907 *Deed*, *v*. *Thresholdgate infra*.

STAMFORD RD, *Stamford gate* 1618 *Ct*, *via de Stamford* 1663 *ib*, *Stamford Way* 1691 *ib*, 17 *Terrier*, 1702 *Ct*, *Stamford road* 1846 White, *v*. **gata**; the road to Stamford L.

STATION RD, 1932 Kelly. It was formerly *Northbackway* 1884 Map westwards from Kilburn Rd junction, and *Oddhouse Lane* 1884 ib from Kilburn Rd eastwards, *v*. **back** and Odd House Tavern *infra*.

UPPINGHAM RD, 1846 White is *Uppingham way* 1634, 1691, 1698 *Ct*. It is probably *Suthgate* c1200 *WDB*, 'the south road', *v*. **sūð, gata** and Uppingham.

WESTFIELD AVENUE recalls the old west open-field of the town, *v*. West Field in f.ns. (a) *infra*.

WESTGATE ST, 1932 Kelly, *Westgate* 1549 Pat, 'the west road', *v*. **west, gata**. It is *Beadhouse Row* 1856 OR, *Bedehouse Row* 1866,

1889 *ib* because leading to the Chapel of St John and St Anne, *v.*
bed-hūs 'a prayer-house, a chapel', **rāw** '(a street lined with) a row
of houses'.

WEST RD is (*le*) *Cow Lane* 1630, 1671, 1674, 1687, 1702 *Ct*, 18
Terrier, cf. *Cowlane end* 1632 *ib*, *Cow Lane End* 1674 *Ct*, *v.* **cū, lane,
ende**[1].

WILLIAM DALBY ST is named from *William Dalby* of Exton,
wool merchant, who built and endowed the Hospital of St John the
Evangelist and St Anne for two chaplains and twelve poor men in
1399 Pat. Formerly its name was Gas Street: the original gas
works were built here in 1840, cf. *Gas Works* 1846 White.

The following street-names have not been identified:

Busbie waie 1624 *Ct*, containing the house of *Magistr' Busbie* 1626
ib.

Castledine's Lane 1785-97 *Ct*, with the surname *Castledine*.

Dark Lane 1733-6, 1755, 1785-97 *Ct*, cf. *Dark Lane End* 1733-6,
1755, 1785-97 *ib*, *v.* **deorc.**

Fengate 15 VCH, 'the road to the marsh', *v.* **fenn, gata.** The marsh
is perhaps to be equated with Catmose *infra*.

le Grenegate 1498 *Ct*, *Green(e)gate* 1624, 1630, 1632 *ib*, 1632 *Terrier*,
1671 *Ct*, *Greene Gate* 1679 *ib*, 'the green way', *v.* **grēne**[1], **gata.**

Little Lane 1691 *Ct*, *v.* **lytel, lane.**

Longe Lane 1611 *Ct, v.* **lang¹, lane.**

Pinfold Lane 1785-97 *Ct, v.* **pynd-fald.**

Rotten Row 1607 *Ct, (le) Rotten Rowe* 1607, 1620, 1723, 1733-6, 1763 *ib, Rotten Roe* 1634 *ib, Rotten Row* 1800, 1803 *ib* '(street lined with) a row of rat-infested houses', *v.* **raton, rāw.**

Tanners Lane 1787 Map.

the Tithebarne lane 1638 *Ct, v.* **tēoða;** Speed's map of Oakham of 1610 shows the Tithe Barn on the east side of a road running north from Northgate St. The site is now built over.

Thresholdgate 1632 *Terrier, Threshaldgate* 1667 *Ct, Threshwellgate* 1671 *ib, Threshold gate* 1691 *ib, Threshwells Gate* 1705 *ib, Threshall gate* 1739-42 *ib,* 'the road at the threshold', *v.* **þerscold, gata.** The name is recorded as that of a furlong in the old south open-field of the town; it is likely to refer to a road running across the southern limit of the early enceinte. Its line may have been that of the eastern stretch of modern South St.

the westende 1590 *Ct, le Westend in dead lane* 1630 *ib, v.* **west, ende¹** and Dean's St *supra.*

No early forms have been found for the following Oakham street-names:

ALEXANDER CRESCENT, ALPINE CLOSE, AVON CLOSE, BALMORAL RD, BARLOW RD, BEECH RD, BOWLING GREEN CLOSE, BROWNING RD, CALGARY CRESCENT, CATMOSE PARK RD, CHATER RD, CHESTNUT RD, CHEVIOT CLOSE, CHILTERN CLOSE, CHURCHILL RD, CRICKET LAWNS, THE DELL, DERWENT DRIVE, DON CLOSE,

EDMONTON WAY, ELM CLOSE, FARSIDE, GLEBE WAY, GLEN DRIVE, GRAMPIAN WAY, HILL RD, HOLYROOD CLOSE, KENNEDY CLOSE, KING'S RD, LONG ROW, MENDIP RD, NENE CRESCENT, PETERBOROUGH AVENUE, PRINCESS AVENUE, QUEEN'S RD, REDLAND RD, ST ALBANS CLOSE, ST PETER'S CLOSE, SANDRINGHAM CLOSE, SHORT ST, SNOWDON AVENUE, SPEY RD, TAY CLOSE, TEES CLOSE, TRENT RD, TYNE RD, THE VALE, VICARAGE RD, WARN CRESCENT, WELLAND WAY, WILLOW CRESCENT, WINDSOR DRIVE, WITHAM AVENUE, WOODLAND VIEW.

Town Buildings

BUTTER CROSS, 1608 VCH. It is *Market Cross* 1765, 1790 OR, cf. *atte Crosse* 1341 NI (p), *v.* **cros**.

THE CASTLE, *in castro de Okeham* 1269 For, *extra Castrum* 1374 *MinAcct, The Castell* 1610 Speed, *the Castle* 1638 *Ct, v.* **castel(l)**. The Inner Bailey is *le Baillie* 1329 *Deed,* 1376 *MinAcct, le Bailie* 1377 *ib, le Bayllie* 1373, 1374 *ib, le Baylye* 1374 *ib, le Bail(l)ye* 1375, 1382 *ib, v.* **baille**. It is *Castle Yard* 1686 *Rental*. The defensive ditch of the castle is *le Casteldyk'* 1373, 1374 *MinAcct, le Casteldich'* 1374 *ib, le Casteldisch* 1377 *ib, le Casteldech* 1382 *ib, v.* **dĩk, dīc**. The castle bridge across its southern ditch and into the town is recorded in *iuxta pontem castri* 1374 *MinAcct, apud pontem Castelli* 1383 *ib, v.* **brycg**. The Norman hall within the Bailey is *le Mothalle* 1373, 1377 *MinAcct, Shire Hall* 1610 Speed, cf. *super aulam* 1285 *MinAcct* (p), *v.* **mōt, scīr**[1], **hall**. To the north is an enclosure surrounded by large banks, possibly a garden, which became known as *Cutte Close* 1610, 1611 *Ct, Cutts Close* 17 *Deed, Cutt's Close* 1795 Nichols, 1868 OR, *v.* **cutte**[1] 'a water channel'. As late as 1868 OR, we learn of *the open ditch through Cutt's Close*, evidently a sewer. The castle stew or fishpond lay along the length of the north wall of the main enceinte: it is *le Fispol* 1344 *MR, le Fishpoll'* 1360 Ipm, *le Fisshpol* 1374, 1375 *MinAcct, le Fyschpool'* 1376 *ib, le Fysshepol* 1377 *ib, le Fischepol* 1381 *ib, le Fyschpol* 1382 *ib, Fyshpole* 1388 Misc, *(le) Fishpool(e)* 1667, 1763 *Ct, Fishpooles* 1632 *Terrier, v.* **fisc, pōl**. The castle gardens are variously *gardinum extra castrum* 14 *Rental, Herbag' gardini infra Castr'* 1374 *MinAcct, Herbag' gardini* *extra Castrum* 1374 *ib* and *fructu Gardini infra castrum* 1285 *ib*: the last is perhaps to be identified with *le Castelorchard'* 1380 *ib, le Castell' Orchard* 1498 *Ct, Castell' orchard'* 1547 *ib, v.* **gardin, orceard**. The castle's vineyard is *Wynnʒerd* 1374 *MinAcct, Vyneryerd'* 1375 *ib, Vyneʒerd* 1376 *ib, v.* **wīn-geard**.

The associated Little Park of the castle, at its eastern side, is *paruo Parco* 1285 *MinAcct, paruus parcus* (sic) 14 *Rental, the Park(e)* 1657, 1686, 1687 *ib, le Parke* 1702 *Ct,* cf. *ad parcum* 1305 OSurv (p), *atte Park'* 1326 *Ct* (p), *v.* **lȳtel, park**.

CATMOSE VALE HOSPITAL is *Union House* 1824 O, *Union Workhouse* 1846, 1863, 1877 White, *Oakham Union* 1855 OR, originally a Poor Law institute, *v.* Vale of Catmose.

FLORE'S HOUSE (34 High St) was built by William *Flore* who was controller of the works of the castle from 1373 to 1380 and Sheriff of Rutland. His son Roger was Speaker of the House of Commons in the parliaments of 1416, 1417, 1419 and 1422 and married the daughter of William Dalby (*v.* William Dalby St *supra*). William Flore extended his house to incorporate the West Bar - 'a solar built over the gate called Le Westbarreyate' 1373 Pat. The solar no doubt was the reason for the West Bar's survival to be illustrated on Speed's town map of 1610. Roger Flore is reputed to have built the church steeple c1425.

HAYNE HOUSE, cf. *Heynes lane* 1494 *Finch, Haynes Lane* 15 VCH, *v.* **hægen** 'an enclosure'. This enclosure was to the south-east of the precinct of the early town. The later *Penn Close* (*v.* **penne²** 'a small enclosure') remembered in Penn St *supra* was nearby to its west.

HOSPITAL OF ST JOHN, 'hospital of St John Evangelist and St Anne, Okeham' 1404, 1406 Pat, *the Old Hospitall* 1684 Wright, *the Hospital of St Ann commonly called the Old Hospital* 1757 *Hotchkin, the Hospital of Saint Ann* 1829 *Anc, Hospital of St John the Evangelist and St Anne in Oakham* 1846 White. Its chapel was *le*

Beadhouse 1622 *Ct, the Old Bead-house* 1689 *Deed, (the) Bedehouse* 18 *Rental,* 1846 White, cf. *le Beadhouse Close* 1677 *Ct, v.* **hospital, bed-hūs.** William Dalby of Exton, wool merchant, founded the Hospital in 1399 for two chaplains and twelve poor men, with a messuage and two acres of land, *v.* VCH **2** 25. The chapel survives.

MILL HOUSE, cf. *a newly erected windmill situated in the North Field* 1833 OR. The mill was known as *Mason's Mill* from the *Mason* family - OR.

OAKHAM CHURCH, *Church (All Saints)* 1846, 1863, 1877 White.

OAKHAM SCHOOL, 1932 Kelly. It is *Free Schole* 1610 Speed, *Free School* 1780 Map, *Free Grammar School* 1846, 1863, 1877 White. Founded in 1584 by Robert Johnson, Rector of North Luffenham, it was one of *the free grammer Scholes of Robert Johnson, clarke ... in Okeham and Uppingham* 1587 Pat, *v.* VCH **2** 26. The *Free Schole,* illustrated on Speed's map of 1610, is now the Shakespeare Building of Oakham School.

RUTLAND COUNTY MUSEUM is *Riding School* 1846, 1863 White.

VICTORIA HALL, 1932 Kelly is *New Agricultural Hall* 1839 OR, *Agricultural Hall* 1846, 1863 White.

The following later buildings are recorded:

Baptist Chapel 1850 Slater, 1932 Kelly; *Patent Steam Brewery* 1846, 1863 White; *Brookfield* 1932 Kelly; *The Callis* 1846 White (which probably recalls the fact that the chief merchants of Oakham belonged to the Staple of Calais until Calais was lost in 1558, *v.* VCH **2** 24 and xxxi; in Stamford, the plural form *callises* was used of certain almshouses built for decayed members of the Staple and it is possible that in Oakham the singular was used of an early almshouse, cf. The Callis (local) in Ashby de la Zouch Lei (*the Callis* 1796 *EnclA, The Calais* 1835 O), *v.* EDD *s.v.* callises); *Congregational Chapel* 1846, 1863 White; *Deanscroft* 1932 Kelly; *Friends' Meeting House* 1850 Slater; *County Gaol and House of Correction* 1846, 1863, 1877 White; *Gas Works* 1846 ib; *The Hollies* (Penn St) 1877 ib; *Independent Chapel* 1850 Slater; *Old Vicarage* 1846 White; *Particular Baptist Chapel* 1932 Kelly; *Pen Villa* (Dean's St) 1846 White; *Police Station* 1877 ib; *Primitive Methodist Chapel* 1932 Kelly; *Railway Station* 1850 Slater, 1877 White; *Rutland Dispensary* 1832 OR, 1846 White; *South Bank Villa* 1932 Kelly; *Springfield* 1932 ib; *Wesleyan Methodist Chapel* 1850 Slater, *Wesleyan Chapel* 1864 OR, *Wesleyan Methodist church* 1932 Kelly.

The following structures either do not survive or have not been identified:

Alletts windmill 1874 OR stood on Brooke Hill and was occupied by John *Allett* 1863 ib.

the Brewhouse 1785-97 *Ct*, cf. *the Brewhouse End* 1785-97 *ib*, *v.* **brew-hous.**

Catmouse mill 1610 Speed, *Catmouse myll, a water myll or corne myll scituate in Okeham* 1611 *Deed, Catmouse Mill* 1620 Map, *Catmouse Mill* 1715 ib, cf. *Catmouse myll close* 1611 *Deed.* It is *ye watermyln* 1482 *MisAccts, v.* **water-mylne.** The mill stood near Swooning Bridge, *v.* Vale of Catmose, and Catmose *infra.*

Estbarreʒate 1494 Finch, *Estbarregate* 15 VCH, cf. *atte Barre orientale* 1305 OSurv (p), *v.* The Town Gates *infra.*

hospitii apud Okham 1376 *MR* refers to the Abbot of Westminster's Hospice. Richard de Berkyn, Abbot of Westminster, bought the

temporalities of Oakham Church and its dependent churches from
the Bishop of Lincoln in 1231. The Hospice was endowed for the
reception of monks sent from Westminster for the service of the
church, *v.* VCH 2 15 and OR 4.

Kilne house 1628 *Ct,* cf. *le Mill Kilne* 1667 *ib, v.* **cyln**. Part of the
former malt mill, *v.* Mill St *supra.*

le Meeting place (*messuag' vocat'* ...) 1723 *Ct,* perhaps to be identified
with 31 Gaol St which was formerly a Quaker meeting house.

vno molendino equino 1381 *MinAcct, ye horsse myln* 1482 *MisAccts,*
v. **horse-mylne** 'a mill worked by a horse'.

The Butchers Shambles 17 *Deed,* (*The*) *Shambles* 1780 Map, 1851,
1867 OR, *v.* **shamel** 'a stall for the sale of meat'; this stood in the
Market Place and was removed in 1880 - OR.

Shoomakers Shop 1614 *Deed,* in the Market Place, it was the
property of Mark Wayne 1614 *ib,* cf. *Shoemakers Stalls* 17. *ib, v.*
shoemaker.

Stamford Bridge 1611, 1614 *Deed,* 1683 *Ct,* a bridge on the road to
Stamford L. It is perhaps to be identified with *Stanbrigge* 1498 *Ct,*
Burley Stone Bridge 1733-6, 1776 *Ct* (*v.* **stān, brycg**) and also *Twiford*
Bridge 1684 Wright, cf. *ad quendam uadum in predicta aqua currente*
inter Burle et Egoluestun qui uadus appellatur Thuiford 1218 *For,*
Twiford' 1269 *ib,* 'double ford', *v.* **twī-, ford** and Burley and Egleton.

Tythe Barne 1610 Speed, *le Tithebarne* 1630, 1638 *Ct, v.* **tēoða** and
the *Tithebarne lane supra.*

Le Westbarreyate 1373 Pat, 1375 *MinAcct, Westbarreȝate* 1381 *MinAcct, v.* The Town Gates *infra.*

ye wyndmyln 1482 *MisAccts, v.* **wind-mylne.**

The Town Gates

Both the east and west gates of medieval Oakham are recorded. The east gate stood near the entrance to the cul-de-sac Bull Lane which was originally the beginning of the old Stamford Road. It is first recorded as *atte Barre orientale* 1305 OSurv (p), *v.* **ēast, barre.** The lost Bull Inn, from which Bull Lane is named, was situated near the gateway: *messuag' iacet apud Estbarreȝate voc' le Bulle inter viam voc' Neugate et Heynes lane* 1494 Finch, cf. *Estbarregate* 15 VCH, *v.* Bull Lane *supra* and Hayne House *supra.* The west gate is illustrated on Speed's town map of 1610. The arched gateway crosses what was to become High St. The gate is *Le Westbarreyate* 1373 Pat, 1375 *MinAcct, Westbarrewate* (sic) 1380 *ib, Westbarreȝate* 1381 *ib, v.* **west, barre,** cf. *a certayne streete called without the west barr gates* 1614 *Deed.* The personal-name forms *a la Barre* 1305 OSurv (p), *atte Barre* 1326 (p), 1329 *Ct* (p), 1331 Cl (p), 1374 *Ct* (p), 14 *Rental* (p), *ad Barram* 1305 OSurv (p), 14 *Rental* (p) probably refer to the west gateway since they all name Robert (? father and son) as distinct from Emma who by contrast is specifically of the east gateway in 1305 OSurv.

The town enceinte appears to have been defended by an outer ditch recorded as *le Barredyk'* 1377 *MinAcct, v.* **barre, dik.** Whether this solitary reference to a defensive ditch relates to the east or west bar is uncertain.

Bargate is recorded on Speed's map of 1610. It may refer to his illustrated gateway or, less likely, it may be the earlier name of Oakham's major thoroughfare for which we have otherwise no name recorded before 1831. If the latter is indeed the case, this road was 'the bar street', *v.* **barre, gata.** The medieval street and road names of Oakham are usually formed with Scand **gata** 'road'. The *gata* of this possible street-name may early have become incorporated into the names of the bars so that eventually we have the pleonastic combination of **barre** 'a barrier closing an entrance to a town' and **geat** 'an entrance through a town wall'. However, early forms for Pockthorpe Gate in Norwich (Nf **1** 19) show just such a compounding of **barre** and **geat** for a medieval town bar. An independently used *barre* for such gateways is more usual, such as in Monk Bar and Bootham Bar in York.

The survival of the west gate in 1610 was no doubt due to its incorporation into the house of William Flore (*v.* Flore's House *supra*) for we learn of his 'solar built over the gate called Le Westbarreyate' 1373 *Pat*. By 1614, the west bar's gates are specifically cited: *a certayne streete called without the west barr gates* 1614 *Deed*.

The north side of the early medieval town's fortifications is formed by the castle (*v. supra*) so that any northern exit would have been part of the castle's defences. There is no record of a south gateway to the town unless the name *Thresholdgate* (*v. supra*) implies a road lying across the threshold of a southern gateway. The solitary form *Suthgate* c1200 *WDB* is to be interpreted as 'south road' (*v.* **sūð, gata**) rather than 'south gateway'.

Oakham Inns and Taverns

ANGEL (Northgate St - lost), 1846, 1863 White.

BELL (Catmos St - lost), 1846, 1863 White.

BLUE BALL (Northgate St - lost), 1862 OR.

BLUE BELL (lost), 1740 OR. This may be the later Blue Ball *supra*.

BOAT (lost - now 44 Ashwell Rd), served the navvies working on the Melton Mowbray-Oakham Canal.

BRITANNIA (Northgate St - lost), - OR.

BULL (High St East/Bull Lane - lost), *messuag' iacet apud Estbarreʒate voc' le Bulle inter viam voc' Neugate et Heynes lane* 1494 *Finch, le Bull* 15 VCH, *the Bull* 1614 *Deed, the Bull Inne* 17 *ib*, cf. *the Bull Lane* 1744 *Asw.*

CROSS KEYS (lost - now 9 New St), - OR.

CROWN HOTEL (High St), *The Crowne, a common Inne* 1611 *Deed, Crown Inn* 1846 White, *Crown Hotel* 1850 Slater, 1881 OR, 1907 *Deed*, 1932 Kelly.

DUKE'S HEAD (Market Place - lost), 1846, 1863 White, *Dukes Head* 1899 OR.

FINCH'S ARMS (lost), 1846 White, 1850 Slater, named from the *Finch* family of Burley on the Hill.

GEORGE HOTEL (Market Place - lost), (*The*) *George Inn* 1739 .OR, 1804 *Deed*, 1842 OR, 1846, 1863 White, 1896 *Anc.* Recently (1991) renamed The Whipper-in.

KING'S HEAD (lost - now 25 Westgate St), - OR.

LORD NELSON (lost - now 11 Market Place), 1846, 1863 White.

ODD HOUSE TAVERN (Ashwell Rd/Station Rd), *Odd House Inn* 1841 OR, *Odd House* 1846 White.

PRINCE OF WALES (New St/John St).

RAILWAY INN (Station Rd), 1846 White, 1850 Slater.

RED COW (lost), 1827 OR; became Odd House Tavern *supra.*

RED LION (High St - lost), *Old Red Lion* 1846, 1863 White, *Red Lion* 1861 OR, 1877 White, 1880 OR.

ROEBUCK (Church St - lost), 1846 White, 1850 Slater.

ROYAL DUKE (West Rd).

ROYAL OAK (High St - lost), 1846, 1877 White.

RUTLAND ARMS (lost - now 4 Cross St), 1832 OR, referring to the Dukes of Rutland.

SUN (lost), *apud le Sonne* 1374 *MinAcct;* evidently gave its name to a furlong, abutting the town in its great south field, called *Vnder the sun* 1691 *Ct, Undersun Furlong* 18 *Terrier.*

SUN (lost), 1830 OR, 1846 White, 1850 Slater; it is uncertain whether this is the same tavern as the early Sun *supra.*

THREE CROWNS INN (Northgate St/Finkey St), 1875 OR.

VINE (lost - now 9 Mill St), - OR.

WHEATSHEAF (Church St/Northgate St), *Wheat Sheaf* 1846 White, *Wheatsheaf* 1850 Slater, 1880 OR.

WHIPPER-IN (Market Place), *v.* George Hotel *supra.*

WHITE LION HOTEL (Melton Rd - lost), 1932 Kelly, *White Lion Inn* 1846, 1877 White.

WINETAVERN (lost), *le Wyntauerne* 1381 *MinAcct,* 'the wine tavern', *v.* **wyn, taverne.**

BANKY MEADOW. BROOKE COVERT, - EAST, *v.* **cover(t)** and Brooke *supra.* BROOKE HILL. CATMOSE (2½"), - FM, - LODGE, *Catmos Lodge* 1824 O, 1850 Slater: south-east of the town and in what was probably once the region of the 'wild-cat bog', cf. *Fengate supra, Catmouse mill supra* and *v.* V.ale of Catmose. CAXMIR COTTAGE, *the Cottage* 1846, 1863 White, 1932 Kelly. THE CLOSE. DOG KENNEL COTTAGES, *le Doggkinnell* 1687 *Ct, v.* **dogge-kenel.** FLITTERIS PARK FM is *Flitteris Lodge* 1846, 1863 White, *v.* Flitteris Park *infra.* THE GLEBE, *v.* **glebe.** THE GRANGE, *grangie de Ocham* 1276, 1296 *MR, Oakham Grange* 1825 Map, *The Grange* 1846 White, *v.* **grange.** HILL TOP FM. THE LODGE, *Oakham Lodge* 1932 Kelly. MELTON MOWBRAY AND OAKHAM CANAL, 1846 White, *the Oakham Canal* 1808 *Anc;* it was completed in 1803 (*v.* VCH 2 10). MOUNT PLEASANT, perhaps an ironical name since it was the site of the town gallows. OUR LADY'S WELL, *Ladies well* 1632 *Terrier, Lady's Well* 1691 *Ct, Ladywell* 1780 Map, *Lady Well* 1801 ib, cf. *Ladies well furlonge* 1632 *Ct, Lady Well Furlong* 1723 *ib, Ladyswell furlong* 1739-42 *ib, Ladywell Furlong* 18 *Terrier,* 'the Virgin Mary's spring or well', *v.* **hlæfdige, wella** and Burley Rd *supra.* SWOONING BRIDGE is so called, according to local lore, because it was the point at which the condemned had their first sight of the gallows at Mount Pleasant.

Oakham Field-Names

Undated forms in (a) are 1943 *Map;* those dated 1800, 1802 and 1803 are *Ct,* 1804 are *ChurchwardensAccts* while those of 1825 and 1832 are *Deed.* Early forms dated 1285, 1374, 1375, 1376, 1380 and 1381 are *MinAcct*; 1290 and 1344 are *MR*; 1300, 1347 and 1360 are Ipm; those dated 1305 are OSurv; 14 are *Rental*; 1501, 1547, 1548, 1590, 1601, 1604, 1607, 1610, 1611, 1618, 1620, 1624, 1626, 1628, 1630, 1632[1], 1634, 1636, 1641, 1663, 1671, 1674, 1676, 1677, 1679, 1681, 1683, 1687, 1691, 1698, 1702, 1705, 1723, 1726, 1730, 1733-6, 1739-42, 1746, 1755, 1758-61, 1763, 1776, 1780 and 1785-97 are *Ct*; 1614, c1685, 1689, 17, 1718, 1724 and 1790 are *Deed*; and those dated 1632[2] and 18 are *Terrier*.

(a) The Acres; 4 Acre, 5 -, 6 -, 7 -, 8 -, 9 Acre (x2), 10 Acre (x2), 11 -, 12 -, 14 Acre (x2), 18 -, 20 Acre (*v.* æcer); The Allotments 1925 *Deed* (noted as 'now known as Twitch Hill' (*q.v.*), referring to allotment gardens); Back Fd; Baines 12 Acre (named from the *Baines* family, cf. John Russel *Baines* 1932 Kelly); Ball's Ploughed Fd; Barleythorpe Rails 1804 (*v.* raile); Barnett's (named from the *Barnett* family, cf. George Edward *Barnett* 1932 Kelly); Belgium (prob. dating from the exile of the King of the Belgians whose royal coaches, horses and grooms were brought to Oakham for the duration of the First World War, the coaches being kept in the Riding School (now the Rutland County Museum) and the horses grazed locally); Bishops Cl 1803, Bishop's - 1832 (*Bishops-Close* 1691, *Bishops Close* 1698, 1730, 1755, 1785-97); Bottom Fd; Bradshaw's Railway Fd (crossed by the railway; the field is named from the local *Bradshaw* family, cf. Arthur M. *Bradshaw* 1932 Kelly); Brick Fd; Broken Back (*v.* Brokenback Furlong in N. Luffenham f.ns. (a) where the name is discussed); Bullimore's (a sum., cf. *Bulimore* in neighbouring Burley f.ns. (b)); Champantes Cl 1908 *Deed*; Church Cl 1804; Clarke's; Bottom -, Middle -, Clifton's; Cole's Well 1804 (*Coles Well* 1611, *iuxta fontem vocat' Coleswell* 1626, *Coleswell* 1632[1], *Coales Well* 1632[2], 1763, 1780, *Coaleswell furlong* 1671, *Coleswell furlong* 1679, 1698, 1702, *Colswell Furlong* 18, poss. from the surn. *Cole*, cf. Thomas *Cole* 1266 *For* whose descendants may have come to be associated with Cole's Lodge in Leighfield, *v.* wella); Copse (*Cop* 1300 Ipm, 1305 OSurv, 1632[2], *le Copp* 1632[1], *le Coppe* 1676, 1698, *the Cops* 1733-6, 1755, 1785-97, 18, *the Copse* 1785-97, *Cop Furlong* 1739-42, 18, *v.* copp, cf. *le Coppede* 1632[1] (*v.* hēafod)); Damm Acres 1803, 1832 (*Damacres* 1691, *Dammacres* 1730, 1755, 1785-97, *Dam Acres* 18, *v.* damme, æcer); Daniel's (prob. named from the *Daniels* family, cf. Miss *Daniels* 1932 Kelly); Doves Nest 1803, Dove's - 1832 (*Doves nest* 1632[2], *Doves-nest* 1691, *Doves Nest* 1730, 1755, 1785-97, *Dove Nest* 18, evidently a name for a pleasant place); Faulk's Fd; Feeding Fd or Scouts Hut Fd (originally grazing ground, pasturage, *v.* feeding); Gallows Peice 1804 (*the gallowes* 1632[2], *v.* galga, pece, cf. Catmos St *supra*); Hart's (the sum. *Hart*, cf. *Hartes acres* in Egleton f.ns. (b) and Harts Cl in Gunthorpe f.ns. (a)); Hell's Hales (prob. a variant of Hills and Hales in Exton f.ns. (a), with dial. *hell* 'hill'); High Mdw 1800, 1802, 1803 (*le hiemeadow*(*e*) 1632[1], *le high meadow* 1667, 1679, 1683, 1691, (*the*) *High Meadow* 1632[2], 1758-61, 1776, 18, *v.* hēah[1], mǣd, cf. *Hymeadow side* 1632[1], *le High Meadow Side* 1723, *v.* sīde); Hill Side; Home Fd (*v.* home); Hovel Cl (*v.* hovel); Big Jackson's; Lady Wood Fd (cf. Lady Wood Piece in Flitteris Park f.ns. (a)); Lewin's Cl (from the family of George *Lewin* 1910 OR); Lewis's Quarter. 1800, Lewis' - 1802 (a quarter of a yard-land so called); Long Gate Side 1803, 1832 (*Long-gate side* 1691, 1755, *Long gate side* 1730, 1785-97, cf. *Longate Furlong* 18, *v.* langet 'a long (narrow) strip of ground', sīde); Long Mdw; the Meere 1804 (*v.* (ge)mǣre); Militia Cl 1907 *Deed* (later Royce's Cattle Market in South St, it takes its name from the Rutland Militia 1791 OR which evidently used the field for mustering); Mill Fd or Covey Lane Fd (adjoins Brooke Covert, *v.* cover(t)); Middle -, Top Needham (from the local *Needham* family, cf. Rowland *Needham* 1932 Kelly); Noll's (*Noll* is a pet-form of *Oliver*, used here prob. as a surn., cf. Thomas *Olyuer* of Belton 1522 MilS and Richard *Olever* of Ayston 1525 SR); North Fd 1802, 1832 (*Nortfeld* 1285, *Northfeld* 1305, 14, *le Northe Feild* 1611, *the north Feild* 1614, *le Northfeild* 1626, 1630, 1636, 1641, *North Feilde* 1635, (*the*) *Northfield* 1733-6, 1739-42, 1762, 1776, 1785-97, *North Field* 18, *in Campo boreali* 1618, 1636, *in boreal' campo* 1632, 1634, one of the great open-fields of the town, *v.* norð, feld); The Parks 1943 (*les Parkes* 1698, *the Parks* c1685, 17), The Park Side 1803, 1832 (*le Park-side* 1691, *le Park side* 1730, *Park Side* 1755, 1785-97, *v.* park, sīde, Little Park *s.n.* The Castle *supra* and Park Lane *supra*); Rawlings Mdw; Round Haystack Fd; 1st -, 2nd Ridge (*le Ridge* 1634, *Rig Furlong* 18, *v.* hrycg, hryggr and *The Rigg* in Egleton f.ns. (b)); Round Hill; Royce (named from the *Royce* family, cf. George *Royce* 1788 OR, David Needham *Royce* 1932 Kelly); The Seeds (alluding to a field of sown grass, *v.* sǣd); Shepcoat Hollow 1800, Sheep Coat Hollow 1802, 1803 (*Sheepecot*(*e*) *Hollow*(*e*) 1630, 1632[2], *Sheepcoat hollowe* 1687, *Shipcote Hollow* 1691, *Sheep Coat Hollow* 1726, 1758-61, 1776, *Sheepcoat Hollow* 1739-42, *v.* scēap-cot, holh); Simpers Cl 1825, Simper - 1829 OR (*Simpers Close* 1718, 1724, from the surn. *Simper*); Slay Fd; Sleath's (prob. from the surn. *Sleath*, cf. Sleath Lane in neighbouring Brooke f.ns. (a)); South Fd 1802, 1832 (*Suthfeld* 1285, 1305, *Sthefeld* 1290, *Southfeld* 14, *the South Feild* 1614, (*le*) *Southfeild* 1626, 1630, 1632[2], 1641, (*the*) *Southfield* 1671, 1689, 1733-6, 1739-42, 1785-97, *South Field* 1763, 18, *in austral' campo* 1611, 1634, *in campo Australi* 1723, one of the great open-fields of the town, *v.* sūð, feld); Spring Fd; Top Fd; Townsend Cl 1803, 1908 *Deed* (*le Townes-end Close* 1687, 1705, *Le ·Townsend* 1702, *Townsend Close* 1733-6, 1755, *v.* tūn, ende[1]; noted as 'now King's Road' 1908 *Deed*); Twitch Hill (Mr J. Field notes that this site was formely called The Allotments, *v.* cwice); Voss's; West Fd 1802, 1832 ((*le*) *Westfeld* 1285, 1305, 14, 1498, *Westesfeld'* 1547, (*le*) *Westfeild* 1620, 1624, 1626, 1630, 1632[2], 1641, *the West field*

1739-42, 1763, 1776, 1785-97, *in occidental' campo* 1632², *in campo occidentali* 1636, one of the great open-fields of the town, *v.* **wēst, feld**); White Wong 1803, 1832, White Worms (sic) 1943 ((*le*) *Whitwong* 1691, *Whitewong* 1691, 1730, 1755, *White Wong* 1785-97, *Whitewonges* 1702, *White Wongs* 18; in eModE, *white* 'infertile' is contrasted with *black* 'fertile', but dial. *white* is also used of dry, open pasture, *v.* **hwīt, vangr**); Wilson's Gorse Fd (*v.* **gorst**); Wood Furlong 1803, 1832 (*Woodfurlonge* 1607, 1620, 1624, 1626, 1630, 1632¹, 1674, *Woodfurlong* 1730, *Wood Furlong* 1632², 1687, 1691, 1702, 1739-42, 1755, 1776, 1785-96, 18, *v.* **wudu**).

(b) *Almeshouse lane end* 1632² (cf. Hospital of St John *supra*); *Armstrong's* 1790 (from the surn. *Armstrong*, cf. Robert *Armystrong* 1522 MilS, - *Armestronge* 1524 SR); *Ashwell bridge* 1632² (evidently a bridge on the road to Ashwell which lies three miles to the north); *Le Balke* 1702 (*v.* **balca**); *Barleythorpe meere* 1632², *Barlythorpe Meare* 1733-6, 1755, 1785-97 ('Barleythorpe parish boundary', *v.* **(ge)mǣre**); *Barrowes* 1632² (if not the pl. of **beorg** 'a tumulus', then a surn., cf. Barrow's in Ridlington f.ns. (a)); *Beadhouse furlong* 18 (*v.* Hospital of St John *supra*); *Beestons Close* 17 (from the surn. *Beeston*); *Billingtons Willows* 1776, 1785-96 (from the surn. *Billington, v.* **wilig**); *Bincks terr'* 1687 (from the surn. *Binks, v.* **land**); *Blofeilds* 1632² (the surn. *Blofield,* cf. Thomas *Blowfeld* 1524 SR of Mkt. Overton); *Boothes headland* 1632² (from the surn. *Booth,* cf. Booth's Cl in neighbouring Burley f.ns. (a) and *Booths-close Furlong* in Cottesmore f.ns. (b)); *Branston gate Furlong* 1676 (Braunston parish adjoins to the south-west, *v.* **gata**); *Brinckes furlonge* 1620 (*v.* **brink**); *in Broad Campo* 1676 (*v.* **brād, feld**); *Burlis Brooke* 1618, *Burley Well* 1698 (Burley parish adjoins to the east, *v.* **brōc, wella**); *Burtons close* 1632² (from the surn. *Burton*); *Carmeadow* 1632² (prob. with ME *ker* 'marsh', *v.* **kjarr**); *Cartley* 1632², 1687, 1691, 1739-42, - *Furlong* 18, *Cartley hill* 1632², 1687, - *furlong* 1676 ('woodland where timber for making carts is got', *v.* **cræt, lēah**, cf. *Cartley* in neighbouring Egleton f.ns. (b)); *Chamberleynes Croft* 1421 (1684) Wright (from the surn. *Chamberlain,* cf. Robert *Chamberlyn* 1522 MilS, 1525 SR of Cottesmore, John *Chamberlyn* 1522 MilS, - *Chamberlen* 1524 SR of Greetham, *v.* **croft**); *Chappel seeke* 1611, *Chappell sike* 1632², *Chapwell Sick* 18 (*v.* **chapel(e), sīk**); *Charnock Hedge* 1739-42 (prob. from the surn. *Charnock,* ultimately from Charnock La, *v.* **hecg**); *Churchfurlonge* 1628, (*le*) *Church Furlong* 1630, 1671, 1683, 1687, 1698, 1705, 1723, 1733-6, 1746, 1776, 18 (*v.* **cirice**); *Cockacres* 1614, *Cockacre* 1632², *Cock Acres* 1733-6, 1755, 1785-97, 18 (*v.* **cocc², æcer**); *the Comon Feilde* 1601, *the Comone fielde* 1607 (*v.* **commun**); *Compe Furlonge* 1634 (poss. a poor form of *Cop Furlong, v.* Copse *supra*); *the Cornfielde* 1607 Ct (*v.* **corn¹**); *the Cow Pasture* 17; *Cowpit* 18 (*v.* **col-pytt**); *Cresswell* 1626, *Creswell* 1632², 1667, *Creswelle* 1679, *Cresswells* 1663, 1739-42,

Creswells 1691 (*v.* **cærse, wella**); *Croslands* 1676 (*v.* **cross**[2]**, land**); *Cur Meadowe* 1607, 1620, *Curr Meadowe* 1626, *Curmeadow* 1632[1], *Curr Meadow* 1691, 1739-42, *Cur Meadow* 18 (*v.* **curre**); *Longedales* 1634, *Long Dales* 18, *Northdales* 1624, *North dales* 1676, 1691, *North Dales* 18, *North dales Close* 1676, *Short Dales* 18, *Stondales* 1632[1], 1632[2], *Stone Dales* 1663 (*v.* **deill**); *long doles, short doles* 1632[2] (these names prob. belong with the previous group of f.ns., otherwise *v.* **dāl**); *East acre* 1632[2]; *East Furlong* 18; *Edgson willowes* 1614 (*Edgson* is a late form of Egleton, the parish adjoining to the south-east which also gave rise to the surn. *Edgson*, cf. Edgson's 2½ Acre in Langham f.ns. (a), *v.* **wilig**); *Eggleton Way Furlong* 18 (Egleton parish adjoins to the south-east); *Elbowes* 1671, *prato vocat' Elbowes* 1705, *Elbows* 18 (*v.* **elbowe** 'an elbow, a sharp bend'); *Far Hill* 18; *atte Felde* 1375 (p) (*v.* **feld**); *Filbarn Furlong* 18 (a complimentary name for high-yielding land); *Fitch pole Furlong* 1679, *Fishpoole Furlong* 1698, *fishpole furlong* 1705, *Fishpool furlong* 1739-42, 1780, 18 (evidently abutting the castle stew, *v.* le Fispol *s.n.* The Castle *supra*); *Flints* 1632[2], *Little -, Flints* 18 (the surn. *Flint,* cf. Flint's Covert in neighbouring Burley and Flint's Fds in Cottesmore f.ns. (a)); *Flithulle* c1200 *WDB* ('hill subject to dispute', *v.* **(ge)flit, hyll,** cf. Flitteris Park *infra*); *atte forde* 1374 (p), *atte Forth'* 1375 (p) (*v.* **ford**); *Foxholes* 1634, *foxhols* 1691, *Fox Holes* 18 (*v.* **fox-hol**); *Furhill* 1630, 1683, 1733-6, 1785-97, *Furr Hill* 1755, 1785-97, *Furrhill* 1687, 1691, *Furhillslade* 1618, *Furhill slade* 1634, *le furrhill slade* 1691 (*v.* **feor, hyll, slæd**); *the Furze hill* 1739-42 (*v.* **fyrs**); *le Garyth* 1285 (*v.* **garðr**); *Gate Furlong* 1691 (*v.* **gata**); *the goare* 1632[2] *(v.* **gāra**); *(le) Hanging Leys* 1614, 1676, 1691, 18, *hanging leies* 1632[2] ('meadowland on a steep slope', *v.* **hangende, lēah**); *Harbottles headland* 1632[2], *Harbottle's* 1790 (from the surn. *Harbottle, v.* **hēafod-land**); *the Hedge* 1723 (*v.* **hecg**); *Helwell'* 1498, *Heylwell'* 1547 (the first el. is either *hæl* 'good fortune' or *hælu* 'healing, cure', hence 'the healing spring' or 'the wishing well', perh. an earlier ' name for Our Lady's Well *supra, v.* **hæl, hælu, wella**); *Hogstyes* 1630, 1634, *Hogstys* 18, *great hogsties* 1632[2], *great Hogstyes* 1676, *Little Hogsties* 1671, 1705, *long hodgstiles* 1676, *Long-Hoggstiles* 1683, *midle hogsties* 1632[2] (*v.* **hogg, stigu**); *in the Holm* 1341 (p), *Midle Holmes* 1687 (*v.* **holmr**); *Hundesbuske* c1200 *WDB* ('Hund's bush', a name which may refer to a boundary marker or else to ground covered with brushwood; the contained pers.n. is either OE *Hund* or Scand *Hundr, v.* **buskr**); *Kimberleys hedland* 1630 (from the surn. *Kimberley, v.* **hēafod-land**); *le Lammas Close* 1683 (*v.* **lammas**); *Lark Catchers Leys* 1739-42 (*v.* **lēah**); *litle acre* 1632[2] (*v.* **lȳtel, æcer**); *(le) Little Sicke* 1630, 1698, 1733-6, 1755, *little sike* 1632[2], *Little Seek(e)* 1691, 1739-42, *(the) Little Seike* 1785-97, *the little Sick Furlong* 18 (*v.* **sīk**); *Long Close* 1667; *long hedge close* 1614 (*v.* **hecg**); *South longlands* 1687, *Westlongland* 1681 (*v.* **lang**[1]**, land**); *Longsicke* 1607, *Long seeke* 1610, *Longe secke* 1611, *long sicke* 1620, *Longsyk* 1624, *long sike* 1632[2], *Longesickeland* 1618 (*v.*

lang[1], sik, land); *Lundes* 1300, *Loundes* 1305, *les Loundes* 1347, *le Loundes* 1376 (*v.* lundr); *Meadow Furlong* 1702; *Mertewell'* 1498, *Mortrewell'* 1547 (the first el. is obscure but may be a lost OE word which gave ME *mort* 'a young salmon', cf. Norw *murt* 'a roach', Icel *murti* 'a young trout', *v.* wella); *Middleton Furlong* 18; *Mikelingge* c1200 *WDB* (a Scand compound, *v.* mikill, eng); *Millhill* 1632[1], 1634, 1667, (*le*) *Mill Hill* 1636, 1681, 1683, 1687, *Millhill Furlong* 18 (the site of a windmill, *v.* myln, hyll); *Mouleholm(e)* 1300, 1305, 1344, 14, *le Moulholm* 1347, *Melleholm'* 1374, 1375, 1376, *le Mulneholm* 1360, *Milneholm* 1375, 1378, 1388, (*le*) *Milleholm(e)* 1380, 1381, *Myllholmes* 1611 (referring to a water-mill, *v.* myln, holmr); *Miltonsons Close* 1634 (prob. with scribal duplication of the possessive of the surn. *Milton*); *Moneybalke* 1691 (perh. referring to the discovery of a coin-hoard, but *Money* was a common Ru surn. (cf. William *Monee* 1522 MilS of Whitwell, Thomas *Monee* 1522 ib and William *Money* 1524 SR, both of Teigh) and *balca* 'a strip of ground left unploughed to mark the boundary between adjacent strips of the common field' is frequently found compounded with a surn., *v.* monie, balca); *le mor ... apud Ocham* 1316 (*v.* mōr[1]); *Moyses Close* 1726, 1758-61 (from the surn. *Moyse(s)*, cf. William *Moysez* 1522 MilS, - *Moyse* 1524 SR of Exton); *Mur Pit Meadow* 18 (*v.* mýrr, pytt); *narrow points* 1632[2], *Narrow Point* 1776 (*v.* nearu, point); *le Nether Close* 1634; *Newfeild* 1632[2], *New Field* 1705, *New Feild Furlong* 1702, *Newfeild side* 1687, 1691, 1698, *New Feild Side* 1702, 1705; *le Oake hill* 1679 (*v.* āc); *Okeham Feild* 1601, *Okehamfeilde* 1607, 1611 (*v.* feld); *le Parke furlong* 1676, *Park Nook* 18 (*v.* park, nōk and Little Park *s.n.* The Castle *supra*); *Peysland* 1501, *Pease Land* 1676 (*v.* pise, land); *Pi(c)kwellsi(c)ke* 1604, 1620, 1630, *Pickwelsi(c)ke* 1607, 1618, *Pykwellsike* 1624, *Pickwelle Sike* 1679, *Pickwellsik(e)* 1632[1], 1632[2], 1702, *Picwellseeke* 1671, *Pick(e)wellseek(e)* 1663, 1687, 1691, 1705, 1739-42, *Pickwell seike* 1702 (perh. 'pike stream', *v.* pīc[1], wella, sīk); *Pindars balk* 1632[2] (from the surn. *Pinder*, *v.* balca); *the pingle* 1614, (*le*) *Pingle* 1632[1], 1632[2], *le Pingle Close* 1687, *Pingle Furlong(e)* 1634, 1663, 1671, 1702, 1705, 1776, 1785-97, 18, *Pingle Bridge Furlong* 18 (*v.* pingel); *in le Pitte* 1305 (p) (*v.* pytt); *Pottles close* 1632[2] (from the surn. *Pottle*); *presgraves close* 1632[2] (from the surn. *Presgrave*, a family which prob. originated from the lost village of *Prestgrave* in Neville Holt, near the Lei border with Ru, cf. Presgraves Far Towns in Ashwell f.ns. (a)); *una virgat' ter' voc' pulters* 1548 (prob. the surn. *Poulter*, itself from OFr *pouletier* 'poultry-dealer'); *le seauen land* 1624, 1630, 1632[1], *le Seauen Lands* 1634 ('the seven selions', no doubt enclosed as an agricultural unit, *v.* seofon, land); *Sortewong* c1200 *WDB* (*v.* sc(e)ort, vangr); *Southacre* 1632[2] (*v.* sūð, æcer); *Suthdale* 1285, 1305, 14, *Southdale* 1344, 1360, 1374 (*v.* sūð, dalr); *le Standford Bridge Close* 1667 (i.e., 'the close beside the bridge on the road to Stamford', *v.* Stamford Rd *supra*); *le Stappe* c1200 *WDB*, *v.* stæpe 'a step', here perh. used topographically of a ledge of land);

stone pits 1632[2], *Stone pitt Furlong* 1702 (*v.* **stän-pytt**); *stone landes* 1632[2] (*v.* **stän, land**); *Stonyland* 1498, 1547, 1630, 1698, *Stonieland* 1624, *Stony Land(e)* 1676, *Stonylands* 1634, 1687, *Ston(e)y Lands* 1691, 1733-6, 1755, 1785-97, *nether -, upper Stonyland* 1679, *Neither -, upper stony Land* 1691, *Short Stony Lands* 1691, 1702, *Stonnyland furlonge* 1663 (*v.* **stänig, land**; the previous f.n. may belong here); *Vnder the sun* 1691, *Undersun Furlong* 18, *v.* Sun in Oakham Inns and Taverns *supra*); *the through ley* 1671, *Thorough Ley* 1689 ('meadow running through' (perh. through an area of arable), *v.* **þurh, lēah**); *le Townes-end Close* 1687, 1705, *Le Townsend* 1702, *Townsend Close* 1733-6, 1755 (*v.* **tūn, ende**[1]); *Tungerode* c1200 *WDB* (*v.* **tunge** 'a tongue of land'; the second el. is either **rod**[1] 'a clearing' or **rōd**[3] 'a rood of land'); *le viccaradge land* 1624 (*v.* **vikerage**); *le Wall Close* 1632, 1674, *Wall Close* 1687, 1726; *Warrens headlond* 1624 (from the surn. *Warren*, cf. *Jamys Waren* 1522 MilS, *v.* **hēafod-land**); (*les*) *Water gaules* 1632[1], 1634, 1636, 1676, 1681, *Watergalls* 1632[2], 1698, 1739-42, 18, *Water Galls* 18 (*v.* **wæter, galla**); *the well* 1671, *Well Close* 1758-61 (*v.* **wella**); *Whetefyllde* 1590, *the Wheatfeild* 1607, 1630 (*v.* **hwǣte, feld**); *Wheat Leyes* 1679 (*v. Wheatleas* in neighbouring Barleythorpe f.ns. (b)); *Whitteway furlong* 1681 (*v.* **hwīt, weg**); *the willowes* 1632[2] (*v.* **wilig**); *Wonders* 1723, 1733-6 (poss. a later form of *Vnder the sun supra* with a development such as *Vnder the sun > Undersun > *Unders > *Wunders > Wonders*; otherwise, simply a complimentary name for high-yielding ground); *Upper -, Yellows* 18 (*v.* **geolu**, presumably alluding to soil colour); *Yewcake* 1632[2], *yulecake hill* 1667, *Ulstrake Hill* 1691, *le Vle Gate Hill* 1698 (the form *Yule Cake hills* 1651 *Surv* appears in neighbouring Egleton f.ns. (b). A *yule-cake* was a spiced cake, shaped like a baby to celebrate Christ's birth, here perh. used fancifully of rising ground of similar configuration. However, the later forms suggest a more mundane origin, with the first el. OE *üle* 'an owl' and the second OE *straca* 'a strip of land', hence 'strip of land frequented by owls' or even 'road frequented by owls', with *gata* ' a road' rather than *straca*. In either of these cases, the earlier forms would then show the influence of folk etymology, but in the interpretation of p.ns., earlier forms are usually more reliable evidence.)

FLITTERIS PARK

    Fly-, Fliteris, -ys 1252, 1287 Pat, 1300 Ipm *et passim* to 1399
        Pat, (- *in Okham*) 1287 ib, *Fli-, Flytteris, -ys* (*parcum de -*)
        1285, 1375 *MinAcct*
    Flitris 1269 For, *Flytrys* 1383 *MinAcct*
    Fliares (*parcum de -*) 1275, 1276 RH
    Fletris, -ys 1296 *MinAcct*, 1340 Pat, *Flettres* 1287 Coram, *Fleteris,*

-*ys* 1305 OSurv, 1380 *MinAcct*, 1384 Fine, 1388 Misc, 1461
Wright
Flitteris 1695 *Map*, *Fliteress Park* 1602, 1607 Map

The first el. is OE **(ge)flit** 'strife, dispute' and the second OE
hrīs 'brushwood'. The area lies beside the county boundary and no
doubt was once subject to territorial dispute, hence 'brushwood
region of disputed ownership', *v.* **(ge)flit, hrī s.** The park is also
Ockham parcus 1252 IpmR, *v.* **park**. Its park gate is recorded in
extra portam de Flyteris 1344 *MR*, *extra port' de flyterys* 1374
MinAcct, *v.* **geat**. The park was created as a deer park by Richard,
Earl of Cornwall, under licence of 1252, *v.* MER 32.

Flitteris Park Field-Names

Undated forms in (a) are 1839 *TA*.

(a) Hill Cl; Home Cl (*v.* **home**); Nether -, Lady Wood Piece (*v.* **hlǣfdige,
wudu, pece**); Little Fd; Great Meadow Piece (*v.* **pece**); Little Mdw; The Great
Pasture; Pasture Close Mdw; Three Cornered Piece (*v.* **pece**); Underhill Cl.

(b) *Fletterette Corner* 1684 Wright (*v.* **corner**); *Stacy quarter* 1388 Pat (from
the surn. *Stac(e)y*, *v.* **quarter**).

Wardley

WARDLEY
Werlea 1067 BM, -*leia*(*m*) 1080-7 Reg, Wm 1 Dugd, *Vuerlia*
Stephen (1340) Ch
Warleie c1125 Dugd, -*leia* c1160 BM, 1199 GildR (p), -*lea*(*m*)
Hy 1 Dugd, 1157 *WDB*, -*le* 1205 P, 1209-34 AllS, 1263
RGrav, -*lee* 1202 Ass, -*leg'* Hy2 Dugd, 1202 Ass, 1235,
1238, 1243 RGros, -*lei* 1199 GildR (p), -*leye* 1249 Cl,
1286 Ass, 1311 *Rut* (p), -*leya* 1223, 1224 RHug, 1254 Val
Wardel' 1241 RGros, *Wardeley*(*e*) 1263 *Ass*, 1265 Misc *et
passim* to 1535 VE, -*le* 1266 *For*, c1291 Tax *et passim*
to 1428 FA, -*legh* 1284 Cl
Wardl' 1239, 1243 RGros, -*leyh* 1235 ib, -*le* 1286 *Ass*, -*ley*

1535 VE, 1610 Speed

The second el. is OE **lēah** 'a woodland glade, a clearing in woodland'. The first is obscure. It is uncertain whether the *d* is intrusive. If it is organic, the first el. may be OE **weard** 'watch' in some sense. Wardley stands on a hillside above Eye Brook with fine westerly views across the Rutland frontier. The hillside would have made a notable vantage point to look out for threatened incursions from the west, *v.* **weard, lēah**.

WARDLEY CHURCH, *Church* (*St Botolph*) 1846, 1863, 1877 White. Botolph, a monastic leader who flourished in East Anglia in the later 7th century, was by the end of the 11th century regarded as a patron saint of boundaries. It may be significant for the church's dedication that Wardley is a border parish, *v.* R. Morris, *Churches in the Landscape*, London 1989, 217-9. The church appears to be an ancient foundation. The earliest surviving masonry is no later than c1175. WARDLEY HO., 1846 White. WARDLEY WOOD, 1586 *DuLa, bosco de Warley* 1253 Cl, *v.* **wudu.** WOOD LANE, 1633 *Bru.*

Field-Names

Undated forms in (a) are 1943 *Map*; those dated 1844 are *TA* and those of 1940 are *Deed.* Early forms dated 1609 and 1633 are *Bru*, those dated 1611 are *SP*, those dated 1626, 1677 and 1694 are *Deed*, while those of 1634 are *Terrier.*

(a) Nine Acres; Andrews Cl 1844, 1940; Ayston Cl 1844, 1940 (named from the adjoining parish of Ayston); Banky Cl 1844, Bankey - 1940; Miss Browns Fd; Bushy Dales c1800, 1806 Map (prob. with **dalr** rather than **deill**); Cants Cl, - Mdw 1844, 1943, Cants Nether Wood 1844 (x2) (from the surn. *Cant*, cf. Cant's Cl in neighbouring Ayston f.ns. (a) and Robert *Cant* 1877 White of Preston); Little -, Chapel Cl 1844, Chapel Cl 1940 (*Chappell Close* 1633, c1635 *Map, Chappell Feild*(*e*) 1633, 1634, *Chappell furlong* 1634; *Chappell Feilde* was one of the open-fields of the village, poss. named from *The Hermitage infra*; the map of c1635 sites *Chappell Close* at about SK 837 005, the poss. position of the hermitage, *v.* **chapel(e), feld**); Chapmans Cl 1844 (1634, from the surn. *Chapman*); Cockatrice Cl 1844, Cockety Hill 1943 (*Cockadie hole* 1633, *Cockadic*

Hole c1635 *Map*, of uncertain meaning; *Cockatrice* is an imaginative reconstruction of an earlier name, originally prob. with $cocc^2$, *v.* hol^1); Coleman's Cl 1844; Ekin's Fd, Little Ekin's; Far -, Near Garbage Holm 1844 (*v.* holmr) (cf. *Garbage Wonge, Garbige Wounge* 1633, *Garbige Wounges* c1635 *Map*, *v.* gorebrode 'broad strip of land in the triangular corner of the common field', vangr); Garner Hill Sale 1844 (*v.* sale); Gravel Pit Cl 1844 (x2); Great Cl 1844; Far -, First -, Middle Grub Sale, New Grub Piece (from the verb 'to grub' (OE *grybban*) in the sense 'to clear the ground of roots and stumps', cf. Grubwoods in Clipsham f.ns. (a), *v.* sale, pece); Ham's Homestead 1844 (*v.* hām-stede); Harris's; Hawthorn Mdw 1844 (x3) (*Hawthorne meaddow* 1633, *v.* hagu-þorn); Headland Sale 1804 Map, 1844 (*Hadland Sale* 1609, 1611, *Eadland Sale* 1609, *Headland Sale* 1633, *v.* hēafod-land, sale); Hemp's Cl 1844, Kemp's Cl 50 Acre 1943; Long -, Hill Cl 1844, Long Hill, - Mdw 1943 (*Long Hill* 1633, cf. *The Hill* (a close) 1633 *Bru*, c1635 *Map*, *The Hylls* 1633, *v.* hyll); Hoby Cross 1844, Hoby Cl 1940 (*Hooby Crosse* 1633, *Hobiecross* 1634, *v.* cros; *Hoby* in this name may well be a surn., cf. John *Hoby* 1522 MilS, 1524 SR of Brooke and *v.* Hooby Lodge in Stretton); (Little - 1844), Home Cl 1844, 1940 (*v.* home); Hospital (since there appear to be no almshouses in or connected with Wardley and since this as a name for a close for the isolation of sick animals seems unlikely, then poss. a memory of land owned here by the Knights Hospitallers who held Stoke Dry, two miles to the south-west, *v.* Fronald in Stoke Dry f.ns. (a) and cf. also Temple Barns in Stretton f.ns. (a) and *Temple Peyse* in Greetham f.ns. (b), lands of the Knights Templars); Hudsons Cl 1844; Klondyke (a fanciful name usually indicating remoteness; it appears also in neighbouring Beaumont Chase, Barleythorpe and Hambleton f.ns. (a)); Little Mdw 1844; Long Cl; Mole's Cl; Monks Hill 1804 Map (*Monkyshill'* 1437 *Deed*, *Mun(c)ks hill* 1633; the early date of the 1437 form suggests that the first el. is munuc 'a monk' rather than the surn. *Monk* (which occurs, however, in Ashwell f.ns.), although there is no surviving record of the association of land here with either Brooke Priory or nearby Launde Abbey Lei, cf. the related *Monks Wood* in neighbouring Beaumont Chase f.ns. (b), *v.* munuc, hyll); Mossender's Mdw 1844, Massender's - 1940 (named from the local *Mossender* family, cf. Rob. *Mosindue* c1635 *Map*); Nether Cl 1844, 1940; Nether -, New Mdw 1844; Little Nether Wood 1844, Nether Wood 1943; Newn's Home (prob. named from the *Noone* family, cf. Rich. and Nich. *Noone* c1635 *Map*, *v.* holmr); Old Sale 1804 Map, 1844, Old Sale Plain 1804 Map (*v.* plain) (cf. *Ould Sale leyes* 1609, 1633, *old sale leaze* 1611, *Old-sale Leyes* 1633, *v.* ald, sale, lēah); Pear Tree Cl 1844 (*Partree* 1634, cf. *Peartree furlong* 1633, *v.* pertre); Far -, First Plain (*v.* plain); Plough Fd; Riding 1844 (*v.* ryding); Road Cl 1844, 1940; Long Slade 1844, 1940, 1943 (*v.* slæd); South West of the River 1844; Spiney (sic) 1844; Nether -, Over Steeping 1844, Steeping Sale

(Plain) 1804 Map, 1844, The Steepings 1943 (*Steping sale* 1611, *Steepinge Sale* 1633, *Steepings Sale* c1635 *Map*, v. **stybbing** 'a place with tree stumps, a clearing', **sale**; the name has been influenced by the adj. *steep*); Swallowsale 1844 (v. **sale**); Townsend Cl 1844 (v. **tūn, ende**[1]); Upper Cl 1844, 1940, - Mdw 1844; Wilson's Cl (x3) 1844 (named from the *Wilson* family, cf. Dan. *Wilson* c1635 *Map*); Woods Cl 1844, Wood - 1943 (cf. *Beneath-woodes* 1633, *Beneathwood* 1634, *Beneath Woodes* c1635 *Map*, *Wood nooke* 1633, v. **wudu, nōk**).

(b) *Ballands* 1633 (perh. 'land near the boundary mound'; a prehistoric barrow is sited at SK 842 008, still visible at ground level, and this may relate to the f.n., v. **ball, land**); *Barne Close* 1633; *Beamont hedge* 1634 (the boundary of Beaumont Chase, v. **hecg**); *Over -, Neather Blackwel* 1634 (v. **blæc, wella**); *ye Breache(s)* 1633, *Breach* 1634, *Breaches Close, Breaches lane* 1633 (v. **brēc**); *Broadway* 1634 (v. **brād, weg**); *Brooke furlong* 1634 (v. **brōc**); *Chappell hill close* 1633, *Chappell hyll Sale* 1609 (cf. Chapel Cl *supra*, v. **sale**); *the coppy close* 1634 (v. **copis**); *cottiers part* 1633 (v. **cottere, part**); *the Cow Close* 1611; *dale close* 1634 (v. **dalr**); *goldney* 1611 (the first el. is OE **gylden**, perh. 'golden-coloured' because of flowers or other vegetation, and the second prob. **ēg** 'land partly surrounded by water', alluding to the course of Eye Brook); *Goodmans Snowte al's Snowte Sale* 1609 (either with the surn. *Goodman* or with the nickname of the Devil, hence 'the Devil's snout' with ME **snūte** 'snout' used of 'a projecting point of land', v. **sale**); *Greengate, greenegate furlong* 1634 (v. **grēne**[1], **gata**); *The Hermitage* 1584 Pat, 1610 Speed, 1645, 1715 Map (v. **hermitage**); *Heywards hill* 1634 (from the surn. *Heyward*); *Kyttan Close* 1611 (v. **kytton**); *New Kyrke* 1611 (evidently land recently endowed to the parish church in contrast to land earlier so endowed (v. **kirkja**) but cf. *New Kirke* in Edith Weston f.ns. (b)); *Laber Sike* 1633 (v. **læfer, sīk**); *the Linche* 1633, *Lynch furlong* 1634, cf. *Weldons Linche infra*, v. **hlinc**); *Wardley lound* 1609, *Lounde sale* 1633, *The Lounde al's Stockinge Sale* 1633 (v. **lundr, sale** and *Stocking hill sale infra*); *March hill* 1633, *Marchill* 1634 ('hill above the marsh', v. **mersc, hyll**); *the moores* 1634 (v. **mōr**[1]); *Nether Feilde* 1633, *Neather Feild* 1634 (one of the open-fields of the village, v. **neoðera, feld**); *the Parke close* 1634 (alluding to Ridlington Park, v. Park Lodge in Ridlington); *Port Waye* 1633 (the road to Uppingham, v. **port-weg**); *Red landes* 1633, *Redlands* 1634 (perh. alluding to clay soil, v. **rēad, land**); *Rough Sale* 1609, 1611, 1633 (here poss. the surn. *Rough/Ruff*, cf. *Rough Maples* in Beaumont Chase f.ns. (b), otherwise **rūh** 'rough', v. **sale**); *Sheepe Lane* 1633 (v. **scēap**); *Slade Acre* 1633, *Longslade* 1634 (v. **slæd**); *Small Roodes* 1633, *Smallroods* 1634 (v. **rōd**[3]); *Snowte Sale* 1609 (v. **sale** and *Goodmans Snowte supra*); *Stockinge Sale* 1633, *Stocking hill sale* 1609, 1611 (v. **stocking, sale**); *Stonelands* 1634 (v. **stān, land**); *the stone meddow* 1634 (v. **stān**); *le towne Close* 1611 (v. **tūn**); *Towne* *furlong* 1634 (*v.* **tūn**); *Trenchsick,* - *slade* 1634 (*v.* **trenche, sīk, slæd**); *Turtle Slade* 1633 (most likely with **tōt-hyll** 'a look-out hill' since this is a border location, cf. the poss. signification of the name Wardley, cf. *Tirtle Meare* in Morcott f.ns. (b) and Turtle Bridge in Barrowden, *v.* **slæd**); *Weldons Linche* 1633 (with the surn. *Weldon, v.* **hlinc,** cf. *Weldons Gibbet s.n.* Gibbet Gorse in Hambleton); *West Feilde* 1633, *Westfeild* 1634 (one of the open-fields of 'the village, *v.* **west, feld**); *Wildegate* 1633, *Wildgate Saile* 1626, *Wild(e)gate Sale* 1677, 1694 (*v.* **wilde, gata, sale**); *the woodhedge* 1634 (*v.* **wudu, hecg**).

EAST HUNDRED

East Hundred was originally part of the hundred of Witchley whose territory was later divided into East Hundred and Wrangdike Hundred. East Hundred comprises the land of *Hwicceslea east hundred* a.1075 (l12) GeldR. It appears as *Esth'dr'* 1166, 1167 P, *Esthundr'* 1168 ib, *Esthundred* 1176 ib *et passim* to 1428 FA, *Thesthundrede* 1546 *SR, East Hundred* 1610 Speed, *v.* **ēast, hundred.**

If the new hundred was assigned a moot-site, its location is unknown. The former Romano-British town at Great Casterton would have been central to its territory.

Great Casterton

GREAT CASTERTON
  Castreton(e) 1086 DB, c1176 Dugd, 1202 Ass (p) *et passim* to
    1371 ELiW, -*tune* 1125-8 LNPetr
  Casterton' 1202 (p), 1206 Ass (p) *et passim* to 1254 Val *et freq*
    to 1610 Speed, *Kasterton'* 1274 RGrav, 1288 *For*
  Chasterton' 1269 For, 1321 Pat, 1332 *FF, Chastirton'* 1352 Cl
  Cestreton 1257 Ch, -*tun'* 1225 Bracton (p)

  Affixes are normally added as:
  Magna - 1218 For, 1234 RHug, 1305, 1428 FA, - *Magna* 1292
    OSut, 1535 VE
  - *Maior* 1254 Val, 1274 RGrav, 1282 Ipm, - *Majori(s)* c1291 Tax,
    1428 FA
  Brigg(e)-, -*y*- 1265 Misc, 1269 For *et passim* to 1476 Pat, *Brig-*

Hy 3 *TT*, 1370 Cl, 1393 *FF et passim* to 1539 *Rut*, 1576 Saxton, *Bridge* - 1610 Speed, 1642 *Recov*, *Great or Bridge* - 1824 O

'The estate at the fortified Roman town', *v.* **ceaster, tūn**. The form of OE *ceaster* here is Angl *cæster*. There are extensive remains of a Romano-British settlement which evidently developed to the south-west of an earlier Roman fort, *v.* Crop Marks 66-7. Ermine Street crosses R. Gwash at this point, hence the affix *Bridge* -, *v.* **brycg** and cf. Little Casterton.

WOODHEAD
> *Wod(e)heved* 1263 *For*, 1272 Ipm, 1286 Ass *et passim* to 1364
> *FF*, 1370 Cl
> *Wod(e)hed(e)* 1327 Ipm, 1392 AD *et passim* to 1510 LP, *Le*
> *Wodehede* 1476 Ipm
> *Woodhed* 1545 *Surv*, -*head* 1695 *Map*, *Woodhead Wood* 1610
> Speed

'Headland or eminence with a wood', *v.* **wudu, hēafod**. This became the name of a neighbouring medieval manor house, a strongly defended moated site whose earthworks are clearly visible. There appears to have been a village here also: 'Within the parish of Brig Casterton lies Woodhead, formerly a village and chapelry, now only one house and that in ruins', *v.* Wright 36. Earthworks east of the manor site may well indicate its former position, *v.* BrownArchSites 13 and MER 17.

CASTERTON BRIDGE, BRIDGE FM, *ad pontem de Casterton* 1269 For (p), *ad pontem de Magne Casterton* Hy 3 Nichols (p), *v.* **brycg**. GREAT CASTERTON CHURCH, *Church* (*St Peter and St Paul*) 1846, 1863 White. CASTERTON LINGS (locally EXETER'S GORSE), *The Lynge* 1545 *Surv*, *East* -, *North* -, *South-Lings* 1798 *Plan*, *Casterton Lings* 1806 Map, 1824 O, *The Lings* 1943 *Map*, 1950 *Burghley*. The Earl of *Exeter* was lord of the manor in 1684 Wright, *v.* **lyng**. CASTERTON MILL, *ad molendinum* 1296 *SR* (p), *the Myll* Edw 6 *Harl*, cf. *Milneholm* 1346 Cl, *v.* **myln, holmr**. COW PASTURE FM, *Cow Pasture* 1876 *Burghley*, 1943 *Map*, 1950

Burghley. THE CROWN P.H. EASTWOOD, *Est Wood* 1610 Speed, *East Wood* 1798 *Plan,* c1800 Map, *v.* ēast, wudu. MOUNTS LODGE, 1950 *Burghley.* THE PLOUGH P.H., 1846 White. THE RECTORY, 1846, 1863 ib. WALK FM, 1846, 1863 ib, 1876, 1950 *Burghley, The Walk* 1876, 1950 *ib, Sheep Walk* 1798 *Plan,* referring to an unenclosed tract of land for pasturing sheep, *v.* sheep-walk.

Field-Names

Undated forms in (a) are 1950 *Burghley,* those dated 1943 are *Map* and those dated 1876 are also *Burghley.* Forms which are identical in 1876, 1943 and 1950 are marked with an asterisk. Undated forms in (b) are 1634 *Terrier,* those dated 1545 are *Surv.*

(a) The Two Acres (x3) 1876, 1950; The Four Acres; The Five Acres 1876, 1950; The Six Acres; Eight Acres 1876, 1943, The Eight - 1950; The Ten Acres 1876, First -, Second Ten Acre 1876, 1943, The First -, The Second Ten Acres 1950; The Eleven Acres 1876, 1950; Twelve Acres 1876, 1943, The Twelve - 1950; Thirteen Acres*; Fourteen Acres*, The Fourteen - 1950; Fifteen Acre 1943, The Fifteen Acres 1876, 1950; The Sixteen Acres*; The Seventeen Acres; The Eighteen Acres 1876, 1950; Nineteen Acres 1876, 1943, The Nineteen - 1950; Twenty Acres 1876, The Twenty - 1950; The Twenty-four Acres*; The Twenty Eight Acres 1876, 1950; Thirty Acres*; The Forty Acres 1876, 1950 (Mr J. Field notes that this has an area of 41a. 3r. 4p., but that *Forty Acres* is occasionally used ironically in Ru and Lei, like *Hundred Acres* elsewhere, as a name for very small pieces of land); Ash Tree Cl*; Badger Holes 1876, Badger Hills 1943, 1950; Barn Cl 1876 (*the Barneclose* 1545), - Lodge 1950; The Battery 1876, 1950 (referring to a platform or fortified work for the positioning of artillery, but at which date prior to 1876 this example was constructed is undocumented); Boil Nook* (cf. *Boyall Waye* 1634, from the surn. *Boyall,* cf. John *Boyeall* 1524 SR of Ketton); Bourne Rd Cl* (alluding to the road to Bourne L); First -, Second Broad Oak* (cf. *Brood Oke Way* 1634, *v.* brād, āc); Clay Hill*; Common Hill* (*v.* commun); Copy Cl* (1798 *Plan,* 'enclosure by a plantation' with *copy* as a reconstructed singular form of *coppice, v.* copis); Cottager's Fd* (*v.* cotager); The (First) Cow Cl*; Dale Hollow* (cf. *The Dale* 1634, *Dalefurlong* 1307 AD, *Dale Furlonge* 1634, *v.* dalr); Bottom Double Gates 1950; East Wood 1876, Great -, Little East Wood Cl 1876, Eastwood Cl 1943, 1950 (*v.* Eastwood *supra*); Bottom -, Middle Flagpole*, Top -*, Little - 1943; Footpath Cl*; Four Score Acre 1876, - Acres 1943, 1950 (*Four Score Acre* 1798 *Plan,* Mr J. Field notes that the actual acreage is given as 67a. 1r. 18p. in 1798 and 24a. in 1943, *v.* æcer); Frith Cl 1943, The - 1876, 1950 (*v.* Frith Fm in Lt. Casterton); Gipsy's Quick 1876, Gypsy's - 1943, Gipsey's - 1950 (prob. alluding to an area with a quickset hedge, *v.* gypsey, cwic); Late Glebe 1943, 1950 (*v.* glebe); The Gorse 1943 (*v.* gorst); The Heath* (*The Heathe* 1634, *v.* hæð); Hill Cl 1943, 1950; The Hill Piece* (*v.* pece); The Hill Side 1876, 1950, Hillside 1943; Home Cl 1950, Home Paddock 1876, 1950 (*v.* home); Hovel Cl* (*v.* hovel); The Narrows, Top Narrows 1876; New Cl*; The Nook 1943 (*v.* nōk); Occupation Road 1876 (with ModE occupation in the sense 'used by occupiers of land', cf. Occupation Road Db 651, naming a green lane used for access to a tenant's strips; the name also occurs in neighbouring Pickworth f.ns. (a)); Paddock 1876 (freq.); Paddys Garden 1876, 1950, Paddy's - 1943 (poss. a derogatory name for neglected land); Parish Pit 1876; Peaches Cl 1876, Peach's - 1943, 1950 (from the surn. *Peach,* cf. Joseph *Peach* 1846, 1877 White); Peak's Cl 1943, 1950 (from a surn., perh. identical with Peats Cl *infra*); Pear Tree Cl 1876 (*the Pertre Close* 1545, *v.* pertre); Peats Cl (from the surn. *Peat,* cf. Samuel and William *Peat* 1877 White, *v.* Peak's Cl *supra*); The Pikelets 1876, 1950 (evidently dial. *pikelet* 'a small round teacake'; this may have been used fancifully of a small patch of ground with a roughly pitted surface reminiscent of that surface of the teacake upon which butter is spread); The Pingle 1876, 1950 (*v.* pingel); Pismire Nook* (*v.* pissemyre, nōk); Pit Cl 1843, 1950 (cf. Parish Pit *supra*); The Pits 1950; The Plain 1950 (annotated 'Exeter Gorse', *v.* plain, cf. Casterton Lings *supra*); Pond; Pond Cl 1876, 1943; Rabbit Cl 1876; Rampart Hill* (poss. the result of popular etymology acting on *Rampittes infra*, otherwise dial. *rampart* 'a causeway'); Red Lands* (*Redlands* 1634, *v.* rēad, land); Bottom -, Top Redstones 1876, 1950, - Redstone 1943 (prob. named from a small outcropping of ironstone, cf. the preceding f.n., *v.* rēad, stān); Ryhall Road Cl (Ryhall parish lies to the east); The Sainfoin Cl 1876, Sanfoin - 1943, 1950 (with *sainfoin,* a perennial herb much grown as a forage plant, *v.* sainfoin); The Sands 1943, 1950; Stackyard Cl* (*v.* stak-ʒard); Stone Pit 1950 (1798 *Plan, v.* stān-pytt); Three Cornered Cl 1943, The - 1876, 1950; Tree Cl*; The Urns 1876, 1950 (perh. referring to the discovery of a Roman or pagan Anglo-Saxon cremation cemetery with urn burials outside the precinct of the Romano-British town); Wall Cl 1943, The - 1876, 1950; Warboys Fen 1950 (with the surn. *Warboy(s), v.* fenn); Willow Tree Cl 1876, 1950, Willow Cl 1943; Wood Head Cl 1876, 1950, Woodhead - 1943 (*Wood Head Close* 1798 *Plan, v.* Woodhead *supra*); The Wood Land 1876, The Woodland 1943, 1950; Woods Cl 1876, 1950.

(b) *Bowles Pitt* (prob. with the surn. *Bowles* since the Ru name for the ball-game bowls is always *bowling, v.* pytt); *Broadbalk Furlong* (*v.* brād, balca);

Cottage Pasture 1798 *Plan, Crosse Furlong* (in the great East Field, cf. *ad crucem* in Lt. Casterton f.ns. (b), *v.* **cros**); *Crosse Waye* (*v.* **cros, weg**); *The Little Dale* (prob. with **dalr**, *v.* **lytel**); *The Dyke* (prob. referring to the defensive ditch of the Roman town, *v.* **dīk**); *Eastfeild* (one of the open-fields of the village, *v.* **ēast, feld**); *Close called the Herbar* 1545 (prob. **erber** 'a grass-covered piece of ground' but poss. *eorð-burg* 'fortification built of earth' with reference to the ramparts of the Roman town); *Kinges Slade* (with the surn. *King, v.* **slæd**); *Ladiakre* 1375 Ipm (at this date, prob. land dedicated to the Virgin Mary for the maintenance of a chapel or shrine in the parish church, *y.* **hlæfdige, æcer**); *in ye Lane* 1360 P (p) (*v.* **lane**); *Meddowe Furlonge* (*v.* **mæd**); *Middle Feilde* (one of the open-fields of the village, *v.* **middel, feld**); *Middle Furlonge* (*v.* **middel**); *Pykworth Ouerfeld* 1545 (referring to land lying above Pickworth Plain to the north, *v.* **ofer²**, **feld**); *The Pounde Close* 1545 (*v.* **pund**); *Rampittes* (perh. dial. *rampart* 'a causeway', otherwise *v.* **ramm, pytt**, cf. The Pits and Rampart Hill *supra*); *Saltergate Furlong* (*v.* **saltere, gata** and *Saltergate* in Tolethorpe (Lt. Casterton) f.ns. (b)); *Street Waye* (*v.* **stræt, weg**); *Tickencoatefeild Side* (Tickencote parish adjoins to the west, *v.* **feld, sīde**); *West Feild* (one of the open-fields of the village, *v.* **west, feld**).

Little Casterton

LITTLE CASTERTON
For forms and interpretation, *v.* Great Casterton *supra*.

Affixes are normally added as:
Parva - 1262 Cl, 1276 RH *et freq* to 1537 MinAcct, - *Parva*
     1298 Ipm *et passim* to 1535 VE
- *Minor* 1254 Val, - *Minori*(*s*) c1291 Tax, 1428 FA
Little - 1610 Speed

TOLETHORPE HALL, - MILL, - OAKS
Toltorp(*e*) 1086 DB, 1212 Cur (p), 1215 P (p) *et passim* to 1327
     SR, -*thorp*(*e*) 1215 ChancR (p), 1273 Ipm *et freq* to 1428
     FA
Toletorp 1202 Ass *et passim* to 1220 *FF*, -*thorp*(*e*) 1249 Cur
     (p), 1273 Ipm
Tolestorp' 1196 ChancR (p), 1220 Cur (p)
Tholtorp' 1220 Cur (p), -*thorp*(*e*) 1305 FA *et passim* to 1405

PRep, 1610 Speed
Tholetorp 1272 *FF,* -*thorp* 1327 Ch (p)

'Tóli's outlying farmstead', *v.* þorp. The OScand pers.n. *Tóli* is a short form of names such as *Þorlakr, Þorleikr* and *Þorlaugr, v.* SPNLY 289. Forms with genitival -*es*- may show the influence of OScand *Tólir,* also a short form of Scand pers.ns. in *Þorl-, v.* SPNLY 290. Substitution of *th* for *t* is the result of AN orthographical interchange between the symbols *th* and *t* for etymological *t, v.* Feilitzen § 96. For - Hall, - Mill and - Oaks, *v. infra.* The deserted medieval village site is at TF 022 104, *v.* MER 26.

LITTLE CASTERTON CHURCH, cf. *Chirchefeld* Hy 3 *TT, Church Meadow* 1796 *Whit, v.* cirice, feld; presumably the 'Church Field' was one of the early open-fields of the village. LITTLE CASTERTON LODGE. THE CHANTRY. THE ENGINE INN (lost), closed 1956 - VR. FRITH FM, 1846, 1863 White is *Thrift House* 1780, 1806 Map, cf. *Frithwod* 1256 *For, Frith Wood* 1610 Speed, *The Frith* 1824 O, *v.* fyrhð, wudu. GLEBE BARN, cf. *Glebe Barn Field* 1943 *Map, The Glebe* 1943 *ib, v.* glebe. NEWTOWN, a late creation which has not appeared by 1824 O. NORTHFIELDS. QUARRY FM. THE RECTORY. THE ROOKERY, *v. Rochaue* in Lt. Casterton f.ns. (b) *infra.* THE SMITHY. TOLETHORPE HALL, cf. *le Oldehall* c1300 Blore, *The Hall Close* 1811 ib, *v.* ald, hall. TOLETHORPE MILL, 1851 *Conant.* TOLETHORPE OAKS, *Tolthorpe Oaks* 1806 Map, *v.* āc.

Field-Names

Undated forms in (a) are 1943 *Map;* those dated 1950 are *Burghley.* The early f.ns. of Little Casterton and Tolethorpe are treated separately in (b). Undated forms in (b) for Little Casterton are 18 *Monson;* those dated Hy 3 are *TT* and 1796 are *Whit.* All forms in (b) for Tolethorpe are c1300 Blore.

(a) Six -, Seven Acre; Ten Acre Above Spinney; Fourteen - (cf. *Old Fourteen Acres* 18), Seventeen Acre 1943, - Acres 1950; Eighteen Acres 1950; Twenty-three -, Twenty-four -, Far Twenty-seven -, Middle Twenty-seven Acres;

Thirty-three Acre; Barn Fd; Bland's Cl (with the surn. *Bland*, cf. Clement *Bland* 1846 White); Botany Bay 1943, 1950 (a frequent name for land which is remote from the village or on which labour is hard as in the former New South Wales penal colony, cf. Botany Bay in S. Luffenham f.ns. (a)); Burnt Bush (*v.* **busc**); Burnt Cl 1950; Chapel Fd (adjoining a Methodist chapel); Corn Fd; Cottage Cl 1943, 1950; Crow Spinney 1943, 1950; Evidences (*Evidence* 18; Mr J. Field observes that this is apparently an abstract f.n. of the same type as Reasonableness in Halstock Do and the editor believes that it may well refer to 18th cent. agricultural improvements); Farm Road Fd; Garden Cl 1943, 1950; Hare's Hill; Hogg's Lee (*Hog Leys* 18, alluding to shearling lambs, dial. *hog, v.* lēah); Home Cl, - Fd (*v.* **home**); Horse Cl; Insthorpe Oaks 1801 Map (referring to Ingthorpe in neighbouring Tinwell, *v.* **āc**); King's Hill, King's Pit (from the surn. *King,* cf. *Kinges Slade* in Gt. Casterton f.ns. (b)); Kitty's Cl (evidently with the pers.n. *Kitty,* the pet-form of *Catherine*); Knight's Fd; Long Cl 1943, 1950 (18); The Marrums (perh. to be identified with *Manholm* Hy 3, poss. 'the communally-held water-meadow', *v.* **(ge)mǣne, holmr**); Big -, New Cl; North Road Cl; Nursery Cl 1943, 1950 (18, 'plot in which young plants are reared until fit for transplantation', *v.* **nursery**); Philpott's (a surn., cf. William *Phellypot* 1522 MilS, husbandman of Langham); Pit Fd; Pond Cl (*Great Pond Close* 18, *Little* - 1796); River Cl 1943, 1950 (adjoining R. Gwash); Old Sanfoin Cl 1943, 1950 (with *sainfoin,* a perennial herb much grown as a forage plant, *v.* **sainfoin**); Smeeth's Mdws (cf. *Smytheholme* in Tolethorpe f.ns. (b) *infra*); Smith Road Cl; Smith's Fd; Stable Fd; Stamford Hill (adjoins the county boundary with Stamford L); Stonepit Cl 1943, Stone Pit - 1950 (freestone quarries were worked in the parish); Tank Cl 1943, 1950 (cf. Tank Cl in neighbouring Ryhall f.ns. (a) and Rommell's Cl in Whissendine f.ns. (a)); Upton's Cl; Waste Boundary Land; White Ground (either from dial. *white* used of 'dry, open pasture' or eModE *white* 'infertile' in contrast to *black* 'fertile, *v.* **grund**); Will Syke (*ad Wellis sike, ad le Wellesikes* Hy 3, *v.* **wella, sīk**; the reference may be to the chalybeate spring mentioned in 1846 White).

(b) Little Casterton: *Abbotispittes, -pittis* Hy 3 (Olveston Abbey Lei held land in nearby Pickworth and may well have done so here, *v.* **abbat, pytt**); *super aquam* Hy 3 ('(furlong) above the water', no doubt alluding to R. Gwash, *v.* **wæter**); *Ash Coppice, Barnes's Meadow, Bochawesti, Bochawsti* Hy 3 (*v.* **bōc**[1], **haga**[1], **stīg**); *Bollands Close* (if not from *ball-land* 'land at the boundary mound' (cf. *Ballands* in Wardley f.ns. (b), also a parish on the Ru boundary), then from the surn. *Bolland,* cf. *Bollands Meadow* in Lyndon f.ns. (b)); *Bucwell', Bukewelle* Hy 3 (prob. 'he-goat spring or stream', *v.* **bucca, wella**); *Bushy Close* (*v.* **busshi**); *Cottagers Close* (*v.* **cotager**); *ad crucem, ex occidentali parte crucis* Hy 3

(v. cros); *Diked Holm, Dikedholm, ad Dikholm* Hy 3 ('a water-meadow, ditched or enclosed by ditches', v. **diked, holm**; the third form may contain **dík** rather than **diked**); *Dilkes's Close* (with the surn. *Dilkes*, v. White Hills *infra*); *Doctor's Close, Dovecote Close, Dry Ground* (v. **drȳge, grund**); *Estcroft* Hy 3 (v. **ēast, croft**); *Five Acres, Friths Sale* (referring to an area of woodland disposed of by sale, v. **sale** and Frith Fm *supra*); *Grenhil* Hy 3 (v. **grēne**[1], **hyll**); *Hag Meadow* (v. **hogg**); *Hauerdale* Hy 3 (either 'valley where oats are grown' or 'valley where the he-goats are pastured'; either compound could have an OE or Scand first el., v. **hæfera, hafri, hæfer**[1], **hafr, dalr**); *Hall Close* 18, *Old Hall Close* 1796, 18 (referring to Tolethorpe Hall *supra*); *Hene Houe, Hennehowong* Hy 3 (v. **henn, haugr, vangr**); *unam rodam contra collem* Hy 3 (v. **hyll**); *Hill Green* (v. **grēne**[2]); *le Lady Wong* 1318 Blore (prob. a field whose revenues were assigned to the upkeep of a chapel or shrine in the local church and referring to Our Lady, the Virgin Mary, v. **hlæfdige, vangr**); *The Lammas, otherwise Town Meadow* 1796 (v. **lammas, tūn**); *Land Close* (an enclosure consolidating selions of an open-field, v. **land**); *super semitan versus occidentem* Hy 3 (v. **lane**); *Linges* Hy 3 (v. **lyng**); *Louth's Leys* 1796, *Louths -* 18 (from the surn. *Louth*, cf. *Louths farm* 1785 in Empingham f.ns. (b), v. **lēah**); *in medio campo* Hy 3 ('the middle field', one of the open-fields of the village, v. **middel, feld**); *Mill Field; Mill Meadow, New Close Field, New Closes* 1796, 18; *The Oaks, Pan Meadow* (alluding either to a circular field or to a circular hollow, v. **panne**); *Pikes Close* (with the surn. *Pike*); *The Pingle* 1796 (v. **pingel**); *Popple Close* (evidently a close on pebbly ground, v. **popel**); *Riholm* Hy 3 (v. **ryge, holmr**); *Risholm, Risceholm* Hy 3 (v. **risc, holmr**); *Rochaue, Rochawe* Hy 3 (if the first el. is *hróc* 'a rook' rather than the OE pers.n. *Hróc(a)*, then The Rookery *supra* may have a long history, so perh. 'enclosure where the rooks nest', v. **hróc, haga**[1]); *Ryhall Heath* (Ryhall parish adjoins to the east, v. **hǣð**); *Saint John's Land* 1796 (Lt. Casterton church is dedicated to St John and this ground may have been an endowment for its upkeep, but v. *St John's Peice* in Greetham f.ns. (b)); *Sale Close* (cf. Frith Sale *supra*); *Schucheved* Hy 3 (perh. 'the goblin's headland', v. **scucca, hēafod**); *Sheep Hill Close* 1796, 18; *Spaw Grounds* (prob. referring to the chalybeate spring mentioned in 1846 White, from **spa** 'a mineral, medicinal spring', v. **grund**); *Spring Close* (may refer to the spring of the previous f.n., v. **spring**); *super viam de Stanford* Hy 3 ('(furlong) above the road to Stamford L'); *Stone Pit* (v. **stān-pytt**); *Sunderland, Sunderlaund, Sundrelond* Hy 3 (v. **sundor-land**); *Town Meadow* 1796 (v. *The Lammas supra*); *Old -, Twelve Acres, Water Field* (no doubt lay beside R. Gwash, cf. *super aquam, supra*); *dimidiam acram ad fontem q' vocat' Welhalfager* Hy 3 ('the half acre at the spring', v. **wella, half, æcer**); *White Hills otherwise Dilkes's Close* 1796 (perh. from dial. *white* 'dry, open pasture' and the surn. *Dilkes*); *in campo occidentali* Hy 3 ('the west field', one of the open-fields of the village', v. **west, feld**).

(b) Tolethorpe: *Almawewonge* (v. **elm, haga**[1], **vangr**, the first el. has been influenced by Scand **almr** 'elm'); *Brechewong* (v. **brēc, vangr**); *le Brydgefurlong* (v. **brycg, furlang**); *Davysyke* (from the surn. *Davy*, common from the 13th cent., v. **sik**); *Dracouncrofte* (from the surn. *Dragon*, cf. Dragon's Hill in Preston f.ns. (a), v. **croft**; Reaney *s.n.* notes that *Dragon* was occasionally a nickname but usually metonymic for *dragoner* (< OFr *dragonier* 'a standard-bearer'). He observes that 'standards were often emblazoned with a dragon and were carried not only in battle but in pageants and processions.' In the latter context, the proximity of medieval Stamford may well be significant.); *Handacre* (perh. with reference to land that could only be tilled with the spade rather than by the plough, v. **hand, æcer**, cf. *Handacre furlong* in Caldecott f.ns. (b)); *Helle* (poss. a term of reproach for land difficult to cultivate, but much more likely simply a local form of **hyll** 'a hill', cf. Big -, Little Hell in Mkt. Overton f.ns. (a), Little Hell in Burley f.ns. (a)); *Litelhawewonge* (v. **lytel, haga**[1], **vangr**); *Mydelfelde* ('the middle field', one of the open-fields of Tolethorpe, v. **middel, feld**); *Midelwonge* (v. **middel, vangr**); *Northcrofte* (v. **norð, croft**); *le Oldefelde* (may indicate the in-field of a former in-field/out-field system as at Pickworth, v. **ald, feld**); *Ounbystye* (Aunby L lies to the north, v. **stig**); *Pallemersacre* (from the surn. *Palmer*, cf. Nicolis *Palmer* 1522 MilS of Langham and Henry *Palmer* 1524 SR of Barrow, v. **æcer**); *Saltergate* (v. **saltere, gata**, cf. *Saltergate Furlong* in Gt. Casterton f.ns. (b); the road ran east to west, cf. Salterford in Burley f.ns. (a)); *Smytheholme* ('the smithy meadow', poss. remembered in Smeeth's Mdws *supra*, v. **smiðð e, holmr**); *le Storth* (v. **storð**); *le Stylle* (v. **stigel**); *Tibwellewonge* ('the in-field by Tibba's well or spring', v. **wella, vangr**, the 7th cent. *Tibba*, patron saint of falconers, is supposed to have spent most of her life in neighbouring Ryhall, v. Tibba's Well in Ryhall f.ns. (a)); *Toftewell* (v. **toft, wella**); *le Watergalle* (v. **wæter, galla**); *le Wro* (v. **vrá**).

Empingham

EMPINGHAM

Epingeham 1086 DB bis, a.1118 RegAnt
Empingeham 1106-10, 1146 RegAnt, 1167, 1168 P *et passim* to 1259 Ipm, *Hempingeham* 1106-10 RegAnt
Empingham, -y- 1140 Reg *et passim* to 1243 FF *et freq* to 1610 Speed, *Hempingham* 1185 Templar
Impingeham 1210 FF, *Impyngham* 1286 Ass

'The village of Empa's people', *v.* -**inga-**, **hām**. The OE pers.n. *Empa* may be a by-name related to OE *ampre* 'dock, sorrel', Du *amper* 'bitter, sour', *v.* PN -ing 147.

HARDWICK COTTAGES, - FM, - WOOD

    Herdewik 1281 Cl, -*wyk(e)* 1315 *Ass*, 1315 Ipm, 1384 Cl,
        Empyngham Herdewyk 1316 FA
    Herdwyk 1295 Ipm, 1318 Pat, 1362 Ipm
    Hardwick 1610 Speed, 1695 *Map*, 1701 *Deed*

'The herd farm', i.e. 'the sheep farm', *v.* **heorde-wīc**. The identification of *Harduic* 1086 DB, a berewick of Archbishop Aldred's vill of Skillington L, with the Rutland Hardwick is suggested in C.W. Foster and T. Longley, *The Lincolnshire Domesday and the Lindsey Survey*, Lincs. Record Society 19 (1924, repr. 1976), xl and 227. Minor names arising appear as *Hardwick Farm* 1795, 1893 *Anc*, *Hardwick Lodge* 1846 White, *Hardwick Wood* c1700 *Rental*, 1795, 1818, 1893 *Anc*. In 1383-4, the whole village is described as waste and destroyed, *v.* Blore 144. Its site may have been at SK 973 123, *v.* BrownArchSites 9.

SHACKLEWELL, - LODGE, - SPINNEY, *Shacklewell* 1698 *Anc*, 1826 G, *Shaklewell* 117 *Anc*, *Shacklewell Spinney* 1893 *ib*, possibly 'the spring or stream where animals are shackled', *v.* **sceacol**, **wella**. However, *sceacol* in this compound may be a much older form of the dial. word *shackle* 'quaking grass' from the OE verb *sceacan* 'to shake' (i.e. referring to something loose, just as a shackle allows 'loose movement') and may allude to quake-fen at the spring or along the stream. Shacklewell rises at a spring on the south-eastern boundary of the parish and then, forming the line of the boundary itself, runs into R. Gwash, *v.* Sr 199-200 *s.n.* Shackleford, cf. Shacklewell Mx 107.

AUDIT HALL ROAD, cf. *Audit Hall Yard* 1979 VR. THE AVENUE, cf. *Avenue Close* 1795 *DC*, 1818 *Anc*, *v.* **avenue**. BECKWORTH SPINNEY, 1893 *Anc*, 1938 *Burghley*, possibly from the surn. *Buckworth*, cf. *Mr Buckworth's Close* c1850 *Anc*. THE

BELT, 1893 *ib*, a narrow strip of woodland planted as game cover for the Earls of Ancaster. BLACK HORSE P.H. (lost), closed c1890 - VR. BLOODY OAKS, c1800, 1806 Map, 1893 *Anc*, a fanciful name for woodland adjacent to the site of, and recalling, the Battle of Empingham (1470), otherwise Horn Field or Losecoat Field, *v.* Losecoat Field *infra.* BULLOCK SPINNEY, 1908 *Anc.* BUNKER'S HILL, cf. *Bunker's Hill Spinney* 1893 *ib*, referring to the Battle of *Bunker Hill* (1775) in the American War of Independence when British victory failed to break the colonists' siege of Boston. CHAPEL FIELD SPINNEY, 1893 *ib*, *le Capell Feilde* 1550 Pat, *Chaplefeild* 1698, l17 *Terrier,* (*Le*) *Chappell Feild* 1712 *Anc,* 1719 *Deed, Chapel Field* 1795 *DC,* 1818 *Anc,* one of the great open-fields of Empingham and named from the former medieval chapel dedicated to St Botolph, *v.* **chapel(e), feld** and South Field *infra.* CHAPEL HILL, 1824 O, 1877 White, in the Chapel Field. CHAPEL SPINNEY, 1893 *Anc,* 1943 *Deed,* sited on Chapel Hill. The stone foundations of the Chapel of St Botolph exist in the spinney at SK 9610 0895, *v.* BrownArchSites 9. CHURCH BRIDGE, 1887 *Anc,* cf. *ad pontem de Empingham* 1269 *For, v.* **brycg.** CHURCH FM. THE CITY (local), an ironical name for a small group of houses. CLIPSHAM FORD SPINNEY, 1893 *Anc,* named from Clipsham which lies to the north-east. COCKED HAT SPINNEY, 1893 *ib*, alluding to the tricorne shape of the spinney. COW CROFT SPINNEY, 1893 *ib, Cow Croft* 1744 *ib, v.* **croft.** CROCKET LANE (local). CROSS ROADS FM, 1893 *ib, Crossroads Farm* 1932 Kelly, cf. *Crossroads Field* 1943 *Map.* The earlier name of the cross-roads was *Gate Shells* l17, *v.* **gate-shadel** 'a cross-roads' and YW 7 192, *s.v.* gate-shadel. THE CROWN P.H., 1846, 1863 White. DEB DALE, *Debdale* 1698, l17 *Terrier, Deepdale* c1850 *Anc, Bottom Deepdales* 1943 *Map,* cf. *Deepdale Spinney* 1892 *Anc, v.* **dēop, dalr.** DOVECOT, cf. *Dovecote Close* 1795 *DC,* 1818 *Anc, Doue House* 1701 *Deed, Dovehouse Yard* 1701 *ib, v.* **dove-cot(e), dove-house.** EMPINGHAM CHURCH, *Church* (*St Peter*) 1846, 1863 White. EMPINGHAM MILL, c1700 *Letter,* 1887 *Anc,* cf. Mill Close Spinney and Mill Fm *infra.* GLEBE FM, 1932 Kelly, *v.* **glebe.** GUNNEL LANE (local), *Gun Hill* c1850 *Anc, Gunwell Stye Way* l17 *Terrier.* Ostensibly a p.n. with OE *wella* 'a spring, a stream' but if so, the first el. presents problems. The Scand pers.n. *Gunni* is the most obvious choice for this but it is rare to find a Scand pers.n. compounded with OE *wella. Gunni* may have replaced an earlier OE pers.n. (as in Bracewell YW 6 38), but as the pers.n. *Gunni* is also probable in *Gundale* in neighbouring Ketton f.ns. (b), it may be that the Empingham name is also *Gundale* 'Gunni's valley', *v.* **sty-way**. HALL CLOSE, 1698 *Terrier*, 1795 *DC*, 1818 *Anc*, *Whitehead's Hall Close* 1785 *ib*, cf. *Hall Closes* 1649 (1729) *ib*, *Hall Close Spinney* 1893 *ib*. Hall Close contains earthworks of a medieval manor house, *v.* MER 14, 17. HIBBITS LODGE, cf. Amos, Robert and William *Hibbitt* 1846 White and Arthur and Cecil *Hibbitt* 1932 Kelly, all of neighbouring Exton. HIGHFIELD CLOSE. HIGHFIELDS. HIGH MOOR, *High Moor(e)* 1698, 117 *Terrier*, 1893 *Anc*, *v.* **hēah**[1], **mōr**[1]. HOT HOLLOW FM (HOLLOW FM 2½"), *Hot Hollow* 1943 *Map*, *The Hott* 1698, 117 *Terrier*, perh. with dial. *ho't* (from *holt*) with the sense 'poor land covered with furze or ling', cf. Warren's Holt in f.ns. (a) *infra*, *v.* **holh**. HORN MILL SPINNEY, 1893 *Anc*, *v.* Horn Mill in Exton. LEE SPINNEY, 1892 *Anc*, *Lea Spinney* 1938 *Burghley*, cf. *Lees Spinney Field* 1938 *ib*, 1943 *Map*, *Leys Farm* 1785 *Anc*, *v.* **lēah**. LINGS SPINNEY, *Ling's Spinney* 1893 *ib*, *The Lings* 1698, 117 *Terrier*, *v.* **lyng**. LITTLE OAKS, - LODGE, *Little Oaks* 1893 *Anc*. LOSECOAT FIELD, *Losecote-field* 1811 Blore, *Losecoat Field* 1893 *Anc*, the local name for the site of the Battle of Empingham, 12th May 1470. Popular lore maintains that it refers to the tradition that the defeated Lancastrians threw off their coats to escape detection after the battle, but the name is no doubt from the more mundane OE *hlōse-cot* 'pigsty cottage' as the 1811 form indicates, *v.* **hlōse**, **cot**, cf. *Loscott* in Leighfield f.ns. (b) and *Loscoat(e)s* in Braunston f.ns. (b). The contemporary name for the battleground was *Hornefeld in Empyngham* 1475 Pat because it was adjacent to Horn, *v.* VCH 2 242. Early references are *Hornefeld* 1472 Blore, 1509 Pat, 1535 VE, and later *Hornefield* 1806 Map, 1846 White. MIDDLE LODGE, 1893 *Anc*. MILL CLOSE SPINNEY, 1925 *Deed*, *Mill Close* 1683, 1698 *ib*, 1698, 117 *Terrier*, 1795, 1818 *Anc*. MILL FM, 1893 *ib*, cf. *atte Suthmylne* 1296 *SR* (p), *atte Suth Milne* 1310 Pat (p), *le Southmylne* 1369 *Deed*, *Mill* 1824 O, *v.* **sūð**, **myln**. Remains of this water-mill survive at SK 957 084, *v.* BrownArchSites 9. MORRIS'S SPINNEY, 1893 *Anc*. MOWMIRES, - SPINNEY, 1893 *ib*, on R. Gwash and probably referring to swampy ground used for mowing grass, *v.* **mýrr**. NEW WOOD, 1824 *Terrier*, *The New Wood* c1800, 1806 Map, 1893 *Anc*, a new plantation named in contrast to Old Wood *infra*. NEW

WOOD LODGE, 1893, 1908 *ib* is *Newwood Farm* 1932 Kelly. THE NOOK, 1932 ib, *Loves Nooke* 1698, 117 *Terrier, Love's Nook* 1795, 1818 *Anc,* from the family name of Thomas *Love* who held a tenement in *Love's Lane* in Empingham c1850 *ib, v.* nōk. NOOK FM. NOOK LANE is probably *Love's Lane* c1850 *ib.* NORMANTON COTTAGES (NEW COTTAGES 2½"), a row of cottages in the south-west of the parish, adjacent to Normanton. NORTH BROOK, 1818, 1893 *Anc, Northbrooke* 1698, 117 *Terrier, North Brooke* 1758 *Surv,* 1795 *DC, v.* norð, brōc. OLD WOOD, 1893 *ib* is *Empingham Wood* 1610 Speed, c1700 *Rental,* 1795 *DC,* 1806 Map, 1818 *Anc,* 1825 Map, *v.* wudu. OLD WOOD LODGE. OLIVE BRANCH P.H. (lost), 1887 *Anc,* 1932 Kelly. PARK HO. PREBENDAL HO., 1932 ib. STONE PIT SPINNEY, cf. *Stone-pit Close* 1795 *DC,* 1818 *Anc, Stonepit Close* 1943 *Map, Stonepit Field* 1943 *ib, Old Stone Pit* 1893 *Anc.* SYKES SPINNEY (SYKE'S - 2½"), *Syke Spinney* 1824 O, *Syke's Spinney* 1893 *Anc, The Sykes* 1698, 117 *Terrier, le Sikes* 1712 *Anc, West Field Sykes* 1795, 1818 *ib, (The) Syke Close* 1683 *Deed,* 1683 (1729) *Anc,* 1698, 117 *Terrier, The Sike Close* 1721 *Deed, Sykes Field* 1938 *Burghley, Old Sykes Field* 1943 *Map, Sykes Field Seven Acres* 1943 *ib, v.* sīk and West Field *infra.* TITHE BARN. THE VICARAGE, 1846, 1863 White is *The Personage House* 1701 *Deed, v.* personage. WARREN SPINNEY, 1806 Map, 1893 *Anc,* 1938 *Burghley, v.* wareine. THE WASHDYKE (local), referring to an old sheep-dip, *v.* wæsce, dīk. WHITE HORSE P.H., 1846 White, c1850 *Anc,* 1863 White, 1887 *Anc.* THE WILDERNESS, 1932 Kelly. WISTERIA HO., 1932 ib.

Field-Names

Undated forms in (a) are 1943 *Map;* those dated 1818, c1850, 1887 and 1893 are *Anc.* Those dated 1925 and 1943 are *Deed* (per Mr D. Tew). Those of 1938 are *Burghley.* Early forms dated 1649 (1729), 1661 (1729), 1683, 1683 (1729), 1712, 1719, 1739, 1741, 1744, 1779 and 1785 are *Anc;* 1673, 1683, 1701, 1714 and 1721 are *Deed;* 1698 and 117 are *Terrier;* c1700 are *Rental;* 1727 are *Plan;* 1758 are *Surv* and 1795 are *DC.* Hardwick f.ns., where known, are marked (H).

(a) The Seven Acres 1938, Seven Acres 1943, Eight -, Nine Acres, Eleven Acre, The Eleven - 1925, The Fourteen Acres 1925, 1943, Fifteen Acres 1818

(1795), Sixteen Acre, The Eighteen Acre, The Twenty-two Acres (v. æcer);
Alexandra Cl; Mr Allen's Cl c1850; Bailey's Fd 1938; Becky's Grave 1943 *Deed*
(alluding to an old excavation here, v. græf, cf. Solomon's Grave in Mkt.
Overton f.ns. (a), Jackson's Grave in Greetham f.ns. (a); poss. with a pet-form
of the surn. *Beckworth*, cf. Beckworth Spinney *supra*, rather than of the pers.n.
Rebecca); Big Fd; Bird-Holme (H) 1818 (1758, 1795, *Bird Holme Close* 1701, v.
bridd, holmr); Mr Bloodworth's Cl c1850; Bottom Lodge 1893, - Cl 1943 (cf.
Top Lodge *infra*); Great -, Little Boyal Leys (H) 1818 (1795, *Boyall Leas* 1673,
Boyal Leys 1758, 1779, from the surn. *Boyall*, cf. John *Boyeall* 1525 SR of
Ketton, v. lēah); Bridge Cl 1818 (*The Bridge Close* 1683, 1795), Bridge Fd 1818
(*Bridge Field and Meadow* 1795) (alluding to Church Bridge *supra*); Broad Water
1818 (*molendin' de Bradewater* 1286 *Ass*, *Broadwater* 1795, a prob. reference to
the early damming of North Brook, v. brād, wæter, myln); Brooms Fd; Bryant's
Fd; Building Fd; Mr Bunning's Cl, Mr Bunning's Home Cl c1850; Carriers Cl
(cf. *Carryers Close* in adjoining Normanton f.ns. (b)); Bottom -, Top Chambers;
Chapel Road c1850; The Chelsea (evidently a transferred name from Chelsea
in London, prob. indicating a field towards the parish limits); Mr Christian's Cl
c1850 (with an old Ru surn., cf. John-, Robert- and William *Cristian* 1522 MilS
of Barrow); Cobler's Cl 1818, Cobblers - 1943, Cobblers Fd (*Coblers Croft vel le*
Chappel Croft 1329 Wright, *Coblers Crofte* 1550 Pat, *Coblers Close* 1727, 1795,
Cobler's Close 1785, *Cobler's row* 1785, *Coblers Row(e) Furlong* 1698, 117; as the
earliest citation in NED for *cobelere* 'a shoe-maker' is 1362, it is poss. that we
have here the name of the trade rather than a surn. formed from it, but in Ru,
early names with *-croft* are frequently compounded with a surn., v. cobelere,
croft, rāw); Coneygree 1818 (1795, *The Coninger End* 1698, ye Coninger end 117,
v. coninger); Revd. L. Cooper's Cl c1850; Cottagers Cl 1818 (*Cotchers Close*
1758, 1785, *Cottager's Close* 1795, v. cottere, cotager); Cow Ground, Cow Pasture;
Cracraft's, - Cl 1818, Crowscroft Fds 1943 (*Crow Croft* 1698, *Crowcroft* 117, *Cray*
Crofts 1785, *Cracrafts, Cracrafts Close* 1795, v. crāwe, croft); Cream Pot Leys (H)
1818 (*the Creame Pott Close* 1673, *Cream Pot Close* 1758, 1779, *Creampot Furlong*
1698, 117, *Cream-pot Leys* 1795 (v. lēah), alluding to rich pasture); The Crofts
1925, 1943; Doctor's Cl; Dry Leys (H) 1818 (1795, 'well-drained pasture', v.
drȳge, lēah); The Dunnels (may be a metathesised modern reflex of *Dullands*
infra); Ellis Cl (with the surn. *Ellis*, cf. *Ellis Nooke* in Greetham f.ns. (b));
Exton Gate Fd 1938, 1943 (v. gata), Exton Road Cl 1938, 1943 (beside the road
to Exton, the adjoining parish to the north-west); Fancourt's Cl (with the surn.
Fancourt, cf. Lionel *Fancourt* 1698, John, Matthew and William *Fancourt* 1846
White); Field Road c1850; First Fd (cf. Second Fd *infra*); Footpath Fd;
Freestone Pit 1818, - Cl 1943 (*freestone* is building stone which is fine grained
and uniform enough to be worked in any direction); Garden Cl; Glebe Fd,

Glebe Fifteen Acres 1938, - Acre 1943 (Mr J. Field observes that a total of 53 acres of glebe is noted in 1846 White, cf. Glebe Fm *supra*); Great Ground (H) 1818 (1795, *v.* **grund**); Grub Cl (H) 1818 (1795, referring to land cleared of trees, i.e. to tree-stumps grubbed out); Far -, Green Hill (117, *Greenhill* 1698, *v.* **grēne**[1], **hyll**); Hare's Fd; The Heath 1818 (1795, *Empingham Heath* 1721, 1727, *v.* **hǣð**); Hog Yard (H) 1818 (1795, *v.* **hogg, geard**); Home Cl 1925, 1943 (*The Home Close* 1714, 1785, *v.* **home**); The Homes 1925, 1943; Horn Hill Fd 1943; Horn Lane Cl (H) 1818 (1795, *Horn Lane* being an 18th cent. local name for Ermine Street, cf. Horn Lane Spinney in Horn parish which adjoins to the west of Hardwick); Horse Pasture; Horse Shoot Fd; The Island 1818 (1795, used of a field completely surrounded by other fields); Mr Islip's Cl c1850, Islip's Fd 1943 (from the family name of John *Islip* 1846 White); Mr D. Keen's Cl, Mr Keen's Home Cl c1850; Keepers Cl (referring to a gamekeeper); Kingston's Cl (from the surn. *Kingston*); The Limekiln; Little Fd 1818, 1943 (*The Little Feild* 1698, 117, 1712, 1719, *The Little Field* 1795); Lodge Fd; Lovell's Fd; Mad Moll's; The Meadows 1925, 1943 (*furlong along the Meadow* 1698, 117); Meer Cl 1818 (1698, 1758, 1795, (*ye*) *Meare Close* 1649 (1729), 117, *v.* **(ge)mǣre**); Mile Post 1893, Milestone Fd 1943; Mill Lane c1850 (*the Mill Lane* 1712), Mill Lane Cl 1818 (1795); Neanton 1818, c1850 (1795), Neanton Cl 1818 (1795) (poss. recording the name of a lost early farmstead, an OE *(*æt*) *Nēowantūne* '(at) the new farm', *v.* **nīwe, tūn**; but the surn. *Neanton* cannot be discounted, although it does not occur elsewhere in Ru); New Row c1850; Paddocks; The Paper Mill 1925, 1943; Park Wall; Parson's Cl; Percival's Cl 1818 (*Percivals Close* 1795, from the family name of Francis *Percival* 1712 of Empingham); Pinfold c1850, 1893 (*v.* **pynd-fald**); The Pingle 1893, 1925, 1943 (*v.* **pingel**); Pope's Spring 1893 (cf. William *Pope* 1522 MilS, 1524 SR of adjoining Tickencote and Pope's Spring in Barrowden f.ns. (a), *v.* **spring**); Prebendal Fd 1979 VR (cf. Prebendal Ho. *supra*); Primrose Hill 1887; Pump House 1893 (the 19th cent. saw the installation of mechanical pumps and rams for water supply); Reservoir Fd; River Fd; Roundabout (*v.* **roundabout**); Mrs Thomas Royce's Cl, Mrs Royce's Home Cl c1850 (*v.* **home**); Rudkins Fds; The Sands; Scott's Garden c1850 (cf. *Scotts Farm* 1785; cf. also Robert *Scott* 1524 SR of neighbouring Hambleton, Henry *Scot* 1522 MilS, - *Scotte* 1524 SR of Ryhall and Thomas *Scott* 1522 MilS, also of Ryhall); Second Fd (cf. First Fd *supra*); Sheep Dike Cl c1850 (a close with a ditch used as a sheep-dip, *v.* **scēap, dīk**); Shelton's Fd; Side Leys (*v.* **sīde, lēah**); South Fd 1925, 1943 (*le Southfeld alias le Capell Feilde* 1550 Pat, (*the*) *South Feild* 1698, 117, 1719, 'the south field', *v.* **sūð, feld**, one of the great open-fields of Empingham, also called Chapel Field, *v.* Chapel Field Spinney *supra*); Spinney Cl 1925, Spinney Fd 1943; Stack-Yard Cl 1818, Stackyard Fd 1925, 1943 (*Stack Yard Close* 1795, *v.* **stak-ȝard**); Stamford Road Fd (cf. *furlong above Stamford*

Way 117, - *below* - 1698, referring to land beside the road to Stamford L); Mr J. Steven's Cl c1850; Stonebridge Hollow; Strong Land ('ground with firm, compact soil', *v.* **strang, land**); Mr Syson's Cl, Mr Syson's Paddock c1850; Top Lodge 1893 (cf. Bottom Lodge *supra*); Town Street c1850 (cf. *The Towngate* 1712, *v.* **tūn, gata**); Mr J. Turner's Cl c1850; The Turnpike (a roadside close, the name anachronistic by 1943, *v.* **turnepike**); Vetchery Cl 1818 (1795, *v.* **vacherie**); Warren Cl 1943; Mr Warren's Cl c1850, Warren's Holt 1943 (*v.* **holt**), Mr Warren's Home Cl, Mr Warren's Fm c1850; The Waste 1818 (1795, *v.* **waste**); Water Mill House and Holm 1818 (*Water Mill House and Holme* 1795, referring to the house and meadow at Empingham Mill *supra, v.* **holmr**); West Field 1818, 1943 ((*the*) *West Feild* 1698, 117, 1712, 1719, *The West Field* 1721, one of the open-fields of Empingham, *v.* **west, feld**); Whitwell Cl, - Fd (*Whitwell Closes* 1712, *furlong above Whitwell Way*, - *below* - 1698, 117; Whitwell parish adjoins to the west); Wood Fd 1818, 1943 (*The Woodfeild* 1698, 117, *The Wood Feild* 1719, *Wood Field* 1795, one of open-fields of the village, *v.* **wudu, feld**); Wood Lane 1818 (1795); Workhouse Yard and Garden 1818 (referring to a Poor Law institute).

(b) *Ash Close* (H) 1649 (1729), c1700 (*v.* **æsc**); *Beavers House Land* 1698, 117 (cf. Thomas *Beaver* 1712 of Empingham); *The Bracke Closes* 1683, 1683 (1729), *Break(e) Closes* 1701, 1712, *The Breakes* 1701, *Brakedale* 1698, *furlong over Brakeway* 1698 (*v.* **bræc**[1]**, dalr, weg**); *Broken Barrow* 117 (poss. a prehistoric burial mound with visible signs of grave robbery, *v.* **brocen, beorg**; it should be noted, however, that early forms of names with *brakni* 'bracken' can mislead, cf. Brakenburgh L 2 224 which records the spellings *brokinborow, brokynborow* 1577); *Bushy Close* (H) 1649 (1729), c1700 (*v.* **busshi**); *Cheesecake Close* (H) c1700 (dial. *cheesecake* is used of the fruit of such wild plants as the common mallow (*Malva sylvestris*) and bird's foot trefoil (*Lotus corniculatus*)); *le Chappel Croft* 1329 Wright, *Chapple Crofts, Chaple Leys, ye Chaple Yard* 117 (all referring to the medieval chapel dedicated to St Botolph, *v.* **chapel(e), croft, lēah, geard**, cf. Chapel Field Spinney *supra*); *Clipsamway* 1698 (Clipsham parish is on the county boundary, north-east of Empingham); *Collingtons* 1785 (a surn. with gen. *s*); *Cow Commons* 1785 ('common land for the grazing of cows', *v.* **commun**); *furlong above* -, *Cringlety Valley* 1698, 117 (*v.* **cringol, tēag**); *ad Crucem* Hy 3 (p), 1288 *Deed* (p), *atte Croos* 1369 *ib* (p), *atte Cross(e)* 1388 *ib* (p), 1401 *Fine* (p) (*v.* **cros**, cf. *Ketton Cross over Luffenham Way infra*); *de la Curt* Hy 3 (p), 1288 *Deed* (p) (*Johannes de la Curt* no doubt lived at the manor house whose earthworks survive in Hall Close *supra, v.* **curt** 'a manorial house'); *Dollacres Furlong* 117 (*v.* **dāl, æcer**); *Dove Wong* 1698, *Doue wong* 117 (poss. the site of an old dovecote, *v.* **dūfe, vangr**); *Dowsetts* 1698, 117 (perh. 'a shelter for doves (or pigeons)' but earlier forms are needed, *v.* **dūfe**, **(ge)set**); *Dry Lake alias Mill Meadows* 1698, 117 (referring to a dried-up water-course or mill pond at the water-mill); *Dullands* 1698, 117 (*v.* **land**); *Dunston* 1698, *Dunstone* 117 (evidently the same name as Great Dunston in neighbouring Ketton f.ns. (a), prob. from **tūn-stall** 'a farmstead'); *furl' butt'* on *Exton Heath* 117 (Exton parish adjoins to the north-west, *v.* **hǣð**); *Extons Old Farm* 1785 (cf. Thomas *Exton*, husbandman of Empingham, 1522 MilS, 1524 SR); *Le Fallow Feild* 1712 (*v.* **falh**); *Fullwellhead* 1698, 117 (*v.* **ful**, **wella**, **hēafod**); *Galways Close* 1521 Ct (Richard *Galway* owned land in Empingham in 1459 Deed); *furlong above Greetham Balke* 117 (this appears to be a Hardwick f.n. since only there does Greetham parish adjoin Empingham, *v.* **balca**); *Grimesholm(e)* 1698, 117 (from the surn. *Grimes, v.* **holmr**, cf. *Grymes Wong Furlong* in neighbouring Greetham f.ns. (b)); *The Hades* 1712 (*v.* **hēafod**); *ye Hadings* 1739 (poss. an alternative form of the preceding name; it denotes places at the ends of an arable field where the plough was turned, cf. *ye headings* L 2 14, *v.* **hēafod, -ing**[1]); *Hambleton Way* 117 (Hambleton parish adjoins to the south-west); *ye Heath Close* 1683 (1729), *the Heath Close* 1701 (*v.* **hǣð**); *High Thorne Nooke* 1698, 117, *Middle High Thorne* 1698, *Midle* - 117 (*v.* **hēah**[1], **þorn**, **nōk**, **middel**); *Hogden Hill* 1712, *Hogdenhill Furlong* 1698, 117 (*v.* **hogg**); *furlong above Horne Way*, - *below* - 117 (Horn parish adjoins to the north); *Hunt's Cottage* 1785; *Incroft Phillipi* 1261, c1261, 1265 Deed ('Philip's inner croft', *v.* **in**, **croft**); *Ingersdale* 1698, 117 (perh. 'Ingvarr's valley', *v.* **dalr**, evidently at the boundary with neighbouring Exton, cf. *Ingresdale Slade* in Exton f.ns. (b)); *Jackson Wall* 1697, 1780 Deed (a close so called, *v.* **wall**); *Ketton Cross over Luffenham Way* 1698 (a wayside cross in that part of the parish towards Ketton and beside the road to N. Luffenham, *v.* **cros**, cf. *ad Crucem supra*); *The Lamass Commons* 1712 (common land used for grazing after 1st August, *v.* **lammas**, **commun**); *Lands End* 1712 (*v.* **land**, **ende**[1]); *in venella* c1250 Deed (p), *in ye Lane* 1477 (e16) *Charyte* (p) (*v.* **lane**); *Leatons Cottage* 1785; *Little Close* (H) 1779; *Little Grass Close* 1785 (prob. referring to a close of sown grass); *Little Heath* 1698, *Litle Heath* 117 (*v.* **hǣð**); *Louths Farm* 1785 (from the surn. *Louth*, cf. *Louths Leys* in Lt. Casterton f.ns. (b)); *Luffenham Way* 1698 (N. Luffenham lies to the south of Empingham); *Makworth(e) Close* 1521 Ct (in the possession of Georgius *Makworthe* 1521 ib, *v.* **clos(e)**); *Manigate Furlong* 1698, *Mannigates Fur'* 117 ('(the furlong at) the place where several roads come together', *v.* **manig**, **gata**); *Mill Holme* 1649 (1729) (*v.* **myln**, **holmr**); *Mill Lane Farm* 1758, 1785; *Mill Meadows* 1698, 117; *Neath Towne Close* 1649 (1729) (*v.* **beneoðan**, **tūn**); *Newfield* (H) 1649 (1729), c1700 Letter, *Lower* -, *Upper New Field Close* (H) c1700 (cf. *The Old Feild infra*); *Normanton Heath* 1727 (Normanton parish adjoins to the south, *v.* **hǣð**); *furlong below Normanton Way* 1698, 117; *The Old Feild* (H) 1661 Deed, *Old Field* 1661 (1729), *v.* **ald**, **feld**, cf. *Newfield supra*); *Old*

Hall 1698, 117 (*v.* **ald, hall**); *The Orchards Gardens* 1701 (*v.* **orceard**); *Outfield* (H) c1700 *Letter, Lower -, Upper Out Field Close* (H) c1700 *ib* ('field on the outskirts', *v.* **ūt(e), feld**); *Peas(e) Broad* 1698, 117 ('broad strip of land on which pease is grown', *v.* **pise, brǣdu**); *The Pease Feilds* 1741 (*v.* **pise, feld**); *Pibbles* 1698, 117 ('pebbly ground', *v.* **pibbil**); *Plantation* 1795; *furlong below Porthades* 117 (*v.* **port²**, **hēafod**); *Ram Close* 1649 (1729), c1700 (*v.* **ramm**); *Redfoard* 117 (prob. 'the ford with a red bottom' since Empingham stands on an ironstone ridge, *v.* **rēad, ford**); *Row Furlong* 1698, 117 (*v.* **rūh¹**); *Scotneys Cottage* 1785, *Scotneys Lands* 1719 (cf. John *Scotney* 1678 *Anc* of Stretton); *The Sheep Walks* 1712 (*v.* **sheep-walk**); *Stocklands* 1698, 117 (*v.* **stocc, land**); *Sweeting Tree Nooke* 1698, 117 ('the nook of land with a sweet-apple tree', *v.* **sweeting, nōk**); *Tenter Hedge* 117 (*v.* **tentour, hecg**); *Three Crofts* 1701 (a close so called, *v.* **croft**); *Tyrespyt* 1261, c1261 *Deed,* *Thyrspyth* c1265 *ib* bis ('the goblin's pit', *v.* **þyrs, pytt**); *Towne Close* 1701 (*v.* **tūn**); *The Wall Close* 1685, 1691, 1693 *Deed* (*v.* **wall,** cf. *Jackson Wall supra*).

Essendine

ESSENDINE

Esindone 1086 DB, *Esindon, -y-* 1316 FA, 1318 Pat, 1324 Cl
Essenden 1222 Cur, 1230 Cl *et passim* to 1316 *MktHPR*
Esinden(e), -y- 1265 Misc, 1276 RH *et passim* to 1400 ELiW
Essenden(e) 1230 Pat (p), 1290 Cl, 1292 OSut
Es(s)ingden(e), -y- 1286 *Ass,* 1286 *FF,* 1324, 1401 Pat *et passim*
    to 1509 LP
Is(s)enden(e) 1185 Dom, 1262 Cl, 1263 *Ass*
Ezenden 1610 Speed, 1618 Wright
Esendyne 1617 *FF, Easondyne* 1665 *SR*

'Esa's valley', *v.* **denu**.

BROADHOLME, 1932 Kelly, *Great -, Little Broad Holme* 1844 *TA,* cf. *Holmes* 1417 Blore, *v.* **holmr**. CHAPEL FM, 1932 Kelly; the chapel of Essendine Castle survives as the parish church. COUZENS HEATH (local), *Cousin's Heath* 1844 *TA,* with the surn. *Cousin,* cf. Richard *Cossyn* 1522 MilS, - *Cosyn* 1524, 1525 SR of Lt. Casterton, *v.* **hǣð**. ESSENDINE CHURCH, *Church (St Mary)* 1846 White. ESSENDINE LODGE FM. THE FREEWARDS, *Frewode*

1417 Blore, *Free Wood Mouth* 1844 *TA* (*v.* **mūða**), *Free Wood Piece* 1844 *ib*, *Free Wood Side* 1844 *ib*, *Freewards Thorns* c1800, 1806 Map, 1824 O, *Freewoods Thorns* 1826 G, 'the free wood', i.e., woodland in which commoners enjoyed certain rights, such as wood-gathering, *v.* **frēo, wudu**. NIGHTINGALE SPINNEY (local). PARK FM, *parcus de Esindene* 1296 Cl, *Esenden Parke* 1548 Pat, *Essendine Park* 1824 O, cf. *Parkelande* n.d. MinAcct, *Park House* c1800, 1806 Map, *Park Lodge* 1846 White, *v.* **park**. RAILWAY INN (lost), 1846, 1863 ib, 1932 Kelly. RAVENSTOCK WOOD (local), *Far -, First Ravenstock* 1844 *TA*; if this is an early name, then probably 'Hræfn's dairy-farm', *v.* **stoc**. STATION, 1863 O, the junction of the *Essendine and Bourn Railway* 1863 ib and the *Stamford and Essendine Branch Railway* 1863 ib.

Field-Names

Undated forms in (a) are 1844 *TA*; those dated 1943 are *Map*. Forms found in both sources are marked with an asterisk.

(a) Five Acre 1943; Six Acre Slip 1943 (*v.* **slipe**); Eight Acre 1943 (cf. Bottom Townsend *infra*); The Ten Acre*; Twelve Acre* (cf. Top Townsend *infra*); Thirteen Acres; The Fourteen Acre 1943; The Fifteen Acres 1943; Top Eighteen Acre or Seventeen Acres, Bottom Eighteen or Sixteen Acres 1943; The Nineteen Acre; The Twenty-one Acre or Peartree Cl 1943; Twenty-five Acres 1943; Thirty Acres; Aunby Cl (in an enclave within Carlby L; VCH 2 250 notes that up to enclosure, part of a common called Aunby Heath was attached to the manor of Essendine and that some fields were exchanged with Carlby in 1803-4 or poss. 1887, cf. North Cl *infra*); Backside (adjoins the west end of the village, *v.* **ba(c)ksyde**); Banthorpe Mdw 1943 (on the county boundary; Banthorpe Wood and Lodge lie in neighbouring Braceborough and Wilsthorpe parish L); Batt Mdw; the Beacon Fd, Beacon Hill (Side), Beacon Mdw (*v.* **(ge)bēacon**, cf. Beacon Fd, - Hill in Glaston f.ns. (a)); Black Lands (Mdw) (in eModE, *black* 'fertile' is contrasted with *white* 'infertile', cf. White Lands *infra*); Bottom Cl; Bottom Mdw 1943; Bullock Cl; Burkett Cl; Burnt Willow; Castle Hill and Moat; Coal Tar 1943 (perh. of black, sticky soil); Cocks and Holes (*v.* Hills and Holes *infra*); Coll Cl (if not with the surn. *Coll*, then with Scand **kollr** 'a hill, a summit'); Copwold Hill (*v.* **copp, wold**); Far Cott (*v.* **cot**); Cottage Cl; First -, Cow Cl 1844, The Cow Cl, Little Cow Cl 1943; Cross Cl; Crossroads Fd 1943; Dog Kennel (*v.* **dogge-kenel**); Drift ((land beside) a cattle way running on through Ryhall and so to Stamford market, v. **drift**); Eddy Croft Mdw (*Edycroft* n.d. MinAcct, from the surn. *Eddy*, cf. *Edycroft* in Lyddington f.ns. (b), v. **croft**); Bottom -, Top Foxholes (v. **fox-hol**); Great -, Little Fullers Leys (with the surn. *Fuller*, v. **lēah**); Garners Cl, - Mdw (with the surn. *Garner*, cf. *Garners grounds* in Tickencote f.ns. (b)); Gravel Pit Cl, Gravels; Great Ground (Mr J. Field notes that this is described as 'pasture' and more than 52 acres in area); Hangmans Cl (may record the site of an ancient gibbet, especially in view of Essendine's medieval castle with its natural association with early law-enforcement); The Hay Fd 1943; the Heath (x5), Top -*, Bottom Heath 1844, Stimpson's Heath 1844 (cf. Couzens Heath *supra*; *Stimpson* is a Ru surn., cf. William *Stimpson* 1785 *Surv* of Hambleton); Hills and Holes 1844, - and Hales 1943 (a widely used term for very uneven land, often the site of medieval quarrying, as at Barnack Nth (now Cambs.)); Home Cl (Mdw)* (v. **home**); Bottom -, Top Homestead (v. **hām-stede**); House Ground; Hunts Mdw (cf. *Hunt's Cottage* in Empingham f.ns. (b) and Anthony *Hunt* 1665 *HT* of Ketton); Intake (v. **inntak**); Lambkin Hall 1801 Map (1780 ib); Lammas Mdw (v. **lammas**); Bottom -, Top Lane Mdw; Langford Bridge c1800, 1801 Map, 1824 O (1780 Map, referring to the ford on the county boundary at TF 061 109, v. **lang^1, ford**); Leveret Leys (prob. from **leveret** 'a young hare', less likely the surn. derived from it, v. **lēah**); Low Mdw; Lower Mdw; Middle of the Field (Mr J. Field notes that the land lies among surrounding closes without obvious access); Mill Green (x2) (v. **grēne^2**); the Mowing Mdw 1943; New Cl, - Nook (v. **nōk**); New Wood 1943; The Nook 1943 (v. **nōk**); North Cl; Over the Line 1943 ('(land) across the railway track'); Picks Cl; Pinfold (v. **pynd-fald**); Pit Fd 1943; Pokes (v. **poke**); Red Lands (x4); Far - 1844, First -*, Rise, Rise Piece; Road Cl 1943; Rough Mdws; Great -, Little Row Syke, Row Syke Mdw (*Roweseke* 1417 Blore, *Rowsike* n.d. MinAcct, v. **rūh^1, sik**); School Fd 1943; Scutt Hill* (prob. a hill frequented by rabbits, v. **scut**); Sheep Cl, - Pasture 1943; Shelf Cl; Hanging Shelf ('a shelf of land on a hillside', v. **hangende, scelf**); Spring Piece 1844, - Fd 1943 (Mr J. Field observes that the sense is poss. 'plantation' as no springs are marked on the map, v. **spring, pece**); Stone Pit Cl*; Tobacco Pipe Piece (poss. a source of pipe-clay, v. **pece**); Bottom Townend or Eight Acre, Top Townend or Twelve Acre 1943 (v. **tūn, ende^1**); Tups Cl (v. **tup**); Wallis's Piece (v. **pece**); Water Furrows ('land where water tends to lie in the furrows', v. **wæter, furh**); White Lands (cf. Black Lands *supra*); Willow Hedge; The Wise (x2) (perh. 'the willow trees', v. **wīðig (wīðigas** pl.)); Wood Fd 1943.

(b) *le Deynes* n.d. MinAcct (v. **denu**); *Greteley* 1417 Blore (v. **grēat, lēah**); *Lituley* 1417 ib (v. **lȳtel, lēah**).

KETTON

Chetene 1086 DB, *Chetena* 1146 RegAnt, *Chetenea* 1163 ib
Ketene 1174, c1180 France, 1199 *FF et passim* to 1278 *LCDeeds
et freq* to 1322 *Wyg et passim* to 1384 Cl
Keton(*e*) 1322 Ipm *et passim* to 1397 *FF et freq* to 1505 Pat
Ketton 1519 EpCB *et freq* to 1556 *Conant,* 1583 *FF*

According to Ekwall, DEPN *s.n.*, this is an old alternative name
for R. Chater. The second element is OE **ēa** 'a river'. The first is
a derivative of PrWelsh **cę̄d** 'a wood', possibly an OE tribal name
* *Cētan.* The final syllable of the early p.n. form was eventually
dropped. Hence, 'the river of the Cētan', *v.* **ēa.**

GEESTON

Gyston 1286 *Ass, Giston in Keten'* 1316 *Ct*
Geston 1557 *FF, Geeston* 1602 *Recov,* 1610 Speed, 1620 Map,
1624 *Deed*
Geeson 1705 *Anc,* 1811 Blore

Probably 'Gyssa's farmstead', *v.* **tūn,** cf. Gissing Nf. For
illustration of its surviving medieval earthworks, *v.* MER 23-4.

FREGSTHORPE (lost)

Frygisthorp' 1300-20 *DC* (p), *Fregisthorp'* 1322 *Wyg* (p),
Fregisthorpe 1550 Pat
Fregthorp 1610 Speed, 1620 Map
Fregsthorpe Close 1638 *DC*

'Friðegist's outlying farmstead', *v.* **þorp.** According to DB, a
man called *Fredgis* held land in neighbouring Empingham in the
reign of Edward the Confessor. The pers.n. is OScand *Friðgestr*
which appears in late OE sources as *Friðegist,* or, as in the Liber
Vitae of Thorney Abbey, as *Freðegyst, Freþegist, v.* Feilitzen 254-5,
SPNLY 86. The settlement lay at approximately SK 991 049, *v.*
MER 24.

KILTHORPE GRANGE
    Ketelistorp c1250 *Ct, Ketelesthorp* 1296 *SR, Ketillisthorp* 1296 *ib*
    (p)
    Kedilistorp 1316 *Ct, Kedelistorp* 1327 *SR*
    Kelthorp(*e*) 1563 *FF,* 1610 Speed *et passim* to 1824 O
    .*Kilthorp*(*e*), -*y*- c1250 *Ct,* 1263 *Ass,* 1266 *For,* 13 *Wyg* (p), 1332
    Extent et freq to 1456 AD, 1535 VE

'Ketil's outlying farmstead', *v.* þorp, cf. Ab Kettleby and Eye
Kettleby Lei. The OScand pers.n. *Ketill* is an original by-name, cf.
OIcel *ketill* 'a cauldron, a cauldron-shaped helmet'. It was common
in Norway, Iceland and Denmark throughout the medieval period,
v. SPNLY 166-70. The p.n. appears compounded in later minor
forms as *Ketilthorpe Grange* 1516 (1684) Wright, *Kettylthorpphalle*
1539 MinAcct, *Kettlethorpe Hall* 1545 LP, *Kelthorp Farm* 1769
EnclA, v. grange, hall. For f.ns. arising, *v. infra.* For surviving
medieval earthworks, *v.* MER 24.

NEWBOTTLE (lost)
    Neubottle 1297 *Wyg* (p), *Neubotle* 13 *ib* (p) bis, 1332 *Extent*
    (p), *Neubotele de Ketene* 1332 *ib* (p)
    Newbottle 1610 Speed, *Newbotle* 1620, 1715 Map, *New Bottle*
    c1680 *Terrier*
'The new building', *v.* nīwe, bōtl. For f.ns. arising, *v. infra.*

MANTHORPE (lost), *Manthorpe Br*[ ]*e* 1677 *Terrier, Manthorpe Hill*
1919 *Sale.* These two late minor names may record a lost early
farmstead. If so, the first el. is probably a Scand pers.n. *Manni;* a
Scand or OE gen.pl. *manna* 'of the men', i.e. 'of the community' is
unlikely, cf. Manthorpe L (x2). Manthorpe Hill is beside R.
Chater, thus the damaged word in the 1677 manuscript is probably
either - *Bridge* or - *Brigge,* since *Mantle Brigg* 1943 *Map* is no doubt
a reduced form of the same name, *v.* þorp.

SOULTHORPE (lost), *Soulthorpe Lane Close* 1919 *Sale,* 1943 *Map.*
Possibly recording another lost farmstead, but earlier forms are
needed. The first el. could be the ON by-name *Súla, v.* þorp, cf.

Soulby We 2 22. The field and lane are at the western boundary of the parish.

Ketton Inns and Taverns

AVELAND ARMS (lost), closed 1930 - VR. Lord *Aveland* of Normanton Park near Stamford L owned 13,000 acres in Rutland c1875. BARLEY MOW (lost), closed 1918 - VR. BLUE BELL (lost), closed 1962 - VR. THE CROWN (lost), closed 1935 - VR. EXETER ARMS (lost), named from the Marquess of *Exeter*, closed 1945 - VR. GEESTON TAP (lost), closed 1970 - VR, *v.* Geeston *supra.* MIDLAND HOTEL (lost), closed 1941 - VR. NORTHWICK ARMS, named from the family of Lord *Northwick*, local landowners. The last member of the family died in 1887. PIED BULL (lost), 1846, 1863 White, closed 1935 - VR. RAILWAY INN. WHITE HART (lost), 1846, 1863 White, closed 1910 - VR.

ALDGATE, -FM, *Aldgate* 1846 White, 1932 Kelly, *Aldgate Farm* 1846, 1863 White, 1919 *Sale, Aldgate Lodge* 1846 White, 'the old road', *v.* **ald, gata.** The road probably led to the lost *Fregsthorpe, v. supra.* BLACKGROUND, 1943 *Map, Black Ground Close* 1919 *Sale*; in eModE, dial. *black* 'fertile' is contrasted with *white* 'infertile', cf. White Ground Cl in f.ns. (a) *infra, v.* **blæc, grund.** BULL LANE, 1932 Kelly, named from the Pied Bull P.H. *supra.* CATS HILL SPINNEY, cf. *Cattes Hill Furlong* 1638 *DC*, referring to wild cats, *v.* **cat(t), hyll.** THE COTTAGE. CUCKOO LODGE, cf. *Cuckoo Farm* 1932 Kelly. THE FIRS, 1932 ib. GEESTON HO., cf. *Geeson Lodge* 1846, 1863 White, *Geeston Farm* 1919 *Sale, v.* Geeston *supra.* THE GRANGE, *Grange Farm* 1919 *ib, v.* **grange.** THE GREEN, *The Greene* 1638 *DC, v.* **grēne**[2]. THE HOLMES, 1932 Kelly, *le Holme* 1297 *Wyg, v.* **holmr.** HOME FM, 1932 Kelly. HUNT'S LODGE, *Hunts Farm* 1919 *Sale*, perhaps alluding to the family of Anthony *Hunt* 1665 *HT.* KETTON CHURCH, *Church (St Mary)* 1846, 1863 White. KETTON COTTAGE, 1846, 1863 ib. KETTON GRANGE, 1846 ib, *v.* **grange.** KETTON HALL (lost), *Hall* 1846, 1863 ib; demolished 1873, rebuilt, and finally demolished 1926. KETTON HO., 1846,

1863 ib. KETTON PARK. KETTON QUARRIES, 1825 Map, 1846 White, *Ketton Stone Pits* c1800, 1806 Map, *Ketton Stones* 1824 O, *Ketton Stone Quarry* 1919 *Sale*. The quarries 'have long been noted for freestone of superior quality, obtained from the oolite formation' 1932 Kelly. THE LIMES, 1932 ib. LONG BARN FM (local). MANOR FM, 1932 ib. THE MOUNT, 1932 ib. NORTHWICK COTTAGES, cf. Northwick Arms P.H. *supra*. THE NURSERY, *The Nurseries* 1919 *Sale*, v. nursery. OLD HEATH LODGE, cf. *The Heath* 1677 *Terrier*, *Ketton Heath* 1824 O, 1826 G, *Old Heath* 1919 *Sale*, *Old Heath Farm* 1919 *ib*, v. hǽð. OLD WINDMILL, *ye Windmill* c1680 *Terrier*, cf. *Windmill Close* 1774 *Anc*, 1786 Map, 1919 *Sale*, *Windmill Hunt Close* 1919 *ib*, v. wind-mylne and cf. Hunt's Cl *infra*. THE ORCHARDS, 1932 Kelly. THE PRIORY, 1932 ib. ROCK VILLA. RUTLAND HO., 1932 ib. STOCKS HILL (lost), the site of the stocks which were removed in 1890 - VR, v. stocc. THE VALE, 1932 Kelly. THE VICARAGE, *ye Vicaridge* 1677 *Terrier*, cf. *the Parsonage* 1638 *DC*, v. vikerage, personage. WARREN COTTAGES, named from Witchley Warren in neighbouring Edith Weston.

Field-Names

Undated forms in (a) are 1943 *Map*. Those dated 1810 and 1838 are *Anc*; 1919 are *Sale*, while 1979 are VR. Early forms dated 1638 are *DC*; 1677 and c1680 are *Terrier*; 1678 and 1702 are *Deed*; 1705, 1773, 1774 and 1782 are *Anc*; 1717 are *Asw*; 1768 are Map; 1769 are *EnclA*.

(a) Six Acre, Seven Acres, The Eleven Acre (v. Pond Cl *infra*), The Fourteen -, The Nineteen Acre, Twenty Acres (x2), Twenty-six -, Twenty-seven -, Bottom Thirty -, The Forty Acres (v. æcer); First -, Second Allotment Fd (v. allotment); Anchor Fd (*Ancles Close* 1768, perh. alluding to a hermitage, v. ancre); Backside Cl 1919 (1768, v. ba(c)ksyde); Bartles Hollow 1919, Bartle's - 1943 (v. holh); Bennington Cl 1838 (v. Pennington's Pit Cl *infra*); Best Cl; Blackamire Cl 1919 (*Blackamore Close* 1768; adjoining Jackanapes Nook *infra*, hence the intrusive *a* by analogy, v. blæc, mōr[1]); Black Ash Cl 1919, Black Ash 1943 (poss. the site of a burned building); Bottle Hill 1979 (v. bōtl); Breach Cl, Top Breach 1943 (*The Breach* 1638, v. brēc); Broadham Cl 1919 (1768, v. brād, hamm); Broadholmes 1943 (*Holmes* 1768, v. holmr); Bottom Cl; Bushy Cl 1810, 1838; Cabbage Cl (1768); Carrion Pit Lane 1979; Carwell Cl 1919, Carrol - 1943

(*Carwell Close, Carwell Spring* 1768, *v.* **kjarr, wella**); Cart *Leys 1919, 1943 (*le Carte Leye* 1297 *Wyg, v.* **cræt, lēah,** cf. *Cartley* in Egleton f.ns. (b) and Oakham f.ns. (b)); Clay Ground (*v.* **grund**); Cocked Hat (a fanciful name for a triangular close); Creampot Cl 1919, Cream Pott 1943 (a complimentary name, usually indicating rich pasture); Crook Cl 1919 (*Crooks Close* 1768, *Crooke Rods* 1717, *v.* **crōk, rōd³**); Doe Pit(t)s Cl 1810, 1838, Doe Pit - 1943 (perh. alluding to the female rabbit, the *doe, v.* **pytt**); Drift Cl 1919, 1943 (1768, *v.* **drift**); Dry Nook Cl 1919 (*v.* **drȳge, nōk**); Great Dunstan Cl 1810, Great Dunston - 1943, Dunstan's Cl 1810, Dunstone - 1838 (*Dunstall Furlong* 1638; prob. OE **tūn-stall** 'the site of a farm, a farmstead', cf. Dunstall Plantations in Whissendine, *Dunston* in neighbouring Empingham f.ns. (b) and *Dunston Hedge* in Lyddington f.ns. (b) where forms vary principally between *Dunston* and *Dunstall*); Eight Leys 1919 (1768, *v.* **lēah**); Elder Stump Cl 1919 (*v.* **ellern, stump**); The Fishponds 1979; Five Acres Hill 1919; Fleet Cl 1919, 1943 (1768 (x2), *v.* **flēot**); Folly Gardens, Little Folly (prob. alluding to an eccentric or extravagant building, *v.* **folie**); Gate Shakleway Cl 1919 (*v.* **gate-shadel** 'a cross-roads'; the modern form has been influenced by Shacklewell (Spinney) on the boundary of neighbouring Empingham parish); Glebe Cl 1919, 1943 (1768, *v.* **glebe**); Grannum Cl 1919, Grannam's - 1943 (poss. from the surn. *Greneham,* cf. Thomas *Greneham* 1522 MilS, *Greneham's Manor* 1846, 1877 White, but Mr J. Field notes that the reference may be to dower land for the support of the widow of the late owner, *v.* **grandmother**); Great Cl 1979; Haggards Hill Cl 1919 (*Hogards Close* 1768, from the surn. *Hoggard*); Hall Cl 1919 (1768, *v.* **hall**); Harrison's Cl; Far -, Under Hay Cl 1810, 1838, 1943, Homeward Hay Cl 1810, 1838 (*The Hay Close* 1612 *Conant, v.* **hēg**); Great -, Little Hewitts; Home Cl 1838, 1943 (1768), Home Fd 1943 (*v.* **home**); Homedale Cl (most prob. a late corrupt form of *Horne Dale - infra*); Homeward Cl; Horse Cl; House Cl; Hunt's Cl 1943, Hunts Fm 1919, Hunts Lane 1979, Hunt's Mdw 1943 (*v.* Hunt's Lodge *supra*); Jack(a)napes Nook 1919, 1943 (*Jackeynapes Nook* 1768; perh. with *jackanapes* 'a mischievous boy', but *Jackanapes on Horseback* was a 17th cent. name for a proliferous variety of cowslip and this may be present here, *v.* **nōk**); Kelthorpe Cl 1979, Kettlethorpe Mdw 1919 (*Kelthorpe Meadow* 1768, *v.* Kilthorpe Grange *supra*); Land Cl 1810, 1838, 1943 (a consolidation of selions of a former open-field, *v.* **land**); Law's Cl (cf. *lawes close* in neighbouring N. Luffenham f.ns. (b)); Limepits; The Line Fd (adjoining a railway); Little Mdw 1979 (1768); Long Cl; Long Mdw 1979; Luffenham Fd, - Mdw (S. Luffenham parish adjoins to the south-west); March Mdw 1919 (1768, *The Marsh* 1705, *Marsh Spinney* 1774, *v.* **mersc**); The Meadow 1838, 1943; Middle Cl; Mid Leys 1919 (*Midd Leys* 1768, *v.* **midd, lēah**); Mill Bridge Cl 1919, 1943 (1768), - Hill 1919, - Leys 1919 (1768), Mill Brigg 1979, Mill Dam 1979 (*ye Mill* 1677, *the Myll Damme* 1638, *the Myll Holmes* 1638, *v.*

myln, damme, holmr); Mill Fd (the site of Old Windmill *supra*); Money Pit Cl 1919, 1943 (1768; prob. referring to an early discovery of a coin hoard (cf. the finds of· Roman coins in Ketton in BrownArchSites 16), *v.* **monie**); Newbottle Cl 1919 (*New(e) Bottle Feild* 1638, 1677, (*le*) *Newbottle Feild* 1702, 1717, *Newbottle Furlong* 1638, *v. Newbottle supra*); New Plantation 1919; Oak Style Cl 1810, - Stile - 1838, Oakstile Cl or the Home Fd 1943 (*v.* **āc, stigel**); Oddfellows Fd (belonging to the mutual-help society founded in the 18th cent.); Onion Bed (*v.* **bedd**); Osborne Fd; Pennington's Pit Cl 1919, Pennington - 1943 (Bennington Cl *supra* no doubt records an earlier form of the surn.); Petty Green Cl 1919 (with ME **pety** 'small' to distinguish Petty Green from The Green *supra*, *v.* **grēne**[2]); Pile Bridge 1979 (*v.* **pīl**); The Plain 1943, Plain Cl 1919, Redmiles Plain 1919 (*v.* **plain**, cf. Redmiles Fm *infra*); The Planting (the site of a plantation, cf. Plantation Fd or Planting Cl in Teigh f.ns. (a)); Pond Cl or the Eleven Acres; Quarry Fm 1919; Railway 1919 (cf. The Line Fd *supra*); Red Ground 1943, - Cl 1919 (*v.* **grund**); Redmile Lane 1979, Redmiles Fm 1919 (the farm was the property of Mr R. *Redmile* in 1919); Row Mdw 1919 (1768, *v.* **rūh**); Sandfurrows Cl 1919 (*v.* **sand, furh**); Seven Acres Cl 1919; The Sheep Pen; Shelverdale Cl 1810, 1838 (1774, *v.* **dalr**; perh. the Silverdale of neighbouring Tixover f.ns. (a) but retaining the *e* spelling of ME *seluer* 'silver'); Shorthorn Cl 1919 (1768, alluding to shorthorn cattle; the earliest NED citation for the shorthorn is 1826); Sink Lane, - Bridge 1979 (*v.* **sinke**); Slipe 1919 (*v.* **slipe**); Somerton Cl 1810 (prob. from the surn. *Somerton*); Arable -, Grass Soward (*Soward Field and Meadow* 1769, 1773, 1782, *Soward Field Close, Soward Meadow Close* 1774, *v.* **sūðeweard**); Spinney Cl 1810; Sports Fd; Spring Cl (*v.* **spring**); Starthill Pits 1979 (*v.* **steort**); Big -, First -, Second Steadfold 1943, Steadfold Road Cl 1919, 1943 (1768) (*Stedfold* c1680, 1717, *Far -, Homeward -, Middle Steadfold Close* 1768, *Stedfold Feild* 1677, 1702, 1705, *Stetfold Feild* 1705, *Steadfold Hill* 1768, *v.* **stōd-fald** 'horse enclosure', often used generally of ancient enclosures); Stone Pit Hill, Old Stone Pits 1919 (referring to early quarrying); Ten Acres Allotment 1919 (*v.* **allotment**); Timbergate Cl 1919 (*Tymber Gate Furlong* 1638, 'road along which timber is transported', *v.* **timber, gata**); Town (*Town End Close, Town Land* 1768, *v.* **tūn**); Turnpike Cl 1919 (a roadside close, the name anachronistic by 1919, *v.* **turnepike**); Washpikes Cl 1919, Washspokes 1943 (prob. 'land by a pond in which cartwheels are washed', cf. *Washpole infra*); Weston Way Cl 1919 (Edith Weston parish adjoins to the west); Wheatlands Cl; White Bread Cl 1846 White, 1932 Kelly, 1943 (a charitable endowment, prob. originally to provide bread, but later used for more general charitable purposes); White Ground Cl 1919 (in eModE, *white* 'infertile' is contrasted with *black* 'fertile', cf. Blackground *supra*, *v.* **grund**); Williams Cl 1919 (*William's Close* 1768); Witchley Fd 1943, Wychley Way Cl 1919 (named from Witchley (Warren) in neighbouring

Edith Weston).

(b) *Barradon Hayfeild* 1677, *Barrowden Hay Field* 1769, 1773, 1782, (*le*) *Hay Feild* 1702, 1717 (Barrowden parish adjoins to the south-west, v. **(ge)hæg**); *Carlespitt, - Furlong* 1638 (the first el. could be either the surn. *Carl* or *Scand karl* 'a free peasant' from which it is derived, or the Scand pers.n. *Karl* also from *karl*, v. **pytt**); *The Common* 1638, *The Intercommon lying part in the parish of Ketton and part in the parish of Empingham* 1769 (v. **commun, intercommon**); *Dove Coat* 1774, *Dovecote Close* 1768 (v. **dove-cot(e)**); *Dunhills Close* 1768 (from the surn. *Dunhill*); *The Eight Acres* 1638; *The Feeding Ground* 1774 (grazing ground, pasturage, v. **feeding**); *atte Fenne* 1336 Fine (p) (v. **fenn**); *Foxes Close* 1768 (from the surn. *Fox*); *Gundale Furlong* 1638 (perh. 'Gunni's valley', v. **dalr**, cf. Gunnel Lane in neighbouring Empingham); *on the Hill* 1332 Extent (p) (v. **hyll**); *Horne Dale Furlong* 1638 (v. **horn, dalr**); *a messuage called Hutchens or Hutchins* 1678 (from the surn. *Hutchins*); *Ivey House Close* 1768 (v. **ifig**); *Ketendale* 1347 CN (v. **dalr**); *Ketton Feild* 1702; *Kilthorpe Little Field and Meadow* 1769, 1773, *Kilthorpe Old Inclosure* 1774, *Kilthorpe Upper Field* 1774, *Wottons Kilthorpe Farm* 1773 (v. Kilthorpe Grange *supra*; John *Wotton* was resident in Ketton in 1705, Francis *Wotton* in 1769, v. **inclosure**); *in the Lane* 1332 Extent (p) (v. **lane**); *Long Close* 1769, 1773, 1774; *Long Lawn Close* 1774 (v. **launde**); *ye Low Pasture* c1680; *Mayden Balke* c1680 (prob. from the surn. *Maiden, Maydon*, v. **balca**); *May Thorn Bush* 1638, *Meythorne Bush* 1677, c1680 (the hawthorn blooms in May, hence its alternative name the *maythorn*; this was prob. an area of scrubland, v. **busc**); *Medudyk* 113 CN (v. **mæd, dīk**); *Middle Furlong* 1638; *Mikeleng* 113 CN (a Scand compound, v. **mikill, eng**); *Nether Meadow* 1768; *Okeham Way* 1638 ('the road to Oakham', v. **weg**); *ye Pasture* c1680; *Pinfold Green* 1768 (v. **pynd-fald, grēne**[2]); *in le Pyt* 1328 Banco (p), *in the Pitt(e)* 1332 Extent (p) (poss. the name of a 14th cent. quarryman, v. **pytt**); *Richmond Close* 1774 (with the surn. *Richmond*, cf. Robert *Richmond* 1678 *Anc* of Stretton); *Round Close* 1774 (alluding to shape); *Rowls Close* 1768 (with the surn. *Rowles*); *le Southfeld* 1550 Pat (one of the great open-fields of the village, v. **sūð, feld**); *ye Stone Trough* 1677, *Stonetrough* c1680 (used either of a close containing a stone drinking trough or topographically of a stone hollow resembling a trough in form, v. **stān, trog**); *Sprat Pittes* 1638 (from eModE **sprat** 'a kind of rush or rush-like grass', v. **pytt**); *Swyne Pitt Hill* 1638 (the hill named from 'the pit where swine forage', v. **swīn, pytt**); *Tinwell Plank* 1705, *- Plank Close* 1768 (a close containing a plank bridge crossing into Tinwell parish which adjoins to the north-east, v. **planke**); *ye Vicar Pits* 1677 (v. **vikere, pytt**); *Washpole* c1680 (poss. refers to a pool used for washing the wheels of carts, cf. Washpikes Cl *supra*, v. **wæsce, pōl**[1]); *Watry Close* 1769, *Watery Close* 1773 (land by or containing standing water or a stream, *v.* **wæterig**); *atte Welle* 1332 *Extent* (p) (*v.* **wella**); *le Westfeld* 1332 *Wyg* (one of the open-fields of the village, *v.* **west, feld**); *Wi(t)chl(e)y Hedge* 1638, 1677, c1680 (referring to Witchley (Warren) in neighbouring Edith Watson, *v.* **hecg**); *Wortwell Close* 1768, - *Feld* 1769, 1773, 1774, *Wortwell Old Inclosure* 1774 (*v.* **wyrt, wella, inclosure**).

Pickworth

PICKWORTH

    Pichewurða 1170 (p), 1171 P (p), *-wurth'* 1228 Cur, *Pycheworth* 1288 Abbr

    Py-, Pikewurða 1175 P (p), *-wurtha* 1176 (p), 1177 ib (p), *-wurda* 1174 (p), 1178 ib (p) *et freq* to 1187 ib (p), *-worth(e)*) 1219, 1221, 1226 RHug, 1268 RGrav, 1316 FA

    Py-, Pikkeworth' 1263 *Ass*, 1284 OSut, 1300 Ipm, *Pickeworth* 1263, 1294 *Ass*, 1301 Cl, *-wurth'* 1226 RHug, 1292 OSut

    Picworth(e) 1293 AD, 1296 *SR et passim* to 1376 Ipm, *Py-, Pikworth(e)* 1336 *Ass*, 1340 IpmR *et passim* to 1503 Cl

    Py-, Pickworth 1286 Ass, 1495 Ipm, 1695 *Map*

'Pīca's enclosure', *v.* **worð**, cf. Pickworth L.

NEWELL WOOD, *Newhall* 1541 LP, *Newall Wood* 1610 Speed, *Newhall Wood* c1800, 1806 Map, *Newell Wood* 1824 O, 1846 White, 1876 *Burghley*, cf. *Newell Hills* 1876 *ib*. The wood was named from 'the new hall', *v.* **nīwe, hall**.

MOCKBEGGAR, *Pickworth....of which nothing remains at this day but a steeple now known by the name of Mockbegger* 1684 Wright. It is also recorded as *Ruins Mockbeggar* 1780 Map, *Ruins of Mockbeggar* 1801 ib, *Mockbeggar* 1806 ib, 1863 White, *Mock Beggar* 1824 O. At Pickworth in the 17th and 18th centuries, the most obvious ruins of the early village were of the tower and steeple of the medieval church: today, only the entrance into its south porch remains. Mockbeggar is a common name which dates from early in the 17th century when country gentry frequently moved to London to live, leaving their country seats neglected and empty, so that

beggars went hungry from their doors.   One of the Roxburghe
ballads records the beggars' plight:

> Let any poore to such a doore
> Come, they expecting plenty,
>> They there may ask till their throats are sore
>> For mockbegger hall stands empty.

v. mockbeggar, NED *s.v.* mock v., 5.

BIG PITS WOOD. BLUE BELL P.H. (lost), 1846, 1863 White,
Blue Bell Inn 1935 VCH. CHRISTIAN'S LODGE, *Christians Lodge*
c1800, 1806 Map, 1846 White, 1943 *Map*, named from the family
of William *Christian* 1665 *HT*. THE DRIFT, *Drift* 1844 *TA*, a
cattle-road which may have run on eventually to Stamford market,
v. **drift**. FAIRCHILD'S FM is *Fairchilds Lodge* c1800, 1806 Map,
Fairchild's Lodge 1846, 1863 White, named from the family of John
Fairchild 1665 *HT*. HUNT'S BARN, cf. *Hunt's Close* 1876 *Burghley*,
from the surn. *Hunt*. LINCOLNSHIRE GATE is marked on both
the 2½" and 6" maps at the point where the road from Pickworth
enters Lincs.   It presumably recalls a former toll-gate in the
turnpike system rather than being from Scand *gata* 'a road'.
MANOR FM. MANOR HO. PICKWORTH GREAT WOOD,
Pikeworth Wood 1541 LP, *Pickworth Wood* 1710 *Burghley*, 1846
White, *Pickworth Gt. Wood* c1800, 1806 Map, *Great Wood* 1876
Burghley, *v.* **wudu**. PICKWORTH PLAIN, *The Plane* 1710 *ib*, *The*
Plain 1876 *ib*, 1943 *Map*, 1950 *Burghley*, *v.* **plain**. BIG -, LITTLE
SUTIE, *Great -, Little Sutie Wood* 1687 *Map*. TOP PICKWORTH,
1935 VCH. This was an outlying area of settlement at SK 985 135.
Three houses existed here until the 1880s, *v.* MER 32.
TURNPOLE WOOD, 1710 *Burghley*, c1800, 1806· Map, 1876
Burghley. It is *Tornekowe* 1541 LP, *Turnecouse Wood* 1610 Speed,
which is perhaps from OE *þorn* or *þyrne* 'a thorn-tree' with Scand
skógr 'a wood' (with metathesis *-scow* > *-cow*(*s*)), but earlier forms
are needed.   The wood is beside the county boundary, cf.
Harethornes in f.ns. (b) *infra*. WESLEYAN CHAPEL, 1863 White.

Field-Names

The undated forms in (a) are 1943 *Map*; those dated 1710, 1876 and 1950 are *Burghley*. Forms occurring in both 1876 and 1943 are marked with an asterisk. Early forms dated 1313, 1633, 1657 and c1675 are *Deed*.

(a) The Nine Acres* 1950; The Ten Acre 1943, - Acres 1876, 1950; The Twelve Acres* 1950; The Fourteen Acres 1876, Fourteen Acre 1943; The Seventeen Acres 1876; Far -, Middle -, Twenty Acres*, First - 1876; Back Cl 1811 Blore; Bacon Fd* 1950 (*Bacons Field* 1710, cf. Bernard *Bacon* 1678 *Anc* of nearby Stretton); Bakers Cl 1950; Barn Cl 1876, 1950; Baynes Cl 1876, Bayne's - 1943, 1950 (named from the family of Ian- and Susan *Baines* 1710); Bottom -, Far -, First Beaver Ground* 1950 (no doubt with the surn. *Beaver*, cf. Thomas *Beaver* 1712 *Anc* of neighbouring Empingham and *Beavers House Land* 1698 *Terrier* in the same parish, *v.* **grund**); Berridge's Fd* 1950, Far - 1943, Far Berridge's Cl 1950; Burnt Ground 1950 (1710, *v.* **brende²**, **grund**); Bushey Cl 1876 (1710), Bushy - 1943, 1950; Calf Cl* 1950 (cf. *Calf Close Nook* 1710, *v.* **nōk**); Calves Cl*; Close's Cl 1876, - Fd 1950 (from the surn. *Close*); Conington's Cl 1876, Conningtons -, Cunningtons Cl 1950 (from the surn. *Connington*); Coppy Hills 1876, Copy - 1943, 1950 (*Coppy Hill* 1710, *v.* **copis**); Cow Cl* (1710); Dry Fd* 1950 (1710, *v.* **drÿge**); (The) Foundations 1811 Blore, 1876, Bottom -, Top Foundations 1950 (the site of the early manor house); Fox Cover Cl* (*v.* **cover(t)**); Garden Cl 1876, 1950; Grange Fm (*v.* **grange**); High Cl* 1950; Far -, Hill's Cl; Hollow Cl* 1950; Holywell Wood (named from Holywell L which lies just beyond the county boundary); Home Cl* 1950 (x5) (*Home Close* 1710, *v.* **home**); Horse Cl* 1950 (1710); House Cl* 1950; Hunt's Cl* 1950 (cf. Hunt's Barn *supra*); Jarvis' Cl 1876, Jarves' - 1943, Jarveses - 1950 (named from the family of John *Jarvis* 1710); L Nook (so called from its shape, *v.* **nōk**); Land Fd* 1950 (1710, an enclosure consolidating selions of an old open-field, *v.* **land**); The Lings* (*Lyngh'* Hy 4 *Rental*, *v.* **lyng**); Meadow Platt 1876 (*v.* **plat²**); Normans Fd* 1950; The Oaks c1800, 1806 Map, 1824 O; Occupation Road 1876 (with ModE **occupation** 'used by occupiers of land', naming a green lane used for access to a tenant's strips, cf. Occupation Road in Gt. Casterton f.ns. (a)); Over the Way 1876, 1950; Page Cl 1876; The Park 1876, 1950, Pickworth Park 1943; Peas Cl 1950; Pen Cl 1876 (1710, *v.* **penn²**); Pinfold Cl 1950 (*v.* **pynd-fald**); Pocket Cl* 1950 (1710, originally alluding to a round field with a narrow entrance, *v.* **poket**); Rabbit Cl*; South Cl* 1950; Spring Cl 1876; Spring Holt 1943, - Cl 1950 (*v.* **holt**); Stackyard Cl* 1950 (x4) (*v.* **stak-ȝard**); Steeple Fd* 1950, Top - 1943 (poss. referring to an endowment of land to maintain the church steeple, cf. Steeple Cl in Ashwell f.ns. (a) and *Steeple Acre* in Lyddington f.ns. (b), but also *v.* Mockbeggar *supra*); Stone Pit 1950, Stonepit Cl*; Stony Cl 1876 (1710), Stoney - 1943, 1950; Thompsons Fd 1943, - Cl 1876, 1950; Bottom -, Top Turnpole 1943, 1950 (*Turnpole Close* 1710, *v.* Turnpole Wood *supra*); Wades Cl* 1950 (with the surn. *Wade*, cf. William *Wade* 1652 *Surv* of Greetham and William *Wade* 1758 *ib* of Stretton, both neighbouring parishes); Water Cl 1876, 1950 (x2) (1710); West Gate* 1950; Wheatley's Fd 1950 (*Wheatly's home close, Home Close Pat. Wheatly's, Wheatly's Old ground* 1710, named from the family of *Patrick Wheatly* 1710); Wood Cl 1950 (1710); Far -, First Woolfox 1950 (*Woolfox Close No. and So.* 1710 (i.e. - North and South), named from Woolfox Wood in neighbouring Greetham.

(b) *Abbots Stocking* 1537 (1684) Wright, *Pickworth Stocking alias Abbot's Stocking* 1611 (1811) Blore, *Pickworth-Stockinge* 1614 (1684) Wright, *Pickworth Stocking* 1617 (1684) ib (Olveston Abbey Lei held land in Pickworth, *v.* **abbat, stoccing**); *Barkers Close* 1710; *Barley Close* 1633, *great -, little Barley Close* 1657 (*v.* **bærlic**); *Brakeswheyt* 1313 (*v.* *Swythawe Pitts infra*); *in campo orient'* 1313 ('the east field', one of the old open-fields of the village, *v.* **east, feld**); *Harethornes* 1253 Pat ('thorn-trees on the boundary', *v.* **hār², þorn**; Pickworth parish lies on the county boundary); *Pickworth Innfeild* 1657, *Infeild* c1675, *Pikeworth-Infield* 1684 Wright, cf. *Infield Spinney* c1795 *Deed* (*v.* **infeld**); *Lyndwode* 1313 (*v.* **lind, wudu**); *Meadow Close* 1710; *Great -, Little Newell Field* 1710 (cf. Newell Wood *supra*); *in campo aquilon'* 1313 ('the north field', one of the old open-fields of the village, *v.* **norð, feld**); *Outfeild* c1675, *Pikeworth-Outfield* 1684 Wright (*v.* **ūt(e), feld**, cf. *Pickworth Innfeild supra*); *ad portam aule* 1313 (p) (*v.* **hall, geat**); *Stokkyngpittes* 1313 (*v.* **stoccing, pytt**, cf. *Abbots Stocking supra*); *Wheate Close* 1633, *Wheat field close* 1633; *Withawe Pitts* 1537 (1684) Wright, *Swythawe Pitts* 1616 Blore (*v.* **haga¹, pytt**; the first el. may be ME *swite* of uncertain meaning, cf. Swite's Fm, Sr 273 and the second el. of *Brakeswheyt supra*).

Ryhall

RYHALL

    Righale 1042-55 (m12) KCD 927 (S 1481) bis

    Riehale 1086 DB

    Rihala c1121 (s.a. 963) ASC E

    Ry-, Rihal(e) 1107 Reg, 1179, 1195 P, 1204 Cur *et freq* to 1400

        Pat *et passim* to 1415 ELiW, *Ryale* 1230 Pat, 1276 RH *et*

        passim to 1361 Ipm

    Ryhall(e) 1426 Cl, 1535 VE, 1577 *FF*, *Ryall(e)* 1400, 1402 Fine *et passim* to 1539 *Rut*

'The piece of land in the bend of the river, where rye is grown', *v.* **ryge, halh.** R. Gwash makes a big bend here.

BELMESTHORPE

Beolmesðorp 1042-55 (m12) KCD 927 (S 1481) bis
Belmestorp(e) 1086 DB, 1233 AD, *-thorp(e)* c1200 RBE, 1237
Fees, 1303 FA *et passim* to 1610 Speed
Belstropp 1573 *FF*

'Beornhelm's outlying farmstead', *v.* **þorp.** The pers.n. is OE.

BELINSFORD BRIDGE (local), presumably with a much altered form of Belmesthorpe. Belinsford may just possibly represent 'Beornhelm's ford', but earlier forms are needed. BELMISTHORPE GRANGE, *Grange* 1846 White, *v.* **grange** and Belmesthorpe *supra*. CHURCH FM, cf. *atte Kirke* 1296 (p), 1327 *SR* (p), *v.* **kirkja.** CLAY HILL is *Claypit Hill* 1824 O, *Clay Hill* 1826 G, 1943 *Map, v.* **clæg, pytt.** THE DRIFT, *Drift Way* 1806 *Burghley,* a cattle-road running through Essendine, Ryhall, and so to Stamford market, *v.* **drift.** ESSENDINE HILL (local), Essendine parish adjoins to the north-east. GRANGE FM is *Ryhall Lodge* 1824 O. THE HALL, *Hall* 1846, 1863 White, cf. *Hall Yard* 1734 VCH, *Hall Furlong* 1799 *Terrier, Hall Balk Road* 1806 *Burghley, v.* **hall, balca.** HUNGATE FM, 1846, 1863 White, *Hundegate in Ryhale* 13 VCH (p), *Hang Gate* 1943 *Map,* literally 'road frequented by dogs', *v.* **hund, gata;** but such a name is more usual in a town (cf. Hungate in Lincoln, L 1 75, Hounds Gate in Nottingham, Nt 18) and this example may be from a surn., cf. *Mr Hungates Close* 1634 in Uppingham f.ns. (b). However, the 13th century form does imply that Ryhall had its own Hungate. THE LAURELS. MILL FM, *Ryall Mill* 1850 Slater, cf. *le Mylnedamme* 1433 *Deed, Mill banks* 1677 *Ct, Mill Head, - Tail* 1873 *Burghley, Mill Close* 1943 *Map, Mill Lane Road* 1806 *Burghley, Mill Lane* 1943 *Map, v.* **myln, damme, banke, hēafod, taile.** ROSE COTTAGE, 1863 White. RYHALL GRANGE, *Grange* 1846, 1863 ib, *v.* **grange.** RYHALL HEATH FM 18 *Monson,* 1824 O, 1826 G, *Ryhall Heath Lodge* 1824

O, v. hæð. SALTERS LANE (local), *Salters Road* 1799 *Terrier,*
Salters Lane Road 1806 *Burghley,* v. **saltere**.

Ryhall and Belmesthorpe Inns and Taverns

BLUE BELL. CROWN (lost) - VR. FIVE BELLS (lost), closed
1914 - VR. FOUNDRY ARMS (lost), closed 1920s - VR.
GREEN DRAGON, *...the old Manor House ... now partly the Green
Dragon public house* 1846 White. MILLSTONE, 1846, 1863 ib.
TALLY HO (lost), 1846, 1863 ib, closed 1960s - VR.
WHEATSHEAF (lost), closed 1914 - VR.

Field-Names

Undated forms in (a) are 1950 *Burghley,* those dated 1806, 1873 and 1876 are
also *Burghley,* those dated 1943 are *Map.* Forms occurring in both 1943 and
1950 are marked with an asterisk. Early forms dated 1634 and 1799 are *Terrier,*
1677 are *Ct,* 1798 are *Deed.*

(a) The Six Acres 1876, 1950, Six Acres 1943; Eight Acre 1943; The Nine
Acres* 1876; The Ten Acre 1876, (The) Ten Acres*; The Twelve Acres 1876,
1943; Thirteen Acres 1943, The - 1876, 1950; Fourteen Acres 1943, The - 1876,
1950; The Fifteen Acres* 1876; The Sixteen Acres 1876, Top -, Sixteen Acres
1943; Second -, Seventeen Acres; Top -, Eighteen Acre 1943; Nineteen Acre
1943; The Twenty Acres 1876, 1950, - Acre 1943; 27 Acre 1943; The Thirty
Acres 1876, 1950, - Acre 1943; 33 Acres 1943; 40 Acres 1943; The 73 Acres*
1876 (Mr J. Field notes that the area was 72a. 1r. 19p.); Allotment 1873 (*v.*
allotment); Ash Tree Cl* 1876 (cf. *Ash Tree Furlong* 1799); Backside Road 1806
(*v.* **ba(c)ksyde**); Belmesthorpe Lodge 1824 O; Belmisthorpe Fd 1876; Belmisthorpe
3 Acres 1876; Bretland Allotment(s)*, Far Bretland* (*Bretland feild* 1634, *v.* **land,**
cf. Bretland in Whissendine f.ns. (a)); Bridge or Far Home Cl 1943; Far
Broadeng Mdw 1806, Far -, Middle Broaden, Broading 1943 (*Far brodenfeild,
hither Broden* 1634, *v.* **bråd, eng**); Castle Rise 1979 VR; The Chapel Yard 1811
Blore (in Belmesthorpe); Church Headlands 1943 (*Church headland furlong,
Church headland Road* 1798, *v.* **hēafod-land**); Close 1873; Cock Lane 1943;
Bottom -, Top Colonels 1943 (a *Colonel* Pierrepont was in residence in the
manor house in 1813 VCH); Cottage Twenty Acres 1943; Cow Fd 1943; Old Cow
Pasture 1876, The Cow Pasture 1876, Old -, Cow Pasture*; Darnell Fd, - Mdw

1806 (from *darnel* (*Lolium temulentum*), a deleterious grass which grows as weed among corn); Day's Mdw 1943; Elm Cl 1811 Blore; Freewood Cl 1871 *Deed*, Froward 1943 (*v.* The Freewards in neighbouring Essendine); Gandy's Cl 1943 (with the surn. *Gandy*); Garden; Halegreen 1979 VR; Hangman's Cl 1943, Hangman's Corner 1979 VR (prob. the site of a gibbet on the county boundary; Hangman's Cl 1844 *TA* in Essendine refers to the same site, cf. *Gallowtree Hill infra*); East -, West Hill Fd 1943; Hills and Dales (a descriptive name of the same type as Hills and Holes in Essendine f.ns. (a)); Hoe Bridge Mdw 1806 (*How Bridge* 1799, *v.* **haugr**); Home Cl* 1873, 1876 (*v.* **home**); Home Fifteen Acres 1943; Horse Cl 1943; Ivett's Ten Acre 1943 (with the family name of Walter *Ivett* 1932 Kelly); Jacobs Well 1935 VCH (*v.* **wella**); Lincoln Cl* 1876 (cf. *Lincoln Hill* 1799, poss. referring to property of Lincoln Cathedral, but the surn. *Lincoln* also occurs in the county, cf. Richard *Lincoln* 1525 SR of Uppingham); The Long Fd; The Meadow and Two acres 1876, The Meadow*; Middle Ground (*v.* **grund**); Millstone Fd 1979 VR (cf. The Millstone P.H. *supra*); Ness Mdw 1806, 1871 *Deed* (*v.* **nes**); Net Land 1943 (poss. with OE *nēat* 'cattle'); New Broken Pasture 1943; No Mans Ground* (on the boundary of the parish and county, *v.* **nān-mann**); Paddock 1873, The -* 1876; Pear Tree Furlong* 1876; Pinfold Cl 1806 (*v.* **pynd-fald**); Poplar Tree Cl 1943; Post Office Fd 1943; Rabbit Burrows 1943; Red Gate 1943 (*Radgates* 1587 Blore, a messuage so called); Rice Hollow 1979 VR (*v.* **hrīs, holh**); Riddle Fd 1806, 1871 *Deed* (1799, *Riddle Dale Field* 1798), High Riddle 1943 (1799) (perh. 'hill cleared of trees', *v.* **(ge)ryd(d), hyll**, the name of one of the great open-fields of the village); Roberts Cl 1876, 1950, Robert's - 1943; The Shelf Hill (*v.* **scelf**); Shortlands or 33 Acres 1943; The Shred 1943 (*v.* **scrēad**); Six Cow Pastures; Sour Hill 1943 (*v.* **sūr**); South Fd 1806, Bottom -, Middle South Fd 1876, 1950 (*Southfeild* 1634, *South Field* 1798, one of the open-fields of the village, *v.* **sūð, feld**); South Mdw 1806, 1943 (1677, *South Meadow Furlong* 1799); Sow Hills 1876, - Hill 1950 (perh. identical with Sour Hill *supra*); Stablesford Bridge 1935 VCH, Stapleford Bridge 1950 (VCH 2 269 offers the popular etymology of 'St Eabba's Well ford' for Stablesford, St Æbba supposedly being cousin and companion of St Tibba (*v.* Tibba's Well *infra*) and like Tibba, having a well or spring associated with her; however, this name is most prob. the common 'ford marked by a post', *v.* **stapol, ford**); Stackyard Fifteen Acres 1943 (*v.* **stak-ʒard**); Star Fd 1806, Star Leys* (*Starr Field* 1677, *Stare Field* 1798, *Star Field* 1799, cf. *Star Leighs* 1799, *v.* **storr, lēah**, one of the open-fields of the village, cf. *Starr Close* in Burley f.ns. (b)); Station Fd 1943 (beside Ryhall and Belmesthorpe Railway Station); Stone pit Cl 1876, Stonepit -*; Stump Stone c1800, 1806 Map, 1806 *Map*, 1824 O (*Stumpedestone* 1269 For, *le Stubbedèston*' 1299 ib, 'the truncated, broken-off stone' (a cross shaft?); the earliest citation in NED for *stubbed* is 1575, which this example predates by 275 years, *v.* **stubbede, stump, -ede, stān,** cf. *atte Ston* 1292 CN (p), known later as *Rullers -, Rullors Stone* 1610 Speed, *Rollors Stone* 1620 Map, *v.* **roller** 'a cylinder of stone', and *Robin Hoods Stone* 1780, 1801 Map); Taggle's Cl 1811 Blore (from the surn. *Taggle*, cf. Robert *Tagell* 1522 MilS, husbandman of Ryhall); Tank Cl 1943 (*v.* Rommell's Cl in Whissendine f.ns. (a), cf. Tank Cl in neighbouring Lt. Casterton f.ns. (a)); Tibba's Well 1935 VCH (cf. *Tibael Hill* 1677, *Tipple Hill Furlong* 1799, 'Tibba's spring or well', *v.* **wella**; St Tibba (*sanctissimam et piissimam uirginem Tibbam de Riale* m12 Cand, *sancta Tibba* m12 ib), a 7th cent. Anglo-Saxon religieuse, is reputed to have lived the greater part of her life in Ryhall); Tollbar Cl 1943 (*v.* **toll-bar**, an anachronism by 1943); Turnpike Rd 1806 (*v.* **turnepike**); Twelve Cls; Waterside 1979 VR; West Mdw 1806, West Mdw Leys* 1806 (*West Meadow Furlong* 1799); Willow Row 1943; Wind Gate Hill 1876, 1950, Windgate - 1943 (*Wingate Hill* 1799, ostensibly *wind-geat* 'wind-swept gap', but the topography would seem to argue against this, so that Scand *hvin-gata* 'gorse-lined road' may be preferable); Wood Penn, - Cl 1943 (*v.* **penn²**).

Road names in 1806 are: Greatford Rd, Little Bytham and Grimsthorpe Rd, Little Casterton Rd, Pickworth Rd, Stamford and Little Casterton Rd, Uffington Rd, Uffington and Greatford Rd (Greatford, Grimsthorpe, Stamford and Uffington are neighbouring villages in Lincs. For Lt. Casterton and Pickworth, *v. supra*).

(b) *Breadth Land furlong* 1799 (poss. identical with Bretland *supra*); *Brokemell -, Brokenell Wood* 1610 Speed; *Dale Acres* 1799 (*v.* **dāl**); *Five Land Acre* 1799 (*v.* **land**); *Gallowtree hill* 1634, *Gallotree Hill* 1799 (*v.* **galg-trēow**; the site of a gallows, cf. Hangman's Cl *supra*); *Guildings* 1799 (*v.* **gylde, eng**); *Hilley Green* 1799 (*v.* **grēne²**); *Howinge Meadow* 1677 ·('meadow containing a mound or tumulus', *v.* **haugr, eng,** evidently another burial mound sited near the Ru territorial boundary, cf. Hoe Bridge Mdw *supra*); *Litwood Hill* 1677 (*v.* **hlið¹, wudu**); *Long three Rood* 1799 (*v.* **rōd³**); *atte Margetes* 1445 Fine (p), *Margetts lands* 1587 VCH (by 1587, *Margetts* was a capital messuage; apparently this is the surn. *Margetts,* derived from the pers.n. *Margaret,* but ME *atte* 'at the' was normally used to form surnames of local toponymic origin and if this were the case here, *Margetes* must remain unexplained); *New Close Nook* 1799 (*v.* **nōk**); *Overdike Close* 1799 (*v.* **dīk**); *Ryhall Brook* 1798; *Short Leas furlong* 1799 (*v.* **lēah**); *Stamford Way* 1634 ('the road to Stamford L'); *Surmedue* 14 DuDCCh (*v.* **sūr, mǣd**); *Tenpenny Acre* 1798 (perh. alluding to rental for the land); *Tollthorp way* 1634 ('the road to Tolethorpe'; Tolethorpe lies in Lt. Casterton); *White Ingle Dale* 1799 (perh. from a Scand pers.n. such as *Ingjaldr* or *Ingulfr,* with dial. *white* 'dry, open pasture', *v.* **dair**, cf. Ingthorpe in nearby Tinwell, which perh. records the same individual); *White Lands* 1799 (in eModE, *white* 'infertile' is contrasted with *black* 'fertile', *v.* **land**); *Upper Wye sike* 1677, *Wysike Close, Wysike furlong* 1799 (the first el. is poss. OE *wigga* 'a beetle' used of the water-beetle, *v.* **sik**, cf. *le wyȝesike* in Seaton f.ns. (b)).

Tickencote

TICKENCOTE

Tichecote 1086 DB
Tichencote Hy 3 Dane, *-cota* l12 ib (p), *-chote* 1184 ib
Ty-, Tikencot(e), *-k-* 1199 *FF*, 1202 Ass (p), 1234 RHug *et freq* to 1550 Fine
Ty-, Tikincot(e), *-y-* 1202 Ass, 1234 RHug *et passim* to 1553 *Conant*
Thicencote 1185 Templar, *Thikencot* 1253 Ipm
Tekencote, -yn- 1288 *FF*, 1432 ELiW, *Tekyngcote* 1553 *FF*
Tykyngcote 1553 *Conant, Tyckyngcote* 1552 ib, *Tyckingecote* 1553 ib
Tickencote 1610 Speed

'The shelter or shed where young goats are kept', *v.* **ticcen**, **cot**.

FLOWER POT INN (lost), closed 119 cent. - VR. MILL DAM, cf. *the Mill Close* 1673 *Deed, Mill Field* 1943 *Map, v.* **myln**. TICKENCOTE HALL, *Hall* 1824 O, 1846, 1863 White. TICKENCOTE LAUND, c1800, 1806 Map, 'an open space in woodland, woodland pasture', *v.* **launde**. TICKENCOTE LODGE, *The Lodge* 1673 *Deed,* 1824 O, *Lodge* 1846, 1863 White. TICKENCOTE PARK. TICKENCOTE WARREN, *The Warren* 1673 *Deed,* 1846, 1863 White, *Tickencote Warren* 1824 O, *v.* **wareine**. WARREN PLANTATION. WILD'S FORD, 1824 O, named from the family of Robert *Wylde* 1296 *SR.* WILD'S LODGE, 1846, 1863 White, *Lodge* 1824 O, *v.* Wild's Ford *supra.* WING PLANTATIONS.

Field-Names

Undated forms in (a) are 1943 *Map*. Early forms dated 1632 are *Terrier* and 1673 are *Deed*.

(a) Six Acre, Nine -, Twelve -, Eighteen -, Twenty-two -, Thirty Acres (*v.* **æcer**); Becky's Grave (partly in Empingham parish, alluding to an old excavation, *v.* **græf**); Boundary Fd; Bowlands Gibbet c1800, 1806 *Map*, 1824 O (the site of a gallows on Ermine Street at SK 973 114; *Bowland* is poss. *bŏga-land* 'ground in a bow-shaped recess in a hillside' which suits local topography, *v.* **gibet**); Clothesline Cl (Mr J. Field observes that this was prob. a laundry drying ground); Cocked Hat (named from its tricorne shape, cf. Cocked Hat in Ketton f.ns. (a)); Corner Fd; Cottage Cl, - Fd; Cow Cl; Crabtree (*v.* **crabtre**); D Close (a semicircular field in the bend of R. Gwash); Dry Fd (*v.* **drȳge**); East Hill; Far -, First Elm Tree Cl; Faraway Cl; Footpath Cl; Ford Cl; Gorse Fd (*v.* **gorst**); Hollow Back; Horse Cl; Far -, Letter Box (so called from its rectangular shape); First Low Road; The Meadow (*the Meadow Close* 1673); First -, Second -, Top Millington (Bryan *Millington* was miller in Tickencote in 1851 WR, Edwin *Millington* from 1855 to 1859 ib); New Plantation; Far -, First No Name; Nova Scotia (a 'remoteness' name, the land being on the extreme south-west edge of the parish); Paddock; Pit Fd; Plank Cl (*v.* **planke**); Quarry Fd; Rectory Fds 1935 VCH; Far -, First Roundabout (with streams on two sides, *v.* **roundabout**); Sanfoin Cl (*v.* **sainfoin**); Shacklewell Hollow (Shacklewell flows into R. Gwash near Wild's Lodge, *v.* **holh** and Shacklewell in Empingham); Spinney Cl; Stackyard Fd (*v.* **stak-ȝard**); Steel's Cl; Straw Gall (*v.* **galla**); Twixendykes ('between the ditches', *v.* **betweox(n)**, **dīk**; this land adjoining the river is liable to flooding); Wood Cl; Young Covert Cl (*v.* **cover(t)**).

(b) The Ash Close 1673 (*v.* **æsc**); Barbers Close 1673 (from the surn. *Barber*, cf. John *Barber* 1524 SR of nearby Ryhall); The Great Barne Close 1673; *Beanon feild* 1632, *Beanham* 1673 (one of the open-fields of the village, *v.* **bēan, hamm**); Bitterlys Close 1673; *Bowwood* 1585 Will, *Bowwoode, Bouwood* 1605 Conant (the first el. appears to be *boga* 'a bow' in some sense, either topographically and referring to a curve in a hillside, or literally and indicating a wood where materials for bow-making could be got, *v.* **boga, wudu**, cf. Bowlands *supra*); The Bowling Alley Close 1673 (*v.* **bowling, aley**); *Boyal Wood* 1610 Speed, *Bowyowe Wood* 1632 VCH (from the surn. *Boyall*, cf. John *Boyeall* 1525 SR of Ketton); the Brose Close, Brose meadow 1673 ˙(*v.* **brouse**); The Bullocke Close 1673; The Calves Nooke 1673 (*v.* **calf, nōk**); *Cattlespring* 1632 (*v.* **cat(t)el, spring**); The Close Yard 1673 (*v.* **geard**); The Cottagers Close 1673 (*v.* **cotager**); Empingham highway

1632 (Empingham parish adjoins to the west); *Exton highway* 1632 (Exton lies four miles north-west); *Garners grounds* 1673 (from the surn. *Garner*, v. **grund**); (*The*) *Hanging Peice* 1632, 1673 ('piece of land on a steep slope', v. **hangende, pece**); *Hocroft* 1632 (v. **hōh, croft**); *horse Leies* 1632, *Horsleys Close* 1673 (v. **hors, lēah**); *the long Balk* 1632 (v. **balca**); *Longstreete furlong* 1632 (lying beside Roman Ermine Street, v. **strǣt**); *Midle feild* 1632 (one of the open-fields of the village, v. **middel, feld**); *Mowbreies headland* 1632 (from the surn. *Mowbray*, v. **hēafod-land**); *the Oake Close* 1673 (v. **āc**); *pease close* 1632, *the two Pease Closes* 1673 (v. **pise**); *The Pingle* 1673 (v. **pingel**); *the plash* 1632 (v. **plæsc**); *short buts* 1632 (v. **butte**); *Stevens headland* 1632 (cf. John *Stevens* 1627 LML of Tickencote, v. **hēafod-land**); *stone pits* 1632 (v. **stān-pytt**); *The Turnbull Sike* 1673 (v. **sīk**; *Turnbull* is doubtlessly a surn.); *the Three Turrett Closes* 1673; *wrongsdale* 1632 (v. **wrang, vrangr, dalr**).

Tinwell

TINWELL

Tedinwelle 1086 DB
Tineguella 1125-8 LNPetr bis
Tiningewelle m13 Swaff
Tineuuell(e) m12 Cand, m12 (m13) Swaff, *Tinewell(e)* 1220, 1221
    RHug *et passim* to 1237 Cl (p) *et freq* to 1347 ib
Ty-, Tinwell(e) 1221 RHug, 1283 OSut *et passim* to 1395 Cl *et*
    freq to 1553 Pat

Possibly 'the spring or stream of Tȳni's people', v. -**inga-**, **wella**. The DB form has AN *e* for *i* and its *d* for *n* appears to be erratic. The mid 13th century form *Tiningewelle* is recorded by Robert de Swaffham in a footnote to his transcript of the 12th century Chronicle of Hugh Candidus. This footnote incorporates a valuation of 3s. 4d for Tinwell which suggests that Robert had access to early records. Thus the spelling may perhaps be accepted as authentic and significant. An unrecorded OE pers.n. *Tȳni* would be a short form of pers.ns. in *Tūn-* such as *Tūnhere* or *Tūnfrið*.

INGTHORPE

Ingelthorpe 1189 (1332) Ch
Ingeðorp ? m12 BCS 22 (S 68), -*torp* 1203 Ass, -*thorpe* 1227 Ch,

m13 CN, 1286 *Ass et passim* to 1327 *SR, Hingethorp'* 1263
Ass
Ingthorp(e) 1370 Pat, 1432 ELiW *et passim* to 1610 Speed
Inglethorp(e) 1547, 1553 Pat

Possibly 'Ingi's outlying farmstead', *v.* þorp. If the early form
Ingelthorpe is significant (and cf. the late *Inglethorp(e)* spellings),
then the first el. could be the OScand pers.n. *Ingjaldr* or *Ingulfr*
(possibly also present in *White Ingle Dale* in nearby Ryhall f.ns. (b)).
More likely, however, is OScand *Ingi*, a short form of masculine
pers.ns. in *Ingi-* such as *Ingimarr, Ingimundr.*

BREDCROFT
 Bradecroft 1180-1200 BM, 1209 Pap, 1224 *FF et passim* to 1263
  Ass et freq to 1403 Pat, (- *iuxta Staunford*) 1332 Extent
 Bradcroft 1521 Ct, 1547 Pat
 Bredcroft 1491 Ipm, 1494 Pat, (- *iuxta Staunford*) 1491 Ipm
 Breede Croft c1545 Leland, *Bread Croft* 1844 *TA*

'The spacious enclosed field', *v.* brād, croft. The village lay at
the boundary with Stamford L.

GRACE DIEU (lost), *Grace Dieu Nunnery in Rutlandshire* 1786
CR. There is fragmentary evidence for a convent for nuns of the
Cistercian order in Tinwell (not to be confused with Grace Dieu
Priory in Belton Lei, a foundation for Augustinian canonesses). No
early p.n. or f.n. evidence for a convent survives for Tinwell, but cf.
None Stalls in Braunston f.ns. (a) and *Nunesland* in Exton f.ns. (b)
which may refer to land owned by such a foundation, *v. Churches in
Rutland*, Rutland Local History Society Vol. 11 (1988), *s.n.*

BREDCROFT HO., 1846, 1863 White, *v.* Bredcroft *supra.* THE
COTTAGE, *Tinwell Cottage* 1846, 1863 ib, cf. *Cottage Field* 1844
TA, 1877, 1950 *Burghley.* THE CROWN P.H., 1846 White, *Crown
Inn* 1877 ib. EMPINGHAM ROAD COTTAGES. GLEBE FM.,
cf. *Ingthorpe Glebe* 1844 *TA, Glebe Close* 1844 *ib, Glebe Meadow*
1877 *Burghley, v.* glebe. THE GRANGE, *v.* grange. MANOR FM

is *The Hall* 1846 White. MANOR HO., 1846, 1863 ib, cf. *The Manor Place* 1546 VCH, *v.* **maner, place.** THE MILL is *Water Corn Mill* 1844 *TA*, cf. *Mill Holmes* 1844 *ib*, *Mill Close* 1877, 1950 *Burghley, Mill Field* 1943 *Map, v.* **holmr.** MURRAY LODGE, cf. *Mount Murray Wood* 1806 Map. The only Mt. Murray which the editor has been able to trace is in the former Australian territory of Papua. Australia's eastern and north-eastern coast was explored only in 1770 by Captain Cook which leaves little time for the transference of the name to Rutland by 1806. If colonial exploration is not the source of this name, then an attachment of *Mount* to the surname *Murray* with reference to a minor feature of local topography is possible; compare, perhaps, with Mt. Alstoe in Burley parish, roughly of the same date. THE RECTORY, 1846, 1863 White. THE ROOKERY, 1846 ib. SOUTH VIEW FM is *Prospect House* 1846 ib. STEDFOLD LANE (local), *v.* **stōd-fald.** TINWELL CHURCH, *Church* (*All Saints*) 1846 ib. TINWELL HO. TINWELL LODGE, 1824 O, 1846 White.

Field-Names

Undated forms in (a) are 1844 *TA*; those dated 1877 and 1950 are *Burghley,* 1943 are *Map.* Early forms dated 1225-9, 1292, 113 and 1347 are CN. Fields in Ingthorpe, where known, are marked (I).

(a) The Acre 1877, The Four Acres 1844, 1877, 1950, The Six -, The Eight -, The Nine Acres 1877, 1950, The Ten Acre 1877, - Acres 1950, The Eleven Acres 1950, The Twelve Acres 1877, Twelve - 1943, 1950, The Thirteen Acres 1877, Thirteen - 1943, 1950, The Fourteen Acres 1877, Fourteen - 1943, The Seventeen Acres 1877, Seventeen - 1943, The Eighteen Acres 1877, The Twenty Acres 1877, 1950, North -, South Twenty Acres 1877, 1943, 1950, The Twenty-one Acres 1877, The Thirty Acres 1844, 1877, 1943, The Thirty-four Acres 1877, 1943, The Thirty-seven Acres 1950, The Forty Acres 1943, Forty-seven Acres 1943 (*v.* **æcer**); Baines Orchard (I); Bottom Cl; Great -, Little Brickennook (I) (*v.* **brakni, nōk**); Broadeng Mdw 1877, - Mdw(s) 1950 (*Brodyngg* 1347 CN, 'the broad meadow', *v.* **brād, eng**); Cave's Cl 1844, Close over Cave's 1877, - over Caves 1950 (cf. *Caves Mill* 1546 VCH, *v.* **myln**); Cherry Cls 1844, Cherry Holt 1877, 1943, 1950 (*v.* **holt**); The Close (x2); Coppice Cl (*the coppice close* 1796 *Deed*); Dead Man's Ground (perh. referring to the discovery of an ancient burial site, *v.* **dede-man, grund**); Dry Cl (*v.* **dryge**); The Fox Cover 1844, - Covert 1877, 1943 (*v.* **cover(t)**); Front Mdw 1877, 1950; Grass Bake Nook 1877, 1943 (prob. alluding to the practice of burn-baking, the systematic slow combustion of herbage on fallow land to create potash on the field so treated, *v.* **nōk**); Grass Cl (prob. referring to sown grass, *v.* **gærs**); The Green 1844, 1877, 1943, High Green 1844, 1877, 1943, Low Green 1844 (cf. *atte Grene* 1292 CN (p), *v.* **grēne²**); Bottom Heath (I) 1844, 1877, 1943, Top Heath (I) 1844; High Ground (I); Hill Cl 1877, 1943, 1950; The Holmes (I) (*v.* **holmr**); Home Cl 1844, - and the Pound 1950 (*v.* **pund**), Home Fd 1877 (*v.* **home**); Horse Cl 1844, 1877, 1943, 1950; House Cl 1877, 1950; Hoverdale 1877 (*v.* **ofer³**, **dalr**); Inclosed Road 1877; Intake (*v.* **inntak**); Lowth Cl (I) (from the surn. *Louth*, cf. *Louth's Leys* in Lt. Casterton f.ns. (b) and *Louths farm* in Empingham f.ns. (b)); Maxwell Mdw; Great Mdw (I) 1844, 1847, 1943 (perh. to be identified with *Mykeleng* 113 in Ingthorpe, *v.* **mikill, eng**, a Scand compound); Little Mdw 1877, 1943, The Meadow 1877, 1950, Meadow Cl 1844; Oakham Road Cl 1877, 1943; Ozier Bed 1844, - Holt 1844, 1877, Osier Holt 1950 (*v.* **oyser, bedd, holt**); The Pasture 1877, 1943 (*the Pasture 1796 Deed*); Piece by Gwash Brook; Pingle 1844, 1877 (*v.* **pingel**); The Ram Cl 1877; Red Ground and Garden 1844, Red Ground 1877, 1950, (*v.* **rēad, grund**); Road Cl; Robbs Fd 1877, 1950, Robbs Pingle 1877 (*v.* **pingel**); Robert's Home Cl; Old Sanfoin Cl 1844, Sainfoin - 1877, (Old) Saintfoin 1943 (*v.* **sainfoin**); Shacklewell 1943, - Foldyard 1950, - Piece 1844 (*v.* Shacklewell in Empingham which adjoins to the north-west); Short Trees Cl 1844, 1877; Shortacres 1943, Short Acres 1950; Slipe 1877 (*v.* **slipe**); Speed's Mdw (I); Spinney Cl 1844, 1877, 1950; Spring Cl 1844, 1877, 1950, - Fd 1844, 1877, 1943 (*v.* **spring**); Old Stone Pit 1877, Stone Pit and Rubbish Dump 1950, Stone Pit Cl 1950, - Fd 1877, Stonepit Cl 1844, 1877, - Fd 1943, 1950, - Piece 1877; The Sykes 1877, 1943 (*v.* **sik**); Sykes Cl (I) 1844; Tickencote Mdw 1877 (Tickencote parish adjoins to the north); Tollbar Cl 1844, - Fd 1943, Toll Bar Cl 1950, - Cl and Fd 1877 (alluding to the former turnpike system, *v.* **toll-bar**); Top Cl (x2); Townend Cl 1877, 1950 (*v.* **tūn, ende¹**); Triangular Piece; Twixen Dykes ('(land) between the ditches', *v.* **betweox(n), dik**); Waste in Fox Covert 1877, - in Sainfoin Cl 1877, - in Shacklewell Hollow 1950 (*v.* **waste** and Shacklewell Hollow in Tickencote); Well Cl 1844, The - 1877.

(b) *ad crucem* 1292 (p), 1347 (p) (*v.* **cros**; *Henricus ad crucem* (1292) and *Ricardus ad crucem* (1347) were both of Ingthorpe; a medieval cross shaft, prob. that which gave them their names, survives built into a wall south of the farm at Ingthorpe at SK 9960 0888, *v.* MER 42 and BrownArchSites 26); *le Estfeld* 1347 ('the east field', one of the great open-fields of the village, *v.* **ēast, feld**); *Lynghau* 1225-9 ('heather-covered tumulus', *v.* **lyng, haugr**, a Scand compound, prob. naming a burial mound on the territorial boundary); *Nomanislond* 1225-9 ('no man's land, deserted land', v. **nān-mann, land**; a piece of ground lying near the parish boundary with Stamford L); *Tynewell Lynges, Tynnewell Lyngis* 1347 (v. **lyng**); *Tunkeacre* 1225-9 ('the plot of arable on the tongue of land', v. **tunge, æcer**); *in uenella* 1292 (p) (v. **lane**); *le Westfeld* 1550 Pat ('the west field', one of the open-fields of the village, v. **west, feld**); *le Westlane* 1292 (p) (I) (v. **west, lane**).

MARTINSLEY HUNDRED

Martineslei(e), *-yn-* 1086 DB bis, *-leia* 1199, 1200, 1201 P, *-lea* 1169, 1179 ib *et passim* to 1202 ib, *-le* 1263 *Ass,* 1265 Misc *et passim* to 1346 FA, 1403 Pat
Martinsle, -yn- 1275 RH bis, *-ley* 1535 VE, 1536 Denb, 1610 Speed

The division is styled:

> *wapentac* 1086 DB bis, 1190 P, 1202 Ass, *-tagio* 1179, 1188 P
> *hundred* 1199, 1200 P *et passim*

'Martin's woodland glade or clearing', v. **lēah, vápnatak, hundred.** The OE pers.n. *Martin* (originally MedLat *Martinus*) appears also in Martinsthorpe, in the earlier *Martinestoch* and in *martines hó* (v. Ayston f.ns. (b)), all in Martinsley Hundred. These p.ns. are, no doubt, to be assoociated with the same Martin who gave his name to the hundred. The moot-site of the original hundred was at the lost *Martinsley* in Martinsthorpe. Whether this continued as the moot-site after the remodelling of the hundred is unknown.

Ayston

AYSTON
    Æthelstanestun 1046 (12) *SAL* (S 1014), (*into*) *Æthelstanes tune* 1046 (12) *ib*
    Adelstaneston' 1203 Cur

Hadestanestun 1186 P
Athestaneston 1284 OSut, *Athestanston* 1254 Val
Astaneston' 1293 OSut, *Asteneston'* 1204 ClR, 1299 For, 1300
    DC, *Astoneston* 1256 For, *Astonston* 1319 FF
Atheston 1275 Pat, c1291 Tax
Aston(*e*) 1269 For, 1286 *Ass*, 1305 FA *et passim* to 1477 Banco
Ayston 1535 VE, 1564 SR, 1610 Speed

'Æðelstān's estate', *v.* **tūn.** The sole surviving Anglo-Saxon
charter with boundary clauses for Rutland describes a grant of land
at Ayston by Edward the Confessor to Æðelstān (*ministro mihi* ....
fideli). Ayston is thus a p.n. of late manorial type identifying a
possession of a king's thane who, presumably, spent the majority of
his time away from his estate. For discussion of the charter
bounds, *v.* The Ayston Charter *infra*.

AYSTON CHURCH, *Church* (*St Mary*) 1846, 1863 White.
AYSTON HALL, 1846, 1863 ib, *The Hall* 1568 *Bru.* It is (*the*)
Manner house 1607, 1608 *ib*, *Ayston House* 1801 Map, *v.* **hall,
maner.** AYSTON SPINNEY, 1806 ib, 1940 *Deed.* THE GREEN
(local), *v.* **grēne²**. SEWELL'S BARN, William *Sewell* is *late of
Wardley* in 1758 *Deed.*

Field-Names

Undated forms in (a) are 1943 *Map.* Forms dated 1849 are *TA*; those dated
1940 are *Deed.* Early forms dated 1046 (12) are *SAL*; 1606, 1607, 1608, 1609,
1633 and 1667 are *Bru*; 1631 are *Terrier.*

(a) Four Acres 1849, - Acre 1943; Twelve Acre; Ayston Cl; Baines's Cl, -
Mdw, - Hill 1849, Baine's Hill 1940 (from the family name of Jos. *Baines* 1849
of Ayston); Banier's Cl 1849; Barn Cl, - Fd; Barnett's Cl 1940, - Hill 1849, 1940,
New -, Old Barnett's 1943; Brown's Mdw 1849; Butt Cl; Cant's Cl, - Mdw 1849,
1940 (from the surn. *Cant*, cf. Cants Cl, - Mdw, - Nether Wood in neighbouring
Wardley f.ns. (a) and Robert *Cant* 1877 White of adjoining Preston); Clement's
Cl, - Mdw 1849 (cf. John-, Thomas- and William *Clement* 1522 MilS of nearby
Belton); Cottagers Cl 1940, Cottagers 1943 (*v.* **cotager**); Crofts 1849, 1943; Dale
Cl 1849, 1940, Dale's - 1940; Deals Close Covert 1806 Map, - Cover 1824 O (*v.*

cover(t)); Deep Dale Cl 1849, Deepdale 1940 (*Debdale* 1606, 1609, 1633, *Depdale* 1607, 1608, *Depdale Close* 1633, cf. *Debdale Lodge* 1667, v. **dēop, dalr**); Elliott's Cl 1940, - Hill 1849, 1940, - Mdw 1849, 1940, 1943; Footpad Fd ('field with or near a footpath', v. **pad**); The Glebe (v. **glebe**); Gorse, - Cl (v. **gorst**); High Road Cl 1849, 1940, Road Cl 1943; Hills; Home Cl 1849, 1940, - Fd, - Grass Fd 1943, - Mdw 1940 (v. **home**); Hopkins, - Mdw; Hornsby's Cl 1940 (with an old Ru surn., cf. William *Horneby* 1524 SR of Empingham); Hudson's Cl 1940; Humphrey's 1943, - Cl, - Mdw 1940; Land Cl (an enclosure consolidating selions of an open-field, v. **land**); Lockwood's Mdw 1849 (cf. Lockwoods Cl in neighbouring Martinsthorpe f.ns. (a)); Martins (prob. a surn., cf. Martins House in neighbouring Uppingham, but cf. also perh. *martines hō* in the Ayston Charter *infra*); Meadow Cl 1940, - Fd 1943; Middle Cl 1849, 1940; The Nether Part 1849, The Netherpart 1943; Parliament Cl, - Mdw 1849 (Mr J. Field notes that this poss. refers to land enclosed by act of Parliament, cf. Parliament (Leese parish) Ch 2 229); Perkin's Cl 1940; Peter's Middle Mdw; Close called the Pines 1940, Pines 1943; The Pingle 1849, Pingel 1943 (v. **pingel**); Poor Fds (poss. land endowed for charity); Pretty Gorse (v. **gorst**), Bottom -, Prettys (with the surn. *Pretty*, cf. Willm. *Pritty* 1663 *Asw* of nearby Glaston); First -, Second -, Third -, Fourth Roberts; Rudkin's Hill 1849; Scott's Cl 1849, 1940, - Hill 1849, - Mdw 1849, 1940, Bottom -, Middle -, Top Scotts 1943 (with the family name of John *Scott* 1932 Kelly); Sismey's Mdw 1849, Sismey's 1940 (from the surn. *Sismey*, cf. John *Sismay* 1522 MilS of Lyddington); Sprigg's Cl, - Mdw 1849; Terrewest's Cl, - Mdw 1849, Terrewest, - Cl 1940 (John *Terrywest* owned *Terrywest's Cottage* in neighbouring Bisbrooke in 1760 *Will* and a John *Tyrriwest* was resident in adjoining Preston in 1706 *Anc*); Toll Bar (adjacent to a former turnpike road, v. **toll-bar**); Wade's Hill 1849, 1940, Waits Hills 1943 (cf. Wades Hill in Thistleton f.ns. (a), William *Wade* 1652 *Surv* of Greetham and William *Wade* 1758 *ib* of Stretton; while the surn. must remain the obvious choice of origin of the name of the hill, the coincidence of two examples of Wades Hill in Ru suggests the possibility that the names record a local superstition which associated these hills with the legendary *Wade* whose earliest appearance is as a hero in the OE poem *Widsith* but who in the Scand *Þidrekssaga* has been transformed into a giant, cf. Wat's Dyke where Wade is associated with a major Anglo-Saxon defensive earthwork); Washpit Mdw (alluding to a sheep-wash, v. **wæsce, pytt**); Watts's Cl 1849, Watts' - 1940, Watt's Hill 1849, Watts' - 1940; William's Cl 1849, 1940 (cf. William's Lane Cl in neighbouring Wing f.ns. (a)).

(b) *Aston Mill* 1633 (v. **myln**); *Balland* 1606, 1607, 1608, *Balland Closes* 1633 (v. **ball, land**); *Pisbrooke Close* 1633, *Bisbrook lound* 1609, *Pisbrooke Lounde* 1633 (Bisbrooke parish adjoins to the east, v. **lundr**); *brocholes* 1046 (12) (prob. the common boundary marker *brocc-holu* 'badger setts', but *brōc-holu* 'the burrows at the brook' is poss., *v.* **brocc-hol, brōc, hol**[1]); *Childeslund'* 1218 *For* (the first el. is OE *cild* 'a young person', but by the 11th cent. *cild* was being used as a title of honour and this gen. sg. construction suggests some such function here. Reaney *s.n.* Child notes that '(in the earliest examples) it probably denotes one comparable in status to the drengs of the northern Danelaw.' The dreng was a man holding land by a particular form of free tenure, combining service, money payments and military duty, *v.* **cild, lundr**); *Colepit Corner* 1633 (*v.* **col-pytt, corner**); *the Common Feild* 1607, *Ayston Common feild* 1684 Wright (*v.* **commun, feld**); *the Cowpasture* 1633, *Cow Pasture* 1667; *Damfeild* 1631, *Dam(m) Feild, Damme Feilde* 1633 (one of the great open-fields of the village, *v.* **damme, feld**; a medieval stone-faced dam survives in part on the north side of the stream at SK 871 007, *v.* MER 6-7); *Dovecote Close* 1631 (*v.* **dove-cot(e)**); *Eastfeild* 1631, *East Feilde* 1633 (one of the open-fields of the village, *v.* **ēast, feld**); *Haddisly* 1607, *Haddisley* 1633, *Hadslie Corner* 1633 (perh. 'Hæddi's woodland clearing', but *Headd,* a short form of OE pers.ns. in *Heard-,* is also formally poss., *v.* **lēah, corner**); *Hawthorne hill* 1607, *Hawthornehill* 1633, *Hawthorne hill Cowpasture* 1633 (*v.* **hagu-þorn**); *holebroc* 1046 (12) (*v.* **hol**[2]**, brōc**); *molendino equino* 1519 *Bru* ('the horse-driven mill', *v.* **hors, myln**); *Kilne close* 1607, 1633 (*v.* **cyln**); *Lammas Close* 1631, 1633 (a close used for grazing after August 1st, *v.* **lammas**); *Lound close* 1633 (*v.* **lundr**); *Maltmill* 1608 (*v.* **malte-mylne**); *martines hô* 1046 (12) ('Martin's headland', *v.* **hōh,** perh. remembered in Martins *supra.* The Martin of the early f.n. is doubtlessly the Martin of Martinsley (Hundred) and Martinsthorpe); *Midle grounde* 1633 (*v.* **middel, grund**); *Mill Close* 1609 (*v.* **myln**); *New close by Preston brooke* 1633 (Preston parish adjoins); *The New Inclosures* 1633 (*v.* **inclosure**); *Oxe yard* 1607, *Oxeyard* 1667 (*v.* **oxa, geard**); *the Parsonage House* 1667 (*v.* **personage**); *Pecks Oake close* 1633 (with the surn. *Peck,* cf. John *Peyke* 1525 SR of Ayston, Richerd *Pek* 1524 ib of Ridlington and *Pexoke Close* 1681 *Anc* in adjoining Bisbrooke f.ns. (b), *v.* **āc**); *Pen yard* 1607, *Penyard* 1609, *Pen Yarde* 1633 (*v.* **penn**[2]**, geard**); *Pond Close* 1609 (*v.* **ponde**); *Preston brooke* 1633 (the brook forming the parish boundary with Preston, *v.* **brōc**); *Preston Close* 1633 (Preston parish adjoins to the north-east); *rædwege* 1046 (12) ('road suitable for riding upon', *v.* **rǣde-weg**); *Ridlington brooke* 1607 (Ridlington parish adjoins to the north-west, *v.* **brōc**); *Ridlington Way* 1667; *þornham broc* 1046 (12) (perh. 'the brook running through Thornham, i.e., through the estate where thorn-bushes grow', *v.* **þorn, hām, brōc,** but a name with **hamm** 'an enclosure, a water-meadow' cannot be discounted, *v.* The Ayston Charter *s.n. infra); þureslege broc* 1046 (12) (prob. 'the brook at Thursley, i.e. the grove sacred to the god Þunor', *v.* **lēah, brōc;** an Anglo-Scand pers.n. *Þōr* or *Þūr* is less likely, *v.* The Ayston Charter *s.n. infra); Town(e) Closes* 1633, 1667 (*v.* **tūn**); *Uppingham Close*

1633 (Uppingham parish adjoins to the south); *Uppingham Meere* 1667 (*v.* **(ge)mǽre**); *Westfeild* 1631, *West Feilde* 1633 (one of the great open-fields of the village, *v.* **west,** `feld`); (*into*) *wenge forde* 1046 (12) (either 'the ford to the field' or 'Wing ford', *v.* **vengi, ford** and The Ayston Charter *s.n. infra*); *the windmill* 1608, *Wind Myll* 1633 (*v.* **wind-mylne**).

THE AYSTON CHARTER

The only surviving Anglo-Saxon charter for Rutland with boundary clauses is that granting three *cassati* of land at Ayston to Æðelstan by Edward the Confessor in 1046. The charter is in Latin with OE bounds. These bounds are preserved only in a 12th century copy of the charter in Society of Antiquaries, London, MS 60, folio 32 verso. They read as follows:

þis sind þa land ge mære into Æthelstanes tune. þæt is of þornham broc[1] into þureslege broc.[2] swa in to martines hó.[3] swa in to holebroc.[4] of holebroc swa into brocholes.[5] swa into rædwege.[6] of rædwege swa into wenge forde[7] and swa eft into þornham broc.

The diacritic of bound 3 (*martines hó*) is the only one surviving. Five of the seven bounds present ambiguity in interpretation.

1. *þornham broc*, 'the brook running through Thornham'. *Thornham* may mean either 'the estate or village growing with thorn-bushes', i.e. with the second el. *hām*, or 'promontory, river-meadow or enclosed plot with thorn-bushes' with the second el. *hamm*. It is likelier that the name records a lost larger Anglo-Saxon land-unit (a *hām*), later divided to become at least the parishes of Glaston, Wing and Bisbrooke. The brook may be the nameless stream running between Glaston and Wing to a confluence with R. Chater at South Luffenham, *v.* **þorn, hām, hamm, brōc.**

2. *þureslege broc*, probably 'the brook at Þunor's sacred grove', recording a shrine dedicated to the pagan Anglo-Saxon god *Þunor*. This lost site was in close proximity to Holyoaks, originally OE *hālig-āc* 'the holy oak', which together with 'Þunor's grove' suggests

a small woodland area in which pagan rites survived for a time after the introduction of Christianity to the region. The monolithic pre-Germanic mother goddess surviving in the churchyard at Braunston, four miles away, may be further evidence of this. However, the first el. of *pureslege* could formally be an Anglo-Scand pers.n. *Þūr* or *Þōr*, although pers.ns. of Scand origin are not commonly compounded with OE *lēah* and would be unlikely in territory where Norse influence seems so limited. If indeed the first el. is a late Anglo-Scand pers.n., then *lēah* would mean rather 'clearing in woodland', *v.* **lēah, brōc.**

3. *martines hó*, 'Martin's headland or promontory', *v.* **hōh.** The MedLat pers.n. *Martin* is also found in the name of Martinsley Hundred in which Ayston is situated, as well as in the early *Martinestoch* which was probably remodelled as Martinsthorpe in the same hundred. The chapel and church at Martinsthorpe and Lyndon (also in Martinsley Hundred) were both dedicated to St Martin. However, the names *martines hó* and *Martinestoch* 'Martin's outlying farmstead' suggest that it was an early secular Martin whose name later inspired the two church dedications in the hundred rather than the church dedications which gave rise to such minor p.ns. as *martines hó* and *Martinestoch* and the name of the hundred *Martinsley*. The modern f.n. Martins in Ayston f.ns. (a) may record the same individual.

4. *holebroc*, 'the brook running in a hollow', *v.* **hol^2, brōc.**

5. *brocholes*, either 'the badger setts' or 'the burrows at the brook', *v.* **brocc-hol, brōc, hol^1.** However, most likely this bound was originally OE *brocc-holu* 'the badger-setts', a common bounds marker.

6. *rædwege*, probably 'road suitable for riding upon', *v.* **ræde-weg.** The vowel in the first el. would seem to preclude interpretation as OE *rēad* 'red' alluding to red soil, although Ayston does lie on an outcropping of the ironstone which produces Rutland's red soils. This road may be that whose name survives in Uppingham as Redgate (with Scand *gata* 'a road' substituted for OE *weg* 'a way').

7. (*into*) *wenge forde*, either 'the ford to the field' or 'Wing ford', *v.*

vengi, ford. It is difficult to decide whether, at the date of the charter, *vengi* 'a field' had become the fixed name of a developed settlement of Wing or whether the word simply alluded to a field across the stream from Glaston.

The identifications of these bounds are discussed in C.R. Hart, *The Early Charters of Eastern England*, Leicester 1966, 108-19, in C. Phythian-Adams, 'Rutland Reconsidered', *Mercian Studies*, ed. A. Dornier, Leicester 1977, 81-2 and in Barrie Cox, 'Rutland and the Scandinavian Settlements: the Place-Name Evidence', *Anglo-Saxon England* 18 (1989), 138.

Beaumont Chase

Previously extra-parochial, Beaumont Chase became a parish in 1799 by Act of Parliament, part of its territory being annexed to Uppingham.

BEAUMONT CHASE
    Bellomonte 1203 PatR, *(foresta de -)* 1203 ib
    Beumund' 1254 Cl, *-munt* 1255 Pat
    Beaumund 1266, 1286 *For*, *-munt* 1257 Cl, *-mount* 1344 *For*,
      -mond 1365 *ib*, 1375 Cl
    Beamund 1286 *Ass*, 1302 Cl, *-mond* 1510 *MinAcct*, 1611 *SP*,
      -mount 1551 Pat, 1610 Speed
    Beamount Chase 1633 *Bru*, *the Chase or Forest called Beamont*
      1665 *Deed*, *Beamont Chase* 1670 *Rental*, 1684 *FF*

'Beautiful hill', *v.* **beau, mont**, cf. Beaumont Leys Lei. The area was once a chase for breeding and hunting wild animals, *v.* **chace.**

CASTLE HILL, 1633 *Bru*, 1736, 1763 *Bir*, 1846 White, *a wood called Castle Hills* 1575 *For*, *Castle Hills* 1688 *Anc*, cf. *Castle Hill Close* 1728 *Asw*, *Castle Hill Leyes* 1746 *Bir*, *Castle Hills leys* 1688 *Anc* (*v.* lēah). The hill takes its name from the motte and bailey castle at the tip of the headland, *v.* **castel(l), hyll.** KING'S HILL,

1799 *Deed, Lower -, Upper Kings Hill* 18 *Surv,* cf. *Lower Kings Hill Meadow* 18 *ib.* KING'S HILL LODGE is *The Kings lodge* 1610 Speed, 1620 Map, *le Kinges lodge* 1611 *SP, Kings Lodge* 1780, 1801 Map, *Kings Hill Lodge* 1824 O. It is *Beamonte lodge* 1575 *For, Beaumont Lodge* 1804 *Map, The Lodge* 1634, 1705, 1720, 1723 *Terrier.* King's Hill (Lodge) is so called because the forest of Rutland was royal forest, *v.* **loge.** STOCKERSTON ROAD is *le Kingsway* 1278 (16) *SlCart, Kings Road* 1610 Speed, *v.* **cyning, weg.** WOOD'S LODGE (lost) was demolished in 1925 - UR.

Field-Names

Undated forms in (a) are 1804 *Map,* those dated 1943 are also *Map.* Early forms dated 1373 and 1575 are *For,* 1611 are *SP,* 1633 are *Bru,* 1634, 1705, 1720, 1723 and 1730 are *Terrier,* 1746 and 1763 are *Bir,* 1799 are *Deed.*

(a) Armsley Quarter (*Armondesleye, Armondele* 1373, *Armslie* 1633, *Armley Sale* 1799, 'Earnmund's woodland clearing', *v.* **lēah;** the use of *sale* 'division or quarter of a wood, of which the underwood is cut down and sold' is frequent in the parish. This woodland term is tentatively discussed in Nth 157, *v.* **sale, quarter**); Broughton's Plain (1799, *v.* **plain**); Candlemakers Road (*Candlemakers Roade* 1633; it is unclear why the road is associated with candlemakers unless *Candlemaker* is here a surn., *v.* Fransson 73 *s.n.*); Castle Hill Sale (1799, *v.* **sale** and Castle Hill *supra*); Nether and Upper Catwell Sale (*Catwell saile* 1575, cf. *Bisshop' catwell'* 1510 *MinAcct, v.* **cat(t), wella, sale;** the quarter was a possession of the *Bishop* of Lincoln in 1510 *ib*); Crabtree Hill (1728 *Asw, Crabtree hill Sale* 1799, *v.* **crabtre, sale**); Garner Hill Sale; Far -, Middle -, New Great Sale 1943; Headland Sale (*v.* **hēafod-land**); Kings Hill Riding (*v.* **ryding** and King's Hill *supra*); Klondyke 1943 (a name indicating remoteness and associated with the gold rush in Canada in and after 1896; at the parish boundary in Beaumont Chase, the name also appears in Barleythorpe, Hambleton and Wardley f.ns. (a)); Lady Sale (1799, *v.* **hlǣfdige, sale**); Far -, Middle Lawn (*le Launde, le lownde* 1611, cf. *Laund' Chase* 1677, 1694 *Deed, v.* **launde, chace**); Lower and Upper Lodge Quarter (*Lodge Quarter* 1633, *Lower -, Upper Lodge Sale* 1799, *v.* **quarter, sale** and King's Hill Lodge *supra*); Lodge Road (1799); Little Maples (1728 *Asw,* 1799, cf. *Rough Maples* 17 *Deed,* 1729, 18 *Surv,* 18 *Rental, Ruffmaplehill* 1677 *Deed, Ruffmaple Hill* 1694 *ib, v.* **mapel;** *Ruff* is prob. a surn., cf. Barbara *Ruffe* c1685 *Deed* of Burley); Maple Stile Sale (*Maplestile Sale* 1799, *v.* **mapel, stigel, sale**); Lower and Upper Miry Quarter (*Lower -, Mirey Quarter* 1799, prob. 'the muddy quarter', *v.* **myry, quarter,** but (*ge*)*mǽre* 'a boundary' is poss. as the first el.); Mountjoy Thick (*Mountioy thicke, Monioye Thicke* 1611, *Mount Joy Thick* 1799, *Greenwood alias Mountjoy Thicke* 1600 Moulton, *Mounioy plaine alias Mounioy Thicke* 1665 *Deed*; Lord *Mountjoy* held land in nearby Belton in 1522 MilS; the early alias of Mountjoy Thick appears to be a topographical compound meaning 'the young wood' (*v.* **grēne**[1], **wudu**); for this absolute use of *thick* 'the densest part of a wood', *v.* NED *s.v.* (B); *v.* **þicce**[1], **plain**); Pole Sale (1799, *v.* **sale**); Sallow Sale (*v.* **salh**); Great -, Little Warwick Sale (1728 *Asw*, 1799, *Warwike Sale* 1575, with reference to the Earl of *Warwick* who also held land in nearby Uppingham and Preston 1527 *Surv* and in Barrowden 1551 Pat, *v.* **sale**); Woodland Bushes (1799).

(b) *Beamond Closes* 1611, *Beamont Closes* 1665 *Deed*, *Beamount Close* 1633, *Beamont Close* 1723, *Beaumont Close* 1705, 1720, 1733, 1746 (*v.* Beaumont Chase *supra*); *Beaumont Sale* 1684 Wright (*v.* **sale**); *Beamont Walk* 1622 *Deed* (referring to unenclosed sheep pasture, *v.* **walk**); *Lower* -, *Upper Catlow* 1799 ('wild-cat hill', *v.* **cat(t), hlāw,** cf. Catwell *supra*); *Chiseldine banke* 1633 (with the Ru surn. *Cheseldine, v.* **banke**); *Kings Oake Hills* 17 *Deed, Kings Oakhil* 18 *Rental, Kings Oak Meadow* 18 *Surv, Kings Oake Sale* al's *Kings Oake* al's *Kings Oake Hill* al's *Kings Oake Hill Sale* al's *Fair Oake Hill* al's *Laund Chase* al's *Faire Oake Hill Coppice* 1677 *Deed, Kingsoke sale* al's *Kings Oke* al's *Kings Oke hill* al's *Kingsoke hill sale* al's *Faire Oake hill* al's *Laund Chase* al's *Faire Oake Coppice* 1694 *ib* (it is presumed that this group of forest names belongs to the region of King's Hill *supra* although the *Laund Chase* alias may refer it to the Leighfield area near Launde Lei, *v.* **fæger, āc, sale, launde, chace**); *Lodge Hole* 1705, 1720, 1723, 1730, *Lodge Leyes* 1634, 1746, *lodgleys* 1688 *Anc, Lodge Leys* 1705, 1720 (*v.* **hol**[1], **lēah** and King's Hill Lodge *supra*); *Monks Wood* 1728 *Asw, Monkwood Sale* 1799 (*v.* **munuc, wudu, sale** and cf. *Monkyshill* in neighbouring Wardley f.ns. (b)).

Hambleton

HAMBLETON, UPPER -, MIDDLE -, NETHER -

Hamelduna 1067 *WDB,* -*dunam* 1157 *ib,* -*don'* 1231 RegAnt, 1241 *FF,* 1256 *For,* 1283 *FF,* 1312 Pat

Hameldun(e) 1086 DB bis, 1232 RegAnt, -*don(e)* 1212 RBE, 1227 RHug *et passim* to 1241 RGros *et freq* to 1413, 1423, 1427 *Comp et passim* to 1556 Chap

Hamildon, -*y*- 1235 RGros, 1275 RH bis, 1327 *SR et passim* to 1513 LP

Hamelton 1289, 1290 OSut
Hambuldon c1538 Farnham, *Hambledon* 1549, 1553 Pat,
　1655 *FF*
Hamleyton 1610 Speed
Hambleton 1684 Wright, *Hambleton alias Hamildon* 1701 DKR

The first element of Hambleton is OE *hamol* 'mutilated' used topographically of a flat-topped hill, one which appears to have been sliced off; the word was also used in the sense 'bare, treeless'. The second el. is OE *dūn* 'a large hill'. The hill here is imposing, *v.* hamol, dūn.

The original settlement, possibly the early *caput* of Anglo-Saxon Rutland, was on the hilltop at Upper Hambleton, known earlier as *Magna* - 1288 *Ass*, 1344 Inqaqd, *Great* - 1684 Wright. Nether Hambleton was *le Nethertowne of Hambledon* 1549 Pat, but the affix was normally *Parua* -, *-v-* c1200 BM, 1241 *FF et passim* to 1442 BM (*Little* - 1632 *Anc*, 1655 *FF*, *Nether* - 1549 Pat, 1684 Wright). *Middle Hambleton* appears by 1824 O.

Middle and Nether Hambleton were demolished in 1975 to make way for Empingham Reservoir, now Rutland Water, which was completed in 1977.

APRIL COTTAGE. ARMLEY LODGE, *v.* Armley Wood in Exton. BARNHILL SPINNEY. BEECH FM. BEEHIVE COTTAGE. BULL BRIDGE, *Bulbrigg* 1632 *Anc*, *Bull Bridge* 1726 *ib*, *Bulbridge* 1792 *ib*, cf. *Bulbrigg Close* 1632 *ib*, *Bulbridge Close* 1758, 1785 *Surv*, 1792 *Anc*, *Widow Bridges Bull Bridge Meadow* 1726 *ib*, *Bulbridge Meadow* 1758, 1785 *Surv*, *Bull Bridge Meadow* 118 *ib*, *Bulbridge Cottage Meadow* 1729 *Anc*, *Empingham Bull Bridges* 1726 *ib*. Probably named from the family of John *Bull* 1785 *Surv* and William *Bull* 118 *ib*. The most recent bridge (now submerged in Rutland Water) was of stone and built in the 18th century. It may well have replaced an earlier structure recorded as *Stanbrigge* 1269 For, *Stanbrigghe* 1269 ib, cf. *ad pontem* 1289 OSut (p), although this early stone bridge may have been on the site of the present Fox Bridge on the northern boundary of the parish with Exton, *v.* stān, brycg. DUKES WELL (local), cf. *Dukes Close* 1729, 1785, 118 *Surv*, from the surname *Duke*. EAST VIEW. FINCH'S ARMS P.H., 1846, 1863 White, named from the *Finch* family of Burley on the

Hill. GIBBET GORSE, 1943 *Map* is *Gibbet Cover* 1824 O, named from *Weldons Gibbet* 1806 Map, the site of a gallows, *v.* **gibet, cover(t)**, **gorst**. *Weldon* is a surname, cf. *Weldons Linche* in Wardley f.ns. (b). HALF MOON SPINNEY, 1943 *Map*, named from its semicircular shape. HAMBLETON CHURCH, *Church (St Andrew)* 1846, 1863 White. HAMBLETON HALL, 1846, 1863 ib. HAMBLETON LODGE (LODGE FM 6"), *Hambleton Lodge* 1824 O, *The Lodge* 1846, 1863 White, *Healeys Lodge* 1806 Map. Peter *Healy* farmed land in the parish in 118 *Surv.* HAMBLETON MANOR, *Manor House* 1846, 1863 White. HAMBLETON WOOD, 1806 Map, *Hamleytonwood* 1610 Speed, *Hambledon Wood* 1628 *MisAccts*, *v.* **wudu**. HILL TOP FM. HOME FM. IVYDENE. KEEPER'S LODGE, a gamekeeper's house. LAX HILL, 1729, 1785, 118 *Surv*, possibly with ModE *lax* in the sense 'loose in texture, loosely compacted', referring to the nature of the soil, cf. Lax Hill in Barrowden. LAX HILL COVERT. THE LIMES. MANOR FM. NEW PARK, *The New Park* e19 *Anc*, *New Park* 1943 *Map*, *The Park* 1933 *Deed*. An earlier park is recorded as *le Park* 1360 Ipm, *v.* **park**. OLD HALL is *The Hall House* 1735 *Conant*, cf. *the Hall Wood* 1628 *MisAccts*, *Hall Wood* 1729, 1785, 118 *Surv*, *the hallwood side* 1605 *Deed*, *hall Wood close* 1629 *Rental*, *Hallwood Close* c1685 *Deed*, 1686 *Rental*, 17 *Deed*, *v.* **hall, wudu**. ORCHARD HO., cf. *Orchard Close* 1943 *Map*. PINFOLD HO. (local), *v.* **pynd-fald**. THE RED HO. SCHOOL HILL (local), cf. *National School* 1846, 1863 White. STANNYFORD (local), cf. *Stanwell Ford Close* 1685, 1690, 1795 *Anc*, originally 'ford in the stony stream', *v.* **stān, wella, ford**, but the modern form means 'ford with a stony bottom', *v.* **stānig**. THE VICARAGE, 1846 White is *the Vicarage House* 118 *Surv*, cf. *ye Parsonage House* 1675 *DC*, 1676 *Terrier*, *v.* **personage**. WOODBINE HO.

Field-Names

Undated forms in (a) are 1943 *Map*. Those dated 1906, 1915, 1920 and 1933 are *Deed* (per Mr D. Tew); 1848 are *TA*. Early forms dated 1495, 1526 and 1540 are *Finch*; 1585, 1611, 1626, 1661, 1672, 1727, 1735 and 1760 are *Conant*; 1598, 1601, 1605, c1630, 1653, 1659, 1663, c1685, 1692, 17 and 1716 are *Deed*; 1626 (1729), 1632, 1632 (1729), 1635, 1662, 1685, 1690, 1726, 1748, 1772, 1792 and 1795 are *Anc*; 1628 are *MisAccts*; 1629, 1686, 1781 and 1795 are *Rental*; 1675,

1700, 1719 and 1762 are *DC*; 1676 are *Terrier*; 1729, 1758, 1785 and 118 are *Surv*, while 1747 are *Hotchkin*.

(a) Three Acre (*Three Acre Close* 1729, *Three Acre Meadow* 1727, 1735, 1760), Four -, Five -, Seven Acre (*Seven Acre Piece* 118), The Eight Acres, Nine -, Ten Acre, Twelve Acres (1785, 118, *Twelve Acre Close* 1729), Nineteen Acre (*v.* **æcer**); Top Adcock's (cf. *Adcock's Lyndon Hill* 1785, 118, held by Joseph *Adcock* 1762, Francis *Adcock* 118); Andrew's Mdws (*Andrews Meadow* 118, cf. *Andrews Close* 1727, 1760, *Allen's Close otherwise Andrews Close* 1785, *Allens Close alias Andrews Close* 118, *Andrews Closes* 1735, *v. Allins Close infra*); Ayre's Hill Cl (with a form of the Ru surn. *Eayr*, cf. Eayr's Far Fd in Manton f.ns. (a), Eayr's Big Cl in Martinsthorpe f.ns. (a)); Ballease (*Ball Leys* 1672, 1727, 1735, 1760, *Bald Leys* 118, *v.* **lēah**); Barnsdale Fds (*v.* Barnsdale in Exton); Bell's Cl (*Bell Close* 1729, *Bells* - 1785, 118, *Bell's* - 118, cf. *Bells Orchard* 118, with the surn. *Bell*, cf. Charles *Bell* 1932 Kelly of neighbouring Exton); Big Fd (x2), Big Fd or Sixteen Acres; Brook Fd or River Fd (cf. *Brook Meadow* c1685, 1686, 17, *v.* **brōc**); Bull Cl (perh. to be identified with *Bulls Close* 1747, 1785, 118, *Bull's* - 1748, from the family name of John *Bull* 1785, Widow *Bull* 118, William *Bull* 118); Bunklins (cf. *Bunkland Meadow* 118); Bush Calves (*Bushcrofte* 1626, *Bushcroft with the windmill* 1629, *Bush. Crofts* 1727, 1735, 1760, *Bush Croft* 118, *Little Bush Croft* 1785; *calves* is evidently for *crofts*, cf. *Grass Grarves infra*, *v.* **busc**, **croft**); Cinder Mdw (*Sundermedow* 1338 Ipm, *Sindermeadowes* 1629, *Sinder Meadow* c1685, 1686, 17, also c1700 *Rental*, e18 *ib*, *Sunder Meadow* 1729, *Cynder Meadow* 1729, *Cinder Meadow* 118, 'the meadow detached from the estate', *v.* **sundor**, **mǣd**; the land belonged to Burley); Clarks Cl 1906 (*Clarkes close* 1632, 1632 (1729), 1785, *Clarks Close* 1632, 1727, 1758, 1760, 1785, *John Bloodeth's Clerks Close* 1726, *Clerks Close* 1735, 1748, *Eastward* -, *Westward Clarke's Close* 118, *Clarke's Close alias The Pasture and Meadow* 1792); Cleedale (*Claydale* c1685, 1686, *clay dayel* 17, *Clay Dale* 1729, *Northward* -, *Southward Claydale Meadow* 1785, *North* -, *South Claydale Meadow* 118, *Lower* -, *Upper Claydale* 1785, 118, *Lower Clay-Dale* 1785, poss. with **deill** rather than **dalr**, *v.* **clǣg**); Cow Pasture 1848 (*The Cowe Pasture* 1626, (*The*) *Cowpasture* 1662, 1686, 1762, 118, (*The*) *Cow Pasture* 1663, 1675, 17, 1719, 1729, *v.* **cū**, **pasture**); Lower -, Upper East Cl 1906 (*East Close* 1785, 118); Egleton or Bottom Pastures (cf. *Bottom Close* 1758, 1785, *John · Roulats Bottom Close* 1726, *William Roulats Bottom Close* 1726; Egleton parish adjoins to the west); Eight Leys or Tomblins Cl 1906 (*Eight Leys* 1785, 118 (*v.* **lēah**), *Tomblins Close* 118, *Tomblin's* - 1785, 118; Thomas *Tomblin* 1785, Tobias and William *Tomblin* 118 gave their family name to the close); Far Fd (1758, 1785, *Farfield* 118, - *Close* 1792, *v.* **feor**); Fell's Cl; Finch's (the *Finch* family lived at Burley on the Hill); Bottom Fowler's (cf. *pastur' ... nuper ... Ric'i*

Fowler 1543 *Comp, Fowlers land* 1611, *Fowlers Closes* 1729, - *Close* 118, *Fowlers Lower Close,* - *Upper* - 1785, 118, *Fowlers Meadow* 1785, 118, from the family name of Richard *Fowler* 1543 *Comp,* Roger *Fowler* 1611 and William *Fowler* 1653); Garden Fd; Gorse Cl, - Fd (*v.* **gorst**); Grass Grarves (*Great* -, *littell Grascroft* 1629, *grasscroft* 1659, *Grass crafts* 1729, *Grass Croft* 1785, *Lower Grass Croft* 1785, - *Crofts* 118, *Upper Grass Croft* 1785, - *Crofts* 118, *v.* **gærs, croft;** *grarves* is evidently for *crofts,* cf. Bush Calves *supra*); Gregory's or Top Fowler's (*v.* Bottom Fowler's *supra*); Big -, Middle Guntrup's (cf. *Gunthorpe nooke* 1653, *Gunthorp Nook* c1685, 1686, *Gunthorpe noke* 17, *Gunthorpe Nooks* 1729, *Nether* -, *Upper Gunthorpe Nook* 1785, . 118, *Gunthorpe Nook Meadow* 1785, 118, *Nether* - 118, *v.* **nōk;** Gunthorpe parish adjoins to the south-west); Hale's Gorse (*v.* **gorst**), Hales' Mdw (from the surn. *Hale,* cf. William *Hayle* 1522 MilS of Belton); Hambleton Cow Pastures (*v.* Cow Pasture *supra*); Healy's Mdw (Peter *Healy* was resident in Hambleton in 118); Holwell 1906, 1915 (*Holwell Meadow* 118; poss. 'stream running in a hollow', *v.* **hol², wella,** but cf. *Holywell Meadow infra*); Home Cl (x4) (*Home Close* 1729, 118); Horse Road Cl (cf. *Horse Close* 1729, 1760, 118, *Northward* -, *Southward Horse Close* 1785, 118); New -, Old Hovel Fd (*v.* **hovel**); Klondyke (a name indicating remoteness or some quality (hard work or large profit) associated with the gold-rush in Canada in and after 1896, cf. Klondyke in Barleythorpe, Beaumont Chase and Wardley f.ns. (a)); The Leys 1933 (*v.* **lēah**); Lincoln Pasture or Fd, Lincoln's Hold (*the Lincolne holdlands* c1685, *the Lincoln hold lands* 1692, *Lincoln hold farm* 1686, *Lincolnhold Cowpastures* 118, *Lincolnhold Field* 118, the property of the Dean and Chapter of Lincoln Cathedral, *v.* **holde**); Long Cl (1781, 1785, 118); Long Leaze West Cl 1906 (*Long Leys* 118, *v.* **lēah**); Marriotts (the surn. *Marriott,* cf. John *Mariet* 1522 MilS, 1525 SR of Lyddington); Meadow Cl (1758, 1785, 1792); Mere Cl (*Mear Close* 1729, *Meer* - 1785, 118; near to, but not on the parish boundary, *v.* **(ge)mǣre**); Middle Cl (1785, 118); The Middle Fd (118); Mill Dams 1920, Millums 1943 (*Millhams* 118; cf. *molend' de parua Hameld'* c1200 *AddCh,* the Mill 1686, *the milne balke* 1598 (*v.* **balca**), *Mill feild* c1630, *Mill Close* 1729, 1785, 118, *v.* **myln, hamm**); First -, Second Moor 1920, 1943 (*Moors* 118, *Moor Furlong* 1729, 1785, 118, *v.* **mōr¹**); Lower -, New Cl (*Lower New Close* 118, - *Meadow* 118, *North* -, *South* -, *West New Close* 1792); Bottom -, Top Oakham Road Fd; Old Hills (cf. *Hill Close* 1785, 118); The New Piece (*v.* **pece**); Pasture Cl (*East* -, *West Pasture Close* 1792, cf. *The Pasture and Meadow* 1792); Pawlett's Cl, - Lower Cl (*Pawlet's* -, *Pawletts Close* 118, *Pawlet's House and Close* 1785, in the possession of John *Pawlett* 118); Plank Cl (1685, 1729, 1785, 1795, 118, *Planck Close* 1690, referring to a plank bridge, *v.* **planke** and cf. *Planke Meadow* in neighbouring Gunthorpe f.ns. (b)); Ploughed Cl; Bottom -, Top Pond Mdw (adjoining a fishpond by a ford in the river); Pony Paddock; Poor Cl (poss.

land endowed for charity); River Cl; Sevrells (*v.* **severall**); Sharpe's Fd or Wheat Cl 1943 (*Wheat Close* 1729, 1785, 118), Sharplands Hill 1824 O, 1826 G, 1943 (*Sharp Lands* 1729, 118, *Sharplands* 1785, cf. *Sharplins Gorse* c1800 Map, *Sharplands Gorse* 1806 ib (*v.* **gorst**); with the surn. *Sharp(e)*, cf. *Robert Sharpe* 1677 *Conant* of neighbouring Lyndon); Sysons Cl; Townsend (*Townsend Close* 1729, 118, *Town's End Close* 1781, *Townend Close* 1785, *Townsend Lower* -, - *Middle* -, - *Upper Close* 1785, 118, *Townsends Lower* -, - *Middle* -, - *Upper Close* 118, *v.* **tūn, ende**[1]); Tween Brooks (1727, 1735, 1760, 118, *Tween Brookes* 1672; land lying between two tributaries of R. Gwash); Underhills; (Big -, Little -) Wall Cl (*Wall Close* c1685, 1686, 17, 118, *Jacksons wall close* 1785, *Great Wall Close* 1785, 118, *Great Wall Close Meadow* 1785, *Great Wall Meadow* 118, *Little Wall Close* 1785, 118, *Little Wall Close and Meadow* 1795, *Little Wall Close Meadow* 1785, 118, *Little Wall Meadow* 118, *v.* **wall**); Washdykes (*Wash Dyke* 118, *Washdyke Meadow* 118, referring to a sheep-dip, *v.* **wæsce, dīk**); Well Cl (1672, 1727, 1735, 1760, 1785, 118, *Well Close Bottom Part, - Top Part* 1792); Water Mdw 1829 *Anc* (1785, 118); Lower -, Middle -, Upper West Cl 1906, 1943 (*West Close* 118); The Wood Cl 1848, (Far -, Near -) Wood Cl 1943 (*Wood Close* 1729, 1758, 1785, 118, *John Bloodeth's Wood Close* 1726, *Bridges's Wood Close* 1726 (cf. Widow *Bridges* 1726), *Love's Wood Close* 1785, *Loves* - 118, *Widow Parkers Wood Close* 1726, *Wing's Close otherwise Wood Close* 1785, *Wing's Close* als. *Wood Close* 118, *Wings Close alias Wood Close* 118 (*v. Wing's Close infra*), *William Roulats Wood Close Meadow* 1726, *Beyond Wood Close* 1729, *Lower* -, *Middle* -, *Upper Wood Close* 1785, all adjoining Armley Wood in Exton); Under Wood (*Underwood* 118, adjoining Hambleton Wood).

(b) *Allins Close* 1729, *Allens Close* 118, *Allen's Meadow* 118 (John *Allen* in possession in 118); *Bankes Close* 1672; *John Bloodeths Barn Close* 1726, *Royce Barn Close* 1758 (with the surn. *Royce*), *Barn Close* 1792; *Barn Ground* 1785, 118 (*v.* **grund**); *Beclane* 1495, 1540, *Bekelane* 1526, *Beklane* 1540 (*v.* **bekkr, lane**, cf. *Henbecke infra*); *Benetshouse* 1675, 1676 (with the surn. *Bennett*, cf. John *Bennet*, - *Benytt* 1522 MilS, 1524 SR of Oakham and Rafe *Benet* 1524 ib, also of Oakham); *Berridges Great Close* 118, *Berridges Meadow* 1785, 118 (Widow *Berridge* lived in Hambleton 118); *Berryhill* 1626, *Berie hill* 1629 (prob. 'the hill where berries grow', although 'the hill with the fortified site' is poss.; there is a moated site at SK 923 072, *v.* **berige, burh** (**byrig** dat.sg.), **hyll**, and cf. the following f.n.); *Berycroft* 1495, *Berecroft* 1526, *Berycrofte* 1540 (prob. 'the croft where berries grow', although 'the croft at the fortified site' is poss., *v.* **berige, burh** (**byrig** dat.sg.), **croft**, cf. *Berryhill supra*); *Bingham's Close* 1785, 118, *Binghams* - 118 (with the surn. *Bingham*); *Birdin Close* 1729 (with the surn. *Burden*); *Blewits Close* 1785, 118, *Blewets* - 118 (from the family name of John *Blewett* 1675 and Richard

Blewett c1685); *John Bloodeth's Meadow* 1726, *Bloodworths Close* 1747, *Bludworth's* -, *Bloodworth* - 1748 (Thomas *Bloodworth* is cited as the previous owner in 1748); *le Blynde Lane* 1549 Pat, *the Blynde Lane* 1611 ('the lane with a dead end', *v.* **blind, lane**); *Bortolphs Close* c1685 (apparently the saint's name *Botolph*, Hambleton church is dedicated to St Andrew but the now ruined medieval chapel of neighbouring Empingham was dedicated to St Botolph and this f.n. prob. alludes to an endowment for the chapel's maintenance); *Bowling Green* 1729, 1785, 118 (for the sport of bowls, *v.* **bowling, grēne**^{2}); *Bradleyes homeplott* 1653, *Bradleys farm* 1686 (with the surn. *Bradley*, cf. Thomas *Bradley* 1522 MilS, 1524 SR of Hambleton, *v.* **home, plot**); *Bradshaw Close* 1729, *Bradshaws* -, *Bradshaw's* - 118 (with the surn. *Bradshaw*); *John Friers Brake Close* 1726, *Brake Close* 118 (*v.* **bræc**^{1}); *Breeches* 1626, *Breaches* 1629, *the Breaches* 1653, 1692, *ye Breaches* 1675, 1676, *the Briaches alias Cowpasture* 1662, *the Breaches or Cow pasture* 1663, *the Breeches or Cow Pasture* 1719 ('land broken up for cultivation', *v.* **brēc**; the arable was obviously later given over to pasture); *John Roulats Bridge Close* 1726, *Bridge Close* 1758, 1792, 118, *Hobs brigg Close* 1729, *Hobb's Bridge Close* 1785, *Hobs* -, *Hobbs* - 118 (with the surn. *Hobbs*), *Brigfurlong* 1727, 1735, *Bridge Furlong* 1760, 118, *Bridge Meadow and Lane* 1792 (*v.* **brycg**); *Bridges Meadow* 1758, 1785 (Widow *Bridges* was resident in Hambleton in 1726); *John Bloodeths Broom Close* 1726, *Broom Close* 1758, 1785, 1798 (*v.* **brōm**); *Brown's Close* 1785, 118, *Browns* - 118; *Burgess's Close* 1785, 118, *Burgess* - 118 (with the surn. *Burgess*, cf. William *Burges* 1522 MilS, 1524 SR, - *Burgeys* 1525 ib of Hambleton); *Burleigh parke wall* 1659 (referring to the neighbouring park of Burley on the Hill, *v.* Burley); *Bush Close* 1729, *Little Bush Close* 118; *Bushcrofts* 1735, 1760 (*v.* **busc, croft**); *Buttocks Close* 118 (alluding to the contours of the land, reminiscent of the human posterior, *v.* **buttuc**); *Chantry Close* 1685, 1690, 1795, *le Chanterie House* 1549 Pat, *the Chauntrey house of Whitwell scituate in Hambleton Magna* 1632, *the Chantry house* 1684 Wright (*v.* **chaunterie**; Whitwell parish adjoins to the north-east); *Cheesecake Close* 1626 (1729), *Cheescake close* 1635, *Wm. Collingtons Cheesecake Close* 1726, *East* -, *West Cheese Cake Close* 1792 (dial. *cheesecake* is used of the fruit of such wild plants as the common mallow (*Malva sylvestris*) or the bird's foot trefoil (*Lotus corniculatus*)); *Chisledine's Close* 1785, 118, *Cheseldines Close* 118, *Chesledine's Meadow* 1785, *Cheseldines* - 118 (Anthony *Cheseldine* lived in the parish in 1653); *Christophers Close* 1716 (Goody *Christopher*'s holding in 1716); *Cooks Close* 1747, 1758, *Cookes* - 1748, 1795; *J. Roulats Copy Close* 1726, *Coppie Close* 1758, *Copy* - 1785, *Coppice* - 1792, *Coppice Meadow* 1792 (*v.* **copis**); *Cordwell Close* 1729, 118, *Cordwell Lower Close*, - *Upper* - 1785, 118 (*v.* **cald, wella**); *Lower Cottage Close* 118, *Reeve's Cottage Close* 1785, *Reeves* -, *Reeves's* - 118, *Swanson's Cottage Close* 1785, 118, *Swansons* - 118 (cf. John- and Richard *Swanson* 1522 MilS of Mkt.

Overton), *Woodcock's Cottage Close* 1785, 118, *Wood Cocks* - 118 (cf. George *Woodcock* 118 of Hambleton); *cottiers close* 1653, *ye Cottiers Close* 1675, 1676, *Cottyers Close* 1692, *Cottager's Close* 1700, 1781, *Cottagers* - 1729, 1785, 118 (*v.* cottere, cotager); *a close called Dalbies* 1626 (1729), *Dalbies Close* 1635 (from the surn. *Dalby*); *Dwpwelleholmes* 1338 Ipm (the first el. of this unsupported form may represent Scand *djúpr* 'deep', *v.* dēop, djúpr, wella, holmr); *John Bloodeth's Dry Close* 1726, *Dry Close* 1758, 1785 (*v.* drȳge); *theste feild* 1598, *ye E. feild'* 1675, 1676 ('the east field', one of the great open-fields of the village, *v.* ēast, feld); *Egleston Meere* 1659, *Egletonmeere* 1675, *Egleton Meer* 1676 (*v.* (ge)mǣre; Egleton parish adjoins to the west); *Ewes Close* 1632, 1632 (1729) (*v.* eowu); *Farr Close* 1729 ('the distant close', *v.* feor); *the Five Closes* 1632 (*v.* fīf); *Flower Lands* 1585 (named from the family of John *Flower* 1585 and John *Flowers* 1632, *v.* land); *Edward Lees Furr Close* 1726, *Furr Close* 1729 (*v.* feor); *Furze Close* 1785, 1792, 118, *Furry Close* 1729, *Furzy Close* 1785, 118, *Furze Meadow* 118 (*v.* fyrs, fyrsig); *Fryer's Close* 118 (cf. John- and Francis *Fryer* of Hambleton 118); *Georges Lane Close* 1785; *Gibbs Bitt* 1632, *Gibbs Pitt* 1632 (1729) (*v.* bit); *Girnam* 1685, *Girnholme alias Girnam* 1690, *Gernholm al's Girnam* 1690, *Girnholm* 1735, *Girn Holm Close* 1772 (the first el. is difficult, but perh. grēne[1] 'green', cf. Girnhill YW 2 87, *v.* hamm, holmr); *Berridges Great Close* 1785, 118 (Widow *Berridge* in residence 1785); *Great Close* 118, *Needham's Great Close* 118; *Great Meadow* 1785, 118; *the Green* 1716 (*v.* grēne[2]); *the Harts* 17, *Harts Close* 1686, 1785, 118 (with the surn. *Hart*, cf. Harts Cl in Gunthorpe f.ns. (a) and *Hartes̗ acres* in neighbouring Egleton f.ns. (b); William *Hart* held land in Edith Weston in 1681 *Hotchkin*); *Haunton Meadow* 1785, 118, *Haunton Town Close* 1729 (with the surn. *Haunton v.* tūn); *Henbecke* 1585, 1601, *Henbeck* 1601 ('water-hen stream', *v.* henn, bekkr); *Highway Close* 1729, - *otherwise Long Close* 1785, - *al's Long Close* 118; *a certain place called the hill towne in Hambleton* 1601 (*v.* hyll, tūn); *Peter Hiltons Close* 1632; *Hippisley's Close* 1785, 118, *Hippisley's Piece* 1785, *Hippisleys* - 118 (named from the family of Toby *Hippisly* 1675 and Tobias *Hippisley* 118, *v.* pece); *Hob Close* 1729 (perh. 'close with tussocks or hummocks', *v.* hobb(e), although the surn. *Hobbs* cannot be discounted, cf. Hobs brigg Close (1729) *supra*); *Holdmedow* 1338 Ipm (prob. an early example of holde 'a holding' as in Lincoln's Hold *supra*, *v.* NED *s.v.* hold sb[1], 1, and mǣd); *The Holme* 1785, 118 ·(*v.* holmr); *John Roulats Holy Well Close* 1726, *Holliwell Close* 1758, *Holywell Close* 1785, 1792, *Holywell Meadow* 1792 (*v.* hālig, wella; it is poss. that Holwell *supra* is a later reflex); *Homefield* ('field near home', *v.* home); *hook medows* 1629, *Tomblin's Lower* -, - *Middle* -, - *Upper Hook* 1785, 118, *Tomblins* - 118 (cf. William *Tomblin* 118 of Hambleton) ('a hook, a projecting piece of ground', *v.* hōc); *How bush Close* 1729, *Howbush* - 1785, *Howebush* - 118 (*v.* haugr, busc); *How Close* 1729, *Howes* - 1785, 118, *Howe's* - 118, *Howes Meadow* 1785, 118 (*v.*

haugr); *Hungerford farm* 1686; *Irelands Close* 1785 (from the surn. *Ireland,* cf. Robert *Ireland* 1758); *Jarvice Close* 1729, *Jarvis's* - 1785, *Jarvi(e)s* - 118 (from the surn. *Jarvis,* cf. Henry *Jervis* 1522 MilS, - *Jarves* 1524 SR of Oakham); *Kings pasture* c1685, 1686 (from the surn. *King, v.* **pasture**); *Lamplees* 1626, *lamp leayes* 1629, *Lampeleyes* 1653, *Lamp Layes* 1661, *Lampleys* 1675, 1676, 118, *Lamp Leys* 1729, 1758, 1785, 118, *Nether -, Upper Lampleys* 1727, 1735, 1760, *Long Lampleys* 118, *Round Lampleys* 118, *Bell's Lamp Leys* 1785, 118, *Bells* - 118, *Hippisleys Lampleys* 1785, 118, *Hippisley's* - 118 (Tobias *Hippisley* 118), *Needhams Lampleys* 1785, 118, *Needham's* - 118 (Joseph *Needham* 118), *Lamp Leas Close* 1685, *Lamp Leys* - 1690, *Lampleys* - 1795 (originally land endowed for the upkeep of the altar lamp in the parish church, *v.* **lampe, lēah**); *Lampolmedow* 1338 Ipm ('clay pool meadow', *v.* **lām, pōl¹, mǣd**); *William Collington's Land Close* 1726 (*v.* **land**); *Lane Close* 1729, 1785, 118; *Ley Close* 1729 (*v.* **lēah**); *Little Meadow* 1785, 118; *Long Close* 1781, 1785, 118; *Loves Home Close* 118, *Love's Lower -, - Upper Close* 1785, *Loves* - 118, *Loves Meadow* 118 (from the family name of Christopher *Love* 1785, Thomas- and Jane *Love* 118); *Lower Close* 1785, 118; *Linden Hill* 1653, 1661, 1675, 1676, *Lindon Hill* 1762, *Lyndon Hill* 1785, 118, *Adcock's Lyndon Hill* 1785, 118, *Adcocks* - 118 (Joseph *Adcock* 1762), *Furzy Lindin Hill* 1729, *Furzy Lyndon Hill* 1785, 118 (*v.* **fyrsig**), *Great Lindin hill* 1729, *Great Lyndon Hill* 1785, 118 ('the hill towards Lyndon'; Lyndon parish adjoins to the south); *Manton Field* c1685, *Manton feild* 1686 (Manton parish adjoins to the south-west); *Mare's close* 1632, *Mares Close* 1632 (1729), 1635; *Matthews Meadow* 118; *Mitchell's Piece* 1785, *Mitchell -, Mitchel's* - 118 (William *Mitchell* was resident in the parish in 1675, *v.* **pece**); *Needham's Close* 1785, 118, *Needhams* - 118, *Needham's Meadow* 118 (Joseph *Needham* was resident 118); *the Nether Meadow* 1748; *North brigg* 1729, *North Bridge Close* 1792, *North brig Meadow* 1729 (North Bridge was poss. an earlier name of Fox Bridge, Exton parish, *v.* **norð, brycg**); *North Close* 1785, 1795, 118, *Hobb's North Close* 1785, 118, *Hobbs* - 118 (with the surn. *Hobbs*); *North Meadow* 1785, 118; *Oakham Yard* 1729 (from the surn. *Oakham,* cf. Henrie *Okeham* 1601 of neighbouring Burley, *v.* **geard**); *Oat Close* 1632, 1758, 1785, 118, *Oate Close* 1632 (1729), 1729, *Widow Bridges Oat Close* 1726 (cf. *Bridges Meadow supra*) (*v.* **āte**); *Oatemeale Meadowe* 1650 Cl, 1653, *Oatmealemeadow* 1675, *Oatemeal meadow.* 1676 (poss. with reference to dry, flaky soil, *v.* **ote-mele**); *Palmers Close* 1626 (1729), 1632, 1632 (1729), *Palmer's closes* 1635 (from the surn. *Palmer,* cf. Nicolis *Palmer* 1522 MilS of Langham and Henry *Palmer* 1524 SR of Barrow); *Nether -, Over Parkfield* 1632, 1635, *Nether -, Over Parke Feild* 1632 (1729) (*v.* **park**); *Partition Closes* 1729, - *Close* 1785, *Lower -, Upper Partition Close* 1785, 118 (perh. referring to an early enclosure, but the f.n. may be a later form of *Petitioners Close infra,* at present unexplained); *The Pasture and Meadow* 1792 (*v.* Clarks Cl *supra*); *Percivalls Close* 1716 (Vincent Percivall held this in 1716); *Petitioners Close* 17 (unexplained); *The Pightle* 1785, 118 (*v.* **pightel**); *plashin, plashing* 1628, *Plashin Wood* 1628 (either 'the meadow with a pool' or 'the pool place', *v.* **plæsc, eng, -ing²**); *Plowright's Close* 118 (Widow *Plowright* was resident in Hambleton 118); *Posternes close* 1629 (perh. a surn. taken from OFr *posterne* 'a postern-gate', *v.* Reaney *s.n.* Postan; there is no indication that there was once a postern-gate to any fortified building in Hambleton unless the f.n. records an earlier defended manor house, but *postern* is to be noted also in unexplained f.ns. in Brk 1 42 and L 2 56); *The Pound* 1785, 118 (*v.* **pund**); *Punch Leas Closes* 1685, 1690, *Punchleas Close* 1795 (prob. an early instance of *punch* 'a draught horse with thickset body and short legs', unrecorded otherwise until 1813 NED, *v.* **lēah**); *The Ram close* c1630, *Ram Close* 118 (*v.* **ramm**); *widdow Richardsons close* 1653 (a *Widow Richardson* is otherwise recorded in Hambleton in 1675); *Road Ground* 1785, 118 (*v.* **grund**); *Rough Close* 118, *Lower -, Upper Rough Close* 1785, 118, *Rough Meadow* 1785, 118 (perh. later forms for *Ruffs Closes infra*, otherwise **rūh** 'rough'); *Rudkin's Close* 118, *Rudkin's Meadow* 118; *Ruffs Closes* 1729 (Barbara *Ruffe* was resident in Burley c1685); *Salters Lane* 1729 (*v.* **saltere**, cf. Salters Lane in Ryhall and Salter Ford Lane in Ashwell); *Upper -, Sanam Close* 1729, *Sanam's Lower -, - Upper Close* 1785, 118, *Sanams -* 118 (poss. 'water-meadow subject to dispute', *v.* **sænna, holmr**, cf. *Senholme* in Mkt. Overton f.ns. (b) and Sanham House in Frisby Lei 290); *Scantive Acre* 1785, 118 (either 'a unit of land barely an acre in size' or 'an acre with poor yield', from ON **skamt** 'stinted in measure' with the adjective-forming suffix -*ive* 'having a tendency to, having the nature, character or quality of', *v.* **skammr**); *William Collingtons Sheppards Close* 1726, *Shepherds Close* 1758, 1785, *Shepherd's -* 1792; *Six Acres* 118; *Six Leys* 1785, 118 (*v.* **lēah**); *Smythie close* 1626 (1729), 1635 (*v.* **smiððe**); *South Close* 1785, 1795, 118, *Hobb's South Close* 1785, *Hobs South Close, Hobbs -* 118 (from the surn. *Hobbs*); *the sowthe feild* 1598, *the Southfeild* 1653, *South Field* 1729 (one of the great open-fields of the village, *v.* **sūð, feld**); *South Meadow* 1785, 118; *Spencers Close* 1747, 1758, 1785, 1795, *Spencer's -* 1792 (late in the tenure of Wm. *Spencer* in 1748); *Staffords Close* 1747, 1748, 1758, 1795, *Stafford -* 1785, 1792 (with the surn. *Stafford*); *Stimson's Close* 1785, 118, *Stimsons -* 118 (in the tenure of Wm. *Stimson* 1785); *Taylor's Close* 1785, 118, *Taylors -* 118; *Thompsons Meadow* 1785, *Tomsons -, Tomson's -* 118 (in the possession of Thomas *Tomson* 118, cf. *Tomson's Lount* in neighbouring Egleton f.ns. (b)); *Thornborow Hill* 1661 ('hill or mound covered by thorn-bushes', *v.* **þorn, beorg**); *thorny close* c1630 (*v.* **þornig**); *Toby's Close* 1785, 118, *Tobys Close and Meadow* 118 (cf. *Toby* Hippisly 1675 and *Tobias* Hippisley 118 of Hambleton); *Tomblin's Yard* 1785 (Thomas *Tomblin* lived in Hambleton in 1785, *v.* **geard**); *one close next Tookeys* 1675 (cf. Nehemiah *Tookey* 1688 *Anc* of Uppingham); *Towels Close* 118; *the Towneship meadow* c1630 (*v.* **tūn-scipe**);

Turners Close c1685, 1686, 17; *Twelve Acre Close* 1729, *Twelve Acres* 1785, 118; *Tyler's Close* 1785, 118, *Tylors* - 118 (cf. Tyler's Homestead in neighbouring Lyndon f.ns. (a)); *Upper Close* 1785, 118; *Vynes farm* 1686 (with the surn. *Vine*, cf. John *Vine* 1685 *Anc* who held land in Bisbrooke); *Wall Gressons* 1650 Cl, *Wallgressings* 1675 (evidently 'the grassy places at the wall', *v.* **wall, gærs, -ing**[2] and cf. Wall Cl *supra*; the wall may be *Burleigh parke wall supra*); *Walkers Close* 118, *Walker's* - 118 (in the tenure of Elizabeth *Walker* 118); *the Waste* 118 (*v.* **waste**); *Water Close* 1729, 118 (beside R. Gwash); *Watkin's Meadow* 1785, *Watkins* - 118 (Edw. *Watkins* in possession 118); *Wells's Close* 1747, *Wells* - 1748, 1758, 1795 (a rare surn. in Ru, cf. Robert *Wells* 1522 MilS of Stretton); *the west feild* 1598, *the Westfeild* 1675, 1676, 1692, *West field* 1729 (one of the open-fields of the village, *v.* **west, feld**); *Weston Brooke* 1632, *Weston Close* 1792, *Weston Town Close* 1748 (Edith Weston parish adjoins to the south-east, *v.* **brōc, tūn**); *Westwell seeke* 1598, *West Well Spring* 1650 (*v.* **west, wella, sīk, spring**); *White Acres alias Bulbrigg* 1632, 1632 (1729) (in eModE, *white* 'infertile' is contrasted with *black* 'fertile', but dial. *white* is also used of 'dry open pasture', *v.* **hwīt, æcer** and Bull Bridge *supra*); *Whitwell Close* 1792 (Whitwell parish adjoins to the north-east); *the windmill* 1626 (*v.* **wind-mylne**); *Wing's Close* 1729 (with the surn. *Wing*, cf. Widow *Wing* c1685 and *v.* The Wood Cl *supra*); *Woodcocks Close* 1795, 118 (in the tenure of George *Woodcock* 118); *Woodwards Cottage* 1675, 1676; *Wright's Close* 1785, 118, *Wrights* - 118.

Lyndon

LYNDON

Ly-, Lindon(e) 1167, 1197 P, 1202 (p), 1203 Ass (p) *et freq* to
    1543, 1552, 1553 *Conant, -dun(e)* 112 Dane (p), 1205 *FF* (p)
Ly-, Linden' 1535 VE, 1540 *Conant*, 1610 Speed

'The hill with lime-trees upon it', *v.* **lind, dūn**.

GREAT GROUND BARN, cf. *Great Ground Meadow* 1748 *Conant*, *v.* **grund**. LYNDON CHURCH, *Church (St Martin)* 1846, 1863 White. LYNDON HALL, 1841 *Hotchkin*, 1846, 1863 White. This hall was built 1671-3. Its predecessor is recorded as *the manor house* 1601 *Conant*, *manor house of Lyndon* 1662 *ib*, *the Hall* 1612, 1614 *ib*, *v.* **hall, maner**. LYNDON WOOD, 1806 Map, 1840 *TA*. It is *Lyndon Spinney* 1824 O. TOP HALL is *Upper Hall* 1824 ib,

1846, 1863 White, cf. *Upper Hall Home Close* c1794, 1795 *DC.*
WESTON BARN, cf. Weston Cl *infra,* from the name of the
adjacent parish of Edith Weston.

Field-Names

Undated forms in (a) are 1840 *TA;* those dated 1841 are *Hotchkin.* Early forms
dated 1319 and 1335 are *Deed;* those dated 1601, 1605, 1629, 1632, 1634, 1637,
1648, 1652, 1654, 1655, 1658, 1662, 1667, 1679, 1681, 1691, 1704, 1715, 1720, 1738
and 1748 are *Conant;* those of 1612 and 1614 are *Terrier,* whilst those of 1731,
1794, c1794 and 1795 are *DC.*

(a) Three Acre Cl; Allen's Upper Cl, Allen's Nether Cl or West
Dunmore's (*Allens close* 1677 (held by Edward *Allen* 1677), *Greater -, Lesser -,
Dunmore's* 1795, *Nether Tomlyns now Dunmores* c1794 (with the surn. *Dunmore*));
Austin's Cl (1661, *Austins Meadow* 1681 (in the tenure of George *Austin* 1681),
Nether -, Upper Austins c1794; Anthony *Austin* was resident in Lyndon 1612);
Baine's Cl or Sharp's Nether Cl (*Baines's* 1731, 1795, *Baine's* c1794 (John *Baynes*
lived in neighbouring Hambleton in 1605 *Deed*), *Sharps close* 1677 (held by
Robert *Sharpe* of Lyndon 1677)); Baker's Cl (1794, held by Thomas *Barker* (sic)
1794); Barsby's Cl (1794, held by John *Barsby* 1794); Upper Breach, Lower
Breach Mdw (*The Breach* 1601, 1605, 1612, 1634, 1652, 1655, 1658, 1662, c1794,
1795, *the Breche* 1614, *Breache* 1654, *Breach Close* 1634, 1637, 1652, 1654, 1662,
1681, *breche hedge* 1614, *Breach(e) Side, Breatch Side* 1612, *Breache syde, Breche
side* 1614, *v.* **brēc, hecg, sīde**); Bulls Cl (*Bulls* c1794, *Bulls Meadow* 1704, from
the family name of John *Bull* 1785 *Surv,* Widow *Bull* and William *Bull* 118 *ib* of
Hambleton); Cardies Piece (1794, *v.* **pece**); Church Road and Strip (*v.* **strīp**);
Upper Cottage Cl; Elm Tree Homestead (*Elmtrees Homestead* 1794, *v.*
hām-stede); Little -, West Furze Cl (*Furze Close* 1648, 1654, 1658, 1662, 1681,
1715, *furzes close* 1634, *v.* **fyrs**); Goddards Nether Cl, Goddard's Upper Cl or
West Dunmore (with the surn. *Dunmore,* cf. William *Dunmore* 1524 SR of
Barrowden); Goodman's · Nether Cl or Bull's Cl (*Goodmans Close* 1677; John
Goodman in possession 1677, cf. Robert- and Thomas *Goodman* 1522 MilS of
neighbouring N. Luffenham); Grants Cl (1794, cf. Grants Mdw in neighbouring
Normanton f.ns. (a)); The Grove; (West) Upper Hall Cl, Upper Hall Mdw (*v.*
Top Hall *supra*); Hand's Cl (c1794, held by Andrew *Hand* c1794); Hop Yard
(1794, *the Hoppyard* 1654, 1662, *v.* **hop-yard** 'a hop-yard, a hop-garden, an
enclosure where hops are grown'); North -, South -, West Land Cl (*Lande Close*
1634, *Land Close* 1648, 1654, 1658, 1662, 1715, *Walter's Land Close* 1731, 1795

(William *Walter* was in possession in 1795), an enclosure consolidating selions of
a former open-field, *v.* **land**); Lincoln Yard (1795, *Lincolne hold yard* 1677,
Lincoln Houlde 1612; a holding of the Dean and Chapter of Lincoln Cathedral,
cf. Lincoln's Hold in Hambleton f.ns. (a), *v.* **holde, geard**); Love's Nether Cl,
Love's Upper Cl or Peache's Cl (*Loves Close* 1677, *Loues Hose* 1677 (*v.* **hūs**)
(the *Love* family was living in neighbouring Hambleton in the 18th cent., e.g.
Christopher *Love* 1785 *Surv*, Thomas- and Jane *Love* 118 *ib*), *Peaches* 1731, c1794,
1795, *Peaches Meadow* 1748, 1795 (from the surn. *Peach*)); Luffen Great Cl,
Luffen Mdw (*Luffenham alias Lufnam close* 1632, *Luffenham Close* 1648, 1654,
1658, 1662, 1679, 1691, 1738, cf. *Luffenham Hedge* 1612, 1614, *Northluffenham
hedge 1629* (*v.* **hecg**); N. Luffenham parish adjoins to the east); Middle Cl
(Mdw), East -, West Middle Cl or Sharps Cl (*Middle Close* 1648, 1654, 1658,
1662, 1679, *Sharps Close* 1677 (held by Robert *Sharpe* 1677)); East Notwells
1840, 1841, Notwell's NE -, NW -, SE -, SW -, - Middle Ground (*Notwelles,
Nottwelles* 1612, *Notwells* 1614, *Not(t)wells Close* 1629, 1634, 1637, 1654, 1658,
1662, *Notwell Close* 1634, 1681, *another close called Notwells Close* 1681; there is
no Ru evidence for *Notwell* as a surn., so apparently here 'the stream where the
nuts grow', *v.* **hnutu, hnot, wella**, cf. (the) Notwells in neighbouring Edith
Weston f.ns. (a)); Oak Leys, Oak Leys (Little) Mdw (*Oke Leayes, Oak Layes*
1612, *Oake Leaze Close next the Breache* 1654, *Oakelease next the Breach* 1658,
Oak Lease Close next the Breach 1662, *Oak Leyes Meadow* 1679, 'open pasture
with oak trees', *v.* **āc, lēah** and Upper Breach *supra*); The Park, Park Hill (*The
Park* 1748); Pear Tree Cl (*Paretree close* 1652, *Pearetree Close* 1658, *Peartree -*
1655, 1662, 1720, *Pear Tree -* 1794, *v.* **pertre**); A Piece of Ground on the South
Side of the river Chater Open to the Parish of Pilton (cf. *the feild towards
Pilton* 1633; Pilton parish adjoins to the south); Pinfold Cl (1652, 1654, 1655,
1658, 1662, 1794, *v.* **pynd-fald**); Ricks Cl (*v.* **hrēac**); Sharps Upper Cl (*v.*
Baine's Cl *supra*); Sidneys Homestead (*v.* **hām-stede**, cf. *Sidney's Close* 1794,
Richard *Sidney* in possession 1794); Smiths Cl (*Smith's Close* 1794); Sponholm or
Pilton Mdw (*Spongham* 1612, 1748, *Sponngham* 1614, *Spongholme* 1677,
Spongholm 1748, 1795, *Spongholm (West and East)* 1731, c1794, *Great Spongham*
1748, *Great Spongholm* 1748; OE *spang* 'a clasp, a buckle' was prob. used
topographically in the same sense as its reflex, dial. *spong* 'a long narrow strip
of ground', but it is uncertain whether we have the earlier or later word here.
The second el. appears to have been originally OE *hamm* 'a water-meadow', but
later varying with and then replaced by Scand *holmr* of the same meaning, *v.*
spang, hamm, holmr); Townsend Mdw (1795, *Townsend Meadow or Path Close*
1794, *Townsend Close* c1794, *v.* **tūn, ende**[1]); Tyler's Homestead (with the surn.
Tyler, cf. *Tyler's Close* in Hambleton f.ns. (b), *v.* **hām-stede**); Near Upper Cl,
Upper Cl Garden, Upper Cl or Cottage Cl, Upper Cl or West Devits (*Great*

Dewit's 1731, c1794, *Upper Dewit's* 1731, *Upper Dewit's now East Dewit's* c1794, *East Dewit's* 1795, *West Dewit's* c1794, 1795, from the Dutch surn. *de Witt*, no doubt a legacy of the presence of Dutch drainage engineers following Cornelius Vermuyden in the East Midlands in the 17th cent.); Walter's Far -, - Middle -, - Nether Cl, Walter's Orchard (*Walters Close* 1677, *Walters Hose* 1677 (v. **hūs**) (both in the possession of Norwich *Walters* 1677), *Walters Nether* -, - *Upper Close* 1720 (in the possession of William *Walters* 1720), *Walters Orchard* 1794 (held by a later William *Walters* 1794)); Water Mdw (1748, beside R. Chater); West Well Plantation (*Westwell(e)*, *West Well* 1612, *Westwellemedewe* 1335, 'the west stream', v. **west, wella, mǣd**); Little -, Middle -, South Weston Cl 1840, Weston Cl 1841 (*Weston Close* 1648, 1654, 1658, *Weston close feild* 1662; Edith Weston parish adjoins to the north-east); Wheat Cl; Lower -, Upper Wing Bridge Cl (*Wingbridge, Wyng bridge* 1612, *Winge Bridge* 1629, *Wingebridge furlong* 1614, *Wing-land bridge Leyes* 1612 (v. **lēah**), *Wingbridge Close* 1654, 1662, 1679; in the extreme south-west corner of the parish at SK 897 037, a small bridge crosses R. Chater into Wing parish, v. **brycg**; (note that *pontis de Veynge* 1409 PRep, cited for Crown Well Bridge in adjoining Manton, may rather be an early reference to this bridge)); Woodward Gorse 1806 Map (v. **gorst**) (*Woodwards Close* 1794, cf. *Woodwards Cottage* 1675 in adjoining Hambleton f.ns. (b)).

(b) *Acre Rigges* 1612 (v. **æcer, hrycg**); ye *Arbour* 1612 (v. **erber**); ye *Backehouse land* 1612 (v. **bæc-hūs**); *Bannill dale* (v. **dalr**), *Bannill hill* 1614 (originally 'hill where beans are grown', v. **bēan, hyll**, with a later *hill* added after the meaning of the compound had been forgotten); *Blackstones* 1614 (presumably referring to the nature of the soil , v. **blæc, stān**); *Bollands Meadow* c1794 (prob. from the surn. *Bolland*, cf. John *Bolland* 1522 MilS of S. Luffenham); *Breaky Close* 1748 (v. **bræc**[1], **-ig**[3]); *Bridge Close* 1704, *Brig close* 1748 (v. **brycg**); *Brimlands* 1614 ('selions at the margin' of something such as water, v. **brimme, land**); *the Broade, the Brode* 1614 ('a broad stretch of ground, a broad cultivation strip in the common field', v. **brǣdu**); *the broad bushe* 1614 (either 'scrubland at *the Broade*' and referring to the previous f.n. or 'broad patch of scrubland', v. **busc**); *the brook(e)* 1612, 1614, ye *brooke* 1612, *the Brook* 1748 (v. **brōc**); *Bushy Close* 1748 (v. **busshi**); *Buskwells* 1614 ('spring or stream lined with bushes', v. **buskr, wella**; an OE *busc* has been Scandinavianized); *Cattayles* 1612, *Caittells* 1614 (dial. *catstails* may refer to the catkins of hazel or willow or to spires of Timothy Grass (*Phelum pratense*), an important fodder plant); *Schapelfeld* 1335 ('the chapel field', v. **chapel(e), feld**); *Church Yard* 1794; *Cothers Close* 1652, *Cottiers* - 1704, *Cottagers Close* 1658, c1794, *Cottager's* - 1795 (v. **cottere, cotager**); *Cow Pasture* 1654, 1662; (le) *Crosfeld* 1319, 1335 ('the field at the cross', v. **cros, feld**); *Crowebeck waye* 1614 ('the road to Crowbeck, i.e. the stream frequented by crows', v. **crāwe, bekkr, weg**; the second el. is Scand); *Cutskirts* 1614 (v. **cutte², skirt**, cf. Cut Skirt Cl in Ridlington f.ns. (a)); *Drie lees* 1614 (v. **drȳge, lēah**); *Eastern Close* 1795; *East -, Est Feild* 1612, *the feild formerly called East Feild now North and South Feild* 1654, v. **ēast, feld**); *East Meadow* 1748; *Empty House Close* 1794; *Finningley* 1794 (a surn., cf. Richard *Fyn(n)yngley* 1524, 1525 SR of Whitwell); *Forked Bushes, the forked bushes* 1612, *forked bushe* 1614 (evidently alluding to scrubland with a bifurcate spread, v. **forked, busc**); *Furr Close* 1691, 1738, *Furr Close Meadow* 1738 (v. **feor**); *Lyndon Glebe Close* c1794, *the Glebe* 1795 (v. **glebe**); *Gose Roode* 1612, - *Roodes* 1614 (v. **gōs, rōd³**); *Goslyms* 1614 (the surn. *Goslin*, cf. *Goslin(g) Lane* in neighbouring N. Luffenham f.ns. (b)); *Greate Close* 1629, *Great -* 1632, *Walter's great close* 1731, *Walters Great Close* c1794 (a William *Walters* was resident in Lyndon in both 1720 and 1794); *the Green* 1652, *ye Greene* 117 DC (v. **grēne²**); *Greengate(s), Greengate Way* 1612 (v. **grēne¹, gata**); *Greenhill* 1612, *Greenehill* 1612, 1614 (v. **grēne¹, hyll**); *ye Hale* 1612, *the hale mylne yard* 1612 (v. **halh, myln, geard**); *the Halewell* 1612 (v. **halh, wella**); *Hall Gardens* 1794; *the Hall Pen(n), Hallpen* 1612, *the hall pen* 1614 ('the hall fold', v. **hall, penn²**, referring to a hall earlier than either Lyndon Hall or Top Hall which are both of c1670); *the half Handkerchief* 1748 (alluding to a very small plot); *Hawfords yardland* 1654, 1662 (v. *Wymarkes land infra*); *Helpitt dale* 1614, *Helepitt layes* 1612, *Helpitt slade* 1614 (presumably a derogatory 'hell-pit', v. **hell, pytt, dalr, lēah, slæd**); *Heige Meadow, Heigh Meadowe, Hye Meadow(e)* 1612, *Highe Meadowe* 1614 (v. **hēah¹, mǣd**); *ye highway* 1612, *Highway Closes* c1794, 1795, - *Close* 1795 (v. **hēah-weg** 'a main road'); *The Hills* c1794, 1795; *Holme Close* 1704 (v. **holmr**); *Home Close* 1637, 1654 (v. **home**); *Homefeild* 1654, 1662 (v. **home**); *Irelandes house* 1634 (William *Ireland* was resident in Lyndon 1612); *Kirks* 1731, *Kirk's* c1794, 1795 (prob. the surn. *Kirk*, cf. John *Kyrke* 1522 MilS of nearby Morcott, but v. *New Kirke* in Edith Weston f.ns. (b)); *The Lynges* 1612, *the Linges* 1614 (v. **lyng**); *Little Close* 1662; *long brook landes* 1614 (v. **lang, brōc, land**); *Long Landes* 1612, *Longlands* 1614, 1748 (v. **lang, land**); *ye Lords balke* 1612 (v. **hlāford, balc**); *North Luffenham Close* 1677, *West Luffenham Close* c1794, 1795, *Luffenham Close Meadow* 1679, 1681, 1738, 1748, *Luffenham Hedge* 1612, 1614, *Northluffenham hedge* 1629 (v. **hecg**), *Luffenham way(e)* 1612, 1614 (N. Luffenham parish adjoins to the east, *Luffenham Hedge* marking the boundary); *Mans leyes* 1614 (with the surn. *Mann*, cf. William *Man* 1524 SR of Cottesmore, v. **lēah**); *Meadows Close*. 1679; *the Me(e)re* 1612, 1614, *Manton mere* 1614, *Meere furlonge* 1612 (v. **(ge)mǣre**; Manton parish adjoins to the west); *Middle Furlong(e)* 1612, *Midle Furlonge* 1614; *ye Mylne* 1612, *Milne close alias furzes Close* 1634, *Mill Close* 1654, 1662 (v. **myln** and Furze Cl *supra*); *ye halfe Mylnegate* 1612 (referring to a small plot beside the road to the mill, *v.* **half, myln, gata**); *Moore Dale, Moordale* 1612, *More Dale* 1614, *Moore Dale head* 1612, *More dale hadd* 1614 (*v.* **hēafod**) ('the moorland valley', *v.* **mōr**[1], **dalr**); *Nether Forlange* 1612, - *Furlonge* 1612, 1614 (*v.* **furlang**); *Nixons Sponk* 1748 (the surn. *Nixon* with dial. *spong* 'a long narrow strip of ground', *v.* **spang**); *Northfeild* 1614, 1655, *North Feild* 1652, 1654, *Northfeilde* 1658 (*v.* **norð, feld**; created by the division of the old *East Feild supra*); *Ockham Ford* 1612 ('ford on the road to Oakham', *v.* **ford**); *Old Orchard* 1794; *Mistress Ormes House* 1655, *Ormes House* 1658, *Mrs Ormes house* 1662 (John *Orme* was resident in Lyndon 1612); *thovre furlonge* 1614 ('the upper furlong', *v.* **uferra**, cf. *Nether Forlange supra*); *Palmers* 1794 (William *Palmer* resident 1794); *the Parsonage land* 1612, - *lands* 1614, *Parsonage Lees* 1612 (*v.* **personage, lēah**); *Parsons Close* 1654, 1655, 1658, *Parsons swathes* 1614, 1633, (*v.* **persone, swæð**); *Path Close* 1794 (*v.* **pæð**); *Peasehill plott* 1614 (*v.* **pise, hyll, plot**); *Pegs House* 1704 (presumably the surn. *Pegg* rather than the pers.n. *Peg*, pet-form of Margaret); *the Pen* 1634, *the Penn End* 1612 (*v.* **penn**[2], **ende**[1]); *Rushey Banke* 1612 (*v.* **riscig, banke**); *the Sandes* 1614 ('sandy ground', *v.* **sand**); *Shelakers Close* 1794 (Mr R. *Shelaker* was resident in Lyndon 1794); *South Feild* 1652, 1654, 1655, *Southfeilde* 1658 (*v.* **sūð, feld**; created by the division of the old *East Feild supra*); *the Spinney* 1655, 1658, 1662 (*v.* **spinney**); *ye Stonepittes* 1612 (*v.* **stān-pytt**); *Nether Tomlyn's* 1731, *Nether Tomlyns now Dunmores* c1794, *Upper Tomlyn's* 1731, c1794 (Thomas *Tomblin* was resident in neighbouring Hambleton in 1785 *Surv; Dunmore* is a surn., cf. William *Dunmore* 1524 SR of Barrowden); *The Town* c1794, *The Town Close* 1795, *the towne streete* 1677 (*v.* **strǣt**) (referring to the village itself, *v.* **tūn**); *the Water gutter, the gutter* 1614 (*v.* **wæter, goter**); *Westfeelde, Westfeild* 1612, *West Feild* 1614, 1633 (one of the open-fields of the village, *v.* **west, feld**); *Weston mere syde* 1614 ('(land) beside Edith Weston parish boundary', *v.* **(ge)mǣre, sīde**); *Weston Way* 1614 (Edith Weston parish adjoins to the north-east); *the Whites* 1614 (in eModE, *white* 'infertile' is contrasted with *black* fertile', although dial. *white* was used of dry open pasture, *v.* **hwīt**); *the Windmilne, - Wyndmilne* 1614 (*v.* **wind-my/ne**); *Wing Close* 1648 (Wing parish adjoins to the south-west); *the Wrinckles* 1612, 1614, *ye Wrinkles* 1612 (*v.* **wrinkel** 'a slight narrow ridge'); *Wymarkes land, Wymarkes yardland* 1634, *Wymarkes alias Hawfords yardland* 1654, 1662 (*v.* **gerd-landes** 'a square measure of a quarter of a hide' (about 30 acres); cf. Anthony *Wymarke* 1572 PR of neighbouring N. Luffenham and Mr *Halford* 1655 of Lyndon).

Manton

MANTON

Mannatonam 1120-9 Reg, Manneton 1123-9 CartAnt, 1209-19
    RHug (p)
Manatona ?1131 Reg, 1130-3 France
Manenton' 1275 RHug
Manetun' 1218 For, -ton(e) 1219 RHug et passim to 1278
    RGrav
Manton(e) 1244 Cl, 1263 Ass et passim to 1345 Hazlerigg (p)
    et freq to 1610 Speed
Maynton 1579, 1683 FF

The first element is probably the OE pers.n. Manna. For the
Ru, Nt and W examples of Manton, Ekwall DEPN prefers OE
(ge)mæne 'common, communally owned', but for the Ru p.n., early
spellings with nn and the surviving gen.sg. of the 1275 form favour
the pers.n. Of the Manton in Nt, Gover, Mawer and Stenton note,
'Ekwall's suggestion (DEPN) 'common tun' (from OE (ge)mæne
'common') is, from the historical point of view, most unlikely', v. Nt
107. Their stricture applies here also, hence 'Manna's farm', v.
tūn.

LUFFEWYKE (lost). In 1401 Cl, the manor of Manton is called
Luffewyke maner. Recorded for Manton also are Luffwick 1325
VCH (p) and Luffwyk 1330 ib (p). It is uncertain whether the
manor simply takes its name from a Luffwyk family or whether both
the name of the family and the name of the manor represent an
otherwise unrecorded farmstead in Manton. If the latter is the
case, we have 'Luffa's dairy farm', v. wīc. The relationship of such
a site to nearby (North) Luffenham, 'Luffa's village', would then be
significant and Luffewyke as a settlement name may thus predate
Manton.

BLUE BALL P.H. (lost), 1846 White, 1850 Slater. CHANTRY
(lost), 1846, 1863 White, v. chaunterie. CROWN WELL BRIDGE
is probably from OE crumb-wella 'crooked stream' with reference
to the twisting of R. Chater along this stretch, cf. the Croome in

f.ns. (b) *infra*. An earlier bridge at this site on the Manton-Wing
boundary may be referred to in *ad pontem sub Manetun'* 1218 For
and *pontis de Veynge* 1409 PRep, *v.* **crumb, wella, brycg**. FOX
COVERT, cf. *Cover Field* 1943 *Map*, *Covert Close* 1943 *ib*, *v.*
cover(t). HORSE AND JOCKEY P.H., 1846, 1863 White.
MANTON CHURCH, *Church (St Mary)* 1846, 1863 ib. MANTON
HALL is *Manton House* 1846 ib. MANTON LODGE (- FM 6"),
Manton Lodge 1824 O. THE PINFOLD (local), 1749 *Terrier*, *v.*
pynd-fald. STOCKS HILL was the site of the village stocks - VR,
v. **stocc**. STONEFIELD FM. WELLFIELD. THE WOODEN
HO.

Field-Names

The undated forms in (a) are 1943 *Map*. Those dated 1920 are *Deed*. The
undated forms in (b) are 1749 *Terrier*, early forms dated 1730 and 1753 are *Bir*
and those of 1772 and 1774 are *Deed*.

(a) Four Acres, Seven -, Nine -, Fourteen -, The Twenty-seven -,
Thirty-five Acres; Ball's Mill *(Balls Mill, - Furlong* 1749, from the surn. *Ball*, *v.*
myln); The Barn Cl 1920, Top Barn Cl 1943; Black Mdw (poss. eModE *black*
'fertile' in contrast to *white* 'infertile'); Bottom Fd, - Mdw; Bridge Fd; Chestnut
Tree Fd; Corner Fd; Cricket Fd (alluding to the game of cricket); Eayr's Far Fd
(with the surn. *Eayr*; Edwin *Eyre* was resident in Preston 1877 White, cf. Eayr's
Five Acre, - Eight Acre etc. in adjoining Martinsthorpe f.ns. (a))); Far Mdw;
Fowler's Middle Fd (cf. Roger *Fowler* 1611 *Conant* and William *Fowler* 1653
Deed, both of neighbouring Hambleton); Glaziers (the surn. *Glazier*); Glebe (*v.*
glebe); Holbrooks; Hovel Fd (*v.* **hovel**); Bottom -, Top Langholmes *(Long
Holm(e), Longholm* 1749, 'the long water-meadow', *v.* **lang, holmr**); Left-Hand -,
Right-Hand Manton Fd (perh. alluding to parts of the great North Field before
enclosure); Middle Fd; Bottom Milking Cl (*v.* **milking**); Mill Cl 1920, 1943, Mill
Pit 1943; (Big) Mires; Pebbles *(the Pibbles* 1749, *v.* **pibbil**); First Ploughed Fd;
North Redlands and South Redlands forming one close called Redlands 1920,
West Redlands South, - North 1920 *(Redlands, Redland Close* 1749, 'red land(s)',
alluding to the colour of the soil, *v.* **rēad, land**); Robinson's; Seed Cl (an area
of sown grass, *v.* **sǣd**); Shoulder of Mutton (so called from its shape); East -,
West Sideholmes, Sideholmes Mdw 1920 *(Side Holm* 1749, *v.* **sīd, side, holmr**);
Spinney Fd; Stone Bridge; Stone Cl; Store Pit; Story's Fifty Acre, - Five Acre
(with the surn. *Storey*, cf. Arthur John *Storey* 1932 Kelly, grazier); Taylor's (the

surn. *Taylor*, cf. Henry and Nathaniel *Taylor*, resident in Manton 1877 White); Top Fd; Townend Cl (*v.* **tūn, ende**[1]); Tyler's Fourteen Acre (named from the *Tyler* family, cf. George and Henry *Tyler* of Manton 1877 ib and Tyler's Homestead in Lyndon f.ns. (a), *Tyler's Close* in Hambleton f.ns. (b)); West Holme 1906 *Anc*, 1939 *Deed*, Westholme 1932 Kelly (*the Holmes* 1795 *Anc*, *v.* **holmr**); Wilson's Seven Acre, - Nine Acre (from the surn. *Wilson*, cf. George *Wilson* 1932 Kelly, grazier); Wing Mdw (Wing parish adjoins to the south-west).

(b) *the Great Allottment* 1774 (referring to land allocated to a tenant at enclosure in exchange for holding and rights under the open-field system, *v.* **allotment**); *Amos Butt* (*v.* **butte**); *Appletree Bushes, Appletree Furlong, Appletree Slade* (*v.* **æppel-trēow, busc, slæd**); *Beanhill* (*v.* **bēan, hyll**); *Blind Roods* ('secluded or hidden roods of land', *v.* **blind, rōd**[3]); *Bowling Leys Furlong* ('(furlong beside) the meadows where bowls are played', *v.* **bowling, lēah**); *Bradleys yard Land* 1753 (with the surn. *Bradley*, cf. Thomas *Bradley* 1522 MilS, 1524 SR of neighbouring Hambleton, *v.* **gerd-landes**); *the Brakes* (*v.* **bræc**[1]); *Brentley* ('the burnt clearing', *v.* **brende**[2]**, lēah**); *Brightley Bridge, - Hide* (prob. 'bright clearing in woodland', *v.* **beorht, lēah, hīd**); *Broadarse* (alluding to the conformation of the ground, *v.* **brād, ears**); *Brooms Bushes* (from the surn. *Broom*, cf. William *Brome* 1522 MilS, 1524 SR of Wardley and *Brooms Folly* in neighbouring Edith Weston f.ns. (b), *v.* **busc**); *Bullpiece Furlong* (*v.* **bula, pece**); *Burnebys Hedge Furlong* (from the surn. *Burnby*, cf. William *Burnby* and John *Burneby* 1522 MilS, *v.* **hecg**); *Cheseldens Pen* (Francis *Cheselden* held *the Great Allottment supra* in 1774, cf. Richard *Chysylden* 1524 SR, husbandman of Manton, *v.* **penn**[2]); *Clements House* (with an early Ru surn., cf. John -, Thomas - and William *Clement* 1522 MilS of Belton); *the Cow Pasture; the Croome* ('(land in) the bend of the stream', *v.* **crumbe**, cf. Crown Well Bridge *supra*); *Childs Cross Furlong* (*v.* **cros**); *Crosswell Gutter, Crosswell Spring, Crosswell Way, Far Crosswell, - Hill* ('the spring or well with a cross', *v.* **cros, wella, goter, spring**); *Cut(t)grave Leys* (*v.* **cutte**[2]**, græfe, lēah**); *the Dales* (*v.* **deill**); *Deadmore* 'infertile moorland', *v.* **dēad, mōr**[1]); *Deephouse* ('house in a deep hollow', *v.* **dēope, hūs**); *Elbow Leys, Elbow Rood* (*v.* **elbowe, lēah, rōd**[3]); *Elde Stump* (*v.* **ellern, stump**); *Folding Furlong* (*v.* **falding**); *Fulhill, - Close* (the first el. is either *fugol* 'bird' or *fūl* 'foul, dirty, filthy', *v.* **hyll**); *the Gauls* ('the wet places in the field', *v.* **galla**); *Girnham* (in the North Field and referring to the same feature as *Girnam* in adjoining Hambleton f.ns. (b)); *Greenhill, - Furlong, v.* **grēne**[1]**, hyll**); *Greengate Way* ('the grassy road', *v.* **grēne**[1]**, gata**); *Hangcock Well Gutter* (with the surn. *Hancock, v.* **wella, goter**); *the Hole* (*v.* **hol**[1]); *Hollowgate Way* ('the road in the hollow', *v.* **holh, gata**); *Holywell Gutter* (*v.* **hālig, wella, goter**, cf. *Crosswell Gutter supra*); *the Homestead or Old Inclosure* (*v.* **hām-stede, inclosure**); *Julians*

Headland (from the surn. *Julian,* cf. *Julians Rode* in Leighfield f.ns. (b), *v.* hēafod-land); *Lamas pastures* 1730 (*v.* lammas); *Lambert Slade* (from the surn. *Lambert,* cf. Robert *Lamperte* 1525 SR of Morcott, *v.* slæd); *Langley balk* (*v.* lang, lēah, balca); *Linden Gate, Linden Way* ('the road to Lyndon', *v.* gata, weg; Lyndon parish adjoins to the east); *Linden Hill* ('the hill towards Lyndon', *v.* hyll); *the West field or Martinsthorpe Field* (one of the great open-fields of the village; Martinsthorpe parish adjoins to the west, *v.* feld); *Martinsthorpe hades (v.* hēafod); *Meadow Balk* (*v.* balca); *Meadow Shank(e)* (*v.* scanca); *the Mear* (*v.* (ge)mǣre); *Mett Meadow* ('meadow at the boundary', *v.* mete, mǣd); *Mill Furlong* (*v.* myln), *Mill hades* (*v.* hēafod); *Millholme Leys* (*v.* myln, holmr, lēah); *Moorgate, - Furlong* (*v.* mōr[1], gata); *Nether Furlong,* (*the*) *North Field* 1749, 1772, 1774 (one of the open-fields of the village, *v.* norð, feld); *Old Inclosure* (*v. the Homestead supra*); *the old pasture, - hedge* (*v.* ald, pasture, hecg); *the Patch of Grass* (*v.* pacche); *Peasehill, - Slade* (*v.* pise, hyll, slæd); *Priest Gore* ('the priest's point of land'. *v.* prēost, gāra); *Prestons Yard Land* 1730 (with the surn. *Preston,* cf. Robert *Preston* 1522 MilS, *v.* gerd-landes); *Rascalhill* (ME *raskayl* was used of 'a young deer'; otherwise, but less likely, *rascal* here may allude to mischievous children, *v.* raskayl, hyll; cf. however *Raskellgate* L 2 115 for which the surn. *Raskell* < *?Raskelf* is postulated); *Redset* (prob. 'the fold on red soil'; because of the need for dry shelter for animals, *hrēod* 'a reed, a reed-bed' is unlikely as the first el. here, *v.* rēad, (ge)set); *Redwell* (prob. with hrēod 'a reed, a reed-bed', although since Manton stands on an outcropping of ironstone, rēad 'red' cannot be discounted, *v.* wella and cf. Redwells in neighbouring Gunthorpe f.ns. (a)); *Shortham piece* (*v.* sc(e)ort, hamm, pece); *Short Sett, Shortsett, Shortset Furlong* (*v.* sc(e)ort, (ge)set); *South Field or Wingfield* 1749, *South Field* 1749, 1772, 1774 (one of the open-fields of the village, lying towards Wing parish which adjoins to the south-east, *v.* sūð, feld); *Susanna Smith's Quarter Land* 1753 (computed to be a quarter of one yardland); *the thorow Land* (*v.* þurh, land); *the Tyth Meadow* (*v.* tēoða, mǣd), *the Great Tyth Meadow peice* 1774 (*v.* pece); *the upper Furlong* (*v.* upper); *Uppingham Way* ('the road to Uppingham', *v.* weg); *Waterfield Syke, - Furlong, Waterfield Syke Leys* (*v.* wæter, feld, sīk, lēah); *West field or Martinsthorpe Field* 1749, *West field* 1749, 1774 (one of the open-fields of the village lying towards Martinsthorpe parish which adjoins to the west, *v.* west, feld); *Whitehill* (perh. eModE *white* 'infertile' used in contrast to *black* 'fertile', but dial. *white* was also used of 'dry, open pasture', *v.* hwīt); *Wig Acres* (with dial. *wig* 'buttermilk', used of rich pasture); *old Willow Leys* (*v.* ald, wilig, lēah); *Willow Spring* ('spring at the willow(s)', *v.* wilig, spring); *Wing brook leys* (Wing parish adjoins to the south-east, *v.* brōc, lēah); *South Field or Wingfield* (one of the open-fields of the village lying towards Wing parish, *v.* feld); *Wingate, Wing gate* ('the road to Wing', *v.* gata); *Wing Plank Furlong* (ME *planke* is probably used here of a plank bridge crossing Wing Brook; otherwise of 'a thin strip of cultivated land', v. **planke**); *Winnow dale Slade* (prob. for *Willow dale Slade,* cf. *old Willow Leys* and *Willow Spring supra,* v. **wilig, dalr, slæd**); *Wipesnest, the Wipes nest* ('the wasps' nest', v. **wæps, nest** and cf. *Wipesnest fur'* in Egleton f.ns. (b)).

Martinsthorpe

MARTINSTHORPE
> *Martinestorp'* 1206 Cur (p), 1211 P (p), 1218 For, 1230 Cur
> (p), 1250 Cl, *-thorp(e), -yn-* 1209 *For,* 1272 *FF,* 1274 RGrav,
> 1296 *SR et passim* to 1428 FA
> *Martinstorp'* 1254 Val, 1286 *Ass, -thorp(e), -yn-* 1286 *ib,* 1327
> *SR,* 1463 *FF,* 1610 Speed, *Martensthorp(e)* 1497 *Braye,*
> 1510 LP, 1536 Denb
> *Mastorpe* 1510 LP, *-troppe* 1598 *FF, -trop* 1720 *Recov, -thorp*
> 1463 *FF,* 1506 Cl, 1510 LP, *-thrope* 1608 *Bir*

The name's present form means 'Martin's outlying farmstead', v. **þorp**. However, recorded also are the spellings *Martinestoch* 1176 P (p) and *Martinstok* 1286 *Ass,* 1286 QW, which probably represent an earlier name for the same settlement site, with OE **stoc** 'a place, a religious place, a secondary settlement' as the generic. If so, this name was later reshaped through Scandinavian linguistic influence. The pers.n. *Martin,* originally MedLat *Martinus* and entering OE via the Church, also appears in *Martinsley infra* and in *Martines hó* in the 1046 A.D. charter bounds of Ayston, a village lying some three miles to the south-west. These names clearly represent the same Martin. The earthworks of the deserted medieval village are sited at SK 867 047, v. MER 27-8, BrownArchSites 19.

MARTINSLEY (lost)
> *Martensley ... a passel off my manor off Martynsthorpe* 1536
> Denb, *Martinsley* 1536 ib

'Martin's woodland glade or clearing in woodland', v. **lēah.** This was no doubt the moot-site of the Martinsley Hundred which took its name.

There are obvious problems to be faced with this group of place-names. First, there is the uncertainty of whether *Martinstok*, the name of which survived until at least 1286, refers to the same settlement as Martinsthorpe, whose earliest recording is eighty years earlier than this. *Martinstok* is, of course, first recorded thirty years earlier than Martinsthorpe. Then there is the question of what precisely the *stoc* of *Martinstok* represents. If it were simply 'a secondary settlement', the replacement of OE *stoc* by Scand *þorp*, with the same meaning, is easily understandable. But its compounding with the saint's name *Martin* suggests that *stoc* here could originally have meant 'a religious place', conforming to a pattern of religious associations of *stoc* in English place-names (*v.* Elements *s.v.* **stoc** (2)). The dedications of the churches at Martinsthorpe and Lyndon (both in Martinsley Hundred) were to St Martin, but we do not know from what period these dedications date. However, *Martin* is compounded also in the topographical names *Martines hó* 'Martin's headland', some three miles to the south-west of Martinsthorpe, and *Martinsley* 'Martin's woodland glade or clearing', evidently somewhere within Martinsthorpe's bounds. It is difficult to see in what circumstances such topographical names containing a saint's name could have been created and how a saint could have been associated with as large a tract of land as their locations indicate: but a secular Martin as landowner would present no such problems. It should be noted that Martin was used as an everyday OE personal name. For example, one Martin, a mill owner in *Esctun* in the East Midlands, sold his mill in the years between 972 and 992 (BCS 1130).

The weight of the evidence as we have it at present favours a secular, landowning Martin whose secondary settlement of *Martinstok* had its name reshaped during the thirteenth century by the Scandinavian word for farmstead in the ME dialect of the East Midlands and whose woodland glade or clearing was the meeting-place for the men of the Martinsley Hundred.

Field-Names

Undated forms in (a) are 1943 *Map*. Forms dated 1844 are *TA*. Those dated

1939 are *Deed* (per Mr D. Tew).

(a) Three Acre; The Five Acre 1939, Five Acres 1943; Bottom Eight Acre 1939; Ten Acres Cl 1844; Long Thirteen Acre 1939, 1943; Top Twenty-one Acres; Top Twenty-four Acre 1939; Bottom Cl; Bottom Mdws 1939; Bradshaw's Cl 1939, 1943; Bridge Fd; Briggs's Cl 1844; Clarke's Cl 1939, - Fd 1943, Clark's Thirteen Acre 1943; Close North Part, - South Part 1844; Cramps Cl 1844; Great -, Little Dry Hill 1844 (*v.* dryge); Eayr's Big Cl 1939, - Fd 1943, Eayr's Five Acre, - Eight Acre 1939, - Lane Cl 1939, - Far Mdw, - Near Mdw 1943 (with the surn. *Eayr;* Edwin *Eyre* was resident in Preston in 1877 White); Fox Cover Lane 1939 (runs beside Fox Covert inside Manton parish boundary, *v.* cover(t)); Gwash Mdw 1939 (beside R. Gwash); Hinch's Cl 1939, Finch's - 1943; Home Five Acres (*v.* home); Hop Ground 1844, 1939, West - 1844; Horse Cl North, - South 1844; Hovel Fd (*v.* hovel); Lane Cl; Lawrence's Cl, - Mdw 1844; Little Mdw; Lockwoods Cl and Hop Ground 1844, Lockwoods Mdw 1844 (cf. Lockwood's Mdw in neighbouring Ayston f.ns. (a)); Long Spinney 1939; First -, Middle -, Third Meadow Cl 1844; Middle Cl 1939, 1943; Neals Nine Acres; New Plantation 1939; North Ground 1844, - or Willow Cl 1943; Oak Tree Cl; The Park 1844, Bottom -, Top Park 1943; Road Piece 1844 (*v.* pece); Royce's Cl, - Mdw 1844 (a Ru surn., cf. George *Royce* 1788 OR of Oakham); Upper Sheilds (sic) 1844, Lower Shields Cl East Part, - West Part 1844 (to be associated with the *Sheild* family, cf. Edward - and William *Sheild* 1713 *Anc* of Preston, Robert *Sheild* 1846 White); Spinney Cl 1939, 1943; Square Spinney 1939; Three Corner Cl 1939 (alluding to its triangular shape); Top Cl 1844, 1943, - Ground 1943; Willow Cl 1939.

(b) *Martinsthorpe House* 1684 Wright.

Normanton

NORMANTON
   Normanton(e) 1183 P, 1205 RFinib (p), 1234 RHug *et freq* to
       1610 Speed, *Normenton'* 1180 P (p)
   Northmanton 1295 Ipm, *Nortmanton* 1327 *SR*
   Normanneton 1375 Misc

'The farm or estate of the Norwegians', *v.* Norðman (-manna gen.pl.), tūn. The village was depopulated in 1764 when Normanton Park was laid out by Sir Gilbert Heathcote and the inhabitants were moved to Empingham. Earthworks of the old village survived at SK 921 063 until the creation of Rutland Water, *v.* MER 28-9.

THE BELT, *Belt* 1908 *Anc, v.* **belt.** BRACKNELL COTTAGE, BRACKNELL HO. (both 6"), *Bracknell House* 1935 *ib,* cf. *Bracknel(l) Lane* 1726 *ib,* 1824 *Terrier, John Bloodeth's Braknell* 1726 *Anc* (with the surn. *Bloodworth*). Most likely, the source-name means 'bracken-covered hill', *v.* **brakni, hyll,** although OE *halh* 'a nook, a corner of land' is possible as its second element. FISH POND, *the Pond* 1661, 1662 *Deed, v.* **ponde.** The pond was a broadening of R. Gwash at SK 929 066, now drowned by Rutland Water. NORMANTON CHURCH, *Church (St Matthew)* 1846, 1863 White, now disused and embanked from Rutland Water. NORMANTON GARDENS is *Hall Garden* 1726 *Anc.* NORMANTON HO., 1684 Wright; it is *the Mannor house* 1662 *Deed, Normanton Hall* 1908 *Anc, v.* **maner.** The great Palladian house was pulled down after the Second World War. NORMANTON LODGE, 1824 O, *The Lodge* 1906 *Anc.* NORMANTON PARK, 1801 Map, *the Park* 1758 *Surv,* 1906 *Anc.* OAK FM. RECTORY, 1846, 1863 White. STOKE'S SPINNEY, *Stokes Spinney* 1908 *Anc.*

Field-Names

Forms dated 1824 in (a) are *Terrier;* those dated 1906, 1908 and 1935 are *Anc* and those of 1943 are *Map.* Early forms dated 1631 and 1684 are *Terrier;* those dated 1661 and 1662 are *Deed;* those of c1700 are *Letter;* those of 1702 and 1758 are *Surv;* those of 1661 (1729), 1726, 1739, c1750 and 1785 are *Anc;* those dated 18 are *Plan.*

(a) Thirteen -, Eighteen -, Twenty-four -, Twenty-six Acre Cl 1943; Alexander's Fm 1824; Alfin's House 1824; Allen's Fm 1824; Black Spinney 1908; Church Cl 1935, 1943, East -, West - 1906; Field Cl 1906; Glovers Fd 1908; Grants Mdw 1906 (cf. Grants Cl in neighbouring Lyndon f.ns. (a)); the Heath 1824, 1906 (*Normanton Heath, Heath Furlong* 1726, *v.* **hæð**); Iliff's House 1824; King's House 1824 (cf. *Kings Pasture* in neighbouring Hambleton f.ns. (b)); Lodge Fd 1943 (*v.* Normanton Lodge *supra*); Lucas's House 1824 (Thomas *Lucas* was miller of adjoining Empingham 1791-1811 - WR); High Moor 1943; Newman's Fd

1908, 1943 (named from the *Newman* family, cf. Joseph *Newman* 1877 White); Old · Plantation 1824; Paddock 1943 (*The Paddock* 1726, *the Paddock Crofts* 1758, 1785 (*v.* **pearroc**); Park Mdw 1908, 1943, Park Wall 1906, - Fd 1943 (*v.* Normanton Park *supra*); Pleasure Grounds 1908; Three Cornered Cl 1908 (with reference to its triangular shape); Tewson's House 1824 (cf. Tewson's Fm in Edith Weston f.ns. (a)); New Wood Fd 1908, 1943 (*v.* New Wood in Empingham parish).

(b) *Widow Bridges Meadow* 1726 (*Widow Bridges* was resident in adjoining Hambleton 1726 *Anc*); *Bridle Gate Close* 1739 (*v.* **brigdels, gata** and cf. *The Twenty Acres infra*); *Butt Furlong* 1726 (*v.* **butte**); *Carryers Close* 1661, 1661 (1729), 1758, *Carriers Close* c1700, 1726, 1758, 18, *Carriers Meadow* 1726, 1758, 1785, 18 (with the surn. *Carrier*); *Clarkes Close* 1758; *Corner Furlong* 1726 (*v.* **corner**); *Cow Pasture* 1726; *ad Crucem* 1296 ChancW (p) (*v.* **cros**); *Old Douecoat, the old Dovecoat* 1758, *Old Dovecote* 1785 (*v.* **dove-cot(e)**); *Duports Close* 1661, 1661 (1729), 1662, *Duport -* 1726, 1758, *Duports Meadow* 1684, *Duport -* 1726, 1758, *Duports Close and Meadow* c1700, 1702, *Duport -* 1785 (with the surn. *Duport*); *East Feild* 1631, *the feild next to Empingham* 1684 (*v.* **ēast, feld**; Empingham parish adjoins to the north-east); *John Bloodeths Empingham Hedg Close* 1726, *Empingham Hedge Close* 1739, *Empingham Hedg Furlong* 1726 (*v.* **hecg**); *Fat(t) Sheep Close* c1700, 1758, *Ne(a)ther -* 1726, 1758, *Upper -* 1726, 1758, 18 (descriptive of rich pasture, *v.* **fætt**); *Middle -, South Field Lane Furlong* 1726 (*v.* **feld**); *Fowlers Close* 1661, 1661 (1729), 1662 (cf. William *Fowler* 1653 *Deed* of neighbouring Hambleton); *Fox hols* 1684, *Foxhole Furlong* 1726 (*v.* **fox-hol**); *Frears Farm in the Park* 1758, *John Friers Meadow* 1726 (a *John Frier* was resident in neighbouring Hambleton in 1726 *Anc*); *John Bloodeths Freemans Close* 1726 (with the surn. *Freeman*, cf. John *Freeman* 1736 *Bir* of Uppingham); *Glebe Close* 1726 (*v.* **glebe**); *Great Field* 1739; *Hall Crofts* 1726, *Hall Yard* 1726, *Close above ye House* c1700, *Close below the House* 1799 (*v.* **hall**; referring to Normanton House *supra*); *Hedge Furlong* c1750 (*v.* **hecg**); *Home Close* 1758, *John Bloodeths Home Close* 1726, *William Collingtons Home Close* 1726 (*v.* **home**); *Hovel Close* 1799 (*v.* **hovel**); *Hunting Gate* c1750 (presumably a gate in the park wall for ease of passage when fox-hunting); *Ketton Way* 1684 (Ketton lies three miles to the south-east); *John Bloodeths Lamass Close* 1726 (*v.* **lammas**); *John Friers Land Close* 1726 (a close consolidating selions of a former open-field, *v.* **land**); *John Bloodeths Lane Close* 1726, *the Lane Close* 1739, (*ye*) *Lane End* 1684, c1750, *Lane Furlong* 1739 (*v.* **lane, ende**[1]); *Lime Kill Furlong* 1726 (*v.* **lim-kilne**); (*the*) *Little Close* 1661, 1662, 1758; *Little Wood Furlong* 1726, *Littlewood Furlong* 1739 (*v.* **lytel, wudu**); (*the*) *Long Furlong* 1684, 1739; *Long Leeds* 1726 (*v.* **lēah**); (*the*) *Mear(e) Close* 1661, 1661 (1729), 1662, 1726 (*v.* **(ge)mǣre**); *Middle Close* 1684,

1799; *Middle Feild* 1631, 1684, - *Field* 1739 (*v.* **middel, feld**); *Mill Close* 1684 (*v.* **myln**); *Neather Furlong* 1684 (*v.* **neoðera**); *North Furlong* 1726; *Outside Furlong* 1726; *Plank Close* 1726 (*v.* **planke**, used either of a narrow strip of cultivated land or of a plank bridge); *John Bloodeths Pasture Close* 1726; *Russell(s) Close* c1700, 1702 (from the surn. *Russell*); *Row Furlong* 1726 (*v.* **rūh**[1]); (*The*) *St Foin Close,* - *Foyn* - c1700, 1726, 1758, *Saint Foin close,* - *Foyn* - 1702, 1785 (the leguminous herb *sainfoin* (*Onobrychis sativa*) was once much grown for fodder); *Short Butt* 1726 (*v.* **butte**); *Short Furlong* 1726; *Short Leeds* 1726 (*v.* **lēah**); *South Furlong* 1726; *John Bloodeths Style Close* 1726, *ye Stile Close* c1750 (*v.* **stigel**); *Top Close* 1799; *John Bloodeths 20 Acre Close* 1726, *ye 20 acr Close* c1750, (*the*) *Twenty Acres or Bridle Gate Close* 1739 (*v. Bridle Gate Close supra*); *Tyke Close* 1726 (*v.* **tike**); *Wad(d) Close* 1726, 1758 (*v.* **wād**); *Wellban(c)ks* 1661, 1662, 1758, 1785, *Well Banks* 1661 (1729), *Welbanks* 1684, 1758, *North -, South Well Bank* 1726 (poss. a surn., cf. Adam *Walbancks* 1634 *Terrier* of Uppingham and John *Wallbanks* c1750 *Anc* of S. Luffenham; otherwise, *v.* **wella, banke**); *Well Close* 1758, *Wells* - 1785; *West Feild* 1631, *the feild next to Weston* (*v.* **west, feld**; Edith Weston parish adjoins to the south and west); *White Wong Furlong* 1726 (*v.* **hwīt, vangr**; in eModE, *white* 'infertile' is used in contrast to *black* 'fertile').

Preston

PRESTON
  Prestetona 1130 P
  Preston(e) 1208 PatR, 1217 ClR, 1222 *MiD et passim* to 1260
    Rut (p), 1263 *Ass*, 1270 *Rut* (p) *et freq* to 1610 Speed, (-
    on the Hulle 1397 Pat), *-tun* 1218 For

'The estate of the priests', *v.* **prēost, tūn**; land set aside for the endowment of clergy. Preston is a hill-top settlement, hence the affix - *on the Hulle, v.* **hyll**.

CROSS LANE, cf. *crucem ad finem oriental' ville de Preston* 1566 *Ct, v.* **cros**. FOX AND HOUNDS P.H. HOLLY FM. KINGFISHER P.H. was until c1975 *New Inn* 1846, 1863 White. PRESTON CHURCH, *Church* (*St Peter and St Paul*) 1846, 1863 ib. PRESTON HALL, *Hall* 1846 ib, 1850 Slater, cf. *terre ... vocat' the halls* 1560 *Ct, the Hall partes* 1648 *Deed, the Hall land* 1708 *ib, Hall Close* 1713 *Anc, v.* **hall, part**. RECTORY is *Rectory House* 1846,

1863 White. WESTFIELD HO.

Field-Names

Undated forms in (a) are 1943 *Map*; those dated 1804 are *Deed*, those dated 1806 are Map and those of 1824 are O. Early forms dated 1634, 1648, 1657, 1665, 1705, 1708, 1746, 1757, 1758, 1763 and 1774[1] are *Deed*; those of 1713 are *Anc*, while those of 1774[2] are *TA*.

(a) Four Acre, Ten Acres (x2), Far -, Twelve Acres; Ackins; Andrews Bush (*v.* **busc**); Ayston Bridge Cl; Barn Fd; Big Fd or Peak's Cl; Bridge Fd, - Mdw (a footbridge crosses R. Gwash here); Brook Mdw; Butcher's Cl; First -, Second -, Third Cant's (cf. Robert *Cant*, one of 'the principal owners of the soil' 1877 White); Coombs (*v.* **cumb**, cf. Coombe Cl in adjoining Ridlington f.ns. (a)); Cow Cl; Cricket Fd (referring to the game of cricket); Nether -, Upper Deepdale 1804 (*v.* **dēop, dalr**, cf. Deepdale in neighbouring Ayston f.ns. (a)); First -, Second Dexter or Pridmore (the surn. *Pridmore*, cf. *Pridmores Pitt* in Uppingham f.ns. (b)); Under Dikes (*v.* **dīk**); Dragon's Hill (prob. from the surn. *Dragon*, cf. *Dracouncrofte* in Tolethorpe (Lt. Casterton) f.ns. (b)); Firs (*the Furze* 1713, *v.* **fyrs**); Fishpond Mdw; Fox Cover (*v.* **cover(t)**); Glaston Road Cl; Gorse Cl (*v.* **gorst**); Great Cl; Headlands (*v.* **hēafod-land**); Home Fm (*v.* **home**); Horse Cl; Hovel Cl (*v.* **hovel**); Lady Spinney (*v.* **hlǣfdige**); Little Mdw; Long Cl; Mill Cl 1804, 1943, Mill Fd 1943 (*v.* Preston Mill *infra*); Oak Tree Mdw; Parker's (named from the *Parker* family, cf. John *Parker* 1846, 1877 White); Pastures (cf. *le neate pasture* 1562 *Ct*, *v.* **nēat, pasture**); Peasehills (*v.* **pise, hyll**); Pen Mdw (*v.* **penn**[2]); The Piece (*v.* **pece**); The Plain (*v.* **plain**); Preston Mill 1824 (a windmill, demolished in 1926 - VR); Reeves (cf. *Reeves's Cottage Close* in Hambleton f.ns. (b)); Rushden (presumably a surn., originally the Nth p.n. Rushden; otherwise 'rush valley', *v.* **risc, denu**); Scotch Fens 1806, Cotch Ferns 1824, Scotch Fen 1943 (*v.* **cot, fenn** and Cotch Platt in Ridlington f.ns. (a); *cotch* is a Ru dial. form of *cot*); New -, Old Seeds (areas of sown grass, *v.* **sǣd**); Side Mdw; Smith's Mdw; Spinney Fd; Bottom -, Top Swashills (*v.* **swash** 'watery'); Ten Lands (a close created by the consolidation of ten selions of a former open-field); Top Cl, - Fd; Top -, Torr's; Top Town Cl (*v.* **tūn**); Uppingham Road Cl 1804; West Meers 1804, - Mere 1943 (*v.* **(ge)mǣre**); Wing Fd (adjoins the boundary with Wing parish to the east), Wing Gorse c1800 Map, 1806 (*v.* **gorst**), Wing Cover 1824 (*v.* **cover(t)**).

(b) *Ann Banbury's Close formerly Brown's Close* 1774[2]; *Mr Basset's Close*

1774[2]; *the demeasne lands* 1758 (*v.* **demeyn**); *the East field* 1774[1]; *Edwards acre* 1713 (*v.* **æcer**); *the kilne howse* 1566 Ct (*v.* **cyln, hūs**); *Medwells Yard Land* 1757 (from the surn. *Medwell, v.* **gerd-landes**); *the North field* 1774[1]; *Pastmore hyde* 1713 (*v.* **hīd**); *the Porters Lodg or Gate house* 1713 (i.e. to Preston Hall); *Preston Leyes* 1634, 1665, 1705, *Preston Leaze* 1746 (*v.* **lēah**); *Sewells Yard Land* 1758 (*v.* **gerd-landes**; William *Sewell* is described as *late of Wardley* in 1758); *the Sixteen leys* 1657 (*v.* **lēah**); *the South field* 1713, 1774[1]; *Thorn hill* 1713 ('hill growing with thorn-bushes', *v.* **þorn**); *Preston vnderwoods* 1665, *Preston Underwoods* 1684 Wright ('(land) beneath the wood', *v.* **under, wudu**); *Robert Watkin's Close formerly Totman's Close* 1774[2].

Ridlington

RIDLINGTON
    Redlinctune 1086 DB, *-ton'* 1275 RH
    Redelington', -yng- 1257 Cl, 1265 Misc, 1286 *Ass*, 1327 *SR et passim* to 1422 Fine
    Redelinton, -yn- 1266 *For*, 1316 FA, *Reddelinton'* 1220 Cur (p), 1226 ClR, *Reddillinton* 1265 Misc
    Redlington', -yng- 1227 ClR, 1286 *Ass*, 1329, 1371 *FF et passim* to 1505 Pat
    Redlinton', -yn- 1225 ClR, 1373 Pat
    Ry-, Ridelington', -yng- 1253 Pat, 1264 RGrav *et passim* to 1286 *Ass*, 1290 *FF et freq* to 1332 Pat *et passim* to 1428 Fine, *Ridilington'* 1254 Val
    Ridelinctona 1209-19 RHug.
    Ry-, Ridelinton, -yn- 1167 P, 1217 ClR *et passim* to 1296 *For*, *Riddelynton* 1315 Ipm
    Ry-, Ridlington(e), -yng- 1209-19, 1221 RHug *et passim* to 1437 Peake *et freq*

'The estate called after or associated with Rĕdel', *v.* **-ingtūn**, cf. Ridlington Nf and Rillington YE 138. An OE pers.n. *Rĕdel* is unrecorded but this would be the normal Anglian form of the recorded *Rǣdel*, with the vowel eventually shortening to *e* before *dl*. *Rĕdel* is a shortened form of dithematic names in *Rǣd-/Rĕd-*. Names in *-ingtūn* may well belong to the eighth and ninth centuries. The type of place-name formation appears to represent politically a manorial structure in which a king's thane, perhaps based at a royal centre, held estates on which he was not always resident. Here the estate was associated with or named from Rĕdel, who perhaps resided at an Anglian court at Hambleton. Ridlington is a royal vill in DB, having seven unnamed attached outliers. The other royal vills in the Martinsley Hundred were Oakham with five berewicks and Hambleton itself with seven. Ridlington is sited on the attractive soils of the Northampton Sands formation. At SK 845 026 in the village is an unexcavated defended enclosure surrounded by substantial surviving ditches.   It may have been an Anglo-Saxon stronghold.

TWITCH HILL (FM)
>*Toteshulgate* 1332 *Extent*
>*Great Tutshill'* 1670 *Rental,* 17 VCH, *grate Tutshull* 1670 *Rental,*
>*Little Tutshill* 1670 *ib*, 17 VCH, *Tutshill' meddowe* 1670
>*Rental*
>*Touchill Covert* 1806 Map, 1824 O
>*Twitch Hill* 1943 *Map, Twitch Hill Close* 1838 *TA, Great -,*
>*Little Twitch Hill Meadow* 1838 *ib*

'The look-out hill', *v.* **tōt-hyll**. The medial -(*e*)*s*- may well be inorganic and due to AN influence in this royal vill (*v.* R.E. Zachrisson 'The French Element' in *The Survey of English Place-Names*, EPNS Vol. 1 (1924), 114, § 13). Note the close proximity of such Norman centres as Oakham, Brooke Priory, Launde Abbey Lei and Sauvey Castle (in Withcote Lei) as well as neighbouring Braunston (with AN *au* for *a*). Otherwise we must assume that this is an example of the uncommon use of the genitive with an appellative first element and thus more precisely meaning 'the hill of the look-out place' (*v.* E. Tengstrand, *A Contribution to the Study of Genitival Composition in Old English Place-Names*, Uppsala 1940), *v.* **tōt, hyll**. The name in the earliest recorded form is compounded with Scand **gata** 'a road'.

BANCROFT LODGE. FROG HALL, 1961 *Sale,* cf. *Frog Lands* 1943 *Map*. The site lies between R. Chater and a tributary stream, so the presence of frogs is not unexpected, but whether *hall* is an ironical development of *halh* 'a water-meadow, a nook of land' is uncertain, *v.* **frogga.** HANNAH'S FIELD. HOLLYGATE LODGE, *le Haloughyate* 1373 *For*, cf. *Halh*' 1249 Cl, 'the opening to the nook of land', *v.* **halh, geat.** JUBILEE LODGE FM. LEES BARN, cf. *Lease Close* 1838 *TA, Lease Meadow* 1838 *ib, v.* **lēah.** MANOR HO. (formerly OLD HALL), cf. *atte Hall de Redelynton* 1316 FA (p), *v.* **hall.** NOELS ARMS P.H. (lost), *Noel's Arms* 1846 White; named from the *Noel* family of Exton, the inn closed c1960 - VR. PARK FM is *Burgess Lodge* 1806, 1820, 1822 Map, *Ridlington Lodge* 1818 ib, 1824 O. *Burgess* is an old Ru surn., cf. William *Burges* 1522 MilS of Hambleton. PARK LODGE, 1961 *Sale, Ridlington Park Lodge* 1594, 1597 Moulton, 1842 Map, *v.* **loge.** The royal deer park is recorded as *parcus de Ridelinton*' 1254 Cl, 1269 *For, parcus domini regis de Ridelington*' 1269 ib, *Riddlington Park* 1567 LAHS, *Ridlington Park(e)* 1610 *Conant*, 1610 Speed, 1715 Map, 1772 *Chat, Park* 1846, 1863 White, *v.* **park.** PATEMAN'S LODGE, *Patemans Lodge* 1961 *Sale*, from the family name of Richard *Pakeman* 1701 VCH of Ridlington. The family was earlier in Uppingham, cf. Richard *Pateman* 1637 *Anc*, Richard *Pakeman* 1688 *ib.* QUAKER'S SPINNEY. RAVENSCROFT FM. If Ravenscroft is an early name, then 'Raven's small enclosed field', with *Raven* a probable ME surn. rather than the OE pers.n. *Hrœfn* or the Scand pers.n. *Hrafn, v.* **croft.** Otherwise Ravenscroft in entirety is a surname. RECTORY, 1846, 1863 White. RIDLINGTON CHURCH, *Church (St Mary and St Andrew)* 1846, 1863 ib, cf. *atte Kirke* 1332 *Extent* (p), *v.* **kirkja.** ROWELL'S LODGE, 1961 *Sale.* SCHOOL, 1863 White, cf. *ye hall school* 1670 *Rental, v.* **scole.** SWANS LODGE (lost), 1780, 1801 Map.

Field-Names

Undated forms in (a) are 1943 *Map*; forms dated 1838 are *TA*. Early forms dated 1634 are *Terrier*; those of 1670 are *Rental*; those of 1725 are *Deed*; those dated 1714, 1739, 1779 and 1782 are *Anc* while those of 1772 are *Chat.*

(a) Four Acre 1943, Five Acre Cl 1838 (x2), (Page's) Five Acre 1943, Six Acre Cl 1838, Baker's Six Acre 1943, Seven -, Eight Acre, Nine -, Bottom Twelve -, Top Twelve -, Seventeen -, Nineteen Acres (*v.* **æcer**); Aldergate (*v.* **gata**); Back Lane Cl; Backside Cl 1838 (perh. identical with the preceding, *v.* **ba(c)ksyde**); Baker's Hill; Bottom -, Top Banks; Barn Cl 1943, - Mdw 1838;

Barrow's (poss. the surn. *Barrow*, cf. Robert *Borow* 1522 MilS of nearby Braunston, but there is a surviving tumulus at SK 832 017 (*v.* Crop Marks 62-3), now barely perceptible from the ground, which this f.n. may record); Bassetts Cl 1838 (cf. Mr *Basset* 1774 *TA* of neighbouring Preston); Bellmear c1800 Map, Bellmeer 1806 ib, 1824 O, Bell Moor Cl, - Mdw 1838 (*Belmere* 1634; on the parish boundary, its first el. is poss. OE *belle* 'a bell-shaped hill', *v.* (ge)mǣre); Big Fd (Mr J. Field notes that it is of 99 acres); Bottom Mdw; Bridge Cl 1838; Broad Lane 1838; Brook Fds, - Mdw; Bryan's (named from the *Bryan* family, cf. Charles and William *Bryan* 1877 White); Bull Pasture 1838; Burgess' (*v.* Park Fm *supra*); Bushy Dales 1824 O (*v.* deill); Cabin Cl, - Mdw (with cabin 'a shed for workmen'); Clark's Cl (from the surn. *Clark(e)*, cf. perh. Samuel *Clarke* 1877 White); Cole's Cl; Coombe Cl 1838 (*v.* cumb, cf. Coombs in Preston f.ns. (a)); Cotch Platt, Nether Cotch Fern 1838 (*v.* cot, plat^2, fenn and Scotch Fens in Preston f.ns. (a), cf. dial. *cotcher* 'cottager'); Cottage Cl; Cottier's Cl, - Platt (Cl) 1838 (*v.* cottere, plat^2); Cow Cl 1838, 1943; Cricket Paddock (for the game of cricket); Cut Skirt Cl 1838, Cut Skirt's Cl, - Mdw 1943 (*Cut Skirts meddow* 1670, *v.* cutte^2, skirt, mǣd, cf. *Cutskirts* in Lyndon f.ns. (b)); Lower Dale 1838, Middle -, Upper Dale Cl 1838, First -, Second Dale 1943 (*la Dale* 1269 For, *v.* dalr); Dirty Back Cl 1838 (*v.* back); Dockey Cl 1838 (prob. a close with many dock plants growing in it, *v.* docce); East Lees (*v.* lēah); Everett's; Far Cl 1838, Far Part 1943; Feather Bed Lane c1800 Map (with dial. *feather-bed* 'a quagmire'; the lane ran into Leighfield parish); Feeding Cl (grazing-ground, pasturage, *v.* feeding); Flats (*v.* flat); Fountains Mdw and Cl 1838 (from the surn. *Fountain*); Fox Cover (*v.* cover(t)); Franks Cl 1838 (with the surn. *Frank*, cf. John *Frank* 1522 MilS, 1524 SR of Morcott, Franks Cl in Morcott f.ns. (a)); Frisby's Cl 1838 (from the surn. *Frisby*); Furzy Cl 1838 (*v.* fyrsig); Gands Cl 1838; Gardners Cl 1838; West Glebe 1838, Glebes 1943 (*v.* glebe); Goode's Gorse Cl (*v.* gorst); Gray's; Hall Cl 1838, 1943 (*v.* Manor Ho. *supra*); Great Hern Cl 1838, Herne's Far Land (*Great* -, *Middle Hearn* 1670, *v.* hyrne); Hickman's; Home Cl 1838, 1943, Home Cl Thirty Acre 1943 (*v.* home); Homefield Cl (*v.* home); Honey Pot Cl 1838, Honey Pots 1943 (prob. alluding to sticky soil); Horse Cl 1838; Hovel Cl 1838 (*v.* hovel); Huits Cl 1838; Husbandmans Cl 1838 (*Husbandmans meadow* 1725; most prob. husbandman in its 17th cent. sense 'tenant farmer, smallholder, customary tenant', in contrast to 'the cottager' of Cottier's Cl *supra*); Issits; Kings Cl 1838; Kit's Cl (with the surn. *Kitt*, cf. John *Kytte* 1522 MilS of nearby Lyddington); Lockhaye Cl (perh. an early 'enclosure that can be locked', *v.* loc, (ge)hæg); Long Cl 1838, - Piece 1943 (*v.* pece); Longland Cl 1838; Lound, Lounts (*the Lount* 1634, 1714, 1725, *the Lownd* 1739, *the Lound Close* 1779, 1782, *v.* lundr); Lower Cl 1838; Mackley (the surn. *Mackley*); Meadow, - Cl 1838; Middle Cl 1838 (*the middle close* 1725);

Naps Cl (either from *nēp* 'turnip' or from the surn. *Napp*); Nether Cl 1838 (*the nether close* 1725); New Cl (1725); Newlands; Old Fd; Oven Cl 1838; Pease Hill Cl 1838 (*v.* pise); Pegs Cl 1838 (from the surn. *Peg*, cf. *Pegs House* in Lyndon f.ns. (b)); Penn Cl 1838 (*v.* penn²); Picks Cl 1838; Piggery Fd; Pines or Ferry Cl 1838; Pookery's or Home Cl 1838 (*v.* home); Preston Mdw (Preston parish adjoins to the east); Pynes Nook 1838 (*v.* nōk); Robinson's Barn Cl, Robinson's Mdws (named from the *Robinson* family, cf. John C. *Robinson* 1877 White); Round Hill; Russell's Hern Cl (cf. Great Hern Cl *supra* and Robert *Russell* 1522 MilS, 1525 SR, Thomas *Russell* 1525 ib, both of nearby Caldecott); Rye Cl (*v.* ryge); First Seeds (an area of sown grass, *v.* sǣd); Spinney Lount (*v.* lundr); Spot's Cl (poss. named from a horse); Stackyard Cl (*v.* stak-ȝard); Big Tenter's (*v.* tentour, cf. *Tentar Lane* in Edith Weston f.ns. (b)); Bottom -, Tompkin's; Top Mdw; West Fd; White's Parks (*v.* Park Fm *supra*).

(b) *Brenles* 1238 Pat, 1282 Cl (a wood so called, *v.* brende², lēah); *Chappell-close* 1634 (*v.* chapel(e)); *Colts Close* 1772 (*v.* colt); *conygreene* 1670 (*v.* coninger, coni, grene²); *Fole Close* 1772 (*v.* fola); *Fridwod* 1253 Pat, 1254 Cl, *Fritwode* 1255 Pat (the first el. may be OE friðr 'protection', perh. referring to woodland subject to special conditions, such as commoners' access to game, otherwise fyrhð 'scrub' *v.* wudu); *Harethornes* 1253 Pat, 1254 Cl, 1255 Pat (a wood so called; either 'the lichen-covered thorns' or 'the boundary thorns', *v.* hār², þorn); *super Montem* 1332 Extent (p) (*v.* hyll); *Lady-holme* 1670, *Lady Holme* 1725 (*v.* hlǣfdige, holmr); *the Little Close* 1670; *Little Meadow and Dale* 1772; *Lowskirts* 1670 ('low-lying land on the outskirts', *v.* la(g)h, skirt); *ye Mault Mill* 1670, *the Great Mill Close* 1714, 1739, *the Mill Close* 1779, 1782 (*v.* malte-mylne); *the Parkstile* 1634 (*v.* park, stigel and Park Lodge *supra*); *Twheresgate* 1332 Extent (perh. '(furlong) lying athwart the road', *v.* þvers, gata).

Uppingham

UPPINGHAM

> *Yppingeham* 1067 BM, Wm 1 Dugd
> *Ippingeham* 1157 *WDB*
> *Uppingeham* 1080-7 Reg, 1167, 1190 P, 1201, 1245 *FF*,
>   *Huppingeham* 1235 Ch
> *V-*, *Uppingham*, -*y*- 1198 Abbr, 12 *Peake*, 1200 Cur *et passim*
>   to 1221, 1222 *MiD et freq* to 1610 Speed, *Upingham* 1199
>   *FF*, *Huppingham subtus Biaumund* 1253 Pat
> *Oppingham*, -*y*- 1254 Cl, 1255 Pat, 1286 *Ass*, (- *subtus Beumunt*)

1255 Pat

'The village of the Yppingas', *v.* **yppe, upp, -inga-, hām.** The folk-name *Yppingas means 'the people of the upland'. Uppingham stands on a long, high ridge beside Beaumont Chase. Hence the affix - *subtus Beumunt.*

Uppingham Street-Names

ADDERLEY ST, 1901 UR, named from Mr *Adderley*, later Lord Norton. ALLIN ROW (lost), from the family name of Henry *Allin* 1822 UR and William *Allin* 1855 ib. It is *Ragmans Row* 1839 *Plan.* AYSTON RD is *Alston Way* 1634, 1705 *Terrier, Aston way(e)* 1634 ib, 1688 *Anc, Ayston(e) highway* 1723, 1730 *Terrier, v.* **weg** and Ayston. BAYLEY CLOSE. BEAST HILL is *Cow Markett Hill* 1753 *Bir, the Cow Market* 1754 ib, *Beast Market Hill* 1844 UR, *Beast market* 1846, 1863 White; the cattle market was held here, *v.* **best(e).** BINNETTS ENTRY (lost), 1839 *Plan.* BRANSTON RD, *v.* Braunston. BULLOCK'S YARD (lost), 1850 Slater. CASTLE CLOSE takes its name from the motte and bailey castle on Castle Hill in neighbouring Beaumont Chase. CEDAR CLOSE. CHAPEL LANE (lost), 1839 *Plan*; the *Ebenezer Chapel* 1839 *ib* was sited here. CHESTNUT CLOSE. CHURCH HILL, *v.* Scale Hill *infra.* CHURCH LANE (lost), 1735 UR, 1850 Slater. CONSTITUTION HILL (lost), 1839 *Plan.* Mr J. Field points out that this 'is almost certainly, like the street of the same name in Birmingham, an imitation of the London name.' COTTESMORE RD, *v.* Cottesmore. FARLEIGH GARDENS. FINCH CLOSE, named from the *Finch* family of Burley on the Hill. FIRS AVENUE. FISHER'S YARD (lost), *v.* Printer's Yard *infra.* GAINSBOROUGH RD, named from the Noel family, the Earls of *Gainsborough.* GAS HILL was the site of the Uppingham Gas Works, *v. infra.* GLASTON RD is *glaston waye* 1634 *Terrier, Glaston way* 1688 *Anc,* 1705 *Terrier, Glaiston Way* 1720, 1723 ib, *v.* **weg** and Glaston. HIGH ST, 1839 *Plan,* 1846, 1863 White. HOG HILL (local), *the hog hill* 1688 *Anc, Hog Hill* 1746, 18 *Bir,* 1839 *Plan, Hog Markett Hill* 1753 *Bir;* the pig market was held here. HOG LANE (lost), *v.* Norton St *infra.* HOPE'S YARD. JOHNSON RD, named from the benefactor Robert *Johnson,* rector of North Luffenham from 1574, who founded Uppingham School in 1584, cf. *Schools and Hospitals of the Foundation of Robert Johnson in Oakham and Uppingham* 1846, 1863 White. LEAMINGTON TERRACE, 1839 *Plan*, 1846, 1863 White; alluding to Leamington Spa because of the adjacent local spring, *v.* Spring Back Way and Springfield *infra*. LEICESTER RD is *Lestr wey* c1650 *Bir*, *Leicester Road* 1846, 1863 White, *Lester Turnpike* 1886 *Anc*, *v.* weg, turnepike. LODGE CLOSE. LONDON RD, 1846, 1863 White, formerly Redgate *infra*. LYDDINGTON RD, *v.* Lyddington. MARKET PLACE, *in Mercat' de Vppyngham* 1510 *MinAcct*, *in loco Mercati de Vppyngham* 1527 *Surv*, *Market Place* 1839 *Plan*, 1846, 1863 White, cf. *The Market Cross* 1740 UR, *v.* market. MEETING LANE (local), 1846, 1863 White, *Meeting House Lane* 1825 UR, named from the Nonconformist chapel situated here. MOUNT PLEASANT, 1839 *Plan*, a complimentary name which is sometimes given ironically. NEWTOWN CRESCENT, NEWTOWN RD. NORTH ST. NORTON ST is named from Lord *Norton*, previously Mr Adderley, *v.* Adderley St *supra*. It was earlier *Hog Lane* - UR. ORANGE ST is *Orrange Lane* 1727 *Anc*, *Orange Lane* 1736, 1781 *Bir*, 1839 *Plan*, 1846, 1863 White; leading into Market Place and possibly named from the traditional site of vendors' stalls selling China Oranges in the later 17th and early 18th centuries. POPLAR CLOSE. PRINTER'S YARD (formerly Fisher's Yard) was owned by John Hawthorn, printer, in the 19th cent. and earlier by James *Fisher* from 1808 to 1820 - UR. THE QUADRANT, so called from its shape. QUEEN ST, 1846, 1863 White; it is *Horne Lane* 1734 UR, *Horn Lane* 1839 *Plan*: in local lore, Horn Lane was named from the horns of the guards of the London Mail coaches who blew warning for change of horses as they climbed the incline into the town from the south. However, the horn-shaped curve of the road from London Rd into Queen St may also be thought of as the origin of the name. QUEENS RD. RAGMANS ROW (lost), *v.* Allin Row *supra*. REDGATE, *le Redegate* 1290, 1376 *For*, *Redgate* 1610 Speed, 1620 Map; either 'road suitable for riding on' or 'red road', *v.* ræde, read, gata and rædweg in Ayston f.ns. (b). RED HILL, *Redd hill* 1634 *Terrier*, *Red Hill* 1688 *Anc*, 1705, 1720, 1723 *Terrier*, 1728 *Asw*, 1736, 1746, 1751, 1763 *Bir*, *v.* read, hyll. REEVES YARD. RUTLAND CLOSE. SCALE HILL (or CHURCH HILL), perhaps from OWScand skáli 'a temporary hut or shed', a word associated with Norwegian rather than Danish settlement in England. SCHOOL LANE, 1839 *Plan*, 1846, 1863 White, leading to *Free School* 1839 *Plan*. SEATON RD is *Seaton high way* c1650 *Bir*, *Seaton Lane* 1776 *ib*, *v*. Seaton. SHEILD'S YARD (lost), 1846, 1863 White, from the *Sheild* family, prominent landowners in the 18th and 19th centuries, cf. Edward- and William *Sheild* of Preston 1713 *Anc* and Robert *Sheild* 1846 White. SHEPHERDS WAY. SOUTH ST (locally SPRING BACK WAY and SOUTH BACK WAY) leads to Town Spring, cf. Springdale and Springfield *infra*. SOUTH VIEW. STAMFORD RD. STATION RD. STOCKERSTON CRESCENT. STOCKERSTON RD, 1846 White. It is *Stockerston Way* 1746 *Bir*, leading to Stockerston Lei, *v*. Stockerston Rd in Beaumont Chase. WARDLEY LANE, 1763 *Bru*, *Wardley Lane Way* 1746 *ib*, *v*. Wardley. WHEATLEY AVENUE.

Uppingham Buildings

THE BEAR HOUSE (lost), 1863 White, for the safe-keeping of performing bears. It became The Bethesda Chapel - UR. BROOKLANDS, 1846, 1863 White. BUTLER'S COTTAGE was occupied by Peter *Butler* c1660 - UR. CHRIST'S HOSPITAL (lost), *the hospitalle of Christe in Uppingham* 1625 Ep. DOVECOAT HOUSE (lost), 1753 *Bir*, *v*. **dove-cot(e)**. GAS WORKS, 1841 UR, 1846 White; the town was first gaslit in December 1839 - UR. HEALALL COTTAGE (lost), 1839 *Plan*; evidently the abode of a quack doctor or a 'wise woman'. HILLAM'S COTTAGE was occupied by William *Hillam* c1660 - UR. MR LOWITH'S COTTAGE (lost), 1705 *Terrier*, cf. Widow *Louthe* 1634 *ib*. MARTINS HOUSE (lost), 1685 *Deed*, *Martins Cottage* 1705 *Terrier*. PARSONAGE HO., *the parsonage* 1525 SR, *the Parsonage House* 1634, 1705, 1720, 1723 *Terrier*, *v*. **personage**. RECTORY, *The Rectory of Uppingham* 1705, 1720, 1723 *ib*, *Rectory* 1846, 1863 White. RECTORY FM. UNION SCHOOL (lost), 1846, 1863 *ib*. UNION WORKHOUSE (lost), 1846, 1863 *ib*; this Poor Law institution was closed in 1914 - UR. UPPINGHAM CHURCH, *Church* (*St Peter and St Paul*) 1846, 1863 White. UPPINGHAM SCHOOL is *free Gramar schoole in Uppingham* 1625 Ep, *Free School* 1839 *Plan*, *Free Grammar School* 1846, 1863 White, cf. *the free grammer Scholes of Robert Johnson, clarke … in Okeham* *and Uppingham* 1587 Pat. UPPINGHAM TOLLHOUSE (lost), 1830 UR, cf. *le Tolbothe* 1527 *Surv, v.* **toll-bothe.** THOMAS VICARS COTTAGE (lost), 1705 *Terrier.* VINE HOUSE (lost), 1735 *Add,* possibly from the surn. *Vine,* cf. John *Vine* 1685, 1706 *Anc* who held land in neighbouring Bisbrooke, but cf. also *Le Vyne,* Uppingham Inns and Taverns *infra.* WESLEYAN CHAPEL.

Uppingham Inns and Taverns

BLACK BULL (lost), became the Horse and Trumpet (High St West) - UR. CATHERINE WHEEL (lost), 1762 UR. CHEQUERS (London Rd - lost), 1846, 1863 White. CROSS KEYS (High St - lost), pulled down in 1862 to make way for Uppingham School chapel - UR. CROSS KEYS (Queen St), 1850 Slater, *Cross Keys Inn* 1875 UR. CROWN (High St West), *Crown Inn* 1982 ib. EXETER ARMS (Leicester Rd), named from the Marquess of *Exeter.* FALCON (High St East), *The Faulcon* 1740 ib, *The Falcon Inn* 1781, 1785 ib, *Falcon Inn* 1846, 1863 White. FLUDYER'S ARMS (lost), 1846 ib, from the family name of George *Fludyer* of Ayston Hall 1846 ib. GEORGE (lost), *sign of the George* 1660 *Deed,* cf. *the George landes* 1638 *Anc,* possibly the forerunner of the GEORGE AND DRAGON (Market Place - lost), 1822 UR, 1839 *Plan,* 1846, 1863 White, which became the Horse and Trumpet - UR. HORSE AND JOCKEY (lost), 1783 ib. HORSE AND TRUMPET (High St West - lost), 1792 ib, 1846 White. HORSE AND TRUMPET (Market Place - lost), demolished 1960 - UR. KING'S HEAD (lost), 1640 ib; it became The White Hynde - UR. OSTLERS ARMS (lost), 1890 ib. PUMP (Market Place - lost), *the Pump* 1799 *Deed, Pump Inn* 1822 UR; it became the George and Dragon - UR. ROSE AND CROWN (Beast Hill - lost), 1846, 1863 White. ROYAL OAK (Queen St - lost), 1846, 1863 ib. SWAN (Market Place - lost), *Swan Inn* 1844 UR, *Swan Tap* 1846, 1863 White, now 5 Market Place - UR. UNICORN (High St - lost), *The Unicorn* 1827, 1880 ib, *Unicorn Inn* 1846, 1863 White, closed 1974 - UR. VAULTS (Market Place). LE VYNE (lost), *cotag' vocat' le vyne* 1562 *Ct,* possibly an early tavern, *v.* **vine.** WAGON AND HORSES (High St East). WHITE HART (High St West - lost), 1774 UR; it became The Black Bull - UR. WHITE HART (High St West), 1846, 1863 White. WHITE

HYNDE (lost), 1650 UR. WHITE SWAN (lost), 1846 White.

WILKERSHAW (lost)
    Wulgareshag 1238 Pat, *Wulgareshagh* 1282 Cl
    Wilgershaw 1414 Pat, *Wyllgeshaw* 1560 Ct
    Wilkershaw 1688 *Anc,* 1696 *Bir,* 1728 *Asw,* 1736, 1746 *Bir,* 1799
        Deed
    Wilk(e)sawe 1634 *Terrier, Wilkeshaw* 1705 *ib*
    Wilkersey c1725, 1781 *Bir, Willcausey* 1720, 1723, 1749 *Terrier,*
        Wilcausey 1730 *ib, Wilkcausey* 1744 *ib*
    Wilkershaw Cowpasture 1804 Map

    Probably 'Wulfgār's enclosure', with OE **haga**[1] as the second
element. However, OE **scaga** 'a copse, a small wood' is possible as
the generic, although this is rarely compounded with personal names
and early spellings with *-ss-* indicating the genitive plus the *s* of
scaga are absent, *v.* Elements **2** 100 *s.v.* **sceaga,** *Shy Close* in f.ns.
(b) *infra* and *Shaw Hills* in Lyddington f.ns. (b).

    ARCHFIELD probably refers to a cattle arch in a railway
embankment. AYSTON MILL, *Aston Mill also calld Wind Mill*
1633 *Bru, the Windmill* 1608 *ib,* 1720, 1723, 1744 *Terrier.* It is
Peppers Mill 1688 *Anc,* 1763 *Bir,* cf. *the Mill furlong* 1720 *Terrier,*
Peppers Mill Furlong 1728 *Asw, Wind Mill Furlong* 1763 *Bir.* Richard
Pepper 1720, 1723 *Terrier* and Henry *Pepper* 1744 *ib* were the
millers at this windmill which stood in the old West Field towards
Ayston, *v.* **wind-mylne.** BREACH FM, *le Breche* 1344 *For, the*
Breach c1725 *Bir,* 1728 *Asw,* 1736, 1746, 1763 *Bir, The Breech* 1776
ib, 'land broken up for cultivation', *v.* **brēc.** CONSTABLES.
FARLEIGH.   FIRCROFT.   GIPSY   HOLLOW   LANE.
HIGHFIELD.   LAUNDE FM, cf. *de la Launde* 1359 *FF* (p),
Lawnde Park 1572 *Deposition, close of Lawnde* 1572 *ib, Lawn Close*
1799 *Deed, v.* **launde, park.** MANY BUSHES, *Manny bushes* 1688
Anc, Many Bushes 1736, 1746, 1763, 1781 *Bir,* 1799 *Deed,* cf. *Many*
Bushes Dyke 1763 *Bir, Many Bushes Cowpasture* 1804 *Map, v.*
manig, busc, dīk. MEADHURST. MILL COTTAGES, MILL HO.,
the site of *Uppingham Mill* 1824 O, a windmill demolished 1912 -
UR. This mill is probably to be identified with *the New Mill* 1763

Bir. Close by was *the Nether Mill* 1736 *ib, the Old Mill* 1763 *ib,* cf. (*the*) *Myll furlong*(*e*) 1634 *Terrier, the Mill Furlong* 1705, 1723 *ib,* c1725, 1746 *Bir, Neather Mill Furlong* 1688 *Anc,* 1746 *Bir, Nether* - 1736 *ib, Neither* - 1781 *ib, Old Mill furlong* 1763 *ib, Mill Peice* 1728 *Asw, the Mill Field* 1799 *Deed, v.* **myln, neoðera, pece.** THE PITTS, *the Ston pittes, stonepittes* 1634 *Terrier, the Stone Pitts* 1688 *Anc,* 1705, 1720, 1723 *Terrier,* c1725, 1746 *Bir, Stone Pit Holes* 1763 *ib, v.* **stān-pytt.** SPRINGDALE, SPRINGFIELD, cf. *Town Spring* 1839 *Plan, v.* **spring.** SUNNYBANK. TODDS PIECE, *Todds Peice* 1720 *Anc,* 1746 *Terrier, Tods Piece* 1763 *Bir,* with the surn. *Todd, v.* **pece.** TWITCHBED LANE, *v.* **cwice, bedd.** WEST BANK. WEST DEYNE. WEST END.

Field-Names

Undated forms in (a) are 1943 *Map.* Those dated 1804 are *Map* and 1886 are *Anc.* Early forms dated 1637, 1638, 1688 and 1727 are *Anc;* those dated 1634[1], 1634[2], 1705, 1720, 1723, 1730, 1733, 1744 and 1749 are *Terrier;* those of 1660, 1788 and 1799 are *Deed;* those of 1696, 1697, c1725, 1726, 1736, 1746, 1751, 1753, 1754, 1760, 1763, 1776, 1781 and 18 are *Bir,* while those dated 1728 are *Asw.*

(a) Nine -, Sixteen Acre (*v.* **æcer**); The Bank; Beaumont Leys 18 *TA* (*v.* Beaumont Leys); The Belgrave (Mr J. Field suggests that this may be based on a surn., cf. William *Belgrave* 1785 UR of Uppingham); Brand Fd 1804 (*le Brende* 1436 *Deed, Brente* 1538 LinDoc, *the Brent* 1566 *Ct, the Brand* 1684 Wright, 1781, 1798 Nichols, *Uppingham Brand* 1799, *the Brand Feild* 1660, 1688, 1728, *Le Brand Field* 1697, 1726, (*the*) *Brand Field* 1736, 1746, 1753, 1763, 1781, 1799, *the Brand or South Field* 1763, cf. *the Brand Dyke* 1688, 1746, - *Dike* 1736 (*v.* **dīk**), *Brand Furlong* 1746, 'a place cleared by burning', *v.* **brende**[1]; this was one of the three great open-fields of Uppingham); Cackerony (*Cockroan Close* 1736, *Cockroon* - 1746, *Cockcrown* -, *Cock Crown* - 1763, *Cocroans* - 1781; on the parish boundary, so poss. *cocc-rān* 'boundary strip frequented by (wood)cocks', but forms seem at least to have been influenced by dial. *cock-crowen* 'that which the cock has crowed on, i.e. that which is no longer fresh; stale'); Chapel Cl; Donaby's Fd 1886; Hockey Fd; Home Cl (*v.* **home**); The Innem's (cf. *Bisbrooke Innyms* 1746, *Spisbrook Inhams* 1763, *v.* **innām;** Bisbrook parish adjoins to the east); Lane Fds; Lound Fd 1804 (*the Lounde* 1634[1], 1634[2], *the Lownde* 1723, *the Lownd Feild* 1660, *Lound Feild* 1688, 1728, 1781, *Lound Field* 1736, 1746, 1799, *the North or Lound Field* 1763, *v.* **lundr** 'a small wood'; one of the old open-fields of

Uppingham, cf. *Lound(s) Nook* 1746, 1763, *Easton Lound Nook* 1763, *v.* **nōk;** Ayston parish adjoins to the north); Middle Cl; The Orchard; Plough Fd; Reid's Cl; Sally's Cl (poss. with the pers.n. *Sally*, pet-form of *Sarah*, but *salig* 'a willow, a sallow' may also be thought of); Sewage Grass; First -, Second Slade (*the Slade* 1746, *Slade Acres* 1688, 1696, 1697, 1746, *Slead Acres* 1763, *Slade Acre furlong* 1634, 1705, 1720, 1723, *v.* **slæd**); Taylor's Fd; Wash Pond 1839 *Plan* (1728 UR, perh. cf. *Soap Spring* 1763); Woodfield 1804 (*the Wood feild* 1688, 1728, 1781, (*the*) *Wood Field* 1736, 1746, 1788, 1799, *v.* **wudu, feld,** one of the great open-fields of Uppingham and known also as the West Field, *v. infra*).

(b) *Allins Spring* 1736, *Allens Spring* 1763, 1781, *The Spring* 1746, *Allens Spring Slade* 1746 (*v.* **spring, slæd** and cf. *Allin Row supra*); *Alwoldestie* 1201 *FF* ('Alwald's path', *v.* **stīg** and Feilitzen 154 *s.n.* Alweald); *Aston gapp* 1688, *Aston hedg* 1688, *Ayston Hedge* c1725, 1781, *Aiston hedge* 1736, 1746, *Easton Meer* 1763, *Aston stone* 1688 (apparently all boundary names referring to neighbouring Ayston parish, *v.* **gappe** 'an opening in a (boundary) hedge', **hecg** 'a (boundary) hedge', **(ge)mære** 'a boundary', **stān** 'a (boundary) stone'; presumably the stone preceded the hedge as boundary marker); *at the Back of the Yard* 1746 (*v.* **back, geard**); *the Backside* 1746 (*v.* **ba(c)ksyde**); *Thomas Bains Headland* 1763 (*v.* **hēafod-land**); *Bisbrooke dale* 1634[2], *Bisbrook(e) Horse way* 1736, 1781, *Bisbrooke Meere* 1688, c1725 (Bisbrooke parish adjoins to the east, *v.* **dalr, (ge)mære**); *the Blow(e)s* 1688, 1746, 1763, *East -, West Blowse* 1799 ('cheerless, exposed (ground)', *v.* **blāw**); *the old bowling Ally* 1763, *the Bowling greene* 1688, (*the*) *old Bowling Leys* 1688, 1728, 1746 (for the sport of bowls, *v.* **bowling, aley, grēne**[2], **lēah**); *the Brick Kilnes* 1746, *ye Dike below the Brick-Kilns* 1763 (*v.* **bryke-kyl**); *le Brodegate* 1299 For, 1300 *DC, le Brodgate* 1375 Nichols, *Bradegatt, Bradgate* 1610 Speed, *Bradgatt* 1620 Map (*v.* **brād, gata**); *Browns Breach* 1746 (*v.* **brēc**); *Browns Bridge* 1763 (poss. a corrupted form of the previous f.n.); *Brushfields Close* 1746; *Buckston(e) Ley(e)s* 1634[1], 1634[2], 1705, 1763, *Buxton Ley(e)s* 1688, c1725, 1728, 1730, 1746, 1799, *Bux(s)tone Leys* 1720, 1723, 1733 (prob. from the surn. *Buxton, v.* **lēah**); *Bull Close* 1705, 1763; *the Bull Land* 1688, *Lower Bull Land* c1725 (perh. belonging to the Black Bull Inn, otherwise *v.* **bula, land**); *Bunyons foot path* 1763 (from the surn. *Bunyan*); *at the Bush* 1736 (*v.* **busc**); *Bush(e)y Balk Furlong* 1634[1], 1705, 1720, 1723 (*v.* **busshi, balca**); *Bushy Close* 1728 (*v.* **busshi**); *the buttes* 1688, *Butt Close* 1634[1], 1705, 1720, 1723 (*v.* **butte**); *Chethams Peice* 1746, *- Piece* 1763, 18 (from the surn. *Chetham, v.* **pece**); *the Church Hadland* 1763 (*v.* **hēafod-land**); *Clay-Pit hill* 1763, *Clay Pit Hill Close* 1751, *Cley pit Lane* 1736, *Claypit Lane* 1763, 1781, *Clay Pitt Lane Way* 1746 (*v.* **cley-pytt**); *Clements Lands* 1753 (from the surn. *Clement*, cf. John -, Thomas - and William *Clement* 1522 MilS, 1524 SR of nearby Belton, *v.* **land**); *Collin's Folly* 1763, *The Folley*

1799 (v. **folie**, cf. Thomas *Collins*, a landowner in Uppingham 1763. Gipsy Hollow Lane *supra* was once known locally as Folly Lane - UR); *John Cooks Close* 1763; *Coultons Close* 1781 (from the surn. *Coulton*); *Cowlair* 1799 ('the cow barn', from ModE dial. **lair** 'a barn', cf. Cow Lair in Whissendine f.ns. (a)); *Cow Lane* 1746; *Cow Market Close* 1760 (cf. Beast Hill *supra*); *the Crooks* 1728, 1746, 1763 ('the nooks or secluded corners of land', v. **krókr**); *Daweleys* 1564 *Ct* (perh. 'jackdaw meadows', but the surn. *Dawe(s)* is also poss., cf. Johan *Daue* and Elizabeth *Dawes* 1522 MilS, both of Langham, v. **daw(e), lēah**); *Depedale* 1269 *For*, *Depe dale*, *Deepedale* 1610 Speed, *Debdale* 1634[1], 1634[2], 1705, 1728, 1746, 1763, *Aston Debdale* 1688, *Easton Debdale* 1763, *Deepdale* 1720, 1723, c1725 and 1780 Map, *Deep Dale* 1799 and 1801 Map, *Deepdale Foot(e) Way* c1725, 1736, 1781, *Debdale Way* 1746 ('the deep valley', v. **dēop, dalr**, the valley separated Uppingham from Ayston to the north); *the Demeasnes* 1634[1], 1720 (v. **demeyn**); *the Dike* 1736, 1763, 1781, *the Dyke* 1746, 18 (v. **dík**); *the Dogholes* 1763, *Dog Pitts* 1746 (prob. 'the holes or pits where dock grows', v. **docce, hol**[1], **pytt**); *Drove Ley(e)s* c1725, 1726, 1728, 1753, *Drove Leys Close* 1728, 1746, 1763 (v. **drāf, lēah**); *Dunston Furlong* 1634[1], 1634[2], 1688, 1705, 1736, 1763, *Dunton Furlong* 1723, *Dunstan Furlong* 1720, 1723, c1725, 1781, *Dunstan Long Furlong* 1746 (poss. with the surn. *Dunston*, but cf. *Dunston Hedge* in neighbouring Lyddington f.ns. (b)); *East feilde* 1637, *East Field* 1684 (v. **ēast, feld**); *Estwod'*, *Estwode extra Wppingham* 1269 For (v. **ēast, wudu**); *Mr Lyon Falkeners Close* 1736, *Fawkners Litle Close* c1725; *Floddreacre* 1201 *FF* ('mire acre', v. **flodder, æcer**, cf. *flodder* 'to flood' 1513 NED; Kristensson in SMETT *s.n.* Flodre suggests for OE *flodor, ME flod(d)er a meaning 'channel', the word itself surviving as dial. *flother* 'a swamp', cf. *Floderforlong* Wa 368); *Flyblowne close* c1725, *Flyblown Close* 1746 (a pejorative name, presumably 'fly-blown' because a dumping ground for unusable offal, animal carcases or such); *John Freemans otherwise Yorkes Close* 1736, *John Freemans otherways Yorks Close* 1781 (with the surn. *York*); *Gallow(e) Hill* 1634[1], 1634[2], 1705, 1720, 1723, *Gall(e)y Hill* 1688, 1746, *Gally hill Close* 1763, *gallowe hill furlonge* 1634[1], *Gallow Hill Furlong* 1705, 1720, 1723, *Gally Hill Mortar pitts* 1736, *Gallow Hill Mortar Pits* 1781 (v. **morter-pytt**), *Galley Hill Way* 1746 (evidently 'gallows hill' (v. **galga**) but 'bare hill' (with **calu**) is also poss., v. *Galowe hill furlong* in Caldecott f.ns. (b)); *Gerwaldesholm* 1213 *FF* ('Gǣrwald's water-meadow', v. **holmr**); *atte Grene* 1303 Ipm (p) (v. **grēne**[2]); *Greengate* 1688, 1728, 1746, *Green(e) Gate* 1696, c1725, 1736, 1763, 1799, *Greengate end* 1746 ('the grassy road', v. **grēne**[1], **gata**); *Harrisons Closes* 1751, 1760; *the Hill* 1746; *the Hillybanks* 1746, *Hill(e)y Banks* 1746, 1763 ('slopes covered with mounds', v. **banke**; presumably with reference to early diggings or to ancient ridge and furrow); *Holmes* 1344 *For* ('the water-meadows', v. **holmr**). *Horsecrafts* 1688, *Horse Crafts* 1705, 1720, 1723, *horse croftes* 1634[1],

Horse Crofts 1728, 1746, 1763 (*v.* **hors, croft**); (*the*) *Horse Fair Ley(e)s* 1736, 1746, 1781 (*v.* **feire, lēah**); *Mr Hungates Close* 1634[1], 1705, *Hungates Close* 1634[2], 1720, 1723, *Hungate Close* 1749, *Hungates Hedge* 1746 (*v.* **hecg**); *Jackwell Balke* 1746 (*v.* **balca**), *Jagwell Pond* 1688 (*v.* **ponde**), *Jagwell S(e)i̇(c)ke* 1634[1], 1634[2], 1705, 1720, 1723, 1733, 1744, 1763, - *Seeke* 1637, 1688, - *Sieke* 1697, *Jagwall Sike* 1730, *Jackwell seek* 1728 (*v.* **sīk**), *Jagwell Slade* 1688, 1763, *Jackwell Slade* 1746, *Jagwell Slade Close* 1760 (*v.* **slæd**) ('stream lined with broom or gorse', *v.* **ceacga, wella**, cf. *ceacga broc* 925-39 (11) BCS 726 (S 387)); *the Judges balke* 1688 (*v.* **judge, balca**); *Katterns leyes* 1638 (with the surn. *Cater(e)ns*, cf. Raff *Caterns* 1522 MilS of Empingham, John *Caterns* 1522 ib of Oakham and Clement *Catterens* 1617 PR of N. Luffenham, *v.* **lēah**); *Kites Seeke* 1688, *Kytes Seek* 1728, 1746, *Kite Sike* 1763 ('ditch frequented by kites', *v.* **cȳta, sīk**); *Knightlys Piece* 1763 (with the surn. *Knightley, v.* **pece**); *one Rode of land betwixt My Ladyes Leggs* 1688, *between my Ladys Legs* 1736, *between Ladys Legs* 1763 (the name *My Ladyes Leggs* evidently describes a topographical feature fancifully reminiscent of the spread legs of a woman); *Lampacre Close* 1688, *Laump-Acre -, Lamp Acre -* 1763 (land endowed for the maintenance of the altar lamp in the parish church, *v.* **lampe, æcer**); *Laxtons Peice* 1736, 1781 (with the surn. *Laxton*); *Liddington foot Bridge* 1736, 1781 (Lyddington parish adjoins to the south); *longland furlong* 1634[2] (*v.* **lang[1], land**); *Long Leys* 1746 (*v.* **lēah**); *Marbles sheep-pens* 1763 (with the surn. *Marble*); *the Midle furlong* 1688, *Middle Furlong* 1746, 1763, *Stoney Middle Furlong* 1763 (*v.* **middel, stānig**); *Ambrose Moles Close* 1763; *the Morter holes* 1763 (*v.* **morter, hol[1]**); *Myry peice* 1728 (*v.* **myry, pece**); *the Neather furlong* 1688, 1746, *Nether Furlong* 1763 (*v.* **neoðera**); (*the*) *North Feild(e)* 1634[1], 1634[2], 1688, 1720, 1723, c1725, *North Field* 1705, *North or Lound field* 1763 (*v.* **norð, feld**; one of the great open-fields of the settlement); *Mr Palmers Close* 1638; (*the*) *Parsons Balke* 1696, 1746, *Parsons Baulke* 1763 (*v.* **persone, balca**); *Pearetree hill* 1634[1], 1634[2], *Pairtree hill* 1688, *Pare Tree hill* 1705, *Peartree Hill* 1720, 1723, 1736, 1746, 1763, 1781 (*v.* **pertre**); *Penn Close* 1746 (*v.* **penn[2]**); *Poles Close* 1728; *Preston Footway* c1725, 1746, *Preston Leys* 18 (*v.* **lēah**) (Preston parish lies to the north); *Pridmores Pitt* 1688, 1746 (with the surn. *Pridmore*, cf. Second Dexter or Pridmore in neighbouring Preston f.ns. (a), *v.* **pytt**; *Pye Lane* c1725, 1746 (this appears not to be an urban 'lane where pie-makers trade', hence 'magpie lane', *v.* **pīe[2]**); *the Quickhedge* 1736, *ye Quick Hedge* 1781 (*v.* **cwic, hecg**); *Red Hill Close* 1746 (*v.* Red Hill *supra*); *the Ricke yeard* 1660 (*v.* **hrēac, geard**); *Rite sink* c1725 (*v.* **sinke**); *Rotten Dyke* 1746, - *Dike* 1763 ('ditch infested by (water-) rats', *v.* **raton, dīk**); *Round Hill* 1688, 1763, *Round hill Peice* 1746 (*v.* **rond, hyll, pece**); *Rovey Furlong* 1763; *the landes called Sct. Johns* 1638 (either alluding to land once owned by the Knights of St John or less likely to the site of the local bonfires on St John's Day, 24th June, *v.* **land**, cf. *St Johns Peice* in

220 RUTLAND

Greetham f.ns. (b)); *Seaton Ford* 1776, *Seaton ford Close* 1763, *Seaton Lane end* 1776 (Seaton parish lies to the south-east); *Syortebrech* 1211 Cur, *Sortebrech'* 1212 ib (*v.* **sc(e)ort, brēc**); *Short Hedge* 1763 (*v.* **hecg**); (*the*) *Shy Close* 1728, 1746, *Shea Close* 1763, *Shy close end* 1688 (perh. dial. *shy* 'unprolific', but *shay* 'rough grazing land', ultimately from OE *scaga* 'a copse, a small wood' is also poss. since names in *shaw* and *shay* regularly occur side by side, *v.* 'Shay names - a need for re-appraisal?', *Nomina* 12 (1988-9), 89-104 and cf. *Wilkershaw supra*; however, the forms are too disparate for any certainty); *James Smiths close* 1688, *Smiths Close* 1781, *Smiths hedge* 1746 (*v.* **hecg**); *Soap Spring* 1763, *Spring Close* 1746, 1763 (alluding to a spring where crude soap was manufactured, *v.* **sāpe, spring**, but cf. Wash Pond *supra*); *Southams Close* 1781; *in Austral' campo de Vppingham* 1564 Ct, (*the*) *South Feild(e)* 1634[1], 1634[2], 1688, 1696, 1720, 1723, c1725, - *Field* 1705, 1763, *South Field or Brand Field* 1763 (*v.* **sūð, feld**, one of the old open-fields of Uppingham); *Spicers booth* c1725, *Spices Booth* 1763 (*v.* **bōthe** 'a temporary shelter'; this name should perh. be cited in Uppingham Buildings *supra*); *Square acre Close* 1728; *Square Close* 1728; *Sto(a)ke foot(e) way* 1688, c1725, 1736, 1763, 1781, *Stoke foot path* 1763 (Stoke Dry parish lies to the south-west); *Stone Hill* 1799 (*v.* **stān**); *Stonye furlong* 1634, *stonie furlonge* 1637, *Ston(e)y Furlong* 1688, 1705, 1720, 1723, 1728, 1736, 1746, 1781 (*v.* **stānig**); *Stybbynges* 1373 Ipm ('a place with tree-stumps, a clearing', *v.* **stybbing**); *Teates landes* 1638 (from the surn. *Teate/Teyte, v.* **land**); *Thorpe footeway* c1725 (Thorpe by Water parish lies to the south-east); *Three Acre Piece* 1763 (*v.* **pece**); *Tong Furlong* 1749, *Tongue Land(s)* 1728, 1746, 1763, *tongland furlong* 1634[1], *Tong Land Furlong* 1705, 1723, *Tangland furlong* 1705, *Tongue land furlong* 1730 ('a spit of land', *v.* **tang; land**); *the townes end* 1634[2], *at the Townes End* 1720, 1723, *The Town's end* 1705, *the Towns End* 1736, *Townsend Furlong* 1746 (*v.* **tūn, ende**[1]); *the Turnpike Rails* 1763 (*v.* **turnepike, raile**); *Twigdins* 1763 (a Mr *Twigden* owned land in Uppingham c1725); *Upper Furlong* 1746, 1763; *Uppingham Course* 1781 SM (a reference to the old racecourse); *Vppingham parke* 1610 Speed, 1645 Map, *Vppinham park* 1610 Speed (*v.* **park**); *Walbankes hedge* 1728 (from the family name of Adam *Walbancks* 1634[1], v. **hecg**); *John Wards Close* 1746; *Water Furrows* 1746 (perh. 'land where water tends to lie in the furrows' or else simply 'wet furrows', *v.* **wæter, furh**); *Water Gaules* 1688, *Watergalls* c1725 ('the wet places in the open-field', *v.* **wæter, galla**); *Watermill furlong* 1688, 1736, 1746, *Water Mill furlong* c1725, 1728, 1746, 1781 (*v.* **water-myln**); *le Westfeld* 1550 Pat, *Westfeilde* 1634[2], (*the*) *West Feild(e)* 1634[1], 1688, 1696, 1720, 1723, c1725, - *Field* 1705, 1763 (*v.* **west, feld**; one of the great open-fields, and also known as the Wood Field); *Whetstones Close* 1688; *White acre* 1688, c1725 (in eModE, *white* 'infertile' is contrasted with *black* 'fertile', *v.* **hwīt, æcer**); *White Cross(e)* 1688, 1746 (*v.* **hwīt, cros**); *Willcoxe Gap* 1763 (with the surn. *Wilcox, v.* **gappe**); *Willows*

1736 (*v.* **wilig**); *Wood Close,* - *Corner* 1746, *Wood Close Gapp* 1728 (*v.* **wudu, corner, gappe**); *the Wood footway* 1736; *Woodfield Close* 1728 (*v.* Woodfield *supra*); *Woodpile leyes* 1728 (with ModE **wood-pile** 'a pile or stack of wood, especially for fuel', *v.* **lēah**); *Yelsmores Close* 1746, *Yellsmoor Close* 1763, *Earlsmoor Close* 1763, *Yellsmoor Slade* 1763 (*v.* **slæd**) (perh. originally 'the nobleman's moorland', *v.* **eorl, mōr**[1]; the surn. *Earl* does not appear in f.ns. or in early records for the county); *Yorkes Close* 1736, *Yorks* - 1781 (*v. John Freemans otherwise Yorkes Close supra*).

Edith Weston

EDITH WESTON
> *Weston(e)* 1114, 1115-29 France, 1173 CartAnt, 1189 France *et freq* to 1610 Speed, -*tona* 1113, c1115 Reg, 1167 P, -*tun'* 1230 Cur (p)
> *Veston* 1198 France, 1275 RH, -*tona* 1155-66 France

The affix is normally added as:
> *Edi-, -y-* 1263 *Ass*, 1272 *FF et passim* to 1340 Pat *et freq* to 1610 Speed
> *Edith(e)* - 1309 Inqaqd, 1310 Pat *et passim* to 1378 Fine, 1594, 1634 *FF*
> - *Edith, -y-* 1270 RGrav, 1275 RH, 1294 Pat, 1298 *Deed*
> - *St Edith* 1372, 1375 Fine, 1381, 1386 Pat
> *Nedy-* 1576 Saxton

'The western estate', *v.* **west, tūn**. Edith Weston was a royal estate, once part of the dower lands of Edith (*Ēadgӯð*), queen of Edward the Confessor. Its name indicates its westerly relationship to the royal manor of Ketton. Later 14th century affixes confuse Queen Edith with the Anglo-Saxon saint Edith. For the prosthetic *n* of Saxton's prefix, cf. *N*ed and *N*oll for Edward and Oliver.

WITCHLEY WARREN FM, - SPINNEY
> *Hwicceslea* a.1075 (l12) GeldR, *Hwiccleslea* a.1075 (l12) ib, *Whicchesle* 1290 For
> *Wiceslea* 1086 DB bis, -*le* 1086 ib, *Wicheslea* 1185 P
> *Wicelea* 1086 DB

Phwichel' 1220 Cur
Whicchele(e) 1299 *For*, 1313 *Deed*, 1344 *For*
Wicheley 1309, 1310 Inqaqd, *Wychele(e)* 1310 Pat, 1313 *Deed*,
   1375 Misc, *Wichele* 1373 *For*

The genitival *s* of the earliest forms suggests that the first
element is an unrecorded OE pers.n. *Hwicce* derived from the
major folk-name *Hwicce*. However, these apparent genitival forms
disappear very early and this is unusual. Also unusual is the
presence of four place-names within thirty miles of each other in
which a form of *Hwicce*, be it pers.n. or folk-name, seems to be
present, namely Whissendine, Wichley (in Whissendine), Witchley in
Edith Weston and Whiston Nth. It is very possible that rather than
a pers.n., it is the folk-name which is present here and that the
original form of the p.n. was **Hwicca-lēah* 'the woodland of the
Hwicce', *v.* **lēah**.

Witchley occupies a position beside a probable Roman road
running south from Empingham and through Edith Weston, North
Luffenham, Morcott and Barrowden parishes to cross R. Welland at
Turtle Bridge. Thus, if a folk-group of the Hwicce was early in situ
here, its position on an ancient routeway would parallel that of the
Hwicce in Whissendine on the Roman road running west to Fosse
Way from the major Romano-British settlement at Thistleton.

Witchley is the name of two hundreds in the Northamptonshire
Geld Roll of a.1075, *Hwicceslea east hundred* and *Hwiccleslea west
hundred*. In DB, these are treated as a single hundred: thus
variously *Wiceslea Hund'*, *Wicesle Hund'*, *Wiceslea Wapent'*, *Wicelea
Wapent'*. The hundred is unrecorded after 1086, *v.* **hundred,
vápnatak**.

Minor names arising are: *pro vasto de Wicheslea* 1185 P (*v.*
waste), *Wich(e)ley Heath* 1610 Speed, 1616 *ExchDep*, *Witchley Heath*
1695 *Map* (*v.* **hæð**), *Ketton Common or Wichley Heath* 1616 DKR,
Witchley Common 1780 Map (*v.* **commun**), *Wychley Warren* 1750,
1772 *Hotchkin*, c1800 Map, *Wi(t)chley Warren* c1760, 1769 *Hotchkin*,
1801 Map, 1810 *Hotchkin*, 1846, 1863 White, *Wichley Warren Corner*
1758 *Anc* (*v.* **corner**), *Wychly Warren Farm* c1800 ib, *Warren Spinney*
c1800 Map (*v.* **wareine**).

BERRYBUT SPINNEYS, *Berribut* 1676 (1794) *Hotchkin*, *Berrybutt*

1681 (1794) *ib*, *Berrey But* 1746 *Anc*, *Berry Butt* 1874 *Hotchkin*, *Berr(e)y Butts* 1746, 1842 *Anc*, *Berrybutts* 1829 *ib*, cf. *Little Berry Butts* 1851 *ib*, *Bottom -*, *Top Berrybuts* 1943 *Map*, *Berributt Close* 1682 (1794) *Hotchkin*, 1758 (1829) *Anc*, *Berrybutt Close* 1815, 1824 *ib*, *berry butt hedge* 1634 *Terrier*, *Berrybutt piece* 1651 (1794) *Hotchkin*, *v.* **berige, butte, hecg, pece.** BLUEBOTTLE LODGE. BRAKE SPINNEY, cf. *Bottom -*, *Top Breaks* 1846 *TA*, *Brakehill* 1651 (1794) *Hotchkin*, *Brackhill* 1681 (1794) *ib*, *Brake Hill* 1746 *Anc*, *Brackhill Gate* 1758 *ib*, *Brakehill Gate* 1796 *ib*, *Brakehill Lane* 1796 *ib*, *v.* **bræc**[1], **hyll, gata.** CANDLESTICK SPINNEY, so named because of its shape. CAPTAIN'S COVERT. CHURCH FM. CHURCH LANE. EAST LODGE (lost), 1846, 1863 White. EDITH WESTON CHURCH, *the church of St Mary* 1935 VCH. EDITH WESTON HALL, cf. *Old Hall* 1935 ib. EDITH WESTON QUARRIES. FOOTBALL PIECE, 1943 *Map*. FORTY ACRE BARN. GIBBET LANE, leading to Gibbet Gorse in Hambleton. THE GORSE, *v.* **gorst.** THE GRANGE, *v.* **grange.** THE GREEN (local), 1724 *Hotchkin*, *v.* **grēne**[2]. HOME FM, *v.* **home.** KETTON GORSE, *v.* **gorst.** LONG COVERT. MASONS ARMS P.H. (lost), now Hurstbourne Cottage - VR. NEW BARN LODGE (2½"). THE PRIORY (local), 1863 White. Formerly an alien cell of the Benedictine Abbey of St George de Boscherville in Normandy, it passed to the Carthusian house of St Mary and St Anne of Coventry in 1390 Pat. Only its fish ponds remain at SK 925 055, but half of the site is now beneath Rutland Water, *v.* MER 14. THE NEW RECTORY, *The Rectory* 1935 VR. THE OLD RECTORY, 1935 ib. RECTORY LANE. SLIP INN P.H. (lost), c1750, 1757, 1758 *Anc*. THORN COVERT. WELL CROSS, cf. *ad fontem de Weston* 1298 *Deed* (p), *atte Welle* 1337 Pat (p), 1340 ib (p), 1355 Misc (p), *v.* **wella.** WESTON LODGE (EDITH WESTON LODGE FM 6") is *West Lodge* 1846 White. WHEATSHEAF P.H., 1846, 1863 ib. WHITE HART P.H. (lost), 1846 ib, closed in 1868 - VR. THE YEWS.

Field-Names

Undated forms in (a) are 1943 *Map*. Those dated c1800, 1809 (1829), 1810 (1829), 1811, 1814, 1815, 1817 (1829), 1822 (1829), 1824, 1829, 1842, 1850, 1851, 1855, 1861, 1869, 1872, 1882, 1889 and 1891 are *Anc*; those of 1804, 1810, 1839,

1841, 1874, 1877 and 1878 are *Hotchkin*; those dated 1846 are *TA*. Early forms dated 1621 are VCH; those of 1634 and 1650 are *Terrier*; those of 1651 (1794), 1676 (1794), 1681 (1794), 1682 (1794), 1707, 1724, 1746 (1822), 1750, 1753, 1759, c1760, 1762, 1766, 1769, 1772 and 1795 are *Hotchkin*; those dated 1675, 1711, 1738 (1811), 1742, 1746, c1750, 1757, 1758, 1758 (1829), 1763, 1775 (1811), 1788, 1788 (1829), 1789 and 1796 are *Anc*; those of 1705 are *Deed*.

(a) Acre, Two -, Five Acre, Seven Acres 1846, Ten -, Eleven -, Sixteen -, Eighteen -, Twenty-two -, Twenty-eight Acre (*v.* **æcer**); Barkers Bushes 1814, 1874 (1681 (1794), 1746, from the surn. *Barker*, cf. William *Barker* 1524 SR, husbandman, *v.* **busc**); Barn Cl; Bastard Leys 1814 (*Bastard Leyes* 1757, dial. **bastard** 'unproductive, poor, barren', *v.* **lēah**; this pasture is also recorded in neighbouring N. Luffenham f.ns. (b)); Black Piece (*v.* **pece**); Blind Pit 1874, Blind Pitt Mdw 1842, - Pit - 1874, Blind Pits Great Mdw, - Little - 1809 (1829), 1829, Blind Pits Close 1809 (1829), 1829, Blind Pit Plantation 1874 (with **blind** 'hidden by vegetation', *v.* **pytt**); Branstons Cl 1810, Branstons Meadow Cl 1810 (*Branston's Meadow Close* 1757, c1760, *Branstons Meadow Close* c1760, 1795, in the tenure of John *Branston* 1795), Branstons Lane 1810 (*Branstone's Lane* 1757, *Branstons Lane* c1760, cf. *Thomas Branstons Lane end* 1681 (1794)); Bridge Cl 1842; Bottom -, Top Brooke; Calibut's (*Calibutt* 1681 (1794), *Callibut Close* 1746, *Callibutt* - 1757, *Calybutt* - 1789, *Callibutt Close and Meadow* 1763, *v.* **calu, butte**); Clark's Cl (cf. *Clarkes baulke* 1681 (1794), *v.* **balca**); Bottom -, Top Clenwell (*Clenwel* 1746, *Clenwell* 1788, *Clenwells Spring* 1757, *v.* **clǣne, wella**); The Clinkers 1814 (1757, c1760, referring to a field with **clinker** 'furnace slag' in the soil); Combhead Cl 1814 (*Coomes head* 1651 (1794), *Comes head* 1681 (1794), *Combes head Close* 1757, 'the upper end of the valley', *v.* **cumb, hēafod**); Dalby Cl 1869 (1775 (1811), *Dalbye* - c1760; from the surn. *Dalby*); Edith Weston Fd 1829; First Fd; Fox Cover 1846 (*v.* **cover(t)**); Front Fd; Gold Hills (*Golding* 1621, *Goulding* 1750; either 'meadow with (marsh-) marigolds' or 'the (marsh-) marigold place', *v.* **golde, eng, -ing**[2]); Grandmother's Cl (*v.* **grandmother**); Harlewong 1810, 1877, 1878 (*Harlewonge* 1757, *Harlewong Closes* 1772, cf. *Harle baulke* 1681 (1794); earlier forms are needed to establish the meaning of *Harle-*, *v.* **vangr, balca**); Harnett Hill 1842, 1874, Harnet Hill Cl 1815, Harnett - 1824 (*Harnot hill* 1746, *Harnet* - 1746, *Harnutt Hill Close* c1750, 1757, from eModE dial. *arnut, ernut* 'the earth-nut, the pig-nut', the edible root of *Bunium flexuosum*); Harts Cl 1814 (*William Harts Close* 1681 (1794), *Hart's Close* 1757); the Heath 1810, 1874 (1650, 1651 (1794), 1676 (1794), 1707, c1750, 1757, 1769, 1775 (1811), *Normanton Heath* 1746), Heath Cl 1804, 1811, 1815, 1824, 1842 (*the Heath Close* 1763) (*v.* **hǣð**; Normanton parish adjoins to the west); Home Cl 1814, 1815, 1824, 1842, 1846 (*the Home Close* 1650, 1738 (1811), *v.* **home**); Home Fd 1943 (cf. *Home Meadow* 1788, *v.* **home**); the Hop Yard 1814 (1757, c1760, *v.* **hop-yard**); Horse Cl 1810 (1829), 1829, 1842, 1874, Horse Close Mdw 1829, Horse Cl below the Road

1842, Bottom Horse Cl 1874; Ilfin's Cottage c1800; (The) Irishman's Cl 1842, 1874; Jackson's Cl 1874; Bottom of Ketton Dykes 1821 (1757, *Ketton Dike* 1651 (1794), 1681 (1794), *Ketton Dikes* 1707, 1747, *v.* **dīk**; Ketton parish adjoins to the east); Lamas (x2), Lammas Cl 1810, 1817 (1829), 1842, 1846, 1874, William Lawrences Lamas Cl 1810 (in the tenure of *William Lawrence* 1810) (*Branstone's Lamas Closes* 1757, *Branstons* - c1760 (with the family name of Thomas *Branston* 1681), *Wrights Lammas Close* 1758 (1829), *v.* **lammas**); Lawrence Cl 1804 (cf. William Lawrences Lamas Cl *supra*); Ling Cover 1846 (*v.* **lyng, cover(t)**); Little Mdw 1874; The Lodge Cl 1850, The Lodge House 1842, 1851, Lodge Mdw 1943, The Lodge Pen 1846 (*v.* **penn^2**); Luffenham Fd c1800 (N. Luffenham parish adjoins to the south-east); Lyndon Hill c1800, 1806 Map (Lyndon parish adjoins to the south-west); Manifold Atton, Manifold Cl 1943, Manifold Leys 1809 (1829), 1829 (*Manifold Leys* 1788, 1788 (1829); prob. with the surn. *Manifold*; *Atton* is also a surn., cf. Edward -, Luke - and Mark *Atton* 1932 Kelly, graziers in Braunston, Robert *Atton* 1932 ib, grazier in Brooke); Manton Way 1810, 1814 (1651 (1794), *Mantonway* 1746 '(land beside) the road to Manton', *v.* **weg**); Middle Cl 1811, 1861; Middle Fd 1861; Milking Fd (a field where the cows were milked, *v.* **milking**); Mill Fd 1810, Near -, Far -, First - 1889 (*the Millfeild* 1650, (*the*) *Mill Field* 1651 (1794), 1676 (1794), 1681 (1794), 1682 (1794), 1746, c1750, 1769, 1775 (1811), *v.* **myln, feld**; earlier called *Eastfeild*, one of the great open-fields of the village); Mill Hill 1842, 1874, Far -, First - 1855 (*Mill Hill* 1746); Moor Leys 1814 (*Moore leyes* 1651 (1794), *Moor Lees* 1746, *v.* **mōr^1, lēah**); Naylor's; Nether Mdw 1846, 1943 (1759); Nine Leys 1815, 1824, 1842, - Mdw 1874 (*v.* **lēah**); Nineteen Acre Cl 1815, 1824, Nineteen Acres 1842, 1872; Normanton Nook (*v.* **nōk**; Normanton parish adjoins to the north-east); (the) Notwells 1810, 1841, Knotwell Cl 1810, 1878 (*Notwells* 1681 (1794), *Knotwell Close* 1757, *v.* East Notwells in Lyndon f.ns. (a); 'the stream where the nuts grow' is evidently that which forms the boundary between Edith Weston and Lyndon from SK 922 043 to SK 925 042); Nova Scotia 1804 (a name transferred from Canada, indicating a field remote from the village); Nuts Cl (perh. cf. Harnett Hill and Notwells *supra*); Pages Holme 1846 (*v.* **holmr**; with the surn. *Page*, cf. John *Page* 1522 MilS, 1524 SR and Page's Five Acre in nearby Ridlington f.ns. (a)); The Park 1943, Park Gate c1800, - Cl 1943, Park Leys 1817 (1829), 1829, 1842, 1874 (*Park(e) leyes* 1634, 1650, *Park Leas(es)* 1676 (1794), *Park Leys* 1682 (1794), c1760, *Park Lees* 1746), Park Leys Cl 1829, (the) Park Leys Mdw 1809 (1829), 1829, 1842, 1874, Park Leys Mdw below the Road 1842, Park Leys Top Mdw 1809 (1829), 1829, Top Park Leys Mdw 1874 (*v.* **park, lēah**); (The) Pike Piece 1809 (1829), 1814, 1842, 1874 (dial. *pike* 'land running to a point', *v.* **pīc^1, pece**); Little -, Poor Hills; Prestons Home Cl 1874; the Quick 1814 (1757, 1758 (1829), *a certain fence called the Quick* c1760; *New Quick* 1746, *v.* **cwic** 'a quickset hedge'); Roadside; Saintfoin Cl 1842 (from the leguminous herb *sainfoin* (*Onobrychis sativa*), once much grown for fodder); Sands 1874, (the) East Sands 1804, 1817 (1829), 1839, West Sands 1822 (1829), The Sands Cl

1842, Sand Cl 1882 (the Sands 1634, 1650, 1651 (1794), 1676 (1794), 1746, c1760, East -, West Sands 1788, v. sand); Long Shrubbs 1815, 1824, - Shrubs 1842 (longeshrubs 1634, Long Shrubbs 1681 (1794), 1746, v. lang¹, scrubb); South Cl 1815, 1824; (the) South Field 1810, 1814, 1821, 1842, 1874, Far -, Near - 1891 ((the) Southfeild 1634, 1650, (the) South Field 1651 (1794), 1676 (1794), 1681 (1794), 1682 (1794), 1746, 1769, Great South Field 1788, v. sūð, feld, one of the great open-fields of the village); Little South Field 1829 (1788); Stonehill 1814, Stone Hill 1943 (Stonehill 1651 (1794), Stone Hill 1681 (1794), v. stān, hyll); Stonepit Fd (cf. the stonepitts 1634, v. stān-pytt); Tewson's Fm 1874 (cf. Tewson's House in Normanton f.ns. (a)); Deborah Thorpes Cls 1810 (Deborah Thorpes Close c1760, held by Deborah Thorpe c1760); Tibber's Twenty-one Acre; Top Cl; Town Cl 1809 (1829), 1810, 1814, 1829, 1842 (le Towne Close 1621, (the) Town Close 1681 (1794), 1746, c1760, 1788, 1788 (1829)), Town Close Hill 1809 (1829), 1829, 1874, Town Close Mdw 1809 (1829), 1829, 1842, 1874, Town Close Nook 1814, 1874 (v. nōk), Town Cl on the Heath 1874 (v. tūn); Townside Cl 1842; Twin-gates 1824 (Tweenegates 1634, Twine Gates 1682 (1794), Twingates 1769, '(land lying) between the roads', v. betwēonan, gata); the uninclosed Meer 1841 (a plot of land so called, v. (ge)mǣre); Veazey's Mdw 1874 (cf. Thomas Vesey 1524 SR of Gt. Casterton); West Cl 1815, 1824, 1846, 1874; (The) West Fd 1809 (1829), 1810, 1814, 1842 ((the) Westfeild 1634, 1650, (the) West Field 1651 (1794), 1676 (1794), 1681 (1794), 1682 (1794), 1707, Westfield 1746, v. west, feld, one of the great open-fields of the village); the West Lands 1821 (v. land); Weston Mdws; Weston Town Land c1800 (v. tūn); Whitehead Leys 1814, 1842, 1874, West Whiteseds Leys 1877, Whitead Leys Mdw 1810 (Whitehead leyes 1634, White Heads leys 1676 (1794), Whitehead Leas 1682 (1794), Whitehead Leys 1788, 1788 (1829), Whitehead Lees Meadow 1746, from the surn. Whitehead, cf. Robert Whyethed 1525 SR of neighbouring Empingham, v. lēah); Wigginton Five Acre (with the surn. Wigginton, cf. Robert Wyggenton 1522 MilS of Belton); Wood Hill 1804, Woodhill 1810 (Woodhill 1634, 1746, 1757, Wood Hill 1681 (1794), Wood Hill Close 1795, cf. Edyweston wood 1610 Speed, v. wudu, hyll); the Woodlands 1810 (a close so called).

(b) Ash(e)furlong(e) 1634, 1650, Ash Furlong(e) 1651 (1794), 1681 (1794), 1682 (1794), 1707, 1746 (v. æsc); George Austins headland 1676 (1794) (v. hēafod-land; George Austin was resident in Lyndon in 1681 Conant); Balls house 1753; the Bark Barn 1766 (perh. referring to undressed timber in its construction, but ME bark-house was 'a tanning shed' and this may be the meaning here); Bates Penn 1681 (1794), Bates Pen Furlong 1676 (1794), 1746 (from the surn. Bates, v. penn²); Benysons Land 1675, Benystones land 1742 (William Beneson held land here in 1522 MilS); Richard Billings Land 1681 (1794); Brakey Close 1759 (v. bræc¹, -ig³); Brooms Folly c1750, 1758 (with the surn. Broom, cf. Brooms Bushes in neighbouring Manton f.ns. (b), v. folie); the Bushes 1681 (1794) (v. busc); Cheselden's Gate c1760 (with the surn. Chesildine);

Church Headland 1676 (1794), 1746, - *Furlong* 1746 (*v.* **hēafod-land**); *The Constables Grass* 1681 (1794) (*v.* **conestable, gærs,** cf. *Constables Grass* in Pilton f.ns. (b) and *the Constables Grass* Ca 371); *Miss Cooks Close* 1758; *Joseph Cookes hadland* 1681 (1794), *Thomas Cook's Headland* 1746 (prob. refer to the same headland, *v.* **hēafod-land**); *le Cowe Close* 1621, *Cow Close* 1750, 1772; *Cowpasture Close* 1705; *the Creach* 1650, 1676 (1794), 1681 (1794), 1682 (1794), *the Creach Furlonge* 1681 (1794) (dial. *creach* 'a light sandy or gravelly soil'); *Dud seeke* 1681 (1794) (*v.* **dodde, sik**); *the Earth Close* 1789 (*v.* **crð**); *Eastfeild* 1634 (*v.* **ēast, feld;** an earlier name for Mill Fd *supra*); *the far ford* 1651 (1794) (*v.* **feor, ford**); (*the*) *Far(r) Meadow* 1651 (1794), 1676 (1794), 1788 (*v.* **feor, mæd**); *Field Furlong* 1746, *Field Way* 1746 (*v.* **feld**); *the Forcklese* 1682 (1794), *Forke seek(e)s* 1676 (1794), 1681 (1794) (*v.* **forca, lēah, sik**); *the Four and Twenty Roods* 1651 (1794), 1681 (1794) (*v.* **rōd³**); *Freeman Holt* 1746 (from the family name of Robert *Freeman* 1522 MilS, *v.* **holt**); *Gibbs Pitt* c1750, 1757 (from the surn. *Gibb(s)*, *v.* **pytt**); *the Great Close* 1789; *Hambleton Hedge* 1681 (1794) (the parish boundary hedge of Hambleton, *v.* **hecg**); *Hill Close* 1772; *Hawkeinge hedges* 1634 (with the surn. *Hawking,* cf. William *Haukinge* 1522 MilS of Belton, *v.* **hecg**); *the Hollow* 1772 (*v.* **holh**); *Horseleys Way* 1681 (1794), *Hors(e)ley Way* 1758, c1760, 1775 (1811) (*v.* **hors, lēah**); *Thomas Islipp the smiths hadland* 1681 (1794) (a *Thomas Islip* is also recorded in the village in 1724, *v.* **hēafod-land**); *Jermyns Farm* 1746, 1746 (1822) (cf. William *Jerman* 1522 MilS of N. Luffenham); *Kittam Close* 1621, *Kettons Close* 1750 (Ketton parish adjoins to the east); *New Kirke* 1621, 1750 (apparently with Scand **kirkja** 'church' and thus suggesting newly endowed church land, but it is poss. that both this f.n. and *New Kyrke* in Wardley f.ns. (b) represent 'New Quick', i.e. newly planted quickset hedging, cf. The Quick *supra* where *New Quick* occurs for 1746); *Lamb Close* 1795; *Lees Yard Land* 1711 (with the surn. *Lee, v.* **gerd-landes**); *Linden Close* 1650, *Lindon* - 1651 (1794), *Linden Closes* 1746, *Linden fur Close* 1651 (1794), *Linden furre Close Gate* 1650 (*v.* **feor**), *Linden Furlong* 1746, *Linden gate* 1681 (1794) (*v.* **gata**), *Linden shrubbs* 1682 (1794), *Lyndon Shrubbs* c1750, 1757 (*v.* **scrubb**) (Lyndon parish adjoins to the south-west); *Longlands* 1746, *Long Langelands* 1676 (1794), *Short(e) Langlands* 1634, 1650, 1676 (1794), *Long Land Bushes* 1681 (1794) (*v.* **busc**), *Langland Pitts* 1681 (1794) (*v.* **pytt**) (*v.* **lang¹, land**); *Luffenham Hedge* 1634, 1676 (1794), 1682 (1794), *Luffenham Hedge Furlong* 1746 (*v.* **hecg**), *Luffenham Nook(e)* 1682 (1794), 1746 (*v.* **nōk**), *Luffenham Piece Furlong* 1746 (*v.* **pece**), *Luffenham Way* 1746 (N. Luffenham parish adjoins to the south-east); *the Meadow* 1681 (1794); *the Meere* 1634 (*v.* **(ge)mǣre**); *the Mill* 1676 (1794), *Mill Close* 1763, *Millfurlonge* 1634, *Mill Furlong* 1676 (1794), 1746 (*v.* **myln**); *Mold Meadow* 1681 (1794), *Mooles* - 1681 (1794), *Moyld* - 1682 (1794) (with dial. *mould* 'the mole'); *Moss Holmes* 1676 (1794) (*v.* **mos, holmr**); (*the*) *Nether Furlong* 1651 (1794), 1676 (1794), 1746, *the neather Furlong* 1681 (1794) (*v.* **neoðera**); *Nettle Croft* 1759, 1772, *nether nettle crofte* 1634 (*v.* **netele, croft**); *the new house or the neither house* 1675 (*v.* **neoðera**); *Nine Acre Close* 1789; *Nobles Garden* 1772 (with the surn.

Noble); *Normanton Cawseway, Normanton New Causey Way* 1758 (Normanton parish adjoins to the north-east, *v.* **caucie**); *Normanton Meare* 1681 (1794) (*v.* **(ge)mǣre**); *Notwell's Grasse* 1681 (1794) (eModE *grass* 'a piece of grassland', *v.* **gærs** and (the) Notwells *supra*); *the Oaks* 1746; *Oat Close* 1757; *the Parsons Gleabe Close* 1676 (1794) (*v.* **glebe**); *atte Pertre* 1375 Misc (p) (*v.* **pertre**); *Randike Meer* 1746 (the first el. is either OE *rān* 'a boundary strip' or OE *rand* 'an edge, a border', *v.* **dīk, (ge)mǣre**); *Redbankes* 1634, *Red Banks Meadow* 1746; *Reights Furlong* 1746 (with the surn. *Wr*(*e*)*ight*, John *Wright* was resident in Edith Weston 1810); *John Ridlingtons Hedge* 1676 (1794), *John Ridlington's Holme* c1750, c1760 (*v.* **hecg, holmr**); *the Roe* 1635, *the Row* 1746, 1758 (*v.* **rāw**); *Roughlands* 1634 (*v.* **rūh**[1], **land**); *the Rushes* 1634, 1650, 1746, *Rushes Furlong* 1746 (*v.* **risc**); *the Sandy Close* 1763 (*v.* **sandig**); *Sitten Bush* 1681 (1794) (dial. *sitten* 'stunted in growth', describing scrub, *v.* **busc**); *South Field Close* 1795; *the Long Spinn*(*e*)*y* 1757, *Nether Spyney* 1621, *Over Spyney* 1621 (*v.* **uferra**), *the upper Spinney* 1759 (*v.* **spinney**); *Spring Close* 1759, 1772 (*v.* **spring**); *Stamford Way* 1651 (1794), *- Furlong* 1746 ('(the furlong beside) the road to Stamford'); *Stump Cross* 1676 (1794) (prob. the broken shaft of a medieval cross, *v.* **stump, cros**); *Sweete well dike* 1650, *Sweetwell Dike* 1681 (1794) (*v.* **swēte, wella, dīk**); *Swingate Furlong* 1746 (*swingate* is perh. 'pasturage for pigs' and to be compared with **cow-gate** *q.v.*, cf. also *sheep-gate* 'pasturage for sheep' NED *s.v.* sheep 8; however, the compound is not recorded independently in this sense, but cf. also *galtesgate* in Lyddington f.ns. (b); otherwise, *v.* **swīn**[1], **gata**); *Sudwell, Sudewell Dike* 1676 (1794) (*v.* **sūð, wella, dīk**); *Tentar Lane* 1746, *the Tentars* 1746 (*v.* **tentour**); *Thos. Tomblins Headland* 1746 (*Thomas Tomblin* held land in neighbouring Hambleton in 1785 *Surv, v.* **hēafod-land**); *Top Field Close* 1788 (*v.* **feld**); *Town Balk* 1746 (*v.* **balca**), (*the*) *Towne hadland* 1634, 1681 (1794), *The Town headland* 1651 (1794) (*v.* **hēafod-land**), *the Townsend* 1676 (1794) (*v.* **ende**[1]), *Town-Street* 1746 (*v.* **strǣt**) (*v.* **tūn**); *the Upper Meadow* 1746; *the water furrowes* 1634 (either 'land where water tends to lie in the furrows' or simply 'wet furrows', *v.* **wæter, furh**); *Wells's Peice, Wells - 1746* (*v.* **pece**), *Well's Quarter Land* 1738 (1811) (computed to be a quarter of one yardland and in the possession of Thos. *Wells* 1738 (1811)); *Wheatland Close* 1762; *Whitewall* 1757, 1769; *Wychley Piece Close* 1772 (*v.* **pece** and Witchley Warren Fm, - Spinney *supra*); *Wranglands* 1676 (1794), *Rangland, - Furlong* 1746 (*v.* **wrang, vrangr, land**).

Wing

WING

 Weng(*e*) 1136-9 Reg, 1202 Ass *et passim* to 1209-19 RHug *et freq*
 to 1298 OSut *et passim* to 1394 Rut (p), 1428 FA, *Wenga*

1136-9, 1148-54 Reg *et passim* to c1291 Tax
Wieng' 1203, 1204 P, *Wyenge* 1296 *SR*
Whenge 1315 Ipm, 1403, 1407 Cl, *Wheenge* 1346 *FF*
Weyng 1390 Pat, *Veynge* 1409 ELiW, 1409 PRep
Wyng(e) 1294 *Ass*, 1305 FA *et passim* to 1543 *Conant, Wing*
     1516 EpCB, 1610 Speed

'The field', *v.* **vengi**. OScand *vengi* is a derivative of ON *vangr*
'an in-field'. The earliest reference to this toponym is in the
bounds of the Ayston charter of 1046 where we find *into wenge
forde* (*v.* The Ayston Charter). It is uncertain whether at this date
wenge applied to a field or to a settlement which had developed
there.

WESTHORPE
     Westhorp' 1296 *SR* (p), *Westorp'* 1327 *ib* (p)
     Westhrope 1607 VCH, *Westrops* 1631 *Terrier*

'The western outlying farmstead', *v.* **west, þorp**. At the
western edge of Wing village, this farmstead would appear to be a
comparatively late foundation.

BOTTOM ST.   CHURCH ST, cf. *viam que ducit ad ecclesiam*
c1212-38 (14) *RBT, v.* **cirice**. CITY YARD (local), possibly alluding to
the ancient turf-cut maze *infra*. These mazes were often called City of
Troy or Troy Town or The Walls of Troy. Popular lore derived such
names from the supposedly complicated structure of the walls of Troy,
so formed that an enemy, once inside, could neither find his way into
the city nor out again. However, The City is sometimes used ironically
of a very small group of houses, cf. The City in Empingham.
CROWNWELL FM, *v.* Crown Well Bridge, Manton parish.   THE
CUCKOO P.H.   THE GRANGE, 1935 VCH, *v.* **grange**.   THE
KING'S ARMS P.H. MIDDLE ST. NOEL'S ARMS P.H. (lost), 1846,
1863 White, named from the *Noel* family of Exton.   OLD HALL
(local), cf. *atte Halle* 1358 Pat (p), *v.* **hall**. RAILWAY INN (lost),
1846, 1863 White. RECTORY, 1863 ib, *Rectory House* 1846 ib.   RED
LION P.H. (lost), 1815 *Deed*. REEVES LANE. TOP ST. WING
CHURCH, *Church* (*St Peter and St Paul*) 1846, 1863 White. WING

HALL. WING HOLLOW, v. **holh**. WING MAZE, *Winge Maze* 1631 *Terrier, Maze* 1846, 1863 White, v. **masc**. WINGWELL (local), *iuxta fontem de Weng'* c1212-38 (14) *RBT, Wingewells* 1631 *Terrier, Bottom Wingwell* 1943 *Map*, v. **wella**.

Field-Names

Undated forms in (a) are 1943 *Map*. Undated forms in (b) are c1212-38 (14) *RBT*. Forms dated 1631 are *Terrier* (extracted by Mr G.A. Chinnery).

(a) Four Acres, Five -, Ten Acre (v. **æcer**); Ball's Bottom Cl, Ball's Mdw (cf. Ball's Mill in neighbouring Manton f.ns. (a)); Bottom -, Middle Belgrave (from the surn. *Belgrave*, cf. the Rev. Mr *Belgrave* 1785 SM of Preston and Mill Hole *infra*); Berry's Big Fd (poss. with the surn. *Berry*, but the field borders Wing Burrows in Bisbrooke which may have given the form Berry's -); Bridge Cl; Bridle Fds; Cedar Fd; Clark's Fds; Cramps; Dedmoor 1824 O, 1943 (*Dead more furlong* 1631, 'infertile moorland', v. **dēad, mōr**[1]); Footpad Fd ('enclosure with a footpath', v. **pad**); Gibson's Acres; Bottom -, Glaston Cl; Far -, Near Grammers (with dial. *grammer* 'grandmother', cf. Grandmother's Cl in Edith Weston f.ns. (a), v. **grandmother**); Headlands (v. **hēafod-land**); Hill Cl; Home Cl, - Fd (v. **home**); Lester's Barn Cl, Lester's Water Mdw (cf. Lester's Barnfield in neighbouring Bisbrooke f.ns. (a), Lester's Barn Fd in Glaston f.ns. (a) and Thomas *Leyster* 1522 MilS of Belton); Lotts Covert c1800, 1806 Map, Lotts or Gorse Hill (from the surn. *Lott*, v. **cover(t), gorst**); Mill Cl, (Little) Mill Fd, Mill Hole or Top Belgrave (v. **hol**[1]) (cf. *molendino ventritico de Wenge* c1212-38 (14), v. **wind-mylne**; an early windmill mound survives in part in the hedge-line at SK 8951 0274 and there was another windmill in use more recently across the road at SK 8958 0274, v. MER 48); Bottom -, Top Moles (from the surn. *Mole*, cf. Ambrose *Mole* 1763 *Bir* of nearby Uppingham); Morter Pits (*the Mortar Pits* 1785 *Deed*, v. **morter-pytt**); The Paddock or Bottom Sixteen Acres; Lower Parker's Cl or Ten Acres, Upper Parker's Cl (from the surn. *Parker*); Pit and Style; Pumphouse Fd (the 19th cent. saw the installation of mechanical pumps and rams for water supply); Sharlow's Water Mdw; Side of the Hill; Stanicle or Tomblin's Great Cl (the first el. is presumably OE **stānig** 'stony', perh. with **clæg** 'clay' (cf. Cleedale in Hambleton f.ns. (a)), but earlier forms are needed for a sound etymology); Station Fds; Sutor's Cl, - Mdws; Tomblin's Bottom Cl, - Great Cl (cf. Stanicle *supra*); William's Lane Cl (cf. William's Cl in neighbouring Ayston f.ns. (a)); Wingfield or Sixteen Acres; Wing Pit; Wrangling or Wrangland (*le Wrongelond* c1212-38 (14), 'the crooked selion', v. **wrang, vrangr, land**).

(b) *Abbotts meadow* 1631 (the Abbot of Thorney held land in Wing 1522 MilS, *v.* **abbat**); *Butterwell slade* 1631 (*v.* **butere, wella, slæd**, referring to a valley with rich pasture); *Brightmore home* 1631 (from the surn. *Brightmore*, cf. Wylliam *Bryghtmer* 1524 SR of neighbouring Morcott, *v.* **holmr**); *Gerberdfurlong* (at this early 13th cent. date, prob. from the OFr pers.n. *Gerbert*, *v.* **furlang**); *Glaston gate* 1631 (Glaston parish adjoins to the south-east, *v.* **gata**); *Guns yard* 1631 (with the surn. *Gun(n)*, *v.* **geard**); *hanging Crosse* 1631 (evidently 'cross on a steep slope', *v.* **hangende, cros**); *hither half acre* 1631; *le Holegate* ('road running in a hollow', *v.* **hol²**, **gata**); *semitam de Pilton*' ('the lane to Pilton', *v.* **lane**); *Kirke sike* 1631 (*v.* **kirkja, sik**, cf. Wing Church *supra*); *Langmore* 1631 (*v.* **lang¹**, **mōr¹**); *Linges* 1631 (*v.* **lyng**); *Marefurlong* 1631 (*v.* **(ge)mǣre**); *le Meduegate* (*v.* **mǣd, gata**); *Mooredike* 1631 (*v.* **mōr¹**, **dīk**); *Northfeild* 1631 (one of the open-fields of the village, *v.* **norð, feld**); *Paradise* 1649 *Asw* (*v.* **paradis** 'an orchard, a pleasure garden'); *Parsons Balke, Parsons Close* 1631 (prob. with **persone** 'a parson', *v.* **balca**); *priors medowe* 1565 *Ct*, *Priors meadow* 1631 (the Prior of St Neots held land in the parish 1522 MilS, *v.* **prior, mǣd**); *le Ridgate* (*v.* **ryde, gata**); *le Santfurlong* (*v.* **sand, furlang**); *Southbrookes* 1631 (*v.* **sūð, brōc**); *in campo australi* ('the south field', one of the great open-fields of the village, *v.* **sūð, feld**); *South hill* 1631; *Stanfordehill*' (apparently 'the hill by the stony ford' since Stamford L seems too far distant from Wing for it to feature here and Stamford as a surn. appears not to occur in the county, *v.* **stān, ford, hyll**); *stonewaters* 1631 (either 'stony ground beside a stream' or 'stony ground which regularly retains surface water', *v.* **stān, wæter**); *in campo occident*' de *Winge* 1565 *Ct*, *West feild* 1631 (one of the open-fields of the village, *v.* **west, feld**).

WRANGDIKE HUNDRED

Wrangedich(e) 1166, 1167 P, 1167 ChancR, 1169 P *et freq* to 1197 ib,
    -dik 1275, 1276 RH, *-dyk(e)* 1286 *Ass*, 1550, 1551 Pat, 1610
    Speed
Wrongedich 1168, 1169, 1170 P *et freq* to 1181 ib, *Wronghedich* 1256
    For, *Wrongedik(e)*, *-y-* 1257 Ipm, 1265 Misc, 1302 *AddCh*, 1305
    FA, *Wronggedik* 1296 *SR*
Wrangdych 1428 FA, *-dyk(e)* 1344 Pat, 1369 Ipm *et passim* to 1551
    Pat
Wrongdiche 1291 Abbr, *Wrongdyke* 1295 ib

From its earliest mention, the division is styled as a hundred, never as a wapentake. *Wrangedich* was the name given to the western part of the old Witchley Hundred, *v.* Witchley Warren Fm in Edith Weston. It appears to be OE *wrang-dīc 'crooked ditch', later Scandinavianized. OE *wrang* is not necessarily a loan from ON since it occurs in Berkshire as early as 944 (*on wrangan hylle* 944 (c1240) BCS 801 (S 496)), v. **wrang, dīc**. The whereabouts of the 'crooked ditch' which gave the hundred its name is unknown. The only *wrang-dīc* recorded is in North Luffenham parish, an unlikely position for a moot-site since it is at the very edge of this revised hundredal territory. A site for a hundredal court would have been more likely in Glaston or Seaton, central to the territorial unit. In Seaton, a *Syrepol* is recorded at the beginning of the 15th century. If its first element is OE *scīr* 'a shire, an administrative district', then the name of the pool may indicate the proximity of the hundred's moot-site.

Barrowden

BARROWDEN
>   *Berchedone* 1086 DB, *-dun* e13 *Rut*
>   *Bergedunam* 1141 Reg, *-dona(m)* 1153 ib, *-don'* 1202 Ass, 1220 Cur
>   *Bergendona* 1105-7 Reg, 1130 P (p)
>   *Beregedun* 1201 Ass, *-don'* 1202 ib (p), 1206 (p), 1210 Cur
>   *Berg(h)don* 1316, 1317 Cl, 1349 Ch *et passim* to 1428 FA
>   *Ber(o)ugdon* 1342, 1344 Pat *et passim* to 1431 Fine
>   *Berewedon(e)* 1212 RBE, 1220 *FF et passim* to 1364 Pap,
>   *Berwedon(e)* 1213 *FF*, 1219, 1231 Cur *et passim* to 1377
>   Fine, *Berewdon'* 1205 RFinib (p), *Bereudon(e)* 1321 *FF*,
>   *Berudon'* 1268 Cl, 1268 Ipm *et passim* to 1336 (e15)
>   *BelCartB, Berwdon'* 1272 (e15) *ib, Beroudon'* 1269 (e15) *ib*
>   (p) *et passim* to 1327 *SR, Berowydon* 1556 *Conant*
>   *Barghedon* 1263 *Ass, Barghdon* 1459 Pat
>   *Barugdon* 1428 FA, *Barroghdon* 1459 AD, *Barowghdon* 1486,
>   1551 Pat, *Bar(r)oug(h)don* 1490 ib, 1535 VE *et passim* to
>   1555 *Conant*, 1610 Speed
>   *Barodon* 1471 *Peake*, 1537 *MinAcct, Bar(r)owdon* 1479 Pat,
>   1511 LP *et passim* to 1552 Pat, *Bar(r)adon* 1503 ib, 1621
>   *FF*
>   *Bar(r)oughden* 1479, 1551 Pat, 1552 *Conant*
>   *Bar(r)owden* 1487 Cl, 1498 Ipm, 1695 *Map*

'The hill with burial mounds upon it', *v.* **beorg, dūn.** The barrows, already ancient when the Anglo-Saxons arrived in the region, stood on the ridge overlooking R. Welland. The line of barrows continued in neighbouring Seaton, in Thorpe by Water and in Lyddington. To the north-east, the crop marks of what are probably ploughed-out tumuli lie along R. Welland in Tixover parish, *v.* Crop Marks 64-5, 74-5.

Barrowden Inns and Taverns

CROWN (lost), 1896 White, closed in 1971 - VR.   EXETER ARMS, 1846, 1863 White, 1932 Kelly, named from the Marquess of *Exeter,* lord of the manor.   SWAN (lost), 1896 White, closed 1925 - VR. WHEEL (lost), 1846 White, closed 1925 - VR.   WINDMILL INN (lost, now Windmill House), 1846 White, 1850 Slater, 1932 Kelly.

TURTLE BRIDGE, 1806 Map, *Thurkelbregge* 1298 Ipm, *Turtles Bridge* 1762 *Anc,* cf. *Turtle Bridge Acre furlong, Turtle Brigg (Close) Furlong* 1798 *Burghley, Turtle Bridge (Close) Furlong* 1844 *ib.* The first element appears to be a surn. reflex of the OScand pers.n. *Þorketill, v.* SPNLY 309-11. This bridge across R. Welland connects Harringworth Nth with Barrowden.   One Ralph *Turcle* is mentioned in connection with Harringworth in 1247 *Ass* and the name of the bridge may have become associated with that of his family, *v.* **brycg** and cf. *Tirtle Meare* in Morcott f.ns. (b).

BAPTIST CHAPEL, *General Baptist Chapel* 1846 White. BERCKLEY HO., 1932 Kelly. BROOKLEIGH HO., 1932 ib. COPPICE LEYS, 1844, 1876, 1884, 1901-28 *Burghley, v.* **copis, lēah.** THE DRIFT, 1943 *Map, The Drift Road* 1844 *Burghley,* 'the cattle road', *v.* **drift.** DURANT FARMHOUSE (local), associated with Roland *Durant* (died 1588) whose monument is in St Peter's Church.   THE GREEN (local), *v.* **grēne²**.   THE MILL,· *molend' aquatic'* 1404 *FH, molendin' Aquatic'* 1624 *Deed, molendina aquatica* 1634 *ib, v.* **water-mylne.** THE RECTORY, 1846, 1863 White, 1932 Kelly. RED HILL, - FM, *Red Hill* 1844 *Burghley, Red Hill farm* 1932 Kelly, so called from the colour of the soil based on the

234 RUTLAND

ironstone, v. rēad. SHIRE OAKS, 1844 Burghley, 1849, 1873 Anc;
the oaks lie close to the county boundary, v. scīr¹, āc. ST
PETER'S CHURCH, Church 1863 White, cf. Church leyes 1665
Anc, Church Close, Church Furlong 1798 Burghley. OLD
TANNERY YARD (local). TIPPINGS LANE (local), cf. Tipping's
Close c1840 TA, Tippings - 1844, 1876, 1901-28 Burghley, from the
surn. Tipping of a 19th cent. blacksmith, while John Tippyng 1522
MilS was parish priest of neighbouring Caldecott. VINE
COTTAGE. WELLAND SPINNEY, 1943 Map, lies beside R.
Welland.

Field-Names

Undated forms in (a) are 1943 Map; those dated 1798, 1844¹, 1844², 1876, 1884,
1901-28 and 1950 are Burghley; those of 1839, 1840, 1849 and c1873 are Anc, while
those dated c1840 are TA. Early forms dated c1275 (e15) are BelCartB; 1298 are
Ipm; e14 are BelCartA; 1404 are FH; 1547-53 are Hart; 1626, 1652, 1665, 1720, 1726,
1750, 1776 and c1795 are Anc; 1632 are Terrier; 1748 and 1749 are Asw; 1796 are Surv
and 1798 are Burghley.

(a) The Seven -, The Twelve -, Fourteen Acre (v. æcer); The Allotments;
Barrowden Hay c1800, 1806 Map, 1824 O, Barrowden Heigh 1844¹ (le Esthay 1298, le
Hay 1404, Berowydon haye 1556 Conant, Baroug(h)don hey 1610 Speed; comprising a
finger of land which juts north-eastward between S. Luffenham and Tixover parishes,
v. (ge)hæg 'an enclosure', ēast); Barrowden Heath 1825 Map, The Heath c1840 (v.
hǣð); Barrowden Mdws 1840, - Mdw 1844¹, 1849, 1884 (earlier Woolland meadow
1624, 1629 Conant, a meadow(e) called Wo(o)lland 1626, 1726, Welland 1652, Wolland
1720, Welland al's Barrowden Meadow c1750, Welland otherwise Barrowden Meadows
1776, Barrowden Meadow c1795; beside R. Welland); Barrowden Mill 1824 O,
Windmill balk (v. balca), Wind Mill Cl 1844², - Piece 1844¹ (v. pece) (cf. wind Mill
way 1798); Barrowden Open Field c1873; Barrowden Way 1806 Map; Bellows Piece
1844² (Bellows is a common surn. in neighbouring Lincs., v. pece); Bottom Cl 1844¹,
1844²; Bottom Fd, - Mdws 1943; Bradley Cl 1844¹, 1844²; Bridle Pad Fd ('land with
or beside a bridle-path, i.e. a by-way suitable for a ridden horse but not for a vehicle';
pad, found in Ru and Lei f.ns., is a vagabonds' cant term which became a regular dial.
form in the 19th cent., v. pad); Buck's Acre 1844¹ (1798); Bull Acre 1844²; Bull Holm
1839 (v. holmr); Capeland 1844² (the first el. is obscure, v. land); Cattle Arch (land
beside a tunnel allowing cattle to pass through a railway embankment); Chapel Cl
c1840, 1844¹, 1844², Chapel Club Cl 1943; Cheesecake Piece 1839 (dial. cheesecake is

used of the fruit of such wild plants as the common mallow (*Malva sylvestris*) and the bird's foot trefoil (*Lotus corniculatus*), *v.* pece); Chicken Acre 1844[2] (1798); Church Fd (distant from the church, so perh. originally indicating endowed land); Clarke's Slade 1844[1] (*John Clarke's Slade* 1798, *v.* slæd); Coach Bridge Road 1844[2] (*v.* Coach Bridge in Seaton); The Common c1840 (*v.* commun); The Copstead 1844[2] (*v.* copp, stede); Copthorn Hill 1844[1] (1798, *v.* copped, þorn); The Cow Pasture c1840, 1844[1], Barrowden Cow Pasture 1849, Cow Pasture 1876, 1901-28, 1943, - Pastures or Barrowden Pastures 1943; Crowden's Fd (from the surn. *Crowden*, cf. Crowden Little Fd in Bisbrooke f.ns. (a), Crowden's Mdws in Seaton f.ns. (a)); Dawkinson's Holme c1840, 1844[1], 1844[2], 1950, - and Island 1876, 1901-28 (*v.* holmr; the *island* is in R. Welland); Day's Piece 1844[1] (*v.* pece); Deadmans Holme 1844[2] (*Deadmans Holm* 1798; no doubt alluding to the discovery of an ancient burial in a barrow, *v.* dede-man, holmr and cf. *Dedemansforlang* in Barrow f.ns. (b))); Debdale Cl 1844[1], Deepdale 1943 (*v.* dēop, dalr); Denpit Cl 1844[2], 1943, - Furlong 1844[2], Den Pit Furlong 1943 (*v.* denn, pytt); Doves Cl 1844[1] (*Dove's Close* 1798); Drift Fd 1943 (cf. *Drift Hedge* 1798, *v.* The Drift *supra* and hecg); Dry Cl 1844[1] (*v.* drȳge); East Fd 1840, 1844[2], 1876, 1884, 1901-28, 1943, 1950 (1796, *the East Feild* 1665, one of the open-fields of the village, *v.* ēast, feld); East Mdw c1840, 1844[1] (*Estmede* 1404, *v.* ēast, mǣd); East and West Furlong 1844[1] (1798), East and West 1943; Falkner's Cl 1844[1], Faulkners - 1844[2], 1943 (*Falkner's -, Faulkner's Close* 1798, from the family name of Everard *Falkener* 1623, 1632 *FF*); Feeding Cl (grazing-ground, pasturage, *v.* feeding); First Fd; Football pit 1844[2] (Mr J. Field notes that this is on the site of, or very near the present recreation ground); Fowler's Cl c1840, Fowlers - 1844[2], 1876, 1901-28 (1798); Fox Cover 1876 (*v.* cover(t)); Foxhole Acre 1844[2], Foxholes 1876, Fox Holes 1943 (*Fox-Hole Acre* 1798, *v.* fox-hol); Gate Balk 1844[1] (*v.* balca); Gills Island 1902-28 (Mrs L. Worrall notes that Richard *Gill* owned the unnamed plot No. 31 near the island 1844[1] (cf. Dawkinson's Holme and Island *supra*)); Halffoots Acre 1844[2]; The Hall Cl 1844[2], Hall Cl 1876 (*the Hall Close* 1798, cf. *Halleholm* 1404, *at hall'* 1527 *Surv* (p), *v.* hall, holmr); Second Heart Acre 1844[2]; Hempland 1844[2] (*v.* hempland; the term *hempland* was eventually applied to piece of land held by a small tenant, irrespective of the produce of the soil, and such a plot was often adjacent to a dwelling); Highthorn Furlong 1844[1] (*High Thorne Furlong* 1798, cf. *High Thorn Bush* 1798, *v.* þorn, busc); Hillside; The Holmes 1876 (*The Holm* 1798, *v.* holmr); Home Cl (several) 1844[1], 1876, 1901-28, 1950 (*v.* home); Ketton Spinney 1806 Map (in Barrowden Hay *supra*; Ketton parish adjoins to the north-east); Kittleng hill 1844[2] (*Kittling Hill Acre* 1798; ModE *kitling* 'a catkin of willow or other tree' is poss., otherwise ME *kiteling* 'a young cat'); Lambford furlong 1839, Lanford Mead c1840, - Mdw 1844[2], Lamford Mdw 1849, Lamford Cl 1844[1] (1798), Lamford 1901-28 (*Lamford's Close Furlong, - Close North* 1798, *Lamford -, Lamford's ford* 1798; in both this group of f.ns. and that following, *lām* 'clay' is much likelier than *lamb* 'a lamb', hence 'ford with a clay bottom', v. lām, ford); Lamb Pool 1943, Laumple 1987 (info. per Mrs L. Worrall) (lampole 1547-53, cf. Lampoole way 1632, 'clay pool', v. lām, pōl[1]); Lax hill 1876 (cf. Laxhill Closes 1665, - Close 1798, Laxhill Slade 1665, 1798; prob. with lax 'loose in texture' describing the soil on the hill, v. slæd and cf. Lax Hill in Hambleton); The Leys (v. lēah); Lime Kilne Acre 1844[1]; Little Hill 1943, 1950; the Live Hill 1943, Live Hill 1950 (perh. alluding to slipping earth, cf. Lax hill supra); Long Cl, Long Fd; Lords Acre 1844[2] (Mrs L. Worrall observes that this was owned by the Marquess of Exeter, lord of the manor, but as he was a major landholder in the parish, this is prob. coincidental and hardly a sufficiently specific source for the f.n.); Medley Acre 1844[2], Medley's - 1844[1], Motley's Acre 1844[1] (Medley -, Motley's Acre 1798); Middle Furlong 1844[1]; Mill Holme 1844[2] (cf. Mill Close 1798, v. holmr and The Mill supra); Mole Hills 1844[2], 1849, 1950, - Hill c1873, 1943 (le Moldhills 1665, Mould Hill 1798; prob. with dial. mould 'a mole', but OE molda, ON moldi 'the crown of a head' used as a hill name (as in Norw. p.ns.) is also poss.); Nether Furlong 1839; Pain's Bush 1844[1] (with the surn. Pain(e) and prob. referring to scrubland, v. busc); Pepper's Acre 1844[1] (1798), - Headland 1844[1] (cf. Peppers Balk 1798 (v. balca), with the surn. Pepper, cf. John - and William Peper 1522 MilS of Wing, William Pepeer 1522 ib of Empingham, William Peper 1524 SR of Greetham and Raff Peper 1522 MilS, 1524 SR of Brooke); Pike Acre 1844[2], 1950 (1798, v. pīc[1]); Pope's Willows 1844[1], - Spring 1844[1] (alluding to a spring of water, of which there are many here, cf. Pope's Spring in Empingham f.ns. (a)); Pridemore's Mdws (from the local Pridmore family, cf. Augustine -, Edward - and John Pridmore 1845 Burghley of S. Luffenham); Queeney's Leys 1844[1] (1798, cf. Queeneys Balk 1798 (v. balca); hardly a surn. formed from the fem. pers.n. Queenie (a pet-form of Regina) and not the pers.n. itself; more likely is a surn. based on a p.n., v. lēah); Ransack Dyke 1844[1] (Ransicke Dike 1665, cf. Ransike willowes 1632, v. rān, sīk, dīk, wilig); Ransack Spring 1844[1] (v. spring and cf. Ransack Dyke supra); Richmond's Nook 1844[1], Richmonds - 1844[2] (with the surn. Richmond, v. nōk); Rowgate High Road, - Way 1844[1] (Rogate Way 1632, 1665; the road ran northwards to S. Luffenham, v. rūh[1], gata); Far Rye hill Furlong 1844[1] (The far Rye Hill Furlong 1798), Rye Hill 1943 (Homeward Rye hill 1798, v. ryge); Saint Anns 1839, Saint Anne's Cl c1840 (a St Anne's Well is poss. here, cf. halywelcros infra); Saphill Slade 1844[2] (v. slæd), Satchell Cl 1876, 1901-28, Satchwell - 1950 (Saphill -, Satchell -, Satchwell - may well be forms of Scapwell - following); Scapwell Fd 1839, c1840, 1884, 1901-28, 1950, Scapewell - 1840 (scapwelle c1275 (e15), Schapwellefeld 1298, Scapewellefeld e14, Scapwell feild 1632, Scapwell Field 1665, 1796, cf. Scapwell way 1632, one of the great open-fields of the village, v. scēap, wella, feld; the a spellings throughout are due to AN a for e, cf. Scopwick L in DEPN s.n.); Seaton dyke 1839 (Seaton Dike 1665; Seaton parish adjoins to the south-west, v. dīk); Sharps Copstead Furlong 1844[2] (cf. The Copstead supra); Silver Hill (Silver Hill Furlong 1798, v. seolfor; the application of 'silver' in most toponyms is uncertain); Sismey's Fd (from the surn. *Sismey*, cf. Robert *Sesmey* 1524 SR of neighbouring Seaton); South Leys 1844[1] (*v.* lēah); South Luffenham Mdw 1839, 1901-28, 1950; South Mear in Hell 1844[1] (*v.* (ge)mǣre; in Ru, most f.ns. with *hell* are from *hyll* 'a hill'); Stone Cl 1844[2] (1798); Stone Fd 1840, c1840, 1876, 1943 (*Stonfeld* c1275 (e15), 1298, *Stonfelde* e14, *Stonefeild* 1632, *the Stonefeild* 1665, *Stone Field* 1796; one of the great open-fields of the village, *v.* stān, feld); The Ninety Acre -, Hundred Acre Stone Fd 1943; Stray Pasture (x2) c1840, The -, 1844, 1876 (*v.* stray 'a piece of unenclosed common pasture'); Stripe c1840 (*v.* strīp); Stubb's Twelve Acre (from the surn. *Stubbs*, cf. Stubs Close Furlong in neighbouring Seaton f.ns. (a)); Sty Way 1844[2] (*Styway* 1632, *v.* sty-way); Thompsons Cl 1876, 1901-28, 1950; Top Mdw 1839; Upper Furlong 1839; Warren Bank 1844[1], Warren's Banke 1943; The Weir Cl 1844, Wire Cl 1876, Wier's - 1943 (*The Wire's close* 1798, prob. with ME *weyour* 'a horse-pond'); West Fd 1844[2], 1876; West Mdw c1840, 1876, 1901-28 (*Westmede* 1404, *v.* west, mǣd); Windmill balk, Wind Mill Cl 1844[2], - Piece 1844[1] (*Windemill* 1683, *the Windmill Furlong, the Windmill Way* 1665, *wind Mill way* 1798, *v.* wind-mylne, balca, pece); Wood Cl 1844, 1876, 1901-28 (several in each source), 1943, Wood Nook 1876, - Furlong 1901-28, 1950 (1798, *v.* nōk); The Workhouse Cl 1844[2], Workhouse Cl 1876, 1901-28 (referring to a Poor Law institute); Wrang roods 1839 (*v.* wrang, vrangr, rōd[3]); Wright's Cl.

(b) *Allins hadland* 1665, *Allins or the old Farm* 1749 (from the surn. *Allin*, cf. Henry *Allin* 1822 UR of Uppingham, *v.* hēafod-land); *Baroden mere* 1632 (*v.* (ge)mǣre); *Beresdall'* e14 (*v.* dalr); *le Berues* c1275 (e15), *Brewes* e14 ('the burial mounds' which gave Barrowden its name, *v.* beorg); *Bradwell close* 1632; *le Brodemor* c1275 (e15), e14 (*v.* brād, mōr[1]); *Brokenback hill, Brokenback slade, Brokenback way* 1632 (no doubt describing a humped topographical feature, cf. especially Brokenback Furlong in N. Luffenham f.ns. (a) and *v.* Broken Back in Oakham f.ns. (a)); *the Clay* 1665 (*v.* clǣg); *Cloudstone furlong* 1632 (*v.* clūd, stān); *le Conygher* 1315 Ipm (*v.* coninger); *Roger Cookes hadland* 1665 (*v.* hēafod-land); *the Cross* 1552 Pat (*v.* cros; perh. to be identified with *halywelcros infra*); *Davenports Close* 1748, 1749; *Dodesell* 1404 ('hill with a rounded summit', *v.* dodde, hyll); *le Ferme Place* 1552 Pat (*v.* ferme, place); *le gaplondes* c1275 (e15), *Gapelondes* e14 (*v.* gappe, land); *goswelle* c1275 (e15), *Goswell'* e14 (*v.* gōs, wella); *halywelcros* c1275 (e15), *Hallewellescros* e14 ('the cross at Hallewell,* i.e. the holy well or spring', *v.* hālig, wella, cros); *the Highestrete* 1552 Surv (*v.* hēah[1], strǣt; perh. an early instance of a village main street being thus distinguished since no Roman road is known here, but cf. *Street furlong* and *Street Leys* in neighbouring Morcott f.ns. (b) which seem not to relate to a village street and may represent a lost Roman road from the north which crossed R. Welland at Turtle Bridge); *le holugate* c1275 (e15), *le holwegate* e14, *Hollowgate* 1632, - *Way* 1665 (*v.* holh, gata); *Incrofte* 1547-53 (*v.* in, croft); *Lyncroft* 1404 (*v.* līn, croft, cf. *Lyncroft* in

Caldecott f.ns. (b)); *Meadow endes* 1665 (*v.* **ende**[1]); *the Meadow Gleebe land* 1665 (*v.* **glebe**); *the Redground* 1665 (named from the red soil on the ironstone, *v.* **rēad, grund**); *Red Way* 1798 (cf. the previous name); *le risdale* c1275 (e15) (*v.* **hrīs, dalr**); *robynilpit* c1275 (e15) (*v.* **hyll, pytt**; the first el. is the pers.n. *Robin* and as it is compounded with *hyll* and *pytt,* may be an early reference to Robin-a-Tiptoe alias Robin Goodfellow, the drudging goblin, who threshes corn and does domestic work whilst the farmer and his household are asleep, hence *-a-Tiptoe,* cf. Robin-a-Tiptoe Hill in nearby Tilton Lei, *v.* B. Dickins, 'Yorkshire hobs', *Transactions of the Yorkshire Dialect Society* 7, pt. 43 (1942), 9-23); *Search Hole* 1749 (the object of the search remains obscure); *Seaton Way* 1665 (Seaton parish adjoins to the south-west); *Slawsons Thynge* 1547-53 (with the surn. *Slawson, v.* **þing**); *Stony Bancke* 1665 (*v.* **stānig, banke**); *thyrspit* c1275 (e15), *Thirspit* e14 ('the giant's pit', *v.* **þyrs, pytt**, poss. to be identified with *robynilpit supra*); *tirngore* c1275 (e15) (*v.* **þyrne, gāra**); *Tongue furlong* 1632 (*v.* **tunge**); *Wakerle Brigge* 1298 (a bridge across R. Welland to Wakerley Nth, *v.* **brycg**); *le Westhay* 1298 (*v.* **west, (ge)hæg**); *the Willoes* 1665, *le welugate* c1275 (e15) (*v.* **wilig, gata**).

Bisbrooke

BISBROOKE

    By-, Bitlesbroch 1086 DB, Wm 2 Dugd, *-broc, -is-* e12 ib, 1167, 1168 P, c1200 Dugd, *-brok(e)* 1238 RGros, 1260 *FF,* 1263 *Ass et passim* to 1286 OSut

    Bitlebroc 1186 P (p), *Bitebroc* 1196 ChancR, 1197, 1198 P

    By-, Bittlesbrok' 1263, 1286, 1288 *Ass,* 1328 Banco

    Buttlesbrok 1265 *FF*

    Betelesbrok 1294 *Ass*

    Bittel(l)esbroc, -is- 1321 *Rut,* 1327 *SR, -bro(c)k'* 1254 Val, 1302 BM, 1328 Banco, *-brook'* 1302 *AddCh*

    By-, Bissebrok(e) c1291 Tax, 1297 OSut *et passim* to 1335, 1359, 1367 *Rut et freq* to 1394 *ib et passim* to 1534 *ib, -broc(k)* 1265 RGrav, 1339, 1418 *Rut, -brook'* 1417, 1468 *ib*

    By-, Bisbrok(e) 1394 *Rut,* 1428 *FF et passim* to 1460 *Rut et freq* to 1518, 1530 *ib et passim* to 1557 *ib, -brooke* 1520 *ib,* 1610 Speed

    Bisbrooke al's Pisbrooke 1681 *Anc, Bysbrook or Pisbrook* 1684 Wright

    Pyssebrok' 1427 *Rut*

    Py-, Pisbroke 1442 *Rut,* 1450 *FH,* 1454, 1477 *Rut et passim* to

1555 *DuLa*, 1586 *Recov*, *-brook*(*e*) 1591 *Rut et passim* to 1746 *Anc*

The first element appears initially to be an OE pers.n. in the gen.sg., either *Byttel* (as in Bittesby Lei) or *Bitel* whose weak form *Bitela* is found in *æt Bitelanwyrthe* 956 (12) BCS 952 (S 601). However, the compounding of a pers.n. with *brōc* 'a stream' is rare. A common occurrence is for *brōc* to be prefixed by the name of a creature which haunts it, as in *Padbrok'* (Burley f.ns. (b), with *padde* 'a toad'). In *Bittlewell* (*v*. Leighfield f.ns. (b)), *wella* 'a steam' is most probably compounded with *bitela* 'a beetle', presumably used of the water-beetle, and it is likely that Bisbrooke is a parallel formation, but with a strong noun *bitel*. Such a form is recorded in *þa blacan betlas* 'the black beetles' (Wülcker 456), pointing to a nom.sg. *betel*. Hence, Bisbrooke is possibly 'the stream infested by water-beetles'; otherwise 'Byttel's (or Bitel's) stream', *v*. **bitel, brōc.**

BAULK HILL (local), BAULK RD, cf. *the Meere Balke* 1681, 1682 *Anc*, - *above North Close* 1682 *ib*, *the Meare Balke* 1681 *ib*, *v*. **(ge)mære, balca,** referring to the boundary with Uppingham parish. BISBROOKE HALL, *Hall* 1863 White. BLACK HEDGE (local), *Blacheg'* 1373 *Rut*, *blackhedge* 1685 *Anc*, *Black Hedge* 1781, 1783 *ib*, *over black hedge furlonge* 1597 *ib*, *upon black hedge*, *upon Blackhedge* 1706 *ib*, *Blackhedg*(*e*) *furlong* 1632, 1679 *Terrier*, the hedge was once the boundary of the property of the local *Black/Blake* family, cf. William *Blake* 1522 MilS, 1524 SR of neighbouring Glaston, Rowlond *Blak* 1524 SR, - *Blake* 1525 *ib* of Greetham and cf. also *Blaclondis* and *Black Wong infra*, *v*. **hecg.** THE GATE P.H., 1850 Slater, 1863 White. GRANBY LODGE, 1825 Map, 1846, 1863 White: the Marquis of *Granby* is the title of the eldest son of the Duke of Rutland, lord of the manor (*v*. VCH 2 377). HALES SPINNEY, *in ye holis* 1392 *Rut*, *The holes* 1632 *Terrier*, *ye holes* 1679 *Anc*, *v*. **hol**[1]; *hale* is a local dial. form of *hole*, cf. Hills and Hales in Exton f.ns. (a) and Hell's Hales in Oakham f.ns. (a). MANOR HO. ST JOHN THE BAPTIST'S CHURCH was built in 1871. *Church* 1846, 1863 White refers to its predecessor, cf. *Church Field infra*. SOUTHFIELD LODGE, 1846, 1863 *ib*, *in campo australi* Edw I *Rut*, *the South Feild* 1597, 1679 *Anc*, *the Southfeild* 1685 *ib*, *the South Field* 1706, 1783 *ib*; one of the early open-fields of the village, *v.* **sūð, feld**. THE VICARAGE, cf. *the Vicaridge Land* 1743 *Asw* and *Old Rectory House* 1846 White. WILLESLEY SPINNEY. WING BURROWS, *Beru* 1373 *Rut, le Berugh'* 1442 *ib, le Bergh* 1444 *ib, the Burrough* 1648 *Deed, the Burrowes* 1632 *Terrier,* 1648 *Deed,* 1681, 1682, 1701, 1710 *Anc, the Burrowes abutting against Preston Dike* 1682 *ib* (*v.* **dīk**), *The Barrowes of Pisbrooke* 1710 *ib, the Burrowes of Bisbrooke* 1746 *ib, the Burrows* 1671, 1735 *ib,* 1743 *Asw,* 1769, 1775 *Anc, Burrows* 1850 *Asw,* cf. *the Burrowe house* 1632 *Terrier, v.* **beorg**. This name evidently records a burial mound since Ru p.ns. with *beorg* appear invariably to refer to prehistoric barrows. However, there is now no indication of a tumulus in the vicinity; the name on the O.S. 6" map is sited on the lower eastward slope of the Ayston promontory. The name appears to have acquired its later plural form by analogy with The Barrows in Seaton on the southern boundary of the parish. The surviving forms suggest that this development took place in the 17th century. Wing and Preston parishes adjoin Bisbrooke to the north and north-west.

Field-Names

Undated forms in (a) are 1943 *Map*; those dated 1850 are *Asw,* while those of 1855 and 1888 are *Anc.* Early forms dated Edw I, 1335, 1339, 1373[1], 1373[2], 1392, 1394, 1417, 1438, 1454, 1463, 1488, 1515 and 1591 are *Rut*; those dated Hy 8 are *Surv;* 1610, 1681[2], 1717, 1743 and 1756 are *Asw;* 1632, 1634, 1705, 1720 and 1723 are *Terrier;* 1597, 1636, 1640, 1671, 1676, 1679[1], 1679[2], 1681[1], 1682[1], 1682[2], 1685, 1701, 1706[1], 1706[2], 1710, 1721, 1732, 1735, 1738, 1746, 1758, 1760, 1761, 1769, 1774, 1775, 1781 and 1783 are *Anc;* 1637, 1688 and 1736 are *Bir;* 1648 are *Deed.*

(a) Six -, Nine Acre, Top Sixteen Acres; Backside (*v.* **ba(c)ksyde**); The Breach (cf. *Brownes breach* 1632, *v.* **brēc**); Brick Piece (*v.* **pece**); Clarke's Gorse (*v.* **gorst**; John *Clark* held land in Bisbrooke 1761); Commons (*v.* **commun**); Cow Cl; Crowden Little Fd (with the surn. *Crowden,* cf. Crowden's Fd in Barrowden f.ns. (a) and Exton f.ns. (a), Crowdens Mdws in Seaton f.ns. (a)); East Fd c1840 *TA;* Elms (Corner Fd); The Far Fd; Fox Cover (*v.* **cover(t)**); The Foxes; Garrett's Black Hedge (*v.* Black Hedge *supra*); Gray's Ten -, Gray's Twelve -, Gray's Sixteen Acre (cf. Gerald *Gray* 1932 Kelly of neighbouring Glaston and Gray's Seventeen Acres in Glaston f.ns. (a)); The Great Cl 1855; Helland (prob. with local dial. *hell* 'hill'); The Home Cls 1855, Home Cl 1943 (*v.* **home**); Far Hovel Fd (*v.* **hovel**); Innems Fd (*the Inhams* 1597, *The*

Innoms 1632, *the Innams* 1679[2], 1706[1], 1706[2], 1781, *Innams* 1717, *Inholmes* 1721, *the Inholmes* 1743, 1761, *v.* **innām**); The Kuniger (*v.* **coninger**); Langram's Hill (*Langram Hill* 1632); Far Lee (*v.* **lēah**); Lester's Barnfield (cf. Lester's Barn Cl in neighbouring Wing f.ns. (a) and Thomas *Leyster* 1522 MilS of Belton); Middle Four; New Farm; Newell's Grass (*v.* **gærs**); North Hills 1855, Far -, North Hill 1943 (*Northill* 1373[1], *la northhul* 1392, *v.* **norð, hyll**); Oak Trees; The Orchard 1855; Parsons Farm; Peach's Willow (*Peaches Willows* 1721, *Peache's Willows* 1761, from the surn. *Peach, v.* **wilig**); The Priest's Mere (cf. *Preistmore furlong* 1632, *v.* **prēost, mōr**[1]); Red Ground (*the Red Ground* 1783, *v.* **rēad, grund**; a f.n. occurring at the 300 ft contour in this and neighbouring parishes on the ironstone, cf. Barrowden f.ns. (b) and Seaton f.ns. (a) examples); Rising Ground; East Seaton Lane Cl 1888; South Wells (cf. *Sowell gate* 1632, *the furlongs called Sowell gate* 1721, - *Sewell Gate* 1761, *Sowel Gate* 1783, *v.* **sūð, wella, gata**); Turnpike Cl 1855 (cf. *the Turnpike Road* 1783, *v.* **turnepike**); Warren's Fd; Washpit Fd (containing a sheep-dip, *v.* **wæsce, pytt**); West Fd (*the West Field* 1783); Yellemans Mdw 1855, Yellsmer 1943 (cf. *Yelsmores Close* and *Yellsmoor Slade* in neighbouring Uppingham f.ns. (b)).

(b) *Aswell' Balke* 1597 (poss. with the surn. *Ashwell,* cf. Henry *Aswell* 1678 *Anc* of Stretton, although *Ash-well ditch, - dike* (1602) in nearby Morcott presumably contains a stream-name which may also be present here, *v.* **æsc, wella, balca**); *Barbars Bushe, Barbers bushe* 1597, *barber bush furlong* 1679, *Barberry Bush furlong* 1783 (the early forms indicate a bush or scrubland associated with the *Barber* family, later confused with *barberry* (the shrub *Berberis vulgaris*), *v.* **busc**); *Blaclondis* 1373[1], *Black Wong Acre, - Headland* 1743, *black wong peice* 1743 (all poss. containing the surn. *Black/Blake* rather than referring to black soil, cf. Black Hedge *supra, v.* **blæc, land, vangr, hēafod-land, pece**); *Boygraue* 1339 (one of several minor names in the area which appear to associate *boi(a)* 'a boy, a servant' or even the pers.n. *Boia* with a pit or dell of some kind; it may be that the names allude to a forgotten folklore hobgoblin, *v.* **boi(a), græf,** cf. Boy's Pit Spinney, *boydale* and *Boygreue* in N. Luffenham f.ns. (a) and (b); cf. also *robynilpit* in Barrowden f.ns. (b)); *bradthorn* 1373[2], *Esthalfbradthorn* 1373[1] (*v.* **brād, þorn, ēast, half**); *Brakenhul* 1339 (*v.* **brakni, hyll**); *Brayeshouse* 1488 (from the surn. *Bray, v.* **hūs**); *le broc* Edw 1, *the brooke* 1597, 1648 (*v.* **brōc**); *brygforlong* 1373[2] (*v.* **brycg, furlang**); *Burtch furlong* 1632 (*v.* **bryce**); *Capmans headland* 1632 (with the surn. *Chapman, v.* **hēafod-land**); *careston' hadelond* 1438 (*v.* **hēafod-land**); *Castur Thyng* 1515 (presumably with the surn. *Castor, v.* **þing**); *the Church Feild* 1632, 1679[2], 1682[1], 1682[2], 1685, 1721, *the Church Field* 1681[1], 1681[2], 1738, 1743, 1761, 1781, 1783 (one of the great open-fields of the village, formerly *the Eastfeild infra, v.* **cirice, feld**); *Daglane* 1394, *Dragge Lane* 1454, *the two Dag lane Closes* 1717 (these forms presumably belong together; OE (Angl) *dræg* 'a drag, a portage', either Scandinavianized or replaced by ON *drag* 'a soft slope or valley; a portage' would explain the 1454 form, but if those of 1394 and 1717 more properly represent the original word, then the name must remain obscure, v. lane); *the Dale* 1597, 1632, 1640, 1648, 1681[1], 1681[2], 1682[2], 1732, *le Dale* 1610, *Bisbrooke Dale* 1634, 1705, 1720, 1723, *a certayne place called Bisbrooke dale or Glaston dale* 1636, 1640, *Glaston dale* 1636, 1640, 1679[1], 1679[2], 1774, 1781 (Glaston parish adjoins to the east, v. **dalr**); *the Dale Balke* 1743 (v. **dalr, balca**); *the Dike* 1648, 1676, 1681[1] (v. **dík**); *the Duke of Rutlands peice* 1721, 1761, *the Dukes Headland* 1743 (the Duke of Rutland is lord of the manor of Bisbrooke, v. **pece, hēafod-land**); *Estcroft* 1392 (v. **ēast, croft**); *thestfeld* Hy 8, *the Eastfeild* 1597 (the earlier name of Church Field *supra*, one of the open-fields of the village, v. **ēast, feld**); *yest Peice* 1783 (v. **ēast, pece**); *Faleys* 1339, *Flys* 1373[2], *Follyes Close* 1758 (perh. OE *falh* 'ploughed land' (later 'fallow land') with *lēah* 'a clearing', otherwise with *(ge)fall* 'a felling of trees'; the 18th cent. form with its pl. *s* appears to belong here, there being no evidence for an erstwhile folly building in the parish, cf. The Follies in S. Luffenham f.ns. (a) which seems to be of identical origin); *the great Farm(e) Peece* 1681[1], 1681[2], 1682[1], 1682[2] (v. **ferme, pece**); *the Ford* 1597 (v. **ford**); *the close of John Vine called fourteen(e) acres* 1685, 1706[2], - *acre* 1706[1], *the Close formerly of John Vine now of Mrs Roberts called Fourteen Acres* 1781; *the Galls* 1721, 1761 (v. **galla**); *Glaston Gap* 1736, 1763 (v. **gappe**); *(upon) Glaston Hedge* 1597, 1685, 1706[1], 1706[2], 1781 (v. **hecg**); *the stone called Glaston Stone* 1637, *Glaston Ston(e)* 1688, 1736, 1763 (no doubt a boundary marker, v. **stān**); *Glaston Town End* 1738 (v. **tūn, ende**[1]; Glaston parish adjoins to the east, with the village very close to the boundary); *the Glebe land* 1721, 1761 (v. **glebe**); *gledene* 1373[2] (as OE *glædene* 'iris' is unlikely as a simplex topographical name, then perh. 'valley frequented by kites', v. **gleoda, denu**, but more forms are needed); *le gor'* 1373[2] (v. **gāra**); *Hadmundheg'* 1373[1] ('Edmond's boundary hedge', v. **hecg**, cf. Jamys *Edmond* 1522 MilS, - *Edmounde* 1524 SR, husbandman of Bisbrooke); *Headland Road* 1743 (v. **hēafod-land**); *hennes crofte* 1597, *hencecrofte* 1658, *Hencecroft* 1706[1], 1706[2], *the Henchcroft* 1781, *the Hench Croft* 1783, *Henscrafte furlong* 1632, *Henscroft furlong* 1679[2] (prob. with the surn. *Henn*, although OE *hēns* 'a flock of hens' is poss., v. **croft**); *John Herberts Close* 1783; *Hessecroft* 1373[1] (prob. 'the small enclosure with ash trees', v. **æsc, croft**); *Hill Dike* 1743 (v. **dík**); *hotoft* 1373[2] (v. **hōh, toft**); *Jenkinsons ford Balke, - peice, - Hedge* 1743 (v. **balca, pece, hecg**); *The Knoll* 1743 (v. **cnoll**); *the Laump land Lands of Mr Digby* 1721, *the Lamp land* 1761 (land endowed for the maintenance of a lamp above the altar in the parish church, v. **lampe**); *Ley Meadow* 1769 (v. **lēah**); *the long Close* 1717; *The Lownd* 1591, *Lound balke furlong* 1632 (v. **balca**), *(the) Lound Feild* 1632, 1681[1], 1681[2], 1682[1], 1682[2], *the Loand feild* 1721, *the Lound Field* 1738, 1743, *the Loand Field* 1761, *the Lownd Field* 1783 (one of the great open-fields of the village, formerly *the Northe feild infra*, v. **lundr, feld**); *Lound furlong* 1632, *Lound Hill* 1648 (v. **lundr**); *Luffs Close* 1648, 1743 (from the surn. *Luff*, cf. Richard -, Thomas - and William *Luff* 1522 MilS of Caldecott, William *Luff* 1522 ib of Oakham and Thomas *Luffe* 1524 SR of

Ketton); *Le Lyngges* 1335 (*v.* **lyng**); *Menegate* 1373[1], 1373[2] (*v.* **(ge)mǣne, gata**); *The Millfeild* 1632, *Mill Feild* 1681[1], 1681[2], *Mill Field* 1682[1], 1682[2] (*v.* **myln, feld**; one of the open-fields of the village, also called South Field (*v.* Southfield Lodge *supra*) and the *Nether feild infra*); *le mor* 1392 (*v.* **mōr**[1]); *the morter pittes* 1597, *the Mortar Pitts* 1743 (*v.* **morter-pytt**); *the Nether feild* 1721, *the Neither field* 1761 (*v.* **neoðera**; an alternative name for *The Millfeild supra*); *Netherford* 1632 (*v.* **neoðera, ford**); *new close* 1679, 1685, 1706[1], (*the*) *New Close* 1706[2], 1781; *Nine Lands Ford Dike, Nine Lands Furlong* 1743 (*v.* **land, dīk**); *Pisbrooke Nooke* 1717 (*v.* **nōk**); *North Close* 1632, 1681[1], 1681[2], 1682[1], 1682[2], 1685, 1706[1], 1706[2], 1781; *the Northe feild'* 1597, *the Northfeild* 1640, 1685, *the North Feild* 1679[1], 1679[2], 1706[1], - *Field* 1706[2], 1781 (later *Lownd Field supra, v.* **norð, feld**); *Pexoke Close* 1681[1], 1681[2], 1682[1], 1682[2] (cf. *Pecks Oake close* in neighbouring Ayston f.ns. (b)); *Pike peice* 1743 (*v.* **pīc**[1], **pece**); *Above portway* 1632 ('(furlong above) the road to the market town', i.e. Uppingham), *the Portway* 1632 (*v.* **port-weg**, cf. *Portegate* in Glaston f.ns. (b) and *Portgate* in Seaton f.ns. (b)); *Preston Bridge* 1648, *Preston Dike* 1681[1], 1681[2], 1682[1], 1682[2] (*v.* **brycg, dīk**; Preston parish adjoins to the north-west); *Puttocks Well close* 1640, *Puttywell Close* 1756, *Puttoxwell close end* 1632 (*v.* **puttoc, wella, ende**[1]); *la redegate* 1392 ('the red road', with reference to the soil on the ironstone, *v.* **rēad, gata**); *the Sandes* 1597, *The sands* 1632, *the Sands* 1679[2], 1783, *Nether sands, The over sands* 1632 (*v.* **sand**); *Seytondykes* 1339 (*v.* **dīk**), *vnto Seaton Way* 1685, *into Seaton Way* 1706[1], *abutting upon Seaton Road* 1783, cf. *abutting vpon the way South* 1721 (a furlong abutting the road to Seaton parish which adjoins to the south); *Schirreriuscroft* 1373[1] (prob. with an early surn. form based on OE *scīrgerēfa* 'sheriff', *v.* **croft**); *the Sheep Close* 1717; *the Shepecote of John Presgrave* 1597 (*v.* **scēap-cot**); *Six Lands, - end* 1743 (a land-unit consisting of six selions of one of the old open-fields, *v.* **six, land, ende**[1], cf. *Nine Lands Furlong supra*); *Smithy leas furlong* 1632, *Smithy Leas Nook* 1756 (*v.* **smiððe, lēah, nōk**); (*the*) *South Dike* 1681[1], 1681[2], 1682[2] (*v.* **sūð, dīk**); *Southhillegate* 1417 (*v.* **sūð, hyll, gata**); *the south peeces* 1632 (*v.* **pece**); *Stanbriggate* 1373[1] (*v.* **stān, brycg, gata**); *Sudforlong'* 1373[2], *Suffurlong'* 1372[2], *Suffurlonges* 1392 (*v.* **sūð, furlang**); *Terrywests Cott' lately purchased from John Terrywest* 1760 (cf. John *Tyrriwest* of neighbouring Preston 1706[1]); *the three leys close* 1717 (*v.* **lēah**); *the Town balk* 1597 (*v.* **balca**), *the towne ground* 1679[1] (*v.* **grund**) (*v.* **tūn**); *the tythe barn* Hy 8 (*v.* **tēoða**); *the Wadmill Close* 1783 (*v.* **wadmill**); *Waterfal* 1373[2] (*v.* **wæter-gefall**); *atte Welle* 1463 (p) (*v.* **wella**); *the Weites* 1597, *Nether whites, Overwhites* 1632, *vper Whites* 1679[2], *the vpper whites* 1685, *the Upper Whites* 1706[1], 1706[2], 1781 (poss. the surn. *White*, cf. *whittes furlong* and *Whites House* in neighbouring Glaston f.ns. (b), but eModE *white* 'infertile' was used in contrast to *black* 'fertile', while dial. *white* was used of 'dry, open pasture', cf. *the Whites* in Lyndon f.ns. (b)); *Wing Bridge* 1681[1], 1681[2], 1682[1], 1682[2] (*v.* **brycg**), *Wing Dike* 1681[1], 1681[2], 1682[1], 1682[2] (*v.* **dīk**) (Wing parish adjoins to the north); *Woole Elders* 1632 (the significance of the first el. is unclear although dial. *wool* was used of

downy substances on certain trees and plants, cf. *Wool Slades* in Barleythorpe f.ns.
(b)); *Wylbernecroftes* 1339 (poss. with the ME reflex of an OE pers.n. such as the
recorded *Wulfbeorn* or an unrecorded *Wilbeorn*, v. **croft**).

Caldecott

CALDECOTT
> *Caldecot(ę)* 1086 DB, 1198 FF (p), 12 *Peake* (p), 1246 Ch *et*
> *freq* to 1389 *Win*, 1410 *Wyg* (p), *-cota* 1187, 1188 P, *-cott*
> 1535 VE, 1610 Speed
> *Caldcote* 1586 *DuLa*
> *Calcot(e)* 1426 Pat, 1510 LP *et passim* to 1553 Pat, *-cott* 1516
> ELiW, 1529 Chap, 1546 *SR*, e17 *Conant*
> *Coldecoate* 1673 *Terrier*

Literally 'the cold or bleak shelter', but this common
compound no doubt had the particular meaning 'a place of shelter
for travellers', *v.* **cald, cot**. The village is on the line of a Roman
road from Medbourne Lei to Wansford Nth on Ermine Street.

SNELSTON (lost)
> *Smelistone* 1086 DB
> *Snelleston* 1247 RGros, 1256, 1266 *For*, 1286 *Ass*, 1296 *SR*,
> 1316 FA, 1327 *SR*, 1349 *Queen's*, *Snelliston* 1322 *FH* (p)
> *Snelston* 1684 Wright, 1695 *Map*
> *Snelson* 1551 Pat, 1649 *Terrier*

'Snell's farm', *v.* **tūn**. The OE pers.n. *Snell* is a by-name from
snell 'brisk, active'. The earthworks of the deserted village are in
the field called Long Snelston at SP 865 951, *v.* BrownArchSites 5-6.
Minor names arising are *Snelleston' netherwong* 1349 *Queen's* (*v.*
neoðera, vangr), *Snelson feeld* 1649 *Terrier*, *Snelston Fields* 1684
Wright, *Snelston Ruins* 1780 Map, *v.* Long Snelston in f.ns. (a) *infra*.

BLACK HORSE P.H. (lost), 1850 Slater, 1863 White, closed 1927 -
VR.   BLACK HORSE LANE (local), named from the tavern.
CALDECOTT CHURCH, *Church* 1846, 1863 White.   CASTLE

INN is *Castle Hotel* 1863 ib. ENGINE AND TENDER P.H. (lost) was sited next to the watermill, where traction engines were watered; it was formerly called The Sun - VR. THE GREEN (local), *v.* **grēne**[2]. MILL LANE, cf. *Ancient Wind Corn Mill* 1844 *TA, Windmill Close* 1943 *Map*. BrownArchSites 6 notes a windmill mound 17 yards in diameter at SP 8658 9392, cf. *Kermontwindmuln s.n.* Long Carmen in f.ns. (a) *infra.* THE OLD VICARAGE. PLOUGH P.H. (lost), 1850 Slater, 1863 White, closed 1948 and now 41 Main St - VR. PLOUGH P.H. has replaced the earlier inn of the same name - VR. SUN P.H. (lost), *v.* Engine and Tender P.H. *supra.* WHITE HART P.H. (lost), formerly The King's Head; it was closed c1950 and is now Harelaw Ho. - VR.

Field-Names

Undated forms in (a) are 1943 *Map*; those dated 1844 are *TA* while those of 1979 are VR. Early forms dated 1349 are *Queen's*, 1510 are *MinAcct*, 1649, 1668, 1669, 1673 and 1703 are *Terrier*, 1769 are *Will* and 1799 are *Deed*.

(a) Ten Acre, Bottom -, Middle -, Top Ten Acres, Thirty Acre (*v.* **æcer**); Ashes; Base Dam or Duck's Nest 1979 (*v.* **damme**); Bells Cl 1950 *Burghley*; Benefield 1979 (*v.* **bēan**); Best Cl; Big Mdw; Big Drift (*v.* **drift**); Bridge Cl (cf. *Briggewong* 1349, *Briggefurlong* 1510, *Briggatefurlong* 1673, *Long bridge by Caldecot* 1684 Wright, *v.* **brycg, vangr, gata**); Broadhouse; Long Carmen (*Kermount* 1349, *Long Carmot(e) furlong* 1668, 1669, *Long Carmont furlong* 1673, cf. *Kermontwindmuln'* 1349 (*v.* **wind-mylne**), on a hilltop above Eye Brook; from Scand *kjarr* 'brushwood' which gave ME *ker* 'a marsh overgrown with brushwood' and ME *mont* 'a hill' (from OFr and thus poss. reflecting the manor's proximity to the park and palace of the Bishops of Lincoln at Lyddington), hence 'hill above the brushwood marsh', *v.* **kjarr, mont**; the site of the windmill was much higher than the surviving mill mound at SP 8658 9392); Cave's Cl 1943, - Mdw 1979 (with the surn. *Cave*); Duck's Nest 1979 (*v.* Base Dam *supra*); Fairchild's; First Cl; Little Godley (poss. a surn. based on a p.n., cf. Godley Ch 1 306); Hayr's First, - Second (with the Ru surn. *Eayr*); Big -, East -, West Hobbijohn (named from the local *Hobbijohn* family); Laxton Mdw (with the surn. *Laxton*); Lodge Cl; (Second -, Third Allotment in) Lower Fd 1844 (*v.* **allotment**) (Lower Fd was originally one of the three open-fields of the village, earlier called *the Neither field* and *the South Field*, both *infra*); Marches (*March furlong* 1673, *v.* **mersc**, cf. March Dike Leys and March Mdw in Lyddington f.ns. (a)); Marquis Mdw (the *Marquess* of Exeter is lord of the manor); Middle Cl; (Second -, Third Allotment in)

Middle Fd 1844 (*v.* **allotment**) (*the midle feeld* 1649, *Midle field* 1703, one of the open-fields of the village, also called *the East feild infra, v.* **middel, feld**); (Third Allotment in) The Meadow 1844 (*v.* **allotment**), Old Mdw 1943 (*The Meadow* 1668, *The medow* 1673, cf. *the meadowe furlonge* 1649, *Medowe gate furlong* 1673 (*v.* **gata**), *v.* **mǣd**); Mill Acres (*Millacre Furlong* 1668, *Mill acer furlong* 1673, running down to R. Welland and alluding to a vanished water-mill, *v.* **myln**); Oak Tree Cl 1979; Old Cl 1979; Bottom -, Top Pepper (from the surn. *Pepper,* cf. John *Peper* 1522 MilS, 1524 SR of Wing, Richard *Pepper* 1720 *Terrier* of Uppingham); The Pimpole 1979 (*Pimpile furlong* 1668, 1669, *pimple -* 1673, evidently a topographical use of **pimpel** 'a pimple' to describe a hillock or prehistoric barrow); Bottom -, Top Pitch Furlong (*Piche furlong* 1673, *v.* **piche**); Pitts Mdws 1979; Tyler's Saltmere (*Saltmore* 1799, *Saltmeere furlong* 1668, 1669, *Saltmorefurlong* 1673; adjoining Saltmere in Lyddington f.ns. (a)); Second Cl; Long -, Palmer's -, Rylands - (*v.* **rye-land**) Snelston (*v. Snelston supra*); Spring Cl (there are several springs near the north and south edges of this field); Big -, Little Stockwell (*Stokewell hill furlong* 1668, *Stockwell -* 1669, *Stocwell -* 1673, *Stockwell Hill* 1799, unrelated to the neighbouring settlement of Stoke Dry and with a stream running through Big Stockwell field towards R. Welland; poss. recording the other *stoc* 'dairy farm' from which it was necessary to distinguish Stoke Dry, *v.* **stoc, wella**); Topside; Upper Fd 1844 (*the vpper feelde* 1649, *The Upper Feelde* 1649, one of the open-fields of the village, also called *the North Field infra*); Walton's; Watson's Paddock (with the surn. *Watson,* cf. Edward *Watson* 1525 SR of neighbouring Lyddington); Whiteroods (*whit roods* 1649, *Short Whitrood'* 1649, *White roodes furlong* 1673; in eModE, *white* 'infertile' is contrasted with *black* 'fertile', *v.* **rōd**³); Yoke Crop (*v.* **geoc**¹, **crop(p)**).

(b) *Aling(s)well furlong* 1668, 1669, *Alynwell -* 1673 (from the surn. *Allin/Allen, v.* **wella**); *Ball's Cottage* 1799, *Balls Orchard* 1769; *Botteme* 1349 ('a flat stretch of a river valley floor', *v.* **botm**); *Brengewong* 1349 (*v.* **brink, vangr**); *Brethesik* 1349 (*v.* **breiðr, sík**); *the Brooke* 1649 (i.e. Eye Brook); *Buttesbithesik* 1349 ('butts by the stream or ditch' *v.* **butte, sík**); *Caldecot meadowe* 1649 (*v. Welland Meadow infra*); *Church lease* 1649 (*v.* **lēah** and Caldecott Church *supra*); *Clay field* 1703 (*v.* **clǣg**); *Cole poole furlong* 1673 (the first el. is either OE *cōl* 'cool' or OE *cole* 'a hollow', *v.* **pōl**¹); *Cottage Toft* 1799 (*v.* **toft**); *Crossefurlong* 1349, 1510, *Crosse furlong* 1673 (*v.* **cros, furlang**); *Dures furlonge* 1649 (prob. from the surn. *Doure,* cf. John *Doure* 1524 SR of Cottesmore and *Doris Close* in Barleythorpe f.ns. (b)); *the East field* 1668, *the East feild* 1673 (one of the open-fields of the village, also called Middle Field *supra, v.* **ēast, feld**); *Est longs furlong* 1668, *Est longes -* 1669, *Estlonges -* 1673 ('the eastern long strip of land', *v.* **ēast, lang**²); *Estmedewong* 1349, 1510 (*v.* **ēast, mǣd, vangr**); *Fox holes furlong* 1649 (*v.* **fox-hol**); *Frame furlong* 1668, 1673 (perh. land containing or beside cloth-stretching frames or tenters, cf. *Fram(e)less fur'* in Egleton f.ns. (b));

Fyuacrewong 1349 (*v.* **fīf, æccer, vangr**); *Galowe hill furlong* 1669, *Gallowe* - 1673 (apparently 'gallows hill', *v.* **galga,** but because of the ease of confusion between upper case C and G in manuscripts and without earlier forms, *calu* 'bare of vegetation' may also be thought of, cf. *Galley Hill* in f.ns. (b) of neighbouring Lyddington which doubtlessly refers to the same topographical feature (*Kallowhill* in Morcott f.ns. (b) illustrates the danger of such names being automatically referred to *galga*), cf. also *Caleweho* in Tixover f.ns. (b)); *Gosholm* 1349, *Gooseholme* 1510 (*v.* **gōs, holmr**); *Gregorys Garden* 1769; *Grenefurlong* 1349 (*v.* **grēne²**); *Groue gate furlong* 1673 (prob. 'copse road furlong', *v.* **grāf, gata**); *Handacre furlong* 1668, *Handacre forty furlong* 1669, 1673 (originally perh. an acre of land that could only be worked with the spade rather than with the plough, *v.* **hand, æccer,** cf. *Handacre* in Lt. Casterton (Tolethorpe) f.ns. (b)); *Harryes furlong* 1668, *Harreyes* - 1669, 1673 (perh. simply 'Harry's furlong'); *the Holme* 1799 (*v.* **holmr**); *Horenggewong* 1349 (*v.* **hār², eng, vangr**); *Littelheggegate* 1349 (*v.* **lȳtel, hecg;** the final el. may well be *geat* 'a gap, an opening' rather than *gata* 'a road'); *longfurlong* 1510 (*v.* **lang¹, furlang**); *Longlandfurlong* 1349 (*v.* **lang¹, land, furlang**); *Lyncroft* 1349 (*v.* **līn, croft,** cf. *Lyncroft* in Barrowden f.ns. (b)); *lyndeseyfurlong* 1510 (with the surn. *Lindsey,* no doubt recording an agent from Lindsey of the Bishops of Lincoln who once held the manor; a Mr E. *Lindsey* who died in 1846 WR was miller in nearby Barrowden and may well have been a local descendant); *Marshall's Cottage* 1799; *Mickle Doles* 1799 (*v.* **mikill, dāl**); *Moorewell furlong* 1668, *More well furlong* 1673 (*v.* **mōr¹, wella**); *Neitherfeild* 1649 (*v.* **neoðera;** an alternative name for *the South Field infra,* one of the open-fields of Caldecott); *Newecroft* 1349 (*v.* **nīwe, croft**); *the North Field* 1668, 1669, *the north feild* 1673 (one of the open-fields of the village, also called the Upper Field *supra, v.* **norð, feld**); *Northolmwong* 1349 (*v.* **norð, holmr, vangr**); *Ouer hills furlong* 1673 (*v.* **ofer³, hyll**); *Ouerthwertwong* 1349 (*v.* **ofer-þwart, vangr**); *Ouerwong* 1349 (the first el. could be either *ōfer* 'a river bank' or *ofer* 'a slope, a hill', *v.* **vangr**); *Padox ford* 1649 (*v.* **padduc, ford;** the field lay between Caldecott and Lyddington, *v.* *Padokeford* in Lyddington f.ns. (b)); *Page Marsh* 1799, *Page's Marsh Meadow* 1799 (from the surn. *Page, v.* **mersc**); *Russel's Quick* 1799 (from the surn. *Russell* and referring to a quickset hedge, *v.* **cwic,** cf. Thomas *Russell* 1525 SR and Robert *Russell* 1522 MilS, 1525 SR, both of Caldecott and Russell's Hern Cl in nearby Ridlington f.ns. (a)); *Shorte gore furlong* 1673 (*v.* **sc(e)ort, gāra**); *Schorthorswong* 1349 (*v.* **sc(e)ort, hors, vangr**); *The South Field* 1668, *the south feild* 1673 (one of the open-fields of the village, also called *Neither feild supra, v.* **sūð, feld**); *Spongwong* 1349 (*v.* **spang, vangr**); *Thorne poole furlong* 1673 (*v.* **þorn, pōl¹**); *Threwong* 1349 (*v.* **þrēo, vangr**); *Toftwong* 1349 (*v.* **toft, vangr**); *Welland Meadow alias Caldecott meadow* 1799 (beside R. Welland); *Wellemorheuedlandes* 1349 (*v.* **wella, mōr¹, hēafod-land**); *West homes furlong* 1668, *West home* - 1673 (*v.* **holmr**); *White Five Acres* 1703 (cf. *Whiteroods supra;* poss. with eModE *white* 'infertile').

Glaston

GLASTON [gleistən]

Gladestone 1086 DB
Glathestun c1100 Dugd, m12 Cand, m12 (forgery) BCS 22
    (S 68), -ton(e) 1273 GildR (p), c1320 Cand
Glaðestunne m12 (forgery) BCS 22 (S 68)
Gladston 1203 FF
Glaeston Hy 2 Dugd, c1190 Nichols, Glaest' 1209-34 AllS
Glaston(e) 1225 RHug, 1228 Cur (p) et passim to 1297 Wyg
    (p) et freq to 1557 Rut, -tun(e) 1241 FF, 1241 Cl
Glaceton(e) 1254 Cl, 1286 Ass et passim to 1302 AddCh
Glaiston, -y- 1506 Rut, 1535 VE, 1607 FF et passim to 1695
    Map, 1724 Recov
Glason 1515 Rut, 1620 LML, 1633 Bru, 1646 TB

Probably 'Glaðr's estate', v. tūn. The first element appears to be the Scand pers.n. Glaðr which is otherwise found only in Norw p.ns. (v. LindBN 110-11). The p.n. may reflect the settlement of Norwegians at nearby Normanton. The pagan Anglo-Saxon cemetery in the parish at SK 8946 0055 indicates the replacement of earlier English p.ns. hereabouts.

CHURCH LANE, the Church Lane 1730 Asw. FISH POND, cf. Fish Pond Close 1756 ib, 1772 Anc, Fishpond Close 1841 TA. The rectangular embanked pond at SK 900 007 is thought by BrownArchSites 12 to be a medieval fishpond. GLASTON CHURCH, Church 1846, 1863 White. GLASTON LODGE, cf. Lodge Ley(e)s 1729 Anc, 1756 Asw, v. loge, lēah. GLASTON TUNNEL, constructed 1875-80 with Welland Viaduct in Seaton parish. GRANGE FM, v. grange. LONSDALE FM, named from Hugh Cecil Lowther, 5th Earl of Lonsdale, v. Lonsdale Ho. in Barleythorpe. MONCKTON ARMS P.H., named from the local Monckton family. George Monckton, grandson of the 1st Viscount Galway, acquired the manor of Glaston in the middle of the 19th century. PARK COTTAGES. THE RECTORY, 1846, 1863 White, Glaston Rectory 1838 Anc. SONDES ARMS P.H. (lost), 1846, 1863 White. The Watson family, the Lords Sondes, held the manor of Glaston from 1820 to c1850. SPRING LANE, cf.

Wellegate 14 *Bru,* atte *Welle* 14 *ib* (p), *v.* **wella, gata.** THE SWAN
P.H. (lost), *the Swan or Blackswan* 1697 *Asw, the Swan* 1729, 1738,
1795 *Anc, the name or sign of the Swann* 1738 *ib.* THREE
HORSESHOES P.H. (lost), *Three Horse Shoes* 1850 Slater, *3
Horse Shoes* 1863 White. THE TROOPERS P.H. was until c1980
The Three Crowns.

Field-Names

Undated forms in (a) are 1943 *Map;* forms dated 1841 are TA, 1842 are *TA;* forms of
1838 are *Anc;* of 1850, c1850, 1851, 1853, 1855 and 1856 are *Asw.* Early forms dated 14
are *Bru;* 1635[2] are *Terrier;* 1635[1], 1636, 1638, 1640[1], 1640[2], 1640[3], 1640[4], 1640[5], 1642[2],
1642[3], 1646, 1647, 1648, 1649[1], 1649[2], 1649 (117), 1653, 1661[1], 1661[2], 1663, 1664, 1665,
1670, 1671, 1675[1], 1675[2], 1676[2], 1678[1], 1678[2], 1678[3], 1681[1], 1681[2], c1681, 1684, 1685,
1688, 1690, 1697, 1698[1], 1698[2], 117, 1702, 1709[1], 1709[2], e18, 1714, c1715, 1718[2], 1718[3],
1720, 1723[1], 1724, 1726, 1727, 1728, 1730, 1734, 1736, 1737[2], 1738[3], 1738[4], 1743, 1744,
1748[1], 1748[2], c1750, 1756 and 1770[1] are *Asw;* 1641[1], 1642[1], 1654, 1660, 1676[1], 1682,
1694, 1698[3], 1700, 1707[1], 1707[2], 1709[3], 1718[1], 1723[2], 1729[1], 1729[2], 1737[1], 1738[1], 1738[2],
1770[2], 1772 and 1795 are *Anc,* while 1796 are *Surv.*

(a) Six Acre 1943, Seven Acres 1838, The Seven Acre 1841, Near -, Far -, Seven
Acres 1943 (*Seven Acres Close* 1796), New Eight Acre 1943 (*Eightacres Close* 1772),
Nine Acre (*Nine Acres Close* 1756), Thirteen Acres ((*the*) *Thirteen(e) Acres Close* 1649
(117), 1681[1], c1681, 1737[1], *13 acres Close* als. *Poplin spring Close* 1714, *East -, West
Thirteen Acres Close* 1796 (*v.* Poplin Spring *infra*)), Fifteen Acre, Top Sixteen Acres,
Seventeen Acre (*Seventeen Acres* 1756), Eighteen Acres, Fifty-two Acre (*v.* **æcer**);
Allen's Cl 1841 (*Allins close* 1676[2], *Allens Close* 1685, from the surn. *Allin/Allen*);
Baines Mdw (named from the *Baines* family, cf. Algernon *Baines* 1932 Kelly); Bank
Cl; (Bottom -, Far -, First -, Middle -, Top -) Barn Cl 1841 (1756, *Barn Leys* 1756 (*v.*
lēah)); Beacon 1850, 1853, 1856, - Cl 1856, Beacons 1855 (*the Beacon* 1642[2], 1661[1], *the
place where the Beacon stood* 1671, *the place called the Bacon* 1726, (*the*) *Beacon
Clos(s)e* 1675[1], 1675[2], 1709[1], 1709[3], 1756, *the beacon feild close* 1670, *Beaconfeild*
1642[2], *the Beacon feild* 1647, *Beacon Feild* 1723[1], *the Mill Feild or the East Feild or
Beacon Feild* 1737, *the Beacon hill* 1610 Speed, 1642[2], (*the*) *Becon hill* 1610 Speed,
1620 Map, *the Bacon Hill* 1718[2], *the Beacon Hill* 1718[3], *v.* (**ge**)**bēacon, feld;** Beacon
Field was one of the great open-fields of the village, called also Mill Field and East
Field); Bellair's Cl 1841, Part of Bellairs's Cl 1842 (with the surn. *Bellaers,* cf. John
Bellaers 1845 *BHS* of Stretton and Bellairs Piece in Seaton f.ns. (a)); Bottom Cl 1841,
1943; Bridge Cl 1841 (1748[1], 1748[2], *Midle Muswells or Bridge Close* 1756 (*v.* Muxwells

infra), cf. *Great Bridge Peice* 1756, *Little Briggpeice* 1700 Moulton, *Little Bridge Peice* 1756 (*v.* **pece**), *Little Brig Piece now commonly called Sweet Lips Close* 1772; the bridge crossed Glaston Brook at the parish boundary on the road to Wing and was evidently a favourite spot for lovers); Broughton's Cl 1841; Bryan's Cl 1841 (cf. Charles - and William *Bryan* 1877 White of nearby Ridlington); Chapmans 1855 (cf. *Capmans headland* in neighbouring Bisbrooke f.ns. (b)); Cherry Holt 1850, formerly the Cherry Orchard afterwards Cherry Holt 1853, 1856 ((*the*) *Cherry Orchard* 1636, 1697, 1709[3], *the Cherry Orchyard* 1709[1], *v.* **cheri(e), orceard, holt**); Church Garden 1853 (*the Church Garden*, cf. Glaston Church *supra*); John Clark's Cl (cf. *John Clark* 1761 *Anc* of neighbouring Bisbrooke); Coneygear Cl 1841 (*the Coningre* 1640[2], *the Coney Grey* 1729[2], *Coney Greys* 1756, *v.* **coninger**); Cook's Cl 1841 (*Cookes Close* 1756, *v. Bastard Close infra*); Coppice Cl 1841, Coppice Close Leys 1841, The Coppice 1943 (*Great -, little Coppie leas* 1635[2], *Coppice Leise* 1649, 1681[1], 117, *Little -, Copy Leys* 1756, *v.* **copis, lĕah**); The Corner Cl 1838 (*Corner Close* 1796); Cow Cl 1853, 1943 (*the Cow Close* 1640, *Cowe Close* 1653, *Cow Close afterwards divided into two closes which are now called the Wash Pitt Close and Prettys Close* 1738[3] (*v.* Pretty's Cl and Washpit Cl *infra*)); Nether -, Upper Cuckold Way 1850, 1851, Cuckold Way 1853, Cuckold Way Close earlier divided into two called the Upper Cuckold Way Close and the Neather Cuckold Way 1853, Nether -, Upper Cowholdway 1841, 1856, Part of Cowholding 1943 (*Cuckhouldes way* 1635[2], *Cuckold Way* 1636, 1640[4], 1642[3], 1681[1], e18, *north -, South Cuckold way* 1698[1], *Neather -, Upper Cuckold way* 1748[2], (*the*) *Cuckold Way Close* 1709[1], 1709[3], *Neather -, Upper Cockald Way Close* 1756, prob. with *cokewold* 'cuckold' and thus the name of a lane used for illicit love-making; otherwise with dial. *cuckold* 'the fruit of the burdock', although EDD does not associate this word with the East Midlands; Victorian prudery succeeded in disguising *cuckold* as *cowhold*, cf. the following f.n.); Cuckleys 1855, The Cuckley 1943 (in 1855 *Asw, Nether -, Upper Cuckold Way* of 1853 *ib* are replaced by *Cuckleys* (x2), apparently another attempt to disguise *cuckold* which has succeeded); Dale Cl 1841, Neather -, Upper - 1853, The Dales 1943, Dale Spinney 1850 (*the Dale* 1638, 1640[2], 1665, 1675[1], 1675[2], 1729[1], *the common Feild of Glaston called ye Dale* 1660, *the West Feild or Dale of Glaston* 1682, 1718[1], *Glaston Dale* 1697, *the Dale in the North Feild* 1681[1], *Dayle Close* 1694[1], *Dale Close* 1756, (*the*) *Dale Closes* 1681[2], 1743, *the Dale Close now called the Lings* 1743, 1744, *the Ne(a)ther -, Upper Dale Close* 1709[1], 1709[3], *the Nether Dale Close* 1770[1], *v.* **dalr** and also *the Lings* and *West Field infra*); Dark Lane Cl 1841; Deacon's Drove Cl 1841, 1842 (*v.* **drāf**); Dry Cl 1838, 1841, 1850, 1853, 1943 ((*the*) *Dry Close* 1700, 1729[1], 1729[2], 1738[1], 1738[2], 1756, 1795, *the Westfield Close or Dry Close* 1770[1], *v.* **dryge**); East Cl 1838; The Elm Spinney 1853 (*the Elm Spinny* 1770[1]); Far Cl 1841, 1842; Flax Cl (1756, *v.* **fleax**); Forty Acre Cl (*the Forty Acres* 1756); Fox Cover 1943 (*v.* **cover(t)**); Foxearth Spinney 1841, Fox Hearth Spinney 1850, 1853, Fox Earth Spinney 1856 (*Fox Earth Spinny* 1738[4], with eModE *earth* 'a hole or lair in the earth'); Foxhole Spinney

1824 O, Fox hole 1855 (*v.* **fox-hol**); Fox's Cl 1841 (with the surn. *Fox*, cf. Richard *Fox* 1525 SR of nearby Uppingham); Furze Cl 1841, 1855, Pasture Furze Cl 1855 (*v.* **fyrs**); Gambles (the surn. *Gamble,* cf. Henry *Gambell* 1522 MilS of Bisbrooke); Garden Cl 1856; Gate Cl 1841, 1850, 1855, 1856 ((*the*) *Gate Close* 1698 *Deed,* 1720, c1750, 1756, *the Yate Close* 1727, 1743, 1744, *v.* **geat**); Glaston Gorse c1800, 1806 Map (*v.* **gorst**); Glayston House 1801 Map, Glaston - 1846 White, 1850 Slater; Glaston Pasture c1800, 1806 Map (cf. *the Cow Pasture* 1661[2], *Glaston Cow Pasture* 1743, 1744, *Cow Pasture Close* 1772); Great -, Little -, Top -, Gorgimer Cl 1841 (evidently a late form of *Gochismore* in neighbouring Seaton f.ns. (b)); Gray's Seventeen Acres (named from the local *Gray* family, cf. Gerald *Gray* 1932 Kelly); Bottom -, Top Great Grounds (*the Great Ground* 1734, 1756, *the Great Close now called the Great Ground* 1738[3], *v.* **grund**); The Green (*the Green(e)* 1638, 1756, *v.* **grēne**[2]); Greens 1855 (*the Greens or Green Close* 1772, prob. belongs with the previous f.n.); (The) Green Gate 1850, 1853, 1856, Part of the Green Gate 1842 (*le Grenegate* 14, *Green Gate* 1756, *v.* **grēne**[1], **gata**); Hazlegate 1850, 1853, 1856, Hazle Gate Cl 1841 (*Haslegate* 117, 1756, - *Close* 1732[2], *v.* **hæsel, gata**); Hill Cl 1853 (1756); North Holmes 1850, c1850, South Holmes 1841, 1850, 1853, 1856 (*the holmes* 1664, *the North Holmes* 1681[1], 1681[2], *Little Holme* 1756, *the Holme Pitt Close* 1649 (117), 1681[1] (*v.* **pytt**), *v.* **holmr**); Home Cl 1838, 1841, Home Paddock 1943 (*the. Home Close* 1681[1], 1681[2], 1698, *Home Close* 1796, *the Home Close commonly called Larretts Close* 1737[1], *v.* **home** and cf. Daniel *Larrett* 1640 and Widow *Larrett* 1676, both of Glaston); How Cl 1841, 1842, Hoe - 1943 (*How close* 1649 (117), *Howe Close* 1678[2], 1678[3], *East and Middle How Close, West How Close and Meadow* 1756, *the Farr how closes, the two hither how Closes* 1772, *v.* **haugr**); the Kings 1853 (two closes so called); The L Fds (named from their shape); Launsey Bank 1853 (*Lancey banke* 1638, *Lawncy banck* 1665, *Laund Sea banke* 1675[1], *Laundsea banke* 1675[2], *Launsey bank* 1698[1], 1709[1], *Launsey Banck* 1709[3], *Laundsey Bank* 1756, *Launsey Bank or Wire Close* 1748[2] (*v.* Wier Cl *infra*), *Lancie Banke lane* 1640[4], *Lancey banke Lane* 1642[3], *Lancey banck peice* 1640[5] (*v.* **pece**); the second el. of Launsey may be OE *ēa* 'a stream' (cf. *Mawsey Beck* in Morcott f.ns. (b)), but earlier forms are necessary for more than a guess at the etymology of this name, *v.* **banke**); Laxton's Barn, Laxton's Fox Cl (with the surn. *Laxton*); Lester's Barn Fd (cf. Lester's Barn Cl in Wing f.ns. (a), Lester's Barnfield in Bisbrooke f.ns. (a) and Thomas *Leyster* 1522 of Belton); Lodge Fd; Ling Cl 1850, 1853, Lings 1841, 1850, 1856 (*the Lings* 1743, 1744, *v.* **lyng**); Long Cl 1841, 1842, 1855, 1856, 1943 (*West Musswell(s) or Long Close* 1748[2], 1756, *v.* Muxwells *infra*); Mawford Cl 1838 (prob. a miscopied *Hawford,* a local form of the surn. *Halford,* cf. *Hawfords yardland* in nearby Lyndon f.ns. (b)); Mere Cl 1841, 1850, 1853, 1856 (*the Meare* 1642[2], *the meere close al's the Milne feild close* 1670 (*v.* Mill field *infra*), *the Meare Close* 1681[1], c1681, (*the*) *Meer*(*e*) *Close* 1723[1], 1728, 1756, *North -, South Meer Close* 117, *North and South Meer Closes* 1756, cf. *the meere Hedge* 1649 (117), *the Meare Hedge* 1681[1], c1681 (*v.* **hecg**), *v.* **(ge)mǣre**); Middle Cl 1841, 1943; formerly Mill field, afterwards the Mill Cl 1853 (*Myllne Fielde* 1635[1], *the Milnefeild or Beaconfeild* 1642[2], *the Milne Feild or Beacon feild* 1646, *Milnefeild* 1647, *the Mill Feylde* 1649[2], *the Mill Feild* 1641[2], 1723[1], 1726, - *field* 1671, 1718[2], 1718[3], *the Mill Feild or the East Feild or Beacon Feild* 1723[1], *the Millfield al's the East Field or Beacon Field* 1757[2], *Mill Close* 1756, *v.* **myln, feld**, one of the great open-fields of the village; on this raised site, the mill was obviously a windmill, *v.* Beacon *supra*); Mire Hole (*v.* **mȳrr, hol**[1]); Mortar Pit(t) Cl 1850, 1853 (*the Mortar Pitt Close* 1718[3], *v.* **morter-pytt**); Muxwells 1841, Maxwells 1850, 1853, 1856, Middle -, West Muswells 1853, East Muswells Cl 1853 (*Mouswell* 14, *Muswells furlong* 1635[2], *Muswells* 1661[2], 1670, 1675[2], *East* -, *Middle -, West musswells* 1698[1], - *Muswells* 1709[1], *East* -, *Middle Musswells* 1709[3], *North and South Musswells* 1748[2], *East* -, *North* -, *South Muswells* 1756, *West Muswells* 1770[1], *West Mus*(*s*)*well*(*s*) *or Long Close* 1748[2], 1756, *Midle Muswells or Bridge Close* 1756, 'spring or stream frequented by field-mice', *v.* **mūs, wella**); Nether Cl 1841; Nether Croft 1853 (*v.* **croft**); Nettle Croft 1850, 1856 (*Netle Croft Close* 1756, *v.* **netel**(**e**), **croft**); New Cl 1841, 1853 (*Newe Close* 1636, *new close* 1690); New Spinney 1853; North Cl 1841; North Gate 1850, 1853, 1856, - Spinney 1841, 1850, 1856 (*Northgate* 1756, *North Gate Close* 1756, *v.* **norð, gata**); Oak Tree Cl 1853, Oak Trees 1943 (*Oak*(*e*) *Tree Close* 1698[2], c1750); Oat Cl 1841; Old Cl 1841; the Old Spinney 1853; Far Pan Cl 1841, 1943, Part of Middle Pan Cl 1943 (*the Great Pann* 1727, *Upper or Great Pann* 1735 Deed, *the Upper Pann* 1772, *Little* -, *North* -, *South pann* 1756, *v.* **panne**); Parker's Cl 1841; Pasture Cl 1841, The Pasture (x2), Part of Top Pasture 1842, The Pastures 1943; Paul's Austin (*Paules Austin* 1756, *Pauls* - 1772; *Austin* is the surn. of an earlier owner of the field, cf. Anthony *Austin* 1612 *Terrier* and George *Austin* . 1681 *Conant*, both of nearby Lyndon; *Paul* is also a local surn., cf. Paul's Fd in Stoke Dry f.ns. (a)); Plank Cl 1841 (*v.* **planke**); Pond Gate 1850, 1853, 1855, 1856, Pondgate 1943, Pond Gate Spinney 1841, 1856 (*Pond Gate Close and Spinney* 1756, *v.* **gata** and Fish Pond *supra*); Nether -, Part of Upper Poplin Spring 1842 (*Poplinge Springe furlong* 1635[2], *Poplinge springe* 1640[3], *Pop*(*p*)*ling Spring* 1640[5], 1665, 1675[1], e18, c1715, *Great* -, *Middle -, North* -, *South Poppleing Spring* 1698[1], 1709[3], - *Popling* - 1709[1], *Neather* -, *Upper Poppleing Springs* 1748[2], - *Popling Spring* 1756, *Popling*(*e*) *Spring*(*e*) *Close* 1638, 1640[4], 1642[3], *Neather Poppling Spring Close* 1738[4], *North Popling Spring or Wood Close* 1756, *13 Acres als. Poplin spring Close* 1714, *v.* **poppling, spring**; from the vb. *popple* 'to bubble up, to flow in a tumbling, interrupted manner, as water flowing from a spring or over a pebbly surface'); Pretty's Cl 1853 (*Prettys Close* 1734, 1738[3], from the family name of

Willm. *Pritty* 1663); Pridmores Bean Fd (cf. *Pridmores Close* 1707[2], from the surn. *Pridmore*, cf. *Pridmores Pitt* in Uppingham f.ns. (b) and John *Pridmore* 1732 *Anc* of nearby N. Luffenham); Rising Ground; Sandwells 1850, 1853, Sandy Wells 1855, Sandywells 1856 (*North* -, *South Sandywell* 1748[2], *North and South Sandywells* 1756, 'spring or stream with a sandy bottom', *v.* **sandig, wella**); Seaton Lane, East Seaton Lane Cl 1838 (*Seaton Lane* 1796, Seaton parish adjoins to the south-east); The Several Cl 1853 (*the Severall Closse* 1649, *severall close* 1690, *v.* **severall**); South Gate 1850, 1853, 1856, Part of South Gate 1943 (*South Gate Close* 1795, *v.* **sūð, gata**); Southwells; Spinny 1850, Spinney 1853, Top -, Bottom Spinney Cl 1841, Part of Top Spinney Cl 1842, 1943, Spin(n)ey Cl 1850, 1853, 1855, 1856 (*the Spinney* 1734, *New* -, *Old Spinney* 1756, *Spinn(e)y Close* c1750, 1756); Stable Cl 1841, 1850, 1853, 1856, 1943, North Wire Cl afterwards called the Stable Cl 1853 (*the Stable Close* 1738[4], *Stable Close* 1748[2], 1756, *v.* Wier Cl *infra*); Staffords 1855 (the surn. *Stafford*); Town end Cl 1838, Townsend Cl 1841 (*Townsend* 1756, *Townend Close* 1796, *v.* **tūn, ende**[1]); Tunnel Cl (*v.* Glaston Tunnel *supra*); Wadmill Cl 1838 (*Wad Mill Close* 1700, *Wad(d)mill Close* 1729[1], 1729[2], 1796, *Wadd Mill Close* 1737[1], (*the*) *Woadmill Close* 1736, 1738[1], 1795, (*the*) *Woad Mill Close* 1738[1], 1738[2], 1756, *East Wadmill Close* 1796, cf. *Wad(d)mill Garden* 1729[1], 1729[2], *Woadmill Garden* 1736, 1795, (*the*) *Woad Mill Garden* 1738[1], 1738[2], 1756, *v.* **wadmill**); Washpit Cl 1853 (*Washpitts* 1635[1], *wynge washpitt* 1635[2], (*the*) *Wash Pitt Close* 1684, 1734, 1738[3], 1756, *v.* **wæsce, pytt**; this sheep-dip lay towards Wing and was prob. located in Glaston Brook); West Cl 1838; (The) West Fd 1850, 1853, 1855, 1943 ((*the*) *West Fielde* 1635[1], 1676[1], *the West feylde* 1636, *the Westfield* 1641[1], 1654, (*the*) *Westfeild* 1649, 1675[1], 1690, *the West Field* 1665, 1676[2], 1685, 1698, *the West Feild or Dale of Glaston* 1682, 1718[1], cf. *Six Lands without Westfield Gate* 1756, *West Feild Hedge* 1723[2], *the Westfeild Hedge* 1738[1] (*v.* **hecg**), (*the*) *West feild Close* 1709[2], 1709[3], *the West Field Close* 1709[1], *Round Hole Close now Westfeild Close* 1707[2], *Round Hole Close now called the West Feild Close* 1709[3] (*v.* **hol**[1]), *West Field Close or Well Close* 1756, *the Westfield Close or Dry Close* 1770[1] (*v.* **drýge**), *a certain field formerly called the Westfield and then called the East Field or east part of Westfield* 1770[1], *v.* **west, feld**; West Field was originally one of the open-fields of the village); Wheat Cl 1841, 1850, 1855, 1856, 1943 (1748[2], 1756); Whincup's Grass Fd (i.e. land put down to grass, *v.* **gærs**); Wier Cl 1841, 1856, Far Wier 1841, Cowlair Wier Cl 1855 (*v.* **lair**), the North Wire Cl afterwards called the Stable Cl 1853, the South Wire Cl late called The Wheat Cl 1853, Weir Cl 1842, 1850, 1853, Middle Weir 1842, First -, Second Wires 1943 (*the Wyer Closes* 1678[1], 1678[2], *North* -, *South Wire Close* 1698[1], 1709[1], 1709[3], 1738[4], *Wire Close* 1734, *the Wyer* 1756, *East* -, *West Wyer Close* 1756, *v.* **weyour** 'a pond', with reference to Fish Pond *supra*); Wing Gap 1853 (*wynge gap* 1635,

Wing gappe 1636, *Wing Gapp* 1642[3], *Wingap* e18, *a furlong called next Wing Gap* 1770[1], cf. *Wingap(p) Close* 1681[1], 1681[2], c1715, *Wing Gap Close* c1681, 1756; Wing parish adjoins to the north, *v.* **gappe**).

(b) *Apiltremedou* 14, *Appletree Meadowes* 1649[2], *Apple Tree Meadows* 1756 (*v.* **æppel-trēow, mǣd**); *Atkins's Close* 1756; *Backside Close* 1756 (*v.* **ba(c)ksyde**); *Bastard Close or Cookes Close* 1756 (*bastard* often alludes to abnormal shape, but dial. *bastard* means 'unproductive, poor, barren' as in Bastard Leys in Edith Weston f.ns. (a)); *the Bowling Ally* 1681[1], 1681[2], (*the*) *Bowling Alley* 1698[3], 1729[1], 1729[2], 1738, 1756, 1795, *Bowlinge greene* 1642[3], *the Bowlinge Leys* 1640[2] (for the pastime of bowls, *v.* **bowling, aley, grēne**[2], **lēah**); *the Brakes* 1635[2], *Great Brake Close* 1756 (*v.* **bræc**[1]); *Longbreatches, Shortbreatches* 1635[1] (*v.* **brēc**); (*le*) *Brende* 1327 Ipm, 1491 For, *le Brand* 1491 ib (*v.* **brende**[1]); *Brights Close* 1648 (from the family name of William *Bright* 1642); *Buckles Close* 1756 (Widow *Buckle* held land in Glaston 1770[2]); *Buggs Close* 1756, 1772; *Calouhill'* 14 (*v.* **calu, hyll**); (*the*) *Car(r)ott Close* 1729[1], 1729[2], 1756, *Carrat(t) Close* 1738[1], 1738[2], 1795 (*v.* **carot**); *Chattertons Close* 1756 (from the surn. *Chatterton*); *the Church Lane* 1730 (*v.* Glaston Church *supra*); *the Cley* 14 (*v.* **clǣg**); *Cockhill furlong* 1635[2] (*v.* **cocc**[1], **cocc**[2], **hyll**); *Cophill* 1635[2] (*v.* **copp, hyll**); *Corbetts Close* 1640[2]; *the Crab tree* 1698[2] (*v.* **crabtre**); *the Croft* 14 (*v.* **croft**); *the Desart* 1739 Will, 1756 (*v.* **desert**); *Digby Headland* 1756 (with the surn. *Digby*, Sir John *Digby* held land in the surrounding parishes of Bisbrooke, Morcott and Seaton in 1522 MilS, cf. Mr *Digby* 1721 Anc of Bisbrooke, *v.* **hēadfod-land**); *Dukes Butts* c1750 (with the surn. *Duke*, *v.* **butte** and cf. *Dukes bushe* in N. Luffenham f.ns. (b)); *in campo oriental'* 14, *the East feild* 1675[1], *the East field or Beacon feild* 1723[1], *the East feild or Bacon feild* 1724, *the Mill Feild or the East Feild or Beacon Feild* 1723[1], *the Millfeild al's the East Field or Beacon Field* 1737[2], *East Field* c1750, - *late Wyches* 1756, *a certain field formerly called the Westfield and then called the East Field or east part of Westfield* 1770[1], *v.* **ēast, feld**, one of the open-fields of Glaston); *the Eight Acres* 1756; *the Elm Spinney* 1770[1]; *Fedds Close* 1697, 1729[1], 1729[2], 1738[1], 1756, 1795, *Fedd's* - 1738[1] (with the surn. *Fedd*); *the Fence Closes* 1737[1]; *Five Acres Close* 1756, *The Five Acre Close* 1770[2]; *the ford close* 1664 (alluding to a ford in Glaston/Wing Brook); *the Forty Shillings Close* 1697 (referring to the rental); *the Fourteen Acres* 1756; *Bryan Franklines backside, - close* 1640[2] (*v.* **ba(c)ksyde**); *Georges Close* 1756; *Glastonbrok* c1320 AD (the stream running between Glaston and Wing, *v.* **brōc**); *Glason Feilde* 1633 Bru, *Glaston Field* 1659 Conant, *Glaston Lane* 1734 (leading to Barrowden); *The Glebe Close, East -, Dale Glebe Close* (*v.* **dalr**), *the west and two north Glebe Closes* 1756 (*v.* **glebe**); *Gosemor* 14 (*v.* **gōs, mōr**[1]); *Hall Barn* 1756, *the Hall homestead and Copy* 1756 (*v.* **hall, hām-stede, copis**); *Halls Close* 1756; *le Hangendehill'* 14 (*v.* **hangende,** hyll); *Hare Closes* 1756 (prob. alluding to the animal); *Henneplot* 14 (*v.* **henn,** **plot**); *hickmans headland* 1635[2] (from the surn. *Hickman,* v. **hēafod-land**); *Round* *Hole Close now Westfeild Close* 1707[2], *the Round Hole Close now called the West* *Feild Close* 1709[2], 1709[3] (*v.* **hol**[1]); *Hop Ground* 1756 (*v.* **hoppe, grund**); *Johnsons* *Close* 1654 (cf. George *Johnson* 1522 MilS, - *Jonson* 1524 SR, labourer); *Kirke* *Close* 1640, *Kirks* - 1653, 1688, 1702, *Kirkes* - 1734 (from the surn. *Kirk,* cf. Thomas *Kyrke* 1522 MilS of nearby Ayston and John *Kyrke* 1522 MilS, 1525 SR of the same); *Lamb Pitt Close* 1756 (*v.* **lām-pytt**); *The Lane in Seven Acres Close* 1796; *Daniell Larrettes Close* 1640[2], *Larrett(e)s Close* 1676[2], 1737[1] (Widow *Larrett* is also recorded in 1676[1]); *Longholm* 14 (*v.* **lang**[1], **holmr**); *John Luffes close* 1640[2]; *Thomas Masseyes ground* 1676[2]; *Middle furlong* 1635[2]; *Milnegate* 14 (*v.* **myln, gata**); *the Milne Holme Close* 1649 (117, 1681[1], *the Mill Holmes* 1697 (*v.* **myln, holmr**; suggestive of a water-mill in Glaston as well as the prob. windmill in Beacon Fd); *the Moor* 14 (*v.* **mōr**[1]); *Morcotts Close* c1750 (Morcott parish adjoins to the east); *new hedge* 1676[2] (*v.* **hecg**); *the Nook* 1723[2] (*v.* **nōk**); *in* *campo borial'* 14, (*the*) *North Feild(e)* 1635[2], 1636, 1640[3], 1640[5], 1648, 1664, 1670, 1681[1], *Northe Fielde* 1635[1], *the Northfield* 1649 (117), 1661, 1665, *v.* **norð, feld**; one of the great open-fields of the village); *the North Holmes* 1720, - *Holm* 1727 (*v.* **holmr**); *North West Close* 1756; *Olivers headland* 1698[2] (from the surn. *Oliver,* cf. Richard *Olever* 1525 SR of Ayston, *v.* **hēafod-land**); (*the*) *Parsonage Close* 1653, 1676[2], 1688, 1734, *Personage Close* 1702, *the parsonage lande* 1636 (*v.* **personage**); *the Parsons Close* 1640[1]; *Parsons Penn* 1756 (*v.* **penn**[2]); *the pinfold* *Garden* 1729[2] (*v.* **pynd-fald**); *Portegate* 14, *Portgate* 1409 ELiW, 1409 PRep ('the road to the market town', i.e. Uppingham, *v.* **port**[2], **gata**, cf. *Portgate* in Seaton f.ns. (b) and *Above portway* in Bisbrooke f.ns. (b)); *Prestesmor* 14 ('the moorland of the priest(s)', *v.* **prēost, mōr**[1]); *Preston Lane* 1756 (Preston parish adjoins to the north-west); *Reads close* 1670, 1675[1], - *closse* 1675[2] (from the family name of Ralph *Read* 1648); *Reynaldiscroft* 14 (from the surn. *Reynold,* cf. Richard *Reynold* 1522 MilS, - *Reynolde* 1524 SR of nearby Barrowden, *v.* **croft**); *Robertissike* 14 (from the surn. *Robert(s),* v. **sík**); *the Round Close* 1697 (referring to its shape); *the Sandes* 1635[2] (*v.* **sand**); *Scharpslade* 14, *Sharpeslade* 1635[2] (*v.* **scēarp, slæd**); *the Sheepeclose* 1640, *Sheepe Close* 1653, *the Ship Close afterwards called the Great* *Close and now called the Great Ground* 1738[2] (*v.* **scēap** and *Great Grounds* supra); *Mr Edward Sheilds Close* 1698[2], *Mr Sheilds Close* 1723[1], *Sheilds Close* c1750 (*Edward Sheild* was resident in nearby Preston in 1713 Anc); *Schortdoles* 14 (*v.* **sc(e)ort, dāl**); *Robert Slies close* 1640[2]; *the Smithie Leyes* 1640[2], *the Smithye* *Leas* 1642[1], 1642[3], *Smithy Lees* 1723[3], - *Leys* 1756, *Smiths Leyes* 1681[1], 1681[2], *Smiths Leys* 1698[3] (all prob. referring to the same ground, *v.* **smiððe, smið,** **lēah**); *in campo austr'* 14, *South Fielde* 1635[1], *Southfield* 1649 (117), *South Feild* 1681 (one of the open-fields of the village, *v.* **sūð, feld**); *Stamford Waye* 1649[2] (the road to Stamford L); *Stodfolde* 14, *East Stedfold and Meadow, West Stedfold and Meadow* 1756 (v. **stŏd-fald**); *Stevens acre* 1676[2], 1685, *Steevens headland* 1698[2] (with the surn. *Stevens,* v. **æcer, hēafod-land**); (*the*) *Great and Little Stone Pitt Closes* 1756, *Little Stone Pit Close* 1772 (v. **stān-pytt**); *Sweet Lips Close* 1772 (v. Bridge Cl *supra*); *Swynewik'* 14 ('the pig farm', v. **swīn**[1], **wīc**); *Taylors House and Homestead* 1772 (from the family name of Abel *Taylor* 1682, 1734 and Dennis *Taylor* 1718[1], v. **hām-stede**); *Ten Acres* 1756; *the Tenths* 1756 (v. **tenthe**); *Thirspit* 14 ('the giant's or demon's pit', v. **þyrs, pytt**, cf. *thyrspit* in Barrowden f.ns. (b) and *Tyrespyt* in Empingham f.ns. (b)); *the three Acres Close* 1737[1], *Three Acre Close* 1756; *the Timber Yard* 1748[1]; *Tounmedou* 14 (v. **tūn, mǣd**); *the Towne yard* 1640 (v. **tūn, geard**); *Trespasesike* 14 (the first el. is ME *trespas* 'encroachment', but just what type of encroachment depends on the denotation of *sīk* in the compound; if 'a small stream', it may have been one liable to flooding, but if 'a boundary ditch' or 'a piece of meadow along a stream', then some sort of territorial encroachment must have taken place, v. **trespas, sīk**); *Twelve acres Close* 1649 (117), *the 12 Acres or Wingap Close* c1681, *the Twelve acres Close or Wingapp Close* 1681[1] (v. Wing Gap *supra*); *the Upper House* 1756; *William Velhams close* 1640[2] (*William Vellam* appears again in 1642[2], the surn. being modern *Welham*); *Wakefields Garden* 1756; *Wall Nutt tree Close* 1684, (*the*) *Wallnutt Tree Close* 1688, 17.02, 1734 (v. **walhhnutu**); *welbrakes* 1635[2] (v. **wella, bræc**[1]); *Wellebroc* 14 (v. **wella, brōc**); (*the*) *Well Close* 1729[2], 1756; *Well Nook* 1756 (v. **nōk**); *Wellesike* 14 (v. **wella, sīk**); *whittes furlong* 1635[1], *over whittes* 1635[2] (prob. from the surn. *White*, but cf. *the Weites* in Bisbrooke f.ns. (b) and *the Whites* in Lyndon f.ns. (b)); *Whites House* 1704 Moulton; *Wynge brooke* 1635[2], *Wynge dike* 1635[2], *Winge dike* 1640[3], 1673[1], - *Dyke* 1665, *Wing Dike* 1681[2], *Wing Lane* c1715, 1729[2], *Wing Lane Close* 1756 (Wing parish adjoins to the north, with Wing Brook alias Glaston Brook forming the parish boundary, v. **brōc, dīk**); *Wood Close* 1748[2], 1756, *North Popling Spring or Wood Close* 1756 (v. Poplin Spring *supra*); *Yngedale, Yngdale* 14 (the first el. is either the Scand pers.n. *Ingi* or **eng** 'meadow, pasture', v. **dalr**).

North Luffenham

NORTH LUFFENHAM
> *Luffenham* 1086 DB, 1141 Reg, 1167 P (p) *et passim* to 1206
> Cur *et freq* to 1555 *Conant*, 1610 Speed, *Luffinham, -y-*
> Hy 2 Dane, 1235 RGros, 1275 RGrav *et passim* to 1445
> Pat
> *Luffeham* 1105-7 Reg, 1196 Cur, 1197 *FF et passim* to 1206 Cur

Luffham 1219, 1224 Cur *et passim* to 1250 Misc
Lufenham 1086 DB, 1197, 1199 *FF et passim* to 1213 *ib*
Lufham 1179, 1180 P *et freq* to 1199 *FF et passim* to 1230 Cur
Loffenham 1234 RHug, 1255 Misc, 1286 *Ass et passim* to 1342
   Fine

The affix is normally added as:
   Nor- 1179, 1180, 1181 P *et passim* to 1250 Misc, *Nord-* 1185,
      1186, 1188 P, *Nort-* 1210, 1211 Cur *et passim* to 1302 BM,
      North(e)- 1197 *FF*, 1206 Ass *et freq, v.* **norð**.

'Luffa's village or estate', *v.* **hām,** cf. Luffenhall Hrt 156.
Luffenham is one of a series of Rutland names in *hām* related to the
earlier pattern of Romano-British settlements and routeways. It lies
beside a probable Roman road running south from Empingham to
cross R. Welland at Turtle Bridge in Barrowden. Just to its north, an
early folk-group of the Hwicce may well have been settled near
Witchley in Edith Weston, while in North Luffenham itself, the pagan
Anglo-Saxon cemetery at SK 932 045, in use from c400 A.D., has
produced late Roman military metalwork which has been associated
with Germanic *foederati* (to be compared with similar equipment found
at Clipsham's Roman villa site).

SCULTHORPE SPINNEY
   Sculetorp 1086 DB, *-torp'* 1220 Cur
   Scultorp c1160 Dane, 1199 *FF*, 1220 Cur, *-thorp(e)* 1247
      RGros, 1248 FineR (p) *et passim* to 1552 *Conant, -thrope*
      1554, 1555 *ib, Skulthorp(e)* 1256 *For,* 1302 *AddCh,* 1321 Pat
   Schulthorp 1263 *Ass,* 1286 *Rut* (p), 1313 *Deed* (p), *-thorppe*
      1297 *Ass*
   Scoltorp' 1255 Cl (p), *-thorp(e)* 1255 *ib,* 1288 *Rut* (p), 1313
      Pat (p)

'Skúli's outlying farmstead', *v.* **þorp,** cf. Sculthorpe Nf. The
OScand pers.n. *Skúli* is an original by-name, cf. OIcel *skýla* 'to
screen, to shelter', *v.* SPNLY 254. For later f.ns. arising from
Sculthorpe, *v.* f.ns. (a) *infra.* The site of the deserted village is
'marked at SK 923 038 and SK 927 028 by a series of low banks
and a possible hollow way' BrownArchSites 20.

ACORN SPINNEY. BARKER'S SPINNEY, *Barkers Spinney* c1800, 1806 Map, cf. *Mr Barkers Close* c1700 *BHS*; from an old Luffenham family name, as Robert *Barkere* 1296 *SR*, Bawdwyn *Barker* 1546 *ib*, Bezaliell *Barker* 1596 PR, Christopher *Barker* 1600 ib and Samuel *Barker* 1630 *Conant.* Barker's Spinney is part of *Bushey Closes* in 1824 O. BUTT LANE (local), 1776 *Anc*, cf. *Butlane end* c1700 *BHS*, *Butt Lane End* 1781 *ib* and *Bates Buttes* 1659 *Anc* (with the surn. *Bates*), v. **butte.** CHURCH LANE, (*the*) *Church Lane* 1710, 1732, 1776 *ib*, cf. *Church Lane Close* 1844 *TA*, v. St John the Baptist's Church *infra.* CLAY LANE, cf. *the Clay* e17, 1626, 1709, 1712, 1716 *Anc*, v. **clæg.** COW PASTURE, (*the*) *Cow Pasture* 1660 VCH, 1729 *Terrier*, 1844 *TA*, *Cow Pastures* 1754 *Anc*, *Luffenham Pasture* 1796 *Surv*, 1824 O, *North Luffenham Cow Pasture* 1849 *Anc.* FOX AND HOUNDS P.H., 1846, 1863 White. GREAT CLOSE SPINNEY, *Great Close* 1659, 1686, 1690, 1759, 1761 *Anc*, 1765 *Conant*, 1766 *Anc.* Great Close Spinney is part of *Bushey Closes* 1824 O. HIGH PASTURE, 1844 *TA.* HORSE AND PANNIERS P.H., 1850 Slater, 1863 White, - *Pannier* 1846 ib. LONG HEDGE SPINNEY. LUFFENHAM HALL, 1863 ib, was formerly Digby House (named from the local *Digby* family). The earlier Luffenham Hall was demolished in 1806 and the name transferred, cf. *ad Aulam* 1295 OSut (p), *the Hall Closes* 1711, 1715 *Anc*, 1729 *Deed*, - *Close* 1732, 1765 *Anc*, 1844 *TA*, v. **hall.** MANOR FM, 1846 White. MOOR LANE, 1776 *Anc*, cf. *Moore balke way* 1631 *Terrier* (*v.* **balca**), *v.* **mōr**[1], cf. *batusmore* and Blackmore in f.ns. *infra.* MOOR LANE BRIDGE, *Morebrig* 1615 *Conant*, *the more brigg* 1686 *Anc*, cf. *Moore bridg Close* 1678 *ib*, *Moor(e) Bridge Close* 1710 *Deed*, 1763, 1785, 1796 *Anc*, *Moorbridge Close* c1795 *ib*, *v.* **brycg.** The early spellings with *brig(g)* may represent Scand influence. MORCOTT SPINNEY is on the parish boundary with Morcott to the south. NINE ACRE SPINNEY, cf. *Mr Digbys 9 acre peice* c1700 *BHS* (cf. James *Digby* 1659 *Anc*), *Sir Gilbert Heathcotes Nine Acre Piece* 1781 *BHS*, *v.* **pece.** THE OVAL (local), *the Oval, formerly the approach to the Hall then demolished* 1808 *Anc*, *v.* Luffenham Hall *supra.* THE PASTURES, a house built to the design of C.F.A. Voysey 1901-9. PINFOLD LANE (local), cf. *the Pinfold Piece* 1763 *ib*, *v.* **pynd-fald**, **pece.** RATCLIFFE SPINNEY, cf. *Ratcliffe's Close* 1779 *ib*, from the surn. *Ratcliffe.* RECTORY, 1863 White. ST JOHN THE BAPTIST'S CHURCH, *Church* 1846, 1863 ib, cf. *the Churchyard* 1808 *Anc*, (*the*) *Church Brigg* 1659, 1686, 1690 *ib*, (*the*) *Church Bridge* 1659 *ib*, 1682 *Deed*, 1761 *Anc*. SETTINGS FM, *Settings* 1631 *Terrier*, cf. *Settin leas* 1629 *Conant* (*v.* **lēah**), *Sittings Close, Sixty Acre Settings* 1943 *Map*; perhaps OE *seten* 'land in occupation', later 'buildings necessary for such occupation', *v.* Sx 561-2. If of more recent origin, perhaps *setting* in some such sense as 'land marked out in some way, possibly as allotments under an enclosure agreement'. The word is used in Orkney (EDD) in the sense 'piece of land'. SHELTON'S BARN, 1943 *Map*, is named from the family of Robert - and Matthew *Shelton* 1783 PR. SPRINGTHORPE YARD (local), from the family name of John - and Martha *Springthorpe* 1794 ib. WATERMILL SPINNEY, cf. (*the*) *Water Mill Feild* e17, 1627 *Conant*, 1659 *Anc*, c1700 *BHS*, 1709, 1712 *Anc*, 1729 *Deed*, 1751, 1780, 1796 *Anc*, *the Wartermill Feild* 1751 *ib*, (*the*) *Water Mill Field* e18, 1716, 1763 *ib*, 1781 *BHS*, *Water Mill Close* 1763 *Anc*, *v.* **water-mylne**; Water Mill Field was one of the great open-fields of the village. WYMARK SPINNEY, cf. *Mr Wymarkes Close* 1629 *Conant*, *Wymarks Closes* 1763 *Anc*, named from an old Luffenham family, cf. Alan *Wymark'* 1296 *MinAcct*, John *Wymake* 1565 PR, Anthony *Wymarke* 1572 ib.

Field-Names

Undated forms in (a) are 1943 *Map*; those dated 1805, 1808, 1828 and 1849 are *Anc*; those dated 1809, 1816 and 1828 are *BHS* while those of 1844 are *TA*. Early spellings dated e13 are FacCh; 1257 are *FF*; 1323, 1356, 1358, 1361, 1363, 1366, 1368, 1370, 1371, 1373, 1379, 1385, 1387, 1389, 1403, c1700, c1745, 1781[1] and 1781[2] are *BHS*; 1590, e17, 1621, 1626[1], 1627[1], 1627[2], 1629, 1630, 1636, 1660, 1678[1], 1710[1] and 1765[2] are *Conant*; 1626[2], 1659, 1678[2], 1686, 1690, 1694, 1699, e18, 1705, 1709, 1710[2], 1711[1], 1711[2], 1712, 1715[1], 1715[2], 1716[1], 1716[2], 1719, 1720, 1722[1], 1722[2], 1726, 1728, 1732[1], 1732[2], 1735, 1742, 1751[1], 1751[2], 1754, 1759, 1761[1], 1761[2], 1763, 1764, 1765[1], 1766, 1776, 1779, 1780[1], 1780[2], 1785, 1786, c1795, 1796[1], 1796[2] and 1796[3] are *Anc*; 1631 and 1729[3] are *Terrier*; 1682, 1710[3], 1729[1], 1729[2], 1736 and 1755 are *Deed*.

(a) Twenty-four -, Thirty-five -, The Forty -, Fifty-three Acre, The Eighty-five Acres, One Hundred and Nine Acres (*v.* **æcer**); Ash Cl 1844 (1682, 1781[1], *Hunts* - c1700 (held by a Mr *Hunt* c1700), *Mr Ray's* (*late Hunt*) - 1781[2], *v.* **æsc**); Babes Croft 1844 (*Babscroft* 1682, 1729[2], *Babcroft* 1763, *Babscroft Close* 1711[1], 1711[2], 1764, from the surn. *Babb*(*s*), *v.* **croft**); Baggerly Cl 1844 (from the surn.

Bagley/Baggerley, cf. Elizabeth *Bagley* 1589 PR); Beck Fd 1809, 1844 (*le beck* 1366, *Beckefeild* 1627[2], *Beckfeild* e17, 1627[2], 1659, 1709, (*the*) *Beck Feild* 1678[1], c1700, 1709, 1712, 1729[3], (*the*) *Beck Field* 1631, e18, 1763, 1780[1], 1780[2], 1781[1], 1781[2], 1796[3], one of the open-fields of the village, *v.* **bekkr**); Little Bidwell 1809, Bottom -, Top Bidwells 1943 (*Bedewell'* e13, *Bytwelle* 1368, *Bedwell* 1631, *Bidwell* 1659, c1700, 1781[1], 1781[2], cf. *Budewelleheved* 1257, *Bedwell head* 1631 (*v.* **hēafod**), *Bidwell Close* e17, 1659, 1682, c1700, 1711[1], 1729[3], 1763, 1780[1], 1781[1], 1781[2], - *West* c1700, *Bidwells Close* 1711[2], 1729[2], 1764), Bidwell Spring 1809 (1780[1], 1780[2], *Bidwell Pond* 1659) (prob. 'spring or well with a (drinking) vessel or tub', *v.* **byden, wella** and *Nomina* 12, 123-30, cf. Bidwell's Lodge in Clipsham); Big Buttermilk (a complimentary name for excellent pasture); Big Mdw (x2); Blackmore Furlong 1809, Blackenmore 1943 (*Blackmore hill Furlong* 1659, *Blackmoor Headland* 1781[1], *Blackmoors* - 1781[2] (*v.* **hēafod-land**), *v.* **blæc, mōr**[1]); Bottom Cl 1844 (1732[2]); Brickyard Fd; Brokenback Furlong 1809, Brokenback Cl 1844, Brokenbacks 1943 (*Brokenbagge close* 1621, *Brokenbacke* - 1626[1], 1627[1], *Brokett back Close* 1699, *Broken Back Close* 1627[2], 1710[2], 1729[3], 1732[1], 1736, 1754, 1763, *Broken Back Slade* 1729[3], 1736 (*v.* **slæd**), (*Furlong above*) *Brokenback Way* c1700, 1781[1], 1782[2]; the range of the forms indicates that Brokenback refers to a physical feature such as a ridge with a distinctive profile rather than being an uncomplimentary name for land difficult to till; cf. *Brokenbak* a.1244, 1337, *Brokenback Hill* 1824 in West Rasen, L 3 115, forms which no doubt refer to a large, ditched Bronze Age barrow, later apparently used as a windmill mound, cf. also the ME adj. *broke*(*n*)-*bak*(*ked*) 'hunchbacked', *v.* Broken Back in Oakham f.ns. (a) and *Brokenback Hill* in Barrowden f.ns. (b)); Boy's Pitt Spinney 1809 (*Boy pitte* e17, *Boy Pitt Furlong* c1700, 1781[1], 1781[2], *Boy Pitts furlong* 1709, 1712, 1716[2], *v.* **boi(a), pytt**, cf. *boydale* and *Boygreue infra* and *Boygraue* in Bisbrooke f.ns. (b)); Burnt Cl 1844; Bushey Cls 1824 O (*Bushy Close* 1765); Carters Cl 1805, Carter's - 1828 (*Carters Close* e17, 1678[2], 1710[3], 1719, 1720, cf. *Carters Farme* 1678[2], 1710[3], from the surn. *Carter*); Chapmans Cl; Coleswood Furlong 1809, Coleswood Hill Furlong 1809, Coles Wood or Windmill Fd 1808 (*Coleswood feild* e17, - *Field* 1631, 1780[2], (*the*) *Colewood feild* 1627[3], 1694, - *Field* 1786, *Collswood feild* 1705, *Coleswood Feild alias the Cock pitt Feild* c1700, *Coleswood Field alias the Cock·Pit Field alias the Windmill Field* 1781[1], 1781[2] (one of the great open-fields of the village, *v. Cockpit Field* and Windmill Fd *infra*), Colewood Close 1627[1], 1627[2], *Coleswood Close* 1621, 1626[1], 1761[2], - *Closes* 1682, *Colswood Close* 1659, 1690, *Collswood Close* 1694, 1705, 1759, *Colesworth* 1729[3], - *Close* 1729[1], 1736, *Coleswood pond* e17, 1631 (*v.* **ponde**), *Coleswood way* c1700; Willielmus and Alicia *Colle* were resident in Luffenham in 1356 *BHS* as was Robert *Colle* 1522 MilS, and their family name is most likely to be the first el. here, hence 'Cole's wood', *v.* **wudu**); Deadman's Grave Furlong 1809 (*Deadmans grave* e17, - *way* 1631, *v.* **dede-man, græf**, referring most prob. to an early discovery of part of the pagan Anglo-Saxon cemetery at SK 932 045); Deepdale Hollow 1809 (*Depedale* e13, *ouerdepdale* 1356 (*v.* ofer[3]), *Debdayle* 1631, *Debdale* e18, 1716[2], *depedale hol* 1323, *Debdale Hole* e17, 1709, 1712, 1716, 1729, *Depdell Hole* c1700, 1781[1], 1781[2] (*v.* hol[1]), *Debdale Hollow* 1780[1] (*v.* holh), *v.* dēop, dalr); Digbys Cl 1844 (*Mr Digbys New Close* c1700, cf. James *Digby* of N. Luffenham 1659); Engine Cl 1844 (1732[2], 1779, 1785, land on which agricultural or other machines were sited); Fernham Furlong 1809 (*Fenholme* 1631, *Fenhams* 1729[3], *v.* fenn, holmr); Flaxmans Slade 1808 (*Flackmore Slade* e17, *Flaxmans Slade* 1631, *Flaxman* - c1700, *Flaxland* - c1745, *Flaxman's* - 1781, *Flaxmore slade Furlong* 1659, *Flaxman Slade Furlong* c1700, 1781[1], 1781[2], originally 'marsh or moorland where turves are cut', *v.* flak, mōr[1], cf. Flatmoor C 296, *v.* slæd); Fosters Bridge Cl 1844 (*Foster Bridge Close* c1700, 1729, *Fosters* - 1754, 1761[1], *Foster's Bridge Closes* 1763, 1781[1], *Foster's Bridge furlong* 1781[1], *v.* Foster's Bridge in S. Luffenham); Gibbon's Hollow 1809 (*Gibinses Hollow* 1729[3], from the surn. *Gibbon*, cf. Peter *Gybbon* 1522 MilS of S. Luffenham, *v.* holh); Home Cl 1844 (x3), Nether - 1844 (*Home Close* 1732[2], 1763, 1779, *v.* home); How Cl Furlong 1809 (*How Close* 1780[2], 1786, *How hedge* e17, 1659, *v.* haugr, hecg); Jarminy (apparently a fanciful spelling of *Germany* and thus prob. denoting a field remote from the village, though based on the surn. of William *Jerman* 1522 MilS, - *German* 1524 SR of N. Luffenham); Jericho (a 'remoteness' name, sometimes denoting land on which sick animals were isolated); Lammas (Bottom) Cl 1844 (*Lammas 'Close* c1700, 1796[3], *v.* lammas); Long Cl 1844 ((*the*) *Long Close* 1715[2], 1716[1], 1755); Long Cutts 1844 (*Long Cutt* 1732[2], *Long Cutts and Meadow* 1779, 1785, *v.* cutte[1] 'a water channel'; associated with a 'a square moat-like earthwork, cut in two by a channel, at SK 9347 0280, fed from R. Chater by a cutting' BrownArchSites 19, which suggests that this was poss. an osier bed); Lyndon Head 1979 VR (Lyndon parish adjoins to the west, *v.* hēafod); Mallories Cl 1844 (1765[2], cf. Mr *Mallorie*, a landowner here e17); Matthews Station Fd (alluding to Luffenham railway station); Great -, Little Mdw (*the great meadow* 1627[2], (*the*) *Great Meadow* c1700, 1781[1], 1781[2], 1796[3], (*the*) *Little Meadow* 1627[2], c1700, 1781[1], 1781[2], 1796[3], *the two Little Meadow Closes* 1659, 1690, 1759, 1761[2], 1766, *v.* mæd); Meers next to Pilton 1844 (Pilton parish adjoins to the south-west, *v.* (ge)mǣre); Middle Cl 1844 (1682, 1763, 1785); Middlesey Way Furlong 1809 (*Midlestey furlong* 1631, *Middlese Way* c1700, *Middlestey way* e18, *Middle Sea Way* 1729[3], 1736, *Midlese or Middlesea Way* 1781[2], *Middlesea Way* 1781[1], - *Furlong* 1781[1], 1781[2], 'the middle path or narrow road', *v.* middel, stīg influenced by the ME sb. *sty-way* 'a pathway, a narrow road, a footpath'); Mill Cl 1844 (1711[1], 1711[2], 1729[2], 1763, 1764, 1785); Mill Holme 1844 (*v.* holmr); Moat Cl 1844, The Motts 1943 (the moat is traceable 'in grass at SK 9289 0330, close to R. Chater' MER 28, 30, poss. a decorative or recreational feature related to N. Luffenham Hall); the Nook Piece 1809 (*v.* nōk, pece); Nuts Cl; Orchard 1844 (*the Old Orchard* 1621, 1626[1], 1627[1], 1627[2], *the olde Orchyarde* 1636, ·*v.*

orceard); Parks 1844, Park Spinney 1943; Bottom -, Top Pasture; Penny Holmes 1844, - Piece 1943 (*penny holme* 1686, *Peny Holme* 1722[1], *Penny Holm(e)* 1728, 1742, 1763, 1785, perh. referring to an original penny rent, *v.* **pening, holmr, pece**); Pilton Well (cf. *Wells Close* 1686; Pilton parish adjoins to the south-west, *v.* **wella**); The Pond 1844; Pound Cl 1844 (*v.* **pund**); Price's Little Mdw; Rushby Cl 1816, 1828, Rush -, Rushey Cl 1844 (*Rushy Close* c1700, *v.* **riscig**); Scotland (e17, 1627[2], *Mr Barkers Scotland Close* 1781[2], land subject to the payment of a tax, *v.* **scot, land**); the Great Sculthorpe Cl 1809, the little Top Sculthorpe Cl 1809, Sculthorpe Cl 1844 (Bottom) Scultrups 1944 (*the neither Sculthorpe* 1659 (*v.* **neoðera**), *Sculthorpe Close* 1779, 1796[3], *East* -, *West* - 1796[3], *Sculthorp(e) Lane* c1700, 1781[2], *v.* Sculthorpe Spinney *supra*); Sour Furlong 1809 (*v.* **sūr**); South Fd 1844 (1796[3]); Spinney Fd; Spring Cl 1844 (1765[2], *v.* **spring**); Station Fds (adjoining Luffenham railway station); the Stone Acre 1809 (*v.* **stān**); Three Cornered Cl 1844 (cf. *Three Corner Close* in S. Luffenham f.ns. (b)); The Townsend Cl 1844 (*Townes end* e17, 1631, *Northerns Town end* c1700, *- Towns End* 1781[2], *- Town's End* 1781[1], *Townsend Furlong* c1700, 1781[1], 1781[2], *v.* **tūn, ende**[1]; with the surn. *Northern*, cf. *Northerns Leys* in Egleton f.ns. (b)); the Town Headland Hedge 1809 (*Town(e) Headland* 1631, 1729[3], 1781[1], *the Town hade land* c1700, *v.* **tūn, hēafod-land**); Warren Fd (*ye Waring* 1729[3], *v.* **wareine**); Waterfurrows Furlong 1809 (*the water Furrowes* 1659, 'land where water tends to lie in the furrows' or simply 'wet furrows', *v.* **wæter, furh**); Edith Weston Fd 1943 (*Furlong buting on Weston Feild* c1700), Edithweston Hedge 1809 (*Weston hedg* 1631, *- Hedge* 1780[1], 1780[2], *v.* **hecg**) (Edith Weston parish adjoins to the north); Whichley Warren Furlong 1809 (*Witchl(e)y furlong* 1631, 1709, 1716[2], *v.* Witchley Warren Fm, - Spinney); White Clay Furlong 1809 ((*the*) *White Clay* e17, 1729[3], 1736, *v.* **hwīt, clǣg**); Wilkinsons Cl 1844 (1765[2], from the surn. *Wilkinson*, cf. Margere *Wylkynson* 1524 SR); Windmill Fd 1844 (*the Windmill* 1631, (*the*) *Windmill Feild* 1729[3], - *Field* 1751[1], 1763, 1781[1], 1781[2], 1796[3], *v.* **wind-mylne**; one of the great open-fields of the village, also called Coles Wood Field *supra* and *Cockpit Field*, *v. infra*); Woolsdale 1809 (*Wolfdale* e17, *Woolsdale* c1700, 1781[1], 1781[2], - *North and South* c1700, 'Wulf's valley', *v.* **dalr**); Woottons, Wottons Cl 1844 (with the surn. *Wootton*, cf. John *Wotton* 1705 *Anc* and Francis *Wotton* 1769 *EnclA* of neighbouring Ketton).

(b) *Adams Yard and Close* 1682 (Randall *Adams* was resident in the village in 1722[1]); *Allens Close* 1715, *Allens and Pits's Barne* 1715[1] (from the surns. *Allen* and *Pitts*, cf. Matthew - and Richard *Pitts* 1710[2] and Widow *Pitts* 1732[2] of N. Luffenham); *Avenue* 1763, 1776 (*v.* **avenue**); *at the backside* 1729[3], *the Backside* 1736 (*v.* **ba(c)ksyde**); *Bastard Leys* 1781[1], 1781[2], *North Bastard Ley* c1745 (dial. *bastard* 'unproductive, poor, barren', *v.* **lēah**, cf. Bastard Leys in neighbouring Edith Weston f.ns. (a), no doubt referring to the same pasture); *Bates Close* 1765[2] (from the surn. *Bates*); *batusmore* 1368, *Great* -, *Over* -, *Batesmore* 1621, 1626[1], 1627[1], 1627[2], 1636, *Batesmore End* 1709, 1712, 1716[2], *Great* -, *Little Batesmore Close* 1660, 1678[1] (with the surn. *Bate(s)*, v. **mōr**[1]); *the Beadhouse* 1715[1], 1781[2], *the bead-house farm* 1796[2], *Beadhouse peice* c1700, *the Beadhouse Piece* 1781[2] (v. **pece**), v. **bed-hūs**); *Beckclosse* 1631, *ye Beckclose* 1659 (v. **clos**), *(the) Beck Dike* c1700, 1781[1], 1781[2] (v. **dīk**), v. **bekkr**); *Bidwell Tree* 1781[1], 1781[2] (v. **trēow** and Little Bidwell *supra*); *Blowland* 1631, *Bloland Hedge* e17 (v. **hecg**), 'cold, cheerless land', v. **blāw, land**); *boydale* 1356 (perh. either 'the boy's valley' or 'Boia's valley', but cf. the following f.n., v. **boi(a), dalr**); *Boygreue* 13 VCH (v. **boi(a), græf** and cf. Boy's Pitt Spinney *supra* and *Boygraue* in Bisbrooke f.ns. (b)); *Bradcroft* 1779, 1785 (v. **brād, croft**); *lybrakehil* 1371 (presumably, *ly-* represents the OFr definite article *le* or *la*, v. **bræc**[1], **hyll**); *Bretfeilds Farm* 1715[1] (Abraham *Bretfield* was baptized in N. Luffenham in 1633 PR and a Richard *Bretfeild* was farming here in 1690 and 1766); *Britain's Old Homestead* 1763, *Brittains homestead* 1785 (with the surn. *Brit(t)ain*, v. **hām-stede**); *Broc Holys* 1358, *Brockwells* c1700, 1729[3], 1780[1], 1780[2], 1781[1], 1781[2], *- Close* 1715[2], 1716[1], 1763, 1785 (v. **brocc-hol**, cf. Brockwells in S. Luffenham f.ns. (a) and Brockwell in Lyddington f.ns. (a)); *ye Brooke* e17 (v. **brōc**); *Cants Close* 1761[1], 1785 (from the family name of John *Cant* 1715); *Clapmilleclose* n.d. VCH (a *clap-mill* was a clapper turned by the wind for scaring away birds); *Clarks Cottage* 1763; *Cockpitt* e17, *Cockpitts* 1631, *Cockpitt Feild* c1700, *Cock Pitt Field* 1780[1], *Cockpit Field* 1781[1], 1781[2], *Cockpit(t) Furlong* c1700, 1781[1], 1781[2] (v. **cockpit** 'a pit used for cock-fighting' and Coles Wood or Windmill Fd *supra*); *Coes Close* 1763 (with the surn. *Coe*); *Colebush* 1659 (prob. scrubland belonging to the *Cole* family, v. **busc** and Coleswood *supra*); *Colsons Close* 1715[2], 1716[1], 1755 (with the surn. *Colson*, cf. Thomas *Colson* 1525 SR of Ayston); *Coopers Close* 1682; *Cow Close* 1785; *Cow Commons* (x3) 1796[3] (v. **commun**); *Crabtree peice Furlong* c1700, *- Piece* c1700, 1781[1], 1781[2] (v. **crabtre, pece**); *Craddocks Homestead and Cowpasture* 1763, 1785 (v. **hām-stede**); *ad crucem Benedicti* e13 (a cross either dedicated to St Benedict or associated with a local Benedict, v. **cros**); *Digbies Leyes* 1631 (from the family name of James *Digby* 1659 of N. Luffenham, v. **lēah**); *the Doggkennell Yard and Garden* 1722[2] (v. **dogge-kenel**); *Dovecoat Close* 1765[2] (v. **dove-cot(e)**); *Dukes bushe* 1631, *Duke Bush* e17, *Dukes Bush Furlong* c1700, 1781[1], 1781[2], *dukesbush nook* 1729[3], *Dukes bush nook* 1736 (v. **nōk**) (prob. alluding to ground covered with scrub and owned by a family called *Duke*, cf. *Dukes Butts* in Glaston f.ns. (b), v. **busc**); *Dry Close* 1682 (v. **dryge**); *Eastfeild alias Upper Feild* 1627[2], *East Feild* 1631, *The East or Water Mill Feild* 1729[3], *East Field* c1745 (one of the great open-fields of the village, v. **ēast, feld** and Watermill Spinney *supra*); *East Furlong* 1781[2]; *le Est Meade* 1550 Pat (v. **ēast, mǣd**); *Extons Headland* 1631 (with the surn. *Exton*, cf. Thomas *Exton* 1522 MilS of Empingham, *v.* hēafod-land); *Falkeners House*, - *Yard* 1715[1] (the property of Francis *Falkener* 1715[1]); *Fincett Land* 1710[1] (once the holding of the prior and convent of *Fineshade* Nth; their estate in N. Luffenham was acquired before 1223); *Freeschool(e) house* 1715[2], 1716[1], 1755, *Free School* 1846 White; *Gate Close* c1700; *Gibson's Close* 1763, *Gibsons* - 1785; *Gills Mill* c1700, 1781[1], 1781[2] (with the surn. *Gill*; the mill stood in *Water Mill Field*, *v.* Watermill Spinney *supra*); *the Gleab land* 1709 (*v.* glebe); *Gosholm* 14 VCH (*v.* gōs, holmr); *Goslin(g) Lane* 1715[1] (from the surn. *Goslin*, cf. *Goslyms* in neighbouring Lyndon f.ns. (b)); *ye Grasse* 1659 (evidently identifying land put down to grass, *v.* gærs); *the Great Furlong* 1780[2]; *Hauerland* e13, *Haverlond* 1361, *Havirlond* 1363, *Haverlands* 1659, 1686, 1690, 1709, 1712, 1759, 1761[2], 1766, 1780[2], 1781[2] (*v.* hæfera, hafri, land); *the Hay Closes* 1732[2], 1761[1]; *the nine acres Hedge Feild* 1715[1]; *(the) Hempland* 1715[2], 1716[1], 1755 (the term *hempland* was eventually applied to a piece of land held by a small tenant irrespective of the produce of the soil; such patches of ground were often adjacent to dwellings, *v.* hempland and cf. Hemp Yards in S. Luffenham f.ns. (a)); *Homestead with Clarks Cottage* 1763 (*v.* hām-stede); *the Homeward Acre* 1780[2], 1786 ('the plot of arable towards home', *v.* hāmweard, æcer); *Hunisforlong* 1257, *Honey Furlong* 1631, c1700, 1709, 1712, 1716[2], 1781[1], 1781[2] (although with a large gap in the continuity of forms, these prob. belong together; the ME surn. *Hunn* or the ME reflex of the OE pers.n. *Hūn* is the first el. of the early form (*v.* furlang), while in the later spellings *honey*, used in many f.ns. with reference to sticky or muddy soil, may have replaced the surn./pers.n. through folk etymology or have developed naturally from it); *Horeston* e17, *Whore Stone* c1700, *Hostone* 1729[3], *Hostern* 1780[1], *Hoar Stone* 1781[1], 1781[2], *Horston Hedg* 1631 ('the boundary stone', *v.* hār[2], stān, superseded by a boundary hedge, *v.* hecg); *Horse Close* 1732[2]; *How Close* 1780[2], 1786, *Howhedge* e17, 1659 (*v.* haugr, hecg); *Mr Hunts Close* 1686; *Johnsons Closse* 1631 (cf. *Johnsons Close* 1654 in nearby Glaston); *the Joint* 1781[1] (land held in jointure, implying a co-tenancy of husband and wife, or else entailed property); *Ketenemer* 14 VCH, *Ketton Meir* 1729[3], - *Meare* 1751[1], 1751[2], - *Mear* 1780[1] (*v.* (ge)mǣre), *Ketton ways* 1729[3] (Ketton parish adjoins to the east); *King's house* 1796[1] (with the surn. *King*); *kinges land, kings lande* e17, *Kings Mills* 1686, 1722[1], *King's Mills* 1742, *Kings myll dame* 1590 (*v.* damme), *Kyngmilne Stey* 1368 (*v.* stīg) (the king held Luffenham from DB, but these names are prob. from the common Ru surn. *King*, *v.* myln); *the Knights house* 1692 (with the surn. *Knight*); *knyttyshadlond* 1385 (with the surn. *Knight*, cf. the preceding name, *v.* hēafod-land); *le kydhaker* 1357 (*v.* kide, æcer); *Larretts · house* 1715[1] (cf. John - and George *Larrett* 1654 Anc and Widow *Larrett* 1676 Asw of nearby Glaston);

lawes close 1686, *Laws Close* 1722[1], 1728, 1742 (with the surn. *Law*, cf. Laws Cl in neighbouring Ketton f.ns. (a)); *the leys* 1726 (*v.* lēah); *the Lime Close* 1712 (*v.* līm); *Limekilne balke* c1700, *Lime Kiln Balk* 1781[1], 1781[2], *the lyme Kilne Close* 1709, *Lime Kiln Close* 1763 (*v.* lim-kilne, balca); *Litelhowe* e13, *Little How Gate* 1780[1] (*v.* gata) (*v.* lytel, haugr); (*the*) *Little Meadow* 1627[2], c1700, 1781[1], 1781[2], 1796[3] (*v.* mǣd); *the two little over Closes* 1686 (*v.* ofer[3]); *Longcrofts* 1631 (*v.* lang[1], croft); *Long Furlong* 1631, c1700, 1781[1], 1781[2]; *Luffs Crabtree* e17 (from the surn. *Luff*, cf. George *Luffe* 1585 PR and Edward *Luff* 1729[1], *v.* crabtre); *Luffs hil* c1700, - *Hill* c1700, 1709, 1712, 1716[2], 1781[1], *Luff's Hill* 1781[2] (cf. the preceding f.n.); *abutting on le Mantell'* 1366 (poss. an early use of *mantel* in the sense 'rampart' as in *mantel-wall* (*v.* NED *s.v.* mantel 2) and referring to the fortified site at SK 928 033, cf. *Le Pele infra*); *Medwedik'* 1363, *le Medewedyk* 1366, *medoudike* 1373, *le Medowdik* 1389 (*v.* mǣd, dīk); *Merestones* 1403 ('the boundary-marking stones', *v.* (ge)mǣre, stān); *Middelfurlong* e13, *Middle Furlong* e17, 1631, 1659, c1700, 1781[1], 1781[2] (*v.* middel, furlang); *Middelstow* e13 (*v.* middel, stōw); *morishadlond* 1385 (prob. with the surn. *Morris* rather than *mōr* 'a moor, moorland', *v.* hēafod-land and cf. the following f.n.); *Morris's Close* 1779 (with the surn. *Morris*); *Moubreche* e13 (*v.* mūga, brēc); *Muntons Close* c1700, 1781[1], 1781[2] (from the family name of Thomas *Munton* 1754); *le Mylnedam* 1403 (*v.* myln, damme; perh. to be identified with *Kinges myll dame supra*, but cf. also *molendina aquatica de Sculthorp infra*); *the neate pasture* 1627[2] (*v.* nēat); *Neather Furlong* c1700, *Nether -* c1700, 1781[1], 1781[2] (*v.* neoðera); *the new Dike* 1686 (*v.* dīk); *New Close* 1781[1]; *Oak Tree Close* c1700; *Oldames Headland* 1631 (*v.* hēafod-land), *Odehams Hedge* e17, *Oldhams Hedg(e)* c1700, 1709, 1712, 1716[2], *Oldhames hedges* 1659, *Odams Hedges* 1729, 1736, *Oldham's Hedge* 1781[1], 1781[2], *Oldhams farr hedg* 1709, *Oldhams furr Hedge* 1712, - *Fur hedg* 1716[2] (*v.* feor), *Oldhams Upper Hedge* c1700, 1781[2], *Oldham's -* 1781[1], *Oldhams Hedge Furlong* 1781[2] (from the family name of John *Oldham* 1594 PR, *v.* hecg); *le Ololondes* 1358 (*v.* holh, land); *Mr Hunts Open Close* c1700, *Mr Ray's (late Hunt) Open Close* 1781[1] (a close without permanent gates, sometimes called an 'open gap close', *v.* Open Cl in S. Luffenham f.ns. (a)); *the Parsonage yard* 1715[2], 1716[1]; *le Pele* 1363 (poss. ME pēl 'a palisade, an enclosure formed by a palisade', cf. *le Mantell' supra*); *Pesedale* e13 (*v.* pise, dalr); *Pheasants Close* 1659, 1761[2], 1766, *Fesants Close* 1690, 1759 (from the surn. *Pheasant*, cf. Anna *Phesant* 1572 PR and Dorcas *Phesant* 1576 ib); *Pilton gate* 1370 (Pilton parish adjoins to the south-west, *v.* gata); *Pits's Barne* 1715[1], *Pitt house* 1715[1] (from the family name of Matthew - and Richard *Pitts* 1710[2]); *the poors barne* 1715[2], *the Poor's Barn* 1716[1] (a barn used for charitable purposes); *Pridmores Close* 1686 (from the family name of John *Pridmore* 1732); *Pullens acre* e17 (with the surn. *Pullen*, *v.* æcer); *Randike Meir* 1729[3] (with either *rand* 'a border, a boundary' or *rān* 'a boundary strip', *v.* dīk, (ge)mǣre); *Mr Rays Fur Peice* 1729[3], 1736 (*v.* feor, pece); *Redehille* e13, *Redhill* 1631, 1716[2], *Red Hill* e18, 1709, 1712 (alluding to the colour of the soil on the ironstone, *v.* rēad, hyll); *Reynolds Cottage* 1761 (cf. Richard *Reynold* 1522 MilS, - *Reynolde* 1524 SR of nearby Barrowden); *Rochefurlong* Hy 3 AD (if not an early instance of the surn. *Roche* (> *Roach*), then ME *roche* 'a rock, a cliff'); *Rough Close* 1682 (*v.* rūh[1]); *Sandacre* e13 (*v.* sand, æcer); *sandpits* 1631 (*v.* sand, pytt); *Saxholmes* 1682, *Saxholms* 1763, 1785, *Saxholme* 1779, *Saxhams Close* 1711[1], 1711[2], 1729[2], *Saxums* - 1764 (*v.* holmr); *cepecotehyl* 1358 (*v.* scēap-cot, hyll); *Sheperdsbush* e18 (prob. scrubland belonging to the *Shepherd* family, *v.* busc); *le sondes* 1356 (*v.* sand); *Sowell Sike* e17, *Sewell seek* 1631, *Southwell Syke furlong* 1659 (*v.* sūð, wella, sīk); *Stamford Way* 1729[3] (the road to Stamford L); *the Stone pitts* e17 (*v.* stān-pytt); *le Stoniforlong* 1356, *Stonifurlong(e)* 1356, 1368, 1385 (*v.* stānig, furlang); *the Street* 1763 (perh. referring to the village street, cf. *the towne streete* in Lyndon f.ns. (b) and *Town-Street* in Edith Weston f.ns. (b); but note *the Highestrete* in Barrowden f.ns. (b) and *Street furl', Street Leys* in Morcott f.ns. (b) which may well represent the line of a lost Roman road from the north through Empingham, Edith Weston, N. Luffenham, Morcott and Barrowden parishes to Turtle Bridge across R. Welland); *the swamp* 1659 (*v.* swamp); *Swan(n)s Close* 1659, 1690, 1759, *Swan close* 1761[2], 1766 (from the family name of Edward *Swanne* 1600 PR); *Syms headland* 1631 (from the surn. *Syms, v.* hēafod-land); *thefholm* 1356 (*v.* þefa, holmr); *Thorney Meadow* 1715[1] (*v.* þornig); *Tilton's Piece* 1781[2], *Tiltons Shrubbs* e17 (cf. John *Tilton* 1522 MilS, - *Tylton* 1524 SR, *v.* pece, scrubb); *(the) Town Close* 1751[1], 1751[2], *Town Corner* 1729[3] (*v.* corner), *(the) Town Farm (House)* 1715[2], 1716[1], c1745, 1755, *(the) Town Ley(e)s* 1715[2], 1716[1], 1722[2], 1755 (*v.* lēah) (*v.* tūn); *Tree Topps* 1715[1] (*v.* topp); *Trews close* e17 (with the surn. *Trew*); *Turners headland* 1631 (*v.* hēafod-land); *Umpthorne* 1368 (*v.* impa, þorn); *Upfeld* 13, 15 VCH, *Vpfeild* 1659, *the Upfeild* 1709, 1712 (*v.* upp, feld); *Eastfield alias Upper Feild* 1627[2], *Upper Field* c1745; *Upper Furlong* c1700; *the Upper Gardens* 1732[2]; *Walle close* e17, *Wall Close* c1700 (*v.* wall); *Wards Close* 1763, 1785 (in the possession of John *Ward* 1763); *the water balke* e17 (*v.* wæter, balca); *molendina aquatica de Sculthorpe* 1387 (*v.* water-mylne and Sculthorpe Spinney *supra*); *between the Wayes* e17, 1716[2] ('(furlong) between the roads', *v.* weg); *West Field* c1745; *Weston close* 1659, *Weston Foot way* 1781[1], *Weston Gapp(e)* e17, 1659 (*v.* gappe), *apud Westongat'* 1356, *Westungate* 1379 ('(furlong) beside the road to Edith Weston', *v.* gata), *Weston Town Close* c1700, 1709, 1781[2], *Weston Towne Close Corner* 1712, 1716[2], 1781[1] (*v.* tūn, corner), *Weston Way* e17, 1631, 1659, c1700, 1780[1], 1781[1], 1781[2] (Edith Weston parish adjoins to the north); *le wetlondes* 1356, *long -, Short Wheatlands* 1631, *Short Wheatlandes, Long Wheat Landes Furlong* 1659 ('wet selions', *v.* wēt, land); *(the) Witch Close* 1686, 1763, 1785, *the Wich Close* 1722[1], 1728, 1735 (*v.* wice); *Willow Row* 1776 (*v.* wilig, rāw); *windmill pits* 1631 (*v.* pytt and Windmill Fd *supra*); *Witchley* e17, *- Corner* 1631, 1781[1], 1781[2], *Wickley Corner* c1700 (*v.* corner), *Witchl(e)y Gapp* 1709, 1712, 1716[2] (*v.* gappe), *Wickly Hedg* c1700, *Witchley Hedge* 1781[2] (*v.* hecg), *Witchley*

Piece 1781[1], 1781[2] (*v.* **pece**), *Wichley way* e17, *Witchley Way* 1631 (*v.* Witchley Warren Fm in Edith Weston); *Woodcrosse way* 1631 (*v.* **wudu, cros**); *apud le wodgate* 1356 ('(furlong) beside the road to the wood', *v.* **wudu, gata**); *Wrongedich* 1257, *Wrangdykmere* 15 VCH (*v.* **(ge)mǣre**) (*v.* **wrang, dic, dík** and Wrangdike Hundred; the later form may not belong here, being rather a reference to the Wrangdike Hundred boundary which coincides with the parish boundary along its northern and eastern extents); *Wyleweholm* 1257 (*v.* **wilig, holmr**); *Mr Wimarks yard end* 1631 (*v.* **geard, ende**[1] and cf. Wymark Spinney *supra*).

South Luffenham

SOUTH LUFFENHAM
For forms and interpretation, *v.* North Luffenham.

The affix is normally added as:
Sut- 1210 Cur, 1213 *FF*, 1220 Cur, *Sud-* 1219 ib, 1233 RHug, 1250 Misc, *Suth-* 1209-19 RHug, 1224 Cur, 1254 Val *et freq* to 1324 *Conant et passim* to 1480 Pat, *South-* 1356 ib, 1362 *Conant et freq* to 1555 *ib*, 1610 Speed, *v.* **sūð**.

South Luffenham Inns and Taverns

AXE AND SAW (lost), 1846 White; burnt down in 1874 - VR. BOOT AND SHOE, 1935 VCH; according to VR, a shoemaker's premises in the 19th century, although conflicting local lore has it that the shoemaker's was nearby. CROWN (lost), c1795, 1796 *Anc.* DURHAM OX (lost), 1863 White. HALFWAY HOUSE, 1935 VCH; the halfway coaching inn between Uppingham and Stamford. HEREFORD OX (lost), 1850 Slater. RAILWAY (lost), closed in the 1930s - VR.

FOSTER'S BRIDGE, *Fosters Bridge* 1610 Speed, 1620 Map, 1732 *Anc*, c1800, 1806 Map, 1849, 1873 *Anc*, *- Brigg* 1659 *ib*, *Foster Bridge* 1700 BHS, 1729 *Terrier*, *Foster's Bridge* 1763 *Anc*, 1781 BHS, 1796 *Anc*, cf. *Foster's Bridge Lane* 1809 BHS, *Foster Bridge Spinney* 1943 *Map*. If the early S. Luffenham f.n. form *Fosdeybalk'* 1368 BHS (with **balca** 'a bank') belongs here, then what appears to be the surn. *Foster* may originally have been OE **foss-dīc*. If so, OE *foss* 'a ditch', perhaps a direct loan from Lat *fossa*, had an explanatory OE *dīc* 'an artificial water-course' (later perhaps influenced by Scand *dīk*) added to it, cf. Foss Dyke L and cf. also the reduction *dīk* > *dey* in *Landiegate, Landeygate* (from *land-dīk*) L 2 189. In view of the late Roman military metalwork found in the pagan Anglo-Saxon cemetery here, the name perhaps reflects the antiquity of Germanic settlement at Luffenham. It must be stressed, however, that apart from R. Chater, its derivative Ketton, R. Glen and perhaps R. Welland, Rutland has no surviving names which indicate direct contact between Romano-British and Germanic peoples and this in itself throws serious doubt on a possible derivation from Lat *fossa*. Nevertheless, *Foster* is not a family name associated with either North or South Luffenham in the 16th and 17th centuries, although one John *Foster* was resident in neighbouring Morcott in 1524 SR.

BACK LANE (local). CLAY LANE (local), cf. *Clay Lane Close* 1843 *Anc*. OLD WINDMILL, *the windmill* 1710 *ib, The Wind Mill* 1843, 1844 *ib*, cf. *the Windmill Field* 1803 *ib*. RECTORY, 1846 White, cf. *(the) Parsonage* 1615 *Conant,* 1631 *Terrier*. RED BARN. SOUTH LUFFENHAM CHURCH, *Church* 1863 White, cf. *South Luffenham Churchyard* 1849 *Anc.* SOUTH LUFFENHAM HALL is *the Neither House* 1710 *ib* (*v.* neoðera), *South Luffenham House* 1801 Map, *Hall* 1846 White. SOUTH LUFFENHAM HEATH, 1824 O, *the Heath* 1615 *Conant,* 1796 *Anc,* 1845 *Burghley,* 1849 *Anc, Luffenham Heath* 1873 *ib, v.* hæð. UPPER HALL, *le Uphalle* 1315 Ipm, *Le Uppehall* 1316 ib, *the Vppermost House* 1710 *Anc,* cf. *ad Aulam* 1327 *SR* (p), *atte Hall(e)* 1352 Cl (p), 1356 Pat (p), 1362 *Conant* (p), 1364 *BHS* (p), 1364 Pat (p), 1388 Fine (p), *v.* upp, hall.

Field-Names

Undated forms in (a) are 1943 *Map*; those dated 1803, 1823, 1838, 1843, 1844[3], 1845[1], 1849, 1873 and 1887 are *Anc*; those dated 1844[1] are *TA*; 1844[2] and 1845[2] are *Burghley* and 1953 are *Deed.* Early forms dated 1590, 1615, 1629,

1635, 1649, 1651 and 1729 are *Conant*; those dated 1626, 1652^1, 1652^2, 1671, 1695^1, 1695^2, 1708, 1709, 1710, 1720, 1726, 1729, 1742, c1750, 1766, 1772, c1795 and 1796 are *Anc*; 1631 are *Terrier*.

(a) the Acre 1845^1, 1849 (c1795), Six Acres 1844^1, 1845^2, Seven Acres 1844^2, Ten Acres 1845^2 (*the Ten Acres* c1795), Fourteen -, Eighteen Acres 1943, Twenty Acre Cl 1845^2, Twenty Acres 1844^1 (c1795, *20 Acres Close* 1796), The Seventy Acre 1943 (*v.* **æcer**); Ash Cl 1844^1, 1845^2, Little - 1845^2, Ash Cls 1845^1, 1849 (*Ashclose* 1652^2, *Ash Close* 1652^1, 1652^2, 1796, *v.* **æsc**); Aspin's Grass Fds (i.e. land put down to grass, *v.* **gærs**); Back Gate Piece (*v.* **pece**); Barkers Hey 1873, Barker's Hay 1943 (from the local surn. *Barker*, cf. Barker's Spinney in N. Luffenham, *v.* **(ge)hæg**); Barrowden Balk 1845^2 (*v.* **balca**), - Heath, - Road Fd 1943 (Barrowden parish adjoins to the south); Bassett Acres 1845^2 (cf. *the Mannor of North Luffenham called Bassetts Manor* 1711 *Anc*, *the manor of North Luffenham called Bassetts Manor* 1764 *ib*; Thomas *Basset*, gentleman, held land here in 1522 MilS, while John *Basset* did likewise in 1626 *Anc*); Baxters Garden 1844^1, 1844^2, 1845^2; Bell Ringing Cl 1845^2, Bellringers Fd al. Bell Fd 1979 VR (so called because the land was endowed to pay the sexton to ring the bells at 5.00 a.m. and 8.00 p.m. daily from the end of October to March 25th for the sake of benighted travellers, *v.* VCH 2 207); The Big Fd; Big Mdw; the Blacksmiths Shop 1844^3 (*v.* **sc(e)oppa**); Botany Bay 1844^1, 1845^2 (a common derogatory name for remote land where perh. labour was hard, as in the penal settlement in New South Wales, cf. Botany Bay in Lt. Casterton f.ns. (a)); Bottom Furlong 1843, 1844^3, 1849; Broad Ash Cl otherwise Broads Cl 1843, 1844^3, 1849 (*Broadsclose* 1710); Broad Cl 1823, 1843, 1844^3, 1849 (*the Broad Close* 1710); Little -, Brockwells 1844^1, 1845^2 (*Brockwells* c1750, 1766, *Brockwell's Close* 1796, *Brockwells* - 1796, *Brockwells Meadow* c1795, *v. Broc Holys* in N. Luffenham f.ns. (b)); Bull Piece 1873 (*v.* **pece**); Top -, Cardalls (with the surn. *Cardwell*); Child Furlong 1845^1, 1849 (c1795; poss. with the surn. *Child*, but the f.n. occurs in exactly the same form in Barleythorpe f.ns. (b) for 1746 and it is poss. that an original *cild* 'a young person' may be the source); Church Balk 1845^2 (*v.* **balca**), Church Mdw 1845^2 (*church meadows* 1631, c1795); The Clay 1943 (*the Cley* 1615, *middle furlong in the clay* 1631), Clay Cl 1953, Little - 1844^1, 1844^2, 1845 (*the Clayclose* 1631, *Clay Close* c1795, 1796, *Clay Close abutting on the Heath* 1796, *Clay Close by Short Gate Balk* 1796), Clay Foot 1943 (i.e. land at the foot of Clay Hill, *v.* **fōt**), Clay Hill 1843, 1844^3, - Hills 1843, 1849, Clay Hill Furlong 1845^2, 1849 (*Clayshill* 1631), Clay Lock Cl 1844^1, 1845^2, Claylock - 1844^2 (*v.* **loc**) (*v.* **clæg**); Conygear Lane 1873 (*v.* **coninger**); Cookes Nook 1845^2, Cooks - 1943 (*v.* **nōk**, cf. Home Cl *infra*); Coppice Leys 1873 (*v.* **lēah**); The Cottage Cl or Digby's

Cl (with the surn. *Digby*); Cow Pasture 1873; Crabtree Cl 1845[2] (*Crab tree Close* 1796, *v.* **crabtre**); Digby Oaks 1845[2], Digbys Oakes 1873 (named from the *Digby* family of N. Luffenham, cf. The Cottage Cl *supra*); Dovecote Cl 1844[1], 1844[2], 1845[2] (*Dovecoat(e) Close* 1729, 1766); Little -, Dry Cl 1844[1], 1845[2] (*Dry Close* 1652[1] (x2), 1652[2], c1750, 1766, c1795, 1796 (x2), *Dry Close SW of the Town* 1796 (*v.* **tūn**), *v.* **drȳge**); East and West; East Fd 1803, 1843, 1844[2], 1844[3], 1845[1], 1845[2], 1849, 1873 (*in campo orientali* 1356 BHS, *Est Feld* 15 VCH, *East Feild* 1590, 1615, 1631, 1710, *East Field* c1795, 1796, one of the great open-fields of S. Luffenham, *v.* **ēast, feld**); Eight Butts 1843, 1844[3] (*v.* **butte**); Eight Trees Hollow 1987 (from oral info. per Mrs. L. Worrall); Fancourts Cl 1844[1], 1845[2] (John *Fancourt* was resident in N. Luffenham 1765 *Anc*); Flasket Leys 1844[1], 1849, The - 1845[2], Flasket Leys Common 1873 (evidently a Scandinavianized form of ModE dial. *flaishet* 'swampy or waterlogged land', *v.* **flaishet, lēah, commun**); The Follies 1943, Follies Cl 1845[2], The Folly 1844[2], 1845[2] (*faleys* 1356 BHS, *the Follys* 1631, *Great Follies* 1652[1], *Little Follies* 1652[1], - *Follyes* 1652[2], *Folleys Close* n.d. VCH, *Follies' -, Folly's Close* c1795, *Follies Close* 1796, *Little* - 1796, *Follys hedg(e)* 1631 (*v.* **hecg**); naming a long stretch of meadowland adjoining the river; perh. *falh* 'ploughed land' (later 'fallow land') compounded with *lēah* 'a clearing', otherwise with (*ge*)*fall* 'a felling of trees', cf. *Faleys* in Bisbrooke f.ns. (b) which appears to be identical in origin and development); Foot Ball Cl 1803, 1843, Football - 1843, 1844[1], 1844[2], 1845[2] (an early example of a field set aside for the game); Footpad Piece 1844[1], 1943 (*v.* **pad, pece**); Garden Cl 1844[1]; Bottom -, Top Glebe ((*the*) *Glebe Close* c1795, 1796, *v.* **glebe**); Goodham Cl 1844[1], 1845[2] (*Goodholme* 1590, *Goadholm Close* c1795, *Goodholm* - 1796, *v.* **holmr**); Goodliffe's Cl 1844[1], 1844[2], 1845[2], 1943; The Grove 1844[1], 1845[2]; The Hall Cl 1844[1], 1943 (*Hall Close* 1652[1], 1796, *the Hall Meadowe* 1652[1], 1652[2]), Hall Ridings 1844[1], 1845[2] (*the Rideing* 1652[1], *v.* **ryding**); Hazel Dyke 1845[2], 1943 (alternatively known as Lammas Cl *infra*, *v.* **dīk**); Next the Heath (cf. *Heath Close* 1729, 1766, *v.* South Luffenham Heath *supra*); the Hedges 1844[3], 1849; Heigh Cl 1845[2] (*the Hay Close* 1652[1], *the Hey Closes* c1795, 1796, *v.* (**ge**)**hæg**); Hemp Yards 1844[2], 1845[2], 1943 (*the Hemp Yards* 1742, *Hemp Yard Closes* 1796, *v.* **hemp-yard**); High Cl 1844[1], Great High Cl 1943; The Holme 1844[1] (*the Holm* c1795, *the Holm on the North Side of the River* 1796, *v.* **holmr**); Home Cl (several) 1844[2], 1845[2], 1953 (*Home Close* c1795, 1796), Home Cl and Cooks Nook 1844[1] (*v.* **nōk**), Great -; Little Home Cl 1845[2] (*v.* **home**); The Homeward Land 1843, 1844[3] (1710, *v.* **hāmweard**); The Hop Ground 1844[1], 1845[2] (*v.* **hoppe, grund**); Inclosure 1844[1] (*v.* **inclosure**); Island 1844[1] (used of a field completely surrounded by other fields); Islips Cl 1803, 1838 (with the surn. *Islip*, cf. Thomas *Islipp* 1681

Hotchkin and Thomas *Islip* 1724 *ib*, poss. the same individual, but otherwise both of nearby Edith Weston); Kings Mdw 1844[1] (with the surn. *King*, cf. *King's House* in N. Luffenham f.ns. (b)); The Ladies Cl 1844[1], 1845[2], Ladies Fds 1943 (*v.* **hlǣfdige**); Lammas Cl 1844[2], - or Hazel Dike 1844[1] (*the Lammas Close* 1742, *v.* **lammas**); Land Cl 1843 (*the Landclose* 1710, cf. *Lower Lands* 1710, consolidating selions of an old open-field, *v.* **land**); Lane Cl 1844[1], 1844[2], 1845[2]; Line Fds 1943 (adjoining the railway, cf. Station Fds in Morcott f.ns. (a) *infra*); Little Cl 1844[2] (*Little Close West of the Town* 1796 (*v.* **tūn**)); Little Mdw 1844[1], 1844[2], 1845[2], 1849, 1953; Long Cl 1844[1], 1845[2], 1943 (1652[1], 1729, 1742, c1750, 1766, *East* -, *West* - c1795, 1796); Luffenham Cl 1845[2], 1943 (c1795, 1796); Many Wells 1845[2] (*Maniwelle* 1615, *v.* **manig, wella**); Mead Cl 1844[1] (*v.* **mǣd**); Meadow Cl 1823, 1843, 1844[3], 1849 (1710, c1750, c1795, 1796); Meer Balk 1845[2], 1849 (*v.* **(ge)mǣre, balca**); Mere Holes 1849 (*v.* **(ge)mǣre, hol[1]**); Middle Furlong 1803, 1849; Mill Backwater 1844[1] (*v.* **backwater**), the Mill Balk 1838 (c1795, *v.* **balca**), Mill Cl 1803, 1844[1] (1729, 1766, 1772), - Cls 1843, - Fd 1943, - Furlong 1843, - Holme 1844[3] (c1795, *Millhomes* 1633 VCH, *Millholm* 1796, *v.* **holmr**), - Mdw 1845[2], - Orchard 1844[1], 1845[2] (*v.* Kings Mills in N. Luffenham); Milleys Cl 1844[1], 1845[2] (*v.* **myln, lēah**); Miry Cl 1844[1], 1844[2], Mirey - 1845[2] (*v.* **myry**); Morcott Cl 1844[2], 1845[2] (1742), - Holme 1844[1], 1845[2] (*v.* **holmr**), - Townsend 1844[1], 1849 (*v.* **tūn, ende[1]**) (Morcott parish adjoins to the west, the S. Luffenham boundary passing close to Morcott village); The New Yard 1845[2]; Nine Butts 1843 (1710, *v.* **butte**); Nutts Cl 1845[2] (Mrs L. Worrall notes that James and Thomas *Nutt* owned land in S. Luffenham in 1845[2] but at this date, not this field; the ownership was divided among members of the Pridmore family); Open Cl 1843, 1844[1], 1844[3], 1845[2], 1849 ((*the*) *Open Close* 1710, 1729, 1766, c1795, *Open Gap Close* c1795, 1796, an enclosure without permanent gates); Paddock 1844[2]; Pea Cl 1845[2] (referring to its regular produce); Pen Cl 1844, 1873 (*the penne* 1615, *thother penne* 1615, *Penne Close* 1652[1], *Pennclose* 1652[2], *Pen Close* c1750, 1766, c1795, 1796, *v.* **penn[2]**); Pig Stye 1943, Pigstye Cl 1845[2] (*Pigsty Close* 1796); Pike Piece (roughly triangular; cf. *the Pike Furlonge* c1795, *v.* **pīc[1]**); Pond Cl 1844[1], 1844[2], 1845[2], 1953 ((*the*) *Pond Close* 1709, c1795, 1796); John Pridmores Cl 1803 (poss. named from the *John Pridmore* resident in N. Luffenham in 1732 *Anc*); Priest Croft Cl 1844[1], 1845[2], *Priests* - 1953 (cf. *Priests Pit Close* 1631 belonging to *the Parsonage*, *v.* **prēost, pytt**); the Quick 1843, 1844[3], 1849 (1710, referring to an enclosure with a new quickset hedge, *v.* **cwic**); The Ram Fd; Reeds Cl 1844[1], 1844[2], 1845[2]; Remington Hold Cl 1823, Rimmington Hole Cl 1838, Remingtons Hold 1843, 1844[3], Remington's - 1849, Remingtons Hold Cls 1843 (*Remingtons Hold, - Close* 1710, *Remington Hold* 1710, - *Close* 1766, from the surn. *Rimmington*, cf. *Rimyngton Furlonge* in Barleythorpe f.ns. (b),

Remington Heath in Greetham f.ns. (a), Bottom -, Top Rimmington in Langham
f.ns. (a) and Rimmingtons Hoole in Morcott f.ns. (a), v. **holde**); Rogateway 1843
(the road ran south into Barrowden, v. **rūh**[1], **gata** and Rowgate High Road, - Way
in Barrowden f.ns. (a)); Rudds Cl 1843 (1710, *Rud's* - 1796, with the surn. *Rudd*);
Rushey Piece 1844[1], 1845[2], Rushes - 1849 (v. **riscig, risc, pece**); Sands 1843, 1844[3],
1849 (*the Sonde* 1615, v. **sand**); School Fd; Sheep Hovel Cl 1823, 1843 (*Sheep Hovell
Close* 1710, v. **hovel**); Shockmore Balk 1843 (perh. 'the demon's moor', v. **scucca,
mōr**[1], **balca**); Short Gate 1873, Shortgate Balk 1845[2] (*Short Gate* c1795, *short-gate
balke* 1631, *Short Gate Balk* c1795, 1796, v. **sc(e)ort, gata, balca**); Sour Lands 1843,
1844[3], 1849, 1873, Sow Land Cl 1845[2] (*Sowre Lande* 1615, *Sour Lands Close* 1796, v.
sūr, land, the first el. being used of coarse, worked-out or acid soil); South Fd 1843,
1844[1], 1844[2], 1844[3], 1845[1], 1845[2], 1849 ((*the*) *South Feild* 1615, 1631, 1635, 1710, (*ye*)
South Field 1710, c1795, 1796, one of the great open-fields of the village, v. **sūð,
feld**); South Luffenham Open Fd 1873 (cf. Open Cl *supra*); Spells Cl 1844[1], 1844[2],
1845[2] (1629); The Spinny 1803, - Spinney 1844[1], 1844[2], 1845[2], Spinney Cl 1844[2],
1845[2], Little Spinney 1843; Square Cl 1844[1], 1844[2], 1845[2] (1729, c1750, 1766);
Stackyard Cl (v. **stak-ȝard**); Stamford Way 1843 (*Stanford(e) Way* 1615, 1631,
Stamford Way 1615, 1710, 'the road to Stamford L', v. **weg**); Near Stamford Road Cl
or Wireless Station Fd; Stepping Stone Cl 1845[2], 1943, 1953 (*Steppingstone Close*
1652[1], 1652[2], *Stepping Stones Close* 1796); Stone Pit Cl 1844[2], 1845[2] (*Stone Pitts*
1615, *Stonepit Close* 1615, *Stone Pit Close* 1796, *Stone Pit Furlong* c1795, v. **stān-pytt**);
the Stripe 1844[1], 1844[2], 1845[2] (v. **strip**); Stubbs Two Acres; Swancote Leys 1845[1],
1849, Swan-Cote Leys 1845[2] (*Swancote Leys* c1795, v. **swān**[2], **cot, lēah**); Tailby's Fd
1979 VR (George *Tailby* held land in S. Luffenham 1874, cf. Anne *Taylbye* 1621
PR); Tixover Lane 1873 (Tixover lies to the south-east); Top Cl; Town Land 1943,
Town Street 1843 (cf. *Towns end* 1615, *Town End Furlong* c1795, *Towne roode* 1615,
Town Rood c1795, v. **tūn, ende**[1], **rōd**[3]); the Turnpike Road 1844[3], Stamford
Turnpike Road 1843, Wansford Turnpike Road 1843 (v. **turnepike**; roads leading to
Stamford L and Wansford Nth); the Waggon Hovel 1843 (v. **hovel**); Walkers Cl;
Water Pasture 1873; Waters Cl 1844[2], Watters - 1845[2]; Weldons Cl (with the surn.
Weldon, cf. *Weldons Gibbet* in Hambleton f.ns. (b) and *Weldons Linch* in Wardley
f.ns. (b)); Welthorn Cls 1803, Welthorn 1844[1], Wellthorne Cl 1844[2], Welsthorne
- 1845[2], Weltham Cl 1843, 1849, - Cls 1844[3] (*Wellthorne close* 1635, *Welthorne Close
Gate* 1615, *Weltham Closes* 1710, v. **wella, þorn**); West Fd 1843, 1844[1], 1844[3], 1845
(*West Feild* 1615, 1635, 1710, - *Field* c1795, 1796, originally the name of one of the
great open-fields of the village, v. **west, feld**); West Holmes 1803, - Holme 1844[2],
1845 (v. **holmr**); Wireless Station Fd (v. Near Stamford Road Fd *supra*); Wood Cls
1849, 1873; Wood Slade Hedge 1873 (*woodslade* 1615, *Woodslade Furlong* c1795, v.
wudu, slæd); Wortleys Garden 1844[1], 1845[2] (cf. *Wortleys Yard* 1796, *Wortley's* -
c1795, with the surn. *Wortley*); Yard Cl 1845[2] (v. **geard**).

(b) *Bollands Close* 1729 (with the surn. *Bolland,* cf. John *Bollond* 1522 MilS); *Bridge Close* 1708, c1795, 1796; *Brownes Close* 1649, *Browns* - 1651; *Bushy Close* c1795, 1796; *Cheesecake Piece* c1795 (dial. *cheesecake* was used of the fruit of such wild plants as the common mallow (*Malva sylvestris*) and the bird's foot trefoil (*Lotus corniculatus*), *v.* **pece**); *Church Headland* 1631, c1795, - *Hedland* 1633 VCH (*v.* **hēafod-land,** cf. South Luffenham Church *supra*); *furlong along the Dale* c1795 (*v.* **dalr**); *Douty Close* 1652[1], 1652[2] (with the surn. *Doughty,* cf. Thomas *Dowghty* 1524 SR); *Durants Thing* 1671, 1695[1], 1695[2] (from the family name of Roland *Durant* of Barrowden, *v.* **þing** and Durant Farmhouse in Barrowden); *East Yard Thing* 1671, 1695[1], 1695[2] (*v.* **geard, þing**); *the gateway* 1710; *Great Close* c1795, 1796; *Hemp Lands* 1766 (the term *hempland* was eventually applied to a piece of land held by a small tenant irrespective of the produce of the soil, *v.* **hempland** and cf. Hemp Yards *supra*); *Hill Close* c1795; *the hollowe* 1615 (*v.* **holh**); *le kyrkepittes* 1324 BHS (*v.* **kirkja, pytt** and cf. South Luffenham Church *supra*); *the Little Barne* 1710; *the Little Stable* 1710; *Meadow Close* c1795; *Moor Bridge Close* c1795, 1796 (cf. Moor Bridge in N. Luffenham); *Morcott Meadow* c1795, - *Mere* c1795 (*v.* **(ge)mǣre**), *Morcot moor* 1631 (*v.* **mōr**[1]) (Morcott parish adjoins to the west); *The Neat Yard Close* 1796 (*v.* **nēat**); *Nether Furlong* c1795; *Nixes Thing* 1671, 1695[2] (from the family name of Daniel *Nickes* 1640 PR of N. Luffenham, *v.* **þing**); *Noones Closes* 1729, *Noons* - 1766, *Noon's Close* c1795, 1796 (from the surn. *Noon,* cf. John *None* 1522 MilS of Uppingham, Richard - and Nich. *Noone* c1635 *Map* of Wardley); *North Luffenham Brooke* 1590 (*v.* **brōc**), - *Mere* c1795 (*v.* **(ge)mǣre** 'a boundary') (R. Chater forms the boundary between N. Luffenham and S. Luffenham except for a short stretch north-west of S. Luffenham village); *the Orchard* 1709; *Osier Holt* 1796 (*v.* **oyser, holt**); *Overtons Close* 1729, 1796 (from the surn. *Overton,* cf. *William Overtons Croft* in neighbouring Morcott f.ns. (b)); *Pilton Footpath, Pilton Way* c1795 (Pilton lies to the north-west); *the Rails* 1796, *Rail Close* c1795, *Rail Meadow,* - *Close* 1796 (*v.* **raile**); *Redebrug'* 1356 BHS (poss. referring to a causeway made of reeds running across marshy ground, *v.* **hrēod, brycg**); *St Ann's Meadow* c1795 (this may be identical with Saint Anns in Barrowden f.ns. (a) *q.v.*); *Salters crosse* 1615, *Salter's Cross* c1795 (alluding to an early salt-way, *v.* **saltere, cros**); *Sangate feild* 1615 (*v.* **sand, gata**); *Setting Close* 1729, c1750, 1766 (cf. Settings Fm in N. Luffenham); *Sharpe Lane* 1708 (with the surn. *Sharpe,* cf. Bartilmew - and Robert *Sharpe* 1522 MilS of neighbouring Barrowden); *shortlands* 1631, *Shortlands furlong* c1795 (*v.* **sc(e)ort, land**); *Smockskirts Furlong* c1795 (? with *smock* used of the Greater Bindweed (*Convolvulus sepium*) or of the Ladysmock or Cuckoo Flower (*Cardamine pratensis*), *v.* **smock, skirt**); *South Luffenham Meadow* 1796; *Spencers Thing* 1671, 1695[1], 1695[2] (from the surn. *Spencer, v.* **þing**); *Spring Close* 1729, c1750, 1766, c1795, 1796 (*v.* **spring**); *Stints* c1795, *above the Stints* c1795 (*v.* **stint**); *Stone acre*

1615 (*v.* **stān, æcer**); *Swifts Close* 1796; *Taglock Close* 1652[1], *Tagglocke* - 1652[2] ('a fold or enclosure for young sheep', *v.* **tagga, loca**); *the house called Tallyards place* 1649, *Tallyardes place* 1651, *Tallyards Place* 1709 (with the surn. *Tallyard, v.* **place**); *Three Corner Close* c1795, 1796 (alluding to a triangular enclosure); *Todley Close* n.d.   VCH; *the Upper Yard* 1796; *Walbank's Close* 1729, *Wallbanks* - 1766 (from the family name of John *Wallbanks* c1750 and Henry *Wallbanks* 1766); *Withams house* 1695[1], 1695[2], *Wythams Thing* 1671 (*v.* **þing**) (from the surn. *Wytham,* cf. John *Wytham,* husbandman, 1522 MilS); *Wrangrood* c1795 (*v.* **wrang, vrangr, rōd**[3]); *Mr Wymarkes Close* 1629.

Lyddington

LYDDINGTON
>   *Lidentone* 1086 DB, *-tonam* 1126, 1154-9 RegAnt, *Lydenton'*
>   1286 *Ass,* 1286 QW
>   *Ly-, Lidinton(e), -yn-* 1167, 1187, 1188 P *et freq* to 1286 *Ass,*
>   1294 *RTemple et passim* to 1354 Pat, *-tona(m)* 1215
>   RegAnt, 1221 RHug, *-tun'* 1215 RegAnt
>   *Ly-, Lidington(e), -yng-* 1190 RegAnt, 12 *Peake,* 1215 RegAnt
>   *et passim* to 1263 *Ass,* 1269 *For et freq* to 1547 Chap,
>   *-tun'* 1218 For
>   *Ledingtona* 1163 RegAnt, *Ledyngton'* 1286 *PleaR,* 1324 Cl *et*
>   *passim* to 1450 *Wyg*
>   *Ly-, Liddington', -yng-* 1444 *Rut,* 1506, 1509 *Conant et passim*
>   to 1555 *ib et freq*

Possibly 'the farm or estate called after or associated with a man named Hlȳda', *v.* **-ingtūn**, cf. Lidham Sx 509. This important estate, later to belong to the Bishops of Lincoln, is on the edge of the attractive soils of the Northampton Sands formation. DEPN *s.n.* Liddington prefers a stream-name *Hlȳde* 'the loud one' as the first element, compounded simply with **tūn**. There is a small tributary of R. Welland here which drops some 200 ft in two miles.

PRESTLEY HILL
>   *Presteley* 1249 Cl (p), *Prestesleye* 1284 ib, *Presteleye* 1286 *Ass,*
>   *Prestleys* 1565, 1567 *Conant, Prestleyes* 1567 *ib, Preistleis*
>   1591 *ib*

Prisley Hill 1610 Speed, 1715 Map, *Prestley Hill* c1800, 1806
ib, *Priestly Hill* 1825 ib

'Woodland of the priest(s)'. *v.* prĕost, lĕah. The earliest form,
because constituting a pers.n., indicates that there was once a
habitation site here. The income from this woodland would have
been set aside for the endowment of clergy.

BEDE HOUSE is *Jesus Hospital* 1684 Wright, 1846, 1863 White. It
was a small palace of the Bishops of Lincoln and converted into an
almshouse for a warden, two poor women and twelve poor men by
Thomas, Lord Burghley, in 1602, *v.* hospital, bed-hūs. BEE HILL,
Behull 1349 *Queen's, Bee Hill* 1610 Speed, 1620, 1715, 1780 Map, cf.
Bee Hill Covert c1800, 1806 ib, *Bee Hill Field* 1943 *Map, v.* bĕo, hyll;
evidently a source of wild honey. THE GREEN (local), *v.* grēne^2.
HONEYPOT SPRING, perhaps describing a spring set in boggy
ground, although a compliment to its sweet water is also conceivable.
LORD ROBERTS P.H. (lost - now 4 Main St), closed 1931 - VR.
Named after Earl Roberts of Kandahar (1832-1914), whose successful
campaign in Afghanistan in 1879 included the relief of Kandahar;
Commander-in-Chief against the Boers in South Africa 1899-1900.
LYDDINGTON CHURCH, *Church* 1846, 1863 White.
LYDDINGTON PARK LODGE is *Browns Lodge* c1800, 1806 Map,
1824 O, from the surn. *Brown,* cf. John *Brown* 1522 MilS, 1525 SR of
Lyddington. The Bishops of Lincoln's park is *parcus suus de
Lidington* 1227 ClR, *Olde park* 1349 *Queen's, Lyddington Parke* 1610
Speed, *Liddington Park* 1650 FF, *v.* park. MARQUESS OF
EXETER P.H. is *Exeter Arms* 1846, 1863 White, named from the
Marquess of Exeter, a substantial landowner in Lyddington.
MIDDLE BRIDGE. PIED CALF P.H. (lost - now 13 Main St),
closed 1933 - VR. PREBENDARY HO., 1935 VCH. SWAN P.H.
(lost - now 36 Main St), closed a.1900 - VR. OLD WHITE HART
P.H. is *White Hart* 1846, 1863 White. WHITE SPRING.
WINDMILL HILL (local), *Wyndmuln* 1349 *Queen's,* cf. *Wind Mill
field* 1772 *Terrier,* 1850 *Burghley, Windmill Leas* 1850 *ib* (*v.* lĕah), *v.*
wind-mylne. The only trace of a mill is a mound about 50 ft across,
with a dished top within which is a millstone, noted by
BrownArchSites 17 at SP 8798 9689.

Field-Names

Undated forms in (a) are 1943 *Map*; forms dated 1846 are *TA*; 1849, 1850, 1877 and 1950 are *Burghley*. Early forms dated 1349 are *Queen's* and 1510 are *MinAcct*; those of 1649, 1668, 1669, 1673, 1755 and 1772 are *Terrier*; those dated 1785 and 1799 are *Deed*.

(a) Six Acre 1943, Ten Acres 1950, Sixteen Acre 1943 (*v.* **æcer**); Albines (the surn. *Albin*); Arnesby's Road Fd; Backside Pasture 1849, 1850 (*v.* **ba(c)ksyde**); Banbillings Pad 1849, 1850 (evidently a corrupt form of a pers.n. (? *Ben, Dan*) plus the surn. *Billings*, cf. Thomas *Billyng* 1522 MilS, 1525 SR of Stoke Dry, Oliuer *Billyng* 1525 ib of Morcott and Wylliam *Byllyngs* 1524 ib of Bisbrooke, *v.* **pad**); Barnetts Cl 1850; Far Barrows 1849, 1850, The Barrows 1943 (cf. The Barrows in Seaton, *v.* **beorg**; the crop mark of what is prob. a ploughed-out barrow is recorded at SP 879 954, *v.* Crop Marks 72-3); Under Bay Hill furlong 1849, Under -, Bay Hill 1850 (*v.* Bee Hill *supra*); Beaumont's (the surn. *Beaumont*); Biddle's Lees (either from the surn. *Biddle* or alluding to land allocated to the parish beadle, *v.* **bydel, lēah**); Big Hill; Bisbrook Hill (Bisbrooke parish adjoins to the north-east); Bore Hill 1850 (*Borhull* 1349, *Boor Hill* 1772, *Boar(e)hill Furlong* 1649, 1668, *Borehill* - 1673; prob. 'wild-boar hill', *v.* **bār**[2], **hyll**, especially when associated with the Bishops of Lincoln's park here, but OE *bor* 'a hill, an eminence' is just poss., with pleonastic *hyll* added later); Short Bottom Furlong 1849, - Bottom 1850; The Brand 1849, 1850, 1877, 1950, Brand Cl 1850, Brand's - 1950 (*Liddington Brand* 1755, *v.* **brende**[1], cf. Brand Fd in neighbouring Uppingham f.ns. (a)); Bottom -, Top Breach 1849, 1850 (cf. *Brecheswong* 1349, *v.* **brēc, vangr**); Britton's Cl 1850, Brittons - 1877, Brittain's - 1943, Briton's - 1950 (cf. *Britain's Old Homestead* in N. Luffenham f.ns. (b)); Brockwell 1850, Brookwell 1877, 1950, Bottom Brockwell 1943 (*Brockhols* 1669, *brocholes* 1673, *Brockholls Furlong* 1649, *Brochols* - 1669, *Brockoles* - 1673, *Brockwells* 1772, *v.* **brocc-hol**, cf. *Broc Holys* in N. Luffenham f.ns. (b) and Brockwells in S. Luffenham f.ns. (a)); Brown's Ten Acre, Brown's Mdw 1943 (cf. *Browns Lodge*, an earlier name for Lyddington Park Lodge *supra*); Bumps; Chantry Cl 1850 (1799, *v.* **chaunterie**); Chapmans Piece Furlong 1849, Chapman's Piece 1850 (*v.* **pece**); Churchway Furlong 1849, 1850 (*v.* Lyddington Church *supra*); Clew's Cl; Colley Hill 1824 O, 1850, 1943 (*Colehull* 1349; 'hill where charcoal is made', *v.* **col**[1], **hyll**); Common 1849, Common (Cl) 1850, Far -, Great Common 1943 (*v.* **commun**); Copper hill Cl 1850, Copper Hill (x2), - Fd 1943 (*Copperhill* 1649, 1668, *coper hill* 1673, *Copper Hill* 1799, cf. *Copper Seeke* 1649, 1669, *Copperseeke* 1668, *coperseeke* 1673, *Copper Sike* 1772 (*v.* **sík**); the first el. is poss. *copel* 'a hill rising to a peak' to which *hyll* was later added, *v.* **copel, hyll**); Cow pasture 1877, - Pasture 1950; Crabtree Hedge Furlong 1849 (*Crabtre furlong* 1649, 1673, *v.* **crabtre, hecg**); Deer

Leap 1846 (x4), 1850, Deelips 1943 (v. **deer-leap** 'a low place in a hedge or fence over which deer may jump', cf. The Parks *infra*); Dugden Mdw 1849, 1850 (this is the Dugden Mdw of Thorpe by Water f.ns. (a), cf. Dugden in Seaton f.ns. (a)); Elbow Fd (*Elboes fur'* 1649, *at Elbowes* 1668, *in elboes* 1669, *Abboes* 1673, v. **elbowe** 'an elbow, a sharp bend'); The Folly (x7) 1846, 1850, 1950, The Folley, Folly 1877 (named from *Collin's Folly* in Uppingham f.ns. (b)); The Fronald, Fronald Cl 1850, Fronald Common 1849, 1877, 1950 (v. **commun**), Furnhill 1877, Furn Hill 1950 (*Fronald, Froanld* 1799), Top Funnel (cf. Bottom Funnel in Stoke Dry f.ns. (a); the two closes together make a funnel-shaped area, but this shape may account only for the present form of the f.n. which must be related to the Fronald/Furnhill forms preceding, v. Fronald in neighbouring Stoke Dry f.ns. (a)); Great Garbage (*Garbroad* 1649, 1668, *Garbrode* 1669, *Garbroade* 1673, *Garbige Slade* 1772 (v. **slæd**), 'broad strip of land in the triangular corner of the common field', v. **gorebrode**; the modern form of the name is no doubt the result of popular etymology); Gardens on the Waste 1850 (v. **waste**); Geesemere Cl 1850 (*Geesmore Furlong* 1649, *Geesemore* 1673, *Geese more* 1799 (v. **gōs, mōr**[1])); Green's; Head water 1850 (a body of water kept at a height for supplying a mill, cf. Mill tail *infra*); The Hill 1950, Hill Furlong 1850, Hill Pasture 1849, 1850, 1877 (*the hills* 1673, *Middle Hill Furlong* 1649, 1668, *midle hill furlong* 1673, v. **hyll**); Hoghole 1850, Hog's Hole 1943 (*Hogs hole* 1772, v. **hogg, hol**[1]); Holbrook Fd 1849, Holbrook 1850 (*Holebrok* 1373, *Holebrook* 1649, 1668, *holebrooke* 1673, cf. *Holebrokheued* 1349 (v. **hēafod**), v. **hol**[2], **brōc**); Home Cl (x14) 1850, 1943, Home Paddock (v. **home**); Hover Parks 1850, 1877, 1950 (v. **ofer**[3], **park**); Huffintons Cl Furlong 1849, 1850 (with the surn. *Uffington*, cf. William *Uffyngton* 1522 MilS of neighbouring Thorpe by Water); Big Islip's (from the surn. *Islip*, cf. Robert *Islipp* 1522 MilS of neighbouring Stoke Dry); Jackson's Cl 1850; Jittys Cl 1850, Jitty's - 1943 (*Iudas Closse* 1649, *Jetty's Close* 1799, cf. *Iudas close corner* 1668, 1673, *at Iudes Closs corner* 1669 (v. **corner**); poss. alluding to the elder tree, sometimes known as the *Judas-tree*, or else identifying land regarded as in some way treacherous); The Kell Pits, Kiln Cl 1850, Kelpits 1870, 1950 (v. **cyln, pytt**); Lammas Cl 1850 (v. **lammas**); Langham Balk, - Furlong 1849, 1950, Langham Balk 1950 (v. **balca**); Langland 1850, First -, Second Langlands 1943 (*langlandes al' vocat' Garderobes* 1510, *Longlandwong* 1349 (v. **vangr**), v. **lang**[1], **land**; the alternative name is ME **garderobe** 'a privy, a closet', prob. because of the ground's proximity to the garderobes of the medieval bishops' palace); the Launde 1846, The Lawn 1846, 1850, 1877, 1950, Bottom Lawn 1850, Top Lown (sic) 1950 (*the Laund* 1772, v. **launde** 'enclosed forest glade', such non-commonable enclosures being found within parks, cf. The Parks *infra*); Long Croft 1850, Longcraft 1943 (v. **lang**[1], **croft**); March Dyke Leys, March Mdw 1850 (*March* 1649, 1673, v. **mersc, dīk, lēah**, cf. Marches in Caldecott f.ns. (a)); Middle Fd 1850 (*le Midilfeld'* 1510, *Middle Feild* 1669, *Midlefeilde* 1673, *Middle Field* 1649, 1668, 1772 (one of the open-fields of the village, *v.* **middel, feld**); Middle of the Field 1850; Mill furlong 1850, Mill Fd 1943 (*v.* Windmill Hill *supra*); Mill tail 1850 (a stretch of water so called, *v.* **taile**, cf. Head water *supra* and cf. *molendini aquatic' voc' Fallesmyll'* 1510, evidently a water-mill with a waterfall, i.e. having an overshot wheel, *v.* **(ge)fall, myln**); Mortar Pits 1850 (*morter pitts* 1673, *Mortar Pitts* 1772, *morterpits bush* 1673, *Morter Pitts Bush Furlong* 1649 (*v.* **busc**), *v.* **morter-pytt**); Nether Fd 1850 (*Netherfeld'* 1510, *Nether Feild* 1669, *Netherfeilde* 1673, *Nether Field* 1772, one of the open-fields of the village, *v.* **neoðera, feld**); Nine leys 1850 (*the Nines* 1772, formed from nine pasture units, *v.* **lēah**); Old Stone Pit 1877 (pasture), 1950 (*Stonpites furlang* 1669, *Stone pitts furlong* 1673, *v.* **stān-pytt**); Orchard cl, - furlong 1850; Ox hill furlong 1850; The Parks 1846, 1850 (*Parks* 1799, *Lyddington Parks* 1799), Hills Park 1850, 1877, Hill's Park 1950, Ingram's Park 1943, Little Parks 1850, Long Parks 1850, 1877, 1950, Long Park, Middle -, Top Parks 1943 (noted by BrownArchSites 17 as being on the site of the Bishops of Lincoln's park with which The Launde is also associated); Payne's Corner Fd; Pease holme furlong 1850 (*v.* **pisc, holmr**); Pitchcaps (used perh. of land supporting very uneven growth in crops; the *pitch-cap* was originally a plaster containing pitch, used as a depilatory for scabbed scalps in cases of favus but later adapted in cap form as an instrument of torture); Poor Gardens 1850 (poss. allotments for labourers); Pope's Cl 1850; Racecourse (*v.* *Uppingham Course* in neighbouring Uppingham f.ns. (b)); The Redground 1850, Far -, First Redground 1943 (cf. Red Ground in Bisbrooke f.ns. (a)); Redshaw's farmyard, - Home Cl 1850 (from the surn. *Redshaw*); Roadside 1850; Rylands (*v.* **rye-land**); Saltmere, Saltmere Hollow, - Leys (*v.* **lēah**) (*Saltmore Furlong* 1649, *Saltmoore* 1668, *saltemore* 1673, *salt more* 1673, *Long Saltmoor* 1772, *v.* **salt^2, mere^1**, with typical confusion of *mere* with *mōr* 'moorland' in 17th cent. Ru forms); Seale's Dyke Fd (*v.* **dík**); Seedley Cl 1850; Sheep Cote Cl 1846, 1950, Sheepcote Cl 1850, 1877 (*Shepcote* 1510, *Sheep Coat Close* 1755, 1799, cf. *Schepcoteȝerd* 1349 (*v.* **geard**), *v.* **scēap-cot**); Spencer's First, - Second; Spinney Cl 1850; Spring Cl (cf. *Spring bush* 1673, *v.* **spring, busc**); Stone husk furlong 1850 (unexplained, cf. *Green(e) Huske Furlong* in Barrow f.ns. (b) and Whissendine f.ns. (b)); Sumpter's garden, - home cl 1850; Taylor's Hill (cf. Taylor's Fd in Uppingham f.ns. (a)); Thorough Lands 1850 (prob. 'selions running through', i.e. from one side of an open-field to the other without headland, *v.* **þurh, land**, cf. Throlland Ch 4 200); Three acre corner 1850; Three cornered cl 1877 (Mr J. Field observes that this seems to be identical with the preceding close), The Three Cornered Cl 1950; Twelve Leys furlong 1850 (poss. an arable furlong formed from twelve earlier pasture units, *v.* **lēah**); Twenty lands furlong 1849 (a consolidation of selions of an open-field, *v.* **land**); Tyler's cl (cf. Tyler's Saltmere in Caldecott f.ns. (a)); Upper Fd 1850, 1877, 1950 (*Upper Feild* 1649, *Upper Field* 1772, one of the open-fields of the village, earlier called *le parkefeld'*, *v.* f.ns. (b) *infra*); Van Diemans (a 'remoteness' name, poss. with further disparaging overtones, alluding to the

penal colony in Tasmania, known until 1853 as Van Diemen's Land, cf. Botany Bay
in Lt. Casterton f.ns. (a) and S. Luffenham f.ns. (a)); Vicarage Fd; Wards cl, Wards
Leys 1850 (v. lēah) (named from the *Ward* family, cf. George Henry *Ward* 1932
Kelly); Warrens Holme furlong 1850 (prob. from the surn. *Warren, v.* holmr); West
Cl; Wit Leather Piece 1850 (Mr J. Field notes that this is prob. for 'White Leather'
and alludes to a hard soil of white clay, *v.* pece).

(b) *Alwardescroft* 1349 (from the ME surn. *Al(l)ward*, itself a reflex of
either the OE pers.n. *Ælfweard* or the OE pers.n. *Æðelweard, v.* croft); *Apescrosse*
furlong 1649, 1668, *Apescross* - 1669, *Apes crosse* - 1673 (poss. referring to a
boundary marker of the Bishops of Lincoln's land, 'the cross on the aspen-tree or
white poplar', *v.* æpse, cros, cf. *Whitecroswong infra*); *Barkereswong* 1349 (from the
surn. *Barker*, Dom' *Barcar* is cited 1510, *v.* vangr); *Bernardesbutt'* 1349 (from the
ME surn. *Bernard*, the reflex of OFr *Bernart*, OG *Bernard, v.* butte); *Bishop's Hall*
or Hill Pasture 1799 (cf. Bede House *supra*); *Bonners Yard Land* 1785 (from the
surn. *Bonner, v.* gerd-landes); *Bowestedewong, Bowstedwong* 1349, *Boustedewong* 1510
(*v.* boga, stede, vangr); *bowthis howse* 1517 LinDoc (from the surn. *Booth(e), v.* hūs);
Bredenbriggewong 1349 (*v.* breden, brycg, vangr); *Brethsike* 1510 (*v.* breiðr, sīk; the
name also appears earlier in neighbouring Caldecott f.ns. (b)); *Bryar Land Seeke*
1649, *Breerland Seeke* 1669, *Briarland seeke* 1673, *Brier land Sike* 1772 (*v.* brēr, land,
sīk); *Brooke Furlong* 1649, 1673 (*v.* brōc); *Bulls Nook* 1772 (poss. from the surn.
Bull, cf. Edmund *Bull* 1522 MilS and William *Bull* 1525 SR of neighbouring
Uppingham, but cf. also Bull Nook in Teigh f.ns. (a) and Bull's Nook in Barrow
f.ns. (a), *v.* nōk); *Caldecote bridge furlonge* 1649, *Coldecot bridge* 1668, *Coldicoate*
bridge 1673, *against Caldecot Bridge* 1772 (Caldecott parish adjoins to the
south-west); *Calepitts* 1668, - *furlong* 1649, 1673 (*v.* calu, pytt); *Church acre* 1669,
Churchacer 1673, *Church headland* 1668, 1673, - *hedland* 1669, *Churchland* 1668 (*v.*
æcer, hēafod-land, land, cf. Lyddington Church *supra*); *Coppethornhull* 1349 (*v.*
copped, þorn, hyll); *Coumbes* 1349, *Coumbewell(e)gate* 1349, *Cumwelgate* 1510,
Coumbewellsik 1349, *Cumwelsike* 1510 (*v.* cumb, wella, gata, sīk); *Covermoore* 1668,
Couer more furlong 1673 (prob. an early use of *cover(t)* 'a shelter for game' and
associated with the hunting-park of the Bishops of Lincoln, *v.* cover(t), mōr[1]);
Croefurlonge 1649, *Crowfurlong* 1668, *crofur'* 1669, *Crofurlong* 1673 (poss. with the
surn. *Crow*, cf. the following name); *Croebush Furlong* 1649, *Crowbush furlong* 1668,
crobush furlong 1673 (poss. with the surn. *Crow* and referring to ground covered
with scrub, cf. *Woodcoks Bush infra*; otherwise with *crāwe* 'a crow' and describing
scrubland frequented by the bird, *v.* busc); *alt' Crucem in villa de lidyngton'* 1510
(the principal village cross, the stump of which still survives, *v.* hēah[1], cros); *Darly*
Croft Furlong 1649, *Darley craft* 1668, *Darlecraft* 1669, *Darly croft* 1673 (if the first el.
is not a surn. based on a p.n., then *dēor-lēah* 'woodland (glade) frequented by deer',

v. **croft**); *Dovecoteyarde* 1510 (*v.* **dove-cot(e), geard**); *Dunston hedge* 1649, *at Dunstalls hedg* 1669, *Dunstalls hedge* 1673 (prob. from OE **tūn-stall** 'a farmstead', cf. *Dunston Furlong* in neighbouring Uppingham f.ns. (b), also Dunstall Plantations in Whissendine, *Dunston* in Empingham f.ns. (b) and Great Dunston Cl in Ketton f.ns. (a) where forms vary principally between *Dunston* and *Dunstall, v.* **hecg**); *Yeast Leas, yeastleas* 1649, *East layes* 1668, *east laise* 1673 (*v.* **east, lēah**); *Edycroft* 1510 (from the common ME surn. *Eddy, v.* **croft**); *Eyghacres* 1349 (the first el. is prob. **eahta** 'eight' rather than *ēg* 'well-watered land', cf. *Sefneacrewong infra, v.* **æcer**); *Fluill hill furlong* 1673, *Fleewells hill* 1772 (*v.* **flēoge, wella, hyll**); *Forethers hous* 1517 LinDoc (either with the surn. *Forester* or with *forester* 'an officer in charge of a large tract of woodland or of hunting country', here the forester of the Bishops of Lincoln, *v.* **hūs**); *Long fullwell* 1649, *Short Fulwell* 1649, *Long -, Short fulwell* 1673 (*v.* **fūl, wella**); *Galley Hill* 1799 (*v. Galowe hill furlong* in Caldecott f.ns. (b)); *Galowong* 1349 (prob. 'the gallows meadow', *v.* **galga, vangr**); *Galtesgate* 1510 (perh. 'pasturage for a pig', *v.* **galte**, cf. **cow-gate**, also *Swingate Furlong* in Edith Weston f.ns. (b)); *Grascroft* 1510 (*v.* **gærs, croft**); *Halfacrewong* 1349 (*v.* **half, æcer, vangr**); *Handacre* 1349 (perh. referring to a piece of land that could only be tilled by spade rather than by plough, *v.* **hand, æcer**); *Hangendewong* 1349 (*v.* **hangende, vangr**); *Harresons howse* 1517 LinDoc (with the surn. *Harrison, v.* **hūs**); *hay bridge* 1673, *Little Hay* 1799 (*v.* **(ge)hæg**); *Heuedlandes* 1349 (*v.* **hēafod-land**); *Holdenewong* 1349 (perh. 'an in-field in a deep valley', *v.* **hol², denu, vangr**); *Horscroft* 1349, 1510 (*v.* **hors, croft**); *Horsholm* 1349, *the Short horse home* 1649, *shorthorse homes* 1668, *Short horse holms* 1669, *Horseholm' Acr'* 1510 (*v.* **æcer**) (*v.* **hors, holmr**); *Longhorsewong, Shorthorswong* 1349 (*v.* **hors, vangr**); *Kingshome* 1649, 1673, *- fur'* 1649 (from the surn. *King, v.* **holmr**); *Kirkcroft Flatt* 1649, *Kircraft flatt* 1673 (prob. from the surn. *Kirk,* cf. John - and Thomas *Kyrke* 1522 MilS of nearby Ayston, *v.* **croft, flat**); *Lambecroft* 1349 (*v.* **lamb, croft**); *the East Longe* 1649, *eastelong* 1673 (*v.* **east, lang²**); *Langlane* 1649, *Lang Lanes Balk* 1649 (*v.* **lang¹, lane, balca**); *le Lee* 1349 (*v.* **lēah**); *Long lay* 1649, 1673, *- laye* 1668 (*v.* **lēah**); *Nethirlee* 1349 (*v.* **neoðera, lēah**); *Ley seeke* 1649, *Leay seeke* 1669, *lay seeke* 1673, *Ouerleesik* 1349 (*v.* **ofer³**) (*v.* **lēah, sīk**); *in the Throat of the Lea* 1649, *in the Throte of the leay* 1669, *the throate of the lay* 1673 (*v.* **þrote, lēah**); *laise more* 1673 (*v.* **lēah, mōr¹**); *long meer* 1649 (*v.* **lang¹, (ge)mǣre**); *Lord Exeter's Sheep Walk* 1799 (referring to the Marquess of *Exeter, v.* **sheep-walk**); *Luffs hedge* 1668, 1669, *lufs hedge* 1673 (with the surn. *Luff,* cf. Wylliam *Luffe* 1525 SR of neighbouring Caldecott, *v.* **hecg**); *Marsh Slade* 1772 (*v.* **mersc, slæd**); *the Me(a)dow* 1668, 1669, 1673, 1772, (*at*) *the Meadow dik(e)* 1649, 1668, *the medow dike* 1673 (*v.* **mǣd, dīk**); *Medeplote* 1510 (*v.* **mǣd, plot**); *Mikildole* 1510 (*v.* **mikill, dāl**); *the Nether Pasture* 1772; *at the od willowe* 1649, *at the old Willow* 1668, *at the olde Willowe* 1669, *at the odd willowe* (sic) 1673 (*v.* **ald, wilig**); *Oxemede* 1349, *Oxmede* 1510 (*v.* **oxa, mǣd**); *Padokeford'* 1510 ('frog ford', *v.* **padduc, ford** and *Padox ford* in neighbouring

Caldecott f.ns. (b)); *le parkefeld'* 1510 (one of the open-fields of the village, later known as Upper Field *supra*, *v.* **park, feld** and Lyddington Park Lodge *supra*); *Parck wall Furlong* 1649, *Parke wall furlong* 1673 (*v.* **wall** and Lyddington Park Lodge *supra*); *Peaches Quick* 1772 (from the surn. *Peach*, *v.* **cwic**, cf. Peach's Willow in neighbouring Bisbrooke); *Pesewong* 1349 (**pise, vangr**); *Penn Leas* 1649, *Pen l(e)ayes* 1668, 1669, *Penlaise* 1673 (*v.* **penn**², **lēah**); *Prestleywong* 1349, *Priestly Hill Close* 1799 (*v.* **vangr** and Prestley Hill *supra*); *Rouclout* 1349, *Rough' clouth* 1510 (literally 'coarse cloth, shaggy patch', prob. used of rough meadowland, *v.* **rūh**¹, **clūt**); *Rowlatts Hedge* 1649, *Rowlets hedge* 1673 (*v.* **hecg**), Rowlett's Yard Land 1785 (*v.* **gerd-landes**), Rowlat's Close 1799 (with the surn. *Roulat*); *the rungs* 1649, *south runnge meadow* 1649, *the Wrongs* 1668, *the Rounges* 1669, *the wronges* 1673 (OE **hrung** in some such sense as 'enclosed with poles' or 'logs set rung-wise to form a track over marshy ground'); *Sefneacrewong* 1349 (*v.* **seofon, æcer, vangr**); *le Schar* 1344 *For*, *le Sharre* 1375 Nichols, *Leshare* 1610 Speed (OE **scearu** in its sense 'boundary'; Speed's map shows shows *Leshare* to be north of the village so that it may refer to land at the boundary of the Bishops of Lincoln's park); *Shaw Hills* 1649, *shawhills* 1673 (prob. does not belong with the previous name, but is rather from OE **scaga** 'a small wood', and perh. relates to *Wilkershaw* in neighbouring Uppingham); *shifting Meadow* 1772 (perh. indicating quake-fen, land with an unstable surface, cf. March Mdw *supra*); *the sik* 1349, *la Sike* 1510 (*v.* **sīk**); *sixbutts* 1673 (*v.* **sex, butte**); *the Slade* 1799 (*v.* **slæd**); *Hallofstag* 1516 ELiW, *the hows called hall of stagh* 1517 ib, *hall of stache* 1517 ib ('the hall belonging to the man surnamed Stagg', *v.* **hall**; the genitival construction with surn. here is prob. to be found also in *the Castel of Croydone* Gl 2 135 and *the Castle of Crake* L 1 141); *Steeple Acre* 1799 (so called *for its resemblance to a spired steeple* 1799, but this gloss may be popular etymology disguising the fact that the land was formerly endowed for the maintenance of the steeple of St Andrew's Church, cf. Steeple Cl in Ashwell f.ns. (a) and Steeple Fd in Pickworth f.ns. (a)); *Stentgrass* 1510 (common pasturage to which a limited number of cattle were given access, *v.* NED *s.v.* stint sb.¹, 6, 'the right of pasturage according to a fixed rate', *v.* **stint, gærs**); *atte Stile* 1393 Pat (p) (*v.* **stigel**); *Stoake Meadow* 1649, *against Stoke Mill* 1772, *Stoke Rislonde* 1510 (*v.* **hrīs, land**) (Stoke Dry parish adjoins to the west); *atte Ston' de Lidington* 1322 *FH* (p) (*v.* **stān**; the nature of the stone is uncertain); *On Sunn Furlong* 1649, *Sunn(e) furlong* 1669, 1673 (this may be named from a lost tavern called The Sun, cf. the furlong called *Vnder the sun* in Oakham f.ns. (b)); *Langeswyneslee* 1349, *Schortswynleyes* 1349 (*v.* **swīn**¹, **lēah**); *Thorneyeclose* 1567 Conant (*v.* **þornig**); *three swathe furlong* 1649, *three swathes* 1673, 1772 (*v.* **þrēo, swǣð**); *Wong at ye tounesende* 1349 (*v.* **vangr, tūn, ende**¹); *Town Furlong* 1649 (*v.* **tūn**); *towne langlands* 1673 (*v.* **tūn, lang**¹, **land**); *Trewelmore* 1510 (*v.* **trēow, wella, mōr**¹; cf. Trowell Nt 153); *The Turnpike* 1772 (*v.* **turnepike**); *Walls Herne* 1565 Conant (a messuage; prob. held by the family of Richard *Walles* 1525 SR of Lyddington, *v.* **hyrne**); (*the*) *Wester seeke Furlong* 1649, *westerseek* 1668, *wester seeke* 1673 (*v.* **wester, sīk**); *Whitecross Furlong* 1649, *Whit Cross* - 1669, *White crosse* - 1673, *Whitecroswong* 1349 (prob. referring to a cross of limestone, *v.* **hwīt, cros, vangr**); *Willowesholme* 1510 (*v.* **wilig, holmr**); *Wingate furlong* 1669, *Winnigates Furlong* 1649, 1673 (*v.* **hvin, -ig³, gata**); *Woodcoks Bush* 1649, (*At*) *Woodcockes Bush* 1668, 1669 (poss. referring to scrubland owned by the *Woodcock* family, cf. Thomas *Woodcok* 1522 MilS of Lyddington and Peter *Woodcock* 1639 VCH, grazier in neighbouring Caldecott, *v.* **busc**); *Wolwardisholm* 1349 (from the surn. *Woolward* (originally the OE pers.n. *Wulfweard*), *v.* **holmr**); *the small Yard Land* 1785 (*v.* **gerd-landes**).

Morcott

MORCOTT

> *Morcot(t)* 1086 DB, 1185 Dom, 1203 *FF et freq* to 1362, 1373 *Conant et passim* to 1543 *ib*, -*kot(e)* 1255, 1256 Cl *et passim* to 1354 Pat, -*cott* 1495, 1505 *Rut*, 1518 EpCB, 1535 VE
>
> *Morecot(e)* 1263 *Ass*, 1324 *Conant* (p) *et passim* to 1555 *ib*, -*cott* 1535 VE, 1552 *Conant*, 1610 Speed

'The cottage on the moorland', *v.* **mōr¹, cot.**

BLUE BELL P.H. (lost), 1846, 1863 White, closed c1960 - VR. CROWN P.H. (lost), closed a.1920 - VR. ELMS LODGE. FOX P.H. (lost), closed a.1900 - VR. GILSON'S HOSPITAL is *Morcot Hospital* 1779 *Terrier, Hospital* 1846, 1863 White; almshouses founded in 1612 by George *Gilson* for six poor men and women, *v.* **hospital.** THE GREEN (local), *v.* **grēne².** HAY COTTAGE. MORCOTT CHURCH, *Church* 1846, 1863 White. MORCOTT HALL, *Hall* 1846, 1863 ib. MOUNT PLEASANT (local), a complimentary name, but one which is sometimes given ironically. PRIESTS HO. (local). SMITH'S LANE (local). WHITE HORSE P.H., 1846, 1863 ib. WINDMILL, cf. *Old Mill Hill* 1779 *Terrier, Mill Gate* 1779 *ib* (*v.* **gata**).

Field-Names

Undated forms in (a) are 1943 *Map*; those dated 1815, 1816, 1840, 1846, 1856, 1869 and 1882 are *Anc*; those of 1839 are *TA*, while those of 1841 and 1950 are *Burghley*. Early forms dated 1602 and 1625 are *Burghley*, 1631, 1763[2] and 1779 are *Terrier*, 1709 are *Asw*; 1728, 1733, 1736, 1757, 1759, 1762, 1763[1] and c1795 are *Anc*; 1796 are *Surv*.

(a) Four Acre, Five -, Seven -, Eight -, Nine -, Eleven -, Thirteen Acre (x2), Fourteen Acre (*Fourteen Acres fur'*, *Fourteen Acres Leys* 1779 (v. lēah)), Fifteen Acre (x2), Seventeen Acre (v. æcer); Ancaster Pit (named from the Earl of *Ancaster* who owned land in the parish); Baines Cl (from the surn. *Baines*, cf. Miss *Baines* 1932 Kelly); Barkers Cl 1839 (with the surn. *Barker*); Barrowden Footway, - Road 1841 (Barrowden parish adjoins to the south-east); Blowhill Cl 1839 (perh. with OE blāw 'cold, cheerless', cf. *Blowland* in neighbouring N. Luffenham f.ns. (b), but cf. also *blowe hill*, L 3 11 which is characterized as 'presumably self-explanatory'); Breach furlong 1815 (*the breach furlong* 1602, *Breach Furlong* 1763[1], v. brēc); Broadholmes (*Broad-home furlong* 1602, *Broad-home* 1625, *Broadholm* 1762, v. brād, holmr); Brook Poor Fd 1979 VR (in 1636, Edward Cleypole endowed 20 shillings per annum to the poor of the parish from his lands in Morcott); Bull's Cl (cf. Raff *Bull* 1522 MilS); Near Burnt Wong (1779, v. brende[2], vangr); The Bushes 1815, 1839 (1763[1], 1763[2], v. busc); Butt Lane Road 1815, 1841 (cf. *Butt Balk*, - *Close* 1779, v. butte, balca); Camswell furlong, Camswell Grass 1815 (v. gærs) (*Kemswell* 1631, *Camswell* 1762, *Cams-well Meadow* 1602, *Camswell Meadow* 1757, 1763[1], v. camb, wella); Church Moors 1815 (1762, v. mōr[1], cf. Morcott Church *supra*); Clay Lock 1856 (v. loc) (*the Cley* 1631, v. clǣg); Cock Pit Cl 1839, 1943 (v. cockpit); Cotesbrook Mdw 1815, Codgebrook Mdw 1839, 1950 (*Cotes-brook meadow* 1602, - *furlong* 1602, *Codbrook* 1631, *Cotesbrooke Meadow* 1763[1]; the brook forms the south-western boundary of the parish, v. brōc and Coach Bridge in neighbouring Seaton); Cottage Fd; Cowpasture 1839, 1841 ((*the*) *Cow Pasture* 1762, 1763[2]); Cramps holme furlong 1815 (*Crampshom* 1631, *Cramps Holme* 1757, *Crampsholm* 1763[2], - *Furlong* 1763[1]; prob. from the surn. *Cramp*, v. holmr); Cross furlong 1815; Dark Lane Cl 1815, 1839; Dry Hedge Road 1841; Ell Cl (so called from its L-shape); Far Fd; Fenton Gap 1869, Fenton Grass 1882 (from the surn. *Fenton*, cf. John *Fenton* 1522 MilS, 1525 SR, v. gappe, gærs 'land put down to grass'); Footpad Fds (v. pad, cf. Bridle Pad Fd in Barrowden f.ns. (a)); Forest Wells Furlong 1816, Forest Walls 1943 (*Forrestwells furlong* 1602, *For(r)estwells* 1757, 1762, 1763[1], v. forst, wella); Franks Cl 1846, 1943 (with the surn. *Frank*, cf. John *Frank* 1522 MilS, 1524 SR); Glaston Footway 1841 (*Glaistonway* 17 VCH; Glaston parish adjoins to the west); Good's Home Cl (perh. to be identified with *Gutts home close* 1602, v.

home); Gorsemoor Leys 1816 (*v.* lēah) (*Gosemore furlong* 1602, *Gosmore* 1625, 1757, 1763[1], *Gorsmore Close* 1762, *v.* gōs, mōr[1]); Gray's Cl; Green Headland (*The Green Headland* 1757, 1763[1], 1763[2], *v.* grēne[2], hēafod-land); Green Skirts (1779, - *fur'* 1779, *v.* grēne[2], skirt); Green's; Hade furlong 1815 (*v.* hēafod); Hall Cl 1839 (cf. *The Hall Yard* 1625, *v.* hall, geard and Morcott Hall *supra*); Harp Piece (*Little Harp,* - *Piece* 1772, so called from the shape, *v.* pece); Haringworth Road 1841 (Harringworth lies south beyond R. Welland in Nth); Haseldyke 1839 (*v.* hæsel, dīk); Heck Balk Furlong 1815, 1816 (*Heck-Mill Balke* 1602, *Hec Mill Balk* 1757, 1763[2], *mill balk* 1631, cf. *Heck Gate* 1602, 1757, *Heck Mill Gate* 1763[1] (*v.* gata), *Heck Mill Way* 1757, 1763[1], 1763[2], *Heck-Mill Bush* 1602 (*v.* busc), *Heck-Mill Hill* 1602, *v.* hæc(c), myln, balca; the form *heck* is due to Scand influence); Hell Fd 1950 (*Hell Close* 1737, 1762, *Hell Furlong* 1602, 1757, 1762, *Hell Hill* 1631, with the dial. form *hell* 'a hill' common in Ru f.ns.); Hill Cl 1815, 1943 (x2) (cf. Station Fds *infra*); Hog Hole (*v.* hogg, hol[1]); Home Cl (1779, *v.* home); Hovel Cl (*v.* hovel); Hambleton Hurn (*Hambleton-hern furlong* 1602, *Hambleton Hern* 1763[1], *v.* hyrne; it is unclear why Hambleton, over four miles to the north-west, should appear in Morcott f.ns. since *Hambleton* does not occur as a surn. in the county; it may be explained by a view of Hambleton hill from the f.n. site, cf. also *Hambleton Close* 1779); Islip's Cl 1839, 1943 (from the surn. *Islip*, cf. Robert *Islepp* 1522 MilS, 1525 SR of Stoke Dry); Jacques' Cl 1839; Lammas Cl 1839, 1846, - Cls 1841 (*v.* lammas); Lane End Fd (cf. *in the Lane* 1328 Banco (p), *the Lane* 1779, *v.* lane); Stephen Laxtons Piece 1815, 1816 (*v.* pece); Limekiln Cl (cf. *Kiln House Leys* 1779 (*v.* lēah)); Long Spinney Road 1841; Middle Fd (cf. *Middle fur'* 1779); Midsummer Cl 1839, - Cls 1841 (Midsummer Day is 24th June, evidently the date on which the rental for the close(s) became due); Mill Fd (*v.* Windmill *supra*); Morcott Four Acre; Moulds Cl (if not from a surn., then with dial. *mould* 'the mole'); North Fd 1816, 1846, Morcot North Fd 1824 O) (*North Feild* 1602, *north feeld* 1631, (*The*) *North Field* 1602, 1757, 1762, 1763[1], 1763[2], one of the open-fields of the village, *v.* norð, feld); North Luffenham Footway, - Road 1841 (N. Luffenham parish adjoins to the north); Oak Tree Cl; Old Orchard 1839, 1846; Old Ozier Bed 1839 (*v.* oyser, bedd); Pasture; Pedlar's Garden 1839; Pike Acre Furlong 1816 (*v.* pīc[1]); Pilton (Lodge) Cl, Pilton Corner (*Pilton Corner* 1602, 1757, 1763[1], 1763[2], - *Furlong* 1602, *v.* corner, Pilton parish adjoins to the north-west); Pit Fd; Quicks Cl (*the Quick* 1762, *v.* cwic); Railway Fds (beside the line of the former Rugby and Stamford Railway); Little Red Hill Cl 1839 (cf. *Great Redhill Close* 1762, *v.* rēad); Red Road Fd 1950, Red Way 1815 (*Red way* 1602, c1795, *Red-way* 1757, cf. *bove Redway* 1631, *aboue Redway* 1763[1] (with eModE above 'above, over'), *v.* rēad, weg, from the colour of the soil); Rimmingtons Hoole 1846, - Hole 1943 (from the surn. *Rimmington, v.* holde, cf. Remington Hold Cl in S. Luffenham f.ns. (a)); Rudkins Piece (cf. *Rudkins Land* 1733, held by Thomas *Rudkin* 1733); Sand Nook Furlong 1816, Sand Nooks 1943

(Mr J. Field points out that this is a little to the south of an old sand pit, v. nōk); Sands (the Sands 1762, - furlong 1602, Short Sands Furlong 1763[1]; considerably to the west of the preceding, v. sand); Seaton Dyke, Seaton Footway 1841 (Seaton parish adjoins to the south-west, v. dīk); Simon Ford 1841 (a road so called), Simon Ford Garden 1943 (a lane called Simons Ford 1602, Simonse ford 1631, The Homes at Simons Ford 1602 (v. holmr); poss. with reference to Simon Digby of Morcott, a landowner in 1625, v. ford); Smith's Building Paddock 1839; The South Fd 1815, 1816 ((The) South Field 1602, 1757, 1763[1], 1763[2], 1779, 1796, Southfeeld 1631, one of the open-fields of the village, v. sūð, feld); South Field Corner Piece 1839 (v. corner, pece); South Leys 1846, 1856, 1943 (cf. South Furlong Leys 1779, v. lēah); South Luffenham Tything 1815 (South Luffenham Tythings 1763[1], v. tēoðung; S. Luffenham parish adjoins to the east); Spinney Hollow; Spinney Path Hades (v. hēafod; the path runs from Glaston); Station Fds (Mr J. Field notes that these consist of Swift's House Cl and one of the two Hill Cls, and adjoin the Line Fds in S. Luffenham; cf. Railway Fds supra); Bottom -, Top Stavely (if this is not a surn., then OE stæf-lēah 'wood where staves are got', v. stæf, lēah); Studfold furlong 1815 (Stut-fold furlong 1602, Stutfold Furlong 1631, 1763[1], v. stōd-fald); Swan's Nest; Swift's House Cl (v. Station Fds supra); Swingford Fd; Tenter Gap 1839, 1846, - Furlong 1815, 1816 (cf. The Tenter Leys 1728, v. tentour, gappe, lēah); Thorolds Garden 1839 (the family name Thorold is common in neighbouring Lincs.); Three-Corner Fd (referring to its triangular shape); Top Cl; Tun Lane Cl 1839, 1846 (Turn Lane Close 1796, v. tūn); Turnpike Road to Stamford 1841 (i.e. Stamford L, v. turnepike); Vale of White Horse furlong 1815, Vale of White Horse public drain 1841, Vale of White Horse 1943 (a furlong called Vale of White Horse 1602; this may be a transferred name from the Berkshire Vale of White Horse, the turf-cut White Horse itself being in Uffington parish in that county; a William Uffyngton was resident in Ru in nearby Thorpe by Water in 1522 MilS and poss. the f.ns. are to be associated with his family, although a more likely origin for this family is Uffington near Stamford L rather than Uffington Brk; the White Horse Inn in Morcott has been thus called since at least 1846 and if the presence of the Uffington family in Thorpe by Water has no bearing on the origin of the furlong called Vale of White Horse in Morcott, then one can only speculate on the presence of a lost former turf-cut hill-figure hereabouts which the name of the furlong and the later name of the inn record); Washdyke (a sheep-dip, v. wæsce, dīk); Water furrows 1815, 1816 (1757, 1763[1], a place where water tends to lie in the furrows, or simply 'wet furrows', v. wæter, furh); (The) West Field 1815, 1816, 1841, 1846 (1602, 1757, 1762, 1763[1], 1763[2], 1779, west feeld 1631, in campo occidentali Hy 4 Rental, in campo occident' 1625, one of the great open-fields of the village, v. west, feld); West Lane Fd 1839; Wing Barn, Wing Four Acres, Wing Fd (all named from the adjoining parish of Wing; Mr J. Field notes that Wing Four Acres, with Morcott

Four Acres and another (unnamed) close, appear to have been taken from Wing
Barn, which adjoins the parish boundary, but Wing Fd lies further to the east).

(b) *Alders Close, - Croft* 1625 (prob. with the surn. *Alders*, but *alor* 'the alder'
is poss., *v.* **croft**); *Arber(r)y Gate* 1602, 1757 (perh. '(the road to or near) the
fortification built of earth', with OE **corð-burg**, cf. *Castle Thorns infra*; this is a
tantalizing possibility of a fortified site overlooking Rutland's southern boundary,
and is very unlikely to refer to Harborough Hill in Gretton Nth, four miles away
across R. Welland (*v.* Nth 167); the crop-mark of a ploughed-out large rectangular
enclosure on upland beside the road south of the village is recorded at SK 921 005,
v. Crop Marks 74-5; however, the f.n. spellings are late and the name may otherwise
be a compound of **hār**^{2} and **beorg**, hence 'the boundary barrow' belonging to the
series of burial mounds overlooking R. Welland, *v.* **gata**); *Ash-well ditch, - dike* 1602
(*v.* **æsc, wella, dīc, dīk**); *the Barrows* 1757, 1763^1, 1763^2, *- furlong* 1602 (*v.* **beorg**,
recording prehistoric burial mounds on the hilltops lining the Ru boundary, cf.
Barrowden and The Barrows in Seaton parish; these in Morcott must have stood on
the southern end of the windmill headland); *the Beck* 1779 (*v.* **bekkr**); *Bigotts Croft*
1625, *- Farm, Bygots farm* 1625 (from the surn. *Bigott*); *Black Lands* 1762,
Black-lands furlong 1625 (in eModE, *black* 'fertile' was sometimes used in contrast
to *white* 'infertile', *v.* **blæc, land**); *Bridgeway* 1762 (*v.* **brycg, weg**); *Bridge Wong* 1757,
1763^2, *Bridgewong* 1757, *- Furlong* 1763^2, *Bridge wrong furlong* 1602 (*v.* **brycg, vangr**);
Brightmors Farm 1625 (with the surn. *Brightmore*, cf. Wylliam *Bryghtmer* 1524 SR);
Broad Gate 1779 (*v.* **brād, gata**); *Brogholes* 1757, 1762, 1763^1, *Brog-holes furlong* 1602
(*v.* **brocc-hol**); *Brownseek* 1757, 1763^1, 1763^2, *Brown-seek* 1602 (prob. from the surn.
Brown, v. **sík**); *Bull Holme* 1763^1 (cf. Bull's Cl *supra, v.* **holmr**); *Burton Hill fur'* 1779
(if *Burton* is not a surn., then a lost **burh-tūn** 'a fort-enclosure', cf. *Arber(r)y Gate*
supra); *John Cants Headland* 1762 (*John Cant* held land in neighbouring N.
Luffenham in 1715 Anc, *v.* **hēafod-land**); *Castle Thorn Leys, Castle Thorns* 1779 (*v.*
castel(l), þorn, lēah, cf. *Arber(r)y Gate supra*; any earthworks that may once have
existed are no longer visible); *(the) Church Headland* 1602, 1757, *Church Leys* 1779
(*v.* **hēafod-land, lēah**, cf. Morcott Church *supra*); *Clipshams Quick* 1762 (with the
surn. *Clipsham*, originally a Ru p.n., and referring to a quickset hedge, *v.* **cwic**); *The*
Common 1779 (*v.* **commun**); *Constables baulk* 1762, *Constable Balk, - Gate* 1779 (*v.*
conestable, balca, gata, cf. *Constables Grass* in Pilton f.ns. (b), referring to a Petty
or Parish Constable); *Copie close* 1631 (the assumed popular singular form of *copis*
'a coppice', *v.* **copis**); *Cowards Farm, Cowerds Close* 1625 (from the surn. *Coward*);
Cow Gate 1779 (*v.* **cow-gate**); *Cranehill* 1757, *Crane-hill furlong* 1602, *Crane Hurn*
1779 (*v.* **cran, hyll, hyrne**); *Crook fur'* 1779 (*v.* **crōk** 'a nook, a secluded corner of
land'); *Curtis Farm* 1625; *Dallacres* 17 VCH (*v.* **dāl, æcer**); *Deep-home* 1625 (*v.* **dēop,**
holmr; it is unclear what *dēop* precisely signifies in this compound, since by its very

nature a *holmr* 'a water-meadow' is low-lying, but perh. 'a piece of flat ground in a hemmed-in place' is what was intended); *Dewlands* 1757, 1762, - *furlong* 1602 (*v.* **dēaw, land**); *Simon Digbys Farm* 1625 (cf. perh. Simon Ford *supra*); *drakehome* 1631, *Drake holme* 1757, *Drakesholme* 1763[1], *Drakes-home furlong* 1602 (the first el. is either the surn. *Drake* or ME **drak** 'a drake', cf. Thomas *Drake* 1524 SR of Belton, *v.* **holmr**); *Durrands -, Durrants close* 1625 (from the surn. *Durrant, v.* Durant Farmhouse in Barrowden); *East Field* 1779 (one of the open-fields of the village, *v.* **ēast, feld**); *Fawkners Farm, - place* 1625 (from the surn. *Falkner,* cf. Thomas *Fawkener* and Wylliam *Fawkner* 1524 SR); *Fishers Farm* 1625; *Flaxlandes* 1203 FF, *Flax-lands* 1602, 1757 (*v.* **flēax, land**); *under forde* 1631 ('(land) below the ford', *v.* **ford**); *Gilsons Square Close* 1779 (from the surn. *Gilson,* cf. Gilson's Hospital *supra*); *Glaiston hedge* 1602, *Glason heage* 1631, *Glaston Hedge* 1763[2] (the parish boundary hedge of neighbouring Glaston, *v.* **hecg**); *Gorse Hill fur'* 1779 (*v.* **gorst**); *Grains Lump* 1779 (presumably with ME *lump* ' a lump' in some topographical sense, but poss. an ill-written *lamp*, cf. *Lamp Leys infra, v.* **lump**); *Hastlers Croft, - Farm* 1625 (from the surn. *Hastler*); *Home-hades furlong* 1602, *Homehades* 1757, 1763[2], - *Furlong* 1757, 1762, 1763[1], 1763[2] (*v.* **holmr, hēafod**); *The Homes* 1602 (*v.* **holmr**); *Howhedge* 1762, *How-wrong* 1602, - *Piece* 1602, *How Wong* 1757, 1763[1], 1763[2] (*v.* **haugr, hecg, vangr, pece**); *North -, South Inclay fur'* 1779 (*v.* **in, clǣg**); *Kallowhill* 1631 (*v.* **calu, hyll**); *Lamp Leys* 1779 (land endowed for the maintenance of the altar lamp in the parish church, *v.* **lampe, lēah**); *Ley Lands fur', Ley Lands Leys* 1779 (*v.* **lǣge, land, lēah**); *(the) Leys* 1779, c1795 (*v.* **lēah**); *Long Close* 1779; *the Long Furlong* c1795; *Long Lands* 1757, 1763[1], - *Furlong* 1763[2], *Long-lands furlong* 1602 (*v.* **lang[1], land**); *Long Meadow* 1602, - *Furlong* 1763[1]; *Lymgate* 1602, *Lynsgate Furlong* 1763[1], 1763[2] (*v.* **lind, gata**); *Luff's Yard Close* 1796 (the surn. *Luffe* was common in southern Ru, cf. George *Luffe* 1585 PR of N. Luffenham, John *Luffe* 1640 *Asw* of Glaston); *Mawsey Beck Close, - Furlong, East Mawsey Beck* 1779 (originally perh. 'the moor stream', *v.* **mōr[1], ēa**, with Scand **bekkr** 'stream' added later); *the Meer* 1757, 1763[2], *Meer Balk* 1763[2] (*v.* **balca**), *Mere Meadow* 1602 (*v.* **(ge)mǣre**); *Messengers Farm* 1625 (with the surn. *Messenger,* cf. Johan(e) *Messynger* 1522 MilS, 1525 SR (widow) and John *Messenger* 1524 ib, both of Morcott); *Middle Hill Furlong* 1602, 1763[1], 1763[2]; *Middle seek* 1602, *Middle seeke Close* 1602, *Middleseek(e) Close* 1757, 1763[2] (*v.* **sīk**); *Middleton dike* 1602, - *Dyke* 1757, 1762 (*v.* **dīk**), *Middletons farm* 1625, *Middletons thing* 1625 (*v.* **þing**), *Middleton Willows* 1602, *Middletons Willows* 1625 (*v.* **wilig**) (with the surn. *Middleton*); *Moor fur'* 1779, *East -* 1779, *Moor Meadow* 1779 (*v.* **mōr[1]**); *The Mortar Pitt Furlong* 1763[1] (*v.* **morter-pytt**); *Normantons farm* 1625 (with the surn. *Normanton,* cf. Thomas - and William *Normanton* 1524 SR of Ketton); *North Luffenham Meer(e)* 1602, 1757, 1763[1] (N. Luffenham parish adjoins to the north, *v.* **(ge)mǣre**); *Okes gate* 1602, *Oaksgate* 1763[1], *Okes-gate Furlong* 1602 (*v.* **āc, gata**); *Overtons Close* 1602, *William Overtons*

Croft 1625, *Overtons hedge* 1602, 1757 (*v.* **croft, hecg**, cf. *Overtons Close* in S. Luffenham f.ns. (b); one William de *Overton* (died c1400) is buried in Morcott Church); *the Pen* 1762 (*v.* **penn**^{2}); *Pertrees Farm* 1625 (cf. Agnes *Pertre* 1522 MilS, widow); *Pickerings Close* 1625 (cf. Issabell *Pekryng* 1522 MilS, widow); *pilton balk* 1631 (*v.* **balca**), *Pilton Corner furlong* 1602 (*v.* **corner**), *Pilton Meer* 1763^1, *Pilton Meare furlong* 1602 (*v.* **(ge)mǣre**), *Pilton Way* 17 VCH (Pilton parish adjoins to the north-west); *the Points* 1762 (*v.* **point**); *Pole Meadow* 1602, 1762, 1763^2 (*v.* **pōl**^{1}); *Popes Farm* 1625; *Posses Spring* 1762 (*v.* **spring**); *Ratts Cottage* 1796 (Abraham *Ratt* held land in Morcott 1796); *Reads Close* 1625, *Reads Croft, Reeds* - 1625 (with the surn. *Read*, cf. Ralph *Read* 1648 *Asw* of neighbouring Glaston and *Reads close* in Glaston f.ns. (b)); *Rogate Furlong* 1602, 1757, 1763^2 (prob. 'the rough road', *v.* **rūh**^{1}, **gata**); *Rough Close* 1779 (*v.* **rūh**^{1}); *Round fur'* 1779 (Mr J. Field observes that *round* in modern f.ns. describes areas of land not necessarily circular, but equilateral rather than oblong or irregular polygons); *Rudkins land* 1709 (cf. William *Rudkyn* 1522 MilS of Preston, Henry - and John *Rutkyn* 1522 ib of Manton, Thomas *Rudkin* 1733 *Anc* of Morcott, *v.* **land**); *Saint Thomas's Cross* 1757, 1763^1 (a cross dedicated to St Thomas, *v.* **cros**); *Sculthorpe Meere* 1602 (at this date, Morcott is considered to be adjoining Sculthorpe rather than N. Luffenham, *v.* **(ge)mǣre** and Sculthorpe Spinney in N. Luffenham); *Seaton-balke* 1602, *Seaton Balk* 1763^1 (*v.* **balca**), *seton meare* 1631 (*v.* **(ge)mǣre**) (Seaton parish adjoins to the south-west); *the severall* 1762 ('land held in separate or private ownership', *v.* **severall**); *Shep-worth,* - *Bridge* 1625 (*v.* **scēap, worð**); *(the) Short Furlong* 1757, c1795; *Sink Furlong* c1795 (*v.* **sinke**); *Skyrmers Close* 1625 (from the surn. *Skirmer*); *Smith's Close* 1759 (cf. John - and Richard *Smyth* 1522 MilS, both of Morcott); *the South Ends* 1762 (*v.* **ende**^{1}); *South fur'* 1799; *South Luffenham Field* 1757, - *Gap* 1762 (*v.* **gappe**), - *Hades* 1762 (*v.* **hēafod**), *aboue luffnam headge* 1631 (*v.* **hecg**), *South-luffenham Mear* 1602 (*v.* **(ge)mǣre**) (S. Luffenham parish adjoins to the east); *Square Close* 1779 (perh. identical with *Gilsons Square Close supra*); *First* -, *Second* -, *Bottom* -, *Middle Stint* 1779, *Stint Leys* 1779 (*v.* **lēah**), *Eastern Stints* 1779, *Headley stints fur'* 1779 (with eModE *stint* 'a portion of common pasturage to which a limited number of cattle, according to kind, is assigned for grazing', cf. *Stentgrass* in Lyddington f.ns. (b), *v.* **stint**); *stonpittes* 1631, *Stone pitts furlong* 1602, *the Stone Pitt,* - *Furlong* 1757, *Stonepitt Furlong* 1763^1, 1763^2 (*v.* **stān-pytt**); *Street fur', Street Leys* 1779 (*v.* **lēah**), *Street Open Close* 1779 (*v.* **strǣt**; f.ns. which seem hardly to relate to Morcott village street, cf. *the Highestrete* in Barrowden f.ns. (b), but which may record a lost Roman road running south to cross R. Welland at Turtle Bridge; the third f.n. in this group refers to an open close, one without permanent gates, being shut off when necessary by hurdles); *Suttons Farm* 1625 (with the surn. *Sutton*); *Mag-swans* 1625, *Swans* 1762 (prob. with the surn. *Swan*, cf. Edward *Swanne* 1600 PR of neighbouring N. Luffenham; the earlier form perh. has an abbreviated Lat *magister* 'master, mister' prefixed, cf. *Magistr' Busbie* of *Busbie waie* in Oakham); *Tagland* 1631 (*v.* **tagga, land**); *Thorney Leys* 1779 (*v.* **þornig, lēah**); *Thurndel Ley* 1763[2] (the second el. must remain obscure since Scand *deill* 'a portion of land' does not occur in this area and according to Elements 1 129, OE *dell* 'a dell, a valley' is not found in the Midl and NCy (but cf. perh. *Meredel* in Barrow f.ns. (b)), *v.* **þyrne, lēah**); *Tirtle Meare* 1602, *Turk-well* 1625 (these forms appear to belong together and to relate to Turtle Bridge, a mile to the south in Barrowden (earliest recording *Thurkelbregge* 1298 Ipm). While it seems safe to take the first el. of *Thurkelbregge* as the surn. *Turcle* (*v.* Turtle Bridge in Barrowden), the later forms of the name of the bridge were perh. influenced by a neighbouring *tōt-hyll* 'look-out hill' in Morcott on the promontory overlooking this early crossing point of R. Welland. This *tōt-hyll* may have been the lost *Arberry* in Morcott (if indeed this was an *eorð-burg* 'fortification built of earth'). Hill-forts were sometimes designated *tōt* 'look-out place' in p.ns., *v.* Signposts 146 and cf. *Turtle Slade* in Wardley, also a border village on a high hillside. If *Tirtle* - is from *tōt-hyll*, then the - *Meare* of the 1602 form may represent (*ge*)*mære* 'a boundary'. However, if the Morcott forms are unrelated to Turtle Bridge, perh. *turtla* 'the turtle-dove' and *mere* 'a pool' may be thought of.); *Miss Titley's Close* 1762 (cf. Rev. Charles *Titley* who held land in neighbouring S. Luffenham in 1766); *Towells furlong* 1602 (*v.* **twēgen, wella**); *Middle -, Town End fur'* 1779, *the Town Ground* 1602, 1762, *the Town hedges* 1602 (*v.* **tūn, ende**[1]**, grund, hecg**); *uppingham way* 1631 (the road to Uppingham, *v.* **weg**); *Vicarage Close* 1779; (*East*) *Water Galls, -fur'* 1779, *Water Gall Leys* 1779 (*v.* **wæter, galla, lēah**); *West End Furlong* c1795 (*v.* **ende**[1]); *Wetherleys thing* 1625 (from the surn. *Wetherley, v.* **þing**); *Whetstone Bushes* 1763[1] (*v.* **busc**); *Whitehead's Furlong* c1795; *a furlong called Whites* 1762 (prob. the surn. *White*, cf. Raff *Whit* 1522 MilS of neighbouring Seaton); *Wilesmore* 1625 (the first el. is poss. the pl. of OE *wilig* 'a willow', cf. *Sharpes willes* in Pilton f.ns. (b), *v.* **mōr**[1]); *wilkinson close* 1631 (cf. Margere *Wylkynson* 1524 SR of N. Luffenham and Wylliam *Wylkynson* 1525 ib of Seaton, both adjoining parishes); *Wing Hedge* 1763[2] (*v.* **hecg**), *Wing Meer* 1602, 1762 (*v.* (**ge**)**mære**), *Wingway* 1763[1], *Wingwey 'balke* 1631 (*v.* **weg, balca**) (Wing parish adjoins to the north-west); *yeallow landes* 1631, *Yellow Lands* 1762, *Yellow lands furlong* 1602 (*v.* **geolu, land**; the name presumably alludes to the colour of the soil at the site).

Pilton

PILTON

> *Pilton'* 1202, 1203 Ass *et freq* to 1352 *Peake et passim* to
> 1535 VE, *-tun* 1218 For (p)
> *Pylton'* 1248, 1344 Cl (p), 1346 *RTemple* (p), 1382 Fine *et*

passim to 1513 *Conant*, 1610 Speed
Py-, *Pileton* 1205 (p), 1206 P (p), 1209-35 RHug, c1291
Tax, *Pilleton* 1294 *Ass*

'Farmstead beside the stream', *v.* **pyll, tūn**. The stream to which the name refers is R. Chater in its upper reaches.

BAY HOUSE FM (local), with *bay*, a Rutland dial. form of *bee*, cf. Under Bay hill in Thorpe by Water f.ns. (a), with reference to Bee Hill, Lyddington; for *bee-house*, *v.* NED *s.v.* bee[1], 6.   PILTON FOX COVERT is *Pilton Gorse* c1800, 1806 Map, *Pilton Cover* 1824 O, *Fox Covert* 1943 *Map*, *v.* **gorst, cover(t)**.   ST NICHOLAS CHURCH, *Church* 1846, 1863 White, cf. *The Church Yard* 1796 *Surv*.

Field-Names

Undated forms in (a) are 1943 *Map*; forms dated 1838 are *TA*, 1903 and 1910 are *Anc*. Early forms dated 1613, 1641, 1705, 1720, 1723, 1730, 1733, 1744, 1749, 1758, c1765, 1771, 1774, c1775, 1780, c1785, 1786, c1790 and 1792 are *Terrier*, while 1796 are *Surv*. All forms from *Terrier* extracted by Mr G.A. Chinnery.

(a) Four -, Seven Acres 1903 (*Great -, 7 Acres* 1796), Eight -, Eleven -, Twelve -, Thirteen -, Sixteen Acre (*v.* **æcer**); North Brakey Cl 1838, 1903, Middle - 1838, South - 1903 (*Braky Close* 1796, *v.* **bræc**[1], **-ig**[3]); Brickyard Fds (also in N. Luffenham); Bridge Cl 1910; Bungalow Cl 1910; Clay Cl, Clays 1838 (*Digbys Clay Close* 1720, *Clay Close* 1723, c1765, 1771, 1780, c1785, 1786, c1790, 1792, 1796, *- balke* 1749, *- side* 1774, c1775, *v.* **clæg, balca, side**, cf. John - and Edward *Digby* 1522 MilS); Cocked Hat Piece 1903 (alluding to its tricorne shape, *v.* **pece**); Cow Fd 1943; Cow Pasture 1838, 1903 (1749, 1796, *Cow Pasture Corner* 1796, *v.* **corner**); Crabtree Cl 1838 (1796, *v.* **crabtre**); East -, West Dry Cl 1838 (1796, *v.* **dryge**); East Fd 1838, 1903, Far -, Near East Fd 1903 (*East Feild* 1613, 1641, *- Field* 1720, c1775, c1785, c1790, 1792, 1796, one of the open-fields of the village, *v.* **ēast, feld**); East Mdw 1903 (1720, 1796); Elm Tree Pasture, Elm Tree Plough; Fallow Mdw 1838, 1903 (1796, *v.* **falh**); Far -, First Hill; First Fd; Fox Cover Cl 1903 (*v.* Pilton Fox Covert *supra*); Great Cl 1838, 1903 (1796); Hewitts Cl 1838, Hewitt's - 1903, 1910 (*Hewett's Close* 1796); The Holms 1903 (*Holm under the Cowpasture* 1796, *Holm Hedge* 1796, *v.* **holmr, hecg**); Home Cl 1903, 1943 (*v.* **home**); Horse Cl 1838 (1796); Lammas Ground 1838 (*v.* **lammas, grund**); Little Cl 1838; Long Cl 1838 (*Long Close* *in the cley* 1749 (*v.* **clǣg**), *Long Close* 1771, 1780, c1785, 1786, c1790, 1792, 1796, - *sike* 1771 (*v.* **sīk**)); Luffenham Hedge Cl 1903 (alluding to the old parish boundary hedge of N. Luffenham to the east, *v.* **hecg**); Lyndon Bridge Fd (Lyndon parish adjoins to the north); Misery (Mr J. Field notes that this is a derogatory name of the rare abstract type); Muck Fd (*v.* **muk**); Nether Fd 1838, 1903, Middle - 1943 (*Neather Field* 1723, 1744, 1758, *Neither* - 1730, 1733, *Nether* - 1796, *v.* **neoðera**); New Cl 1838 (1796), South New Cl 1838, 1903, 1910; The Nooks 1903 (*v.* **nōk**); The (Old) Orchard 1838 (cf. *Nether Orchard* 1796); Ozier Holt 1903 (*v.* **oyser, holt**); Penderdocks Holme 1903 (perh. from the surn. *Pender/Pinder* with *docce* 'the dock-plant' or 'the water-lily', *v.* **holmr**); Plank Mdw 1903 (*v.* **planke**); Rickyard Fd; North Side the River 1838 (R. Chater forms the northern boundary of the parish and only where the river has later flowed on a more southerly course is there now Pilton parish land north of the river); Roundabout 1903 (used in f.ns. of a field surrounding a clump of trees or of a field surrounded by a wood, *v.* **roundabout**); Mrs Pridmore's Scultrups Clays (*Sculthorpe* 1720, 1733, - *baulk* c1785, c1790, - *balk* 1792, *Scolthorpe balke* 1780, named from Sculthorpe (Spinney) in N. Luffenham, *v.* **balca**; the modern field is separated by the brickworks from Sculthorpe Cl in N. Luffenham f.ns. (a), its contained surn. being that of the local *Pridmore* family, cf. Harry *Pridmore* 1932 Kelly, farmer, *v.* **clǣg**); Shelton's (cf. Matthew - and Robert *Shelton* 1783 PR of neighbouring N. Luffenham); South Fd 1838 (*South Feild* 1613, - *Field* 1720, 1749, c1765, 1771, 1774, c1775, 1796, one of the open-fields of the village, *v.* **sūð, feld**); Spoil Bank Cl 1903, Spoil Banks (named from spoil banks left by the construction of the railway); Spongham's Mdw 1903 (*Spongham* 1720, *Little Sponghome* 1744, 1749, 1758, c1765, 1771, c1775, 1780, 1786, c1790, 1792, *Great* -, *Little Spongholm* 1796, *v.* **spang**; the generic varies between OE **hamm** 'a water-meadow' and Scand **holmr** of the same meaning, cf. Sponholm in Lyndon f.ns. (a)); Square Bit 1903 (*v.* **bit**); Stackyard 1903 (*v.* **stak-ȝard**); Three Corner Cl 1903, - Fd 1943 (alluding to a triangular shape); Townsend Cl 1838, Town End - 1903 (*Town End* 1723, *Towns end furlong* 1744, 1765, 1774, 1786, c1790, 1792, *Town-end furlong* 1771, *Townend Close* 1796, *v.* **tūn, ende**[1]); Willow Cl 1838 (1796); Wing Stile Cl 1838 (1796, *Wing stile* 1720, 1723, 1733, 1744, *Wing Stile Furlong* c1765, 1771, 1774, c1775, 1780, c1785, 1786, c1790), Wing Stile Plantation 1903 (Wing parish adjoins to the west, *v.* **stigel**).

(b) *Bell Strings* 1720, *Bellstrings* 1744, 1758, 1771, c1790, 1792, - *Baulk* 1749 (*v.* **balca**) (land endowed for the maintenance of the bell-ropes in the parish church); *Brooms Brake Close* 1720, (*the*) *Brake Close* 1744, 1749, 1758, 1771, 1774, c1775, 1780, c1785, 1786, 1792 (*v.* **bræc**[1], cf. William *Brome* 1522 MilS, 1524 SR of Wardley); *Brakeall Close* c1790 (poss. a form of Brakey Cl *supra*, but otherwise a derogatory name for land difficult to cultivate); *the Brook* c1765 (*v.* **brōc**); *Constables Grass*

1796 ('*there is paid for this grass 3.6d every Fallow field year to the Constable*' 1796, *v.* **conestable, gærs**, cf. *Constables Grass* in Edith Weston f.ns. (b) and *Constable Balk* in neighbouring Morcott f.ns. (b)); *Digby's Nook* 1796 (the surn. is that of the family of Edward - and John *Digby* 1522 MilS, *v.* **nōk**, cf. The Nooks *supra*); (*the*) *hanging balk* 1733, 1744, 1749, c1785, 1786, c1790, 1792, *Hanging baulk* 1780 (*v.* **hangende, balca**); (*the*) *holes* 1774, c1775, 1780, c1790, 1792 (*v.* **hol**[1]); *Horners Pit* c1765, 1771, 1774, c1775, 1780, 1786, c1790, 1792 (*v.* **pytt**); *Hunts Meere* 1733, 1771, - *mear* 1792 (from the surn. *Hunt*, cf. Thomas *Hunt* 1522 MilS, - *Hvnte* 1524 SR of neighbouring N. Luffenham, *v.* **(ge)mǣre**); *Ling furlong* 1771, c1775, 1786, c1790, 1792 (*v.* **lyng**); *Long meere* 1758, c1765, 1771 (*v.* **(ge)mǣre**); *the meere* 1641, 1749 (*v.* **(ge)mǣre**); *moorcott feild* 1723, *Morcott Goss* 1720 (*v.* **gorst**), *Morcott Meare* 1720 (*v.* **(ge)mǣre**) (Morcott parish adjoins to the south); *North Feild* 1613, - *Field* 1720 (one of the open-fields of the village, *v.* **norð, feld**); *the north west feilde* 1641; *the Open close* 1749 (a close without gates, sometimes called an open-gap close, closure of which was by hurdles); *Sharpes willes* 1758 (cf. Robert *Sharpe* 1677 *Conant* of neighbouring Lyndon, *v.* **wilig**); *the short meare* 1733 (cf. *Long meere supra*, *v.* **(ge)mǣre**); *the South West Feilde* 1641; *the stonepitts* 1723 (*v.* **stān-pytt**); *Upper feild* 1723, - *field* 1730, 1733; *wellfeild* 1723, *Well field* 1730, 1733 (*v.* **wella**); *West Field* 1749, c1765, 1771, 1774, c1775, c1785, 1786, c1790, 1792 (one of the open-fields of the village, *v.* **west, feld**); *Wing Close* 1796, *wing balk* 1749 (*v.* **balca**), *wingmeirhedg balk* 1744 (*v.* **(ge)mǣre, hecg, balca**), *sidewing balk* 1744 (*v.* **side, balca**) (Wing parish adjoins to the west).

Seaton

SEATON
> *Segentone* 1086 DB, *-tona* 1105-7 Reg, *Seinton* 1197 P
> *Segestone* 1086 DB
> *Segeton* 1178 P (p), *-tona* a.1088 (e15) *BelCartB*, *-tuna* Hy 1 (1333) Ch, Hy 2 (e15) *BelCartB*
> *Seieton* 1086 DB
> *Seiton(e)* 1086 DB, 1185 Dom, 1191, 1192 P *et passim* to 1302 BM, *Seyton(e)* 1232, 1233 Ch *et passim* to 1286 *PleaR* (p) *et freq* to 1549 Pat, 1610 Speed
> *Saieton'* 1167 P, *Saitona* 1167 ChancR, *Sayton* 1313 *FF*, 1316, 1360 Ipm
> *Seton'* 1205, 1206 Cur, 1282 Fine (p), 1355 *MiD* (p)
> *Seaton* 1546 *FF*, 1557 *Rut*

Probably 'Sæga's estate', *v.* **tūn**. The OE pers.n. *Sæga* is unrecorded but may be a short form of names such as *Sægeard, Sægeat*. As an alternative etymology, Ekwall DEPN suggests a stream-name *Sæge* 'the slow-moving one', from an unrecorded OE adjective **sæge*, related to *stgan* 'to descend, to move'. However, the village stands on a south-facing hillside overlooking R. Welland with only a tiny stream separating it from the river. It is difficult to believe that either watercourse provided the name of the settlement, the stream because it is too insignificant and the river because it already had an important ancient name when the settlement was founded. A pers.n. must be the most likely as the first element of the place-name.

COACH BRIDGE, *Coton'* 1322 *FH* (p), *Cotisgrene* n.d. AD, *Coates Bridge* 1665 *Anc, Coates Hill* 1665 *ib, Coach holme* 1646 *Deed, Coach Bridge* 1806 Map, 'the cottages', *v.* **cot** (**cotum** dat.pl.). The cottages were at the crossing of the stream separating Seaton parish from Barrowden. The ME nom.pl. form *cotes* with analogical *-s* replaced the dat.pl. form *cotum* 'at the cottages'. The minor name compounds recorded contain **grēne**[2] 'a grassy place', **brycg** 'a bridge', **hyll** 'a hill' and **holmr** 'land by a stream'.

THE BARROWS, 1824 O, *the Berryges* 16 VCH, *v.* **beorg**. It is apparent that in the south of the parish there was a group of burial mounds above R. Welland continuing those of Lyddington, Thorpe by Water, Morcott and Barrowden. One of these prehistoric burial mounds is recorded early as *Estberge* Hy 4 *Rental*, 'the eastern barrow', *v.* **ēast, beorg**, cf. Far -, Hither Barrows in Thorpe by Water f.ns. (a) for which parallel early forms survive.

ALL HALLOWS CHURCH, *Church* 1846, 1863 White. BAINES LANE (local), cf. *Baines Meadow* 1943 *Map*, named from the *Baines* family, cf. Charles William *Baines* 1932 Kelly. GEORGE AND DRAGON P.H., 1846, 1863 White. MANOR HO. is on the site of *Vphalle* 1429 *TB, Vphall'* 1527 *Surv, Uphall* 1597 *TB*, 'the upper hall', *v.* **upp, hall**, cf. *Downhall* in f.ns. (b) *infra*. RECTORY, 1846, 1863 White. SEATON GRANGE, 1935 VCH, 1943 *Map*, cf. *Grange*

Farm 1932 Kelly, *v.* **grange.** SEATON MILL, 1824 O, cf. *Milne Holme* 16 VCH, *v.* **myln, holmr.** THREE HORSESHOES P.H. (lost - now Croft Ho.), 1850 Slater, 1863 White, closed 1955 - VR. WELLAND VIADUCT was built in 1876-8, with a total length of more than three quarters of a mile, *v.* Cyprus in f.ns. (a) *infra.*

Field-Names

Undated forms in (a) are 1846 *TA*; those dated 1840 and 1908 are *Anc*, 1846 are *Hotchkin* and 1943 are *Map*. Early forms dated 1322 are *FH*; those dated Hy 4 are *Rental*; 1421, 1429, 1597 and 1631 are *TB*; 1527, 1757 and 1796 are *Surv*; 1646 are *Deed*; 1665, 1717, 1754 and 1758 are *Anc*.

(a) Albert Leas 1943 (*Abbott Leyes* 1646, *Abbot Meadow* 1646, *v.* **lēah**); Allens Mdws 1943 (named from the *Allen* family, cf. John *Allen* 1932 Kelly); Annes Bank (poss. with the surn. *Anness*, cf. William *Annes* 1524 SR of Belton, but cf. also Saint Anns in neighbouring Barrowden f.ns. (a)); Ashpool Hedge Furlong; Backside Furlong (*v.* **ba(c)ksyde**); Bassets Close Furlong (cf. Thomas *Basset* 1522 MilS of S. Luffenham, John *Basset* 1626 *Anc* of N. Luffenham); Beast Commons 1840 (referring specifically to cattle at this date, *v.* **bēst(e), commun**); Bellairs -, Bellars Piece (from the Ru surn. *Bellaers*, cf. John *Bellaers* 1845 *BHS* of Stretton, *v.* **pece**); Bisbrook Furze Furlong (*v.* **fyrs**), Far -, Bisbrooke Road Allotment 1903 (*v.* **allotment**) (Bisbrooke parish adjoins to the north); Broadmoor Head -, Heath Furlong (*v.* **brād, mōr**[1]); Little Brook(e) Furlong, Little Brook Slade (Furlong) (*v.* **slæd**); Carrot Garden Furlong (*v.* **carot**); Chancel Furlong (All Hallows Church lies on the eastern fringe of the village); Church Meadow Furlong; Close Furlong; Coach Hedge Furlong 1846, Coach Hedge Fd 1979 VR, Coach Hill Leys (*v.* **lēah**), Coach Hill Nether Furlong 1846 (*v.* Coach Bridge *supra*; the *hecg* 'a boundary hedge' in these f.ns. indicates a recognized boundary for 'the cottages'); The Common, Common Furlong 1846, The Common or Seaton Common 1943 (*v.* **commun**); Coney Gar (*Coniegray Close* 1631, *the Coney-Gray Close* 1646, *the Coney Grey Leys* 1646 (*v.* **lēah**), *v.* **coninger**); Cookes Cl (cf. Roger *Cooke* 1665 *Anc* of neighbouring Barrowden); Cordial-Way Furlong, Cordial Spring Furlong (*Caldwell', Caldewell'* Hy 4, cf. *Caldwelhill'* Hy 4 (*v.* **hyll**), *Caldwelsyke* Hy 4 (*v.* **sīk**), *v.* **cald, wella, spring**); Crowden's Mdws (Rye Hill), Crowdens Pasture 1943 (named from the local *Crowden* family, cf. Mrs Fanny *Crowden* and Sons, farmers, Edward *Crowden*, smallholder and Robert *Crowden*, farmer 1932 Kelly); Cyprus (recorded in VR - the name of the navvies' camp during the building of Welland Viaduct 1876-8; Cyprus was much in the news in these years, with Disraeli's aggressive imperial policy in the Mediterranean securing control of the Suez Canal for Britain in 1875 and Cyprus itself from the Turks in 1878); Dog Bank Furlong (v. **docce**); Dovecote Cl; Drift Furlong (v. **drift**); Dry Cl or Middle Fd 1943 (v. **dryge**); Duckhouse Cl, - Leys (v. **lēah**) (cf. perh. *Ducketts Meadow* 1646 which may belong here, from the surn. *Duckett*, but BrownArchSites 23 identifies an earthwork at SP 9095 9770 in a low-lying marshy position close to R. Welland in Duckhouse Cl as a poss. duck decoy; popular etymology may have transformed the surn. however); Dugden 1846 (cf. Dugden Mdw in Thorpe by Water f.ns. (a) and Lyddington f.ns. (a)); East and West Furlong; Eight Leys Cl 1840, Eight Leys Furlong (Open Close) 1846 (*Eight Leys* 1796, *Eight Leys Close* 1719, 1754, *Eightleys Close* 1758, v. **lēah**; an open-gap close was one whose method of closure was by hurdles rather than by permanent gates); Fallow Cl (v. **falh**); Galls Furlong (v. **galla**); Long Gate Furlong (v. **langet** 'a long strip of land'); Giles Hedge Furlong (v. **hecg**); Glaston Dyke Furlong (Glaston parish adjoins to the north-west, the boundary being *Glastonbrok(e)* c1320, Hy 4 (v. **brōc**) into which this dyke drained, v. **dīk**); Godfreys Bush (prob. referring to scrubland owned by the *Godfrey* family, cf. William *Godfrey* 1619 *Terrier* of Belton, v. **busc**); Greengateway Furlong (*Grenegate* Hy 4, v. **grēne**[1], **gata**); Hall Cl ((*the*) *Hall Close* 1631, 1646, v. **hall**); Hassocks 1846, 1943, - Furlong (*Hassocke Close* 1646, v. **hassuc**); Short Haverhill (*Hauerhill'* Hy 4, v. **hæfer**[1], **hafr, hæfera, hafri, hyll**); Furlong South of Highway; The Hill 1943; Holes Butts, - Furlong (v. **butte**); Nether -, Upper Holywell 1846 (*Halywell'* Hy 4, *Holywell'* 1421 'the holy spring', v. **hālig, wella**, presumably on the boundary with Barrowden where the cross at the spring was sited, v. *halywelcros* in Barrowden f.ns. (b)); Hollowell's 1943 (a field in the north-west of the parish, in a shallow valley and containing a small stream, v. **hol**[1], **wella**); Home Fd 1943 (v. **home**); Hop Ground (v. **hoppe, grund**; Seaton had its own brewhouse in Baines Lane, earlier known as Maltings Lane - VR); Horse Cl (or Hillside) 1943; Horse Commons 1840 (v. **commun**); Hovel Cl (v. **hovel**); Hunting Cl 1943; Land Cl 1840, Land Cl (Open Close) 1846, Lands Cl 1943 (*Land Close* 1754, 1796; an enclosure consolidating selions of an earlier open-field, in this case an open-gap close which had no permanent gate, but which was closed by means of hurdles, v. **land**); Long Leigh Cl 1846, Short Leys Cl 1840, Short Leigh Open Cl, North -, South Leigh Open Furlong 1846 (*Long Lies* 1796, *Long Lyes Close* 1754, *Short Lies* 1796, *Short Leys Close* 1754, v. **lēah**); Bottom -, Top Lithes 1943 (v. **hlið**[1]); Nether -, Little Cl 1840, Little Cl 1846 (*Little Close* 1758); Little Mdw (*the Little Meadow* 1796); Longham Piece Furlong (v. **pece**); The Lots (v. **hlot**); Lound Cl (*the Lownd close* 16 VCH), Lound Cl Allotment 1908 (v. **allotment**), Lound Gate Furlong 1846 (v. **gata**), The Lound, Bottom - 1943 (*The Lound* 1631, 1646, *the Lound Leys* 1646 (v. **lēah**), v. **lundr**); Michaelmas Holme (v. **holmr**; Michaelmas, the Feast of St Michael the Archangel, falls on 29th September, and being a quarter day of the business year, was no doubt that on which the rental for this ground became due); Middle Furlong; Mill Balk Furlong (v. **balca**); West End of Mill Leys (v. **lēah**); Moor Willows 1846, 1943 (v. **wilig**); Nether Cl (Open Close) ((*the*) *Neither Close* 1719, 1754, 1758, 1796, v. **neoðera**; an open-gap close, cf. Land Cl (Open Close) *supra*); Nether Fd 1840, 1846 (1796, one of the later open-fields of the village, cf. Red Fd and Windmill Fd *infra*); New Cl, - Furlong, New Close Mdw (*New Close* 1646); Nineteen Leys Cl, Nineteen Leys Furlong (*Nyneteene Leys* 1646, v. **lēah**); No Mans-Land, No Mans-Plot (referring to land on a boundary, v. **nan-mann**); North Commons 1843 (v. **commun**); Oak Cl 1840, 1846, Great -, Little Oak Cl Allotment 1908 (v. **allotment**) (*Oak(e) Close* 1631, 1646, v. **āc**); Obberd Leys (v. **lēah**, cf. *Hubberdysmore, Huberdesmore* Hy 4; with the surn. *Hubbard*, cf. John - and Thomas *Hubberd* 1522 MilS of Langham, v. **mōr**[1]); One Hundred and Twenty Acres 1943; Ox Hill Furlong (v. **oxa**); Parsons Wall Furlong; Pasture Cl 1846 (1646), Pasture Holme 1846 (v. **holmr**), The Pasture 1943; Pen Cl 1840, Pens Cl 1846 (*Pens Close* 1719, 1754, *Penn's* - 1758, *Pen* - 1796), Penns Hill Butts (v. **butte**), Little Pens Hill (*Pennes Hill* 1631, *Penns hill* 1646, v. **penn**[2]); Randalls Hill Furlong; Red Fd 1840, 1846 (1734 *Ct*, 1796, v. **rēad**, so named from the soil on the ironstone; one of the later open-fields of the village); Red Ground 1943 (a name occurring on the 300 ft contour in this and neighbouring parishes, v. **rēad**, **grund**); Ridgeway Furlong, Below Ridgeway, Furlong over Ridgeway (*le Rigewaye, Rygeway* Hy 4, cf. *Rigegate* Hy 4, v. **hrycg**, **weg**, **gata**); The Ridings 1979 VR (v. **ryding**); Long Row(e) Furlong; Sand Hill Furlong 1846, The Sands 1943 (v. **sand**); Seaton Gorse c1800, 1806 Map (v. **gorst**); The Seeds 1943 (referring to an area of sown grass, v. **sǣd**); Sense Lands Furlong (v. **land**; the first el. must remain unexplained); Sheep Commons (v. **commun**); Short Furlong; Sixteen Leys, - Furlong (v. **lēah**); Spout Water Mdw 1846, Spoutwater 1943 (a water-meadow beside R. Welland); Station Cl (adjoining the railway station); Stone Furlong (v. **stān**); Stone Pit Furlong (v. **stān-pytt**); Stubs Cl Furlong (with the surn. *Stubbs*, cf. Stubb's Twelve Acre in neighbouring Barrowden f.ns. (a)); Sutter Furlong (cf. *Suthorne infra*, of which this f.n. may be a later form); Stripe (v. **strip**); Tinkers Hill Furlong; Top Fd (at the north-western extremity of the parish); Below the Town, Drift North of the Town 1846 (v. **drift**), The Town Land 1840 (v. **tūn**); Uppingham Way Furlong (*vltra viam de Huppyngham* Hy 4, v. **weg**; Lat *ultra* indicates land above or beyond the Uppingham road); Viaduct Cl (at the northern end of Welland Viaduct *supra*); Watermill Furlong (cf. Seaton Mill *supra*, which is beside R. Welland); West of the Bank (cf. Annes Bank *supra*); West Cl (1646); West Leys (*Westlayes* 1646, *Westleys Close* 1719, *Westleys Close or Short Leys Close* 1754, *Westley's Close* 1758, v. **lēah**), West Leys Drift (v. **drift**); Nether -, Windmill Fd 1840, Windmill Fd, Windmill Furlong 1846 (*Windmill Field* 1796).

(b) *Bohill Leyes* 16 VCH (from the surn. of Henry *Bowell* 1524 SR, v.

lēah); *Bottingeshowes* 1320 AD (either with the surn. *Botting* which developed from
an OE pers.n. *Botting 'son of Botta', or with the pers.n. itself, *v.* hōh); *apud
Byrtwell'* Hy 4 (*v.* beorht, wella); *diuisionem de Bytlysbroke* Hy 4 ('the boundary
with Bisbrooke', *v.* (ge)mǣrc; Bisbrooke parish adjoins to the north-west); *Crispe's
Close* 1758, *Crispes house* 1717 (cf. Thomas *Crispe* 1522 MilS of Burley); *Downhall*
1597 (also called *Neather House* 1717 *Conant*, *Neither House* 1754 (*v.* neoðera), 'the
lower hall', *v.* dūne, hall); *in campo Oriental'* Hy 4 ('the east field', one of the early
open-fields of the village, *v.* ēast, feld); *the Eighteene acres* 1646 (*v.* æccr); *the Five
Shillings peece* 1646 (alluding to the annual rental of the land, *v.* pece); *the fower
acres* 1646 (*v.* fēower, æccr); *Greygate* Hy 4 (either alluding to a track frequented by
the badger (OE *grǽg*) or to the colour of the soil or stone; the distribution of
names in *brocc-hol* 'a badger-sett' indicates that the extreme south of Ru was once
badger country, so that the former interpretation is reasonable, *v.* grǣg^2, grǣg^1,
gata); *viam de Glaston* Hy 4 ('the road to Glaston'; Glaston parish adjoins to the
north); *Gochismore* Hy 4 (*v.* mōr^1 and Gorgimer Cl in neighbouring Glaston f.ns.
(a)); *la Grene* Hy 4 (p) (*v.* grēne^2); *Home Close* 1757, 1796 (*v.* home); *Humiscrofte*
Hy 4 (from the surn. *Hum(m)*, *v.* croft); *Ivehall or Ivyehall* 16 VCH, *Ivie Hall* 1631,
1646 ('the ivy-covered hall', *v.* īfig, hall); *lauerockes þing* 1527 (from the surn.
Laverock, *v.* þing); *long furlong* Hy 4 (*v.* lang^1, furlang); *Nether Meadow* 1796;
Newleys Close 1719, *Newleys Close or Long Lyes Close* 1754 (*v.* lēah); *the Nyne acres
1646* (*v.* nigon); *in campo Borial'* Hy 4 ('the north field', *v.* norð, feld, one of the
early open-fields of the village); *the Open Field* 1757 (poss. an open-gap close, cf.
Land Cl (Open Close) *supra*); *Great House Orchard* 1757, *Orchard* 1758 (prob. the
orchard of what is now Manor Ho. *supra*); *Portgate* Hy 4 ('the road to the
(market) town', i.e. to Uppingham, *v.* port^2, gata, cf. *Portegate* in Glaston f.ns. (b)
and *Above portway* in Bisbrooke f.ns. (b)); *Sampsons Holme* 1646 (from the surn.
Sampson, cf. Richard *Sampson* 1522 MilS, 1525 SR, husbandman of neighbouring
Lyddington, *v.* holmr); *Sandhowes* 1320 AD (*v.* sand, hōh); *Selfsownelondys* Hy 4
('selions which have re-seeded without human agency', with the p.part. *gesāwen* of
the OE verb (*ge*)*sawan* 'to sow', *v.* self, land, cf. ON *sjálfsáinn*; the earliest NED
citation for *self-sown* is for 1608); *in campo australi* Hy 4 ('the south field', *v.* sūð,
feld, one of the early open-fields of the village); *Spurres Close* 1547-53 VCH (from
the surn. *Spurr*); *Stonebridge Close* 1719, 1758, - *or Land Close* 1754; *Suthorne
meadow* 1646 (*v.* sūð, þorn, cf. Sutter Furlong *supra*); *ad Syrepol* Hy 4 (a form
from a Rental which, because such documents are likely to conserve early spellings
through transmission in a series of copies, may well retain AN scribal·*s* for *sh*;
hence either '(at) the shire pool', which could indicate the proximity of the
Wrangdike Hundred's moot-site (cf. *The Shirewood* in Burley f.ns. (b)), or '(at) the
clear pool', *v.* scīr^1, scīr^2, pōl^1, cf. *in Wis infra*); *Tanners Close* 1631, 1646 (with the
surn. *Tanner*); *Tubbs Close* 1646, *Tupp's Close* 1758 (with the surn. *Tubb(s)* rather

than with ME *tup* 'a ram, a tup'); *The Turnipp Close* 1758 (*v.* **turnep(e)**); *the Twenty acres* 1646; *super aquam subtus villam de Seyton'* Hy 4 (it is unclear whether this refers to R. Welland or to the small stream which runs between the village and the river, *v.* **wæter**); *atte Welle* 1321 Pat (p), *atte Well'* 1322 ib (p), *ad Fontem* 1322 (p), Hy 4 (p) (*v.* **wella**); *in campo occidental'* Hy 4 ('the west field', one of the early open-fields of the village, *v.* **west, feld**); *in Wis* Hy 4 (perh. from **wisc** 'a marshy meadow'; a Rental form which even at this date may retain AN scribal *s* for *sh*, cf. *ad Syrepol supra*, otherwise from **wise** 'a marsh'); *Wythyrsike* Hy 4 (*v.* **wiðig, sík**); *le wyȝesike* Hy 4 (the first el. is poss. **wigga** 'a beetle' used of the water-beetle, *v.* **sík**, cf. *Wye sike* in Ryhall f.ns. (b)).

Stoke Dry

STOKE DRY
    Stoche 1086 DB, *Stoch'* 1176 P (p)
    Stok(e) 1179 (p), 1180 (p), 1181 P (p), 1205, 1220 *FF et passim* to 1263 *Ass et freq*

The affix is normally added as:
    Dri- 1205 *FF*, 1254 Val *et passim* to 1330 Pat, *Drie-* 1220
        RHug, 1238 RGros *et passim* to 1374 Cl, *Drye-* 1220
        FF, 1263 *Ass et passim* to 1376 Pat, *Drei-* 1263 *Ass, Drey-*
        1304 *FF, Druye-* 1295 *ib, Dry-* 1294 *Ass,* 1413 Pat, 1428
        Fine
    -drie 1281 OSut, 1296 *SR et passim* to 1436 Banco, *-drye*
        1362 Ipm, 1373 *Peake et passim* to 1610 Speed, *-dreye*
        1377 *Peake, -dry* 1492 *MktHPR,* 1510 LP, 1546 Pat

'The dairy farm', later distinguished by the affix 'dry', *v.* **stoc, dryge**. The village is on a hill above the valley of Eye Brook which was marshy when Stoke acquired its qualifying epithet. The other *stoc* from which it was necessary to distinguish Stoke Dry may have been in neighbouring Caldecott, *v.* Big Stockwell in Caldecott f.ns. (a).

HOLYOAKS, - LODGE, - WOOD
    Haliach 1086 DB, 1221 RHug (p), *Haliac, -k* 1163 P, 1330
        (p), 1338 *Peake* (p), *-ack* m13 *ib* (p), *-hac* 12 *ib, Halyack*

m13 *ib* (p), *Halliak* 1318 *ib* (p)
Halioc, -k e13 *Peake et passim* to 1303 Ipm, 1369, 1375 *Peake et passim* to 1535 VE, *Halihoc, -k* 1296 *SR* (p), *Alihoc* 13 *Peake* (p), *Halyo(c)k* 1367 Pat, 1374 Cl, 1394 *Peake et passim* to 1537 MinAcct
Haly(h)oke 1428 Cl, 1480 Hastings, 1560 LeicW
Holyoke 1537 AAS, *Holliock* 1606 *ExchSpC, Holyoake* 1698 LeicW, *-oakes* 1722 ib
Halliok Wood c1800, 1806 Map, *Holyoaks Wood* 1824 O

'The holy oak', *v.* **hālig, āc.** There is no direct evidence that this deserted medieval village was formerly a pagan Anglo-Saxon religious site, but its position on a territorial boundary away from Christian religious centres suggests an enclave where pagan practices flourished for a period after the general acceptance of Christianity in Mercia. Compare the survival of the pre-Germanic mother goddess in the churchyard of nearby Braunston and the possible sacred site dedicated to the pagan Anglo-Saxon god Þunor recorded for neighbouring Ayston.

Holyoaks Liberty, although part of Stoke Dry manor, was added to Stockerston Lei by Local Government Order of 1885. With Stoke Dry, it was held by the Knights Hospitallers as early as 1206 Cur. It is perhaps described as a liberty on account of privileges held by the Hospitallers. The last harvest of the village was gathered in 1496 after which Sir Robert Brudenell evicted thirty people to make way for cattle and sheep pastures.

STOKE DRY WOOD (6") (consisting of STOKE GREAT WOOD and STOKE LITTLE WOOD 2½"), *Stocwod(e)* 1235 Misc, 1254 Cl, 1255 Pat, *Stokewod'* 1269 *For, Coppes called stoke wood within the Forrest of leighe feylde* 1553 *Surv, Stockewod Coppyes* 1553 *ib, Stockwood Copice* 1553 *ib, Stokwood salle sollde this yeare* 1553 *ib, Stokwode salle* 1553 *ib, Stockwood sale* 1611 *SP, Stockwood* 1651 VCH, 18 *Rental, Stockwood Sale alias Stockwood alias Stockwood Coppice* 1677, 1694 *Deed, Stockwoods* 1729 *Surv, Stock Wood* 18 *ib, Stockwood Wood* 18 *ib, v.* **wudu, copis, sale.**

The recorded *Stokwood salle sollde this yeare* is a useful confirmation of the meaning of the woodland term *sale* 'a division of a wood of which the underwood is cut down and sold', *v.* Nth

157.   Stoke Great Wood is *Stoke End* 1824 O, *v.* **ende**[1].

ASSHELOUNDE (lost), *Esschelund* 1266, 1269 *For, Asselund* 1276 RH, *Asshelond* 1282 Cl, 1306 Ipm, *Asshilund* 1290 Cl, *Hasschelownd* 1344 *For, Asshelounde* 1387 Cl, 'the ash-tree copse', *v.* **æsc, lundr**.

THE GRANGE, *v.* **grange**. RECTORY is *Rectory House* 1846, 1863 White. RESERVOIR, constructed in 1935 as a water supply for Corby steelworks. ST ANDREW'S CHURCH, 1846, 1863 ib.

Field-Names

Undated forms in (a) are 1943 *Map*; those dated c1840 are *TA* and 1877 are *Burghley*. Early forms dated 1634 are *Terrier*, 1756 are *Burghley*. Fields in Holyoaks are marked (H) in both (a) and (b).

(a) The Nine Acres c1840, Nether -, Over Twelve Acre c1840, Twelve Acre, Bottom Twelve Acres 1877, 1943, Top - 1943 (*v.* **æcer**); Bottom Cl (H) 1877; Brand Cl (H) c1840, 1877 (*v.* **brende**[1]); Bridge Cl (H) c1840, 1877; Broughton's Plain (*v.* **plain**); The Buildings Fd; Cave's (Mill Cl) (cf. William *Cave* 1540 *Ct* and Robert *Cave* 1566 PR, both of Barrowden and both mill owners.   Charles *Cave* held Barrowden Mill 1870-81 WR); Cliffs Cl 1877, Cliff's Cl, - Mdw 1943 (*West Cliffe* Chas I Nichols, *v.*   **clif**); Coppice (*Coppy* 1756, *v.* **copis**); Cottage Fd; Crabtree Hill 1877, 1943 (*Crabtree hill sale* 1756, *v.*   **crabtre, sale**); Curtis Cl c1840, 1877 (*Curtisses Close* 1756, from the surn.   *Curtis*, cf. William *Curtes* 1522 MilS of Ridlington); Lower Darnell c1840, - Darnels 1877, Over Darnell c1840, Darnell's 1943 (*Lower -, Over Darnel* 1756; *darnel* (*Lolium temulentum*) is a deleterious grass which grows as a weed among corn); Doll's Hole c1840, Dals - 1877 (*Dalls Hole* 1756, *v.* **hol**[1]); Eastwick (H) c1840, 1877 (*Further -, Hither Eastwicks* 1756; poss.   'east farm', *v.* **wic**, but cf.   the Ru surn.   *Estwick* (Stretton 1678)); Nether -, Upper End c1840, Far End 1877 (*v.* **ende**[1]); The Field (H) 1877; Fir Cl; Fronald c1840, Furnwell 1877, Bottom Funnel 1943, Frunnel Fd 1979 VR (*Frunal* 1756, *Fronald* 1799 *Deed*, cf. The Fronald in Lyddington f.ns. (a); this range of late related forms here and in adjoining Lyddington suggests an original **freren-holde* 'the holding of the brothers of the military order', referring to the Knights Hospitallers who held Stoke Dry and Holyoaks from at least 1206, *v.* **frere, holde** and cf.   Hospital in

Wardley f.ns. (a)); Furze Cl c1840 (*Furz -, Fuzz Close* 1756, *v.* **fyrs**); Gladnells c1840 (*Gladnels Coppy* 1756, *v.* **copis**); Old Glebe Cl, - Mdw 1877, The Glebe 1943 (*Glebe Close, - Meadow* 1756, *v.* **glebe**); Goodwins Home Cl c1840 (*v.* **home**); Gorse Fd 1877 (*v.* **gorst**); Great Cl c1840; Nether -, Upper Great Ground (H) c1840 (*v.* **grund**); Great Mdw c1840; Hardy Leys c1840 (1756, *v.* **lēah**); Hill Cl (H) 1877; Holyoaks Spinney (H) c1840, 1877 (cf.   *the Nether Holliock* 1606 *ExchSpC, Nether Halliocke* 1627 *Deed, Nether Hollioakes* Chas I Nichols, *Nether Holliock* 1652 VCH, *the Upper Holliock* 1606 *ExchSpC, the Over Halliock* 1627 *Deed, Over Hollioakes* Chas I Nichols, *Upper Holliock* 1652 VCH, *Over Hallyock* 1657 *Deed, Halliocke brooke* 1634 (referring to Eye Brook), *v.* Holyoaks *supra*); Top -, Home Cl c1840, 1877 (*Home Close* 1756, *v.* **home**); Kelpit Cl c1840, Kelpits 1877, Kelpit's 1943 (*Kilpit close* 1756, *v.* **cyln, pytt**); Lady's Acre c1840, Lady - 1877, 1943 (*Ladys Acre* 1756, cf. *Lady's Sale* 1756, *v.* **hlǣfdige, æcer, sale**); Lane Cl c1840, 1877 (1756); Limbrick (H) c1840, 1877, Limbrick 1843 (a surn.); Nether -, Over Little Cl c1840 (cf. *Nether -, Over Little Field* 1756); Little Fd (1634); Lodge Cl (x2) c1840, 1943, Lodge Fd 1877 (Mr J. Field points out that one Lodge Cl adjoins the lodge by Old Vicarage, the other is south of Stoke Dry Wood); Lowns Nook c1840, 1877 (*v.* **nōk**), Great -, Lowns 1877 (*Lown Close* 1756, *v.* **lundr**, cf. *Asshelounde supra, Sundlund* and *Westlound infra*); The Meadow (H) 1877 (*Meadow* 1756); Mill Cl c1840, 1877 (1756, cf. *The millne feild* 1634, *v.* **myln**); New Mdw c1840; The Nook (cf. *Lower Nook* 1756, *v.* **nōk**); Oliver's Cl c1840, 1877, - Coppice 1877, - Mdw c1840 (*one parcell of grounde or wood grounde called Oliver or Olivoe* 1623 *Deed, Oliver al's Olivo* 1623 *ib, Lower -, Upper Olivers* 18 *Surv, Olivers Close* 1729 *ib, Olyve sale* 1564 *For, Oliver Sale al's Oliver Tonge al's Oliver al's Olive Tonge Coppice al's Olive Sale Coppice* 1677 *Deed, Olivers Sale* 17 *ib,* 18 *Surv, Oliver Sale or Oliver Tongue or Olivo or Olive Tongue Coppice or Olive holt Coppice* 1694 *Deed;* Robert *Oliver* of nearby Belton was purchasing woodland in Leighfield Forest in 1626 *Deed;* cf. also Thomas *Olyuer* 1522 MilS of Belton and Richard *Olever* 1525 SR of Ayston, *v.* **sale, tunge, copis, holt**); Over Fd c1840 (1756), - Mdw c1840, - Cl (H) 1877; Pasture Leys c1840, 1877 (*Pasture leys lane* 1756, *v.* **lēah**); Upper -, Lower Paul's Fd c1840, Bottom -, Top Pauls Fd 1877 (*Pauls Field* 1756, from the surn. *Paul,* cf. *Pauls Closes* in Stretton f.ns. (b)); The Plain 1877 (*v.* **plain**); Pridmore (a surn., cf. John *Pridmore* 1732 *Anc* of N. Luffenham); Ropool Mdw c1840 (*v.* **pōl**[1] 'a pool'; the first el. is either OE *rā* 'a roe-buck' or Scand *rá* 'a boundary' since Stoke Dry was once part of the royal hunting forest of Leighfield but also a border parish with Eye Brook forming the territorial limit); Sandstone Mdw, - Fd c1840; The Seeds (referring to an area of sown grass, *v.* **sǣd**); Sheltons Fd (H) 1877 (cf. Adam *Shelton* 1522 MilS of adjoining Lyddington); Six Leys c1840, 1877 (1756, *v.* **lēah**); Snelstone Sale 1804 Map (1799 *Deed, Snelson Sale* 1756, cf. *Snelsons Field, - Meadow* 1756, *v.* **sale** and *Snelston* in Caldecott); Spinney Cl (H) c1840, 1877; Staffords Mdw c1840 (with the surn. *Stafford*); Steppings (H) 1824 O (*Halliok Stepings* c1800, 1806 Map, v. **stybbing** and Holyoaks *supra*); Swan's Nest Coppice c1840, 1943 (*Swans nest* 1756, v. **swan**[1], **nest**); Taylor's Little Fd (named from the *Taylor* family, cf. George *Taylor* 1932 Kelly); Top Ground c1840 (v. **grund**); Upper Ground (H) c1840, 1877 (v. **grund**); Walnut Tree Leys c1840 (v. **lēah**); West Cl (H) c1840, 1877 (*West Close* 1627 *Deed*, 1652 VCH); West Mdw c1840; Will's Cl c1840, Willis Hill 1943; Great -, Lower -, Upper -, Wood Fd c1840, Far -, Lower -, Short -, Upper Wood Fd 1877 (*Farr -, Woodfield* 1756, *Woodfeild Close* 1632 *Conant, Woodfield hedge* 1634 (v. **hecg**), *Woodfield stile* 1634 (v. **stigel**), v. **wudu, feld**); Wood Hill Fd c1840.

(b) *Blacmyld* (H) 1275 (16) *SlCart, Blacmilde* 13 *Deed, Blackmild* 13 (16) *SlCart* ('the black soil', v. **blæc, mylde**); *Butterie Horne Close* 1632 *Conant* (a complimentary name for land producing rich butter, v. **butere, -ig**[3], **horn**); *Caldecote meere* 1634 (Caldecott parish adjoins to the south, v. **(ge)mǣre**); *Carment Hill Field* 1634 (v. Long Carmen in Caldecott f.ns. (a)); *Crossegate* (H) 1274 (16) *SlCart* (v. **cros, gata**); *Dyngly Lees* (H) 1546 (1687) Wright (named from the preceptory of the Knights Hospitallers at Dingley Nth; they possessed the manor of Stoke Dry with Holyoaks, v. **lēah**); *ford weye* (H) 113 *Deed* (v. **ford, weg**); *Frontenehaue* 1276 RH, *Fruntehawe* 1303 Ipm (the first el. is obscure, v. **haga**[1]); *le Goris* (H) 1278 (16) *SlCart, Goare acre* 1634 (v. **gara**); *high balk acre* 1634 (v. **balca**); *Holme* 1276 RH, *Holmes* 1303 Ipm, *Le Holmes* 1303 ib (v. **holmr**); *Nether Meadowe* 1632 *Conant, Rislonde* 1510 *MinAcct* (v. **hrīs, land**, cf. *Stoke Rislonde* in Lyddington f.ns. (b)); *Stanhill hauedelond* (H) 1275 (16) *SlCart* (v. **stān, hyll, hēafod-land**); *Stockwood Leaze* 1661, 1661 (18), 1680, 1747 *Anc*, - *Leeys* 1670 *Rental, Stockwood close Leaz* 17 *Deed* (v. **lēah** and Stoke Dry Wood *supra*); *le Stuble* 1300 DC (v. **stubbil**); *le Stylegate* 1377 Misc (v. **stigel, gata**); *Sundlund* 1256 *For* (poss. with *sand* as first el., cf. Sandstone Mdw *supra*, v. **lundr**); *Thacholme* (H) 1275 (16) *SlCart* (v. **þak, holmr**); *Wardes coppie* 1634 (with the surn. *Ward*, cf. Richard *Warde* 1525 SR, v. **copis**); *Westlound* 1344 *For* (v. **west, lundr**).

Thorpe by Water

By a Local Government Order of 1885, detached parts of Thorpe by Water parish were added to adjoining Lyddington and to Gretton in Northamptonshire.

THORPE BY WATER

Torp 1086 DB, 1105-7 Reg, 1231 RegAnt, 1296 *SR*

Thorp(e) 1231 RegAnt, 1264 *FF*, 1297 *Ass*, 1302 *AddCh et passim*

The affix is normally added as:
- *iuxta Seyton* 1296, 1297 *Ass*
- *on Welond* 1358 BPR
- *by the Watre* 1428 *FF*, 1429 *TB*, -*bythewatir* 1459 AD,
  - *next the Water* 1549 Pat, - *by Water* 1824 O *et passim*
- *iuxta aquam* 1459 *Peake*, 1610 *TB*, -*juxta aquam de Welland* 1701 *FF*

'The outlying farmstead', later distinguished by its proximity to Seaton and to the waters of R. Welland, *v.* þorp, wæter.

BLACK HORSE P.H. (lost) - VR. THE GREEN, *v.* grēne[2]. MANOR HO. MILL LANE (local). THORPE MILL, *mol' aquatic' in Thorp* 1510 *MinAcct*, cf. *ad stagnum molendini de Thorp* 1399-1413 *Rental, v.* water-mylne, pōl[1].

Field-Names

Undated forms in (a) are 1846 *TA*; those dated 1943 are *Map*. Undated early forms are Hy 4 *Rental*. For later forms of some f.ns. here, *v.* Lyddington f.ns. (a).

(a) Eight -, Twelve -, Forty Acre 1943 (*v.* æcer); Ban Billings Pad, Banbillings Pad (furlong) (*v.* Banbillings Pad in Lyddington f.ns. (a)); Barkers cl 1846, Barker's 1943 (a south Ru surn., cf. Dom' *Barcar* 1510 *MinAcct* of neighbouring Lyddington); Far -, Hither Barrows (*le Norberwe, le Beru, v.* norð, beorg referring to burial mounds on the hill called The Barrows on the parish boundary with Seaton, *v.* The Barrows in Seaton); Basses, - Cl furlong; Under Bay hill, - furlong (*v.* Bee Hill in Lyddington and cf. Bay House Fm in Pilton); Short Bottom furlong; Bottom Cl (cf. Top Cl *infra*); Bottom -, Top Breach 1846, Breach 1943 (*le Breche, v.* brēc); The Butts (*v.* butte); Part of Calves cl; (Next) Chapmans piece furlong (with the surn. *Chapman, v.* pece); Church Fd 1979 VR (at SK 896 967, but there is no church in Thorpe by Water and no record of a lost church; the land was prob. endowed for charitable purposes); Churchway furlong (later appearing as a Lyddington f.n. and poss. indicating that the inhabitants of Thorpe attended Lyddington Church); Great College fd (the college which is referred to in this f.n. remains unidentified); The Common, Common cl 1846, Far -, Second Commons 1943 (all are fields immediately to the south of Seaton Common, v. **commun**); Dugden Mdw (this is the Dugden Mdw of Lyddington f.ns. (a), cf. Dugden in Seaton f.ns. (a)); East and West furlong; Fox Cover 1846, 1943 (v. **cover(t)**); Furrow Cl 1943 (v. **furh**); Huffingtons -, Huffintons cl furlong (from the surn. *Uffington*, cf. William *Uffyngton* 1522 MilS, - *Vffyngton* 1524 SR, - *Uffington* 1525 ib, husbandman of Thorpe); High Trees 1943; Under the hill, Hill furlong, Hills -; Hogs hedge furlong (v. **hecg**); Holes furlong; Home cl (v. **home**); Little lane furlong; Langham balk furlong (v. **balca**); Langley Hill 1943; Ley crofts (v. **lēah, croft**); Lands adjoining Lyddington, Lyddington Road Fd 1943; March mdw, March dyke leys (v. **mersc, dīk, lēah**), Marsh Mdw (v. **mersc**); Mickle mdw (v. **mikill**); Middle of the field; Mill furlong, Mill Tail 1846 (v. **taile** 'the bottom end of a mill pool'), Mill Cl 1943 (cf. Thorpe Mill *supra*); New cl; Nine Leys, Nine leys furlong (v. **lēah**); Old Inclosure little fd (v. **inclosure**); Orchard(s) furlong; Pease holme furlong (v. **pise, holmr**); Road side; Sheepcote furlong (v. **scēap-cot**); Stone husk furlong (unexplained, cf. *Green(e) Huske Furlong* in Barrow f.ns. (b) and Whissendine f.ns. (b)); Thorough lands (prob. 'selions running through', i.e. from one side of an open-field to the other without headland, v. **þurh, land**); Top Cl (Mr J. Field notes that this close adjoins Bottom Cl *supra*, but is on the side further from the village); Trimmers furlong; Twelve leys furlong (v. **lēah**); Twenty lands furlong (v. **land**); Wades holm mdw (with the surn. *Wade*, cf. Richard *Wade* 1525 SR of Glaston, v. **holmr**); Ward leys (with the surn. *Ward*, cf. George *Ward* 1932 Kelly of Lyddington, v. **lēah**); Warrens holme furlong (with the surn. *Warren*, cf. John *Waryn* 1524 SR of Seaton and Henry *Waren* 1525 ib of Caldecott, v. **holmr**).

(b) *Broddole* (v. **brād, dāl**); *le dybbyng Randulphi de Belfago* (v. **dibbing**); *in campo orientali* (v. **ēast, feld**, one of the old open-fields of Thorpe); *Thorpe Meadow* 1796 *Surv*.

Tixover

TIXOVER

Tichesovre, -u- 1086 DB, 1104-6 RegAnt, *-oura(m)* 1104-6
      ib, 1120-9 Reg, 1123-9 CartAnt, Hy 1 Dugd, 1166, 1167 P
Tichesora c1131 Reg, 1130-3 France
Ticesoure 1104-5 RegAnt, *Ty-, Tikesovre, -u-* 1255 (p), 1267
      Pat (p) *et passim* to 1351 Cl (p), *-oura* 1163 RegAnt,

1187, 1188 P *et freq* to 1194 ib (p), *-our'* 1104-6 RegAnt,
-oures 1210 P, *-overe, -u-* 1263, 1286 *Ass et passim* to 1392
FF, -ofre 1203 *ib, -hovere* 1256 *For, -howre* 1286 *Ass,*
Tikessovere 1203 *FF*

Ty-, Tikesor(e) 1205 *FF,* 1267 Pat *et passim* to 1361 Pat *et*
freq to 1423 ib, *-hore* 1258 Cl, *Thikesor* 1285 Pat

Ty-, Tixovere 1343 Pat, *-over, -u-* 1461 Cl, 1468 *Rut,* 1550 Pat,
1556 *FF*

Tyxsore 1382 Pat

Tekesore, -ys- 1347, 1478 Pat, 1535 VE

Texover 1579 *FF*

Tixover or Texover or Tixor or Tekesore 1758 *Recov*

'The ridge where the young goats are grazed', *v.* **ticcen, ofer**[2].
The first el. is the gen sg. *ticcnes* of OE *ticcen* 'a kid', which gives the
voiceless stop [k]. Spellings in *ch* in early forms are AN
representations of this voiceless stop. The generic **ofer**[2] is replaced
in many early forms by OE **ōra**[1] 'an elongated, flat-topped hill', *v.* A.
Cole, 'The origin, distribution and use of the place-name element *ōra*
and its relationship to the element *ofer'*, JEPNS 22 (1989-90), 27-41.

MANOR FM, 1943 *Map.* ST LUKE'S CHURCH, *Church* 1846,
1863 White. TIXOVER GRANGE, 1846, 1863 ib, *v.* **grange.**
TIXOVER HALL, cf. *the Hall Garden* 1723 *Deed, Hall Wong*
1770 *Asw, v.* **vangr.** TIXOVER LODGE, 1824 O.

Field-Names

Undated forms in (a) are 1943 *Map;* those dated 1849 are *TA.* Asterisked
names are those which occur in both documents. Early forms dated 1203 are
FF; those dated 1550 are Pat, 1674 and 1723 are *Deed,* 1751 are *Anc* and 1770
are *Asw.*

(a) Eleven Acres, Fourteen Acre, Sixteen Acres 1849, - Acre 1943, Bottom
-, Top Twenty Acre (*v.* **æcer**); Allotments; Atkins Cl 1849; Bakers Cl; *Far -,
*First Barn Cl; Bridge Cl, *Bridge Mdw (the bridge at Duddington Nth
adjoins the latter); Buckworthies Cl 1849, Buckworth - 1943 (a surn.);
*Calcott's Nook (with the surn. *Calcott,* cf. John *Calcott* 1522 MilS, - *Caldecote*

1524 SR of Ketton whose family no doubt was settled earlier in Caldecott in the south of Ru, v. nōk); Chapel Cl 1849 (*Chapell Close* 1674, *the Chappell Close* 1723, v. **chapel(e)**); *Church Cl (adjoining St Luke's Church), Church Pits 1849 (*the Church Pitts* 1770, v. **pytt**); *Clover Cl; Covert (v. **cover(t)**); Crab Hedge Cl 1849 (v. **crabbe**); *Dairy Cl, (Spinney in) Dairy Cl 1849 (*Dairy Close* 1770); Figg's Green (v. **grēne**²); Front Cl 1849; Grange Mdw (v. Tixover Grange *supra*); Great Hames 1849, Big -, Little Hame 1943 (*the Hame or Bell Holme Close* 1770, v. **holmr**; poss. land endowed for the maintenance of the parish church bell); *Hanging Side (v. **hangende, sīde**); (Spinney in) Hill Side 1849; Home Cl 1849 (1770, - *Closes* 1723, v. **home**); *Honey Hole (*Honey Holes* 1770, an ambiguous name, poss. complimentary, but more likely to refer to an area of sticky, boggy soil in this riverside location); Horsley Ford Hill 1849, - Ford Fd 1943 (adjoins R. Welland, v. **ford**); Great -, Little House Cl 1849; The Island 1849 (used of a field surrounded by other fields and thus with no separate access); Limekiln Cl; The Marshes 1849, Far -, Near Marsh 1943 (*the Marsh Close* 1770, v. **mersc**); The Orchard 1849 (cf. *Coneys Orchard* 1723, v. **coni, orceard**); *(The) Orchard Mdw; The Parish Pound 1849 (cf. *Pinfold Close* 1723, v. **pynd, pynd-fald**); Pitcher Hill Rd 1849, Pitcher Row 1943 (*Pitchill Road* 1770, v. **pightel**); The Plot 1849 (v. **plot**); The Poor's Land 1877 White (about three acres of land, the rent of which provided money for Christmas distribution to the poor); Sainfoin Hill 1849 (v. **sainfoin**); Lower -, Upper Second Cl 1849; Lower -, Upper Shelton's Cl 1849, Shelton's Cl 1943 (with the surn. *Shelton*); Lower -, Upper Short Lane Cl 1849; Silverdale, - East and West 1849 (v. **seolfor, dalr**); Far -, Near Spring Cl; Stone Pit Cl (v. **stān-pytt**); Three Cornered Cl 1849, - Fd 1943 (referring to its triangular shape); Tixover Gorse c1800, 1806 Map (v. **gorst**); *Whitegate Cl; Wilsworth Cl; Wootton's Ground North, - South, - East 1849, Far -, Near Wootton's Ground 1943 (*wootton meadowes* 1674; from the surn. *Wootton*, cf. John *Wootton* 1705 *Anc* and Francis *Wotton* 1769 *EnclA* of neighbouring Ketton, v. **grund**); Wortley's Mdw (with the surn. *Wortley*, cf. Edward *Worteley* 1580 PR and Josiah *Worteley* 1586 ib, both of nearby N. Luffenham).

(b) *Bell Holme Close* 1770 (v. Great Hames *supra*), *Great -, Little Bellum Field* 1770 (v. **holmr**); *the Briery Close* 1723 (v. **brērig**); *Brittins Close* 1723, *Britains* - 1751 (with the surn. *Britain*, cf. *Britain's Old Homestead* in N. Luffenham f.ns. (b)); *the Butt Close* 1723, - *Closes* 1723, 1751 (v. **butte**); *Caleweho* 1203 (v. **calu, hōh**); *Church feild* 1723, *the Churchfield* 1723, 1770 (one of the open-fields of the village, v. **cirice, feld** and cf. St Luke's Church *supra*; the church stands away from the village in a large bend of R. Welland); *the Dovecoat Close* 1723 (the dovecote survives as part of Manor

Fm); *le Estfeld* 1550, *the East feild* 1723 (one of the open-fields of the village, *v.* **ēast, feld**); *Este Meade, le Estmedowe* 1550 (*v.* **ēast, mǣd**); *Grenegatebalke* 1203 (*v.* **grēne**[1], **gata, balca**); *Holfurbalke* 1203 (*v.* **hol**[2], **furh, balca**); *Holly Close* 1723; *the Horse Close* 1770; *Leffildespol* 1203 (with the ME reflex of the OE pers.n. *Lēofhild*, used in late Anglo-Saxon England for both men and women, *v.* **pōl**[1]); *the Leys or Dairy Close* 1770 (*v.* **lēah**); *Maud Pool* 1770 (poss. associated with Queen *Maud*, wife of Henry 1, the *caput* of whose estates in Ru was at neighbouring Barrowden, *v.* VCH 2 170); *Mill Holme Close* 1723 (*v.* **holmr**); *Normandale* 1770 (evidently 'the valley of the Norwegians', *v.* **Norðman** (**-manna** gen.pl.), **dalr**, cf. Normanton and note the Norw pers.n. compounded in Glaston; lack of genitival *s* makes the presence here of the late OE pers.n. *Norðman* unlikely, although the compounding of this pers.n. with *deill* 'a portion of land' rather than *dalr* is just possible); *le Northfeld* 1550, *North Feild* 1723 (one of the open-fields of the village, *v.* **norð, feld**); *Pecks Close* 1723 (with the surn. *Peck*); *the Smiths shop* 1723, *the Smith's Shop* 1770 (*v.* **smið, sc(e)oppa**); *the Town end* 1723 (*v.* **tūn, ende**[1]); *the Water Yard* 1770 (*v.* **geard**).

THE ELEMENTS, OTHER THAN PERSONAL NAMES, IN RUTLAND PLACE-NAMES, STREAM-NAMES AND FIELD-NAMES

This list includes the elements in uncompounded and compounded place-names, stream-names and field-names. The names quoted in each entry are arranged in alphabetical order, with no distinction between uncompounded and compounded names. Names which survive on modern maps and also lost major names are listed first, followed by a summary of the use of the element in field-names. Although a concise translation of each element is provided, for a fuller discussion of its significance and use, reference should be made to *English Place-Name Elements* (EPNS, vols. 25 and 26, amended in JEPNS 1). The elements are often given in an OE, ON or OFr form, but it should be remembered that many of these elements continued as common nouns in the English language and that many of the place-names of Rutland are of more recent origin than the periods represented by the lexical head-forms used. Many terms are included which are not in the Elements volumes, but it has not been felt necessary to distinguish these. Those elements marked * are not independently recorded in the head-forms cited or are hypothetical reconstructions from the place-name evidence.

abbat OFr, ME, 'an abbot'.
Abbotispittes (f.n. Lt. Casterton), *Abbotts meadow* (f.n. Wing), *Abbots Stocking* (f.n. Pickworth), *the abutes close* (f.n. Egleton).
āc OE, 'an oak-tree'.
Holyoaks, Shire Oaks, Tolethorpe Oaks. Fairly freq. in f.ns., e.g. *the Oake Close* (Tickencote), *le Oake hill* (Oakham), *Oake Stockin* (Clipsham), *oke Forl'* (Egleton), *Okes gate* (Morcott), *Okestead Close* (Braunston), *Pecks Oake close* (Ayston).
æcer OE, 'a plot of arable or cultivated land; a measure of land which a yoke of oxen could plough in a day'.
Freq. in f.ns., often with a numeral indicating size, e.g. *Fyuacrewong* (Caldecott), *Halfacrewong* (Lyddington), *Seavenacres* (Teigh). Occasionally with a surn., e.g. *Hartes acres* (Egleton), *Pallemersacre* (Lt. Casterton), *Stevens acre* (Glaston). Reference may be made to the nature or condition of the soil, e.g. *Pottacres* (Egleton), *Sandacre* (N. Luffenham), *Stoneacre* (S. Luffenham); to

features of the landscape, natural or man-made, e.g. *Damm Acres* (Oakham), *Foldehaluacre* (Mkt. Overton), *Tunkeacre* (Tinwell), *Welhalfager* (Lt. Casterton); to fauna, e.g. *Cockacres* (Oakham), *le kydhaker* (N. Luffenham); or to land connected with a church, chapel or altar, e.g. *Church acre* (Lyddington), *Ladiakre* (Gt. Casterton), *Lampacre Close* (Uppingham). The three instances of *Handacre* (Caldecott, Lt. Casterton, Lyddington) may refer to awkwardly sited plots, workable only by the spade.

æppel OE, 'an apple; an apple-tree'.
Appelmede (f.n. Whissendine).

æppel-trēow OE, 'an apple-tree'.
Apiltremedou (f.n. Glaston), *Appletree Bushes* (f.n. Manton).

æpse OE, 'an aspen-tree'.
? *Apescrosse furlong* (f.n. Lyddington).

æsc OE, 'an ash-tree'.
Ashwell, *Asshelounde*. Freq. in f.ns., e.g. *Ash Close* (Empingham, Tickencote), *Ashefurlonge* (Edith Weston), *Ashegate, Ashslade Ford* (Belton), *Parkassh'* (Mkt. Overton), *Stamford Ashe* (Exton).

ald OE (Angl), 'old'.
Aldgate, Oldsale Wood. Occasionally in f.ns., e.g. *le Oldefelde* (Lt. Casterton), *Old Field* (Empingham), *at the od willowe* (Lyddington), *old Willow Leys* (Manton); *(le) Old(e)hall* (Lt. Casterton, Empingham).

aley ME, 'an alley', used in Ru from the 17th cent. of a bowling alley.
the Bowling Ally (Glaston), *the old bowling Ally* (Uppingham), *The Bowling Alley Close* (f.n. Tickencote).

allotment eModE, 'land allocated to a tenant at enclosure in exchange for holding and rights under the open-field system'. Occasionally in f.ns., e.g. *Allotment* (Ryhall), *the Great Allottment* (Manton), *Third Allotment in The Meadow* (Caldecott).

alor OE, 'alder'.
? *Alders Croft* (f.n. Morcott), Alley Wong (f.n. Whissendine).

alren OE, 'growing with alders'.
? Big Olran (f.n. Whissendine).

ancre ME, 'an anchorite, an anchoress'.
? Anchor Fd (f.n. Ketton).

arnut, ernut eModE dial., 'the earth-nut, the pig-nut'.
arnat hyll (f.n. Egleton), *Harnett Hill* (f.n. Edith Weston).

asker ModE dial., 'a newt'.

Asker Syke (f.n. Egleton).
askr ON, 'an ash-tree'.
Asketrow (f.n. Clipsham).
āte OE, 'oats'.
Oat Close (f.n. Hambleton).
avenue ModE, 'a tree-lined approach'.
The Avenue. Avenue (f.n. N. Luffenham), *The Avenue* (f.n. Burley).

back ModE, 'lying behind, hindmost'.
Occasionally in f.ns., e.g. *at the back of the Yard* (Uppingham), Back Mdw (Belton), Dirty Back Cl (Ridlington).
ba(c)ksyde eModE, 'a field at the back of a house, the back premises, the hinder part of an estate'.
Backside Lane. Occasionally in f.ns., e.g. *the Backside* (N. Luffenham, Uppingham), *Backside Close* (Glaston); sometimes defined by the owner's name, e.g. *George Bates's Backside* (Braunston), *Bryan Franklines backside* (Glaston).
backwater eModE, 'water dammed back in the channel of a mill-race'; later 'a piece of water without current, fed from a mill-race at the lower end by a back-flow'.
Mill Backwater (S. Luffenham).
*bæc-hūs OE, 'a bake-house'.
ye Backehouse land (f.n. Lyndon).
bærlic OE, 'barley'.
Barleythorpe. *Barley Close* (f.n. Pickworth).
baille OFr, 'a palisade, a castle courtyard or bailey'.
le Baillie (Oakham).
baillie OFr, 'a bailiff, a steward'.
? *Bayliffe Close* (f.n. Clipsham).
balca OE, 'a ridge, a bank'; later 'a strip of ground left unploughed to mark the boundary between adjacent strips of the common field'.
Baulk Hill. Freq. in f.ns.; often compounded with a village name, e.g. *Seaton balke* (Morcott), *Sculthorpe baulk, wing balk* (Pilton), or with a surn., e.g. *Beebies Baulk* (Belton), *Bettes Baulke* (Greetham), *Peppers Balk* (Barrowden). Reference may be made to local functionaries, e.g. *Constables baulk* (Morcott), *the Judges balke, the Parsons Balke* (Uppingham); to flora or topographical features, e.g. *Crabbtree Balke furlong* (Greetham), *Lound balke*

furlong (Bisbrooke), *Moore balke way* (N. Luffenham); to structures, e.g. *Limekiln balke* (N. Luffenham), *the milne balke* (Hambleton), *Windmill balk* (Barrowden). Other compounds include *Bellstrings Baulk* (Pilton), *Cock Stirrop Balk* (Egleton), *Fosdeybalk'* (N. Luffenham), *Mayden Balke* (Ketton).

*ball OE (Angl), 'a ball', hence 'a rounded hill' and 'a mound set up as a boundary mark'.

Balland (f.n. Ayston), *Ballands* (f.n. Wardley), Ballease (f.n. Hambleton), *?Bollands Close* (f.n. Lt. Casterton).

banke ME, 'a bank, the slope of a hill or ridge'.

Occasionally in f.ns., e.g. *Chiseldine banke* (Beaumont Chase), *Coxhill Bank fur'* (Egleton), *Rushey Banke* (Lyndon), *Stony Bancke* (Barrowden), ? *Wellban(c)ks* (Normanton).

bār² OE, 'a boar'.

Bore Hill (f.n. Lyddington).

barre ME from OFr, 'a barrier closing an entrance, especially to a fortified town'.

atte Barre orientale (p), *le Barredyk', le Westbarreʒate* (Oakham).

bastard OFr 'a bastard'; but in later f.ns. used derogatively of fields of abnormal shape or of land of poor quality.

Bastard(e) Close (f.n. Braunston, Glaston), *Bastard Leys* (f.n. N. Luffenham, Edith Weston).

(ge)bēacon OE, 'a beacon'.

Beacon (f.n. Glaston), Beacon Hill (f.n. Essendine).

bēan OE, 'a bean'.

Occasionally in f.ns., e.g. *Bannil dale* (Lyndon), *Beanham* (Tickencote), *Beanhill* (Manton), Benefield (Caldecott).

beau OFr, 'beautiful'.

Beaumont Chase.

bedd OE, 'a plot of ground where plants grow'.

Twitchbed Lane. Occasionally in f.ns., e.g. Onion Bed (Ketton), Osier Bed (Ashwell, Gunthorpe), (Old) Ozier Bed (Morcott, Tinwell); *Bedsycke* (Egleton).

bed-hūs OE, 'a prayer-house, a chapel, an oratory'.

Bede House. *le Beadhouse, Beadhouse Row* (Oakham), Beadhouse Croft (f.n. Stretton), *Beadhouse peice* (f.n. N. Luffenham).

bekkr ON, 'a stream'.

Holbeck Lodge. Infrequent for streams, for which OE *brŏc* is usual, e.g. *the Beck* (Morcott), *Mawsey Beck Close* (f.n. Morcott),

Beckclosse (f.n. N.   Luffenham), *Beck Leas* (f.n. Thistleton), *Crowebeck waye* (Lyndon), *Henbecke* (Hambleton).

belle OE, 'a bell'; but prob. used in p.ns. in the transferred sense 'a bell-shaped hill'.

? Bellmear (f.n. Ridlington).

belt ModE, 'a belt (of woodland), a screen of trees, a plantation'. The Belt.

beneoðan OE, '(place) beneath, under, below'.

Benethegate (f.n. Langham), *Neath Towne Close* (f.n. Empingham).

bēo OE, 'a bee'.

Bee Hill.

beonet OE, 'bent-grass'.

Bentle (f.n. Mkt. Overton).

beorg OE, **berg** (Angl), 'a tumulus, a hill', used by the Anglo-Saxons to denote prehistoric barrows in contrast to their own *hlǣw* for contemporary burial mounds (*v.* D. Hooke, 'Burial features in West Midland charters', JEPNS 13 (1980-1), 1-40). Barrow, The Barrows, Barrowden, Ranksborough, Wing Burrows. The el. appears as a simplex in f.ns., e.g. *le Beru(es)* (Barrowden, Thorpe by Water), *the Barrows* (Morcott), *Barrowe Hill* (Belton), Far Barrows (Lyddington). It may be compounded with an OE pers.n., e.g. *Budborow* (Greetham), Ranksborough (Langham), with an adj. descriptive of position, e.g. *mydle borrowes* (Egleton), *Netherborrowes* (Braunston), *le Norberwe* (Thorpe by Water), or with an el. indicating vegetation, e.g. *Gosborough* (Whissendine), *Riseberwe* (Leighfield), *Rush Barrow* (Teigh), *Thornborrow Hill* (Hambleton).   Note *Broken Barrow* (Empingham) which may indicate early grave robbery; *v.* also Notes on the Distribution and Usage of some Elements, *s.v.* **beorg.**

beorht OE, **berht** (Angl), 'bright, clear'.

Brightley Bridge (f.n. Manton), *Byrtwell'* (f.n. Seaton).

bercet OE (Angl), 'a birch-copse'.

? Bargate (f.n. Ashwell), Bargate Hill (f.n. Braunston).

bere-ærn OE, 'a barn'.

le Upper Barne (Barleythorpe).

bere-tūn OE, 'a barley-farm', later 'a farm-yard'.

Isaac's Barton (Langham).

berige OE, 'a berry'.

Berrybut Spinneys. ? *Berryhill,* ? *Berycroft* (f.ns. Hambleton).

best(e) ME, 'an animal, a farm-beast'.

Beast Hill. *Beast Commons* (f.n. Seaton).

betwēonan OE, '(the place) between'.

Between Gates (f.n. Greetham), Twin-Gates (f.n. Edith Weston).

betweox(n) OE, '(the place) between'.

Twixendykes (f.n. Tickencote, Tinwell).

biker ME, 'a dispute'.

Bikerwode (Ashwell).

*bircen[1] OE, 'a place overgrown with birches, a birch-copse'.

? Bircham (f.n. Ashwell).

bita OE, 'a morsel, a piece', eModE **bit**, 'a small piece of land'.

Byteleyes, Bytenooke (f.ns. Stretton), Gibbs Bitt (f.n. Hambleton), Square Bit (f.n. Pilton).

*bitel, bitela OE, 'a beetle'.

? Bisbrooke. *Bittlewell* (Leighfield).

blæc OE, 'black, dark-coloured, dark'; in eModE, *black* 'fertile' is contrasted with *white* 'infertile'.

Blackground. Freq. in f.ns., e.g. *Blackholme* (Stretton), *Blacmyld* (Stoke Dry), *Blakroodes* (Belton), *Blackstones* (Lyndon), *Blackwel* (Wardley).

blāw OE, 'blue, cold, cheerless'.

the Blowes (f.n. Uppingham), *Blowland* (f.n. N. Luffenham), ? Blowhill Cl (f.n. Morcott).

bleikr ON, 'pale, white (as with foam), bleak'.

? *Bleksik* (f.n. Mkt. Overton).

blind OE, 'dark, obscure, hidden (by vegetation)'; later of roads, passages 'obstructed, without exit'.

Blind Pitt (f.n. Edith Weston), *le Blynde Lane* (Hambleton).

bōc[1] OE, 'a beech-tree'.

Bochawesti (f.n. Lt. Casterton).

bog ME, 'a bog'.

Hills Cl and Bogg (f.n. Ashwell).

boga OE, 'a bow'; also used in p.ns. with senses 'something curved; a river bend; a curved valley'.

Bowestedewong (f.n. Lyddington), *Bowwoode* (Tickencote).

boi(a) OE, 'a boy, a servant'; in southern Ru, association with pits and hollow places may indicate its local use for 'a hobgoblin'.

boydale, Boygreue, Boy's Pitt Spinney (f.ns. N. Luffenham), *Boygraue* (f.n. Bisbrooke).

*bole ME, 'a place where ore was smelted before the invention of furnaces, usually in a round cavity on a hill top'. Perh. from OE *bolla* 'a bowl'.

Bole howe (f.n. Thistleton).

bombast eModE, 'the soft down of the cotton-plant (*Gossypium*) and related species'.

Bombast Lane (Leighfield).

bōs (**bōsum** dat.pl.) OE, 'a cowstall'.

? Bosomes Cl (f.n. Burley), Boswick Cl (f.n. Teigh).

bōt OE, 'help, remedy; healing'.

Botewell Wood (Leighfield).

bōthe ME, 'a (herdsman's) temporary shelter, a covered market-stall'.

Spicers booth (Uppingham).

bōtl OE, **bottle** ME, 'a dwelling, a house'.

Newbottle. Bottle Hill (f.n. Ketton).

botm OE, 'a bottom, a valley bottom'.

Botteme (f.n. Caldecott).

bowling eModE, 'playing at bowls, the action of rolling a bowl'.

Evidently a popular Ru pastime in the 17th and 18th centuries, hence *the Bowling Ally* (Glaston), *the old bowling Ally, the Bowling greene, the old Bowling Leys* (Uppingham), *The Bowling Alley Close* (f.n. Tickencote), *Bowling Green* (Hambleton), *Bowling Leys Furlong* (f.n. Manton).

brād OE, 'broad, spacious, wide, large'.

Bradley Lane, Bredcroft. Freq. in f.ns., e.g. *Bradcroft* (N. Luffenham), *bradthorn* (Bisbrooke), *Broddole* (Thorpe by Water), *le Brodemor* (Barrowden). Recurring compounds are Broadholme(s) (f.n. Ashwell, Morcott), (Old) Broadway (f.n. Wardley, Whissendine), cf. Broad Gate (f.n. Morcott), Broadeng Mdw (f.n. Tinwell), Broading Mdw (f.n. Ryhall).

bræc[1] OE, 'a brake, a thicket, brushwood'.

Brake Spinney. Freq. in f.ns. in central parishes south-east of Hambleton. Of limited variety in form; simplex are *the Brakes* (Glaston, Manton); also *Brake Close* (Hambleton), *The Bracke Close* (Empingham); *lybrakehil* (N. Luffenham), *Brake Hill* (Whitwell), *Brakehill Furlonge* (Belton). With adj. suffix -ig[3] are *Brakey Close* (Edith Weston), Brakey Cl (Pilton), *Breaky Close* (Lyndon). Cf. also *welbrakes* (Glaston).

brædu OE, **brede, brode** ME, 'breadth', hence 'a broad stretch of land, a broad strip; a broad cultivation strip in the common field'.

the Broade (f.n. Lyndon), *Pease Broad* (f.n. Empingham).

*brakni ON, ***bræcen** OE, **braken** ME, 'bracken, fern'.
Bracknell Cottage. *Brackendale* (f.n. Braunston), *Brakenhul* (f.n. Bisbrooke), *Brickennook* (f.n. Tinwell).
brēc OE (Angl), **brēche** ME, 'breaking, breach, land broken up for cultivation'.
Breach Fm. Common in f.ns. as a simplex, e.g. (The) Breach (Bisbrooke, Lyndon, Thorpe by Water, Whissendine), and earlier *le Brech(e)* (Mkt. Overton), *ye Breache* (Wardley), *Breaches* (Egleton), *Breeches* (Hambleton); Breach Cl (Ketton), - Furlong (Morcott, Stretton), - Mdw (Belton), *Brechewong* (Lt. Casterton). Occasionally with a qualifier, e.g. *Longbreatches* (Glaston), *Syortebrech* (Uppingham), Top Breach (Lyddington).
breden OE, 'made of planks, planked'.
Bredenbriggewong (f.n. Lyddington).
breeder eModE, 'one who breeds cattle or other animals'.
Breeder Leys (f.n. Stretton).
breiðr ON, 'broad, spacious'.
Brethesik (f.n. Caldecott), *Brethsike* (f.n. Lyddington).
*brende¹ OE, 'a burnt place, a place cleared by burning'.
Occasionally in f.ns., e.g. *le Brende* (Glaston), The Brand (Lyddington), Brand Cl (Stoke Dry), Brand Fd (Uppingham), *Brendegate* (Belton).
brende², **brente** ME pa.part., adj., 'burnt, cleared by burning'.
Common in f.ns., e.g. *Brende Dike* (Thistleton), *Brendeʒerdes, Brendhoutecroft* (Mkt. Overton), *Brenles* (Ridlington), *Brentley* (Manton), Burnt Ground (Pickworth), - Land (Horn), - Wong (Morcott).
brēr OE (Angl), 'briers'.
Bryer Bush (f.n. Greetham), *Bryar Bush Furlong* (f.n. Barrow), *Bryar Land Seeke* (f.n. Lyddington).
*brērig OE (Angl), 'growing with or overgrown by briars'.
the Briery Close (f.n. Tixover), Briery Wong (f.n. Whissendine).
brew-hous ME, 'a brew-house, a brewery'.
the Brewhouse (Oakham).
bridd OE, 'a bird; a young bird'.
Bird-Holme (f.n. Empingham).
brigdels OE, 'a bridle' (used in the sense 'fit for a horse to pass').
Bridle Gate Close (f.n. Normanton), Bridle Road Fd (f.n. Cottesmore).
brimme ME, 'an edge, a border'.

Brimlands (f.n. Lyndon).
brink, brenke ME, 'a brink, the edge of a bank'.
Occasionally in f.ns., e.g. *Brengewong* (Caldecott), *Brinkes* (Barley-thorpe), *The Brinks* (Braunston), *Brinckes furlonge* (Oakham), *Priests brink fur'* (Egleton).
brōc OE, 'a brook, a stream', the usual generic in Ru stream-names.
Bisbrooke, Brook Fm, Brooke, Brooke Fm, North Brook. In f.ns., commonly as a simplex, e.g. *le broc* (Bisbrooke), *ye Brooke* (Braunston, N. Luffenham), *the Brook(e)* (Lyndon, Pilton), *Brooke(s)* (Exton). Often compounded with a village name, e.g. *Allaxton Brooke* (Belton), *Burley Brok'* (Egleton), *Glastonbrok* (Glaston), *Ridlington brooke* (Ayston), *Weston Brooke* (Hambleton), *Wynge brooke* (Glaston); or with the names of lost sites, e.g. *Cotesbrook* (Morcott), *pornham broc* (Ayston). It may be prefixed by an el. indicating location, e.g. *Norbrooke* (Langham), *Southbrookes* (Wing), *holebroc* (Ayston), or fauna or flora, e.g. *Padbrok'* (Burley), *Redbroke* (Horn). Note especially *pureslege broc* (in the OE bounds of Ayston) recording a poss. site of pagan Anglo-Saxon worship.
brocc-hol OE, 'a badger-hole, a badger-sett'.
Broc Holys (f.n. N. Luffenham), *Brogholes* (f.n. Morcott), *Brockholes Furlonge* (f.n. Belton), *Brockwell* (f.n. Lyddington), ? *brocholes* (in OE bounds of Ayston).
brocen OE, 'broken'.
? *Broken Barrow* (f.n. Empingham).
brōm OE, 'broom'.
Broom Close (f.n. Tickencote).
brouse eModE, 'fodder for cattle consisting of young shoots; that which can be browsed'.
the Brose Close (f.n. Tickencote).
brusshe ME, 'brushwood'.
Brushfeild (f.n. Barleythorpe), *Brushfield(s)* (f.n. Stretton).
bryce OE, 'breaking', whence 'land newly broken up for cultivation; an assart'.
? *Birchaby. Burtch furlong* (f.n. Bisbrooke).
brycg OE, 'a bridge; a causeway'.
Bull Bridge, Church Bridge, Finchley Bridge, Moor Lane Bridge, Turtle Bridge. Occasionally prefixed by a village name, e.g. *Preston Bridge, Wing Bridge* (Bisbrooke), *Wakerle Brigge*

(Barrowden). May be compounded with an el. indicating the materials of which bridge or causeway was constructed, e.g. *Bredenbriggewong* (f.n. Lyddington), *Redebrug'* (S. Luffenham), *Stanbrigge* (Hambleton, Oakham). Fairly freq. in f.ns., e.g. *le Brydgefurlong* (Lt. Casterton), *Bridge Wong* (Morcott), *Heybryggeholm* (Langham), *Stanbryghyl'* (Cottesmore).

bucc OE, 'a male deer'.

? Buck Hill Cl (f.n. Ashwell).

bucca OE, 'a he-goat'.

Bucwell' (f.n. Lt. Casterton), ? Buck Hill Cl (f.n. Ashwell).

*bula OE, **bule** ME, 'a bull'.

Bullgrassefurlong (f.n. Barleythorpe), *Bull Grass fur'* (f.n. Egleton), Bull Nook (f.n. Teigh), *Bullpiece Furlong* (f.n. Manton), Bull's Nook (f.n. Barrow), ? *Bulls Nook* (f.n. Lyddington).

bulluc, -oc OE, 'a male calf, a bullock'.

Bullock Close (f.n. Greetham), Bullock Cl (f.n. Egleton).

burh, burg (byrig dat.sg.) OE, 'a fortified place'.

Burley, ? Bussack Barn. *Burghsyk'* (f.n. Barrow), ? *Berryhill*, ? *Berycroft* (f.ns. Hambleton).

burh-stall OE, 'the site of a fortification'.

Burstall' medewe (f.n. Teigh).

burh-tūn OE, 'a fort-enclosure'.

? *Burton Hill fur'* (f.n. Morcott).

burna OE, 'a spring, a stream'.

Burnsike (f.n. Ashwell), ? Holborn (f.n. Whissendine).

*busc OE, **bush** ME, 'a bush'; also 'ground covered with bushes, scrubland'.

Burley Bushes, Greetham Bushes, Many Bushes, ? Bussack Barn. Surn. prefixed indicates ownership, e.g. *Barbars Bushe* (Bisbrooke), *Colebush, Sheperds Bush* (N. Luffenham), *Woodcoks Bush* (Lyddington). The prefixed el. may describe species, e.g. *Bryer Bush* (Greetham), *le Gooseberry Bush* (Barleythorpe), *May Thorne Bush* (Ketton); or shape, e.g. *the broad bushe, Forked Bushes* (Lyndon), *Sitten Bush* (Edith Weston). Location is occasionally indicated, e.g. *the Leane wong bush* (Thistleton), *Long Land Bushes* (Edith Weston), *morterpits bush, Spring bush* (Lyddington). F.ns. include *Bushcrofts* (Hambleton), *Crowbush Furlong* (Lyddington), *High Bush fur', Three Bush Furlong, - Wong* (Greetham), *How bush Close* (Hambleton).

*buskr ON, **busk** ME, 'a bush'.

Rare in Ru; *Buskwells* (f.n. Lyndon), *Halffmylle Busk* (Mkt. Overton), *Hundesbuske* (Oakham).

busshi ME, 'bushy; covered with bushes'.

Bushy Wood. *Bushey Balk Furlong* (f.n. Uppingham), *Bushy Close* (f.n. Ashwell, Lt. Casterton, Empingham, Lyndon, Uppingham), Bushy Park Wood (Leighfield).

butere OE, 'butter'.

Butterie Horne Close (f.n. Stoke Dry), *Butterwell slade* (f.n. Wing).

butte ME, 'a strip of land abutting on a boundary'; also 'a short strip at right angles to other strips; a short strip in an angle where two furlongs meet'.

Berrybut Spinneys, Butt Lane. Freq. in f.ns., e.g. *the Butt(e)s* (f.n. Greetham, Uppingham), *Buttes atte Parkwall* (f.n. Mkt. Overton), *Buttesbithesik* (f.n. Caldecott); ownership may be indicated, e.g. *Amos Butt* (f.n. Manton), *Bernardesbutt'* (f.n. Lyddington), *Dukes Butts* (f.n. Glaston), or size, e.g. *Short buts* (f.n. Tickencote), - *Butt* (f.n. Normanton), or number, e.g. *six butts* (f.n. Lyddington), Eight -, Nine Butts (f.ns. S. Luffenham), or location, e.g. *Cophill but fur'* (f.n. Egleton), Penns Hill Butts (f.n. Seaton).

buttuc OE, 'the buttock', used of a rounded slope.

Buttocks Close (f.n. Hambleton).

bȳ ODan, **bȳr** ON, 'a farmstead, a village'.

Very rare in Ru. ? *Birchaby,* ? Hooby Lodge (*v.* Barrie Cox, 'Rutland and the Scandinavian settlements: the place-name evidence', ASE 18 (1989), 135-48).

bydel OE, 'a beadle'.

? *Beadles fur'* (f.n. Greetham), ? Biddle's Lees (f.n. Lyddington).

byden OE, 'a vessel, a tub', topographically 'a hollow'.

Bidwell's Lodge. Bidwell (f.n. N. Luffenham).

cabin ModE, 'a cabin, a shed for workmen'.

Cabin Cl (f.n. Ridlington).

cærse, cresse OE, 'cress, water-cress'.

Cresswell (f.n. Oakham).

calc OE (Angl), 'chalk; limestone' and prob. also 'coarse sand mixed with pebbles; heavy clay'.

Kalkeleys.

cald OE (Angl), **cald, cold** ME, 'cold; inhospitable; uncomfortable, bleak, exposed'.

Caldecott, Cordle Spring. *Cawdwell fur'* (f.n. Egleton), Cordhill

Mdws (f.n. Belton), Cordial-Way Furlong (f.n. Seaton), *Cordwell Close* (f.n. Hambleton).

calf (calfra gen.pl.) OE (Angl), 'a calf'.

Calvercroft (f.n. Cottesmore), *Calves Close* (f.n. Stretton), *The Calves Nooke* (f.n. Thistleton).

calu (cal(e)wan wk.obl.) OE, 'bald, bare; lacking vegetation'. ʹ

Calibut's (f.n. Edith Weston), *Calepitts* (f.n. Lyddington), *Calouhill'* (f.n. Glaston), *Kallowhill* (f.n. Morcott), *Caleweho* (f.n. Tixover), *Caleueldale* (f.n. Barrow), *Callewell Leas* (f.n. Barleythorpe), *Callywell* (f.n. Belton). Because of difficulty in distinguishing upper case C from G in some early scripts, some names attributed to OE *galga* 'a gallows' in p.n. surveys may belong to *calu*; hence the following Ru names are problematical: *Gallow Hill* (Uppingham), *Galowong* (f.n. Lyddington), *Galowe hill furlong* (f.n. Caldecott).

camb OE, 'a comb, a crest', hence topographically 'the crest of a hill, a ridge'.

Camswell (f.n. Morcott).

capun OE, 'a capon'.

? *Capon Acres* (f.n. Greetham), ? *Capun More* (f.n. Stretton).

carot eModE, 'a carrot'.

the Car(r)ott Close (f.n. Glaston), Carrot Garden Furlong (f.n. Seaton).

castel(l) ME, 'a castle, a camp'.

The Castle, Castle Hill. *Castle Thorns* (f.n. Morcott).

catstails ModE dial., 'spires of Timothy Grass (*Phelum pratense*); catkins of hazel and willow'.

Cattayles (f.n. Lyndon).

cat(t) OE, 'a cat'.

Cats Hill Spinney, Vale of Catmose. Cat Cl (f.n. Teigh), *Cathole* (f.n. Braunston), *Catmouse* (f.n. Burley), *Catlow* (f.n. Beaumont Chase), Catwell Sale (Beaumont Chase).

catte (cattena gen.pl.) OE, 'a she-cat'.

Catten Hills (f.n. Ashwell).

cat(t)el ME, 'cattle, livestock'.

Cattlespring (f.n. Tickencote).

caucie ONFr, **cauce, cause** ME, 'an embankment, a raised way across marshy ground; a (raised) paved way'.

Normanton Causeway (Edith Weston).

*ceacga OE, 'broom, gorse, brushwood'.

Jagwell (f.n. Uppingham).

ceaster OE, **cæster** (Angl), 'an old fortification; a Roman site'.

Casterton. ? Chester (f.n. Whissendine).

cęd PrWelsh, 'a wood'; the form **ceto-* in Elements corrected by JEPNS 1 45.

Ketton, R. Chater.

chace, chase ME, 'a chase, a tract of ground for breeding and hunting wild animals'.

Beaumont Chase. *Laund' Chase* (Beaumont Chase).

chapel(e) ME, 'a chapel'.

Chapel Field Spinney. *capell' de Brok'* (Brooke), Chapel Cl (f.n. Tixover, Wardley), *Chappell-close* (f.n. Ridlington), *le Chappel Croft* (f.n. Empingham), *Chappel seeke* (f.n. Oakham), *Schapelfeld* (f.n. Lyndon).

charnel OFr, ME, 'a burial place, a cemetery; a charnel house'.

Canal Hole (f.n. Teigh).

chaunterie ME, 'a chantry'.

Chantry. *Chantry Close* (f.n. Greetham), Chantry Cl (f.n. Lyddington), *le Chanterie House* (Hambleton), *le Chauntryhouse* (Clipsham).

cheesecake ModE dial., 'the fruit of such wild plants as the common mallow (*Malva sylvestris*) and the bird's foot trefoil (*Lotus corniculatus*)'.

Cheesecake (f.n. Langham), *Cheesecake Close* (f.n. Empingham, Hambleton, Stretton), - *Piece* (f.n. S. Luffenham), Cheesecake Piece (f.n. Barrowden).

cheri(e) ME, 'a cherry-tree'.

Cherry Holt (Glaston).

cild OE, 'a child, a young person'.

Childeslund' (Ayston), ? *Child Furlong* (f.n. Barleythorpe), ? Child Furlong (f.n. S. Luffenham).

cirice OE, **chirche, churche** ME, 'a church'.

Chirchefeld (f.n. Lt. Casterton), (*the*) *Church Feild* (f.n. Bisbrooke, Tixover), - *fielde* (f.n. Greetham), - *acre* (f.n. Lyddington), - *Close* (f.n. Mkt. Overton), - *furlong* (f.n. Oakham), *Churche Forl'* (f.n. Egleton), *ad ecclesiam de Berk'* (f.n. Barrow).

clæg OE, 'clay, clayey soil'.

Clay Hill, Clay Lane. Fairly common in f.ns., e.g. *the Cley* (Glaston), *The Clay* (Barrowden), *Clayfield* (Caldecott), *cleay hill'* (Egleton), *Inclay fur'* (Morcott), White Clay Furlong (N.

Luffenham).

clǣne OE, 'clean, clear of weeds etc.'.

Clenwell (f.n. Edith Weston).

clap-mill ModE dial., 'a clapper turned by the wind for scaring away birds'.

Clapmilleclose (f.n. N. Luffenham).

cley-pytt ME, 'a clay-pit'.

Claypithill Barn. *Clay-Pit hill* (f.n. Uppingham).

clif OE, 'a cliff, a bank, a steep hillside'.

Swintley Lodge. ? Cleves Cl (f.n. Greetham), Cliffs Cl (f.n. Stoke Dry), Horse Mdw or Cleeve (f.n. Stretton).

clinker ModE, 'furnace slag'.

The Clinkers (f.n. Edith Weston).

*clōh OE, **clough** ME, 'a deep valley or ravine'.

Cluf Cl (f.n. Greetham).

clos(e) ME, 'a close, an enclosure'.

Cow Close Plantation. Very freq. in f.ns., with forms from the 16th century onwards, e.g. *the abutes close* (1566, Egleton), *Brok close* (1530, Brooke), *ye Lodgeclosse* (1567, Leighfield), *Makworth(e) Close* (1521, Empingham).

closing eModE, 'an enclosure'.

the new closing (f.n. Barleythorpe).

clot(t) OE, 'a lump of earth, a clod'.

Long(e) clotes (f.n. Egleton).

clūd OE, 'a rock, a mass of rock, a rocky hill'.

Cloudstone furlong (f.n. Barrowden).

clūt OE, 'a patch, a piece of cloth, a clout'.

Rouclout (f.n. Lyddington).

cnoll OE, 'a hill-top, the summit of a large hill'.

Knoll (f.n. Brooke), *The Knoll* (f.n. Bisbrooke).

*cobb(e) OE, 'a round lump, a cob', **cob** ModE dial., 'a mound, a hillock, a tumulus'.

Cobdale furlong (f.n. Braunston).

cobelere ME, 'a cobbler, a mender of shoes'.

? Cobler's Cl (f.n. Empingham).

*cocc[1] OE, 'a hillock'.

? *Cockhill furlong* (f.n. Glaston), *Coke stawpe* (f.n. Egleton).

cocc[2] OE, 'a cock, a woodcock'.

Cackerony (f.n. Uppingham), *Cockacres* (f.n. Oakham), ? *Cockhill furlong* (f.n. Glaston), *Cockleys, Kokerode* (f.ns. Leighfield), Cock

Leys (f.n. Whissendine).

cockle-stone eModE, 'a fossil mollusc in limestone'.
Kokelstone furlong (f.n. Greetham).

cockpit ModE, 'a pit for cock-fighting, a cock-pit'.
Cockpitt (f.n. N. Luffenham), Cock Pit Cl (f.n. Morcott), *Cockepitt Wong* (f.n. Greetham).

cokewold ME, 'a cuckold'.
? Cuckold Way (Glaston).

col¹ OE, 'coal, esp. charcoal'.
Colley Hill (f.n. Lyddington).

cōl² OE, 'cool'.
? *Cole poole furlong* (f.n. Caldecott).

cole OE, 'a hollow'.
? *Cole poole furlong* (f.n. Caldecott).

coleseed ModE, 'rape (*Brassica campestris oleifera*)'.
Coleseed Cl (f.n. Burley).

col-pytt OE, 'a coalpit', i.e. a place where charcoal was made.
Colepit Corner (f.n. Ayston), *Cowpit* (f.n. Oakham), *Cowpitt* (f.n. Braunston), Cowpit Holme (f.n. Whissendine).

colt OE, 'a colt'.
Colts Close (f.n. Ridlington), Colt's Fd (f.n. Horn).

commun ME, 'common land'.
Freq. in f.ns., e.g. Common(s) (Bisbrooke, Lyddington), *The Common* (Greetham, Ketton, Morcott), Common Hill (Gt. Casterton), Common Leys (Whissendine), *Common Wood* (Stretton); *Cow Commons* (Empingham, N. Luffenham), Beast -, Horse -, Sheep Commons (Seaton); *The Lamass Commons* (Empingham); Ketton Common (Edith Weston).

conestable ME, 'a constable'.
Constables baulk (f.n. Morcott), (*The*) *Constables Grass* (f.n. Pilton, Edith Weston).

coni ME, 'a rabbit'.
Conie Close (f.n. Whitwell), ? *conygreene* (f.n. Ridlington), *Coneys Orchard* (f.n. Tixover).

coninger, coningre ME, 'a rabbit-warren'.
Common in f.ns., e.g. Coney Gar (Seaton), Coneygear Cl (Glaston), Conygear Lane (S. Luffenham), Coneygree (Empingham), ? *conygreene* (Ridlington), *Coneygrey* (Egleton), Conger Hill (Whissendine), *le Conyngher* (Barrowden), *cunningree feelde* (Teigh), The Kuniger (Bisbrooke).

*copel OE, '(a hill) rising to a peak'.
? Copper hill cl (f.n. Lyddington).
copis ME, 'a coppice'.
The Coppice, Coppice Leys, Prior's Coppice. Esp. freq. in the old
forest area of western Ru, e.g. *Birchley -, Branston -, Cockleyes -,
Dryhill -, Freewood Quarter -, Huntwood -, Lamley -, Loscott -,
Swincliffe -, Todhill -, Tostick -, Water Leaze -, Woodfleet Coppice*
(Leighfield), *Gladnels Coppy, Olive Sale Coppice, Stockewod
Coppyes, Wardes coppie* (Stoke Dry). The two Stoke Dry names
with *coppie, -y* are due to popular reconstruction of a 'singular'
form, hence also, e.g. *Copie close* (f.n. Morcott), *Copy Close* (f.n.
Hambleton), *the coppy close* (f.n. Wardley), Coppy Hills (f.n.
Pickworth).
copp, cop OE, 'the top of a hill, a peak'.
Cop, Cophill but fur' (f.ns. Egleton), *Cophill* (f.n. Glaston), Copse
(f.n. Oakham), The Copstead (f.n. Barrowden), Copwold Hill (f.n.
Essendine).
copped ME, 'pollarded, having the top removed'.
Cob-thorn Furlong (f.n. Cottesmore), *Coppethornhull* (f.n.
Lyddington), Copthorn Hill (f.n. Barrowden).
corn[1] OE, 'corn, grain'.
the Cornfielde (f.n. Oakham).
corner ME, 'a corner, a nook'.
Fairly freq. in f.ns., usually with a prefixed p.n., e.g. *Colepit
Corner, Hadslie Corner* (f.ns. Ayston), *Fletterette Corner* (f.n.
Oakham), *Grinley Corner* (f.n. Belton), *Hawxwell Corner* (f.n.
Exton); occasionally with a surn., as *Jordens Corner*, Torkington's
Corner (f.ns. Stretton).
cot OE, 'a cottage, a shelter'.
Caldecott, Coach Bridge, Losecoat Field, Morcott, Rocott Ho.,
Tickencote. Cotch Ferns (f.n. Preston), Cotch Platt (f.n.
Ridlington), Far Cott (f.n. Essendine), *Loscoat(e)s* (f.n. Braunston),
Loscott sale (Leighfield), Swancote Leys (f.n. S. Luffenham).
cotager eModE, 'a cottager'.
(The) Cottagers Close (f.n. Lt. Casterton, Mkt. Overton,
Tickencote), (The) Cottagers Cl (f.ns. Ayston, Cottesmore, Teigh),
Cottager's Fd (f.n. Gt. Casterton), Cottagers Pastures (f.n.
Ashwell), Cottager's Spinney (Burley).
*cottere OE, 'a cottar, a cottager'.
Cothers Close (f.n. Lyndon), *cottiers close* (f.n. Hambleton), *cottiers*

part (f.n. Wardley). Cottagers Cl (f.n. Empingham) and Cottager's Spinney (Burley) show *cotager* replacing *cottere*.

cover(t) ME, 'a covert, a hiding place, a shelter for game'.
Bottom Mill Covert, Brooke Covert, Fox Covert, Pilton Fox Covert, Purveyor's Covert. Freq. in f.ns., e.g. Fox Cover (Barrowden, Bisbrooke, Glaston, Preston, Ridlington, Thorpe by Water, Tinwell, Edith Weston), (Fox) Cover Cl (Cottesmore, Pickworth); occasionally compounded with a surn., e.g. Adcock's Covert (Whissendine), Lotts Covert (Wing). Note the early *Covermoore* (Lyddington) associated with the hunting-park of the Bishops of Lincoln. Other compounds include *Gibbet Cover* (Hambleton), Gorse Cover (Burley), Pasture Cover (Whissendine).

cow-gate ModE dial., 'pasturage for a single cow'.
Cow Gait (f.n. Ashwell), *Cow Gate* (f.n. Morcott).

crabbe ME, 'a crab-apple, a crab-apple tree'.
Crab Hedge Cl (f.n. Tixover).

crabtre ME, 'a crab-apple tree'.
Crabtree (f.n. Mkt. Overton, Tickencote), *the Crab tree* (Glaston), *le Crab Tree in le Millfeild* (Barleythorpe), *Crabbtree Balke furlong* (f.n. Greetham), Crabtree Cl (f.n. S. Luffenham, Pilton), Crabtree Hedge Furlong (f.n. Lyddington), Crabtree Hill (f.n. Beaumont Chase, Stoke Dry), *Crabtree peice Furlong, Luffs Crabtree* (f.ns. N. Luffenham), *Crab Tree Stockin* (f.n. Clipsham).

*craca OE, **kráka** ON, **crake** ME, 'a crow, a raven'.
Crakepornfurlong (f.n. Barrow).

cræt OE, **carte** ME, 'a cart, a waggon'.
Cartley (f.n. Egleton, Oakham), Cart Leys (f.n. Ketton).

cran OE, 'a crane, a heron'.
Cranehill, Crane Hurn (f.n. Morcott).

crappe ME, **crap** ModE, 'darnel, rye-grass'.
Crap Land (f.n. Barrow).

cráwe OE, 'a crow'.
Cracraft's (f.n. Empingham), *Crowebeck waye* (f.n. Lyndon), ? *Crowfurlong* ? *Crowbush Furlong* (f.ns. Lyddington).

creach ModE dial., 'a light sandy or gravelly soil'.
the Creach (f.n. Edith Weston).

crew-yard ModE, 'a close or yard with sheds for cattle'.
Crewyard (f.n. Seaton).

*cringol OE, 'twisting, crooked'.

Cringlety Valley (f.n. Empingham).
croft OE, 'a small enclosed field'.
Bredcroft, Crow Croft Spinney, Maycroft. Freq. in f.ns. where it is commonly prefixed by a surn., e.g. *Alwardescroft* (Lyddington), *Humiscrofte* (Seaton), *Reynaldiscroft* (Glaston), *Roychards Crofte* (Ashwell), *William Overtons Croft* (Morcott); it may be compounded with an el. specifying flora, e.g. *Bushcrofts* (Hambleton), *Grascroft* (Lyddington), *Lyncroft* (Barrowden, Caldecott), *Nettle Croft* (Edith Weston), or (use for) animals, e.g. *Calvercroft* (Cottesmore), *Horsecrofts* (Uppingham), *Lambyngecrofte* (Leighfield), or location, e.g. *Estcroft* (Bisbrooke, Lt. Casterton), *Northcrofte* (Lt. Casterton), *Incrofte* (Barrowden), *Brendhoutecroft* (Mkt. Overton), *Hocroft* (Tickencote), or size or shape, e.g. *Acrecroft* (Egleton), *Bradcroft, Longcrofts* (N. Luffenham). It is only rarely compounded with an el. denoting a building, e.g. *Chapple Crofts* (Empingham).
*crōh² OE, 'a nook, a corner'.
Crowcut Hades (f.n. Ashwell), *Crow Stockin* (f.n. Clipsham).
crōk ME, 'a bend', usually denoting 'land in the bend of a river', but also in later f.ns. 'a nook, a secluded corner of land'.
Crook Cl (f.n. Ketton), *Crook fur'* (f.n. Morcott), Croke Hill Furlong (f.n. Stretton).
croked ME, 'crooked, twisted'.
Crooked Hasels (f.n. Leighfield).
crop(p) OE, 'a swelling, a mound, a hill'.
Yoke Crop (f.n. Caldecott).
cros late OE, ME, **cross¹** ModE, 'a cross' (Lat *crux*); cf. **cross²**, often difficult to distinguish, which is to be regarded as a separate el.
Butter Cross, Cross Lane. Common in minor names and f.ns.; the el. may be prefixed by an indication of site, e.g. *Fiue Mile Crosse, Sprowridge Crosse, Stretton Gate Crosse* (Greetham), *halywelcros* (Barrowden), *Ketton Cross* (Empingham); individuals, groups or saints may be referred to, e.g. *ad crucem Benedicti* (N. Luffenham), *Ravens Crosse* (Barleythorpe), *Salters Crosse* (S. Luffenham), *Saint Thomas's Cross* (Morcott); local limestone is suggested by *White Cross* (Uppingham) and *Whitecross Furlong* (f.n. Lyddington), while *Stump Cross* (Edith Weston) indicates the broken shaft of an ancient cross.
cross² ModE, 'athwart, lying across, intersecting', cf. **cros (cross¹)**.

Cross Hedges (f.n. Whissendine), *Crosse Horne fur'* (f.n. Greetham), ? *Croslands* (f.n. Oakham).

crumb OE, 'crooked, twisted'.

Crown Well Bridge.

*crumbe OE. 'a bend (esp. in a river or stream)'.

the Croome (f.n. Manton).

cū OE, 'a cow'.

Cow Close Plantation. Occasionally in f.ns., e.g. *the Cow Close* (Wardley), *Cow Hill Feild* (Barrow), *le Cow Lane* (Oakham).

cuckold ModE dial., 'the fruit of the burdock'.

? Cuckold Way (Glaston).

cumb OE, 'a hollow, a valley, a coomb'.

Combhead Cl (f.n. Edith Weston), Coombs (f.n. Preston), *Coumbes* (f.n. Lyddington).

cundite eModE, 'a conduit, an aqueduct'.

Cundict (f.n. Braunston).

curre ME, 'a cur, a dog'.

Cur Meadowe (f.n. Oakham).

curt, court ME, 'a manor house; a house where manorial courts are held'.

de la Curt (p) (Empingham).

cutte^1, cut^1 ME, 'a water channel'.

Cutt Close (f.n. Oakham), Cut Cl (f.n. Clipsham), Long Cutts (f.n. N. Luffenham).

cutte^2 ME, **cut^2** ModE, 'cut off, truncated; having been cut'.

Cuttgrave Leys (f.n. Manton), *Cutskirts* (f.n. Lyndon), Cut Skirt Cl (f.n. Ridlington).

*cwic OE, 'a quickset hedge'.

the Quick (S. Luffenham, Edith Weston), Quicks Cl (f.n. Morcott), *the Quickhedge* (Uppingham), *Clipshams Quick* (Morcott), Gipsy's Quick (f.n. Gt. Casterton), *Peaches Quick* (Lyddington), *Russel's Quick* (Caldecott), *Staffords Quicke* (Whissendine).

cwice OE, 'quitch, couch-grass'.

Twitchbed Lane. Twitch Hill (f.n. Oakham).

cyln, cylen OE, 'a kiln'.

The Kell Pits (f.n. Lyddington), Kelpit Cl (f.n. Stoke Dry), *Kilne close* (f.n. Ayston), *Kilne house* (Oakham), *the kilne howse* (Preston).

cyning OE, **king** ME, 'a king'.

le Kingsway (Beaumont Chase).

cȳta OE, 'the kite (a bird of prey)'.
Kite fur' (f.n. Greetham), *Kites Seeke* (f.n. Uppingham).

dāl OE, **dole** ME, 'a share, a portion; a share in the common field'. *Broddole* (f.n. Thorpe by Water), *Mickle Doles* (f.n. Caldecott), *Mikildole* (f.n. Lyddington), *Schortdoles* (f.n. Glaston), *Langmeadow doles, Stilton meadow doles* (f.ns. Belton), *Dallacres* (f.n. Morcott), *Dale Acres* (f.n. Ryhall), *Dollacres furlong* (f.n. Empingham), ? *long doles* (f.n. Oakham).

dalr ON, 'a valley'; very difficult to distinguish from ON **deill** 'a share, a portion of land' (*q.v.*), except where topographically obvious.
Deb Dale, Loudal Lane. Occasionally in f.ns., often compounded with OE *dēop* 'deep', e.g. *Debdale* (Greetham), Debdale (Cottesmore), Debdales (Ashwell), Deepdale (Ayston, Barrowden, Preston), - Hollow (N. Luffenham), *Depedale* (Uppingham). It may be prefixed by a p.n., e.g. *Bisbrooke dale* (Uppingham), *Clipsham Dale* (Stretton), *Ketendale* (Ketton); it may be compounded with an el. indicating direction from a settlement, e.g. *East Dale* (Greetham), *Suthdale* (Oakham); or flora, e.g. *Brakedale* (Empingham), *Brackendale* (Braunston), *le risdale* (Barrowden). There is a group of names, unfortunately surviving only in late spellings, in which -*dale* appears to be compounded with a pers.n.: in these, *deill* may be present rather than *dalr*, although their occurrence in isolation and away from the apparent distribution of names in *deill* would favour *dalr*, i.e. *Gundale Furlong* (f.n. Ketton), *Ingersdale* (Empingham), *Ingresdale Slade* (Exton), *Yngedale* (Glaston), *White Ingle Dale* (Ryhall), *Woolsdale* (N. Luffenham).

damme ME (*damm, *domm OE, dammr late ON), 'a dam', *v.* Löfvenberg 49, Sandred 100, SMED 2.
Base Dam (Caldecott), Damade (f.n. Mkt. Overton), *Damfeild* (f.n. Ayston), Damm Acres (f.n. Oakham), *Damwongs* (f.n. Thistleton), *Mill Dam* (Greetham), *Kingesmyll dame, le Mylnedam* (N. Luffenham), *le Mylnedamme* (Ryhall), *the Myll Damme* (Ketton).

darnel ME, 'darnel'.
Darnell Fd (f.n. Ryhall), Lower Darnell (f.n. Stoke Dry).

daw(e) ME, 'a jackdaw'.
? *Daweleys* (f.n. Uppingham).

dēad OE, 'dead'; also 'infertile'.
le Dedelane (Oakham); *Deadmoore furlong(e)* (f.n. Belton), *Deadmore* (Manton), Dedmoor (Wing), Dodmore (Greetham).

dēaw OE, 'dew'.
Dewlands (f.n. Morcott).

dede-man ME, 'a dead man, a corpse'.
Deadman's Grave Furlong (f.n. N. Luffenham), Dead Man's Ground (f.n. Tinwell), Deadmans Holme (f.n. Barrowden), *Dedemansforlang* (f.n. Barrow). In the last two instances, the association of corpses with barrows may not be fortuitous.

deer-leap ModE, 'a lower place in a fence or hedge where deer may leap over'.
Deer Leap (f.n. Lyddington).

deill ON, 'a share, a portion of land'.
This is very difficult to distinguish from **dalr** 'a valley' (*q.v.*) in Ru, except where plural forms or a high incidence within a parish occur. Occasionally in f.ns., e.g. Dale's (Egleton), *the Dales* (Manton), Crossdales, Longdales (Clipsham), *Longedales, Northdales* (Oakham), *Le parke Dales* (Leighfield). Note esp. the group in Brooke, not all with the plural signal for *deill*: Big Dale, Dales Cl, Fant's Dale, Ploughed Dales, Rawsons Dales, Robinson's Dale, Rough Dale.

demeyn ME, 'demesne'.
the Demeasnes (Uppingham), *the demeasne lands* (Preston).

den ME, 'a dean'.
Dean's St.

denn OE, 'a den, a wild beast's lair, a pit'.
Denpit Cl (f.n. Barrowden).

denu OE, 'a valley'.
Essendine, Whissendine. *le Deynes* (f.n. Essendine), Mickledine (f.n. Barleythorpe), ? *gledene* (f.n. Bisbrooke), ? *Holdenewong* (f.n. Lyddington).

dēop OE, 'deep'.
Deb Dale. *Debdale* (f.n. Greetham), Debdale(s) (f.n. Ashwell, Cottesmore), Deepdale (f.n. Ayston, Barrowden, Preston), - Hollow (f.n. N. Luffenham), *Depedale* (f.n. Uppingham), *Deep-home* (f.n. Morcott), ? *Dwpwelleholmes* (f.n. Hambleton).

dēope OE, 'a deep place'.
Deephouse (Manton).

dēor OE, 'an animal, a beast', **de(e)r** ME, 'an animal, a deer'.

? *Darley Croft Furlong* (f.n. Lyddington).

deorc OE, 'dark, obscure, gloomy'.

Dark Lane (Oakham).

desert ME, 'a wild, deserted place'.

the Desart (Glaston).

dibbing ME, 'a dibbling', poss. 'a new plantation'.

le dybbyng Randulphi de Belfago (Thorpe by Water).

dīc OE, 'a ditch'.

Wrangdike Hundred (early forms). *Ash-well ditch* (Morcott), *Broad Ditch* (Thistleton), *le Casteldisch* (Oakham), *cope well. Dyche* (Egleton), *Wrongedich* (N. Luffenham).

dīk ON, 'a ditch'; the el. varies with **dīc** in some f.ns. Sheepdyke Lane, The Washdyke. Freq. in f.ns.; a ditch obviously formed the boundary between parishes, hence e.g. *Glaston Dyke Furlong* (Seaton), Ketton Dykes (Edith Weston), *Preston Dike, Seytondykes* (Bisbrooke), Stapleford Dyke (Whissendine), *Wynge dike* (Glaston); or *Randike Meer, - Meir* (Edith Weston, N. Luffenham), Ransack Dyke (Barrowden) with OE *rān* 'a boundary strip' or OE *rand* 'a boundary'. Noteworthy also are *le Barredyk', le Casteldyk'* (Oakham), recording the use of ditches in urban fortification. Late agricultural use is illustrated in Sheep Dike Cl (f.n. Empingham), Sheep Dyke (Thistleton), Washdyke Cl or Sheepdyke Cl (f.n. Exton), Washdyke(s) (f.n. Hambleton, Morcott), Wash Dike Nook (f.n. Gunthorpe). Only rarely does the el. appear initially in a compound, e.g. Dikeham (Clipsham, Greetham) where use for drainage is suggested, as also in *Medudyk* (Ketton), *Medwedik'* (N. Luffenham), *the Meadow dike* (Lyddington) and poss. in *Ruddyngdykefurlang* (f.n. Cottesmore).

diked ME, 'ditched, enclosed with ditches'.

Dikedholm (f.n. Lt. Casterton).

djúpr ON, 'deep'.

? *Dwpwelleholmes* (f.n. Hambleton).

docce OE, 'a dock', poss. also 'a water-lily' when combined with an el. denoting water.

Dockey Cl (f.n. Ridlington), Dog Bank Furlong (f.n. Seaton), *the Dogholes* (f.n. Uppingham), Dogwell (f.n. Whissendine), Loose Dogs (f.n. Ashwell), ? Penderdocks Holme (f.n. Pilton).

dodde ME, 'the rounded summit of a hill'.

Dodesell (f.n. Barrowden), *Dud seeke* (f.n. Edith Weston).

dogge-kenel ME, 'a kennel'.

Dog Kennel Cottages. *the Doggkennell Yard* (f.n. N. Luffenham), *Dogkennell Furlong* (f.n. Belton), Dog Kennel (Essendine), Dog Kennel Spinney (Burley).

dove-cot(e) ME, 'a dove-cote'.

Dovecoat House, Dovecot. Dove Coat (f.n. Ketton), - Cl (f.n. Stretton), *Dovecoat(e) Close* (f.n. Belton, Braunston, N. Luffenham, Whitwell), *Dovecote Close* (f.n. Ayston), *Dovecoteyarde* (f.n. Lyddington), *the Old Dovecoat* (Normanton).

dove-house eModE, 'a dove-cote'.

Doue House (Empingham), Dove House Cl (f.n. Langham).

drāf OE, 'a herd, a drove'; also 'a road on which cattle are driven'.

Drove Cl (f.n. Glaston, Teigh), *Drove Leyes* (f.n. Uppingham).

drak ME, 'a drake'.

? *drakehome* (f.n. Morcott).

drift ModE, 'a track along which cattle are driven'.

The Drift (Barrowden, Pickworth, Ryhall). Big Drift (f.n. Caldecott), Drift (Essendine), - Cl (f.n. Ketton), - Furlong (f.n. Seaton), Drift North of the Town, West Leys Drift (Seaton), *The Drift Way* (Thistleton).

dropi ON, 'a drop, a drip, that which drips', prob. with reference to a stream.

Drop Hills (f.n. Egleton).

drȳge OE, 'dry'; in later f.ns. 'well-drained'.

Stoke Dry. Freq. in f.ns., e.g. *Drie Close* (Burley), *Dry Close* (Hambleton, N. Luffenham, Stretton), Dry Cl (Cottesmore, Glaston, Greetham, Langham, S. Luffenham, Pilton, Teigh, Tinwell), - Fd (Clipsham, Pickworth, Tickencote), *Dry Ground* (Lt. Casterton), Dry Hill (Leighfield, Martinsthorpe), *Drie Lees* (Lyndon), Dry Lees (Empingham), Dry Nook Cl (Ketton), Dry Slight (Braunston).

dußr PrWelsh, 'water'.

R. Chater.

dūfe OE, **dúfa** ON, 'a dove'.

Dove Wong, ? *Dowsetts* (f.ns. Empingham).

dūn OE, 'a hill, a tract of hill country'.

Barrowden, Hambleton, Lyndon. Goddins (f.n. Mkt. Overton), ? *Mickleton Hill Furlong* (f.n. Whissendine).

dūne late OE, 'down, below; a place lower down than another'.

Down Croft (f.n. Teigh), *Downhall* (Seaton).

eā OE, 'a river, a stream'.
Eye Brook, Ketton. *Emedw* (f.n. Barrow), ? *Mawsey Beck* (Morcott).
eahta OE, 'eight'.
Eyghacres (f.n. Lyddington).
earm OE, 'wretched, poor'.
Armley Wood. *Armslades* (f.n. Barleythorpe).
ears OE, 'a buttock; a rounded hill'.
Broadarse (f.n. Manton), ? *Pepinherse* (f.n. Burley).
ēast OE, 'east'.
East Hundred. Freq. in f.ns., e.g. *Estcroft, Esthalfbradthorn* (f.ns. Bisbrooke), *le Estfeld* (f.n. Tinwell), *le Esthawe* (f.n. Stretton), *le Esthay* (f.n. Barrowden), *Estholm, Estmor* (f.ns. Mkt. Overton), *Estmedewong* (f.n. Caldecott), *est syck* (f.n. Egleton).
ēasterra OE, 'more eastern'.
ester syke (f.n. Egleton).
-ede OE adj. suffix, used to form adjs. from nouns (ESt xliii 43 corrects Elements *s.v.* -ed³).
Stump Stone (Ryhall).
ēg OE, 'an island; land partly surrounded by water; well-watered land, a water-meadow'.
? *goldney* (f.n. Wardley).
egg ON, 'an egg'; but also eModE dial. for 'the snowberry (*Symphoricarpus racemosus*)'.
Egg Spinney.
elbowe ME, 'an elbow; a sharp bend' (OE *elnboga* 'an elbow').
Elbowes (f.n. Oakham), Elbow Fd (f.n. Lyddington), *Elbow Leys* (f.n. Manton).
ellern, ellen, elle OE, 'an elder-tree'.
Elde Stump (f.n. Manton), Elder Stump Cl (f.n. Ketton), Eldern Stump, ? *Elgate* (f.ns. Whissendine), *Woole Elders* (f.n. Bisbrooke).
elm OE, 'an elm-tree'.
Almawewonge (f.n. Lt. Casterton).
ende[1] OE, **endi** ON, 'an end, the end of something, the edge of an estate, district or quarter of a village or town'.
Freq. in f.ns., esp. prefixed by *tūn* 'village', e.g. *the Town end* (Tixover), *Towne end close* (Egleton), Townend (Essendine), - Cl (Glaston, Manton, Tinwell, Whissendine), - Fd (Cottesmore), *Town End fur'* (Morcott), *(the) Town(e)s End* (Burley, Greetham, Edith Weston), - *Close* (Oakham), Townsend (Hambleton), - Cl

(Oakham, Pilton), - Mdw (Lyndon), *Townsend Leys* (Belton). Other compounds include *Batesmore End* (N. Luffenham), *the Brewhouse End* (Oakham), *Codslane end* (Braunston), *le Grasse Ends* (Barleythorpe), *Grove End* (Burley), Lands End (Empingham), *the Penn End* (Lyndon), *Street Ende* (Greetham).

eng ON, 'a meadow, pasture'.
Fairly freq. in f.ns., e.g. Broadeng Mdw, *Mykeleng* (Tinwell), *Horenggewong* (Caldecott), Little 'Uns (Mkt. Overton), Middlings (Teigh), West Ings (Whissendine).

eorl OE, 'a nobleman'.
? *Yellsmoor Slade* (Uppingham).

eorð-burg OE, 'an earthwork'.
? *Arberry Gate* (Morcott).

eowu OE, 'a ewe'.
Ewes Close (f.n. Hambleton).

erber, herber ME from OFr, 'a grass-covered piece of ground, a garden, an orchard'.
ye Arbour (f.n. Lyndon), ? *Close called the Herbar* (f.n. Gt. Casterton).

-erie ME noun suffix denoting 'that which is characteristic of, all that is connected with', used mostly with contemptuous implication.
? *Quintrey Lane* (Braunston).

erð OE (Angl), 'ploughed land'.
the Earth Close (f.n. Edith Weston).

estraieure OFr, 'possessions left without an heir and which passed to the lord'.
? *Stray Lands* (f.n. Whissendine).

*estre OE, 'a sheepfold'.
Estrewellewong (f.n. Mkt. Overton).

-et(t) OE, **-et(e)**, **-ett(e)** ME noun suffix denoting 'a place characterized by what is named'.
? *Clagett Rode* (Leighfield), Flasket Leys (f.n. S. Luffenham).

fæger OE, 'fair, beautiful, pleasant'.
Fair Ash Sale (Leighfield), *Fair Oake Hill* (Beaumont Chase).

fætt OE, 'fed up for slaughter, fatted'.
Fatt Sheep Close (f.n. Normanton).

fald, falod OE, 'a fold, a small enclosure for animals'.
Fauldal(l) Wood (Greetham), *Foldehaluacre* (f.n. Mkt. Overton), *Fouldhill* (f.n. Braunston).

*falding OE, 'the act of folding animals'.
Folding Furlong (f.n. Manton).

falh, falg OE (Angl), 'land broken up for cultivation, ploughed land', later 'ploughed land left uncultivated for a year, fallow land'.
? *Faleys* (f.n. Bisbrooke), *Le Fallow Feild* (f.n. Empingham), Fallow Cl (f.n. Seaton), - Mdw (f.n. Pilton), Far Fallow Fd (f.n. Greetham), ? The Follies (f.n. S. Luffenham).

*(ge)fall OE (Angl), 'a falling, a place where something falls', whence 'a felling of trees'.
? *Faleys* (f.n. Bisbrooke), *Fallesmyll'* (Lyddington), *ston fall* (Egleton), ? The Follies (f.n. S. Luffenham).

fearn OE, 'a fern'.
Feernegate, Feernsyke (f.ns. Cottesmore).

feather-bed ModE dial., 'something soft and yielding; spongy ground, a quagmire'.
Feather Bed Lane (Leighfield, Ridlington).

feeding ModE dial., 'grazing ground or pasture land, pasturage'.
Feeding Cl (f.n. Barrowden, Ridlington), - Fd (f.n. Braunston, Oakham), *The Feeding Ground* (f.n. Ketton).

feire ME, 'a fair, a gathering of merchants'.
Horse Fair Leyes (f.n. Uppingham).

feld OE, 'open country', **feld(e)** ME, 'land for pasture or cultivation'.
Chapel Field Spinney, Leighfield, Parkfield, Southfield Lodge. Only in Leighfield does the el. occur in its very early sense 'open country'. Freq. in early f.ns. with the sense 'common arable field', the great open-field of a medieval village. These typically occur in groups of three, e.g. *Nortfeld, Suthfeld, le Westfeld* (Oakham), *le Eastfelde, le Southefeld, le Westfelde* (Clipsham). Early examples of 'east -', 'north -', 'south -', 'west -' and 'middle field' in various combinations occur in the following parishes: Ashwell, Barleythorpe, Barrow, Bisbrooke, Burley, Lt. Casterton, Clipsham, Cottesmore, Egleton, Empingham, Exton, Glaston, Greetham, Hambleton, Ketton, S. Luffenham, Lyndon, Manton, Normanton, Oakham, Mkt. Overton, Pilton, Stretton, Teigh, Thistleton, Tickencote, Tinwell, Tixover, Uppingham, Edith Weston, Whissendine, Wing. Cf. also *Chirchefeld, le Oldefelde* (Lt. Casterton), *le Crosfeld, Schapelfeld* (Lyndon), *Kyrke Fylde* (Greetham), *le parkefeld'* (Lyddington), *Scapewellefeld, Stonfeld* (Barrowden), *Upfeld* (N. Luffenham). In Burley, *Newfeild* of 1601

indicates Elizabethan enclosure.

fen(e)kel ME, 'fennel'.

? Finkey St.

fenn OE, 'a fen, a marsh, marshland'.

Fengate (Oakham), *at(t)e Fenne* (p) (Burley, Ketton), Fernham Furlong (f.n. N. Luffenham), Quake Fen (f.n. Whissendine), Nether Cotch Fern (f.n. Ridlington), Scotch Fens (f.n. Preston), Warboys Fen (f.n. Gt. Casterton).

feor OE, **fur(re)** ME, **fur** ModE dial., **far** ModE, 'far, distant'.

Farr(e) Close (f.n. Ashwell, Hambleton), *the far ford, the Farr Meadow, Linden fur Close* (f.ns. Edith Weston), *Farr Field* (f.n. Clipsham), *Furhill* (f.n. Oakham), *(The) Furr Close* (f.ns. Hambleton, Lyndon, Mkt. Overton), *Mr Rays Fur Peice* (f.n. N. Luffenham).

feorðung, feorðing OE, 'a fourth part, a quarter'.

Farding Green Furlong (f.n. Greetham).

feower OE, 'four'.

the fower acres (f.n. Seaton).

ferme OFr, ME, 'rent', **farme** eModE, 'land held on lease, a farm, an agricultural tenement'.

le Ferme Place (Barrowden), *the great Farme Peece* (f.n. Bisbrooke). Common in modern minor p.ns.

fif OE, 'five'.

the Five Closes (f.n. Hambleton), *Fyuacrewong* (f.n. Caldecott).

finc OE, 'a finch'.

Finchley Bridge.

fisc-pōl OE, 'a fish-pond'.

le Fispol (Oakham), *Fisshepool ʒerd'* (f.n. Barrow).

flak ME, 'a turf'.

Flaxmans Slade (f.n. N. Luffenham).

flaishet, flasket ModE dial., 'swampy or waterlogged land'.

Flasket Leys (f.n. S. Luffenham).

flasshe, flosshe, flask ME, 'a swamp, swampy grassland'.

The Flashes (f.n. Whissendine), *Flush fur'* (f.n. Egleton).

flat ON, 'a piece of level ground', **flat** ModE dial., 'a division of a field'.

(The) Flats (f.n. Ridlington, Whissendine), *Flat Seeks* (f.n. Leighfield), *Kirkcroft Flatt* (f.n. Lyddington), *Mannell Flatt* (f.n. Greetham).

flax-yerde ME, 'an enclosure where flax is grown'.

le Flaxeyerde (f.n. Whissendine).

fleax OE, **flax** ME, 'flax'.

Flax Cl (f.n. Glaston), Flax Hole Mdw (f.n. Teigh), *Flaxlandes* (f.n. Morcott), Flax Leys (f.n. Whissendine).

flēoge OE, 'a fly'.

Fluill hill furlong (f.n. Lyddington).

flēot OE, 'a small stream'.

Fleet Cl (f.n. Ketton), - Mdw (f.n. Braunston), *fleetefurlong, Sowyt Flet, Tyflet* (f.ns. Teigh), *flet landes* (f.n. Egleton).

(ge)flit OE, 'strife, dispute', used in p.ns. of land in dispute.

Flitteris Park.   *Flithulle* (f.n. Oakham).

*flodder ME, 'mire, a boggy place'.

Floddreacre (f.n. Uppingham).

fola OE, 'a foal'.

Foal's Cl (f.n. Stretton), *Fole Close* (f.n. Ridlington).

folie OFr, ME, 'folly; an extravagent or (later) bogus building'.

Brooms Folly (Edith Weston), *Collin's Folly* (Uppingham), The Folly (Belton), Folly Gardens (f.n. Ketton).

forca OE, ' a fork', for 'land shaped like a fork'.

the Forcklese (f.n. Edith Weston).

ford OE, 'a ford'.

Ford, Salters Ford Lane.   Fairly freq. in f.ns.; the el. may be compounded with the names of associated fauna, e.g. *Fynchefordebrig* (Belton), *Padokeford', Padox ford* (Caldecott, Lyddington), or flora, e.g. *Redfoard* (Empingham); the underfoot conditions may be indicated, e.g. *Lamford* (Barrowden), *Staney Ford Willows* (Whissendine), Stanwell Ford Close (f.n. Hambleton), or way-marking, e.g. Stablesford Bridge (Ryhall).   Cf. also *Park Ford* (Egleton), *Thuiford* (Oakham), *into wenge forde* (Ayston).

forest OFr, ME, 'a large tract of woodland or of hunting country; a forest'.

Rutland Forest.   *The Forrest Close* (f.n. Leighfield), *the Forrest hedge* (Belton).

forester ME, 'a forester, an officer in charge of a forest'.

? *Forethers hous* (Lyddington).

forked ME, 'shaped like a fork, bifurcate, branching'.

Forked Bushes (f.n. Lyndon).

*forst OE, 'a ridge'.

Forest Wells (f.n. Morcott).

foss[1] OE, 'a ditch'.

Fosse Lane, ? Foster's Bridge.
fōt OE, 'a foot', used of 'the foot of a hill'.
Clay Foot (f.n. S. Luffenham).
fox-hol OE, 'a fox-hole, a fox's earth'.
Foxhole Acre (f.n. Barrowden), *Foxhol(e)s* (f.n. Normanton, Oakham), - *furlong* (f.n. Caldecott), Foxholes (f.n. Essendine, Whissendine), - Mdw (f.n. Langham), Foxhole Spinney (f.n. Glaston).
frēo OE, 'free from service or charge'.
The Freewards. *Freewoods* (Leighfield).
frere ME, 'a friar, a member of one of the mendicant orders, a "brother" of a military order'.
? (The) Fronald (f.ns. Lyddington, Stoke Dry).
friŏ OE, 'refuge, protection'.
? *Fridwod* (Ridlington).
frogga OE, 'a frog'.
Frog Hall.
fūl OE, 'foul, dirty, filthy'.
Fulcrofte (f.n. Egleton), *Fullwellhead* (f.n. Empingham), *Fulwell* (f.n. Lyddington), - *Sick* (f.n. Belton), *Fulwood* (Greetham).
furh OE, 'a furrow, a trench'.
Occasionally in f.ns., e.g. *the waterforowes* (f.n. Teigh), *(the) Water Furrow(e)s* (f.ns. Edith Weston, Uppingham), Water Furrows (f.n. Essendine, Greetham, Morcott), - Furlong (f.n. N. Luffenham). Cf. also *Gadman Furrow fur'* (f.n. Greetham), *Holefurbalke* (f.n. Tixover), *Hole Furrow* (f.n. Barleythorpe), Sandfurrows Cl (f.n. Ketton); Furrow Cl (f.n. Thorpe by Water).
furlang OE, 'a piece of land the length of a furrow', later 'a division of the common field cultivated as a unit'.
Freq. in f.ns., e.g. *Crakepornfurlong'*, *Dedemansforlang*, *Gluckffurlang* (f.ns. Barrow), *Gerberdfurlang, le Santfurlang* (f.ns. Wing), *Hunisforlang* (f.n. N. Luffenham), *Lyngefurlonges* (f.n. Cottesmore). Many of the 'field-names' in ME sources are furlong-names.
fyrhŏ, (ge)fyrŏe OE, 'land overgrown with brushwood, scrub'.
Frith Fm., ? *Fridwod* (Ridlington).
fyrs OE, 'furze'.
Firs (f.n. Preston), *The Furres Leies* (f.n. Belton), Furze Cl (f.n. Glaston, Gunthorpe, Lyndon, Stoke Dry), the Furze hill (f.n. Oakham).

*fyrsig OE, 'growing with furze'.
Furry Close, Furzy Lindin hill (f.ns. Hambleton), Furzy Cl (f.n. Ridlington).

gadman ME, 'a goadsman'.
? *Gadman fur'* (f.n. Greetham).

gærs, græs, gres OE, 'grass'; in modern f.ns. as **grass** 'land put down to grass, a piece of grassland'.
Fairly freq. in f.ns., e.g. *ye Grasse* (N. Luffenham), *Bullgrass(e) furlong* (Barleythorpe, Egleton), *(The) Constables Grass* (Pilton, Edith Weston), *Stentgrass, Grascroft* (Lyddington), *Grescroft* (Oakham), *Grasse Ground* (Burley). In modern f.ns., occasionally prefixed by the surn. of the owner/tenant, e.g. Newell's Grass (Bisbrooke).

galga OE, 'a gallows'; because of difficulty in distinguishing upper case C from G in some early scripts, some names attributed to *galga* in county p.n. surveys may belong to *calu* 'bare, lacking in vegetation'.
? *Gallow Hill* (Uppingham), Gallows Peice (f.n. Oakham), ? *Galowe hill furlong* (f.n. Caldecott), ? *Galowong* (f.n. Lyddington).

galg-trēow OE, 'a gallows-tree, a gallows'.
Gallowtree hill (Ryhall).

galla OE, 'a sore; a wet place in a field'.
Occasionally in f.ns., e.g. *the Galls* (Bisbrooke), *Stone-gals Furlong* (Manton), Straw Gall (Tickencote), *le Watergalle* (Lt. Casterton), *(les) Watergaules* (Barleythorpe, Oakham, Uppingham).

galte ME, 'a boar, a pig'.
Galtesgate (f.n. Lyddington).

gappe ME, 'an opening in a wall or fence'.
In later minor names, the references appear freq. to be openings through fenced parish boundaries, e.g. Thistleton Gap, cf. *Aston gapp* (Uppingham), *Glaston Gap* (Bisbrooke), *South Luffenham Gap* (Morcott), *Weston Gapp(e), Witchley Gap* (N. Luffenham), Wing Gap (Glaston). *ye Postgapp* (Thistleton) refers to the point at which the post-road crossed the county boundary. Prefixed surnames indicate openings into fenced private properties, e.g. Fenton Gap (Morcott), *Willcoxe Gap* (Uppingham). Cf. also *Open Gap Close* (f.n. S. Luffenham) referring to a type of enclosure with no permanent gates.

gāra OE, 'a gore, a triangular plot of ground, a point of land'.

Occasionally in f.ns., e.g. *le Goris* (Stoke Dry), *Moregore* (Langham), *Priest Gore* (Manton), *tirngore* (Barrowden).

garderobe ME, 'a closet, a privy'.

Garderobes (f.n. Lyddington).

gardin ME, 'a garden, an enclosed plot'.

gardinum extra castrum (Oakham).

garðr ON, **garth** ME, 'an enclosure'.

Garth (f.n. Ashwell), *le Garyth* (f.n. Oakham).

gata ON, 'a way, a road, a street'.

Aldgate, Hungate Fm, Redgate, Ry Gate Plantation. Freq. in f.ns.; it may be prefixed by a village name, e.g. *Burlye gate* (Exton), *Extongate* (Cottesmore), *Gunthorpe Gate* (Egleton), *Pilton Gate* (N. Luffenham); compounded with an el. indicating topography, e.g. *le Hilgate* (Barrow), *le Holgate, le Ridgate* (Wing), *Wellegate* (Cottesmore); or with a minor name indicating location, e.g. *Caudwell gate* (Egleton), *Coumbewellegate* (Lyddington), *Toteshulgate* (Ridlington). The local flora may be indicated, e.g. *Ashegate* (Belton), *Feernegate* (Cottesmore), *Hesilgate* (Barrow), *Lymgate, Okesgate* (Morcott), *le welugate* (Barrowden). Grassy tracks are freq. recorded, e.g. *Grenegate* (Barleythorpe, Oakham, Tixover), *Greengate* (Lyndon, Uppingham, Wardley). Man-made structures are sometimes represented, e.g. *(le) Crossegate* (Barrow, Stoke Dry), *Milnegate* (Glaston), *Stanbriggate* (Bisbrooke), although human occupations are infrequent, e.g. *Constable Gate* (Morcott), *Saltergate* (Gt. -, Lt. Casterton). Many of these road names have survived as furlong-names, even when not specifically so designated; but sometimes a furlong-name is clearly indicated by the compound, as e.g. *Benethegate* (Langham), *ye halfe Mylnegate* (Lyndon), *ouer Stamfordgate* (Cottesmore), *be Westgate* (Mkt. Overton), *apud le wodgate* (N. Luffenham). In Oakham, *gata* was freq. used of a town street, e.g. *le gebutt gate, le Kirkgate, le Neugate, le Northgate, Westgate*.

gate-shadel ME, 'a cross-roads'.

Cross Roads Fm. Gate Shakleway Cl (f.n. Ketton).

geard OE, 'an enclosure, a yard'.

Freq. in f.ns., especially compounded with els. indicating husbandry, e.g. *Dovecoteyarde, Schepcoteȝerd* (Lyddington), *Fisshepoolȝerd'* (Barrow), Hog Yard (Empingham), *Oxe Yard* (Ayston), *the Ricke yeard* (Uppingham). Ownership is sometimes designated, e.g. *Guns yard* (Wing), Lincoln Yard (Lyndon),

Mathew Yard (Whissendine), *Tomblin's Yard* (Hambleton). Cf. also *Brende3erdes* (Mkt. Overton), *Thorntre 3ard* (Thistleton), The Tithe Yard (Whissendine), *the Water Yard* (Tixover).

geat OE, 'an opening, a gap, a gate'.
Hollygate Lodge. Gate Cl (f.n. Glaston), *Cheselden's Gate* (Edith Weston), *extra portam de Flyteris* (Oakham), ? *Littelheggegate* (Caldecott).

geoc[1] OE, 'a yoke, a wooden device for coupling two oxen or beasts together for drawing a plough; something resembling a yoke in appearance; a measure of land, a yoke of land'.
Yoke Crop (f.n. Caldecott).

geolu OE, 'yellow'.
Yeallow landes, Yellow lands furlong (f.ns. Morcott), *Yellows* (f.n. Oakham).

geong OE, 'young'.
Youngwood Sale (Leighfield).

gerd-landes OE (Angl), **yerdland** ME, **yardland** eModE, 'a square measure of a quarter of a hide (about 30 acres)'.
Occasionally in f.ns., principally of the 17th and 18th centuries, usually compounded with a surn. signifying ownership, e.g. *Bonners -, Rowlett's Yard Land* (Lyddington), *Bradleys -, Prestons Yard Land* (Manton), *Medwells -, Sewells Yard Land* (Preston). Cf. also *Ogdens -, Walkers half yard Land* (Belton); *The Great Yard Land* (Belton), *the small Yard Land* (Lyddington), *Two Yard Land* (Mkt. Overton).

gibet ME, 'a gallows, a gibbet'.
Gibbet Gorse. Bowlands Gibbet (Tickencote), *le gebutt gate* (Oakham).

glebe ME, 'glebe'.
The Glebe, Glebe Barn, Glebe Fm (Barrow, Empingham, Greetham, Tinwell), Glebe Farm Ho., Glebe Ho. Freq. in f.ns., e.g. (The) Glebe (Ayston, Burley, Langham, Egleton, Manton), Glebes (Ridlington), *(The) Glebe Close* (Glaston, Normanton), *the Gleab land* (N. Luffenham), *the Glebe Land(s)* (Belton, Bisbrooke), *the Meadow Gleebe land* (Barrowden).

gleoda OE (Angl), 'a kite, a bird of prey'.
? *gledene* (f.n. Bisbrooke).

glug ME, ' a clod'.
? *Gluckffurlang, le Glugg* (f.ns. Barrow).

gorebrode ME, 'a broad strip in a gore of an open-field'.

Garbage Holm (f.n. Wardley), *Garbridge Furlang* (f.n. Barleythorpe), Garbroads (f.n. Egleton), Gt. Garbage (f.n. Lyddington).

golde OE, 'a marigold'.

Gold Hills (f.n. Edith Weston).

gorst, gors OE, 'gorse, furze'. In modern names and f.ns., freq. in the sense 'a piece of ground covered with gorse, a fox-covert of gorse-bushes'.

The Gorse, Cottesmore Gorse, Gibbet Gorse, Ketton Gorse, Watkin's Gorse. In f.ns. and minor names, sometimes prefixed by the parish name, e.g. Glaston -, Gunthorpe -, Seaton -, Tixover Gorse, or by a surn., e.g. Campion's Gorse (Burley), Clarke's Gorse (Bisbrooke), Hale's Gorse (Hambleton), Wilson's Gorse (Oakham). As a f.n., often simplex, e.g. (The) Gorse (Ayston, Gt. Casterton), - Cl (Brooke, Hambleton, Preston, Ridlington, Teigh), - Fd (Stoke Dry, Tickencote). Gorse as animal-covert can be seen in such minor names as Gorse Cover (Burley), Foxearth Gorse, Warren Gorse (Cottesmore). For a detailed discussion of this el. in Rutland, *v.* Barrie Cox, 'Furze, gorse and whin: an aside on Rutland in the Danelaw', JEPNS 20 (1987-8), 3-9.

*gorstig OE, 'overgrown with gorse'.

Gossey Cl (f.n. Stretton), *Gossy Midlongs* (f.n. Teigh).

gōs OE, 'a goose'.

Geesemere Cl (f.n. Lyddington), *Goose Green* (f.n. Greetham), Gorsemoor Leys (f.n. Morcott), *Gosemore* (f.n. Glaston), *Gose Roodes* (f.n. Lyndon), *Gosholm* (f.n. Caldecott, N. Luffenham), *Goswell'* (f.n. Barrowden).

gooseberry eModE, 'a gooseberry'.

le Gooseberry Bush (f.n. Barleythorpe).

goter ME, 'a gutter'.

Croswell Gutter, Hangcock Well Gutter, Holywell Gutter (Manton), *the Water Gutter* (Lyndon).

græf OE, 'a digging, a grave, a pit, a trench'.

Becky's Grave (f.n. Empingham), *Boygraue* (f.n. Bisbrooke), *Boygreue,* Deadman's Grave Furlong (f.ns. N. Luffenham), Jackson's Grave (f.n. Greetham), Solomon's Grave (f.n. Mkt. Overton), *Stonegravehill* (f.n. Thistleton), ? Avenue Cl or Thistle Graves (f.n. Exton).

græfe OE, 'a grove, a copse, a thicket'.

Cuttgrave Leys (f.n. Manton).

grǣg[1] OE, 'grey'.

? *Greygate* (f.n. Seaton).

grǣg[2] OE, 'a badger'.

? *Greygate* (f.n. Seaton).

grāf OE, 'a copse'.

Barleythorpe Grove (Barleythorpe), *Grove End* (f.n. Burley), *Groue gate furlong* (f.n. Caldecott).

grandmother eModE, 'a grandmother, a female ancestor'; in f.ns. sometimes used of dower land for the support of the widow of the late owner.

Grammers (f.n. Wing), Grandmother's Cl (f.n. Edith Weston), ? Grannum Cl (f.n. Ketton).

grange ME from OFr, 'a grange, an outlying farm belonging to a religious house or to a feudal lord, where crops were stored'; also 'a homestead, small mansion or farmhouse, especially one standing by itself remote from others' (*v.* Croxton Grange L 2 100); often used in the names of more recent country houses, usually with an older p.n. prefixed, to convey a pretence of antiquity.

The Grange (Exton, Ketton, Oakham, Stoke Dry, Tinwell, Edith Weston, Wing), Grange Fm (Glaston, Thistleton), Ashwell Grange, Belmesthorpe Grange, Cottesmore Grange, Exton Grange, Ketton Grange, Kilthorpe Grange, Ryhall Grange, Seaton Grange, Tixover Grange. *grangea de Brooke* (Brooke), *grangia de Wenton* (Cottesmore).

grēat OE, 'thick, massive', ME 'big in size'.

Greteley (f.n. Essendine).

grendel OE, 'a gravelly place or stream'.

Grindle (f.n. Whissendine), Grindles Cl (f.n. Langham), *Grindle Syke* (f.n. Barleythorpe).

grēne[1] OE, 'green, grass-grown; young'.

Fairly freq. in f.ns., esp. prefixed to *gata* 'a road', e.g. *Greengate* (Lyndon, Uppingham, Wardley), *Greengateway* (Manton), (*le*) *Grenegate* (Barleythorpe, Oakham), *Grenegatebalke* (Tixover); *Greenhill* (Barleythorpe, Lyndon, Manton), *Grenhil* (Lt. Casterton), *Grenehowe* (Cottesmore), *Greenwood* (Beaumont Chase), *Grinley Corner* (Belton).

grēne[2] OE, 'a grassy spot, a village green'.

The Green (Ayston, Barrow, Barrowden, Braunston, ' Caldecott, Exton, Ketton, Lyddington, Morcott, Mkt. Overton, Thorpe by Water). Freq. in earlier minor names and f.ns., e.g. *atte Grene* (p)

RUTLAND

342

(Egleton, Langham, Tinwell, Uppingham), *la Grene* (Seaton), *The Green* (Greetham, Hambleton, Lyndon, Edith Weston); cf. also *(the) Bowling(e) green(e)* (Glaston, Hambleton, Uppingham), ? *conygreene* (Ridlington), *Goose Green, Farding Green Furlong, Thyckmore Grene* (Greetham), *le Smythie Grene* (Egleton).

grēot OE, 'gravel'.

Greetham.

*grindel-stān OE, 'a grindstone'.

Grindstone (f.n. Stretton).

*groten OE, 'made of particles' (in reference to some kind of sandy or gravelly soil).

grotten forll' (f.n. Egleton).

grund OE, 'ground; a stretch of land', later, 'a piece of land enclosed for agricultural purposes'.

Blackground, Great Ground Barn. Freq. in f.ns., esp. signifying condition or type of soil, e.g. Burnt Ground (Pickworth), Clay Ground (Ketton), Dry Ground (Lt. Casterton), *Light Ground* (Barleythorpe), *the Redground* (Barrowden), Redground (Bisbrooke, Seaton, Tinwell), Rough Ground (Whissendine), White Ground (Lt. Casterton); or location, e.g. *the Hall Grounds* (Burley), *the House Ground* (Greetham), *the Pond Ground* (Brooke), *the Town(e) Ground* (Bisbrooke, Morcott). Ownership/tenancy may be indicated, e.g. Bank's Ground (Leighfield), *Dalbies Ground* (Burley), *Garners grounds* (Tickencote), *Thomas Massyes ground* (Glaston), Wootton's Ground (Tixover); or crops, e.g. *Grasse Ground* (Burley), *Hop Ground* (Glaston), (The) Hop Ground (S. Luffenham, Seaton). Note also such recurring compounds as Great Ground(s) (Empingham, Glaston, Stoke Dry, Teigh), *Midle grounde* (Ayston), Middle Ground (Gunthorpe, Ryhall), Rising Ground (Bisbrooke, Glaston).

*gylde OE, 'a golden flower'.

Guildings (f.n. Ryhall).

gylden OE, 'golden', literally as to colour, figuratively as to fertility.

goldney (f.n. Wardley), *Guilton fur'* (f.n. Egleton).

gypsey eModE, 'a gipsy'.

Gipsey Close (f.n. Egleton), Gipsy's Quick (f.n. Gt. Casterton).

hæc(c) OE (Angl), 'a hatch, a grating, a half-gate, a gate'; also 'a sluice-gate'.

Heck Balk Furlong (f.n. Morcott), *Heckleyn Seeke* (f.n.

Whissendine), *Nuthatch* (f.n. Braunston).

hæfer[1] OE, **hafr** ON, 'a he-goat', difficult to distinguish from ***hæfera** OE, **hafri** ON, 'oats'.

? *Hauerdale* (f.n. Lt. Casterton), ? Haverhill (f.n. Seaton).

*hæfera OE, **hafri** ON, 'oats', difficult to distinguish from **hæfer**[1] OE, **hafr** ON, 'a he-goat'.

? *Hauerdale* (f.n. Lt. Casterton), ? Haverhill (f.n. Seaton), *Haverlands* (f.n. N. Luffenham).

(ge)hæg OE, **hay** ME, 'a fence, an enclosure, a fenced-in enclosure'.

the haies (f.n. Belton), *le Haye* (f.n. Ashwell), *hay bridge* (Lyddington), Barkers Hey, Heigh Cl (f.ns. S. Luffenham), Barrowden Hay, *le Westhay* (f.ns. Barrowden), *Barradon Hayfeild* (f.n. Ketton), *Heybryggeholm* (f.n. Langham), Lockhaye Cl (f.n. Ridlington).

*hægen OE, 'an enclosure'.

Hayne Ho.

hæl OE, 'omen, good fortune', **hælu** OE, 'health, healing, cure'.

Helwell' (f.n. Oakham), *Hellwell medowe* (f.n. Teigh).

hæsel OE, **hesli** ON, 'a hazel'.

Crooked Hasels (f.n. Leighfield), Haseldyke (f.n. Morcott), Hazel's (f.n. Greetham), Hazlegate (f.n. Glaston), *Heseldal'*, *Hesilgate*, *Longhesil* (f.ns. Barrow), *Hesyllgate* (f.n. Cottesmore), *smalheasels* (f.n. Egleton).

hæð OE, 'heath, heather; a heath'.

Heath Lodge, Couzens Heath, South Luffenham Heath, Old Heath Lodge, Ryhall Heath Fm. Common in minor names in the eastern half of the county, esp. prefixed by a village name, e.g. *Exton Heath* (Empingham), *Normanton Heath* (Empingham, Edith Weston), *Ryhall Heath* (Lt. Casterton), *Thistleton Heath* (Greetham, Stretton). Cf. also The Heath (Gt. Casterton, Empingham, Normanton, Edith Weston), *Barrow Heath Piece, New Heath, Old Heath Furlong* (f.ns. Barrow), *on the side of the Heath* (f.n. Cottesmore).

hafoc OE, 'a hawk'.

Hawkswell Spring. ? *Hawkeslands* (f.n. Greetham), *Hawkswell Close* (f.n. Barrow).

haga[1] OE, 'a hedge, an enclosure'.

Wilkershaw. *Almawewonge, Bochawesti, Litelhawewonge, Rochaue* (f.ns. Lt. Casterton), *le Esthawe, Lyttilhawe, Westhawewong* (f.ns. Stretton), *Frontenehaue* (f.n. Stoke Dry), *Withawe Pitts* (f.n. Pickworth), ? Lullhaugh Cl (f.n. Whissendine).

hagu-þorn OE, 'the hawthorn, the whitethorn'.
Hawthorne hill (f.n. Ayston), Hawthorn Mdw (f.n. Wardley).
half OE, 'a half'.
Halfacrewong (f.n. Lyddington), *ye halfe Mylnegate* (f.n. Lyndon), *Halffmylle Busk, Foldehaluacre* (f.ns. Mkt. Overton), *Esthalfbradthorn* (f.n. Bisbrooke), *Welhalfager* (f.n. Lt. Casterton).
halh OE, 'a nook; a corner of land; a water-meadow; a piece of land almost enclosed by a bend of a river; a secluded valley' etc.
Hollygate Lodge, Ryhall. *ye Hale* (f.n. Lyndon).
hālig OE, 'holy, sacred'; perhaps *hali-welle, holi-welle* ME, 'holy spring' could be considered a common el.
Holyoaks. *Halywelcros* (Barrowden), *Hollywell slades* (f.n. Barleythorpe), Holywell (Seaton), *Holy Well Close* (f.n. Hambleton), *Holywell Gutter* (Manton).
hall OE (Angl), 'a hall, a large residence, a manor house'.
Ayston Hall, Barleythorpe Hall, Brooke Hall, Luffenham Hall, Lyndon Hall, Preston Hall, Tixover Hall, Tolethorpe Hall, Wing Hall; Hall Close, Moorhall, Newell Wood, Old Hall (Exton, Hambleton, Mkt. Overton, Ridlington, Wing), Old Hall Fm, Upper Hall. Cf. also *Hallofstag* (Lyddington), *Downhall, Ivyehall, Vphalle* (Seaton). Occasionally in f.ns., e.g. *the halls* (Preston), The Hall Cl · (Barrowden), Hall Wong (Whissendine).
hām OE, 'a village, an estate, a homestead', (*v.* Barrie Cox, 'The significance of the distribution of English place-names in *-hām* in the Midlands and East Anglia', JEPNS 5 (1972-3), 15-73).
Clipsham, Empingham, Greetham, ? Langham, Luffenham (N. and S.), Oakham, Uppingham. ? *þornham broc* (Ayston).
hamm OE, 'an enclosure, a water-meadow, land in the bend of a river' etc. (*v.* J. McN. Dodgson, 'Place-names from *hām*, distinguished from *hamm* names, in relation to the settlement of Kent, Surrey and Sussex', ASE 2 (1973), 1-50).
? Langham. Very freq. in f.ns., invariably as a second el., e.g. *Beanham* (Tickencote), Broadham Cl (Ketton), Girnam, *Millhams* (Hambleton), Longham (Greetham), *Millam Bridg* (Braunston), *Pansham Mead,* The Thackhams (Langham), *Shortham piece* (Manton), *Spongham* (Lyndon), Spongham's Mdw (Pilton), *thackham medowe* (Teigh), ? *þornham broc* (Ayston). Uniquely as a simplex, Ham (Whissendine).
*hamol OE, 'flat-topped'.
Hambleton.

hām-stede OE, 'a homestead'; later 'a house with its dependent buildings, esp. a farmstead'.

Britain's Old Homestead, Craddocks Homestead, Homestead with Clarks Cottage (N. Luffenham), Elm Tree Homestead, Sidneys Homestead, Tyler's Homestead (Lyndon), *the Hall homestead, Taylors House and Homestead* (Glaston), Ham's Homestead (Wardley), Homestead (Brooke), the Homestead or Old Inclosure (Manton), *Homesteads or Old Inclosures* (Barleythorpe), Top Homestead (Essendine).

hāmweard OE, 'towards home'.

The Homeward Acre (f.n. N. Luffenham), The Homeward Land (f.n. S. Luffenham).

hand OE, 'a hand'; in f.ns., possibly used with reference to land tilled by spade rather than by plough.

Handacre (f.n. Lt. Casterton, Lyddington), - *furlong* (f.n. Caldecott).

hangende OE, 'hanging', of places on steep slopes.

le Hangendehill' (f.n. Glaston), *Hangendewong* (f.n. Lyddington), *hanging balk* (f.n. Pilton), Hanging Balk (f.n. Whitwell), *hanging Crosse* (Wing), *le Hanging Leys* (f.n. Oakham), *Hanging Peice* (f.n. Stretton, Tickencote), Hanging Shelf (f.n. Essendine), Hanging Side (f.n. Tixover).

hār² OE, 'grey, hoar', esp. 'grey through being overgrown with lichen'; also 'boundary'.

Harethornes (f.n. Pickworth, Ridlington), Harton (f.n. Clipsham), *Horenggewong* (f.n. Caldecott), *Horeston* (f.n. N. Luffenham), ? *Arberry Gate* (f.n. Morcott).

hara OE, 'a hare'.

? Haremouth Cl (f.n. Teigh), Hare Park (f.n. Stretton).

hassuc OE, 'a clump of coarse grass'.

Hassocks (f.n. Seaton), Hassock's Holme (f.n. Whissendine).

haugr ON, 'a natural height, a hill, a heap, an artificial mound, a burial mound'.

Fairly freq. in f.ns. in the eastern half of the county, e.g. *Bole howe* (Thistleton), *Grenehowe* (Cottesmore), *Hene Houe* (Lt. Casterton), *Litelhowe* (N. Luffenham), *Lynghau* (Tinwell); occasionally as the initial el. in a compound, e.g. *Howhedge, How-wrong* (Morcott), *Howinge Meadow* (Ryhall).

hēafod OE, 'a head; the (top) end of something, a headland, a promontory; the source of a stream'.

Woodhead. Freq. in f.ns., e.g. *Bedwell head* (N. Luffenham),

Fullwellhead (Empingham); *Fulcroft Hades* (Egleton), *Godyehades* (Ashwell), *Martinsthorpe hades, Mill hades* (Manton), *Morehead* (Braunston), *Porthades* (Empingham), *Schucheved* (Lt. Casterton).

hēafod-land OE, 'a strip of land at the head of a furlong, left for turning the plough'.
Freq. in f.ns., usually with a surn. prefixed, e.g. *George Austins headland, Joseph Cookes hadland, Thomas Islipp the smith's hadland* (Edith Weston), *Harbottles headland, Kimberleys hedland, Warrens headlond* (Oakham), *knyttyshadlond, morishadlond* (N. Luffenham). Common also is a prefixed p.n. or f.n., e.g. *Black Wong Headland* (Bisbrooke), *Stanhill hauedelond* (Stoke Dry), *Wellemorheuedlandes* (Caldecott). Common is *Church Hadland* (Uppingham), *- Hedlond* (Greetham), *- Headland* (S. Luffenham, Morcott, Edith Weston), *Church Headlands* (Braunston). The simplex *Heuedlandes* (Lyddington), *Headlands* (Preston, Wing) is rare.

hēah[1] (**hēan** wk. obl.) OE, **hēh** (Angl), **high** ModE, 'high, tall, important; lying high up, standing in a high place, prominent'.
High Moor, - Fm. *High Bush fur'* (f.n. Greetham), *The Heigh Feild* (f.n. Burley), *Heighe Meadow* (f.n. Lyndon), *the Hyghe meddowe* (f.n. Egleton), *Braunston high meadow* (f.n. Braunston), *the High Rodes* (f.n. Leighfield), *the Highestrete* (Barrowden), *High Thorne Nooke* (f.n. Empingham); with **hēan**, *Heynwyk'* (Stretton).

hēah-fore OE, 'a heifer'.
Heif(f)er Close (f.n. Greetham).

hēah-weg OE, 'a highway, a main road'.
ye highway (Lyndon).

hecg OE, 'a hedge'.
Black Hedge. Freq. in f.ns.; often compounded with parish names since hedges, esp. in the 17th cent., defined parish boundaries, e.g. *Clipsham Hedge* (Stretton), *Glaiston hedge* (Morcott), *Luffenham Hedge* (Lyndon, Edith Weston), *wingmeirhedg* (Pilton), cf. *le Meare hedge* (Barleythorpe), *the meere Hedge* (Glaston). Surnames are often compounded, indicating a landowner's boundary; examples date from the 14th and 15th centuries, e.g. *Hadmundheg'* (Bisbrooke), *Bylleshegge* (Cottesmore), but like parish boundary-hedges, are more common in the 17th cent., e.g. *John Ridlingtons Hedge* (Edith Weston), *Rowlatts Hedge* (Lyddington). Occasionally, a hedge's flora is specified, e.g. Crabtree Hedge Furlong (Lyddington), Gorse Hedges, *Swynetre Hedge Furlong* (Greetham), *the Quickhedge* (Uppingham).

hēg OE, 'hay, mowing grass'.
Hay Cl (f.n. Ketton), ? *Haye gatte* (Exton).
hell OE, 'hell'.
Helpitt dale (f.n. Lyndon).
hempland eModE, 'land appropriated to the growth of hemp; later
'a piece of land held by a small tenant, irrespective of the produce
of the soil'.
Hempland (f.n. Barrow), *the Hempland* (f.n. N. Luffenham), *Hemp
Lands* (f.n. S. Luffenham).
hemp-yard ME, 'an enclosure in which hemp is grown'.
Hemp Yards (f.n. S. Luffenham).
henn OE, 'a hen (esp. of wild birds); a water-hen' etc.
Henbecke (f.n. Hambleton), *Hene Houe* (f.n. Lt. Casterton),
Henneplot (f.n. Glaston), *Henn Hill fur'* (f.n. Greetham).
*hēns OE, 'poultry, a flock of hens'.
? *hennes croft* (f.n. Bisbrooke).
heorde-wīc OE, 'a herd farm'.
Hardwick Cottages.
hermitage ME from OFr, 'a hermitage'.
heremitagium de Nordwude (Clipsham), *The Hermitage* (Wardley).
*herse OE, 'a hill top'.
? *Pepinherse* (f.n. Burley).
hesli ON, 'a hazel', *v.* **hæsel**.
hīd OE, 'a hide of land; an amount of land for the support of one
free family and its dependents'.
Hide. Brightley Bridge Hide (f.n. Manton), *Pastmore hyde* (f.n.
Preston).
hlæfdige OE, **ladi** ME, 'a lady; a nun; Our Lady, the Virgin Mary';
often alluding to a female proprietor or a dowager or the lady of a
manor.
Lady Wood, Our Lady's Well. *Ladiakre* (f.n. Gt. Casterton), Lady's
Acre (f.n. Stoke Dry), *Ladie Close* (f.n. Burley), The Ladies Cl (f.n.
S. Luffenham), Lady Cl (f.n. Barleythorpe), *Lady-holme* (f.n.
Ridlington), Lady's Mdw (f.n. Whissendine), Lady Sale (Beaumont
Chase), Lady Spinney (Preston), *le Lady Wong* (f.n. Lt. Casterton),
Lady Wood Piece (f.n. (Oakham).
hlāford OE, 'a lord'.
ye Lords balke (f.n. Lyndon).
hlāw OE, 'a mound, a hill'.
Catlow (f.n. Beaumont Chase), *le Spellow* (f.n. Barleythorpe).

hlinc OE, 'a ridge, a bank; a ledge of ploughland on a hillside; an unploughed strip between fields'.
the Linche, Weldons Linche (f.ns. Wardley).

hliδ¹ OE, 'a slope, a hillside'.
Lithes (f.n. Seaton), *Litwood Hill* (f.n. Ryhall).

hlōse OE, 'a pig-sty', originally 'a shed, a shelter'.
Losecoat Field. *Loscoat(e)s* (Braunston), *Loscott sale* (Leighfield).

hlot OE, **lot** ME, ModE, 'a lot, a share, an allotment'.
The Lots (f.n. Seaton).

*hlȳde OE, ' a noisy stream' (literally 'the loud one').
? Lyddington.

hnutu OE, **hnot** ON, 'a nut', whence 'a nut-bearing tree'.
Notwells (f.n. Lyndon, Edith Weston), *Nuthatch* (f.n. Braunston).

hob, hobbe ME, 'a hobgoblin'.
? *Hob Hole* (f.n. Greetham).

hobb(e) OE, 'a tussock, a hummock'.
? *Hob Close* (f.n. Hambleton), ? *Hob Hole* (f.n. Greetham).

hōc OE, 'a hook, a projecting piece of ground'.
hook medows (f.n. Hambleton).

hog ModE dial., 'a shearling lamb'.
? *Hogg Home* (f.n. Whissendine), *Hog Leys* (f.n. Lt. Casterton).

hogg OE, 'a hog, a pig'.
Hogden Hill (f.n. Empingham), Hog's Hole (f.n. Braunston), Hog Hole (f.n. Lyddington, Morcott), *Hogstyes* (f.n. Oakham), Hog Yard (f.n. Empingham), ? *Hogg Home* (f.n. Whissendine).

hogg ON, 'a cutting or felling of trees', **hag(g)** ModE dial., 'a copse'.
Hag Meadow (f.n. Lt. Casterton).

hōh (**hōs** nom.pl.) OE, 'a spur of land'.
? Hooby Lodge. *Caleweho* (f.n. Tixover), *martines hó* (f.n. Ayston), *Hocroft* (f.n. Tickencote), *hotoft* (f.n. Bisbrooke); *Bottingeshowes, Sandhowes* (f.ns. Seaton).

hol¹ OE, 'a hole, a hollow'.
Hales Spinney. Freq. in f.ns., e.g. (*the*) *Holes* (Barrow, Pilton), *Cathole* (Braunston), *Cockadie Hole* (Wardley), *the Dogholes* (Uppingham).

hol² OE, 'lying or running in a hollow'.
Holbeck Lodge. Occasionally in f.ns., e.g. *holebroc* (Ayston), *le Holegate* (Wing), *Holfurbalke* (Tixover), *Holgate* (Stretton), ? Holwell (Hambleton).

holde ME, 'a possession, a holding'.
(The) Fronald (f.ns. Lyddington, Stoke Dry), *Holdmedow*, Lincoln's
Hold (f.ns. Hambleton), *Lincoln hold yard* (f.n. Lyndon), Remington
Hold Cl (f.n. Luffenham), Rimmingtons Hoole (f.n. Morcott).
holh (**holwe** dat. sg.) OE, 'a hole, a hollow'.
Hot Hollow Fm, Wing Hollow. Occasionally in f.ns., e.g. *the
Hollow(e)* (S. Luffenham, Edith Weston), *le Ololondes* (N.
Luffenham), Rice Hollow (Ryhall), Shacklewell Hollow (Tickencote).
holmr ON, 'a small island, a water-meadow'.
Broadholme, The Holmes. Very freq. in f.ns.; as a simplex, e.g. (*the*)
Holme (Belton, Caldecott, Hambleton, Stoke Dry), *Holmes*
(Essendine, Uppingham); compounded with owner's or tenant's name,
e.g. *Gerwaldesholm* (Uppingham), *Grimesholme* (Empingham),
Osbernholm (Whissendine), *Wolwardisholm* (Lyddington); with an el.
indicating flora, e.g. *Moss Holmes* (Edith Weston), *Risceholm* (Lt.
Casterton), *Thacholme* (Stoke Dry), *Wyleweholm* (N. Luffenham); or
fauna, e.g. *Bull Holme* (Morcott), *Gosholm* (Caldecott, N. Luffenham),
Horsholm (Lyddington), *Padholne, Piggs Holme* (Egleton). Size may
be indicated, e.g. Broadholme(s) (Ashwell, Morcott), *Great Holme*
(Greetham), *Longholm* (Glaston); or direction from a village, e.g.
Estholm, Northholm (Mkt. Overton), *Northolmwong, West homes
furlong* (Caldecott). It is esp. common in compound with **myln** 'a mill'
(as in Barrowden, Belton, Gt. Casterton, Empingham, Glaston,
Greetham, Ketton, N. and S. Luffenham, Manton, Oakham, Seaton,
Teigh, Tinwell, Tixover). Varieties of human suffering are suggested
by Deadmans Holme (Barrowden), *Sanam* (Hambleton), *Senholm*
(Mkt. Overton).
holt OE, 'a wood, a thicket, a holt'.
Cherry Holt (Glaston, Tinwell), *Freeman Holt* (Edith Weston), *Olive
holt Coppice* (Stoke Dry), *Osier Holt* (S. Luffenham), Ozier Holt
(Pilton, Tinwell), Spring Holt (Pickworth), Warren's Holt
(Empingham).
home ModE, 'near home'.
Occurs in most parishes in modern f.ns., esp. in the forms Home
Cl, Home Fd. The earliest instances date from the beginning of
the 17th cent., e.g. *Gutts home close* (Morcott), *Home Close*
(Ashwell, Greetham, Lyndon, Edith Weston), *Home Field*
(Clipsham), *Home Meadow* (Stretton).
hoppe ME, 'the hop-plant'.
Hop Ground (f.n. Glaston), (The) Hop Ground (f.ns. S. Luffenham,

Seaton).

hop-yard ModE, 'a hop-yard, a hop-garden, an enclosure where hops are grown'.

(the) Hop Yard (f.ns. Belton, Lyndon, Edith Weston).

horn OE, ON, ***horna** OE, 'a horn; a projection, a projecting feature; a horn-shaped feature'.

Horn. *Butterie Horne Close* (f.n. Stoke Dry).

hors OE, 'a horse'.

Horscroft, Horsholm, Longhorsewong (f.ns. Lyddington), *Horsecrafts* (f.n. Uppingham), *horse dales* (f.n. Barleythorpe), *horse Leies* (f.n. Tickencote), *Horseleys Way* (Edith Weston), *ye horsse myln* (Oakham), *Schorthorswong* (f.n. Caldecott).

hospital ME, 'a hospital'.

Bede Ho. (Lyddington), Hospital of St John (Oakham).

hovel eModE, 'a hovel, a shed; a frame or stand on which a stack of corn is built' (*v.* Db 757, YW 7 208).

Very freq. in f.ns.; the earliest form is *le upper Houel* (1667, Barleythorpe), but usually found as Hovel Cl (Ashwell, Belton, Gt. Casterton, Clipsham etc.); occasionally Hovel Fd (Manton, Martinsthorpe), Far - (Bisbrooke), Old - (Hambleton). Cf. also Hovel (Egleton), Bell's Hovel (Exton), Sheep Hovel Cl, the Waggon Hovel (S. Luffenham), Tin Hovel Fd (Mkt. Overton).

hrēac OE, 'a rick'.

the Ricke yeard (f.n. Uppingham).

hrēod OE, 'a reed, a rush'; also 'a reed-bed'.

Redebrug' (f.n. S. Luffenham), *Redespires* (f.n. Braunston), ? *Redbroke* (f.n. Horn), ? *Redwell* (f.n. Manton), ? Redwells (f.n. Gunthorpe).

hrīs OE, **hrís** ON, 'shrubs, brushwood'.

Flitteris Park. *Rice Furlong* (f.n. Greetham), Rice Hollow (f.n. Ryhall), *le risdale* (f.n. Barrowden), *Riseberwe* (f.n. Leighfield), *Rislonde* (f.n. Stoke Dry), *Stoke Rislonde* (f.n. Lyddington).

hrōc OE, **hrókr** ON, 'a rook'.

Rochaue (f.n. Lt. Casterton), Rook Cl (f.n. Ashwell).

*hrōst OE, 'a roost, a perch'.

The Roost (f.n. Egleton).

hrung OE, 'a rung, a pole'; used in p.ns. in some such sense as 'enclosed with poles' or 'logs set rung-wise to form a track over marshy ground'.

the rungs (f.n. Lyddington).

hrycg OE, 'a ridge, a long narrow hill'; in ME f.ns., 'a cultivated strip of ground'.
Acre Rigges (f.n. Lyndon), 1st -, 2nd Ridge (f.ns. Oakham), *Oakeham Ridgg* (f.n. Braunston), Ridgeway Furlong (f.n. Seaton), *Sprouridge* (f.n. Greetham).
hryggr ON, 'a ridge', used in the same way as **hrycg** which it sometimes replaces.
Acre Riggs (f.n. Teigh), *the Rigg* (f.n. Egleton).
hund OE, **hundr** ON, 'a hound'.
Hungate Fm.
hundred OE, 'an administrative division of a county, prob. consisting originally of 100 hides' (*v.* **hīd**).
Alstoe Hundred, East Hundred, *Hwicceslea east hundred, Hwiccleslea west hundred,* Martinsley Hundred, Oakham Soke Hundred, Wrangdike Hundred.
hunig OE, 'honey'.
Honey Holme (f.n. Egleton).
hūs OE, 'a house, a building'.
Woolfox. *bowthis howse, Forethers hous, Harresons howse* (Lyddington), *Brayeshouse* (Bisbrooke), *Deephouse* (Manton), *Irnhouse Sick* (f.n. Whissendine), *the kilne howse* (Preston), *Loues Hose, Walters Hose* (Lyndon), *le Slathouse, le White howse* (Egleton); *Hooss Piece* (f.n. Belton), *House Holme* (f.n. Egleton).
husbandman ModE, 'a tenant farmer; a smallholder'.
Husbandmans Cl (f.n. Ridlington).
hvarf ON, 'a bend, a nook, a corner'.
? Waffs (f.n. Whissendine).
*hvin ON, **whin** ME, 'whin, gorse'.
Wingate Furlong (f.n. Lyddington), Winsell (f.n. Mkt. Overton), ? Wind Gate Hill (f.n. Ryhall).
hwǣte OE (Angl), 'wheat'.
Whetefylde (f.n. Oakham), *Wheytlondes* (f.n. Cottesmore).
hwerfel OE (Angl), 'a circle'; used in p.ns. to denote something circular, such as 'a circular or round-topped hill'.
? *Far Wherles* (f.n. Barleythorpe).
Hwicce OE, a tribe which settled mostly in Gl and Wo.
? Whissendine, ? Witchley Warren Fm. ? Wichley Leys (f.n. Whissendine).
hwīt OE, 'white'; in eModE, *white* 'infertile' is contrasted with *black* 'fertile'. ModE dial. *white* is used of dry, open pasture.

Whitwell. *the Whites* (f.n. Lyndon), *White acre, White Cross* (f.ns.
Uppingham), *White Acres* (f.n. Hambleton), White Clay Furlong (f.n.
N. Luffenham), *Whitecross Furlong, Whitecroswong* (f.ns. Lyddington),
White Ground (f.n. Lt. Casterton), - Cl (f.n. Ketton), *Whitehill* (f.n.
Manton), *White Ingle Dale, White Lands* (f.ns. Ryhall), White Leys (f.n.
Burley), *White Five Acres,* Whiteroods (f.ns. Caldecott), *Whitteway
furlong,* White Wong (f.ns. Oakham), *White Wong Furlong* (f.n.
Normanton), *Whitthele* (f.n. Braunston); *the White howse* (Egleton).
hyll OE, 'a hill'.
Bee Hill, Mill Hill, Twitch Hill Fm. Very freq. in f.ns.; soil type may
be indicated, e.g. *cleay hill'* (Egleton), Clay Hill (Barleythorpe), *Stanhill*
(Stoke Dry), *Stonhill* (Thistleton); or size, shape, aspect, e.g. *Micle Hill*
(Belton), *Smallhill* (Braunston), *Cophill, Calouhill', le Hangendehill'*
(Glaston); or animals, e.g. Boar Hill (Lyddington), Cow Hill (Barrow);
or flora, e.g. *arnet hyll* (Egleton), *Brakenhul* (Bisbrooke), *lybrakehil* (N.
Luffenham), *Coppethornhull* (Lyddington); or birds, e.g. *Kite Hill fur'*
(Greetham). Ownership is sometimes indicated, e.g. *Monkyshill'*
(Wardley), *Willeshulles* (Mkt. Overton); or usage, e.g. *cepecotehyl* (N.
Luffenham), *Fouldhill* (Braunston), *Stonegravehill* (Thistleton), *Toft
Hill* (Cottesmore), *Wakehull* (Mkt. Overton). In Ru, the dial. form
hell developed from the 14th cent., hence *Helle* (Lt. Casterton), *Hell
fur', lytle hell* (Egleton), Little Hell, Winsell (Mkt. Overton), Hell Fd
(Morcott), Helland (Bisbrooke), *Dodesell* (Barrowden).
hyrne OE, 'an angle, a corner; a recess in a hill, a corner in a
valley; a projection of land'.
The Hurn. Cart Run (f.n. Stretton), *Crane Hurn,* Hambleton Hurn
(f.ns. Morcott), *Herne Meadow* (f.n. Egleton), Herne's Far Land,
Russell's Hern Cl (f.ns. Ridlington), Irnhouse Sick (f.n. Whissendine),
Walls Herne (f.n. Lyddington).

ifig OE, 'ivy'.
Ivyehall (Seaton), *Ivey House Close* (f.n. Ketton).
-ig³ OE suffix, mainly adjectival, **-i(e), -y(e)** ME, **-y** ModE adj.
suffix.
Brakey Close (f.n. Edith Weston), Brakey Cl (f.n. Pilton), *Breaky
Close* (f.n. Lyndon), *Butterie Horne Close* (f.n. Stoke Dry),
Winnigates Furlong (f.n. Lyddington).
impa OE, 'a young shoot'.
Umpthorne (f.n. N. Luffenham).
in OE preposition, 'in', sometimes with adj. force 'inner'.

Inclay fur' (f.n. Morcott), *Incrofte* (f.n. Barrowden), *Incroft Phillipi* (f.n. Empingham).

inclosure eModE, 'an inclosing, an enclosure'; a variant form of *enclosure*, being the statutory form in reference to the inclosing of waste lands, commons etc.

· Inclosure (f.n. S. Luffenham), *The New Inclosures* (f.n. Ayston), *the Homestead(s) or Old Inclosure(s)* (f.ns. Barleythorpe, Brooke, Manton), *Kilthorpe Old Inclosure, Wortwell Old Inclosure* (f.ns. Ketton), Old Inclosure little fd (f.n. Thorpe by Water).

infeld ME, 'an in-field, a field near a homestead'.

Pickworth Innfeild (f.n. Pickworth).

-ing¹ OE noun suffix.

ye Hadings (f.n. Empingham).

-ing² OE place-name-forming suffix.

Gold Hills (f.n. Edith Weston), *plashing, Wall Gressings* (f.ns. Hambleton).

-inga- OE, gen. of **-ingas**, 'of the people of -, of the people called after -'.

Empingham, Tinwell, Uppingham, ? Whissendine.

-ingtūn OE, added to a pers.n. to indicate an estate associated with that person.

Lyddington, Ridlington, *v.* **tūn.**

inhōke ME, 'land temporarily enclosed from fallow land for cultivation'.

Hanex (f.n. Clipsham).

*innām OE, **innám** ON, 'a piece of land taken in or enclosed'.

Innems (f.n. Braunston), - Fd (f.n. Bisbrooke), The Innem's (f.n. Uppingham), *Under Innammes* (f.n. Belton).

inntak ON, 'a piece of land taken in or enclosed'.

Intake (f.n. Essendine, Tinwell).

intercommon eModE, 'a common shared by two or more villages'.

The Intercommon lying part in the parish of Ketton and part in the parish of Empingham (*v.* Ketton f.ns. (b)).

jackanapes eModE, 'a mischievous boy, a 'monkey''; but also *Jackanapes · on horseback* was a 17th cent. name for a proliferous variety of cowslip (and daisy).

Jackanapes Nook (f.n. Ketton).

judge ModE, 'a judge'.

the Judges balke (f.n. Uppingham).

kide ME, 'a kid, a young goat'.
le kydhaker (f.n. N. Luffenham).
kirkja ON, 'a church'.
Church Fm, Ridlington Church. *le Kirkemedou* (f.n. Whissendine), *Kirke Meadow* (f.n. Thistleton), *Kirke sike* (f.n. Wing), *le Kirkgate* (Oakham), Kirk Hole (f.n. Mkt. Overton), Kirk Leys (f.n. Langham), *Kyrke Fylde* (f.n. Greetham), *Kyrkelane* (Clipsham), *le kyrkepittes* (f.n. S. Luffenham), ? *New Kirke* (f.n. Edith Weston), ? *New Kyrke* (f.n. Wardley).
kiteling ME, 'a cub, a whelp; a young cat'.
? Kittleng Hill (f.n. Barrowden).
kjarr ON, 'brushwood', **ker** ME, 'marsh; marshland overgrown with brushwood'.
Carrmeadow (f.n. Oakham), Long Carmen (f.n. Caldecott), Carwell Cl (f.n. Ketton).
kollr ON, 'a hill, a top, a summit'.
? Coll Hill (f.n. Essendine).
krókr ON, 'a crook, a bend; a nook, a secluded corner'.
the Crooks (f.n. Uppingham), *Crook Stockin* (f.n. Clipsham).
kytton ME, 'a kitten'.
Kyttan Close (f.n. Wardley).

*læc(c), ***læce** OE, **lache, leche** ME, 'a stream, a bog'.
Southeleche (f.n. Teigh).
læfer OE, 'a rush, a reed'.
Laber Sike (f.n. Wardley).
*læge OE, 'fallow, lying untilled'.
Ley Lands fur' (f.n. Morcott).
læs OE, 'pasture, meadow-land'.
Leasewell Seeke (f.n. Braunston), *v.* **lēah** and Notes on the Distribution and Usage of some Elements, *s.v.* **læs** and **lēah**.
la(g)h ME, 'low, low-lying'.
Lowskirts (f.n. Ridlington).
lair ModE dial., 'a barn, a resting-place for animals'.
Cowlair (Uppingham), Cow Lair (Whissendine), Cowlair Wier Cl (f.n. Glaston).
lām OE, 'loam, clay'.
Lamb Pool, Lamford ford (f.ns. Barrowden), *Lampolmedow* (f.n. Hambleton).
lamb OE, 'a lamb'.

Lambley Lodge. *Lambecroft* (f.n. Lyddington).
lambing eModE, 'the parturition or yeaning of lambs'.
Lambyngecrofte (f.n. Leighfield).
lammas eModE. The 1st of August; in the early English Church, observed as a harvest festival, at which loaves of bread made from the first ripe corn were consecrated. In f.ns., referring to land which was under cultivation until harvest and reverted to common pasture from Lammas-tide until the following Spring.
Common in f.ns., e.g. Lamas (Edith Weston), *The Lamass Commons* (Empingham), *Lamas pastures* (Manton), Lamas Pen (Thistleton), *Lamass Close* (Normanton), *Lames fur'* (Egleton), *The Lammass* (Lt. Casterton), *(le) Lammas Close* (Ayston, Barleythorpe, Belton, Oakham), Lammas Cl (N. and S. Luffenham, Lyddington, Morcott, Whissendine), Lammas Ground (Pilton), - Mdw (Essendine).
lampe ME, 'a lamp'; in f.ns. referring to land endowed for the maintenance of an altar lamp in the parish church.
Lampacre Close (f.n. Uppingham), *le Lampe* (f.n. Mkt. Overton), *Lamplees* (f.n. Hambleton), *Lamp Leys* (f.n. Morcott), *the Laump land Lands of Mr Digby* (f.n. Bisbrooke).
lām-pytt OE, 'a loam-pit'.
Lamb Pitt Close (f.n. Glaston).
land, lond OE, 'land', either in the general sense 'ground, part of the earth's surface' or as 'a "land", i.e. a strip of arable in a common-field'.
Rutland, Westland Wood. Very freq. in f.ns. The nature of the soil may be indicated, e.g. *Blaclondis* (Bisbrooke), Sour Lands (S. Luffenham), *Stonyland* (Oakham), *le wetlondes* (N. Luffenham), *White Lands* (Ryhall), *yeallow landes* (Morcott); or crops, e.g. *Bandlandes* (Exton), *Flaxlandes* (Morcott), *Haverlands* (N. Luffenham), *Peys(e)land* (Cottesmore, Oakham), *Wheytlondes* (Cottesmore); or animals, e.g. *Shipland Furlong* (Barrow), *Tagland* (Morcott). Ownership may be specified, e.g. *Bruseslonde, Musgroseslonde* (Cottesmore), *Clements Lands* (Uppingham), *Nunesland* (Exton), *Prestlands* (Barleythorpe), *Smythlond* (Burley). Position is often indicated, e.g. *Brimlands* (Lyndon), *le gaplondes* (Barrowden), *more landes, Tongue Lands fur'* (Egleton). Shape or size is freq. indicated, esp. as *Long Land(s)* (Barleythorpe; *v.* also Belton, Caldecott, Egleton, Lyddington, Lyndon, Morcott, Thistleton, Uppingham, Edith Weston), *Shortlands* (S. Luffenham), *Ranglands*

(Braunston), *Longwrangelondes* (Cottesmore), *(W)rangland(s)* (Whissendine, Wing). In later f.ns., units formed from specified numbers of selions of the open-fields appear, e.g. *Five Land Acre* (Ryhall), *Six Lands, Nine Lands Furlong* (Bisbrooke), *le seauen land* (Oakham), Ten Lands (Preston), Fourteen Lands (Belton), Twenty lands furlong (Lyddington). Esp. common is the enclosure formed from unspecified numbers of selions of the old open-field, e.g. *Land Close* (Burley, Lt. Casterton, Hambleton, Normanton, Stretton), Land Cl (Ashwell, Ayston, Barrow, Brooke, Ketton, Langham, S. Luffenham, Lyndon, Mkt. Overton, Seaton), - Fd (Clipsham, Pickworth), - Mdw (Teigh). Cf. also *Selfsownelondys* (Seaton), *Twopenny Lands Furlong* (Belton), *le viccaradge land* (Oakham).

lane OE, 'a lane, a narrow road'.
Beclane, le Blynde Lane (Hambleton), *Codslane end, in quondam venella....vocat' Fosters* (Braunston), *Daglane* (Bisbrooke), *le Dedelane* (Oakham), *Kyrkelane* (Clipsham), *Langlane* (Lyddington), *le Westlane* (Tinwell), *Lanes-end Furlong* (f.n. Cottesmore), *Lane Stockin* (f.n. Clipsham).

lang¹ OE, 'long'.
Langham. Freq. in f.ns., esp. in compound with **land** (*v. supra*) referring to the shape of the selions in a furlong. Cf. also the f.ns. *Langele* (Leighfield), *Langmerewong, Long(e)wong, Northlong furlong* (Mkt. Overton), *Longborough Nook, Longemore Hedge Furlong* (Greetham), *Long(e) clotes* (Egleton), Long Cl, Longdales (Clipsham), *longfurlong* (Caldecott, Seaton), *Longhesil* (Barrow), *Long Hedge* (Thistleton), *Longholm* (Glaston), *Long lay* (Lyddington), *Long Leys* (Uppingham), *longeshrubs* (Edith Weston), *Longsicke* (Oakham), *Longthorne leas* (Burley), *Longwrangelondes* (Cottesmore) and Langford Bridge (Essendine).

lang² ME, 'a long strip of land'.
the East Longe (f.n. Lyddington), *Est longs furlong* (f.n. Caldecott).

*langet OE, **langate** ModE dial., 'a long (narrow) strip of ground'.
Longate furlong (f.n. Egleton), *Long Gate Furlong* (f.n. Seaton), Long Gate Side (f.n. Oakham).

launde OFr, ME, 'an open space in woodland, a forest glade, woodland pasture'.
Launde Fm, Tickencote Launde. *Berchley Laund Sale* (f.n. Belton), Bottom Lawn (f.n. Lyddington), Far -, Middle Lawn, *Launde Chase* (f.ns. Beaumont Chase), *Long Lawn Close* (f.n. Ketton).

lax ModE, of soils 'loose in texture, loosely compacted'.
? Lax Hill.   ? Lax hill (f.n. Barrowden).
lēah OE, **lǣh** (Angl), 'a wood, woodland, a woodland glade, a clearing in a wood' etc. (*v.* Elements 2 18-19).   Professor K. Cameron argues that most later f.ns. with *ley(e)s* (sg. *ley*) are probably from **lēah** in its developed sense 'a meadow, a piece of meadow, an open pasture' rather than from **lǣs** 'pasture, meadow-land', *v.* L 2 66 *s.n.* Carr Leys Wood.   Also *v.* Notes on the Distribution and Usage of some Elements *infra, s.v.* **lǣs** and **lēah.**

Armley Wood, Bradley Lane, Burley, *Kalkeleys,* Lambley Lodge, The Leas, Lees' Barn, Lee Spinney, Leighfield, Martinsley, Mill Hill, Morkery Leys, Priestley Hill, Tunneley Wood, Wardley, Witchley Warren.   Fairly freq. in f.ns., e.g. Armsley Quarter (Beaumont Chase), *Bentle* (Mkt. Overton), *Brenles* (Ridlington), *Brentley, Brightley Bridge, Langley balk* (Manton), *Cartley* (Oakham), *Cockleys, Langele* (Leighfield), *Curtley, Mapeley Cross furlong* (Egleton), *Greteley, Lituley* (Essendine), *Grinley Corner* (Belton), *Haddisly, þureslege broc* (Ayston), *Nethirlee, le Lee, in the Throat of the Lea* (Lyddington).
lēoht OE, 'light, light-coloured'.
Light Ground (f.n. Burley).
lesser ME, 'smaller'.
Lesser Wood (Greetham).
leveret ME, 'a young hare'.
? Leveret Leys (f.n. Essendine).
leyne, lain ME, 'a layer, a tract of arable land'.
Heckleyne Seeke (f.n. Whissendine), ? *the Leane wonge bush* (Thistleton).
līm OE, 'lime'.
the Lime Close (f.n. N. Luffenham).
lim-kilne ME, 'a lime-kiln'.
Lime Kill Furlong (f.n. Normanton), *Limekilne balke* (f.n. N. Luffenham), *Lyme Kilne fur'* (f.n. Greetham).
līn OE, **lín** ON, 'flax'.
Lyncroft (f.n. Barrowden, Caldecott).
lind OE, ON, 'a lime-tree'.
Lyndon.   *Lymgate* (f.n. Morcott), *Lyndwode* (Pickworth).
loc OE, 'a lock, a bolt; a fold', **loca** OE, 'an enclosure'.
Clay Lock (f.n. Morcott), - Cl (f.n. S. Luffenham), ? Lockhaye Cl

(f.n. Ridlington), *Taglock Close* (f.n. S. Luffenham).

loge OFr, **log(g)e** ME, 'a hut, a small house'; later 'a house in a forest for temporary use (a forester's house or a hunting lodge), a house at the entrance to a park'.

Glaston Lodge, King's Hill Lodge, Lambley Lodge, Leighfield Lodge, Park Lodge.

lug ModE dial., 'a projection, a protuberance'.

? *Lugmoor* (f.n. Belton).

lugg eModE, of surface 'a square pole or perch'.

? *Lugmoor* (f.n. Belton).

lumber ME, 'lumber, odds and ends'.

Lumber Nook (f.n. Greetham).

lump ME, 'a lump'.

? *Grains Lump* (f.n. Morcott).

lundr ON, 'a small wood, a grove'.

Asshelounde.   Bisbrooke lound, Childeslund' (Ayston), *Lound close* (f.n. Ayston), *Farr Lound* (Clipsham), Lound, Spinney Lount (Ridlington), Launde Lees (f.n. Belton), Lound Cl (f.n. Seaton), - Fd (f.n. Uppingham), Lounds (f.n. Egleton), *The Lownd* (Bisbrooke), *Lundes* (f.n. Oakham), *Sundlund, Westlound* (Stoke Dry), *Wardley lound* (Wardley).

lyng ON, 'ling, heather'.

Casterton Lings, Lings Spinney. Ling Cl (f.n. Glaston), Ling Cover (f.n. Edith Weston), *Ling(e) furlong* (f.n. Barrow, Pilton), *Linges* (f.n. Lt. Casterton, Wing), Lingmore Cl (f.n. Ashwell), The Lings (f.n. Pickworth), *Lyngefurlonges* (f.n. Cottesmore), *The Lynges* (f.n. Lyndon), *Le Lyngges* (f.n. Bisbrooke), *Lynghau, Tynewell Lynges* (f.ns. Tinwell).

lytel, lytel, lĩtel OE, **lítill** ON, 'little, small'.

Littleworth. Occasionally in f.ns., e.g. *Litelhawewonge* (Lt. Casterton), *Litelhowe* (N. Luffenham), *litle acre* (Oakham), *Lituley* (Essendine), *Lyttilhawe* (Stretton).

mæd (**mǽdwe** dat.sg.) OE, **mēd** (Angl), 'a meadow'.

Fairly freq. in f.ns.; sometimes as a first el., e.g. *Medeplot* (Lyddington), *le Meduegate* (Wing), *Medwedik'* (N. Luffenham), but usually as a second el., e.g. *Apiltremedou, Tounmedou* (Glaston), *Appelmede, le Kirkemedou, Odmelmedou* (Whissendine), *Emedw* (Barrow), *Goddemade* (Burley), *Holdmedow, Lampolmedow* (Hambleton), *le Milnetymbermede* (Stretton), *Priors medowe* (Wing),

Roluesmedowe (Whitwell), *Surmedue* (Ryhall). *Meadow* from dat.sg.
mædwe is freq. in modern f.ns.

mægð OE, 'a maiden'.

? *mayde Crofte* (f.n. Egleton).

mægðe OE, 'may-weed'.

? *mayde Crofte* (f.n. Egleton).

(ge)mæne OE, 'common, communal (land)'.

? *Manholm* (f.n. Lt. Casterton), *Menegate* (f.n. Bisbrooke).

(ge)mære OE, 'a boundary, a border'.

Mere Lane. Freq. in f.ns., occasionally as a simplex, e.g. *the Meer(e)* (Barrow, Lyndon, Morcott, Pilton, Edith Weston), also *the Meare Close* (Normanton), *Mere Meadow* (Morcott), *Meare Wong* (Greetham); but more often prefixed by a village name, e.g. *Bisbrooke -, Easton Meer(e)* (Uppingham), *Greetham -, Orton -, Thistleton Meer(e)* (Stretton), *Morcott Meare, wingmeirhedg balk* (Pilton), *Pilton -, Sculthorpe -, Wing Meer(e), seton meare* (Morcott). It is probable that the el. came to denote 'a piece of land on a boundary', e.g. Meers next to Pilton (N. Luffenham), the uninclosed Meer (Edith Weston), *Hunts Meere* (Pilton), *Jackson's Meer* (Greetham) and perh. *Long meere, the short meare* (Pilton), *Long meer* (Lyddington). Cf. also *Wrangdykmere* (N. Luffenham) which may record the boundary of Wrangdike Hundred.

malte-mylne ME, 'a malt-mill'.

Mill St. *Barlythorpe Mault myll, Mault Milne way* (Barleythorpe), *Maltmill* (Ayston), *Mault Mill* (Exton, Ridlington).

maner ME, 'a manor (house), a mansion'.

Ayston Hall, Clipsham Hall, Lyndon Hall, Manor Ho., Normanton Ho.

manig OE, 'many'.

Many Bushes. *Manigate Furlong* (f.n. Empingham), *Maniwell Spring* (f.n. Greetham), Many Wells (f.n. S. Luffenham).

mann OE, **maðr** (**manna** gen.pl.) ON, 'a man'; in some p.ns. denoting in the pl. 'community'.

? *Manthorpe.*

mantel ME, 'a rampart'.

le Mantell' (f.n. N. Luffenham).

*mapel, *mapul OE, 'a maple-tree'.

Mapeley Cross furlong (f.n. Egleton), Little Maples, Maple Stile Sale (Beaumont Chase), *Maple stubbe* (f.n. Belton).

market late OE, ME, 'a market, a market-place'.

Market Overton, Market Place (Oakham, Uppingham).

mase ME, 'a maze'.

Wing Maze.

maythorn eModE, 'the hawthorn'.

May Thorne Bush (f.n. Ketton).

mearc OE, 'a boundary'.

? *Morkery Leys.*

mere[1] OE, 'a pool'.

ate Mere (p) (Burley), *the mear* (Egleton), *Saltmere* (Lyddington), ?
Tirtle Meare (Morcott).

mersc OE, 'watery land, a marsh'; in Ru, appears in a late dial.
form *march*.   Although most of the following names are of
locations beside streams forming the county boundary, OE· *mearc* 'a
boundary' would normally have given unpalatalized *mark* in the East
Midlands, not *march*, and thus derivation from *mersc* is preferable.
Marches (f.n. Caldecott), March Dyke Leys, March Mdw (f.ns.
Lyddington, Thorpe by Water), *March hill* (f.n. Wardley), March
Mdw (f.n. Ketton), Marsh Mdw (f.n. Thorpe by Water), *Marsh
Slade* (f.n. Lyddington), Page Marsh (f.n. Caldecott), *Perotesmersh,
le Westmers(s)h* (f.ns. Whissendine).

mesne ME, 'demesne land'.

les Mesnes (f.n. Barleythorpe).

mete ME, 'a boundary'.

Mett Meadow (f.n. Manton).

micel, mycel OE, 'big, great'.

Michell dale (f.n. Thistleton), *Mickleton Hill Furlong* (f.n.
Whissendine), *Midle muckle hill* (f.n. Belton).

midd OE, 'middle'.

Mid Leys (f.n. Ketton), *Midleyes* (f.n. Teigh).

middel OE, 'middle'.

Occasionally in f.ns., most freq. with **feld** 'field' (as in Barleythorpe,
Burley, Lt. Casterton, Lyddington, Teigh).   Cf. also *Middelfurlong,
Middelstow* (N. Luffenham), *Mid(d)le Close* (Greetham),
Midlebrinkes (Teigh), *Middle seek* (Morcott), *Midil syke* (Barrow),
Midle Furlong, Midle muckle hill (Belton), *Midle grounde* (Ayston),
mydle borowes (Egleton).

mikill ON, 'big, great'.

Mickledine (f.n. Barleythorpe), *Mickle Doles* (f.n. Caldecott),
Micklehill, East Micklings, *Midle muckle hill* (f.ns. Belton), Mickle
mdw (f.n. Thorpe by Water), *Mickleton Hill Furlong* (f.n.

Whissendine), *Mikeleng* (f.n. Ketton), *Mikelingge* (f.n. Oakham), *Mikildole* (f.n. Lyddington), *Mykeleng* (f.n. Tinwell).

mīl OE, 'a mile'.

Halffmylle Busk (f.n. Mkt. Overton).

milking eModE, 'the act of milking', denoting a place where cows were milked, or where milch-cows were specially pastured.

Milking Cl (f.n. Egleton, Manton, Whissendine), - Fd (f.n. Greetham, Edith Weston).

molde OE, 'earth, soil'.

Black Mould (f.n. Whitwell).

monie ME, 'money'.

? *Moneybalke* (f.n. Oakham), Money Pit Cl (f.n. Ketton).

mont OFr, ME, ' a mount, a hill'.

Beaumont Chase. Long Carmen (f.n. Caldecott).

mōr[1] OE, **mór** ON, 'moor, marshland, barren wasteland'.

Cottesmore, High Moor, High Moor Fm, *Moorhall*, Moor Lane (N. Luffenham, Whissendine), Moor Plantation, Morcott, *Rutmore*, Westmoor Lane. Freq. in f.ns., occasionally as a simplex, e.g. *the Moor(es)* (Glaston, Wardley), *le Mor* (Oakham, Mkt. Overton) or as a first el., e.g. *Mooredike* (Wing), *Moorewell furlong* (Caldecott), *Moorgate* (Manton), *Moregore, Morehead* (Braunston); but usually as a second el. In these compounds, ownership may be indicated, e.g. *batusmore* (N. Luffenham), *Bondesmore* (Belton), *Hubberdysmore* (Seaton), or the neighbouring village specified, e.g. *Morcot moor* (S. Luffenham), *Whyttewell more* (Exton), *Witham Moore* (Thistleton). Direction from a settlement may be indicated, e.g. *Estmor(e)* (Mkt. Overton, Whissendine), *Westmore* (Exton), or size or shape, e.g. *le Brodemor* (Barrowden), *Longemore* (Greetham), *Lugmoor* (Belton). Associated fauna may be specified, e.g. Geesemere (Lyddington), *sparrowmore* (Teigh), or flora, e.g. Lingmore (Ashwell), *Thicke Moore* (Greetham). Recurring is *Deadmo(o)re* (Belton, Manton), Dedmoor (Wing), Dedmore (Greetham), probably indicating infertility. Cf. also *Smeeth More* (Burley), *Trewelmore* (Lyddington), *Yellsmoor* (Uppingham).

mork ON, 'a boundary, a border'.

? Morkery Leys.

morter ME, 'mortar'.

the Morter holes (f.n. Uppingham), cf. **morter-pytt**.

morter-pytt ME, 'a mortar-pit'.

Gally Hill Mortar pitts (f.n. Uppingham), Mortar Pits (f.n.

Lyddington), Mortar Pit(t) Cl (f.n. Glaston), *The Mortar Pitt Furlong* (f.n. Morcott), Morter Pits (f.n. Wing), *Morterpitt Close* (f.n. Egleton), *the morter pittes* (f.n. Bisbrooke), *Morter Pitts fur'* (f.n. Greetham).

mos OE, **mosi** ON, 'moss, lichen'; also 'a bog, a swamp, a moss'.
Vale of Catmose. *Catmouse* (f.n. Burley), *Moss Holmes* (f.n. Edith Weston).

mōt OE, 'a meeting'.
le Mothalle (Oakham).

mote OFr, 'an embankment', **mote** ME, 'a protective ditch (filled with water) around a building'.
Moat Cl (f.n. N. Luffenham), ? *Mott Close* (f.n. Clipsham).

mould ModE dial., 'the mole'.
Mold Meadow (f.n. Edith Weston), ? Mole Hills (f.n. Barrowden).

mūga OE, 'a stack, a heap'.
Moubreche (f.n. N. Luffenham).

muk ME, 'dung, muck, dirt'.
Muck Fd (f.n. Pilton).

munuc OE, **monke** ME, 'a monk'.
Monks Hill (f.n. Wardley), Monks Wood (Beaumont Chase).

mūs OE, **mús** ON, 'a mouse, a field-mouse'.
Muxwells (f.n. Glaston).

mūða OE, 'a mouth'; in early p.ns., transferred to 'the mouth of a river', later 'a valley mouth' etc.
Free Wood Mouth (f.n. Essendine), Haremouth Cl (f.n. Teigh).

***mylde** OE (Angl), 'soil, earth'.
Blacmyld (f.n. Stoke Dry), *Blakmyld'* (f.n. Cottesmore), ? Blakemiles (f.n. Whissendine).

myln OE, 'a mill'.
Brooke Mill, Casterton Mill, Horn Mill, Mill Close Spinney, Mill Cottages, Mill Dam, Mill Fm, Millfield Spinney, Mill Hill, Mill Ho., Seaton Mill. Freq. in f.ns., usually as a first el., e.g. *Mill nook* (Cottesmore), *Milne Furlong* (Whissendine), *Milnegate* (Glaston), *le Milnetymbermede* (Stretton), *Milnewongk'* (Barrow), *Mouleholme* (Oakham), *le Mylnedam* (N. Luffenham). Cf. also *Fallesmyll'* (Lyddington), *Kyngmilne Stey* (N. Luffenham), *le Newmill* (Greetham), *atte Suthmylne* (p) (Empingham).

myrge OE, 'pleasant'.
? Merry Acres (f.n. Teigh).

mȳrr ON, 'a mire, a bog, swampy ground'.
Mowmires. Mire Hole (f.n. Glaston), *Mur Pit Meadow* (f.n. Oakham).
myry ME, 'miry, muddy'.
Miry Cl (f.n. S. Luffenham), Miry Quarter (Beaumont Chase), *Myry peice* (f.n. Uppingham).

nan-mann OE, 'no man, nobody'.
Nomanislond (f.n. Tinwell), No Mans Ground (f.n. Ryhall), No Mans-Land, No Mans-Plot (f.ns. Seaton).
nearu OE, 'narrow'.
Narrow Point(s) (f.ns. Barleythorpe, Oakham).
nēat OE, 'cattle'.
(le) neate pasture (f.ns. N. Luffenham, Preston), *The Neat Yard Close* (f.n. S. Luffenham), ? Net Land (f.n. Ryhall).
neetherd ME, 'a cowherd'.
Neatherd Close (f.n. Belton).
neoðera OE, 'lower'.
Occasionally in f.ns., esp. with **feld** 'a field'. Cf. also (*The*) *Neather Close* (Barrow), - *Furlong* (Normanton), Neather Mdw (Whissendine), *Neather Mill Furlong* (Uppingham), *neither closse, the Neither meadowe, Nether micle hill* (Belton), *the Nether Furlong* (Edith Weston), *Netherford* (Bisbrooke), Netherlands (Mkt. Overton), *Nethirlee* (Lyddington).
nēp OE (Angl), 'a turnip'.
? Naps Cl (f.n. Ridlington).
nes ON, 'a headland, a promontory'.
Ness Mdw (f.n. Ryhall).
nest OE, 'a nest'.
Swan's Nest Coppice (Stoke Dry), *Wipesnest, -fur'* (f.ns. Egleton, Manton).
netel(e) OE, 'a nettle'.
Nettle Croft (f.n. Edith Weston), Nettle Croft (f.n. Glaston).
nigon OE, 'nine'.
Nine Lands Ford Dike (f.n. Bisbrooke), Nine leys (f.n. Lyddington), *the Nyne acres* (f.n. Seaton).
nīwe, nēowe (**nēowan** wk.obl.) OE, 'new'.
Newbottle, Newell Wood. *le Neugate* (Oakham), *Newecroft* (f.n. Caldecott), Newell Hills (f.n. Stretton), *Newfeild* (f.n. Burley), *le Newmill* (Greetham). Cf. also Neanton Cl (f.n. Empingham),

originally from the wk.obl. **nēowan.**

nōk ME, 'a nook; a nook of land, a triangular plot of ground'.
The Nook. Freq. in f.ns., occasionally simplex, e.g. *the Nook*
(Glaston), The Nook (Gt. Casterton, Essendine, Stoke Dry,
Whissendine), but usually as a second el. It may be compounded
with a prefixed surn., e.g. *Digby's Nook* (Pilton), *Ellis Nooke*
(Greetham), *Shermans Nooke* (Stretton); or with a village name, e.g.
Gunthorpe nooke (Hambleton), *Luffenham Nooke* (Edith Weston),
Pisbrooke Nooke (Bisbrooke). Associated animals may be specified,
e.g. *Bull Nook, cunnigree nooke* (Teigh), *The Calves Nooke*
(Tickencote); or flora, e.g. *High Thorne Nooke, Sweeting Tree Nooke*
(Empingham). Cf. also *Bytenooke* (Stretton), *dukesbush nook* (N.
Luffenham), *Longborough Nook, Lumber Nook* (Greetham), *Lound
Nook* (Uppingham), *Mill nook* (Cottesmore), *Park Nook* (Oakham),
Well Nook (Glaston), *Wood nooke* (Wardley).

nooked ME, 'nooked; having corners'.
Three Nook'd Cl (f.n. Ashwell).

norð OE, ON, 'northern, north'.
North Brook. Freq. in f.ns., esp. with **feld** 'a field' (Burley,
Egleton, Exton, Greetham, Oakham, Pilton, Thistleton, Tixover,
Whissendine). Cf. also *le Norberwe* (Thorpe by Water), *Norbrooke*
(Langham), *Nordwude* (Clipsham), *Northings Close* (Egleton),
Northholm, Northlongfurlong, Norton' Wod' (Mkt. Overton),
Northolmwong (Caldecott), *Northwode* (Stretton).

Norðman late OE, 'a Norwegian'.
Normanton. ? *Normandale* (f.n. Tixover).

nunne OE, 'a nun'.
? None Stalls (f.n. Braunston), ? *Nunesland* (f.n. Exton).

nursery ModE, 'a plot of ground in which young plants or trees are
reared until fit for transplantation'.
The Nursery. Nursery Cl (f.n. Lt. Casterton), *Home Close (called
the Nursery)* (f.n. Gunthorpe).

ōfer¹ OE, 'a bank, a river-bank'.
? *Ouerwong* (f.n. Caldecott).

ofer² OE, 'a flat-topped ridge'.
Market Overton, Tixover. ? *Ouerwong* (f.n. Caldecott), *Pykworth
Ouerfeld* (f.n. Gt. Casterton).

ofer³ OE, 'over, above'.
Hover Parks (f.n. Lyddington), Hoverdale (f.n. Tinwell), *ouerdykes,*

ouergates, ouerholmes (f.ns. Barleythorpe), *Ouer hills furlong* (f.n. Caldecott),˙ *Over Batesmore, the two little over closes* (f.ns. N. Luffenham), *ouer Stamfordgate* (f.n. Cottesmore).

ofer-þwart ME, 'across'.
Ouerthwertwong (f.n. Caldecott).

ōra[1] OE, 'a flat-topped ridge with a shoulder at one or both ends'.. Tixover.

orceard, ort-geard OE, 'a garden', later in OE 'an orchard'.
le Castelorchard' (f.n. Oakham), *Cherry Orchard* (f.n. Glaston), (The) Orchard (f.ns. N. Luffenham, Tixover), *The Orchards Gardens* (f.n. Empingham), *South Orchard* (f.n. Ashwell).

ote-mele ME, 'oatmeal'.
Odmelmedou (f.n. Whissendine), · *Oatemeale Meadowe* (f.n. Hambleton).

oxa (oxan gen.sg., **exen** nom.pl., ***exna** gen.pl.) OE, 'an ox'.
? Exton. *Oxemede* (f.n. Lyddington), *Oxe yard* (f.n. Ayston), Ox Piece (f.n. Brooke).

oyser ME, 'osier, willow'.
Osier Bed (f.n. Ashwell, Gunthorpe), *Osier Holt* (f.n. S. Luffenham), (Old) Ozier Bed (f.ns. Morcott, Tinwell), Ozier Holt (f.n. Pilton).

pacche ME, 'a patch of ground'.
the Patch of Grass (f.n. Manton).

pad eModE, ModE dial., 'a path, a track'.
Banbillings Pad (f.n. Lyddington, Thorpe by Water), Bridle Pad Fd (f.n. Barrowden), Footpad Fd(s) (f.ns. Ayston, Morcott), - Piece (f.n. S. Luffenham).

*padde OE, **padda** ON, 'a toad'.
Padbrok' (f.n. Burley), Padfields (f.n. Braunston), *Padholme* (f.n. Egleton), Padholme (f.n. Brooke).

*padduc OE, **paddok** ME, 'a frog'.
Padokeford' (f.n. Lyddington), *Padox ford* (f.n. Caldecott).

pæð OE, 'a path'.
Path Close (f.n. Lyndon).

pale ME, 'a fence, a park-pale'.
the Parke Pale (Brooke).

panne OE, 'a pan; a pan-shaped thing'; perh. topographically used of a hollow.
(Far) Pan Cl (f.ns. Ashwell, Glaston, Whissendine), *Pan Meadow*

(f.n. Lt. Casterton), *The Panne* (f.n. Burley).

paradis ME, 'an orchard; an enclosed pleasure ground'.

Paradise (f.n. Wing).

park ME, 'an enclosed tract of land for beasts of the chase'.

Burley Park, Clipsham Park, Exton Park, Flitteris Park, Lyddington Park, New Park, Park Fm, Parkfield, Parkfield Rd, Park Lane, Park Lodge, Town Park. *Barnsdale Park* (Exton), Hare Park, *The Parke Feild,* The Parks, *Parkwall* (f.ns. Stretton), *Lawnde Park* (Uppingham), *Le park Dales* (f.n. Leighfield), *le parkefeld'* (f.n. Lyddington), *le Parke furlong, The Parks* (f.ns. Oakham), *the Parke Pale* (Brooke), *Park Ford* (Egleton), Park Leys (f.n. Edith Weston), Park Platt (f.n. Brooke), *Parks* (f.n. Mkt. Overton), *the Parkstile* (Ridlington), Pug's Park Spinney (Horn), *Vppingham parke* (Uppingham).

parlur ME, 'a secluded rendezvous'; in later f.ns., 'a small secluded piece of ground'.

The Parlour (f.n. Belton), Stafford's Parlour (f.n. Langham).

part ME, 'a part, a portion'.

cottiers part (f.n. Wardley), *the Hall partes* (f.n. Preston).

pasture ME, 'a pasture, a piece of pasture land'.

Cow Pasture, *Kings pasture* (f.ns. Hambleton), *the old pasture* (f.n. Manton), *Pasture Closes* (f.n. Whitwell), *- Leyes* (f.n. Thistleton), Pastures (f.n. Greetham, Preston).

pearroc OE, 'a small enclosure', **paddock** ModE, 'a paddock'.

Paddock (f.n. Normanton).

pece ME, 'a piece or plot of land', sometimes referring to a consolidation of strips acquired by piecemeal enclosure.

Todds Piece. Very freq. in f.ns., as: *black wong peice, the Duke of Rutlands peice, the great Farme Peece, Jenkinsons ford peice, Pike peice, the south peeces, yest Peice* (Bisbrooke), *Knightlys Piece, Laxtons Peice, Three Acre Piece* (Uppingham), *Mr Rays Fur Peice, Tilton's Piece, Witchley Piece* (N. Luffenham). The earliest recorded examples are *Temple Peyse* (1556, Greetham), *How Piece* (1602, Morcott), *The Furres Peice* (1619, Belton), *Hanging Peice* (1632, Tickencote), *Green end peece* (1633, Thistleton), *the Five Shillings peece* (1646, Seaton); but most belong to the 18th cent.

peddere ME, 'a pedlar'.

Pedderstyle (Cottesmore).

pel ME, 'a palisade, a palisaded enclosure'.

le Pele (f.n. N. Luffenham).

pening OE, **peni** ME, 'a penny; a penny rent'.

Penny Holmes (f.n. N. Luffenham).

penn² OE, 'a small enclosure, a fold'; later 'an enclosure for animals'.

Penn St. *Bates Penn*, The Lodge Pen (f.ns. Edith Weston), *Cheseldens Pen* (f.n. Manton), *the Hall Pen* (f.n. Lyndon), Lamas Pen (f.n. Thistleton), *Parsons Penn* (f.n. Glaston), *the Pen* (f.n. Morcott), Pen(n) Cl (f.n. Ashwell, S. Luffenham, Pickworth, Ridlington), - Mdw (f.n. Ashwell, Leighfield, Preston), *Penn Close* (f.n. Uppingham), *the Penn End* (f.n. Lyndon), *Penn Leas* (f.n. Lyddington), Penns Hill Butts (f.n. Seaton), *Pen Yard* (f.n. Ayston).

personage ME, 'a parsonage'.

Parsonage Ho., The Rectory, The Vicarage (Empingham, Hambleton, Ketton). *The Parsonage* (Greetham), - *hedge* (Belton), - *House* (Ayston), - *land* (f.n. Glaston, Lyndon), - *Piece* (f.n. Braunston).

persone ME, 'a parson, a beneficed cleric'.

(*the*) *Parsons Balke* (f.n. Uppingham), *Parsons Close, Parsons swathes* (f.ns. Lyndon).

pertre ME, 'a peartree'.

Pearetree hill (f.n. Uppingham), Pear Tree Cl (f.n. Gt. Casterton, Greetham, Lyndon, Wardley), *atte Pertre* (p) (Edith Weston).

pety ME, 'little' (<OFr *petit*).

Petty Green Cl (f.n. Ketton).

pibbil ME, 'a pebble'.

Pebbles (f.n. Manton), *Pibbles* (f.n. Empingham).

pīc OE, 'a point, a pointed hill'; also 'a pike' (i.e. the fish).

Pike Acre (f.n. Barrowden), - Furlong (f.n. Morcott), *Pike peice* (f.n. Bisbrooke), Pike Piece (f.n. S. Luffenham, Edith Weston); *Pikwellsicke* (f.n. Oakham).

piche ME, 'a pitch, a small plot of land marked out'.

Pich Close (f.n. Thistleton), Pitch Furlong (f.n. Caldecott).

pīe² ME, 'a magpie'.

? *Pye Lane* (Uppingham).

pigga OE, **pigge** ME, 'a young pig'.

Piggs Holme (f.n. Egleton).

pightel, pichel ME, 'a small enclosure, a croft'.

Pightle (f.n. Langham), *The Pightle* (f.n. Hambleton), Three-Cornered Pightle (f.n. Clipsham); Pitcher Hill (f.n. Tixover).

pīl OE, 'a shaft, a pile'.

Pile Bridge (Ketton).

pimpel eModE, 'a pimple'; topographically 'a small mound'.

The Pimpole (f.n. Caldecott).

pingel ME, 'a small plot of ground'.

Ireland's Pingle (f.n. Whissendine), Pingel (f.n. Teigh), *le Pingle* (f.n. Barleythorpe), (*The*) *Pingle* (f.ns. Lt. Casterton, Egleton, Greetham, Oakham, Tickencote), (The) Pingle (f.ns. Ayston, Gt. Casterton, Tinwell, Whissendine), - Plantation (Clipsham), Pingles (f.n. Brooke), Robbs Pingle (f.n. Tinwell), Stadfolds and Pingle (f.n. Ashwell), Tingle Mdw (f.n. Leighfield).

*pipere OE, 'a spring'.

? *Piper Pitt Furlong* (f.n. Greetham).

pise OE, 'pease'.

Occasionally in f.ns., e.g. *Pease Broad, The Pease Fields* (Empingham), *pease close* (Tickencote), *Peasehill* (Manton), - *plott* (Lyndon), *Peaselands fur'* (Egleton), *Peasewell seeke* (Whissendine), *Peaze hill* (Thistleton), *Pesedale* (N. Luffenham), *Pesewong* (Lyddington), *Peys(e)land* (Cottesmore, Oakham).

pissemyre ME, 'an ant'.

Pismire Nook (f.n. Gt. Casterton).

place OFr, **place, plas** ME, 'a town-house; a residence, a mansion house'.

Manor Ho. *Carterplase, Jekes plase* (Whissendine), *Fawkners place* (Morcott), *le Ferme Place* (Barrowden), *the house called Tallyards place* (S. Luffenham).

*plæsc OE, 'a pool'.

Clash Wongs (f.n. Greetham), *the plash* (f.n. Tickencote), *plashing* (f.n. Hambleton).

plain ME, 'a piece of flat ground, a large open tract'; **plain** eModE, 'open ground beside woodland'.

Pickworth Plain. Broughton's Plain (f.n. Beaumont Chase, Stoke Dry), The Plain (f.n. Gt. Casterton, Ketton, Preston, Stoke Dry), Far Plain (f.n. Wardley).

planke ME, 'a plank, a plank bridge'; **plank** ModE dial., 'a narrow strip of cultivated land'.

Planke Close (f.n. Normanton), Plank Cl (f.n. Glaston, Hambleton, Tickencote), *Planke Meadow* (f.n. Gunthorpe), Plank Mdw (f.n. Pilton), *Tinwell Plank* (f.n. Ketton), *Wing Plank Furlong* (f.n. Manton), ? Blank Piece (f.n. Clipsham).

plat² ME, 'a plot, a small piece of ground'.

Barrow Platt (f.n. Mkt. Overton), Berry's Platt (f.n. Greetham), Berrys Plott Fd, Clipsham Platt, Grants Platt, Hall Platt, Moneys Plat(t), Old Moor Platt, The Platt, *Wards Platt* (f.ns. Stretton), Cotch Platt (f.n. Ridlington), House Platt, Road Plat, Roberts Plat, Well Plat (f.ns. Teigh), Lows Plat (f.n. Langham), Meadow Platt (f.n. Pickworth), Merrimans Plat, Middle Platt, New Platt Piece, Park Platt, Platts, West Platt (f.ns. Brooke).

plot late OE, ME, 'a small piece of ground'.
The Plot (f.n. Tixover), *Aswells Plot*, Yard Plott (f.ns. Stretton), *Bradleyes homeplott* (f.n. Hambelton), *Henneplot* (f.n. Glaston), *Medeplot* (f.n. Lyddington), *Peasehill plott* (f.n. Lyndon), *Scotneys Plot* (f.n. Gunthorpe).

plover ME, 'a plover, a peewit'.
(Plovers) New Fd (f.n. Teigh).

point eModE, 'a promontory, a pointed headland, a point of land'.
Narrow Point(s) (f.ns. Barleythorpe, Oakham), *the Points* (f.n. Morcott).

poke ME, 'a bag, a pouch', alluding to a round field in later f.ns.
Pokes (f.n. Essendine).

poket ME, 'a pocket', alluding to a round field with a narrow entrance.
Pocket Cl (f.n. Pickworth), Pocket Nook (f.n. Barleythorpe), *Pocket Piece* (f.n. Braunston).

pōl¹ OE, 'a pool'.
Cole poole furlong, Thorne poole furlong (f.ns. Caldecott), Lamb Pool (Barrowden), *Lampolmedow* (f.n. Hambleton), *Leffildespol, Maud Pool* (Tixover), *Pole Meadow* (f.n. Morcott), *Pole Stockin* (f.n. Clipsham), Ropool Mdw (f.n. Stoke Dry), *Shirt Pole Dale* (f.n. Greetham), *Syrepol* (Seaton), *Washpole* (Ketton).

ponde ME, 'a pond, an artificial or natural pool'.
Fish Pond. *Coleswood pond* (N. Luffenham), *crospond* (Burley), Great Pond Cl (f.n. Brooke), *Jagwell Pond* (Uppingham), *Pond Close* (f.n. Ayston).

*popel OE, 'a pebble'.
Popple Close (f.n. Lt. Casterton), ? *Popples Farm* (Greetham).

poppling eModE, 'bubbling up, flowing in a tumbling, interrupted manner'.
Poplin Spring (Glaston).

port² OE, 'a market-town, a market', cf. **port-weg**.
Port(e)gate (Glaston, Seaton), *Porthades* (f.n. Empingham).

port-weg OE, **port-wey** ME, 'a road to a (market-) town, a public road, a road to a market'.
Port Waye (Wardley), *the Portway* (Bisbrooke).

post-way ModE, 'a road on which a series of post-houses or stations for post-horses is established, a road on which mails are carried'.
The Post Way (Thistleton), *Post Way fur'* (f.n. Greetham).

pot(t) late OE, 'a pot'.
Pottacres (f.n. Egleton).

pounce eModE, 'a hole cut out for decoration'; also 'a powder (such as powdered pipe-clay) used in preparing parchment'.
? *Pounce Pits* (f.n. Belton).

prēost OE, 'a priest'.
Preston, Priestley Hill. *Prestesmor* (f.n. Glaston), *Prestlands* (f.n. Barleythorpe), *Preist Wood* (Greetham), Priestwells (f.n. Greetham), Priest Croft Cl (f.n. S. Luffenham), *Priest Gore* (f.n. Manton), The Priest's Mere (f.n. Bisbrooke), ? Priestwell's (f.n. Barleythorpe).

prior late OE, ME, 'a prior of a religious house'.
Prior's Coppice. *priors medowe* (f.n. Wing).

pug ModE dial., 'a hare'.
Pug's Park Spinney (Horn).

*pull OE, a pool'.
? *Pulpit Dale Furlong* (f.n. Stretton).

pumpe ME, 'a pump'.
Pump Close (f.n. Stretton), Pump Cl (f.n. Teigh).

punch ModE, 'a short, thickset horse, a heavy draught horse'.
Punch Leas Closes (f.n. Hambleton).

*pund OE, **pund** ME, 'a pound, an enclosure into which stray cattle are put'.
Lea pounde (f.n. Barleythorpe), *The Pound* (f.n. Hambleton), *The Pounde Close* (f.n. Gt. Casterton), The Pound (f.n. Tinwell, Whissendine), - Cl (f.n. N. Luffenham).

purveyor eModE, 'a steward; a domestic officer who makes purveyance of necessaries for a great personage'.
Purveyor's Covert.

*puttoc OE, 'a kite'.
Puttocks Well close (f.n. Bisbrooke).

pyll OE, 'a pool in a river; a small stream'.
Pilton.

pynd OE, 'a pound, an enclosure'.
The Parish Pound (f.n. Tixover).

*pynd-fald OE, 'a pinfold'.

Pinfold, Pinfold Ho., Pinfold Lane (N. Luffenham, Mkt. Overton), The Pinfold (Cottesmore, Manton). *The Pinfold* (f.n. Greetham), (The) Pinfold (f.ns. Clipsham, Empingham, Essendine), *Pinfold Close* (f.n. Tixover), Pinfold Cl (f.n. Burley, Lyndon, Pickworth, Ryhall), *the pinfold Garden* (f.n. Greetham), *Pinfold Green* (Ketton), *Pinfold Lane* (Oakham).

pytt OE, 'a pit, a natural hollow, an excavated hole'.

Rushpit Wood. Freq. in f.ns., almost invariably as a second el. Local superstitions are suggested in *Helpitt dale* (Lyndon), *Robynilpit* (Barrowden), *Thirspit* (Barrowden, Glaston), *Tyrespyt* (Empingham). Ownership is specified in *Abbotispittes* (Lt. Casterton), *Bowles Pitt* (Gt. Casterton), *Gibbs Pitt* (Edith Weston), *Horners Pit* (Pilton), *Pridmores Pitt* (Uppingham), *ye Vicar Pits* (Ketton); mineral extraction in *Claypitt Hill* (Ryhall), *sandpits* (N. Luffenham); associated livestock in *Swynpit* (Mkt. Overton), ? *Rampittes* (Gt. Casterton); flora in *Dog Pitts* (Uppingham), *Rushpitt* (Burley), *Sprat Pittes* (Ketton); nearby buildings in *le kyrkepittes* (S. Luffenham), *windmill pits* (N. Luffenham). Cf. also Washpit Cl (Glaston), - Fd (Bisbrooke), - Mdw (Ayston, Leighfield), evidently referring to sheep-dips.

quake ME, 'the act of quaking', **quake** ModE, 'a stretch of quake-ooze'.

Quake Fen (f.n. Whissendine).

quarriere OFr, **quarrere** ME, 'a quarry'.

New Quarry Fm. *Quarrie Pastures*, Quarry Dale (f.ns. Clipsham).

quarter ME, 'a quarter; a division of, or locality in, a larger area'.

Armsley -, Lodge -, Miry Quarter (Beaumont Chase), *Berchby -*, *Braniston -*, *Cockleys -*, *Lamley -*, *Loscott -*, *Toftsike Quarter*, *Freewood Quarter Coppice* (Leighfield), *Stacy quarter* (Flitteris in Oakham).

queinte ME, 'the female pudendum'.

? *Quintrey Lane* (Braunston).

rā¹ OE, **rá** ON, 'a roe, a roe-buck'.

? Ropool Mdw (f.n. Stoke Dry).

rá² ON, 'a boundary'.

Rocott Ho. ? Ropool Mdw (f.n. Stoke Dry).

ræde OE, 'suitable for riding on'.

? Redgate.
ræde-weg OE, 'a road broad enough for riding along'.
rædwege (Ayston).
raile, reille ME, 'a fence, a railing'.
Barleythorpe Rails (f.n. Oakham), Rail Mdw (f.n. Leighfield), *the Rails* (f.n. S. Luffenham), *the Turnpike Rails* (f.n. Uppingham).
ramm OE, 'a ram'.
(The) Ram Close (f.ns. Empingham, Hambleton), Ram Fd (f.n. Teigh), ? *Rampittes* (f.n. Gt. Casterton), Rams Cl (f.n. Gunthorpe).
rampart ModE dial., 'a causeway'.
The Ramparts. ? Rampart Hill (Gt. Casterton).
*rān OE, 'a boundary strip'.
Ransack Dyke, Ransack Spring (f.ns. Barrowden), ? *Randale Baulke* (f.n. Braunston), ? *Randike Meer* (f.n. Edith Weston), ? *Randike Meir* (f.n. N. Luffenham).
rand OE, 'a border, an edge'.
? *Randale Baulke* (f.n. Braunston), ? *Randike Meer* (f.n. Edith Weston), ? *Randike Meir* (f.n. N. Luffenham).
raskayl ME, 'a young deer', **rascal** ModE, 'a rogue, a scamp'.
Rascalhill (f.n. Manton).
raton OFr, **ratoun** ME, 'a rat'.
Rotten Dyke (f.n. Uppingham), *Rotton Row* (Oakham).
rāw OE, 'a row', either of trees or esp. of houses.
Westgate St (earlier *Beadhouse Row*). *Coblers Rowe Furlong* (f.n. Empingham), *the Roe* (Edith Weston), *Rotton Row* (Oakham), *Willow Row* (N. Luffenham).
rēad OE, 'red'.
? Redgate, Red Hill (Barrowden, Uppingham). Occasionally in f.ns., e.g. *Red(e)hill(e)* (N. Luffenham, Thistleton), *La redegate* (Bisbrooke), *Redfoard* (Empingham), *le Redground* (Barrowden), Red Ground (Bisbrooke, Seaton, Tinwell), *Redlands* (Wardley), Redlands (Gt. Casterton, Manton), *Redset,* ? *Redwell* (Manton), ? Redwells (Gunthorpe).
respas eModE, 'raspberries'.
Respas Springe (f.n. Belton).
rickstead ModE dial., 'an enclosure containing ricks, a rickyard, a stackyard'.
Brackles Reekstead (f.n. Braunston), *Gunthorpe rickstede* (f.n. Gunthorpe), Rickstead (f.n. Belton), *Ricksteads fur'* (f.n. Egleton).

Three of these forms belong to the 17th century., one to the 18th century..

risc OE, 'a rush'; in the simplex plural, 'a place where rushes grow, a rush bed'.

Rushpit Wood. *Risceholm* (f.n. Lt. Casterton), Rush Barrow (f.n. Teigh), *Rushpitt* (f.n. Burley); *the Rushes* (f.n. Edith Weston).

*riscig OE, **rushy** ModE, 'rushy, growing with rushes' (*v.* **risc, -ig³**).

Rushey Banke (f.n. Lyndon), Rushey Cl (f.n. N. Luffenham), Rushey Piece (f.n. S. Luffenham).

rīð OE, 'a stream'.

? Morkery Leys.

roche¹ OFr, ME, 'a rock, a cliff'.

? *Rochefurlong* (f.n. N. Luffenham).

*rod¹, *rodu OE, 'a clearing'.

Branston Rode, Brooke Rode, Clagett Rode, Gillians al's Julians Rode, Kokerode, the High Rodes, Sharpes Rode (Leighfield), *Rhode Sike* (f.n. Braunston), ? *Tungerode* (f.n. Oakham).

rōd³ OE, 'a rood of land, a rood measure'.

blake Roudes, White Roods (f.ns. Egleton), *Blakroodes* (f.n. Belton), *Broad Roods Furlong* (f.n. Cottesmore), *Crooke Rods* (f.n. Ketton), *Elbow Rood* (f.n. Manton), *the Four and Twenty Roods* (f.n. Edith Weston), *Gos Roodes* (f.n. Lyndon), *Long Roods* (f.n. Barleythorpe), *Long three Roods* (f.n. Ryhall), *Small Roodes* (f.n. Wardley), *Towne roode, Wrangrood* (f.ns. S. Luffenham), Whiteroods (f.n. Caldecott), Wrang roods (f.n. Barrowden), ? *Tungerode* (f.n. Oakham).

roller eModE, 'a cylinder of stone'.

Stump Stone (earlier *Rollors Stone*, Ryhall).

rond OFr, **round** ME, 'round'.

Round Hill (f.n. Uppingham).

roundabout ModE; used in f.ns. of a field surrounded by a wood or of a field with a clump of trees in its middle.

Roundabout (f.n. Empingham, Pilton, Tickencote).

rūh¹ OE, 'rough'.

Rogate Furlong (f.n. Morcott), Rogateway (f.n. S. Luffenham), *Rouclout* (f.n. Lyddington), *Rough Close* (f.n. N. Luffenham, Morcott), Rough Cl (f.n. Ashwell, Burley), - Dale (f.n. Brooke), - Ground (f.n. Whissendine), *Roughlands* (f.n. Edith Weston), *Row Furlong* (f.n. Empingham, Normanton), Rowgate High Road (Barrowden), Row Mdw (f.n. Ketton), Row Syke (f.n. Essendine).

*rūh² OE, 'a rough place' (a sb. use of **rūh¹**, *v.* Löfvenberg 169). Bartram's Rough (f.n. Langham).

rūm¹ OE, 'an open space'.
parcell' terr' vocat' le yard roome (f.n. Barleythorpe).

(ge)ryd(d) OE, 'cleared (of trees)'.
Riddle Fd (f.n. Ryhall).

*ryde OE, 'a clearing'.
le Ridgate (Wing).

*ryding OE, 'a clearing'.
Eight Riding Tree. Hall Ridings (f.n. S. Luffenham), Kings Hill Riding (f.n. Beaumont Chase), Riding (f.n. Wardley), The Ridings (f.n. Seaton), Ridings Furlong (f.n. Stretton), *Ruddyngdykefurlang* (f.n. Cottesmore).

rye-grass ModE dial., 'rye-grass (*Lolium perenne*)'.
Ryegrass (f.n. Barrow).

rye-land eModE, 'a selion or piece of ground suitable for growing rye', cf. **ryge, land.**
Rylands (f.n. Lyddington), - Cl (f.n. Langham), Rylands Snelston (f.n. Caldecott).

ryge OE, 'rye', cf. **rye-land.**
Ry Gate Plantation, Ryhall. Rialls (f.n. Belton), *Riholm* (f.n. Lt. Casterton), *le Rydale* (f.n. Barrow), Rye Cl (f.n. Ridlington), *Rye furlong* (f.n. Barleythorpe).

rynel OE, **rundle** ModE dial., 'a runnel, a small stream, a rivulet'.
the well rundell (Thistleton).

sǣd OE, 'seed'; in f.ns., used of areas of sown grass.
First Seeds (f.n. Ridlington), Old Seeds (f.n. Preston), Seed Acre (f.n. Braunston), *Seed Close* (f.n. Egleton), Seed Cl (f.n. Manton), Seed Grass Cl (f.n. Stretton), Seed Moor (f.n. Teigh), (The) Seeds (f.ns. Barleythorpe, Burley, Oakham, Seaton, Stone Dry, Whissendine).

sænna ODan, **senna** ON, 'a dispute, a quarrel'.
? *Sanam Close* (f.n. Hambleton), *Senholm* (f.n. Mkt. Overton).

sainfoin ModE, 'the fodder plant sainfoin (*Onobrychis sativa*)' and occasionally 'lucerne (*Medicago sativa*)'.
Old Sainfoin Close (f.n. Greetham), The Sainfoin Cl (f.n. Gt. Casterton), Sainfoin Hill (f.n. Tixover), Saintfoin Cl (f.n. Edith Weston), *St. Foin Close* (f.n. Normanton), Sanfoin Cl (f.n. Tickencote), Old Sanfoin Cl (f.n. Lt. Casterton, Tinwell).

sale eModE dial., 'a division or "quarter" of a wood, of which the underwood is cut down and sold' (*v.* Nth 157 and EDD *s.v.*). Common in the old forest parishes of western Rutland, where the earliest recorded instances date from the mid 16th cent. Principally found in Beaumont Chase, Leighfield, Stoke Dry and Wardley, e.g. *Armley* -, *Beaumont* -, *Crabtree hill* -, *Kings Oake* -, *Monkwood Sale* (Beaumont Chase), *Bittlewell sail*, *Branston* -, *Burtchbie* -, *Cockleyes* -, *Fair Ash* -, *Free Wood* -, *Hunts* -, *Loscott* -, *Rosell* -, *Withcock* -, *Woolfitt* -, *Youngwood Sale* (Leighfield), *Lady's* -, *Olyve sale*, *Stokwood salle* (Stoke Dry). Note *Friths Sale* (Lt. Casterton), the only recorded example in the east of the county.

salh, salig OE, 'a willow, a sallow'.
Sallow Sale (Beaumont Chase), *Salow Tre Leyes Fur'* (f.n. Greetham), ? *de la Sale* (p) (Exton).

salt² OE (Angl), 'salty, brackish'.
Saltmere (f.n. Lyddington), Saltwells (f.n. Greetham).

saltere OE (Angl), 'a salter, a salt-merchant'.
Salters Ford Lane, Salters Lane. *Saltergate* (f.n. Lt. Casterton), - *Furlong* (f.n. Gt. Casterton), *Salters crosse* (S. Luffenham), *Salters Lane* (Hambleton), ? *Salter Leys* (f.n. Greetham).

sand OE, 'sand, a tract of sandy ground, a place where sand is got, a sand-bed'.
Occasionally in f.ns., e.g. *Sandacre, sandpits, le sondes* (N. Luffenham), *the Sandes* (Bisbrooke, Glaston, Lyndon), *Sandhowes* (Seaton), *Sangate feild* (S. Luffenham), *le Santfurlong* (Wing).

sandig OE, 'sandy'.
the Sandy Close (f.n. Edith Weston), *Sandye Peece fur'* (f.n. Greetham), Sandy Wells (f.n. Glaston).

sand-pytt OE, 'a sand-pit'.
the Sandpitt (f.n. Belton), *Sandpitts* (f.n. Egleton).

sāpe OE, 'soap, salve'.
Soap Spring (Uppingham).

scanca OE, 'a shank, a leg'; figuratively, used of long, narrow, bent fields.
Meadow Shanke (f.n. Manton).

sceacol, scacol OE, 'a shackle', in p.ns. used esp. in the sense 'a place where animals are tethered or shackled'; also **shackle** ModE dial., 'quaking grass', which may have a long history (*v.* Elements 2 98-9).
Shacklewell.

sceaft OE, 'a shaft, a pole', in p.ns. prob. used of a pole acting as a landmark or a boundary-post.
? Shaft Nook (f.n. Whissendine).
sceaga, scaga OE, 'a small wood, a copse'.
? *Wilkershaw.*   ? *Shaw Hills* (f.n. Lyddington).
scēap, scēp, OE, 'a sheep'.
Sheepdyke Lane.   Only occasionally in f.ns., e.g. Scapwell Fd (Barrow), Sheep Dyke (Thistleton), *the Sheepeclose* (Glaston), *Sheepe Lane* (Wardley), *Shep-worth* (Morcott), *Shipland Furlong* (Barrow).
*****scēap-cot** OE, 'a shed for sheltering sheep, a sheepcote'.
Arme Strong Sheepcoate (Braunston), *cepecotehyl* (f.n. N. Luffenham), *Sheepcoate* (Egleton), Sheep Cote Cl (f.n. Lyddington), Sheepcote furlong (f.n. Thorpe by Water), Shepcoat Hollow (f.n. Oakham), *the Shepecote of John Presgrave* (Bisbrooke).
scearn, scarn OE, 'dung, muck'.
? Shorne Hill.
scēarp OE, 'sharp, pointed', **scharp** ME, 'a pointed piece of land'.
Scharpslade (f.n. Glaston).
scearu OE, 'a share, a division'.
le Schar (f.n. Lyddington).
scelf OE, 'a ledge, shelving terrain'.
Hanging Shelf (f.n. Essendine), The Shelf Hill (f.n. Ryhall).
sc(e)oppa OE, 'a shop, a booth, a shed'; in ME, chiefly of 'a building for the manufacture or sale of goods'.
Shop End Cl (f.n. Stretton), *the Smiths shop* (Tixover).
sceort OE, 'short'.
Schortdoles (f.n. Glaston), *Schorthorswong, Shortegore furlong* (f.ns. Caldecott), *Short fur'* (f.n. Greetham), *Shortham piece, Short Sett* (f.ns. Manton), *shortlands* (f.n. S. Luffenham), *Sortewong* (f.n. Oakham), *Ssortwong'* (f.n. Mkt. Overton), *Syortebrech* (f.n. Uppingham).
scīr[1] OE, 'a shire, an administrative district'.
Shire Oaks.   *Shire Hall* (Oakham), *The Shirewood* (Burley), ? *Syrepol* (Seaton).
scīr[2] OE, 'bright, gleaming, clear of weeds'.
? *Syrepol* (Seaton).
scite OE, 'shit, dung'.
? *Shirt Pole Dale* (f.n. Greetham).
*****scofl-brǣdu** OE, 'a narrow strip of land' (*v.* YW 7 242, cf. **scofl**

Elements 2 112).
Shovelboards Furlong (f.n. Whissendine).
scole ME, 'a school'.
School.
scot ME, 'a tax, a payment'.
Scotland (f.n. N. Luffenham).
scrape, sheep-scrape ModE dial., 'a bare place where turf has been
scraped off by sheep on a steep hillside'.
Scrape Hills (f.n. Stretton).
scrēad OE, 'a scrap, a shred', used figuratively of a small patch of
land.
The Shred (f.n. Ryhall).
***scrubb** OE, 'a shrub, brushwood, a place overgrown with brush-
wood'.
Linden shrubbs, Long Shrubbs (f.ns. Edith Weston), *Tiltons Shrubbs*
(f.n. N. Luffenham).
scucca OE, 'a goblin, a sprite, a demon'.
? Shockmore Balk (f.n. S. Luffenham), ? *Shucheved* (f.n. Lt.
Casterton).
scut ModE, 'a short tail, esp. that of a rabbit'.
Scutt Hill (f.n. Essendine).
scyt(t)els, scyt(t)el OE, 'a bolt, a bar; a gate which bolts shut'; also
'an arrow'.
? Shuttlewood (Barleythorpe).
self OE, 'self'.
Selfsownelandys (f.n. Seaton).
seofon OE, 'seven'.
le seauen land (f.n. Oakham), *Seavenacres* (f.n. Teigh),
Sefneacrewong (f.n. Lyddington).
seolfor OE, **seluer** ME, 'silver'.
Silverdale (f.n. Tixover), Silver Hill (f.n. Barrowden).
(ge)set OE, 'a place for animals, a fold, a stable'.
Redset, Short Sett (f.ns. Manton), *Sett Closse* (f.n. Burley), ?
Dowsetts (f.n. Empingham).
seten OE, 'land in occupation'; also 'a plantation' (*v.* Elements 2
121, Sx 561).
? Settings Fm.
severall eModE, 'privately owned', referring to land in individual
ownership as opposed to common land.
The Several Cl (f.n. Glaston), *the severall* (f.n. Morcott), *Severall*

Leys (f.n. Stretton), Sevrells (f.n. Hambleton).
sex, seox, six OE, 'six'.
sixbutts (f.n. Lyddington).
shamel ME, 'a stall for the sale of meat'.
The Butchers Shambles (Oakham).
sheep-walk ModE, 'a range of pasture for sheep'.
Walk Fm. *Lord Exeter's Sheep Walk* (Lyddington), *The Sheepe Walke* (Stretton, Whissendine), Sheep Walk (Clipsham), *Sheep Walk* (Gt. Casterton), *the Sheep Walk in the Forrest of Lee* (Leighfield), *The Sheep Walks* (Empingham).
shoemaker ModE, 'a maker of shoes'.
Shoomakers Shop (Oakham).
shorthorn ModE, 'one of a breed of cattle with short horns'.
Shorthorn Cl (f.n. Ketton).
sīc OE, 'a small stream', **siche** ME, 'a piece of meadow along a stream'. Rarely survives in Ru f.ns., but sometimes varies with, and was no doubt often replaced by, **sīk** ON 'a ditch, a trench' (*v.* **sīk**).
Asker Syche, Bed Syche, Little Syche, Narrow Syche, Syche, Between the Syches (f.ns. Egleton), Peaseland Sich (f.n. Whissendine).
sīd OE, 'large, spacious, extensive, long'.
? Side Hills (f.n. Stretton), ? *Sideholmes* (f.n. Manton), ? *sydehome* (f.n. Teigh).
side OE, 'a side; the long side of a slope or hill, a hill-side; the land alongside a river, wood, village etc.'
Freq. in f.ns., e.g. *Breache Side* (Lyndon), *brooke side close* (Whitwell), *Churchside fur', Okeham field side, Side of the Hill* (Egleton), *Heath Side, Town Side fur', Wood Side* (Greetham), *sidewing balk* (Pilton).
sīk ON, 'a ditch, a trench'; the equivalent of **sīc** OE (*v. supra*) which it no doubt often replaced in Ru f.ns.
Sykes Spinney. Very freq. in f.ns., occasionally as a simplex, e.g. *Seek* (Egleton), *the sik* (Lyddington), (The) Syke(s) (Exton, Mkt. Overton, Tinwell). It is commonly compounded with spring- or stream-names, e.g. *Caldwelsyke* (Seaton), *Coumbewellsik* (Lyddington), *Grindle Syke* (Barleythorpe), *Jagwell Seike* (Uppingham), *Pikwell sicke* (Oakham), *Sowell Sike* (N. Luffenham), *Westwell seeke* (Hambleton). Size and shape are sometimes indicated, e.g. *Brethesik(e)* (Caldecott, Lyddington), *Forke seekes* (Edith Weston), *le Little Sicke, Longsicke* (Oakham); or position, e.g. *est syck, ester syke* (Egleton), *Midilsyke* (Barrow), *Wester seeke*

Furlong (Lyddington). Flora may be specified, e.g. *Feernsyke* (Cottesmore), *Laber Sike* (Wardley), *Wythyrsike* (Seaton); or associated buildings, e.g. *Chappel seeke* (Oakham), *Hallesik'* (Mkt. Overton), *Kirke sike* (Wing), *Toft Seeke* (Leighfield). The el. compounded with a surn., e.g. *Mr Chiseldines Sike* (Braunston), *Davysyke* (Lt. Casterton), *Robertissike* (Glaston), *The Turnbull Sike* (Tickencote) and such compounds as *Burntseeke* (Ashwell), *Flat Seeks* (Leighfield), *Row Syke* (Essendine) and *Tythstacke Seeke* (Whissendine), may indicate the later use of sík to denote pieces of land (cf. sīc).

sinder OE, 'cinder, slag'.
? Cindrell (f.n. Brooke).

sinke ME, 'a cesspool, a bog, a sump'.
Rite sink (f.n. Uppingham), *Sinke Furlong* (f.n. Morcott), Sink Lane (Ketton).

sitten ModE dial., 'stunted in growth'.
Sitten Bush (f.n. Edith Weston).

skáli ON, 'a temporary hut or shed'.
? Scale Hill.

skammr (skamt neut.) ON, 'short, brief, stinted in measure'.
Scantive Acre (f.n. Hambleton).

skirt ModE, 'the edge, the outskirts, the periphery' (<ON *skyrta* 'a shirt, a skirt').
Cut Skirt Cl, *Lowskirts* (f.ns. Ridlington), *Cutskirts* (f.n. Lyndon), Green Skirts (f.n. Morcott), *Smockskirts Furlong* (f.n. S. Luffenham).

skógr ON, 'a wood'.
? Turnpole Wood.

slæd OE, 'a valley'.
Fairly freq. in f.ns., e.g. *Allen Spring* -, *Jagwell* -, *Yellsmoor Slade* (Uppingham), *Appletree* -, *Lambert* -, *Peasehill* -, *Winnowdale Slade* (Manton), *Armslades, Hollywell slades, mikeldenslade, Wool Slades* (Barleythorpe), *Trenchsick slade, Turtle Slade* (Wardley). Cf. also *Butterwell slade* (Wing), *Helpitt slade* (Lyndon), *Ingresdale Slade* (Exton).

*slæget, *sleget OE, 'a sheep pasture'.
Dryslight (f.n. Braunston).

slang ModE dial., 'a long, narrow piece of land'.
Longslang (f.n. Burley).

slash ModE dial., 'a piece of wet or swampy ground overgrown with bushes'.

the Slash (f.n. Belton).

slate, sclate ME, 'slate; roofing slates'.

le Slathouse upon the Smythie Grene (Egleton).

*slēa OE, 'a grassy slope'.

? *Sleadike Lease* (f.n. Thistleton).

slipe, slippe ME, 'a slip, a narrow strip of land'.

(The) Slip ˙(f.ns. Barleythorpe, Braunston, Mkt. Overton, Whissendine), Slipe (f.n. Ketton, Tinwell), Six Acre Slip (f.n. Essendine).

smæl OE, 'narrow, thin'.

Smallhill (f.n. Braunston), *smalstones* (f.n. Thistleton).

smeoru OE, 'fat, grease, lard', **smjǫr** ON, 'grease, butter', alluding to rich pasture, productive of butter etc.

Smear Hill (f.n. Belton).

smēðe[1] OE, 'smooth'.

Smeeth More (f.n. Burley).

smið OE, **smiðr** ON, 'a smith, a worker in metal'.

Smiths Leyes (f.n. Glaston), *the Smiths shop* (Tixover), *Smythlond* (f.n. Burley), *terre fabri* (f.n. Langham).

smiððe OE, **smiðie** ME, 'a smithy, a metal-worker's shop'.

the Smithie Leyes (f.n. Glaston), *Smithy Leas Nook* (f.n. Bisbrooke), *Smytheholme* (f.n. Lt. Casterton), *Smythie close* (f.n. Hambleton), *le Smythie Grene* (f.n. Egleton).

smock ModE dial., used of both the Greater Bindweed (*Convolvulus sepium*) and the Ladysmock or Cuckoo Flower (*Cardamine pratensis*).

? *Smockskirts Furlong* (f.n. S. Luffenham).

*snār OE, 'brushwood'.

Snarlings (f.n. Mkt. Overton), *Snarlings* (f.n. Thistleton).

snūte ME, 'a snout', used topographically in the sense 'a projecting point of land'.

Goodmans Snowte (f.n. Wardley).

sōcn OE, **soke** ME, 'jurisdiction, the district over which a right of jurisdiction is exercised'.

Oakham Soke Hundred, Rutland (*Roteland sokene*).

spa eModE, 'a spa, a mineral medicinal spring'.

Spa Cl (f.n. Mkt. Overton), *Spaw Grounds* (f.n. Lt. Casterton).

spang OE, 'a clasp, a buckle', prob. used in some topographical sense like **spong** ModE dial., 'a long, narrow strip of land'.

Sponge fur' (f.n. Egleton), Spongham's Mdw (f.n. Pilton), *Spongwong* (f.n. Caldecott), Sponholm, *Nixons Sponk* (f.ns. Lyndon).

spearwa OE, 'a sparrow'.

sparrowmore (f.n. Teigh).

spell OE, 'speech, discourse', used in p.ns. esp. of places where speeches were made in assemblies and freq. denotes a hundred- or other meeting-place.

le Spellow (f.n. Barleythorpe).

spinney ME, 'a copse, a small plantation, a spinney'.

Nether Spyney (Edith Weston), *the Spinney* (Lyndon).

spīr OE, 'a spike, the blade of a_plant', **spire** ModE dial., 'reeds, rushes'.

Redespires (f.n. Braunston), Reed Spire Mdw (f.n. Langham).

sprat eModE, 'a rush, rush-like grass'.

Sprat Pittes (f.n. Ketton).

spring, spryng OE, 'a spring, a well, the source of a stream'. Springfield. Freq. in f.ns., e.g. *Spring Close* (Lt. Casterton, S. Luffenham, Edith Weston), Spring Cl (Burley, Clipsham, Ketton, N. Luffenham, Lyddington, Mkt. Overton, Tinwell), - Hades (Whissendine), - Mdw (Belton), - Piece (Ashwell, Teigh); *Cattlespring* (Tickencote), *Crosswell Spring* (Manton), *Maniwell Spring* (Greetham), *Respas Springe* (Belton), *West Well Spring* (Hambleton), ? *Willow Spring* (Manton). Cf. also *Allins Spring, Soap Spring* (Uppingham), Pope's Spring (Empingham), Poplin Spring (Glaston). In ME, a second meaning of 'a young plantation, a copse' is found and this may be present in *Willow Spring* (Manton), although the willow is naturally associated with water. Poss. also in Spring Piece (f.n. Essendine).

*sprogh ODan, 'brushwood', poss. in ablaut relationship to ***spræg** OE, 'brushwood, twigs' (*v.* K. Hald, *Nudansk Ordbog,* 2 vols., 6th ed., Copenhagen 1969, *s.n.* Sprogǿ).

Sprouridge (f.n. Greetham).

stæf OE, 'a stave, a rod'.

? Stavely (f.n. Morcott).

*stæfer OE, 'a pole, a stake'.

? Stover Hill (f.n. Whissendine).

stæpe OE, 'a step'.

le Stappe (f.n. Oakham).

*stak-ȝard ME, **stack-yard** ModE, 'a stack-yard, an enclosure for ricks'.

Stackyard (f.n. Exton, Pilton, Ryhall, Stretton, Teigh, Thistleton), - Cl (f.n. Barrow, Gt. Casterton, Empingham, Langham, S. Luffenham, Pickworth, Ridlington, Teigh), - Fd (f.n. Ashwell, Tickencote, Whissendine), The Rectors Stackyard (f.n. Stretton), *le Stakeyard* (f.n. Barleythorpe).
stakkr ON, 'a stack', cf. **stak-ʒard.*
Tythstacke Seeke (f.n. Whissendine).
stall OE, 'a place', esp. 'a standing-place, a stall for cattle etc.'; also 'the site of a building' (*v*. Sandred 37-41).
None Stalls (f.n. Braunston), Stall Cl (f.n. Barleythorpe).
stān OE, 'a stone, stone, rock'.
Freq. in f.ns., e.g. *Blackstones* (Lyndon), *smalstones* (Thistleton), *Stone acre* (S. Luffenham), - *Meadow* (Clipsham), *Stone-gals Furlong* (Cottesmore), *Stonelands* (Wardley), *stonewaters* (Wing), *Stonwongk'* (Barrow). Larger rock formations are suggested by *Cloudstone furlong* (Barrowden), *Stonegravehill* (Thistleton), *ston fall* (Egleton). The el. recurs in compound with **hyll** 'a hill', e.g. *Stanhill hauedelond* (Stoke Dry), *Stone Hill* (Uppingham), - *Furlong* (Barrow); and with **brycg** 'a bridge', e.g. *Stanbriggate* (Bisbrooke), *Stanbrigge* (Hambleton, Oakham), *Stanbryghyll'* (Cottesmore). Stone boundary markers are sometimes recorded, e.g. *Aston Stone* (Uppingham), *the stone called Glaston Stone* (Bisbrooke), *Horeston, Merestones* (N. Luffenham), as well as stone crosses and their remains, e.g. *Stompstone* (Cottesmore), *stone cross dale* (Thistleton), Stump Stone (Ryhall).
stānig OE, 'stone, rocky'.
Stannywell. *Staney Ford Willows* (f.n. Whissendine), *Stanicle* (f.n. Wing), *Stoney Middle Furlong, Stonye furlong* (f.ns. Uppingham), *le Stoniforlong* (f.n. N . Luffenham), *Stony Bancke* (f.n. Barrowden), *Stonyland* (f.n. Oakham).
*stān-pytt OE, ***stan(e)pytt** ME, **stone-pit** ModE, 'a stone-pit, a pit from which stone is got, a quarry'.
Fairly freq. in f.ns., e.g. *(the) Ston(e)pitt(e)s* (N. Luffenham, Lyndon, Morcott, Pilton, Uppingham), *Stone Pitt Closes* (Glaston), - *Furlong* (Barrow, Oakham), - *Hill* (Stretton), Old Stone Pit (Lyddington, Stretton), Stone Pit (Gt. Casterton, Thistleton), - Cl (Greetham, S. Luffenham), - Fd (Edith Weston), - Furlong (Seaton).
stapol OE, 'a post, a pillar'.
Stablesford Bridge.
staup ON, 'a steep declivity'.

? *Coke stawpe* (f.n. Egleton).
stede OE, 'a place, a site'.
Bowestedewong (f.n. Lyddington), The Copstead (f.n. Barrowden), *Okestead Close* (f.n. Braunston).
steort OE, 'a tail'; in p.ns., 'a tail of land, a projecting piece of land'.
Starthill Pits (f.n. Ketton).
stīg OE, 'a path, a narrow road', cf. **sty-way**.
Alwoldestie (Uppingham), *Bochawesti, Ounbystye* (Lt. Casterton), *Kyngmilne Stey*, Middlesey Way (N. Luffenham).
stigel OE, 'a stile'; also 'a steep ascent'.
Occasionally in f.ns., e.g. *the Parkstile* (Ridlington), *Pedderstyle* (Cottesmore), *le Stylle* (Lt. Casterton), *Woodfield stile* (Stoke Dry), *ye Stile Close, Woodstyle Close* (Braunston); *le Stylegate* (Stoke Dry).
stīg-rāp OE, 'a stirrup', used in p.ns. in some undetermined sense, poss. from a fancied resemblance.
? *Coke stawpe* (f.n. Egleton).
stigu, stig OE, 'a sty, a pen'.
Hogstyes (Oakham), *Stye3* (Cottesmore).
stint eModE, 'a portion of common pasturage to which a limited number of cattle, according to kind, is assigned for grazing'.
Stentgrass (f.n. Lyddington), *Stint(s)* (f.ns. S. Luffenham, Morcott).
stoc OE, 'a place, a religious place; a secondary settlement'.
Martinsthorpe (*Martinestoch*), Stoke Dry, ? Ravenstock Wood. Stockwell (f.n. Caldecott).
stocc OE, 'a tree-trunk, a tree-stump, a stock'; also '(a pair or set of) stocks as an instrument of punishment'.
Stocks Hill (Ketton, Manton). *Stocke Wong* (f.n. Greetham), *Stocklands* (f.n. Empingham).
*stoccing OE, **stocking** ME, 'a clearing of stumps, a piece of ground cleared of stumps'.
Stocken Fm, Stocken Hall. *Abbots Stocking, Stokkyngpittes* (f.ns. Pickworth), *Apple Tree Stockin* (f.n. Clipsham), Bottom Stocking (f.n. Exton), *North Stockings* (f.n. Greetham), *Stockinge Sale* (f.n. Wardley).
stōd OE, 'a stud, a herd of horses'.
Stud Ho.
stōd-fald OE, 'a stud-fold, a horse-enclosure'.
Stedfold Lane. Stadfolds (f.n. Ashwell), Steadfold (f.n. Ketton), *Stodfolde* (f.n. Glaston), Studfold Furlong (f.n. Morcott).

stomacher eModE, 'a kind of waistcoat worn by men; a triangular panel in a woman's dress', used figuratively in f.ns. of closes of irregular shape.
Stomacher Close (f.n. Egleton).
storr² ON, **star** ODan, **star(r)** ModE dial., 'sedge', later 'bent-grass, marram-grass'.
Star Fd (f.n. Ryhall), ? *Starr Close* (f.n. Burley).
storð ON, 'a young wood'.
le Storth (Lt. Casterton).
stōw OE, ' place, a place of assembly, a holy place'.
Alstoe. *Middelstow* (N. Luffenham).
strǣt OE, **strēt** (Angl), 'a Roman road, a paved road; an urban road, a street (of houses)'; freq. in modern urban street-names.
Stretton. *the Highestrete* (Barrowden), *High Street, Nottingham streete* (Thistleton), *Lyngcolne Strete, Nottyngham Strete* (Greetham), *the Street* (N. Luffenham), *Streete-Waye* (Gt. Casterton), *le Strete* (Barrow), *Town-Street* (Edith Weston). Occasionally in f.ns., e.g. *Longstreete furlong* (Tickencote), *Street Ende* (Greetham), *Street furl'* (Morcott), *le wong be west the Strete* (Mkt. Overton).
strang OE, 'strong'; in f.ns. 'with firm, compact soil'.
Strong Land (f.n. Empingham).
stray ME, 'a piece of unenclosed common pasture'.
? Stray Lands (f.n. Whissendine), Stray Pasture (f.n. Barrowden).
*strīp OE, 'a narrow tract of land; a small stream'.
Church Road and Strip (f.n. Lyndon), (the) Stripe (f.ns. Barrowden, S. Luffenham, Seaton).
stubb OE, 'a stub, a tree-stump'.
Maple stubbe (f.n. Belton), *stubbe furlonge* (f.n. Barleythorpe).
stubbede ME, 'reduced to a stub, cut off or broken near the ground' (NED 1575).
Stump Stone (*le Stubbedeston'*, Ryhall).
stubbil, stuble ME, 'stubble'.
le Stuble (f.n. Stoke Dry).
stump OE, 'a stump, a tree-stump'.
Elde Stump (f.n. Manton), Elder Stump Cl (f.n. Ketton), Eldern Stump (f.n. Whissendine); *Stompstone* (Cottesmore), *Stump Cross* (Edith Weston), Stump Stone (Ryhall).
*stybbing OE, 'a place with tree-stumps, a clearing'.
Steeping (f.n. Wardley), Steppings (f.n. Stoke Dry), *Stybbbynges* (f.n. Uppingham).

stȳr OE, 'a rule, a regulation'; also 'a penalty, a fine'.
Sturrock's Nooks (f.n. Belton).

*sty-way ME, 'a pathway, a narrow road, a footpath' (*v.* **stīg, weg**).
Gunnel Lane. Middlesey Way (N. Luffenham), Sty Way
(Barrowden).

sundor, synder OE, 'asunder, apart', alluding to land or property
detached or separated from an estate, or to land or property of a
special kind, e.g. private or privileged; cf. **sundor-land.**
Cinder Mdw (f.n. Hambleton).

sundor-land OE, 'land set apart for some special purpose, private
land, detached land', cf. **sundor.**
Sinderlands (f.n. Braunston), *Sunderland* (f.n. Lt. Casterton).

sūr OE, 'sour, damp, coarse' (of land).
Sour Hill, *Surmedue* (f.ns. Ryhall), Sour Lands (f.n. S. Luffenham).

sūð OE, 'south, southward'.
Southfield Lodge. Freq. in f.ns., esp. compounded with **feld** 'a field'
(Barleythorpe, Clipsham, Egleton, Exton, Greetham, Oakham, Pilton,
Whissendine). Cf. also *Southbrookes* (Wing), *South Hill*
(Barleythorpe), *Southton'* (Mkt. Overton), *Sudforlong'* (Bisbrooke),
Sudwell (Edith Weston), *Suthdale, Suthgate* (Oakham) etc.

sūðeweard OE, 'southward, south, southern'.
Grass Soward (f.n. Ketton), *Sowyt Flet* (f.n. Teigh).

swæð, swaðu OE, 'a track, a pathway', **swathe** ME, 'a strip of
grassland'.
Parsons swathes (f.n. Lyndon), Swarth Mdw (f.n. Belton), *three
swathe furlong* (f.n. Lyddington).

*swalg OE, 'a pit, a pool'.
Swallow Hole (f.n. Greetham), - Cl (f.n. Stretton), - Furlong (f.n.
Barrow), Swallow Pit Cl (f.n. Thistleton).

swan[1] OE, 'a swan'.
Swan's Nest Coppice (Stoke Dry).

swān[2] OE, 'a herdsman, a swine-herd, a peasant'.
Swancote Leys (f.n. S. Luffenham).

swash ModE, 'a rush of water, a flooding; watery'.
Swashills (f.n. Preston).

sweeting eModE, 'a sweet-apple tree'.
Sweeting Tree Nooke (f.n. Empingham).

swēte OE, 'sweet, pure, pleasant'.
Sweete well dike (f.n. Edith Weston).

swīn[1] OE, **svín** ON, 'a swine, a pig'.

Swintley Lodge. *Longeswyneslee* (f.n. Lyddington), *Swine Tree fur'* (f.n. Greetham), *Swingate Furlong* (f.n. Edith Weston), *Swynewik'* (f.n. Glaston), *Swynpit* (f.n. Mkt. Overton).

*tagga, *tegga OE, **tag, teg** ModE dial., 'a teg, a young sheep'.
Tagland (f.n. Morcott), *Taglock Close* (f.n. S. Luffenham).
taile eModE, 'the part of a mill-race below the wheel, the tail-race'.
Mill Tail (Ryhall), Mill Tail (Lyddington, Thorpe by Water).
tang, *tong OE, 'tong, forceps', but usually in the sense of **tangi** ON, 'a tang, a spit of land'.
tongland furlong (f.n. Uppingham).
tan-yard ModE, 'a yard or factory where tanning is carried on, a tannery'.
Tan Yard (Egleton).
taverne ME, 'a tavern'.
The Winetavern (Oakham).
tēag OE, 'a close, a small enclosure'.
Teigh. *Cringlety Valley* (f.n. Empingham), ? *Overbothtys* (f.n. Barrow), *Tyflet* (f.n. Teigh).
temple ME, 'a temple', usually in allusion to the properties of the Knights Templars.
Temple Barns (f.n. Stretton), *Temple Peyse* (f.n. Greetham).
tenthe ME, 'a tenth part; a tenth part of produce or profits appropriated as an ecclesiastical due'.
the Tenths (f.n. Glaston).
tentour ME, 'a tenter, a frame for stretching cloth'.
Big Tenter's (f.n. Ridlington), *Tentar Lane* (Edith Weston), Tenter Gap (f.n. Morcott), *Tenter Hedge* (f.n. Empingham), Tenters Cl (f.n. Langham).
tēoða OE, 'a tithe, a tenth'.
The Tithe Barne (Braunston), *the Tithebarne lane, Tythe Barne* (Oakham), Tithe Mdw, The Tithe Yard (f.ns. Whissendine), *the tythe barn* (Bisbrooke), *Tythe Close* (f.n. Greetham), *Tyth Meadow* (f.n. Manton), *Tythstacke Seeke* (f.n. Whissendine).
tēoðung OE, 'a tenth, a tenth part, a tithing', used either of 'land set apart for the payment of tithes' or 'a small administrative district'.
South Luffenham Tything (Morcott).
þæc OE, 'thatch, materials for thatching'.

thackham medowe (f.n. Teigh), The Thackhams (f.n. Langham).
þak ON, 'thatch, materials for thatching'.
Thacholme (f.n. Stoke Dry).
*þefa OE, 'brushwood, bramble'.
thefholm (f.n. N. Luffenham).
þerscold OE, 'a threshold, a border, a limit'.
Thresholdgate (Oakham).
þicce[1] OE, 'a thicket, dense undergrowth'.
Thicke Moore (f.n. Greetham), Mountjoy Thick (Beaumont Chase).
þing OE, 'a possession, property'.
Castur Thyng (Bisbrooke), *Durants -, East Yard -, Spencers -,
Wythams Thing* (S. Luffenham), *lauerockes þing* (Seaton), *Middletons
-, Wetherleys thing* (Morcott), *Slawsons Thynge* (Barrowden).
þistel OE, 'a thistle'.
Thistleton.
*þistlig OE, thist(e)ly ME, 'thistly'.
Thistley Gore (f.n. Whissendine).
þorn OE, ON, 'a thorn-tree, a hawthorn'.
? Turnpole Wood. Fairly freq. in f.ns., usually as a second el., e.g.
bradthorn (Bisbrooke), *Castle Thorns* (Morcott), *Coppethornhull*
(Lyddington), *Crakepornfurlong'* (Barrow), *Harethornes* (Pickworth,
Ridlington), *Umpthorne* (N. Luffenham), *Wdebindthornwong*
(Cottesmore); but occasionally as a first el., e.g. *Thornborrow Hill*
(Hambleton), *pornham broc* (Ayston), *Thorntre ʒard* (Thistleton).
þornig OE, 'thorny, growing with thorns'.
Thorn(e)yclose (f.n. Lyddington, Hambleton), *Thorney Leys* (f.n.
Morcott), *Thorney Meadow* (f.n. N. Luffenham).
þorp ON, 'a secondary settlement, a dependent outlying farmstead
or hamlet'.
Alsthorpe, Barleythorpe, Belmesthorpe, *Fregsthorpe,* Gunthorpe,
Ingthorpe, Kilthorpe Grange, *Manthorpe,* Martinsthorpe, Sculthorpe
Spinney, *Soulthorpe,* Thorpe by Water, Tolethorpe Hall, Westhorpe.
For the el. in Ru, *v.* Barrie Cox, 'Rutland and the Scandinavian
settlements: the place-name evidence', ASE 18 (1989), 135-48.
þrēo OE, 'three'.
Three Bush Furlong (f.n. Greetham), *three swathe furlong* (f.n.
Lyddington), *Threwong* (f.n. Caldecott).
þrote OE, 'a throat', eModE throte, 'a throat, a narrow passage'.
in the Throat of the Lea (f.n. Lyddington).
Þunor OE, the name of a pagan Anglo-Saxon god, corresponding to

Scand *Þórr*.
? *pureslege broc* (Ayston).
þurh OE, 'through'.
Thorough Lands (f.n. Lyddington, Thorpe by Water), *the thorow Land* (f.n. Manton), *the through ley* (f.n. Oakham).
þvers ON, 'athwart'.
Twheresgate (f.n. Ridlington).
þynne OE, 'thin, not dense, poor', used in minor names to indicate sparse growth.
Branston Thins (Leighfield).
þyrne OE, **þyrnir** ON, 'a thorn-bush'.
Thurndel Ley (f.n. Morcott), *Thurn dike, tirngore* (f.ns. Barrowden).
þyrs OE, 'a giant, a demon', ME **thirs**, 'a goblin, a hobgoblin'.
Thirspit (f.n. Barrowden, Glaston), *Tyrespyt* (f.n. Empingham).
ticcen OE, 'a kid, a young goat'. ·
Tickencote, Tixover.
tike, tyke ModE, 'a low-bred dog'.
Tyke Close (f.n. Normanton).
timber OE, 'timber, trees'.
le Milnetymbermede (f.n. Stretton), Timbergate Cl (f.n. Ketton).
tod-hole ME, 'a fox's earth, a fox-hole'.
Todhols (f.n. Leighfield).   ·
toft ODan, **topt** ON, **toft** late OE, 'a building site, a curtilage, a messuage'.
Cottage Toft, Toftwong (f.ns. Caldecott), *hotoft* (f.n. Bisbrooke), *Toftewell* (f.n. Lt. Casterton), Tofts (f.n. Cottesmore), *Toft Seeke* (f.n. Leighfield).
toll-bar ModE, 'a toll-bar'.
Toll Bar (f.n. Ayston), Tollbar Cl (f.n. Ryhall, Tinwell).
toll-bōthe ME, 'a toll-booth'.
Uppingham Tollhouse (*le Tolbothe*).
topp OE, 'top, the top of a bank or hill'.
Tree Topps (f.n. N. Luffenham).
*tōt OE, **tote** ME, 'a look-out hill'.
Twitch Hill Fm.
*tōt-hyll OE, 'a look-out hill'.
Twitch Hill Fm.   ?   *Tirtle Meare* (f.n. Morcott), *Turtle Slade* (f.n. Wardley).
trenche ME, 'a cutting, a ditch'.
Trenchsike (f.n. Wardley).

trēow, trēo OE, 'a tree'.

Asketrow (f.n. Clipsham), *Bidwell Tree* (f.n. N. Luffenham), *Thorntre-ȝard* (f.n. Thistleton), *Trewelmore* (f.n. Lyddington), *Salow Tre Leyes Furlong, Swine Tree fur'* (f.ns. Greetham).

trespas OFr, ME, 'a transgression, a breach of law'.

Trespasesike (f.n. Glaston).

trog OE, 'a valley, a trough; a long, narrow vessel'.

ye Stone Trough (f.n. Ketton).

tūn OE, 'an enclosure, a farmstead, a village, an estate' (*v.* **-ingtūn**).

Ayston, Belton, Braunston, Casterton, Egleton, Exton, Geeston, Glaston, Lyddington, Manton, Normanton, Mkt. Overton, Pilton, Preston, Ridlington, Seaton, *Snelston*, Stretton, Thistleton, Town Park, *Wenton*, Edith Weston. Freq. in f.ns., e.g. Town (Ketton), *The Town* (Lyndon), *Town(e) Close* (Ayston, Egleton, Empingham, N. Luffenham, Wardley, Whissendine), Town Cl (Ashwell, Preston, Edith Weston), *(the) Town(e)(s)end* (Burley, Greetham, Morcott, Tixover, Uppingham), Town(s)end (Essendine, S. Luffenham, Hambleton), *Towne end close* (Egleton), Town(s)end Cl (N. Luffenham, Manton, Oakham, Pilton, Thistleton, Tinwell, Whissendine), - Fd (Cottesmore), *Townsend Leys* (Belton), *Town Meadow* (Lt. Casterton) etc. Cf. also *Norton' Wod', Southton'* (Mkt. Overton), Harton (Clipsham).

tunge OE, 'a tongue, a tongue of land'.

Oliver Tonge (f.n. Stoke Dry), *Tongue furlong* (f.n. Barrowden), *Tongue Lands fur'* (f.n. Egleton), *Tungerode* (f.n. Oakham), *Tunkeacre* (f.n. Tinwell).

tūn-scipe OE, 'a township; the population of a village'. Greetham Township Furlong (f.n. Cottesmore), *the Towneship meadow* (f.n. Hambleton).

*tūn-stall OE, 'the site of a farm, a farmstead'.

Dunstall Plantations. *Dunstalls hedg* (Lyddington), *Dunston* (f.n. Empingham), Great Dunston Cl (f.n. Ketton), *Dunston Furlong* (f.n. Uppingham).

tup ME, 'a ram, a tup'.

Tups Cl (f.n. Essendine).

turnep(e) eModE, 'a turnip'.

The Turnipp Close (f.n. Seaton).

turnepike ME, 'a turnpike'.

Leicester Rd (*Lester Turnpike*). *The Turnpike* (Lyddington), The Turnpike (Empingham), - Cl (f.n. Bisbrooke, Ketton), *the Turnpike*

Rails (f.n. Uppingham), *Turnpike Road* (S. Luffenham), Turnpike Rd (Ryhall).

turtla OE, 'a turtle-dove'.

? *Tirtle Meare* (f.n. Morcott).

twēgen OE, **twey** ME, **two** ModE, 'two'.

Tolands (f.n. Barrow), *Towell Hill* (f.n. Whissendine), *Towells furlong* (f.n. Morcott).

twī- OE prefix, 'double, two'.

Thuiford (Oakham).

-uc, -oc OE noun suffix.

? Bussack Barn.

uferra OE, 'higher, upper'.

Overmicle Hill (f.n. Belton), *Over Spyney* (Edith Weston), *The Over Pasture* (f.n. Whissendine), *thovre furlonge* (f.n. Lyndon).

under OE, 'under, beneath, below'.

Preston vnderwoods (f.n. Preston).

upp, ūp, uppe OE, 'up, higher up'.

Upper Hall, Uppingham. *Upfeld* (f.n. N. Luffenham), *Vphalle* (Seaton).

upper ME, 'higher'.

the upper Furlong (f.n. Manton).

ūt(e) OE, 'outside, on the outskirts; outer, more distant'.

Brendhoutecroft (f.n. Mkt. Overton), *Outfeild* (f.n. Pickworth), *Outfield* (f.n. Empingham).

vacherie ME, 'a dairy farm, cow-pasture, a place where cows are kept or pastured'.

Vetchery Cl (f.n. Empingham).

vangr ON, 'a garden, an in-field'.

Very freq. in f.ns., invariably as the final el. of a compound. Typical parish groups from the 14th cent. show their great variety, e.g. *Almawewonge, Brechewong, Hennehowong, le Lady Wong, Litelhawewonge, Midelwonge, Tibwellewonge* (Lt. Casterton), *Barkereswong, Bowestedewong, Brecheswong, Bredenbriggewong, Galowong, Halfacrewong, Hangendewong, Holdenewong, Longhorsewong, Longlandwong, Pesewong, Prestleywong, Sefneacrewong, Whitecroswong* (Lyddington), *Brengewong, Briggewong, Estmedewong, Fyuacrewong, Horenggewong, Northolmwong, Ouerthwertwong, Ouerwong, Schorthorswong, Spongwong, Threwong,*

Toftwong (Caldecott), *Estrewellewong, Langmerewong, Mellewong',
Morwong, Southton' wong, Ssortwong', Swynpitwong, Walwortwong'*
(Mkt. Overton).

vápnatak ON, **wæpengetæc** late OE, **wapentac** ME, 'a wapentake, a
subdivision of a county', corresponding to OE **hundred**.
(Early forms for) Alstoe Hundred, Martinsley Hundred; *Wiceslea
Wapent'*.

veche ME, 'vetch', a plant grown for fodder.
Viche Close (f.n. Thistleton).

vengi ON, 'a field'.
Wing.

vikerage ME, 'a vicarage'.
The Vicarage. *le viccaradge land* (f.n. Oakham).

vikere ME, 'a vicar'.
Vicar Cl (f.n. Stretton), *ye Vicar Pits* (f.n. Ketton), *Vicar Pyttes* (f.n.
Exton), *Vicker Lane* (Stretton).

vine ME, 'a vine'.
Le Vyne.

vrá ON, **wro** ME, 'a nook, a corner of land'.
le Wro (f.n. Lt. Casterton).

*wacu OE, 'a watch', used in p.ns. of a watching-place.
Wakehull (f.n. Mkt. Overton).

wād OE, 'woad', cultivated for dye.
Wadd Close (f.n. Normanton).

wadmill ModE dial., 'a mill for the processing of woad'.
the Wadmill Close (f.n. Bisbrooke), Wadmill Cl (f.n. Glaston,
Langham).

wægn OE, 'a wagon, a cart'.
? *Wenton*.

wæps OE, 'a wasp'.
Wipesnest (f.n. Manton), *-fur'* (f.n. Egleton).

(ge)wæsc OE, 'a washing, a flood'.
R. Gwash.

wæsce OE, 'a place for washing'.
The Washdyke. Wash Dike Nook (f.n. Gunthorpe), Washdyke(s)
(f.ns. Hambleton, Morcott), - Cl (f.n. Exton), Washpit Cl (f.n.
Glaston), - Fd (f.n. Bisbrooke), - Mdw (f.n. Ayston, Leighfield),
Washpole (f.n. Ketton).

wæter OE, 'water, an expanse of water; a stream or river'; or as first el., 'near to a stream; wet, watery'.

Thorpe by Water. Fairly freq. in f.ns., esp. as a first el. compounded with **furh** 'a furrow' (Essendine, Greetham, Morcott, N. Luffenham, Teigh, Uppingham, Edith Weston); or with **galla** 'a wet place in a field' (Barleythorpe, Lt. Casterton, Egleton, Morcott, Oakham, Uppingham). Cf. also *the water balke* (N. Luffenham), *the Water gutter* (Lyndon), *Waterfield Syke* (Manton), *Water Wong fur'* (Greetham). Rarely appears as a second el., e.g. Broad Water (Empingham), *stonewaters* (Wing).

wæter-gefall OE, 'a waterfall'; prob. also 'a place where a stream disappears into the ground'.

Waterfal (f.n. Bisbrooke), *Waterfall Dale* (f.n. Stretton).

wæterig OE, 'watery'.

Watry Close (f.n. Ketton).

walhhnutu OE, 'a walnut (-tree)'.

Wall Nutt tree Close (f.n. Glaston).

walhwyrt OE, 'the dwarf elder, the wallwort'.

Walwortwong' (f.n. Mkt. Overton).

walk ModE, 'a range of pasture', cf. **sheep-walk**.

Beaumont Walk (f.n. Beaumont Chase), *Walkleys* (f.n. Ashwell).

wall OE, 'a wall'.

Jackson Wall, The Wall Close (f.ns. Empingham), *Parck wall Furlong* (f.n. Lyddington), Wall Cl, *Wall Gressons* (f.ns. Hambleton), *Walle close* (f.n. N. Luffenham).

wareine ME, 'a piece of ground for the breeding of rabbits, a warren'.

Tickencote Warren, Warren Fm, Warren Spinney, Witchley Warren Fm. The Warren(s) (f.ns. Braunston, Stretton), Warren Fd (f.n. N. Luffenham).

waste ME, 'wasteland'; frequently used of rough pasture.

the Waste (Egleton, Greetham, Hambleton), - *Way* (Barrow), (The) Waste (Empingham, Lyddington), - in the Fox Covert (Tinwell).

water-mylne ME, 'a water-mill'.

The Mill (Barrowden), Thorpe Mill, Watermill Spinney. *Watermill* (Belton), - *furlong* (f.n. Uppingham), *ye watermyln* (Oakham).

weard OE, 'watch'.

? Wardley.

weg OE, 'a way, a road'.

Common in Ru, but Scand **gata** 'a road' is more freq. in earlier road names at a ratio of almost 3 : 1. Freq. appears with a village name, e.g. *Gonthorpe* -, *Hambleton* -, *Manton* -, *Okeham* -, *Stamford Way*(*e*) (Egleton), *Pilton* -, *uppingham way*, *Wingway* (Morcott). Local minor features may also be compounded, e.g. *Bridgeway* (Morcott), *Crosse Waye* (Gt. Casterton), *ford weye* (Stoke Dry), *Woodcrosse way* (N. Luffenham). Recurring compounds include *Broadway* (Wardley, Whissendine) and *Street*(*e*) *Way*(*e*) (Barrow, Gt. Casterton). Cf. also *le Kingsway* (Beaumont Chase). Occurs only once as a first el., in *Way Dikeham* (f.n. Clipsham).

wella, well(e) OE (Angl), 'a well, a spring, a stream (fed by a spring)'.
Ashwell, Bidwell's Lodge, Cordle Spring, Crown Well Bridge, Hawkswell Spring, Our Lady's Well, Shacklewell, Tinwell, Well Cross, Wells St, Whitwell, Wingwell. Very freq. in f.ns.; it may be compounded with els. indicating associated flora, e.g. *Cresswell* (Oakham), Dogwell, *Peasewell* (Whissendine), *Jagwell* (Uppingham), *Wortwell* (Ketton); or birds, e.g. *Goswell'* (Barrowden), *Hawkswell* (Barrow), *Puttocks Well* (Bisbrooke); or fish, e.g. *Mertewell'*, *Pikwellsicke* (Oakham); or animals, e.g. *Bucwell'* (Lt. Casterton), Catwell (Beaumont Chase), Muxwells (Glaston), Scapwell (Barrowden). Springs were often considered to be holy or had religious associations, e.g. *Crosswell* (Manton), *halywelcros* (Barrowden), *Holy Well* (Hambleton), Tibba's Well (Ryhall); or were known for their efficacy in healing, e.g. *Botewell* (Leighfield), *Hel*(*l*)*well* (Oakham, Teigh). *Butterwell* (Wing), *Byrtwell'* (Seaton), Clenwell, *Sweete well* (Edith Weston) suggest approval of the spring's quality, Saltwells (Greetham) disapproval. *Northwell* (Oakham), *Sudwell* (Edith Weston) and *Westwell* (Hambleton) indicate the direction of the well, spring or stream from the settlement, and *Maniwell Spring* (Greetham), Many Wells (S. Luffenham), *Towells* (Morcott), Towell Hill (Whissendine) the number of springs. Ownership is sometimes specified, e.g. *Alingwell* (Caldecott), *Hangcock Well* (Manton). Recurring els. in compound with **wella** are **cald** 'cold' (Belton, Egleton, Hambleton, Seaton), **calu** 'lacking in vegetation' (Barleythorpe, Barrow, Belton) and **fūl** 'foul, dirty' (Belton, Empingham, Lyddington). The el. only very occasionally appears ˙ initially in a compound, e.g. *Wellemorheuedlandes* (Caldecott), *Welhalfager* (Lt. Casterton), *Wellheadland Field* (Whissendine).

welle-heved ME, 'the place at which a spring breaks out of the ground'; **well-head** eModE retains the ME denotation, but in

addition signifies '(a structure erected over) the top of a draw-well'.
Drywell Head, Parker's Well Head (f.ns. Thistleton).
west OE, 'west'.
Westhorpe, Westmoor Lane, Edith Weston. In f.ns., freq. compounded with **feld** 'a field' (Ashwell, Barleythorpe, Barrow, Burley, Clipsham, Cottesmore, Egleton, Exton, Oakham, Mkt. Overton, Stretton, Thistleton, Wing). Cf. also *be Westgate* (Mkt. Overton), *le Westhay* (Barrowden), West Ings, *le Westmers(s)h* (Whissendine), *West lands* (Barleythorpe), *West Meades fur'* (Egleton), *Westmore* (Exton), *Westwode3* (Cottesmore).
*wester OE, 'west, western'.
Westland Wood. *Wester seeke Furlong* (f.n. Lyddington).
wēt OE (Angl), 'wet, damp'.
le wetlondes (f.n. N. Luffenham), *Wheat(e) Moore* (f.n. Greetham), ? *Wheatleas* (f.n. Barleythorpe).
weðer OE, 'a castrated ram, a wether'.
le Wedare furlong (f.n. Barleythorpe).
weyour ME, 'a pond'.
The Weir Cl (f.n. Barrowden), Wier Cl (f.n. Glaston), ? *Wyers Town End Close* (f.n. Whissendine).
wheelhouse ModE, 'a building containing a horsewheel as motive power for farm machinery'.
Wheelhouse Cl (f.n. Ashwell, Teigh).
wīc OE, 'a building or collection of buildings for a special purpose; a farm, a dairy farm', cf. **heorde-wīc.**
Luffewyke. Boswick Cl (f.n. Teigh), ? *Eastwick* (f.n. Stoke Dry), *Heynwyk'* (f.n. Stretton), *Swynewik'* (f.n. Glaston).
wice OE, 'a wych-elm'.
the Witch Close (f.n. N. Luffenham).
wig ModE dial., 'buttermilk', used of good pasture.
Wig Acres (f.n. Manton).
*wigga OE, 'a beetle'.
? *Wye sike* (f.n. Ryhall), ? *le wy3esike* (f.n. Seaton).
wilde OE, 'wild, desolate'.
Wildegate (f.n. Wardley).
*wilig OE, 'a willow'.
Fairly freq. in f.ns.; occasionally as a simplex, e.g. *the Willoes* (Barrowden), *(the) Willow(e)s* (Oakham, Uppingham), the el. is more often prefixed by an owner's name, e.g. *Billingtons Willows*

(Oakham), *Brownes Willow* (Egleton), *Middleton Willows* (Morcott), *Peach's Willow* (Bisbrooke), *Sharpes willes* (Pilton), or appears as a first el., e.g. *Willowesholme* (Lyddington), *Willow Row, Wyleweholm* (N. Luffenham), *Willow Spring* (Manton), *Wyllowong* (Cottesmore). Cf. also *Ransike willowes* (Barrowden), *Staney Ford Willows* (Whissendine).

*wind-geat OE, 'a wind-swept gap'.
? Wind Gate Hill (f.n. Ryhall).

wind-mylne ME, 'a windmill'.
Old Windmill, Windmill, Windmill Hill. Recorded in Ru from the early 13th cent., e.g. *molendino ventritico de Wenge* (c. 1212-38, Wing), *Kermontwindmuln'* (1349, Caldecott), *ye wyndmyln* (1482, Oakham). Most instances belong to the 17th cent., e.g. *(the) Windmill* (Ayston, Braunston, Hambleton, Thistleton), *the Windmilne* (Lyndon) and those of Windmill Cl (f.n. Barrowden) and Windmill Fd (f.n. N. Luffenham). Note also *molendinum ventriticum de Langham* (1305, Langham), another early example. Old Windmill *supra* is earlier *Wyndmuln* (1349, Ketton), while Windmill (Whissendine) and Windmill Hill (Lyddington) both record 17th cent. examples.

wīn-geard OE, **vinȝerd** ME, 'a vineyard'.
Wynnȝerd (f.n. Oakham).

wisc OE, 'a marshy meadow'.
? *in Wis* (f.n. Seaton).

*wise OE, poss. 'a marsh, a marshy meadow'.
? *in Wis* (f.n. Seaton).

*wisp, *wips OE, 'a wisp', used topographically as 'a thicket, brushwood'.
The Wisp.

wīðig (**wīðigas** nom.pl.) OE, 'a withy, a willow'.
Wythyrsike (f.n. Seaton), ? The Wise (f.n. Essendine).

wold ME, 'a hill'.
Copwold Hill (f.n. Essendine).

wood-pile ModE, 'a pile or stack of wood, esp. for fuel'.
Woodpile leyes (f.n. Uppingham).

wool ModE dial., 'thistledown'.
? *Woole Elders* (f.n. Bisbrooke), ? *Wool Slades* (f.n. Barleythorpe).

worð OE, 'an enclosure'; possibly also 'a fortified enclosure'.
Pickworth, ? Littleworth. *Shep-worth* (f.n. Morcott).

wote, vote eModE, 'a vote, the collective assent of a body of persons'.

Vote Land (f.n. Thistleton).

wrang OE, **(v)rangr** ON, 'crooked, twisted in shape'.

Wrangdike Hundred. Occasionally in f.ns., most commonly as a first el. compounded with **land** in its sense 'a strip of arable in the common field' (Braunston, Cottesmore, Edith Weston, Whissendine, Wing); cf. also *Wrangrood* (S. Luffenham), Wrang roods (Barrowden), *Wrongedich* (N. Luffenham), *wrongsdale* (Tickencote).

wrinkel ME, 'a slight narrow ridge, a corrugation'; also 'a twisting, a winding'.

the Wrinckles (f.n. Lyndon).

wudu OE, 'a wood'; also 'timber'.

Burley Wood, Clipsham Park Wood, Eastwood, The Freewards, Greetham Wood, Hambleton Wood, Pickworth Gt. Wood, Rushpit Wood, Stoke Dry Wood, Stretton Wood, Wardley Wood, Woodhead. Occasionally in f.ns. as a first el., e.g. *Wodegate* (Cottesmore), *The Wood Close* (Brooke), *Wood Fylde* (Greetham), *Woodstyle Close* (Braunston), *Woodcrosse way* (N. Luffenham). Freq. as a second el., e.g. *Bikerwode* (Ashwell), *Bowwoode* (Tickencote), *Estwode* (Uppingham), *Fridwod* (Ridlington), *Lyndwode* (Pickworth), *The Shirewood* (Burley), *Westwode 3* (Cottesmore).

wudubinde OE, 'woodbine, convolvulus'.

Wdebindthornwong (f.n. Cottesmore).

wulf-pytt OE, 'a wolf-pit, a wolf-trap'.

Woolfit (Leighfield).

wyn ME, 'wine'.

The Winetavern (Oakham).

wyrt OE, 'a plant, a vegetable'.

Wortwell Field (f.n. Ketton).

yppe OE (Angl), 'a raised place, a hill'.

Uppingham.

NOTES ON THE DISTRIBUTION AND USAGE
OF SOME ELEMENTS

āc is confined to the south-west of the county beyond a line from Oakham to Barrowden and to the east beyond a line from Stretton to Ketton.

æsc. There is a western strip of names with **æsc** west of the line Market Overton to Stoke Dry, and a south-eastern triangle of such names defined by Exton, Morcott and Tickencote.

ba(c)ksyde. This is a local dialectal feature which, apart from two outlying instances in the east in adjoining Essendine and Ryhall, is limited to the south of the county, south of a line from Braunston to Ketton.

banke. Apart from one instance at Ryhall in the east, Scand **banke** is limited to the south-western half of the county beyond a line from Langham to Barrowden.

bekkr. Despite Rutland's location within the Danelaw, the distribution of Scand **bekkr** is limited to 9 parishes only, and in these only 13 names are recorded. They are present in the north-west in the parishes of Ashwell, Braunston, Langham, Thistleton and Whissendine (6 names), indicating the linguistic influence of the Scandinavians of Leicestershire; and in a small triangle of parishes in the south-east comprising Hambleton, Morcott, North Luffenham and Lyndon (7 names), which may reflect Scandinavian settlement in Normanton and Glaston/Wing. The usual word for a Rutland stream is OE **brōc**.

beorg. This element in Rutland appears to have been used of pre-Anglo-Saxon burial mounds rather than of natural hills. Names with **beorg** occur sporadically in the interior of the county, as in Bisbrooke, Egleton, Empingham and Hambleton. But what is apparent is their predominance in those parishes which line Rutland's borders. The precise locations of the majority of names in **beorg** are not known. But in the upland west, names in **beorg** are found in Belton, Leighfield, Braunston, Langham and Whissendine. A probable earlier northern frontier appears to be demarcated by **beorg** names in the line of the adjoining parishes of Teigh, Barrow and

Greetham. While in the eastern border parishes, names with
beorg may have been replaced by Scand **haugr** 'a burial mound, a
hill', the south-eastern border parishes of Barrowden, Morcott,
Seaton, Thorpe by Water and Lyddington all have names with
beorg, principally related to the higher ground overlooking R.
Welland. Barrow mounds remain visible in Wardley and
Ridlington on raised land above Eye Brook. The recorded names in
beorg in the western and south-eastern border parishes may well
have survived because the barrows themselves survived medieval
cultivation on their more upland sites. Those barrows on the
eastern borders have in large measure been ploughed out, but their
sites survive as crop marks.

Crop Marks 60-74 lists Rutland ring-ditches recorded from the
air. The locations of the ring-ditches in the eastern parishes are in
harmony with the distribution of names with **beorg** in the west and
south-east. The county boundary in Essendine, Ryhall, Ketton and
Tixover is lined with groups of ring-ditches: additional ring-ditches
appear in border locations in Lyddington, Beaumont Chase,
Whissendine and Teigh. Perhaps significantly, the easternmost
parish bound of Essendine follows the line of a Bronze Age
triple-ditched linear earthwork between TF 061 115 and TF 062
119, combining with a barrow which survived until recent times at
TF 062 118 and three ring-ditches between TF 061 112 and TF 061
115.

It is most unlikely that Rutland barrows are of the Iron Age.
Iron Age barrows are comparatively rare in England. If, as seems
a distinct possibility, the barrows/ring-ditches/names in **beorg** are
recognizing Rutland's boundaries, then it follows that Rutland as a
territory may well have had its origins in the Bronze Age.

There is a series of caveats to bear in mind in evaluating this
distribution. All names in **beorg** may not relate to barrows: the
automatic equation of **beorg** with barrow rather than with hill is not
entirely secure and in any case, some natural features may have
been thought to be ancient burial mounds and so called. The
survival of actual barrows may have been conditioned by their
position and in the west, south-west and south-east, they appear to
be related to the higher ground along which the county boundary
marches. Thus an artificial 'boundary' line of barrows may have
been created by chance. All ring-ditches which survive as crop
marks may not be those of barrows (single Iron Age moated

farmsteads, windmill sites, Second World War gun emplacements, for example, may be thought of). The distribution of ring-ditches in the east may depend in part on the gravel spreads along the streams and on the limestones which are favourable for the appearance of crop marks. Elsewhere, they may not show up because of the nature of the soils. Streams may have been the principal factor in the siting of the barrows rather than boundaries. Were such burial sites placed where they did not interfere with agriculture? That is to say, were they placed simply at the edge of the arable rather than on boundaries as such? Another variable may have been the intensity of medieval cultivation throughout Rutland. Finally, the distribution patterns *beyond* Rutland's boundaries need to be analysed. Do they respect, indicate these boundaries? Unfortunately, detailed field-name studies of the encircling parishes in Leicestershire, Lincolnshire and Northampton-shire have not yet been published.

All that can be said in the present state of our knowledge is that, apart from the limits created by the apparent later northern extension of the territory, a Bronze Age date for Rutland's boundaries is a distinct possibility and that names in **beorg** appear to relate significantly to these boundaries.

bræc[1]. Apart from an outlier in the west at Belton, all names with this element are confined to a tight group of 9 parishes in central Rutland, namely Empingham, Glaston, Hambleton, North Luffenham, Lyndon, Manton, Pilton, Edith Weston and Whitwell.

brōc is common throughout the county in contrast to Scand **bekkr**.

brocc-hol. This compound is limited to the south of the county, south of a line from Belton to North Luffenham; obviously this area was once badger country.

burh. This important element does not occur as a generic in the county and is only certainly present in 3 names, i.e. in Burley, in the lost *Burghsyk'* in Barrow and in *Burstall* (the OE appellative compound **burh-stall** 'the site of a fortification') recorded in Teigh. While the names in Barrow and Teigh may refer to the same *burh*, Burley appears to be so called because of its relationship to the *burh* of the probable Angian *caput* of Hambleton.

bȳ is very rare. It may occur in the lost *Birchaby* in the western border parish of Belton and possibly in Hooby Lodge in the northern border parish of Stretton. The absence of place-names in **bȳ** compared with their ubiquity in surrounding Leicestershire, Lincolnshire and Northamptonshire appears to be an indicator of lack of Danish settlement in Rutland.

clæg. Names with this element occur principally in a broad belt running south-east from Langham, widening towards R. Welland.

cot. Of the 10 instances of place-names with **cot** as a generic, 8 are in border parishes or in parishes very close to the county boundaries. 3 instances are recorded as DB vills, including Caldecott, originally a shelter for travellers on a former Roman road, and Morcott, once a cottage on poor land. 5 other names indicate original lowly status: Tickencote (a DB vill) 'a shelter for young goats', 3 examples of *hlōse-cot* 'pigsty shelter', and Swancote 'swineherd's shelter'.

dalr. ON **dalr** is fairly frequent in hilly Rutland, although some names apparently with this element no doubt contain rather ON **deill**. An earlier OE (Angl) *dœl* 'a valley' is unlikely to have survived. As an early place-name-forming element, it does not appear to occur with great frequency anywhere in England.

dede-man is recorded only 4 times in Rutland, but it is significant that 2 instances occur in settlement names with OE **beorg** 'a tumulus', namely Barrow and Barrowden, and a third belongs to North Luffenham, the site of a pagan Anglo-Saxon cemetery. A fourth is in Tinwell, an eastern border parish where Scand **haugr** 'a tumulus' may have replaced **beorg**.

deill. This element occurs only with certainty in Oakham and its immediately surrounding parishes of Barleythorpe, Braunston, Brooke and Egleton in the extreme west of the territory. No doubt this reflects Oakham's linguistic contact as a market with the Scandinavian settlers of the Wreake Valley to its north-west. The element appears to occur also in Clipsham and Stretton, parishes which border Scandinavian Lincolnshire. In Rutland names, it is extremely difficult to distinguish names with **deill** from those with

dalr except where the latter relate obviously to topography. Spellings are always in -*dale*(*s*). In neighbouring Lincolnshire, the later reflex of **deill** very frequently is *dail*(*e*), *dayl*(*e*) (*v*. K. Cameron, *Place-Names of Lincolnshire*, Part 2, *passim*) but this indication of origin does not occur in the forms collected for Rutland. Even the plural -*dales* here is no sure guide to **deill**, e.g. Debdales in Ashwell, which is simply a plural form of **dalr**.

denu. There are only 4 certain survivals of place-names with this element. Of these, Essendine and Whissendine are ancient settlement sites and were DB vills. The element, as with OE *dæl*, may have been replaced by Scand **dalr**.

dīc survives only in 5 scattered parishes, in which a few field-name forms in **dīc** vary with Scand **dīk**.

dīk is common throughout Rutland.

drift. The patterns formed by this element in Rutland field-names indicate a cattle-droving route to Stamford along the north bank of R. Welland, through Caldecott, Seaton, Barrowden and Ketton, and another through Essendine and Ryhall, also to Stamford.

dūn. Only 4 certain examples of this ancient place-name-forming generic are present in the county; of these, 3 survive as the names of modern parishes. 2 were DB vills. Hambleton (OE *hamol-dūn*) was probably the *caput* of an Anglian kingdom of Rutland and it seems significant in this context that this settlement is still sited on the crown of the great hill, the natural location for a fortified *burh*. In contrast, the villages of both Barrowden and Lyndon are now situated on the lower southern slopes of the major hill formations whose names they perpetuate. The lost *Godwynnisdon* (Market Overton) may have been the early name for the northern section of the dramatic western scarp of the Cottesmore Upland.

eng. 10 parishes contain unambiguous examples of field-names with this Scand element. Of these, 9 are border parishes, namely Belton, Caldecott, Ketton, Oakham, Market Overton, Ryhall, Teigh, Tinwell and Whissendine. Only Greetham is divorced from the border and this is only one mile from it.

feld as an early settlement generic is absent from Rutland. It was used in the sense 'open country' only once when added to Leigh to give Leighfield in the 14th century.

fenn. There are only 4 occurrences of this element in Rutland, i.e. in field-names in Great Casterton, North Luffenham, Oakham and Whissendine. It also occurs in 2 early personal names of residents in Burley and Ketton.

flēot is rare and only occurs in field-names in 4 scattered parishes, namely Braunston, Egleton, Ketton and Teigh.

ford is a common element in minor - and field-names in the southern half of the county but not in the north. It does not occur as an element in settlement names.

fyrs is present only in the south-western quarter of the county (*v.* Barrie Cox, 'Furze, gorse and whin: an aside on Rutland in the Danelaw', JEPNS 20 (1987-8), 3-9).

gappe. Apart from an outlier in the north at Thistleton, local names in **gappe** of the 17th, 18th and 19th centuries (presumably named from gaps in parish boundary fences and hedges) are confined to a contiguous group of parishes in the south of the county, stretching from Uppingham in the west to North - and South Luffenham in the east.

gara. Names with this element are confined to the south-western half of the county, apart from an outlier at Stretton in the north.

gata. This Scand element is common throughout the county as a feature of the ME dialect of the region.

gerd-landes is a compound which is confined in surviving field-names to the southern half of the county, except for an isolated example in Market Overton in the north.

hǣð. Names in **hǣð** are limited to the eastern half of Rutland, east of a line from Barrow to Barrowden.

hām. Of the 6 certain names with **hām**, all survive as modern parishes. 2 (Empingham and North Luffenham) are associated with pagan Anglo-Saxon burial sites; 2 (Clipsham and Greetham) are associated with Romano-British settlements. From Clipsham and North Luffenham has come late military metalwork of the type attributed by some scholars to Germanic *foederati*. 2 (Uppingham and Empingham) are names in **-ingahām**. 4 (Empingham, Greetham, Luffenham and Oakham) were DB vills.

hamm. Names in **hamm** are distributed in the northern half of Rutland. Langham is the only settlement which we can reasonably suppose to have a generic in **hamm**. It was not a DB vill and is unrecorded until the reign of Henry II. However, it could possibly be a name in **hām** and if so, would remove **hamm** entirely from settlement-name-forming generics.

hām-stede. Apart from an outlier in Essendine in the extreme east, this compound is to be found only in the south-western half of the county. The instances are sited south-west of a line from Barleythorpe to North Luffenham and all are late formations.

haugr. 11 parishes contain field-names with this element; 6 line the south-eastern border of the county. 3 of the parishes lie on the north and north-western borders. The only inland example of **haugr** is in Hambleton, the probable ancient *caput* of the territory.

hlāw. Only 2 examples are recorded in Rutland, both in western border parishes. In Barleythorpe, *le Spellow* ('the mound where speeches are made, the moot-mound') is possibly a particular example of a pre-Saxon tumulus on the Rutland-Leicestershire boundary, otherwise recognized as a **beorg**, but in this case used as a moot-site.

hōh is rare in the county, with only 6 certain instances, 4 of which are used as generics.

holmr. Scand **holmr** is common throughout the county, in contrast to OE **hamm** of similar meaning and usage.

holt has a limited distribution, south-east only of a line Stoke Dry,

Empingham, Pickworth.

hop and **hop-yard** are limited to the south of the county.

hyll is common, except in the east of Rutland. It is applied generally to small features, in contrast to **dūn**. No names in **hyll** refer to settlements, again in contrast to **dūn**.

-inga-. There are 3 (plus 1 possible) place-names with this genitive of the folk-name-forming ending **-ingas**. All are the names of modern villages, of which Empingham and Uppingham are major settlements. Empingham, Tinwell and Whissendine are closely related to the Roman road system. All three were DB vills while Uppingham is no doubt referred to as a berewick of Ridlington in that survey.

-ingtūn. Ridlington is the only certain example of this formation, with Lyddington as a probable addition. Both are in the south-western half of the county. Ridlington was an important DB vill with 7 outliers, one of which was probably Uppingham, while Lyddington became a major estate of the Bishops of Lincoln.

innām is restricted to the south-west of the county, cf. **inntak**.

inntak is limited to the far east of Rutland. No doubt **inntak** reflects the Scandinavians of Lincolnshire while **innām** was the English word for the same feature of husbandry.

kirkja. With the exception of an instance in Wing and another in Edith Weston, **kirkja** is present only in parishes on or close to the county boundary. 8 of the 13 parishes in which the element appears line Rutland's borders.

læs (**læswe** gen., dat.sg.). No examples of dialectal *leasowe* (from the oblique **læswe**) occur in Rutland field-names. It is thus rarely possible to identify **læs** in the later field-names of the county, *v.* **lēah** *infra*.

lēah. Major early place-names with this element as a generic (or simplex) are concentrated in the south-west of the county in the old

Forest of Rutland area. 3 only are parish names, and of these, Leighfield and Wardley are in the south-west. A small group, including Burley, records woodland at the southern end of the Cottesmore Upland.

The element **lēah**, originally meaning 'a wood, woodland' and 'a woodland glade, a clearing in woodland' came later to signify 'a meadow, an open pasture', similar to the meaning of the early OE **lǣs** 'pasture, meadow-land'. This causes great difficulty in ascertaining the etymology of later minor names and field-names with *ley(e)s* in Rutland (variant spellings *layes, leas(e), leaze, lees, leez, leies, leighs*). Professor K. Cameron's evidence from neighbouring Lincolnshire, earlier and more concrete than from Rutland, indicates that although *ley(e)s* may sometimes be a later spelling for **lǣs** 'pasture, meadow-land', the plural of **lēah** (Angl **lǣh**) in its later sense is most probably its usual source, *v.* L 2 66 *s.n.* Carr Leys Wood. When compounded with a numeral, the later *ley(e)s* represents grassland units of tenure corresponding to **land** similarly used of arable (as in *The Seven Leas or Severall Leas but now called Stanhopes Close* (Stretton)).

lōge is a feature of the south-west of the county and is related to the Forest of Rutland.

lundr is distributed mainly in the extreme south-west of Rutland in the ancient forest region bordering Leicestershire. There are 2 examples in the far north-east in Clipsham in woodland bordering Lincolnshire. Both areas march on regions of heavy Scandinavian settlement.

lyng. Apart from a small group of names in the north of the county, field-names with **lyng** are concentrated south-east of a line from Wing to Pickworth.

mersc is found only in parishes which line R. Welland and Eye Brook.

mōr[1] is well represented in all parts of Rutland except in the far east beyond a line from Pickworth to Tixover. The names of 2 DB vills, Cottesmore and Morcott, contain this element.

pad is confined to the far southern parishes.

padde is limited to a small group of parishes in the west, namely Braunston, Brooke and Burley.

pingel has a limited distribution. There is a north-eastern group of names confined north-east of a line from Greetham to Tinwell and a western group, west of a line from Teigh to Ayston. The element is absent from central Rutland and from the south-east.

planke is confined to a small group of parishes in the central south-east quarter of the county.

plat² is limited in distribution to the north and to the west of Rutland.

pōl¹ occurs chiefly in parishes bordering R. Welland in the south-east and Eye Brook in the south-west. This suggests that the meaning 'pool in a river or stream' is usual in Rutland, cf. **ponde** *infra.*

ponde is distributed in the central parishes of the county, in contrast to **pōl¹** *supra.*

rēad. The distribution of this element reflects the spread of red soils on the ironstone in the south, east and north of the county.

rickstead is a local dialectal compound, occurring only in the centre-west of Rutland

sǣd. Field-names with this element are distributed in the western half of the county.

sainfoin. Field-names with this element are confined to the east of Rutland.

sale. This woodland element is almost entirely limited to the south-west, in the border parishes of the old forest area, especially in Beaumont Chase, Leighfield, Stoke Dry and Wardley. There is one instance only recorded in the far east, in Little Casterton, another area of old woodland.

sand has two well-defined areas of distribution, namely in the south-east quarter of the county in the adjoining parishes of Bisbrooke, Wing, Glaston, Seaton, Morcott, Lyndon, Edith Weston, North - and South Luffenham and Ketton, and in the north-east in Clipsham and Greetham.

sík is common throughout Rutland. A few spellings which show the presence of the cognate OE **sīc** occur only in Egleton and Whissendine in the north-west quarter of the county and here also **sík** is usual.

stak-ʒard. Apart from examples in Ridlington, Pilton and South Luffenham, field-names with this compound are concentrated in the northern half of the county.

stān-pytt. The two concentrations of this compound are in the south and south-east, and on the Lincolnshire Limestone in the north.

stede. This important element is only represented by 3 field-names, in Barrowden, Braunston and Lyddington. Note, however, the compound **hām-stede** *supra*.

stoc. 3 names are recorded with **stoc** as a generic, 2 of which are settlements which survive as parishes (with Martinsthorpe showing probable replacement of **stoc** by **þorp**). Stoke Dry was a DB vill.

stoccing is almost entirely confined to the north-east of Rutland, reflecting early woodland clearance in this area.

stow occurs twice, once in an early 13th century field-name in North Luffenham and also in the name of Alstoe Hundred.

strǣt. Field-names with this element relate principally to the known Roman roads Ermine Street and Sewstern Lane in the north-east of the county. However, a group of forms in the south, in Edith Weston, North Luffenham, Morcott and Barrowden, suggests a lost Roman road running south to cross R. Welland at Turtle Bridge in

Barrowden.

strīp. A small group of field-names with this element is confined to the south-east.

swalg. This element occurs in a small group of field-names on the Lincolnshire Limestone in the north of the county.

þorp. There are 14 instances of **þorp**, of which 5 were DB vills, namely *Alsthorpe*, Belmesthorpe, Sculthorpe, Thorpe by Water and Tolethorpe. 9 line the south-eastern boundary of the county. Of these, 7 are related closely to Stamford. 2 more, Barleythorpe and Thorpe by Water, are also boundary parishes. For a detailed discussion of Rutland's place-names in **þorp**, *v.* Barrie Cox, 'Rutland and the Scandinavian settlements: the place-name evidence', ASE 18 (1989), 135-48.

tūn. There are 23 certain settlement names in **tūn**, of which 12 are in the south-west quarter of the county, while a further group of 7 is on high ground in the north. 17 survive as modern parishes. The south-western group may represent both assarting in a forested area and renaming of earlier estates. **tūn** is the commonest element in Rutland's major place-names. 10 settlements are recorded as DB vills, namely Casterton, Exton, Glaston, Lyddington, Market Overton, Ridlington, Seaton, *Snelston*, Stretton and Thistleton. Of compounded personal names in place-names with **tūn**, only 2 are of the fully dithematic type, incorporated in names which usually represent estates rather than farmsteads (i.e. in Ayston and Egleton), although Ridlington and Seaton contain shortened forms of dithematic personal names. 5 (plus 1 possible) personal names in place-names with **tūn** are of the earlier monothematic type; 12 (plus 1 possible) place-names in **tūn** have a significant word as first element. Only 3 (*Norton'*, *Southton'* and Edith Weston) are of the geographically related type.

vangr. This Scandinavian element is common throughout the county.

wæsce-dīk and **wæsce-pytt.** These two compounds representing sheep-dips have different distributions; **wæsce-dīk** is limited to central Rutland while **wæsce-pytt** has a south-western distribution.

wella is common throughout the county. Ashwell, Tinwell and Whitwell are modern parishes and all are recorded as DB vills.

wīc is rare in Rutland. Only Boswick in Teigh survives, and possibly Eastwick in Stoke Dry. *Heynwyk'* (Stretton) and *Swynewik'* (Glaston) are lost 14th century instances, while the lost *Luffewyke*, the probable earlier name of the manor of Manton, contains the same personal name as nearby Luffenham and doubtlessly records the same individual. The element occurs also in the compound appellative Hardwick (OE **heorde-wīc**).

wilig. Names with this element are confined to the south-west of the county.

wind-mylne. Apart from an isolated example in Thistleton in the extreme north, all recorded early windmills were south-west of a line from Whissendine to Ketton, i.e. situated on Rutland's higher ground.

worð is rare. There are only 2 certain examples recorded in the county. Pickworth is a boundary parish. (Note that the problematical Littleworth is also in the boundary parish of Belton.) *Shep-worth* is recorded only as a 17th century field-name and was probably never more than an enclosure for sheep. No **worð** appears as a DB vill. However, it may be significant that both Pickworth and Littleworth are at the territorial boundaries. Margaret Gelling in *The Names of Towns and Cities in Britain*, London 1970, *s.n.* Tamworth, and in *The West Midlands in the Early Middle Ages*, Leicester 1992, 147-8, makes the point that *worð/worðig* 'an enclosure' at an early stage may have 'developed a meaning akin to that of *burh*', i.e. 'a fortified place'. Fortified sites on the frontiers at both Pickworth and Belton would conform to the evident pattern of Rutland's territorial defences. Indeed, it is possible that Pickworth was the name of the earthwork now called Castle Dike on the Rutland boundary to the north-east. Littleworth is on rising ground above Eye Brook, some 200 yards from the frontier, while Castle Dike is contiguous with the territorial limits. Littleworth lies beside an obvious route into Rutland's heartlands.

wudu is distributed mainly in the north and north-east of the county, especially north-east of the Roman roads Sewtern Lane and Ermine Street. It is also found in the south-west in the ancient woodland of the Leighfield Forest area. There are a few survivals in the Hambleton/southern Exton region. The element is virtually absent from Wrangdike Hundred.

NAMES WHICH ARE WHOLLY OR PARTLY PRE-ENGLISH

Chater, Glen, Ketton and possibly Welland.

FRENCH PLACE-NAMES

Beaumont Chase.

Elements originally from early French, borrowed into Middle English, and found in place-names and field-names include: **abbat, aley, baille, baillie, barre, bastard, beau, cabin, caucie, chace, chapel(e), chaunterie, cheri(e), clos(e), commun, conestable, coni, coninger, copis, corner, cover(t), cundite, curt, darnel, demeyn, den, desert, erber, feire, ferme, folie, forest, forester, frere, garderobe, gardin, gibet, goter, grange, hermitage, hospital, judge, lampe, launde, leveret, loge, mantel, mesne, monie, mont, morter, mote, oyser, pale, paradis, parlur, pasture, personage, persone, petit, pīe**[2]**, place, plain, planke, point, pounce, purveyor, quarriere, quarter, raile, raskayl, raton, roche**[1]**, rond, slate, spinney, stomacher, stray, taverne, trenche, trespas, vacherie, veche, vikerage, vikere, vine, wareine, weyour.**

CATEGORIES OF FIELD- AND MINOR NAMES

A. Poor land or unpleasant places

Armley Wood (Exton), *Armslades* (Barleythorpe); *Bastard(e) Close* (Braunston, Glaston), Bastard Leys (Edith Weston), *Bastard Leys* (N. Luffenham); *Bedlam Meadow* (Leighfield, *v.* P); Blackamire Cl (Ketton); *the Blowes* (Uppingham), Blowhill Cl (Morcott), *Blowland* (N. Luffenham); Bogg (Ashwell); Botany Bay (Lt. Casterton, S. Luffenham, *v.* P); *Brakeall Close* (Pilton); Carrion Pit Lane (Ketton); *Catmouse* (Burley); *Deadmo(o)re (furlonge)* (Belton, Manton), Dedmoor (Wing); *the Desart* (Glaston); Big Dodmoor (Exton), *Dod-moor Furlong* (Cottesmore), Dodmore (Greetham); Endless (Belton); Feather Bed Lane (Leighfield, Ridlington); *The Flashes* (Whissendine); Flasket Leys (S. Luffenham); *Floddreacre* (Uppingham); *Fluill hill furlong* (Lyddington); *Flush fur'* (Egleton); *Flyblowne close* (Uppingham); Frog Hall (Ridlington, *v.* G); *Fulcrofte* (Egleton), *Fullwellhead* (Empingham), *Fulwell* (Belton), *Fulwood* (Greetham); Gallows Peice (Oakham); Galls (Burley), *the Galls* (Bisbrooke), Galls Furlong (Seaton), *The Gauls* (Manton); *Gluckffurlang* (Barrow); Hangmans Cl (Essendine, Ryhall); Hell Holes (Langham), *Helpitt dale* (Lyndon, *v.* O); Hot Hollow (Empingham); Jittys Cl (Lyddington, *v.* E, O); Mire Hole (Glaston), *Mur Pit Meadow* (Oakham); Miry Cl (S. Luffenham), *Myry peice* (Uppingham); Misery (Pilton); Mockbeggar (Pickworth); Muck Fd (Pilton); Paddys Garden (Gt. Casterton); Quake Fen (Whissendine); Saltmere (Lyddington), *Saltmore* (Caldecott), Saltwells (Greetham); *Scantive Acre* (Hambleton); Scotch Fens (Preston); Shacklewell (Empingham); *shifting Meadow* (Lyddington); Shockmore Balk (S. Luffenham, *v.* O); Shorne Hill (Brooke); *Shy Close* (Uppingham); Silver Diggings (Whissendine); *Sink Furlong* (Morcott), Sink Lane (Ketton); Snarlings (Thistleton), *Snarlings* (Mkt. Overton); Sour Hill (Ryhall), Sour Lands (S. Luffenham), *Surmedue* (Ryhall); Spout Water Mdw (Seaton); Stone Galls (Langham); Straw Gall (Tickencote); Swooning Bridge (Oakham); *Thirspit* (Glaston), *thyrspit* (Barrowden), *Tyrespyt* (Empingham) (*v.* O); Vale of Catmose; Van Diemans (Lyddington, *v.* P); The Waste (Empingham), *The Waste* (Egleton, Greetham, Hambleton), Waste Boundary Land (Lt. Casterton), Waste Piece (Langham), *The Waste*

Way (Barrow); *le Watergalle* (Lt. Casterton), Watergauls (Egleton), *Watergaules* (Barleythorpe, Oakham, Uppingham); *le wetlondes* (N. Luffenham), *Wheate Moore* (Greetham), *Wheatleas* (Barleythorpe); *White acre, White Crofte* (Uppingham), *White Five Acres* (Caldecott), White Ground Cl (Ketton), White Lands (Essendine, Ryhall), Whiteroods (Caldecott), *White Roods* (Egleton), *White Wong Furlong* (Normanton); *Wildegate* (Wardley); (The) Wilderness (Ashwell, Empingham, Langham); *Wipesnest* (Manton), *Wipesnest fur'* (Egleton).

B.   Productive land or pleasant places

ye Arbour (Lyndon); Bee Hill (Lyddington); Blackground (Ketton), Black Holmes (Mkt. Overton), Black Lands (Essendine), *Black Lands* (Morcott), Black Piece (Greetham), Black Wong (Mkt. Overton); *Botewell* (Leighfield); Breeder Leys (Clipsham, Stretton); *Butterie Horne Close* (Stoke Dry); Big Buttermilk (N. Luffenham), *Butterwell slade* (Wing); *Byrtwell'* (Seaton); Cherry Holt (Glaston, Tinwell, *v.* E); Creampot Cl (Ketton), Cream Pot Leys (Empingham); *Cresswell* (Oakham, *v.* F); *Drie Close* (Burley), *Dry Close* (N. Luffenham), Dry Cl (Glaston, Greetham, S. Luffenham, Seaton, Tinwell), Dry Fd (Clipsham, Pickworth, Thistleton, Tickencote), Dry Hill (Leighfield, Martinsthorpe), Dry Leys (Ashwell), Dry Slight (Braunston); *Fatt Sheep Close* (Normanton); Feeding Cl (Barrowden, Ridlington), Feeding Fd (Braunston, Oakham), *the Feeding Ground* (Ketton); *Filbarn Furlong* (Oakham); Gold Hills (Edith Weston), *goldney* (Wardley); Goodfeed's Barnsdale (Exton); *Guilton fur'* (Egleton); *Hellwell medowe* (Teigh), *Helwell'* (Oakham, *v.* O); *the Herbar* (Gt. Casterton); Merry Acres (Teigh); Mount Pleasant (Morcott, Oakham, Uppingham, Whissendine); the Mowing Mdw (Essendine); The Nursery (Ketton), Nursery Cl (Lt. Casterton); (The) Orchard (Bisbrooke, Ketton, Langham, N. Luffenham, Pilton, Thistleton, Tixover, Uppingham), *The Orchard* (Belton, S. Luffenham), Beadhouse Orchard (Stretton), the Cherry Orchard (Glaston), Mill Orchard (S. Luffenham), Old Orchard (Morcott, Pilton), *Balls Orchard* (Caldecott), *Bells Orchard* (Hambleton), *Brown's Orchard* (Belton), *le Castelorchard'* (Oakham), *Great House Orchard* (Seaton), *le New Orchard* (Barleythorpe), *South Orchard* (Ashwell), *le Upper Orchard* (Barleythorpe), *Walters*

Orchard (Lyndon), Orchard Cl (Lyddington), Orchard(s) furlong
(Thorpe by Water), *The Orchards Gardens* (Empingham); *Paradise*
(Wing, *v.* O); *The Parlour* (Belton), Stafford's Parlour (Langham);
Pleasure Grounds (Normanton, *v.* Q); *Respas Springs* (Belton, *v.* F);
Sanctuary (Gunthorpe); Smear Hill (Belton); Smith's Heaven
(Langham); Spa Cl (Mkt. Overton), *Spaw Grounds* (Lt. Casterton);
Steadfast Syke (Langham); Sweet Leys (Brooke), *Sweete well dike*
(Edith Weston); White Leys (Burley); *Wig Acres* (Manton); *Wonders*
(Oakham); *Wynn ȝerd* (Oakham).

C.   Shape, size or appearance

(Modern field-names which simply distinguish acreage are not
listed.)

Acrecroft (Egleton); The Belt (Normanton); Big Drift (Caldecott),
(The) Big Fd (Exton, S. Luffenham), Steel's Big Fd (Langham), Big
Islip's (Lyddington), Big Leighs (Whissendine), Big Mdw (Caldecott,
S. Luffenham), Big Moor (Teigh), Big Olran, Big Pickard's
(Whissendine), Big Tenter's (Ridlington); Bradley (Clipsham),
Bredcroft (Tinwell), *Broadarse* (Manton), Broadback (Ashwell),
Broad Cl (S. Luffenham), *the Broade* (Lyndon), Broadeng Mdw
(Tinwell), Broadham Cl (Ketton), Broadholm(s) (Ashwell,
Essendine, Ketton), Broading (Ryhall), *Broddole* (Thorpe by Water);
Brende ȝerdes, Brendhoutecroft (Mkt. Overton), *Brentley* (Manton);
Brethsike (Lyddington); Broken Back (Oakham), Brokenback Furlong
(N. Luffenham), *Brokenback Hill* (Barrowden); Burnt Cl (Lt.
Casterton), Burnt Ground (Pickworth), Burnt Wong (Morcott),
Burntseeke (Ashwell); *Buttocks Close* (Hambleton); Candlestick
Spinney (Edith Weston); Cocked Hat (Ketton, Tickencote), Cocked
Hat Piece (Pilton), Cocked Hat Spinney (Empingham, Exton);
Cocks and Holes (Essendine); Cow Gait (Ashwell); *Cringlety Valley*
(Empingham); *Crooked Hasels* (Leighfield, *v.* E); D Close
(Tickencote); Egg Spinney (Burley, *v.* E); *Elbowes* (Oakham), Elbow
Fd (Lyddington), *Elbow Leys, Elbow Rood* (Manton); Ell Plantation
(Stretton); *Farding Green Furlong* (Greetham); *Five Land Acre*
(Ryhall), *Five Lands fur'* Greetham); Flat Mdw (Langham), Flats
(Ridlington), *Flat Seeks* (Leighfield); Four Score Acre (Gt.
Casterton); Funnel (Lyddington, Stoke Dry); Great Garbage

(Lyddington), Garbage Holm (Wardley), *Garbroads* (Egleton); *the goare* (Oakham), *le gor'* (Bisbrooke), *Goare acre* (Stoke Dry), *Priest Gore* (Manton), Red Gore (Whissendine), *Shorte gore furlong* (Caldecott), Thistley Gore (Whissendine), *timgore* (Barrowden, *v.* E); *the Great Allotment* (Manton), Great Cl (Langham, Pilton, Preston, Stoke Dry), Luffen Great Cl (Lyndon), *(the) Great(e) Close* (Egleton, Glaston, S. Luffenham, Lyndon, Edith Weston), *the great Farme Peece* (Bisbrooke), Great Ground (Empingham, Essendine, Stoke Dry, Teigh), *the Great Ground* (Glaston), Great Hames (Tixover), Greatholme (Ashwell, Greetham), (The) Great Mdw (Belton, N. Luffenham, Stoke Dry, Tinwell), Big Pits Great Mdw (Edith Weston), *Great Meadow* (Leighfield), The Great Yard Land (Belton), *Greteley* (Essendine); *the half Handkerchief* (Lyndon), Half Moon Spinney (Hambleton); Harp Piece (Morcott); Hassock's Holme (Whissendine); Hell Holes (Langham), Hell's Hales (Oakham); *Hide* (Egleton) *Pastmore hyde* (Preston); Hills and Hales (Exton), Hills and Holes (Essendine); *the Hillybanks* (Uppingham); *Hob Close* (Hambleton); Great Horn Cl (Brooke); Humps and Hollows (Whissendine); (The) Island (Empingham, S. Luffenham, Tixover); The L Fds (Glaston); Langholms (Manton), Langings (Belton), Langland (Lyddington), *Langley balk* (Manton), *Langmeadowe* (Belton); Letter Box (Tickencote); *litle acre* (Oakham), Little Cl (S. Luffenham, Pilton, Seaton, Stoke Dry, Stretton, Teigh), *Little Close* (Lyndon), Little Fd (Ashwell, Oakham, Stoke Dry), Little Holme (Greetham), *Little Holme* (Glaston), Little Ing (Whissendine), Little Mdw (Ketton, N. Luffenham, Martinsthorpe, Oakham, Seaton, Tinwell, Edith Weston, Whissendine), - Mdws (Cottesmore), *Lit(t)le Meadow* (Hambleton, Langham, N. Luffenham, Stretton, Teigh), Little Moor (Teigh), Little One (Greetham), *le Little Sicke* (Oakham), Little 'Uns (Mkt. Overton), Little Wood (Stretton), *Lituley* (Essendine), *Lyttilhawe* (Stretton); Long Acre (Greetham), *the long Balk* (Tickencote), Long Cl (Barrowden, Lt. Casterton, Clipsham, Greetham, Ketton, N. Luffenham, Pilton, Stretton), *Long Close* (Burley, Egleton, Hambleton, Ketton, Morcott, Oakham, Teigh), *Rubbins's Long Close* (Stretton), *Longe clotes* (Egleton), Long Croft (Lyddington), Long Cutts (N. Luffenham), Longdales (Clipsham), *Long(e)dales* (Egleton, Oakham), *long doles* (Oakham), Long Fd (Barrowden), *(the) Long Furlong* (Morcott, Normanton), *Longhesil* (Barrow, *v.* E), *Longholm* (Glaston), *Longland(e)(s)* (Barleythorpe, Egleton, Lyndon, Morcott,

Oakham, Edith Weston), *Long lay* (Lyddington), Long Leaze (Hambleton), *Long Leeds* (Normanton), Long Mdw (Ashwell, Cottesmore, Gunthorpe, Ketton, Oakham), *Long Meadow* (Burley), *Long Roods* (Barleythorpe), Long Rotten (Egleton), *Long seeke* (Oakham), Long Shrubbs (Edith Weston), *Longslade* (Wardley), Longslang (Burley), Long Spinney (Martinsthorpe), *the Long Spinney* (Edith Weston), *long syk* (Egleton), *Longewong* (Mkt. Overton); *Est longs furlong* (Caldecott); *Longate furlong* (Egleton), Long Gate Side (Oakham); *Lugmoor* (Belton); *Mickle Doles* (Caldecott), *Mikildole* (Lyddington), Mickling (Belton), *Mikeleng* (Ketton), *Mykeleng* (Tinwell), Mickle Mdw (Thorpe by Water); The Narrows (Gt. Casterton), *Narrow Close* (Egleton), *Narrow point(s)* (Barleythorpe, Oakham), *Narrow Syche* (Egleton); Open Cl (S. Luffenham); The Oval (N. Luffenham); *Oxe livers* (Brooke), Ox Liver (Braunston); *The Panne* (Burley), Pan Cl (Ashwell, Glaston, Whissendine), *Pan Meadow* (Lt. Casterton); *The Parlour* (Belton, *v.* B), Stafford's Parlour (Langham); *the Patch of Grass* (Manton); *Pease Broad* (Empingham, *v.* H); Petty Green Cl (Ketton); *Pich Close* (Thistleton); Pightlé (Langham); Pitcher Hill (Tixover); Pike Acre (Barrowden), Pike Piece (S. Luffenham), *Pike peice* (Bisbrooke); The Pikelets (Gt. Casterton); Pingel (Teigh), (The) Pingle (Ashwell, Ayston, Gt. Casterton, Empingham, Greetham, Tinwell), Ireland's Pingle (Whissendine), Robbs Pingle (Tinwell), Pingles (Brooke), *le Pingle* (Barleythorpe), *The Pingle* (Lt. Casterton, Egleton, Oakham, Tickencote), Pingle Plantation (Clipsham); The Platt (Stretton), Platts (Brooke), Barrow Plat(t) (Mkt. Overton), Berry's - (Greetham), Clipsham -, Grants -, Hall - (Stretton), House - (Teigh), Merrimans -, Middle - (Brooke), Moneys -, Old Moor - (Stretton), Park - (Brooke), Road -, Roberts -, Well - (Teigh), West Platt (Brooke), *Wards Platt* (Stretton), New Platt Piece (Brooke); *Aswells Plot*, Yard Plott, Berrys Plott Fd (Stretton); Pocket Cl (Pickworth), Pocket Nook (Barleythorpe); Pokes (Essendine); Pudding Bag End (Exton); The Quadrant (Uppingham); Redcap Hill (Thistleton); *Acre Rigges, Rigged Baulke* (Whissendine); Ring Fd (Barleythorpe); The Roost (Egleton); *Rouclout* (Lyddington), Bartram's Rough (Langham), *Rough Close* (Hambleton, Leighfield, N. Luffenham), Rough Dale (Brooke), Rough Fd, - Ground, - Hill (Whissendine), *Roughlands* (Edith Weston), *Rough Meadow* (Hambleton), Rough Mdws (Essendine); *(the) Round Close* (Glaston, Ketton), Round Fd (Braunston), *Round fur'* (Morcott), Round Haystack Fd (Oakham), *Round Hill* (Uppingham), Round Piece (Brooke); Roundabout (Empingham, Pilton, Tickencote); *Row Furlong* (Empingham), Row Syke (Essendine); *Scantive Acre* (Hambleton, *v.* A); Shortacres (Tinwell), *Syortebrech* (Uppingham), *short buts* (Tickencote), *S(c)hortdoles* (Glaston, Oakham), *Short fur(long)* (Greetham, Normanton), *Shortham piece* (Manton), *Short Hedge* (Uppingham), Short Hollow (Cottesmore), Shortlands (Ryhall), *shortlands* (S. Luffenham), *Short Leeds* (Normanton), *Shortsett* (Manton), *Sortewong* (Oakham), *Ssortwong'* (Mkt. Overton); Shoulder of Mutton (Manton); *Shovelboards Furlong* (Whissendine); The Shred (Ryhall); (The) Slip (Barleythorpe, Braunston, Mkt. Overton, Whissendine), Six Acre Slip (Essendine), Slipe (Ketton, Tinwell); *smalheasell* (Egleton, v. E), Small Plantation (Stretton), *Small Roodes* (Wardley), *the small Yard Land* (Lyddington); *Smeeth More* (Burley); *Goodmans Snowte (v.* O); *Sponge fur'* (Egleton), *Nixons Sponk* (Lyndon); *Square acre Close* (Uppingham), Square Cl (S. Luffenham), *Square Close* (Morcott, Uppingham), Square Plantation (Stretton), Square Spinney (Martinsthorpe); *Stomacher Close* (Egleton); *ye Stone Trough* (Ketton); Strip (Lyndon), (the) Stripe (Barrowden, S. Luffenham, Seaton); Three Corner Cl (Greetham, Pilton), *Three Corner Close* (S. Luffenham), Three Corner Fd (Cottesmore, Exton, Greetham, Morcott), Three Cornered Cl (Gt. Casterton, N. Luffenham, Lyddington, Normanton, Tixover), Three-Cornered Pightle (Clipsham); Three Nook'd Cl (Ashwell); *Tinwell Plank* (Ketton); Tobacco Pipe Piece (Essendine, *v.* D); Triangle Cl (Stretton); Triangular Piece (Tinwell); Wide Hole (Cottesmore), Barrow Wide Hole (Barrow); *Wrangland* (Wing), *(W)ranglands* (Braunston, Edith Weston), *Wrang roods* (Barrowden), *Wrangrood* (S. Luffenham), *Wrongedich* (N. Luffenham); *ye Wrinkles* (Lyndon).

D.   Soil type or geological formation

Black Acres (Brooke), Black Ash Cl, Blackground (Ketton), Black Holme(s) (Mkt. Overton, Thistleton), *Blackholme* (Stretton), Black Lands (Essendine), *Black Lands* (Morcott), *Blaclondis* (Bisbrooke), Black Mdw (Gunthorpe, Manton), Black Mould (Whitwell), *Blacmyld* (Stoke Dry), *Blakmyld'* (Cottesmore), Black Piece (Greetham, Edith Weston), *Blackroodes* (Belton), *blake Roudes*

(Egleton), *Blackstones* (Lyndon), Black Wong (Mkt. Overton), *Black Wong* (Bisbrooke) (cf. B); *Cake Makers* (Greetham); The Clay (S. Luffenham), *the Clay* (Barrowden), *the Cley* (Glaston), Clays (Pilton), Clay Cl, - Fd (Stretton), *Clay field* (Caldecott), Clay Foot (S. Luffenham), Clay Ground (Ketton, Stretton), Clay Hill (Barleythorpe, Gt. Casterton, S. Luffenham, Ryhall), *cleay hill'* (Egleton), Clay Hill Cl (Langham), Clay Lane (S. Luffenham), Clay Lock (Cl) (S. Luffenham, Morcott), Clay Piece (Teigh), *Claypit Hill* (Thistleton, Uppingham), Cleedale (Hambleton); The Clinkers (Edith Weston); Coal Tar (Essendine); *the Creach* (Edith Weston); *the Earth Close* (Edith Weston); Gravels (Essendine), Gravel Pit (Belton, Egleton), - Cl (Clipsham, Wardley, Whissendine); *grotten forll'* (Egleton); Honey Furlong (N. Luffenham), Honey Hole (Mkt. Overton, Tixover), Honey Holme (Egleton), Honey Pots (Ridlington), Honeypot Spring (Lyddington); Ironstone Cl (Cottesmore); *Kalkeleys* (Leighfield); *Kokelstone furlong* (Greetham, v. N); Lambford furlong (Barrowden), *Lamb Pitt Close* (Glaston), Lamb Pool (Barrowden), *Lampolmedow* (Hambleton); Lax Hill (Barrowden, Hambleton), *Laxmore fur'* (Greetham); *Light Ground* (Barleythorpe); Limepit Fd (Exton); Live Hill (Barrowden); *Longe clotes* (Egleton); Long Rotten (Egleton); Loose Dogs (Ashwell); *Oatmealemeadow* (Hambleton), *Odmelmedou* (Whissendine); Pebbles (Manton), *Pibbles* (Empingham); *Popple Close* (Lt. Casterton), *Popples Farm* (Greetham); *Pounce Pits* (Belton); *Redbankes* (Edith Weston), Red Fd (Seaton), *Redfoard* (Empingham), *La redegate* (Bisbrooke), Red Ground (Bisbrooke, Ketton, Lyddington, Seaton, Tinwell), *the Redground* (Barrowden), Red Hill (Barrowden, Morcott, Uppingham), - Hills (Stretton), *Red(e)hill(e)* (N. Luffenham, Thistleton), Red Lands (Gt. Casterton, Essendine, Manton), *Red landes* (Wardley), *Redset* (Manton), Redstones (Gt. Casterton), Red Way (Morcott), *Redwell* (Manton); (The) Sands (Gt. Casterton, Empingham, S. Luffenham, Morcott, Seaton, Edith Weston), *the Sandes* (Bisbrooke, Glaston, Lyndon), *le sondes*, *Sandacre* (N. Luffenham), *le Santfurlong* (Wing), Sandfurrows Cl (Ketton), *Sangate feild* (S. Luffenham), *Sandhowes* (Seaton), Sand Nook (Morcott), *the Sandpitt* (Belton), Sandpits (Whissendine), *Sandpit(t)s* (Egleton, N. Luffenham), Sandstone Mdw (Stoke Dry), Sandwells (Clipsham); Sandy Cl (Greetham), *the Sandy Close* (Edith Weston), Sandy Leys (Ashwell), *Sandye Peece fur'* (Greetham), Sandywells (Glaston); *smalstones* (Thistleton);

Standlands (Whissendine), the Stone Acre (N. Luffenham), Stone Cl (Manton), *Stondales* (Oakham), Stone Fd (Barrowden), *Stonhill* (Thistleton), *stone landes* (Oakham), *Stone Meadow* (Clipsham), *ye Stone Trough* (Ketton, *v.* C), *Stone Wong fur'* (Greetham); Stanicle (Wing), *Stannyford* (Hambleton), *Stony Bancke* (Barrowden), *le Stoniforlong* (N. Luffenham), *Stonye furlong* (Uppingham), *Stonyland* (Oakham), Stony Lands (Whissendine); Strong Land (Empingham); Tobacco Pipe Piece (Essendine, *v.* C); Treadwell (Greetham); Waltham Clays (Mkt. Overton), White Clay Furlong (N. Luffenham); Wit Leather Piece (Lyddington); *yeallow landes* (Morcott), *Yellows* (Oakham).

E. Trees

Alders Close, - *Croft* (Morcott), Alley Wong, Big Olran (Whissendine); *Apescrosse furlong* (Lyddington); *Appelmede* (Whissendine), *Apiltremedou* (Glaston), *Appletree Furlong* (Manton), Appletree Moor (Ashwell), *Apple Tree Stockin* (Clipsham); The Ashes (Braunston), *Parkassh'* (Mkt. Overton), *Stamford Ashe* (Exton), Ash Cl (S. Luffenham, Whitwell), (*The*) *Ash Close* (Empingham, Tickencote), *Fair Ash Close* (Belton), *Ash Coppice* (Lt. Casterton), *Ash(e)furlong(e)* (Cottesmore, Edith Weston), *Ashegate* (Belton), *Asshelounde* (Stoke Dry), Ash Plantation (Exton), Ashpool Hedge Furlong (Seaton), *Ashslade* (Belton), Ash Tree Cl (Exton, Ryhall), *Ash Tree Furlong* (Greetham), *Ash-well ditch* (Morcott), Ash Wood (Greetham), *Hessecroft* (Bisbrooke); Bargate (Ashwell), Bargate Hill (Braunston); Beech Fm (Hambleton); Bircham (Ashwell); Blackthorn Covert (Cottesmore); Cedar Fd (Wing); Cherry Cls, Cherry Holt (Tinwell), *Cherrytree Close* (Belton); Chestnut Fm (Braunston, Burley), Chestnut Tree Fd (Manton); Crab Hedge Cl (Tixover), Crabtree (Mkt. Overton, Tickencote), *the Crab tree* (Glaston), *Luffs Crabtree* (N. Luffenham), Crabtree Cl (S. Luffenham, Pilton), *Crabtree Furlonge* (Belton), *Crabb Tree fur'* (Greetham), Crabtree Hedge Furlong (Lyddington), Crabtree Hill (Beaumont Chase, Stoke Dry), *Crabtree Peice* (N. Luffenham), *Crab Tree Stockin* (Clipsham); *Woole Elders* Bisbrooke), *Elde Stump* (Manton), Elder Stump Cl (Ketton), Eldern Stumps, Elgate (Whissendine); The Elms (Braunston), Elm Cl (Ryhall), Elms Lodge (Morcott), The Elm Spinney (Glaston), *Almawewonge*

(Lt. Casterton), Elm Tree Cl (Tickencote), Elm Tree Homestead (Lyndon), Elm Tree Pasture (Pilton); The Firs (Ketton), Fircroft (Uppingham); Hazel's (Greetham), *Crooked Hasels* (Leighfield), *Longhesil* (Barrow), *smalheasels* (Egleton), Haseldyke (Morcott), Hazel Dyke (S. Luffenham), Hazlegate (Glaston), *Heseldal'*, *Hesilgate* (Barrow), *Hesyllgate* (Cottesmore); *Holly Close* (Tixover), Holly Fm (Preston); Hollytree Cottage (Brooke); Jittys Cl (Lyddington, *v.* A, O); The Laurels (Ryhall, Whissendine); The Limes (Hambleton, Ketton), *Lymgate* (Morcott), *Lyndwode* (Pickworth); Little Maples (Beaumont Chase), *Mapeley Cross furlong* (Egleton), Maple Stile Sale (Beaumont Chase), *Maple stubbe* (Belton); The Oaks (Pickworth), *The Oaks* (Lt. Casterton, Edith Weston), Bloody Oaks (Empingham), Digby -, (S. Luffenham), Insthorpe - (Lt. Casterton), Little - (Empingham), Shire - (Barrowden), Tolethorpe Oaks (Lt. Casterton), Oak Cl (Seaton), *the Oake Close* (Tickencote), *Pecks Oake close* (Ayston), *oke Forl'* (Egleton), *Okes gate* (Morcott), *le Oake hill* (Oakham), *Kings Oake Hills* (Beaumont Chase), Oak Leys (Lyndon), *Okestead Close* (Braunston), *Oake Stockin* (Clipsham), Oak Trees (Bisbrooke), Oak Tree Cl . (Caldecott, Glaston, Martinsthorpe, Morcott), *Oak Tree Close* (N. Luffenham), Oak Tree Mdw (Preston); Osier Bed (Gunthorpe), *Osier Holt* (S. Luffenham), (Old) Ozier Bed (Morcott, Tinwell), Ozier Holt (Pilton, Tinwell); Pear Tree Cl (Gt. Casterton, Lyndon), *Peartree Close* (Stretton), Pear Tree Furlong (Ryhall), *Peartree hill* (Uppingham), Peartree Lane (Thistleton); Pines (Ayston, Ridlington), Pynes Nook (Ridlington); The Poplars (Whissendine), Poplar Tree Cl (Ryhall); the Quick (S. Luffenham, Edith Weston), Russell's Quick (Caldecott), *Gipsy's* - (Gt. Casterton), *Peaches* - (Lyddington), *Staffords Quick(e)* (Whissendine), *the Quickhedge* (Uppingham), Quicks Cl (Morcott); Sallow Sale (Beaumont Chase), *Salley Tree Leas* (Greetham); *Sweeting Tree Nooke* (Empingham); *le thorn in campo occidentali* (Barleythorpe), *bradthorn* (Bisbrooke), *Castle Thorns* (Morcott), *Cob-thorn Furlong* (Cottesmore), *Coppethornhull* (Lyddington), *Crakepornfurlong'* (Barrow), *Harethornes* (Pickworth, Ridlington), Hawthorn Mdw (Wardley), *Hawthorne Hill* (Ayston), Highthorn Furlong (Barrowden), *High Thorne Nooke* (Empingham), *Longthorne leas* (Burley), *May Thorne Bush* (Ketton), *Suthorne meadow* (Seaton), *Umpthorne* (N. Luffenham), Thorn Covert (Edith Weston), *Thornborow Hill* (Hambleton), *pornham broc* (Ayston), *Thornhill*

(Preston), *Thorne poole furlong* (Caldecott), *Thorntre ȝard* (Thistleton); *Thorneyeclose* (Lyddington), *thorny close* (Hambleton), *Thorney Leys* (Morcott), *Thorney Meadow* (N. Luffenham); *Thurndel Ley* (Morcott), *Thurn dike* (Braunston), *timgore* (Barrowden); *Wall Nutt tree Close* (Glaston), Walnut Tree Leys (Stoke Dry); *Walwortwong'* (Mkt. Overton); *at the old Willow* (Lyddington), The Willows (Exton), *the Willoes* (Barrowden), *(the) Willow(e)s* (Oakham, Uppingham), Burnt Willow (Essendine), Peach's Willow (Bisbrooke), Moor Willows (Seaton), Pope's Willows (Barrowden), *Billingtons Willows* (Oakham), *Brownes Willow* (Egleton), *Edgson willowes* (Oakham), *Middletons Willows* (Morcott), *Ransike willowes* (Barrowden), *Sharpes willes* (Pilton), *Staney Ford Willows* (Whissendine), *le welugate* (Barrowden), Willow Cl (Martinsthorpe, Pilton), Willow Hedge (Essendine), *Willowesholme* (Lyddington), *Wyleweholm* (N. Luffenham), *old Willow Leys* (Manton), Willow Row (Ryhall), *Willow Row* (N. Luffenham), *Willow Spring* (Manton), Willow Tree Cl (Gt. Casterton), *Wyllowong* (Cottesmore); *the Witch Close* (N. Luffenham); *Wythyrsike* (Seaton); The Yews (Edith Weston), Yew Tree Ho. (Exton).

F. Vegetation

Bentle (Mkt. Overton); Bombast Lane (Leighfield); *the Brakes* (Manton), *welbrakes* (Glaston), *The Bracke Close* (Empingham), *Brake Close* (Pilton), *lybrakehil* (N. Luffenham), *Brake Hill* (Whitwell), - *Furlonge* (Belton), Brake Spinney (Edith Weston); Brakey Cl (Pilton), *Breaky Close* (Lyndon); *Brackendale* (Braunston), Bracknell (Normanton), *Brakenhul* (Bisbrooke), Brickennook (Tinwell); *Bryar Bush Furlong* (Barrow), *Bryar Land Seeke* (Lyddington); *.the Briery Close* (Tixover), Briery Wong (Whissendine); Brown Broom (Clipsham); *Brushfeild* (Barleythorpe), *Brushfields* (Stretton); *Cattayles* (Lyndon); Cheesecake (Langham), - Cl (Greetham, Stretton), *Cheesecake Close* (Empingham, Hambleton), Cheesecake Piece (Barrowden), *Cheesecake Piece* (S. Luffenham); Clover Cl (Greetham, Tixover), - Fd (Braunston); *Crap Land* (Barrow); *Cresswell* (Oakham); Cuckold Way (Glaston, *v.* Q); Darnell (Stoke Dry), - Fd, - Mdw (Ryhall); Loose Dogs (Ashwell), Dog Bank Furlong (Seaton), *Dog Pitts* (Uppingham), Dogwell (Whissendine); Dockey Cl (Ridlington); Egg Spinney (Burley, *v.* C);

Feernegate, Feernsyke (Cottesmore); Firs (Preston), *The Furze* (Belton), Furze Cl (Glaston, Gunthorpe, Lyndon, Stoke Dry), *Furze Close* (Hambleton), *the Furze hill* (Oakham), Furze Mdw (Gunthorpe), Bisbrooke Furze Furlong (Seaton); *Furzy Lyndin Hill* (Hambleton); Gold Hills (Edith Weston), *Guildings* (Ryhall); *le Gooseberry Bush* (Barleythorpe); (The) Gorse (Ayston, Gt. Casterton), Campion's Gorse (Burley), Clarke's - (Bisbrooke), Cottesmore - (Cottesmore), Glaston - (Glaston), Gunthorpe - (Gunthorpe), Hale's - (Hambleton), Henton - (Burley), Hopkinson's - (Mkt. Overton), Pilton - (Pilton), Pretty - (Ayston), Seaton - (Seaton), Sharplins - (Hambleton), Tixover - (Tixover), Watkin's - (Burley), Wing - (Preston), Woodward Gorse (Lyndon), *Mill Gorse* (Burley), *Morcott Goss* (Pilton), *Warren Gorse* (Cottesmore), Gorse Cl (Brooke, Hambleton, Preston, Ridlington, Teigh), Gorse Cover (Burley), Gorse Fd (Hambleton, Stoke Dry, Tickencote), Dixon's Gorse Fd (Whitwell), Gorse Hedges (Greetham), Gorse Hill (Wing), *Gorse Hill fur'* (Morcott), The Gorse Pit (Mkt. Overton), Gasby Sick (Whissendine); *ye Grasse* (N. Luffenham), *the Patch of Grass* (Manton), *Bullgrass(e) fur(long)* (Barleythorpe, Egleton), Camswell Grass (Morcott), Far - (Ashwell), Fenton - (Morcott), Highmoor - (Exton), Newell's - (Bisbrooke), Sewage Grass (Uppingham), (*The*) *Constables Grass* (Pilton, Edith Weston), *Notwell's Grasse* (Edith Weston), *Stentgrass* (Lyddington), Grass Cl (Tinwell), Grass Crofts (Langham), *Grascroft* (Lyddington), *le Grasse Ends* (Barleythorpe), Aspin's Grass Fds (S. Luffenham), Home Grass Fd (Ayston), Whincup's Grass Fd (Glaston), Grass Grarves (Exton), *Grass Ground* (Burley), Grass Soward (Ketton); *arnat hyll* (Egleton), Harnett Hill (Edith Weston); Hassocks (Seaton), Hassock's Holme (Whissendine); Ivy Bridge, Ivy Cottage (Cottesmore), Ivydene (Hambleton), *Ivyehall* (Seaton); Jack(a)napes Cl (Ketton); *Jagwell* (Uppingham); *Laber Sike* (Wardley); Lavender Fm (Mkt. Overton); The Lings (Pickworth), *Linges* (Lt. Casterton, Wing), *Le Lyngges* (Bisbrooke), *The Lynges* (Lyndon), Casterton Lings (Gt. Casterton), *Tynewell Lynges* (Tinwell), Ling Cl (Glaston), Ling Cover (Edith Weston), *Ling furlong* (Pilton), *Lyngefurlonges* (Cottesmore), *Lynghau* (Tinwell); *Moss Holmes* (Edith Weston); The Mushroom Cl (Whissendine); Nettle Croft (Glaston), *Nettle Croft* (Edith Weston); *Redbroke* (Horn), *Redebrug'* (S. Luffenham), Reed Spire Mdw (Langham), *Redespires* (Braunston), Redwells (Gunthorpe), *Redwell* (Manton); *Respas Springe* (Belton); Rice

Hollow (Ryhall), *Rice Furlong* (Greetham), *Riseberwe* (Leighfield), *le risdale* (Barrowden), *Rislonde* (Stoke Dry), *Stoke Rislonde* (Lyddington), Flitteris Park (Oakham); Rose Cottage (Ryhall); *the Rushes* (Edith Weston), Rush Cl (N. Luffenham), *Ris(ce)holm* (Lt. Casterton), *Rushpitt* (Burley), Rushpit Wood (Exton); *Rushey Banke* (Lyndon), Rushey Piece (S. Luffenham); *Smockskirts Furlong* (S. Luffenham); Snarlings (Thistleton), *Snarlings* (Mkt. Overton); *Sprat Pittes* (Ketton); *Sprouridge* (Greetham); Star Fd (Ryhall), *Starr Close* (Burley); Thistle Graves (Exton); Thistley Gore (Whissendine); Twitchbed Lane (Uppingham), Twitch Hill (Oakham); Wind Gate Hill (Ryhall), *Wingate furlong* (Lyddington), Winsell (Mkt. Overton); Wisteria Ho. (Empingham); Woodbine Ho. (Hambleton), *Wdebindthornwong* (Cottesmore); *Wool Slades* (Barleythorpe).

G.   Wild fauna: animals, birds, fishes and amphibians, insects

Badger Holes (Gt. Casterton); Bore Hill (Lyddington); *brocholes* (Ayston), *Broc Holys* (N. Luffenham), *Brogholes* (Morcott), *Brockholes Furlonge* (Belton), Brockwell(s) (S. Luffenham, Lyddington); Buck Hill Cl (Ashwell); Cat Cl (Teigh), *Cathole* (Braunston), *Catlow* (Beaumont Chase), *Catmouse* (Burley), Cats Hill Spinney (Ketton), Catterhills (Ashwell), Catwell Sale (Beaumont Chase); *Conie Close* (Whitwell), Coney Gar (Seaton), Coneygree (Empingham), The Kuniger (Bisbrooke), *le Conyngher* (Barrowden), *conygreene* (Ridlington), *cunningree* (Teigh), Coneygear Cl (Glaston), *Coneygrey Close* (Egleton), Conger Hill (Whissendine), Conygear Lane (S. Luffenham); Deer Leap (Lyddington), Red Deer Park (Brooke); Doe Pitts Cl (Ketton); Fox Cover (Glaston, Preston, Ridlington, Thorpe by Water), - Covert (Tinwell), Fox Cover Cl (Pilton), - Lane (Martinsthorpe), Foxearth Spinney (Glaston), Foxholes (Ashwell, Barrowden, Essendine, Langham, Whissendine), *Foxhol(e)s* (Normanton, Oakham), Foxhole Spinney (Glaston); Greygate (Seaton); Haremouth Cl (Teigh), Hare Park (Stretton); Kittleng hill (Barrowden), *Kyttan Close* (Wardley); Leveret Leys (Essendine); Mole Hills (Barrowden), *Mooles Meadow* (Edith Weston); Muxwells (Glaston); Rabbit Burrows (Ryhall), Rabbit Cl (Gt. Casterton, Pickworth); *Rascalhill* (Manton); *Rotten Dyke* (Uppingham), *Rotten Row* (Oakham); Scut Hill (Essendine); *Todholes* (Leighfield); *Woolf Pitt* (Leighfield).

Cockacres (Oakham), Cock Leys (Whissendine), *Cockleys* (Leighfield); *Crakepornfurlong'* (Barrow); *Cranehill* (Morcott); *Crow Croft* (Empingham), *Crowfurlong* (Lyddington), Crow(s) Spinney (Lt. Casterton, Horn), *Crowebeck waye* (Lyndon), *Crowbush furlong* (Lyddington); Cuckoo Lodge (Ketton), Cuckoo Spinney (Exton); Finchley Bridge (Belton); *gledene* (Bisbrooke); *Hawkeslands* (Greetham), *Hawkswell Close* (Barrow), Hawkswell Spinney, - Spring (Exton); *Kite Hill fur'* (Greetham), *Kites Seeke* (Uppingham); *Lark Catchers Leys* (Oakham); Nightingale Spinney (Essendine); (Plovers) New Fd (Teigh); *Puttocks Well close* (Bisbrooke); *Pye Lane* (Uppingham); Rook Cl (Ashwell), The Rookery (Lt. Casterton, Cottesmore, Stretton, Tinwell); *sparrowmore* (Teigh); *Tirtle Meare* (Morcott).

Mertewell' (Oakham); *Pikwellsike* (Oakham); Frog Hall (Ridlington); *Padbrok'* (Burley), Padholme (Brooke), *Padholme* (Egleton); *Padokeford'* (Lyddington), *Padox ford* (Caldecott).

Bittlewell sail (Leighfield); Pismire Nook (Gt. Casterton); *Wipesnest* (Manton), *- fur'* (Egleton); *le wyȝesike* (Seaton).

H.   Crops

Bandale (Mkt. Overton), *Bandlandes* (Exton), *Bandlands Furlong* (Whissendine), *Bannill dale* (Lyndon), *Beanham* (Tickencote), *Beanhill* (Manton); *Barley Close* (Pickworth); *the Brose Close* (Tickencote); Cabbage Cl (Ketton); *Carott Close* (Glaston), Carrot Garden Furlong (Seaton); Coleseed Cl (Burley); Corn Cl (Thistleton), *Corn Close* (Burley), Corn Fd (Gunthorpe); Flax Cl (Glaston), Flax Hole Mdw (Teigh), *Flaxlandes* (Morcott), Flax Leys, *le Flaxeyerde* (Whissendine); *Hauerdale* (Lt. Casterton), *Hauerland* (N. Luffenham), Short Haverhill (Seaton); Hay Cl (Ketton), *the Hay Closes* (N. Luffenham), Hay Croft (Langham), The Hay Fd (Essendine), *Haye gatte* (Exton), *Hay Hill* (Barleythorpe); Hempland (Barrowden), *(the) Hempland(s)* (N. Luffenham, S. Luffenham), Hemp Yards (S. Luffenham); (The) Hop Ground (S. Luffenham, Martinsthorpe, Seaton), *Hop Ground* (Glaston), (The) Hop Yard (Belton, Lyndon, Edith Weston); *Lyncroft* (Barrowden, Caldecott); Oat Cl (Glaston), *Oat Close* (Hambleton, Edith Weston); Onion

Bed (Ketton); *Pease Broad* (Empingham), Pea(s) Cl (S. Luffenham, Pickworth), *pease close* (Tickencote), *The Pease Feilds* (Empingham), Pease Hill(s) (Preston, Ridlington), *Peasehill* (Manton), *Peaze hill* (Thistleton), *Peasehill plott* (Lyndon), Pease holme furlong (Lyddington), Peasland (Mkt. Overton), *Peyseland'* (Cottesmore), *Peaselands fur'* (Egleton), Peaseland Sick, *Peasewell seeke* (Whissendine), *Pesewong* (Lyddington); Rye Cl (Ridlington), *le Rydale* (Barrow), *Rye furlong* (Barleythorpe), *Rygate* (Exton), Rye Hill (Barrowden, Belton, Seaton), *Riholm* (Lt. Casterton), Rylands (Langham, Lyddington); Rye-grass Cl (Barrow); (The) Sain(t)foin Cl (Gt. Casterton, Edith Weston), *St Foin Close* (Normanton), *Old Saintfoin Close* (Greetham), Sanfoin Cl (Tickencote), Old Sanfoin Cl (Lt. Casterton, Tinwell), Sainfoin Hill (Tixover); (The) Seeds (Barleythorpe, Oakham, Preston, Seaton, Stoke Dry, Whissendine), Big Seeds, Great Seeds (Braunston), First Seeds (Ridlington), Middle Seeds (Burley), Seed Acre (Braunston), Seed Cl (Braunston, Manton), *Seed Close* (Egleton), Seed Grass Cl (Stretton); *The Turnipp Close* (Seaton); *Vich Close* (Thistleton); *Wad(d) Close* (Normanton); Wheat Cl (Glaston), *Wheate Close* (Pickworth), Pond Wheat Cl (Braunston), *Whetefyllde* (Oakham), *Wheytelondes* (Cottesmore), *Wheatland Close* (Edith Weston).

I.   Agricultural practice, custom and land tenure

Allotment (Barrow, Caldecott, Ryhall), Bisbrooke Road Allotment (Seaton), Bretland - (Ryhall), Lound Cl -, Oak Cl - (Seaton), Ten Acres Allotment (Ketton), *the Great Allottment* (Manton), Allotment Fd (Ketton, Langham, Mkt. Overton); (The) Allotments (Barrow, Exton, Oakham, Tixover); *Bayliffe Close* (Clipsham); *Beadles fur'* (Greetham), Biddle's Lees (Lyddington); *Childeslund'* (Ayston); (The) Common (Barrowden, Ketton, Lyddington, Seaton, Thorpe by Water), *The Common* (Morcott), Beast Commons (Seaton), Cow Commons (Empingham, Greetham), *Cow Commons* (N. Luffenham), Horse -, Sheep Commons (Seaton), *The Lamass Commons* (Empingham, v. L), *the Com(m)on Feild(e)* (Ayston, Oakham), - *Field* (Whitwell), Common Hill (Gt. Casterton), Common Leys (Whissendine), .Common Wood Cl (Stretton); *Constables baulk* (Morcott), (*The*) *Constables Grass* (Pilton, Edith Weston); (The) Cottagers Cl (Ayston, Cottesmore, Empingham,

Teigh), (*The*) *Cottagers Close* (Lt. Casterton, Mkt. Overton, Tickencote), Cottager's Fd (Gt. Casterton), Cottagers Pastures (Ashwell), Cottager's Spinney (Burley); *Cothers Close* (Lyndon), Cottiers Cl, - Platt (Ridlington), *cottiers close* (Hambleton), *cottiers part* (Wardley); Crewyard (Stretton); *Cure Close* (Burley); Dairy Cl (Tixover), - Fm (Barleythorpe); (The) Drift (Barrowden, Essendine, Pickworth, Ryhall, Seaton), Big Drift (Caldecott), West Leys Drift (Seaton), Drift Cl (Ketton), *The Drift Way* (Thistleton); Drove Cl (Teigh), *Drove Leyes* (Uppingham); Engine Cl (N. Luffenham), - Fd (Mkt. Overton); Nether Fallow (Langham), Fallow Cl (Seaton), Far Fallow Fd (Greetham), *Le Fallow Feild* (Empingham); *Folding Furlong* (Manton); Freeholds Cl (Ashwell); The Freewards (Essendine), *Freewoods* (Leighfield); Grandmother's Cl (Edith Weston), Grammers (Wing), Grannum Cl (Ketton); Grass Bake Nook (Tinwell); Grub Cl (Empingham); *Handacre* (Lt. Casterton, Lyddington), - *furlong* (Caldecott); Herd Cl (Ashwell); Horse Drills (Barleythorpe); *Invention Meadow* (Egleton); Jericho (N. Luffenham); The Joint (N. Luffenham); Lady's Acre (Stoke Dry), *Ladiakre* (Gt. Casterton), (The) Ladies Cl, - Fds (S. Luffenham), *Ladie Close* (Burley), *Lady-holme* (Ridlington), Lady's Mdw (Whissendine), *Lady Meadow* (Burley), Lady Sale (Beaumont Chase), Lady Spinney (Preston), *le Lady Wong* (Lt. Casterton), Lady Wood (Stretton), - Fd, - Piece (Oakham) [note that some of these f.ns. may refer to Our Lady, the Virgin Mary, and so should be listed in K]; *Lambyngecrofte* (Leighfield); The Lots (Seaton); *les meanes* (Barleythorpe); Milking Cl (Egleton, Whissendine), Bottom Milking Cl (Manton), Milking Fd (Greetham); Mowmires (Empingham); No Man's Ground (Ryhall), - Land, - Plot (Seaton), *Nomanislond* (Tinwell); *the Open Close* (Pilton), *Mr Hunts* - (N. Luffenham), *Street Open Close* (Morcott), *Open Gap Close* (S. Luffenham), *the Open Field* (Seaton); (The) Pasture (Brooke, Glaston, Morcott, Seaton, Tinwell), *ye Pasture* (Ketton), *The Pasture and Meadow* (Hambleton), Pastures (Preston), Backside Pasture (Lyddington), Cottagers Pastures (Ashwell), (The) Cow Pasture (Barrowden, Empingham, Hambleton, Langham, N. Luffenham, S. Luffenham, Lyddington, Morcott, Pilton), (*the*) *Cowpasture* (Ayston, Barleythorpe, Lyndon, Normanton), Cow Pastures (Egleton, Greetham), Hambleton Cow Pasture (Hambleton), Old Cow Pasture, Six Cow Pastures (Ryhall), *Cowpasture Close* (Edith Weston), Cow Pasture Fm (Gt. Casterton), Elm Tree Pasture

(Pilton), Glaston - (Glaston), High - (N. Luffenham), Horse - (Empingham), Lincoln - (Hambleton), Stray - (Barrowden), Water Pasture (S. Luffenham), Pasture Cl, - Holme (Seaton), *Pasture Closes* (Whitwell), Pasture Leys (Stoke Dry); Piggery Fd (Ridlington); The Planting (Ketton), Planting Cl (Exton, Teigh); Rickstead (Belton), *Brackles Reekstead* (Braunston), *Gunthorpe rickstede* (Gunthorpe), *Ricksteads fur'* (Egleton); *the Ricke yeard* (Uppingham), Rickyard Fd (Pilton); *Sanam Close* (Hambleton), *Senholm* (Mkt. Overton); *the severall* (Morcott), Sevrells (Hambleton), The Several Cl (Glaston), *Severall Leys* (Stretton); Sheep Dyke (Thistleton), - Cl (Exton), - Lane (Greetham), Sheep Dike Cl (Empingham); Sheep Walk (Clipsham), *The Sheepe Walke* (Stretton, Whissendine), *the Sheep Walk in the Forrest of Lee* (Leighfield), *The Sheep Walks* (Empingham), Lord Exeter's Sheep Walk (Lyddington), *Beamont Walk* (Beaumont Chase), Walk Fm (Gt. Casterton), Walkleys (Ashwell); Cinder Mdw (Hambleton), *Sinderlands* (Braunston), *Sunderland* (Lt. Casterton); Stackyard (Exton, Pilton, Stretton, Teigh, Thistleton), *le Stakeyard* (Barleythorpe), *The Rectors Stackyard* (Stretton), Stackyard Cl (Barrow, Gt. Casterton, Empingham, Langham, S. Luffenham, Pickworth, Ridlington, Teigh), - Fd (Ashwell, Thistleton, Tickencote, Whissendine), Stackyard Fifteen Acres (Ryhall); Stadfolds (Ashwell), Steadfold (Ketton), *Stodfolde* (Glaston), Studfold furlong (Morcott), Stedfold Lane (Tinwell); *Stirwood* (Belton); Stray Lands (Whissendine); Tan Yard (Egleton); *Trespasesike* (Glaston); Vetchery Cl (Empingham); Vote Land (Thistleton); (The) Washdyke (Empingham, Morcott), - Cl (Exton), Wash Dike Nook (Gunthorpe); Washpikes Cl (Ketton); Washpit Cl (Glaston), - Fd (Bisbrooke), - Mdw (Leighfield), *Washpole* (Ketton).

J.   Rents and values

Penny Holmes (N. Luffenham), *Twopenny Lands Furlong* (Belton), *Tenpenny Acre* (Ryhall); *the Five Shillings peece* (Seaton), *the Forty Shillings Close* (Glaston); Scotland (N. Luffenham).

K. Land for (1) Church or (2) charitable use

(1) *the abut(t)es close,* - *leas* (Egleton), *Abbotts meadow* (Wing), *Abbotispittes* (Lt. Casterton), *Abbots Stocking* (Pickworth); *Bell Holme Close* (Tixover), Bell Piece (Langham), Bell Ringing Fd (S. Luffenham), Bell Strings (Pilton); *Bisshop' catwell'* (Beaumont Chase); *Bortolphs Close* (Hambleton); Chantry Cl (Lyddington), *Chantry Close* (Greetham, Hambleton); The Chapel Yard (Ryhall); Chapter Fm (Braunston); Church Fd (Barrowden), *Churchland* (Lyddington), Church Yard (Ashwell, S. Luffenham, Stretton, Teigh), *(The) Church(e) Yard* (Egleton, Lyndon, Pilton); College Fm (Leighfield); *Fincett Land* (N. Luffenham); (The) Glebe (Burley, Egleton, Langham, S. Luffenham, Oakham), Late Glebe (Gt. Casterton), West Glebe (Ridlington), Glebe Barn Fd (Lt. Casterton), Glebe Cl (Ketton, Stretton), East -, West - (Clipsham), Old Glebe Cl (Stoke Dry), *(The) Glebe Close* (Glaston, Normanton), *Lyndon Glebe Close* (Lyndon), *the Parsons Gleabe Close* (Edith Weston), Glebe Fm (Barrow, Tinwell), - Ho. (Burley), Glebe Fd (Empingham, Thistleton), *The Glebe Land(s)* (Belton, Bisbrooke), *the Meadow Gleebe land* (Barrowden); *Ladiakre* (Gt. Casterton), *le Lady Wong* (Lt. Casterton) etc. (*v.* f.ns. with Lady - in I); *le Lampe* (Mkt. Overton), *Lampacre Close* (Uppingham), *the Laump land* (Bisbrooke), *Lamplees* (Hambleton), *Lamp Leys* (Morcott); Lincolns Cl (Ryhall), Lincoln's Hold, Lincoln Pasture (Hambleton), Lincoln Yard (Lyndon); *New Kirke* (Edith Weston), *New Kyrke* (Wardley); None Stalls (Braunston); *Organs Close* (Burley); *The Parsonage* (Greetham), *the parsonage land(e)* (Belton, Glaston, Lyndon), *the Parsonage Yard* (N. Luffenham); *(the) Parsons Close* (Glaston, Lyndon), - *Penn* (Glaston), - *swathes* (Lyndon); Prebendal Fd (Empingham); *Priest Gore* (Manton), *Prestlands* (Barleythorpe), Prestley Hill (Lyddington), *Prestesmor* (Glaston), Priestwell(s) (Barleythorpe, Cottesmore, Greetham), *Preist Wood* (Greetham), Priest Wong (Whissendine); *Priorage Close* (Greetham); Prior's Coppice (Brooke), *priors medowe* (Wing); Great Queen's Cl (Teigh); *Saint John's Land* (Lt. Casterton); Sanctuary (Gunthorpe); The Rectors Stackyard (Stretton); *Steeple Acre* (Lyddington), Steeple Cl (Ashwell), - Fd (Pickworth); Tithe Barn (Empingham), *The Tythe Barn(e)* (Bisbrooke, Greetham, Oakham), *The Tith Barne and Close* (Braunston), *Tythe Close, The Tythe House* (Greetham), Tithe Mdw (Belton), *Tyth Meadow* (Manton), *Tythstacke Seeke,* The Tithe Yard

(Whissendine); Vicar Cl (Stretton), *ye Vicar Pits* (Ketton); *le viccaradge land* (Oakham), *the Vicaridge Land* (Bisbrooke).

(2)   *le Beadhouse Close* (Oakham), Beadhouse Croft, - Leys (Stretton), *the bead-house farm, Beadhouse peice* (N. Luffenham); *Dyngly Lees* (Stoke Dry); (The) Fronald (Lyddington, Stoke Dry); Hospital (Wardley); Oddfellows Fd (Ketton); *the poors barne* (N. Luffenham), Poor Cl (Hambleton), Poor Close Covert (Burley), Poor Fds (Ayston), Brook Poor Fd (Morcott), Poor Gardens (Lyddington), The Poor's Land (Tixover); *Saint John's Land* (Lt. Casterton), *the landes called Sct. Johns* (Uppingham), *St Johns Peice* (Greetham) (*v.* L); Temple Barns, *Temple Field* (Stretton), *Temple Peyse* (Greetham); White Bread Cl (Ketton); Workhouse (Uppingham), The Workhouse Cl (Barrowden), Workhouse Yard and Garden (Empingham).

L.   Seasons and festivals

Lamas (Edith Weston), *The Lammas* (Lt. Casterton), Lammas Cl (N. Luffenham, S. Luffenham, Lyddington, Morcott, Whissendine), (*le*) *Lammas Close* (Ayston, Barleythorpe, Belton, Oakham), *The Lammas Commons* (Empingham), *Lames fur'* (Egleton), Lammas Ground (Pilton), *Lammas Grounds* (Whissendine), Lammas Mdw (Essendine), *Lamas pastures* (Manton), Lamas Pen (Thistleton); Michaelmas Holme (Seaton); Midsummer Cl (Morcott); *Saint John's Land* (Lt. Casterton), *St Johns Peice* (Greetham), *the landes called Sct. Johns* (Uppingham).

M.   Structures (excluding buildings and bridges)

Arberry Gate (Morcott); Beacon (Glaston), the Beacon Fd (Essendine); *the Brick Kilnes* (Uppingham), Brickkiln Cl (Ashwell), - Spinney (Burley); *Clapmilleclose* (N. Luffenham); Cundict (Braunston); Dams (Langham), Base Dam (Caldecott), Mill Dam (Ketton, Tickencote), *le Mylnedam(me)* (N. Luffenham, Ryhall), Damm Acres (Oakham), Damade (Mkt. Overton), *Damfeild* (Ayston, Thistleton), *Damwongs* (Thistleton); Engine Fd (Mkt. Overton), - Pond (Burley); *Frame furlong* (Caldecott); *Gallow Hill*

(Uppingham), *Galowe hill furlong* (Caldecott), *Gallows Peice* (Oakham), *Gallowtree hill* (Ryhall), *Galowong* (Lyddington); *Gibbet Gate* (Oakham), Gibbet Gorse (Hambleton); Glaston Tunnel (Glaston); Kelpit Cl (Stoke Dry), *Kiln(e) Close* (Ayston, Egleton), *the kilne howse* (Preston); Limekiln (Mkt. Overton), Limekiln Cl (Morcott), *Lime Kiln Close* (N. Luffenham), Limekiln Spinney (Cottesmore); The Line Fd (Ketton), Line Fds (S. Luffenham), Over the Line (Barrow, Essendine); *le Mantell'* (N. Luffenham); Moat Cl (N. Luffenham), *Mott Close* (Clipsham); *the Navigation* (Mkt. Overton), Navigation Cl (Barrow); *le Pele* (N. Luffenham); Railway (Ketton), - Fds (Morcott), Bradshaw's Railway Fd (Oakham), Piece by the Railway (Gunthorpe); The Ramparts (Egleton), Rampart Hill (Gt. Casterton); Reservoir Fd (Exton); Stocks Hill (Ketton, Manton); *the Strete* (Mkt. Overton), *Street Ende*, Street Fd (Greetham), *Street fur'*, - *Leys* (Morcott), *the Streete Way* (Barrow), *the Highestrete* (Barrowden), *High Street* (Thistleton), *Longstreete furlong* (Tickencote), *Lyngcolne -*, *Nottyngham Strete* (Greetham); *Stile Close* (Normanton), *Pedderstyle* (Cottesmore), Wing Stile Cl (Pilton), *Woodfield stile* (Stoke Dry); *the Tentars* (Edith Weston), Big Tenter's (Ridlington), Tenters Cl (Langham), Tenter Gap (Morcott), - Hedge (Empingham); Toll Bar (Ayston), - Cl (Ryhall, Tinwell); The Wharf (Mkt. Overton); Barrow -, Wide Hole (Barrow, Cottesmore); *Winge Maze* (Wing).

N. Names referring to objects found

Charnellhoale (Teigh); The Clinkers (Edith Weston); *Dedemansforlang* (Barrow), Deadman's Grave Furlong (N. Luffenham), Dead Man's Ground (Tinwell), Deadmans Holme (Barrowden); The Foundations (Pickworth); *Kokelstone furlong* (Greetham); *Moneybalke* (Oakham), Money Holes (Greetham), Money Pit Cl (Ketton); *Pottacres* (Egleton); The Urns (Gt. Casterton).

O. Allusions to Bible, religion, folklore, superstition

Bloody Oaks (Empingham); *Botewell* (Leighfield); *Boygraue* (Bisbrooke), *Boygreue*, Boy's Pitt Spinney (N. Luffenham);

Goodmans Snowte (Wardley); *Healall Cottage* (Uppingham); *Helwell'* (Oakham), *Hellwell medowe* (Teigh); *Helpitt dale* (Lyndon); *Hob Hole* (Greetham); Holywell (Seaton), *Halywelcros* (Barrowden), *Hollywell slades* (Barleythorpe), *Holywell Close* (Hambleton); Jittys Cl (Lyddington, *v.* A, E); Our Lady's Well (Oakham); *Paradise* (Wing); *robynilpit* (Barrowden); Robin Hood's Cave (Exton), *Robin Hoods Stone* (Ryhall); Saint Ann's (Barrowden), *St Ann's Meadow* (S. Luffenham); *Schucheved* (Lt. Casterton), Shockmore Balk (S. Luffenham); *Thirspit* (Glaston), *thyrspit* (Barrowden), *Tyrespyt* (Empingham) (*v.* A); *þureslege broc* (Ayston); Tibba's Well (Ryhall), *Tibwellewonge* (Lt. Casterton); Wade's Hill (Ayston), Wades Hill (Thistleton).

P.   Transferred names: (1) foreign or (2) British

(1)   America (Cottesmore), - Lodge (Brooke); Belgium (Oakham); Botany Bay (Lt. Casterton, S. Luffenham, *v.* A); Bunker's Hill (Empingham); The Canada (Stretton); Cyprus (Seaton); Jarminy (N. Luffenham); Jericho (N. Luffenham); Klondyke (Barleythorpe, Beaumont Chase, Hambleton, Wardley); Nova Scotia (Edith Weston, Tickencote), Scotia Cl (Stretton); Van Diemans (Lyddington, *v.* A).

(2)   *Bedlam Meadow* (Leighfield); The Chelsea (Empingham); Constitution Hill (Uppingham); Jersey Hill (Whissendine); Scotland Voyage (Thistleton); *a furlong called Vale of White Horse* (Morcott).

Q.   Recreation

the Bowling Ally, Bowlinge greene, the Bowlinge Leys (Glaston), *the old bowling Ally, the Bowling greene, the old Bowling Leys* (Uppingham), *The Bowling Alley Close* (Tickencote), *Bowling Green* (Hambleton), *Bowling Leys Furlong* (Manton); Cock Pit Cl (Morcott), *Cockpitt* (N. Luffenham), *Cockepitt Wong* (Greetham); Cricket Fd (Barleythorpe, Belton, Langham, Preston), Cricket Paddock (Ridlington); Dog Kennel (Essendine), - Cottages (Oakham), *Dogkennell Furlong* (Belton), Dog Kennel Spinney (Burley), *the Doggkennell Yard* (N. Luffenham), Kennels Fd

(Langham); Football Cl (S. Luffenham), - Fd (Mkt. Overton), - Piece (Edith Weston), Football pit (Barrowden); Hockey Fd (Uppingham); Hunting Gate (Normanton) [and note the range of names in Fox Cover listed in G]; Pleasure Grounds (Normanton); Racecourse (Barleythorpe, Lyddington); Sports Fd (Ketton); Tennis Court (Whissendine); *Uppingham Course* (Uppingham).

R.   Dalliance

Cuckold Way (Glaston, *v*. F); *Quintrey lane* (Braunston); *Sweet Lips Close* (Glaston).

S.   Field-names which may be derived from older place-names

Burton Hill fur' (Morcott); Eastwick (Stoke Dry); Henton (Burley, Cottesmore); *Islington* (Thistleton); Neanton Cl (Empingham); Ravenstock Wood (Essendine); *Stilton meadowe* (Belton).

T.   Miscellaneous unexplained minor names and field-names

The following, through lack of sufficient early forms or through absence of pertinent supporting information, remain unexplained in part or in entirety: Addah Wood (Clipsham), *Archdales* (Mkt. Overton), *Beresdall'* (Barrowden), *Boddilie Meadow* (Burley), Boy Fd, Boyfields Cl (Ashwell, Teigh), *Brakeswheyt* (Pickworth), Bretland (Ryhall, Whissendine), Bunklins (Hambleton), Capeland (Barrowden), *careston' hadelond* (Bisbrooke), Cockatrice Cl (Wardley), Doll's Hole (Stoke Dry), *Dullands* (Empingham), *Flealscroft* (Egleton), *Frontenhaue* (Stoke Dry), *Gochismore* (Seaton), *Green(e) Huske Furlong* (Barrow, Whissendine), Harlewong (Edith Weston), Launsey Bank (Glaston), Loudal Lane (Ashwell), *Mount Murray Wood* (Tinwell), *Pastmore hyde* (Preston), *Petitioners Close* (Hambleton), *Raslingdike* (Thistleton), *Rite sink* (Uppingham), *Rovey Furlong* (Uppingham), *Search Hole* (Barrowden), Sense Lands Furlong (Seaton), Stone husk furlong (Thorpe by Water), Big -, Little Sutie (Pickworth), *Todley Close* (S. Luffenham), Tunneley Wood (Exton).

PERSONAL NAMES IN RUTLAND
PLACE-NAMES AND FIELD-NAMES

This list includes personal names incorporated in place-names and field-names. In some cases it is uncertain that the examples contain the personal name but they are listed here if there is a possibility that they do contain it. The discussions of the individual place-names should be consulted in all cases. Some field-names are entered more than once in this list, as alternative etymologies involving different personal names are given for them. Some personal names which are cited in their OE or Scandinavian forms continued in use in ME and it is often impossible to say whether a field-name or minor name originated in an earlier or later period. Names not independently attested are marked with an asterisk. The unindexed field-names containing personal names are assigned to their parishes.

A. OLD ENGLISH

Ælfnoð (Alstoe Hundred), *Æðelstān* (Ayston), *Alwald* (*Alwoldestie* (Uppingham)), *Anna* (*Anwell Bryg'* (Egleton)), *Beornhelm* (Belmesthorpe), *Bitel (Bisbrooke), *Boia* (*Boygraue* (Bisbrooke), *boydale, Boygreue,* Boy's Pitt Spinney (N. Luffenham)), *Botting (*Bottingeshowes* (Seaton)), *Brant* (Braunston), *Bud(d)a* (*Budborow* (Greetham)), *Byttel (Bisbrooke), *Cott (Cottesmore), *Cylp (Clipsham), *Ēadgȳð* fem. (Edith Weston), (*E*)*alhstān* (*Alsthorpe*), *Earnmund* (Armsley Quarter (Beaumont Chase)), *Ecgwulf* (Egleton), *Empa* (Empingham), *Ēsa* (Essendine), *Gǣrwald* (*Gerwaldesholm* (Uppingham)), *Godda* (*Goddemade* (Burley)), *Gōdwine* (Goddins (Mkt. Overton)), *Gyssa (Geeston), *Hǣddi* (*Haddisly* (Ayston)), *Headd* (*Haddisly* (Ayston)), *Hlȳda (Lyddington), *Hræfn (*Ravens Crosse* (Barleythorpe), Ravenstock Wood), *Hūn* (*Hunisforlong* (N. Luffenham)), *Hund* (*Hundesbuske* (Oakham)), *Hwicce (Whissendine, Wichley Leys (Whissendine), Witchley Warren), *Lēofhild* (*Leffildespol* (Tixover)), *Luffa (Luffenham, *Luffewyke*), *Lulla* (Lullhaugh Cl (Whissendine), *Lull Hill* (Greetham)), *Manna* (Manton), *Martin* (from MedLat *Martinus*) (*martines hō* (Ayston), *Martinsley*, Martinsthorpe, *Martinestoch*), *Oc(c)a* (Oakham), *Pīca (Pickworth), *Ranc (Ranksborough), *Rēdel

RUTLAND

(Ridlington), *Rōta* (Rutland, *Rutmore*), **Sǽga* (Seaton), *Snell* (*Snelston*), *Tibba* fem. (Tibba's Well (Ryhall), *Tibwellewonge* (Lt. Casterton)), **Tȳni* (Tinwell), **Wenna* (*Wenton*), *Wifel* (*Wyueleshell'* (Mkt. Overton)), *Wulf* (Woolsdale (N. Luffenham)), *Wulfa* (Woolfox), *Wulfbeorn* (*Wylbernecroftes* (Bisbrooke)), *Wulfgār* (*Wilkershaw*).

B. SCANDINAVIAN

Ásbjǫrn (*Osbernholm* (Whissendine), Osbonall Wood), *Friðgestr* (*Fregsthorpe*), *Glaðr* (Glaston), *Gunni* (*Gundale Furlong* (Ketton), Gunnel Lane, Gunthorpe), *Hrafn* (*Ravens Crosse* (Barleythorpe)), *Hrolfr* (*Roluesmedowe* (Whitwell)), *Hundr* (*Hundesbuske* (Oakham)), *Ingi* (Ingthorpe, *Yngedale* (Glaston)), *Ingjaldr* (*White Ingle Dale* (Ryhall)), *Ingulfr* (*White Ingle Dale* (Ryhall)), *Ingvarr* (*Ingersdale* (Empingham), *Ingresdale Slade* (Exton)), *Ketill* (Kilthorpe Grange), *Manni* (*Manthorpe*), *Skúli* (Sculthorpe Spinney), *Súla* (Soulthorpe Lane Close (Ketton)), *Þór* (Anglo-Scand) (*þureslege broc* (Ayston)), *Þūr* (Anglo-Scand) (*þureslege broc* (Ayston)), *Tóli* (Tolethorpe Hall).

C. MIDDLE ENGLISH AND CONTINENTAL

Benedict (from MedLat *Benedictus*) (*ad crucem Benedicti* (N. Luffenham)), *Bernard* (OGer) (Barnsdale), *Gerbert* (OFr, OGer) (*Gerberdfurlong* (Wing)), *Herbert* (OFr) (*Herbertmer* (Stretton)), *Maud* (from OGer *Mahthildis* > *Matilda* of which a common vernacular form was *Mahald* > *Maud*) (*Maud Pool* (Tixover)), *Randulf* (OFr) (*le dybbyng Randulphi de Belfago* (Thorpe by Water)), *Robin* (diminutive of *Rob*, a pet-form of OFr *Robert*) (*robynilpit* (Barrowden)).

THE SURNAMES RECORDED IN RUTLAND MINOR NAMES AND FIELD-NAMES

Each surname is cited with the parishes in which it appears. Occasionally it is impossible to be certain whether a field-name contains a surname or an otherwise unrecorded place-name (e.g. *Headley stints fur'* 1799 (Morcott), *Islington* 1633 (Thistleton)). Also, ambiguity between a surname and an occupation or office may occur (e.g. *Salter Leys* 1652, *Beadles fur'* 1652 (both Greetham)). Where such ambiguity exists, the names have been included.

Abbey (Cottesmore), *Ackins* (Preston), *Adams* (N. Luffenham), *Adcock* (Hambleton, Whissendine), *Albin* (Lyddington), *Alder(s)* (Morcott), *Alexander* (Normanton), *Alfin* (Normanton, Stretton), *Allen* (Belton, Caldecott, Clipsham, Empingham, Hambleton, N. Luffenham, Lyndon, Normanton, Seaton, Stretton), *Allett* (Oakham), *Allin* (Caldecott, Uppingham), *Almond* (Langham), *Alward* (Lyddington), *Andrews* (Hambleton, Preston, Stretton), *Anness* (Exton, Seaton), *Armstrong* (Braunston, Oakham), *Ashwell* (Bisbrooke, Stretton), *Askew* (Stretton), *Aspin* (S. Luffenham), *Atkin(s)* (Glaston, Tixover), *Atton* (Braunston, Edith Weston), *Austin* (Glaston, Lyndon, Edith Weston).

Babb(s) (N. Luffenham), *Bacon* (Pickworth, Stretton), *Bag(ger)ley* (N. Luffenham), *Bailey* (Empingham, Teigh), *Baines* (Barleythorpe, Egleton, Glaston, Lyndon, Morcott, Oakham, Pickworth, Seaton, Tinwell, Uppingham), *Baker* (Pickworth, Ridlington, Stretton, Teigh, Tixover), *Ball* (Caldecott, Manton, Oakham, Edith Weston), *Banbury* (Preston), *Bancroft* (Cottesmore, Ridlington), *Banier* (Ayston), *Banks* (Hambleton, Leighfield), *Bannister* (Stretton), *Barber* (Bisbrooke, Tickencote), *Barfoot* (Leighfield, Mkt. Overton), *Barker* (N. Luffenham, S. Luffenham, Lyddington, Lyndon, Morcott, Pickworth, Edith Weston), *Barnes* (Lt. Casterton), *Barnett* (Ayston, Egleton, Lyddington, Oakham), *Barrow* (Exton, Oakham, Ridlington), *Barsby* (Lyndon), *Bartle* (Ketton), *Basset(t)* (S. Luffenham, Preston, Ridlington, Seaton), *Bates* (Braunston, N. Luffenham, Edith Weston), *Baxter* (Langham, S. Luffenham), *Bayliffe* (Clipsham), *Beadle* (Greetham), *Beadman* (Braunston), *Beaumont* (Lyddington), *Beaver* (Empingham, Langham, Pickworth), *Beeby* (Belton), *Belgrave*

(Uppingham, Wing), *Bell* (Caldecott, Exton, Hambleton), *Bellaers* (Glaston, Greetham, Seaton, Stretton), *Bellamy* (Whissendine), *Bellows* (Barrowden), *Belton* (Stretton), *Bennett* (Hambleton, Teigh), *Bennington* (Ketton), *Bennison* (Edith Weston), *Beran* (Langham), *Bernard* (Lyddington), *Berridge* (Hambleton, Pickworth), *Berry* (Greetham, Stretton, Wing), *Bett* (Barleythorpe, Greetham), *Biddle* (Lyddington), *Biggs* (Egleton), *Bigott* (Morcott), *Billings* (Lyddington, Thorpe by Water, Edith Weston), *Billington* (Oakham), *Bill(s)* (Cottesmore, Whitwell), *Bingham* (Hambleton), *Binks* (Oakham), *Binnett* (Uppingham), *Birchnell* (Teigh), *Bishop* (Oakham), *Bitterley* (Tickencote), *Blair* (Ashwell), *Blake* (Bisbrooke), *Blakemile* (Whissendine), *Bland* (Lt. Casterton), *Blaze* (Stretton), *Blewett* (Hambleton), *Blofield* (Oakham), *Blood* (Barleythorpe), *Bloodworth* (Empingham, Hambleton, Normanton), *Blunfield* (Stretton), *Board* (Ashwell), *Bolland* (Lt. Casterton, S. Luffenham, Lyndon), *Bo(u)nds* (Barleythorpe), *Bonner* (Lyddington), *Booth* (Burley, Cottesmore, Lyddington), *Bossom* (Burley), *Botting* (Seaton), *Bowell* (Seaton), *Bowles* (Gt. Casterton), *Boyall* (Gt. Casterton, Empingham, Stretton, Tickencote), *Boyer* (Brooke), *Bradley* (Belton, Hambleton, Manton), *Bradshaw* (Barleythorpe, Egleton, Hambleton, Martinsthorpe, Oakham), *Brampton* (Brooke), *Branston* (Edith Weston), *Bray* (Bisbrooke), *Bretfield* (N. Luffenham), *Bridges* (Hambleton, Normanton), *Briggs* (Martinsthorpe), *Bright* (Glaston, Leighfield), *Brightmore* (Morcott, Wing), *Brindle* (Langham), *Brinkley* (Burley, Teigh), *Britain* (N. Luffenham, Tixover), *Broadhouse* (Caldecott), *Bromley* (Ashwell), *Broom* (Empingham, Manton, Pilton, Edith Weston), *Broughton* (Beaumont Chase, Glaston, Stoke Dry), *Brown(e)* (Ayston, Belton, Bisbrooke, Cottesmore, Hambleton, Leighfield, S. Luffenham, Lyddington, Morcott, Preston, Stretton, Thistleton, Uppingham, Wardley, Whissendine), *Bryan* (Glaston, Ridlington), *Bryant* (Empingham), *Buck* (Barrowden), *Buckle* (Glaston), *Buckworth* (Empingham, Tixover), *Bugg(s)* (Glaston), *Bull* (Hambleton, Langham, Lyddington, Lyndon, Morcott, Whitwell), *Bullimore* (Burley, Langham, Oakham), *Bullock* (Uppingham), *Bunning* (Empingham), *Bunyon* (Uppingham), *Burden* (Hambleton, Teigh), *Burgess* (Hambleton, Ridlington), *Burke* (Brooke), *Burkett* (Essendine), *Burneby* (Manton), *Burnman* (Exton), *Burton* (Belton, Burley, Egleton, Langham, Morcott), *Butcher* (Ashwell, Burley, Cottesmore, Greetham, Langham, Preston), *Butler* (Langham, Preston), *Buxton* (Uppingham).

Calcott (Tixover), *Camm* (Stretton), *Campion* (Burley), *Candlemaker* (Beaumont Chase), *Cant* (Ayston, N. Luffenham, Morcott, Preston, Wardley), *Cannon* (Belton), *Capon* (Greetham, Stretton), *Cardwell* (S. Luffenham), *Cardy* (Lyndon), *Carrier* (Empingham, Normanton), *Carter* (Egleton, N. Luffenham, Stretton, Whissendine), *Castledine* (Oakham), *Castor* (Bisbrooke), *Catherines* (Langham, Uppingham), *Cave* (Caldecott, Stoke Dry), *Cawshaw* (Stretton), *Chamberlain* (Burley, Oakham), *Chambers* (Empingham), *Champante* (Oakham), *Chapman* (Ashwell, Bisbrooke, Glaston, Greetham, N. Luffenham, Lyddington, Thorpe by Water, Wardley), *Charity* (Greetham), *Charnock* (Oakham), *Chatterton* (Glaston), *Cheriton* (Mkt. Overton), *Cheseldine* (Beaumont Chase, Braunston, Hambleton, Leighfield, Manton, Edith Weston), *Chetham* (Uppingham), *Child* (S. Luffenham, Manton), *Christian* (Barrow, Empingham, Mkt. Overton, Pickworth), *Christopher* (Hambleton), *Clark(e)* (Ashwell, Barrowden, Bisbrooke, Burley, Cottesmore, Glaston, Hambleton, N. Luffenham, Martinsthorpe, Normanton, Oakham, Mkt. Overton, Ridlington, Stretton, Edith Weston, Wing), *Clement* (Ayston, Gunthorpe, Manton, Uppingham), *Cleve* (Greetham), *Clew* (Lyddington), *Clifton* (Oakham), *Clipston* (Belton), *Close* (Pickworth), *Cobbler* (Empingham), *Codd* (Braunston), *Coe* (N. Luffenham), *Cole* (Langham, Leighfield, N. Luffenham, Oakham, Ridlington), *Coleman* (Wardley), *Coll* (Essendine), *Collington* (Empingham, Hambleton, Normanton), *Collins* (Greetham, Uppingham), *Colson* (N. Luffenham), *Colt* (Egleton), *Compton* (Burley), *Connington* (Pickworth), *Cook(e)* (Ashwell, Barrowden, Brooke, Glaston, Hambleton, S. Luffenham, Seaton, Uppingham, Edith Weston), *Cooper* (Braunston, Brooke, Empingham, Langham, N. Luffenham), *Corbett* (Glaston), *Cottle* (Mkt. Overton, Whissendine), *Coulton* (Uppingham), *Coundry* (Brooke), *Couzens* (Essendine), *Coward* (Morcott), *Cox* (Burley, Egleton, Langham, Teigh), *Cramp* (Martinsthorpe, Morcott, Wing), *Cresswell* (Cottesmore), *Crispe* (Seaton), *Crow* (Lyddington, Mkt. Overton, Thistleton), *Crowden* (Barrowden, Belton, Bisbrooke, Exton, Seaton), *Cumbrey* (Greetham, Stretton), *Cunnington* (Brooke), *Cup* (Cottesmore), *Curtis* (Morcott, Stoke Dry).

Dalby (Ashwell, Burley, Hambleton, Langham, Edith Weston), *Dane* (Exton), *Daniels* (Oakham), *Darby* (Langham), *Davenport* (Barrowden), *Davis* (Mkt. Overton), *Davy* (Lt. Casterton), *Dawe(s)*

(Langham, Uppingham), *Dawkinson* (Barrowden), *Day* (Ashwell, Barrowden, Ryhall), *Deacon* (Glaston), *Dennison* (Barleythorpe), *Dent* (Whitwell), *de Witt* (Lyndon), *Dexter* (Preston), *Dickie* (Thistleton), *Dickman* (Braunston), *Digby* (Bisbrooke, Glaston, N. Luffenham, S. Luffenham, Morcott, Pilton, Stoke Dry), *Dilkes* (Lt. Casterton), *Ding* (Mkt. Overton), *Dixon* (Whitwell) *Donaby* (Uppingham), *Dorman* (Langham), *Doughty* (S. Luffenham), *Doure* (Barleythorpe, Caldecott), *Dove* (Barrowden), *Dragon* (Lt. Casterton, Preston), *Drake* (Morcott), *Duckett* (Seaton), *Dugden* (Lyddington, Seaton, Thrope by Water), *Duke* (Glaston, Hambleton, N. Luffenham), *Dunhill* (Ketton), *Dunmore* (Lyndon), *Duport* (Normanton), *Durant* (Barrowden, S. Luffenham, Morcott).

Eayr (Caldecott, Gunthorpe, Hambleton, Manton), *Eddy* (Essendine, Lyddington), *Edgson* (Langham), *Edwards* (Preston, Whissendine), *Ekins* (Wardley), *Elliott* (Ayston), *Ellis* (Empingham, Greetham), *Emmanuel* (Clipsham), *Estwick* (Stretton), *Everett* (Ridlington), *Exton* (Empingham).

Fairchild (Caldecott, Pickworth), *Falkener* (Barrowden, N. Luffenham, Morcott, Uppingham, Whissendine), *Fancourt* (Burley, Empingham, S. Luffenham, Stretton), *Fant* (Brooke), *Faulk* (Oakham), *Fawcett* (Ashwell), *Fedd* (Galston), *Fell* (Hambleton), *Fenton* (Morcott), *Figg* (Tixover), *Finch* (Hambleton, Martinsthorpe), *Finningley* (Lyndon), *Fisher* (Morcott, Stretton, Uppingham), *Fleming* (Belton), *Flint* (Burley, Cottesmore, Oakham), *Flore* (Oakham), *Flower* (Hambleton, Whissendine), *Forester* (Lyddington), *Forster* (Thistleton), *Foster* (Braunston, Burley), *Fountain* (Cottesmore, Exton, Ridlington), *Fowler* (Barrowden, Exton, Hambleton, Manton, Normanton), *Fox* (Glaston, Ketton), *Frank* (Morcott, Ridlington), *Franklin* (Glaston), *Freeman* (Braunston, Normanton, Uppingham, Edith Weston), *Frisby* (Ridlington), *Fryer* (Hambleton, Normanton).

Galway (Empingham), *Gamble* (Glaston), *Gand* (Ridlington), *Gandy* (Ryhall), *Gann* (Mkt. Overton, Stretton), *Gardner* (Ridlington), *Garner* (Beaumont Chase, Essendine, Tickencote, Whissendine), *Garrett* (Bisbrooke), *Gascoigne* (Mkt. Overton, Teigh), *George* (Glaston, Hambleton), *Gibb(s)* (Greetham, Hambleton, Edith Weston), *Gibbon* (N. Luffenham), *Gibson* (N. Luffenham, Whissendine, Wing), *Giles* (Seaton), *Gill* (Barrowden, N.

Luffenham), *Gilson* (Greetham, Morcott), *Gladnell* (Stoke Dry), *Glazier* (Manton), *Glover* (Cottesmore, Normanton, Whissendine), *Goddard* (Lyndon), *Godfrey* (Belton, Seaton), *Goodacre* (Thistleton), *Good(e)* (Burley, Morcott, Ridlington), *Goodliffe* (S. Luffenham), *Goodman* (Greetham, Lyndon, Stretton, Teigh, Wardley), *Goodwin* (Stoke Dry), *Goody* (Ashwell), *Gordon* (Thistleton), *Goslin* (N. Luffenham, Lyndon), *Grant* (Lyndon, Normanton, Stretton), *Gray* (Bisbrooke, Glaston, Ridlington), *Green* (Belton, Lyddington, Morcott, Whissendine), *Greenham* (Ketton), *Gregory* (Caldecott, Hambleton), *Griffin* (Belton), *Grimes* (Empingham, Greetham), *Gunby* (Barleythorpe), *Gunn* (Wing).

Hack (Stretton), *Hale* (Hambleton), *Haley* (Burley), *Halffoot* (Barrowden), *Halford* (Lyndon), *Halliday* (Greetham, Stretton, Thistleton), *Ham* (Wardley), *Hancock* (Manton), *Hand* (Lyndon), *Hannah* (Ridlington), *Harbottle* (Oakham), *Harbuck* (Exton), *Hardy* (Barrow, Stoke Dry), *Harley* (Clipsham), *Harris* (Langham, Mkt. Overton, Wardley), *Harrison* (Ketton, Lyddington, Uppingham), *Hart* (Egleton, Gunthorpe, Hambleton, Edith Weston), *Haselwood* (Belton), *Hastler* (Morcott), *Hasty* (Ashwell), *Haunton* (Hambleton), *Hawking* (Edith Weston), *Headley* (Morcott), *Healey* (Burley, Hambleton), *Heathcote* (N. Luffenham), *Henn* (Bisbrooke), *Henton* (Burley, Cottesmore), *Herbert* (Bisbrooke), *Herring* (Teigh), *Hewitt* (Pilton, Ridlington), *Hibbitt* (Brooke, Empingham, Horn), *Hickman* (Glaston, Ridlington), *Hill* (Braunston), *Hillam* (Uppingham), *Hilton* (Hambleton), *Hingley* (Langham), *Hippesley* (Burley, Hambleton), *Hobbijohn* (Caldecott), *Hobbs* (Hambleton), *Hoby* (Wardley), *Hogg* (Thorpe by Water), *Hoggard* (Ketton), *Hope* (Uppingham), *Hopkins* (Ayston), *Hopkinson* (Mkt. Overton), *Horner* (Pilton), *Horn(s)by* (Ashwell, Ayston, Langham), *Horton* (Whissendine), *Hubbard* (Langham, Seaton), *Hudson* (Ayston, Wardley, Whissendine), *Humm* (Seaton), *Humphrey(s)* (Ayston, Langham), *Hungate* (Uppingham), *Hungerford* (Hambleton), *Hunn* (N. Luffenham), *Hunt* (Empingham, Essendine, Ketton, Leighfield, N. Luffenham, Pickworth, Pilton), *Hurst* (Stretton), *Hutchins* (Ketton), *Hutton* (Brooke).

Idle (Cottesmore), *Ilfin* (Edith Weston), *Illif* (Normanton), *Ingram* (Lyddington), *Inman* (Ashwell, Barrow, Stretton), *Ireland* (Egleton, Hambleton, Lyndon), *Isaac* (Langham), *Islip* (Empingham, S.

Luffenham, Lyddington, Morcott, Edith Weston), *Issit* (Ridlington), *Ivett* (Ryhall).

Jackson (Burley, Cottesmore, Empingham, Greetham, Hambleton, Lyddington, Oakham, Edith Weston, Whissendine), *Jacques* (Morcott), *Jarvis* (Egleton, Hambleton, Pickworth), *Jeeks* (Whissendine), *Jenkinson* (Bisbrooke), *Jerman* (N. Luffenham, Edith Weston), *Johnson* (Brooke, Glaston, N. Luffenham), *Jones* (Langham), *Jordan* (Langham, Stretton), *Julian* (Leighfield, Manton).

Keen (Empingham), *Kemp* (Wardley), *Kettle* (Barrow), *Kidd* (Clipsham), *Kimberley* (Oakham), *King* (Gt. Casterton, Lt. Casterton, Exton, Glaston, Hambleton, N. Luffenham, S. Luffenham, Lyddington, Normanton, Ridlington, Stretton), *King(s)ton* (Braunston, Empingham), *Kirk* (Glaston, Lyddington, Lyndon), *Kitt* (Ridlington), *Knight* (Lt. Casterton, N. Luffenham), *Knightley* (Uppingham).

Lambert (Manton), *Lank* (Thistleton), *Larrett* (Glaston, N. Luffenham), *Laverock* (Seaton), *Law* (Ketton, N. Luffenham), *Lawrence* (Martinsthorpe, Edith Weston, Whissendine), *Laxton* (Burley, Caldecott, Glaston, Greetham, Morcott, Uppingham), *Leason* (Barrow), *Leaton* (Empingham), *Leaverland* (Barrow), *Lee* (Hambleton, Edith Weston), *Lester* (Bisbrooke, Glaston, Wing), *Lewin* (Braunston, Oakham), *Lewis* (Oakham), *Limbrick* (Stoke Dry), *Lincoln* (Ryhall), *Lindsey* (Caldecott), *Lock* (Cottesmore, Greetham), *Lockwood* (Martinsthorpe), *Lott* (Wing), *Louth* (Lt. Casterton, Empingham, Tinwell, Uppingham), *Love* (Empingham, Hambleton, Lyndon), *Lovell* (Empingham), *Lucas* (Normanton), *Luff* (Bisbrooke, Clipsham, Glaston, N. Luffenham, Lyddington, Morcott).

Mackley (Ridlington), *Mackworth* (Empingham), *MacTurk* (Belton), *Maddison* (Barrow), *Mallory* (N. Luffenham), *Manifold* (Edith Weston), *Mann* (Lyndon), *Marble* (Uppingham), *Margetts* (Ryhall), *Marks* (Langham), *Marley* (Teigh), *Marriott* (Hambleton, Mkt. Overton, Thistleton), *Marshall* (Caldecott, Langham), *Marsham* (Langham), *Martin* (Uppingham), *Massey* (Glaston), *Mason* (Burley, Whissendine), *Masson* (Exton), *Matthews* (Clipsham, Hambleton, N.

Luffenham, Whissendine), *Maud* (Tixover), *Maxey* (Stretton), *May* (Ashwell), *Meadows* (Egleton), *Meakin* (Burley), *Medwell* (Preston), *Merrill* (Braunston, Brooke), *Merriman* (Brooke, Exton), *Merry* (Stretton), *Messenger* (Morcott), *Metcalf(e)* (Whissendine), *Mickley* (Langham), *Middleton* (Barleythorpe, Morcott), *Millington* (Tickencote), *Mills* (Stretton), *Milton* (Oakham), *Mitchell* (Hambleton), *Mitcheson* (Thistleton), *Mole* (Uppingham, Wing), *Molson* (Ashwell), *Money* (Cottesmore, Greetham, Oakham, Stretton, Thistleton), *Monk* (Ashwell, Beaumont Chase, Wardley), *Morris* (N. Luffenham, Teigh), *Mossender* (Wardley), *Mould* (Morcott), *Mowbray* (Tickencote), *Moyse* (Exton), *Munday* (Barleythorpe), *Munton* (N. Luffenham).

Napp (Ridlington), *Naylor* (Stretton, Edith Weston), *Neal* (Martinsthorpe), *Neanton* (Empingham), *Needham* (Belton, Braunston, Hambleton, Oakham), *Nelson* (Langham), *Newell* (Bisbrooke), *Newman* (Normanton), *Newton* (Belton), *Nix* (S. Luffenham, Thistleton, Whitwell), *Nixon* (Lyndon), *Noble* (Edith Weston), *Noel* (Cottesmore, Exton), *Noon* (S. Luffenham, Wardley), *Normanton* (Morcott), *Northern* (Egleton, N. Luffenham), *Norton* (Braunston), *Nunn* (Exton), *Nutt* (S. Luffenham).

Oakham (Burley, Hambleton), *Ogden* (Belton), *Oldham* (N. Luffenham), *Oliver* (Glaston, Oakham, Stoke Dry), *Organ* (Burley), *Orme* (Lyndon), *Ormond* (Thistleton), *Orson* (Whissendine), *Osborn(e)* (Egleton, Ketton, Whissendine), *Overton* (S. Luffenham, Morcott), *Owen* (Burley).

Pacey (Braunston), *Page* (Caldecott, Ridlington, Edith Weston), *Payne* (Barrowden, Lyddington), *Palmer* (Brooke, Caldecott, Lt. Casterton, Hambleton, Leighfield, Lyndon, Teigh, Uppingham), *Parker* (Cottesmore, Glaston, Greetham, Hambleton, Preston, Thistleton, Wing), *Parsons* (Belton, Empingham), *Partridge* (Barleythorpe), *Pateman* (Ridlington), *Paul* (Glaston, Stoke Dry, Stretton), *Pawlett* (Hambleton), *Peach* (Bisbrooke, Gt. Casterton, Lyddington, Lyndon, Whissendine), *Peak* (Preston), *Peartree* (Morcott), *Peat* (Gt. Casterton), *Peck* (Ayston, Bisbrooke, Tixover), *Pedlar* (Morcott), *Pegg* (Lyndon), *Pender* (Pilton), *Pepin* (Burley), *Pepper* (Barrowden, Caldecott, Uppingham), *Percival* (Empingham, Hambleton), *Perkins* (Ayston), *Perott* (Whissendine), *Peter(s)*

(Ayston), *Pettifer* (Thistleton), *Pheasant* (Greetham, N. Luffenham), *Phillips* (Clipsham), *Philpott* (Ashwell, Lt. Casterton, Gunthorpe), *Pick* (Essendine, Ridlington, Teigh), *Pickard* (Whissendine), *Pickering* (Morcott), *Pike* (Lt. Casterton), *Pilkington* (Cottesmore, Langham), *Pilley* (Belton), *Pinder* (Oakham), *Piper* (Whissendine), *Pitt*(*s*) (Caldecott, N. Luffenham), *Plowright* (Hambleton), *Pole* (Uppingham), *Pool* (Belton), *Pope* (Barrowden, Empingham, Lyddington, Morcott), *Porter* (Braunston), *Postan* (Hambleton), *Pottle* (Oakham), *Poulter* (Oakham), *Presgrave* (Ashwell, Bisbrooke), *Preston* (Manton, Edith Weston), *Pretty* (Ayston, Glaston), *Price* (N. Luffenham), *Pridmore* (Barrowden, Glaston, N. Luffenham, S. Luffenham, Pilton, Preston, Uppingham), *Proctor* (Langham), *Pullen* (N. Luffenham).

Queeney (Barrowden), *Queniborough* (Clipsham).

Raison (Burley), *Raiterley* (Langham), *Randall* (Seaton), *Ratcliffe* (N. Luffenham, Stretton), *Ratt* (Braunston, Morcott), *Raven* (Barleythorpe, Ridlington), *Ravenscroft* (Ridlington), *Rawson* (Braunston, Brooke), *Ray* (N. Luffenham), *Read* (Glaston, Morcott), *Reddish* (Stretton), *Redmile* (Barleythorpe, Burley, Ketton), *Redshaw* (Ashwell, Lyddington), *Reeves* (Belton, Hambleton, Preston, Uppingham, Wing), *Reid* (Uppingham), *Revell* (Greetham), *Reynold*(*s*) (Belton, Glaston, N. Luffenham), *Richards* (Ashwell), *Richardson* (Hambleton), *Richmond* (Barrowden, Ketton, Stretton, Whissendine), *Ridlington* (Langham, Edith Weston), *Riley* (Burley), *Rimmington* (Barleythorpe, Greetham, Langham, S. Luffenham, Morcott), *Rippin* (Ashwell, Egleton), *Roadley* (Braunston), *Robb* (Tinwell), *Roberts* (Ayston, Bisbrooke, Braunston, Glaston, Ryhall, Teigh, Tinwell), *Robinson* (Braunston, Brooke, Cottesmore, Manton, Ridlington), *Robley* (Barrow), *Roher* (Langham), *Rose* (Exton), *Rowell* (Ridlington), *Rowlatt* (Hambleton, Lyddington), *Rowles* (Ketton), *Royce* (Barrow, Empingham, Greetham, Hambleton, Martinsthorpe, Oakham), *Rubbins* (Stretton), *Rudd* (S. Luffenham), *Rudkin* (Ayston, Empingham, Hambleton, Langham, Morcott), *Ruff* (Beaumont Chase, Burley, Hambleton, Wardley), *Rushden* (Preston), *Russell* (Caldecott, Langham, Normanton, Ridlington).

Salter (Greetham), *Sampson* (Seaton), *Scotney* (Empingham, Gunthorpe, Stretton), *Scott* (Ayston, Empingham), *Seale*

(Lyddington), *Sealy* (Thistleton), *Sewell* (Ayston, Preston), *Sewerby* (Stretton), *Shaft* (Belton, Whissendine), *Sharlow* (Wing), *Sharman* (Greetham, Langham, Stretton), *Sharp(e)* (Barleythorpe, Egleton, Greetham, Hambleton, Leighfield, S. Luffenham, Lyndon, Pilton), *Sharrard* (Langham), *Sheild* (Glaston, Martinsthorpe, Uppingham), *Shelaker* (Lyndon), *Shelton* (Empingham, N. Luffenham, Pilton, Stoke Dry, Tixover), *Shepherd* (Greetham, N. Luffenham), *Sheriff* (Bisbrooke), *Shipman* (Ashwell), *Sidney* (Lyndon), *Sill(s)* (Belton), *Simper* (Oakham), *Simpson* (Braunston), *Sismey* (Ayston, Barrowden), *Sisson* (Clipsham, Langham, Thistleton), *Sivers* (Clipsham, Stretton), *Skillington* (Stretton), *Skirmer* (Morcott), *Skirtley* (Whitwell), *Slawson* (Barrowden), *Sleath* (Brooke, Oakham), *Sly* (Glaston), *Smith* (Belton, Lt. Casterton, Cottesmore, Gunthorpe, Langham, Manton, Morcott, Mkt. Overton, Preston, Stretton, Thistleton, Uppingham, Whitwell), *Sneath* (Thistleton), *Solomon* (Burley, Mkt. Overton), *Somerton* (Ketton), *Speed* (Tinwell), *Spells* (S. Luffenham), *Spencer* (Hambleton, S. Luffenham, Lyddington), *Sprigg* (Ayston), *Springthorpe* (N. Luffenham), *Spurr* (Seaton), *Squire(s)* (Burley), *Stac(e)y* (Oakham), *Stafford* (Glaston, Hambleton, Stoke Dry, Teigh, Whissendine), *Stagg* (Lyddington), *Stanhope* (Stretton, Whissendine), *Stanley* (Stretton), *Steel* (Langham), *Steven(s)* (Burley, Empingham, Glaston, Tickencote), *Stimson* (Essendine, Gunthorpe, Hambleton), *Stokes* (Normanton, Thistleton), *Storer* (Stretton), *Storey* (Burley, Manton), *Strickland* (Leighfield), *Stubbs* (Barrowden, Greetham, Seaton), *Sturgess* (Stretton), *Sumpter* (Lyddington), *Sutton* (Morcott), *Swann* (Langham, N. Luffenham, Morcott), *Swanson* (Hambleton), *Swift* (Morcott), *Swingler* (Belton, Clipsham), *Syms* (N. Luffenham), *Syson* (Empingham, Hambleton).

Taggle (Ryhall), *Tailby* (S. Luffenham), *Tallyard* (S. Luffenham), *Tanner* (Seaton), *Taylor* (Belton, Glaston, Hambleton, Lyndon, Manton, Stoke Dry, Stretton, Uppingham), *Teat* (Uppingham), *Templeman* (Teigh), *Terrywest* (Ayston, Bisbrooke), *Tewson* (Normanton, Edith Weston), *T(h)om(p)son* (Barrowden, Belton, Egleton, Hambleton, Pickworth, Teigh), *Thorold* (Morcott), *Thorpe* (Edith Weston), *Tibber* (Edith Weston), *Tim(p)son* (Gunthorpe), *Tilton* (N. Luffenham), *Tipping* (Barrowden), *Titley* (Morcott), *Todd* (Stretton, Uppingham), *Tom(b)lin* (Hambleton, Lyndon, Thistleton, Edith Weston, Wing), *Tompkins* (Ridlington), *Tookey* (Belton, Hambleton), *Topper* (Burley), *Torkington* (Stretton), *Torr* (Preston),

Totman (Preston), *Trew* (N. Luffenham), *Trimmer* (Thorpe by Water), *Tubb(s)* (Seaton), *Tucker* (Whitwell), *Turl* (Langham), *Turnbull* (Tickencote), *Turner* (Belton, Empingham, N. Luffenham, Mkt. Overton, Stretton), *Twigden* (Uppingham), *Tyler* (Caldecott, Exton, Hambleton, Lyddington, Lyndon, Manton), *Tyth* (Belton).

Uffington (Lyddington, Thorpe by Water).

Veasey (Edith Weston), *Vicar(s)* (Uppingham), *Vine* (Bisbrooke, Hambleton, Uppingham), *Voss* (Oakham).

Wade (Ayston, Greetham, Pickworth, Thistleton, Thorpe by Water), *Wakefield* (Glaston), *Wales* (Barleythorpe, Clipsham, Mkt. Overton), *Walker* (Greetham, Hambleton, Langham, S. Luffenham, Thistleton), *Wallbanks* (S. Luffenham, Normanton, Uppingham), *Wallis* (Essendine), *Walls* (Lyddington), *Walters* (Lyndon), *Waltham* (Mkt. Overton), *Walton* (Caldecott), *Warboys* (Gt. Casterton), *Ward* (Brooke, N. Luffenham, Lyddington, Stoke Dry, Stretton, Thorpe by Water, Uppingham), *Warren* (Bisbrooke, Empingham, Lyddington, Oakham, Thorpe by Water), *Waters* (Burley, S. Luffenham), *Watkins* (Burley, Hambleton, Preston, Stretton), *Watson* (Caldecott), *Watts* (Ayston), *Wayte* (Whissendine), *Webster* (Belton), *Weldon* (Hambleton, S. Luffenham, Wardley), *Welham* (Glaston), *Wells* (Hambleton, Stretton, Edith Weston), *Wetherley* (Morcott), *Wheatley* (Pickworth), *Whincup* (Glaston), *White* (Glaston, Morcott, Ridlington, Thistleton), *Whitehead* (Morcott, Edith Weston), *Whittle* (Ashwell), *Wigginton* (Edith Weston), *Wilcox* (Uppingham, Whissendine), *Wild* (Tickencote), *Wilkinson* (N. Luffenham, Morcott), *Williams* (Ayston, Ketton, Wing), *Williamson* (Langham), *Wills* (Stoke Dry), *Wilson* (Braunston, Manton, Oakham, Wardley), *Wilsworth* (Tixover), *Wing* (Hambleton), *Wingfield* (Burley), *Winkley* (Stretton), *Winterton* (Burley), *Witham* (S. Luffenham), *Wolney* (Brooke), *Woodcock* (Hambleton, Lyddington), *Woods* (Beaumont Chase, Burley), *Woodward* (Hambleton, Lyndon), *Woolward* (Lyddington), *Wootton* (Ketton, N. Luffenham, Tixover), *Wortley* (S. Luffenham, Tixover), *Wright* (Ashwell, Barrowden, Exton, Hambleton, Edith Weston), *Wyles* (Stretton), *Wymark* (N. Luffenham, S. Luffenham, Lyndon).

York (Uppingham).

The limited movement of medieval family groups or individuals is illustrated by the fact that at least eleven major Rutland settlements gave rise to surnames in use *within* the county itself. The dates indicate the earliest surviving recordings of such surnames:

Ashwell (1637), Belton (1678), Braunston (*Branston* 1681), Caldecott (*Calcott* 1522), Egleton (*Egyston* 1524), Exton (1522), Normanton (1524), Oakham (*Okeham* 1601), Preston (1522), Ridlington (1676), Wing (c. 1685).

To these may possibly be added: Barrow, Hoby, Overton, Thorpe.

THE NAMES OF IDENTIFIED PERSONS OR FAMILIES
WITH MINOR NAMES AND FIELD- NAMES
IN WHICH THEY OCCUR

Individuals are listed in alphabetical order, together with their places of abode and dates of recording. Sample field-names containing a person's surname in his/her parish of residence follow in brackets. Where field-names are located in parishes other than that of an individual's place of abode, as, for example, when a major landowner's properties were located in several parishes, these parishes are specified with the field-names. Occasionally in the parish lists of field-names in the body of the survey, an individual with a markedly rare and recognizable surname has been cited for the sake of comparison with the surname occurring in an otherwise unattributable field-name in a parish at some distance from the individual's place of abode. Such individuals are also listed here, together with the relevant field-names and parishes. Field-names in italic type are to be found in sections (b) of the parish lists, those in roman type in sections (a). These sections should be consulted for a full list of the field-names containing the surnames of each cited person. Minor names (except those lost) are in roman type.

Randall *Adams* 1722 of N. Luffenham (*Adam Yard and Close*); Francis *Adcock* 118 and Joseph *Adcock* 1762 of Hambleton (Top Adcock's, *Adcocks Lyndon Hill*); Edward *Allen* 1677 of Lyndon (Allen's Upper Cl); John *Allen* 118 of Hambleton (*Allens Close*); John *Allen* 1932 of Seaton (Allens Mdws); Mr *Allen* c. 1850 of Empingham (Mr Allen's Cl); John *Allett* 1863 of Oakham (*Alletts windmill*); Henry *Allin* 1822 and William *Allin* 1855 of Uppingham (Allin Row, *Allins hadland*); Thomas *Andrews* 1678 of Stretton (*Thomas Andrews Close*); William *Annes* 1524 of Belton (Annecy's Well (Exton), Annes Bank (Seaton)); Robert *Armystrong* 1522 of Oakham (*Armstrong's*); Henry *Ashwell* 1637 of Stretton (*Henry Ashwells Closes*); Edward -, Luke - and Mark *Atton* 1932 of Braunston (Bob Atton); Robert *Atton* 1932 of Brooke (Manifold Atton (Edith Weston)); Anthony *Austin* 1612 and George *Austin* 1681 of Lyndon (Austin's Cl (Lyndon), Paul's Austin (Glaston), *George Austins headland* (Edith Weston)).

Bernard *Bacon* 1678 of Stretton (*Bacons East Common Wood Close* (Stretton), Bacon Fd (Pickworth)); Elizabeth *Bagley* 1589 of N. Luffenham (Baggerly Cl); Algernon *Baines* 1932 of Glaston (Baines Mdw); Charles William *Baines* 1932 of Seaton (Baines Mdw); John Russell *Baines* 1932 of Oakham (Baines 12 Acre (Oakham), Baines' (Barleythorpe)); Jos. *Baines* 1849 of Ayston (Baines's Cl); Susan *Baines* 1710 of Pickworth (Baynes Cl); Miss *Baines* 1932 of Morcott (Baines Cl); Thomas *Bains* 1763 of Uppingham (*Thomas Bains Headland*); Ann *Banbury* 1774 of Preston (*Ann Banbury's Close*); Thomas *Banes* 1522 of Braunston, Hew *Banys* 1524 of Wing, Thomas *Banys* 1524 of Manton (Middle -, Top Baines (Egleton)); John *Banyster* 1522 of Lyddington (Bannister's Cl (Stretton)); John *Barbor* 1524 of Ryhall (*Barbers Close* (Tickencote)); Dom' *Barcar* 1510 of Lyddington (*Barkereswong* (Lyddington), Barkers Cl (Thorpe by Water)); Rev. H. *Barfoot* 1830 of Lyddington (Barfoot Cl (Mkt. Overton), Barfoots Wood (Leighfield)); Bawdwyn *Barker* 1546, Bezaliell *Barker* 1596, Christopher *Barker* 1600 and Samuel *Barker* 1630 of Luffenham (Barker's Spinney, *Mr Barkers Close* (N. Luffenham), Barkers Hey (S. Luffenham)); Thomas *Barker* 1794 of Lyndon (Baker's Cl (sic)); William *Barker* 1524 of Edith Weston (Barkers Bushes); Robert *Barkere* 1296 of Luffenham (Barker's Spinney (N. Luffenham)); George *Barnett* 1932 of Oakham (Barnett's); John *Barsby* 1794 of Lyndon (Barsby's Cl); John *Basset* 1626 of N. Luffenham, Thomas *Basset* 1522 of S. Luffenham (Bassett Acres (S. Luffenham), Bassets Close Furlong (Seaton)); Mr *Basset* 1774 of Preston (*Mr Basset's Close* (Preston), Bassetts Cl (Ridlington)); George *Bates* 1726 of Braunston (*George Bates's Backside*); John *Baynes* 1605 of Hambleton (Bain's Cl (Lyndon)); George *Beadman* 1932 of Braunston (Beadman's Pountry Fm); Thomas *Beaver* 1712 of Empingham (*Beavers House Land*); Henry *Beebie* 1619 of Belton (*Beebies Baulke*); Randulph *de Belfago*, landowner in Thorpe by Water t. Hy 4 (*le dybbyng Randulphi de Belfago*); Rev. Mr *Belgrave* 1785 of Preston (Bottom -, Middle -, Top Belgrave (Wing)); William *Belgrave* 1785 of Uppingham (The Belgrave); Edward Charles *Bell* 1932 of Exton (Bell's Hovel (Exton), Bell's Cl, *Bell's Lamp Leys* (Hambleton)); John *Bellaers* 1845 of Stretton (Bellaers Cl (Stretton), Bellair's Cl (Glaston), Bellases Hollow (Greetham), Bellairs Piece (Seaton)); Robert *Bellamy* 1522 of Whissendine (Bellamy Cl); Christopher *Belton* 1678 of Stretton (*Christopher Beltons Closes*); William *Beneson* 1522 of

Edith Weston (*Benysons Land*); Rafe *Benet* 1524 and John *Bennet*
1522 of Oakham (*Benetshouse* (Hambleton)); Widow *Berridge* 118 of
Hambleton (*Berridges Great Close*); John *Bett* 1522 of Cottesmore
and Stephen *Bett* 1522 of Greetham (*Betts Balke* (Greetham), Bett's
Barn (Barleythorpe)); Richard *Billing* 1681 of Edith Weston
(*Richard Billings Land*); Oliuer *Billyng* 1525 of Morcott, Thomas
Billyng 1522 of Stoke Dry and William *Byllyngs* 1524 of Bisbrooke
(Banbillings Pad (Lyddington and Thorpe by Water)); Lt.-Col. F.G.
Blair 1932 of Ashwell (Colonel Blair's Big Fd); William *Blake* 1522
of Glaston (*Black Hedge* (Bisbrooke)); Clement *Bland* 1846 of Lt.
Casterton (Bland's Cl); John *Blayes* 1678 and Stephen *Blaze* 1732 of
Stretton (*John Blayes Closes, Blazes Common Wood Close*); John
Blewett 1675 and Richard *Blewett* c1685 of Hambleton (*Blewits
Close*); Thomas *Blowfeld* 1524 of Mkt. Overton (*Blofeilds*
(Oakham)); Johane *Blood* 1522 and John *Bloode* 1524 of Ryhall
(Blood Cl (Barleythorpe), Blood's Cl (Langham)); John *Bloodworth*
1726 and Thomas *Bloodworth* 1748 of Hambleton (*John Bloodeths
Barn Close* (Hambleton), Mr Bloodworth's Cl (Empingham), *John
Bloodeth's Braknell* (Normanton)); Clement Blunfield 1758 of
Stretton (*Clems Closes*); John *Bolland* 1522 of S. Luffenham
(*Bollands Close* (S. Luffenham), *Bollands Meadow* (Lyndon));
Robert *Borow* 1522 of Braunston (*Barrowes* (Oakham), Barrow's
(Ridlington)); Henry *Bowell* 1524 of Seaton (*Bohill Leyes*); John
Boyeall 1524 of Ketton (Boil Nook, *Boyall Waye* (Gt. Casterton),
Boyal Leys (Empingham), *Boyalls* (*North*) *Bite Nooke* (Stretton),
Boyall Wood (Tickencote)); James *Bradley* 1932 of Belton
(Bradley's); Thomas *Bradley* 1522 of Hambleton (*Bradleyes
homeplott* (Hambleton), *Bradleys yard Land* (Manton)); Arthur M.
Bradshaw 1932 of Oakham (Bradshaw's Railway Fd); Mrs F.
Bradshaw 1932 and John Robert *Bradshaw* 1932 of Egleton
(Bradshaw's Paddock (Egleton), *Bradshaws Close* (Hambleton));
John *Brampton* 1522 of Barrowden (Bramton Piece (Brooke)); John
Branston 1795 and Thomas *Branston* 1681 of Edith Weston
(Branstons Cl, *Branstons Lamas Closes*); Abraham *Bretfield* 1633,
Richard *Bretfield* 1690 and Richard *Bretfield* 1766 of N. Luffenham
(*Bretfeilds Farm*); Widow *Bridges* 1726 of Hambleton (*Bridges
Meadow* (Hambleton), *Widow Bridges Meadow* (Normanton));
William *Bright* 1642 of Glaston (*Brights Close*); William *Brome* 1522
of Wardley (*Brooms Bushes* (Manton), *Brooms Brake Close* (Pilton),
Brooms Folly (Edith Weston)); John *Brown* 1522 of Lyddington

(*Browns Lodge*); Elizabeth *Brown* 1713 and Samuel *Browne* 1676 of Stretton (*Browns Close, Widdow Brownes Meadow*); Henry *Browne* 1592 and Thomas *Browne* 1522 of Whissendine (Browne's Lodge); Bernard *de Brus*, landowner in Exton 1280 (*Bruseslonde* (Cottesmore)); Charles - and William *Bryan* 1877 of Ridlington (Bryan's (Ridlington), Bryan's Cl (Glaston)); William *Bryghtmer* 1524 of Morcott (*Brightmors Farm* (Morcott), *Brightmore home* (Wing)); Widow *Buckle* 1770 of Glaston (*Buckles Close*); Mr *Buckworth* c1850 of Empingham (Beckworth Spinney, *Mr Buckworth's Close*); Edmund *Bull* 1522 of Lyddington (*Bulls Nook*); John *Bull* 1785, Widow *Bull* 118 and William *Bull* 118 of Hambleton (Bull Bridge, *Bulls Close* (Hambleton), Bulls Cl (Lyndon)); Raff *Bull* 1522 of Morcott (Bull's Cl, *Bull Holme*); Mr *Bunning* c1850 of Empingham (Mr Bunning's Cl); William *Burges* 1522 of Hambleton (*Burgess's Close* (Hambleton), Burgess', *Burgess Lodge* (Ridlington)); John *Burneby* 1522 and William *Burnby* 1522 of Manton (*Burnebys Hedge Furlong*); Peter *Butler* c1660 of Uppingham (Butler's Cottage).

John *Calcott* 1522 of Ketton (Calcott's Nook (Tixover)); John *Cant* 1715 of N. Luffenham (*Cants Close* (N. Luffenham), *John Cants Headland* (Morcott)); Robert *Cant* 1877 of Preston (Cant's (Preston), Cant's Cl (Ayston), Cants Cl (Wardley)); Ann *Carter* 1790 of Egleton (*Carter's Close*); John *Caterns* 1522 of Oakham, Raff *Caterns* 1522 of Empingham, Clement *Catterens* 1617 of N. Luffenham (*Katterns leyes* (Uppingham), *Katherines Closes* (Langham)); Charles *Cave* 1870, Robert *Cave* 1566, William *Cave* 1540 of Barrowden (Cave's Cl (Caldecott), Cave's Mill Cl (Stoke Dry)); Robert *Chamberlen* 1524 of Greetham, Robert *Chamberlyn* 1522 of Cottesmore (*Chamberlains Close* (Burley), *Chamberleyns Croft* (Oakham)); Thomas *Charity* 1787 of Greetham (*Charitys Home Close*); Francis *Cheselden* 1774 and Richard *Chysylden* 1524 of Manton (*Cheseldens Pen*); John *Cheselden* 1747, Kenelm *Cheselden* 1596 and Robert *Chesilden* 1392 of Braunston (Cheseldyne Ho., *Mr Chiseldines Sike* (Braunston), *Chiseldine banke* (Beaumont Chase), *Mr Cheseldines closes* (Leighfield)); Anthony *Cheseldine* 1653 of Hambleton (*Chisledine's Close* (Hambleton), *Cheselden's Gate* (Edith Weston)); William *Christian* 1665 of Pickworth (Christian's Lodge (Pickworth), Mr Christian's Cl (Empingham)); Goody *Christopher* 1716 of Hambleton (*Christophers Close*); John *Clark*

1761 of Bisbrooke (Clarke's Gorse (Bisbrooke), John Clark's Cl (Glaston)); John *Clarke* 1798 of Barrowden (Clarke's Slade); Samuel *Clarke* 1877 of Ridlington (Clark's Cl); Widow *Clarke* 1678 of Stretton (Clarke's Cl, *Mills's Clerk Close*); William *Clarke* 118 of Burley (*Clarkes Paddock* (Burley), Clarks Cl (Ashwell), *Clarks headland Furlong* (Cottesmore)); John -, Thomas - and William *Clement* 1522 of Belton (Clement's Cl (Ayston), Clement's Nook (Gunthorpe), *Clements House* (Manton), *Clements Lands* (Uppingham)); Thomas *Cole* 1266 (Cole's Lodge (Leighfield), Cole's Well (Oakham), Cole's Cl (Ridlington)); Widow *Cole* c1685 of Burley (*Coles Cottage* (Burley), Cole's Mdw (Langham)); Alicia *Colle* and Willielmus *Colle* 1356 of Luffenham, Robert *Colle* 1522 of N. Luffenham (Coles Wood, *Colebush* (N. Luffenham)); William *Collington* 1726 of Hambleton (*Wm. Collingtons Cheesecake Close* (Hambleton), *William Collingtons Home Close* (Normanton)); Thomas *Collins* 1763 of Uppingham (*Collin's Folly*); Thomas *Colson* 1525 of Ayston (*Colsons Close* (N. Luffenham)); John *Cook* 1763 of Uppingham (*John Cooks Close*); Joseph *Cook* 1681 and Thomas *Cook* 1746 of Edith Weston (*Joseph Cookes hadland, Miss Cooks Close*); Roger *Cooke* 1665 of Barrowden (*Roger Cookes hadland* (Barrowden), Cookes Cl (Seaton)); Richard *Cossyn* 1522 of Lt. Casterton (Couzens Heath (Essendine)); Thomas *Crispe* 1522 of Burley (*Crispe's Close* (Seaton)); John -, Robert - and William *Cristian* 1522 of Barrow (Christian's Cl (Barrow), Christian Cl (Mkt. Overton)); Edward -, Fanny - and Robert *Crowden* 1932 of Seaton (Crowden's Mdws (Seaton), Crowden's Fd (Barrowden), Crowden's Fd (Belton), Crowden Little Fd (Bisbrooke)); Robert *Cumbrey* 1739 of Greetham (*Robert Cumbreys Hadelond* (Greetham), *Cumbry and Boyalls Closes* (Stretton)); William *Curtes* 1522 of Ridlington (Curtis Cl (Stoke Dry)).

William *Dalby* 1399 of Exton (Dalby Cl (Ashwell), *Dalbies Ground* (Burley), *Dalbies Close* (Hambleton), Dolby Great Cl (Langham)); Miss *Daniels* 1932 of Oakham (Daniel's); Johan *Daue* 1522 and Elizabeth *Dawes* 1522 of Langham (*Daweleys* (Uppingham), *Dawes's Close* (Greetham)); Robert *Dicman* 1522, (- *Dykman* 1524) of Braunston (Dickman's); Edward *Digby* and John *Digby* 1522 of Pilton (*Digbys Clay Close*); James *Digby* 1659 of N. Luffenham (Digbys Cl, *Digbies Leyes*); Sir John *Digby* 1522, landowner in Bisbrooke, Morcott and Seaton (*the Laumplands of Mr Digby*

(Bisbrooke), *Digby Headland* (Glaston)); Simon *Digby* 1625 of Morcott (*Simon Digby Farm*); John *Doure* 1524 of Cottesmore (*Doris Close* (Barleythorpe), *Dures furlonge* (Caldecott)); Thomas *Dowghty* 1524 of S. Luffenham (*Douty Close*); Thomas *Drake* 1524 of Belton (*Drakesholme* (Morcott)); William *Dunmore* 1524 of Barrowden (West Dunmore (Lyndon)); Roland *Durant* 1588 of Barrowden (Durant Farmhouse (Barrowden), *Durants Thing* (S. Luffenham), *Durrants close* (Morcott)); John *Dyng* and Robert *Dyng* 1522 of Teigh (Ding Hades (Mkt. Overton)).

Geoffrey *Eayr* and William *Eayr* 1932 of Burley, Edwin *Eyre* 1877 of Preston (Hayr's First (Caldecott), Eayr's Far Fd (Gunthorpe), Ayre's Hill Cl (Hambleton), Eayr's Far Fd (Manton), Eayr's Big Cl (Martinsthorpe)); William *Edgson* 1932 and Robert *Egyston* 1524 of Langham (Edgson's 21½ Acre); Stephen *Estwick* 1678 of Stretton (*Stephen Estwicks Closes*); Thomas *Exton* 1522 of Empingham (*Extons Old Farm* (Empingham), *Extons Headland* (N. Luffenham)).

John *Fairchild* 1665 of Pickworth (Fairchild's Fm); Everard *Falkener* 1623 of Barrowden (Falkner's Cl); Francis *Falkener* 1715 of N. Luffenham (*Falkeners House*); Lyon *Falkener* 1736 of Uppingham (*Fawknrs Litle Close*); John *Fancourt* 1765 of N. Luffenham (Fancourts Cl (S. Luffenham)); Lionel *Fancourt* 1698, John -, Matthew - and William *Fancourt* 1846 of Empingham (Fancourt's Cl (Empingham), *Fancutt's Cottage* (Burley)); Thomas *Fawkener* 1524 and Wylliam *Fawkner* 1524 of Morcott (*Fawkners Farm*); John *Fenton* 1522 of Lyddington (Fenton Gap (Morcott)); James *Fisher* 1808 of Uppingham (Fisher's Yard); John *Flint* 1846 of Cottesmore (Flint's Fds (Cottesmore), Flint's Covert (Burley), *Flints* (Oakham)); William *Flore* 1373 of Oakham (Flore's Ho.); John *Flower* 1585 and John *Flowers* 1632 of Hambleton (*Flower Lands*); Roger *Flower* 1522 of Oakham (Flowers Cl (Whissendine)); George *Fludyer* 1846 of Ayston (*Fludyer's Arms* (Uppingham)); Richard *Fountain* 1932 and William *Fountain* 1846 of Cottesmore (Fountain's Barn (Cottesmore), Fountain's Barn (Exton), Fountains Mdw (Ridlington)); Richard *Fowler* 1543, Roger *Fowler* 1611 and William *Fowler* 1653 of Hambleton (Bottom Fowler's (Hambleton), Fowler's Middle Fd (Manton), *Fowlers Close* (Normanton)); Willingham *Fowler* 1877 and Willoughby *Fowler* 1846 of Exton (Fowler's Park);

Richard *Fox* 1525 of Uppingham (Fox's Cl (Glaston)); John *Frank* 1522 of Morcott (Franks Cl.(Morcott), Franks Cl (Ridlington)); Bryan *Franklin* 1640 of Glaston (*Bryan Franklines backside*); Harry *Freeman* 1932 of Braunston (Harry Freeman's); John *Freeman* 1736 of Uppingham (*John Freemans otherwise Yorkes Close*); Robert *Freeman* 1522 of Edith Weston (*Freeman Holt* (Edith Weston), *John Bloodeths Freemans Close* (Normanton)); John *Frier* 1726, Francis *Fryer* 118 and John *Fryer* 118 of Hambleton (*John Friers Brake Close, Fryer's Close* (Hambleton), *John Friers Land Close* (Normanton)); Richard *Fynnyngley* 1524 of Whitwell (*Finningley*).

Richard *Galway* 1459 of Empingham (*Galways Close*); Henry *Gambell* 1522 of Bisbrooke (Gambles (Glaston)); John *Ganne* 1524 of Ryhall (*Ganns Close* (Mkt. Overton), Gan's Cl (Stretton)); Richard *Gill* 1844 of Barrowden (Gills Island); George *Gilson* 1612 of Morcott (Gilson's Hospital, *Gilsons Square Close*); William *Gilson* 1787 of Greetham (*Gilsons Home Close*); William *Glover* 1522 of Whissendine (Glover's Fd); William *Godfrey* 1619 of Belton (*Godfreyes headland* (Belton), Godfreys Bush (Seaton)); John *Goodman* 1677 of Lyndon, Robert *Goodman* and Thomas *Goodman* 1522 of N. Luffenham (Goodman's Nether Cl (Lyndon)); Henry *Grant* and John *Grant* 1678 of Stretton (Grants Platt); Gerald *Gray* 1932 of Glaston (Gray's Seventeen Acres (Glaston), Gray's Ten Acre (Bisbrooke)); Thomas *Greneham* 1522 of Ketton (Greneham's Manor); John *Gunby* 1522 of Gt. Casterton and Robert *Gunby* 1522 of Oakham (Gunby's (Barleythorpe)); Peter *Gybbon* 1522 of S. Luffenham (Gibbon's Hollow (N. Luffenham)).

Mr *Halford* 1655 of Lyndon (*Hawfords yardland*); John *Halliday* 1776 of Stretton (Hallidays Home (Stretton), Halliday (Greetham), Halliday's Cl (Thistleton)); Andrew *Hand* c1794 of Lyndon (Hand's Cl); Philip *Harris* 1932 of Langham (Harris's Top); William *Hart* 1681 of Edith Weston (Harts Cl); Thomas *Haselwood* 1559 of Leighfield Forest and Thomas *Hayslewood* 1619 of Belton (*Haslewoods Lands* (Belton)); William *Haukinge* 1522 of Belton (*Hawkeinge hedges* (Edith Weston)); Sam. *Hauley* 1729 of Burley (*Haleys Close*); William *Hayle* 1522 of Belton (Hale's Gorse (Hambleton)); Peter *Healy* 118 of Hambleton (Healy's Mdw, *Healeys Lodge*); Sir Gilbert *Heathcote* 1781, landowner in N. Luffenham (*Sir Gilbert Heathcotes Nine Acre Piece* (N. Luffenham));

John *Herbert* 1783 of Bisbrooke (*John Herberts Close*); Richard *Heryng* 1522 of Ashwell and Thomas *Heryng* 1522 of Cottesmore (Herrings Mdw (Teigh)); Amos -, Robert - and William *Hibbitt* 1846, Arthur -, Cecil - and Frederick *Hibbitt* 1932 of Exton (Hibbits Lodge (Empingham), Hibbitt's Thirty-six Acre (Horn)); John *Hill* 1932 of Braunston (Hill's Fd); William *Hillam* c1660 of Uppingham (Hillam's Cottage); Peter *Hilton* 1632 of Hambleton (*Peter Hiltons Close*); Philip *Hinman* 1678, Philip *Hinman* 1758 and Wright *Hinman* 1678 of Stretton (*Philip Hinmans Close* (Stretton), Inmans Cl (Ashwell), Hinmans (Barrow)); Toby *Hippesley* 1716, Tobias *Hippisley* 118 and Toby *Hippisly* 1675 of Hambleton (*Hippisleys Lampleys* (Hambleton), *Hippisley's Close* (Burley)); John *Hoby* 1522 of Brooke (Hoby Cross (Wardley)); William *Horneby* 1524 of Empingham, Capt. *Hornsby* 1943 of Ashwell (Capt. Hornsby Cl (Ashwell), Hornsby's Cl (Ayston), Hornby Cl (Langham)); Herbert *Hubbard* 1932, Richard *Hubbard* 1524, John *Hubberd* 1522, Thomas *Hubberd* 1522 and Henry *Hubbert* 1524 of Langham (Big Hubbard's); Mr *Hungate* 1634 of Uppingham (*Mr Hungates Close*); Anthony *Hunt* 1665 of Ketton (Hunt's Lodge (Ketton), Hunt's Cottage (Empingham)); Thomas *Hunt* 1522 of N. Luffenham (*Hunts Ash Close, Mr `Hunts Open Close* (N. Luffenham), *Hunts Meere* (Pilton)).

Edward *Inkley* 1678 of Stretton (Winkleys Cl); George *Ireland* 118 and Robert *Ireland* 1758 of Hambleton (*Irelands Close* (Hambleton), *Ireland Hill* (Egleton)); William *Ireland* 1612 of Lyndon (*Irelandes house*); Alice *Isaac* 1932 of Langham, William *Isak* 1524 of Braunston (Isaac's Barton (Langham)); Robert *Islepp* 1522 of Stoke Dry (Big Islip's (Lyddington), Islip's Cl (Morcott)); John *Islip* 1846 of Empingham (Mr Islip's Cl); Thomas *Islip* 1724 and Thomas *Islipp* 1681 of Edith Weston (*Thomas Islipp the smith's hadland*); Walter *Ivett* 1932 of Ryhall (Ivett's Ten Acre).

Henry *Jarves* 1524 of Oakham (*Jarvis's Close* (Egleton), *Jarvice Close* (Hambleton)); John *Jarvis* 1710 of Pickworth (Jarvis' Cl); William *Jerman* 1522 of N. Luffenham (Jarminy (N. Luffenham), *Jermyns Farm* (Edith Weston)); George *Johnson* 1522 of Glaston (*Johnsons Close*); Hew *Jorden* 1524 and John *Jorden* 1524 of Barleythorpe (Jordans Cl (Langham)).

Mr D. *Keen* c1850 of Empingham (Mr Keen's Home Cl); John *Kyrke* 1522 and Thomas *Kyrke* 1522 of Ayston (*Kirkcroft Flatt* (Lyddington)); John *Kyrke* 1522 of Morcott (*Kirke Close* (Glaston), *Kirks* (Lyndon)); John *Kytte* 1522 of Lyddington (Kit's Cl (Ridlington)).

Robert *Lamperte* 1525 of Morcott (*Lambert Slade* (Manton)); Daniel *Larrett* 1640, George *Larrett* 1654, John *Larrett* 1654 and Widow *Larrett* 1676 of Glaston (*Daniell Larrettes Close* (Glaston), *Larretts house* (N. Luffenham)); John *Laurence* 1522 of Langham, Richard *Laurens* 1524 of Whissendine (*Lawrence Moor* (Whissendine)); William *Lawrence* 1810 of Edith Weston (Lawrence Cl); Robert *Laxston* 1522 of Greetham (*Laxton Balke* (Greetham), Laxton's Cl (Burley)); Stephen *Laxton* 1815 of Morcott (Stephen Laxtons Piece (Morcott), Laxton's Barn (Glaston)); William *Leaverland* 1846 of Barrow (Leaverlands); Edward *Lee* 1726 of Hambleton (*Edward Lees Furr Close*); George *Lewin* 1910 of Oakham (Lewin's Cl); Thomas *Leyster* 1522 of Belton (Lester's Barnfield (Bisbrooke), Lester's Barn Fd (Glaston), Lester's Barn Cl (Wing)); Richard *Lincoln* 1525 of Uppingham (Lincolns Cl, *Lincoln Hill* (Ryhall)); E. *Lindsey* 1846 of Barrowden (*lyndeseyfurlong* (Caldecott)); Robert *Loke* 1522 of Exton (Lock's Cl (Cottesmore), Lock's Cl (Greetham)); Widow *Louthe* 1634 of Uppingham (*Mr Lowith's Cottage* (Uppingham), *Louths Farm* (Empingham), *Louth's Leys* (Lt. Casterton)); Christopher *Love* 1785 and Thomas *Love* 118 of Hambleton (*Loves Home Close* (Hambleton), Love's Nether Cl (Lyndon)); Thomas *Love* c1850 of Empingham (Love's Lane, *Loves Nooke*); Thomas *Lucas* 1791 of Empingham (Lucas's House (Normanton)); Edward *Luffe* 1729 and George *Luffe* 1585 of N. Luffenham (*Luffs Crabtree* (N. Luffenham), *Luff's Yard Close* (Manton)); John *Luffe* 1640 of Glaston (*John Luffes close* (Glaston), *Luffs Close* (Bisbrooke)); John *Luffe* 1524 of Empingham (Luffs Cl (Clipsham)); Wylliam *Luffe* 1525 of Caldecott (*Luffs hedge* (Lyddington)).

George *Mackworthe* 1521 of Empingham (*Makworth Close*); Mr *Mallorie* e17 of N. Luffenham (Mallories Cl); William *Man* 1524 of Cottesmore (*Mans leyes* (Lyndon)); John *Mariet* 1522 of Lyddington (Marriotts (Hambleton), Marriotts (Mkt. Overton), Marriott's Cl (Thistleton)); Thomas *Massey* 1676 of Glaston (*Thomas Masseyes ground*); Thomas *Masson* 1522 of Exton (Messons Fd); William *Maxy* 1678 of Stretton (*William Maxyes Close*); William *May* 1524 and John *Maye* 1522 of Langham, John *Maye* 1522 of Teigh (Maycroft (Ashwell)); Edward *Meadows* 1790 of Egleton (*Meadow's Nine Acres*); William *Meryell* 1524 of Braunston (Merrill's (Braunston), Merrall's Fd (Brooke)); John *Messenger* 1524 and Johane *Messynger* 1522 of Morcott (*Messengers Farm*); John *Middleton* 1522 of Langham (*Middletons Lands* (Barleythorpe)); Bryan *Millington* 1851 and Edwin *Millington* 1855 of Tickencote (Millington); Nicholas *Mills* 1678 of Stretton (*Mills's Triangle Close*); William *Mitchell* 1675 of Hambleton (*Mitchell's Piece*); Ambrose *Mole* 1763 of Uppingham (*Ambrose Moles Close* (Uppingham), Bottom Moles (Wing)); Thomas *Monee* 1522 of Teigh, William *Monee* 1522 of Whitwell, Richard *Money* 1678, Richard *Money* 1732, Thomas *Money* 1758 and Widow *Money* 1723 of Stretton (Money's Cl, *Widow Moneys Meadow* (Stretton), *Money Furlong* (Cottesmore), *Moneis Peice* (Thistleton)); Rob. *Mosindue* 1635 of Wardley (Mossender's Mdw); William *Moyse* 1522 of Exton (*Moyses Close* (Oakham)); Robert *de Mucegros* 1276, landholder in Cottesmore (*Musgroseslonde*); Thomas *Munton* 1754 of N. Luffenham (*Muntons Close*).

Thomas *Naylor* c1700 of Stretton (*Thomas Naylors Close*); Joseph *Needham* 118 of Hambleton (*Needham's Great Close*); Rowland *Needham* 1932 of Oakham (Middle Needham (Oakham), Big Needham's (Braunston)); Joseph *Newman* 1877 of Normanton (Newman's Fd); Daniel *Nickes* 1640 of S. Luffenham (*Nixes Thing*); Mr *Nixe* 1717 of Thistleton (*Mr Nixes Home Peice* (Thistleton), *Nixe's Close* (Whitwell)); Mrs *Noel* 1932 of Cottesmore (Mrs Noel's Fd (Cottesmore), Noels Cl (Exton)); Joseph *None* 1522 of Uppingham, Nicholas *Noone* c1635 and Richard Noone c1635 of Wardley (Newn's Home (Wardley), *Noones Closes* (S. Luffenham)); Thomas *Normanton* 1524 and William *Normanton* 1524 of Ketton (*Normantons farm* (Morcott)); Arthur *Norton* 1932 of Braunston (Norton's); James *Nutt* and Thomas *Nutt* 1845 of S. Luffenham (Nutts Cl).

John *Ogden* 1619 of Belton (*Ogdens Half Yard Land*); Henrie *Okeham* 1601 of Burley (*Henrie Okehams Closse* (Burley), *Oakhams Yard* (Hambleton)); John *Oldham* 1594 of N. Luffenham (*Oldames*

Headland); Richard *Olever* 1525 of Ayston, Robert *Oliver* 1626 and Thomas *Olyuer* 1522 of Belton (Oliver's Cl (Stoke Dry), *Olivers headland* (Glaston)); Joseph *Ormand* 1871 of Whissendine (Ormond's (Thistleton)); John *Orme* 1612 and Mistress *Orme* 1655 of Lyndon (*Ormes House*); William *Overton* 1625 and William *de Overtoun* c1400 of Morcott (*Overtons Close* (Morcott), *Overtons Close* (S. Luffenham)).

John *Page* 1522 of Edith Weston (Pages Holme (Edith Weston), *Page Marsh* (Caldecott), Page's Five Acre (Ridlington)); Richard *Pakeman* 1701 of Ridlington, Richard *Pakeman* 1688 and Richard *Pateman* 1637 of Uppingham (Pateman's Lodge (Ridlington)); Henry *Palmer* 1524 of Barrow, Nicolis *Palmer* 1522 of Langham (*Palmers Close* (Hambleton), Palmers Moor (Teigh)); William *Palmer* 1794 of Lyndon (*Palmers*); Mr *Palmer* 1638 of Uppingham (*Mr Palmers Close*); John *Parker* 1846 of Preston (Parker's); Widow *Parker* 1726 of Hambleton (*Widow Parkers Wood Close*); William *Parker* 1706 of Greetham (*William Parkers Tyth Close*); John *Partridge* 1814 of Whissendine (*partridge Furlong* (Barleythorpe)); John *Pawlett* 118 of Hambleton (Pawlett's Cl); Joseph *Peach* 1846 of Gt. Casterton (Peaches Cl (Gt. Casterton), Peach's Willow (Bisbrooke), Peaches Quick (Lyddington)); Samuel *Peat* and William *Peat* 1877 of Gt. Casterton (Peats Cl); Richard *Pek* 1524 of Ridlington, John *Peyke* 1525 of Ayston (*Pecks Oake close* (Ayston)); Issabell *Pekryng* 1522 of Morcott (*Pickerings Close*); John *Peper* and William *Peper* 1522 of Wing, Raff *Peper* 1522 of Brooke, Richard *Pepper* 1720 of Uppingham (Pepper's Acre (Barrowden), Bottom Pepper (Caldecott), *Peppers Mill* (Uppingham)); Francis *Percival* 1712 of Empingham (Percival's Cl); Vincent *Percival* 1716 of Hambleton (*Percivalls Close*); Agnes *Pertre* 1522 of Morcott (*Pertrees Farm*); William *Phellypot* 1522 of Langham (Philpots Cl (Ashwell), Philpott's (Gunthorpe)); Anna *Phesant* 1572 and Dorcas *Phesant* 1576 of N. Luffenham (*Pheasants Close*); Matthew *Pitts* and Richard *Pitts* 1710, Widow *Pitts* 1732 of N. Luffenham (*Pits's Barne*); Widow *Plowright* 118 of Hambleton (*Plowrights Close*); William *Pope* 1522 of Tickencote (Pope's Spring (Empingham)); John *Presgrave* 1597 of Bisbrooke (*the Shepecote of John Presgrave*); Robert *Preston* 1522 of Manton (*Prestons Yard Land*); Augustine -, Edward · - and John *Pridmore* 1845 of S. Luffenham, John *Pridmore* 1732 of N. Luffenham (Pridmore's Mdws (Barrowden), Pridmores Bean Fd

(Glaston), *Pridmores Close* (N. Luffenham), John Pridmores Cl (S. Luffenham)); Harry *Pridmore* 1932 of Pilton (Mrs Pridmore's Scultrups Clays); Willm. *Pritty* 1633 of Glaston (Pretty's Cl (Glaston), Prettys (Ayston)); Richard *Procter* 1524 of Oakham (Proctor's Cl (Langham)); John -, Richard - and William *Pylkyngton* 1522 of Barleythorpe (Pilkington's (Cottesmore)).

John *Queneborow* 1522 of Stretton, Thomas *Queneborow* and William *Queneborow* 1522 of Teigh (Quanbury Cl (Clipsham)).

Robt. *Rason* 1729 of Burley (*Rason Close*); Abraham *Ratt* 1796 of Morcott (*Ratts Cottage*); George *Ratt* 1943 of Braunston (Ratts Lane); Fred *Rawson* 1932 of Braunston (Rawson (Braunston), Rawson's Dale (Brooke)); Mr *Ray* 1729 of N. Luffenham (*Mr Rays Fur Peice*); Ralph *Read* 1648 of Glaston (*Reads close* (Glaston), *Reads Croft* (Morcott)); Thomas *Reddish* 1678 of Stretton (*Redishes Common Wood Close*); Mr R. *Redmile* 1919 of Ketton (Redmiles Plain); Edmund *Reeves* 1619 of Belton (*Edmund Reeves Landes*); Richard *Reynold* 1522 of Barrowden (*Reynaldiscroft* (Glaston), *Reynolds Cottage* (N. Luffenham)); Widow *Richardson* 1675 of Hambleton (*widdow Richardsons close*); Robert *Richmond* 1678 of Stretton (*Richmonds Bush Close* (Stretton), *Richmond Close* (Ketton), Richmond Leys (Whissendine)); John *Ridlington* 1676 of Edith Weston (*John Ridlingtons Hedge*); Alice *Rippin* 1790 of Egleton (*Rippin's Close*); John *Rippin* 1932 of Ashwell (Rippins Bottom Fd); Mrs *Roberts* 1781 of Bisbrooke (*the Close...of Mrs Roberts called Fourteen Acres*); John C. *Robinson* 1877 of Ridlington (Robinson's Barn Cl); Cecil *Rose* 1932 of Exton (Rose's Fd); John *Roulat* and William *Roulat* 1726 of Hambleton (*John Roulats Bottom Close, William Roulats Wood Close Meadow);* George Royce 1788 of Oakham, Richard *Royse* 1524 of Greetham, John *Rasse* 1522 of Thistleton, Richard *Raysse* 1524 of Egleton (Hardy's Rayces (Barrow), Mrs Thomas Royce's Cl (Empingham), *Royse fur'* (Greetham), *Royce Barn Close* (Hambleton), Royce's Cl (Martinsthorpe), Royce (Oakham)); John *Rubbins* 1678 of Stretton (*Rubbins Common Wood Close*); Thomas *Rudkin* 1733 of Morcott (Rudkins Piece, *Rudkins land*); William *Rudkin* 1932 of ·Langham (Rudkins Cl); Barbara *Ruffe* c1685 of Burley (*Ruffs Close* (Burley), *Ruffmaplehill* (Beaumont Chase), *Ruffs Closes* (Hambleton)); Robert *Russell* 1522 and Thomas *Russell* 1525 of Caldecott (*Russel's Quick*

(Caldecott), Russell's Hern Cl (Ridlington).

Richard *Sampson* 1522 of Lyddington (*Sampsons Holme* (Seaton)); John *Scotney* 1678 of Stretton (Scotneys Fd, *Scotneys Common Wood Close* (Stretton), *Scotneys Lands* (Empingham), *Scotneys Gunthorpe* (Gunthorpe)); Henry *Scot* 1522 and Thomas *Scott* 1522 of Ryhall, Robert *Scott* 1524 of Hambleton (Scott's Garden, *Scotts Farm* (Empingham)); Robert *Sesmey* 1524 of Seaton, John *Sismay* 1522 of Lyddington (Sismey's (Ayston), Sismey's Fd (Barrowden)); William *Sewell* 1758 of Ayston (Sewell's Barn (Ayston), *Sewells Yard Land* (Preston)); Bartilmew *Sharpe* 1522 and Robert *Sharpe* 1522 of Barrowden (*Sharpe Lane* (S. Luffenham)); Robert *Sharpe* 1677 of Lyndon (Sharps Upper Cl, *Sharps close* (Lyndon), Sharpe's Fd (Hambleton), *Sharpes willes* (Pilton)); Thomas *Sharpe* 1522 and Harry *Sharp* 1932 of Egleton (Sharp's 9 Acres (Egleton), Sharp's Hill Fd (Barleythorpe), Sharpes Cl, Sharpes Rode (Leighfield)); Edward *Sheild* and William *Sheild* 1713, Robert *Sheild* 1846 of Preston (*Mr Edward Sheilds Close* (Glaston), Sheilds (Martinsthorpe), Sheild's Yard (Uppingham)); Mr R. *Shelaker* 1794 of Lyndon (*Shelakers Close*); Adam *Shelton* 1522 of Lyddington (Sheltons Fd (Stoke Dry)); Matthew *Shelton* and Robert *Shelton* 1783 of N. Luffenham (Shelton's Barn (N. Luffenham), Shelton's (Pilton)); Thomas *Shereman* 1665 of Greetham (Sharman's Lodge); Thomas *Sherman* 1678 of Stretton (*Shermans Nooke*); Richard *Sidney* 1794 of Lyndon (Sidneys Homestead, *Sidney's Close*); George *Simpson* 1932 of Braunston (Simpson's); Stephen *Sivers* 1724 of Stretton (*Sivers his Bite Nooke* (Stretton), Sivers Cl (Clipsham)); Henry *Skillington* c1720, William *Skillington* 1678, John *Skillyngton* and Robert *Skillyngton* 1522 of Stretton (*Skillingtons Bite Nooke*); Robert *Sly* 1640 of Glaston (*Robert Slies close*); James *Smith* 1688 of Uppingham (*James Smiths close*); Susanna *Smith* 1753 of Manton (*Susanna Smith's Quarter Land*); William Henry *Smith* 1932 of Langham (Smith's Heaven); John *Smyth* and Richard *Smyth* 1522 of Morcott (*Smith's Close*); Robert *Sneth* 1522 of Cottesmore (Sneath's Fd (Thistleton)); Wm. *Spencer* 1748 of Hambleton (*Spencer's Close*); John *Springthorpe* and Martha *Springthorpe* 1794 of N. Luffenham (Springthorpe Yard); John *Stevens* 1627 of Tickencote (*Stevens headland*); William *Stimson* 1785 of Hambleton (*Stimson's Close* (Hambleton), Stimpson's Mdw (Gunthorpe)); Humphrey *Storer* and Robert *Storer* 1678 of Stretton

(*Storers Common Wood Close*); Arthur John *Storey* 1932 of Manton (Story's Fifty Acre); John *Stryckland* 1524 of Lyddington, Edmund *Strykland* 1524 of Barrowden (*Strickland Lodge* (Leighfield)); Edward *Swanne* 1600 of N. Luffenham (*Swanns Close* (N. Luffenham), *Swans* (Morcott)); John *Swanson* and Richard *Swanson* 1522 of Mkt. Overton (*Swansons Cottage Close* (Hambleton)); Albert *Swingler* 1932 of Belton (Swingler's (Belton), *Swingler Stockin* (Clipsham)); Mr *Syson* c1850 of Empingham (Mr Syson's Cl).

Robert *Tagell* 1522 of Ryhall (Taggle's Cl); George *Tailby* 1874 and Anne *Taylbye* 1621 of S. Luffenham (Tailby's Fd); Abel *Taylor* 1682 and Dennis *Taylor* 1718 of Glaston (*Taylors House and Homestead*); George *Taylor* 1932 of Stoke Dry (Taylor's Little Fd); Henry *Taylor* and Nathaniel *Taylor* 1877 of Manton (Taylor's); John *Terrywest* 1760 of Bisbrooke, John *Tyrriwest* 1706 of Preston (Terrewest's Cl (Ayston), *Terrywests Cott'* (Bisbrooke)); William *Thompson* 1619 of Belton (*William Thompsons baulk*); Deborah *Thorpe* c1760 of Edith Weston (Deborah Thorpes Cls); John *Tilton* 1522 of N. Luffenham (*Tilton's Piece*); John *Tippyng* 1522 of Caldecott (Tippings Lane (Barrowden)); Charles *Titley* 1766 of S. Luffenham, Miss *Titley* 1762 of Morcott (*Miss Titley's Close* (Morcott)); Thomas *Tomblin* 1785, Tobias *Tomblin* and William *Tomblin* 118 of Hambleton (Tomblins Cl, *Tomblin's Yard* (Hambleton), *Nether Tomlyn's* (Lyndon), Thos. *Tomblins Headland* (Edith Weston), Tomblin's Bottom Cl (Wing)); Thomas *Tomson* 1790 of Egleton (*Tomson's Lount* (Egleton), *Tomson's Meadow* (Hambleton)); John *Tokey* 1619 of Belton, Henry *Tokey* 1524 and Jane *Toky* 1522 of Seaton, Nehemiah *Tookey* 1688 of Uppingham (*John Tokeyes headland* (Belton), *Tookeys* (Hambleton)); James *Torkington* 1845 of Stretton (Torkington's Corner); J. *Turner* c1850 of Empingham (Mr J. Turner's Cl); John *Turner* and Robert *Turner* 1932 of Belton (Turner's Home Cl); Thomas *Turner* 1678 of Stretton (*Thomas Turners Close*); Mr *Twigden* c1725 of Uppingham (*Twigdins*); George *Tyler* and Henry *Tyler* 1877 of Manton (Tyler's Fourteen Acre (Manton), *Tyler's Close* (Hambleton), Tyler's Homestead (Lyndon)); Alexander *Tyth* 1524 of Barrowden (Tuth Leys (Belton)).

William *Uffyngton* 1522 of Thorpe by Water (*Huffintons close furlong* (Thorpe by Water), Huffinton's Close Furlong (Lyddington)).

William *Vellam* 1642 of Glaston (*William Velhams close*); Thomas *Vesey* 1524 of Gt. Casterton (Veazey's Mdw (Edith Weston)); Thomas *Vicar(s)* 1705 of Uppingham (*Thomas Vicars Cottage*); John *Vine* 1685 of ? Hambleton (*Vynes farm* (Hambleton), *the close of John Vine called fourteen acres* (Bisbrooke)).

Richard *Wade* 1525 of Glaston (Wade's Hill (Ayston), Wades holm mdw (Thorpe by Water)); William Wade 1652 of Greetham (*Wades Lane* (Greetham), Wades Cl (Pickworth)); William *Wade* 1758 of Stretton (Wades Hill (Thistleton)); Adam *Walbancks* 1634 of Uppingham (*Walbankes hedge*); Willelmus *Waleys* 1371 of Mkt. Overton (*Walescroft*); Harry *Wallbanks* 1766 and John *Wallbanks* c1750 of S. Luffenham (*Walbank's Close*); Elizabeth *Walker* l18 of Hambleton (*Walker's Close*); George *Walker* 1665 of Greetham (Walker's Lodge, *Walkers Farm*); John *Walker* 1932 of Langham (Walker's Top); Richard *Walles* 1525 of Lyddington (*Walls Herne*); Norwich *Walters* 1677, William *Walters* 1720 and William *Walters* 1795 of Lyndon (*Walters Close*); John -, Laurence - and Richard *Waltham* 1522 of Teigh, Lawrence *Waltham* 1525 of Ashwell (Waltham Clays (Mkt. Overton)); George Henry *Ward* 1932 of Lyddington (Wards Leys); John *Ward* 1678 and William *Ward* 1758 of Stretton (Wards Homestead, *Wards Platt*); John *Ward* 1746 of Uppingham (*John Wards Close*); John *Ward* 1763 of N. Luffenham (*Wards Close*); Thomas *Ward* 1522 and William *Ward* 1524 of Brooke (Wards Great Cl); Richard *Warde* 1525 of Stoke Dry (*Wardes coppie*); Henry *Waren* 1525 of Caldecott, John *Waryn* 1524 of Seaton (Warrens holme furlong (Thorpe by Water)); Jamys *Waren* 1522 of Oakham (*Warrens headlond*); Mr *Warren* c1850 of Empingham (Warren's Holt); Edward *Watkins* l18 of Hambleton (*Watkin's Meadow*); Robert *Watkins* 1774 of Preston (*Robert Watkin's Close*); Edward *Watson* 1525 of Lyddington (Watson's Paddock); John *Wayte* 1522 and Richard *Wayte* 1524 of Whissendine (White Headlands); Robert *Wells* 1522 of Stretton (Wells Cl); Thomas *Wells* 1738 of Edith Weston (*Wells's Peice* (Edith Weston), *Wells's Close* (Hambleton)); Patrick *Wheatly* 1710 of Pickworth (Wheatley's Fd); Raff *Whit* 1522 of Seaton (*a furlong called Whites* (Morcott)); Robert *Whyethed* 1525 of Empingham (Whitehead Leys (Edith Weston)); Robert *Wilcokes* and John *Wilkokes* 1522 of Ashwell (*Wilcocke Meadow* (Whissendine)); Christopher *Williamson* and Fred *Williamson* 1932 of Langham (Williamson's 9 Acre); Bernard *Wilson* 1932 of Braunston (Big Wilson's); Dan. *Wilson* 1635 of Wardley (Wilson's Cl); George *Wilson* 1932 of Manton (Wilson's Seven Acre); Widow *Wing* c1685 of Hambleton (*Wing's Close*); Mr *Wingfield* 1729 of Burley (*Wingfield's Close*); Samuel *Winterton* 1729 of Burley (Winterton's Cl); George *Woodcock* 118 of Hambleton (*Woodcock's Cottage Close*); Peter *Woodcock* 1639 of Caldecott, Thomas *Woodcok* 1522 of Lyddington (*Woodcoks Bush* (Lyddington)); Edward *Worteley* 1580 and Josia *Worteley* 1586 of N. Luffenham (Wortley's Mdw (Tixover)); John *Wotton* 1705 and Francis *Wotton* 1769 of Ketton (*Wottons Kilthorp Farm* (Ketton), Wottons Cl (N. Luffenham), Wootton's Ground (Tixover)); John *Wright* 1810 of Edith Weston (*Reights Furlong*); William Edward *Wright* 1877 of Exton (First Wright's); Robert *Wyggenton* 1522 of Belton (Wigginton Five Acre (Edith Weston)); Robert *Wylde* 1296 of Tickencote (Wild's Ford); Thomas *Wyles* 1758 of Stretton (Wyles Cl); Margere *Wylkynson* 1524 of N. Luffenham (Wilkinsons Cl); Wylliam *Wylkynson* 1525 of Seaton (*wilkinson close* (Morcott)); Alan *Wymark'* 1296, Anthony *Wymarke* 1572, John *Wymake* 1565 of Luffenham, Mr *Wymark* 1631 of N. Luffenham (Wymark Spinney, *Mr Wymarkes Close* (N. Luffenham), *Wymarkes Close* (S. Luffenham), *Wymarkes yardland* (Lyndon)); John *Wytham* 1522 of S. Luffenham (*Wythams Thing*).

INDEX OF THE PLACE-NAMES OF RUTLAND

This index includes all the major names and minor names in the Introduction and in the main body of the work, but not in the Phonology of Rutland Place-Names or in the analyses of names.

Field-names are not indexed unless they are noted in the Introduction. Parish names are printed in small capitals and lost names in italics. Field-names are also printed in italics.

Acorn Spinney 258
Addah Wood 81
Adderley St 211
Aldgate 152
Aldgate Fm 152
All Hallows Church 293
Allin Row 211
Alsthorpe xxxix, lv, 11
Alstoe Ho. xlvii, 11
Alstoe Hundred/Wapentake
  xlvi, xlvii, 4
America Lodge 78
Anchorage, The 17
Angel 116
Annwell liii, 85
April Cottage 180
Arberry Gate xxxvi, 286, 289
Archfield 215
Armley Lodge 180
Armley Wood 20
Ash Plantation 21
ASHWELL xiv, xxvi, lvii, 4
Ashwell Church 4
Ashwell Grange 4
Ashwell Hall 4
Ashwell Hill 4
Ashwell Lodge 4
Ashwell Rd (Oakham) 102
Ash Wood 25
Asshelounde 300
Audit Hall Rd 139
Aveland Arms 152
Avenue, The 139
Axe and Saw 267
AYSTON xxi, xxvii, xxx, xxxi, xxxii,
  xxxvi, liii, lix, 171
Ayston Church 172
Ayston Hall 172
Ayston Mill 215
Ayston Rd (Uppingham) 211

Ayston Spinney 172

Back Lane (Langham) 92
  (S. Luffenham) 268
Backside Lane 69
Baines Lane 293
Bancroft Lodge 207
Banky Meadow 119
Baptist Chapel (Barrowden) 233
  (Belton) 69
  (Langham) 92
Bargate 115
Barker's Spinney 258
Barley Mow 152
BARLEYTHORPE xvii, xxvi, xl,
  xliii, liii, liv, lviii, 64
Barleythorpe Hall 65
Barleythorpe Rd (Oakham) 102
Barnetts Fm 84
Barnhill Spinney 180
Barnsdale xv, xxx, xlv, lvi, 20
Barnsdale Avenue 20
Barnsdale Hill 20
Barnsdale Lodge 20
Barnsdale Wood 20
Barredyk' li, 115
BARROW xvii, xviii, xxi, xxii, xxiv,
  xxvi, xxviii, xxix, xxxiv, xxxv, xliv,
  xlix, liv, lx, 7
Barrow Ho. 8
BARROWDEN xiv, xvii, xxi, xxii,
  xxv, xxxi, xxxv, xxxvi, l, liii, liv,
  lviii, 232
Barrowe Hill xvii, 72
Barrow leayes xvi, 23
Barrows, The (Seaton) xvii, 293
Barrows, The (Lyddington) xvii, 276
  (Morcott) xvii, 286
Barrow Wide Hole lix, 8

Baulk Hill 239
Baulk Rd 239
Bay House Fm 290
Bear House 213
Beast Hill 211
BEAUMONT CHASE xv, xviii, xxxvi,
    xlii, xliv, lvi, 177
Beckley Ho. 233
Beckworth Spinney 139
Bede House 275
Beech Fm 180
Bee Hill 275
Beehive Cottage 180
Belinsford Bridge 161
Bell 116
Belmesthorpe xxxix, 161
Belmisthorpe Grange 161
Belt, The (Empingham) 140
    (Normanton) 202
BELTON xiii, xiv, xxvii, xxxvi,
    xxxix, lv, lx, 68
Belton Church 69
Belton Ho. 70
Berrybut Spinneys 222
Beru (Thorpe by Water) xvii, 303
Berues (Barrowden) xvii, 237
Bidwell's Lodge 81
Big Pits Wood 158
Big Sutie 158
Binnetts Entry 211
Birchaby xxxix, lv, 69
BISBROOKE xvi, xxi, xxxii, xxxiii,
    xxxviii, xlv, lviii, 238
Bisbrooke Hall 239
Black Bull (Mkt. Overton) 34
Black Bull (Uppingham) 214
Blackground 152
Black Hedge 239
Black Horse (Caldecott) 244
    (Greetham) 25

    (Langham) 92
Black Horse (Barleythorpe) 65
    (Belton) 70
    (Empingham) 140
    (Thorpe by Water) 303
Black Horse Lane 244
Blacksmiths Lane 21
Blackthorn Covert 17
Blakewell Cottage 57
Bloody Oaks 140
Blue Ball (Braunston) 74
Blue Ball (Manton) 195
    (Oakham) 116
Blue Bell (Ryhall) 162
Blue Bell (Ketton) 152
    (Morcott) 282
    (Oakham) 116
    (Pickworth) 158
Bluebottle Lodge 223
Boat 116
Bolaresthorp xliii, 64
Boot and Shoe 267
Bottom Fm 52
Bottom Mill Covert 11
Botwell liii, 100
Bracknell Cottage 202
Bracknell Ho. 202
Bradley Fish Pond 81
Bradley Lane 81
Brake Spinney 223
BRAUNSTON xvi, xvii, xxxi, liii, 74
Braunston Church 74
Braunston Lodge 75
Braunston Rd (Oakham) 102
Braunston South Lodge 75
Breach Fm 215
Bredcroft lv, 168
Bredcroft Ho. 168
Brick Kiln Spinney 11
Bridge Fm (Brooke) 78

466

(Gt. Casterton) 131
Britannia 116
Broadholme 147
Broken Barrow xvi, 145
Brook Fm (Egleton) 84
 (Exton) 21
BROOKE xxxii, xxxiii, lvii, 78
Brooke Church 78
Brooke Covert 119
Brooke Covert East 119
Brooke Fm 12
Brooke Hall 78
Brooke Hill 119
Brooke House Fm 75
Brooke Lodge 78
Brooke Lodge West 78
Brooke Mill 78
Brooke Parke lvii, 79
Brooke Priory liii, 78
Brooke Rd (Oakham) 103
Brooklands 213
Brookleigh Ho. 233
Browne's Lodge 57
Brownswell's Covert 12
Buck Hill lvii, 5
Buckingham Rd 103
Budborow xvii, 28
Bull li, 117
Bull Bridge 180
Bull Lane (Ketton) 152
 (Oakham) li, 103
Bullock Spinney 140
Bullock's Yard 211
Bungalow, The (Brooke) 78
Bungalows, The (Gunthorpe) 89
Bunker's Hill 140
Burghsyk' xxxiv, 8, 9
BURLEY xiv, xv, xxii, xxiv, xxvi, xxix,
 xxxii, xxxix, xlvii, xlix, lv, lvii, lix, 10
Burley Bushes (Burley) 12

(Exton) 21
Burley on the Hill 12
Burley Park 12
Burley Rd (Oakham) 103
Burley Wood 12
Burstall' medewe xxxiv, 8, 51
Busbie waie 108
Bushy Close 98
Bushy Wood 98
Bussack Barn xxxiv, xxxv, 8
Butt Lane 258
Butler's Cottage 213
Butter Cross 110

CALDECOTT xiii, xiv, xvii, xx, xxvii,
 xxxi, xxxv, xxxvi, l, lv, 244
Caldecott Church 244
Callis, The 112
Canal Hole lix, 50
Candlestick Spinney 223
Captain's Covert 223
Casteldyk' li, 110
Castledine's Lane 108
CASTERTON, GREAT xv, xx, xxi,
 xxii, xxiii, xxv, xxvii, xxx, xliii,
 xliv, xlviii, xlix, l, liv, lv, 130
Casterton Bridge 131
Casterton Church, Great 131
Casterton Lings 131
Casterton Mill 131
CASTERTON, LITTLE xxx, xxxix,
 xliii, xliv, liii, lv, lviii, 134
Casterton Church, Little 135
Casterton Lodge, Little 135
Castle Close 211
Castle Dike (Lincs.) xxxv
Castle Hill xxxvi, 177
Castle Inn 244
Castle Thorns xxxvi, 286

Catherine Wheel 214

Catmose 119

Catmose, Vale of xiii, xiv, 3

Catmose Fm 119

Catmose Lodge 119

Catmose Vale Hospital 111

Catmos Lodge 49

Catmos St 103

Cats Hill Spinney 152

Caxmir Cottage 119

Channel Meadow lix, 50

Chantry, The (Lt. Casterton) 135

Chantry (Manton) 195

Chapel Fm (Burley) 12

(Essendine) 147

Chapel Field Spinney 140

Chapel Hill 140

Chapel Lane 211

Chapel Spinney 140

Chapter Fm 75

Charnellhoale lix, 50

Chater, River xxii, xxxi, xxxvii, xli, 1

Chequers 214

Cheseldyne Ho. 75

Chester xxxiv, 58

Chestnut Fm (Braunston) 75

(Burley) 12

Christian's Lodge 158

Christ's Hospital 213

Church Bridge 140

Church Fm (Empingham) 140

(Ryhall) 161

(Edith Weston) 223

Church Lane (Glaston) 248

(Greetham) 25

(N. Luffenham) 258

(Thistleton) 52

(Edith Weston) 223

Church Lane (Uppingham) 211

Church St (Oakham) 104

(Wing) 229

City, The 140

City Yard 229

Clay Hill 161

Clay Lane (N. Luffenham) 258

(S. Luffenham) 268

Claypithill Barn 52

CLIPSHAM xxi, xxiii, xxiv, xxv, xxvii, xxviii, xxix, xxxv, xlviii, lxi, 80

Clipsham Church 81

Clipsham Ford Spinney 140

Clipsham Hall 81

Clipsham Lodge 81

Clipsham Park lvii

Clipsham Park Wood 81

Close, The 119

Coach Bridge lv, 293

Cocked Hat Spinney (Empingham) 140

(Exton) 21

Cold Overton Rd 104

Cole's Lodge 98

College Fm 98

Constables 215

Constitution Hill 211

Coppice, The 25

Coppice Leys 233

Cordle Spring 34

Cotes lv, 293

Cottage, The (Ketton) 152

(Stretton) 40

(Tinwell) 168

Cottage Fm 92

COTTESMORE xxii, xxiv, xxvi, xxix, xliv, liv, lv, lix, 16

Cottesmore Bridge 17

Cottesmore Church 17

Cottesmore Gorse 17

Cottesmore Grange 17

Cottesmore Hall 17

Cottesmore Ho. 17

Cottesmore Lodge 17
Cottesmore Wood 17
Couzens Heath 147
Cow Close Fm 12
Cow Close Plantation 81
Cow Croft Spinney 140
Cow Pasture (N. Luffenham) 258
Cow Pasture Fm (Gt. Casterton) 131
Crocket Lane 140
Crossegate (Barrow) liv, 9
   (Stoke Dry) liv, 302
Crosse Way liv, 134
Cross Keys (Uppingham) 214
Cross Keys (Oakham) 117
   (Uppingham) 214
Cross Lane liv, 204
Cross Roads Fm 140
Cross St 104
Crosswell liv, 197
Crown (Gt. Casterton) 132
   (Empingham) 140
   (Oakham) 117
   (Tinwell) 168
   (Uppingham) 214
Crown (Barrowden) 233
   (Ketton) 152
   (S. Luffenham) 267
   (Morcott) 282
   (Ryhall) 162
Crown and Anchor 25
Crown Well Bridge 195
Crownwell Fm 229
Crow Spinney (Burley) 12
Crows Spinney (Horn) 33
crucem Benedicti liv, 263
Cuckoo 229
Cuckoo Fm 21
Cuckoo Lodge 152
Cuckoo Spinney 21
Cyprus lx, 294

Dairy Fm 65
Dark Lane 108
Dean's St 104
Deb Dale 140
Digby Drive 104
Dog Kennel Cottages 119
Dog Kennel Spinney 12
Dovecoat House 213
Dovecot 140
Drift, The (Barrowden) 233
   (Pickworth) 158
   (Ryhall) 161
Duke's Head 117
Dukes Well 180
Dunstall Plantations 57
Durant Farmhouse 233
Durham Ox (Gunthorpe) lix, 89
   (S. Luffenham) lviii, 267
Durham Ox Fm 89

East End 25
East Hundred xlviii, 130
East Lodge 223
East View 180
Eastwood 132
Egg Spinney 12
EGLETON xxvi, xxvii, xxx, xxxi,
   xxxiii, liii, lv, lvii, lviii, 84
Egleton Church 84
Eight Riding Tree 12
Elms, The 75
Elms Lodge 282
EMPINGHAM xiv, xx, xxi, xxii, xxiii,
   xxv, xxvi, xxxv, liii, lv, lix, 138
Empingham Church 140
Empingham Mill 140
Empingham Reservoir xx, lx
Empingham Road Cottages 168
Engine and Tender 245

Engine Close lviii, 261
Engine Inn 135
Engine Pond 12
Ermine Street xiii, xv, xx, xxi, xxiv,
   xxxv, li, lix
ESSENDINE xiii, xviii, xxii, xxiv, xxvi,
   xxxiv, xxxv, xxxvi, xlv, l, lvi, lviii, lx, 147
Essendine Castle xxxv
Essendine Church 147
Essendine Hill 161
Essendine Lodge Fm 147
Estbarreȝate li, 113
Evidence lviii, 136
Exeter Arms (Barrowden) 233
   (Uppingham) 214
Exeter Arms (Ketton) 152
Exeter's Gorse 131
EXTON xv, xxiv, xxix, lvi, 19
Exton, Little 21
Exton Church 21
Exton Grange 12
Exton Hall 21
Exton Park 21
Eye Brook xiii, xviii, xxx, xxxvi, xli, 1

Fairchild's Fm 158
Falcon 214
Farleigh 215
Fengate 108
Ferrers Close 104
Finch Avenue 105
Finch Close 211
Finchley Bridge 69
Finch's Arms 180
Finchs Arms (Burley) 12
   (Egleton) 84
   (Oakham) 117
Finkey St 105
Fircroft 215

Firs, The (Exton) 21
   (Ketton) 152
Fisher's Yard 211
Fish Pond (Glaston) 248
   (Horn) 33
   (Normanton) 202
   (Stretton) 40
Fiue Mile Crosse liv, 29
Five Bells 162
Flint's Covert 12
Flitteris xiii, lvi
Flitteris Park lvii, 125
Flitteris Park Fm 119
Flore's House 111
Flower Pot Inn 165
Fludyer's Arms 214
Football Piece 223
Ford (Whissendine) 57
Forest of Rutland lvi, 97
Fort Henry 33
Forty Acre Barn 223
Fosse Lane 52
Foster's Bridge 267
Foundry Arms 162
Fountain's Barn 17
Fox 282
Fox and Hounds (Exton) 21
   (N. Luffenham) 258
   (Preston) 204
Fox and Hounds (Cottesmore) 17
Fox Bridge 21
Fox Covert 196
Freewards, The 147
Fregsthorpe xl, lv, 150
Frith Fm 135
Frog Hall 207
Fronald (Stoke Dry) liv, 300
Fronald, (The) (Lyddington) liv, 277

Gainsborough Rd 211
Gaol St 105
Gas Hill 211
Gas Works 213
Gate 239
Gate House Bridge 12
Geeston xxx, lv, 150
Geeston Ho. 152
Geeston Tap 152
George (Oakham) 117
    (Uppingham) 214
George and Dragon (Seaton) 293
George and Dragon (Uppingham) 214
Gibbet Gorse 181
Gibbet Lane 223
Gilson's Hospital 282
Gipsy Hollow Lane 215
GLASTON xiv, xix, xxi, xxii, xxiv, xxv,
    xxxi, xxxii, xxxiii, xxxviii, xli, l, liii,
    lviii, 248
Glaston Church 248
Glaston Lodge 248
Glaston Rd (Uppingham) 211
Glaston Tunnel lx, 248
Glebe, The 119
Glebe Barn 135
Glebe Fm (Barrow) 8
    (Empingham) 140
    (Greetham) 25
    (Tinwell) 168
Glebe Farm Ho. 12
Glebe Ho. 17
Glen, River xxii, 2
Gosborough xvii, 59
Grace Dieu liv, 168
Granby Lodge 239
Grange, The (Exton) 21
    (Ketton) 152
    (Oakham) 119
    (Stoke Dry) 300

(Tinwell) 168
    (Edith Weston) 223
    (Wing) 229
Grange Fm (Glaston) 248
    (Ryhall) 161
    (Thistleton) 52
    (Whissendine) 57
Gravel Pit 70
Great Close Spinney 258
Great Ground Barn 189
Great Lane 25
Green, The (Ayston) 172
    (Barrow) 8
    (Barrowden) 233
    (Braunston) 75
    (Caldecott) 245
    (Exton) 21
    (Ketton) 152
    (Lyddington) liv, 275
    (Morcott) 282
    (Mkt. Overton) 35
    (Thorpe by Water) 303
    (Edith Weston) 223
Green Dragon 162
Green Lane 75
Greensborough xvii, 59
Green's Lodge 57
GREETHAM xv, xvii, xviii, xx, xxi,
    xxii, xxiv, xxv, xxvii, xxviii, xxix, liii,
    liv, lv, lvii, lix, 24
Greetham Church 25
Greetham Ho. 25
Greetham Wood Far 25
Greetham Wood Near 25
Grenegate 108
Greyhound 57
Gunnel Lane 140
GUNTHORPE xxxiii, xl, lv, lix, 89
Gunthorpe Hall 89
Gwash, River xiii, xxxv, xli, 2

Hales Spinney 239
Half Moon Spinney 181
Halfway House 267
Hall, The (Barleythorpe) 65
 (Belton) 70
 (Ryhall) 161
Hall Close 141
Hallewellescros liv, 237
Hall Fm 21
HAMBLETON xiv, xx, xxii, xxv, xxvi,
 xxx, xxxi, xxxii, xxxiii, xxxviii, xxxix,
 xlii, xliii, xlvi, xlviii, l, lv, lvii, 179
Hambleton, Middle 179
Hambleton, Nether lv, 179
Hambleton, Upper 179
Hambleton Church 181
Hambleton Hall 181
Hambleton Lodge 181
Hambleton Manor 181
Hambleton Wood 181
Hanbury Close 105
Hannah's Field 208
Hardwick xxi, lv, 139
Hardwick Cottages 139
Hardwick Fm 139
Hardwick Wood 139
Harewood Ho. 92
Harrington Way 105
Harton xxix, 82
Hawkswell Spinney 21
Hawkswell Spring 21
Haycock Spinney 98
Hay Cottage 282
Hayne Ho. 111
Healall Cottage 213
Heath Lodge 25
Heath Spinney 25
Helwell (Oakham) liii, 123
 (Teigh) liii, 51
Hereford Ox lviii, 267

Hermitage, The 12
Hibbits Lodge (Brooke) 78
 (Empingham) 141
Hide lv, 84
Highfield 215
Highfield Close 141
Highfields 141
High Ho. 75
High Moor 141
Highmoor Fm (Exton) 21
High Moor Fm (Whissendine) 63
High Moor Spinney 63
High Pasture 258
High St (Oakham) 105
 (Uppingham) 211
Hillam's Cottage 213
Hill Top Fm (Hambleton) 181
 (Oakham) 119
Hob Hole liii, 30
Hog Hill 211
Hog Lane 211
Hog Pond 84
Holbeck Lodge 92
Hollow Close Covert 12
Hollow Fm 141
Holly Fm 204
Hollygate Lodge 208
Holly Ho. 57
Hollytree Cottage 78
Holmes, The 152
Holyoaks lii, liv, lv, 298
Holyoaks Lodge 298
Holyoaks Wood 298
Home Fm (Brooke) 78
 (Egleton) 84
 (Hambleton) 181
 (Ketton) 152
 (Edith Weston) 223
 (Whitwell) 63
Honeypot Spring 275

Hooby Crosse liv, 128
Hooby Fm 52
Hooby (Lodge) xxxix, lv, 38
HORN xxi, xxvi, lv, lviii, 33
Horn Ho. 33
Horn Lane Spinney 33
Horn Mill 21
Horn Mill Spinney 141
Horse and Groom (Burley) 12
Horse and Groom (Barleythorpe) 65
Horse and Jockey (Manton) 196
Horse and Jockey (Langham) 92
   (Uppingham) 214
Horse and Panniers 258
Horse and Trumpet (High St West,
   Uppingham) 214
   (Market Place, Uppingham) 214
Horse Drills lviii, 66
Horsepool Lodge 98
Hortons Lane 57
Hospital liv, 128
Hospital of St John 111
Hot Hollow Fm 141
Hungate Fm 161
Hunt's Barn 158
Hunt's Lodge 152
Hurn, The 57
Hwicceslea east hundred xlviii, 222
Hwiccleslea west hundred xlviii, 222

Ingthorpe xl, liv, 167
Invention Meadow lviii, 87
Islington xxix, 54
Ivy Bridge 17
Ivy Cottage 17
Ivydene 181

Johnson Rd 211

John St 106
Jubilee Lodge Fm 208

Kalkeleys 98
Keeper's Cottage 21
Keeper's Lodge 181
KETTON xviii, xx, xxii, xxv, xxx, xl, xlii,
   xlviii, l, lv, lix, lx, 150
Ketton Church 152
Ketton Cottage 152
Ketton Gorse 223
Ketton Grange 152
Ketton Hall 152
Ketton Ho. 152
Ketton Park 153
Ketton Quarries 153
Kilburn Rd 106
Kilthorpe (Grange) xl, lv, 151
Kingfisher 204
King's Arms 229
King's Head (Oakham) 117
   (Uppingham) 214
King's Hill 177
King's Hill Lodge lvi, 178

Lady Wood 40
Lamb 70
Lambley Lodge lvi, 97
LANGHAM xiii, xvii, xxvi, 91
Langham Brewery 92
Langham Church 92
Langham Lodge 92
Langham Place (Ashwell) 4
   (Langham) 92
Launde Fm 215
Laurels, The (Ryhall) 161
   (Whissendine) 57
Lavender Fm 35

Lawnde Park lvii, 215
Lax Hill 181
Lax Hill Covert 181
Leamington Terrace 212
Leas, The 17
Lees Barn 208
Lee Spinney 141
Leicester Rd (Uppingham) 212
Lings Spinney 141
Leigh xxxii, 96, 97
LEIGHFIELD xv, xvii, xxxii, liii, lv,
    lvi, lviii, 96
Leighfield Forest xv, lvi, 97
Leighfield Lodge 98
Leigh Lodge xxxiii, lvi, 98
Limekiln Spinney 17
Limes, The (Hambleton) 181
    (Ketton) 153
Lincolnshire Gate 158
Line Fields lx, 123
Little Lane 108
Little Oaks 141
Little Oaks Lodge 141
Little Pits Wood 81
Little Sutie 158
Littleworth xxvii, 70
Lodge, The (Oakham) 119
    (Mkt. Overton) 35
Lodge Fm 181
London Rd (Uppingham) 212
Long Barn Fm 153
Long Covert 223
Longe Lane 109
Long Hedge Spinney 258
Lonsdale Fm 248
Lonsdale Ho. 65
Lonsdale Way (Oakham) 106
Lord Nelson 117
Lord Roberts 275
Losecoat Field 141

Loudal Lane 4
LUFFENHAM, NORTH xiv, xxi, xxiii,
    xxiv, xxxi, xxxv, xxxix, xliii, xliv, xlviii,
    liv, lv, lviii, lx, 256
Luffenham Hall 258
LUFFENHAM, SOUTH xxiv, xliii, xliv,
    liii, liv, lviii, lix, 267
Luffenham Church, South 268
Luffenham Hall, South 268
Luffenham Heath, South 268
Luffewyke xxxi, 195
LYDDINGTON xv, xvii, xviii, xxx, xxxi,
    xxxii, xxxix, liv, lvi, lvii, lix, 274
Lyddington Church 275
Lyddington Park Lodge 275
LYNDON xxv, xxxi, 189
Lyndon Church 189
Lyndon Hall 189
Lyndon Wood 189

Manor Fm (Ashwell) 4
    (Barleythorpe) 65
    (Hambleton) 181
    (Ketton) 153
    (N. Luffenham) 258
    (Pickworth) 158
    (Tinwell) 168
    (Tixover) 305
    (Whissendine) 57
Manor Ho. (Ashwell) 4
    (Bisbrooke) 239
    (Braunston) 75
    (Egleton) 84
    (Greetham) 25
    (Langham) 92
    (Pickworth) 158
    (Ridlington) 208
    (Seaton) 293
    (Thorpe by Water) 303

474

(Tinwell) 169
(Whissendine) 57
Manor Lane 65
Manthorpe xl, lv, 151
MANTON xxxi, liii, liv, lvii, 195
Manton Church 196
Manton Hall 196
Manton Lodge 196
Manton Lodge Fm 196
Many Bushes 215
Market Place (Oakham) 106
 (Uppingham) 212
Market St (Oakham) 106
Marquess of Exeter 275
Martines-stoc/Martinestoch xxxiii, 199
Martins House 213
Martinsley xlviii, 199
Martinsley Hundred/Wapentake xliii,
 xlvi, xlviii, 171
MARTINSTHORPE xxxiii, xl, xlviii,
 lv, lvi, 199
Masons Arms 223
Maycroft 4
Meadhurst 215
Meeting Lane 212
Melton Rd (Oakham) 106
Mere Lane 4
Middle Bridge 275
Middle Fm 53
Middle Lodge 141
Midland Hotel 152
Mill, The (Barrowden) 233
 (Tinwell) 169
Mill Close Spinney 141
Mill Cottages 215
Mill Dam (Exton) 21
 (Tickencote) 165
Mill Fm (Empingham) 141
 (Pickworth) 161
Mill Field Manor 92

Millfield Spinney 12
Mill Hill 65
Mill Ho. (Greetham) 25
 (Oakham) 112
 (Uppingham) 215
Mill Lane (Caldecott) 245
 (Cottesmore) 17
 (Thorpe by Water) 303
Millstone 162
Mill St (Oakham) 106
Mr Lowith's Cottage 213
Mockbeggar 157
Monckton Arms 248
Moorhall xxxiii, xxxiv, xxxv, 56
Moor Lane (N. Luffenham) 258
 (Whissendine) 57
Moor Lane Bridge 258
Moor Plantation 81
MORCOTT xvii, xxi, xxvii, xxxvi, lix,
 lx, 282
Morcott Church 282
Morcott Hall 282
Morcott Spinney 258
Morkery Leys xxxiv, 39
Morris's Spinney 141
Mott Close xxxv, 83
Mount, The 153
Mount Alstoe 12
Mount Pleasant (Greetham) 25
 (Morcott) 282
 (Oakham) 119
 (Uppingham) 212
 (Whissendine) 57
Mounts Lodge 132
Mowmires 141
Mowmires Spinney 141
Murray Lodge 169

Navigation, The lix, 36

Navigation Close lix, 9
Navvys Yard lx, 60
Netherborrows xvii, 77
Netherfield Ho. 70
New Barn Lodge 223
Newbottle lv, 151
New Cottages 142
Newell Wood xxxv, 157
New Field Rd 21
New Garden Spinney 22
New Inn 25
New Inn Fm 26
New Park lvii, 181
New Quarry Fm 81
New Rectory, The 223
New Row 35
New St (Oakham) 106
Newtown 135
New Wood 141
New Wood Lodge 141
Nightingale Spinney 148
Nine Acre Spinney 258
Noel Avenue 106
Noel Arms (Langham) 92
Noel Arms (Whissendine) 57
Noel's Arms (Whitwell) 63
Noels Arms (Ridlington) 208
Noel's Arms (Wing) 229
Nook, The 142
Nook Fm 142
Nook Lane 142
Norberwe xvii, 303
Normandale xlii, 307
NORMANTON xxi, xxv, xxx, xxxi,
   xxxviii, xxxix, xlii, lv, 201
Normanton Church 202
Normanton Cottages 142
Normanton Gardens 202
Normanton Ho. 202
Normanton Lodge 202

Normanton Park lv, lvii, 202
North Brook 142
Northfields 135
Northgate St 106
North Road Spinney 33
Northwick Arms 152
Northwick Cottages 153
Norton xxix, xlii, lv, 37
Norton St 212
Nursery, The 153
Nursery Close lviii, 136

Oak 25
Oak Fm 202
OAKHAM xiii, xiv, xv, xxii, xxvi,
   xxx, xxxi, xl, xliii, xlviii, xlix, l,
   liii, lvii, lviii, lix, lx, 102
Oakham Canal, Melton Mowbray
   and lix, 119
Oakham Castle lvii, 110
Oakham Church 112
Oakham School 112
Oakham Soke xlviii, 64
Oakham Soke Hundred xlviii, 64
Odd House Tavern 117
Okeham cum Martynesley, Hundreda
   de xlviii, 64
Old Hall (Ashwell) 4
   (Belton) 70
   (Exton) 22
   (Hambleton) 181
   (Langham) 92
   (Mkt. Overton) 35
   (Wing) 229
Old Hall (Ridlington) 208
Old Hall Fm 63
Old Heath Lodge 153
Old Leicester Lane 75
Old Plough 75

Old Quarry Fm 81
Old Rectory, The 223
Oldsale Wood 98
Old Tannery Yard 234
Old Vicarage, The 245
Old White Hart 275
Old Windmill (Greetham) 26
   (Ketton) 153
   (S. Luffenham) 268
Old Wood 142
Old Wood Lodge 142
Olive Branch (Clipsham) 81
Olive Branch (Empingham) 142
Orchard Close 84
Orchard Ho. 181
Orchards, The 153
Orange St 212
Osbonall Wood 81
Ostlers Arms 214
Our Lady's Well liii, 119
Oval, The 258
Over the Line (Barrow) lx, 9
   (Essendine) lx, 149
OVERTON, MARKET xiii, xiv, xv,
   xx, xxi, xxii, xxiii, xxvii, xxviii,
   xxix, xxxiv, xxxvi, xl, xlii, xliii,
   xlviii, xlix, l, lvi, lix, lxi, 34
Overton Church, Mkt. 35
Overton Quarry, Mkt. 35

Pacey's Lodge 75
parcus de Esindene lvi, 148
Park, le (Hambleton) lvii, 181
Park, The (Lyndon) lvii, 191
   (Whissendine) lvii, 57
Park Cottages 248
Park Fm (Burley) 12
   (Essendine) 148
   (Ridlington) 208

Parkfield 70
Parkfield Rd 107
Park Ford lvii, 88
Park Ho. (Empingham) 142
   (Whissendine) 57
Park Lane lvii, 107
Park Leyes lvii, 225
Park Lodge lvi, 208
Parsonage Ho. 213
Pasture Lane 65
Pastures, The 258
Pateman's Lodge 208
Peartree Lane 53
Penn St 107
PICKWORTH xxvi, xxxv, l, 157
Pickworth, Top 158
Pickworth Great Wood 158
Pickworth Plain 158
Pied Bull 152
Pied Calf 275
PILTON xxii, xxxi, lx, 289
Pilton Fox Covert 290
Pimpole, The xvii, 246
Pinfold, The (Cottesmore) 17
   (Egleton) 84
   (Manton) 196
Pinfold Ho. 181
Pinfold Lane (N. Luffenham) 258
   (Mkt. Overton) 35
Pinfold Lane (Oakham) 109
Pitts, The 216
Plough (Bisbrooke) 245
   (Gt. Casterton) 132
   (Greetham) 25
Plough (Bisbrooke) 245
Pond Lane 26
Poor Close Covert 12
Poplars, The 57
Portegate l, 255
Portgate l, 297

Portland (Stamford, Lincs.) 1
Post Way, The lix, 55
Post Way Furlong lix, 31
Prebendal Ho. 142
Prebendary Ho. 275
Prestley Hill xxxii, 274
PRESTON xxxi, xxxii, liv, 204
Preston Church 204
Preston Hall 204
Prince of Wales 117
Printer's Yard 212
Prior's Coppice 78
Priory, The (Ketton) 153
  (Edith Weston) liii, 223
Pudding Bag End 22
Pudding Bag Lane 22
Pug's Park Spinney 33
Pump 214
Pump Close (Stretton) lviii, 47
  (Teigh) lviii, 50
Purveyor's Covert 12

Quadrant, The 212
Quaker's Spinney 208
Quarry Fm 135
Queen St 212

Ragman's Row 212
Railway lx, 155
Railway Fields lx, 284
Railway Inn (Ketton) 152
  (Oakham) 118
Railway Inn (Essendine) 148
  (S. Luffenham) 267
  (Wing) 229
Ram Jam Inn lix, 25
Ramparts, The 84
Ranksborough xvii, 91

Ranksborough Gorse 91
Ranksborough Hill 91
Rascalhill lvii, 198
Ratcliffe Spinney 258
Rattling Jack Spinney 22
Ratts Lane 75
Ravenscroft Fm 208
Ravens Crosse liv, 67
Ravenstock Wood 148
Rectory, (The) (Ashwell) 4
  (Barrowden) 233
  (Gt. Casterton) 132
  (Lt. Casterton) 135
  (Clipsham) 82
  (Cottesmore) 17
  (Exton) 22
  (Glaston) 248
  (N. Luffenham) 258
  (S. Luffenham) 268
  (Normanton) 202
  (Mkt. Overton) 35
  (Preston) 204
  (Ridlington) 208
  (Seaton) 293
  (Stoke Dry) 300
  (Stretton) 40
  (Teigh) 49
  (Tinwell) 169
  (Uppingham) 213
  (Whitwell) 63
  (Wing) 229
Rectory Fm (Brooke) 79
  (Uppingham) 213
Rectory Lane 223
Red Barn 268
Red Cow 118
Red deere Parke lvii, 80
Redgate 212
Red Hill (Barrowden) 233
  (Uppingham) 212

Red Hill Fm 233
Red Ho., (The) (Hambleton) 181
    (Whissendine) 57
Red Lion (Oakham) 118
    (Wing) 229
Reeves Lane 229
Reservoir (Stoke Dry) 300
RIDLINGTON xiv, xviii, xxx, xxxi,
    xxxvi, xliii, lvi, 206
Ridlington Church 208
Risberwe xvii, 101
Robin Hood's Cave 22
Robynilpit liii, 238
Rock Villa 153
Rocott Ho. 92
Rocott Spinney 92
Roebuck 118
Rogues Lane 17
Roman Well 53
Rookery, The (Lt. Casterton) 135
    (Cottesmore) 17
    (Tinwell) 169
Rose and Crown (Whissendine) 57
Rose and Crown (Uppingham) 214
Rose Cottage 161
Rotten Row 109
Rowell's Lodge 208
Royal Duke 118
Royal Oak (Oakham) 118
    (Uppingham) 214
Rush Barrow xvii, 51
Rushpit Wood 22
Rutland xiii, 1
Rutland Arms 118
Rutland County Museum 112
Rutland Forest 3
Rutland Ho. 153
Rutland Water xx, lx
Rutmore xiii, xvii, xxvii, xxviii, xxxiv,
    xlv, 49

Ry Gate Plantation 22
RYHALL xiii, xviii, xxii, xxvi, xxvii,
    xxxix, l, liii, lix, 160
Ryhall Grange 161
Ryhall Heath Fm 161

St Andrew's Church (Stoke Dry) 300
    (Whissendine) 57
St John the Baptist's Church
    (Bisbrooke) 239
    (N. Luffenham) 258
Saint John's Land liv, 137
Sct. Johns, landes called liv, 219
St John's Peice liv, 31
St Luke's Church 305
St Nicholas Church 290
St Peter's Church 234
Salters Crosse liv, 273
Salters Ford Lane 4
Salters Lane 162
Scale Hill 212
School (Ridlington) 208
School Hill 181
School Lane (Langham) 92
    (Uppingham) 213
Sculthorpe (Spinney) xxxix, lv, 257
SEATON xiv, xvii, xxiv, xxxi, xlix, l,
    liii, lv, lviii, 292
Seaton Grange 293
Seaton Mill 294
Seedgrass Close lviii, 44
Settings Fm 259
Sewell's Barn 172
Sewstern Lane xv, xx, xxi, xxii, xxiv,
    xxxiv, xxxvi, xlix, lix
Shacklewell 139
Shacklewell Lodge 139
Shacklewell Spinney 139
Sharman's Lodge 26

Sheepdyke Lane 26
Sheild's Yard 213
Shelton's Barn 259
Shire Oaks 234
Shockmore liii, 272
Shorne Hill 79
Shucheved liii, 137
Simper St 107
Slip Inn 223
Smith's Lane 282
Smithy, The 135
Snelston xxxi, lv, 244
Solomon's Hut 13
Sondes Arms 248
Soulthorpe lv, 151
South Back Way 213
Southfield Lodge 239
South Lodge Fm 75
South St (Oakham) 107
    (Uppingham) 213
Southton xxix, xlii, lv, 37
South View Fm 169
Spellow xvii, 68
Spoil Banks lx, 291
Spring Back Way 213
Springdale 216
Springfield 216
Springfield Ho. 65
Springfield Lane 35
Spring Lane 248
Springthorpe Yard 259
Stamford (Lincs.) xiii, xxxv, xl, xlii,
    xlvi, xlvii, xlix, l, lx, lxiii, lxiv, lxv
Stamford End 22
Stamford Rd (Oakham) 107
Stannyford 181
Station (Essendine) 148
Station Fields lx, 262
Station Rd (Oakham) 107
    (Whissendine) 57

Stedfold Lane 169
Stocken Fm 26
Stocken (Hall) lv, 39
Stocken Park 40
Stockerston Rd (Beaumont Chase) 178
    (Uppingham) 213
Stocks Hill (Manton) 196
Stocks Hill (Ketton) 153
STOKE DRY xiv, xv, xxx, liv, 298
Stoke Dry Wood 299
Stoke Great Wood 299
Stoke Little Wood 299
Stoke's Spinney 202
Stompstone liv, 19
Stonefield Fm 196
Stone Park lvii
Stone Pit 22
Stone Pit Spinney 142
STRETTON xiii, xx, xxi, xxix, xxxiv,
    xxxix, xlviii, liv, lv, lvii, lviii, lix, 37
Stretton Lodge 40
Stretton Wood 40
Stud Ho. 65
Stump Cross liv, 228
Sun (Belton) 70
    (Cottesmore) 17
Sun (Bisbrooke) 245
    (Oakham (1)) 118
    (Oakham (2)) 118
Sunnybank 216
Swan (Barrowden) 233
    (Glaston) 249
    (Lyddington) 275
    (Uppingham) 214
Swans Lodge 208
Swintley Lodge 97
Swooning Bridge 119
Sykes Spinney 142
Syrepol xlix, 297

480

Tally Ho 162

Tanners Lane 109

TEIGH xiii, xvii, xviii, xx, xxi, xxii,
xxvii, xxviii, xxix, xxxiv, xliii, liii, lviii,
lix, lx, 48

Teigh Church 49

Teigh Cottages 49

Teigh Gate Ho. 49

Teigh Hill 49

Teigh Lodge 49

Temple Barns liv, 45

Temple Peyse liv, 32

Terrace, The 26

Thirspit (Barrowden) liii, 238
  (Glaston) liii, 256

THISTLETON xv, xvi, xx, xxi, xxii,
xxv, xxviii, xxix, xlviii, xlix, l, lix,
lxi, 52

Thistleton Church 53

Thistleton Gap 53

Thomas Hill 57

Thomas Vicars Cottage 214

Thorn Covert 223

Thornham xxv, xxxii, xxxviii

þornham broc xxxii, 174, 175

THORPE BY WATER xiv, xxxix, xliii,
302

Thorpe Mill 303

Three Crowns Inn 118

Three Horse Shoes (Mkt. Overton)
35

Three Horseshoes (Whissendine) 57

Three Horseshoes (Glaston) 249
  (Seaton) 294

Thresholdgate li, 109

þureslege liii, 174, 175

Tibba's Well liii, 164

TICKENCOTE xxvii, lxiii, 165

Tickencote Hall 165

Tickencote Laund 165

Tickencote Lodge 165

Tickencote Park 165

Tickencote Warren lviii, 165

TINWELL xiii, xxii, xxv, xxvi, xl, xlv,
liv, lix, lxiii, 167

Tinwell Church 169

Tinwell Ho. 169

Tinwell Lodge 169

Tippings Lane 234

Tirtle Meare xxxv, 289

Tithe Barn (Empingham) 142

Tithebarne lane (Oakham) 109

TIXOVER xviii, xx, xxi, xxii, xxv,
xxvi, xlii, 304

Tixover Grange 305

Tixover Hall 305

Tixover Lodge 305

Todds Piece 216

Tolethorpe (Hall) xxxix, lv, 134

Tolethorpe Mill 134

Tolethorpe Oaks 134

Toll Bar 13

Top Hall 189

Top House Fm 53

Top Lodge 22

Town Gates (Oakham) 115

Town Park lvii, 79

Troopers 249

Tunneley Wood 21

Turnover Bridge 13

Turnpole Wood 158

Turtle Bridge xxi, xxiv, xxv, xxxv,
233

Turtle Slade xxxvi, 130

Twitchbed Lane 216

Twitch Hill xxxvii, 207

Twitch Hill Fm 207

Tyler's Corner 22

Tyrespyt liii, 147

Unicorn 214

Union School 213

Union Workhouse 213

Upper Hall 268

UPPINGHAM xiv, xxii, xxiv, xxv, xxxi, xxxvi, l, liv, lvii, lviii, lix, 210

Uppingham Church 213

Vppingham parke lvii, 220

Uppingham Rd 107

Uppingham School 213

Uppingham Tollhouse 214

Urns, The xxiii, 133

Vale, The 153

Vaults 214

Vicarage, The (Belton) 70

   (Bisbrooke) 240

   (Braunston) 75

   (Burley) 13

   (Empingham) 142

   (Greetham) 26

   (Hambleton) 181

   (Ketton) 153

   (Whissendine) 57

Vicarage Cottage 57

Vicarage Ho. 57

Vicarage Lodge 57

Victoria Hall 112

Vine 118

Vine Cottage 234

Vine House 214

Vyne, le 214

Wagon and Horses 214

Wakehull xxxiv, xxxvi, 37

Walker's Lodge 26

Walk Fm 132

WARDLEY xviii, xxxii, xxxvi, liii, liv, 126

Wardley Church 127

Wardley Ho. 127

Wardley Lane 213

Wardley Wood 127

Warren Cottages 153

Warren Fm 17

Warren Plantation 165

Warren Spinney 142

Washdyke, The 142

Water Mill (Greetham) 26

Watermill Spinney 259

Watkin's Gorse 13

Welland, River xiii, xx, xxi, xxii, xxxv, xli, xlii, l, 2

Welland Spinney 234

Welland Viaduct lx, 294

Well Cross 223

Wellfield 196

Wells St 92

Wenton xxix, lv, 16

Wesleyan Chapel (Pickworth) 158

   (Uppingham) 214

West Bank 216

Westbarreyate' li, 115, 116

Westbourne Ho. 70

West Deyne 216

West End (Exton) 22

   (Greetham) 26

   (Uppingham) 216

westende (Oakham) 109

Western Fm 82

Westfield 4

Westfield Avenue 107

Westfield Ho. 205

Westgate St 107

Westhorpe xl, lv, 229

Westland Wood 21

Westmoor Lane 92

Westmoor Lodge 92

WESTON, EDITH xxi, xxv, xxx, xxxi,
    xxxix, xlii, xliii, xlviii, liii, liv, lvii,
    221
Weston Church, Edith 223
Weston Hall, Edith 223
Weston Lodge Fm, Edith 223
Weston Quarries, Edith 223
Weston Barn 190
Weston Lodge 223
West Rd 108
William Dalby St 108
Wharf, The lix, 35
Wheatsheaf (Greetham) 25
    (Langham) 92
    (Oakham) 118
    (Edith Weston) 223
Wheatsheaf (Ryhall) 162
Wheat Sheaf (Stretton) 40
Wheel 233
Wheelhouse Close lviii, 7
Whipper-In 119
WHISSENDINE xiii, xiv, xvii, xviii,
    xx, xxii, xxv, xxvi, xxvii, xxxiii,
    xxxiv, xxxv, xxxvii, xlv, lvii, lviii,
    lx, 55
Whissenthorpe 58
White Hart (Uppingham) 214
    (Edith Weston) 223
White Hart (Bisbrooke) 245
    (Ketton) 152
    (Uppingham) 214
White Horse (Empingham) 142
    (Morcott) 282
White Horse (Stretton) 40
White Hynde 214
White Lion (Whissendine) 57
White Lion (Oakham) 119
White Spring 275
White Swan 215
WHITWELL xv, xxii, xxvi, 62

Whitwell Church 63
Wichley Leys xxv, 61
Wide Hole lix, 18
Wilderness, The 142
Wild's Ford 165
Wild's Lodge 165
Wilkershaw 215
Willesley Spinney 240
Willows, The 22
Windmill (Morcott) 282
    (Whissendine) 58
Windmill Hill 275
Windmill Inn 233
WING xxi, xxxii, xxxiii, xxxviii, xl,
    xliv, lv, 228
Wing Burrows xvi, 240
Wing Church 229
Wing Hall 229
Wing Hollow 230
Wing Maze 230
Wing Plantations 165
Wingwell 230
Wisp, The 74
Wisteria Ho. 142
Witchley Hundred/Wapentake xxv,
    xlvi, xlvii, xlviii, 222
Witchley Warren xxv, xxx, xlv, 221
Witchley Warren Fm 221
Witchley Warren Spinney 221
Woodbine Ho. 181
Wooden Ho. 196
Woodhead lv, 131
Woodlands Fm 63
Wood Lane (Braunston) 75
    (Wardley) 127
Woodside 4
Wood's Lodge 178
Woolfox Lodge 24
Woolfox (Wood) lv, 24
Wrangdike Hundred xv, xlviii, xlix, 231

Wymark Spinney 259
Wyntauerne, le 119

Yews, The 223
Yew Tree Fm 49
Yew Tree Ho. 22